Clinical Negligence
A Practical Guide

To my wife Victoria

Clinical Negligence

A Practical Guide

Eighth Edition

General Editor of the Eighth Edition
Andrew Buchan, LLB (Hons)
Barrister, Cloisters

Contributors

Rachel Barrett
Barrister, Cloisters

Neil Block QC
39 Essex Chambers

Dr Thomas Boyd
General Practitioner

Andrew Buchan, LLB (Hons)
Barrister, Cloisters

Tamar Burton
Barrister, Cloisters

Dr Jonathan Cook
Barrister, Cloisters

Emma Corkill
39 Essex Chambers

Romilly Cummerson
39 Essex Chambers

Gemma Daly
Barrister, Doughty Street Chambers

Sarah Fraser Butlin
Barrister, Cloisters

Tom Gillie
Barrister, Cloisters

Caron Heyes
Solicitor, Fieldfisher

Patricia Hitchcock QC
Cloisters

Linda Jacobs
Barrister, Cloisters

Hugh Johnson
Solicitor Stewarts Solicitors

Nick Knowles
Solicitor Stewarts Solicitors

William Latimer-Sayer QC, LLB (Hons), MA
Cloisters

Chesca Lord
Barrister, Cloisters

Martyn McLeish
Barrister, Cloisters

Sophy Miles
Barrister, Doughty Street Chambers

Lisa O'Dwyer
Director of Medico-Legal Services / Action against Medical Accidents (AvMA)

Catriona Stirling
Barrister, Cloisters

Lisa Sullivan
Barrister, Cloisters

Aswini Weereratne QC
Barrister, Doughty Street Chambers

The First to the Sixth Editions were written by Charles Lewis, of the Middle Temple, Barrister, former open classical scholar of Oriel College, Oxford.

Bloomsbury Professional

LONDON • DUBLIN • EDINBURGH • NEW YORK • NEW DELHI • SYDNEY

BLOOMSBURY PROFESSIONAL
Bloomsbury Publishing Plc
41–43 Boltro Road, Haywards Heath, RH16 1BJ, UK

BLOOMSBURY and the Diana logo are trademarks of
Bloomsbury Publishing Plc

First published in Great Britain 2019

British Library Cataloguing-in-Publication Data

A catalogue record for this book is available from the British Library.

ISBN:	PB:	978 1 52650 533 0
	ePDF:	978 1 52650 535 4
	ePub:	978 1 52650 534 7

Typeset by Evolution Design & Digital Ltd (Kent)
Printed and bound by CPI Group (UK) Ltd, Croydon, CRO 4YY

To find out more about our authors and books visit
www.bloomsburyprofessional.com. Here you will find extracts, author
information, details of forthcoming events and the option to sign up for our
newsletters

Foreword

Much has changed in the field of clinical negligence litigation since the previous edition of this invaluable book, but for all those who work in this specialist field, this litigation continues to pose particular challenges. It remains as true today as when I wrote the Foreword for the last edition, that the process governing the judicial determination of allegations of negligent medical treatment is complex, time-consuming and not infrequently traumatic.

Judges called upon to try these cases have much cause to be grateful to those experienced practitioners who have mastered the medical issues, legal principles and procedural and funding requirements, and who therefore ensure that clinical disputes are explored and determined thoroughly and efficiently. And the skill and experience of those practitioners continue to owe much to the information, practical guidance and wise advice of the kind to be found in this eighth edition of *Clinical Negligence: A Practical Guide*, all of it written by well known and highly respected experts in the field.

The reader has access to comprehensive guidance on every aspect of this litigation, including a detailed analysis of the relevant legal principles governing breach of duty, causation, consent and the calculation of compensation, funding and costs, the way in which clinical services are delivered in this country, complaints procedures, and procedures in the Court of Protection. The way in which human rights are engaged and protected in this area is also considered, together with an insightful analysis of the important role played by expert witnesses. This new edition carefully analyses the recent changes to the structure of the NHS and to delivery of healthcare services; and the recent authorities on informed consent, on vicarious liability and on the categories of personnel by whom and to whom the duty of care is owed. In the brave new world of legal aid cuts and of CFAs after the Jackson reforms, the minefield of costs provisions is clearly and authoritatively explained. And there is an important new chapter on product liability.

The authors are once again to be commended for delivering such an accessible, informative and comprehensive account of the current state of play in relation to every aspect of clinical negligence litigation. This book is undoubtedly the go-to text for everyone who works in this area, or who is interested in understanding more about the way in which disputes concerning medical treatment are conducted and resolved.

Dame Laura Cox DBE
Cloisters
April 2019

Acknowledgements

I would like to thank Charles Lewis for writing the first six editions of this excellent work and for choosing me to carry on the editorship.

Lastly I would like to thank my fellow authors and the staff at Bloomsbury Professional (particularly Kiran Goss and Marianne Lee) who were very supportive and showed great patience.

Andrew Buchan
Cloisters
September 2019

Contents

The authors

ANDREW BUCHAN – GENERAL EDITOR

Author of Chapter 1 Introduction, co-author of Chapter 9 The proof of negligence, Chapter 10 Consent, Chapter 14 Psychiatric injury, Chapter 21 The medical records, and Appendices

Practitioner publications

1   General Editor and co-author of *Clinical Negligence* (8th edn, 2019, Bloomsbury Professional).
2   He conceived and wrote the first draft of *Personal Injury Schedules – Calculating Damages* (4th edn, 2018, Bloomsbury Professional), the leading practitioner textbook on schedules of loss.
3   General Editor and co-author of *Personal Injury Practice* (6th edn, 2014, Bloomsbury Professional).

He has written numerous articles on clinical negligence and personal injury. He has lectured widely on both subjects. For the last four years he has spoken on webinars for personal injury and schedules of special damage.

Experience in clinical negligence

Andrew was called to the Bar in 1981. In 1987 he specialised in clinical negligence after he was put on the AvMA expert database for counsel. This resulted in him advising upon a wide variety of cases with many reported in Clinical Risk. He has tried not to specialise in particular types of clinical negligence and has therefore accumulated a wide experience of different types of clinical negligence cases. These include multi-party actions at a generic and case counsel level.

He brought the first successful case for the negligent sterilization of a woman with no children. He probably brought the first successful case for damages caused by a twisting masonoeuve fracture during childbirth; negligent stillbirth; failure to diagnose a subarachnoid haemorrhage; cervical cancer treatment causing infected tissue and fistula formation; failed sterilization due to failure of the filshie clip. His limitation cases included cases on knowledge and s 33 discretion. The appropriate test for a compulsory patient detailed under the Mental Health Act 1983. Whether knowledge that an operation had been unsuccessful was the same as knowledge of injury caused by negligence. Section 33 discretion exercised for misleading medical advice.

He acted for a US Air Force Sergeant who had received negligent medical treatment in a UK hospital whilst on service in the UK. International law questions of jurisdiction and the Status of Forces Act. He has had several successful claims for the negligence treatment by orthopaedic surgeons. He has conducted successful cases against ambulance services for delay. He has conducted many cases concerning consent to treatment involving from posterior cruciate ligament repair to consent to stereotactic radiosurgery.

Andrew has been generic and case counsel in several multi-party actions, from Myodil to Volclay.

More recently he has succeeded in several cases involving the failure to diagnose and/or treat malignant melanoma, meningitis, and non-Hodgkin's lymphoma.

Andrew has been a CEDR accredited mediator since 2000.

He is a member of PIBA, AvMA, Inquest Lawyer's Group, PNBA, ELBA, and BIICL. He was on the Bar Council from 1995–2003.

RACHEL BARRETT

Co-author of Chapter 14 Psychiatric injury

Rachel Barrett is a barrister at Cloisters. She has a background and special interest in mental health, and is instructed in psychiatric clinical negligence and coronial matters raising mental health issues. She is named researcher on the sixth edition of Baroness Hale's Mental Health Law.

NEIL BLOCK QC

Co-author of Chapter 16 Product liability in a medical context

Neil is Head of 39 Essex Chambers. He has been instructed in many of the leading product liability cases over the past 30 years. Notable cases include the Court of Appeal cases of *Ide v ATB Sales* [2008] EWCA 424, and *Pollard v Tesco Stores* [2006] EWCA 393. More recently he acted for the Secretary of State of Health in the Metal on Metal Hip Litigation and in particular in *Gee v Depuy International Limited* [2018] EWHC 1208 (QB).

DR THOMAS BOYD

Co-author of Chapter 21 The medical records

Dr Boyd is a general practitioner in Bushey, Hertfordshire. He trained in Cambridge and at University College Hospital. He has over 30 years of clinical experience and has been extensively involved in educating and examining general practitioners, which gives him an insight into the standard of care expected of a minimally competent doctor. He was Associate Dean of Postgraduate General Practice and is a senior examiner for the Royal College of General Practitioners. He is an experienced expert, having provided reports in over 1000 cases for claimants' solicitors, medical defence organisations, the General Medical Council, the Crown Prosecution Service and the Treasury Solicitor. He has given evidence in court in civil and criminal proceedings and to the General Medical Council. He has addressed AvMA's annual clinical negligence conference, contributed to the AvMA Medical and Legal Journal and to another textbook. He has delivered seminars on medical negligence issues to many groups of doctors and lawyers.

TAMAR BURTON

Co-author of Chapter 10 Consent

Tamar Burton was called to the Bar in 2012 and is a tenant at Cloisters. She acts exclusively for claimants in her clinical negligence and personal injury work.

She is often led in complex clinical negligence claims, involving injuries at birth and spinal injuries. She also acts as sole counsel in claims against GPs, dentists, private hospitals as well as against NHS Trusts. She has a particular interest in representing families at inquests concerning deaths in hospital and mental health-related deaths.

In 2018 she was appointed as a junior counsel to the Infected Blood Inquiry, chaired by Sir Brian Langstaff.

DR JONATHAN COOK

Author of Chapter 9 The proof of negligence and Chapter 23 Human rights

Jonathan is a tenant in Cloisters. He specialises in personal injury, clinical negligence and employment law. Jonathan represents claimants in personal injury and clinical negligence claims and has assisted in complex High Court proceedings. He acts for both claimants and respondents in his employment law practice and has acted as sole counsel in the Employment Appeal Tribunal. Jonathan has experience of high value psychiatric injury claims and the cross-over between employment law and personal injury. He has been a contributor to PLC Magazine.

Before coming to the Bar, Jonathan undertook a PhD in Politics and International Studies at the University of Cambridge, where his research focused on the foreign policy of the United States during the Cold War. He is also a keen athlete, and formerly represented England at senior international level in track and field.

EMMA CORKILL

Co-author of Chapter 16 Product liability in a medical context

Emma practises at 39 Essex Chambers. She has a split personal injury and clinical negligence practice, acting for both claimants and defendants. In clinical negligence cases, Emma is regularly instructed by the NHSLA and private insurance companies as well medical and dental defence organisations. Her experience includes cases involving negligent diagnosis, failure to refer, negligent treatment and lack of consent. Her extensive advisory practice has seen her deal with claims covering a broad spectrum of medical complaints, such as birth injuries, cancer, gynaecological conditions, sub-standard plastic surgery and negligent optical treatment.

Emma is a member of the Executive Committee of PIBA and an advocacy trainer for Inner Temple. She is a contributor to the Personal Injury section of *Bullen & Leake & Jacob's Precedents of Pleadings*.

ROMILLY CUMMERSON

Co-author of Chapter 16 Product liability in a medical context

Romilly practises at 39 Essex Chambers. She is recommended as a leading junior in clinical negligence and personal injury in the *Legal 500*. Her clinical negligence practice covers a wide variety of claims, involving all branches of the medical profession, including those relating to surgical error, delayed diagnosis, issues of consent, prescribing errors, the inadequate provision of nursing care and/or hospital facilities, and the defective design/manufacture of medical and healthcare products. Romilly is instructed by NHSR in a large number of claims arising out of the use of prostheses with metal-on-metal bearing surfaces in total hip replacement surgery.

GEMMA DALY

Contributor to Chapter 24 Court of Protection and issues involving capacity

Gemma Daly is a tenant at Doughty Street Chambers. She is a specialist in mental capacity and mental health law, inquests, and public law. She regularly appears in the Court of Protection, challenges detentions under the Mental Health Act, and represents families at inquests. Before being called to the Bar and joining Doughty Street Chambers, Gemma specialised in social security law, representing clients at First tier and Upper Tribunals.

SARAH FRASER BUTLIN

Author of Chapter 12 Wrongful birth and Chapter 13 The Congenital Disabilities Act 1976

Sarah Fraser Butlin is a tenant at Cloisters and is a clinical negligence practitioner. She is experienced in all types of clinical negligence claims, but has a particular interest in birth accidents, including high value cerebral palsy cases and stillbirths causing psychiatric injury. Sarah has a strong academic profile and combines her practice at the Bar with a Fellowship at Selwyn College, Cambridge. Consequently she is regularly instructed in matters raising difficult and novel issues of law, including claims relating to unlawful killing claim and Articles 2 and 8, and negligent misstatement and intended beneficiary points. She is currently junior counsel to the Infected Blood Inquiry.

Recent highlight cases include:

- K: Inquest dealing with the failure to recognise occlusion of a prosthetic mitral valve arising out of the deceased's pregnancy and under anti-coagulation. Following submissions, a Report to Prevent Future Deaths was made. Clinical negligence claim settled for substantial sum.
- ENE: successful settlement of hypoxic brain injury claim for £8million; junior to Patricia Hitchcock QC.
- ETS: successful settlement of cerebral palsy claim for £8.1million; junior to Simon Taylor QC.
- Z: successful settlement of cerebral palsy claim for over £9 million; junior to Simeon Maskrey QC.

TOM GILLIE

Co-author of Chapter 22 Experts

Tom Gillie is barrister at Cloisters. He has a particular interest in clinical negligence claims, in which he acts exclusively for claimants. Tom represents clients in high value claims in the High Court and County Court, including in cases of wrongful diagnosis, necrotising fasciitis and negligent surgical procedures.

CARON HEYES

Author of Chapter 2 The structure of the National Health Service, and contributed to Chapter 19 The inquest – the law, procedure and funding (Funding and the recoverability of costs' section)

Caron Heyes is a senior associate in Fieldfisher's medical negligence team, based in their London office. She has 18 years' experience bringing claims for children and adults who have been left catastrophically injured as a result of medical negligence. She is a member of the Law Society

Clinical Negligence Accreditation Panel and APIL. Chambers rates her as a Star Associate.

Caron's cases include claims for birth injury, failings in treatment of neonate and children, fatal accident claims arising from errors in GP and surgical treatment and maternal deaths, and claims arising out of failings in fertility treatment. She advises on inquests and provides representation at the hearings.

In the last 15 months Caron has recovered in excess of £39m for her clients by way of interim and final damages awards most recently obtaining a six-figure settlement for a woman who sustained a life-changing perineal injury at birth and £19.6 m for a child with an acquired brain injury caused by substandard treatment at the age of five months.

She has often spoken at legal courses provided by AvMA and CLT, provided in-house training for charities, and regularly comments in the press on important issues. In parallel with her case work, Caron works extensively with charities such as the Children's Trust and Child Bereavement UK, Inquest and Changing Faces, and chaired Fieldfisher's Charity Committee until very recently. Caron has also worked voluntarily with Action against Medical Accidents (AvMA) and helped set up their Inquest Project in 2010. AvMA were a core participant at the Mid Staffordshire NHS Foundation Trust Public Inquiry, and Caron worked with their Chief Executive reviewing and analysing the evidence as it was produced.

Caron writes articles for legal press and on occasion for the national press. For instance, discussing lack of regulation in the fertility industry, estimated to be worth £15 billion a year, Caron commented in *The Times* that the terrible emotional impact of mistakes by fertility clinics leaves people devastated when they are at their most vulnerable, whilst also usually leaving them significantly out of pocket and with little right of redress.

Describing the work of Fieldfisher's clinical negligence team, Caron says:

> 'Being part of a team that consistently takes on cases where people's lives have been shattered following mistakes in medical treatment is a privilege. As lawyers, we can make certain that everything possible is done to help such people rebuild their lives and to live as best they can.

> We can't turn back time but we can put in place funding to provide specialist care and treatment and, just importantly, provide financial security to families who work like superheroes and give everything to their disabled children.'

Memberships held: Law Society Panel for Clinical Negligence, APIL.

PATRICIA HITCHCOCK QC

Co-author of Chapter 22 Experts

Patricia is one of the most senior of the strong team of silks who head the Cloisters Clinical Negligence and Personal Injury group. She is a specialist in catastrophic injury resulting from clinical negligence or accidents, both liability and quantum, as well as related administrative and regulatory matters. She is a trained mediator (CEDR-accredited 2003) and also sits as a Recorder in crime. Regularly instructed for many years by leading specialist solicitors in multi-million pound cases, she is especially interested in brain and spinal injuries, oncology and mental health, and cases involving child and adolescent claimants.

Before coming to the Bar, Patricia worked as a non-fiction book editor, and discovered an aptitude for advocacy when elected Mother of the NUJ Chapel at Hutchinson Books. She was called to the Bar in 1988 and embarked initially on a broad-based common law practice – personal injury, employment, discrimination, education – dominated by criminal defence, with around 100 Crown Court trials. In 1996 she specialised in medical law and took silk in 2011. She has chaired three AvMA medico-legal conferences and is a long-term AvMA member and supporter, as well as a member of APIL, MIND and Inquest. She is also co-author of the Catastrophic Injury Division of *Butterworths Personal Injury Litigation Service*. She is married to a sculptor, with two adult children and a granddaughter.

LINDA JACOBS

Author of Chapter 19 The inquest – the law, procedure and funding, and Chapter 25 Wales

Linda Jacobs is a tenant at Cloisters who specialises in clinical negligence, personal injury, and healthcare law; inquest and professional regulatory law; and First-tier Tribunal (Criminal Injuries Compensation) Appeal claims. Linda has extensive advisory and advocacy experience in a broad range of clinical negligence cases, including injuries of maximum severity (birthing injury, spinal and neurological injury, delayed diagnosis of cancer, and fatal injuries), to claims including hip and knee replacement surgeries, abdominal, gynaecology and urological/renal injuries, cardiothoracic negligence and limb amputation. Linda has particular expertise in representing families at inquests (including jury inquests) often preceding successful civil litigation claims. In addition, Linda has experience of appellate advisory work following inquests. Linda has been instructed by healthcare practitioners in cases before the General Medical Council and the Nursing and Midwifery Council. Linda is ranked in *Chambers and Partners* and *Legal 500 Clinical Negligence*, and *Legal 500 Inquests and Inquires*. Prior to being called to the Bar, Linda was a Sister in intensive care in one of London's leading teaching hospitals. Her specialist medical knowledge and experience means that she is comfortable dealing with complex medical facts and legal issues, expert evidence, and complex quantum cases.

HUGH JOHNSON

Author of Chapter 17 Procedure to service of proceedings and Chapter 18 Procedure from service to trial

Hugh Johnson is a Partner at Stewarts. The 'black sheep' in a family of medics, he qualified as a solicitor in 2005 and has now undertaken clinical negligence litigation for some 14 years. He trained at a large regional firm, before moving to Stewarts in 2008 to specialise in catastrophic injury claims. Hugh has a particular interest in spinal injury and claims arising from the mismanagement of mental health conditions.

Hugh is an APIL senior litigator and is Coordinator of the APIL spinal injuries special interest group. He has been recommended in *Chambers and Partners* as 'sought after for his expertise in claims relating to spinal injuries' (2015) and noted to be a practitioner that 'provides good client care and prepares his work to the highest standard' (2018). He has secured numerous substantial settlements on behalf of clients with permanent, life-changing injuries.

NICK KNOWLES

Author of Chapter 26 Funding

Nick Knowles has been a partner at Stewarts for 20 years handling catastrophic clinical negligence claims, mainly brain and spinal cord injury. He often represents children and protected parties and is instructed by the Official Solicitor. He has secured many multi-million pound settlements for his clients over the years. He represented the claimant in the important case of *Masterman-Lister* which formulated the basis of the test for mental capacity.

Nick is a member of the AvMA Specialist Clinical Negligence Panel, he is Fellow of the Royal Society of Medicine and a Fellow of APIL.

He regularly appears in both the *Legal 500* and *Chambers and Partners*, being commonly described in terms such as, 'a leader in his field', 'unflappable', 'with a sure touch and excellent judgement', 'who inspires a great deal of confidence in clients'.

WILLIAM LATIMER-SAYER QC

Author of Chapter 15 Economic loss

William specialises in catastrophic personal injury and clinical negligence. He has a special interest in quantum and the majority of his work is related to contested assessment of damages hearings. He is consistently highly-rated by the independent legal directories, being ranked by *Chambers and Partners* in band 1 for both personal injury and clinical negligence.

William is the General Editor of *Schedules of Loss: Calculating Damages* (4th edn, 2018, Bloomsbury Professional), the leading practitioner textbook on schedules of loss; a co-editor of *Facts & Figures* (2019/2020, Sweet & Maxwell) and the current Chairman of the Ogden Working party, which is responsible for drafting the Ogden Tables, used by all practitioners and judges to assess damages in personal injury and clinical negligence cases.

William won Chambers and Partners' Personal Injury silk of the year in 2018 having previously won Personal Injury junior of the year in 2008 and 2010.

CHESCA LORD

Author of Chapter 7 Causation and damage and Chapter 8 Foreseeability and remoteness

Chesca is a barrister at Cloisters. She specialises in quantum-only catastrophic injury cases, and has been involved in the successful recovery of over £150 million for injured clients. She has particular expertise in negligently inflicted cerebral palsy at birth or during the neonatal period, including acting as junior counsel in a recent case which settled for a capitalised value in excess of £38 million. Other recent work includes claims involving amputation, spinal injuries, acquired brain injuries, vision loss and fatal accidents cases arising from delayed cancer diagnoses.

MONIQUE MARINO

Research Assistant for Chapter 2 The structure of the National Health Service in England

Monique is in the medical negligence department at Fieldfisher LLP. She graduated from the University of Exeter with a First Class law degree. Monique is a competitive sportswoman. She has also worked closely with several charitable organisations, including Shilhay Community, which enables homeless or vulnerably housed people to improve their quality of life. Monique is passionate about social responsibility and has been involved in, and led, many charitable projects.

MARTYN MCLEISH

Author of Chapter 5 The duty of care, Chapter 6 Breach of duty and strict liability, and Chapter 27 Costs

Martyn is Joint Head of Cloisters. He is recommended in *Chambers & Partners* and the *Legal 500* for clinical negligence. His practice covers a wide range of high value clinical negligence cases. He is a Vice-Chairman of the Bar Council Remuneration Committee and is on the Executive Committee of the Personal Injuries Bar Association.

CATHERINE MEENAN

Catherine is, at the time of writing, a pupil at Cloisters who assisted with compiling a summary of the important changes since the 7th edition for publicity purposes.

SOPHY MILES

Co-author of Chapter 24 Court of Protection and issues involving capacity

Sophy is a tenant at Doughty Street Chambers. She qualified as a solicitor in 1989. She was a founding partner at Miles and Partners LLP where she led the mental health and capacity team for 16 years, before becoming a consultant in 2012. Sophy has a busy and varied Court of Protection practice which includes personal welfare, international adult protection, medical treatment and property cases, as well as challenges against deprivation of liberty authorisations. She advises in all areas of mental health and mental capacity law, and is an accredited mediator (Regent's University London).

Sophy is co-author of the Court of Protection Handbook: *A User's Guide* (2nd edn, 2016, Legal Action Group, 3rd edn forthcoming) and of the *Mental Health Tribunal Handbook* (1st edn, 2014, Legal Action Group). She regularly writes and trains on the Mental Health Act, the Mental Capacity Act and on the Court of Protection.

LISA O'DWYER

Author of Chapter 3 Non legal remedies; and Director of Medico-Legal Services/Action against Medical Accidents (AvMA) (AvMA is the UK charity for patient safety and justice)

Lisa qualified as a solicitor in 1993 and specialised in claimant clinical negligence claims before joining AvMA in March 2009. Lisa pioneered AvMA's Pro Bono Inquest Service in 2010. The inquest service is now an integral part of AvMA's client services. Lisa manages both AvMA's client services and lawyers service.

Lisa sits on various committees aimed at improving the patient experience when things go wrong including the Health Innovation Networks (HIN) group on 'Speaking Out' which looks at why healthcare workers are reluctant to speak up; 'Safety for Patients through Quality Review' committee (SPQR) which looks at evaluating the Medical Examiners review of patient records to identify potentially avoidable deaths due to problems in care as well. Lisa is a member of the Civil Justice Council (CJC) working party on fixed costs in clinical negligence claims where her focus is on how any process or scheme of fixed recoverable costs might affect issues of patient safety and access to justice.

CATRIONA STIRLING

Author of Chapter 4 Legal remedies

Catriona is a specialist clinical negligence barrister at Cloisters. She has developed a substantial practice encompassing the whole range of liability and quantum work across this area. She has acted in multiple maximum severity spinal and brain injury cases and amputation cases. She has particular expertise in quantum matters and co-authors one of the leading practitioner textbooks on the calculation of personal injury damages.

LISA SULLIVAN

Author of Chapter 20 Limitation

Lisa Sullivan is a tenant at Cloisters and is a specialist in clinical negligence and personal injury.

Lisa is experienced in a wide range of clinical negligence claims, including high-value cerebral palsy and acquired brain injury, spinal injury cases including cauda equina, claims involving wrongful birth, and delayed diagnosis of cancer. She also has experience of a full range of quantum issues and in particular local authority care issues.

She is recommended in both *Chambers UK* and *Legal 500* for clinical negligence.

Lisa is an advocacy trainer for the Inner Temple and has trained on the South Eastern Circuit Advanced Advocacy Course. She is also a Deputy Queen's Bench Master.

ASWINI WEERERATNE QC

Co-author of Chapter 11 Adults without capacity and Chapter 24 Court of Protection and issues involving capacity

Aswini is a tenant in Doughty Street Chambers. She is an acknowledged expert in human rights, mental health and capacity law, focusing, in particular, on the protection of vulnerable adults, children and young people in many different spheres of life. She utilises her expertise in a wide range of practice areas and cases, in contentious and non-contentious matters. For example, health and welfare cases in the Court of Protection, and concerning public and private law issues, actions against state and private bodies such as sporting bodies, including assault and unlawful detention claims, historic child abuse claims, inquests and inquiries, reporting restrictions and international law. She appears in interventions for NGOs in cases before the higher courts, and advises on proposed legislation.

In addition, she has a strong background in investigatory and regulatory work, and is a qualified mediator. Aswini chairs the Investigating Committee of the General Pharmaceutical Council. She has chaired and produced published reports for six independent inquiries into homicides by patients within mental health services. She acts for core participants in several strands of investigation being undertaken by the Independent Inquiry into Child Sexual Abuse, chaired by Professor Alexis Jay.

Acronyms

BMLR   Butterworths' *Medico-Legal Reports*, published from June 1992.

JPIL   *Journal of Personal Injury Litigation.*

Med LR   The *Medical Law Reports*. From the beginning of 1998 the series has been published by Lloyds of London Press (the citation has been changed to [2001] Lloyd's Rep Med).

ML   *Medical Litigation*: this is the journal that since the beginning of 1998 kept practitioners up to date with all the latest developments in the medical negligence field – judgments with commentaries, writs, settlements, appeals set down, news and views, articles, etc. It ceased hard copy publication at the end of 2004. Its management continues to run two websites: www.medneg.com for practitioners, and www.medicalclaims.co.uk for the public.

MLC   *Medical Litigation Cases*: this is the invaluable database of full transcripts on the Internet at *www.medneg.com*, originally conceived by *Medical Litigation* and now run by *Medical Litigation Online*. Access is by subscription and every UK judgment relevant to medical claims since the end of 1997, as well as many overseas judgments, is posted in full transcript. Also, significant older medical cases are currently being posted all the while. In addition, every other UK medical negligence decision from every available hard copy source appears in summary form in the medical negligence index section. In line with the switch to electronic publishing and citation, MLC will be dropping the citation of the year and will only read, eg, *A* v *B* MLC 00999, rather than *A* v *B* [2001] MLC 00999. For that reason some MLC cases in the text are given a year reference and others are not. Where I have given only a MLC reference for a case I have in any event added the year as I think that information is helpful. The website also contains many articles, news items, and indexed lists of lawyers and experts. The site has an excellent search engine. Anyone practising in the field of medical claims needs to subscribe to this website.

Table of Statutes

References at the right-hand side are to page numbers.

Table of Statutory Instruments

References at the right-hand side are to page numbers.

Table of Cases

References at the right-hand side are to page numbers.

B

F

R

W

Quotations

On law

In law, what plea so tainted and corrupt,
But, being seasoned with a gracious voice,
Obscures the show of evil?

The Merchant of Venice (Bassanio)

I must say that, as a litigant, I should dread a lawsuit beyond almost anything else, short of sickness and death.

Judge Learned Hand

The definition of the duty of care is a matter for the law and the courts. They cannot stand idly by if the profession, by an excess of paternalism, denies their patients a real choice. In a word, the law will not permit the medical profession to play God.

Sir John Donaldson MR

The problem with Bolam *is that it inhibited the courts exercising a restraining influence. The courts must recognise that theirs is essentially a regulatory role and they should not interfere unless interference is justified. But when interference is justified they must not be deterred from doing so by any principle such as the fact that what has been done is in accord with a practice approved of by a respectable body of medical opinion.*

Lord Woolf (January 2001)

On medicine

Physicians of all men are most happy. What good success soever they have, the world proclaimeth, and what faults they commit, the earth covereth.

Francis Quarles (1592-1644)

In the practice of surgery particularly, the public are exposed to great risks from the number of ignorant persons professing a knowledge of the art, without the least pretensions to the necessary qualifications, and they often inflict very serious injury on those who are so unfortunate as to fall into their hands.

Baron Garrow (1822)

The doctor is often more to be feared than the disease.

Old French proverb

Doctors are men who prescribe medicine of which they know little to human beings of whom they know nothing.

Voltaire

The primary function of the doctor is to entertain the patient while he gets better on his own.

Voltaire

Proper treatment will cure a cold in not more than seven days, but left to itself it will hang on for a week.

HG Felsen

It is unwise to place any profession or other body providing services to the public on a pedestal where their actions cannot be subject to close scrutiny. The greater the power the body has, the more important is this need.

Lord Woolf (January 2001)

Chapter 1

Introduction

Andrew Buchan

No one wants to sue or complain about a doctor. However the medical law reports attest to situations where doctors have been so negligent that no responsible body of medical opinion can defend them. On the one hand defendant's lawyers see themselves as the bastions of the NHS and claimant's lawyers are greedy whingers. On the other hand claimant's see themselves as seeking justice for patients injured by the system.

A detailed discussion about these two positions is beyond the scope of this chapter but there can be no doubt that despite the best of intentions – medical practitioners cause considerable harm and suffering to many of their patients. This was emphasised recently by none other than the Secretary of State for Health.

On BBC's Radio 2: 'Political Thinking'[1] Jeremy Hunt (Secretary of State for Health), was asked by Nick Robinson what makes him and angry and his reply was telling. He said:

> 'Well, let me tell you what has been the biggest jolt in my time in my time in the cabinet. When I just arrived at the Department of Health and that job you are dealing with a crisis like every month somethings going wrong and the first thing I had to deal with was Mid-Staff's. And I remember Sir David Nicholson who was the Chief Executive of the NHS taking me aside and saying:
>
>> "Jeremy you have to understand that in medicine it's just the way it works – 10% of patients are harmed through medical error" and I said:
>>
>>> 'well how many die?'
>
> and the Department of Health dug up the research, being the good old NHS we've done lots of research and they said:
>
>> "3.6% of hospital deaths have a 50% or more chance of being avoidable."
>
> It sounds like a statistic but I did the numbers and said:
>
>> "does that mean that we have 150 avoidable deaths every week in the NHS?" and they said:
>
> 'yes' and I said:
>
>> "why isn't anyone talking about this?" ... '

---

1   31 May 2019. For more amusing examples of how things can go wrong I recommend 'This is going to hurt (Secret Diaries of a Junior Doctor' by Dr Adam Kay (2017).

The conversation then changed to other matters but it is not difficult to understand why the experienced mandarin[2] might not want to broadcast such human suffering from our cherished institution.

Despite this, the claimant's lawyers are still being accused of being greedy and milking the system.

It is not the job of this textbook to attempt to answer why this is happening. Just to say that the scholar who has studied and relied upon the last six editions of this book will realise how the emphasis has changed from a necessarily litigious approach (where the claimant's lawyers were truly on the back foot against well organised and experienced defendant's lawyers) to the current state of affairs where there is greater equality of arms as a large number of claimant's legal battles have been won and claimant's lawyers are also more experienced. As a result, the emphasis has to be on recognising and dealing with complaints as soon as practicable and avoiding litigation if at all possible. The advice and principles set out in this book apply for conciliation as well as litigation.

This Eighth Edition reflects this modern approach. I have deliberately chosen a large selection of experienced clinical negligence practitioners to update and supplement the chapters of the Seventh Edition.

A FASCINATING SUBJECT

There is arguably no area of law that provokes such public interest, and so immediately, from the non-lawyer as clinical negligence.

Within the legal profession, the work has a cachet that ordinary personal injury does not. This is bemusing because some personal injury cases can be extremely complicated with respect to liability. Some clinical negligence cases less so. Lawyers, particularly counsel, are quick to say that they specialise in the field, even if their involvement is modest. Many of the solicitors who are qualified to do the work form a tight-knit group, striving to outdo their rivals with some striking victory, and ever on the look-out for new ways of extending the boundaries of the clinical negligence claim.

Why does this branch of the law attract such interest and evoke so keen, often so emotional, a response from the lay person? It is partly because it is almost everyone's experience to have at one time or another been in the hands of the doctors, but, more importantly, it stems above all from the nature of the doctor's role. The patient looks to the physician on the one hand as the comforter and healer who will make him well and happy; he has the learning and the magic that will bring relief from fear and pain. The patient, whether consciously acknowledging it or not, longs to be relieved or comforted. All this gives the physician a hierophantic status. On the other hand, the patient resents his dependence and is not averse to debunking the myth; a myth, be it noted, that he has himself created. This relationship is not entirely dissimilar to the emotional duality that a child feels towards his parents. In an age where the child has learnt that obedience to parents is not necessarily the norm, parental control is less and less effective, and for today's children anything is permissible, it is not surprising that the divine aspect of the medical profession has taken

---

2   As opposed to politician.

a beating (aided enormously by their own well-publicised malpractices). There is perhaps something of a temptation when specialising in cases against the medical profession to regard it as a sort of crusade, as do many of those who specialise in actions against the police, as if not only policemen but also doctors represent some sort of authority figures with which one has not within oneself completely come to terms; and when that happens one forgets too easily the marvellous skills and devoted care that generally characterise the practice of medicine. But this is not a textbook on psychology; the issues raised here are merely by way of explanation for the fascination that lawsuits against the medical profession have for the ordinary member of the public and for the almost emotional response that they can arouse in lawyer and non-lawyer alike.

THE GROWTH OF LITIGATION

There is no doubt that clinical negligence litigation has grown enormously over the last 40 years. In earlier times,[3] such a claim was unusual and stood little chance of success. That was partly because it was not within the current ethos to accuse the 'god-like' doctors (or any professional for that matter) of incompetent treatment: patients shrank from such a course and judges (themselves coming from professional practice) did not approve of it. Lord Denning used to say that to prove a doctor guilty of negligence required a higher standard of proof than if the accusation was levelled against a non-professional.[4] In 1953 Finnemore J said:

> It is the duty of a doctor to exercise reasonable skill and care, but a simple mistake in diagnosis or treatment is not of itself negligence. The court is not bound to shut its eyes to the fact that there are quite a few cases at the present time in which doctors are sued for negligence. That may arise from the changing relationship between doctor and patient, but *it* matters not. There is a considerable onus on the court to see that persons do not easily obtain damages simply because there is some medical or surgical mistake made. But the court will not shrink from facing the issue if it finds that the doctor has failed to give to a case the proper skill and care which patients have a right to expect.[5]

That represented the traditional view: insistence that medical mistakes did not necessarily involve negligence, regardless of the consequences, and a friendly nod in the direction of the patient.

Practicalities, both social and legal, were also against the patient. Few doctors were prepared to give evidence for the patient. It took years to create lists of fair-minded specialists who would give an impartial opinion on the standard of care. Even now, if the patient goes to the wrong expert, s/he will get a whitewash (whitewashes are still the forte of a fair number of oft-appearing defence experts, regardless of their parroting

---

3   At least prior to the mid-1980's and the inception of AvMA.
4   In *Hucks v Cole* [1993] 4 Med LR 393, CA, Lord Denning said that a charge of negligence against a professional man was serious. It stood on a different footing to a charge of negligence against the driver of a motor car. The consequences were far more serious. It affected his professional status and reputation. The burden of proof was correspondingly greater. As the charge was so grave, so should the proof be clear.
5   *Edler v Greenwich and Deptford Hospital Management Committee* (1953) Times, 7 March.

their impartial duty owed to the court). In earlier years statements of witnesses and the evidence of experts were not disclosed until they came to the witness box. It was trial by ambush. Gradually the scene changed, thanks to the persistent efforts of those, like Action for Victims of Medical Accidents (now known as Action against Medical Accidents – AvMA) and the lawyers who supported it, who fought unrelentingly for the rights of the patient. Now, due particularly to the Woolf reforms, a cards-on-the-table approach is a living and mandatory reality. But there are still one or two judges, usually appointed from a successful defence practice at the Bar, who are unreasonably slow to find for the patient and who will always, if at all possible, 'prefer' the evidence of the defence expert to that of the claimant's expert.

THE EXPENSE OF LITIGATION

Whoever wins a clinical negligence action against the NHS, the taxpayer, and/or other patients, are the losers. The lawyers always get something out of it, but who would begrudge them that? If the patient achieves compensation the NHS has to pay the costs of both sides as well as the compensation.

All the recent changes to funding and to the NHS generally, as well as to legal procedures, are dealt with in more detail in the next few chapters. But however clinical negligence litigation is funded and whatever the rules of procedure, it will always be expensive because every medical claim with apparent potential requires from the outset that the medical records be obtained, sorted and carefully investigated, that at least one and probably more than one expert report be obtained from carefully selected independent experts, and that then, unless liability is admitted, the claim be subjected to protracted and complex argument over the content, acceptability and consequences of the medical care afforded to the patient.

ON THE OTHER HAND

The cry is often heard from certain quarters to the effect that greedy patients, over-indulgent judges and, worst of all, unprincipled lawyers, are bringing the NHS to its knees, to the general detriment of the public, and that something has to be done about the growth of clinical negligence claims and the huge rise in the number and the quantum of compensation awards. Yet some of the foremost authorities on the subject offer a different view. In January 2001 at University College, London, Lord Woolf said that in the past courts had been excessively deferential to the medical profession but that this automatic assumption of beneficence had been dented. He said it was unwise to place any profession or other body providing services to the public on a pedestal where their actions could not be subject to close scrutiny. The courts should take a more robust view of negligence by the medical profession and not be deterred by the accepted test for negligence that asked whether what had been done was in accord with a respectable body of medical opinion. He said he could not help believing that the behaviour of the medical personnel involved in recent scandals betrayed a lack of appreciation of the limits of their responsibility. Though not motivated by personal gain, they had lost sight of their power and authority, and had acted as though they were able to take any action they thought desirable, irrespective of the views of others. That over-deferential approach was captured by the phrase 'doctor knows best'. The contemporary approach was a more critical one. It could be said that doctor knows best if he acted reasonably and logically and got his facts right. Lord Woolf also pointed out the increase of more than 30% over the previous year in the number of complaints to the General Medical Council and said this had called the very future of that body into question. He said other factors had made judges less deferential: the difficulties people had in bringing successful claims; increasing awareness of patients' rights; the closer scrutiny of doctors by courts in places such as Canada and Australia, and the scale of medical negligence litigation, which was a 'disaster area'. Lord Woolf said all this indicated that the health service was not giving sufficient priority to avoiding medical mishap and treating patients justly when mishaps occurred (for the full text, see (2001) 9 *Medical Law Review*).

At about the same time, Sir Donald Irving, the then chairman of the GMC, accused doctors of 'deep-seated flaws', including excessive paternalism, secrecy and lack of respect for patients. Dr Michael Wilkes, chairman of the BMA's medical committee, responded, saying that no one in the medical profession expected the public – or the courts – to put doctors on a pedestal, and that the medical profession was working very hard to improve the quality of practice and to ensure that cases of incompetence were dealt with swiftly and fairly.

Over the last few years the element of hostility between lawyers and doctors has reduced to an appreciable extent owing to better liaison, communication and association. In other words, the two professions talk to each other more, rather than just waving their assegais. There is now a greater understanding that the litigation war arises principally from medical mistakes rather than greedy lawyers or ungrateful patients and that therefore eradicating mistakes by a combination of risk assessment, clinical governance and proper training (and not overworking the staff) is the way to turn a war into an alliance, which would benefit not only the public coffers but also the patients.

So the truth lies somewhere between the opposing views. The medical profession is largely good, often marvellous, but sometimes less than satisfactory. The lawyers, on both sides, are largely fair-minded and responsible, but sometimes too quick and too keen to sue or to defend. The judges are on the whole astute and impartial, but sometimes neither one nor the other. However, the practice of the courts in assigning medical trials to whomever is available, rather than to a judge with at least some experience of medical claims, is not conducive to an informed judgment, but only to a guaranteed lottery. But at least the inexperienced judges usually demonstrate a degree of humility in the face of the wide experience of the lawyers appearing before them.

In the Seventh Edition I wrote:

As of 22 January 2012 the fate of the National Health Service appears to stand in the balance.

How times change. Instead the NHS funding was used as a political tool in the BREXIT referendum campaign. The NHS appears now to be more secure than ever or at least until the economy dives after any BREXIT.

Part One

Chapter 2

The structure of the National Health Service in England

Caron Heyes with research by Monique Marino

INTRODUCTION

Understanding the chain of command in the NHS can often be essential to extract the correct disclosure to build a case. This will apply not just in civil negligence claims against the NHS and private health care practitioners, but also in rationing cases, Human Rights Act 1998 claims, and Disability Discrimination Act 1995 claims.

The purpose of this chapter is to provide a short introduction to the structure of the NHS, and the government bodies that exist to regulate and support it. Further information can be found in publications such as the NHS Guide 2017–18: A clear and concise overview of the NHS.[1]

The NHS headcount in January 2018 was 1,205949. Professionally qualified staff make up 54% of the workforce.[2] It is a massive organisation with a heavy burden of care. It is also a constantly evolving and dynamic organisation, of limited resources. At the same time it is an immensely complex organisation requiring a structure that provides chains of accountability, provision and oversight of funding, manages contracting, commissioning of services, and a robust regulatory framework alongside the provision of healthcare services.

The NHS is the responsibility of parliament which in turn devolves its responsibility to the state Department of Health (DoH), and three other bodies: NHS England (NHSE); Public Health England (PHE); and Health Education England (HEE).

The DoH develops and drives healthcare delivery in England, and also provides funding for services. It therefore produces national policies and legislation, plans for the future, and accounts to parliament. The DoH funds NHSE, PHE and HEE. NHS Improvement also works with NHS England to develop long term planning for the NHS.

---

1   NHS Guide 2017–18; A clear and concise overview of the NHS, published by Wilmington Healthcare.
2   See statistics (PDF) at https://digital.nhs.uk/data-and-information/publications/statistical/nhs-workforce-statistics/nhs-workforce-statistics---january-2018.

NHSE runs four regional teams (London, South of England, Midlands and East of England and North of England). Clinical commissioning groups (CCGs) report to the regional teams as well as to Healthwatch England and Health and Wellbeing Boards. CCGs are scrutinised directly by NHSE and the regional teams. However, they are responsible for their own pot of funding, with NHSE directly funding secondary care providers.

PHE is responsible for and funds local authorities and Health and Wellbeing Boards. HEE is responsible for local education and training boards, and funds them.

Thus a chain of accountability runs from local bodies up through the regions to government, ending with the Health Secretary ultimately being accountable to parliament for the NHS.

What follows is a short description of the different bodies and functions that coalesce into the NHS.

PARLIAMENTARY OVERSIGHT OF THE NHS

The NHS is funded by the taxpayer, and parliament scrutinises the service through the medium of parliamentary debates, and a range of Select Committees, in particular the Health and Social Care Committee and the Public Accounts Committee. For instance an inquiry was launched in June 2018 by the Health and Social Care Committee about the implications of the latest five year funding plan.[3]

THE DEPARTMENT OF HEALTH AND SOCIAL CARE (DOH)

The Department of Health and Social Care (DoH) is the state body which is responsible for leadership and setting the strategic direction of the NHS in England. It is managed by the ministerial team led by the Secretary of State for Health. The Secretary of State is supported by the Minister of State, the Parliamentary Under Secretary of State, the Executive Board, the Permanent Secretary and the Board (made up of six board members and including the Chief Medical Officer and Chief Scientific Officer).

The DoH provides political leadership and is responsible for making the main executive decisions on strategy, policy framework priorities, and provision of overall resources. However they do not become involved in local decisions. Its responsibilities include: NHS operations and performance; overall financial control; strategic policy; healthcare quality regulation; failing hospitals; patient safety; workforce (and its pay and pensions); as well as leading the Care Quality Commission; Health Education England and NHS Improvement; NHS Resolution; NHS Property services; and the Human Tissue Authority. Responsibilities are split between different ministers. They are advised by various boards and committees. There is an Executive Committee that considers all major policy and operational issues that have a significant impact on the work of the DoH. The Audit and

---

3   See https://www.parliament.uk/business/committees/committees-a-z/commons-select/ health-and-social-care-committee/inquiries/parliament-2017/nhs-funding-inquiry-17-19/.

Risk Committee advises on risk management, corporate governance and assurance in the DoH and its subsidiary bodies. There is a management committee that oversees the financial and assurance side of projects.

The Ministerial team and the Executive Board are advised by a number of advisory groups that give expert advice to help form policies. They are advised by the National Medical Directorate. That is headed by the National Medical Director who leads a team of National Clinical Directors and their clinical advice is used amongst other duties to drive improvement and transformation of services, identify and deliver clinical priorities and support commissioning. As well as the directors there is a body of chief officers in different medical disciplines who advise the government on their areas of speciality. These chief officers have moved out of the DoH and are now part of NHS England.

ARM'S LENGTH BODIES (ARMS)

An ARM is a standalone national organisation that provides regulation of an aspect of the NHS, is tasked with improving standards and protecting the public, and supporting local services. It falls under the aegis of the DoH. Reform in 2013 has reduced significantly the number of ARMs, and the NHS now has executive agencies responsible for a particular business area, such as PHE. There are also executive non-departmental public bodies that feed not the process of national government but are not part of any government department, and the Care Quality Commission is an example of this type of ARM. Finally, there are also Special Health Authorities (SHAs) that are independent but subject to government and therefore ministerial direction. The Health Research Authority is an example of a SHA.

NON-DEPARTMENTAL PUBLIC BODIES

Care Quality Commission (CQC)

The CQC is the independent regulator of health and social care providers in England. It maintains a register for providers. This includes providers of mental health services, dental, ambulance, primary medical care providers (including GPs). It applies the 'fundamental standards' to all organisations it inspects.

The fundamental standards include the right:

- to receive person-centred care;
- to have dignity and respect maintained;
- for the patient, or anybody legally acting on their behalf, to have given consent prior to any care or treatment being given;
- for the patient not to be given unsafe care or be put at risk of harm that could be avoided;
- for the patient not to suffer any form of abuse or improper treatment while receiving care;
- for the provider to be open and transparent with patients about their care and treatment including telling them if something had gone wrong.

The CGQ publishes its findings. Any report that may be published by the CQC about individual institutions may be of great use in understanding how a healthcare provider may have failed a particular client. However there is often quite a time lag between action and publication.

The CQC is empowered to use enforcement powers such as requirement or warning notices setting out improvements to be made and by what date. It can impose conditions on the registration of any provider of healthcare services, and can also cancel their registration. It can hold the provider to account by issuing cautions and fines, and/or prosecuting cases where people are harmed or placed in danger of harm. It can also intervene when it considers a care provider is going to be forced to exit the market, to encourage other providers and commissioners of services to put in place alternative provision.

NHS England (NHSE)

NHSE is a non-departmental public body which is accountable to the Secretary of State for Health. NHSE leads the NHS in England and is mandated to ensure that the money that is spent on NHS services delivers the best possible care for patients. NHSE provide leadership, coordination and support to the organisations operating in tandem with it and the other ARMs.

At a national level, NHSE acts as commissioner in certain areas (such as specialised services, primary care, offender healthcare and some services for armed forces). It has four regional teams but it is one single organisation operating to a single model with a single board. Each regional team will work closely with the relevant CCGs.

NHSE may also stand in the shoes of now defunct trusts and NHS providers (where their function has not been merged with another provider) for the purposes of naming a defendant.

NHS Improvement (NHSI)

NHSI is responsible for overseeing foundation trusts and NHS trusts, as well as independent providers that provide NHS-funded care. It should offer support to providers to give patients consistently safe, high quality, compassionate care within local health systems that are financially sustainable. It has powers to hold providers to account and, where necessary, intervene, and is focused on offering support to providers and local health systems to help them improve.

It was formed on 1 April 2016 and brought under one roof the functions of:

- monitoring;
- the NHS Trust Development Authority;
- patient safety;
- the Advancing Change Team;
- the intensive support teams.

NHSI has a number of focus areas which include the following categories:

- emergency care (improving quality, safety and patient flow);

- patient safety (improving patient safety and learning from past mistakes;)
- cancer resources (improving waiting times and diagnostic capacity for cancer services);
- workforce (improving staff retention and staff satisfaction);
- finance and use of resource (developing ways to restore the financial position of the NHS and providing support to trusts to identify savings via the Carter review and locum and agency work);
- mental health (improving mental health access and waiting-time standards);
- operational performance (improving and maintaining core standards across all service providers);
- elective care (improving the way service providers manage demand, capacity and operational management);
- culture and leadership (implementing collective leadership strategies);
- maternity and neonatal (making measurable improvements in safety outcomes for women, their babies and families and developing ways to reduce the rates of maternal deaths, stillbirths, neonatal deaths and brain injuries that occur during or soon after birth);
- patient experience and involvement (improving access and input for patients, carers and their families);
- quality improvement (providing advice and support on how to use quality improvement approaches and methodologies);
- learning disabilities (improving and providing resources to help make a sustainable difference to the quality and consistency with which safe and therapeutic services for people with learning disabilities, autism or both, are delivered).

In each of its focus areas, NHSI works with service providers providing them with additional support and issuing guidelines, frameworks and materials to assist them in making the above improvements. This shows an increasing move towards a collaborative approach to providing healthcare services in England.

Of particular importance is NHSI's focus on patient safety by learning from past mistakes. To do this, the NHSI uses a number of tools, such as:

- a reporting system to spot emerging patterns at a national level, so that appropriate guidance can be developed and issued to protect patients from harm in the future;
- an alert system where patient safety alerts are issued via the Central Alerting System (CAS) (a web-based cascading system for issuing alerts, important public health messages and other safety critical information and guidance to the NHS and other organisations, including independent providers of health and social care). The patient safety alerts are developed with input from the National Patient Safety Response Advisory Panel. The National Patient Safety Response Advisory Panel brings together frontline healthcare staff, patients and their families, safety experts, royal colleges and other professional and national bodies;
- patient safety review and response reports which cover six month periods, outlining issues and risks in that period which have been put

together by reviewing confidential patient safety incident reports, and the actions taken as a direct result of those incident reports.

Health and Social Care Information Centre (HSCIC)

HSCIC[4] is a national information and technology partner to the health and social care system which first, supervises and organises the collection, analysis and dissemination of national data and statistical information. Second, it is responsible for delivering national IT systems and services to support the health and care system. HSCIC's primary functions can be summarised as:

- collecting, analysing and publishing health and care data;
- designing processes to make submitting data more simplistic for health care service providers;
- providing national information technology for health and care services;
- producing information standards;
- improving the quality of health and care information and data;
- publishing national indicators for health and care, to measure quality of care and progress against policy initiatives;
- giving advice and support to health and care organisations on information and cyber security.

National Institute for Health and Care Excellence (NICE)

NICE is a non-departmental governmental body set up in 1999 providing evidence based guidance, standards and information to help clinicians and health and social care professionals deliver best care.

The nice guidelines should always be consulted to identify what guidance they may have issued about a particular medical treatment or practice. Whilst these are generally not mandatory treatment protocols, but guidelines only, that does not underplay the importance of these guidelines in setting benchmarks for treatment standards and guidance as to prevailing acceptable practices.

NICE guidelines come into being after a period of consultation. During the consultation period all affected treatment centres should be aware of the proposed changes and actively involved in contributing to the changes being drafted. Therefore a trust/clinician may not be able to defend failure to take account of guidelines because they came into play after the index event, if it can be shown that they participated in any part of the consultation process. Often the ethics committees of NHS Trusts and PCTs will have responsibility for dealing with these consultations.

Human Tissue Authority (HTA)

The HTA is a watchdog that supports public confidence by licensing organisations that store and use human tissue for purposes such as

---

4   Previously NHS Digital.

research, patient treatment, post-mortem examination, teaching, and public exhibitions. It also gives approval for organ and bone marrow donations from living people.

The HTA's aim is to create a regulatory system for the removal, use and disposal of human tissue and organs that is clear, consistent and proportionate and in which professionals, patients, families and members of the public have confidence. Its strategic objectives and information on how the HTA plans to achieve them are included in the strategic plan and annual business plans.

The HTA was established on 1 April 2005 under the Human Tissue Act 2004 (HTA 2004) which extends to England, Wales and Northern Ireland. The HTA is an Executive Non-Departmental Public Body (ENDPB) sponsored by the Department of Health. Its day-to-day operations are managed by a small core team, split into four directorates and led by a Chief Executive. The professional members of the HTA board come from medical and scientific backgrounds and lay members will typically have a wide range of business, commercial and public sector experience.

Human Fertilisation and Embryology Authority (HFEA)

The HFEA is the UK's independent regulator of treatment using gametes and embryos, and embryo research. The HFEA both sets standards for this treatment, and regulates it. It is responsible for licensing fertility clinics and all UK research involving human embryos. Relevant statutory provisions are the HFEA Code of Practice, and the Human Fertilisation and Embryology Act 2008.

When it has held a licensing hearing and made adjudications it will publish its findings. It also provides information for the public, in particular for people seeking treatment, donor-conceived people and donors.

The HFEA has a key role in determining the England policy framework for fertility issues, which are sometimes ethically and clinically complex.

Specific responsibilities when providing guidance and advice include:

- investigation of serious adverse incidents and reactions;
- maintaining a register of serious adverse incidents and serious adverse reactions;
- production and maintenance of a Code of Practice, providing guidelines to clinics and research establishments about the proper conduct of licensed activities;
- licensing the provision of treatment services and activities governed by the Human Fertilisation and Embryology (HFE) Acts 1990 and 2008;
- licensing research into human embryos and developments in research involving human embryos;
- maintenance of a formal register of information about donors, licensed treatments and children born as a result of those treatments including servicing the statutory right of access to register information;
- publication of the HFEA's role;
- provision of relevant advice and information to donor-conceived people, donors, clinics, research establishments and patients;

- advising the Secretary of State for Health on developments in the above fields where appropriate.

EXECUTIVE AGENCIES

Public Health England (PHE)

PHE is a distinct organisation to the DoH with operational autonomy to protect and improve the nation's health and wellbeing, reduce health inequalities and respond to and protect against public health. It does this by:

- providing national leadership;
- providing expert services to support locally led initiatives and respond to public emergencies – for instance it led the initiative to manage avian influenza in 2014;
- providing advice and information to the general public, to health professionals (such as doctors and nurses), and to national and local government;
- researching, collecting and analysing data to improve the public's understanding of public health challenges;
- finding solutions to public health problems.

Medicines and Healthcare products Regulatory Agency (MHRA)

The MHRA regulates medicines and medical devices and equipment. This encompasses a wide range of materials from medicines and medical devices to blood and therapeutic products/services that are derived from tissue engineering.[5] Its functions include:

- authorising NHS use and prescriptions of new drugs (before a medicine can be prescribed by a doctor it must be given a product licence (or 'marketing authorisation') by a regulator. In the UK, the Medicines and Healthcare products Regulatory Agency (MHRA) is the regulator);
- assessing the safety, quality and efficacy of medicines, and authorising their sale or supply in the UK for human use;
- operating post-marketing surveillance and other systems for reporting, investigating and monitoring adverse reactions to medicines and adverse incidents involving medical devices and taking any necessary action to safeguard public health, for example through safety warnings, removing or restricting the availability of products or improving designs;
- operating a proactive compliance programme for medical devices;
- operating a quality surveillance system to sample and test medicines and to address quality defects, monitoring the safety and quality of imported unlicensed medicines and investigating internet sales and potential counterfeiting of medicines;
- regulating clinical trials of medicines and medical devices;

---

5   See www.mhra.gov.uk/Aboutus/index.htm.

- monitoring and ensuring compliance with statutory obligations relating to medicines and medical devices through inspection, and taking enforcement action where necessary;
- promoting good practice in the safe use of medicines and medical devices;
- managing the Clinical Practice Research Database (CPRD) and the National Institute for Biological Standards and Control and contributing to the development of performance standards for medical devices;
- offering scientific, technical and regulatory advice on medicines and medical devices; and
- providing the public and professions with authoritative information to enable informed dialogue on treatment choices.

The MHRA website lists all alerts issued about equipment failures and adverse drug reactions. They distribute their alerts to the NHS through the CAS system (see above). The reports do not simply identify product errors, they also identify common operator errors that, if avoided, will avoid injury to patients.

There is a duty upon trusts to report an adverse event involving a medicine or product. Thus in a case where the defendant relies on a defence of product failure rather than operator error, there should also be a report by them to the MHRA, which should be disclosed.

SPECIAL HEALTH AUTHORITIES

Health Research Authority (HRA)

The HRA protects patients and the public from unethical research, and streamlining and simplifying the process for ethical research. Its primary functions are as follows:

- ensuring research is ethically reviewed and approved;
- promoting transparency in research;
- providing independent recommendations on the processing of identifiable patient information where it is not always practical to obtain consent, for research and non-research projects; and
- overseeing a range of committees and services, including the confidentiality advisory group and Research Ethics Service and Research Ethics Committees.

Board meetings of the HRA are held in public and board papers and minutes are available on its website.

NHS Blood and Transplant (NHSBT)

The NHSBT has responsibility for supply of blood, organs, plasma and tissues and raising the quality, effectiveness and efficiency of blood and transplant services.

NHSBT is responsible for:

- encouraging people to donate organs, blood and tissues;
- optimising the safety and supply of blood, organs and tissues;

- helping to raise the quality, effectiveness and clinical outcomes of blood and transplant services;
- facilitating clinical trials and influencing clinical practise;
- providing expert advice to other NHS organisations, the Department of Health and devolved administrations;
- providing advice and support to health services in other countries;
- commissioning and conducting research and development; and
- implementing relevant EU statutory frameworks and guidance.

NHS Resolution[6]

The NHS Resolution is the organisation that clinical negligence lawyers will deal with most. The NHS Resolution handles negligence claims made against NHS bodies through five schemes that relate to clinical negligence claims, as follows:

- Clinical Negligence Scheme for Trusts ('CNST');
- Clinical Negligence Scheme for General Practice ('CNSGP'), a state indemnity scheme covering NHS services provided by general practice where the negligence occurs on or after 1 April 2019. This will supersede:
  - Existing Liabilities Scheme ('ELS') for incidents occurring before 1 April 1995; and
  - the ex-RHAs Ex-Regional Health Authority Scheme ('EX_RHAS') covering claims against former Regional Health Authorities abolished in 1996;
- Department of Health and Social Care Clinical ('DHSC Clinical') covering clinical negligence claims transferred to the Secretary of State for Health and Social Care following the abolition of health bodies.

There are also schemes that cover non-clinical risks, such as liability for injury to staff and visitors along with property damage (under the Risk Pooling Schemes for Trusts ('RPST')).

The CNST handles all clinical negligence claims against member NHS bodies where the incident in question took place on or after 1 April 1995 (or when the body joined the scheme, if that is later) and the majority of claims will fall under that scheme. Membership of the scheme is voluntary for NHS Trusts but all NHS Trusts in England currently belong to the scheme. In addition since 1 April 2013, independent sector providers of NHS care have also been able to join CNST. Cover under CNST also includes the cost of representation at inquests.

The CNSGP is a new scheme that came into place on 1 April 2019, and all claims made against GP practices or other entities providing NHS primary medical services or ancillary health services will be covered under the scheme if the negligent act complained of occurred on or after 1 April 2019. This includes claims made in respect of liabilities that arise as a consequence of the acts or omissions of employees and others engaged to carry out activities connected to the provision of such services. All claims arising from incidents that occurred before 1 April 2019 will continue to

---

6   Previously known as the NHS Litigation Authority (NHSLA).

be covered by the individual GP's medical defence organisation (MDO)/ indemnity provider.

The scheme applies to any liability in tort (civil wrongdoings such as negligence) that arises as a consequence of a breach of a duty of care owed by a GP contractor or GP sub-contractor to a third party in connection with the provision of primary medical services or ancillary health services where:

1 an act, or omission, on the part of the GP/contractor/sub-contractor (or any employee or other person engaged by them) results in personal injury or loss to the third party;
2 the act, or omission, is in connection with the diagnosis of an illness or the provision of care or treatment to the third party; and
3 the act or omission occurs *on or after 1 April 2019*.

In terms of who is covered under this scheme, all providers of NHS primary medical services will be covered under CNSGP, including out of hours providers. The scheme will extend to all GPs and others working for general practice who are carrying out activities in connection with the delivery of primary medical services – including salaried GPs, locums, students and trainees, nurses, clinical pharmacists and other practice staff.

As well as handling negligence claims, NHS Resolution runs the Family Health Service Appeals Unit settling contractual disputes. It actively deploys alternative models for dispute resolution and explores what drives the costs of harm to patients. Thus it works to improve risk management practices in the NHS. It is also responsible for resolving disputes between practitioners and Primary Care Trusts, giving advice to the NHS on human rights case law and handling equal pay claims on behalf of the NHS.

A highly influential organisation in any negotiations with bodies such as the Civil Justice Council, MoJ and the judiciary, and with strong media support, the NHS Resolution is able to influence the whole manner in which clinical negligence litigation is undertaken. Prior to its inception nearly 80 firms acted for the various NHS trusts in the UK. Now there are a handful of firms on its panel and it is also increasing its in-house provision. Freedom of choice of solicitors for a Trust is generally only allowed for inquest work.

Under NHS indemnity, NHS employers are ordinarily responsible for the negligent acts of their employees where these occur in the course of the NHS employment. The NHS Resolution is therefore representing the Trusts, not the individual doctors who are indemnified by their employers.

An individual may also be separately represented through their defence organisation. This is likely where there is, for instance an inquest where a question is raised regarding their fitness to practice.

In terms of its approach to claims handling, the NHS Resolution adopts a somewhat commercial insurance based approach. They have a remit, as set out in the Framework Document 13, to ensure that claims made against the NHS are handled fairly and consistently, with due regard to the interests of both patients and the NHS. As mentioned above, they operate a legal panel of [12] firms. The panel is dynamic, and subject to change. In addition to the legal panel for clinical cases, there are NHS procurement hubs that appoint law firms for a variety of roles particularly in commercial, real estate and PFI finance work.

NHS Business Services Authority (NHSBSA)

NHSBSA provides critical business support services to NHS organisations, NHS contractors, patients and the public. This includes:

- management of the NHS Supply chain;
- management of the NHS Pension Scheme in England and Wales which has over two million members and receives contributions of over £7 billion per annum;
- administration of the European Health Insurance Card (EHIC) scheme in the UK (until the transitional provisions (if any) of Brexit, presumably);
- provision of NHS Counter Fraud and Security Management services in England and Wales;
- management of a ten-year outsourced contract for the delivery of supply chain services to the NHS in England and Wales;
- payments to pharmacists in England for prescriptions dispensed in primary care settings;
- payments to dentists for work undertaken on NHS contracts in England and Wales;
- provision of management information to over 25,000 registered NHS and DoH users on costs and trends in prescribing and dental care in England and Wales;
- administering a range of health benefit schemes across the UK, including a low income scheme, medical and maternity exemption schemes, tax credit NHS exemption cards (in the UK) and prescription pre-payment certificates (in England). In total they process over six million claims per annum;
- management of schemes for NHS Student Bursaries and NHS Social Work Bursaries in England;
- management of the NHS Injury Benefit Scheme in England and Wales; and
- provision of a range of hosted employment, human resources and financial services, employing staff and administering payments on behalf of various DoH teams and programmes.

Health Education England (HEE)

The HEE is the lead on the education, employment and development of the NHS workforce. It recruits doctors, health providers and dentists into training, and funds and supports the training of a range of multi-professional staff and apprentices. The HEE must account to the DoH which sets the strategic objectives of the HEE and puts in place the education and training outcomes for the system.

DELIVERY OF HEALTHCARE SERVICES

Commissioning

Clinical commissioning groups (CCGs) are groups of local GP practices whose governing bodies include GPs, others clinicians (for example, nurses and secondary care consultants, patient representatives, general managers and, in some cases, practice managers and local authority representatives).

Commissioning involves deciding what services are needed for diverse local populations, and ensuring that those services are provided. The NHS commissioning system was previously made up of primary care trusts and specialised commissioning groups. However, under recent reforms, most of the NHS commissioning is managed by the 207 clinical commissioning groups.

At a local level, the CCGs commission most of the hospital and community NHS services in the local areas for which they are responsible. At a national level, NHSE commissions specialised services. It works closely with the local CCGs in delivering its commissioning functions. CCGs and NHSE are supported by commissioning support units which carry out transactional commissioning functions (for example, market management, risk stratification, information analysis). Public Health England commissions public health services, sometimes devolving its powers to do so to NHSE.

CCGs were brought into being by the Health and Social Care Act 2012.

Broadly, the different organisations bear responsibility for commissioning the following services:

- CCGs:
  - most planned hospital care;
  - rehabilitation;
  - urgent and emergency care;
  - most community health services; and
  - mental health and learning disability services.
- NHSE commissions:
  - dentistry;
  - community pharmacy;
  - primary ophthalmic services;
  - primary care;
  - offender healthcare;
  - military and veteran healthcare; and
  - specialised services defined as a service provided in few hospitals, accessed by comparatively small numbers of patients, such as renal dialysis services.
- Public Health England commissions:
  - national immunisation programmes (via NHSE);
  - national screening programmes (via NHSE);
  - public health services for offenders in custody (via NHSE); and
  - public health services for children aged 0–5 such as health visitors.

Contracts are held directly with the providers. CCGs can also partner up with local authorities to commission services. Also they are increasingly partnering with NHS England to commission primary care services.

PRIMARY CARE PROVIDERS

Community based health care is provided by GPs, community nurses, health visitors and health professionals, pharmacists, dentists and opticians, walk-in centres, and NHS Direct, community nursing, community therapy and midwifery services. It will be the first contact with a healthcare professional for most patients. Primary care services can be provided by any qualified provider (AQP) whether employed directly by the NHS and may provide their services under contract. To be an AQP the provider must be licensed by the CQC. This has expanded the choice of providers for patients who can find all licensed providers in a directory on NHS Choices. The CCGs monitor AQPs for quality of care and can introduce contractual quality standards.

AQPs include private providers, charities and social enterprises.

The third sector

This term encompasses a range of institutions that fit neither the public nor private organisation definition. They include small local community and voluntary groups, large and small charities, cooperatives and social enterprises. They usually provide inpatient and outpatient mental health services, sexual health services, drug rehabilitation and palliative care. There would appear to be an intention by the Department of Health to increase participation by third sector partners in the provision of care. In practical terms it is therefore essential to identify who has actually provided care to the client, who funds it, and who makes the decisions about who was entitled to treatment and what they are entitled to.

GPs

Most GP practices are independent contractors, and formed in partnerships, although they also employ salaried GPs. They are required to provide essential services which include advising people who are ill, making referrals, managing the terminally ill and those with chronic diseases. They have the option of also providing additional services such as contraception or childhood immunisations. Some surgeries also provide enhanced services such as minor surgery units.

In addition to this, commissioning is in the hands of GPs now as all GPs are members of their local CCG. CCGs have further increased the range of services GPs can offer.

Seven day services

The current government target is for seven day out of hours community based care. Thus new incentives have been offered to GP practices to offer access to GP appointments in the evenings and at weekends. Seven day services are also provided via NHS 111, and there is a drive to make consultant assessment and review available every day of the week in the next two years. The strategy is overseen by NHS England.[7]

---

7   See https://www.england.nhs.uk/seven-day-hospital-services/our-ambition/.

NHS 111

NHS 111 is a 24-hour telephone health advice and information service staffed by nurses. Staff use a computer-based decision support system to suggest the best course of action and can pass calls directly to emergency services.

Walk-in centres/minor injuries unit

These are treatment centres that are open seven days a week from 7 am to 10 pm. They may offer assessment for patients needing urgent medical attending but who are not in a life threatening situation. From December 2019 they will all be renamed as urgent treatment centres.

Assessment may be by an experienced NHS nurse as well as an out of hours GP, and they often will offer dental and local pharmacy services as well. Patients can self-refer or may be referred by their GP or NHS 111. Service level varies from centre to centre, but many offer elective surgical procedures. The centres may be staffed by NHS staff or independent contractors but they are funded locally by the local CCG. Whether treated in an NHS or independent sector treatment centre all patients remain NHS patients.

Dentistry services

Dental services in primary care are provided through contracts with individual, self-employed dentists. If there is an issue with dental care provided, NHS England will be the institution with primary responsibility for commissioning that dentist's services, and will be involved in any complaint process. However, usually liability for the treatment will rest with the individual dentist because she is providing services under a contract.

Community pharmacies

Over recent years there has been a significant increase in the use of community pharmacies to provide medicine and some essential treatment without the intervention of the GP. Dispensing and providing medication support is deemed part of essential services, but a number of advanced services may also be provided, such as smoking cessation services.

All pharmacies provide:

- dispensing;
- repeat dispensing;
- disposal of old or out of date medicines; and
- advice on treatment of minor health concerns and healthy living.

Some also offer other services such as vaccinations and a minor ailment service.[8]

---

8   See   https://www.nhs.uk/using-the-nhs/nhs-services/pharmacies/what-to-expect-from-your-pharmacy-team/.

When suing the pharmacy, the pharmacy may be represented by the National Pharmaceutical Association. This is a trade body. Full membership includes legal defence costs and it may be their legal department that has to be dealt with for the majority of independent pharmacists.

Opticians

Optometrists carry out eye tests, prescribe glasses and contact lenses, and identify the presence of eye disease. They are independent contractors and can treat patients who would otherwise have to be seen in hospital. Where they work under contract for local foundation trusts, they work to an agreed protocol, and undertake specified clinical procedures designed to relieve GPs and hospital eye services, as well as providing patient care in the community. They have to be registered with the General Optical Council.

CCGs will not commission NHS eye care services, this will fall under the commissioning remit of NHS England.

In addition, there are dispensing opticians who fit and sell glasses, interpret prescriptions but do not test eyes. They may be qualified to provide contact lenses under instruction from an optometrist. If operating privately rather than under contract to the NHS, it will be necessary to identify their insurer.

Ophthalmic medical practitioners are doctors specialising in eyes and eye care and offer the same terms of service as optometrists do.

Finally, ophthalmologists are doctors specialising in eye diseases and who perform eye surgery, working in hospital eye departments.

Community health services

Community health services can provide more personalised care, closer to patients' homes. Community health services are a major part of the NHS, and encompass a diverse range of statutory registered practitioners known as allied health professionals, including: art therapists; drama therapists; occupational therapists; prosthetists; paramedics; physiotherapists; speech and language therapists; community nurses; district nurses with a post-graduate qualification; registered nurses and nursing assistants; and health visitors. As of 1 May 2017 there were approximately 350,688 allied health professionals registered with the Health and Care Professionals Council and working in a range of surroundings.

Services offered predominantly include care to the elderly and new mothers, as well as district nursing. There is also provision of specialist nursing care, for instance with expertise in stoma care, continence services and midwifery services.

Midwifery services are principally provided under contract to a local trust provider or through a particular GP surgery. Careful consideration needs to be had as to who employs those midwives and who sets the protocols and procedures by which they carry out their work. Although they may be technically employed by their midwifery practice, it may be that the healthcare trust or community trust they are attached to, for instance, has a say in the appointment of new midwives and provides greater control than is immediately apparent. This may create a vicarious responsibility on the part of the contracting trust for the actions of the midwifery practice.

Community health services also provide continuing care. Continuing care is care provided over an extended period to someone, aged 18 or over, to meet physical and mental health needs that have arisen as a result of disability, accident or illness. These services may be provided by a combination of NHS and local authorities. If the patient lives in a care home, the NHS will contribute to the cost of registered nursing care. Financial issues are not taken into account when deciding eligibility for NHS continuing care, though they are for non-medical care.

It is of note that clinical psychology services are often provided by specialist Mental Health Trusts with more than 40% of referrals coming from general practice. These services are more likely to be attached to hospitals, though working in community settings. Community rehabilitation may be delivered by specialist teams drawn from both intermediate care and community hospital care. Where the case arises out of the standard of community care, ascertain who held final responsibility for the actions and care provided by a community care provider, and who set up the care plans.

DELIVERY OF URGENT AND EMERGENCY CARE

The system for delivering urgent and emergency care includes: NHS 111; community pharmacies and self-care; GP services; walk-in centres and minor injuries units; ambulance services; hospital A&E departments; and critical care services.

Ambulance services

Ambulance services have changed significantly in the last 20 years and the intention is to transform ambulance services further to provide more diagnosis, treatment and care in people's homes.

There is an argument that in some cases survival rates are better in specialist centres than in A&E departments. Hence by increasing the amount of paramedical care provided in people's homes or in specialist centres, it is hoped unnecessary A&E admissions will be reduced. For instance, in some areas paramedics are trained specifically in the resuscitation and testing of people with heart pain so that those patients, instead of being taken to emergency departments, are taken directly to a cardiac unit. In other words, ambulance services are improving their ability to assess, diagnose and treat patients. Crews now use satellite navigation systems, and emergency ambulances carry ECG machines and telemetry, which lets the crew send detailed information about a patient's condition directly to the receiving hospital.

On 13 July 2017, NHS England announced a new set of performance targets for the ambulance service which will apply to all 999 calls for the first time.[9] These performance targets include:

---

9   See https://www.england.nhs.uk/urgent-emergency-care/arp/.

- response targets will apply to every single patient, not just those in immediate need;
- call handlers will change the way they assess cases and will have slightly more time to decide the most appropriate clinical response;
- rather than sending multiple vehicles to one call and having to stand crews down, the ambulance service will now send one vehicle;
- 90 per cent of calls are to be reached in the target times (below) rather than 75 per cent under the old system;
- there will now be four classes of 999 calls:
  - Category 1: calls from people with life-threatening illnesses or injuries (for example, cardiac arrest/serious allergic reactions);
  - Category 2: emergency calls (for example, a serious condition, such as stroke or chest pain, which may require rapid assessment and/or urgent transport);
  - Category 3: urgent calls (for example, an uncomplicated diabetic issue, which requires treatment and transport to an acute setting); and
  - Category 4: less urgent calls (for example, stable clinical cases, which require transportation to a hospital ward or clinic);
- the new target response times for each of the four categories of calls are:
  - Category 1: 7 minutes;
  - Category 2: 18 minutes;
  - Category 3: at least 9 out of 10 times within 120 minutes;
  - Category 4: at least 9 out of 10 times within 180 minutes;
- the 'clock' starts on receiving a 999 call to the point of the vehicle arriving at the patient's location.

Response time targets are reported to NHS England by all NHS Ambulance Trusts, which NHS England then publish on its website.

A&E departments

Accident and emergency departments account for around 20% of all admissions to hospital. It is well recognised that A&E departments often suffer from long delays because of the lengthy chain of tests, decisions and treatment that may be invoked in trying to diagnose what is wrong with the patient. As a result, the accident and emergency department will often work from protocols which will need to be referred to if intending to pursue a claim arising out of any treatment in A&E.

SECONDARY CARE

NHS trusts

Under the major 2013 restructuring, the old NHS trusts (such as acute trusts, ambulance trusts, and mental health trusts) were primarily replaced by NHS foundation trusts and NHS trusts providing ambulance services, emergency care services, or mental health services.

Foundation Trusts

The majority of hospitals in England are now managed by NHS foundation trusts.

The Health and Social Care (Community Health and Standards) Act 2003 enabled some NHS trusts to end government control of them by turning them into competing independent corporations called foundation trusts. The Act allows both NHS and non-NHS bodies, including private companies, to apply to become foundation trusts. Although their principal purpose is to provide goods and services to the NHS, they are able to carry out any type of business. With guaranteed independence from direct government control, their sole statutory general duty is to operate 'effectively, efficiently, and economically'. They do not have shareholders but are expected to make and retain surpluses for new investment or for servicing loans raised on the financial markets. The scale of such borrowing will depend on their ability to make surpluses. The government has given them several powers to generate surpluses, including buying and selling land and assets, and retaining the proceeds, creating commercial arms or joining existing commercial ventures, and subcontracting clinical services to commercial companies.

Foundation trusts are free from central government control. The intention behind establishing foundation trusts had been to establish a new NHS service with local delivery and accountability, yet working to national standards. They are independent public benefit corporations, and remain part of the NHS. Therefore they remain subject to NHS standards, performance ratings, and inspection systems. They are accountable to parliament, to their regulator, NHS Improvement and to their governors who are elected by local foundation trust members.

Foundation trusts are accountable to local people and are overseen by NHS Improvement.

Independent providers

The term 'independent providers' means private sector companies, voluntary organisations and social enterprises. The aim is to increase the offering of choice to NHS patients by using such providers. Since 2008, health service patients have freedom of choice of any hospital treatment centre in England that meets NHS standards and costs, including those in the independent sector. The NHS increasingly subcontracts care out to private providers. For instance hip replacements and cataract surgery are commonly outsourced.

Concerns have arisen, however, as to who is responsible for the care provided by independent providers. Is the trust who referred the patient then responsible in a civil claim or is it always the independent provider? Identifying responsibility will depend in part upon obtaining the contract between the parties to assist in identifying whether the independent providers provided a blanket indemnity to the NHS. Reference may need to be had to regulatory frameworks as well. Notwithstanding who bears responsibility for the treatment, it is expected the independent providers will adopt the same NHS standards; therefore protocols that are applied within the NHS should also apply to the independent provider. It is also worth investigating the ownership structure of the private provider in case the trust has any investment or ownership role in it (eg in the provision of laboratory services).

Private sector companies have begun to carry out elective surgery and diagnostic tests of NHS patients under five-year contracts. They are gradually playing an increasing role, and the volume of services they provide the NHS have risen rapidly over recent years.

OTHER CARE PROVIDERS

Mental health

NHS England has responsibility for overseeing the commissioning of specialised services in mental health but they are commissioned locally by CCGs. Typically an area will have inpatient treatment provision alongside community mental health teams running clinics, home visits and case worker support, and a crisis care team.

Under the aegis of mental health services are included services for drug problems and alcohol problems, as well as psychological therapies.

Children are supported through the Child and Adolescent Mental Health services.

Prison healthcare

People in prison have poorer health generally than the population at large. Historically, there have often been some great failings in the care provided to prisoners, and responsibility for commissioning healthcare for regional prisons has been passed to NHSE. In theory this means that all prisoners receive the same quality and range of healthcare services as they would if free civilians with access to the NHS.

There is also a national partnership agreement between the DoH and the Home Office on behalf of the prison service that underpins local partnership arrangements.

Prison services usually now employ a GP and provide in-prison primary care. Specialist care will be provided to the prisoners through their local trusts and other specialist services by contract.

SUMMARY

The NHS is an enormous and complex institution made up of a diverse range of institutions, practitioners and systems. It continues to evolve, as it has from the first day of its creation. As a clinical negligence lawyer, awareness of what service provided your client's care remains important. In any case you undertake involving NHS services, it is important to recognise where information can be found and whether it might be held as part of the patient's personal records (in which case you access it under the Data Protection Act 2018 or Access to Health Records Act 1990) or public statistics, in which case you will have to use the Freedom of Information Act 2000.

Chapter 3

Non legal remedies

Lisa O'Dwyer

INTRODUCTION

Non-legal remedies are increasingly recognised as having an important part to play in resolving clinical negligence disputes and the trend is likely to continue. By way of illustration, in April 2017 the former National Health Service Litigation Authority (NHSLA), was renamed National Health Service Resolution (NHS Resolution); its emphasis is said to be on delivering fair resolution, learning from harm to improve safety, with a focus on early intervention. The NHS is looking to mediation and other forms of Alternative Dispute Resolution (ADR) in recognition of the fact that a more effective solution can be found when the court process is set aside.

It should be noted however that many of the processes discussed in this chapter are not alternatives to litigation in the truest sense, the exceptions perhaps being mediation and arbitration. However, even with mediation the process, if unsuccessful, does not rule out reverting to litigation. By contrast, arbitration does have scope to be a real alternative to litigation and whilst it has proved to be effective in other areas of litigation, especially commercial, it has not been tested to the same extent in clinical negligence litigation. Nonetheless arbitration continues to attract increasing levels of interest and attention and at least one provider, the Personal Injury claims Arbitration Service (PIcARBS), has developed an arbitration process specifically for use in personal injury and clinical negligence work.

However, many of the processes described in this chapter, if used properly, can and do serve to avoid litigation. They do this primarily by putting the emphasis on treating the patient who is complaining with respect, dignity, and by taking their concerns seriously. Most patients who complain want answers; they want to understand what, if anything, went wrong with their care or the care provided to their loved one. Patients rarely start out looking to be part of the litigation process; what they want is open, honest answers to their concerns and for a thorough investigation to be carried out impartially and in a way that makes them feel like they are part of the process.

It has long been acknowledged that there are a number of benefits associated with avoiding litigation. From both the patient and the medical professional's point of view, litigation is a lengthy, stressful and expensive process which is not for the faint hearted. It is much better for the service provider and the patient to avoid litigation altogether, if possible.

The stress of litigation on the parties concerned, for the healthcare provider and for the patient, are weighty enough reasons to avoid it. However, there are also now more compelling economic reasons, notably the rising cost of clinical negligence litigation and the reduction in the number of clinical negligence claims that are eligible for public funding through the Legal Aid Agency (LAA). The importance of non-legal remedies needs to be looked at in the context of these factors.

THE COST OF CLINICAL NEGLIGENCE LITIGATION

In recent years there has rightly been increased focus on the cost of clinical negligence litigation. According to NHS Resolution's most recent annual report (2017/18) its clinical negligence provision has increased significantly; the report estimates that the annual cost of harm is circa £7–8 billion. This figure is 'roughly double the figure prior to 2016/17 partly as a result of the reduced discount rate'.[1] The 2017/18 report also states that 'Clinical claim numbers have stabilised after many years of significant growth'. The number of new claims received in 2016/17 was 10,686; new claims received in 2017/18 are reported to be 10,673.

Although the number of clinical negligence claims received may have stabilised, they are still a cause for concern. There is the very real and inescapable human cost of an injury caused by negligent treatment as well as the financial cost of paying compensation for the injuries received. From a claimant's point of view an award of damages, no matter how large or small, is a blunt tool for compensating a physical or psychiatric injury which has been sustained in this way. As a public body, the cost of the NHS mistakes is ultimately picked up by the public purse, arguably an unnecessary cost if these mistakes could and should have been avoided in the first place.

There may be many reasons why the number of clinical negligence claims being received by NHS Resolution has plateaued and a detailed examination of those reasons goes beyond the remit of this chapter. However, the reduction in the scope of public funding for clinical negligence claims since 2013 is likely to be one factor. Another possible factor is the courts' hardline approach to the actual costs incurred by solicitors in proving the claim and whether those costs can be said to be proportional to the damages recovered.

There is a real and pressing need for the reasons why clinical negligence occurs at all to be properly and thoroughly examined, the reasons need to be fully identified and addressed. It is rarely the case that negligence occurs because of the actions of one individual clinician or healthcare worker, it is more usually a combination of factors including a hospital's own systemic failings. AvMA (Action for victims of Medical Accidents) take the view that the reasons why treatment fell below an acceptable standard of care should be explored regardless of whether the negligence

---

1   NHS Annual report and accounts 2017/18, Chairs welcome, p 8.

gave rise to physical and/or psychiatric injury. The failure to identify the causes of negligence and address them properly tends to result in substandard care repeating itself. Substandard medical care that does not give rise to harm must be treated as a lucky escape, it is as important for these issues to be identified and addressed as any treatment which is substandard and gives rise to physical and/or mental injury and which may then go on to form the basis of a clinical negligence claim.

A failure to deal with the root causes of clinical negligence is to allow an ongoing risk to the public to persist. They are clinical negligence claims waiting to happen. When clinical negligence occurs it causes great distress to the patient and to the doctors, nurses and health professionals involved. Health professionals do not choose their profession with a view to causing harm; on the contrary, they are individuals who often consider their choice of profession a vocation which calls them to help and heal the sick; when something goes wrong health professionals can feel an acute sense of failing, professional embarrassment and personal disappointment, it can seriously rock their confidence. Clinical negligence is lose-lose; there are no winners and is to be avoided for the sake of all the parties.

Undoubtedly, some of the factors giving rise to negligence claims are complex; the inherent and unaddressed failings of some hospital systems often contribute and in some cases may be the catalyst for failings in care. When negligence happens healthcare providers should be taking the initiative and carrying out robust and impartial investigations. Where compensation is due, this should be paid without delay, payments should be fair and reflect the awards made by the courts. Patients should have the opportunity to obtain independent advice on the circumstances of the injury and the offer of compensation, should they choose to, sadly, this does not tend to happen in practice.

THE NATIONAL AUDIT OFFICE (NAO)

The National Audit Office (NAO) is an independent Parliamentary body which is responsible for scrutinising public spending for Parliament; the NAO looked at the NHS handling of clinical negligence claims in England in 2001. They identified that as at 31 March 2000 there were estimated to be some 23,000 outstanding claims. The total budget for clinical negligence claims at that time stood at £3.9 billion.[2]

To put the rising costs in perspective, the NAO reported again in September 2017, at which time it noted that the NHS provision for existing or potential clinical negligence claims stood at £60 billion in 2016/17.[3]

The 2017 NAO report also identified that the time taken by NHSR to settle claims had increased from an average of 300 days in 2010/11 to 426 days in 2016/17. The NAO calculate that each extra day taken to resolve a case costs £40.00. If that figure is correct then the effect of increasing the average settlement time by 126 days is an additional cost of £5,040

---

2 *Handling Negligence Claims in England* HC 403 Session 2000–2001: 3 May 2001, p 1.
3 *Managing the Costs of Clinical Negligence in Trusts* HC 305 Session 2017–2019: 7th September 2017, p 1, para 4.

per case. The fact that the report[4] also identifies that NHSR does not sufficiently understand what motivates people to bring a claim suggests that there is a great deal more for NHS Resolution to understand and act on.

LEGAL AID

Legal aid has been seen as a corner stone to accessing justice since the Legal Aid and Advice Act 1949 was introduced. The body of law and procedures pertaining to clinical negligence litigation really developed and grew from the end of the 1980s onward, the availability of legal aid for clinical negligence was instrumental in enabling that development.

Up until April 2013, legal aid was comparatively widely available for clinical negligence claims subject to the claimant satisfying a means and merits test set by the body overseeing legal aid funding. The body has been known by different names, including the Legal Aid Board, the Legal Services Commission (LSC) and currently the Legal Aid Agency (LAA). These tests were, and continue to be imposed, to ensure that the claimant is in receipt of a sufficiently low income to warrant the grant of public funds and to demonstrate that a prima facie case exists. Legal aid provides an opportunity to investigate the claim further and explore in more detail the prospect of the claim succeeding.

As clinical negligence case law and practice developed so too did the LAA's increasingly stringent criteria for lawyers considered eligible to offer legal aid in this field of work. Of particular importance was the requirement that only firms holding a legal aid contract (formerly referred to as a franchise) in clinical negligence could offer public funding for this work.

One of the criteria for securing a franchise was, and continues to be, that the firm employs at least one solicitor who is an accredited member of a clinical negligence panel. Historically there were two separate panels, the AvMA panel and the Law Society panel – the LAA now also recognises the Association of Personal Injury Lawyers (APIL) clinical negligence accreditation scheme. All accreditation schemes work on the basis that lawyers can only achieve accreditation by demonstrating that they have sufficient expertise and experience in clinical negligence work to meet the standards set out by the accrediting body. The AvMA panel was the first accreditation scheme and is the longest running; as well as demonstrating expertise and experience in clinical negligence cases AvMA requires its members to demonstrate they have the necessary client care skills, medical knowledge and understanding that are crucial to helping injured patients in this area of work.

As a result of the LAA's demanding criteria, including the requirement that at least one practitioner at the firm was accredited as a clinical negligence specialist, so a clinical negligence legal aid franchise came to be synonymous with a quality mark in proficiency.

---

4   *Managing the Costs of Clinical Negligence in Trusts* HC 305 Session 2017–2019: 7 September 2017, p 44, para 3.16.

Legal Aid, Sentencing and Punishment of Offenders Act 2012 (LASPOA 2012)

In April 2013, the LASPOA 2012 was introduced; LASPOA 2012 restricted the scope and therefore the availability of legal aid in clinical negligence claims. Legal aid is now only available to people who have suffered a neurological injury believed to have been caused as a result of negligent treatment occurring in utero, during birth or within the first eight weeks of life. The requirement to hold a legal aid contract to be able to offer public funding for this work continues.

By restricting the scope of legal aid, those members of the public who may have been eligible for legal aid prior to April 2013 are now only able to bring a claim if they can find a lawyer who is prepared to run their case on a Conditional Fee Agreement (CFA). Any lawyer can offer a CFA in clinical negligence work, there is no requirement to show expertise or experience. LASPOA 2012 opened up the clinical negligence market to any lawyer, regardless of their experience to conduct claims in this highly specialised and complex area of work. As a result, NHS Resolution, and in particular its predecessor the National Health Service Litigation Authority (NHS LA), has been faced with a barrage of claims that lacked merit and were often poorly drafted; despite this, NHS Resolution has had to investigate these claims at considerable cost.

Whilst it cannot be said that all non-specialist lawyers undertaking clinical negligence work have achieved bad outcomes for their clients, it stands to reason that the less experience and expertise the lawyer has, the greater the likelihood that the patient will be badly advised; claims will be under settled or struck out for not being properly handled, the wrong experts will be instructed and/or poorly instructed. Inexperienced firms often do not manage the client's expectations properly or at all. Where a lawyer is unable to proceed with a case, the injured patient can end up feeling that they have been let down twice, once by the medical profession and then again by the legal profession.

To complicate matters further, changes to the Civil Procedure Rules (CPR), in particular CPR 44 (General rules about costs) means that costs incurred by lawyers seeking to prove their client's case need to be proportionate to the value of the claim. The courts have shown that they are interpreting this strictly so that even if costs have been reasonably and necessarily incurred, if the costs claimed far exceed the value of the claim then proportionality will trump necessity and the costs will not be allowed.[5]

The emphasis on proportionality has proved to be particularly problematic in low value clinical negligence cases. The burden of proving the claim remains with the claimant; gathering the evidence to prove the claim is often onerous; the issues in low value claims can be complex and, as a result, a low value claim can be as costly to run as a higher value claim. Given this background it is not surprising that experienced clinical negligence lawyers are now far more circumspect about investigating and/or bringing clinical negligence cases in claims where the value is relatively low.

---

5   *Hobbs v Guy's & St Thomas' NHS Foundation Trust* [2015] EWHC B20.

Given the emphasis on the relationship between costs and damages, it is easy to understand why solicitors are driven to only taking on cases that have a good prospect of success and are therefore more likely to be resolved quickly. The longer a case runs on, the more expensive it becomes – complex, low value claims are likely to be expensive and unless they are settled early are likely to run into difficulties on proportionality. As a result, lawyers are more reluctant to take the chance of not recovering their costs on such cases and shy away from them; this has resulted in an access to justice issue as some clients with valid but low value claims have had trouble finding legal representation.

There is no formal definition of what constitutes a lower value claim and we should not lose sight of the fact that there are circumstances where even a modest award of £5,000 can make a significant difference especially to a low income family. From a commercial point of view, firms increasingly view claims with damages valued up to £25,000 as low value. Given the issues around proportionality, it is not unusual to find practitioners using £50,000 or higher as the benchmark for low value. With the reduction in the availability of legal aid and the fact that there are restrictions on the recoverability of after the event (ATE) insurance premiums there are fewer opportunities to find funding for the disbursements associated with clinical negligence.

The ability to instruct independent medical experts to report on clinical negligence cases is a crucial part of proving the claimant's claim, in particular identifying what breaches of duty, if any, exist and what harm has been caused. A clinical negligence case is only as good as the independent expert or experts involved in the case; most of the best experts remain in full time medical practice and write reports in their own time. Medical expert reporting is an important and responsible job which can result in the expert putting his or her professional reputation on the line. The issues need to be properly considered, the medical records carefully read and examined, and the medical practice under scrutiny researched thoroughly.

There is no escaping the fact that medico-legal report writing is expensive; most patients are unable to afford the cost of commissioning an expert or experts to prepare such reports and in any event experts are reluctant to accept instructions directly from members of the public. Although some claimants may have the benefit of before the event (BTE) insurance, this form of funding is not as popular as perhaps initially anticipated prior to 2013. Furthermore, BTE insurance carries with it restrictions on the claimant's choice of solicitor, the insurers preferring to refer clients to their own panel of lawyers in the first instance, rather than the solicitor of the claimant's choice. Insurers often see specialist, accredited lawyers in clinical negligence work as being too expensive and prefer to bypass them for cheaper alternatives.

Some specialist firms will carry the cost of the claimant's disbursements themselves. Usually these firms will take a very strict view on the type of cases they will fund and the prospects of the case succeeding – often the case is expected to have a greater than 60% chance of succeeding before a firm will embark on carrying the disbursements for their client. Some of the smaller, specialist clinical negligence firms are not able to fund their client's disbursements at all and again this can affect a firm's ability to compete and restricts the number of lawyers willing and able to represent claimants, in turn this limits consumer choice. Either way, where a client is unable to fund the required disbursements it restricts the pool of lawyers available to them and in the more extreme cases it is an absolute bar to pursing the claim and accessing justice.

ALTERNATIVES TO LITIGATION

Currently, in England there is no formal forum or process to settle low value claims outside of litigation by contrast Wales has the Welsh Redress Scheme. AvMA has for many years called for consideration to be given to a scheme which will enable swift settlements at a reasonable cost. AvMA is keen to ensure that such claims remain attractive to accredited lawyers so the patient/client has the best and most appropriate representation possible. Equally, it is crucial that the client is able to retain the majority of their award of damages. If most of the damages end up being retained to cover legal and other costs of litigation there ceases to be any point in a patient enforcing their rights to redress whether that is through litigation or otherwise. In turn, this simply results in the ability to access justice being reduced and a loss of learning for trusts and hospitals.

Avoiding litigation

The NHS Constitution and the complaint procedure

One of the starting points for potentially avoiding litigation is the NHS constitution and the NHS complaints procedure. The NHS constitution sets out a number of promises and pledges about the standards and service patients can expect to receive when things go wrong. These pledges are key indicators of the type of service patients should receive.

The NHS constitution establishes the principles and values of the NHS in England; all NHS bodies are required by law to take account of the constitution. The NHS is accountable to the public and the patients it serves; the system for accountability and responsibility for taking decisions in the NHS should be clear and user friendly. Under the constitution there is a right to have any complaint made about an NHS service properly investigated. The level of investigation does in practice tend to vary although the addition of a statutory duty of candour (see below) should create a greater emphasis on the investigation process being open and honest, particularly where the matter complained of is considered to be a notifiable safety incident.

The NHS constitution makes clear that there is a right to compensation where harm has been caused by negligent treatment. The NHS commits to ensuring that when mistakes happen and/or where harm has been caused to a patient whilst receiving health care under the NHS, an appropriate explanation will be given and pledges that lessons will be learned to help avoid a similar incident occurring again.

The NHS complaint procedure is rooted in the NHS constitution and in the Local Authority Social Services and National Health Service Complaints (England) Regulations 2009, SI 2009/309 (the Regulations). The Regulations do not offer any definition of what constitutes a complaint although the *Oxford English Dictionary* refers to a complaint as being a statement of grief, an utterance of a grievance, a statement of an injustice suffered and a statement of injury or grievance laid before a court for the purposes of prosecution and redress.

The Regulations apply to both the local authority social services and to the NHS; the Regulations refer to these bodies as the 'responsible body'. For the purposes of this chapter reference will be made to the NHS only but note the Regulations do extend beyond the NHS and the provisions apply to both NHS primary care as well as secondary care.

Under reg 4, the NHS is obliged to appoint a responsible person for ensuring compliance with the Regulations. That person is equally obliged to act, if necessary, in light of the outcome of any complaint.

The Regulations prescribe that the NHS must appoint a complaints manager to be responsible for managing the procedures for handling and considering complaints in accordance with the Regulations.

Regulation 13, states that complaints may be made orally, in writing, or electronically. The complaint can be made by anyone who receives services from the NHS or who is affected by an action, omission, or decision of the NHS which is the subject of the complaint. A person who is affected in this way also has a right to appoint someone to act on their behalf. Complaints which are made orally must be written down and a copy of the written notice provided to the complainant. In other cases the NHS must acknowledge safe receipt of the written complaint within three working days after the date it was received.

A person acting on behalf of someone who has died as a result of services received may make a complaint about the deceased's care, as can a person acting for a child or person suffering from a physical or mental incapacity.

Having made a complaint, reg 14 creates a duty to investigate the complaint in an appropriate manner and resolve it speedily and efficiently. The complainant should be kept informed about the progress of the investigation and be sent a written response setting out the conclusions reached including any remedial action to be taken.

The NHS is not obliged to investigate complaints which are made orally but are then resolved to the complainant's satisfaction the next working day after the complaint was made. Once a complaint has been investigated under the Regulations or any preceding regulations (2004 and 2006 Regulations), the NHS is not required to deal with the subject matter of that complaint again.

The complaints procedure cannot be used to complain of a failure to respond to a request under the Freedom of Information Act 2000, or by an employee of the NHS who has a grievance about their employment.

Complaints must not be made any later than 12 months after the date the subject of the complaint occurred or the date the complainant knew of it. The time may be extended if the NHS are satisfied that the complainant had good reason for not making the complaint in time and that despite the delay in bringing the complaint, the NHS are still able to investigate the matter effectively and fairly.

Once the NHS has received a complaint they must investigate the matter complained of with a view to resolving the issue speedily and efficiently. The complainant should be kept advised of the progress of the investigation and at its conclusion be sent a written response which sets out an explanation of how the complaint has been considered and any conclusions reached, including any remedial action to be taken.

There has been a long standing tension around whether there is a right to have a complaint investigated when litigation is being considered or undertaken. The situation is not helped by the fact that the Regulations are silent on the approach to be taken in such circumstances. It is AvMA's experience that in practice it has not been uncommon for trusts to refuse to carry out an investigation into a complaint where the patient was also seeking independent legal advice.

The issue has been taken up by AvMA and is one which has been discussed with the Department of Health (DH) on several occasions in the past. Despite repeated verbal reassurances, AvMA was made aware that the issue continued to rear its head from time to time; lawyers and members of the public reported that some trusts continued to see the patient's decision to seek independent legal advice as a bar to an investigation under the NHS complaints procedure. In October 2013, AvMA sent the DH a letter of claim setting out its intention to bring judicial review proceedings if written clarification on this issue was not forthcoming. In response, the DH published a clarification note in the Clinical Commissioning Group (CCG) Bulletin dated 20 March 2014 in which it stated:

> where the complainant is taking, or plans to take legal proceedings, a complaint may only be put on hold where there are exceptional reasons to justify it, or the complainant has requested that the investigation be delayed".

To date it would appear that the definition of exceptional reasons has not been tested. However, following further discussions with the DH, it is understood that exceptional reasons in this context may include a formal request by the police, a coroner or a judge to put the complaint investigation on hold. The situation appears to have improved considerably in recent years and is thankfully rarer now than it once was.

A complaint is an opportunity for the NHS healthcare provider concerned to: investigate the issue complained of; offer an explanation of the conclusions arrived at; provide information; identify any action that needs to be taken as a result of the complaint; and give an assurance that lessons have been learned to help avoid similar incidences occurring again thereby improving NHS services.

NHS England's most recent complaints policy document is dated June 2017. At para 1 it commits to investigating complaints in an 'unbiased, non-judgmental, transparent, timely and appropriate manner'. At para 2 it states that when dealing with complaints they will adhere to principles of: 'openness and transparency ... evidence based complainant led investigations and responses' as well as a logical and rational approach. Those aims and standards are laudable; unfortunately too many patients feel that approach is not reflected in their experience of the complaints process.

The complaints process is potentially a powerful and valuable tool; used properly by committed and trained complaints staff it should provide the best alternative to litigation. It is true, some trusts do operate a better and more effective complaints process than others, but all too often patients tell us that they feel stonewalled by the complaints process and unable to obtain answers to their concerns. The result is that experience all too often drives patients to the door of the clinical negligence lawyer – this is not what the patient wants, and is certainly not what the trust or NHS Resolution wants. The answer is to give greater kudos to the complaints process, improve communication between the patient and the trust, investigate once and investigate well by using the principles extolled by NHS England and the NHS constitution.

It follows that if the complaints process is used properly there is a greater chance that it will identify failings in care early on either through a complaint or patient safety investigation. In turn this provides an opportunity for the trust in consultation with NHS Resolution to consider whether it is appropriate for compensation to be paid. Generally, this is not the approach being taken in practice, as such it amounts to a missed opportunity to resolve claims as swiftly and as inexpensively as possible and can often act as one of the catalysts for driving patients towards litigation. The NHS complaints process is essentially a two tier process. If the complainant, having followed the NHS complaints procedure (often referred to as local resolution), remains dissatisfied with the conclusions reached and/or the level of investigation then they may be able to refer the matter to Parliamentary Health Service Ombudsman (PHSO). The PHSO is the second tier of the complaints process and will consider the nature of the complaint and the way it has been handled.

Parliamentary Health Service Ombudsman (PHSO)

The PHSO exists to help resolve complaints against the NHS, government departments and other public organisations. They make judgments on the complaints and help to put things right if they have gone wrong; they describe themselves as leading the way to make the complaints process better. The PHSO often become involved because the NHS has offered a poor explanation of what went wrong with the care complained of or because they have failed to acknowledge that a mistake or mistakes were made.

There are separate ombudsmen for England, Scotland and Wales. The Scottish Public Services Ombudsman oversees NHS complaints in Scotland (Scottish Public Service Ombudsman Act 2002); the Public Services Ombudsman has jurisdiction over complaints about the NHS in Wales (Public Services Ombudsman (Wales) Act 2005). There is also a separate ombudsman for Northern Ireland (Public Services Ombudsman Act (Northern Ireland) 2016). The relevant statutory provisions for the ombudsman in England can be found in the Health Service Commissioners Act 1993 (as amended).

The PHSO in England will consider a complaint laid by a complainant who has exhausted local resolution providing the complaint did not originate before April 1996. Details of the where to send a complaint are available from the PHSO website but the PHSO must acknowledge the complaint within two days. The PHSO will investigate all areas of NHS healthcare provision including hospitals, GPs, dentists, opticians, pharmacists and the ambulance service.

Complaints to the ombudsman should be made within one year from the date the matter first came to the notice of the complainant. The ombudsman may waive this requirement if he/she thinks fit. The ombudsman for England is currently Robert Frederick Behrens CBE, he has held this post since April 2017.

When the PHSO first receives a complaint it will potentially go through several stages. First, the PHSO will check to make sure that they can investigate the organisation being complained of; if the complaint is about the NHS this will be straightforward. They will also check to make sure that the complainant has accessed and exhausted the NHS complaints process. Those checks should be carried out within five working days.

The PHSO will decide whether the complaint should be investigated by them. There are several factors taken into account at this point, these include how the complainant has been personally affected by what happened, whether the complaint has been lodged within 12 months of knowing about the issue, whether legal action is an option and whether it appears that the organisation may have got its complaint handling and or investigation wrong. The decision on whether the PHSO intends to investigate should be communicated within 20 working days of receipt of the complaint.

It should be noted that the PHSO considers about 8,000 cases a year for this stage although it only investigates about 50% of those cases. In practice there are often difficulties around the issue of whether an alternative legal remedy is an option. AvMA has engaged with the ombudsman on this issue on a number of occasions.

Where litigation has commenced or is contemplated the ombudsman is expected to look at the facts of the case to see whether it would be appropriate to investigate. The ombudsman is unlikely to investigate if the subject of the complaint is also the subject of the litigation as this would potentially amount to a duplication of investigation of the same or similar points. However, where the complainant is bringing or has brought litigation but the matters and issues referred to the PHSO do not form part of the litigation, then these will be considered for the purposes of an investigation. Factors such as time scales and whether the ombudsman's decision is likely to impact on the outcome of the litigation will be taken into consideration.

The PHSO does not have jurisdiction to investigate a complaint where the complainant can obtain a legal remedy. However, the investigation will take place in circumstances where it would be unreasonable to force a complainant to resort to litigation. In practice this issue does cause difficulties and AvMA has raised and continues to raise concerns with the Ombudsman about decisions that have been taken to refuse investigation because legal action was contemplated or taken.

The PHSO have confirmed that they do not operate a blanket policy of not investigating patient concerns at the same time as they are, or may be, taking legal action. The PHSO will consider what has happened and what effect the legal action may have on any investigation they may carry out. However, in practice there are often problems with the way in which the PHSO interprets the availability of alternative legal remedy and there are times when AvMA has become involved in challenging the PHSO's decision to refuse an investigation on these grounds; AvMA has successfully overturned the PHSO's initial decision on several occasions.

Having carried out an investigation the PHSO can recommend financial redress, although is not obliged to do so, each case is considered on its own merits. Some of the factors the PHSO will take into account when considering financial redress are: the way in which the trust has handled the complaint; the impact of the complaint on the individual; and the length of time it has taken to deal with the complaint.

The awards suggested by the PHSO are not calculated with reference to legal principles of assessing quantum.

Complaining about private healthcare

As with NHS care, patients receiving private healthcare have a right to complain about treatment they have received in a private hospital or clinic. However, in the first instance patients and or their families should approach the consultant responsible for the care provided in order to obtain an explanation and advice. If this does not resolve the issue then the patient should follow the hospital or clinic's formal complaints procedure.

Under the Health and Social Care (Community Health and Standards) Act 2003, private hospitals and clinics are obliged to operate a complaint procedure; it should be similar to that offered by NHS hospitals.

The Independent Healthcare Sector Complaints Adjudication Service (ISCAS) has a code of practice for dealing with patient complaints. The ISCAS code of practice can be found at: https://www.iscas.org.uk. ISCAS provides an adjudication service for unresolved complaints about private healthcare provided by its members, however, not all private healthcare providers are members of ISCAS and the code only applies to members and patients treated by a practitioner who is a member of an independent doctors federation.

There are various difficulties with private health care complaints, especially as ISCAS is not a statutory body and private patients have no right to refer their complaint to the PHSO which will only look at complaints made by public bodies.

The CQC are responsible for regulating and inspecting independent healthcare providers who are registered with them in England. The CQC will not look into complaints about the health or social care provided but they do invite patients to let them know of any concerns they have about the care received and may use that information to check whether the healthcare provider is meeting the expected quality and safety standards. The CQC does have legal powers to demand improvements in services.

The duty of candour

Initially, the introduction of a statutory duty of candour met with some resistance; doctors referred to the professional duty already included in their own General Medical Council (GMC) code of conduct. AvMA had long campaigned for the introduction of a statutory duty of candour however Sir Robert Francis' extensive investigations and findings as Chairman of the Mid Staffordshire public inquiry left little doubt that such a duty was indeed necessary.

The duty of candour applies to healthcare providers in both the public and private sectors.

The statutory duty of candour came into force for NHS bodies in November 2014 under of the Health and Social Care Act 2008 (Regulated Activities) Regulations 2014, SI 2014/2936, reg 20. It became a requirement for all other organisations in April 2015 under the Health and Social Care Act 2008 (Regulated Activities) (Amendment) Regulations 2015, SI 2015/64.

The duty of candour is not an alternative to litigation, it does not provide for compensation to be paid to a patient where the care provided has failed them. However, it does place a considerable burden on health care providers to ensure that matters are fully identified, investigated and information is provided to the patient. This is a considerable step forward in that the emphasis is on the quality and quantity of information provided to the patient being as good as possible.

The introduction of the statutory duty of candour is an important step to ensuring that all health and social care organisations registered with the Care Quality Commission (CQC) are open and honest with patients when something has gone wrong with their care. The obligation to be open and transparent is triggered as soon as reasonably practicable after the relevant care provider has become aware that a 'notifiable safety incident' has occurred. The obligation is to notify the patient or relevant person about the incident and to provide them with reasonable support.

However, it is worth noting that under the Health and Social Care (Safety and Quality) Act 2015[6] there is a more general duty for services provided in the course of regulated activity not to cause avoidable harm to people relying on the service. Further, under that Act there is a duty to share information. Helpfully, the Social Care Act 2008 (Regulated Activities) Regulations 2014 define what is meant by a 'notifiable safety incident'. Regulation 20(8) states that a notifiable safety incident means 'any unintended or unexpected incident that occurred in respect of a service user during the provision of a regulated activity that, in the reasonable opinion of a health care professional, could result in, or appears to have resulted in, ...' death or moderate or severe harm to the service user. It also covers the situation where the injury constitutes prolonged psychological harm.

Not only must the patient or service user be notified of the incident and given a true account of the facts according to the information available at the time but written notification must also be given. The written notification must set out the facts and circumstances of the incident, explain what enquiries are being undertaken, and the results of any enquiries undertaken at the time the letter is written. An apology should be given to the patient. The patient must be continually updated on any additional information that comes to light, for example, following completion of any outstanding enquiries.

The regulations only apply if the incident occurred after they came in to force. In the case of NHS care that is on or after November 2014, and in the case of private care on or after April 2015.

The statutory duty of candour is evolving and there are examples of good practice and not so good. It is important that the CQC monitor this situation rigorously to ensure that the duty of candour is embedded in healthcare. It is crucial that the duty is able to satisfy the public that things have changed and are changing in the NHS's approach to being open and honest when something goes wrong. The public need to have

6   See http://www.legislation.gov.uk/ukpga/2015/28/pdfs/ukpga_20150028_en.pdf.

confidence that if something does go wrong with their healthcare those concerns will be addressed fairly and compassionately.

This change in approach will not happen overnight, it needs to be underpinned by good training which sets out the obligations and expectations under the statutory duty and its implementation needs to be monitored. The statutory duty demonstrates that change can happen. However these are still early days and there is room for improvement. In August 2016 AvMA published a report 'Regulating the duty of candour'[7] by Hannah Blythe which identified that there was an inadequate and inconsistent approach by the CQC to regulating candour. In response, the CQC has committed to improve its monitoring of how trusts are implementing the duty of candour as part of their inspections.

In AvMA's experience most people who complain about their healthcare simply want answers; they want to know what went wrong and why. They want to be reassured that measures have been taken to prevent the same thing happening to someone else or to another family, litigation on its own cannot deliver this. The duty of candour should be resonating throughout all healthcare processes and procedures available to a patient, whether that is a trust preparing a serious incident report (SIR) or the handling of a complaint through a healthcare provider's complaint procedure. It should also resonate throughout the litigation process.

Relevant organisations should have policies and procedures in place to support a culture of openness and ensure that their staff are aware of them; staff should be properly trained in the application of the duty and follow it in all aspects of their work.

It is worth remembering that there is an obligation to provide a written record of the account given to the patient, an account which should include all of the known facts around the notifiable safety incident. This written account, often referred to as a duty of candour letter, is a useful document for the purposes of considering whether a patient and/or their family has a legal claim, and if so to help resolve that claim. It is also a document that should be disclosed to the coroner as part of their investigation into how a person died.

Serious Incident Reports (SIR)

Serious incidents are defined by NHS England[8] as events in health care where the potential for learning is so great, or the consequences to patients, families and carers, staff or organisations are so significant, that they warrant using additional resources to mount a comprehensive response.

NHS England also makes it clear that 'Serious incidents can extend beyond incidents which affect patients directly and include incidents which may indirectly impact patient safety or an organisation's ability to deliver ongoing healthcare.'

---

7   See https://www.avma.org.uk/?download_protected_attachment=Regulating-the-duty-of-candour.pdf.

8   See https://improvement.nhs.uk/documents/920/serious-incidnt-framwrk.pdf.

Where NHS treatment is concerned a serious incident must be declared where acts and/or omissions have occurred as part of NHS-funded healthcare (including in the community) that has resulted in:

1 **unexpected or avoidable death** of one or more people. This includes suicide/self-inflicted death; and homicide by a person in receipt of mental health care in the recent past;

2 **unexpected or avoidable injury** to one or more people that has resulted in *serious harm*; or

3 **unexpected or avoidable injury** to one or more people that requires *further treatment* by a healthcare professional in order *to prevent* the death of the service user, or serious harm;

4 **actual or alleged abuse**. There are a number of situations where this applies but in the context of clinical negligence the most relevant ones might be considered to be: sexual abuse; physical or psychological ill-treatment; acts or omissions which constitute neglect, self-neglect. It will also apply where healthcare did not take appropriate action/ intervention to safeguard against such abuse occurring or where the abuse occurred during the provision of NHS-funded care;

5 **a 'never event'**. All never events are defined as serious incidents although not all never events necessarily result in serious harm or death. For further information a list of never events can be found at https://www.england.nhs.uk/wp-content/uploads/2015/03/never-evnts-list-15-16.pdf;

6 **an incident (or series of incidents) that prevents, or threatens to prevent, an organisation's ability to continue to deliver an acceptable quality of healthcare services**. This includes incidents in population-wide healthcare activities like screening or inappropriate enforcement/care under the Mental Health Act 1983 and the Mental Capacity Act 2005 including the Mental Capacity Act, Deprivation of Liberty Safeguards (MCA DOLS);

7 **systematic failure to provide an acceptable standard of safe care**. This *may* include incidents, or a series of incidents, which necessitate ward/unit closure or suspension of services.

In practice it can be difficult to identify whether a serious incident has occurred, outcome alone will not determine whether an incident is serious or not. Serious incidents may be identified in a number of ways including any allegations made by a patient or third party or through the complaints process.

Serious incidents must be reported without delay and in any event no longer than two working days after the incident is identified. NHS trusts should have effective systems and processes in place to report, investigate and respond to serious incidents in line with national policy and best practice. The healthcare provider's Chief Executive Officer (or equivalent) is responsible for identifying a senior manager or clinician or other officer with relevant delegated authority to gather and secure evidence, identify witnesses, and ensure safety of patients and staff.

If a situation arises where there is some doubt as to whether an event amounts to a serious incident then health care providers must discuss the circumstances with the commissioners to agree the appropriate response. It is important that those discussions are open and honest. If there is still doubt, then an investigation should take place so a conclusion can be reached as to whether the incident was serious.

There are three levels of investigation which may be carried out:

1 **concise investigations**: these investigations are suited to complex incidents engaged at local level by a small group of individuals;
2 **comprehensive investigations**: these are suited to complex issues which should be managed by a multidisciplinary team (MDT) involving experts or specialist investigators;
3 **independent investigations**: these are normally reserved for situations where the integrity of the internal investigation is likely to be challenged or it will be difficult for the organisation to be objective.

Healthcare providers should tell families or patients that a serious incident report is underway. The duty of candour and the NHS principles of being open and honest envisage families or patients being involved in the process.

Where an investigation is carried out, it should focus on three key questions: (i) What were the problems?; (ii) How did the incident happen? This will involve looking at the factors that contributed to the problem/s; (iii) Why did the incident occur? This is the key question.

It is important to note that since April 2019, trusts are no longer responsible for carrying out serious incident reports and investigations into any maternity incident that qualifies for an investigation by the Healthcare Safety Investigation Branch (HSIB) – please see below for more details of HSIB and the criteria for an HSIB maternity investigations. However, if a case does not meet the HSIB criteria for an investigation by them then the trust must carry out an investigation and report under the SIR framework.

In AvMA's experience the principles behind serious incident reporting are sound although there are problems in practice. Some of the most usual problems are: SIRs are not always called when they ought to be; the correct level of investigation is not always employed; the family is not always made aware of the investigation, or involved in the investigation or given a copy of the final report; the reports are not always robust, failing to be either sufficiently objective or comprehensive enough in scope.

The SIR can be used to identify whether something has gone wrong with care provided. It may also help to identify whether the care provided contributed to a patient's death. If an inquest has been called then the healthcare provider should be asked to confirm whether the SIR has been prepared.

Regardless of whether a patient wants to consider legal action or just wants their questions answered, the SIR may be a useful source of information. More information on SIRs can be found in the NHS England national framework. The NHS England frequently asked questions document on SIR is also helpful[9] although it is understood that the SIR framework is currently under review.

---

9   See https://www.england.nhs.uk/wp-content/uploads/2015/03/serious-incident-framwrk-15-16-faqs-fin.pdf.

National Health Service Resolution (NHS Resolution) – formerly the NHSLA

In April 2017 the National Health Services Litigation Authority (NHSLA) changed its name to National Health Services Resolution (NHS Resolution). It is intended that NHS Resolution will be more involved in incidents at an earlier stage. The focus of NHS Resolution is to be on prevention, learning and early intervention. The aim is that NHS Resolution will help to avoid unnecessary court action by resolving 'concerns and disputes fairly and effectively to deliver resolution in its broadest sense, which is about more than just money.' It also aims to drive improvement in healthcare and patient safety; identify solutions to prevent harm, share learning, and save money.

Additionally, NHS Resolution has confirmed that it will be taking a new approach to infants who are brain damaged at birth. Trusts are expected to report all maternity incidents that occur after 1 April 2017 to NHS Resolution so they can increase the level of support offered. This reporting process is known as the Early Notification Scheme (ENS). Helen Vernon, Chief Executive of NHS Resolution has said:

> ... we will work with the family, healthcare staff and the trust, right from the start to ensure that we learn from what went wrong and share this rapidly across the NHS. Increased support to the NHS in delivering candour in practice and in sharing learning for improvement will be coupled with a fresh approach to resolution which reduces the need for costly and stressful court proceedings.

Clearly, if NHS Resolution is able to achieve its aims then this could prove to be an effective non-legal remedy to litigation. It is still early days for NHS Resolution and it is too soon to say whether they can effectively deliver improvements for patients and service users.

The Early Notification Scheme (ENS)

The ENS was introduced by NHS Resolution in April 2017 and applies to all maternity incidents likely to result in severe brain injury. It is now a requirement for all NHS trusts to complete the standard report form which has been drafted specifically for this purpose. Details of the ENS can be found on the NHS Resolution website[10] which also directs individuals to the report form.

NHS Resolution requires that the early notification report form is completed in circumstances where, following labour, a baby is diagnosed within the first seven days of life with a potentially serious brain injury. NHS Resolution looks to the Royal College Obstetricians and Gynaecologists (RCOG) guidelines to help identify a potentially serious brain injury. The first requirement is that the baby is at or past 37 weeks gestation; having met that requirement the key criteria are that the baby was diagnosed with a Grade III Hypoxic Ischaemic Encephalopathy (HIE); alternatively or in addition that the baby underwent therapeutic cooling. The other trigger is where the baby has decreased central tone and has experienced seizures and is comatose.

---

10   See https://resolution.nhs.uk/early-notification-scheme/.

If the criteria are met then the early notification report form must be completed. The form does not ask the author of the form to confirm that the family has been advised of their legal rights and their avenues for redress but it does require the author to state whether or not the family have been advised that the relevant records and investigation documents are to be shared with the NHS Resolution. It also seeks confirmation from the author as to whether the family agree to share the documents with NHS Resolution.

The report form also asks for a preliminary assessment of risk to be shared. The risk is expressed as one of the following: that substandard care was unlikely; that there is a less than 10% chance of substandard care occurring; possible substandard care is put at a greater than 25% chance and likely substandard care is put at 50% or more.

Once the report has been completed it should be sent to the trust's legal services department within 14 days of the notifiable brain injury occurring. The trust's legal department is then expected to report to NHS Resolution within 30 days of the incident occurring.

NHS Resolution say the ENS will enable them to increase the level of support to teams where incidences occur and it aims to create national support networks. They also say that the scheme will enable them to introduce mediation with a view to maintaining relations between the trust and the family and will allow a preliminary investigation into legal liability.

The ENS is less clear on what information is given to the family about their right to seek independent advice and information on what the process and ongoing investigations may mean for them. This is an issue which AvMA has raised with NHS Resolution on several occasions since April 2017. For the ENS process to be fair, it is only right that a family is made aware at the outset what the avenues for redress are and how they work; this information needs to be made available to families when the ENS process commences. Many families may want to wait for NHS Resolution to complete their investigations before seeking independent legal advice, some may not want legal advice at all, but the choice must be theirs. Families cannot make proper choices without knowing what their options are; they should be aware that organisations like AvMA exist and provide a free, independent and impartial explanation of what the process means and what the family's options are. AvMA is concerned that this is not happening.

There are good reasons why NHS Resolution should be carrying out investigations into legal liability at an early stage, however there is no good reason for a family whose child may have been injured not to be aware that they too have a right to seek independent advice and to carry out their own legal investigations into liability, should they choose to.

It is too early to say what difference the ENS has made or will make. What is clear though is that by completing the early notification report form and submitting it, it opens the door to these serious, complex and potentially valuable legal claims being subject to other new processes, including investigations by the Health Service Investigation Board (HSIB).

Health Service Investigation Branch (HSIB)

On 31 January 2017, the Public Administration and Constitutional Affairs Committee (PACAC) published a report: 'Will the NHS never learn?' Follow-up to PHSO report 'Learning from mistakes[11] on the NHS in England; the report found that a fear of blame inhibits open investigations, learning and improvement. It also identified that the DH, NHS Improvement, and Care Quality Commission (CQC) acknowledged the need for the 'investigative culture to be transformed into one in which open minded, learning-focused investigations can routinely take place' and stated that this was a critical issue which affected complaint handling and clinical incident investigations in the NHS.

The report also noted that despite a number of initiatives to improve NHS investigations there was also a 'distinct lack of coordination and accountability for how these initiatives might coalesce'. It recommended that, in an attempt to overcome the diffuse ministerial responsibility for clinical incident investigations in the NHS that it should fall to the Secretary of State for Health to be accountable to Parliament for delivering the coordinated shift towards a learning culture in the NHS in England.

Significantly, the report also accepted a previous recommendation from March 2015 to introduce a new Healthcare Safety Investigation Branch (HSIB). It is worth noting that HSIB started life as the Independent Patient Safety Investigation Service (IPSIS), it then evolved into what is now known as the Healthcare Safety Investigation Branch (HSIB). HSIB's aim is to carry out investigations with a focus on developing a learning practice for investigations in the NHS in England.

Essentially, there are two types of investigation carried out by HSIB; the first type became operational in April 2017 and operates using the principles of 'safe space'. The second type, HSIB maternity, became operational in April 2018 and was fully rolled out to all NHS trusts in England by April 2019; HSIB maternity is to operate under the duty of candour, not the 'safe space' principle.

HSIB intends to carry out a small number of non-maternity investigations, estimated to be about 30 per annum. It is intended that HSIB will set the national standards by which all clinical investigations are conducted and serve as a model of how investigations should be carried out. It will also provide support and guidance to NHS organisations when carrying out their own investigations and local NHS providers will be responsible for delivering the HSIB standards according to the serious incident framework. It is understood that the CQC as regulator will assess the quality of the investigations according to those standards at local level.

What is unique and controversial about HSIB's role is that it intends to address the NHS's blame culture by carrying out all of its non-maternity clinical investigations in a 'safe space'. A safe space is where people directly involved in the most serious clinical incidents can speak honestly and openly in the interests of learning. It is envisaged that staff, families and patients will discuss clinical incidents without fear of reprisals and

---

11   See https://publications.parliament.uk/pa/cm201617/cmselect/cmpubadm/743/743.pdf.

that this approach will override the defensive culture which currently prevails and which prevents open and learning-focussed discussions.

Although HSIB came into being in April 2017 there is still insufficient evidence to identify how effective this body will be.

The Health Service Safety Investigations Bill (HSSI Bill) was published on 14 September 2017; The Bill sets out that HSIB's function is to investigate 'qualifying incidents' which occur during NHS services; a qualifying incident is one which has implications for patient safety. The HSIB investigation should also address risks to the safety of patients by recommending improvements to systems and practices within the NHS.

HSIB must publish a report on the outcome of their investigation. The report 'may' include any information or reference to a document or documents to which the prohibition applies but not the documents. The Bill proposes that documents will only be disclosed by order from the High Court and even then it is suggested that the order should only be made where it can be shown that disclosure is necessary in the interests of justice and where the interests of justice outweigh any adverse impact on future HSIB investigations. The effect of this is that key documentation and information relied upon in an HSIB investigation, other than a maternity investigation, will be protected from disclosure and inadmissible in civil proceedings. On 4 December 2018, the DH responded to a joint committee report on the HSSI Bill. The government response confirms their support for non-disclosure of documents unless there is an order from the High Court. The government is considering an appropriate form of wording so HSIB can disclose documents and information to bodies such as the police and regulators to further their investigations without compromising the 'safe space' principle; at the time of writing the draft wording is not available.

The HSSI Bill also proposed that HSIB develop guidance on supporting a measured expansion to safe space investigations by and on behalf of local NHS trusts, NHS foundation trusts and other providers of NHS funded health care.

It proposed that trusts should be able to apply to HSIB to become accredited to carry out its own investigations. Thankfully the joint committee report rejected this proposal. AvMA has put considerable effort into lobbying against the proposed safe space approach to investigations; written and verbal evidence was put before the Joint Committee who described AvMA's evidence as 'compelling'. AvMA's view is that the 'safe space' approach to investigations is an affront to the statutory duty of candour and the NHS constitution on being open and honest when things go wrong. It will prevent the injured person and or their family from accessing information that is relevant to the care they received; it will directly infringe patient's rights. It risks encouraging trusts to retreat behind a closed door which will only serve to exacerbate mistrust between the parties and create a more adversarial atmosphere. This would be a retrograde step and the last thing the NHS needs.

HSIB maternity investigations

HSIB maternity investigations were introduced very recently in April 2018. By contrast, the maternity investigations are being carried out under the duty of candour principles. HSIB maternity investigations are now fully rolled out in England and from 1 April 2019 apply to all trusts. HSIB is expected to undertake one thousand maternity investigations each year. The maternity investigations will include brain injuries arising at birth, stillbirths, neonatal deaths and maternal deaths that occur within 12 months of the birth.

As referred to above, the HSIB maternity investigations will now replace the need for trusts to carry out SIR investigations into this category of case. Given the standard of some SIRs this may not be a bad thing. Perhaps HSIB will demonstrate that it can identify the patient safety risks that the trust needs to address, thereby driving learning and improvements within the NHS healthcare system. It may also prove that it can involve the families in their investigation taking note of the information and evidence they can give and make them feel part of the process, a factor that has all too often been overlooked by a SIR prepared by a trust.

It is understood that HSIB aims to prepare a draft report on the outcome of their investigation and make recommendations for change within 60 days of being notified of the incident. Only one report will be produced and that same report will be available to trusts, staff and the family.

As stated, the HSIB is tasked with undertaking investigations into maternity incidents including brain injured babies. HSIB maternity investigations into brain injured babies look to the RCOG guidelines referred to above (see the section on ENS), further details can be found on HSIB website.[12] To this extent there appears to be a neat overlap between the NHS Resolution's own ENS and HSIB maternity investigations.

AvMA's discussions with the HSIB have tried to explore what safeguards are in place to ensure families are made aware of what their rights are at the point where ENS and HSIB investigations commence. AvMA does not suggest that every family should be sent to a lawyer for legal advice, however AvMA does say that families especially those faced with the daunting prospect that their child may have sustained a lifelong, serious brain injury, should be made aware of their potential rights, options for redress and access to independent advice. The HSIB take the view that they are not under a duty or obligation to advise the family of their rights, but they do expect that trusts comply with their obligations under the duty of candour.

It should be noted that the duty of candour does not extend beyond advising a patient that something may have gone wrong with their care. It appears therefore that there is no obligation on anyone to do anything other than direct a family to the ENS or HSIB investigation process. There is a real risk that this approach will not create a level playing field or instil confidence that the HSIB investigation is independent of the trust and that HSIB investigations are expected to be impartial and robust.

There is a potential link between the HSIB investigations and a new proposed alternative to litigation: rapid resolution and redress (RRR). More information on RRR is available below.

12　See https://www.hsib.org.uk/maternity/what-we-investigate/.

NHS England

NHS England is an executive non-departmental public body (NDPB) of the DH. NHS England oversees the budget, planning, delivery and day-to-day operation of the commissioning side of the NHS in England as set out in the Health and Social Care Act 2012.

NHS England holds organisations to account for spending public money effectively for patients. They are responsible for commissioning the contracts for GPs, pharmacists, and dentists, and support local health services that are led by groups of GPs called Clinical Commissioning Groups (CCGs). CCGs plan and pay for local services such as hospitals and ambulance services. NHS England's complaints policy covers the handling of complaints or concerns relating directly to commissioned services or services provided by NHS England.

NHS England defines a complaint as 'an expression of dissatisfaction about an act, omission or decision of NHS England, either verbal or written, and whether justified or not, which requires a response' (NHS England Complaints Policy).

Complaints can be made by any person who is affected by the action, or by someone who is acting on behalf of a patient who has died, or who is under the age of 18, or has mental or physical incapacity. A complaint can also be made where the patient/complainant has given consent to a third party to act on their behalf or to someone who has appropriate power of attorney. A member of parliament instructed on behalf of a constituent may also complain.

As with the NHS hospital complaints process, complaints must not be made more than 12 months after the date the incident complained of occurred or the date the incident came to the notice of the complainant. However, complaints will be considered outside of the 12 month time limit if they can be investigated effectively and fairly.

Complaints should be acknowledged within three working days after receipt and should be investigated and responded to within 40 days; it may be longer if the investigation process has been discussed and a timetable agreed with the complainant. Where the complaint involves input or investigation from parties or organisations outside of NHS England, the complainant will have to give their consent to NHS England to engage with those organisations.

The complainant will have a named contact throughout the process and should be provided with information on the independent advocacy services provider in their region, however there are reports of waiting lists for help and limited services in some areas. They should also be provided with an update on the progress of the investigation every ten working days within the agreed investigation period.

Once an investigation report has been prepared, the complainant should receive a response to their complaint; the response will be based on the content of the investigation report and should be signed off by the national director or nominated regional sign off. The response must include an explanation of how the complaint has been considered, an apology if appropriate, an explanation based on facts and whether the complaint is upheld in full or in part. The response to the complaint should also set out any remedial action considered to be necessary and confirmation that it is satisfied that the service will implement the recommendations. It will also respond to people about any lessons learned.

The complainant should receive details of the Parliamentary and Health Service Ombudsman (PHSO) as the next stage of the complaint process. This information is provided in the event that they wish to take matters further.

In AvMA's experience the public are rarely aware of the potential to involve NHS England and the use of the complaints process does appear to be underutilised. It is suggested that trusts and primary care providers are unaware of the potential for NHS England to be involved or are deliberately not involving these groups.

Healthwatch England

Healthwatch England is a body established under the Health and Social Care Act 2008 (as amended by the Health and Social Care Act 2012) as an independent consumer champion for health and social care. It provides leadership for the local Healthwatch network but its primary role is to identify the views, experiences and needs of the people who use health and social care services and to communicate these to NHS England and other organisations. It relays whether the standard of health and social care provision should be improved and if so, how. It aims to put people at the centre of health and social care.

In order to help achieve Healthwatch England's aims the Act allowed it to create a local Healthwatch in every local authority area across England.

Although Healthwatch is not a non-legal remedy as such, it does represent the views of the public by identifying worries and or concerns about health and social care services and tries to ensure that those concerns are addressed.

Healthwatch was hailed as the new consumer champion but again, in AvMA's experience, there appears to be a general lack of awareness of the support they might provide.

REQUESTS FOR INFORMATION

Data Protection Act 1998, Freedom of Information Act 2000, General Data Protection Regulations (EU) 2016/679

The type of non-legal remedy an individual might seek to explore is largely dependent on what it is they wish to achieve. Many patients and or their families just want to know what happened, how it happened and why it happened. While that may seem a very straightforward wish, in practice it can be difficult to achieve.

It may be possible to clarify the facts around an incident by requesting information under the Data Protection Act 1998 (DPA 1998), the Freedom of Information Act 2000 (FOIA 2000) or under the General Data Protection Regulation (EU) 2016/679 (GDPR) which were introduced in May 2018.

Under the FOIA 2000 public authorities have to publish certain information about their activities and every citizen has the right to request public information. The Act covers all recorded information held by a public authority; it is not limited to official documents and it may cover, for example, drafts, emails, notes, amongst other things. However, there is no blanket right to information, there may be good reasons not to release information and there are a number of specific exemptions under both the FOIA 2000 and DPA 1998. For example, a request under the FOIA 2000 may be refused if the cost of providing the information will take up too much staff time or is too expensive. A request may also be refused if it is considered vexatious or repeats a previous request from the same person.

Where a FOIA 2000 request is made in relation to a PHSO investigation the PHSO has to consider whether any other Act exempts the disclosure of that information. The PHSO has to balance its duty to operate openly and transparently with other legislative duties, in particular the need to protect the privacy of personal and other information given to the PHSO in confidence.

Under the DPA 1998, every individual has a right to request access to their own data; this is referred to as a subject access request. However, as with the FOIA 2000, there are exemptions to the right to access information about yourself. It should be noted that the DPA 1998 only applies to people who are living, it cannot be used to access information about someone who has died. Organisations responding to a request for personal information are entitled to charge a maximum fee of £10.00 or a maximum of £50.00 in the case of a request for paper based health records, for example: medical records; or education records.

As with FOIA 2000 requests, when the PHSO receives a request under the DPA 1998 it must weigh up whether the substance of the request comes into conflict with their duty to protect the privacy of its investigations.

Where there is a dispute over whether documents are disclosable under the FOIA 2000 or under the DPA 1998, then a referral may be made to the Information Commissioners Officer (ICO). More details on requesting information under either of these Acts and the exemptions can be found at: https://ico.org.uk.

The GDPR also enables individuals to obtain information about themselves. A person can seek information about themselves from any organisation which processes information about them. The request for that information is referred to as a subject access request.

Once a request has been received the person making the request for information about themselves (the data subject) must receive the information held in a concise and intelligible way. The information should include an explanation about the purpose of the processing; the categories of data concerned; the categories of recipient to whom the personal data has been disclosed; and details of how long the information is to be stored. Under the regulations there is a right to request rectification or erasure of personal data, restriction of processing, or object to data being processed.

The information must be provided as soon as possible and in any event within 28 days of the request being made.

Where the response to a subject access request includes other data subjects ie third parties this information should be redacted before it is sent. The only exception to this is where the third party has consented to their details being passed on.

Individuals will find that there are advantages to relying on the GDPR when seeking to obtain copies of their medical records; copies of those records must be provided free of charge, but note the obligation is to provide copies not the original documents. If a hospital or healthcare provider holds a large quantity of information they are allowed to ask the person making the request to specify the information the request relates to, for example they may be asked to specify the period of time the request pertains to.

ALTERNATIVES TO LITIGATION

The Pre-Action Protocol for the Resolution of Clinical Disputes

The Pre-Action Protocol for the Resolution of Clinical Disputes (PAP) is set out in the Civil Procedure Rules 1998.[13]

The PAP aims to resolve as many disputes as possible without the need to resort to litigation. It has long emphasised the need to restore trust and a relationship between patient and healthcare providers, reduce delay and ensure costs are proportionate.

Part 5 of the PAP is dedicated to alternative dispute resolution (ADR). ADR covers a number of mechanisms, other than litigation, by which resolution might be reached, it includes: discussion and negotiation; mediation; arbitration (a third party deciding the dispute); early neutral evaluation (a third party giving an informed opinion on the dispute); and ombudsmen schemes.

Mediation

One of the stated objectives of the PAP is to enable parties to explore the use of mediation (PAP para 2.2(g)). Mediation is defined by the Centre for Effective Dispute Resolution (CEDR) as:

> A flexible process conducted confidentially in which a neutral person actively assists parties in working towards a negotiated agreement of a dispute or difference, with the parties in ultimate control of the decision to settle and the terms of resolution.[14]

The process can be a very powerful tool in resolving claims; one of its key strengths is that it allows patients and or families to fully express their emotions, raise their concerns and to have their say in a managed but less formal way than that offered by litigation. By contrast litigation will only really 'hear' the claimant's concerns through exchange of witness statements and by oral evidence at trial if the case proceeds that far; many claimants find giving evidence at trial an overwhelming and not very positive experience.

The extent to which emotions can get in the way of settlement cannot be underestimated; many claimants are motivated to bring claims through frustration that those earlier processes such as serious incident investigations and/or complaints have not been open and honest. Another key driving factor for patients is the need to ensure that the same thing

---

13 See http://www.justice.gov.uk/courts/procedure-rules/civil/protocol/prot_rcd#alternative.
14 See https://www.cedr.com/about_us/library/glossary.php.

does not happen to anyone else. These motives cannot always be satisfied through litigation or through an award of damages, no matter how significant the award might be. Mediation may offer a solution.

The cost of mediation is often considered prohibitive; recently NHS Resolution has committed itself to the process in a more meaningful way. Following a public tender the NHS LA (now NHS Resolution), announced in December 2016 the launch of a mediation service that was:

> designed to support injured claimants, their families and healthcare staff in working together towards resolution without the need to go to court.[15]

For more information about these services contact:

CEDR
020 7536 6060
adr@cedr.com
www.cedr.com
Contact: Graham Massie, Chief Operating Officer, via gmassie@cedr.com.

Trust Mediation
020 7353 3237
www.trustmediation.org.uk
Contact: Tim Wallis, Chairman, via tim.wallis@trustmediation.org.uk.

CADR
020 3282 7565
www.costs-adr.com
Contact: Hannah Rawlins, Registrar, via hannah.rawlins@costs-adr.com.

It should be noted that CADR (Costs Alternative Dispute Resolution) was set up for the specific purpose of mediating cost disputes. The cases of *Reid v Buckinghamshire Healthcare NHS Trust*[16] and *Bristow v Alexandra Hospital NHS Trust*[17] are cases which demonstrate the importance of taking mediation in costs seriously. In the *Reid* case, Master O'Hare ordered the party which had refused to mediate (the NHS) to pay the claimant's costs on an indemnity basis for failing to engage in the process.

When the NHSLA first launched their mediation services they also published an information leaflet entitled 'Mediating claims in the NHS': that leaflet stated that many people chose to have a lawyer attend the mediation with them however this is not obligatory. It is understood that NHS Resolution has withdrawn that leaflet.

Whilst it is true that mediation can be a powerful tool its strength is in the process being voluntary and that the parties come to it willingly. If mediation is made compulsory then it simply renders it part of the litigation process. Mediation should not be prescriptive and there is no right time to mediate. This will depend on the case and the point at which the claimant lawyer believes that settlement might be achieved; it also depends on what the client wants. Other factors will include the cost of mediation; the process can be expensive and does not guarantee settlement. Other forms of ADR are already widely used in clinical negligence claims, such as round table meetings (RTM) or telephone

---

15   See http://www.nhsla.com/CurrentActivity/Pages/News.aspx.
16   [2015] 10 WLUK 752, 28 October 2015, Master O'Hare.
17   [2015] 11 WLUK 67, 4 November 2015, Master Simons.

discussions, both of which are often thought to be more cost effective and just as likely to achieve resolution.

AvMA take the view that patients or families entering into the process unrepresented or without the benefit of any previous legal advice should obtain independent advice beforehand. Litigants in person are highly likely to be disadvantaged by entering into the mediation process without medical records, independent medical reports, any of the trusts' own investigation documents and in circumstances where they may not have used the NHS complaints process. Ordinary members of the public may not be aware of the existence of these documents and will not necessarily be in a position to ask for them, neither will they have any idea of what might represent a fair and reasonable settlement for their case. A level playing field is required. AvMA may be able to help and offers free advice and information on a helpline.[18]

Arbitration

The Ministry of Justice increased the cost of court fees in March 2016, in some cases by as much as 600%. This increase has caused the legal profession to pause and consider alternatives. Arbitration has become more of a considered option in clinical negligence work although it is still not widely used.

The advantages of arbitration are that parties agree to use this mode of settlement and identify their terms at the outset. The arbitration fee is usually shared by both parties although this can be negotiated. The terms of the arbitration will be in writing and will typically identify who the arbitrator will be and the applicable hourly rate. It is understood that in practice the hourly rates are often lower than the market rate but are still economically viable. Agreeing the rate in this way avoids the need for cost budgeting and keeps the costs at a reasonable and predictable level.

Arbitration gives parties the opportunity to identify and agree an experienced clinical negligence practitioner to act as arbitrator; there is nothing to prevent parties agreeing more than one arbitrator although clearly this will increase the cost. The arbitrator is appointed in place of a judge who may have little or no clinical negligence experience. The mode of identifying and appointing the arbitrator is left to the parties; they are also free to agree any circumstances in which the authority of the arbitrator or arbitrators may be revoked.

The arbitration process is governed by the Arbitration Act 1996. Section 1(a) of the Act states that: 'the object of arbitration is to obtainthe fair resolution of disputes by an impartial tribunal without unnecessary delay or expense'. The Act will apply rules in circumstances where the parties' agreement is silent on a particular point.Parties entering into arbitration can agree to allow the arbitrator to decide either part of, or the entire dispute. They are also free to agree that the arbitrator be responsible for exercising the appropriate remedy or remedies including an award of interest. An award made by the arbitrator is final and binding on both parties unless they have agreed to the contrary, or where it is alleged that there was a serious irregularity affecting the arbitration process.

---

18 AvMA helpline is open Monday to Friday from 10.00 am to 3.00 pm, or see www.avma. org.uk.

Parties are entitled to use any appeal process that may be written into the arbitration agreement or in accordance with the Arbitration Act 1996.

The Personal Injury claims Arbitration Service (PIcARBS) has been offering arbitration services in personal injury and clinical negligence matters since 2015.[19] Some clinical negligence specialist chambers also offer arbitration services. By way of illustrating how the interest in arbitration is growing, the Arbitration (Scotland) Act 2010 was recently amended to include an option for resolving personal injury and medical negligence disputes.

Early neutral evaluation

CEDR defines early neutral evaluation as a process in which the parties or their counsel present their cases to a neutral third party (usually an experienced and respected lawyer with expertise in the substantive area of the dispute) who renders a non-binding reasoned evaluation on the merit of the case.

Parties who agree to arbitration may also agree to ask the arbitrator to carry out a neutral evaluation. However, the person providing the evaluation may also be a mediator. When this happens the evaluator is often referred to as Med-Arb. The object of the exercise is to help parties identify the strengths and weaknesses of their case and from there make an assessment of how likely the claim is to succeed either at arbitration or in civil proceedings.

Although the evaluator's view is usually an informal and impartial evaluation of the merits of the case it can help parties focus their minds on settlement and resolution. In turn, this provides certainty for the parties and can help to avoid the unpredictable nature of litigation and the burden of additional costs.

Rapid Resolution and Redress (RRR)

Although this section has been included, at the time of writing it has not been introduced and is not an alternative to litigation. However, the government has consulted on this scheme and it is possible that RRR or something similar to it may be adopted at some point in the future and offer an alternative to litigation in cases involving severe avoidable birth injury.

The government consulted on a rapid resolution and redress scheme for severe avoidable birth injury in early 2017; it offered a response to that consultation in November 2017.[20] At about the same time, the Parliamentary Under-Secretary, Lord O'Shaughnessy, said in a statement to the house:[21]

> My intention is that in incidents of possibly avoidable serious brain injury at birth, successfully establishing the new independent HSIB investigations

---

19   Details of this service can be found at: http://www.picarbs.co.uk/index_files/thePIcARBS arbitrators.htm.
20   See https://consultations.dh.gov.uk/rapid-resolution-and-redress/maternity-litigation/results/rrr_consultation_response-final.pdf.
21   See https://hansard.parliament.uk/Lords/2017-11-28/debates/BA366EF3-78F1-4AF8-BF27-C7C2ADE7B0B2/MaternalSafetyStrategy.

will be an important step on the road to introducing a full rapid resolution and redress scheme in order to reduce delays in delivering support and compensation for families.

He went on to say that he was looking to launch the scheme ideally from 2019. To date, the government has been silent on introducing the RRR scheme or a variation of it; the government is currently preoccupied with Brexit and as a consequence nothing is expected to happen on this in the near future.

The RRR consultation proposed a voluntary scheme which would allow a family qualifying for entry into the scheme to opt out at any stage. It also proposed introducing a different test to the legal test for clinical negligence claims by applying a test of 'avoidable harm'. Potentially, this would have opened up the scheme to families who cannot satisfy the legal test required to bring a clinical negligence claim. This would make the scheme very expensive, it is AvMA's view that this is one of the reasons the scheme has not been introduced.

The main objectives of the scheme are stated to be: emphasising a learning culture through non adversarial delivery of compensation; shortening the length of time between the avoidable incident occurring and when an award of compensation is made, thereby improving the experience for families when things do go wrong. All of these are laudable aims.

AvMA fully supports an optional alternative to litigation, however there are problems with the proposals, not least the fact that the government was working on the basis that the average settlement for a neurological injury case was £6.25 million. Another key concern for us is that the proposals were modelled on total compensation awarded under the scheme being at 90% of the average court award.

It is not clear how the government has identified the figure for the average settlement; it is the view of the author that if RRR or a similar scheme is to go forward this figure needs to be revisited, not least because of the reduction in the discount rate to -0.075% as announced in February 2017. Neither is it clear how the scheme identifies that justice can be achieved by granting a severely damaged child only receiving 90% of the compensation due to it.

The RRR consultation proposed operating a two stage test. Stage one was to be based on administrative eligibility, that is, if the brain injury met the criteria set out in the RCOG Guidelines. Stage two was more complicated and looked to a panel to decide on the child's eligibility for compensation. The timing of the second stage of the assessment was to be based on the extent and nature of the injury; it was noted that the timing would vary and be determined on a case-by-case basis. An early payment was intended to be made to the injured child when it reached four years of age at which time they would become eligible for a £50–£100,000 payment to cover the cost of things like adaptations to accommodation. The intention was that further lump sums would be awarded along with periodical payments in line with the child's needs; the aim was for 50% of the compensation payable to be made through periodical payments.

Although RRR has not been introduced and there is no certainty that it will be, or if it is, what it will eventually look like, it is still worth a mention as some of the suggestions around stage one, in particular the reference to eligibility based on the RCOG guidelines, appear to have been picked up and are currently reflected in both the NHS Resolution ENS process and HSIB's maternity investigation criteria.

There can be no doubt that families find litigation an extremely stressful and intrusive process. AvMA is confident that there must be a better way of resolving these cases and RRR offers an opportunity to open up a dialogue on what this should look like. However, provision would need to be made for families to obtain independent advice and support on their options.

Professional regulation

Most health professions have a regulatory body which maintains a register of those qualified to work in that particular professional capacity. The most well-known regulatory bodies are the General Medical Council (GMC) which is responsible for regulating doctors and the Nursing and Midwifery Council (NMC) responsible for the regulation of nurses and midwives.

There are a number of other regulatory bodies for other areas of the medical profession such as dentists, pharmacists, opticians and chiropractors.

Other allied health professionals may be covered by the Health and Care Professions Council (HCPC) which covers 16 other professions including speech and language therapists, physiotherapists, chiropodists and so on. HCPC is a regulator and looks to ensuring compliance with regulation, standards, training and behaviour; it does not resolve disputes or complaints.

It is the role of the regulatory body to investigate serious complaints about individual practitioners' fitness to practice. The sort of issues frequently investigated are around serious professional misconduct, criminal offences and repeated poor performance which call into question a person's professional competence.

Complaints to a regulatory body should be made in writing and set out the reasons why it is alleged that the individual is not fit to practise. Usually the regulatory body follows a system that involves screening the complaint to identify the nature of the complaint and satisfying itself that the issue is urgent or concerns a matter they are able to investigate. If the screening suggests that there is an issue which requires further investigation then it will be considered further, however both the GMC and NMC are in the process of changing how cases are going to be handled. Following investigation the matter may be referred for a formal hearing and the complainant may be called as a witness to give evidence. If following the hearing the individual is found wanting then the regulatory body will impose a sanction. The sanctions most commonly used are: removal from the professional register; temporary suspension from the register; and or directions as to further training required.

For further details you should contact the relevant regulatory body.

Public inquiries

Public inquiries are governed by the Public Inquiries Act 2005. A public inquiry can be called in circumstances where a minister of the United

Kingdom, Scotland or Northern Ireland considers that particular events have caused or are capable of causing public concern. They may also be called where there is public concern that particular events may have occurred.

A public inquiry has no power to determine any individual's civil or criminal liability. The inquiry may be undertaken by a chairman acting alone or a chairman acting with one or more other members of an inquiry panel. It is a requirement that any chairman or inquiry panel is impartial and that they possess the necessary expertise to undertake the inquiry.

Members of an inquiry panel and any assessors, counsel or solicitor to the inquiry have immunity from suit for any acts or omissions made during the course of the inquiry. An inquiry comes to an end when the terms of reference have been fulfilled and a report of the inquiry has been delivered to the minister. Reports of an inquiry must be published in full unless it is considered to be in the public interest that some sections of the report are withheld.

In practice, public inquiries are difficult to secure and will not be available for most individual cases of clinical negligence. As we have seen from Stafford Hospital, public inquiries will be held into issues concerning health care where they are considered to be so serious that they cause sufficient public concern.

The Care Quality Commission (CQC)

The CQC is an executive non-departmental public body of the DH. It was first established in 2009 and its function is to regulate, inspect and monitor health and social care services in England.

The CQC are responsible for ensuring health and social care services are providing the public with safe, effective, compassionate and high quality services. Where services fall short of this standard they are encouraged to improve.

Complaints about a service provider should be made directly to the service provider. The CQC will not take up a complaint for a member of the public. The only exception to this is people whose rights are restricted under the Mental Health Act 2007.

However, the CQC do encourage patients or families to make them aware of any complaint being made as the issue may be considered at the time the CQC inspects the relevant hospital trust.

The NHS Redress Act 2006

The NHS Redress Act was enacted in 2006. It gives the Secretary of State power to establish a scheme for the purposes of redress in tort without recourse to civil proceedings for cases involving the health service in England. The scheme is able to make such provisions as the Secretary of State thinks fit but it must be a scheme that provides for the ability to make an offer of compensation in satisfaction of any right to bring civil proceedings. It also requires the giving of an apology, an explanation of what went wrong with the care, and a report on the action that has been, or will be taken to prevent similar cases arising.

The Act does provide a platform for a low value scheme to be developed; despite this no scheme has been set up under it. There would of course be upfront costs associated with implementing the NHS Redress Act 2009 but it is possible that this Act with some adaptations, including the provision of independent advice to the client might offer an appropriate, low cost way of resolving many lower value claims.

CONCLUSION

AvMA recognises that litigation is a difficult process for patients, clinicians and medical staff and remains fully committed to finding a quicker, cheaper and easier resolution to claims that all too often end up in litigation. However, it is equally important that any alternative allows the injured person and or their family to fully engage in the process and to be aware of all their options and rights to redress at the earliest opportunity; they must be treated fairly and with dignity.

Healthcare providers need to learn from their mistakes and take steps to address the problems giving rise to substandard care and unnecessary injury, in practice that can mean many different things, from providing an individual or individuals with appropriate training to changing systems that have shown themselves to be unfit for their purpose. It is only by accepting that poor care and avoidable harm has occurred, being willing to do something about it and sharing that learning with other hospitals, that the cycle of repetitious claims seen in clinical negligence litigation will be broken.

AvMA is open to genuine discussions about workable alternatives to litigation for clinical negligence. Following Jackson LJ's most recent *Review of Civil Litigation Costs: Supplemental Report Fixed Recoverable Costs* (July 2017), the Civil Justice Council (CJC) has set up a working party (AvMA is currently a member) to explore whether an improved process for handling clinical negligence can be developed specifically for claims with damages valued up to £25,000. The working party's terms of reference include the need to draw up a structure for fixed recoverable costs which can be attached to the new process. Additionally, the working party is to have regard to how any improved process might affect issues of patient safety, including the way in which case outcomes are reported back to healthcare providers for learning purposes. At the time of writing the work of the CJC working party is confidential and ongoing.

Chapter 4

Legal remedies

Catriona Stirling

VICARIOUS LIABILITY

Traditionally, an employer was vicariously responsible for the negligent acts or omissions of his servant committed within the scope of the employment, but, generally, not for the negligence of an independent contractor, provided he showed due care in selecting the contractor; an employment relationship was needed in order to establish vicarious liability. However, the position has been developed in recent years by a large amount of appellate case law, which is explored further below.

General principles

The general principles of vicarious liability, that is the liability of one person for the negligence of another, are as follows (they are stated in summary form). Vicarious liability means that, with regard to third parties, the employer, although personally blameless, stands in the shoes of the wrongdoer employee for the purpose of liability to the claimant. Vicarious liability is substitutional, not personal.

The law of vicarious liability has developed very significantly in recent years, with a large number of cases reaching the Court of Appeal, House of Lords and now the Supreme Court. The direction of travel has been in favour of expanding the scope of the doctrine, in some cases considerably. Older, pre-2016 (*Cox v Ministry of Justice*,[1] see below) case law concerning vicarious liability must therefore be treated with some caution.

THE NECESSARY RELATIONSHIP

Employees

To establish that the doctrine of vicarious liability applies, the claimant will often need to show first that the negligence complained of was due to the act or omission of an employee of the defendant. An employee is

---

1   [2016] UKSC 10.

one who is engaged upon a contract of service. The test of employment has varied through the years. Basically, a man is not an employee if the person who engaged him has no say in how he does his work, but only in what work he is to do. It is often not easy to decide, on applying this test, whether there is a situation of employment. A good reference point is the judgment of MacKenna J in *Ready Mixed Concrete (South East) Ltd v Minister of Pensions and National Insurance*.[2]

Despite recent developments, in many cases it will remain necessary to establish who the employer of the alleged wrongdoer is. This used to be fairly easy in the medical field, but has become more complicated in recent years.

The correct defendant in respect of allegations of negligence at a hospital is the body in charge at the time of the negligence (ie the health authority for older claims and the NHS Trust for more recent ones). The trust or health authority is liable for the negligence of any of its staff, including all medical personnel it engages to carry out the necessary treatment upon the patients, both because it is under a primary non-delegable duty of care to see that the patient receives proper treatment and because of the principle of vicarious liability. However, an NHS Trust is not responsible for the negligence of a doctor who has been selected and employed by a private patient (or his GP).

A private clinic is probably responsible only for the negligence of its resident staff, though where it selects and engages the surgeon itself a court may these days find a primary duty of care, just as with an NHS hospital.

The majority of GPs are self-employed; thus, a GP is liable for his own negligent acts. If a GP practices within a partnership, then all of the partners are jointly and severally liable for the negligent acts of any of the partners. The GP (together with the partners, if there are any) is also liable for the acts of anyone they have employed and may possibly be liable for outside services they have engaged to look after patients in during times of absence.

A number of salaried GPs, however, are employed and some GPs who work for out-of-hours services to supplement their income are also employed. In such cases, the employer will be vicariously liable for negligent acts.

The position has been complicated by the number of different types of Trust that now exist. These include Hospital Trusts, Community Trusts and Foundation Trusts.

A health visitor, for example, may be employed by a GP, by a Community Trust, by a Foundation Trust. A GP may even be employed by a Trust. Clinics may be run as part of a GP practice, or by a Trust or a health authority. Who will be responsible for walk-in centres? Who is responsible for telephonic advice given by NHS Direct or other out of hours services? A claimant has to be careful, far more than before, to identify the source of the alleged negligence and ascertain who, if anyone, is the relevant employer. See below under 'Naming the wrong defendant'.

---

2   [1968] 2 QB 497.

Other relationships

While establishing an employment relationship remains the quickest and easiest route to arguing that the doctrine of vicarious liability should apply, it is not necessary to do so in all cases. It remains the case that there is in general no liability for the acts of an independent contractor, ie one who is free to perform the work contracted for in his own way.

For example, in *Kapfunde v Abbey National plc*,[3] a GP had a contract with Abbey National whereby she assessed the health of any prospective employee. She had, upon written material, not an examination, declared that the claimant was unsuitable to be employed as she had sickle cell disease and so was at risk of having a lot of time off work for illness. Having unsuccessfully sued for racial discrimination, the claimant went on to allege in this action that the GP owed her a duty of care, which she had breached. The Court of Appeal upheld, inter alia, the judge's findings that the GP was on a contract for services and not a contract of service and therefore Abbey National would not in any event be vicariously liable for any breach of duty by her. In *North Essex Health Authority v Dr David-John*,[4] the Employment Appeal Tribunal held that the GP was not in any contractual relationship with the health authority, but that, if he was, it was as an independent contractor. This is the normal position for self-employed GPs.

The general principle was confirmed by the Court of Appeal in *Biffa Waste Services Ltd v Maschinefabrik Ernst Hese GMBH*.[5]

However, if an employee is subject to the control and directions of a person other than his employer in respect of the manner in which the work is to be done, that other person will be responsible for the worker's negligent acts (the leading case is *Mersey Docks and Harbour Board v Coggins and Griffith (Liverpool) Ltd*[6]).

Sometimes, employees are loaned or hired to other employers temporarily for the purposes of carrying out a particular task or transaction. The employee remains under a contract of employment with his original employer, but in some circumstances a principle of deemed employment can apply such that vicarious liability can be attributed to the third party.

Viasystems v Thermal Transfer[7] concerned work on an air conditioning system in a factory. The first defendants had been engaged to do the work. They subcontracted the work to the second defendants, who contracted with the third defendants for the provision of a fitters' mate. The fitters' mate negligently damaged the ducting system, causing the factory to flood. At the time of his negligence, he was under the supervision of both the fitter who was employed by the third defendants, and the second defendants' supervisor. The Court of Appeal held that both the employer, and the third party exercising day-to-day control over the employee, could be vicariously liable for the employee's negligence. The question was: 'Who was entitled, and in theory obliged, to control the employee's relevant negligent act so as to prevent it?' Entire and absolute control was not a

---

3   [1999] ICR 1, CA.
4   [2003] Lloyd's Rep Med 586.
5   [2008] EWCA Civ 1257, [2009] BLR 1, CA.
6   [1947] AC 1, HL.
7   [2005] EWCA Civ 1151, [2006] 2 WLR 428.

necessary precondition of vicarious liability and dual vicarious liability was legally possible. However, the court noted that such situations would be rare.

In *Hawley v Luminar Leisure Ltd*,[8] a doorman had been supplied to the defendant nightclub by a third party, under a contract for the supply of security services. He assaulted a member of the public. The Court of Appeal held that the owners of the nightclub were vicariously liable for the assault. Although the doorman was not directly employed by the nightclub, he could properly be deemed to be an employee of the nightclub for vicarious liability purposes. On the facts, only the nightclub and not the doorman's employer could be held liable for the assault, on the basis that there had been a total transfer of control to the nightclub. Sometimes, the factual matrix within which the question of 'independence' and control arises is complex. In *P v Harrow London Borough Council*,[9] a local education authority which, in furtherance of its duty under the Education Act 1981 to make provision for children with special educational needs, sent boys with emotional behavioural difficulties to an independent school approved by the Secretary of State for Education and Science, was held by Potter J not liable in negligence for sexual abuse committed on the boys by the headmaster of the school while the boys were in his charge. The contact between the local authority and the boys was said by the court to have been wholly in the context of assessment and place provision and not in the context of physical control or direction, which was at all times in the charge of the parents and the staff of the school.

There has been much litigation regarding the employment status of agency workers. Agency workers have, in recent years, been much used by the NHS, thus the question of vicarious liability in relation to agency workers has been an important one for the clinical negligence practitioner. The traditional position if a worker is supplied by an agency to its client on a temporary basis is that the client is regarded as a user of the worker's services and not his employer. Most agency workers are not employed by the agency but have a mere 'contract for services'. The agency undertakes only to look for work for the worker and facilitate any engagement. Thus, it has often been found that an agency worker does not have an employer.

Even if there is no express contract between a worker and an agency client, if the worker works consistently for, and under the direction of, the client, ie the client controls what the worker does and how he does it, it may be possible to imply a contract between the worker and the client. However, following *James v London Borough of Greenwich*,[10] such a contract will only be implied where necessary to do so. This requires some words or conduct which indicate that the true nature of the relationship is no longer one of agency, as it originally was. Even once the existence of a contract is established, it is still necessary to establish that its nature is that of employment. The court approved observations made by the EAT to the effect that in the usual agency relationship there were no mutual

---

8   [2006] EWCA Civ 18, [2006] IRLR 816.
9   [1993] 2 FCR 341, QBD.
10 [2008] EWCA Civ 35, [2008] ICR 545, CA.

obligations between the worker and the client. In addition, mere length of service could not justify the implication of a contract.

Hawley and *Viasystems* are both cases which provide examples of the imposition of vicarious liability on a non-employer to whom a worker is provided by his employer. The Court of Appeal in these cases clearly regarded the determining factor in relation to vicarious liability as being control of the employee rather than a technical relationship of employment.

Subsequently, in recent years, there has been a significant expansion in the types of relationship to which the doctrine can apply and it is no longer necessary to fit strictly within the category of employment or one of the small extensions from employment described above.

Many of the leading cases which have heralded this expansion have been child abuse cases in which it is being argued that churches and other religious organisations can be held vicariously liable for abuses committed by their priests.

In one of the earlier cases in this vein, *Maga v Birmingham Roman Catholic Archdiocese Trustees*,[11] the Court of Appeal held that church trustees were vicariously liable for the sexual abuse of a minor by an assistant priest. They concluded that it was fair and just to impose vicarious liability because a number of factors showed that there was a sufficiently close connection between the employment at the church of the assistant priest and the abuse which had been inflicted. A central consideration of the court was the fact that it was the wrongdoer's role as a priest which gave him the status, authority and opportunity to sexually abuse the minor in question.

In *JGE v Trustees of the Portsmouth Roman Catholic Diocesan Trust*,[12] a similar result was reached, with the Court of Appeal holding that the fact that the relationship between the diocese and the priest was not an employment relationship per se did not prevent the Trust being vicariously liable for the priest's conduct. The court considered that the relationship between the parish priest was sufficiently close in character to that of employee and employer to make it just and fair to hold the diocese vicariously liable for the wrongful acts of the priest.

The Supreme Court then held in *Various Claimants v Institute of the Brothers of the Christian Schools*,[13] that the Institute, an unincorporated association of lay brothers, was vicariously liable for alleged abuse perpetrated by brothers who were supplied by the Institute as some of the teaching staff of a particular school, even though the Institute had not managed the school. The alleged abusers included non-Institute members of staff. The Supreme Court therefore imposed vicarious liability on a body which did not employ the wrongdoers, in circumstances where another body did employ them (and had been found to be vicariously liable for the same tort).

The court held that vicarious liability involved a two-stage test. First, it was necessary to consider the relationship between the defendant and the tortfeasor to see whether it was one that was capable of giving rise to vicarious liability. Second, regard should be had to the connection that

---

11 [2010] EWCA Civ 256.
12 [2012] EWCA Civ 938.
13 [2012] UKSC 56.

linked the relationship between the defendant and the tortfeasor and the act or omission of the latter (this second part of the test is considered further below).

In relation to the first part of the test, the court noted that the relationship that gives rise to vicarious liability is in the vast majority of cases that of employer and employee under a contract of employment, with the employer vicariously liable when the employee commits a tort in the course of their employment. They identified a number of policy reasons (or incidents of the relationship between employer and employee) that usually make it fair, just and reasonable to impose vicarious liability on the employer when these criteria are satisfied:

1   the employer is more likely to have the means to compensate the victim than the employee and can be expected to have insured against that liability;
2   the tort will have been committed as a result of activity being undertaken by the employee on behalf of the employer;
3   the employee's activity is likely to be part of the business activity of the employer;
4   the employer, by employing the employee to carry on the activity, will have created the risk of the tort committed by the employee;
5   the employee will, to a greater or lesser degree, have been under the control of the employer.

They went on to hold that, where the defendant and tortfeasor are not bound by a contract of employment, but their relationship has the same incidents, that relationship can properly give rise to vicarious liability on the ground that it is 'akin to that between an employer and an employee'.[14]

The relationship between the teaching brothers and the Institute was sufficiently akin to that of employer and employees to satisfy the first stage of the test:

• the Institute was subdivided into a hierarchical structure and conducted its activities as if it were a corporate body;
• the teaching activity of the brothers was undertaken because the Provincial directed them to undertake it;
• although the brothers entered into contracts of employment with those managing the school, they did so because the Provincial required them to do so;
• the teaching activity undertaken by the brothers was in furtherance of the objective, or mission, of the Institute;
• further, the manner in which the brother teachers were obliged to conduct themselves as teachers was dictated by the Institute's rules.

The Supreme Court gave further consideration to vicarious liability, this time outside the context of religious organisations and sexual abuse, in the leading case of *Cox v Ministry of Justice*,[15] in which it again expressly considered and set out the approach to be adopted in deciding whether a relationship other than one of employment can give rise to vicarious liability. It held that the Ministry of Justice (MoJ) was vicariously liable for injury caused by a negligent act of a prisoner undertaking paid

---

14   [2012] UKSC 56 at [47].
15   [2016] UKSC 10.

kitchen work to a catering manager who worked in the prison kitchen. It endorsed the five factors that had been set out in the *Christian Brothers* case (see above), but expanded upon them, holding that they were not all of equal significance.

The court held that the first factor, that the defendant is more likely than the tortfeasor to have the means to compensate the victim and can be expected to have insured, is unlikely to be of independent significance. A deeper pocket or insurance cover is not a principled justification for imposing vicarious liability. Employers insure themselves because they are (or may be) liable: they are not liable because they are insured. They did not rule out, however, circumstances in which the availability of insurance might be a relevant consideration. Moreover, the fifth factor, that the tortfeasor will, to a greater or lesser degree, have been under the control of the defendant, no longer has the significance that it was sometimes considered to have in the past. It was not realistic in modern life to look for a right to direct how an employee should perform his duties as a necessary element in the relationship between employer and employee. The significance of control was that the defendant can direct what the tortfeasor does, not how he does it. It is therefore a factor which is unlikely to matter in most cases, although the absence of even a vestigial degree of control might negative any vicarious liability.

The remaining three factors were interrelated. The essential idea was that the defendant should be liable for torts that may fairly be regarded as risks of his business activities, whether they are committed for the purpose of furthering those activities or not. He will not be liable where the tortfeasor's activities are entirely attributable to the conduct of a recognisably independent business of his own or of a third party.

The importance of focusing upon the business activities carried out by a defendant and their attendant risks were that they directed attention to the issues which are likely to be relevant in the context of modern workplaces, where workers may in reality be part of the workforce of an organisation without having a contract of employment with it. Defendants could not avoid vicarious liability on the basis of technical arguments about the employment status of the individual who committed the tort.

The court also rejected any distinction between abuse cases and others, or between public, private and charitable employers, noting that the defendant did not need to be carrying on activities of a commercial nature. It had long been established that vicarious liability could apply to public authorities and hospitals, which made it clear that there need not be a business or enterprise in any ordinary sense. Nor did the benefit which the organisation derived from the tortfeasor's activities need to take the form of a profit.

It summarised the position by saying that it was sufficient that there is a defendant which is carrying on activities in the furtherance of its own interests. The individual for whose conduct it may be vicariously liable must carry on activities which were assigned to them by the defendant as an integral part of its operation and for its benefits. The defendant must, by assigning those activities to him, have created a risk of his committing the tort. It noted that a wide range of circumstances could satisfy those requirements.

The court agreed that the requirements laid down in the *Christian Brothers* case were met in Mrs Cox's case. It rejected the argument that the primary aim of setting prisoners to work in a prison was not to advance any enterprise of the prison, but to support the rehabilitation of the prisoners as an aim of penal policy. The activities of prisoners were of benefit to themselves, but also to the Prison Service. It was not essential to liability that a defendant should seek to make a profit; nor did it depend upon an alignment of the objectives of the defendant and of the individual tortfeasor. Nor did the fact that the Prison Service was under a statutory duty to provide useful work for prisoners and had a restricted choice of workers exclude vicarious liability.

Lastly, the court held that where the criteria in the *Christian Brothers* case were satisfied, it should not generally be necessary to re-assess the fairness, justice and reasonableness of the result in the particular case. But the criteria were not to be applied slavishly. Where a case concerned circumstances which had not previously been the subject of an authoritative judicial decision, it may be valuable to consider whether the imposition of vicarious liability would be fair, just and reasonable.

It can be seen from the Supreme Court's judgment in *Cox* that there has been a huge expansion of the doctrine of vicarious liability. Its scope has moved far beyond technical arguments about employment. It is now clear that the key criterion is whether the commission of the wrongful act is a risk created by the defendant, by assigning activities to the wrongdoer which are an integral part of its business activities, carried out for its benefit. The presence of control and ability of a defendant to compensate are less important than previously thought.

The reach of vicarious liability now appears to extend to an extremely wide range of environments and circumstances (subject, always, to the second, 'close connection' part of the test which is considered below).

It is likely to apply to most representatives of a business, as it will apply not only to employees, but also to workers and agency workers in many circumstances, unless they are truly independent contractors operating on their own account. It may also cover volunteers.

And the nature of the organisation which uses the labour of the wrongdoer is neither here nor there. It is sufficient that the organisation is carrying on activities which are in furtherance of its own interests (which would appear to apply to virtually all bodies) and that it has assigned some integral part of those activities to the wrongdoer (which is in practice likely to be the determining factor).

The organisation's interests do not need to be economic: they could be charitable; the interests of a religious institute (as in the *Christian Brothers* case); or the interests of complying with a statutory duty (in the case of a public authority or hospital).

The Supreme Court considered vicarious liability yet again in the case of *Armes v Nottinghamshire County Council*.[16] It applied its reasoning in *Cox* to decide that a local authority was vicariously liable for the abusive way in which a foster child had been treated by his foster parents. In doing so, it took into account a number of factors: the torts were committed in the course of an activity carried out for the local authority's benefit; the placement of children with foster parents created a relationship of

---

16   [2017] UKSC 60.

authority and trust which rendered the children particularly vulnerable to abuse; the local authority's powers of approval, inspection and removal did not have any parallel in ordinary family life; the local authority exercised a significant degree of control over what the foster parents did and how they did it; and local authorities could more easily compensate the victims of abuse.

It now seems clear that relationships such as an agency worker working in a hospital will be regarded as 'akin to employment' and will fall within the scope of the doctrine. However, other situations may be less clear-cut and litigation in this area is likely to continue.

Some other more recent cases will be of particular interest to clinical negligence practitioners.

In *Razumas v Ministry of Justice*,[17] a defendant sued the MoJ as being responsible for healthcare provision at various prisons where he had been an inmate. Healthcare services in the prisons had been contracted out to private providers. This had been done by the relevant PCTs (who were not defendants), not by the MoJ or the prison governors. The court dismissed the argument that the MoJ was vicariously liable for the negligent acts and omissions of the private healthcare providers, mainly because it was the PCTs and not the prisons or MoJ who had engaged the private healthcare providers.

In *Barclays Bank v Various Claimants*,[18] the Barclays Bank was held to be vicariously liable for the sexual assaults of a doctor it had engaged, as an independent contractor, to carry out medical examinations on employees and applicants for employment. The court noted that the bank exercised a significant degree of control over the doctor's assessments, which included requesting that he should carry out a particular set of tests and assessments and stressed that degree of control in reaching its conclusion as to vicarious liability.

It contrasted the particular facts of the case it was considering with the more usual medical examination conducted on behalf of others, noting that most examinations would be on a particular part of the body or a particular facet of mental health. In all such cases, the commissioning party would not normally be in a position to specify the particular tests, results or modes of physical examination to be performed and it was doubtful that the necessary degree of control over the medical expert would often be found.

Following the *Barclays Bank* case, clinical negligence practitioners may seek further to expand the boundaries of vicarious liability, for example by arguing that a cosmetic surgery clinic should be liable for the actions of a surgeon; such claims are usually defended currently on the grounds that the surgeon is an independent contractor.

However, in *Brayshaw v Partners of Apsley Surgery*,[19] there was held to be no vicarious liability for a defendant GP surgery for the actions of a locum GP who had been negligent in introducing a vulnerable patient to his faith and his Christian practices; his religious dealings with the patient had been no part of the surgery's business activity.

---

17   [2018] EWHC 215.
18   [2018] EWCA Civ 1670.
19   [2018] EWHC 3286.

The necessary connection with the act of wrongdoing

Once it is established that the relationship between the wrongdoer and the defendant can sustain vicarious liability (typically, but not always, an employment relationship, as set out above), the next question is whether the defendant is vicariously liable for particular conduct by the wrongdoer.

The traditional method of looking at this was that the claimant must show that the negligence complained of was committed within the course or scope of the employee's employment. The traditional test was referred to as the 'Salmond test', from *Salmond and Heuston on the Law of Torts*:

> An employee's wrongful conduct is said to fall within the course and scope of his or her employment where it consists of either (1) acts authorised by the employer or (2) unauthorised acts that are so connected with acts that the employer has authorised that they may be rightly regarded as modes – although improper modes – of doing what has been authorised. (Salmond and Heuston (19th edn, 1987), p 220)

Around the beginning of this century, the test began to be refined, again prompted by cases of sexual abuse in institutions. The change in the English courts was preceded by the decision of the Supreme Court of Canada in *Bazley v Curry*,[20] which introduced a more liberal test, considering that 'close connection' with employment was a more appropriate test than the Salmond test.

This was followed in this country by the leading case of *Lister v Hesley Hall Ltd*.[21] The claimants in *Lister*, who had been resident some years earlier at the defendant's school for boys with emotional and behavioural difficulties, sued for personal injury in respect of sexual abuse by the warden employed by the defendants. The House of Lords said that it was important to avoid becoming involved in the simplistic and erroneous task of trying to determine whether the acts for which an employer was sought to be held vicariously liable were modes of doing authorised acts. So far as intentional torts were concerned, they did not consider that the Salmond test was especially useful any longer. They held that the starting point should be the judgments in *Bazley*. The proper approach was to adopt a broad assessment of the nature of the employee's employment and the test was whether 'the torts were so closely connected with [the wrongdoer's] employment that it would be fair and just to hold the employers vicariously liable', ie a test of 'close connection' was introduced. The defendant had undertaken to care for the boys in its charge through the services of the warden. The warden's torts were sufficiently closely connected with his employment that it would be fair and just to hold the defendant vicariously liable.

The courts sought to apply the 'close connection' test in subsequent cases. This test made it more likely that vicarious liability would be found in cases of intentional torts.

In *Mattis v Pollock*,[22] a nightclub was held vicariously responsible for the stabbing of a customer by its doorman, where the fight began in the club but the stabbing took place later after the doorman had gone home,

---

20   (1999) 174 CLR (4) 45.
21   [2002] 1 AC 15, HL.
22   [2003] EWCA Civ 887, [2003] 1 WLR 2158, CA.

armed himself with a knife and found his enemy on the street. It was found that the doorman's use of violence in the performance of his duties was encouraged by the club's management. The Court of Appeal said that the doorman was employed to keep order and to act in an aggressive and intimidatory manner. It considered the assault to have been directly linked to the earlier events at the club. It therefore found that it would be fair and just to hold the club vicariously responsible for the assault.

In another nightclub case, *Naylor v Payling*,[23] a customer was assaulted by a doorman. The doorman was employed by a security agent who had a contract with the club to provide security. The agent had failed to take out any public liability insurance, so the customer sued the club instead of the agent. The customer did not seek to argue that the agent was an employee rather than an independent contractor, but that the club owed customers a duty to ensure that the agent was properly insured. The Court of Appeal rejected his claim, saying that the agent had reasonably appeared competent to the club, both originally and over the period of some 18 months prior to the assault, and it was not incumbent on the club to ensure that he was properly insured.

In *Attorney-General v Hartwell*,[24] the Privy Council considered a claim against the Government of the British Virgin Islands as being vicariously liable for the injuries accidentally received by the claimant, a British holidaymaker, who was unfortunately in the line of fire when a policeman employed by the Government discharged a loaded firearm in a bar in pursuance of a personal vendetta against his wife and her suspected lover. The claimant succeeded in that the court said that the defendants were in breach of a duty of care in issuing the policeman with a firearm when they had failed to investigate two complaints that had earlier been made against him of violent behaviour. However, the point here is that they held the Government *not* to be vicariously liable for the assault, saying that the acts of the employee (he had travelled to a neighbouring island, not on duty, but with the express intent of seeking his wife out) were not sufficiently closely connected with those acts which he was authorised to do.

Hartwell was applied in *N v Chief Constable of Merseyside Police*,[25] where the Chief Constable was not vicariously liable where a police officer who was wearing his uniform and held himself out as a police officer, took an intoxicated woman to his home and raped her. The judgment made it clear, however, that the circumstances as a whole must be looked at, and that the result may have been different if the policeman had been exercising a police function, such as making an arrest.

In *Gravill v Carroll*,[26] the Court of Appeal held that a rugby club was vicariously liable when one of its players assaulted another player. The altercation had started during a scrum and culminated in an assault which took place after the whistle had been blown. The Court of Appeal held that the assault was so closely connected to the player's employment that it would be fair and just to hold the club liable.

---

23 [2004] EWCA Civ 560, [2004] PIQR P36, CA.
24 [2004] UKPC 12, [2004] 1 WLR 1273, PC.
25 [2006] EWHC 3041 (QB), [2006] All ER (D) 421 (Nov).
26 [2008] EWCA Civ 689, [2008] ICR 1222, CA.

In *Maga v Birmingham Roman Catholic Archdiocese Trustees*,[27] the claimant, a minor, had been sexually abused by an assistant priest. The alleged victim was not a Catholic and had no connection to the church. However, Lord Neuberger held that the archdiocese was vicariously liable for such abuse because of the status, authority and evangelical duties conferred on the priest, which gave him the opportunity to draw the claimant into a position where he could abuse him, even though he had no particular responsibilities towards the claimant. Lord Neuberger also applied the 'close connection' test.

In *Weddall v Barchester Healthcare Ltd; Wallbank v Wallbank Fox Designs Ltd*,[28] the Court of Appeal considered two cases involving violent assaults by work colleagues. In the former, it reasoned that the violence was 'an independent venture' of the assailant, who was off-duty and drunk at the time, so the employer was not liable. In the latter case, conversely, it concluded that because the violence was a spontaneous reaction to a lawful instruction in a factory setting, it was sufficiently close to the course of employment to give rise to vicarious liability.

In *Various Claimants v Institute of the Brothers of Christian Schools*,[29] vicarious liability was imposed where a defendant, whose relationship with the abuser put it in a position to use the abuser to carry on its business or to further its own interests, had done so in a manner which had created or significantly enhanced the risk that the victim or victims would suffer the relevant abuse. The essential closeness of connection of the relationship between the defendant and the tortfeasor and the acts of abuse thus involved a strong causative link. Those were the criteria that established the necessary 'close connection' between relationship and abuse. It was not right to say that creation of risk was simply a policy consideration and not one of the criteria. It was not enough, of itself, to give rise to vicarious liability for abuse but it was always likely to be an important element in the facts that gave rise to such liability. Both the necessary relationship between the brothers and the Institute and the close connection between that relationship and the abuse committed at the school had been made out. As to the former, the relationship between the Institute and the brothers enabled the Institute to place the brothers in teaching positions and, in particular, in the position of headmaster at the school. The standing that the brothers enjoyed as members of the Institute led the managers of that school to comply with the decisions of the Institute as to who should fill that key position. It was particularly significant that the Institute provided the headmasters, for the running of the school was largely carried out by the headmasters. The brother headmaster was almost always the director of the Institute's community, living on the school premises. There was thus a very close connection between the relationship between the brothers and the Institute and the employment of the brothers as teachers in the school. There was also a very close connection between the brother teachers' employment in the school and the sexual abuse that they committed or must be assumed to have committed. There was no Criminal Records Bureau at the time, but the risk of sexual abuse was recognised, as demonstrated by the

27 [2010] 1 WLR 1441.
28 [2012] IRLR 307.
29 [2012] UKSC 56.

prohibition in the Institute's rules on touching children. The placement of brother teachers at the school, a residential school in the precincts of which they also resided, greatly enhanced the risk of abuse by them if they had a propensity for such misconduct.

Vaickuviene v J Sainsbury plc[30] was a tragic case arising from a man's murder at work by a colleague, Mr McCulloch. Both the victim and the assailant had been employed by the defender to stack shelves. McCulloch had a known history of racist and aggressive conduct. Unlike in *Wallbank*, the fatal incident was not connected to the giving or receiving of management instructions. The Court of Session reversed the Lord Ordinary and allowed the supermarket's motion to dismiss. It concluded that it was not possible to hold that the defender's business, or the engagement of shelf-stackers, carried any additional risk of harm from the violence of fellow employees.

In *GB v Stoke City Football Club*,[31] a claim was brought by an apprentice footballer complaining of degrading assaults, as part of an initiation ritual, by a professional player employed by the club. The claim failed on its facts, but the court went on to determine that the club would not have been vicariously liable in any event because the player 'had no express or implied power or duty or discretion conferred upon him by the club to train, discipline or chastise the apprentices'. This is perhaps in line with the reasoning in the old case of *Warren v Henlys Ltd*,[32] which was expressly approved by Lord Millett in *Lister*. In *Warren,* the defendant was held not to be vicariously liable for an assault on a customer committed by its employee, a petrol pump attendant. The assault occurred after the petrol had been delivered and paid for. The court relied upon this fact in applying the Salmond test, concluding that the assault 'had no connection whatever with the defendant's discharge of any duty for the defendants'.

The Supreme Court has most recently considered this issue again in the case of *Mohamud v WM Morrison Supermarkets plc*.[33] Mr Mohamud entered the petrol station to check the tyre pressure on his car. He also asked if it was possible to print some computer documents which he had stored on a memory stick. In response, the employee, Mr Khan, was verbally abusive towards him. He left the kiosk and walked to his car. The employee was told by his supervisor not to follow Mr Mohamud but nevertheless did so. He then violently assaulted Mr Mohamud. Mr Mohamud failed to establish vicarious liability at first instance or in the Court of Appeal, but appealed to the Supreme Court.

In the Supreme Court, Lord Toulson gave the leading speech, which involved an examination of the doctrine of vicarious liability as it has evolved over centuries and a careful analysis of the case law pre- and post- *Lister*. He held that the 'close connection' test adumbrated in *Lister* had stood the test of time and struck the right balance.

That test involves asking two questions:

1 What functions or 'field of activities' have been entrusted by the employer to the employee; or, in everyday language, what was the nature of his job? This is to be addressed broadly.

---

30 [2013] CSIH 67.
31 [2015] EWHC 2862.
32 [1948] 2 All ER 935.
33 [2016] UKSC 11.

2   Was there a sufficient connection between the position in which
     he was employed and his wrongful conduct to make it right for the
     employer to be held liable?

In applying the *Lister* test, the Supreme Court came to the opposite
conclusion to the Court of Appeal. Lord Toulson held that:[34]

> In the present case it was Mr Khan's job to attend to customers and to respond
> to their enquiries. His conduct in answering the claimant's request in a foul-
> mouthed way and ordering him to leave was inexcusable but within the 'field
> of activities' assigned to him. What happened thereafter was an unbroken
> sequence of events. It was argued by the respondent and accepted by the
> judge that there ceased to be any significant connection between Mr Khan's
> employment and his behaviour towards the claimant when he came out from
> behind the counter and followed the claimant onto the forecourt. I disagree for
> two reasons. First, I do not consider that it is right to regard him as having
> metaphorically taken off his uniform the moment he stepped from behind the
> counter. He was following up on what he had said to the claimant. It was
> a seamless episode. Secondly, when Mr Khan followed the claimant back to
> his car and opened the front passenger door, he again told the claimant in
> threatening words that he was never to come back to the petrol station. This
> was not something personal between them; it was an order to keep away from
> his employer's premises, which he reinforced by violence. In giving such an
> order he was purporting to act about his employer's business. It was a gross
> abuse of his position, but it was in connection with the business in which he
> was employed to serve customers. His employers entrusted him with that
> position and it is just that as between them and the claimant, they should be
> held responsible for their employer's abuse of it.

The Supreme Court did not attempt to reconcile the tension between some
of the divergent decisions in cases such as *Wallbank* and *Vaickuviene*
(both considered above), although the rhetorical question of how both of
those cases could have been correctly decided was asked. The court also
expressly approved *Warren v Henlys* (referred to above), reasoning that
the violence in that case occurred after the claimant had left the garage,
such that the misbehaviour by the petrol pump attendant, in his capacity
as petrol pump attendant, was past history by the time that he assaulted
the claimant.

The decision in *Mohamud* is a recognisable relaxation of the 'close
connection' test. It is now clear that a sufficiently close connection between
employment and tort can apply to the kind of situation – unprovoked
violence by an employee in a workplace context – in which previously
the courts have been reluctant to impose liability, save where there was
some enhanced risk of violence, or where the employee's duties involved
the potential use of force. Nevertheless, *Mohamud* also makes it clear
that the nexus between the wrongdoing and the employment remains
important. Unless there are unusual circumstances, assaults and other
misdeeds committed by employees who are off-duty and away from the
workplace setting will not incur vicarious liability.

Subsequent case law has made it clear that the question of closeness
of connection will be very heavily fact dependent, depending on all the
circumstances of each case.

---

34   [2016] UKSC 11 at [47].

In *Axon v Ministry of Defence*,[35] an employee had disclosed information about a Naval officer to a newspaper. The action was held not to be wrongful in itself, as the disclosed information was not private or confidential. However, it held obiter that had the employee's actions been unlawful, it would have imposed vicarious liability upon the Ministry of Defence, because the functions entrusted to the employee included protecting the confidentiality of any confidential information to which she had access as an employee.

In *Various Claimants v WM Morrison Supermarkets plc*,[36] the Court of Appeal held that an employer was vicariously liable for a disgruntled employee's unlawful misuse of payroll data by disclosing that data online on the grounds that he had been acting in the course of his employment (the common law test applied for the reasons set out below). The common law remedy of vicarious liability of an employer for its employee's misuse of private information and breach of confidence was not expressly or impliedly excluded by the Data Protection Act 1998, notwithstanding that the Act itself excluded an employer's liability for wrongful processing of personal data by an employee. The employer was vicariously liable for the employee's acts away from the workplace where those acts formed a sequence of planned events leading to the commission of the wrongdoing.

In *Bellman v Northampton Recruitment Ltd*,[37] a company was held to be vicariously liable for an assault committed by its managing director on an employee after a Christmas party. Although the assault occurred at a separate drinking session after the party, which was not a seamless extension of the Christmas party, it had to be seen against the background of the evening's events. It was not just an impromptu drinks party between work colleagues which might happen on any night after work. The drinks occurred on the same evening as the work event paid for and orchestrated by the managing director. He had already been fulfilling his managerial duties for a large part of the evening. The wrongdoer was not present merely as a fellow reveller but as managing director. There was sufficient connection between the position in which he was employed and his wrongful conduct so as to make the employer liable under the principle of social justice.

The common law tests outlined above do not apply where a statute makes express provision in relation to vicarious liability (see *Jones v Tower Boot Co Ltd*[38]). The Equality Act 2010 provides in s 109 that an employer will be vicariously liable for acts of unlawful discrimination covered by the Act, which are done by employees or agents. However, it will be necessary to show that the worker was acting as an employee or agent within the meaning of s 109 of the Equality Act 2010 (see *Mahood v Irish Centre Housing Ltd*[39] and even if a sufficient degree of control could be established over a worker to render an employer liable at common law in tort for his actions, in the context of torts based on anti-discrimination legislation, it may be necessary to take account of statutory defences.

---

35 [2016] EWHC 787.
36 [2018] EWCA Civ 2339.
37 [2018] EWCA Civ 2214.
38 [1997] ICR 254.
39 (22 March 2011, unreported), EAT.

If an employee contravenes a statute which does not make express provision regarding vicarious liability, the common law tests are relevant to determining whether the employer may be vicariously liable. In the leading case of *Majrowski v Guys and St Thomas' NHS Hospital Trust*,[40] the House of Lords held that an employer could be vicariously liable for harassment committed by an employee in contravention of the Protection from Harassment Act 1997. However, note the decision of the Court of Appeal in *Fecitt v NHS Manchester*,[41] where it was held that the doctrine of vicarious liability could not operate to make an employer liable under s 47B of the Employment Rights Act 1996. The doctrine required a legal wrong on an individual employee's part, and an employee could not be personally liable for acts of victimisation against whistleblowers (in contrast to discrimination cases, where employees could be personally liable for acts of victimisation).In *Various Claimants v WM Morrison Supermarkets plc*,[42] the High Court held that the Data Protection Act 1998 did not expressly or impliedly exclude the application of common law vicarious liability where an employee, who was acting in his own capacity as data controller, unlawfully misused third party personal data. This was upheld on appeal.

The 'scope of employment' principle could assume significance in a clinical negligence context. This doctrine means that negligence by medical personnel falling outside the scope of their employment would not render the health authority or trust vicariously liable (for example, staff playing a game of cricket on the lawns and carelessly hitting the ball at a patient sitting in the sun, or an off-duty nurse running down a patient as she drives out of the grounds). However, as we shall see, there is a primary non-delegable duty of care imposed upon a trust or health authority.

PRIMARY LIABILITY

Generally, if an employer has employed an independent contractor to do work on his behalf, the rule is that the employer will not be responsible for any wrong committed by that contractor in the course of carrying out the work (assuming that vicarious liability cannot be established). However, there is an exception to this if the employer has a non-delegable duty to perform an act. If that is the case, then the employer cannot discharge that duty by delegating performance of the work in question to an independent contractor. The employer will be liable if the agent in the performance of that act, whether independent contractor or not, performs the act negligently.

Liability is, however, restricted in all cases to acts which fall within the duty of care of the employer: the employer is not liable for the collateral negligence of the independent contractor, ie for acts which are not in fulfilment of the activity in respect of which the primary duty of care

40   [2006] UKHL 34, [2007] 1 AC 224, HL.
41   [2011] EWCA Civ 1190.
42   [2017] EWHC 3113.

is imposed on the employer (a leading case is *Padbury v Holliday and Greenwood Ltd*[43]).

Such non-delegable duties can be contrasted from an ordinary duty to take reasonable care which might be discharged by employing a contractor who is reasonably thought to be competent.

A non-delegable duty might arise by virtue of statute or under the common law.

It is a matter of statutory construction whether a statute requiring a person to do a particular act creates a non-delegable duty upon that person or not.

Beyond such statutory duties, it was until recently not generally clear to what extent a non-delegable duty exists in respect of respect of an activity, although it was relatively clear that in respect of hazardous activities, the employer is liable for the negligence of an independent contractor.

Some clarity regarding non-delegable duties under the common law has been provided in recent years by two Supreme Court judgments, which have laid down helpful guidance in this respect.

In *Woodland v Swimming Teachers Association*,[44] the child claimant had suffered a severe brain injury during a school swimming lesson held at a local authority swimming pool. The swimming lesson was organised and provided by an independent contractor. The claimant alleged that the local education authority was under a non-delegable duty to her. The Supreme Court found in her favour and considered that cases concerning highways and hazards needed to be considered separately (and these are not considered further here) but offered general guidance regarding when a non-delegable duty to exercise reasonable care will be imposed. Lord Sumption held that cases where a duty will be imposed are characterised by five defining features:

1   the claimant is a patient or a child, or for some other reason is especially vulnerable or dependent on the protection of the defendant against the risk of injury;
2   there is an antecedent relationship between the claimant and the defendant, independent of the negligent act or omission itself, which (a) places the claimant in the actual custody, charge or care of the defendant; and (b) from which it is possible to impute to the defendant the assumption of a positive duty to protect the claimant from harm, and not just a duty to refrain from conduct which will foreseeably damage the claimant;
3   the claimant has no control over how the defendant chooses to perform those obligations, ie whether personally or through employees or through third parties;
4   the defendant has delegated to a third party some function which is an integral part of the positive duty which the defendant has assumed towards the claimant; and the third party is exercising, for the purpose of the function thus delegated to them, the defendant's custody or care of the claimant and the element of control that goes with it;

---

43   (1912) 28 TLR 494, CA.
44   [2013] UKSC 66.

5   the third party has been negligent not in some collateral respect but in the performance of the very function assumed by the defendant and delegated by the defendant to the third party.

It can be seen from these criteria that it will not be easy to establish that a non-delegable duty exists.

Following *Woodland,* in *GB v Home Office,*[45] it was held that the Home Office owed a non-delegable duty to immigration detainees in respect of the provision of medical care while being held in an immigration removal centre. The judge noted that persons in such detention were vulnerable and that there was a positive duty to protect them from harm which included a duty to provide medical care.

However, the Supreme Court subsequently heard the case of *Armes v Nottinghamshire County Council.*[46] This case concerned children in local authority care, who were admitted to be vulnerable. The Supreme Court held that a local authority does not come under a non-delegable duty owed to children placed with foster parents, as such a duty would create a potential conflict between the local authority's duty towards a child under the Child Care Act 1980, s 18 and the local authority's interests in avoiding exposure to liability.

In *Razumas v Ministry of Justice,*[47] the healthcare services in prisons had been contracted out to private providers by the relevant PCTs (rather than the MoJ or the prison governors). It was held that the MoJ did not owe a non-delegable duty to ensure that reasonable treatment was afforded to inmates. While there was a very limited direct duty of care owed by the MoJ to the claimant, this extended only to matters arising out of custody and access to healthcare, such as if a PCT made provision for GP services for a prison, but no arrangements were made for the prisoners to attend the GPs at all. Cockerill J, in rejecting the wider non-delegable duty for which the claimant contended, considered the five factors laid out by Lord Sumption in *Woodland* and held as follows:[48]

> It is clear (see Lord Sumption [24]) that the distinguishing feature of the non-delegable duty cases is 'control over the claimant for the purpose of performing a function for which the defendant has assumed responsibility'...
>
> What this part of the analysis makes clear is that there is a nexus between the control of the claimant by the target and the purpose of that control/placing, and the care inherent in that relationship. That facet can be easily seen in a hospital, as regards healthcare – a patient gives himself over to the hospital for the very purpose of healthcare. Or as Lord Sumption put it at [30] the claimant, as well as being in the target's care should be 'receiving a service which is part of the institution's mainstream function'. To similar effect is Baroness Hale's point at [40 and also 42] that the conundrum in the *Woodland* case resulted from 'outsourcing of essential aspects of [public authorities'] functions.'
>
> Here the reasoning breaks down in the current case: the reason for the prisoner being in the hands of the prison is not for, and does not comprehend, healthcare. Healthcare is not (at least since 2003) part of the prison institution's mainstream (or essential) function. It has not been outsourced

---

45   [2015] EWHC 819.
46   [2017] UKSC 60.
47   [2018] EWHC 215.
48   [2018] EWHC 215 at [149]–[151].

by the defendant. Here the position is a fortiori that in the case of *A (A Child) v Ministry of Defence* [2005] QB 183, discussed in detail in *Woodland* and endorsed by Lord Sumption at [24], where a non-delegable duty on the part of the Army for healthcare was not made out because (Lord Phillips at [28]) there was 'no sound basis for any finding ... that secondary treatment in hospital ... was actually provided by the Army (MoD) as opposed to arranged by the Army.'

Even prior to the *Woodland* case, it was beyond argument that under English law an NHS Trust is under a primary non-delegable duty of care in respect of the treatment that is afforded the patient under its auspices. This issue is considered in more detail below.

However, recent developments in how the National Health Service operates have made it less clear when treatment is actually under a Trust's auspices. For example, if an NHS Trust refers a patient to be seen privately because of waiting lists, does it still have a non-delegable duty towards that patient? This issue is considered further below.

Trust or health authority as defendant

The appropriate defendant when the action arises out of NHS treatment in hospital is the health authority or NHS Trust (whichever was in charge of the hospital at the time of the alleged negligence).

However, it should always be borne in mind that the body responsible for any negligent conduct in NHS treatment is the body in charge of the hospital at the time of the alleged negligence. This body may have changed its name or even disappeared as a separate body. It may have merged, or it may have been subsumed into an existing body or into a new body entirely. Although the legislature will always have provided for another body to have taken over the pre-existing liabilities of the old body (the NHS Litigation Authority – now known as NHS Resolution – if all else fails). Again, it is not difficult to find out the name of the body running the hospital at the time of the alleged negligence, and it is just as easy to find out, if that body is no longer extant under the same name, what body is now responsible for the pre-existing liabilities of the original body.

Action may be brought for an act or omission that is directly the responsibility of the authority, such as a failure to provide appropriate medical facilities (see, for example, *Bull and Wakeham v Devon Health Authority*,[49] where the court found that the system of obstetric cover provided was not acceptable in that it gave rise to a real inherent risk that an obstetrician might not attend reasonably promptly); or for an act or omission that is directly the responsibility of the hospital, such as a failure to take appropriate general anti-infection measures (*Lindsey County Council v Marshall*[50] and see *Miller v Glasgow Health Board*[51]); or for specific acts of negligence by its staff. By and large, all medical personnel working at the hospital may be regarded as employed by the health authority or Trust. Obviously, the nursing staff are and the resident doctors and technicians, but, even though, strictly speaking, senior staff and consultants are probably not 'employed', the point is, rightly, not taken (except in the case of private hospitals).

---

49 [1993] 4 Med LR 117, CA.
50 [1937] AC 97, HL.
51 [2010] CSIH 40, 2010 GWD 20-402, CS.

There is no point in adding the particular doctor as defendant where the health authority or trust is in any event clearly liable for any negligence on the doctor's part. It increases costs, delays the trial, and it may be unfair on a young doctor unnecessarily to turn the spotlight and put the pressure on him when he may have been doing his overworked best, perhaps also when he had been, for lack of better qualified staff, required to discharge a responsibility for which he was not yet properly trained.

Suing two defendants

The situation often arises that there appear to be two different parties potentially liable, for example GP and hospital, or two different hospitals run by different Trusts. Liability may be in the alternative or both may be severally liable. One is then anxious about costs in the event of succeeding against one only. This topic is considered in Chapter 27.

Naming the wrong defendant

It is, of course, better to sue the correct defendant from the outset. In appropriate cases, the correct defendant may properly raise a plea of limitation where the claimant seeks to add or substitute the defendant at a later stage. The rules on adding a new defendant in the context of limitation are not easy to understand (see Chapter 20 under 'Amending a claim'). However, it may not be necessary to enter the treacherous waters of limitation simply because a claimant seeks to change the name of the defendant. For example, the NHS Trust is unlikely to object if the claimant gets the wrong title when they are clearly intending to sue the right body. Perhaps that body now has a new name or has been subsumed into another already existing or newly created body. If, however, the claimant has named a completely different NHS Trust instead of the body that was in charge of the hospital at the relevant time, there may be a little more difficulty. On the other hand, it would be surprising if, for example, a health authority raised a plea of limitation where the mistake was to have sued the NHS Trust in respect of negligence occurring at a time when the health authority was still in charge of the hospital.

In some cases, if the wrong defendant has been sued, the mistake can be corrected pursuant to CPR 19.2, 19.5 or CPR 17.4. In *Gregson v Channel Four Television Corp*,[52] the court said, echoing the previous law, that CPR 19.5 applied where the application was to substitute a new party for a party who was named in the claim form in mistake for the new party, and CPR 17.4(3) applied where the intended party was named in the claim form but there was a genuine mistake as to the name of the party and no-one was misled. The court said there was no significant conflict between the two rules. In this case CPR 17.4 applied: it was not a question of substituting a new party, and the judge's discretion in favour of the claimant had been correctly exercised.

In *Adelson v Associated Newspapers Ltd*,[53] the Court of Appeal clarified the law. The court said that mistakes as to the name of a party divide into two categories: errors of identification (where the wrong party is

---

52   [2000] CP Rep 60, (2000) Times, 11 August, CA.
53   [2007] EWCA Civ 701, [2008] 1 WLR 585.

erroneously identified as the proper party) and errors of nomenclature (where the correct party is identified, but erroneously called by the wrong name). CPR 17.4 and CPR 19.5 cover mistakes of nomenclature rather than identification.

The court considered the problems which arise where a claimant knows the attributes of the person they wish to sue (for example their landlord), but does not know the actual identity of that person:

> If on inquiry he is incorrectly informed that a named third party has those attributes and he commences an action naming that third party as defendant but describing in the pleading the attributes of the person intended to be sued, is the case one of misnomer of the person intending to be sued or error of identification?

Such a situation could arise where a patient had seen a GP at the relevant time but did not know which GP in the practice had seen the patient. The Court of Appeal considered that such a mistake would be remediable under CPR 17.4 and CPR 19.5, but that the court may not exercise its discretion to allow such a change if the correct defendant was unaware of the claim until the limitation period had expired. In such a situation, therefore, it would be best to sue the practice as a whole, or to plead liability on the ordinary principles of partnership.

In *Lockheed Martin Corp v Willis Group Ltd*,[54] the Court of Appeal held that where a claimant had sued the wrong defendant by mistake and applied under CPR 19.5 to substitute a new party as defendant, the claimant did not have to show that the mistake had not misled the other party or had not caused reasonable doubt as to the identity of the party it intended to sue.

In *Armes v Godfrey Morgan Solicitors Ltd*,[55] the Court of Appeal further considered the interrelationship between CPR 17.4(3) and CPR 19.5(3) (a). It held that when considering an application under CPR 17.4(3) the court must be satisfied as to each of three matters: (i) whether the mistake was genuine; (ii) whether it was a mistake which would not have caused reasonable doubt as to the identity of the claimant; and (iii) if those matters are answered in favour of the applicant, whether the court should exercise its discretion in favour of the applicant.

Cases under the old rules (RSC)

In *Adelson,* the Court of Appeal said that, when interpreting the provisions of the CPR in respect of the substitution of parties, it is necessary to have regard to the jurisprudence under RSC, Ord 20, r 5. The old rule which permitted an amendment to correct the name of the party when there had been a mistake, provided the mistake did not cause any reasonable doubt as to the identity of the person intending to sue, was RSC, Ord 20, r 3 and the courts will presumably continue to have regard to the jurisprudence under this rule as well. Thus, amendments will continue to be permitted where there is a simple mistake in the identification of a party, for example, an error in spelling, or a correct surname but wrong first name. The seminal case regarding RSC, Ord 20, r 3 was *Evans Construction*

---

54 [2010] EWCA Civ 927.
55 [2017] EWHC Civ 323.

Co Ltd v Charrington & Co Ltd.[56] In *Ritz Casino Ltd v Khashoggi,*[57] an amendment was permitted where the claimant had sued in the wrong company name upon two dishonoured cheques. In *Hibernian Dance Club v Murray,*[58] the court held that a mistake in suing the members and/or proprietors of the club under a collective title apt to describe them but devoid of personality at English law, as opposed to suing individually named defendants, was not such as to cause any reasonable doubt that the claim was being asserted against the membership as a whole. The provisions of RSC, Ord 20, r 5 were apt to cover such a case where the action had been hitherto a nullity because the claimant had sued an entity which did not exist in law.

The private patient

The private claimant has to be careful. Though a private clinic is responsible for its resident staff, on the basis that they are employed by the clinic, a consultant may be an independent contractor, engaged on a contract for services rather than a contract of service. In that instance, the clinic may not be vicariously liable for the consultant's negligent actions. So the private patient will probably have to sue the consultant concerned if it is that consultant's acts or omissions that are alleged to be negligent. It is, however, arguable that, provided it was the clinic and not the patient that engaged the surgeon, albeit upon a contract for services, the clinic should be under the same primary duty of care as an NHS hospital. Where a clinic, specialising in a particular form of treatment, eg liposuction or ophthalmic laser treatment, contracts with a patient to provide medical treatment, it is highly likely that the court would find that the clinic had a primary non-delegable duty of care in tort, or a similar duty on a proper construction of the contract.

Contract

The private patient's relationship with her doctors and hospitals will depend on the contracts made with them.

An attempt to establish a general principle that an NHS patient has a contract with their GP has failed in a number of cases and it appears that the better view is that the NHS patient has no contract.

It is in any event clear that, given a contract, the duty of care is owed both in contract and in tort (see *Midland Bank Trust Co v Hett Stubbs & Kemp*[59]), and that the claimant can elect which remedy to pursue.

The GP

Most GPs and dentists practising in the NHS are independent contractors. If negligence is alleged against such a GP or dentist or anyone they have employed (eg nurses, receptionists, secretaries), including any locum they have engaged, it is the GP or dentist who is the appropriate defendant.

---

56   [1983] QB 810, CA.
57   [1996] CLY 890.
58   [1997] PIQR P46, CA.
59   [1979] Ch 384.

Any partners of the GP or dentist will be jointly and severally liable for the negligence of one partner and may occasionally need to be sued as well. However, it may not be necessary practically to sue the partners (or practice as a whole), as the doctor or dentist will normally be indemnified through their defence organisation or the NHS Clinical Negligence Scheme for Trusts (CNST). The circumstances when it may be necessary to bring in other defendants are when a defendant is uninsured or there is a refusal to indemnify the defendant.

Probably, the GP does not have a contract with a patient, unless the patient is a private patient (see above under 'Contract'). A GP is not permitted to act privately for a patient who is on his NHS list (although the GP may refer the patient to a consultant who may treat privately). It might occasionally be the case that certain services carried out upon the premises of a general practice are performed by agents of the health authority or of some trust, rather than employees of the doctor, for example, immunisation services.

Care always needs to be taken in identifying the employer (or body who may otherwise be held vicariously liable). For example, the health visitor, the community nurse and the community midwife, though working closely with the GP, are usually employed by the health authority or nowadays by some Trust or other, and although they may be acting at times under the direction of the GP, it may be the health authority (or Trust) in such cases and not the GP who will be responsible for any mistakes they personally make.

The primary duty of care

The most important point about NHS hospital treatment is that it is not necessary to prove the facts that would give rise to vicarious liability, because the hospital has a primary non-delegable duty of care to provide proper treatment.

While the courts were still strictly applying the distinction between employees and others for the purpose of establishing liability on the part of a hospital for the negligence of medical personnel, the old distinctions of the common law as regards vicarious liability mentioned above (eg as to whether the employer could control the manner in which the work was done) were important. So in *Hillyer v St Bartholomew's Hospital*,[60] Kennedy LJ expressed the view that a hospital, though responsible for the exercise of due care in selecting its professional staff, whether surgeons, doctors or nurses, was not responsible if they or any of them acted negligently in matters of professional care or skill:[61]

> I see no ground for holding it to be a right legal inference from the circumstances of the relation of hospital and patient that the hospital authority makes itself liable in damages if members of the professional staff, of whose competence there is no question, act negligently towards the patient in some matter of professional care or skill, or neglect to use or use negligently in his treatment the apparatus or appliances which are at their disposal.

---

60 [1909] 2 KB 820, CA.
61 [1909] 2 KB 820, CA at 829.

It was even said that as soon as the nurses enter the operating theatre, the health authority was no longer liable for any errors they may make because they were then under the control of the surgeon, for whose errors the health authority was not responsible.

In *Gold v Essex County Council*,[62] the Court of Appeal was concerned to distinguish between different types of staff: the hospital would not be responsible for the acts of a consulting surgeon or physician, but the position of a house physician or surgeon was left open. Goddard LJ said that responsibility for the position of doctors on the permanent staff would depend on whether the doctor was engaged on a contract for services or a contract of service. On the facts, the defendants were responsible for the negligence of a radiographer who was a full-time employee.

In *Collins v Hertfordshire County Council*,[63] Hilbery J considered that a hospital was responsible for the acts of a house surgeon but not for the acts of a part-time surgeon.

In *Cassidy v Ministry of Health*,[64] it was left to Lord Denning, as ever, to direct the law onto a path more appropriate to modern social needs. In that case, Somervell LJ was prepared to hold a hospital liable for the acts of permanent medical staff, those who were employed to provide the patient with nursing and medical treatment, but not for the acts of a visiting or consulting surgeon or physician. Both he and Singleton LJ decided for the claimant on the basis that, even though the claimant could not pinpoint the employee who had been negligent, there had clearly been negligence by one or more employees of the hospital.

Denning LJ said that the hospital was under a duty to take reasonable care of all patients, whether private or not. They would be discharging that duty through their staff, and it was no answer for the hospital to say that the staff concerned were professionals who would not tolerate any interference with the way they did their work. When hospitals undertook to treat a patient, and themselves selected, appointed and employed the professionals who were to give the treatment (as opposed to the patient himself selecting and employing the staff – which he would be doing if he were to ask a consultant to operate on him privately), the hospital was responsible for any negligence, no matter whether of doctors, surgeons, nurses or anyone else; and 'it does not depend on the fine distinction whether the medical man was engaged under a contract of service or a contract for services'.

> I take it to be clear law as well as good sense that where a person is himself under a duty to use care, he cannot get rid of his responsibility by delegating the performance of it to someone else, no matter whether the delegation be to a servant under a contract of service or to an independent contractor under a contract for services.[65]

In *Roe v Minister of Health*,[66] McNair J at first instance[67] had held himself bound by the majority in *Cassidy*'s case to find that a specialist anaesthetist who carried on a private anaesthetic practice but was under

---

62   [1942] 2 KB 293.
63   [1947] KB 598.
64   [1951] 2 KB 343, MLC 0001, CA.
65   [1951] 2 KB 343, MLC 0001, CA at 363.
66   [1954] 2 QB 66.
67   [1954] 1 WLR 1280.

an obligation to provide a regular service to the hospital concerned, and on the occasion in question had been assisting the theatre staff of the hospital, was not a person for whose acts the hospital could be held liable. On appeal, Somervell LJ said that he regarded the anaesthetist as on the permanent staff of the hospital and therefore it would be liable for his errors. Morris LJ said that the hospital had undertaken to provide all the necessary facilities and equipment for the operation and the obligations of nursing and anaesthetising. This was going some way towards Denning LJ's concept of a primary non-delegable duty of care, but Morris LJ was still basing himself on the maxim of vicarious liability, *respondent superior.*

Once again, it was Denning LJ who brushed aside nice distinctions with a robust and lucid exposition:[68]

> I think that the hospital authorities are responsible for the whole of their staff, not only for the nurses and doctors, but also for the anaesthetists and surgeons. It does not matter whether they are permanent or temporary, resident or visiting, whole-time or part-time. The hospital authorities are responsible for all of them. The reason is because, even if they are not servants, they are the agents of the hospital to give the treatment. The only exception is the case of consultants or anaesthetists selected and employed by the patient himself.

As stated above, the early cases were important in the context of vicarious liability, when it mattered on whom the claimant could fix liability. Vicarious liability in the context of clinical negligence may well still assume significance for the private patient, eg in the case of a private clinic, where the clinic may be able to avoid liability for the mistakes of a visiting consultant, though probably only where the patient has chosen and privately contracted with that consultant, or, if the consultant is being personally sued, they may be able to avoid responsibility for the mistakes of others not under their control at the time.

The interaction between vicarious responsibility and the non-delegable duty of care, and the significance of the distinction between these two bases of liability, was considered by the Court of Appeal in the case of *Wilsher v Essex Area Health Authority*[69] (reversed on another ground by the House of Lords).

In *X (minors) v Bedfordshire County Council*,[70] Lord Browne-Wilkinson said:

> This allegation of a direct duty of care owed by the authority to the plaintiff is to be contrasted with those claims which are based on the vicarious liability of the local authority for the negligence of its servants, ie for the breach of a duty of care owed by the servant to the plaintiff, the authority itself not being under any relevant duty of care to the plaintiff ...

> This distinction between direct and vicarious liability can be important since the authority may not be under a direct duty of care at all or the extent of the duty of care owed directly by the authority to the plaintiff may well differ from that owed by a professional to the patient. However, it is important not to lose sight of the fact that, even in the absence of a claim based on vicarious liability, an authority under a direct duty of care to the plaintiff will be liable for the

---

68   [1954] 2 QB 66 at 82.
69   [1987] QB 730.
70   [1995] 2 AC 633, HL at 739–740.

negligent acts or omissions of its servant which constitute a breach of that direct duty. The authority can only act through its servants.

The position can be illustrated by reference to the hospital cases. It is established that those conducting a hospital are under a direct duty of care to those admitted as patients to the hospital (I express no view as to the extent of that duty). They are liable for the negligent acts of a member of the hospital staff which constitute a breach of that duty, whether or not the member of the staff is himself in breach of a separate duty of care owed by him to the plaintiff.

Thus, it was clear by this time at the latest that there was a primary non-delegable duty of care to provide proper care to hospital patients, albeit that the boundaries and extent of the primary duty perhaps remained unclear.

The duty is perhaps best framed as a duty to provide a safe environment and the effective provision of services. For example, in *Bull v Devon Health Authority*,[71] the claimant was a second born twin who was severely brain damaged, as there was a delay of 68 minutes before he was born, due to difficulty in tracing a suitably qualified medical practitioner to assist in the delivery. The Court of Appeal held that the defendant was in breach of its primary duty to provide an adequate system for securing the attendance of an appropriately qualified doctor to deal with obstetric emergencies.

In *Darnley v Croydon Health Services NHS Trust*,[72] the Supreme Court confirmed that the primary duty of care included a duty to take reasonable care not to cause physical injury to those who presented themselves at A&E departments complaining of illness or injury and that it existed before the patient was treated. In determining whether there was a duty of care in such a case, it was not appropriate to distinguish between medically qualified professionals and administrative staff. The Trust had charged its non-medically qualified staff with being the first point of contact for those seeking assistance. The Trust's duty of care had to be considered in the round. The scope of the duty extended to taking reasonable care not to provide misleading information, whether given by medical or non-medical staff, about how long patients might have to wait before seeing a clinician.

Independent providers

The NHS increasingly subcontracts care out to independent providers, which can be private sector companies, voluntary organisations or social enterprises. Such programmes aim to create additional capacity within the NHS, to reduce waiting times and to increase patient choice.

Who is the correct defendant if something goes wrong when a patient is treated by an independent provider in such circumstances? Is it the body who referred the patient or will it be the independent provider? There is no clear legal authority on this point. The referring body will only be liable if it owes a non-delegable duty of care that extends to treatment in another hospital.

---

71   [1993] 4 Med LR 117, CA.
72   [2018] UKSC 50.

M v Calderdale and Kirklees Health Authority,[73] was, before being overruled, a case of great interest. A girl of 17, an NHS patient, was sent by her NHS consultant to a private clinic for a termination. She did not choose the clinic. She simply went where she was told to go. She remained pregnant, gave birth to a child, and obtained judgment for the negligence of clinic and surgeon. The surgeon was not insured, and the clinic was being wound up. Naturally, she looked to the NHS for her damages. The defendants claimed that they had no liability for the errors of the private clinic and surgeon as they were independent contractors who had been chosen with all due care. The judge rejected their argument, holding that, both by virtue of s 1 of the National Health Service Act 1977 and at common law, they had a continuing primary non-delegable duty of care to the patient which was not discharged by their selection of a private clinic to perform the operation (the judge also found that they had not used due care in their selection of a clinic). He approved of the passage in *Clerk and Lindsell on Torts* (17th edn, 1995) para 5.16, to the effect that the hospital authority itself is under a duty to its patients which it does not discharge simply by delegating its performance to someone else, no matter whether the delegation be to an employee or an independent contractor.

However, the Court of Appeal expressly disapproved of *Calderdale* in *A v Ministry of Defence*.[74] Negligence in a German hospital caused brain injury at birth to the child of a serving British soldier. Guy's and St Thomas' Hospital had undertaken to the MoD in 1996 to procure secondary medical care for servicemen in Germany and their dependants. The German medical units were called Designated German Providers (DGPs). The Court of Appeal held that there was no basis in law for imposing on the MoD a non-delegable duty of care in this context, ie a duty to ensure proper skill and care by the German hospital. The duty, as with the engagement of any independent contractor, was confined to an obligation to provide access to an appropriate system of hospital care provided by another, which duty was fulfilled by the exercise of reasonable care by the MoD in its selection of an agent (here Guy's and St Thomas') to procure DGPs.

In *Farraj v King's Healthcare NHS Trust*,[75] the Court of Appeal overturned a decision by the High Court that a hospital was partially liable to the claimants in respect of the genetic testing of a tissue sample which was sent to be cultured by a reputable independent cytogenetics laboratory. The mother's obstetrician had taken the Trust's report as confirming that maternal contamination had been completely excluded. However, the report recognised that there was a very small background risk of maternal contamination. The person who had carried out the culturing process had expressed doubts about whether she was setting up a culture of foetal cells. The High Court held that the laboratory should have informed the Trust of those doubts and were accordingly liable for a breach of duty of care owed to the claimants. However, the Trust should have proactively asked for information about the sample. In the circumstances, liability was established against both defendants.

---

73 [1998] Lloyd's Rep Med 157, CC.
74 [2004] EWCA Civ 641, [2005] QB 183, CA.
75 [2009] EWCA Civ 1203, [2010] PTSR 1176, CA.

The Court of Appeal held that the hospital and the laboratory had a clearly understood arrangement by which the hospital was entitled to assume that the sample was satisfactory unless the laboratory informed it to the contrary. The hospital and Trust had therefore not been negligent. The general rule was that where a person under a duty of care entrusted the performance of the duty to an apparently competent contractor, they were not under a duty to check the contractor's work, being entitled to rely on its proper performance. Even assuming (without deciding) that the concept of a non-delegable duty extended to hospital cases, this did not justify the conclusion that, on the facts of this case, the hospital owed a non-delegable duty to the parents in respect of genetic testing. There was a significant difference between treating a patient who was admitted to hospital for that purpose and carrying out tests on samples. The special duty that existed between a hospital and a patient arose because the hospital undertook the care, supervision and control of persons who, as patients, were in special need of care. The parents in this case were not admitted to the hospital for treatment. There was no need to depart from the general rule and find that any special duty was owed.

Thus, there was held to be non-delegable duty, either in relation to the independent testing of samples by a laboratory, or where medical treatment in Germany was arranged. *Farraj* and *A* were approved by the Supreme Court in *Woodland* (considered above in relation to non-delegable duties). The Supreme Court in *Woodland* noted that control of the environment in which injury is caused is not an essential element, because the defendant is not usually in control of the environment in which injury is caused by an independent contractor. The essential element is not control of the environment in which injury is caused, but control over the claimant for the purpose of performing a function for which the defendant has assumed responsibility. Thus, the result in *A* was correct in that the MoD was not responsible for the negligence of a hospital with whom it contracted to treat soldiers, but this was because the secondary treatment was arranged by the army rather than being provided by it, and there was therefore no delegation of any function which the MoD had assumed personal responsibility to carry out and no delegation of any custody exercised by the MoD over soldiers and their families. *Farraj* was approved on similar reasoning.

The courts may consider that these existing authorities should not be followed in a case where, for example, a patient has been referred to another organisation in an effort by the NHS to reduce waiting lists. There would be a strong policy argument for imposing a primary non-delegable duty upon the NHS in such cases and it is arguable that the NHS in those circumstances has assumed responsibility for providing care to the patient. However, this issue does not appear to have been tested in the courts.

The question of who the correct defendant is may not be quite as significant as might otherwise be thought, however. The NHSLA's Clinical Negligence Scheme for Trusts (CNST) provides indemnity cover for NHS bodies in England who are members of the scheme against clinical negligence claims made in relation to NHS patients who are treated by or on behalf of those NHS bodies. It may not therefore be necessary to explore the specific terms under which any given healthcare professional was working.

The contract between the parties should, however, always be carefully examined, as the independent provider may have provided an indemnity to the NHS. Furthermore, different arrangements may apply to one-off waiting list initiatives, where the indemnity terms of the relevant contract are likely to be paramount.

When a claim is made against a member of CNST, the NHS body remains the legal defendant. However, the NHSLA (now known as NHS Resolution) takes over full responsibility for handling the claim and meeting the associated costs.

SUING OVER POLICY DECISIONS

The following section looks at claims that are not rooted in alleged clinical negligence but relate more to policy decisions or alleged system or administration failures, whether by government, the NHS or a particular health body. In this context fall claims over the allocation of resources, refusals to authorise a particular treatment, and so forth. The grounds for any such claim may now be more extensive thanks to the human rights aspect, though lawyers need to handle this aspect of any proposed claim with caution (see Chapter 23, Human Rights).

It is useful to consider a bit of background. The Health and Social Care Act 2012 (HSCA 2012) established the NHS Commissioning Board, which since 1 April 2013 has been known as NHS England. The function of NHS England is to assist the Secretary of State with the provision of services under the NHS Act 2006. NHS England commissions primary care and specialised services, as well as some services for prisons and the armed forces. The NHS commissioning budget is managed by clinical commissioning groups (CCGs), which have the task of commissioning the best health services for the populations in their areas.

Of course, resources are restricted, and difficult decisions must be taken about priorities and how to allocate the resources. This can involve consideration of how to measure the benefit of allocating resources in particular ways.

An important player in this area is the National Institute for Health and Clinical Negligence (NICE), which came into being following the HSCA 2012. It is an amalgamation of two former agencies: the National Institute for Clinical Excellence; and the Health Development Agency.

The HSCA 2012 provides that the core purposes of NICE are the preparation of standards on provisions of NHS services, public health services and social care in England, and provision of advice and guidance to the Secretary of State on any quality matter. In meeting these purposes, it must have regard to: (i) the broad balance of benefits and costs; (ii) the degree of need of persons; and (iii) the desirability of promoting innovation. It must do this 'effectively, efficiently and economically' (see ss 233–236).

One of the ways in which NICE meets its purposes is by appraising new and existing technologies in terms of their clinical effectiveness and their cost-effectiveness. A measure it often uses in doing so is the cost per quality adjusted life year (QALY), which is a way of measuring how long a treatment offers an enhanced quality of life. It then considers whether to approve a new treatment or refuse its use.

Once NICE has approved a new treatment, it is then up to the relevant commissioning groups to decide whether or not that treatment should be made available to those in its area. While a 2008 review of the Health Service carried out by Lord Darzi recommended that patients should have a legal right to all drugs approved by NICE if a doctor says that they are clinically appropriate, this recommendation was never put in place.

The only obligation upon health authorities is to provide such therapy as is positively recommended by NICE. Individual CCGs are otherwise free to set out those drugs or other aids that it will only provide in exceptional circumstances in its own policies. Application for treatment that is not thereby routinely available through the NHS is submitted to the relevant CCG by the patient's doctor in the form of an individual funding request. The request is then referred to a multidisciplinary panel. There is a process of appeal, but the decision made is ultimately subject to judicial review on the ordinary principles of public law, including reasonableness and justice. Such principles often involve the need to judge each case on its own merits. In *R v North West Lancashire Health Authority, ex p A, D and G*,[76] it was held that a blanket rule is unlikely to be approved.

The Department of Health or other government bodies may also make recommendations and/or issue guidance about the use of particular treatments.

If NICE or a government body is wrong in the decision it reaches about the clinical or cost effectiveness of a particular treatment, then there may be liability if the decision is *Wednesbury* unreasonable or can otherwise be attacked in line with general principles of public law. (The situation can be distinguished from attacking the decision of a CCG not to pay for a particular treatment.) However, there have been few if any successful challenges to NICE or the government on those grounds.

In *R (on the application of Bristol-Myers Squibb Pharmaceuticals Ltd) v National Institute for Health and Clinical Excellence*,[77] Blake J held that there had not been a breach of Directive 89/105 where NICE had refused to recommend using a drug in the NHS, in accordance with criteria notified to the European Commission, as the drug was not cost-effective when there was a high demand for it and resources were scarce.

And in *R v Secretary of State for Health, ex p Pfizer Ltd*,[78] Collins J held that Department of Health Circular 1998/158 advising that doctors should not prescribe Viagra was unlawful both as seeking to override a doctor's professional judgment as to what treatment would best benefit a patient, and also as being in breach of the European Directive 89/105/EEC (which required that publicity be given to the criteria applied in measures to restrict or exclude from the public domain medicinal products for human use).

An area where such decisions have been challenged however, sometimes successfully, is in relation to the procedures that the relevant body followed.

In *R (on the application of Eisai Ltd) v National Institute for Health and Clinical Negligence*,[79] the Court of Appeal held that NICE had acted

---

76   [2000] 1 WLR 977.
77   [2009] EWHC 2722 (Admin), [2010] 1 CMLR 31.
78   [1999] MLC 0103, 51 BMLR 189.
79   [2008] EWCA Civ 438, (2008) 11 CCL Rep 385.

unfairly during a consultation process by making available to consultees only a read-only version of an economic model used to assess the cost-effectiveness of drugs, and refusing to make available a fully executable version of the model. The model was central to the appraisal committee's determination of a drug's cost-effectiveness. The robustness or reliability of the model was therefore a key question.

In *R (on the application of Servier Laboratories Ltd) v National Institute and Clinical Excellence*,[80] the Court of Appeal held that NICE had failed to give adequate reasons why it had rejected an analysis, taken from a post hoc sub-group of a larger randomised trial group, which was central to a pharmaceutical company's case in support of one of its drugs as a treatment of choice for osteoporosis. NICE had refused to recommend the drug but was required to make a fresh decision.

There have also been a number of challenges to decisions of commissioning groups not to fund drugs where they have been approved or recommended by NICE or others. As a matter of general public law, it is necessary for commissioning groups to have regard to guidance, whether issued by NICE or otherwise, when considering the funding of treatment.

For example, in *R v North Derbyshire Health Authority, ex p Fisher*,[81] the NHS Executive had issued a circular asking all health authorities to facilitate the introduction of a drug, beta interferon, into the NHS and to continue prescribing it in hospitals. The health authority stated that its policy was to fund the drug only as part of a proposed national random trial or a local trial, but later stated that it would not participate in any trials. It argued that it had insufficient resources to fund the drug for the claimant. It was held that although the circular merely provided guidance and was not mandatory, the policy implemented was unlawful as the authority had failed in its duty to give serious consideration to the advice given in the circular; an unlawful blanket ban on the drug had been in place. Its decision was quashed, and it had to formulate and implement a new policy.

The legal position has recently been considered and summarised by the High Court in *R (on the application of Elizabeth Rose) v Thanet Clinical Commissioning Group*.[82] The claimant was a long-standing sufferer of Crohn's disease. She was due to receive chemotherapy which carried a high risk of making her infertile. She therefore wanted to access egg preservation therapy before the chemotherapy began but was repeatedly turned down by her CCG. She argued that the CCG had unlawfully ignored NICE guidance from 2013 that cryopreservation should be offered in her kind of case. The CCG's only reasoning for not following NICE was that it disagreed with its scientific basis.

Jay J held, applying the *North Derbyshire* case, that NICE was a national body and its guidelines were intended to have nationwide application. NICE recommendations were based on an evaluation of the evidence, health benefit and cost, and nothing else. Although NICE guidelines did not have to be followed, a CCG was under a public law obligation to have regard to the relevant NICE guideline and to provide clear reasons for any general policy that did not follow it. Thanet CCG's

---

80   [2010] EWCA Civ 346.
81   [1997] 8 Med LR 327.
82   [2014] EWHC 1182.

sole basis for not following the NICE guidelines was that it disagreed with its evidence on the effectiveness of oocyte cryostorage. Thanet CCG might not legitimately disagree with NICE on matters concerning the current state of medical science. Thus Thanet CCG could not lawfully disagree with the medical or scientific rationale for NICE's recommendation in relation to oocyte cryopreservation. It could have found other reasons for not following the NICE recommendation, but not the one that it relied on. Since no basis or reasoning on grounds of exceptionality had been put forward, it followed that Thanet CCG's new policy was unlawful.

What is the position with regard to challenges to the allocation of resources in the provision of medical services more widely?

Pursuant to s 3B of the National Health Service Act 2006, the Secretary of State has a duty '... to require the Board to arrange, to such extent as it considers necessary to meet all reasonable requirements' very broad provision as part of the health service. However, a service or facility may be prescribed in this way only if the Secretary of State considers that it would be appropriate for the Board (rather than CCGs) to arrange for its provision as part of the service.

They have been few successful challenges to the way in which scarce resources have been allocated. Generally, a test of reasonableness is applied in accordance with ordinary public law principles. Thus, unless a decision is so unreasonable that no reasonable body could have reached it (in accordance with the principles laid down in *Associated Provincial Picture Houses Ltd v Wednesbury Corp*[83]), the court is unlikely to interfere.

One of the earliest cases to consider the allocation of scare resources was *R v Secretary of State for Social Services, ex p Hincks*.[84] Four orthopaedic patients at a Birmingham hospital, who were being obliged to wait longer than was medically advisable for treatment because of a shortage of facilities due in part to a policy decision not to build a new hospital block for economic reasons, applied for declarations against the Minister and Regional and Area Health Authorities that the statutory duties imposed by ss 1 and 3 of the National Health Service Act 1977 had not been discharged. The patients needed to establish in the first place that they had a *locus standi* to bring the action; if they had, they asked for a declaration that the authorities were in breach of their statutory duties, and they sought both an order requiring them to perform their duties, and also damages for the pain and suffering caused to them by the delay in treatment. They failed. Wien J said that the Minister's duty was to provide such services as he considered necessary and that such a wording gave him discretion as to how financial resources were to be used. If there was not enough money then all needs could not be met. In those circumstances, it was impossible to say that the Minister, or any other body, was in breach of statutory duty. The court would only interfere where the Minister had acted as no reasonable Minister could possibly act, or had acted so as to frustrate the policy of the Act. Nor did he take the view that the Act gave any right of action to the individual patient to sue in respect of an alleged breach of the Minister's general duties.

The Court of Appeal agreed with the trial judge; Bridge LJ pointed out that the Minister must be entitled to make policy decisions about

83   [1948] 1 KB 223.
84   (1979) 123 Sol Jo 436, affd (1980) 1 BMLR 93, CA.

the allocation of financial resources in the light of overall long-term planning or he would be called upon to disburse funds that were not in fact available.

In *R v Central Birmingham Health Authority, ex p Walker*,[85] an unsuccessful application was made for judicial review of the health authority's decision that, although it was agreed that baby Walker needed a certain operation, it could not carry it out at that time for resource reasons. The Master of the Rolls said:[86]

> It is not for this court, or indeed any court, to substitute its own judgment for the judgment of those who are responsible for the allocation of resources. This court could only intervene where it was satisfied that there was a *prima facie* case, not only of failing to allocate resources in the way in which others think that resources should be allocated, but of a failure to allocate resources to an extent which was '*Wednesbury* unreasonable', to use the lawyers' jargon, or, in simpler words, which involves a breach of a public law duty. Even then, of course, the court has to exercise a judicial discretion. It has to take account of all the circumstances of the particular case with which it is concerned.

Stephen Brown LJ said:[87]

> In the absence of any evidence which could begin to show that there was [a failure so unreasonable as to come within the jurisdiction of the court] to allocate resources in this instance ... there can be no arguable case ... It does seem to me unfortunate that this procedure has been adopted. It is wholly misconceived in my view. The courts of this country cannot arrange the lists in the hospital ... and should not be asked to intervene.

In another case against the same health authority less than two months later, the father of four year old Matthew Collier failed to persuade the Court of Appeal to intervene where desperately needed open-heart surgery was delayed for months, even though Matthew had been placed at the top of the waiting list, due to shortage of intensive care beds and nurses. The court said that there was no evidence that the health authority had acted unreasonably or in breach of any public duty (*R v Central Birmingham Health Authority, ex p Collier*[88]).

In *R v North West Thames Regional Health Authority, ex p Daniels*[89] the Divisional Court, despite sympathising with the predicament of the boy, Rhys Daniels, and actually finding that the District Health Authority had failed, contrary to reg 19(1) of the Community Health Councils Regulations, SI 1985/304, to consult the community health council before closing the bone marrow unit at Westminster Children's Hospital, was, predictably, unwilling to order the reopening of the unit because making an order would not benefit the boy. The court said it was sure that the unit at Bristol would do all it could. Although one understands that the proceedings had the useful effect of getting the NHS to ensure that appropriate treatment was speedily made available, the parents, most sadly, had to decide in September 1997 that no further treatment should be attempted, and Rhys died just before Christmas 1998, aged nearly eight.

---

85 (1987) 3 BMLR 32, CA.
86 (1987) 3 BMLR 32, CA at 44.
87 [1988] CA, transcript, 6 January.
88 (1987) 3 BMLR 32, CA at 47.
89 [1993] 4 Med LR 364.

In *R v Sheffield Health Authority, ex p Seale*,[90] Auld J held that it was not unreasonable for the health authority to limit IVF treatment to women between the ages of 25 and 35 in view of their limited budget. He said that although they had undertaken to provide such treatment for patients within their area, that did not mean they were bound to provide the service on demand and regardless of financial and other concerns.

In *R v Cambridge District Health Authority, ex p B*,[91] the father of a ten-year-old girl, who had already been treated with two courses of chemotherapy, applied for an order compelling the health authority to fund a third course and a second bone marrow transplant when she suffered a relapse of her acute myeloid leukaemia. The health authority had declined to treat, principally on the basis that the proposed treatment, being of an experimental nature, was not in the child's best interests, and also on the ground that the huge expense involved would not be an appropriate use of their limited resources. The trial judge, Laws J, while not being prepared to order the health authority to treat, required them to reconsider their decision on the ground that their reasoning had been flawed because the treatment was not experimental and because they had not properly explained their funding priorities. The Court of Appeal reversed his decision. The Master of the Rolls provided what at that time might have been thought to be the last word on the attitude of the courts to decisions on funding by health authorities:[92]

> I have no doubt that in a perfect world any treatment which a patient, or a patient's family, sought would be provided if doctors were willing to give it, no matter how much it cost, particularly when a life was potentially at stake. It would however, in my view, be shutting one's eyes to the real world if the court were to proceed on the basis that we do live in such a world. It is common knowledge that health authorities of all kinds are constantly pressed to make ends meet. They cannot pay their nurses as much as they would like; they cannot provide all the treatments they would like; they cannot purchase all the extremely expensive medical equipment they would like; they cannot carry out all the research they would like; they cannot build all the hospitals and specialist units they would like. Difficult and agonising judgments have to be made as to how a limited budget is best allocated to the maximum advantage of the maximum number of patients. That is not a judgment which the court can make. In my judgment, it is not something that a health authority such as this authority can be fairly criticised for not advancing before the court.

And Sir Stephen Brown said:[93]

> After the most critical, anxious consideration, I feel bound to say that I am unable to say that the authority in this case acted in a way that exceeded its powers or which was unreasonable in the legal sense. The powers of this court are not such as to enable it to substitute its own decision in a matter of this kind for that of the authority which is legally charged with making the decision.

While the above case law might make the situation appear hopeless, there have been a number of situations in which the courts have been prepared

---

90   (1994) 25 BMLR 1.
91   [1995] 1 WLR 898, CA.
92   [1995] 1 WLR 898, CA at 906.
93   [1995] 1 WLR 898, CA at 907.

to find that a decision is so unreasonable that no reasonable decision maker would have made it or to impugn the decision on other grounds.

In *R v North West Lancashire Health Authority, ex p Miss A, D and G*,[94] the Court of Appeal upheld a decision of Hidden J, invalidating a decision by the health authority in relation to the treatment it was or was not prepared to provide to transsexuals, ie a decision on the allocation of its limited resources. The health authority had refused the applicants' gender reassignment surgery, from male to female. Suffering as they did from an inability to accept the gender they were born with, they were in principle entitled to be considered for treatment under the NHS. However, the health authority had decided upon a policy that such surgery would be refused unless there were exceptional circumstances over and above the clinical need.

The court said that the allocation and weighting of priorities in funding different treatments from finite resources was a matter of judgment for the health authority; that it was proper for an authority to adopt a general policy; that a policy to allocate a low priority to gender reassignment surgery was not in principle irrational; but that in this case the policy was undermined and invalidated by evidence which showed that the health authority did not in fact regard gender dysphoria as a genuine illness requiring more than psychiatric reassurance, an approach that did not reflect its own medical judgment. The court therefore quashed the relevant resource allocation policies and all decisions based on them and required the health authority to give proper weight to its acknowledgement that gender dysphoria was an illness, to address the clinical evidence as to the need for and effectiveness of gender reassignment procedures, to indicate reasons in broad terms for the priority to be given to providing such treatment, and to make effective provision for exceptions in individual cases from any general policy restricting funding for such treatment.

Hidden J's approach at first instance is worth studying. He accepted that it was for the health authority and not the court to allocate limited budgets to the maximum advantage for the number of patients. Nevertheless, he said, in formulating or applying policy to any particular case before it, the authority had to consider whether there was a demonstrable medical need for the treatment in question. Although the court would not seek to allocate scarce resources in a tight budget, it would ensure that the health authority had asked the right questions and had addressed the right issues before arriving at its policy. In this case the authority was unable to define or exemplify what it meant by the proviso of 'overriding clinical need'. The judge said that it was not entitled to limit its treatment to counselling and so to exclude hormone treatment and surgery. Therefore, its decision was unlawful and irrational, arrived at without consideration of relevant matters such as the question of what the proper treatment was or what was actually recognised as the illness of gender identity dysphoria. Relevant considerations were not taken into account and irrelevant ones were. The policy unlawfully fettered the discretion of the health authority in its duty towards each particular patient of providing treatment and facilities for the prevention of illness and the cure of persons suffering from gender identity dysphoria.

---

94 [2000] 1 WLR 977, [1999] MLC 0111, CA.

In *R (on the application of Rogers) v Swindon NHS Primary Care Trust*,[95] the Court of Appeal allowed an appeal against the decision of Bean J that the defendant Trust's policy not to provide Herceptin to early stage breast cancer sufferers who were HER2 positive, save in exceptional circumstances, was lawful. The Court of Appeal held that the policy to refuse funding for treatment with an unlicensed drug, save where exceptional personal or clinical circumstances could be shown, was irrational, as the policy could not be rationally explained.

The defendant had funds available to provide the drug for all patients who fulfilled the clinical requirements and whose clinician had prescribed it, but its policy was to refuse funding save where exceptional personal or clinical circumstances could be shown. It was held that a policy of withholding assistance save in unstated exceptional circumstances would be rational in the legal sense provided that it was possible to envisage, and the decision maker did envisage, what such exceptional circumstances might be. If it was not possible to envisage any such circumstances, the policy would be in practice a complete refusal of assistance and as such would be irrational because it was sought to be justified not as a complete refusal but as a policy of exceptionality. In deciding whether the defendant's policy was rational or not, the court had to consider whether there were any relevant exceptional circumstances that could justify it granting treatment to one patient but refusing it to another within the eligible group. There was no rational basis for distinguishing between patients within the eligible group on the basis of exceptional clinical circumstances any more than there was on the basis of personal circumstances. Once the defendant had decided, as it had, that it would fund Herceptin for some patients and that cost was irrelevant, the only reasonable approach was to focus on the patient's clinical needs and to fund patients within the eligible group who had been properly prescribed Herceptin by their physicians. The defendant's policy was irrational and therefore unlawful and was quashed.

However, it is notable that this was not a case about the allocation of scarce resources. The defendant had funding available to treat all eligible patients; therefore, the case was about the denial of reasonable access to available resources, rather than rationing. In fact, counsel for Mrs Rogers, and the court, agreed that it would have been a very different case if the Trust's policy had been founded on budgetary considerations.

The decision of the Trust to refuse to fund the treatment of the claimant with Herceptin was quashed. The Court of Appeal was going to hear further submissions, which were not reported, but at the stage of giving the judgment was of the view that it could not and should not order the Trust to fund the treatment, but that the Trust should reconsider its policy and formulate a lawful policy upon which to base decisions in particular cases, including that of the claimant, in the future.

In *R (on the application of Otley) v Barking and Dagenham NHS Primary Care Trust*,[96] Mitting J held that it was unlawful for the defendant NHS Trust to refuse to fund a treatment for cancer, which included the use of an anti-cancer drug not available for normal prescription, where

---

95   [2006] EWCA Civ 392, [2006] 1 WLR 2649.
96   [2007] EWHC 1927 (Admin), (2007) 10 CCL Rep.

the treatment produced beneficial results and the patient's case was exceptional.

The claimant had been privately prescribed a combination of three anti-cancer drugs that included Avastin, which was not available from the NHS. The funds available to the claimant allowed for five courses of treatment. The response to treatment was positive and a further prescription of Avastin was applied for. A panel of the defendant Trust held that sanctioning the use of Avastin would not significantly prolong the claimant's life or be cost effective. Upon being asked to reconsider its decision, a critical analysis of the drug was subsequently prepared, which held that Avastin should be authorised in exceptional circumstances and set out the exceptionality criteria. One member of the panel queried the precise ratio of Avastin to the other drugs in the treatment. He found that the claimant had not received Avastin for several months and that her disease did not appear to have significantly progressed in that time. The panel held that the claimant did not fit the exceptionality criteria and refused to fund the treatment.

It should be noted that, in contrast with *Rogers*, where there were no budgetary constraints, the policy of the Trust, which included consideration of the impact of funding 'on the health of the whole population' was assessed as being rational and sensible.

However, Mitting J held that the reasoning and decision of the panel in relation to the particular case of Mrs Otley was irrational and unlawful on *Wednesbury* grounds.

The query about the ratio of the drugs in the treatment was irrelevant. It was a simple fact that the treatment that had been prescribed, including Avastin, produced beneficial results and there were no other treatments available to the claimant that could be prescribed within normal NHS standards that were likely to have any benefit to her. Further, the panel had not taken into account the slim but important chance that treatment including Avastin could prolong the claimant's life for more than a few months. What the panel had in mind was the short-term effect on the claimant's life of the prescription of Avastin. It was held that, on any fair-minded view of the exceptionality criteria, the claimant's case was exceptional. The case was not one in which the availability of scarce resources was a decisive factor. The panel's decision was quashed, and the defendant gave an undertaking that funding of a further five cycles of treatment would be provided to the claimant, after which her situation would be reviewed.

In *R (on the application of Ross) v West Sussex Primary Care Trust*,[97] Grenfell J held that the refusal of the defendant NHS Trust to provide funding to a cancer sufferer for a potentially life-extending drug was a decision that no reasonable Trust could have made having regard to the exceptional circumstances of the patient's case, in particular his intolerance to other forms of treatment and the clinical efficacy and cost effectiveness of allowing him access to that treatment. The Trust had refused to fund the treatment on the basis that it was neither clinically efficacious nor cost effective and that the claimant's need was not exceptional within the meaning of that term as contained in the Trust's in-house policy. It was held that the Trust had, in attempting to

---

97 [2008] EWHC 2252 (Admin), (2008) 11 CCL Rep 787.

formulate fair guidelines as to what would amount to an exceptional case, introduced an unnecessary element of confusion. The Trust's policy was unlawful because it contained a contradiction in terms. It was not, as it purported to be, a policy for exceptional cases because a person was automatically disqualified if they was likened to another. In reality, in order to qualify, the patient had to demonstrate uniqueness rather than exceptionality. Once a patient had established that they fell within a category of exceptionality, the Trust still had to have regard to principles of clinical efficacy and cost effectiveness before sanctioning funding for treatment, but, once an exceptional case was made out, particularly where matters of extending life were concerned, the Trust should take a less restrictive approach to cost effectiveness when considering the case for funding.

In *R (on the application of AC) v Berkshire West Primary Care Trust*,[98] Bean J held that a policy adopted by the defendant, under which breast augmentation was classified as a 'non-core' procedure in terms of treatment for gender identity disorder and was not therefore routinely funded by the NHS, was not irrational and nor did it discriminate against transsexual patients. The Trust had due regard to the need to eliminate discrimination against transsexual patients and to the need to promote equality of opportunity between transsexual and non-transsexual patients, and its gender identity disorder policy had been drafted with great care and after extensive consultation.

While breast augmentation had been funded in the case of a natal woman who had a congenital absence of breast tissue, in that case the psychological distress suffered had been far more significant, making that situation exceptional. It was well known that NHS budgets were under severe pressure from the increasing longevity of the population and the development of expensive new drugs and surgical procedures. It was therefore lawful for the Trust to have policies about which treatments would, and which would not, be routinely funded. It was equally proper for the Trust to adopt a general policy for the exercise of its discretion, and to allow for exceptions to it in exceptional circumstances.

It can therefore be seen that there are some circumstances in which refusals to fund a particular treatment or allocate resources can be successful. However, it remains difficult to succeed in such actions and it needs to be borne in mind that even where a decision has been quashed, for example by reason of some procedural irregularity, the same decision may result from a subsequent fair decision process. The courts would be highly unlikely to, for example, make a direct order for allocation of resources to a particular purpose or treatment.

Is there any mileage for potential claimants in arguing that their rights under the Human Rights Act 1998 have been infringed by a refusal to provide a particular treatment?

In *R (on the application of McDonald) v Kensington and Chelsea RLBC*,[99] the Supreme Court held that the local authority, which provided home-based community care to a person with limited mobility who suffered from bladder problems requiring her to urinate several times during the night, was entitled to withdraw the provision of an overnight

---

98   [2010] EWHC 1162 (Admin).
99   [2011] UKSC 33.

carer who helped her access a commode where it had assessed that her needs could equally be met by the provision of incontinence pads or absorbent sheets. Such a decision did not violate her rights under Art 8 of the European Convention on Human Rights (ECHR). The local authority had respected her personal feelings as well as taking account of her safety, her independence and its own responsibilities towards other care recipients. Its proposal regarding the use of pads was proportionate and in the interests of other service users.

In *R (on the application of Condliff) v North Staffordshire Primary Care Trust*,[100] the claimant was morbidly obese and wished to have gastric by-pass surgery funded by the NHS. He did not qualify for the surgery under the relevant policy of the defendant, but he made an individual funding request on the ground of exceptionality. The defendant's individual funding request policy stated that, when determining exceptionality, 'social factors', which were non-clinical factors, would not be taken into account. The request was refused. The claimant contended that the policy breached his rights under Art 8 of the ECHR by excluding social or non-clinical factors from consideration. The Court of Appeal held that the policy did not breach Art 8. The defendant was entitled to refuse funding for the gastric by-pass. The claimant's state of health was having a seriously adverse effect on his private and family life in the most basic way which, without surgery, would continue. However, the application of the policy did not involve a lack of respect for the claimant's private and family life. The policy of allocating scarce medical resources on a basis of the comparative assessment of clinical needs was intentionally non-discriminatory. Performing the function of allocating limited resources strictly according to the defendant's assessment of medical need was to do no more than to apply the resource for the purpose for which they were provided without giving preferential treatment on non-medical grounds. Attempts made to impose a positive obligation on the state to provide support for an individual under Art 8 had been unsuccessful. Article 8 could not be relied on as giving rise to a positive duty to take into account welfare considerations wider than the comparative medical conditions and medical needs of different patients. The Trust was entitled to set an individual funding request policy which reflected what it reasonably considered to be the fairest way of treating patients. There was nothing in the authorities leading to the conclusion that the defendant's policy was to be regarded as showing a lack of respect for the claimant's private and family life so as to bring Art 8 into play. However, even if Art 8 were applicable, there were legitimate equality reasons for the Trust to adopt the policy and its decision was well within the area of discretion or margin of appreciation open to it. In other words, a reasonable rejection of a funding request would not breach Art 8.

The *McDonald* case was subsequently taken to the European Court of Human Rights. In its judgment, reported at *McDonald v United Kingdom*,[101] the court reiterated that nation states enjoy a wide margin of appreciation in determining how or whether to allocate scarce resources involving social, economic and health care policy. Moreover, it pointed out that the margin is particularly wide when resources are limited.

---

100 [2011] EWCA Civ 910.
101 (2015) 60 EHRR 1.

It therefore appears unlikely that human rights give any wider grounds for challenge than those available under domestic law. While the ECHR is likely to require that decisions are made with regard to due process requirements and to claims to equality and proportionality, it is difficult to see that this adds much to the domestic law. See for example *R (on the application of Rogers) v Swindon NHS Primary Care Trust.*[102]

---

102 [2006] 1 WLR 2649.

Part Two

Part Two

Chapter 5

The duty of care

Martyn McLeish

INTRODUCTION

In everyday life the word 'negligence' is used in different ways. 'Negligence' is commonly associated with carelessness but lack of care alone will not found a cause of action. The jurisprudence that determines the limit and extent of legal liability ('legal negligence') is the product of an historical evolution with inevitable anomalies, contradictions, and complexities that require explanation.

In broad terms 'legal negligence' has three constituent parts:

1   duty – a situation or relationship in which one party has an obligation to another;
2   breach – the failure of the defendant to discharge the standard expected of someone exercising reasonable skill and care in fulfilling his or her obligation; and
3   damage – loss or injury to a party caused by breach.[1]

In terms of liability the relationship between clinician and patient has to be understood within the general concept of legal negligence. When we ask 'Has the clinician been negligent?' we are asking a much more specific question: whether he or she has been in breach of a duty to take reasonable care of the patient that has resulted in a foreseeable loss. Many cases will fail because the claimant cannot show that the alleged failure of the clinician 'caused' injury. In others the court will find that the duty has not been breached because the treatment given was reasonable. In some cases the court may find that the injury sustained was not foreseeable and, therefore, there was no breach of duty. However, in most cases the existence of a duty of care itself is not in issue.

It is important to understand what we mean when we say that a duty of care is owed by a clinician to a patient. In some factual scenarios the existence of a duty is clear and well established, but the organisation and nature of medical practice changes over time and the law of negligence must develop accordingly and be applied to 'novel' situations.

---

1   Of course the link between the breach and the damage has to be proved: legal causation. This is the subject of Chapter 7.

THE DUTY OF CARE TO THE PATIENT

A doctor or a nurse owe to a patient a duty to exercise the skill and care expected of a reasonable doctor or nurse. Those who operate a hospital casualty department and employ or otherwise engage nurses, doctors, or other medical personnel owe the same duty of care as would be expected of their clinicians.[2] An ambulance service is a part of the health service and owes a duty to provide health care to a patient rather than the care that would be provided by an 'emergency serivce' such as the police or fire service.[3] In establishing the existence or non-existence of a duty of care the court will apply a tripartite test:

1   the foreseeability of harm;
2   the closeness or proximity of the relationship between the parties; and
3   the imposition of a duty of care in the circumstances is consistent with public policy, what is fair, just, and reasonable

This follows the test established in the House of Lords in *Caparo Industries plc v Dickman*.[4]

When the courts have already established the existence or non-existence of a duty of care, it is unnecessary and inappropriate to reconsider whether or not the duty is fair, just and reasonable.[5] It is only in 'novel' cases that the courts will have to consider the *Caparo* test and look at issues of wider principle. The application of such an approach precludes deciding cases by reference to their own particular merits: all cases are decided on their own facts, but where those circumstances comply with established categories of negligence, an appeal to the justice or fairness of an individual case could not justify a departure from the principle already decided.[6] In cases which do give rise to novel questions, where established principles do not provide an answer, *the Caparo* criteria should be developed 'incrementally and by analogy with established authority';[7] *Robinson v Chief Constable of West Yorkshire Police*.[8]

The appplication to clinical negligence cases was considered by the Supreme Court in the case of *Darnley v Croydon Health Services NHS Trust*.[9] Following an assault the claimant attended hospital where he was seen by a receptionist at A&E. The claimant gave a history of sustaining a head injury. The receptionist told him to wait and that there was an estimated waiting time of 4–5 hours. The claimant waited for 19 minutes before leaving A&E. He went home, later that evening he became distressed and an ambulance was called. Despite surgery the claimant suffered brain damage. The claimant's case was that he should have been told that the appropriate waiting time for a head injury assessment was

---

2   *Barnett v Chelsea & Kensington Hospital Management Committee* [1969] 1 QB 428, CA.
3   *Kent v Griffiths* [2001] QB 36, CA.
4   [1990] 2 AC 605.
5   *Robinson v Chief Constable of West Yorkshire Police* [2018] UKSC 4, per Lord Reed at [24].
6   See Hobhouse LJ (as he then was) in *Perrett v Collins* [1999] PNLR 77, CA at [90]–[91].
7   Per Lord Reed in Robinson at [27].
8   [2018] UKSC 50.
9   [2018] UKSC 4.

30 minutes. The trial judge found as a matter of fact that had he been provided with this information he would have waited 30 minutes, would have been assessed, and would have avoided injury.

The hospital trust argued that neither it nor the receptionist owed a duty of care to advise the claimant about waiting times, the damage was outside the scope of the duty owed, and that there was no causal connection between the breach of duty and the injury. The hospital was successful at first instance and in the Court of Appeal, but the claimant won in the Supreme Court. In giving the judgment of the court, Lord Lloyd-Jones rejected the suggestion that imposing a liability on the trust for the acts of the receptionist amounted to 'a new head of liability for NHS health trusts'. The present case fell within an established category of duty of care, in particular the duty owed by the hospital to run an A&E department, following *Barnett v Chelsea and Kensington Hospital Management Committee*.[10] As soon as the claimant had 'booked in' he was a patient and the trust owed him a duty of care. In considering the nature of the duty of care it was not appropriate to distinguish between medically-qualified and non-medically qualified staff: this distinction might be relevant to whether or not that had been a breach of duty where a trust had devolved a role to non-medically qualified staff to provide information, a duty was owed to ensure that the information provided was accurate.

The doctor-patient relationship

The existence of the duty is not based on the 'foreseeability' of harm but on the relationship between doctor and patient. The duty is to be understood within the context of that relationship and the 'status' of the parties: a doctor exercises reasonable skill and care in the treatment of another who becomes a 'patient' as a result of the doctor's assumption of responsibility for his well-being. The relationship is integral to the existence of the duty of care: the relationship would not exist but for the doctor's assumption of responsibility.

The duty of care is a duty to take all reasonable steps, including the duty to commence activity, where appropriate, for the proper medical care of the patient. Where there is an existing doctor-patient relationship negligent omissions, as well as the failure to take appropriate steps, will found a cause of action. In *Barnett v Chelsea and Kensington Hospital Management Committee*,[11] Nield J held that a hospital owed a duty to a person who presented himself at the casualty department, notwithstanding that he had not yet been received into the hospital. Similarly, once a 999 call requesting the dispatch of an ambulance was accepted the ambulance crew owed a duty to take reasonable care to the injured party; see *Kent v Griffiths, Roberts and London Ambulance Service*.[12]

---

10   [1969] 1 QB 428, CA.
11   [1969] 1 QB 428.
12   [2000] 2 WLR 1158, CA.

Medical treatment of non-patients

The rescuer cases

In order for the duty to arise there must be a doctor-patient relationship. A doctor does not owe a duty to intervene when a medical emergency is encountered outside professional life. If a bleeding man comes to one's door for help, one is not legally obliged to lend assistance. Likewise a doctor is not legally obliged to assist in the aftermath of a car accident or if medical care is required on an aeroplane.[13]

Of course in many situations both doctors and non-medical bystanders will help. In lending assistance an ordinary member of the public owes a duty to act reasonably, see *Harrison v British Railways Board*.[14] The ordinary man or woman in the street cannot be taken to have any specialised knowledge, and his or her actions cannot be measured by the standard of a professional rescuer. A first aider owes a duty to assist in giving first aid, but the standard of care provided is that of a first aider and not a doctor, see *Cattley v St John's Ambulance Brigade*.[15]

Confronted with an emergency situation a doctor who decides to act assumes a duty of care to the victim. The duty of care arises from the decision of the doctor to act. At this point the relationship of rescuer to victim is analogous to that between doctor and patient. In assuming such a duty the doctor must consider and if necessary embark upon some form of treatment, as in the absence of the doctor-patient relationship an omission to act will not found a cause of action. A doctor may assist in a way that falls short of providing medical treatment. So a doctor who tells relatives that a patient has died does not assume a doctor-patient relationship, see *Powell v Boldaz*.[16] However, once a decision is taken to act, the doctor will be in breach of duty if they fail to take reasonable care in treating the victim. Circumstances may place a limit on what a doctor can practically do in such circumstances and there are judicial statements to the effect that the duty is limited to not making the victim's condition worse, see *Capital and Counties plc v Hampshire*. A doctor may make the victim's condition worse either by activity or the failure to take reasonable steps. In either event if he or she fails to take reasonable care the victim will have a cause of action.

THE DOCTOR'S DUTY TO OTHERS

Family members

The extension of a clinician's duty of care extending to family members who are not patients is a possibility, but is likely to be limited to very specific circumstances. In *ABC v St George's Healthcare*[17] the claimant's father had shot and killed her mother. He was detained pursuant to mental health legislation under the care of the defendant. He was subsequently

---

13   *Capital and Counties plc v Hampshire CC* [1997] QB 1004, CA.
14   [1981] 3 All ER 679.
15   (1988, unreported).
16   [1998] Lloyd's Rep Med 116, CA.
17   [2017] EWCA Civ 336.

diagnosed with Huntington's Disease, an inherited condition. The claimant's father told others about his condition but not the claimant. Those with care of the claimant's father considered whether or not they should override patient confidentiality and inform the claimant of his condition. The claimant informed her father that she was pregnant, and at a meeting with his clinicians he opposed informing the claimant who could have been advised to take a predictive test for Huntington's Disease. The claimant gave birth to a daughter and discovered that she had Huntington's disease. The issue in this case was whether or not the trust clinicians owed a duty of care to their patient's daughter. She should have been informed of her father's diagnosis. At first instance Nicol J struck out the claim on the basis that there was no reasonably arguable duty of care. The Court of Appeal allowed the claimant's appeal and remitted the case for trial. In giving judgment of the court, Irwin LJ reflected on the policy reasons put forward by the trust that no duty could be owed to the claimant as a 'third party'. He considered that the facts had to be properly considered in the context of the development of the law that had come to emphasise patient autonomy, and in particular the circumstances in which a clinician could withhold information from parties, who were not patients, which may influence decisions they may take about medical treatment. Any decision taken by clinicians would have to be considered within the framework of the *Bolam* and *Bolitho* tests, and whether the actions of the clinicians involved were in accordance with a reasonable body of medical opinion. A determination of this issue could only be resolved by consideration of expert evidence. Such evidence is particularly important in the case of advice given by geneticists, and therefore the issue of opening potential 'floodgates' was limited.

Insurers and employers

It may seem contradictory that if the basis for the duty of care is the relationship between doctor and patient, the scope of the duty should encompass the rights of others to bring an action against a doctor. However, in practice it does. If negligent medical treatment results in the death of a patient the estate of the deceased and dependents have a right of action against the doctor. This is a claim brought under statute – the Fatal Accidents Act 1976 and the Law Reform (Miscellaneous Provisions) Act 1934 – but the common law has also developed a more expansive approach to the doctor-patient duty. For example, a doctor may be liable for psychological shock provoked by the sight of a family member's injuries caused by the doctor's negligence notwithstanding the absence of any relationship between the doctor and the victim.[18]

A doctor's duty of care goes beyond causing or failing to prevent physical injury. Just as a doctor assumes a responsibility in his clinical treatment of the patient, he or she assumes further responsibility in providing other forms of professional service, in particular conducting health examinations and preparing reports for employers, prospective employers, insurance companies, and for the purposes of legal proceedings.

---

18 This is the 'aftermath' principle as set out by the House of Lords in *McLaughlin v O'Brian* [1983] 1 AC 410.

No simple statement of general application can be made in relation to these cases, in part because the factual circumstances and obligations with which they are concerned vary from case to case. For example, non-treating medical practitioners may examine an employee's medical records and prepare a report without any physical examination of the actual employee. The failure to observe a serious health problem may result in a condition going untreated that should have been detected. The failure to record such a condition may result in financial loss to both employee and employer but the failure to treat may also result in physical injury. What happens if the opposite occurs: a serious health condition is wrongly diagnosed as a result of which a job applicant is denied the position? What remedy would unsuccessful applicants have against the doctor whose negligent advice effectively cost them the job? Does it make a difference if the doctor conducts an examination as well as writing a report? Does the 'purpose' of the report, to whom it is made and what it is to contain, determine the extent of any liability?

In *Roy v Croydon Health Authority*[19] the defendant required the claimant to undergo a medical examination as a prospective employee. The defendants' radiologist failed to note that an X-ray disclosed a serious pathology. In this case the defendant admitted that it owed a duty of care in these circumstances. In *Baker v Kaye*[20] Robert Owen QC (as he then was) held that a doctor retained by a company for the purpose of examining a potential employee's medical fitness owed him a duty of care in carrying out his examination and in interpreting the results when reporting to the company.

There is a significant distinction between *Roy v Croydon* and *Baker v Kaye*. In *Roy* the failure to detect the condition caused physical injury to the claimant, in *Baker* the claimant's loss was economic, the financial consequence of not securing prospective employment. The importance of this distinction between physical injury and economic loss is made clear in *Kapfunde v Abbey National Plc*,[21] when the Court of Appeal held that *Baker v Kaye* was wrongly decided. In *Kapfunde* a GP had a contract with Abbey National whereby she assessed the health of a prospective employee on the basis of written materials, not an examination. She considered that the claimant was unsuitable to be employed as she had sickle cell disease so was at risk of having a lot of time off work for illness. The Court of Appeal held that the doctor did not owe a duty of care to the claimant. The GP was working under a contract with Abbey National. The purpose of her recommendation related to selecting potential employees. She had never seen the claimant and there was no close relationship between them. The claim was one for economic loss not physical injury.

The crucial consideration in these cases is not the doctor-patient relationship. These are not clinical situations when an examination is carried out and recommendations made as part of on-going treatment. In these cases the medical practitioner reports upon the patient in a particular situation: what responsibilities the doctor assumes and to whom the resultant duties are owed vary according to the circumstances. So in *Kapfunde* the GP had a duty to Abbey National to give advice

---

19   [1997] PIQR P444.
20   [1997] IRLR 219.
21   [1999] Lloyd's Rep Med 48.

applying reasonable skill and care, but owed no duty to the claimant in providing her advice to Abbey National. Doctors carrying out examination for insurance companies owe a duty of care in making appropriate recommendations to the insurance company not to the patient. The doctor is contracted to make recommendations to the insurance company, not to treat the patient.[22]

Other remedies may be available to an employee if loss arises out of the employee-employer relationship. Cases such as *Kapfunde* may fall foul of the Equality Act 2010. An employer can stipulate essential health requirements but may need to justify doing so, and show that it would not be reasonable to waive them in an individual case. This means that an employer should always consider whether suitable adjustments can be made to facilitate the individual's employment.

The duty of care owed to patients in these situations may be limited only to conducting the examination itself with reasonable skill and care and not causing any injury to the patient in carrying it out.[23]

Advice given in legal proceedings

Two particular issues arise in relation to medical practitioners providing advice in relation to legal proceedings. The first is when a party relies upon such advice to undertake activity or treatment that may result in injury or loss. In *Landall v Dennis Faulkner & Alsop*[24] an orthopaedic surgeon giving advice in a personal injury claim advised the claimant to have spinal fusion surgery. The claimant alleged that this advice was negligent and that he suffered serious injury as a result. At trial it was held that there was no liability. The advice given by the orthopaedic surgeon was given for the purposes of legal proceedings and not as part of the claimant's treatment.

Landall is also an example of the second issue. Because the orthopaedic surgeon was also acting in contemplation of litigation his advice was covered by expert witness immunity. Historically the immunity extends to witness statements and experts' reports made in contemplation of both civil and criminal proceedings. In *Evans v The London Hospital's Medical College (University of London)*[25] Drake J struck out a claim against a pathologist for negligent preparation of a report that led to criminal proceedings.

In *M v Newham London Borough Council*[26] Lord Browne-Wilkinson said that a psychiatrist would have witness immunity where, having been instructed by the local authority to examine a child by way of an inquiry into sexual abuse and its possible perpetrators, she would naturally know that her report might found proceedings.

In *Jones v Kaney*[27] Blake J struck out a claim against a psychologist who radically and allegedly negligently changed her opinion after joint discussion with the defendant's expert. However, he certified that the

---

22 The point has been made obiter: see *M (a minor) v Newham LBC* [1995] 2 AC 633 and *E (a minor) v Dorset CC* [1995] 2 AC 633.
23 *Re N* [1999] Lloyd's Rep Med 257, CA.
24 [1994] 5 Med LR 268.
25 [1981] 1 WLR 184.
26 [1995] 2 AC 633.
27 [2010] EWHC 61 (QB).

issue of expert witness immunity was a suitable subject for consideration by the Supreme Court. The Supreme Court decided that the immunity could not be justified and allowed the appeal.[28] Although the law of expert immunity has been transformed by this decision existing case law gives some indication of how it may impact upon practice.

A medical practitioner's liability in negligence for pre-litigation acts is clearly established. In *Hughes v Lloyds Bank plc*[29] a claimant settled her personal injury claim based upon letters she obtained from her GP about her condition. Although these letters had been used in connection with legal proceedings the GP was not immune from suit. Proceedings had not been issued. The letters had been provided for the purposes of negotiation not as part of disclosure. The claim for negligence against the GP would not be struck out.

Hughes is a strike-out case and it is important to consider that claims against medical practitioners providing advice in connection with legal proceedings are likely to be beset with difficulty. In *N v Agrawal*[30] the claimant alleged that the defendant, who examined her following her complaint of sexual assault and made a report upon this examination, owed her a duty to attend court and give evidence at the trial of her alleged assailant. The failure to give evidence had resulted in an exacerbation of psychological trauma. The Court of Appeal struck out the claim on the ground that a witness was not under a duty to any person to give evidence.

Immunity has been waived in other circumstances. In *Meadow v General Medical Council*[31] the Court of Appeal held that expert witnesses had no immunity against disciplinary proceedings before professional tribunals where fitness to practice was in issue. In *Phillips v Symes (No 2)*[32] Peter Smith J held that expert witnesses were not immune from being held liable to wasted costs orders.

A treating doctor does not have to foresee the consequences of his advice on legal proceedings. In *Stevens v Bermondsey and Southwark Group Hospital Management Committee*,[33] a casualty officer negligently diagnosed the claimant as having suffered a minor injury. She was not liable to the claimant for the financial loss sustained as a result of undersettling her claim for damages for personal injury.

THE DUTY OF DOCTORS EXERCISING STATUTORY POWERS

The notion that a doctor owes a duty of care to a patient is uncontroversial. Doctors will also owe a duty of care when, in certain situations, they assume responsibility for the care of others who are not their patients. In providing reports to employers, insurers, and lawyers, the scope of the doctor's duty of care is limited by the circumstances of the case. Many doctors or other health care professionals are employed by or contracted to public authorities in the provision of social and education services.

---

28   *Jones (appellant) v Kaney (respondent)* [2011] UKSC 13.
29   [1998] PIQR P98, CA.
30   [1999] Lloyd's Rep Med 257, CA.
31   [2007] QB 462.
32   [2004] EWHC 2330 (Ch), [2005] 1 WLR 2043.
33   (1963) 107 Sol Jo 478.

The liability of public bodies for injury and loss caused by failures in the exercise of statutory powers is one of the most complex and controversial issues in contemporary jurisprudence. The central issues involved can only be briefly outlined for the purposes of this chapter.

The distinctive feature of these cases is that the duty of care arises from the statutory function itself and is not based on the relationship between the claimant and defendant, unless a duty is also owed as a result of some other relationship such as that between employer and employee, see *Connor v Surrey County Council*.[34]

In *X (minors) v Bedfordshire County Council*[35] the House of Lords was concerned with test cases where a local authority, exercising its statutory powers, took children into care. Lord Browne-Wilkinson held that a common law duty of care might arise in the performance of such functions, however, a distinction had to be drawn between situations when a public body's decision was based on the exercise of a discretion or judgment or there were administrative failings leading to injury or damage. For example, the decision to close a school might not give rise to a private law cause of action, but the failure to keep a school reasonably safe would found a claim for damages for injury arising as a result of the neglected conditions of the building.

A clear distinction between operational and 'policy' decisions may become more difficult when we are concerned with the judgment of professionals not only exercising their judgment but also balancing competing considerations and risks, including limited public resources. In *X v Bedfordshire* the House of Lords held that a psychiatrist or social worker examining or investigating evidence of sexual abuse on behalf of the local authority in the exercise of statutory child care functions does not owe a duty of care to a child or her mother. However, the possibility that professionals exercising such judgment could have a practical immunity from suit was not accepted by the European Court of Human Rights, see *Z v United Kingdom*.[36]

The House of Lords had to reconsider the issues in *X v Bedfordshire* through the lens of the Strasbourg jurisprudence in *Barrett v Enfield*.[37] In this case the claimant alleged the local authority had failed in its duty of care while he was in care. Their Lordships drew a distinction between decisions taken for policy reasons and those taken as part of the local authority's 'operational' function. The court was not equipped to adjudicate on the policy decisions of statutory bodies which had to be allowed a wide discretion in allocating resources and prioritising care. However, where decisions did not involve issues of policy the traditional common law of negligence could apply. The courts could consider the circumstances of the case, weigh the evidence, and determine whether a decision fell within the policy or operational functions of the local authority. In this way the development of the common law has avoided 'blanket' immunity defeating valid claims against public authorities. However, the existence of a duty of care will be determined according to the three stage test of foreseeability, proximity, and what is fair, just and reasonable.

---

34 [2010] EWCA Civ 286 (CA).
35 [1995] 2 AC 633.
36 (2002) 34 EHRR 3.
37 [2001] 2 AC 550.

The most important example of the three stage test being applied is *JD (FC) v East Berkshire Community Health NHS Trust*.[38] The claimants were parents who were wrongly suspected of child abuse as a result of the misdiagnosis of their children by doctors. Their claims were struck out by the House of Lords. This decision was not based on the foreseeability of injury or the 'proximity' or closeness of the relationship between the parties involved. Both of these limbs of the test were satisfied. The claims were struck out on public and legal policy grounds. First, if a doctor investigating the question of abuse should be liable to parents if he acted without due care, there was no reason why a negligent surgeon should not be liable for psychiatric harm suffered by parents in all cases when negligence results in the injury or death of a child. Second, the floodgates would be open to parents if a doctor with the medical charge of a child also owed a duty of care to the parents. Third, the doctor was charged with the protection of the child, not the parent. Fourth, the interests of the child in these situations were not identical with those of the parent. Fifth, in these particular cases the interest of the child and parent were in conflict: indeed there could only ever be a conflict of interest in such cases as in carrying out their duty of investigation the doctors had regard only to the interests of the children.

The education cases

The European Court of Human Rights has been the midwife to a more liberal approach to the liability of statutory bodies. In *Phelps v Hillingdon London Borough Council*[39] the House of Lords considered the liability of professionals employed by education authorities exercising statutory duties under the Education Acts. Lord Slynn held that in these cases the court had to consider: (a) why that person should *not* owe a duty of care; and (b) why, if the duty is breached by that person, the authority should *not* be liable.

An educational psychologist employed by a local education authority will, or is likely to, owe a duty of care to a pupil, and the local education authority owes a general duty through its teachers to provide a suitable education for its pupils. In *E v Dorset County Council*[40] the House of Lords refused to strike out claims against a local education authority for the failure of its psychologists, teachers and officials to identify the special educational needs of the claimant. In *D N v Greenwich London Borough Council*[41] the Court of Appeal held that a local education authority was liable for the negligence of an educational psychologist who had failed, among other things, to identify the claimant's complex social and communication needs.

The interests of professionals have to be considered as well as the right of a child to claim damages in negligence. In *Devon County Council v Clarke*[42] the Court of Appeal held that it was wrong to characterise all educational negligence cases as being single claims for a failed education

---

38 [2005] 2 WLR 993.
39 [2001] 2 AC 619.
40 [1995] 2 AC 633.
41 [2004] EWCA Civ 1659.
42 [2005] EWCA Civ 266.

over a period of time as if special rules applied to them. The jurisdiction to award damages in cases of this sort was not to be seen as a charter for claimants to make allegations against all the professionals who had been involved in a child's education, secure in the knowledge that, provided they succeeded in one allegation against one professional, they would recover all their costs from the local education authority. In *Carty v Croydon London Borough Council*[43] the court said there were two areas of potential enquiry in such a case. The first was whether the issue was justiciable at all, the second was the application of the three-stage *Caparo* test – foreseeability of damage, proximity, and whether it was fair, just and reasonable that the law should impose a duty of care. In *Nuttall v Mayor & Burgesses of Sutton London Borough Council*[44] an educational psychologist owed a duty to a child with special educational needs to assess the needs of the child with the care and skill to be expected of a reasonably competent educational psychologist. However, in practical terms, it would only be if an educational psychologist conducted an assessment negligently or formulated a recommendation negligently, or both, that any liability would arise. In order to recover damages for negligence, the claimant had also to prove that he had suffered loss as a result of the matters of which he complained.

THE DUTY OWED TO MEMBERS OF THE PUBLIC

The notion that a clinician owes a duty of care to a patient is uncontroversial. A doctor who reacts to an emergency to assist members of the public in an emergency will also owe those treated a duty to take reasonable care. In some cases the treatment a doctor recommends for a patient will involve wider considerations of the patient's well-being and the safety of others. Legal liability in such situations will depend on the circumstances of the case and, in particular, whether or not injury to a specific individual or a particular group of individuals was foreseeable. For example, in *Goodwill v British Pregnancy Advisory Service*[45] the Court of Appeal found that a doctor carrying out a vasectomy does not owe a duty of care to all women with whom the patient will have sexual intercourse in the future.

Different considerations may arise when the risk of injury to members of the public is imminent and not merely theoretical. Earlier cases suggest that a doctor was under a duty of care to potential victims of a dangerous patient who was not properly contained: see *Holgate v Lancashire Mental Hospitals Board*[46] and *Ellis v Home Office*.[47] In *Hill* v *Chief Constable of West Yorkshire*[48] the House of Lords held that no claim could be brought by the victim's estate against the police for its failure to apprehend her murderer. The Court of Appeal applied *Hill* in *Palmer v Tees Health Authority*.[49] In this case the mother of a murdered child was unable to bring a claim against the health authority alleging negligence in failing

---

43 [2005] EWCA Civ 19.
44 [2009] EWHC 294 (QB).
45 [1996] 1 WLR 1397.
46 [1937] 4 All ER 19.
47 [1953] 2 All ER 149, CA.
48 [1988] 1 WLR 1049.
49 [1999] Lloyd's Rep Med 351.

to diagnose the perpetrator of the crime as a risk to children. A health authority owed no duty of care to the public generally in respect of its care of such patients. There was no relationship between the defendant and the victim. Neither the claimant nor her daughter could have been identified as potential victims before the crime was committed. In *Palmer* the Court of Appeal applied the three stage test following *Caparo* and found that there was no 'proximity'.

A complicating factor in these cases is that in most situations the act of violence causing injury or death is a crime. Two issues arise. The first is whether or not the illegal act itself can found a cause of action. The second is whether a doctor or health authority can be liable for an illegal act perpetrated by a patient who may or may not commit such acts while under their control.

In *Clunis v Camden and Islington Health Authority*[50] the plaintiff had been detained in hospital for treatment of a mental disorder. The hospital discharged him and he stabbed a man to death. The plaintiff sued the health authority, alleging that it had been negligent in discharging him. The health authority applied to strike out the action on the ground that damages could not be recovered for the consequences of the plaintiff's own unlawful act. The court accepted this submission. The plaintiff has been convicted of a serious criminal offence. The court ought not to allow itself to be made an instrument to enforce obligations alleged to arise out of the plaintiff's own criminal act.

The House of Lords considered the issues further in *Gray v Thames Trains Ltd.*[51] In this case the claimant was a passenger on a train involved in a major railway accident. He suffered post-traumatic stress disorder which he alleged had been caused by the accident. Whilst suffering from that disorder he killed a man. His plea of guilty to manslaughter on the ground of diminished responsibility was accepted by the Crown and he was ordered to be detained in a hospital under the Mental Health Act 1983. The claimant brought an action in negligence against the defendants, including damages for loss of earnings, loss of liberty and post-traumatic stress disorder. The House of Lords ruled that in order to avoid inconsistency in the justice system a civil court would not award damages to compensate a claimant for an injury or disadvantage which the criminal courts had imposed for a criminal act for which he was responsible; the criminal court by its sentence had found the claimant to have had personal responsibility even if he had acted with diminished responsibility.

Cases involving detention

Earlier cases seem to establish a duty of care on a doctor when recommending the admission of a patient to hospital for mental disorder (*Everett v Griffiths;*[52] *de Freville v Dill*[53]). In cases involving detention under s 3 of the Mental Health Act 1983 the state, through the health

---

50   [1998] QB 978, CA.
51   [2009] UKHL 33.
52   [1920] 3 KB 163, CA.
53   (1927) 96 LJKB 1056.

authority, owes an operational duty to patients.[54] A health authority is under a duty to take steps to prevent a patient from committing suicide where it knows or reasonably ought to have known that there was a real and immediate risk of suicide. This is the case regardless of whether the patient is detained under the Mental Health Act 1983, or whether they are receiving treatment voluntarily, see *Rabone v Pennine Care NHS Foundation Trust*.[55]

---

54 *Savage v South Essex NHS Trust* [2008] UKHL 74.
55 [2012] UKSC 2.

Chapter 6

Breach of duty and strict liability

Martyn McLeish

INTRODUCTION

A medical clinician has a duty to take reasonable care of a patient. This duty will be breached if the clinician fails to provide care which conforms to the standard reasonably expected. The inability of a clinician to treat a patient successfully is not by itself enough to found a claim in negligence. A doctor in general practice cannot be expected to have the skill and expertise of a surgeon. Nevertheless, an inexperienced doctor will be judged by the standards of an experienced doctor. The standard is that which is reasonable in the circumstances of the case. Two questions arise: what is the standard of care in a particular case, and how is the claimant to prove that the defendant has failed to come up to that standard?

Determining the standard of care expected of a clinician depends upon a legal analysis of the facts of the case and is highly dependent upon expert medical evidence. As with all professionals, the law has to accord medical practitioners a degree of respect. In many cases evidence of good practice will provide sufficient evidence of reasonable care. However, in all branches of science and learning there will be differences of opinion as to what is or is not reasonable practice. A doctor may hold a minority view, but so long as this view is held by a respectable body of medical opinion, it is reasonably held, and his treatment of a patient in line with such opinion, no liability will arise.

THE *BOLAM* TEST

The standard of care that is required of a person undertaking an activity is that which is reasonable. Every person who enters into a learned profession undertakes to exercise a reasonable degree of care and skill. The seminal statement of this approach to clinical negligence is that of McNair J in *Bolam v Friern Hospital Management Committee*:[1]

---

1   [1957] 1 WLR 582 at 586.

Where you get a situation which involves the use of some special skill or competence, then the test as to whether there has been negligence or not is not the test of the man on the top of a Clapham omnibus, because he has not got this special skill. The test is the standard of the ordinary skilled man exercising and professing to have that special skill. A man need not possess the highest expert skill ... it is sufficient if he exercises the ordinary skill of an ordinary competent man exercising that particular art.

A doctor's duty is to exercise skill and care according to the ordinary and reasonable standards of those who practice in the relevant field of medicine. *In Ashcroft v Mersey Regional Health Authority*,[2] Kilner Brown J said that the question was whether it had been established on a balance of probabilities that the doctor had failed to exercise the care required of a man possessing and professing special skill in circumstances which required the exercise of that special skill.

The standard of care to be applied is that of the reasonable practitioner, there is no allowance for inexperience (see *Wilsher v Essex Area Health Authority*[3]). In *FB v Rana*,[4] an inexperienced SHO was negligent in failing to ask appropriate questions which would have elicited a patient history consistent with a diagnosis of pneumococcal meningitis. The court concluded that there is a basic standard required of doctors in taking a history that they should be able to establish the reason for the patient attending A & E, see in particular the judgment of Jackson LJ at [57]–[67]. In ordinary circumstances a doctor following a generally approved practice will not be held to be negligent (*Marshall v Lindsey County Council*[5]). In *Arkless v Betsi Cadwaladr University Local Health Board*,[6] the doctor's method of examining the patient's wrist was not one recognised by a reasonable body of medical opinion and the examining doctor should have undertaken the three tests required to detect scaphoid fractures.

In *Taaffe v East of England Ambulance Service NHS Trust*,[7] the court held that the *Bolam* test applies to the ambulance services as well as to medical professionals.

A court cannot choose between two approved practices, ie between two schools of thought (*Maynard v West Midlands Regional Health Authority*[8]). So in *Adderley v North Manchester Health Authority*[9] a diagnosis of schizophrenia, though wrong, was not negligent, applying *Bolam*. The appeal court was bound by the judge's finding that it was a 'two schools of thought' case. If a respectable body of medical opinion, albeit a minority one, would at the time of the alleged negligence have approved of the course taken by the defendant, there is no negligence. In determining whether the opinion of a body of doctors constitutes a responsible body for the purposes of the *Bolam* test it is not simply a matter of counting heads: in appropriate circumstances the judge could find that a small number constituted the necessary defence. In

---

2   [1983] 2 All ER 245.
3   [1987] QB 730.
4   [2017] EWCA Civ 334.
5   [1935] 1 KB 516, CA at 540 per Maugham LJ.
6   [2016] EWHC 330 (QB).
7   [2012] EWHC 1335 (QB).
8   [1984] 1 WLR 634, HL.
9   (1995) 25 BMLR 42, CA.

Defreitas v O'Brien,[10] both an orthopaedic surgeon and neurosurgeon avoided liability by showing that their management was acceptable to a responsible body of medical opinion.

Following *Montgomery v Lanarkshire*[11] the application of the *Bolam* case will not be decisive in cases involving full and informed consent (see Chapter 10).

Recent examples

In *Haywood v University Hospitals of North Midlands NHS Trust*,[12] *Bolam* was applied. The standard of care meant no reasonable doctor would have discharged the claimant, who had recently undergone an emergency C section, without performing further tests to determine the cause of her temperature and elevated pulse. In *Anderson v North West Strategic Health Authority*[13] a responsible body of medical opinion would have opted not to give the claimant's mother an emergency C section, so the claim failed.

Bolam does not apply to the facts

The *Bolam* test applies to the issue of whether or not a doctor's actions were in accordance with reasonable practice. It is not concerned with the actual facts of the case which have to be established in the ordinary way on the balance of probabilities. Where there is an issue of factual causation, such as whether treatment which was not given would have cured the patient or otherwise reduced or avoided injury, a dispute between the experts does not involve the *Bolam* test. In *Fallows v Randle*[14] Stuart-Smith LJ said:

> In my judgment that principle has really no application where what the judge has to decide is, on balance, which of two explanations – for something which has undoubtedly occurred which shows that the operation has been unsuccessful – is to be preferred. That is a question of fact which the judge has to determine on the ordinary basis on a balance of probability. It is not a question of saying whether there was a respectable body of medical opinion here which says that this can happen by chance without any evidence, it is a question for the judge to weigh up the evidence on both sides, and he is, in my judgment, entitled in a situation like this, to prefer the evidence of one expert witness to that of the other.

Situations where the court has considered not applying a simple *Bolam* analysis

There are cases where the court has been concerned that common practice itself may not be reasonable. In *Clarke v Adams*,[15] the judge found that the standard warning given by radiologists before giving heat treatment

---

10   [1995] 6 Med LR 108, CA.
11   [2015] UKSC 11, [2015] AC 1430.
12   [2017] EWHC 335 (QB).
13   [2015] EWHC 3563 (QB).
14   [1997] 8 Med LR 160, CA.
15   (1950) 94 Sol Jo 599.

was negligent because it did not give the patient a clear indication as to when the danger point in the treatment might be reached.

In other cases the court has been concerned with the reasons given for a particular practice. In *Hucks v Cole*,[16] a doctor who failed to treat a patient with penicillin was held negligent even though responsible doctors testified that they would have acted as the defendant had. Sachs LJ said that if the court was satisfied that there was a gap in professional practice whereby the patient was exposed to unnecessary risks, the court would expect the professional practice to be altered accordingly. It was not conclusive of proper practice that other practitioners would have acted as the defendant did. The judge was not satisfied that their reasons for so doing stood up to analysis.

In *Knight v Home Office*,[17] Pill J rejected a claim that a mentally disordered prisoner who committed suicide had not been properly looked after by the prison hospital staff on the ground that the decision to observe him at 15-minute intervals had been a decision that ordinary skilled medical staff in their position could have made. However, in the course of his judgment he said that the reasons given by the doctors for their decision should be examined by the court to see if they stood up to analysis.

The courts have also been willing to impose their own view of what is reasonable and what is not upon professions other than the medical profession. In *Nye Saunders & Partners v Bristow*[18] the trial judge found on the evidence that at the relevant time there was no body of responsible professional opinion among architects that would have failed to give a warning as to inflation when estimating building costs, but that, even if he was wrong, he was prepared to hold that no prudent architect would have omitted such a warning. The Court of Appeal refused to interfere with either of those findings. In *Edward Wong Finance Co Ltd v Johnson Stokes & Master*[19] the Privy Council found an established conveyancing practice among Hong Kong solicitors to be unacceptable. In *Deeny v Gooda Walker Ltd*,[20] Phillips J (as he then was) considered that if 'a profession collectively adopted extremely lax standards in some aspect of its work' the court 'would not acquit practitioners of negligence simply because they had complied with those standards.'

The application of these authorities to medical negligence is not straightforward. In *AB v Leeds Teaching Hospital NHS Trust*,[21] Gage J held that the practice of not informing the parents of deceased children that their child's organs had been removed and retained by the hospital was not acceptable. One consequence of the operation of the *Bolam* test is the implausibility of a judge holding that a respected body of medical opinion is flawed. However, another crucial aspect of the test is how it applies to the facts. The court will find on the balance of probabilities what steps a doctor took in treating a patient. The court will then have to decide whether or not those actions were in accordance with the exercise of ordinary skill and care. In clinical practice a patient may present with

16 A 1968 case reported at [1993] 4 Med LR 393, CA.
17 [1990] 3 All ER 237.
18 (1987) 37 BLR 92, CA.
19 [1984] AC 296.
20 [1996] LRLR 183.
21 [2005] QB 506 (QBD).

a variety of symptoms and a number of potential diagnoses, there may be a range of possible treatments, giving rise to a genuine divergence of view about how to proceed. Applying *Bolam* no claim can succeed where the treatment option selected is considered reasonable by a recognised body of medical opinion, even a minority one. However, in every case evidence given about what a doctor should have done is counter-factual: it is an exposition of what a practitioner may have done in the same circumstances as the defendant.

BOLITHO

Respect for medical practitioners and appropriate deference to their skill and expertise cannot determine liability in every case. In *Bolitho v City and Hackney Health Authority*[22] the House of Lords considered the *Bolam* test within the context of the court's objective of doing justice in the case by the application of its own logical analysis of the expert evidence.

In *Bolitho* the defendant admitted negligence on the basis that a doctor failed to attend the claimant while he was in hospital with an obstruction in his bronchial air passage. Had the doctor attended she said she would not have intubated the claimant. There were two schools of thought about whether or not the doctor should have intubated. The defendant called evidence from one expert who would not have intubated; the claimant called evidence from five experts saying that they would have done.

Such evidence gives cause for concern for several reasons. The first is the patient's fear that medical practitioners may 'close ranks': that the simple marshalling of supportive evidence from doctors will be enough to defeat the claim. However, the courts have always been sensitive to this possibility. In *Chapman v Rix*,[23] the House of Lords indicated that a doctor could not necessarily escape liability merely by calling colleagues to say they would have done the same as he had done. The same point was made by Lord Browne-Wilkinson in *Bolitho*:[24]

> The court is not bound to hold that a defendant doctor escapes liability for negligent treatment or diagnosis just because he leads evidence from a number of medical experts who are genuinely of opinion that the defendant's treatment or diagnosis accorded with sound medical practice.

The judge may take the view that, whatever the defence experts say about what they would have done at the time, they are wrong, ie faced with the actual situation, they would not have acted as the impugned doctor did. An example of this can be found in the dissenting judgment of Simon Brown LJ in *Bolitho* in the Court of Appeal. However, if the defendant's case were accepted it would still need to satisfy the judge that the practice involved was responsible.

A second concern is that cases are decided by judges, applying the law to the facts, and not by medical experts' opinion of good practice. The decision reached has to withstand analysis. However, a practical difficulty lies in determining the basis for such analysis. The court

---

22   [1998] AC 232.
23   A 1960 decision reported in [1994] 5 Med LR 239.
24   [1998] AC 232, at 241G–H.

may have heard from careful and thoughtful witnesses who gave their evidence honestly, based on considerable experience. Although the case for unreasonable treatment will usually be argued by the claimant's experts, judges are understandably reluctant to say that one body of opinion was 'unreasonable'.

The third issue, therefore, is the basis upon which the court can hold expert opinion open to scrutiny. In *Bolitho* Lord Browne-Wilkinson held that the task of the judge was to be satisfied that the experts had directed their minds to the question of comparative risks and benefits and reached a reasonable, logical, and defensible conclusion. Having considered *Hucks v Cole* and *Edward Wong Finance Co Ltd v Johnson Stokes & Master* Lord Browne-Wilkinson concluded:[25]

> These decisions demonstrate that in cases of diagnosis and treatment there are cases where, despite a body of professional opinion sanctioning the defendant's conduct, the defendant can properly be held liable for negligence ... In my judgment that is because, in some cases, it cannot be demonstrated to the judge's satisfaction that the body of opinion relied upon is reasonable or responsible. In the vast majority of cases the fact that distinguished experts in the field are of a particular opinion will demonstrate the reasonableness of that opinion. In particular, where there are questions of assessment of the relative risks and benefits of adopting a particular medical practice, a reasonable view necessarily discloses that the relative risks and benefits have been weighed by the experts in forming their opinions. But if, in a rare case, it can be demonstrated that the professional opinion is not capable of withstanding logical analysis, the judge is entitled to hold that the body of opinion is not reasonable or responsible.

He continued:

> I emphasise that in my view it will very seldom be right for a judge to reach the conclusion that views genuinely held by a competent medical expert are unreasonable. The assessment of medical risks and benefits is a matter of clinical judgment which a judge would not normally be able to make without expert evidence ... it would be wrong to allow such assessment to deteriorate into seeking to persuade the judge to prefer one of two views both of which are capable of being logically supported. It is only where a judge can be satisfied that the body of expert opinion cannot be logically supported at all that such opinion will not provide the bench mark by reference to which the defendant's conduct falls to be assessed.

APPLYING *BOLITHO*

From a practical perspective cases are more likely to be won by undermining the credibility of the other side's expert witnesses. The judge is permitted to take the view that an expert is simply wrong, perhaps because not all the relevant factors have been considered, or the opinion expressed does not represent a responsible body of medical opinion. (See also Chapter 22, Experts.) In *Midland Bank Trust Co Ltd v Hett Stubbs & Kemp*[26] Oliver J said at 402:

---

25   [1998] AC 232, at 243A–B.
26   [1979] Ch 384.

Clearly, if there is some practice in a particular profession, some accepted standard of conduct which is laid down by a professional institute or sanctioned by common usage, evidence of that can and ought to be received. But evidence which really amounts to no more than an expression of opinion of a particular practitioner of what he thinks he would have done had he been placed, hypothetically and without the benefit of hindsight, in the position of the defendants, is of little assistance to the court.

Where a judge finds in favour of one expert rather than another he must give proper reasons for the decision. In *Ratty v Haringey Health Authority*[27] the Court of Appeal reversed the judge's finding in favour of the plaintiff on the ground that, given that he accepted the evidence and the standing of the defendants' experts, he was not entitled to hold that no responsible practitioner would have acted as the accused surgeon did without giving proper reasons. A finding that an expert's opinion represents the view of an acceptable body of opinion is not enough: *Smith v Southampton University Hospitals NHS Trust*.[28] *Pullen v Basildon and Thurrock University Hospitals NHS Foundation Trust*[29] applied *Smith v Southampton*: where there is a difference of medical opinion, the court should not simply state which opinion it prefers, but give reasons why it prefers one expert's view. The judge must subject the opinion expressed to proper analysis. In *Marriott v West Midlands Regional Health Authority*[30] the trial judge found that, if the GP expert's evidence did in fact establish that there was a body of GPs who would not have referred the patient to hospital, 'then such approach is not reasonably prudent'. The Court of Appeal said that the judge was entitled, following *Bolitho,* to subject a body of opinion to analysis to see whether it could properly be regarded as reasonable, and she had been entitled to conclude that it could not be reasonable to fail to refer the patient in such a condition. In *Penney, Palmer and Cannon v East Kent Health Authority*[31] the judge found that the *Bolam* principle did not apply because there was no dispute about acceptable or unacceptable practice, only a factual dispute about whether screeners had given the wrong classification to smears. Even if the principle had applied he was satisfied that the evidence of the three experts called by the defence did not stand up to logical analysis because the screeners did not have the ability to draw a distinction between benign and pre-cancerous cells, and so should have classified the smears as borderline. On appeal the court said that the *Bolam* test did apply as the screeners were exercising skill and judgment in determining what report they should make, but they agreed with the judge that the logical analysis test was applicable, and that it led to the conclusion that the exonerating opinion of the defence experts did not stand up to analysis. In *Muller v King's College Hospital NHS Foundation Trust,*[32] the court discussed whether *Bolam* applied to a pure diagnostic as opposed to treatment decision. It held that it did, through the prism of *Bolitho.* The doctors' failure to diagnose the malignant melanoma fell below the

---

27   [1994] 5 Med LR 413.
28   [2007] EWCA Civ 387.
29   [2015] EWHC 3134 (QB).
30   [1999] Lloyd's Rep Med 23, CA.
31   [1999] Lloyd's Rep Med 123 (QBD), [2000] Lloyd's Rep Med 41, CA.
32   [2017] EWHC 128 (QB).

standard of care to be expected of them, and the opinion of the defendant's expert did not stand up to logical analysis.

In *Reynolds v North Tyneside Health Authority*,[33] Gross J said that, even if there was a body of opinion which would support not performing a vaginal examination immediately upon the admission of a pregnant woman following spontaneous rupture of the membranes. The only justification offered for that view, which was the increased risk of infection, could not withstand scrutiny, because it was illogical and indefensible.

A definitive and helpful account of how to apply *Bolitho* was given by Green J in *C v North Cumbria University Hospitals NHS Trust*:[34]

1   where a body of appropriate expert opinion considers that an act or omission alleged to be negligent is reasonable a court will attach substantial weight to that opinion;

2   this is so even if there is another body of appropriate opinion which condemns the same act or omission as negligent;

3   the court in making this assessment must not however delegate the task of deciding the issue to the expert. It is ultimately an issue that the court, taking account of that expert evidence, must decide for itself;

4   in making an assessment of whether to accept an expert's opinion the court should take account of a variety of factors including (but not limited to): whether the evidence is tendered in good faith; whether the expert is 'responsible', 'competent' and/or 'respectable'; and whether the opinion is reasonable and logical;

5   good faith: a *sine qua non* for treating an expert's opinion as valid and relevant is that it is tendered in good faith. However, the mere fact that one or more expert opinions are tendered in good faith is not per se sufficient for a conclusion that a defendant's conduct, endorsed by expert opinion tendered in good faith, necessarily accords with sound medical practice;

6   responsible/competent/respectable: 'competence' is a matter which flows from qualifications and experience. In the context of allegations of clinical negligence in an NHS setting particular weight may be accorded to an expert with a lengthy experience in the NHS. 'Respectability' is also a matter to be taken into account. A 'responsible' expert is one who does not adapt an extreme position, who will make the necessary concessions and who adheres to the spirit as well as the words of his professional declaration (see CPR 35 and the PD and Protocol);

7   logic/reasonableness: a judge should not simply accept an expert opinion; it should be tested both against the other evidence tendered during the course of a trial, and, against its internal consistency. An expert's report will lack logic if, at the point in which it is tendered, it is out of date and not reflective of the evidence in the case as it has unfolded. If on analysis of the report as a whole the opinion conveyed is from a person of real experience, exhibiting competence and respectability, and it is consistent with the surrounding evidence,

---

33   [2002] Lloyd's Rep Med 459.
34   [2014] EWHC 61 at [25].

and of course internally logical, this is an opinion which a judge should attach considerable weight to.

FACTORS AFFECTING THE STANDARD OF CARE

Errors of judgment

Modern professionals are subject to continuing professional education and are obliged to keep up to date with advances in understanding. The professions learn from their mistakes. The admission of a mistake or an error of judgment on its own will not found a claim in negligence: unless the mistake is one which does not require the exercise of skill and judgment such as where the doctor mistakenly provides the wrong medicine (see, for example, *Penny* above). The treatment a doctor gives must be considered in the light of *Bolam* and the test to be applied is whether or not in the circumstances of the case the care provided fell below the standard to be expected of a competent practitioner exercising reasonable skill and care. So in *Ashton v Alexander and Trent Regional Health Authority*[35] the Court of Appeal held that the admission of a mistake by a surgeon did not equate to negligence and the trial judge had to apply the appropriate test: whether or not the error was one a reasonably competent professional would have made exercising proper care.

There are many aspects of invasive medical treatment that result in recognised complications even though all proper care has been taken. The fact that a patient does not recover as anticipated does not of itself indicate negligence. However, a distinction has to be drawn between a clinical judgment which proves to be erroneous and one which was mistaken at the time it was made. Both may be negligent. If the doctor failed to foresee potential consequences he should reasonably have foreseen his assessment may have been at fault, the treatment chosen may have been mistaken, and the advice given to the patient may have been wrong. If, however, this was a clinical judgment when there were a number of factors that had to be weighed in the balance, and a reasonable body of medical opinion would have proceeded in the same way, there is no negligence subject to the treatment prescribed withstanding logical scrutiny.

Departing from usual practice

A doctor is entitled to use his common sense, experience and judgment in the way he decides to treat any patient. A slight departure from the textbook does not establish negligence (*per* Streatfeild J in *Holland v Devitt & Moore Nautical College*[36]). It has to be shown that the defendant took a course which no physician of ordinary skill would have taken if acting with reasonable care. However, where a doctor departs from standard methods of treatment there must be good reasons for doing so.

Where there was a departure from normal practice in performing a colporrhaphy operation (to remedy stress incontinence) within three

35   (1988, unreported).
36   (1960) Times, 4 March.

months of birth, which proved to be unsuccessful, it was held that such a departure had not been shown to have been justified and therefore constituted a breach of the duty of care owed to the patient (*Clark v MacLennan*[37]).

However, there will be situations where the variety of symptoms with which a patient appears and the need for the development of new techniques mean that novel approaches are justified. In *Wilsher v Essex Area Health Authority*[38] Mustill LJ said that:

> Where the doctor embarks on a form of treatment which is still comparatively untried, with techniques and safeguards which are still in the course of development, or where the treatment is of particular technical difficulty ... if the decision to embark on the treatment at all was justifiable and was taken with the informed consent of the patient, the court should ... be particularly careful not to impute negligence simply because something has gone wrong.

In *Hepworth v Kerr*[39] the judge was satisfied that the defendant anaesthetist had been negligent in adopting a new anaesthetic technique which, as he knew, had never been attempted routinely before by anyone else. Although he had practised the technique previously on some 1,500 patients to a greater or lesser extent, he had never attempted to make any proper scientific validation of it, and without that validation he was not justified in involving the patient in such a fundamental departure from conventional practice.

State of knowledge

It is a doctor's duty to keep reasonably abreast of medical knowledge, and for that purpose needs to be aware of recent developments published in the medical press. Where a medical practitioner continues to use an obsolete procedure, he may well be negligent in continuing to employ it (cf *Roe v Minister of Health*[40]).

However, new techniques do not necessarily prove old methods are negligent unless it can be shown that they are wrong or carry an unacceptable risk to the patient that is no longer justified. In *Newbury v Bath District Health Authority*[41] the patient unsuccessfully claimed damages for a lumbar fusion. Ebsworth J said that neither the claimant's nor the defendant's expert witnesses would have performed the surgery using the technique employed by the surgeon. His choice of technique was unwise, but that was not the correct legal basis for the assessment of liability. The question was whether, on a logical analysis of the decision, it was one a reasonably competent consultant could have made at the time. A competent consultant would keep abreast of the field and adjust procedures appropriately in the light of information received, but would be entitled to keep an old, tried method for use where properly judged to be suitable. That other surgeons might use different methods with success did not render the use of well-tried methods negligent. The surgeon was

---

37 [1983] 1 All ER 416.
38 [1987] QB 730, CA.
39 [1995] 6 Med LR 139.
40 [1954] 2 QB 66.
41 (1998) 47 BMLR 138.

entitled to make the judgment which he had made and was not negligent in so doing, nor had the surgery been carried out negligently.

The length to which a doctor must go to keep abreast of the latest knowledge will depend on the level of speciality. A doctor is not expected to read and ingest every available item. In *Crawford v Charing Cross Hospital*[42] a surgeon was not expected to know that a particular placing of a patient's arm during a blood transfusion was dangerous, as the only evidence of that fact had been one article in a recent medical journal. In the first case on industrial deafness, *Thompson v Smiths Shiprepairers (North Shields)*,[43] Mustill J said:

> One must be careful when considering documents culled for the purpose of a trial, and studied by reference to a single isolated issue, not to forget that they once formed part of a flood of print on numerous aspects of industrial life, in which many items were bound to be overlooked. However conscientious the employer, he cannot read every textbook and periodical, attend every exhibition and conference, on every technical issue which might arise in the course of his business; nor can he necessarily be expected to grasp the importance of every single item which he comes across.

A gynaecologist had to keep himself aware of general developments in the mainstream literature. He did not need to be familiar with the content of more obscure journals (*Gascoine v Ian Sheridan & Co*[44]).

Practices adopted in another country were not necessarily evidence of the appropriate standard in the UK. In *Robb and Unitt v East London and City Health Authority*,[45] Ebsworth J considered evidence of US research and international practice. It did not follow that a particular technique was negligent simply because it could be shown that things were done differently elsewhere. It was a matter of degree and common sense. However, in some cases the field of expertise may be so narrow that it will be necessary to obtain expert opinion from abroad.

(In)Experience

The same standard of care is expected from the learner driver as from any other driver on the road (*Nettleship v Weston*[46]). However, a learner driver chooses to drive on the highway; it is not a matter of necessity. Learner doctors are an essential part of the health service. They will treat patients, though they should be supervised. Following *Nettleship* the courts expect them to show the same level of care and skill as their experienced colleagues. The patient does not choose an inexperienced doctor.

The issue was considered in the medical context at the Court of Appeal stage in *Wilsher v Essex Area Health Authority*.[47] Mustill LJ said that he did not accept the notion of a duty tailored to the actor rather than the act which he elects to perform. If hospitals abstained from using

---

42　(1953) Times, 8 December, CA.
43　[1984] QB 405, CA.
44　[1994] 5 Med L R 437.
45　[1999] MLC 0102.
46　[1971] 2 QB 691, CA.
47　[1987] QB 730.

inexperienced personnel they could not staff their wards and theatres and the junior staff could never learn, but:

> ... it would be a false step to subordinate the legitimate expectation of the patient that he will receive from each person concerned with his care a degree of skill appropriate to the task which he undertakes, to an understandable wish to minimise the psychological and financial pressures on hard-pressed young doctors ... In a case such as the present the standard is not just that of the averagely competent and well-informed junior houseman (or whatever the position of the doctor), but of such a person who fills a post in a unit offering a highly specialised service.

Glidewell LJ said that the law required the trainee or learner to be judged by the same standard as his more experienced colleagues. If it did not, inexperience would frequently be urged as a defence to an action for professional negligence.

Direct liability – system failure

In *Bull and Wakeham v Devon Area Health Authority*[48] there was a medically unacceptable delay of one hour in securing the attendance of a suitably qualified doctor to deal with an emergency arising in the delivery of a second twin, as a result of which he suffered brain damage. On the question whether the defendants should have had in place a system which guaranteed prompt attendance, Slade LJ said the evidence pointed strongly either to inefficiency in the system for summoning the assistance of the registrar or consultant or to negligence by some individual in the working of that system. Dillon LJ said that any hospital which provided a maternity service for expectant mothers ought to be able to cope properly with premature delivery of twins, and there should have been at the hospital a staff reasonably sufficient for the foreseeable requirements of the patient. He described the hospital's system for providing senior attendance where the need arose as 'unreliable and essentially unsatisfactory'. Mustill LJ said that the system fell short of the required standard, which demanded at the least that a doctor of suitable experience be available within 20 minutes to handle any emergency. It was not a question of an 'ideal' solution appropriate to 'centres of excellence', nor a question of highly specialist techniques or advanced new instrumentation which it would be unrealistic to expect in provincial hospitals, but just a question of getting the right people together in the right place at the right time.

In *Robertson v Nottingham Health Authority*[49] there were significant breakdowns in the defendant's systems of communication in respect of obstetric care which were proved to constitute breaches of proper practice. Brooke LJ said that a health authority had a non-delegable duty to establish a proper system of care just as much as it had a duty to engage competent staff and a duty to provide proper and safe equipment, safe premises and a reasonable regime of care, ie a regime of a standard that could reasonably be expected of a hospital of the size and type in question – in the present case a large teaching centre of excellence. It

---

48 [1993] 4 Med LR 117, CA.
49 [1997] 8 Med LR 1, CA.

mattered not whether those at fault could be individually identified. If they could, the hospital would be vicariously liable for their negligence, but, if not, the hospital would be in breach of its own duty of care for failing to provide a proper system.

In *FE (Represented by his litigation friend PE) v St George's University Hospitals NHS Trust*[50] it was held that a poor standard of record keeping at the hospital and poor communication between the midwifery and obstetric teams constituted a breach of duty to the claimant, who suffered brain damage as a result of late delivery.

In *Macaulay v Karim*,[51] it was held that the hospital had been negligent in failing to contact the claimant, who had been waiting many hours for a blood test, to get him to return to hospital, which would have identified the underlying problem. In *Gallardo v Imperial College Healthcare NHS Trust*,[52] it was held that the defendant's duty to the claimant continued after he ceased to be an NHS patient, and that the defendant had a duty to inform the claimant of the outcome of his surgery and of the need for regular monitoring. This duty was not discharged when the claimant was moved to the private wing of the hospital, and it was a necessary concomitant of the surgery the defendant had undertaken.

Lack of funds

A hospital may be unable to deliver as high a standard of care as it would wish or as normal standards would dictate because it does not have the equipment, doctors, and the staff. If there is a failure in care is it any defence for the hospital to say that the staff worked as hard and as long, and with as much expertise, as they could, but economies prevented further care or more experienced doctors from being provided?

In *Ball v Wirral Health Authority*,[53] where the claim (in part) was that the health authority failed to have adequate facilities for the care of babies suffering from respiratory distress syndrome, Simon J said that the fact that an area of medicine might be underfunded or that a particular hospital might not have the same facilities as another might give rise to public concern but did not necessarily provide the basis for a successful claim in negligence, as English public and private law in general left decisions on funding and facilities to those who had legal responsibility for making them.

In *Hardaker v Newcastle Health Authority*,[54] where a diver claimant contended that he had suffered injury because the hospital had failed to keep its decompression chamber manned adequately and at all proper times, Burnton J said that the court was not competent to adjudicate upon a health authority's system for dealing with such a rare medical event as decompression illness, where the issue was one of allocation of resources; and it was not, in any event, enough for the claimant to criticise the system without suggesting a more suitable alternative.

---

50   [2016] EWHC 553 (QB).
51   [2017] EWHC 1795 (QB).
52   [2017] EWHC 3147 (QB).
53   [2003] Lloyd's Rep Med 165.
54   [2001] Lloyd's Rep Med 512.

Emergencies

The standard of care to be expected may vary with the specific circumstances prevailing at the time. One can hardly expect the same meticulous attention in a hospital that is coping with a rail disaster or an epidemic as at normal times. In *Wilsher v Essex Area Health Authority*[55] Mustill LJ said:

> ... in what may be called 'battle conditions' ... an emergency may overburden the available resources, and if an individual is forced by circumstances to do too many things at once, the fact that he does one of them incorrectly should not lightly be taken as negligence.

Alternative therapies

Claims against alternative practitioners create a difficulty when it comes to assessing the standard of care given. Is it the standard that others practising in the same field consider to be appropriate, or is it to be judged by a more orthodox standard? If the management is to be judged by others practising in the field, the level of care acceptable to those practitioners might outrage orthodox practitioners. If it is to be judged by orthodox practitioners, there would be no scope for alternative practitioners.

Cases have been brought against physiotherapists, osteopaths, chiropractors and other practitioners of robust massage and manipulation. Some of these disciplines have regulatory bodies, and it may be possible to prepare a claim based on the opinion of an expert well-versed in that field with the support also of an orthodox expert, such as an orthopaedic consultant.

In *Shakoor v Situ*[56] the defendant was a properly trained, well-qualified and experienced practitioner of Chinese herbal medicine. He prescribed a remedy to a patient who then suffered a fatal idiosyncratic reaction by way of acute liver failure. It was alleged that the defendant had been negligent because papers in orthodox medical journals warned of such a risk. The widow did not adduce any evidence from an expert in Chinese herbal medicine, but relied only on the published matter and on evidence from orthodox consultants that they had no reason to believe that the treatment was effective. The defendant himself had a supportive opinion from a fellow practitioner. The judge (Bernard Livesey QC) said that, even if practitioners in the relevant art agreed that the care was proper, a claimant could still succeed by showing that the prevailing standard of skill in that art was deficient in the UK, having regard to risks which were not (but should have been) taken into account. It was not enough that orthodox practitioners might condemn the management. It was an important consideration that the patient had chosen to go to an alternative practitioner. 'Why should the patient later be able to complain that the alternative practitioner has not provided him with skill and care in accordance with the standards of those orthodox practitioners whom he has rejected?' Neither assessment was conclusive – neither that

---

55   [1987] QB 730 at 749.
56   [2000] 1 WLR 410, CA.

afforded by orthodox practitioners, nor that from practitioners in the impugned art. The judge said that an alternative practitioner practising his art alongside that of orthodox medicine must take account of the implications of that fact. The defendant had a duty to ensure that the remedy prescribed was not merely believed to be beneficial, but he had also a duty to ensure that it was not harmful. He had to keep abreast of relevant publications in the orthodox field as well, to the extent that a similar practitioner in the orthodox field would be expected to keep abreast. A similar practitioner would be a GP. The judge went on to conclude that the published material relied on by the claimant was not sufficiently unambiguous to have deterred a competent GP from prescribing such a remedy. The defendant was found to have acted in accordance with the standard of care appropriate to traditional Chinese herbal medicine as properly practised in accordance with the standards required in the UK.

Self-inflicted injury

Leaving a suicide-risk patient unobserved and with an open window behind his bed was held to constitute a lack of proper care, so that the hospital was liable when the patient got out of the window and threw himself off a roof. A high degree of surveillance was required in the care of patients with suicidal tendencies. The duty of care extended to a duty to protect the patient from the risk of self-inflicted injuries: *Selfe v Ilford and District Hospital Management Committee*.[57] In *Lepine v University Hospital Board*,[58] a hospital was held negligent for not having a constant watch on a patient suffering from a dangerous condition of post-epileptic automatism, who jumped from a window. However, when a patient of suspected suicidal tendencies managed to elude the nurses, went home and killed herself, the hospital was found not to have been negligent: *Thorne v Northern Group Hospital Management Committee*.[59] In *Mahmood v Siggins*,[60] a GP was held to have been negligent for not referring a manic depressive to the local community mental health team. The patient later jumped from a third floor balcony. In *D v South Tyneside Healthcare NHS Trust*[61] the Court of Appeal dismissed a claimant's appeal where a patient, put on hourly observation, had left the hospital, swallowed medication and suffered brain injury. The court said that there was a reasonable body of professional opinion that supported the contention that hourly observation was sufficient and that observation every 15 minutes was not called for. In *Nyang v G4S Care and Justice Services Ltd*,[62] the court considered that the question is whether the risk ought to have been realised. Unless the person is receiving psychiatric treatment, the standard is with reference to non-specialist staff, not a psychiatrist.

---

57   (1970) 114 Sol Jo 935.
58   (1964) 50 DLR (2d) 225; affd (1965) 54 DLR (2d) 340.
59   (1964) 108 Sol Jo 484.
60   [1996] 7 Med LR 76.
61   [2004] PIQR P150.
62   [2013] EWHC 3946 (QB).

Children

Children require a watchful eye. Where a seven-year-old boy was left without supervision near an open window and fell out, the hospital was liable (*Newnham v Rochester and Chatham Joint Hospital Board*[63]). But where the injury occurs in a non-medical context, ie it does not give rise to considerations about care and treatment, the conclusion may be different. Thus a hospital was not negligent where a girl of nine injured herself when she ran into glass swing doors in the hospital, at a time when the orderly was momentarily absent. The hospital's duty in the non-medical context was said to be that of an ordinary prudent parent (*Gravestock v Lewisham Group Hospital Management Committee*[64]). It was not negligent to leave a partially disabled child to manage a jug of hot inhalant in bed on her own (*Cox v Carshalton Hospital Management Committee*[65]).

THE BURDEN OF PROOF

In negligence generally the existence of a duty of care is closely associated with the foreseeability of injury. Where an employee suffers asbestosis as a result of his employer's breach of statutory duty, there may be a presumption that damages will be recovered. Otherwise the non-liability of the employer will 'empty the duty of its content'.[66]

The relationship between breach of duty of care and the foreseeability of harm is more difficult in a clinical negligence context as there may well be 'injury' in the absence of negligence: as a result, for example, of well recognised complications associated with a certain medical procedure. Medicine is also a science, developing and changing over time. There will always be limitations on what can be known and, therefore, on what can be 'proved'.

The ordinary case: the claimant's burden

In the ordinary case the burden of proving negligence rests with the claimant. The circumstances in which that burden may shift to the defendant in clinical negligence cases are very limited. In *Clark v MacLennan*,[67] Pain J said that where there had been a failure to take a generally recognised precaution which had been followed by damage of the kind that that precaution was designed to prevent, the burden of proof shifted to the defendant to show either that he was not in breach of duty or that the damage was not caused by the breach. In that case there had been a departure from the usual practice of not performing an operation for stress incontinence within three months of delivery. That departure was found to have been unjustified and therefore constituted a breach of the duty of care. It was followed by a consequence that that

---

63 (1936) Times, 28 February.
64 (1955) Times, 27 May.
65 (1955) Times, 29 March.
66 See the comments of Lord Bingham in *Fairchild v Glenhaven Funeral Services Ltd* [2002] UKHL 22.
67 [1983] 1 All ER 416.

precaution was designed to prevent: a breakdown of the repair effected in the operation. The judge held that in such circumstances the defendants had to satisfy the court that damage had not flowed from their breach of duty to the patient.

The approach is most probably wrong. In *Wilsher v Essex Area Health Authority*[68] the House of Lords expressly denied that the burden shifted in such circumstances. In *Gregory v Pembrokeshire Health Authority*,[69] Rougier J rejected the suggestion that whenever the fault complained of was a fault in omission the burden of proving causation shifted to the defendants: 'the burden of proof on the balance of probabilities remains on the plaintiff throughout'. In *Defreitas v O'Brien*,[70] Otton LJ said the *Bolam* test did not impose any burden of proof on the defendant to establish that his diagnosis or treatment would be acceptable to a responsible body of medical opinion. The burden of proof was on the claimant.

Shifting the burden of proof

Res ipsa loquitur

[The facts speak for themselves]

In the ordinary case a judge will hear the lay and expert evidence, decide the facts, and apply his analysis of the expert evidence and the law to them. However, there may also be cases in which the facts themselves are indicative of a failure to take reasonable care. If a bag of flour falls on my head it is reasonable to infer that whoever was responsible for the flour has failed to take proper care.

The legal formulation of such a simple proposition is nonetheless somewhat cumbersome: if an accident is such as in the ordinary course of things does not happen if those who have the management use proper care, it affords reasonable evidence, in the absence of explanation by the defendant, that the accident arose from want of care.[71] This is the classic formulation of the maxim *res ipsa loquitur* in the context of the law of negligence.

Res ipsa loquitur has a role to play in clinical negligence cases but the circumstances are limited, and the maxim is often invoked incorrectly and inappropriately. In *Cassidy v Ministry of Health*,[72] Denning LJ explained the possible application of the maxim by the example of the patient who arrives in hospital to be cured of two stiff fingers and leaves with four. In such circumstances the hospital would have to show how the deterioration in the claimant's condition was not caused by any want of care on its part. He considered that in such a situation the patient had a *prima facie* case against the hospital authorities. He applied this analysis in *Roe v Minister of Health*.[73] Where patients in hospital for minor operations were paralysed by the spinal anaesthetic each was given the defendant had to explain how this could have come to pass.

---

68   [1988] AC 1074.
69   [1989] 1 Med LR 81 at 85.
70   [1995] 6 Med LR 108, CA.
71   Per Erle CJ in *Scott v London and St Katherine Docks Co* (1865) 3 H & C 596, Ex Ch.
72   [1951] 2 KB 343.
73   [1954] 2 QB 66.

When we consider this legal formulation it is important to draw out several strands that limit its application. First, there must be an adverse outcome. Second, the principle only applies where the precise cause of the accident cannot be specified, whether upon direct evidence or by inference: I do not know why a bag of flour fell on my head, but I do not need to show why it happened: the fact of the accident is enough to satisfy the law that I have cause for complaint. Third, the facts of the accident must be such that it would be fair and reasonable for the court to make an inference: 'the circumstances are more consistent, reasonably interpreted without further explanation, with ... negligence than with any other cause of the accident happening' (*per* Kennedy LJ in *Russell v London and South-western Rly Co*[74]). These are accidents that 'in ordinary circumstances' do not happen. Fourth, even where the principle applies the defendant is able to defend the claim successfully if it can show that the injury could have occurred without negligence; see for example the comments of Otton LJ in *Hooper v Young*.[75] Sometimes the court will say that the inference gives rise to a *prima facie* case: a case that the defendant not only has to meet but has the burden of proving.

Proving an adverse outcome

The claimant has to establish the facts upon which to base a plea of *res ipsa loquitur*. So in *Ludlow v Swindon Health Authority*,[76] when the claimant alleged she had been awake during a Caesarean section as a result of what must have been the negligent administration of the anaesthetic, the judge said that for the doctrine of *res ipsa loquitur* to apply, the claimant had first to establish that she had indeed been awake during the operation. As the judge was not satisfied of these facts the doctrine could not help her.

The facts proven will not give rise to a proper plea of *res ipsa loquitur* if such injury could have occurred with the exercise of reasonable care. A surgeon performing a laminectomy may penetrate too far and injure the nerve or the spinal cord. One cannot say that 'the matter speaks for itself'. The question is whether or not a surgeon exercising due care would make that mistake. However, the situation may be different if the risk of such injury was so small as to indicate want of care. In *Betts v Berkshire Health Authority*[77] the fact that the risk of damage to the testicle during the procedure was less than 0.03% was indicative that the surgery had been negligent on the balance of probabilities.

The absence of non-negligent explanation

A distinction has to be made between cases in which the facts are known and the courts are able to infer negligence from the circumstances, and those cases where the court applies the maxim when there is no other non-negligent explanation for the injury. If the facts are sufficiently established the question may be whether negligence is to be inferred or

---

74　(1908) 24 TLR 548, CA at 551.
75　[1998] 2 Lloyd's Rep Med 61, CA.
76　[1989] 1 Med LR 104.
77　[1997] 8 Med L Rep 87.

not.[78] For example, where there is evidence of habitual careless behaviour which could have caused it, the court may infer that to be the cause in the absence of any other explanation.[79]

One must draw a distinction between the situation where there is more than one possible cause for the injury and the situation where the precise cause is unknown. In the second situation one may be able to take advantage of the maxim. In the first situation it is simply a matter for the judge to decide what was the operative cause, and, in doing this, he is entitled to prefer the evidence of one expert to another. He may also draw inferences from the evidence. In *Skelton v Lewisham and North Southwark Health Authority*,[80] Kay J decided that the only possible explanation on the facts for the administration of certain drugs preoperatively was an episode of hypotension causing brain injury. In *Bull v Devon Area Health Authority*,[81] Slade LJ said that the trial judge had gone further than he needed when he found that the claimant had excluded all possible causes of his injury other than that for which he contended, because it would have been sufficient to make the less unqualified finding that the cause for which he contended was established on the balance of probabilities.

Examples

In *Mahon v Osborne*,[82] where the surgeon was sued when a swab was left inside the patient, the majority of the Court of Appeal was of the view that the principle did not apply in the case of a complex operation where a number of medical staff took part, but it is now clear that the correct view was that taken by Goddard LJ when he said if a swab is found in the patient's body the surgeon is called upon for an explanation 'not necessarily why he missed it but that he exercised due care to prevent its being left there'; see also *Urry v Bierer*.[83]

In *Clarke v Worboys*,[84] the patient's buttock was burnt in electro-coagulation treatment; the Court of Appeal reversed the judge's finding and held that the evidence showed that such an accident would not happen if reasonable care were used.

The maxim was successfully invoked by the widow of a man who was asphyxiated when he swallowed a dental throat pack in *Garner v Morrell*.[85]

In *Leckie v Brent and Harrow Area Health Authority*,[86] it was held that a 1.5 cm cut on the cheek of a baby delivered by Caesarian section would not happen without some lack of care.

In *Woodhouse v Yorkshire Regional Health Authority*[87] the patient's ulnar nerves were severely damaged in an operation for a subphrenic

---

78 Per Lord Porter in *Barkway v South Wales Transport Co Ltd* [1950] 1 All ER 392, HL at 395.
79 *Clowes v National Coal Board* (1987) Times, 23 April.
80 [1998] Lloyd's Rep Med 324.
81 [1993] 4 Med LR 117, CA.
82 [1939] 2 KB 14.
83 (1955) Times, 15 July.
84 (1952) Times, 18 March.
85 (1953) Times, 31 October.
86 [1982] 1 Lancet 634.
87 [1984] 1 Lancet 1306.

abscess. The judge said that the evidence established that this sort of injury would not occur if the standard precautions to avoid this recognised hazard had been taken. The Court of Appeal upheld his decision.

In *Coyne v Wigan Health Authority*[88] the defendants agreed that *res ipsa* applied when hypoxia leading to brain damage occurred during recovery from a routine operation.

In *Saunders v Leeds Western Health Authority and Robinson*[89] the heart of a four-year-old girl stopped for some 30 minutes during an operation under anaesthetic to remedy a congenitally deformed hip. The defendants agreed that did not normally happen without want of care.

Rebuttal

It is always open to a defendant to rebut a case of *res ipsa* either by giving an explanation of what happened which was inconsistent with negligence or by showing that all reasonable care had been taken. So, for example in *Roe v Minister of Health* the hospital gave an explanation of the accident which was accepted by the court as absolving them from any negligence.

In *Jacobs v Great Yarmouth and Waverney Health Authority*[90] the Court of Appeal said that *res ipsa loquitur* meant no more than that on the facts that a claimant was able to prove, although he might not be able to point to a particular negligent act or omission on the part of the defendants, the fair inference to draw was that there had been negligence of some sort on the part of the defendants. If there were further evidence presented by the defendants, those facts might be shown in an entirely different light so that it would not be possible to draw the inference of negligence.

It is not entirely clear on the authorities how far the defendant must go to shift the onus of proof back to the claimant, in particular, whether he has to show a possible or a likely cause of the accident that would not involve negligence. In *Moore v R Fox & Sons*[91] it was not sufficient for the defendants to show several hypothetical causes consistent with the absence of negligence and that the accident might have occurred without negligence on their part; to discharge the onus they had to go further and either show that they had not been negligent or give a reasonable explanation of the cause of the accident which did not connote negligence.

Examples

In *Howard v Wessex Regional Health Authority*,[92] Morland J said that *res ipsa* could not help the patient where she had sustained tetraplegia following maxillo-facial surgery by way of a sagittal split osteotomy, because her injury was most likely due to a fibro-cartilaginous embolism, which would not connote negligence.

In *Moore v Worthing District Health Authority*,[93] Owen J rejected a plea of *res ipsa* where a patient was left with bilateral ulnar nerve palsy following a mastoidectomy. He absolved the defendants from failing

88   [1991] 2 Med LR 301.
89   [1993] 4 Med LR 355.
90   [1995] 6 Med LR 192.
91   [1956] 1 QB 596, CA.
92   [1994] 5 Med LR 57.
93   [1992] 3 Med LR 431.

to protect the arms properly while the patient was under anaesthetic by accepting their contention that the patient had been abnormally vulnerable to such an injury.

In *O'Malley-Williams v Governors of National Hospital for Nervous Diseases*[94] it was held that the maxim did not apply where partial paralysis was sustained by the claimant because the injury sustained was recognised as an inherent risk of the treatment undergone.

Reasonable traction could have caused the claimant's lesion of the musculocutaneous nerve, as could also excessive traction, and so the maxim could not help him, in the case of *Levenkind v Churchill-Davidson*.[95]

In *Brazier v Ministry of Defence*[96] the defendants satisfied the judge that he should not infer negligence on the part of a person giving an injection to the claimant as the cause of the needle breaking, because the actual cause could properly be inferred to be a latent defect in the shaft of the needle (similarly in *Corner v Murray*[97]).

Thomas v Curley[98] is not a strict application of *res ipsa*, but the Court of Appeal concluded that the first instance judge was right to conclude that the case presented by the claimant demanded an explanation of how the injury occurred (which occurred at a site other than when the original surgery was meant to take place, and the surgery itself was an uncomplicated procedure), and none had been put forward by the defendant.

In *O'Connor v Pennine Acute Hospital NHS Trust*[99] the Court of Appeal concluded that the trial judge was entitled to make a finding of fact as to the cause of the injury in the absence of any other plausible explanation, and that this was not an application of *res ipsa*, because the court had concluded that the claimant's conclusion was the most plausible on the balance of probabilities, and not simply that there was an absence of alternative explanation (see paras [83]–[86]).

STRICT LIABILITY

Consumer Protection Act 1987

Strict liability for injury is imposed on the producers and certain suppliers of any product falling within the Consumer Protection Act 1987 supplied after 1 March 1988. The definition of 'product' covers medical products, equipment and drugs. It may also cover blood and blood-based materials.

Section 2 of the Act provides that where any damage is caused wholly or partly by a defect in a product to any person 'the relevant party' shall be liable for the damage. The relevant party may be the producer of the product, an importer, or the supplier. If he can identify the producer he will not be liable even if the producer cannot satisfy a judgment.

Section 3(1) of the Act defines the meaning of 'defect':

---

94 (1975) 1 BMJ 635.
95 [1983] 1 Lancet 1452.
96 [1965] 1 Lloyd's Rep 26.
97 [1954] 2 BMJ 1555.
98 [2013] EWCA Civ 117.
99 [2015] EWCA Civ 1244.

Subject to the following provisions of this section, there is a defect in a product for the purposes of this Part if the safety of the product is not such as persons generally are entitled to expect; and for those purposes 'safety', in relation to a product, shall include safety with respect to products comprised in that product and safety in the context of risks after damage to property, as well as in the context of risks of death or personal injury.

What persons are generally entitled to expect is considered in s 3(2):

In determining for the purposes of subsection (1) above what persons generally are entitled to expect in relation to a product all the circumstances shall be taken into account, including—

(a) the manner in which, and purposes for which, the product has been marketed, its get-up, the use of any mark in relation to the product and any instructions for, or warnings with respect to, doing or refraining from doing anything with or in relation to the product;

(b) what might reasonably be expected to be done with or in relation to the product; and

(c) the time when the product was supplied by its producer to another;

and nothing in this section shall require a defect to be inferred from the fact alone that the safety of a product which is supplied after that time is greater than the safety of the product in question.

Liability depends upon what members of the public are likely to expect; what warnings should be given; and what the scale and nature of any potential risks are. So a user's expectation is that a condom will not fail. However, where there were no claims made by the manufacturer that a condom will never fail and no-one has ever supposed that any method of contraception will be 100% effective, a fracture in a condom was not proof of a defect (*Richardson v LRC Products*[100]). However, the transfusion of infected blood was evidence of a product defect (*A v The National Blood Authority*[101]). The public had a right to expect that such products would be 100% safe. As the product in *A v The National Blood Authority* was defective, the claimants did not have to prove any fault on the part of the defendant.

Another example of a successful claim brought under the Consumer Protection Act is *Abouzaid v Mothercare (UK) Ltd*.[102] The claimant injured his eye when attempting to fasten a sleeping bag to his young brother's pushchair by means of elasticated straps. The strap slipped from his grasp and the buckle hit him in the eye. The judge said that the product was unsafe due to failure to provide proper instructions, particularly in the case of younger children, and the manufacturer should have appreciated the risk. Expert evidence was to the effect that the hazard had not been recognised by anyone in the business in 1990, but ten years later such a product could be said to have a safety defect. The judge said that if it had one now, it had one then. The public's expectation had not changed since 1990. The Court of Appeal was not satisfied that there was liability at common law, but endorsed the finding of liability under the Act. The defence under s 4(1)(e) (that the state of scientific and technical knowledge at the time was not such that the defect could be discovered),

---

100 [2000] Lloyd's Rep Med 280.
101 [2001] Lloyd's Rep Med 187.
102 (2001) Times, 20 February, CA.

relying as it did on the absence of any record of similar accident, was not valid, as such evidence did not fall within the meaning of scientific and technical knowledge.

Vaccine Damage Payments Act 1979

The Act was passed as a result of anxiety arising in the early 1970s over the possibility that the whooping cough vaccine could cause brain damage.[103]

In *Loveday v Renton*,[104] the claimant sought to establish that the whooping cough vaccine could cause brain damage. Stuart-Smith LJ found, after a long and complex trial, that it had not been established that the whooping cough vaccine was capable of causing permanent brain damage in young children. He said that all four of the suggested mechanisms for the nexus between the vaccine and the damage were improbable. He also added, *obiter*, that even if that nexus had been established, the claimant would surely find it impossible to show that the GP had been negligent in vaccinating. *Loveday* also attempted to pursue compensation through the Vaccine Damage Tribunal (*R v Vaccine Damage Tribunal, ex p Loveday*[105]).

Few claims are made to the scheme and even fewer succeed. The number of claims received and successful payments made under the Act, in each financial year from April 2000 to 7 June 2006 was as follows:

1 April to 31 March	*Number of claims received*	*Number of claims successful*
2000/01	205	0
2001/02	146	2
2002/03	417	5
2003/04	165	4
2004/05	111	4
2005/06	106	4
2006/07 (to 7 June 2006)	14	2
Total	1,164	21

Source: Vaccine Damage Payments Unit Database.[106]

---

103 A DWP publication on the operation of the scheme is available at www.direct.gov.uk/ en/MoneyTaxAndBenefits/BenefitsTaxCreditsAndOtherSupport/Disabledpeople/ DG_10018714.
104 [1990] 1 Med LR 117.
105 [1985] 2 Lancet 1137.
106 HC Deb, 16 June 2006, c1482W; www.theyworkforyou.com/wrans/?id=2006-06-16c.76172.h.

Chapter 7

Causation and damage

Chesca Lord

INTRODUCTION

The claimant in a negligence action has to show that as a result of the defendant's negligence, ie there has been a breach of a duty of care owed to the claimant, and that claimant has suffered damage. The damage may be physical (to person or property), mental or financial, but it must:

- amount to an actionable personal injury;
- be caused by the breach of duty – a patient who cannot show that an admitted act of negligence contributed to his present condition has not proved a causative link between the negligence and his injury;
- come within the scope of the duty to avoid the injury;
- be a type of damage which is recognised by the law – certain types of damage are not recognised by the law, at any rate if they stand alone, eg distress and disappointment, mental strain or nervous shock not amounting to a psychiatric disorder or illness. Mere financial loss is not recoverable if it stands alone, ie not accompanied by any physical injury to person or property and did not arise in the context of a fiduciary or proximate relationship between the parties; and
- come within the foreseeable area of risk created by the breach of duty. The damage will not be the subject of compensation, even if directly caused by the breach of duty, if it is of a completely different type or caused in a completely different way than that which was foreseeable: see Chapter 8.

The different factors in negligence are not clearly separate from one another, they shade off into and overlap each other. A woman who loses wages looking after a lover who has gone to bed because the doctor wrongly and negligently told him he was ill and needed bed-rest may be told by the court that her claim cannot succeed because the doctor owed her no duty of care, or that she cannot recover for mere economic loss, or that the damage she suffered was too remote, or not foreseeable, or that it was not caused by the breach of duty because her decision to look after her friend broke the chain of causation; or the court may even, as a last resort, pray in aid public policy. In the final analysis, a claim that does not clearly come within the body of case law created by the courts in the past, ie a claim that presents a novel quality, will be accepted or rejected by the courts according to the judge's overall view as to whether it is appropriate that it should succeed or not (what has been called 'the judicial hunch'); and if the judge feels that the claim should not succeed, he or she will hang their decision on one or other of the legal pegs that are available.

The issue of causation can raise notoriously difficult intellectual issues, eg as to the cause, or operative or significant cause, of an injury, and in what circumstances the chain is broken, but on the whole the courts give pragmatic answers depending on their assessment of the factual situation.

> Causation is to be understood as the man in the street, and not as either the scientist or the metaphysician would understand it. Cause here means what a ... man would take to be the cause without too microscopic analysis but on a broad view (*per* Lord Wright in *Yorkshire Dale Steamship Co v Minister of War Transport*[1]).

And Lord Denning once said:

> ... it is not every consequence of a wrongful act which is the subject of compensation. The law has to draw a line somewhere. Sometimes it is done by limiting the range of persons to whom duty is owed, sometimes it is done by saying there is break in the chain of causation. At other times it is done by saying that the consequence is too remote to be a head of damages. All these devices are useful in their way. But ultimately it is a question of policy for the judges to decide ... (*Lamb v Camden LBC*[2]).

However, what is the common sense answer in any situation often admits of divergent views (see, for example, the varying views of the Law Lords about the cause of an accident when an unsafe roof fell on a miner in *Stapley v Gypsum Mines Ltd*[3]).

Actionable personal injury

The claimant has, of course, to show that he has suffered some damage (negligence is not actionable without proof of damage). What amounts to injury in the context of the personal injury action was considered by the House of Lords in *Rothwell v Chemical and Insulating Co Ltd.*[4] The House of Lords held that asymptomatic pleural plaques were not actionable physical damage. Furthermore, the argument that psychiatric damage caused by the anxiety provoked by knowing that a clamant might go on to develop mesothelioma or other asbestos-related disease was not actionable either. It was held that such damage was not a reasonably foreseeable consequence of having asymptomatic pleural plaques in a person of normal fortitude. A limited scheme making plural plaques compensatable was introduced in August 2010. However, the scheme closed a year later and, at present, pleural plaques are not compensatable in England and Wales – although it is perhaps worth noting that the Northern Ireland Assembly and the Scottish Parliament have both enacted legislation restoring the right to claim compensation for pleural plaques.

---

1   [1942] AC 691 at 706, HL.
2   [1981] QB 625, at 636.
3   [1953] AC 663, HL.
4   [2008] 1 AC 281.

Rothwell was recently distinguished by the Supreme Court in *Dryden v Johnson Matthey Plc*,[5] which held that the concept of 'actionable personal injury' was broad enough to include sensitisation to platinum salts even though such sensitisation was asymptomatic. A distinction was drawn between pleural plaques, which were nothing more than a marker of exposure to asbestos dust; they were symptomless in themselves and neither led nor contributed to any condition that would produce symptoms, even if the sufferer were to be exposed to further asbestos dust. On the other hand, sensitisation to platinum salts constituted a change in the individual's physiological make-up which meant that further exposure carried the risk of an allergic reaction and meant that sensitised individuals had to make changes to their everyday lives to avoid further exposure.

Lady Black referred to Lord Hoffmann's comments about the nature of damage at para 7 of *Rothwell*:

> Damage in this sense is an abstract concept of being worse off, physically or economically, so that compensation is an appropriate remedy. It does not mean simply a physical change, which is consistent with making one better, as in the case of a successful operation, or with being neutral, having no perceptible effect upon one's health or capability.

She found, in the single judgment of the court, that the claimants' bodily capacity for work had been impaired and they were therefore 'significantly worse off'.

A worsened prognosis, eg where there is a delay in diagnosing cancer, can constitute compensatable injury (see, for example, *Judge v Huntingdon Health Authority*[6]). But see below, *Gregg v Scott*,[7] under 'loss of a chance'.

In *Tahir v Haringey Health Authority*,[8] Otton LJ said that where the claimant alleges their condition has been made worse by medical negligence, it is not sufficient to show that delay materially increased the risk of injury or that delay could cause injury, because the claimant had to go further and prove that damage was actually caused. More significantly, it was not sufficient to show a general increment of injury from the delay because 'some measurable damage' had to be proved. The Lord Justice went on to say that in the absence of any evidence before the trial judge which either identified or qualified additional deficit, it was not possible to assess damages. However, Sir Ralph Gibson said that:

> If it was common ground, or if the judge held upon evidence which she accepted, that in probability each hour of delay caused significant aggravation of, or addition to, the residual disability suffered by the plaintiff, then I would agree that the judge could properly assess damages as she did. The fact that the doctors could not identify any particular form of residual disability resulting from such delay, or precisely quantify any worsening of any form of residual disability as a result of that delay would not, in my judgment, deprive the plaintiff of the right to appropriate damages. I cannot accept, however, that any such common ground existed.

Leggatt LJ said that neither expert had identified any respect in which the plaintiff was actually worse off on account of the delay, and in the

---

5 [2018] UKSC 18.
6 [1995] 6 Med LR 223.
7 [2005] UKHL 2.
8 [1998] Lloyd's Rep Med 104, CA.

absence of any identification of any individual disability that occurred or
was increased, and of any attempt to define the extent of any increase,
the plaintiff's claim failed because there was no evidence before the judge
that any damage caused by the defendants' negligence was more than
minimal. He added the interesting observation that:

> When a doctor has been at fault no court wishes to send his patient away
> empty-handed. But where the fault is not shown to have resulted in any
> particular loss of amenity, there is nothing which the court can legitimately
> translate into money by way of compensation.

It is understandable that the claimant in this case found himself in
difficulty because the case was presented on the basis that the negligence
had been responsible for the whole of a substantial injury and it only
became apparent during the trial that it was not going to be possible to
prove more than a relatively minor increment.

PROOF OF CAUSATION

The claimant has to prove that, on the balance of probabilities, the
breach of duty caused their injury. In clinical negligence cases, this very
often entails the claimant proving what would have happened (and that
whatever that was, the claimant would be better as a result) had there
been no negligence. Proving hypothetical past events is therefore an
essential part of proving factual causation. Commonly the question of
what would have happened is dealt with by the experts based on their
experience of similar situations in their own hospitals and practices. This
evidence can of course be displaced by direct evidence of the particular
circumstances and practices of the doctors who treated the claimant.
A close eye has to be kept on this issue.

An interesting and useful case involving the proof of a series of
hypothetical past events is *Bright v Barnsley District Hospital*.[9] Mr
Recorder Burrell QC sitting as a High Court judge found for the claimant
on the following facts. (Incidentally this case was decided before the
House of Lords decision in *Gregg v Scott*.[10]) The child claimant (Billy-
Joe) was born with cerebral palsy. She had suffered profound hypoxia
lasting between ten and 25 minutes at some time after the 36th week of
pregnancy. There had been a negligent omission to carry out ultrasound
monitoring to check foetal growth at 32 weeks. It was agreed between the
experts that this scan would probably (60% chance) have shown foetal
growth at the fifth centile. This result would have triggered a second scan
that would have confirmed growth retardation (80% chance) which would
have led to a controlled delivery at 37 weeks with an 80% chance of birth
without brain damage.

The defendants argued that the cumulative chance of delivering an
undamaged child was $60 \times 80 \times 80 = 38.4\%$. The claimant had therefore
failed to prove on the balance of probability that she would have been
born without brain damage. The judge rejected this approach, he said
(see p 460):

9   [2005] Lloyd's Law Reports 449.
10 [2005] UKHL 2.

After establishing breach, in the absence of a known person about whom there is evidence to indicate what he or she might actually have done, the question is what would a reasonable radiographer at the hospital have found at the first 32 week scan which should have been carried out? In my judgment it is settled and conventional law that this has to be answered on the balance of probabilities and it is agreed that on balance that such a scan would probably have revealed a foetus at the 5th centile. This is a question of (hypothetical) fact to be decided on the balance of probability. Thereafter for the purpose of deciding what would then have happened, this finding (ie 32 weeks' scanning revealing 5th centile baby) is something which is to be treated as though it would have occurred in fact.

Further at p 460:

> It seems to me that there should be no difference in approach where the court is deciding a hypothetical fact ie deciding on what would have happened as opposed to deciding whether something had or had not actually happened ...

When considering past hypothetical facts the court should take the same approach as past actual events. On the balance of probabilities, would the hypothetical event have happened or not? If yes, it is to be treated as though it was a certainty, and then one turns to consider each subsequent hypothetical event on the same basis. The chances of each happening are only relevant in so far as they are above or below 50%; they are not to be taken cumulatively.

Burden of proof

In considering factual causation the courts should not be too ready to resort to the burden of proof. As noted by Auld LJ at [19] of *Verlander v Devon Waste Management*:[11]

> ... a judge should only resort to the burden of proof where he is unable to resolve an issue of fact or facts after he has unsuccessfully attempted to do so by examination and evaluation of the evidence.

Further, at [24]:

> ... such resort is only necessary where on the available evidence, conflicting and/or uncertain and/or falling short of proof, there is nothing left but to conclude that the claimant has not proved his case. The burden of proof remains part of our law and practice – and a respectable and useful part at that – where a tribunal cannot on the state of the evidence before it rationally decide one way or the other.

However, there may be rare cases where a court is unable to identify the likely operative cause and it is appropriate to decide the case on the burden of proof. A recent example is *Barnett v Medway NHS Foundation Trust*,[12] where the Court of Appeal found that the considerable uncertainty in the medical evidence meant the trial judge was justified in his inability to resolve an issue of fact about whether blood cultures would have revealed an infection. Not only was the medicine particularly difficult, but the expert evidence had been expressed in difficult and shifting terms. Taken

---

11 [2017] EWCA Civ 835.
12 [2017] EWCA Civ 235.

as a whole, the claimant's expert evidence fell short of establishing the probability of infection. He had failed to discharge the burden of proof.

Similarly in *Saunders v Central Manchester University Hospitals NHS Foundation Trust*,[13] Yip J held that the claimant had failed to establish on the balance of probabilities that damage to the blood supply of his bowel had been caused by surgery rather than by natural causes. His expert had not offered a clear explanation of the likely mechanism of surgical injury, and the delay of four days before the onset of symptoms did not fit with an acute event during surgery.

Presumption of competent treatment

The test is what probably would have happened were it not for the negligence. The *Bolam* test is usually irrelevant to this enquiry, except if, as in *Bolitho v City and Hackney Health Authority*[14] for example, it is said that the impugned doctor would not have done the thing (in that case intubated the claimant) that would have made a difference in any event, ie regardless of her negligence in failing to attend, because that was not her practice. Then and only then does the question arise: 'Would the hypothetical conduct of the doctor concerned in the absence of negligence have been negligent itself?' If it would, the defendant cannot rely upon it.

The Bolitho *case*

In *Bolitho v City and Hackney Health Authority*,[15] a child was ill in hospital; it was agreed that it was negligent that during the night no doctor had responded to a call made by the night sister; it was agreed that, if a doctor had come and had intubated the child, the cardiac arrest and brain damage that he went on to suffer would have been avoided. One might think that the defendants would have paid up on these facts, but no. They chose to argue (successfully) that the claimant could not prove that, if a doctor had come, they would probably have intubated. The claimant's expert said that it would have been mandatory to intubate; the defendant's expert said that he would not have intubated. The doctor (Dr Horn) who should have responded to the call from the sister said that she would not have intubated. Faced with this conflict of medical opinion, the judge held that the claimant had not proved that the outcome would probably have been different if the doctor had responded to the nurse's call. By a majority, the Court of Appeal upheld this decision.

Pending appeal to the House of Lords in *Bolitho*, the Court of Appeal considered a not dissimilar situation in *Joyce v Merton, Sutton and Wandsworth Health Authority*.[16] It was agreed that if a vascular surgeon had been called to the ward to review the patient following the initial operation on his arm and had operated within 48 hours, the injury (by way of thrombosis leading to brain stem infarction) would probably

---

13   [2018] EWHC 343 (QB).
14   [1993] 4 Med LR 381, CA, affd [1997] 4 All ER 771, HL.
15   [1993] 4 Med LR 381, CA, affd [1997] 4 All ER 771, HL.
16   [1996] 7 Med LR 1.

have been avoided. But the defendants argued successfully that, even if a vascular surgeon had been called in, the findings of the judge on causation could not be overturned. Those findings were that there was no relevant deterioration in the condition of Mr Joyce during the 48 hours following the procedure; that it was not mandatory to call for a vascular surgeon; and, most significantly, even if a vascular surgeon had monitored the condition of the patient, no vascular surgeon at that hospital would or should have seen a need to operate. In other words:

1   the course that would have ensued would in any event have been conservative treatment; and
2   it could not be said that such a conservative course was unacceptable.

In the *Bolitho* case, the claimant could not show that the doctor would have intubated, nor that it would have been mandatory to intubate. In the *Joyce* case, the claimant could not show that a vascular surgeon would have operated within the crucial 48-hour period, nor that it would have been mandatory for him to have done so.

The House of Lords upheld the decision of the Court of Appeal and for the same reasons.[17] Lord Browne-Wilkinson gave the only speech (although Lord Slynn expressed a degree of anxiety at the actual result). Their conclusions can be shortly expressed. The judge had asked the right two questions:

1   Would Dr Horn (or her junior) have intubated? Answer: the judge's acceptance of her evidence that she would not have intubated could not be interfered with.
2   Would it have been negligent if she had not intubated? Answer: the judge was impressed with the expert evidence called for the defence. He had no grounds for rejecting it as illogical or unreasonable, nor, said the House of Lords on reviewing the evidence and pointing out that the condition of the child at the relevant time did not appear on the evidence to have deteriorated to the point where intubation would have been necessary, had they done so.

Further cases applying this principle

In *Gouldsmith v Mid Staffordshire General Hospitals NHS Trust*,[18] the claimant suffered occlusions in the blood vessels in her left hand. She went to hospital but was not referred as she should have been to a specialist centre. She was treated with anticoagulants. Her fingers were amputated. It was her case that had she been referred on she would have had an operation to repair the lesion and she would not have lost her fingers. The defence argued that surgery was not the correct treatment and that anticoagulation was appropriate. The trial judge found that she should have been referred and that had she had the operation her fingers would have been saved. But he found that causation had not been made out by the claimant because he did not know the identity of the specific surgeon or hospital that would have operated, and was not satisfied that *every* specialist exercising proper care would have operated on her.

---

17   [1998] AC 232, [1997] 4 All ER 771.
18   [2007] EWCA 397.

The Court of Appeal rejected this reasoning and allowed the claimant's appeal (Maurice Kay LJ dissenting) stating that the relevant question was simply, what would have happened on referral to the specialist hospital? The claimant's expert evidence (which the judge purported to accept) was that 'most' specialists would have operated. On the balance of probabilities, the operation would therefore have been conducted. The question of whether it would have been negligent to fail to operate does not then arise. The trial judge had not followed the *Bolitho* questions in the correct sequence.

Where a GP negligently failed to make a referral, a presumption exists in favour of the claimant that they would have received the correct treatment in the event that the referral had been made. It was for the GP to demonstrate, where appropriate, that the hospital's subsequent treatment would have been negligent in any event: *Wright v Cambridge Medical Group*.[19]

In that case Lord Neuberger MR stated at [57]:

> It appears to be a generally accepted proposition that a doctor cannot escape liability for damage caused to a patient by his breach of duty by establishing that, if he had not committed that breach, the damage would have been suffered anyway because he would have committed a subsequent breach of duty.

And later at [75]:

> I think that the judge misdirected himself on the burden of proof. When considering the claimant's argument that different doctors might have attended her if she had been admitted on 15 April from those who did attend her following her admission on 17 April, he said [2010] EWHC 1507 at [60] that 'that is to an extent a speculative argument and the burden of proof is on the claimant at this stage of the case'. It is true that the burden of establishing causation in a negligence claim is, in principle, as with every other ingredient of the claim, on the claimant. However, once the claimant established that (i) she could and should have been referred to the hospital on 15 April, and (ii) she would not have suffered the damage now complained of had she been so referred and been treated competently at the hospital, *she had the benefit of a presumption that she would have been competently treated thereafter. In the absence of evidence to the contrary, the court will assume that professional and other service providers would have or have performed their functions competently.* Of course, provided that I am wrong in my view that this presumption is effectively irrebuttable as a matter of law in a case such as this, that presumption can be discharged by evidence, but it is, as it were, the right starting point. (emphasis added)

Dame Janet Smith largely agreed, stating at [124]:

> In my view, where the condition in question is not difficult to diagnose and the correct treatment is simple and uncontentious, there must be a presumption that a hospital will probably provide a correct diagnosis and treatment. Lord Neuberger MR is of the view that that presumption cannot be rebutted as a matter of law. I am uncertain whether I agree with that conclusion but that matters not because I agree with him that it has not been rebutted on the facts of this case.

---

19   [2011] EWCA Civ 669.

MEDICAL CASES

Causation is tremendously important in medical cases, and always needs careful consideration. This is because the aetiology of medical conditions is often unclear and because the situation will often be complicated by the presence of an underlying illness or other pre-existing vulnerabilities.

In every case, the chain of causation, whether only one link long or more, must be carefully considered. For example, it is all very well to prove that a GP should have visited, but one is likely also to need to consider what that GP would have found, what action they would or should have taken, and what result that would probably have had. It is probable that one would need to ask a specialist what the GP would have found if such an examination had been conducted as the GP expert requested. One then has to ask the GP expert whether finding what the specialist says would have been found at that time required immediate hospital referral, or whether a review in a few hours or advice to the patient or parents to call if the situation deteriorated would suffice. One then asks the specialist whether, assuming the GP had taken the least urgent action which would have remained within the bounds of reasonable management, the outcome would probably have been different. This may involve further links in the chain of causation by way of analysing what the hospital or specialist to which the patient should have been referred would probably have done and when. In a cancer case, one may find the expert unable to say whether earlier diagnosis and treatment would have produced a better outcome. If that is so, one cannot establish causation. In an obstetric case it is not infrequently possible, without too much difficulty, to establish a failure of care. But it is a quite different matter to prove that proper care, usually involving earlier delivery (often by Caesarean section), would have avoided the injury. The expert evidence on that issue may well be extremely technical and speculative. One may be unable to show that the injury was not sustained considerably earlier in the pregnancy, or, at the other end of the spectrum, one may be unable to show that the period of perinatal hypoxia would have been sufficiently curtailed by earlier delivery to avoid damage. An unfortunate example is *De Martell v Merton and Sutton Health Authority,* where the patient had already won an important preliminary hearing establishing the right at common law to sue for pre-natal injury.[20]

The possible scenarios on causation in medical negligence claims are legion, as the cases show. All one can do is make a careful analysis of what probably would have happened, step by step, if proper management, as certified by the appropriate experts, had taken place. Many and varied are the possible defences on causation. It is an unusual case that does not offer some opportunity for such a defence. Hence the fascination of the subject for defendants. The reports are full of cases where the defence has succeeded on some causation argument or other. One surprising example is *Pearman v North Essex Health Authority,*[21] where the defence expert convinced the judge, contrary to common sense (as the judge admitted), that the claimant could not prove that earlier treatment of cauda equina syndrome would have produced a better outcome. And there are plenty

---

20 [1993] QB 204, CA.
21 [2000] Lloyd's Rep Med 174.

of cerebral palsy claims that have failed on causation (an example is *Matthews v East Suffolk Health Authority*[22] – and a further defendant in that case succeeded in a different causation defence in respect of a failure to administer antibiotics). The same goes for most orthopaedic claims (along the lines of 'proper treatment would not have made any difference to the outcome'[23]). Where damage appears post-operatively, other causes can often be postulated.[24]

Further examples of cases on causation

The significance of causation in medical negligence cases is indicated by the number of times it has been an issue in reported cases every year, and the manifold ways in which medical claims can be contested by causation defences, whether valid or trumped up. A glance through the headnotes for any of the series of medical reports online or in hard copy will demonstrate this.

If failure to treat a patient made no difference because that patient would have died anyway, their death is not caused by the negligence. Thus in *Barnett v Chelsea and Kensington Hospital Management Committee*,[25] a casualty officer was negligent in not treating a night watchman who complained of vomiting after drinking tea. He later died of arsenic poisoning. His widow's claim failed on the ground that the workman would have died even if he had received all due care, because the judge concluded on the evidence that there was no chance that the only effective antidote could have been administered in time.

In *Robinson v Post Office*,[26] a doctor was found to be negligent in not administering a test dose of an anti-tetanus serum before injecting it in a patient who had cut his leg. The patient was allergic and developed encephalitis which led to brain damage and paralysis. The Court of Appeal said that the question (on this issue) was whether the negligence of the doctor had 'caused or materially contributed' to the claimant's injury, and that the onus was on the claimant of proving on the balance of probabilities that it had. The Court of Appeal said that the judge had been right to conclude on the evidence before him that even if the test dose had been administered there would have been no observable reaction in the patient and that therefore the doctor would in any event have gone on to administer the injection. So the injury would have happened anyway. The old case of *Rich v Pierpont*[27] was to similar effect: the wrongful administration of tartaric acid made no difference to the outcome – it 'turned out to be of no consequence.'

In *Vernon v Bloomsbury Health Authority*,[28] the court held that, even if the defendants had been negligent in failing to monitor the patient while on Gentamicin, further assays would probably not have revealed any danger signals.

---

22   [1999] MLC 0170.
23   As an example of a typical defence raised in these types of claim.
24   For example *Gray v Southampton and South West Hampshire Health Authority* [2000] MLC 0209.
25   [1969] 1 QB 428, MLC 0005.
26   [1974] 1 WLR 1176, CA.
27   (1862) 3 F & F 35.
28   [1995] 6 Med LR 297.

In *Hotson v East Berkshire Area Health Authority*,[29] the House of Lords denied compensation to an infant claimant on the basis that his injury would not on the balance of probabilities have benefited from the treatment which the defendants negligently failed to afford him (see below for a full discussion of that case and 'loss of a chance').

Then there was the House of Lords decision in *Wilsher v Essex Area Health Authority*,[30] (considered in more detail below) where it was alleged that administration of excessive oxygen had caused neonatal blindness. The House of Lords held that the claimant had not proved causation. The House was unanimously of the view that there had to be a retrial for the simple enough reason that on the evidence there were a number of possible causes for the injury to the child and the judge had not at any time made any finding that excess oxygen was the actual cause, the effective cause, or even the most likely cause (that omission seems to have been due to the judge's misunderstanding of part of the expert evidence). Had he made that finding, his conclusion would have been unassailable. But he did not and so a retrial before another judge on the issue of causation was unavoidable.[31]

In *Gregory v Pembrokeshire Health Authority*,[32] the claimant delivered a child suffering from Down's syndrome. She alleged, correctly, that the consultant had been negligent in not telling her that the sample from her amniocentesis had not produced sufficient cultures to determine whether her child would suffer from Down's syndrome. She contended that, had she been so informed, she would have had the test repeated, the result would have been positive and she would have arranged for an abortion. The judge accepted that she could have obtained a legal abortion, but he concluded that she would have discussed the matter first with the consultant and would as a result have accepted what would have been his advice, namely not to undergo a second amniocentesis (amniocentesis always carries a risk to the foetus; there was no reason to suspect at that time that something was actually amiss, and the statistical chance of chromosomal abnormality was 1 in 800). So the outcome would have been the same even had the defendants not been negligent; therefore the claim for the cost of raising the child failed. The Court of Appeal saw no reason to criticise the judge's conclusion, arrived at on the evidence and his assessment of the witnesses, that the claimant would not have proceeded to a second amniocentesis. A claim similarly failed in *Deriche v Ealing Hospital NHS Trust*[33] where Buckley J held that, even if a pregnant woman had been properly counselled about the risk of foetal damage from her chicken pox, she would not have decided to terminate the pregnancy.

Compare *Rance v Mid-Downs Health Authority*:[34] here a mother of a child born suffering from spina bifida alleged that the defendants should have discovered the defect in the foetus and she would then have had an abortion. Brooke J said that, even if he were satisfied that negligence

---

29 [1987] AC 750.
30 [1988] AC 1074, HL.
31 There was in fact no retrial as an amicable settlement was reached about the end of 1990, under which a proportion of the total damages claimed was paid to the claimant.
32 [1989] 1 Med LR 81.
33 (2003) MLC 1083.
34 [1991] 1 QB 587, [1990] 2 Med LR 27.

had been made out, any abortion would have had to take place when the gestational age was more than 27 weeks; this would have been a crime by virtue of the Infant Life (Preservation) Act 1929 because the child would then have been capable of being born alive; and a claim for damages which depended for its success on establishing a chain of causation which included the commission of a criminal offence could not be accepted by the court. The situation was as if the mother had failed to prove that she would have proceeded to an abortion, so the outcome would have been the same. If the facts of this case were repeated at the present time, the judge would not find that the proposed abortion would be a crime, thanks to s 37(1)(d) of the Human Fertilisation and Embryology Act 1990, which permits the termination of a pregnancy at any stage where there is a substantial risk that if the child were born it would be seriously handicapped. Similarly in *Briody v St Helens and Knowsley Area Health Authority*,[35] where a claimant had been made infertile through medical negligence the Court of Appeal held that a claim for the costs of surrogacy which would involve breach of the Surrogacy Arrangements Act 1985 was not recoverable.

Sellers v Cooke and East Dorset Health Authority[36] is interesting: although the claimant succeeded in persuading the Court of Appeal that certain fresh evidence suggesting a negligent termination of her pregnancy could not reasonably have been obtained by her for the trial (which she had lost), the court went on to hold that, even if that evidence were to establish that her pregnancy had been negligently terminated, that would not have affected the outcome, because the judge had found that the foetus would probably not in any event have survived.

Causation also proved the stumbling block for the claimants who sought to allege that the pertussis vaccine caused brain damage to their children (see *Loveday v Renton*[37]).

In *Marsden v Bateman*,[38] the claimant failed to establish that her brain damage was due to untreated neonatal hypoglycaemia rather than a congenital condition.

In *Stockdale v Nicholls*,[39] the claim failed because the judge held that earlier admission to hospital would not have affected the outcome, in that the claimant would still have been admitted for observation only, and the unavoidable and unpredictable onset of septicaemia resulting in fitting and brain damage would have occurred in hospital at the same time and with the same results.

In *Smith v Barking, Havering and Brentwood Health Authority*,[40] the claimant proved that the defendants had been negligent in not warning her of the risks of a difficult operation on the cervical canal but failed in her claim for damages for serious injury suffered in the operation because the judge was satisfied that, even if warned, she would still have agreed to the operation as it was her only chance of avoiding the onset of

---

35   [2002] QB 856.
36   [1990] 2 Med LR 13 and 16, CA.
37   [1990] 1 Med LR 117.
38   [1993] 4 Med LR 181.
39   [1993] 4 Med LR 190.
40   [1994] 5 Med LR 285.

tetraplegia. However, in *Chester v Afshar*,[41] the usual rules on causation in consent cases were altered: see a further discussion below.

In *Robertson v Nottingham Health Authority*,[42] the trial judge held that the period of culpable delay during labour had made no difference to the outcome because the foetal brain injury had been sustained before the mother had been admitted to hospital. The Court of Appeal held that the judge should have found a more extended period of delay, but, despite that and the fact that he had not dealt in his judgment with the significance of an apparently normal first CTG trace, his conclusion on causation would probably have been the same.[43]

In *Brown v Lewisham and North Southwark Health Authority*,[44] the trip a patient was obliged to undertake by train and taxi from Guy's Hospital in London back to his Blackpool hospital following his negligent discharge with a chest infection was not a cause of later vascular gangrene leading to amputation of a leg. An idiosyncratic reaction to Heparin at the Blackpool hospital was the cause; it would have happened in any event.

In *Brock v Frenchay Healthcare Trust*,[45] there had been a negligent delay in administering Mannitol, but earlier administration would not have helped.

In *Windyk v Wigan Health Authority*,[46] a claim for a negligently-advised operation on a man with little sight (he then lost what little he had), the defendants failed to show that he would in any event have progressed to complete loss of vision.

In *Hossack v Ministry of Defence*,[47] no causal connection was found between a negligent failure to downgrade a soldier for training status and the development of chronic medial tibial syndrome. The court imported into the tortious context the well-known contractual principle that an event which simply provides the opportunity for something else to happen is not thereby the cause of it (the 'Galoo' principle[48]).

In *C v A Health Authority*,[49] a negligent failure to offer a booking appointment was not causative of the birth of a congenitally handicapped child because the consultant, reasonably, would not in any event have recommended the sort of scan which might have shown the defect.

In *Coffey-Martin v Royal Free Hampstead NHS Trust*,[50] Foskett QC, the mother proved breach of duty in that the defendants did not examine her anal sphincter following the birth of her child, but failed on causation as the court concluded that examination would probably not have detected the damage, and, even if it had, repair procedures would probably not have avoided much of the injury.

---

41 [2004] UKHL 41.
42 [1996] 7 Med LR 421.
43 [1997] 8 Med LR 1.
44 [1999] Lloyd's Rep Med 110, [2000] MLC 0081.
45 [1999] MLC 0101.
46 [1999] MLC 0088.
47 [2000] MLC 00185, CA.
48 See [1994] 1 WLR 1360, CA.
49 (3 November 1998, ML 12/98 p. 7).
50 (15 December 2000, unreported), QBD.

Where a solicitor fails to serve a writ in a medical claim but the claim is adjudged hopeless, there will be no causation and the claim against the solicitor will be struck out.[51]

In *Birch v University College London Hospital NHS Foundation Trust*,[52] the failure to obtain consent to the risk of angiogram (ie the risk of stroke which eventuated) as opposed to other alternative tests was held to be causative of injury as the claimant would probably not have consented had he been warned.

In *ST v Maidstone and Tunbridge Wells NHS Trust*,[53] the claimant suffered from congenital haematological conditions. The defendant trust negligently delayed a blood transfusion, failed to administer IV fluids and administered Frusemide during both transfusions. The claimant suffered seizures and strokes resulting in brain damage. He was left with permanent and severe disabilities. However, Swift J held that the claimant had failed to prove on the balance of probabilities that his injuries were caused by the breaches of duty; the primary cause of the strokes was a focal cerebral arteriopathy caused by the upper respiratory tract infection from which he was suffering. The claimant's alternative causation argument, relying on *Bailey* also failed; there was no objective evidence that his dehydration, acute-on-chronic aemolysis and severe anaemia contributed to the arteriopathy to cause his strokes.

In *Baynham v Royal Wolverhampton Hospitals NHS Trust*,[54] the Court of Appeal upheld a finding that at 25-minute (admittedly negligent) delay in performing a Caesarean section had not caused or materially contributed to the child's cerebral palsy.

In *Choudhury v South Central Ambulance Service NHS Trust*,[55] the claimant suffered a rare form of stroke resulting in locked-in syndrome. The defendants admitted various breaches of duty but disputed causation. Cox J held that the claimant had not established on the balance of probabilities that earlier treatment would have avoided further catastrophic deterioration.

Similarly in *Clements v Imperial College Healthcare Trust*,[56] the evidence had not demonstrated on the balance of probabilities that the claimant had been suffocated by her mother's breast during breastfeeding when she was left by a midwife with her parents alone to bond with her. The baby's collapse shortly after her birth and the acute hypoxic insult that she sustained as a result of that collapse remained unexplained. May J concluded that no-one was to blame for the claimant's collapse shortly after her birth, or her disabilities resulting from the acute hypoxic insult that she sustained as a result of that collapse. She considered this was akin to a *Wilsher*-type case where no definitive cause or causes had been identified, but only many risk factors generating hypothesised causes.

Finally, in *NAX v King's College Hospital HNS Trust*,[57] the claimant patient had not established that defendant hospital's breaches of duty in treating her when she fell ill after brain surgery had caused her brain

---

51   *Harris v Bolt Burdon* (2 February 2000, unreported), CA.
52   [2008] EWHC 2237.
53   [2015] EWHC 51 (QB).
54   [2016] EWCA Civ 1249.
55   [2015] EWHC 1311 (QB).
56   [2018] EWHC 2064 (QB).
57   [2018] EWHC 1170 (QB).

damage. On the balance of probabilities, earlier intubation would not have made a material difference to the outcome.

The *Chester v Afshar* exception

In *Chester v Afshar*,[58] the defendant neurosurgeon failed to inform the claimant of the small risk of cauda equine syndrome developing during an operation. The operation was performed non-negligently. Cauda equine syndrome developed. The trial judge found that it was not possible to say whether the claimant would have gone ahead with the surgery although she would probably have sought a second opinion first and the operation which was not urgent may therefore have taken place on a later date. The House of Lords held by a majority (Lords Bingham and Hoffmann dissenting) that the claimant could not prove that the failure to warn of the small risk was the cause of the cauda equine syndrome because she could not say that she would not have gone ahead with the surgery if she had been told of the risk. However, for policy reasons, ie for the duty to obtain consent before operating to have any meaning, the usual rules of causation had to be altered to allow the claimant to recover damages. At para 87 of *Chester* Lord Hope of Craighead said that:

> The function of the law is to enable rights to be vindicated and to provide remedies when duties have been breached' and that unless that was done the right to be consented before an operation would be 'a hollow one, stripped of all practical force and devoid of all content.

This departure from traditional causation principles has been the subject of much discussion (and criticism), but remains binding on lower courts unless and until the Supreme Court revisit the issue.

In *Marshall v Hull and East Yorkshire Hospitals NHS Trust*,[59] the claimant developed an infection after an arthroscopy. She required a total knee replacement, which also became infected. A series of complications ensued involving in excess of 20 operations. The claimant was left barely able to walk and was largely wheelchair dependent. The trust admitted it had managed the original infection negligently, but denied that its actions resulted in the claimant requiring a total knee replacement six years earlier than she otherwise would have, and for all the consequences of that operation.

The defendant argued that the infection risk was not increased by the negligence; on traditional causation principles damages should be restricted to injury loss and damage from the acceleration. It relied on dicta from *Chester*, including Lord Bingham's comments (at paras 8–9) that the timing of operation was irrelevant; the injury was likely to occur whenever the surgery was performed and whoever performed it, and Lord Hope's comment at para 61: 'the failure to warn cannot be said in any was to have increased the risk of surgery. That risk was inherent in the operation itself.'

The defendant argued that, whenever the total knee replacement surgery was performed, the claimant would always have been in the 1–2% of patients at risk of developing an infection.

---

58 [2004] UKHL 41.
59 [2014] EWHC 4326 (QB).

HHJ Reddihough rejected these arguments and distinguished *Chester*. Crucially he considered that the timing of the operation *would* have made a difference to the likely outcome.

He accepted that actual events could potentially displace statistics, relying on *Wardlaw v Farrar*.[60] In that case, a GP negligently failed to diagnose and treat a pulmonary embolism. However, when the deceased was finally admitted to hospital she did not respond as expected to anti-coagulant treatment. The Court of Appeal held that the trial judge was entitled to take into account the failure of treatment when deciding that, on the balance of probabilities, the negligence was not causative of death. Brooke LJ said at [35]:

> While judges are of course entitled to place such weight on statistical evidence as is appropriate, they must not blind themselves to the effect of other evidence which might put a particular patient in a particular category, regardless of the general probabilities.

In *Marshall* however, HHJ Reddihough was not persuaded that there was an identifiable factor giving rise to a susceptibility to infection. On the balance of probabilities the infection following the knee replacement was related to tissue damage arising from the negligent treatment of the post-arthroscopy infection, which a significant contributory factor to the wound breakdown. Therefore, on a balance of probabilities, if the claimant had had the total knee replacement six years later at age 49, when some years would have passed without surgery, she would not have fallen into the very small percentage of patients who develop total post total knee replacement infection and would not have suffered the wound breakdown. If followed that there was a 'link or continuum between the total knee replacement infection and all of the subsequent problems which the claimant suffered (at [69]).

He further held (at [79]) that an alternative way of approaching the issue was to apply *Wright* (considered above). There was a presumption that, had the total knee replacement been carried out at age 49, she would not have been in the 1–2% at infection risk. It was for the defendant to rebut that presumption and it failed to do so.

In *Meadows v Khan*,[61] a doctor negligently failed to determine that the claimant was a carrier for haemophilia. She gave birth to a child who suffered haemophilia, and was also later diagnosed with autism. Yip J allowed the additional costs of raising a child with both autism and haemophila, despite the fact they were unconnected.

The defendant sought to rely on Lord Hoffmann's mountaineer's knee analogy in *South Australia Asset Management Corp v York Montague Ltd (SAAMCO)*,[62] cited here in full:

> A mountaineer about to undertake a difficult climb is concerned about the fitness of his knee. He goes to a doctor who negligently makes a superficial examination and pronounces the knee fit. The climber goes on the expedition, which he would not have undertaken if the doctor had told him the true state of his knee. He suffers an injury which is an entirely foreseeable consequence of mountaineering but has nothing to do with his knee.

---

60 [2014] EWHC 4326 (QB).
61 [2017] EWHC 2990 (QB).
62 [1997] AC 191.

On the Court of Appeal's principle, the doctor is responsible for the injury suffered by the mountaineer because it is damage which would not have occurred if he had been given correct information about his knee. He would not have gone on the expedition and would have suffered no injury. On what I have suggested is the more usual principle, the doctor is not liable. The injury has not been caused by the doctor's bad advice because it would have occurred even if the advice had been correct.

... Your Lordships might, I would suggest, think that there was something wrong with a principle which, in the example which I have given, produced the result that the doctor was liable. What is the reason for this feeling? I think that the Court of Appeal's principle offends common sense because it makes the doctor responsible for consequences which, though in general terms foreseeable, do not appear to have a sufficient causal connection with the subject matter of the duty. The doctor was asked for information on only one of the considerations which might affect the safety of the mountaineer on the expedition. There seems no reason of policy which requires that the negligence of the doctor should require the transfer to him of all the foreseeable risks of the expedition.

However, Yip J held (at [55]) that the facts of Ms Meadows' case bore a closer analogy to *Chester* than the mountaineer's knee in *SAAMCO*. The risk of autism was an inevitable and natural risk of any pregnancy, but it could not be said that it would probably have materialised in another pregnancy. Although the autism was unrelated to the haemophilia, both conditions were a natural consequence of a pregnancy that would not have continued but for the negligence. Thus, the scope of the doctor's duty extended to preventing the child's birth and all its consequences.

The Court of Appeal disagreed, allowing the defendant's appeal.[63] It found that Yip J had erred in reverting to the 'but for' causation test, rather than applying the *SAAMCO* test. The latter required there to be an adequate link between the breach of duty and the particular type of loss claimed. It was insufficient for the court to find that there was a link between the breach and the stage in the chain of causation, in the instant case the pregnancy itself, and thereafter to conclude that the doctor was liable for all the reasonably foreseeable consequences of that pregnancy (at [29]).

Chester has also been reviewed by the Court of Appeal in two recent post-*Montgomery* consent cases (see Chapter 10 for a more detailed discussion of recent developments in this area, and causation in consent cases): *Correia v University Hospital of North Staffordshire NHS Trust;*[64] and *Duce v Worcestershire Acute Hospitals NHS Trust.*[65]

Correia concerned the treatment of a painful recurrent neuroma in the claimant's right foot. The surgeon proposed a rare three-stage procedure, but ended up only performing the first two stages. The claimant alleged that the operation had been negligently performed and that she had not been warned of the material risks of an operation that omitted the third and crucial step. Simon LJ noted that the facts of *Chester* were 'unusual.' It was, he said at [28] a 'crucial finding' of that case that, if warned of the risk, the appellant would have deferred

---

63 [2019] EWCA Civ 152.
64 [2017] EWCA Civ 356.
65 [2018] EWCA Civ 1307.

the operation. If 'the exceptional principle of causation' established by *Chester* was to be relied upon it was necessary to plead and prove that, if warned of the risk, the claimant would have deferred the operation. In the present case there was no such contention in the pleadings or witness statements.

In *Duce*, the claimant alleged the defendant failed to warn her of the risk of developing chronic post-surgical pain following a total abdominal hysterectomy and bilateral salpingo-oophorectomy, which materialised. The claim failed on liability applying *Montgomery* principles, but the trial judge and Court of Appeal found that the claim would have failed on causation in any event. The judge rejected the claimant's evidence that had a warning been given, she would not have had surgery on that day. Before the Court of Appeal she submitted that as a matter of law there was no need to prove this, arguing that Lord Hope's comments at [86]–[87] of *Chester* created an alternative pathway to causation in consent cases, subject to three requirements:

1   the injury was intimately involved with the duty to warn;
2   the duty was owed by the doctor who performed the surgery to which the patient had consented;
3   the injury was the product of the very risk that the patient should have been warned about when they gave their consent.

The defendant argued that, if correct, this would amount to a wholesale disapplication of conventional causation principles in consent cases.

Hamblen LJ considered (at [66]) that, viewed in context of the rest of the judgment:

> it is clear that [Lord Hope] is not setting out a free-standing test, as the appellant contends, but rather the circumstances which justify the normal approach to causation being modified. That modification was to treat a 'but for' cause that was not an effective cause as a sufficient cause in law in the 'unusual' circumstances of the case.

He held that the majority decision in *Chester* did not negate the requirement for a claimant to demonstrate a 'but for' causative effect of the breach of the duty. In this case the factual finding (not successfully challenged on appeal) was that the claimant would still have had the operation *at the same time* even if she had received the warning.

Leggatt LJ was critical of *Chester*, but acknowledged that policy considerations including the importance of vindicating a patient's right to make an informed choice could perhaps be invoked in this context to justify departure from the normal rule (see [87] and [91]). He said at [92]:

> These are all matters which may be thought ripe for further consideration by the Supreme Court when the opportunity arises. They do not, however, assist Mrs Duce in this case, as there is no reasonable interpretation of the decision of the House of Lords in *Chester* which justifies extending liability for negligent failure to warn of a material risk of a surgical operation to a situation where, as here, it has been found as a fact that, if she had been warned of the risk, the claimant would still have proceeded with the operation as and when she did.

It is clear from these recent authorities that *Chester* represents a very narrow exception to traditional causation principles, and must be properly pleaded and evidenced if it is to succeed.

'Material contribution'

It is trite law that any contribution to the injury which is not negligible (ie does not fall within the *de minimis* principle) may be taken to have 'materially contributed' to the injury (see *Bonnington Castings Ltd v Wardlaw*[66], *per* Lord Reid, and *Clarkson v Modern Foundries Ltd*[67]).

It is not always easy to be confident about applying the 'material contribution' test. It may feel more logical to ask the question: would the injury have been sustained if the alleged negligence had not taken place? In some circumstances, the tests may give different answers. That is because injury may be caused by more than one factor. Where a patient suffers brain damage from an underlying illness and also as a result of wrong medication, the 'but for' test might yield the result that the patient had not shown causation because the underlying illness would probably have resulted in the injury in any event, while the 'material contribution' test would establish causation. In other cases, the inability to satisfy the 'but for' test might also lead to the conclusion that the other factor did not play a material part in the injury. The 'but for' test could obviously not be applied in the case of joint tortfeasors, because each defendant could escape liability by pleading that even if he had not been negligent the injury would nevertheless have been sustained. It is also important to bear in mind the rule that joint tortfeasors are individually liable for the whole of the relevant damages in the context where there is a negligent late referral to hospital or to a specialist, and the hospital or specialist is also negligent in the management of the patient. In those circumstances, it should not be open to the first defendant to plead that the injury was caused only by the second failure of management (but see below under 'Divisibility/Apportionment' and 'Breaking the chain of causation'). The 'but for' test gives a wrong answer also in the context of a loss-causing event where the negligent act had no more synergistic connection with the event than that it afforded it an opportunity to occur (see *Hossack* v *Ministry of Defence* (above)).

Examples of cases decided on the 'material contribution' basis

In *Murray v Kensington and Chelsea and Westminster Area Health Authority*,[68] a baby's sight was lost due to excessive oxygen. The trial judge had found one incident only of negligence on the part of the doctors, namely in administering extra oxygen in the first 36 hours of life, but had found for the defendants nevertheless on the basis that it was not proved that it was that particular quantity of oxygen that had caused the injury, for it could have been caused by later doses, in respect of which no negligence was found. The Court of Appeal upheld his decision. It seems hard on the claimant that the judges were not prepared to conclude on the evidence that the initial excess had probably made a material contribution to the injury.

In the Scottish case of *Kay v Ayrshire and Arran Health Board*,[69] a child suffering from pneumococcal meningitis was negligently given three times

---

66   [1956] AC 613, MLC 0003.
67   [1958] 1 All ER 33.
68   (11 May 1981, unreported), CA.
69   [1987] 2 All ER 417, HL.

the proper dose of penicillin. Liability was admitted for the short-term effects of convulsion and temporary paralysis, but denied in respect of the permanent deafness that later occurred. The House of Lords, confirming the appeal court's reversal of the trial judge's award of damages for the deafness, said that there was no evidence which would support a finding that the overdose caused the deafness or even materially increased the risk of its occurring. On the evidence, the probability was that it was the original meningitis that caused the deafness.

In *Page v Smith (No 2)*,[70] the Master of the Rolls said:

> ... it was argued that the judge had erred in asking whether on the balance of probabilities the defendants' negligence had materially contributed to the recrudescence of the plaintiff's symptoms. He should, it was said, have asked himself whether on the balance of probabilities the plaintiff would have suffered the injury for which he was claiming compensation but for the defendant's negligence. I do not for my part accept these criticisms. In a case in which other causes could have played a part in the causation of the defendant's exacerbated symptoms, it was in my view entirely appropriate for the judge to direct himself in the way that he did, reminding himself that a cause was only to be regarded as material if it was more than minimal or trivial or insignificant. I cannot in any event see that in a case such as this the outcome would be different whichever test is formulated. The judge had already accepted the view expressed by one of the medical experts that the plaintiff's recovery would probably have continued but for the accident. The judge adopted a straightforward, pragmatic approach which was in my judgment entirely appropriate in the circumstances.

This was a claim for the exacerbation of a psychiatric injury (chronic fatigue syndrome) caused by a road traffic accident. The issue whether a psychiatric injury had to be foreseeable in the context of a road traffic accident had already gone to the House of Lords, where it had received a negative response.[71]

In *Hutchinson v Epsom and St Hellier's NHS Trust*[72] the defendant's failure to carry out liver function tests on the deceased and their consequent failure to advise him to stop drinking made a material contribution to his death. The deputy High Court judge held that the widow was entitled to recover in full.

In *King v Samsung Heavy Industries Ltd*,[73] the Court of Appeal said that, where the finding had been that an employer's breach of duty, though not necessarily the main or sole cause of the claimant's carpal tunnel syndrome, had been a material cause contributing to the injury, that was sufficient for a finding of liability against the employer.

In *Simmons v British Steel plc 2002*,[74] the House of Lords held that the defendant employer was liable for the claimant's psychiatric illness where one of the causes had been the claimant's anger following an accident at work for which the employer was liable.

In *Bailey v Ministry of Defence*,[75] the claimant was admitted to hospital for an operation to remove a gallstone. After the operation, the

70   [1996] 1 WLR 855, CA.
71   [1996] AC 155.
72   [2002] MLC 1072.
73   (10 April 2002, unreported).
74   [2004] PIQR P33.
75   [2008] EWCA Civ 883.

claimant became very weak and developed pancreatitis. She was sent to the intensive care unit. The claimant's condition stabilised and she was transferred to the ward. There she was given a drink, vomited and was unable to clear her throat. She aspirated the vomit causing a cardiac arrest which led her to suffer hypoxic brain damage. The judge found that the cardiac arrest had been caused by the claimant's weakness which had two cumulative causes: the first defendant's lack of care; and the claimant's pancreatitis, which was not the result of the first defendant's negligence. He held that since the negligent lack of care had contributed materially to the claimant's overall weakness, causation had been established. Critically, he said:[76]

> I cannot say whether the contribution made by this component was more or less than that made by the pancreatitis and it follows that I cannot say whether the contribution made by the pancreatitis was greater or smaller than the contribution of the other component. All I can say is that the natural inference is that each contributed materially to the overall weakness and it was the overall weakness that caused the aspiration.

The Court of Appeal dismissed the defendant's appeal, Lord Justice Waller held at [46]:

> I would summarise the position in relation to cumulative cause cases as follows. If the evidence demonstrates on a balance of probabilities that the injury would have occurred as a result of the non-tortious cause or causes in any event, the claimant will have failed to establish that the tortious cause contributed.

> *Hotson's* case exemplifies such a situation. If the evidence demonstrates that 'but for' the contribution of the tortious cause the injury would probably not have occurred, the claimant will (obviously) have discharged the burden. In a case where medical science cannot establish the probability that 'but for' an act of negligence the injury would not have happened but can establish that the contribution of the negligent cause was more than negligible, the 'but for' test is modified, and the claimant will succeed.

Bailey was followed by Walker J in his *obiter* judgment in the case of *Ingram v Dr Williams*.[77] The judge held that (had the claim succeeded in respect of the breach) the claimant would have established the causation of all his losses and recovered damages in full where it had been agreed between the experts that the alleged negligence had made 'a material but unquantifiable reduction in the degree of disability suffered'. The apportionment approach (the *Holtby* approach) between causes argued for by the defendants was specifically rejected. As will be seen below, much in reality depends upon the type of evidence adduced. If there can be a logical and reasoned apportionment, then the *Holtby* approach may still be adopted.

Another example of the robust application of the material contribution exception to the 'but for' test in clinical negligence cases is *Boustead v North West Strategic Health Authority*.[78] In that case there were a number of potential causes of brain damage in a new born infant. One was the delay in delivery by caesarean section. Others included his prematurity.

---

76   [2007] EWHC 2913 (QB) at [60].
77   [2010] EWHC 758 (QB).
78   [2008] EWHC 2375 (QB).

Mr Justice Mackay held that the negligent delay was one of concurrent cumulative causes and since it had materially contributed to the hypoxia but to an unknown and unknowable extent, the claimant was entitled to recover.

Where, on the balance of probability, therefore, the negligently caused hypoxia had materially contributed to the brain damage, but to an unknown or unknowable extent, liability is established. If, on the other hand, the hypoxia was one of a number of potential causes and it was impossible to say on the balance of probability whether it had caused or materially contributed to the injury, then liability would not be established.

In *Leigh v London Ambulance Service NHS Trust*,[79] a passenger had been trapped on a bus with a dislocated knee for 50 minutes and as a result developed post-traumatic stress disorder. The court accepted that there was a causative link between the admittedly negligent delay of 17 minutes in the attendance of an ambulance and the development of that psychological damage. Globe J found that this was a case where medical science could not establish that PTSD would not have happened 'but for' the delay, but found that the contribution of the delay was more than negligible.

In *E v Somerset Partnership NHS Trust*,[80] the trust admitted it had provided negligent mental health care to a 14 year-old girl, F, including failures to involve her family in the treatment of her eating disorder and premature discharge by the community psychiatric nurse. F committed suicide. HHJ Denyer QC could not accept the assertion of the claimant's expert that on the balance of probabilities, 'but for' the breach F would not have committed suicide, but nor could he accept the defendant's expert evidence that the suicide would have occurred in any event as a result of an impulsive act unrelated to F's eating disorder. He concluded at [17]:

> In my view it is impossible to separate out the eating disorder from the mood disorder: common sense suggests that they must be related. The evidence from the diary shows a deeply disturbed and unhappy young girl and one still in the grip of her eating disorder. In my view, the failure to continue the treatment, the premature ending of the treatment and the failure to involve the family in what was going on, *inevitably contributed to her ongoing problems which led her to take her own life*. In other words, *those failures did materially contribute* to the ultimate decision by F to take her own life, whatever the immediate trigger for that decision might have been. (Emphasis added.)

In *Williams v The Bermuda Hospitals Board*,[81] the plaintiff attended hospital with abdominal pain. He was suffering from acute appendicitis. A negligently delayed CT scan resulted in a delayed appendectomy. There were complications, causing injury to his heart and lungs as a result of sepsis, which had developed incrementally over the six hours leading up to his operation. The trial judge found that by the time the claimant arrived at hospital his appendix had ruptured leading to widespread pus and infection. This process had commenced before surgery would have been performed on the 'but for' scenario, and he was not satisfied that the complications would have been avoided had the surgery been performed

---

79   [2014] EWHC 286 (QB).
80   (12 January 2016, unreported).
81   [2016] UKPC 4.

earlier. He awarded limited damages for the plaintiff's extra suffering during the period of delay.

The Court of Appeal for Bermuda allowed the plaintiff's appeal, holding that the breach of duty by the defendant had materially contributed to the injury. Lord Toulson summarised their findings (at [19] in the PC):

> He [Ward LJ] held, at para 36, that the trial judge was in error 'by raising the bar unattainably high' in his finding that Mr Williams had failed to prove his case. The proper test of causation, he said, was 'not whether the negligent delay and inadequate system caused the injury to [Mr Williams] but rather whether the breaches of duty by [the hospital board] contributed materially to the injury.' That the breaches contributed materially to the injury was in his view beyond argument. He stated that the 'but for' test is sometimes relaxed to enable a claimant to overcome the causation hurdle when it might otherwise seem unjust to require the claimant to prove the impossible, and he referred to *Bailey* [...] as a case in which the 'but for' rule was modified.

The Privy Council dismissed the defendant's appeal. Lord Toulson rejected the defendant's argument that the 'material contribution' approach only applies in concurrent or simultaneous cases, stating:

> 39. The sequence of events may be highly relevant in considering as a matter of fact whether a later event has made a material contribution to the outcome (as *Hotson* [...] illustrates), or conversely whether an earlier event has been so overtaken by later events as not to have made a material contribution to the outcome. But those are evidential considerations. As a matter of principle, successive events are capable of each making a material contribution to the subsequent outcome.

> 40. A claim will fail if the most that can be said is that the claimant's injury is likely to have been caused by one or more of a number of disparate factors, one of which was attributable to a wrongful act or omission of the defendant: *Wilsher* [...]. In such a case the claimant will not have shown as a matter of probability that the factor attributable to the defendant caused the injury, or was one of two or more factors which operated cumulatively to cause it. In *Wilsher* [...] it was held by the House of Lords that it was not enough to show that the defendant's negligence added to the list of risk factors to which he was exposed. The fact that the administration of excess oxygen was negligent did not warrant an inference that it was a more likely cause of the RLF than the various other known possible causes. The House of Lords distinguished the case from *Bonnington's* case [...] in which the injury was caused by a single known process (the inhalation of dust).

Incidentally it should be remembered that 'material contribution' has been defined as something more than de minimis: see *Bonnington Castings v Wardlaw*.[82] It is not necessary for the claimant to prove that the negligent cause was the sole cause or even the main cause of injury.

Materially increasing the risk

Pursuant to *McGhee v National Coal Board*,[83] it had been thought that even if the claimant could not show that what was done materially contributed to his injury (because the state of medical knowledge at the time was not sufficiently advanced to demonstrate the connection), it

---

82 [1956] AC 613.
83 [1973] 1 WLR 1.

was nevertheless enough if he showed that what was done materially increased the risk of injury. In those circumstances, the court would be entitled to infer, as a matter of fact, that what was done did play a part in the causing of the injury.

All that the claimant could prove in that case by his expert medical evidence was that the employer's failure to provide showers had increased the risk of his contracting dermatitis; he could not prove that the provision of showers would probably have prevented the disease, ie that he probably would not have contracted it if there had been no negligence. The speeches of the House of Lords giving judgment in his favour were understood at the time to be pronouncing a rule of causation to the effect that there was 'no substantial difference between saying that what the defendant did materially increased the risk of injury to the claimant and saying that what the defendant did made a material contribution to his injury' (*per* Lord Reid at 5).

This principle was extended by a majority of the Court of Appeal in *Wilsher v Essex Area Health Authority*,[84] where the fact that the administering of an excess of oxygen was only one of the possible causes of loss of sight in a neonate did not preclude the court from attributing the injury to that cause. The principle was also applied in *Bryce v Swan Hunter Group plc*[85] and *Fitzgerald v Lane*.[86]

However, it was established from the judgment of the House of Lords, allowing the appeal in the *Wilsher* case, that the interpretation put upon Lord Reid's words in the *McGhee* case was misconceived, and that that case added nothing to the traditional rules on causation: it was up to the claimant to show on the balance of probabilities that the act or omission complained of caused or materially contributed to his injury. So the matter stood until the important House of Lords decision in *Fairchild v Glenhaven Funeral Services Ltd*.

The Fairchild *case*

The House of Lords in *Fairchild v Glenhaven Funeral Services Ltd*[87] held that where two (or more) employers have been similarly negligent in failing to protect an employee from the risk of contracting a disease (mesothelioma in this instance) and the employee contracts that disease but it is not possible in the current state of medical and scientific knowledge to show during which employment the disease was probably contracted, both employers are to be held to have caused the disease and so both are liable to the employee. The disease in this case is apparently not cumulative and is contracted once and for all at a single moment when a fibre enters the respiratory system. It was not possible to tell under whose employment that fibre was ingested.

An analogy may posit two independent hunters each negligently discharging identical bullets in the direction of a jogger with the result that one only of the bullets cripples the jogger. It is impossible to show whose bullet caused the damage. No sensible person would deny the

---

84   [1987] QB 730.
85   [1988] 1 All ER 659.
86   [1987] QB 781, CA.
87   [2002] 3 WLR 89, MLC 0786.

jogger his claim, but would say that, as both the hunters had negligently created the identical risk of an injury which in fact materialised, they should both be liable. That is the effect of the House of Lords judgment. Incidentally, it is worth noting on the side that neither counsel nor the court suggested that each individual employer should only be liable for part of the compensation due to the injured employee.

Despite Lord Bridge's comments in *Wilsher* that *McGhee* did not introduce any new principle of causation because the conclusion of the House of Lords was merely based on a factual inference that they drew in the circumstances of the case (to the effect that the evidence established to their satisfaction that the failure to provide showers had in fact made a material contribution to the claimant contracting the dermatitis) a large part of the speeches of the House in *Fairchild* was devoted to a minute analysis of what the judges in *McGhee* had and what they had not said. Their conclusion (by a clear majority of four to one) was that the *McGhee* decision was not based on any inference from the evidence but did indeed propose a new principle of causation, albeit in the limited circumstances that the House was now prepared to endorse.

What then are those limited circumstances?

Lord Bingham said that such injustice as there might be in imposing liability on a duty-breaking employer, who might not in fact have been the one responsible for injuring the claimant, was heavily outweighed by the injustice of denying redress to a victim (and all his brethren went on to agree with him). However, this attribution of liability to a defendant where he had not on traditional legal principles been proved to have caused the claimant's injury was limited, for the present time at any rate, to a scenario where certain conditions were satisfied. The conditions specified by Lord Bingham are tightly based around the facts of the instant case, and require that an employee should have contracted mesothelioma from inhaling asbestos dust at some time while working for one or other of a number of different employers, all of whom had been negligent in relation to the risk of contracting such an injury, and that because of the current limits of human science the claimant should be unable to prove within whose employment he had in fact contracted the injury. Clearly the rule as so defined is of no use in medical negligence claims. However, Lord Bingham said that it would be unrealistic to suppose that the principle that he was affirming would not over time be the subject of incremental and analogical development, but he did not suggest more specific possibilities.

Lord Nicholls, agreeing in effect with the full tenor of Lord Bingham's judgment, said that the principle must be closely confined in its application or it could become a source of injustice to defendants. There must be good reason for departing from the normal threshold 'but for' test, and the reason must be sufficiently weighty to justify depriving the defendant of the protection that test normally and rightly afforded him. Policy questions would loom large. It was not possible to be more specific.

Lord Hoffmann said that it was open to the House to formulate a special rule of causal relationship in the type of case with which they were dealing. Otherwise guilty employers would escape all liability and negligently injured claimants would never achieve compensation. He, too, made it clear that this exceptional rule was being limited to the salient facts of the instant case. But he, like the House of Lords in *Wilsher*, rejected the reasoning of the Court of Appeal in that case, which was based on their belief that *McGhee* established a general principle that, where a defendant had materially increased the risk of a claimant sustaining a particular injury, that was enough to prove that he had made a material contribution to the injury. He said that, unlike the instant case, it could not be said that the duty to take reasonable care in treating patients would be virtually drained of content unless the creation of a material risk of injury were accepted as sufficient to satisfy the causal requirements for liability. The political and economic arguments involved in the massive increase in liability of the NHS which would have been a consequence of the broad rule favoured by the Court of Appeal in *Wilsher*'s case were far more complicated than the reasons given in *McGhee* for imposing liability upon an employer who failed to take simple precautions. Nevertheless he too indicated that the rule might well be capable of development and application in new situations.

Lord Rodger concluded that the claimants should be taken in law to have proved a material contribution to their injury by defendants who had been shown to have by their negligence materially increased the risk of them contracting mesothelioma. Then he, alone of the judges, went on to suggest the more general conditions within which the new principle should apply. This is useful because the new rule obviously has to be definable in terms not restricted to an employee developing mesothelioma from being exposed to asbestos while in more than one employment. There must be a more general rule underlying that specific instance of it. In essence he proposed the following:

- the necessary causation must be unprovable by current science;
- the defendant's conduct must have materially increased the risk of injury to the claimant and must have been capable of causing the injury;
- significantly, the claimant must prove that his injury was in fact caused by the sort of risk that the defendant had negligently created. So if other risks of a different nature could have caused the injury the principle would not apply. *Wilsher* is an example of this. The agencies implicated in creating the risks must operate in substantially the same way. He said that the principle applied where the other source(s) of the injury involved lawful conduct by the same defendant but *quaere* if the conduct was that of another person or a natural occurrence.

The reason the principle would not apply in a case like *Wilsher* is that there were a number of different agents that could have caused the RLF (retrolental fibroplasia, an ophthalmic disease) and excess oxygen was only one of them. The other possible causes were of a completely different nature. The defendants were only implicated in respect of the excess oxygen risk. Had the trial judge made a finding of fact that excess oxygen was the most likely cause, the claimant would have succeeded. But he did not – probably because there was no evidence on which such a finding could properly be based. He merely applied the *McGhee* principle, as did the Court of Appeal. The House of Lords said, as they have also done in the *Fairchild* case, that such an application was not permissible. As Lord Rodger said at [107]:

The principle does not apply where the claimant has merely proved that his injury could have been caused by a number of different events, only one of which is the eventuation of the risk created by the defendant's wrongful act or omission. This will usually mean that the claimant must prove that his injury was caused, if not by exactly the same agency as was involved in the defendant's wrongdoing, at least by an agent that operated in substantially the same way.

In speaking to the Personal Injury Bar Association in 2002, Lord Hope said:

> It is clear that the law will not soften its demands without a clear and compelling reason. So it must be demonstrated by evidence that there was only one possible cause, that in subjecting the claimant to that cause the defendant was in breach of its duty of care and that by doing so it materially increased the risk of injury. But it must also be demonstrated that it is not possible to go further and establish the causal link which the law normally requires. If that is the case, a material increase in the risk will be sufficient to satisfy the causal requirements for liability.

Cases applying Fairchild

The application of the *Fairchild* principle to clinical negligence cases may be limited (see below). The House of Lords have been at pains to point out that the principle is applicable only to mesothelioma cases or to those that are closely analogous: see *Novartis Grimsby v Cookson*[88] where exposure to amines doubled the risk of bladder cancer; and *Heneghan v Manchester Dry Docks Ltd*,[89] where the Court of Appeal held that lung cancer contracted from asbestos was indistinguishable in law from mesothelioma, ie an indivisible disease in respect of which causation could not be established either by the 'but for' or material contribution to the disease. Although compare *Brown v Corus (UK) Ltd*,[90] where the Court of Appeal held an employer liable for causing a vibration syndrome where it had materially increased the risk of the claimant contracting the disease, even though the precise reduction in the exposure that proper management would have brought about could not be known. Note that there was no question of more than one possible cause here. There was only the proof that the employer was in breach for not having taken steps to reduce the exposure.

The House of Lords considered another mesothelioma case in *Barker v Corus*.[91] The main issue in this case was apportionment, an issue not raised in *Fairchild*. It was held (reversing the decision of the Court of Appeal) that a defendant should only be liable to the extent that it had materially increased the risk of injury. This decision has been reversed as far as mesothelioma cases is concerned by s 3 of the Compensation Act 2006, so that in effect, as against the claimant, all defendants who have materially increased the risk of the claimant developing mesothelioma are jointly and severally liable to compensate him for his entire loss. However, all other cases that fall within the *Fairchild* exception are

---

88 [2007] EWCA Civ 1261.
89 [2016] EWCA Civ 86.
90 [2004] PIQR P476.
91 [2006] 2 AC 572.

governed by *Barker* and therefore subject to apportionment. This leads to the potentially anomalous position that a tortfeasor who materially contributes to an injury is liable for the whole injury (assuming it is not possible to prove the extent of the contribution), whereas a tortfeasor who materially increases the risk of injury is only liable for the extent to which he has increased the risk (in practice the percentage of total duration of exposure to the noxious agent for which the defendant is responsible).

In *Hull v Sanderson*,[92] the Court of Appeal made it clear that the *Fairchild* exception would only operate in a personal injury case where it was impossible to show which of two or more causes had resulted in injury. In this case, an infection contracted in a turkey factory by a claimant could have occurred in several different ways, any of which was capable of proof on the balance of probabilities.

The Supreme Court more recently revisited the *Fairchild* exception when considering the issue of whether the rule can apply in cases where only one defendant is proved to have exposed the victims to asbestos, but where the victims themselves were also at risk of developing the disease from environmental exposure. In *Sienkiewicz v Greif (UK) Ltd*; *Knowsley MBC v Willmore*,[93] it was held that the exception applies to cases of mesothelioma involving a single defendant so long as it can be demonstrated that the single defendant 'materially increased the risk' of the victim contracting mesothelioma. Lord Phillips stated at [108] that:

> I doubt whether it is ever possible to define, in quantitative terms, what for the purposes of the application of any principle of law, is de minimis. This must be a question for the judge on the facts of the particular case. In the case of mesothelioma, a stage must be reached at which, even allowing for the possibility that exposure to asbestos can have a cumulative effect, a particular exposure is too insignificant to be taken into account, having regard to the overall exposure that has taken place.

He further went on to state at [111]:

> The reality is that, in the current state of knowledge about the disease, the only circumstances in which a court will be able to conclude that wrongful exposure of a mesothelioma victim to asbestos dust did not materially increase the victim's risk of contracting the disease will be where that exposure was insignificant compared to the exposure from other sources.

Subsequent cases have confirmed that even relatively small contributions to the risk are material. In *Carder v Secretary of State for Health*[94] an asbestosis sufferer was entitled to damages from a former employer who had been responsible for just 2.3% of his total exposure to asbestos dust. Although that contribution was very small, it made a material contribution to the claimant's condition. He was awarded damages worth 2.3% of what would have been the full liability value of his claim. In *Mayne v Atlas Stone Co Ltd*[95] the deceased was exposed to asbestos by three employers. He served proceedings against the single insured one (responsible for 8.16% of the exposure). His death was unrelated to the asbestos-induced pleural thickening, which represented 5% of his overall disability. Cox J

---

92   [2009] PIQR P114.
93   [2011] UKSC 10.
94   [2016] EWCA Civ 790.
95   [2016] EWHC 1030 (QB).

held, applying *Carder* that an 8.16% contribution to 5% disability was small but still material. The correct approach to assessing damages was to assess the damages otherwise awardable for the 5% disability and then to apportion an amount to the second defendant relative to its contribution to the overall asbestos exposure. The appropriate award was 8.16% of £12,600, namely £1,208.

One additional aspect of the *Sienkiewicz* decision worth noting is that the Supreme Court rejected the epidemiological argument that in a single exposure case there was a requirement to demonstrate that the defendant's breach of duty doubled the risk of developing the disease. Lord Phillips addressed when it was appropriate to use epidemiological evidence and stated at [90]–[93]:

> ... I see no scope for the application of the 'doubles the risk' test in cases where two agents have operated cumulatively and simultaneously in causing the onset of a disease. In such a case the rule in *Bonnington* applies. Where the disease is indivisible, such as lung cancer, a defendant who has tortiously contributed to the cause of the disease will be liable in full. Where the disease is divisible, such as asbestosis, the tortfeasor will be liable in respect of the share of the disease for which he is responsible.

> Where the initiation of the disease is dose related, and there have been consecutive exposures to an agent or agents that cause the disease, one innocent and one tortious, the position will depend upon which exposure came first in time. Where it was the tortious exposure, it is axiomatic that this will have contributed to causing the disease, even if it is not the sole cause. Where the innocent exposure came first, there may be an issue as to whether this was sufficient to trigger the disease or whether the subsequent, tortious, exposure contributed to the cause. I can see no reason in principle why the 'doubles the risk' test should not be applied in such circumstances, but the court must be astute to see that the epidemiological evidence provides a really sound basis for determining the statistical probability of the cause or causes of the disease.

> ... Where there are competing alternatives, rather than cumulative, potential causes of a disease or injury, such as in *Hotson,* I can see no reason in principle why epidemiological evidence should not be used to show that one of the causes was more than twice as likely as all the others put together to have caused the disease or injury.

Lord Toulson also cautioned against the 'doubling the risk' approach in a medical context (*Williams* above, at [28]):

> Finally, reference was made during the argument to the 'doubling of risk' test which has sometimes been used or advocated as a tool used in deciding questions of causation. The Board would counsel caution in its use. As Baroness Hale of Richmond JSC said in *Sienkiewicz* [...], evaluation of risk can be important in making choices about future action. This is particularly so in the medical field, where a practitioner will owe a duty to the patient to see that the patient is properly informed about the potential risks of different forms of treatment (or non-treatment). Use of such evidence, for example epidemiological evidence, to determine questions of past fact is rather different. That is not to deny that it may sometimes be very helpful. If it is a known fact that a particular type of act (or omission) is likely to have a particular effect, proof that the defendant was responsible for such an act (or omission) and that the claimant had what is the usual effect will be powerful evidence from which to infer causation, without necessarily requiring a detailed scientific explanation for the link. But inferring causation from proof of heightened risk is never an exercise to apply mechanistically. A doubled tiny risk will still be very small.

Relevance to medical cases

There are many scenarios where proof that proper management would have avoided the injury is lacking. Up until now such a claim has been lost for failure to prove causation. Strictly interpreted, it seems that for a *Fairchild* argument to succeed, there would have to be more than one possible cause, proof that the defendant materially increased the risk of the injury, and that the limits of science made it impossible to establish causation in the normal way. However, if we allow ourselves a broader base for the rule, it does not take much imagination to envisage how the more usual claim where, simply, causation is weak could have a chance now of succeeding with the aid of a cleverly formulated argument based on 'material increase in risk'. One awaits such an event with eager anticipation.

Divisibility/apportionment

If it is proved that a cause made a material contribution to an injury, recovery can be made for the whole of the injury, leaving the tortfeasors (if more than one) to sue each other for contribution. So if an injury is caused by negligent cause A or non-negligent cause B and the claimant is unable to establish on the balance of probability that cause A rather than B is the effective cause of the injury, then the claimant will fail to establish causation. However, if the claimant can establish that the cause of the injury is a combination of causes, ie A *and* B and that it is not possible to say to what extent each cause has contributed to injury, then the claimant has established causation and should recover in full. The rationale for full recovery is presumably that it would not be just to an injured claimant to simply guess the extent of the contribution made by the negligent cause. In practice, the potential effects of negligent and non-negligent causes in clinical negligence cases are often argued about and the subject of compromise in the form of apportionment of damages between respective causes. Experts are often asked to say how much better the claimant would have been, for example, without the negligence. Very often there is little or no scientific basis for the answers that are given. Cases proceed on informed guesswork as to what might have been without the negligence.

In *Holtby v Brigham & Cowan (Hull) Ltd*,[96] Stuart-Smith LJ held at [20]:

> The onus of proving causation is on the claimant; it does not shift to the defendant. He will be entitled to succeed if he can prove that the defendant's tortious conduct made a material contribution to his disability. Strictly speaking the defendant is liable only to the extent of that contribution.

Around a similar time, Lord Bingham stated at [142] of *Chester*:

> It is trite law that damage is the gist of the action in the tort of negligence. ... A claimant is entitled to be compensated for the damage which the negligence of another has caused to him or her. A defendant is bound to compensate the claimant for the damage which his or her negligence has caused the claimant. But the corollaries are also true: a claimant is not entitled to be compensated,

---

96   [2000] Lloyd's Rep Med 254, [2000] PIQR Q293.

and a defendant is not bound to compensate the claimant, for damage not caused by the negligence complained of.

These comments are not easy to reconcile with the established law on material contribution in causation (ie that if a material contribution to an injury is proven as against one tortfeasor, they are liable to compensate for the whole of the injury). It might be taken to mean that where two separate agencies (hospitals, doctors, etc) are responsible for a patient's injury, only a percentage of the damages can be recovered from each.

However, *Holtby* need not and should not be interpreted so widely. The key to its proper interpretation (if there is one) lies in the concept of a *divisible injury*, ie one where it is clear that the defendant could not have been responsible for more than a part of the injury *and* it is just that he should not pay for the whole of the injury. The facts in this claim for injury from exposure to asbestos dust were that the claimant had only spent half the period of exposure at the defendant's site. It appeared from the medical evidence that the claimant's condition would have been better if he had only been exposed while working for the defendant. It was therefore successfully argued that a part of the injury had not been caused by the defendant. Obviously, apportioning the injury could only be a matter of impression (the trial judge was said to have been generous when he applied a discount of only 25%). But this concept of apportionment of injury (and hence of compensation) is ripe for abuse. If applied at all, it should only be applied in cases where: (a) it is reasonable to discern different injuries or at any rate different levels of injury as having been caused by different tortfeasors (or a tortfeasor and a non-tortfeasor); and (b) it is reasonable to deny the injured party full compensation from a particular defendant.

The limits of the *Holtby* principle were described by the Court of Appeal in the personal injury case of *Environment Agency v Ellis*.[97] In that case the claimant suffered a back injury at work. Liability was established without contribution. He was also diagnosed with symptomless degenerative change in his back which would have developed in any event regardless of injury. Subsequently the claimant fell at home and suffered further injury. The defendant submitted that there should be an apportionment between the various causes (70% pre-existing condition, 20% to the accident at work, and 10% to the fall at home). The trial judge awarded the claimant 90% of his damages. The defendant appealed and the claimant cross appealed. The Court of Appeal dismissed the appeal and allowed the cross appeal, awarding the claimant 100% of his damages. It was held that the asymptomatic back condition had not been proven to be a cause at all on the evidence and that the 10% reduction for the fall at home was not a truly divisible injury. The *Holtby* principle was usually to be confined to cases where there is successive harm caused by a number of different agencies where the harm is divisible.

In *AB v Ministry of Defence*,[98] Foskett J pointed out at [227] that 'whether damage is divisible or indivisible is a matter of fact and that there may be debatable borderline cases where that which is divisible or indivisible may not be immediately recognisable'.

---

97   [2009] PIQR P5.
98   [2009] EWHC 1225.

However, it is essential that the application of the divisibility concept be restricted to appropriate cases. Even where divisibility is discernible, it must be up to the good sense of the judge whether or not to apply the concept.

The Rahman *case*

In *Rahman v Arearose Ltd and University College London NHS Trust*,[99] the Court of Appeal was asked to decide on apportionment of liability in the unfortunately far too common situation where a non-medical negligent act causes a patient to present at hospital and then negligent medical treatment adds to the hitherto foreseeable adverse consequences of the original injury. Perhaps the original injury was sustained at work, or in a road traffic accident. It should have been minor, but negligent medical treatment, whether of commission or omission, has made it much worse. This scenario also raises the issue of 'breaking the chain of causation'. The two issues overlap; breaking the chain has a section to itself below. The facts can be simply stated: a manager at Burger King was viciously assaulted as a result of his employer not taking proper measures to protect him. Among his injuries was serious damage to one eye. However (this is not explicitly stated in the judgment but it must be so), he would probably not have lost the sight of that eye if he had not received admittedly negligent treatment at the hospital.

This is a type of situation that arises time and again in medico-legal practices. Is the answer to any suggestion for division of responsibility and compensation that the employer is not responsible in law for loss of the eye, as negligent medical treatment should not be deemed by the law (even though a common enough occurrence these days!) to be a foreseeable consequence, and is therefore a *novus actus*? If that is the correct answer, one has to apportion both general and special damage, so that the employer pays only for the foreseeable consequences of the injury, just as, if the initial injury had been a non-negligent accident, the hospital would only be liable for the extra slice of injury that it had caused (and the consequences of that extra slice).

Or should one hold both defendants liable in full, on the doctrine of material contribution, leaving apportionment to be defined as between the defendants?

Although this sort of situation is common, it seems never to have been the subject of litigation before (maybe such claims are virtually always settled by amicable division of responsibility). The nearest one can get to it are the many old cases under the Workmen's Compensation Act 1925 (eg *Hogan v West Hartley Bentinck Collieries (Owners) Ltd*[100]), where the injured workman had to prove that his disability had been caused by the accident rather than by the hospital's negligent treatment. Those cases are not particularly helpful as the social and policy considerations of the time would have been very different and because they were not straightforward tort cases, but involved decisions from arbitrators as to whether a disability fell within the words of the Act or not ('... results from the injury').

---

99   [2000] 3 WLR 1184.
100   [1949] 1 All ER 588, HL.

In the *Rahman* case, the parties appear to have expected the court to divide up the injury, or perhaps only as between the defendants. The psychiatrists had been asked to prepare a joint report which attempted in particular the extraordinary task of attributing different *aspects* of the very substantial psychiatric injury to the different torts (the assault and the medical treatment).

The salient issue in such a situation must be whether the doctrine of 'material contribution' is displaced by the doctrine of *novus actus*. However, at no point in the *Rahman* judgment (given only by Laws LJ) is there any reference to the doctrine of material contribution. In *Rahman*, the court, having declared for the purposes of apportionment under the Civil Liability (Contribution) Act 1978 that the two defendants were not concurrent tortfeasors, was then concerned to fix the proportion of liability which each defendant should bear *vis-à-vis* the claimant, there being no question of each being liable for the whole of the injury subject to apportionment among themselves.

Laws LJ said more than once that it would be wrong for a defendant to pay for any part of the injury or its consequences which, on the evidence, he clearly was not responsible for. In *Rahman*, the court went to infinite pains to divide up responsibility down to the last small head of special damage. After complex analysis of the different aspects of what was really an indivisible injury, the Court of Appeal upheld the judge's original apportionment of 25% to the employer and 75% to the hospital.

Dr John's case

A useful analysis of the material contribution to damage and material contribution to risk cases is the recent case of *John v Central Manchester & Manchester Children's University Hospitals Trust*,[101] where the claimant GP suffered a head injury falling down the stairs. There were negligent delays in performing a CT scan and requesting a transfer ambulance, such that neurosurgery was delayed by nearly six hours. Dr John was left with cognitive and neuropsychological deficits and suffered an adjustment disorder. It was agreed he would never work as a doctor again. Dr John claimed damages contending that the delay in undertaking the CT scan resulted in a period of raised intracranial pressure which had caused or materially contributed to his brain damage. He acknowledged that the classic 'but for' test could not operate since the expert medical analysis did not permit a 'but for' analysis to be made out.

The defendant said Dr John could not rely on the approach in *Bonnington, Bailey* and *Williams* as they were all cases in which a 'single agency' was involved. They were not multiple factor cases. This was a *Wilsher* type case of multiple possible causes. In oral argument the defendant's counsel modified this position and accepted that 'material contribution' would be sufficient in Dr John's case, but argued that he should only be permitted to recover to the extent that the defendant's negligence had materially contributed to the injury. It invited the court to apportion damages between the tortious and non-tortious causes.

Picken J held that this was a material contribution to *damage* not to *risk* case. Whereas 'material contribution to risk' cases required a single

---

101 [2016] EWHC 407 (QB).

causative agent, the 'material contribution to damage' could apply to both single agency and multiple factor cases (at [97]).

Further, in 'material contribution to damage' cases (as opposed to 'material contribution to risk' cases) the claimant was able to recover in relation to the entirety of his or her injury without the need for apportionment. He could not accept that an apportionment exercise of the sort carried out in *Holtby* could be right. He distinguished *Holtby* on the basis that there, apportionment was merely difficult to work out. He stated at [98]: 'I am quite clear that apportionment is not appropriate where it is not merely difficult but is impossible to allot particular loss to a particular cause.'

He considered that *Wilsher* had been wrongly understood by the defendant; it is not a barrier to claimants succeeding in multiple cause cases, but rather requires them to prove, on the balance of probabilities, that an individual cause materially contributed to the injury. If on the medical evidence, the claimant in *Wilsher* had been able to demonstrate that the excess oxygen had caused or materially contributed to his condition, there was no suggestion that he would not have been able to recover the full amount claimed.

Accordingly, in view of the expert evidence, the period of damaging raised intra-cranial pressure had made a material contribution to the claimant's brain injury and, causation having been established, the claimant was entitled to recover without deduction (at [101] and [105]).

BAE Systems

BAE Systems (Operations) Ltd v Konczak[102] began as an employment tribunal sex and disability discrimination case. Following a comment about her ability to cope as a woman, the claimant suffered a mental breakdown and was certified as unfit for work. In relation to assessment of damages, the claimant acknowledged that she had a history of stress and problems at work before the line manager's comment. However, the tribunal found that it was inappropriate to apportion damages because the psychiatric injury was indivisible and had been triggered by a discriminatory comment.

The Employment Appeal Tribunal and Court of Appeal both dismissed the employer's appeals. The Court of Appeal held that in cases where there were multiple extrinsic causes of psychiatric injury, a sensible attempt should be made to apportion the harm, but there might be cases where the harm was indivisible and apportionment would be wrong. Applying the reasoning of Laws LJ in *Rahman*, Underhill LJ held (at [56]):

'For our purposes it is enough to refer to two essential propositions, as follows.

(1) At common law wrongdoers who together cause 'a single indivisible injury' are each liable to compensate the claimant for the whole of the injury suffered: see para 17.
(2) An injury is to be regarded as single and indivisible 'where there is simply no rational basis for an objective apportionment of causative responsibility for [it]': see para 19.

---

102 [2017] EWCA Civ 1188.

He went on to say, relying on parts of the Court of Appeal decision in *Hatton v Sutherland*[103] that had been endorsed by the House of Lords, that in the case of psychiatric injury, where a claimant suddenly tipped over from being under stress into being ill, the tribunal should seek to find a rational basis for distinguishing between a part of the illness due to the employer's wrong and a part due to other causes. However, if there was no such basis, the injury would be truly indivisible, and the claimant was required to be compensated for the whole of the injury.

Where the tortfeasor's breach of duty has exacerbated a pre-existing disorder or accelerated the effect of pre-existing vulnerability, the award of damages will reflect only the exacerbation or acceleration. It is often appropriate to look closely, particularly in a case where psychiatric injury proved indivisible, to establish whether the pre-existing state might not nevertheless demonstrate a high degree of vulnerability to, and the probability of, future injury in any event.

Underhill LJ preferred the suggestion in *Hatton* that psychiatric injury could, as a matter of principle, be divisible, to the views expressed by Smith LJ in *Dickins v O2*[104] that psychiatric injury was always indivisible. This would accord with the approach taken in *Rahman* (made easier by the approach of the medical experts).

He concluded at [72]:

> That distinction [ie apportioning liability] is easy enough to apply in the case of a straightforward physical injury. A broken leg is 'indivisible': if it was suffered as a result of two torts, each tortfeasor is liable for the whole, and any question of the relative degree of 'causative potency' (or culpability) is relevant only to contribution under the 1978 Act. It is less easy in the case of psychiatric harm. The message of *Hatton* is that such harm may well be divisible. In *Rahman* the exercise was made easier by the fact (see para 57 above) that the medical evidence distinguished between different elements in the claimant's overall condition, and their causes, though even there it must be recognised that the attributions were both partial and approximate. In many, I suspect most, cases the tribunal will not have that degree of assistance. But it does not follow that no apportionment will be possible. It may, for example, be possible to conclude that a pre-existing illness, for which the employer is not responsible, has been materially aggravated by the wrong (in terms of severity of symptoms and/or duration), and to award compensation reflecting the extent of the aggravation. The most difficult type of case is that posited by Smith LJ in her article, and which she indeed treats, rightly or wrongly, as the most typical: that is where 'the claimant will have cracked up quite suddenly; tipped over from being under stress into being ill.' On my understanding of *Rahman* and *Hatton*, even in that case the tribunal should seek to find a rational basis for distinguishing between a part of the illness which is due to the employer's wrong and a part which is due to other causes; but whether that is possible will depend on the facts and the evidence. If there is no such basis, then the injury will indeed be, in Hale LJ's words, 'truly indivisible', and principle requires that the claimant is compensated for the whole of the injury—though, importantly, if (as Smith LJ says will be typically the case) the claimant has a vulnerable personality, a discount may be required in accordance with proposition 16.

---

103 [2002] ICR 613.
104 [2008] EWCA Civ 1144.

Conclusion

In many medical negligence cases, the most that the patient is given by his causation expert is that proper treatment would probably have reduced the injury. It is then important to achieve some sort of definition of the extra slice of injury, partly in order to be able to assess general damages, and partly (and usually more significantly) in order to define what special damage (whether in the form of care, transport needs, accommodation or whatever) can be attributed to the extra slice of injury. In that particular context, it is surely necessary to establish that the aids, equipment and care etc claimed for would not have been necessary without the extra slice of injury.

The recent authorities indicate that a claimant will recover damages in full in the case of a truly indivisible injury but in cases of divisible injury, the court should make a sensible attempt to apportion damages only for that part of the injury that was attributable to the defendant's negligence.

BREAKING THE CHAIN OF CAUSATION

As we have seen, an intervening act or event occurring after the original act of negligence may operate to break the chain of causation, with the result that the wrongdoer is not liable for loss caused by that event. There is no clear test or formula for deciding whether an act, which may be of a third party or of the claimant himself, and may be lawful or unlawful, voluntary or involuntary, will break the chain of causation. As held by Lord Neuberger MR in *Wright* (above, at [32]):

> ... where there are successive tortfeasors, the contention that the causative potency of the negligence of the first is destroyed by the subsequent negligence of the second depends very much on the facts of the particular case. In many cases where there are successive acts of negligence by different parties, both parties can be held responsible for the damage which ensues, so that the issue is not which of them is liable, but how liability is to be apportioned between them. The mere fact that, if the second party had not been negligent, the damage which subsequently ensued would not have occurred, by no means automatically exonerates the first party's negligence from being causative of that damage.

The most useful test is to ask whether the act was reasonably foreseeable at the time of the original negligence, but that is not conclusive of the issue. The court will in any event judge each case on its own facts and decide the question according to its own view of whether justice requires the tortfeasor to compensate the claimant for the additional damage suffered from the intervening act.

The court will adjudge an effect too remote where it regards it as inappropriate that the wrongdoer should be made liable in respect of it. In such cases it may be said that the effect is not to be regarded in law as having been caused by the original negligence. This may be so even though the effect appears to be both directly and foreseeably caused by the negligence, without any intervening act that could be said to have broken the chain of causation. Where, however, there is such an intervening act, whether of human agency, lawful or unlawful, voluntary or involuntary, or whether of a third party or of the claimant himself, or whether it be an event which is not of human origination, the court is free, if it chooses, to say that the intervening act, which in the case of a third party's act and sometimes in the case of the claimant is described by the Latin tag of *novus actus interveniens* (an independent supervening act), breaks the chain of causation, so that the damage flowing from it cannot be regarded in law as having been caused by the original negligence.

It is by no means easy to predict when such an intervening act will be regarded as breaking the chain of causation. At times, the test applied seems to have been whether the intervening act was reasonable in the circumstances, but currently the question seems to turn on foreseeability, though that is not necessarily conclusive of the issue. Was it reasonably foreseeable that the intervening act would occur? On that basis, the courts have several times ruled on a wrongdoer's liability for the criminal acts of third parties (*Stansbie v Troman*;[105] *Lamb v Camden London Borough Council*;[106] *Ward v Cannock Chase District Council*;[107] *P Perl (Exporters) Ltd v Camden London Borough Council*;[108] *King v Liverpool City Council*;[109] *Smith v Littlewoods Organisation Ltd*[110]). Compare also *Topp v London Country Bus (South West) Ltd*,[111] with *Grand Metropolitan plc v Closed Circuit Cooling Ltd*[112] (vehicles left with keys in ignition: an unlawful taking was not a *novus actus*).

Lord Reid said in *Home Office v Dorset Yacht Co*[113] that for a *novus actus* not to break the chain of causation, it would have to be an act which was likely or probable to happen; but Lord Denning and Watkins LJ took a contrary view in *Lamb*'s case (above), where a judicious mix of 'reasonable foreseeability' and 'policy' was applied to deny recovery. Watkins LJ said that a robust and sensible approach to the question of remoteness would often produce an instinctive feeling that the event or act being weighed in the balance was too remote to sound in damages (this is the 'judicial hunch' or 'gut reaction' referred to, from time to time, above). Lord Denning said at 636–637:

> ... it is not every consequence of a wrongful act which is the subject of compensation. The law has to draw a line somewhere. Sometimes it is done by limiting the range of persons to whom duty is owed. Sometimes it is done by saying that there is a break in the chain of causation. At other times it is done by saying that the consequence is too remote to be a head of damage. All these devices are useful in their way. But ultimately it is a question of policy for the judges to decide ...

> It seems to me that it is a question of policy which we, as judges, have to decide. The time has come when, in cases of new import, we should decide them according to the reason of the thing. In previous times, when faced with a new problem, the judges have not openly asked themselves the question: what is the best policy for the law to adopt? But the question has always been there

---

105 [1948] 2 KB 48, CA.
106 [1981] QB 625, CA.
107 [1985] 3 All ER 537.
108 [1984] QB 342, CA.
109 [1986] 1 WLR 890, CA.
110 [1987] AC 241, HL.
111 [1993] 1 WLR 976, CA.
112 [1997] JPIL 191.
113 [1970] AC 1004, HL.

in the background. It has been concealed behind such questions as: Was the defendant under any duty to the plaintiff? Was the relationship between them sufficiently proximate? Was the injury direct or indirect? Was it foreseeable or not? Was it too remote? And so forth. Nowadays we direct ourselves to considerations of policy.

But the guidelines of foreseeability, remoteness etc, must still serve a purpose. Policy is an unruly and unpredictable steed. It may tip the balance in many cases, but if it is the only criterion the law becomes fearfully uncertain, and depends only on the view of the particular tribunal. It is still necessary and appropriate for cases to be argued on the lines of the law as set out in the precedents, as far as the legal principles can be gleaned therefrom, and even if that is not very far it is better than nothing.

Where an injury is subsumed into a later injury (eg a broken leg is then severed in a later accident), the original tortfeasor remains liable for the damage he did, and cannot take advantage of the later event to reduce his liability (*Baker v Willoughby*[114]); but a supervening serious illness which was unconnected with the accident and which was already dormant within the claimant at the time of the accident will go to reduce the damages payable (*Jobling v Associated Dairies Ltd*[115]). If a car is already damaged so that a wing needs respraying, a defendant who crashes into that wing cannot be held liable for the cost of the respraying, only for any extra cost he puts the owner to (*Performance Cars Ltd v Abraham*[116]).

This issue of supervening cause, like all aspects of causation, is a fruitful source of academic disputation, and for the practitioner admits of no easy formula. Lord Wilberforce said in *Jobling's* case (above) that no general, logical, or universally fair rules could be stated, which would cover, in a manner consistent with justice, cases of supervening events, whether due to tortious, partially tortious, non-culpable or wholly accidental events. The courts could only deal with each case as best they could to provide just but not excessive compensation.

In *Hogan v West Bentinck Hartley Collieries (Owners) Ltd*,[117] where an injury at work to a workman's thumb was followed by an ill-advised amputation of the thumb, it was held by a bare majority in the House of Lords that that unreasonable operation broke the chain of causation (Lord Simonds said that the question of *novus actus* could only be answered on a consideration of all the circumstances and, in particular, the quality of the later act or event). In *Roberts v Bettany*,[118] the court said it was a question of whether the intervening act was of so powerful a nature that the conduct of the defendants was not a cause at all but merely part of the surrounding circumstances.

In the Australian case of *Martin v Isbard*,[119] where after being involved in an accident, the claimant contracted an anxiety and litigation neurosis because she was wrongly told by her doctor that she had suffered a fracture of the skull, it was held that the advice given by the doctor broke the chain of causation as it was a *novus actus*.

---

114 [1970] AC 467, HL.
115 [1982] AC 794, HL.
116 [1962] 1 QB 33, CA.
117 [1949] 1 All ER 588.
118 (22 January 2001, unreported), CA.
119 (1946) 48 WALR 52.

It was held in *Robinson v Post Office*,[120] that where the Post Office had through their original negligence caused the minor leg injury of their employee, the claimant, the doctor's negligence in failing to administer a test dose before injecting with an anti-tetanus serum did not break the chain of causation. They had to take the claimant as they found him, which included his allergy to the anti-tetanus serum.

Where the act is that of the claimant himself, a number of other factors come into play. If that act is so unreasonable as to eclipse the defendant's wrongdoing, then it will have broken the chain of causation and the defendant will not be liable for the ensuing damage. An odd example of this is the South African case of *Alston v Marine and Trade Insurance Co Ltd*,[121] where the fact that the claimant, who had suffered brain injury in a motor accident, ate cheese while on a certain drug and as a result suffered a stroke, was held to break the chain of causation even though the claimant could not have known it was dangerous to do that.

An example of a case where the conduct of the claimant did not break the chain of causation is *Emeh v Kensington and Chelsea and Westminster Area Health Authority*,[122] where the Court of Appeal in no uncertain terms reversed the trial judge's finding that the refusal of an abortion by a woman who had become pregnant after a negligently performed sterilisation was so unreasonable an act that it eclipsed the original negligence. However, compare this with *Sabri-Tabrizi v Lothian Health Board*,[123] where Lord Nimmo-Smith held at first instance that a woman's decision to continue intercourse with the protection of a condom after she knew that her sterilisation had failed was a *novus actus,* so that the defendants were not liable for a pregnancy that occurred despite the condom.

There is considerable material on *novus actus* in *Reeves v Metropolitan Police Comr*,[124] where the police were found to be negligent in closing the flap on the door of a cell where they were holding a prisoner who was known to be a suicide risk (despite being sane). By a majority, the Court of Appeal held that the voluntary act of the deceased in committing suicide was not a *novus actus*. The House of Lords agreed, stating that a deliberate and informed act intended to exploit a situation created by a defendant did not negative causation where the defendant was in breach of a specific duty imposed by law to guard against that very act. Neither the defence of *novus actus* nor that of *volenti non fit iniuria* (meaning that the claimant took upon himself by his deliberate and conscious act the risk of harm) could succeed. But a defence of contributory negligence did succeed to the tune of 50% of the compensation otherwise due (see the section below on contributory negligence). In *Gill v Home Office*,[125] there was held to be no *novus actus* where an inadequately detained prisoner with a history of violence assaulted a prison officer when allowed to go to slop out unaccompanied. The court said that the injury sustained was the very kind of injury that was foreseeable if he were let out.

---

120 [1974] 1 WLR 1176, CA.
121 1964 (4) SA 112.
122 [1985] QB 1012.
123 1998 SC 373.
124 [1998] QB 169, CA, revsd [2000] 1 AC 360, HL.
125 (6 July 2000, unreported), CA.

In *Spencer v Wincanton Holdings*,[126] a claimant who had suffered a road accident leading to amputation of his leg who then tripped and suffered further injury some three years later was held by the Court of Appeal not to have broken the chain of causation from the original accident by his own act. The finding of 33% contributory negligence was not appealed.

In *Dalling v Heale*,[127] the claimant suffered a head injury for which the defendant was 75% liable. His injury reduced his ability to control his excessive drinking. Three and a half years later he suffered further head injuries when he fell over intoxicated. The judge held that the head injuries sustained in the first accident had had a causative effect in relation to the second accident. The judge also held that it was fair and just that the defendant be held liable. However, he also held that the claimant had failed to take reasonable care so that damages in respect of the second accident fell to be reduced by one third to reflect D's contributory negligence. The Court of Appeal dismissed the appeal; the defendant's tort had impaired the claimant's ability to control his drinking so that when the second accident occurred it was not an act of free volition, but an act for which both parties were partly responsible.

We may here add to our treatment of the 'divisible injury' in this way: given that a fairly common scenario in the medical context where a defendant seeks to take advantage of a plea of *novus actus* is where both GP and hospital have been negligent, the former for not making earlier referral and the latter for not treating the injury or disease competently, it is clear that the GP should not be heard to say that he can escape liability because the hospital should have cured the problem. That is tantamount to resurrecting the ancient doctrine of 'last opportunity' (under which only the person who had the last opportunity to avoid the accident was liable). The correct answer is that they are both tortfeasors and both responsible, in such proportion as the court directs, for the relevant compensation. A more subtle argument on the part of the GP would be to contend that it would have made no difference if he had referred earlier because the patient would have received the same incompetent and ineffective treatment from the hospital. One answer to that contention would be to satisfy the court that the patient would probably have received competent treatment (ie competent and curative treatment; see the section on the presumption of this above). Even if the GP proved that, although the patient could have been cured by competent treatment, the hospital would on earlier referral probably still have provided incompetent treatment, one would hope that the court would nevertheless find that both GP and hospital played a material part in causing the injury for which compensation is claimed, rather than finding that in the circumstances the GP's negligence was not causative of injury.

In the common dual liability situation for a patient's claim, where the original accident, whether road traffic, or employment or whatever, is mistreated at hospital, it appears from the material we have considered above under 'Divisibility/apportionment' that a court would not simply hold that the medical negligence broke the chain of causation. More likely, it would apportion the damages as between the two defendants in such proportion as it considered was merited by their respective fault.

126 [2009] EWCA 1404.
127 [2011] EWCA Civ 365.

In *Webb v Barclays Bank plc and Portsmouth Hospitals NHS Trust*[128] the claimant fell and injured herself through the negligence of the first defendant, an injury which led to amputation through the negligence of the second defendant. The Court of Appeal said that, on the point of contribution as between the defendants, the question was whether, when an employee was injured in the service and by the negligence of her employer, his liability to her is terminated by the intervening negligence of a doctor brought in to treat the original injury, but who in fact made it worse. The answer was that the chain of causation in such a case would only be broken where the medical treatment was of such a degree of negligence as to be an entirely inappropriate response to the injury. Such was not the instant case. Perhaps then it can be said that only gross clinical negligence will break the chain of causation from the original negligent event. Responsibility was assessed at 25% for the first and 75% for the second defendant. In *Panther v Wharton*,[129] the deputy High Court judge came to a similar conclusion where the chain was from GP to hospital ('Dr Wharton's negligence [at the hospital] was not a *novus actus interveniens*: it did not cause the need for the amputations, he failed to act so as to prevent them. That omission did not constitute an event of such impact that it obliterated the wrongdoing of Dr Adegoko [the GP]').

In *Wright* (see above), Lord Neuberger MR did not consider that the hospital's failure to treat the claimant once she was admitted (such admission had been delayed by earlier negligence by the GP) justified a finding that the GP's negligence was not causative of the claimant's injury, or indeed a finding that it broke the chain of causation between the defendants' negligence and the claimant's injury. He said at [37]:

> It was not such an egregious event, in terms of the degree or unusualness of the negligence, or the period of time for which it lasted, to defeat or destroy the causative link between the defendants' negligence and the claimant's injury.

In *Razumas v Ministry of Justice*,[130] Cockerhill J held that, had the claimant succeeded on liability in respect of negligent medical care by the prison service, he would have found that his deliberate failure to seek medical attention during periods when his was not in custody would have amounted to an intervening cause, preventing recovery for any established breach during his time in prison. He noted, at [202]:

> It seems likely that his reason for doing so was that he did not want to bring himself to the attention of the authorities, given that he had reverted to criminal behaviour. That may be understandable (as was argued on his behalf) on an empathetic level, it is not however, as a matter of law, reasonable behaviour. His actions therefore in my judgement amount to an intervening cause, preventing recovery for any established breach relating to this period.

In *Darnley v Croydon Health Services NHS Trust*,[131] the Supreme Court held that the that the claimant's reasonably foreseeable decision to leave the accident and emergency department after 19 minutes (which had been made in reliance on negligent advice about waiting times) had not broken the chain of causation which had resulted in his injury.

---

128 [2001] MLC 0400, [2002] PIQR P61.
129 [2001] MLC 0358.
130 [2018] EWHC 215 (QB).
131 [2018] UKSC 50.

DUTY TO MITIGATE

Another principle that falls to be considered in this context is the rule
that a claimant is under a duty to take reasonable steps to minimise
his loss; if those steps include submitting to medical examination and
accepting medical treatment, then failure so to do will go to reduce
the award (*Selvanayagam v University of West Indies*[132]). In *Geest plc v
Lansiquot*,[133] the Privy Council said that if a defendant intends to contend
that a claimant has failed to act reasonably to mitigate his loss, notice of
such contention should be clearly given long enough before the hearing
to enable the claimant properly to prepare to meet it, and the onus of
proving unreasonable refusal of medical treatment is on the defendant.

CONTRIBUTORY NEGLIGENCE

Where some blameworthiness attaches to the claimant's conduct, in
that he has shown a failure to take proper care for his own safety, the
matter can be dealt with by a proportionate reduction in the award on
the principle of contributory negligence. That is not very likely to arise
in medical negligence cases, but an example is *Brushett v Cowan*,[134]
where the Newfoundland Court of Appeal held that the claimant, who
was a registered nursing assistant with some experience in orthopaedics,
was 50% to blame for her injury when she fell while using crutches and
broke her leg, because she had failed to seek instructions regarding the
proper use of the crutches. Or a patient may be held negligent for failing
to report to his GP when the hospital had advised him to do so or for
failing to attend review appointments. In the end, it is simply a matter
of common sense whether the patient has been irresponsible in regard to
his own health and safety.

We noted above a case where the House of Lords found contributory
negligence by virtue of a deliberate act of self-harm by a rational prisoner
in police custody (*Reeves v Metropolitan Police Comr*).

In *Pidgeon v Doncaster Health Authority*,[135] the County Court judge
at Sheffield held that the health authority was liable for the negligent
evaluation of a cervical smear test which failed to reveal a pre-cancerous
condition, but the claimant was two-thirds responsible (contributorily
negligent) for the development of cervical cancer as she had failed to
attend screenings in the following nine years. The case of *Sabri-Tabrizi*
(above) was distinguished as the claimant's failure in *Pidgeon* was not so
utterly unreasonable as to break the chain of causation entirely.

Where a claim is pursued for professional negligence for loss of the
chance of suing, any contributory negligence likely to have been found
at the original trial must be factored in when assessing the percentage
of total damages to be awarded (*Sharpe v Addison*[136]). See the following
section for further explanation.

---

132 [1983] 1 WLR 585, PC.
133 [2002] Lloyd's Rep Med 482.
134 [1991] 2 Med LR 271.
135 [2002] Lloyd's Rep Med 130.
136 [2003] EWCA Civ 1189, CA.

In *St George v Home Office*,[137] the trial judge awarded a 15% reduction to the damages of a claimant whose drink and drug addiction had contributed to his fall from a prison bunk bed. However, the Court of Appeal reversed this and held that although he was at fault for becoming addicted to drugs and alcohol as a teenager, adopting a common sense approach it was not a potent cause of the injury suffered. In any event, it would not be just and equitable to reduce the claimant's damages given that he had presented himself as a person suffering from addiction.

In *Badger v Ministry of Defence*,[138] Mr Justice Stanley Burton reduced the claimant's damages for lung cancer by 20% because he had continued to smoke despite warnings since 1971 on cigarette packets.

In *Horsley v Cascade Insulation Services Ltd,*[139] a mesothelioma case with a lifetime smoker claimant, it was held by Eady J that the question of smoking reduced the overall damages by 20% for contributory negligence.

In *Blackmore v Department for Communities and Local Government*,[140] the deceased died of lung cancer having smoked throughout his adult life and been employed for 20 years in a dockyard where he had come into significant contact with asbestos. The judge found the risk from smoking was probably between two and three times the risk from asbestos exposure, but having regard to the relative blameworthiness and causative potency, assessed contributory negligence at 30%. The defendant appealed, arguing that 'responsibility' under the Law Reform (Contributory Negligence) Act 1945, s 1 was limited to considerations of causation. The Court of Appeal dismissed the appeal – 'responsibility' was a broad concept that did have to take relative blameworthiness into account – trial judge right to reject apportionment on proportions by which had increased the risk.

Whether such reductions could be applied for similar conduct in clinical negligence cases is perhaps open to doubt particularly if the purpose of treatment is to cure cancer and that treatment has been negligently delayed for example.

The defendant unsuccessfully ran such an argument in the dental negligence case of *Haughton v Patel*.[141] There, the claimant suffered periodontal disease for a number of years while under the care of the defendant dentist, which resulted in the development of recurrent mouth abscesses and loss of several teeth. She subsequently developed a cerebral intracranial abscess in the right side of her brain. It was common ground between the parties that her brain abscess was secondary to her mouth abscesses and so was a consequence, albeit a rare one, of the periodontal disease. The defendant admitted a number of breaches of duty but disputed causation and alleged the claimant had been contributorily negligent by reason of poor oral hygiene and continuing to smoke.

Holroyde J accepted the claimant's evidence that she was aware of general risks to her health of smoking, but had never received clear advice as to just how bad the dental outcome might be if she persisted in her smoking. Her evidence was that if the risk of losing her teeth

---

137 [2008] EWCA Civ 1068.
138 [2006] 3 All ER 173.
139 [2009] EWHC 2945.
140 [2017] EWCA Civ 1136.
141 [2017] EWHC 2316 (QB).

had ever been brought home to her by Dr Patel, she would have acted differently and would have stopped (or at least reduced) smoking. He found in the claimant's favour and declined to make any contributory negligence finding, stating at [95]:

> 'I have found that she was at no stage properly advised as to the risks involved if she did not alter her conduct in those two respects. I find it difficult to see how she can be criticised if she was not advised by the person to whom she looked for advice about those risks.

The judge found that there had been a 'very poor standard of care' in this case. Perhaps his findings on contributory negligence would have been more in line with the blameworthiness attributable to claimants in the asbestos cases above if his perception of the treatment had been less critical.

LOSS OF A CHANCE

This section considers what a patient has to prove where the admitted breach of duty involves a failure to treat. This limited aspect of causation deserves special consideration because the complaint arises time and again: 'I was denied the proper treatment for my condition. They admit negligence. I might have been cured.' (Or, in the appropriate case: 'My wife/husband/child might have lived'.)

What is the problem?

The problem is that, according to traditional jurisprudence, one has to prove that, on the balance of probabilities – ie more likely than not or at least a 51% chance, the outcome would have been better. Why should it not be enough, it is often asked (especially by the patient or his family), given that proper treatment was neglected, to show a chance (let us say, a more than minimal chance) that the treatment would have been successful, and so to award a proportion of total damages dependent upon the percentage chance of the treatment being successful?

What is the modern origin of the rule that the likelihood of a successful outcome must be shown to have been more than evens? For that we turn to the seminal case of *Hotson v Fitzgerald*.[142]

Hotson v Fitzgerald

The facts can be simply stated. The defendant's doctor failed to treat the young claimant at the proper time and so he developed a permanent disability of the hip. The evidence established that, even if he had been properly treated, he would still probably (a 75% chance) have contracted the disability. The defendant said that therefore the claimant had not proved on the balance of probabilities that he had suffered an injury. The claimant argued that he had been deprived of the chance of recovery and should therefore receive one-quarter of full compensation for his injury. The defendant's argument was in accord with traditional jurisprudence,

---

142 [1987] AC 750, CA, MLC 0012, HL.

but both at first instance and in the Court of Appeal the claimant's contention was accepted. The Master of the Rolls said:

> ... it is unjust that there should be no liability for failure to treat a patient, simply because the chances of a successful cure by that treatment were less than 50%. Nor by the same token can it be just that if the chances of a successful cure only marginally exceed 50%, the doctor or his employer should be liable to the same extent as if the treatment could be guaranteed to cure. If this is the law, it is high time that it was changed, assuming that this court has power to do so ... the essence of the plaintiff's claim is that he has lost any benefit which he would have derived from timely treatment.

The court said that this benefit sounded in damages, subject to proper evaluation. The categories of loss were never closed, and it was not only financial or physical injury that were fit subjects for compensation.

In the House of Lords

But the House of Lords unanimously decided that the finding by the trial judge that there had been only a 25% chance that any treatment would have been beneficial, ie would have prevented the necrosis, was equivalent to a finding that the claimant had not proved on the balance of probabilities that the admitted negligence had caused the necrosis, and so the claim could not succeed. The correct approach was to decide first as a matter of fact and in the usual way what was the condition of the claimant when he arrived at the hospital. In this particular case, the question could be framed as: 'Had the blood vessels running along the claimant's leg been injured to such an extent that necrosis was in any event inevitable?' The court said that the finding of only a one in four chance of benefit meant that the claimant would not have benefited from treatment. They applied the traditional rule that a court can only conclude that something would have happened if it is more likely than not that it would have happened.

Lord Bridge said that unless the claimant proved on the balance of probabilities that the delayed treatment was at least a material contributory cause of the avascular necrosis, he failed on the issue of causation and no question of quantification could arise.

Lord Ackner said that to follow the principle of proportionate deduction for the chance of benefit was 'a wholly new doctrine which has no support in principle or authority and would give rise to many complications in the search for mathematical or statistical exactitude'.

In this way the House of Lords affirmed the traditional jurisprudence.

Let us assume that we can prove that treatment should have been given at a certain (earlier) time. As we have seen, we are constrained by the *Hotson* decision to prove that, more likely than not, treatment would have produced a substantially better outcome (we use the word 'substantially' in order to give the claim sufficient financial expectations to justify proceedings).

Do not confuse

We should not confuse the question of showing a percentage chance of there having been a better outcome with the question of by what percentage an assuredly better outcome would have been better. If one can show that the outcome would probably (ie on the balance of probabilities) have been better, it does not matter that the degree of betterment can only be expressed as a percentage and that that percentage may itself be less than 50%. In many cases involving a failure to give timely treatment for cancer, the most the experts can do is suggest statistics for survival, ie as it would have been and as it now is, given the delay in diagnosis and treatment. Provided one can achieve some clarity on the degree of worsened outcome, given that the experts are satisfied that on the balance of probability the prognosis would have been better, the case on causation is proved. All one then has to do (although this may not be easy) is to evaluate for the purposes of quantum the difference between the two prognoses. If a claimant expert is able, instead of relying on survival data, to express the worsened outcome in terms of a specified likely extent of reduced life expectancy, this could help avoid recovery being precluded by *Gregg v Scott* principles. In *Taylor v West Kent Health Authority*,[143] Kay J found that delay in diagnosing breast cancer did not substantially alter the outcome, but that there was a degree of injury in that the claimant would probably have lived 18 months longer. Damages were left to the parties to agree. See also for example the case of *JD* below where an alternative claim on this basis succeeded.

In *Judge v Huntingdon Health Authority*,[144] a breast cancer case, Titheridge QC, sitting as a High Court judge, found that on the balance of probability breast nodes had not been involved in the cancer at the time when diagnosis and treatment should have taken place, and that therefore there had been, on the statistics, an 80% chance of a cure at that time. However, he went on, wrongly in our view, to indicate that the claimant was entitled to 80% of full damages. An 80% probability of survival should have been taken as proof of survival and therefore full damages awarded.

Gregg v Scott and the loss of a prognosis

Introduction

The basic facts of this case[145] are capable of fairly short summary, though also capable of well-nigh endless legal argument. The judges of the House of Lords took months to reflect and research and finalise their views. Even then, the result in this extremely important case comes to us only by a bare majority.

Diagnosis of cancer (lymphoma in the left axilla) was delayed by GP negligence for nine months. In that time, it made further progress (invading the pectoral muscles) causing the patient additional pain and suffering, requiring more intensive treatment, and possibly affecting the prognosis.

Two things need to be made clear at this point. The first is that the original claim was based on the assertion that the patient would probably have survived (ie survived ten years, which is taken by the medical

---

143 [1997] 8 Med LR 251.
144 [1995] 6 Med LR 223.
145 [2005] MLC 1202.

profession, and accepted by the lawyers, to equate with a cure) but now, as a result of the negligent delay, would not. This had to be changed as it was discovered shortly before trial that his cancer was particularly malignant so that, instead of the hitherto claimed probability of survival he had in fact had from the outset, even if treated timeously, a less than even chance of survival. Undeterred, his advisers amended his claim to what was in effect loss of a chance, or – more precisely – injury by way of a diminished chance of survival. Note that each time the case was tried the outlook for the patient, by reason of his survival up to the respective time, had grown better, so that by the time the matter came before the Lords one had to wonder if he would have done any better anyway.

The second point, commented upon by their Lordships, is that, although there was clearly a (relatively small) claim for the additional physical suffering caused by the spread of the cancer during the period of delay, that was not a head of claim being pursued by the claimant. He put all his eggs in the basket of loss of prognosis, ie reduced chance of survival.

One further preliminary note: the whole case was done on statistics, by way of evidence from medical experts. By the time of the trial at first instance, the original statistic (above 50%) for likely cure if treated timeously had fallen to 42%, whereas the actual prospect of cure, given the delay in diagnosis, was only 25%. Bear in mind again that it does not necessarily follow that the chances of survival would have suffered that reduction if there had been no delay.

Approaches

If one accepts this statistical basis for judging a claim (artificial in so many ways), there are two possible approaches. The first is the traditional one: to succeed the claimant need prove that he would have been cured but now will not be, issues which are to be decided on the balance of probabilities. The 45% statistic means that probably he would not have survived ten years (would not have been cured) anyway; so he has suffered no injury. This was the basis of the *Hotson* decision in the Lords. However, as we have seen, that decision, that the child's leg would not have been 'cured' in any event, was based on a finding of fact by the trial judge that so many blood vessels had been lost by the time he came to hospital that the failure to treat him properly at the hospital caused no loss as the leg was doomed in any event. The statistics offered a 25% chance of survival for the leg if properly treated, but the judge did not base his finding that the leg would have been lost on that (at any rate not on that alone). He had this physical fact on which to base his finding, ie the physical fact that the condition of the leg, which was vitally relevant to its prospect of survival, was such that there could be no prospect of survival. In the case of *Gregg* the evidence of statistical chance was paramount, making it more purely a claim for loss of a chance. There was no evidence to allow the sort of physical finding that was possible in *Hotson*. The only relevant evidence was what the experts gave by way of statistics culled from 'this or that' series in the literature, which is very unsatisfactory.

On the traditional approach (and ignoring the unreliability of statistics when applied to a specific case) the only response could be that the claimant had lost nothing as he would not on the balance of probability have been cured in any event.

The *second approach* would be to admit in circumstances of this sort an exception to the traditional legal test, as was done twice in recent years: in the *Fairchild* case (see the section so titled earlier in this chapter) and in *Chester v Afshar*. Two of the judges supported this approach, but three were not prepared to modify the traditional approach. (The trial judge had dismissed the claim; so had the Court of Appeal but only by a majority.)

So the House, which had showed such imagination in carving out new paths to yield the just result in *Fairchild* and in *Chester*, baulked at the final fence in this third recent test of their judicial creativity.

The dissenting minority

LORD NICHOLLS

Lord Nicholls, for allowing the claimant's appeal, said that a remedy for a claimant in this situation was essential. The loss of a 45% prospect of recovery was just as much a real loss for the patient as the loss of a 55% prospect of recovery. In both cases, the patient was worse off. He lost something of importance and value. This gets perilously close to the clearly inadmissible claim of persons who, living in the neighbourhood of a factory when a noxious emission negligently occurs, claim for their reduced prospects of survival, at a time when there is no reason to believe they have suffered anything at all apart from now being at risk where they were not at risk before.

So the question is not whether a chance has been lost – clearly it has – but whether such a 'loss' is recognisable by the law as a claimable head of damages. In some circumstances, of course, loss of a chance is recognised as a claimable loss. Loss of a chance to try for a job or role or whatever, loss of a chance of bringing a successful claim, loss of a chance where the loss would hinge on what a third party might have done; but note that these claims are all for loss of a chance involving financial loss, not physical injury. As already remarked, the law has for years recognised a consequential or parasitic loss of chance of physical integrity, as when something is added to general damages for the chance of osteo-arthritis or epilepsy developing. But none of these scenarios are much similar to an isolated (standalone) medical claim for loss of a chance of surviving (wholly or in relation to a part of the body).

Nevertheless, Lord Nicholls said that, where there is substantial uncertainty about whether the desired outcome would have been achieved (and there surely is uncertainty, it should be added, where the whole question turns on what statistic the experts manage to derive from a study of what reports are available about what may have happened to a limited number of other patients whose situation may have been in some respects similar to that of the claimant), the law would do better to define the claimant's actionable damage more narrowly by reference to the opportunity the claimant lost. The judge said that medical science would often be uncertain as to what the outcome would have been, and so loss of a chance of favourable outcome should be the basis for damages. The doctor's duty, here breached, was to promote the patient's prospects of recovery (not to reduce them). He went on to point to the inherently limited usefulness of statistics (about other patients) when used to predict what would have happened to a particular patient. But 'in the present context use of statistics for the purpose of evaluating a lost chance makes good sense'. Lord Nicholls also emphasised the difference between a *Hotson* case, where a finding of fact about the physical condition of the patient at the time of the negligence determined in itself a certain enough conclusion about the likely outcome, and a *Gregg* case where there was no such prior finding of fact possible. It is interesting to note that as long ago as 1987 (in *Hotson*) Lord Bridge had recognised the distinction between these two sorts of cases.

Lord Nicholls argued strongly for the recognition of a lost chance as a head of damage in cases where medical opinion could only assess the patient's original prospects of recovery on a statistical basis ('fraught with a significant degree of medical uncertainty').

Clearly there is much force in this argument. A law which permits recovery when the chance of survival has gone from 60% to 45% but not when it has gone from 45% to virtually nil does not command respect. The problem, of course, lies in the introduction into these cases of statistics. That is what gives the whole argument of the majority such an unrealistic flavour. Once you say that the statistics show that this particular patient had only a less than 50% chance of recovery, the case is lost, as the traditional approach moves to dominate the debate. But if you allow that the statistics cannot reasonably be used in that way and that they only show various possibilities, it becomes easier to accept that the traditional approach should not be followed.

Lord Hope

Lord Hope agreed that the claimant's appeal should be allowed. He was not the only judge to comment in some surprise on the fact that the claimant was not pursuing any injury claim except the loss of a chance of recovery. But he used the fact of the unclaimed physical injury to support his view that the significant reduction in the prospects of recovery which the claimant had suffered could and should be claimable in damages. He said that the physical injury, in addition to pain and suffering, caused a reduction in the prospects of a successful outcome and this loss of prospects was consequential on the physical injury and so was a proper subject for damages. Not quite the way Lord Nicholls put it, but yielding the same overall conclusion.

Clearly, the question of recognising loss of prospects as a stand-alone claim is one of policy. In *Fairchild* and in *Chester*, the House was prepared on policy grounds to declare for the patient. Here they were not. This is perhaps unsurprising given the significant potential impact on the NHS (as described above, *Chester* represented only a limited exception to ordinary causation principles).

The majority

Lord Phillips

Lord Phillips, in a detailed study, argued that the statistics had been misinterpreted by all except him. He said the position had been complicated by the better than expected progress of the patient during the long course of the litigation. He was unconvinced that the progress of the cancer during the nine months' delay was due to the negligence of the defendant doctor. He said (surely rightly) that the expert's model was a very inadequate tool for assessing the effect of delay in treatment on the claimant's progress and that his subsequent clinical progress was of critical significance in re-assessing the issue. He said that the closer the claimant became with the passage of time to being a survivor (ie surviving ten years) the smaller the likelihood that the delay in commencing his treatment had had any effect on his expectation of life. Analysis of statistics was very difficult in medical cases. That was a reason for adopting the easier and more robust method of traditional valuation. (But that was being based on 'unreliable' statistics too.) Lord Phillips said he was well aware of the need for justice but he was not persuaded that justice demanded that this sort of statistical loss should sound in damages. As he had already explained, the difficulties in evaluating such a case on the chance basis rather than the traditional probability basis ('the complications of this case') had persuaded him that the traditional basis should not be abandoned for any sort of special rule. 'Awarding damages for the reduction in the prospect of a cure where the result of treatment is still uncertain is not a satisfactory exercise.'

LORD HOFFMANN

Lord Hoffmann did not see any clear way in which a new rule for cases of this sort could be formulated. He did not favour the "consequential" hook proposed by Lord Hope. He said that the various control mechanisms proposed to confine liability for loss of a chance within artificial limits were not attractive. A wholesale adoption of possible rather than probable causation as the criterion of liability would be so radical a change in our law as to amount to a legislative act, which would have enormous consequences for insurance companies and the NHS.

BARONESS HALE

Baroness Hale said that she was for a long time attracted by the principal argument submitted for the claimant, namely that the loss of prognosis was simply consequential on the physical damage, ie the spread of the cancer during the period of delay. But, she said, on a proper interpretation of what the trial judge had written, he did not find that the delay caused the spread. She agreed that the instant case was not covered by *Hotson* as the outcome in *Hotson* was determined inevitably by the poor condition of the leg on arrival at hospital, whereas the outcome for the cancer could not be so determined but remained uncertain, capable of expression only on a statistical basis. It was, as accepted by the claimant, a question of policy whether the traditional approach should be modified in cases of this sort by allowing a claim for loss of or reduction in the chance of a successful outcome. There were attractions in allowing an award of damages for loss of such a chance where physiological changes were provable, but such an approach would be difficult to apply, particularly in showing that the delay had caused the loss of chance.

It is thought that the strongest objections of Baroness Hale were seen in the following passages. She was particularly affected by the prospect that any claim for personal injury could be drafted as a claim for loss of chance of a better outcome, and she did not see how the two bases for a claim – loss of chance and balance of probability – could co-exist. It would not make sense if the claimant could at more than 50% go for probability and so get 100% damages and at 49% go for loss of a chance and so get substantial damages. Defendants would lose out either way. But if loss of a chance was adopted and probability had to be dropped, claimants who would now get 100% damages would in future be limited to a proportion unless they showed 100% probability (ie certainty). Expert evidence and trials would be far more complex and costly, and recovery far less predictable. Further, there would be no reason to limit the change in the basis of recovery to medical claims.

Baroness Hale summarised her view by saying that 'the complexities of attempting to introduce liability for the loss of a chance of a more favourable outcome in personal injury claims have driven me, not without regret, to conclude that it should not be done'.

Comment

There appears to be no reason why loss of chance, in appropriate cases, should not go to swell general damages where it is shown that it arises from physiological changes which are due to the negligence. In other words it is a consequential loss, consequential on negligence causing physical injury. The courts, as we well know, have no problem in saying in effect to a claimant: 'You have suffered a physical injury which has meant (*inter alia*) that you are now at a 15% risk of developing epilepsy whereas before the negligence the risk was minute or non-existent. Your chance of remaining free of epilepsy has therefore been reduced from close to 100% to 85%. You may never contract epilepsy but there is that risk now due to the negligence. We will take that factor into account when assessing general damages.' Why then should a court not say in the appropriate case: 'It is proved that if your cancer had been treated timeously you would have had a 45% chance of no relapse and so of keeping your breast/womb (or whatever). It is also proved that the negligent delay has impaired that prospect, to the extent that now there is virtually no chance (or only a 20% chance). The risk of your suffering that injury has been appreciably increased, [just as the risk of possible epilepsy is increased in the earlier example]. We will take that factor into account in assessing general damages.'

The court might find it hard to assess quantum, particularly in cases where potential loss of working years is involved, but plenty of quantum assessments are difficult without causing the court to throw up its hands in despair (or the towel in). There does not seem to be anything in the *Gregg* speeches which could outlaw that approach, which is consistent with the traditional law. Indeed Baroness Hale, given proper causation, would seem to accept it.

Further examples – no award for lost chance

Many further examples could be given of a patient failing on causation because he could not prove on the balance of probabilities that proper treatment would have resulted, in one way or another, in a better outcome.

In *Gregory v Pembrokeshire Health Authority*,[146] the judge said there was no question of assessing the chances that the claimant, had she been properly advised, would have proceeded via a second amniocentesis to an abortion – he had simply to decide on the evidence whether on the balance of probabilities she would or would not.

There is an interesting gloss on the subject in an informative article on the human growth hormone litigation by Mark Mildred.[147] The defendants argued that the question whether treatment would have been stopped if the clinicians had been given certain information fell to be evaluated on percentage terms. Morland J rejected that argument (judgment 22 May 1998), saying that once a claimant had proved on the balance of probabilities that treatment would have been stopped, he was entitled to succeed. A discount was appropriate only in relation to quantification of uncertain damages, for example the likelihood of promotion to a higher paid job or the like.

In *Hardaker v Newcastle Health Authority*,[148] Burnton J held that the claimant failed on causation as the expert evidence as to whether immediate decompression would have produced a better outcome for the claimant diver proved only an unquantified chance of a better but unidentified outcome. Therefore the claimant had failed to prove he had suffered any damage, as a chance of a better recovery below 50% did not sound in damages. It is interesting to note that Burnton J (rightly) viewed the observations of Andrew Smith J in *Smith v NHS Litigation Authority*,[149] as made *per incuriam*. Andrew Smith J had said that, even if the congenital displacement of the hip, which was the subject of the action he was trying, would probably not have been discovered by a competent examination, the claimant would have been able to claim percentage damages.

In *Wright* (above), Lord Neuberger considered that, at least in the Court of Appeal, a loss of a chance argument: 'should probably be treated as foreclosed by the views expressed by the majority of the *House of Lords in Gregg v Scott*.' He continued, at [84]:

> 'I accept that the reasoning of the House of Lords on this point does not conclusively shut out, as a matter of strict logic, this court from applying a loss of a chance approach in this case, which is concerned with rather a different point. However, certainty and consistency are of great importance in this difficult area, and, while the question would be appropriate for reconsideration by the Supreme Court, I consider that, at this level, we should probably not expand the loss of a chance doctrine into the realm of clinical negligence.

Elias LJ dissented on the appeal but agreed on this point (at [93]) that:

> ... this is not an appropriate case to apply the loss of chance principles enunciated in *Allied Maples Ltd v Simmons & Simmons* [1995] 1 WLR 1602. I agree that *Gregg v Scott* [...], even if it is not strictly determinative of this aspect of the case, effectively precludes this court from applying those principles to personal injury—and particularly clinical negligence—cases.

---

146 [1989] 1 Med LR 81.
147 At [1998] JPIL 262.
148 MLC 0395, [2001] Lloyd's Rep Med 512.
149 [2001] Lloyd's Rep Med 90.

JD v Mather[150] involved a delayed diagnosis of a malignant melanoma. By the time it was removed it had spread to the claimant's lymph nodes, and subsequently to his lungs. Bean J rejected his primary case based on lost chance of survival. On the facts he found that the tumour had already become ulcerated and spread to one lymph node by the date of failed diagnosis and so the claimant's chances of surviving ten years were already less than 50%: *Gregg* applied. However, on the balance of probabilities the delayed diagnosis had reduced C's life expectancy by three years and he was entitled to damages (to be assessed if not agreed) accordingly.

In *Oliver v Williams*[151] there was a negligent delay in diagnosing ovarian cancer but the claimant failed to establish that the breach had made a material or measureable difference to her life expectancy. Given that the claimant's expert could not assess the difference in volume of residual material, his estimate of her diminished life expectancy was nothing more than a hunch or belief that she had lost the chance of improvement. The bulk of her symptoms would have occurred but for the delay, although she was entitled to £2,500 damages for pain and suffering and £5,000 for psychiatric injury attributable to the delay in diagnosis.

In *Hague v Dalzell*[152] a delayed diagnosis of cancer resulted in pain and suffering, made worse by the anguish of knowing that the cancer could have been detected earlier. To that extent the claim for negligence on the part of the deceased's estate succeeded. On the balance of probabilities, however, the cancer would have recurred and she would not have survived for five years but would, sadly, have died. That aspect of the claim for negligence, and the claim under the 1976 Act did not succeed. It does not appear that an alternative 'reduction in life expectancy' claim was run here.

Scenarios involving 'chance'

The most obvious 'chance' scenario for our purposes is where a solicitor is sued for not having properly processed a claim. It is clear law that in such a context the court will award damages in proportion to the chance of success of the original action (the right to sue is regarded, quaintly, as a chose in action and it is that asset which falls to be valued). The seminal case is *Kitchen v Royal Air Forces Association*;[153] and a medical example is *Gascoigne v Ian Sheridan & Co and Latham*,[154] where 60% of the total damages relevant to the original medical claim was awarded.

In *Harrison v Bloom Camillin*,[155] a claim against solicitors for failing to process an action against accountants for negligent advice, Neuberger J carefully assessed every aspect of the mooted claim against the accountants to arrive at an estimate of the chances of success and the likely damages. He ended with a deduction of 35% for the risk of losing on negligence and a further 20% for the risk of losing on causation.

---

150 [2012] EWHC 3063 (QB).
151 [2013] EWHC 600 (QB).
152 [2016] EWHC 2753 (QB).
153 [1958] 1 WLR 563, CA.
154 [1994] 5 Med LR 437.
155 [1999] 45 LS Gaz R 32.

In *O'Shea v Weedon & Co*,[156] Alliott J found that the original claim for a failed sterilisation that the defendant solicitor had failed to progress had not stood a 'real and substantial rather than merely a negligible prospect of success', and so the claim against the solicitor failed. In *Hatswell v Goldsbergs (a firm of solicitors)*,[157] the Court of Appeal endorsed the judge's conclusion that the claimant's chances of success in his original medical negligence claim were nil. He would have been seeking to prove by his own recollection some 14 years after the event that he had made complaints to his GP which were completely inconsistent with the contemporaneous medical notes.

In *Sharpe v Addison*,[158] the Court of Appeal, holding that the claim of a victim of a road traffic accident would not have been 'of no real value', said the test as to whether a claim was worthless was very similar to the test for striking out.

In *Perry v Raleys Solicitors*[159] the claimant sued solicitors for the loss of the opportunity to pursue a services award in a vibration white finger case. The Supreme Court confirmed at [20]–[21] that the correct approach to proving the loss that has been caused by a breach of duty in such a case, following *Allied Maples Group Ltd v Simmons & Simmons*,[160] is to require a claimant to prove what he or she would have done on the balance of probabilities, while what others would have done (if relevant) depends on a loss of chance evaluation.

Another example is that a dependent in a Fatal Accidents Act claim will be awarded compensation in proportion to the chances she/he had of financial support from the deceased.

It is also relevant that in a normal personal injury action a percentage chance (often as little as 10%) of some further injury arising in the future (eg osteo-arthritis developing in an injured joint) will be assessed and a suitable addition made to the award.

Further, in claims brought under the Human Rights Act 1998 (see Chapter 23 for further discussion on bringing such claims in a clinical negligence context), a 'looser' approach to causation is adopted and loss of a chance will suffice. As Lord Bingham pointed out in *R (Greenfield) v Secretary of State for the Home Department*,[161] claims under the European Convention on Human Rights have very different objectives from civil actions. Where civil actions are designed essentially to compensate claimants for their losses, Convention claims are intended rather to uphold minimum human rights standards and to vindicate those rights.

Lord Brown, at [138] of *Van Colle v Chief Constable of Hertfordshire*[162] confirmed that:

> Whereas [English tort law] requires the claimant to establish on the balance of probabilities that, but for the defendant's negligence, he would not have suffered his claimed loss—and so establish under Lord Bingham's proposed liability principle that appropriate police action would probably have kept the

156 ML 8/98, p 8.
157 [2001] EWCA Civ 2084.
158 [2003] EWCA Civ 1189.
159 [2019] UKSC 5.
160 [1995] 1 WLR 1602 (CA).
161 [2005] 1 WLR 673.
162 [2008] UKHL 50.

victim safe—under the Convention it appears sufficient generally to establish merely that he lost a substantial chance of this.

Mackay J applied this 'looser' test after the House of Lords had remitted the case of *Savage v South Essex Partnership NHS Foundation Trust*[163] for trial. In that case, Carol Savage suffered from paranoid schizophrenia and had committed suicide after absconding from a hospital run by the trust. An inquest had found that the precautions taken by the trust to prevent her from absconding were inadequate.

Mackay J held at [82] that when considering whether the defendant did all that could reasonably have been expected of it to avoid or prevent a 'real and immediate risk to the life' of Carol Savage from self-harm:

> the test for causation is not the English 'but for' test, but a looser one; the claimant does not have to show to show that had the trust acted appropriately there would probably have been no death, but merely that she has 'lost a substantial chance of this'.

In *Sarjantson v The Chief Constable of Humberside Police*,[164] the Court of Appeal appeared to go further, holding that causation is not a necessary ingredient of a claim under the Human Rights Act 1998, so that even if the defendant police's earlier attendance would have made no difference, the claim could still succeed. However, Lord Dyson MR noted that a finding that, with the benefit of hindsight, a prompt response by the police would still have been too late to prevent the attack on the victim might mean that there was no right to damages, but was not relevant to liability.

Daniel v St George's Healthcare NHS Trust[165] is an example of a Human Rights Act 1998 claim that failed on causation in spite of this looser test. The claim concerned a death in custody following a heart attack. Lang J found the claim failed on liability, but in any event the claimants had not established, on the balance of probabilities, that, even if the defendant had called an ambulance earlier, or an ambulance had been dispatched sooner, there would have been a 'real prospect of altering the outcome' or that the deceased 'lost a substantial chance of avoiding the outcome'.

Conclusion

Given the House of Lords decision in *Gregg v Scott, and the comments in Wright and other subsequent cases,* loss of a chance of a better outcome is dead in the water for the normal medical negligence claims, unless it can be joined as parasitic or consequential damage to another head of claim, probably general damages, in which case there is still hope it might succeed.

---

163 [2010] EWHC 865 (QB).
164 [2013] EWCA Civ 1252.
165 [2016] EWHC 23 (QB).

Chapter 8

Foreseeability and remoteness

Chesca Lord

INTRODUCTION

Even if the claimant has established a duty of care, a breach of that duty, and loss of a type recognised by the law and caused by the breach, the defendants will only be liable to compensate for that loss if it was reasonably foreseeable at the time of the breach that it could arise. In other words, the basic principle (though subject, as we shall see, to substantial exceptions) is that you cannot recover for an injury that was not foreseeable.

Damages are recoverable only in respect of injury of a type that was foreseeable (though no definition of 'type' is available). However this must be read subject to the important rule that the wrongdoer must take the claimant as he finds him, so that the fact that the injury develops unexpected complications or, through hypersensitivity, more harm is suffered than was to be expected is no bar to recovery. Nor is the fact that the injury did not arise in the precisely foreseeable manner.

Strictly, injuries which are of an unforeseeable type and do not come within the rule that the wrongdoer must take the claimant as he finds him are not subjects for compensation. An example would be where a brick is thrown from a window and there is a foreseeable risk from it striking someone, but in fact it hits an electricity cable and in a manner not to be foreseen causes a person in the vicinity to be electrocuted – injury from impact would seem of a different kind from injury by electrocution. A judge would be entitled to hold the wrongdoer not liable for the injury suffered, but in practice he might well find a way to implement his 'gut reaction' to the situation and award compensation, eg by 'finding' that there was in fact some slight degree of foreseeability of electrocution.

TOO REMOTE

The principle is sometimes expressed as a statement that the loss must not be too remote. But that catch-all expression is also used to mean that no duty was owed to the particular claimant (the claimant was too remote, not being within the area of foreseeable risk created by the defendant's actions, and therefore so was the damage he suffered); or that no duty was owed to take care not to inflict the particular sort of harm suffered, or not to inflict it in that particular way; or that the chain of causation was broken; or that policy militates against recovery. Thus a mother who suffers nervous shock on being told of the death of her son and is denied damages on the basis that she does not come within the 'aftermath' principle (see Chapter 14) may be told that the damage she suffered was too remote. This may mean that no duty was owed to her by the tortfeasor, or that the intervening act of her informant broke the chain of causation, or that the law or policy forbids recovery in the particular circumstances.

To assist clarity of thought on this issue, it is better therefore to avoid the expression 'too remote' (it is in fact unhelpful in any context), and say simply that the loss must be reasonably foreseeable. Foreseeability of harm, though a prerequisite for a duty of care, does not of itself prove the existence of a duty. It is a prerequisite for a duty of care because, if there is no reasonable foreseeability of harm arising from an act there can be no duty of care in relation to it. Here, however, we consider the essential requirement of foreseeability in the context of recoverability of loss. We assume therefore in the discussion that follows that duty and breach have been proved.

FORESEEABILITY OF HARM

The basic principle is that a tortfeasor is liable only for the natural and probable consequences of his actions, namely those that he, as a reasonable man, could have foreseen as likely to occur, and which should therefore have caused him to hold his hand. Damage which occurs directly from the breach is not the subject of compensation, as a general rule, unless it was also foreseeable. This is the result of the Privy Council decision in *Overseas Tankship (UK) Ltd v Morts Dock and Engineering Co Ltd (also known as The Wagon Mound)*,[1] which overruled the long-standing decision to the contrary of the Court of Appeal in *Re Polemis*.[2]

A more recent medical case provides a good example of the operation of the principles of remoteness and foreseeability. In *R v Croydon Health Authority*,[3] the claimant, a trained nurse, married and of child-bearing age, had to undergo a medical check with a view to taking employment with the defendant. The defendant's radiologist who interpreted her X-rays was admittedly negligent in not referring her for specialist opinion. It was admitted that, had that been done, the serious pathology of primary pulmonary hypertension would have been diagnosed, she would have been warned of the serious risk to her health if she were to become pregnant, and she would have chosen not to become pregnant, particularly as pregnancy might shorten her life and therefore leave her child without a mother. As it was, the negligence of the radiologist deprived her of that warning and therefore a few months later she became pregnant, giving birth in due course to a healthy child. It was understandable that she claimed compensation for, among other things,

---

1   [1961] AC 388.
2   [1921] 3 KB 560.
3   MLC 0019, [1998] Lloyd's Rep Med 44, CA.

the trauma of the pregnancy and the cost of upkeep of her daughter. She succeeded at first instance,[4] but on appeal the Court of Appeal held that, as far as the radiologist was concerned, a decision to become pregnant fell outside the area of foreseeability. In other words, it was too remote. The court said that the radiologist never actually saw the claimant and knew very little about her except her age (this in itself is unconvincing, as the defendant would have had detailed knowledge of her and they should be taken in this context to stand in the shoes of their radiologist). Kennedy LJ said that the claimant's domestic life fell outside the scope of the radiologist's duty. The damage was too remote. 'The express obligations assumed by the radiologist did not, as it seems to me, extend to the plaintiff's private life.' Chadwick LJ said:

> ... a proper examination of the facts in the present case leads to the conclusion that, whatever duty of care was owed to the plaintiff by the health authority as a prospective employer, the scope and extent of that duty stopped short of responsibility for the consequences of the decision by the plaintiff and her husband that she should become pregnant. I think it essential to keep in mind that the relationship between the plaintiff and the health authority was that of prospective employee and employer. There was nothing in the evidence before the trial judge to suggest the relationship between the plaintiff and her prospective employer had anything to do with whatever plans the plaintiff and her husband may have had for starting a family.

Whatever semantic analysis one likes to construct, the reality of the matter is that the trial judge thought the employers should pay for the child because without their negligence the child would not have been born, whereas the Court of Appeal thought otherwise. However one dresses one's reasons up in the terminology of remoteness or foreseeability, this sort of decision turns on a question of policy, or, less elegantly, gut reaction. (The issue of liability for the cost of upkeep of a child born in such circumstances is dealt with in Chapter 12.)

In another clinical negligence example, *Thompson v Bradford*,[5] an eight year old boy attended his GP for his polio vaccination. He also had a suppurating perianal abscess. The GP advised that the vaccination should go ahead. This was found to be appropriate advice by the trial judge. The contraction of polio was not a foreseeable consequence of the immunisation. The parents were not advised, however, that the abscess might require surgery and that there might be an adverse reaction to the vaccination occurring at the same time as the need for surgery (which eventuated). This was held by the trial judge to be negligent. The trial judge found the GP liable because if had he given the correct advice, ie that there may be an adverse reaction at the same time as the need for surgery, the parents would have delayed the vaccination until after the surgery. The polio would then not have developed. The Court of Appeal overturned the trial judge's decision on the ground that the polio did not flow from any relevant breach of duty. In other words, because the increased risk of polio when combined with an operation was not reasonably foreseeable it is not a relevant breach of duty for the GP to have failed to warn of another risk (ie discomfort due to an adverse reaction at the time of the requirement for other surgery) which

---

4   [1997] PIQR P444.
5   [2006] Lloyd's Rep Med 95.

might have caused as a matter of fact the parents to delay and therefore avoid the polio. The only foreseeable consequence of the failure to advise against immunisation was the discomfort that the claimant might suffer from an adverse reaction to it.

In *Meadows v Khan*,[6] the defendant negligently failed to refer a pregnant woman for genetic testing for haemophilia. Her child was born with haemophilia and also autism. The Court of Appeal, reversing the first instance decision, held that the defendant was not liable for all the additional costs of raising a disabled child, merely those of a haemophiliac child. Only the negligence that was well within the scope of the duty to warn was recoverable: *South Australia Asset Management Corp v York Montague Ltd* (SAAMCO) applied.[7]

The Supreme Court recently held in *Darnley v Croydon Health Services*[8] that it was reasonably foreseeable that a patient who was given incorrect advice about A&E waiting times would leave without being treated and that, in some cases, harm may result. In that case the claimant, presenting at A&E with a suspected head injury was told by a receptionist that the likely wait to be seen by a member of medical staff was four to five hours. In fact he would have been seen by a triage nurse within 30 minutes. He left after 19 minutes. His condition subsequently deteriorated at home. Had his deterioration occurred at the hospital the experts agreed he would have been treated promptly and made a near full recovery. As a result of the delayed treatment he was left with permanent brain damage in the form of a severe and disabling left hemiplegia. The Supreme Court, overturning the decisions below, held that scope of the duty to take reasonable care not to act in such a way as foreseeably to cause such a patient to sustain physical injury clearly extended to a duty to take reasonable care not to provide misleading information which might foreseeably cause physical injury.

DEGREE OF FORESEEABILITY

In *The Wagon Mound (No 2)*,[9] the Privy Council's view was that once some foreseeability of fire was proved that was sufficient, however remote that possibility. This was reiterated by the House of Lords in *The Heron II*.[10] Lord Reid said (at 385–386):

> The defendant will be liable for any type of damage which is reasonably foreseeable as liable to happen even in the most unusual case, unless the risk is so small that a reasonable man would in the whole circumstances feel justified in neglecting it.'

Lord Upjohn came to a similar view at 422:

> The test in tort, as now developed in the authorities, is that the tortfeasor is liable for any damage which he can reasonably foresee may happen as a result of the breach however unlikely it may be, unless it can be brushed aside as far-fetched.'

---

6   [2019] EWCA Civ 152.
7   [1997] AC 191, [1996] 6 WLUK 227.
8   [2018] UKSC 50.
9   [1967] 1 AC 617.
10   [1969] 1 AC 350.

These propositions, however, are hardly consistent with what is generally understood to be the law, ie that the loss has to be reasonably foreseeable – unless we are being told that reasonable foreseeability of harm is appropriate for establishing a duty of care but any degree of foreseeability short of the far-fetched is enough in the context of compensation.

EXCEPTIONS

Policy

To the basic rule that the wrongdoer is liable for the natural and probable consequences of his wrongful act, and for no other consequences, there are a number of very substantial exceptions. In the first place, the law will draw a line at some point as a matter of policy to prevent over-extensive recovery.

> The law cannot take account of everything that follows a wrongful act; it regards some subsequent matters as outside the scope of its selection, because 'it were infinite for the law to judge the cause of causes' or consequence of consequences ... In the varied web of affairs the law must abstract some consequences as relevant, not perhaps on grounds of pure logic but simply for practical reasons (per Lord Wright in *Liesbosch, Dredger (Owners) v SS Edison (Owners)* [1933] AC 449 at 460, HL).

It is always difficult to predict and impossible to define the line where liability stops. It is left to the good sense of the judge in each particular case to decide where practical convenience and policy dictate that it be drawn.

> 'It is something like having to draw a line between night and day; there is a great duration of twilight when it is neither night nor day; but ... though you cannot draw the precise line, you can say on which side of the line the case is (per Blackburn J in *Hobbs v London and South Western Rly Co* (1875) LR 10 QB 111 at 121).

The legal basis for drawing the line is variously expressed:

> In order to limit liability ... the courts sometimes say either that the damage claimed was 'too remote' or that it was not 'caused' by the defendant's carelessness or that the defendant did not 'owe a duty of care' to the plaintiff (*per* Thesiger J in *SCM (UK) v Whittall* [1970] 1 WLR 1017 at 1031).

Or it may simply be said that justice or social convenience demands that a limit be placed upon the defendant's liability. For a good example of policy invalidating a claim where logic would allow it, see *McFarlane v Tayside Health Board*,[11] which is treated in detail in Chapter 12.

'You must take the claimant as you find him': the 'egg shell skull' principle

The most comprehensive exception to the foreseeability principle that goes to extend a defendant's liability is the rule that a tortfeasor must take the claimant as he finds him, in relation both to his physical condition and to his financial circumstances. If you carelessly knock a

---

11   [2000] 2 AC 59, HL.

man over in circumstances where you could reasonably expect a slight injury and a claim for average earnings lost over a relatively short period, you will nevertheless be liable for full damages if he turns out, through an inherently weak physical condition, to suffer far greater damage and for a longer period, and also to be a very high earner, perhaps with several extremely lucrative contracts lined up which he cannot now fulfil.

> One who is guilty of negligence to another must put up with idiosyncrasies of his victim that increase the likelihood or extent of damage to him; it is no answer to a claim for a fractured skull that its owner had an unusually fragile one (per Mackinnon LJ in *Owens v Liverpool Corpn* [1939] 1 KB 394 at 400–1, CA).

It is not only if the foreseeable injury proves more serious than could have been anticipated that the tortfeasor must pay, but also if a different type of injury arises out of the foreseeable injury. Thus, in *Robinson v Post Office*,[12] where a claimant developed encephalitis as a result of an allergic reaction to an anti-tetanus injection, the defendants, whose negligence was responsible for the original slight injury that led to the need for an injection, were held liable to compensate him for the full extent of his injury. The Court of Appeal held that a person who could reasonably foresee that a victim of his negligence may need to seek medical attention is liable for the consequences of that treatment, even if those consequences and their seriousness were not foreseeable (see, however, the discussion of when medical treatment is capable of breaking the chain of causation in Chapter 7).

There have been very many cases where unforeseeable complications involving a different type of physical injury from that which could have been foreseen have been the subject of compensation. For example, in *Warren v Scruttons*,[13] a defendant had to compensate for the unforeseeable aggravation of an existing eye condition that developed after the claimant had hurt his finger on a frayed rope. A cancer which unforeseeably developed from a foreseeable burn on the lip was held to be a proper subject for compensation in *Smith v Leech Brain*.[14] Where a woman had to wear a surgical collar as a result of a foreseeable physical injury she was able also to recover compensation for injury suffered when she fell down stairs due to the fact that she could not see so well with the collar on (*Wieland v Cyril Lord Carpets Ltd*[15]). Eveleigh J said:[16]

> ... in determining liability for ... possible consequences of personal injury, it is not necessary to show that each was within the foreseeable extent or foreseeable scope of the original injury in the same way that the possibility of injury must be foreseen when determining whether or not the defendant's conduct gives a claim in negligence.

In *Woodhouse v Yorkshire Regional Authority*,[17] the claimant suffered foreseeable digital contracture deformity from a carelessly performed operation. The defendants were held liable also for a hysterical condition

---

12 [1974] 1 WLR 1176, CA.
13 [1962] 1 Lloyd's Rep 497.
14 [1962] 2 QB 405.
15 [1969] 3 All ER 1006.
16 [1969] 3 All ER 1006 at 1009–1010.
17 [1984] 1 The Lancet 1306.

that developed because they had damaged a claimant with a hysterical personality and they had to take her as they found her.

In the road traffic case of *Giblett v P & NE Murray Ltd*,[18] the court said that the claimant did not have to prove that her psychiatric injury in the form that it took or its sequelae were reasonably foreseeable by the defendants. Even in the context of nervous shock, or any other attributable psychiatric condition, the defendant had to take the primary victim as he found him: it would avail the defendant nothing that the victim had a psychologically vulnerable 'egg shell' personality.

Similarly, in *Brice v Brown*,[19] the nervous shock sustained was particularly severe due to the claimant's pre-existing hysterical personality disorder, but damages remained recoverable. There is also relevant material in the judgments of the Court of Appeal in *Vernon v Bosley*.[20]

In *Simmons v British Steel*,[21] the House of Lords held that a claimant who suffered a minor head injury at work was entitled to recover damages for the psychiatric harm partly caused by his anger at the treatment he had received by his employers following the accident. Since he had sustained physical injury which was foreseeable it was unnecessary for him to prove that his psychiatric injury was foreseeable. It was held that the defenders had to take their victim as they found him.

The House of Lords in *Ladger v O'Connor*[22] held that the previous rule preventing recovery of losses caused by a claimant's impecuniosity (see *Liesbosch Dredger v SS Edison*[23]) was no longer good law. A defendant must now take his victim as he finds him physically, mentally and financially.

'TYPE' OF INJURY SUFFERED

Of course, if no injury could be foreseen then the fact that an abnormally susceptible claimant suffered some injury does not give rise to a claim; there would probably be neither a duty nor a breach in those circumstances, but even if there were, there would be no liability where no injury could reasonably be foreseen from the acts in question. For an injury to be claimable, it must, if it does not accompany a foreseeable injury, at least be of the same type as the foreseeable injury (although, as we see below, it is quite unclear what is meant by 'type'). Thus, in *Bradford v Robinson Rentals Ltd*,[24] a driver was negligently exposed to freezing conditions in an unheated vehicle as a result of which he developed the unforeseeable injury of frostbite. Rees J made it clear that recovery was permissible in respect of the frostbite as the foreseeable injury, ie common cold, pneumonia, chilblains, was of the same type as that which was in fact suffered. In *Ogwo v Taylor*,[25] the House of Lords held that injury caused

---

18   [1999] 22 LS Gaz R 34, CA.
19   [1984] 1 All ER 997.
20   [1997] 1 All ER 577.
21   [2004] UKHL 20.
22   [2004] 1 AC 1067.
23   [1933] AC 449.
24   [1967] 1 WLR 337.
25   [1988] AC 431.

to a firefighter from the steam that arose when he sprayed water on to a fire was not different in kind from injury caused directly by the flames.

The apparent necessity for a connection between the type of damage that was foreseeable and the type of damage that was suffered arises from the decision of the Privy Council in *The Wagon Mound* (above). That case arose out of the careless spillage of oil on the waters of Sydney harbour. Damage to slipways by pollution was foreseeable, but the damage by fire that occurred was not. The Privy Council said that as the damage that occurred was of a different type from what was foreseeable (ie damage by fire and not damage by pollution), recovery was not permitted. Ironically, in *The Wagon Mound (No 2)*,[26] which concerned the same facts, a contrary decision was reached as to liability, but that was because the evidence given in that trial established, as we saw above, that there was a slight possibility to be foreseen of damage by fire.

What is meant by 'type' of damage in the context of physical injury is not wholly clear. A claimant is assisted by the rules that the defendant must take him as he finds him, and that neither the extent of the damage has to be foreseeable nor the precise manner in which it arose, and it is hard to see what practical scope is left for a rule that restricts liability by providing that the injury suffered has to be of a type that was foreseeable. In *Thurogood v Van den Berghs and Jurgens*,[27] the Court of Appeal permitted recovery by an injured workman when he caught his fingers in a fan even though the foreseeable injury was by catching his necktie in it (a decision that seems good sense); but that was upon an application of the principle derived from *Re Polemis*,[28] that all damage directly caused was claimable for, and that principle was rejected by the Privy Council in *The Wagon Mound* (above). In *Tremain v Pike*,[29] Payne J refused relief to a herdsman who contracted a rare disease from rats' urine because the only foreseeable consequence from exposure to rats was rat-bite or food-poisoning, which was said to be 'entirely different in kind'. This decision must surely have been wrong (see, to an apparently contrary intent, *H Parsons Livestock Ltd v Uttley Ingham & Co Ltd*[30]).

In *H v Royal Alexandra Hospital*,[31] the fact that a haemophiliac given Aids-contaminated blood products was infected with a retro-virus and not with a virus (which alone was foreseeable when the negligent act took place) was of no assistance to the defendants as the damage was of the same kind as what was foreseeable.

In *Wood v Bentall Simplex Ltd*,[32] a farmer was held not to have contributed to his own death by building a grid of a non-approved pattern across the entrance to his slurry tank because the consequence of death by asphyxiation after he entered the tank to clear a blockage resulting from the unorthodox construction was not foreseeable. All that was foreseeable was that a person entering the tank to cure the (foreseeable) blockage might slip and fall. The Court of Appeal said that the test of liability for injury by asphyxiation was foreseeability of injury by asphyxiation.

---

26   [1967] 1 AC 617.
27   [1951] 2 KB 537.
28   [1921] 3 KB 560, CA.
29   [1969] 1 WLR 1556.
30   [1978] QB 791, CA.
31   [1990] 1 Med LR 297.
32   [1992] PIQR P332.

In *Page v Smith*,[33] the House of Lords was principally concerned with the question of whether a claimant involved in a road traffic accident could recover damages for psychiatric injury where only physical injury was foreseeable. The Court of Appeal had held that possibility of psychiatric injury was essential and that in the instant case it had not been foreseeable. The House of Lords by a bare majority restored the decision of the trial judge.

Lord Lloyd held that psychiatric injury in a road traffic accident was foreseeable. But he went further than that. He said that, whereas possibility of psychiatric injury was a crucial ingredient where the claimant was the secondary victim (for discussion of primary and secondary victims see Chapter 14), it would not be sensible in the case of a primary victim, in an age when medical knowledge is expanding fast and psychiatric knowledge with it, to commit the law to a distinction between physical and psychiatric injury which might already seem somewhat artificial, and might soon be altogether outmoded. 'Nothing will be gained by treating them as different "kinds" of personal injury, so as to require the application of different tests in law'.

Lord Browne-Wilkinson held that in the instant circumstances psychiatric injury was foreseeable, and, further, expressly endorsed Lord Lloyd's remarks about the dangers of seeking to draw hard and fast lines between physical and psychiatric illness. He said that for the courts to impose different criteria for liability depending on whether the injury was physical or psychiatric was likely to lead to a growing complication in straightforward personal injury cases. The law would be more effective if it accepted that the results of being involved in a collision might include both physical and psychiatric damage.

Lord Ackner was for allowing the appeal on the basis that psychiatric injury was foreseeable. He did not go further than that. On the other hand, Lord Jauncey, in a long and carefully reasoned judgment, concluded that for recovery for psychiatric injury foreseeability of psychiatric injury was essential, and he was not satisfied that in the circumstances of this accident there was such foreseeability. Lord Keith supported that view.

It therefore appears that not only were the *dicta* to the effect that foreseeability of personal injury would suffice for a claim for 'mere' psychiatric injury arising out of a road traffic accident *obiter* but, further, such a view was endorsed by only two of the judges. Two were of a contrary view and one was silent on the issue. Nevertheless it is now accepted law that this decision established the following principles (*per* the Court of Appeal in *Donachie v Chief Constable of the Greater Manchester Police*[34]):

- A defendant owes a duty of care to a person where he can reasonably foresee that his conduct will expose that person to a risk of personal injury.
- For this purpose, the test of reasonable foreseeability is the same whether the foreseeable injury is physical or psychiatric or both.
- However, its application to the facts differs according to whether the foreseeable injury is physical or psychiatric; in the latter case, if the claimant is not involved in some sort of 'event' caused by the

---

33   [1996] AC 155.
34   [2004] EWCA Civ 405.

negligence, he is a 'secondary' victim and liability is more difficult to establish.

- If the reasonably foreseeable injury is of a physical nature but such injury in fact causes psychiatric injury, it is immaterial whether the psychiatric injury was itself reasonably foreseeable. Equally if, as in the instant case, the breach of duty causes psychiatric injury causing in turn physical injury, it is immaterial that neither the psychiatric injury nor the particular form of the physical injury caused was reasonably foreseeable.

In *Hepworth v Kerr*,[35] the judge was satisfied that, although the specific risk of anterior spinal artery syndrome from the deliberately induced anaesthetic hypotension was not one which could reasonably have been foreseen, it was enough that risk of major organ under-perfusion was reasonably foreseeable and it mattered not that that source of danger acted in an unpredictable way. The mechanism and the source of danger were the same, and the defendant had run the unnecessary and foreseeable risk of causing injury to the claimant by under-perfusion of major organs of the body. What happened was 'but a variant of the foreseeable' and 'within the risk created by the negligence'.

In *Corr v IBC Vehicles*,[36] the claimant's husband was struck on the head by a machine at work. Despite reconstructive surgery he remained disfigured and developed PTSD and depression. He committed suicide nearly six years after the accident. The House of Lords held that his widow's claim under the Fatal Accidents Act 1976 was not barred by principles of causation, remoteness and foreseeability. Lord Bingham stated at [13]:

> Here, the inescapable fact is that depression, possibly severe, possibly very severe, was a foreseeable consequence of the breach. The Court of Appeal majority were right to uphold the claimants' submission that it was not incumbent on her to show that suicide itself was foreseeable but, as Lord Pearce observed *in Hughes v Lord Advocate* [1963] UKHL 8, 'To demand too great a precision in the test of foreseeability would be unfair to the pursuer, since the facets of misadventure are innumerable'. The principle that a tortfeasor who reasonably foresees the occurrence of some damage need not foresee the precise form which the damage may take, in my view, applies. I can readily accept that some manifestations of severe depression could properly be held to be so unusual and unpredictable as to be outside the bounds of what is reasonably foreseeable, but suicide cannot be so regarded. Whilst it is not, happily, a usual manifestation, it is not that it is uncommon; that is enough for the claimant to succeed.

More recently, and in a clinical negligence context, the suicide of a 14-year-old girl who had negligently been prematurely discharged from an NHS Trust's child and adolescent mental health service following negligent treatment for an eating disorder had been foreseeable: *E v Somerset Partnership NHS Trust*.[37] The defendant argued that although self-harm was foreseeable, the suicide itself was not. HHJ Denyer QC applied the principles in *Simmons*, *Corr* and *Jolley* that if the injury is

---

35 [1995] 6 Med LR 139.
36 [2008] 1 AC 884.
37 (12 January 2016, unreported).

of a type that was foreseeable, a defendant is liable even if the particular manifestation of the way it comes about is not. He said at para 18:

> My view is that given that both psychiatrists accept self-harm was a foreseeable consequence of F's condition and that that risk persisted once treatment had been wrongfully terminated, it seems to me that, although extreme, suicide falls within the definition of self-harm for foreseeability purposes. In other words the suicide was within the ambit of the type of damage which could have been foreseen.

THE 'PRECISE MANNER'

We have already adverted to the rule that it does not help a defendant to argue that, although the type of damage could be foreseen, the precise manner in which it arose could not. In *Hughes v Lord Advocate*,[38] where a child picked up a lighted Post Office paraffin lamp and entered an unguarded manhole, damage by burning was foreseeable, so that although the manner in which that damage arose was not foreseeable (the child was burned not by the oversetting of the lamp but by an explosion), that did not prevent recovery. In *Stewart v West African Terminals*,[39] the Court of Appeal said that as long as a result is within the general sphere of contemplation, and not of an entirely different kind, the precise chain of events need not be foreseeable.

> It is not necessary that the precise concatenation of circumstances should be envisaged. If the consequence was one which was within the general range which any reasonable person might foresee (and was not of an entirely different kind which no-one would anticipate) then it is within the rule that a person who has been guilty of negligence, is liable for its consequences (per Lord Denning in *Stewart*).

> ... the precise mechanics of the way in which the negligent act results in the original injury do not have to be foreseen (*per* Eveleigh J in *Wieland v Cyril Lord Carpets* [1969] 3 All ER 1006).

The question of the manner in which the damage arose overlaps with the question whether the damage was of a type that was foreseeable. The difficulties that can arise over these subtle distinctions when injury occurs in an unforeseen manner and one has then to ask whether it still remains within the type of injury foreseeable is illustrated by *Doughty v Turner Manufacturing Co Ltd*.[40] There, the fact that there was a foreseeable risk only of damage from splashing when a cover was carelessly let slip from a height of a few inches into molten liquid prevented recovery for injury caused when the liquid erupted due to an unforeseeable chemical reaction a few moments later. Such subtle distinctions were eschewed in *H Parsons Livestock Ltd v Uttley Ingham & Co Ltd*,[41] where the Court of Appeal said that as long as some illness to the claimant's pigs was foreseeable as a result of the defendant's negligence, they were liable for the unforeseen illness that did in fact develop, the consequence being of

---

38   [1963] AC 837.
39   (1964) 108 Sol Jo 838.
40   [1964] 1 QB 518, CA.
41   [1978] QB 791.

the same type as that which was foreseeable (this was a claim in contract but the court said that the law as to the amount of damages recoverable was the same in contract as in tort).

In *Jolley v Sutton London Borough Council*,[42] a boat was left abandoned on land by the defendants. Children played with it. They propped it up; it fell off the prop; the claimant was injured. The defendants admitted they should not have left it there and that some injury was foreseeable from children playing on it and falling through rotten planking. The Court of Appeal decided that injury from the boat falling over after having being propped up was not foreseeable and was of a different type and kind from an injury caused by simply falling through rotten planking. The House of Lords, pointing out that the wider risk could have been eliminated without any more expense than that involved in eliminating the narrower risk (ie by removing the boat), restored the judgment of the trial judge in favour of the claimant. Lord Hoffmann said:[43]

> It is also agreed that what must have been foreseen is not the precise injury which occurred but injury of a given description. The foreseeability is not as to the particulars but of the genus, and the description is formulated by reference to the nature of the risk which ought to have been foreseen.

In *Wisniewski v Central Manchester Health Authority*[44] the claimant suffered cerebral palsy as a result of partial strangulation by an umbilical cord during childbirth. The judge found that the clinician was negligent in failing to respond to an abnormal cardiotacograph trace, which ought to have led the clinicians to perform a caesarean section. The judge found that the actual mechanism that led to the hypoxia (a knot in the cord wrapped around the neck) could not have been foreseen. He found:[45]

> I am, however, satisfied that there clearly was a foreseeable risk of damage by hypoxia to Philip. The damage that occurred was caused by hypoxia and of the kind that was foreseeable; as the damage was of the kind foreseeable, it makes no difference that the precise mechanism by which the hypoxia arose was not foreseeable.

Dismissing the defendant's appeal, Brooke LJ could:[46]

> find no fault with this approach, and it would in my judgment be regarded as an affront to common sense, and the law would look an ass, if we reached any different conclusion.

In *London Borough of Islington v UCL Hospital NHS Trust*,[47] where the local authority who had to provide care for a patient negligently injured by the hospital sought to recover the cost of that care from the hospital, the Court of Appeal said that the defendant must be taken to have known that the range of patients whom it treated would have a range of care requirements and financial needs. Care by a local authority in a case in which it could not recover the cost of the care could not be seen as so unusual as to fall outside that range. The precise manner in which the injury would occur did not have to be foreseeable, so the defendant did

---

42 [2000] 1 WLR 1082.
43 [2000] 1 WLR 1082 at 1091.
44 [1998] PIQR 324.
45 [1998] PIQR 324 at 344.
46 [1998] PIQR 324 at 344.
47 [2005] EWCA Civ 596, MLC 1254.

not have to know that Mrs J would require local authority care and would not be able to pay for it; but only to have institutional knowledge that some patients with Mrs J's disability would fall into that category.

In *Loraine v Wirral University Teaching Hospital NHS Foundation Trust*,[48] the claimant suffered cerebral palsy caused by foetal asphyxia that he had sustained when his mother suffered a profound placental abruption shortly before his birth. Plender J found that the hospital failed to retrieve the records of the mother's earlier pregnancies. Had her history of fibroid and footling breech been known, a prudent consultant would have admitted her to hospital so that she could be observed and could receive prompt attention in case of an emergency. The claimant would have been born uninjured if the mother had been in hospital when she suffered the placental abruption.

The defendant argued that the immediate cause of hypoxia (placental abruption) was not foreseeable; since the mechanism that caused the claimant's condition was not reasonably within the contemplation of those caring for his mother, it could not incur liability for any act or omission that caused it. However the judge found that the foreseeable consequence of the defendant's breach was the exposure of the claimant to cerebral palsy. The damage foreseeable in the event of a cord prolapse was precisely the same in kind as the damage suffered by reason of the placental abruption. The fact that the route by which the claimant came to suffer that outcome was not the same as the route that was to be foreseen at the time of the breach did not allow the defendant to escape liability.

CONCLUSION

For the purposes of the medical negligence action, we may sum up (remembering that we are here only dealing with the question what damage may be compensated for, given a breach of duty, and also bearing in mind that the law is far from clear in this area) as follows.

If there was no foreseeability of harm on the facts that the defendants knew or ought to have known, then recovery for any injury occasioned will not be permitted.

If there was foreseeability of physical damage, however slight the chance and however slight the injury to be foreseen, then compensation may be got for all physical injury resulting from the breach of duty that is of the same type as the injury to be foreseen, plus any injury, however unforeseeable, that is consequent upon the foreseeable injury. Unforeseeable injury not consequent upon a foreseeable injury is not compensatable, but this is subject to the rule that the tortfeasor must take the claimant as he finds him.

Subject to that rule, some injury must actually be suffered that falls within the type of injury to be foreseen, ie within the area of risk created (in *The Wagon Mound* (above), the Privy Council said that foreseeability must be of 'the damage that happened – the damage in suit'). Whether a court these days is likely in practice to say that the injury suffered was of a different type or kind from the injury that could have been foreseen

---

48   [2008] EWHC 1565 (QB).

and thus deny recovery to a person injured through another's admitted negligence may be doubted.

On this aspect of negligence as on every other, the determining factor will be the judge's view as to whether justice dictates recovery. He will then find a legal peg on which to hang his decision. That is particularly easy in the field of negligence, where so much is uncertain and lacks precision. As Lord Wright said in *Hay (or Bourhill) v Young*,[49] '... negligence is a fluid principle, which has to be applied to the most diverse conditions and problems of human life.' It may well be that, as RWM Dias has said, 'the principles of the future will be that a negligent person shall be liable according as the court thinks reasonable in the circumstances'. The progress of law within a society is always from formalism to flexibility, albeit that in the common law tradition judicial activism is usually disguised by an artfully contrived appearance of deference to authority.

---

49 [1943] AC 92 at 107, HL.

Chapter 9

The proof of negligence

Andrew Buchan and Dr Jonathan H Cook

INTRODUCTION

There are a number of difficulties a claimant faces in proving negligence. They include the problem of ascertaining exactly what was done in the course of treatment, of securing expert evidence which will allege and substantiate a want of due care, of proving a causative link between the treatment and the injury, and of overcoming any possible judicial deference to the medical profession, and, if the matter goes further, the appeal court.

The burden of proving negligent conduct resulting in injury is upon the claimant. Where there is no direct or circumstantial evidence which permits a conclusion to be drawn as to how the accident happened, the claimant may pray in aid the maxim *res ipsa loquitur* (the matter speaks for itself). This applies where what happened is not the sort of thing that would normally happen in the absence of negligence in some form or another. The court may then find that there was negligence even though it is not known what form that negligence took. If the defendants give a reasonable explanation as to how the accident might have happened without negligence, or show that they had in fact taken every possible care of the patient, the court will not be entitled to rely on the maxim.

DIFFICULTIES IN CAUSATION

Another obstacle to proving a claim for compensation is that, even if one knows what specific acts or omissions were alleged to have been negligent, one has to prove that not only did they constitute a less than reasonable standard of care, but also that they were the cause of injury or loss to the patient. Negligence is not actionable without proof of loss or injury arising from the negligent acts or omissions. But the aetiology of medical conditions is notoriously complex and obscure. Would correct or timely treatment have prevented death or resulted in the patient being better off than he actually is? How to prove that a particular act or omission caused any part of the claimant's present condition? Can one give, and is it relevant to give, an estimation of the chances of proper treatment having saved or helped him? The problem of causation, of showing that what was done or omitted was not only negligent by professional standards but also caused or may have caused a deterioration in the condition of the patient that would not otherwise have occurred, is considered above in Chapter 7.

BURDEN OF PROOF

The burden of proving what needs to be proved to establish a case rests on the claimant. It historically has been said that there are no special rules about the burden or standard of proof in cases involving professional negligence, but that it must necessarily be harder to prove negligence where a case concerns the 'complicated and sophisticated professional activities of a doctor, lawyer or architect' (*Dwyer v Roderick*[1]).

In *Hucks v Cole*,[2] Lord Denning said that:

> A charge of negligence against a professional man was serious. It stood on a different footing to a charge of negligence against the driver of a motor car. The consequences were far more serious. It affected his professional status and reputation. The burden of proof was correspondingly greater. As the charge was so grave, so should the proof be clear.

It is clear that statement does not represent the modern law.[3]

In *Ashcroft v Mersey Regional Health Authority*[4] the judge said that the question was whether it had been established on a balance of probabilities that the physician had failed to exercise the care required of a man possessing and professing special skill in circumstances which required the exercise of that special skill. No added burden of proof rested on the claimant. The more skilled a person was the more care which was expected of him. That test should be applied without gloss either way (Kilner Brown J).

The claimant has to persuade the court that the only explanation for the injury that can reasonably be accepted is one that involves negligence. If the court cannot select between two explanations for complications following treatment, only one of which involves negligence, then the claimant has not proved his case (*per* Beldam J in *Harrington v Essex Area Health Authority*[5]).[6]

In *Clark v MacLennan*,[7] Pain J said that where in the context of a general duty of care there had been a failure to take a generally recognised precaution which had been followed by damage of the kind

---

1   (1983) 80 LS Gaz R 3003, 127 Sol Jo 805, CA.

2   (1968) reported [1993] 4 Med LR 393, CA.

3   The same thing may be said for the odd pronouncement from Lord Denning in *Bater v Bater* [1950] 2 All ER 458, CA (approved by the Court of Appeal in *Hornal v Neuberger Products Ltd* [1956] 3 All ER 970) to the effect that the degree of probability required to establish proof could vary with the gravity of the allegation. As a matter of logic, it cannot be right that 51% probability is enough to prove negligence against a shopkeeper or builder, but 75% is required against a doctor; and this approach is no longer applied in practice.

4   [1983] 2 All ER 245.

5   (1984) Times, 14 November.

6   A judge is entitled to conclude that he simply does not know what happened, in which case, if *res ipsa loquitur* does not apply, the claim fails (*Ratcliffe v Plymouth and Torbay Health Authority* [1998] Lloyd's Rep Med 162, CA).

7   [1983] 1 All ER 416.

that that precaution was designed to prevent, the burden of proof shifted to the defendant to show either that he was not in breach of duty or that the damage was not caused by the breach. In that case there had been a departure from the usual practice of not performing a certain operation for stress incontinence within three months of delivery. That departure was found to have been unjustified and therefore constituted a breach of the duty of care. It was followed by a consequence that the precaution was designed to prevent, ie breakdown of the repair effected in the operation, and it was therefore up to the defendant to satisfy the court that that damage had not flowed from their breach of duty to the patient. However, it was expressly denied by the House of Lords in *Wilsher v Essex Area Health Authority*[8] that the burden shifted in such circumstances. In *Gregory v Pembrokeshire Health Authority*,[9] Rougier J rejected the suggestion that whenever the fault complained of was a fault in omission the burden of proving causation shifted to the defendants:

> the burden of proof on the balance of probabilities remains on the plaintiff throughout.

In *Defreitas v O'Brien*,[10] Otton LJ said the *Bolam* test did not impose any burden of proof on the defendant to establish that his diagnosis or treatment would be acceptable to a responsible body of medical opinion. The burden of proof was on the claimant.

Lost records

It is a sad reality that if, as not uncommonly transpires, vital records are 'missing' a claim that could otherwise be proved may fail. However, Latin may help here. In *Malhotra v Dhawan*,[11] the Court of Appeal, considering the maxim *omnia praesumuntur contra spoliatorem ('all things are presumed against the individual who destroys evidence')*, indicated that inferences could be drawn against a party who had destroyed relevant evidence (although the court said the maxim only applied where that had been done to stop the other party showing how much of his property had been taken).[12] In *Le Page v Kingston and Richmond Health Authority*,[13] John Samuels QC, sitting as a deputy judge of the High Court, said that the defendant could not properly complain if he drew inferences from surviving documentation which might have been contradicted by other records which they had improperly destroyed.

In *Skelton v Lewisham and North Southwark Health Authority*,[14] the inadequacy of the anaesthetic notes (brief, unsigned, without a record of key events and pressures), although not causative of the damage, was said by the judge to be indicative of an unexplained carelessness. In *Rhodes v Spokes and Farbridge*,[15] Smith J said:

---

8   [1988] AC 1074.
9   [1989] 1 Med LR 81 at 85.
10   [1995] 6 Med LR 108, CA.
11   [1997] 8 Med LR 319.
12   In *Dobson v North Tyneside Health Authority* [1997] 1 WLR 596, the Court of Appeal said that for the maxim to apply it had to be shown that the spoliator was a 'wrongdoer'.
13   [1997] 8 Med LR 229.
14   [1998] Lloyd's Rep Med 324.
15   [1996] 7 Med LR 135.

A doctor's contemporaneous record of a consultation should form a reliable evidential base in a case such as this. I regret to say that Dr Farbridge's notes of the plaintiff's attendances do not provide any such firm foundation. They are scanty in the extreme. He rarely recorded her complaints or symptoms; he rarely recorded any observations; usually he noted only the drug he prescribed … The failure to take a proper note is not evidence of a doctor's negligence or of the inadequacy of treatment. But a doctor who fails to keep an adequate note of a consultation lays himself open to a finding that his recollection is faulty and someone else's is correct. After all, a patient has only to remember his or her own case, whereas the doctor has to remember one case out of hundreds which occupied his mind at the material time.

In the recent case of *Re (a child) v Calderdale and Huddersfield NHS Foundation Trust*,[16] Goss J found that the defendant had destroyed relevant medical records after the claim began in clear breach of its duties under CPR Pt 31 PDB para 7. While the records were destroyed as a result of 'negligent failings' rather than in a deliberate attempt to destroy evidence, the situation caused difficulties for the judge, and ultimately for the defendant. Goss J said the following at [6]:

> The Claimants contend that where there are ambiguities or uncertainties on the face of the documents, the court ought to resolve them in the claimants' favour. Given that the defendant failed in their duty to maintain the records, where, by reason of the quality of the relevant record now available compared to what would have been expected to have been clearer on the originals, I consider that it is appropriate to proceed on the rebuttable assumption that my reading of the entries should be the most favourable to the claimants that is reasonable on the face of the available documents.

Witness evidence

A number of recent cases illustrate the difficulties that can ensue when witnesses fail to 'come up to proof'.

The recent High Court case of *Britchford v Staffordshire and Stoke-on-Trent Partnership NHS Trust*[17] illustrates the problems that can ensue for both parties in circumstances where significant time has elapsed since the alleged negligence. An important issue in the case was what was said during the claimant's consultation at a health centre. The claimant's case was that she had a 'cold blue hand' when she attended. The claimant did not give oral evidence but did serve a written statement. The claimant's partner, who attended the health centre with her, did give evidence. The treating medical practitioner could not recall the incident, but relied upon his notes. The defendant's case was that if the claimant had indeed had a cold blue hand it would have been mentioned in the notes. In oral evidence, the claimant's partner changed his account and accepted that the claimant did not have a cold blue hand at the time of the consultation. Consequently, in the absence of any evidence that the defendant had negligently failed to diagnose a vascular or surgical problem, the claim failed.

---

16 [2017] EWHC 824 (QB), [2017] Med LR 390.
17 [2018] EWHC 2109 (QB).

In *Jaciubek v Gulati*[18] the court considered the problems that can ensue in circumstances where a witness, in this case the claimant, has an honest but mistaken belief that events have unfolded in a certain way. While the medical records of the claimant's hospital consultation were incomplete, Foskett J determined at [90] that medical records should not be subjected to a 'contextual and linguistic interpretation that the circumstances of their creation do not justify'. Ultimately, Foskett J concluded that while the claimant genuinely believed she had articulated specific complaints to the hospital which would have strengthened her case, he could not accept that the recollection was accurate. Consequently, the claimant had failed to come up to proof and the negligence action failed accordingly.

RES IPSA LOQUITUR

What is considered here is a situation that often arises, where not merely is it unclear why the patient's condition has deteriorated or what the cause must have been of the injury suffered, but where the patient cannot even point to any act or omission and say that it was wrong, and in all probability caused the present condition. In these circumstances the only acts or omissions known to have taken place are unimpugnable. Therefore, all that can be said is that something must have been done which should not have been done, because the injury could not have arisen without something having been done wrong. This is the principle of evidence known as *res ipsa loquitur*, 'the matter speaks for itself'.

There must be reasonable evidence of negligence. But where the thing is shown to be under the management of the defendant or the defendant's servants, and the accident is such as in the ordinary course of things does not happen if those who have the management use proper care, it affords reasonable evidence, in the absence of explanation by the defendant, that the accident arose from want of care (*per* Erle CJ in *Scott v London and St Katherine Docks Co*[19]).

The maxim applies where 'the circumstances are more consistent, reasonably interpreted without further explanation, with ... negligence than with any other cause of the accident happening' (*per* Kennedy LJ in *Russell v London and South-western Rly Co*[20]).

The court is in any event entitled to draw an inference as to how an accident happened upon the evidence before it. It may be that no one can give direct evidence of how it happened, but, if the evidence that is given permits a reasonable inference to be drawn as to the cause, the court in drawing such an inference is not applying the principle of *res ipsa loquitur*, for that principle only applies where the cause cannot be specified, whether upon direct evidence or by inference.

> If the facts are sufficiently known the question ceases to be one where the facts speak for themselves, and the solution is to be found by determining whether on the facts as established negligence is to be inferred or not (*per* Lord Porter in *Barkway v South Wales Transport Co Ltd* [1950] 1 All ER 392 at 395, HL).

---

18   [2016] EWHC 269 (QB).
19   (1865) 3 H & C 596, Ex Ch.
20   (1908) 24 TLR 548 at 551, CA.

The maxim is misapplied if it is deployed where it is known what the doctor did and the dispute is as to whether that constituted negligence. A surgeon performing a laminectomy may penetrate too far and injure the nerve or the spinal cord. One cannot say: 'Of course it was negligent; the matter speaks for itself.' That is simply a misunderstanding of what the maxim means in law. It would be up to expert evidence to establish whether or not any surgeon exercising due care could make that mistake.

It is standard practice when drafting the Particulars of Claim that the claimant will pray in aid the principle of *res ipsa loquitur*. However, *that is strictly* unnecessary if the pleading is otherwise complete as to the facts alleged (see *Bennett v Chemical Construction (GB) Ltd*[21]). *Bennett* identified three fundamental conditions which must be met before *res ipsa loquitur* can be successfully invoked:

1   the event is one that would ordinarily not occur in the absence of negligence/fault;
2   the thing causing the damage must have been under the control of the defendant;
3   there is no evidence as to why or how the accident occurred.

The maxim has often been applied where a defendant is carrying out lifting or building operations and the claimant is injured by a falling article. It is not known what made it fall, but the court declares that it would be unlikely to have happened without negligence.

In *Howard v Wessex Regional Health Authority*,[22] Morland J said that *res ipsa* could not help the patient where she had sustained tetraplegia following maxillo-facial surgery by way of a sagittal split osteotomy, because her injury was most likely due to a fibro-cartilaginous embolism, which would not connote negligence. As the helpful note by Margaret Puxon QC at the end of the report of *Howard* shows, it appears that the defendants, as not infrequently happens in medical cases, advanced their explanation for the injury very late in the day. It seems surprising that the judge accepted it.

In *Delaney v Southmead Health Authority*[23] the patient alleged that she had sustained damage to her arm as a result of negligent placing during surgery. The Court of Appeal upheld the finding of the judge in favour of the defendants. They said that, even if *res ipsa* applied, it was always open to a defendant to rebut a case of *res ipsa* either by giving an explanation of what happened which was inconsistent with negligence or by showing that he had exercised all reasonable care. Stuart-Smith LJ doubted that the principle was useful in medical negligence actions, at least not where 'all the evidence in the case has been adduced',[24] and Dillon LJ said:[25]

> I cannot for my part accept that medical science is such a precise science that there cannot in any particular field be any room for the wholly unexpected

21   [1971] 3 All ER 822, CA.
22   [1994] 5 Med LR 57.
23   [1995] 6 Med LR 355.
24   Judge Thompson QC commented on this observation in *Ritchie v Chichester Health Authority* [1994] 5 Med LR 187 at 206.
25   [1995] 6 Med LR 355 at p 10.

result occurring in the human body from the carrying out of a well-recognised procedure.[26]

In *Jacobs v Great Yarmouth and Waverney Health Authority*,[27] a case of anaesthetic awareness, the Court of Appeal said (in 1984) that *res ipsa loquitur* meant no more than that on the facts that a claimant was able to prove, although he might not be able to point to a particular negligent act or omission on the part of the defendants, the fair inference to draw was that there had been negligence of some sort on the part of the defendants; but if there were further evidence presented by the defendants, those facts might be shown in an entirely different light so that it would not be possible to draw the inference of negligence.

In *Hooper v Young*,[28] Otton LJ said that it was a pity *res ipsa* had ever entered the case because it had no place where the event that caused the injury (damage to a ureter by kinking of the suture) could have happened without negligence.

In *Girard v Royal Columbian Hospital*,[29] where the patient had suffered permanent paralysis of both legs after a spinal anaesthetic, the Canadian judge, Andrews J, exonerating the anaesthetist, used words similar to Dillon LJ in the *Delaney* case (above):

> The human body is not a container filled with a material whose performance can be predictably charted and analysed. It cannot be equated with a box of chewing tobacco or a soft drink. Thus, while permissible inferences may be drawn as to the normal behaviour of these types of commodities, the same type of reasoning does not necessarily apply to a human being. Because of this, medical science has not yet reached the stage where the law ought to presume that a patient must come out of an operation as well as or better than he went into it.

In *Bull and Wakeham v Devon Area Health Authority*[30] two of the Lords Justices differed on the question whether *res ipsa* applied to the failure of the hospital to have an obstetrician attend the mother at the vital time, Mustill LJ taking the view (at 142) that as the facts of the accident were largely known the principle did not apply.

Even if the three conditions set out in *Bennett* (see above) are met, a defendant may rebut the presumption of negligence. However, the defendant cannot do so merely by showing the general precautions they have taken. The authorities are not entirely clear on how far the defendant must go to shift the burden of proof back to the claimant, in particular, whether the defendant has to show a possible or a likely cause of the accident that would not involve negligence. It was said in *Moore v R Fox & Sons*[31] that it was not sufficient for the defendants to show

---

26　Stuart-Smith LJ offered further thoughts on the principle of res ipsa in *Fallows v Randle* [1997] 8 Med LR 160 at 163, CA where he cited a passage from Megaw LJ in *Lloyde v West Midlands Gas Board* [1971] 1 WLR 749 at 755, CA. The Court of Appeal decision in *Ratcliffe v Plymouth and Torbay Health Authority* [1998] Lloyd's Rep Med 162 repays study. It shows that a judge is entitled to conclude that he simply does not know what happened, and that in such circumstances there is no presumption that res ipsa applies.
27　[1995] 6 Med LR 192.
28　[1998] 2 Lloyd's Rep Med 61, CA.
29　(1976) 66 DLR (3d) 676.
30　[1993] 4 Med LR 117, CA.
31　[1956] 1 QB 596, CA.

several hypothetical causes consistent with the absence of negligence and that the accident might have occurred without negligence on their part. To discharge the onus they had to go further and either show that they had not been negligent (it would seem to be enough in this connection if the defendants satisfied the court that all possible precautions had been taken) or give a reasonable explanation of the cause of the accident which did not connote negligence.

It was said in *Ng Chun Pui v Lee Chuen Tat*,[32] that the burden of proving negligence remains upon the claimant, despite the applicability of the doctrine of *res ipsa loquitur*.

The cases make it clear that one must draw a distinction between the situation where there is more than one possible cause for the injury and the situation where the precise cause is unknown. In the second situation one may be able to take advantage of the maxim. In the first situation it is simply a matter for the judge to decide what was the operative cause, and, in doing this, the judge is entitled to prefer the evidence of one expert to another (*see eg Betts v Berkshire Health Authority*[33]). Inferences may also be drawn from the evidence. In *Skelton v Lewisham and North Southwark Health Authority*,[34] Kay J decided that the only possible explanation on the facts for the administration of certain drugs preoperatively was an episode of hypotension causing brain injury. In *Bull v Devon Area Health Authority*,[35] Slade LJ said that the trial judge had gone further than he needed when he found that the claimant had excluded all possible causes of his injury other than that for which he contended, because it would have been sufficient to make the qualified finding that the cause for which he contended was established on the balance of probabilities.

More recent authorities have attempted to clarify the role of the doctrine of *res ipsa loquitur* in clinical negligence cases. In *Thomas v Curley*[36] the claimant sustained an injury during surgery in an area other than the site of the surgery. Lloyd Jones LJ held at [33] that this fact 'called for an explanation as to how that might have occurred in the absence of negligence'. As no evidence was forthcoming from the defendant, the trial judge assessed the weight of the evidence and determined on the balance of probabilities that the claimant had proved the defendant's negligence. That had, in Lloyd Jones LJ's view 'nothing to do with the reversal of the burden of proof and nothing to do with *res ipsa loquitur.*'

Subsequently, in *O'Connor v Pennine Acute Hospitals NHS Trust*,[37] Jackson LJ said the following at [60]:

> More recent authority has tended to the view that res ipsa loquitur is not a principle of law at all. There is no reversal of the burden of proof. The so-called res ipsa loquitur cases are merely cases in which, on the totality of the evidence, the court was able to make a finding of negligence. It has always been the position that courts can make findings of fact by means of inference when there is no direct evidence of the events in issue.

---

32 [1988] RTR 298, PC.
33 [1997] 8 Med LR 87.
34 [1998] Lloyd's Rep Med 324.
35 [1993] 4 Med LR 117, CA.
36 [2013] EWCA Civ 117.
37 [2015] EWCA Civ 1244.

However, Jackson LJ then went on to find that the defendant's failure to provide an explanation for the claimant's injuries was a factor which it was permissible for the trial judge to have taken into account in determining that the defendant's negligence had been proven.

The current position, it appears, is that the doctrine of *res ipsa loquitur* does still have a role to play in clinical negligence cases. The principle merely appears to have been relabelled such that in circumstances where a defendant cannot provide an explanation for a claimant's injuries in circumstances where such an explanation is called for that failure will be considered in the round, and appropriate inferences drawn, as part of a broader assessment of the evidence available.

Whose negligence?

In some of the older cases, the issue has been whether it can be shown that the negligence the court is asked to infer must have been that of the defendant himself or one of his agents rather than that of someone for whom the defendant was not responsible. One would, therefore, encounter the problem as to who was the servant or agent of the surgeon and who was the servant or agent of the hospital (see Chapter 4). Now that most cases are brought against the NHS Trust or health authority, which is responsible for all the medical personnel involved in the treatment of the patient, this particular issue is unlikely to arise frequently (though it could still be relevant in the field of private practice and in cases against a GP). Suffice it to say that the claimant must show that the accident could not reasonably have happened without some want of care on the part of the defendant himself or his agents.

Examples

When one considers the number of times *res ipsa* has been accepted by a court as an aid to its decision, one can only wonder why it has come in for such bad press recently. The answer may be that it is due to unnecessary and inapposite recourse to the maxim by claimant lawyers in many cases.

Whether or not the accident is one which the court will find would not usually happen without some negligence somewhere will depend on expert evidence. Things can go wrong in operations without there being any negligence. Denning LJ had this to say in *Cassidy v Ministry of Health*:[38]

> If the plaintiff had to prove that some particular doctor or nurse was negligent he would not be able to do it. But he was not put to that impossible task: he says, 'I went into the hospital to be cured of two stiff fingers. I have come out with four stiff fingers, and my hand is useless. That should not have happened if due care had been used. Explain it if you can.' I am quite clearly of the opinion that that raises a *prima facie* case against the hospital authorities: see *per* Goddard LJ in *Mahon v Osborne* [1939] 2 KB 14, 50. They have nowhere explained how it could happen without negligence. They have busied themselves in saying that this or that member of their staff was not negligent. But they have not called a single person to say that the injuries were consistent with due care on the part of all the members of their staff. They called some of the people

---

38   [1951] 2 KB 343 at 365.

who actually treated the man ... but they did not call any expert at all to say that this might happen despite all care. They have not therefore displaced the *prima facie* case against them ...

Both Somervell and Singleton LJJ agreed that the facts disclosed a *prima facie* case of negligence on the basis of *res ipsa loquitur*.[39]

In *Roe v Minister of Health*,[40] patients in hospital for minor operations were paralysed by the spinal anaesthetic each was given:

The judge has said that those facts do not speak for themselves, but I think that they do. They certainly call for an explanation. Each of these men is entitled to say to the hospital: 'While I was in your hands something has been done to me which has wrecked my life. Please explain how it has come to pass' (*per* Denning LJ at 81).

Morris LJ said:

When [the claimants] proved all that they were in a position to prove they then said *res ipsa loquitur*. But this convenient and succinct formula possesses no magic qualities: nor has it any added virtue, other than that of brevity, merely because it is expressed in Latin. There are certain happenings that do not normally occur in the absence of negligence, and upon proof of these a court will probably hold that there is a case to answer.

However, in this case, the hospital gave an explanation of the accident which was accepted by the court as absolving them from any negligence (the ampoules of anaesthetic had been kept in a solution of phenol, which seeped into the anaesthetic after the ampoules had developed in some way or another tiny, undetectable cracks or molecular flaws. At that time such a possibility and the danger arising therefrom was not foreseeable).

In this case Lord Denning also referred to the position where both hospital and private doctor deny negligence but give no explanation for the patient's injury. He said:[41]

I do not think that the hospital authorities and [the doctor] can both avoid giving an explanation by the simple expedient of throwing responsibility on to the other. If an injured person shows that one or other or both of two persons injured him, but cannot say which of them it was, then he is not defeated altogether. He can call on each of them for an explanation.

In *Saunders v Leeds Western Health Authority and Robinson*[42] the heart of a four-year-old girl stopped for some 30 minutes during an operation under anaesthetic to remedy a congenitally deformed hip. The defendants agreed that did not normally happen without a want of care somewhere but they offered an explanation as to how the accident might have happened. Mann J rejected their explanation and said:

The plaintiff's reliance on *res ipsa loquitur* makes it unnecessary for her to suggest a specific cause for the cardiac arrest. It is plain from evidence called on her behalf that the heart of a fit child does not arrest under anaesthesia if proper care is taken in the anaesthetic and surgical processes.

This decision has been thought to constitute a helpful departure for claimants in the court's willingness to infer negligence, at any rate in

---

39 [1951] 2 KB 343 at 348, 353.
40 [1954] 2 QB 66.
41 [1954] 2 QB 66 at 82.
42 [1993] 4 Med LR 355.

the context of injury under or from anaesthetic; but, though the case is certainly not without significance as a precedent, it is important to note that the defendants admitted here that the principle of *res ipsa* applied to the facts. See also *Glass v Cambridge Health Authority*.[43]

In *Moore v Worthing District Health Authority*,[44] Owen J rejected a plea of *res ipsa* where a patient was left with bilateral ulnar nerve palsy following a mastoidectomy. He absolved the defendants from failing to protect the arms properly while the patient was under anaesthetic by accepting their contention that the patient had been abnormally vulnerable to such an injury, despite the absence of any real evidence of such a condition.

Other examples

In *Mahon v Osborne*,[45] where the surgeon was sued when a swab was left inside the patient, the majority of the Court of Appeal was of the view that the principle did not apply in the case of a complex operation where a number of medical staff took part, but it is now clear that the correct view was that taken by Goddard LJ when he said:

> There can be no possible question but that neither swabs nor instruments are ordinarily left in the patient's body ... If therefore a swab is left in the patient's body, it seems clear that the surgeon is called upon for an explanation. That is, he is called upon to show, not necessarily why he missed it but that he exercised due care to prevent its being left there.

This view was endorsed by the Court of Appeal in *Urry v Bierer*,[46] where there was a dispute as to whether the surgeon or the nurse had the responsibility for seeing all the swabs were removed after an abdominal operation. As mentioned above, now that the hospital will be liable in almost all cases for the negligence of any of those who treat the patient, this sort of tedious analysis of who had what responsibility and who was whose agent is unlikely to regularly arise.

Reference may also be made to *Cavan v Wilcox*,[47] where the maxim was applied to the situation of a patient who developed gangrene after he had been given an injection in his arm; and to *Fish v Kapur*,[48] where it was held that the maxim did not apply where a patient's jaw was broken during a dental procedure.

In *Clarke v Worboys*,[49] where the patient's buttock was burnt in electro-coagulation treatment, the Court of Appeal reversed the judge's finding and held that the evidence showed that such an accident would not happen if reasonable care were used.

In *Ludlow v Swindon Health Authority*,[50] where the claimant alleged she had been awake during a Caesarean section as a result of what must have been the negligent administration of the anaesthetic, the judge said

---

43   [1995] 6 Med LR 91.
44   [1992] 3 Med LR 431.
45   [1939] 2 KB 14.
46   (1955) Times, 15 July.
47   (1973) 44 DLR (3d) 42.
48   [1948] 2 All ER 176.
49   (1952) Times, 18 March.
50   [1989] 1 Med LR 104.

that for the doctrine of *res ipsa loquitur* to apply the claimant had first to establish that she had indeed been awake during the operation. As he was not satisfied of that, the doctrine could not help her.

In *Leckie v Brent and Harrow Area Health Authority*,[51] it was held that a 1.5 cm cut on the cheek of a baby delivered by Caesarean section would not happen without some lack of care. The matter spoke for itself.

The claimant was successful in *Woodhouse v Yorkshire Regional Health Authority*.[52] She was a pianist whose ulnar nerves were severely damaged in an operation for a subphrenic abscess. The judge said that the evidence established that this sort of injury would not occur if the standard precautions to avoid this recognised hazard had been taken. The Court of Appeal upheld his decision. *However, for a contrary decision see O'Malley-Williams v Governors of National Hospital for Nervous Diseases*,[53] where it was held that the maxim did not apply where partial paralysis was sustained by the claimant (who was also an accomplished pianist) because the injury sustained was recognised as an inherent risk of the treatment undergone, namely an aortagram for recurrent episodes of loss of vision in the right eye.

In *Brazier v Ministry of Defence*[54] the defendant satisfied the judge that he should not infer negligence on the part of a person giving an injection to the claimant as the cause of the needle breaking, because the actual cause could properly be inferred to be a latent defect in the shaft of the needle (see also *Corner v Murray*[55]).

In the Scottish case of *Fowler v Greater Glasgow Health Board*[56] a court of first instance was unable to infer negligence in treatment from the fact that the doctors had failed later to give the parents of a dead child an explanation of what had happened.

In *Coyne v Wigan Health Authority*[57] the defendant agreed that *res ipsa* applied when hypoxia leading to brain damage occurred during recovery from a routine operation, but they failed to satisfy the judge that it was due to the (non-negligent) cause of silent regurgitation of gastric content. Therefore the matter did 'speak for itself' and the claimant succeeded.

APPEALS AND THE BURDEN OF PROOF

The principles of appeal

The two most significant principles of law affecting appeals are:

1   the trial judge has the great advantage of seeing and hearing the witnesses, whether lay or expert, and so the appeal tribunal must be very slow to interfere with those findings (as opposed to the *inferences* which the judge drew from his findings or from facts not in dispute); and

51   [1982] 1 Lancet 634.
52   [1984] 1 Lancet 1306.
53   (1975) 1 BMJ 635.
54   [1965] 1 Lloyd's Rep 26.
55   [1954] 2 BMJ 1555.
56   1990 SLT 303n.
57   [1991] 2 Med LR 301.

2   the exercise of a discretion by the judge should not be invalidated merely because the appeal tribunal would have exercised their discretion differently.

The second principle comes to the fore in medical negligence claims in the context of the exercise of discretion under s 33 of the Limitation Act 1980, which is considered at length in Chapter 20. Here we consider the extent to which the Court of Appeal has on occasions interfered with the findings and conclusions of the trial judge and how it has justified that interference. In *Pickford v ICI*,[58] Stuart-Smith LJ said:

> I am well aware of the inhibitions laid upon this court in interfering with and reversing the trial judge's findings of fact, especially primary findings. The law is succinctly summarised in the Annual Practice at paragraph 59/1/55 and is very familiar to any member of this court. I do not propose to set it out *in extenso*. We were also referred by Mr Hytner to a passage in the speech of Lord Bridge of Harwich in *Wilsher* v *Essex Area Health Authority* [1988] AC 1074 where he reminded the court that similar principles apply in relation to the evaluation of disputed medical evidence. But it is our duty to reconsider the matter, paying great weight to the opinion of the trial judge, especially where there is a conflict of evidence and the demeanour and bearing of the witness plays a significant part in the judge's decision.

In *Briody v St Helens and Knowsley Health Authority*,[59] Ward LJ said:

> Although this court is well able to consider the medical records as they stand, the case depended on more than drawing inevitable inferences from those statements and the judge had the unenviable task of assessing the witnesses and deciding, if there were a conflict, which evidence he preferred. Although I do not shrink from overruling him if, on full consideration, I come to the conclusion that he was wrong, nonetheless, due weight is to be given to the decision of the judge at first instance and I need to be satisfied that his overall conclusion was *plainly* wrong. That requires a close look at the whole of the evidence.

The advantage enjoyed by the trial judge extends to the hearing of expert witnesses. In *Wilsher v Essex Area Health Authority*,[60] Lord Bridge said (at 1091):

> Where expert witnesses are radically at issue about complex technical questions within their own field and are examined and cross-examined at length about their conflicting theories, I believe that the judge's advantage in seeing them and hearing them is scarcely less important than when he has to resolve some conflict of primary fact between lay witnesses in purely mundane matters.

In *Wardlaw v Farrar*,[61] a fatal accident claim over the death of the defendant GP's patient arising out of a failure to consider a diagnosis of pulmonary embolism and arrange hospital admission, the Court of Appeal said that the judge had evidently been much more impressed by the expert cardiological evidence called for the defendant. There was clear authority that an appellate court should be very slow to interfere with a trial judge's views on the quality of the evidence of expert witnesses whom

---

58   [1997] 8 Med LR 270, CA.
59   [1999] Lloyd's Rep Med 185.
60   [1988] AC 1074, HL.
61   [2004] Lloyd's Rep Med 98.

he had had the advantage of seeing and hearing; so the court would not interfere with the judge's assessment and the appeal was dismissed.

In *Gray v Southampton & South West Hampshire Health Authority*,[62] a claim for brain damage sustained in or around a surgical procedure, the Court of Appeal said that where the trial judge had not rejected the evidence of the attending anaesthetist it was not open to them to reach conclusions of primary fact, the effect of which would be to reject such evidence.

More recently, in *Barnett v Medway NHS Foundation Trust*,[63] the claimant appealed against a decision where the trial judge had found it impossible to resolve key factual disputes between the two parties. Consequently, he had relied upon the burden of proof, and found that the claimant had failed to prove his case on the balance of probabilities. Irwin LJ, dismissing the appeal, said the following at [55]:

> ... having now conducted the exercise of examining and evaluating the evidence given before the judge, I for my part understand why he reached the conclusion he did on this issue. Not only was the medicine particularly difficult, but the evidence of the two microbiology experts was expressed in difficult and shifting terms. The excerpts from the transcript set out above are relatively long for an appellate judgment, but represent a small part of the relevant evidence. Both experts shifted position. The evidence of both experts was somewhat rebarbative. I consider the judge was justified in saying Professor Wilson considered bacteraemia in the blood was a 'possibility'. Taken as a whole his evidence fell short of establishing probability. It is clear from an exchange with counsel after the close of evidence that the judge was seeking help to find firm ground in all this. I am not surprised he was unable to do so. In my view this was indeed one of those rare cases where the judge was justified in his inability to resolve an issue of fact consistent with the approach laid down in *Stephens v Cannon* ([2005] EWCA Civ 222) and *Verlander v Devon Waste Management* ([2007] EWCA Civ 835).

Must a judge give reasons for his conclusions?

A judge does not always have to spell out his reasons for every conclusion to which he comes (*Abada v Gray*,[64] a personal injury claim where the trial judge was held to have been entitled to prefer the defendant's medical evidence, even though he had made no express findings of fact). But where no inference as to the judge's reasoning can reasonably be drawn from a judgment that did not make express findings on relevant issues, a retrial will be ordered (*Sewell v Electrolux Ltd*[65]).

In *Eckersley v Binnie*,[66] Bingham LJ said:

> In resolving conflicts of expert evidence the judge remains the judge; he is not obliged to accept evidence simply because it comes from an illustrious source; he can take account of demonstrated partisanship and lack of objectivity. But, save where an expert is guilty of a deliberate attempt to mislead (as happens

---

62   (2002) 67 BMLR 1.
63   [2017] EWCA Civ 235, [2017] Med LR 217.
64   (1997) 40 BMLR 116, CA.
65   (1997) Times, 7 November, CA.
66   (1988) 18 Con LR 1 at 77, CA.

only very rarely), a coherent reasoned opinion expressed by a suitably qualified expert should be the subject of a coherent reasoned rebuttal, unless it can be discounted for other good reason.

Many, if not most, medical negligence trials are decided by the judge's preference for the evidence of one expert rather than another. Consequently, awareness of an expert's reputation, and knowledge of any critical judicial comment on a particular expert, is fundamental for any clinical negligence lawyer. Of course, it does not follow that an expert is not a good expert simply because a judge does not accept his evidence. He may have failed to impress the judge for any number of peripheral reasons. But if he is explicitly criticised by the judge, as is not uncommon, perhaps for being partial or lacking independence, or 'going too far', or it is said that he vacillated or changed his tune, there is usually a good reason for such criticism.

One example is the case of *Hussein v Bradford Teaching Hospitals NHS Foundation Trust*.[67] In that case, which concerned an allegedly negligent failure to diagnose cauda equina syndrome, Coulson J formed a negative opinion of the evidence given by the claimant's orthopaedic expert. At [15] Coulson J noted that the expert's evidence was 'an important element of [the Claimant's] case against the First Defendant, so my conclusion as to his credibility has an inevitable bearing upon my conclusions as to the Claimant's case as a whole'.

In *Stefan v General Medical Council*[68] the Privy Council said that, although at common law there was no general duty to give reasons universally imposed on all decision-makers, the trend of the law had been towards an increased recognition of the duty upon decision-makers of many kinds (the case involved a challenge to a decision of the health committee of the GMC that the appellant's fitness to practice was seriously impaired due to a mental health condition and the consequent indefinite suspension of his registration).

In *English v Emery Reimbold & Strick*,[69] a personal injury claim where the critical issue was whether a disabling dislocation of the claimant's spine was attributable to an injury for which the defendant was responsible, the Court of Appeal gave guidelines on how and when to appeal on the ground that the trial judge's reasons for his decision were inadequate. The court said:

1   It was the judge's duty to produce a judgment that gave a clear explanation for his order.

2   An unsuccessful party should not seek to upset a judgment on the ground of inadequacy of reasons unless, despite the advantage of considering the judgment with knowledge of the evidence given and submissions made at trial, that party was unable to understand why it was that the judge had reached an adverse decision.

3   The effect of the human rights legislation and Strasbourg jurisprudence was that a decision should be reasoned; however the extent of the reasoning did not go further than that required under domestic law.

---

67   [2011] EHWC 2914 (QB).
68   (1999) 49 BMLR 161.
69   [2002] 1 WLR 2409.

4   The practice of giving no reasons for a decision as to costs could only comply with Article 6 of the European Convention on Human Rights if the reason for the decision was implicit from the circumstances in which the award was made.

5   The following course was recommended to deal with cases where inadequacy of reasons was at issue:

When an application for permission to appeal on the ground of lack of reasons was made to the trial judge, the judge should consider whether his judgment was defective. If he concluded that it was, he should set out to remedy the defect by the provision of additional reasons, refusing permission to appeal on the basis that he has adopted that course. If he concluded that the reasons were adequate he should refuse permission to appeal. If an appellate court found an application for permission to appeal well founded, it should consider adjourning the application and remitting the case to the trial judge with an invitation to provide additional reasons for his decision or, where appropriate, his reasons for a specific finding. Where the appellate court was doubtful as to the adequacy of the reasons it was appropriate to adjourn to an oral hearing on notice. Where permission to appeal was granted the appellate court should review the judgment in the context of the evidence and submissions at trial in order to determine whether it was apparent why the judge reached his decision. If satisfied that the reason was apparent then the appeal should be dismissed. If the reason for the decision was not apparent then the appeal court should decide whether itself to proceed to a new hearing or to direct a new trial.

Examples

In the surveying professional negligence case of *Flannery v Halifax Estate Agencies*,[70] Henry LJ said that the professional judge today owed a duty to give reasons, although there were some exceptions (not relevant for our purposes). He said it was not a useful task to attempt to make absolute rules as to the requirement for the judge to give reasons, because issues were so infinitely various. But with expert evidence it should usually be possible to be more explicit in giving reasons (he cited *Eckersley v Binnie* (above)). The parties should be left in no doubt why they had won or lost. Further, a requirement to give reasons concentrated the mind of the judge, so that his deliberations would probably be more soundly based on the evidence. The extent of the duty depended on the subject matter. Where the dispute involves something in the nature of an intellectual exchange, with reasons and analysis advanced on either side, the judge must enter into the issues canvassed before him and explain why he preferred one case over the other. This was likely to apply particularly in litigation where, as in the instant case, there was disputed expert evidence. The court said that in the instant case the judge's preference for the defendant's expert, which was decisive, should have enabled him to give his reasons in the form of the 'coherent reasoned rebuttal' referred to by Bingham LJ in the *Eckersley* case. So the judge had been under a duty

---

70   [2000] 1 WLR 377, CA.

to give reasons but had not done so. The court could not know whether he had had adequate or inadequate reasons for his conclusion. In the circumstances the appeal by the claimants was allowed.

On the other hand, consider the medical case of *Polson v de Silva*.[71] This had been a successful claim against a GP for failing to respond to a mother's request to visit her sick child at home, with the result that the child sustained hearing loss from meningitis. The court said that the judge had carefully considered the evidence and had been fully entitled to prefer the expert evidence of the two consultant physicians for the claimant over that of the defendant's expert witness. There was an ample basis for the judge to conclude that earlier treatment would have avoided the deafness. Clearly, in this case the court was satisfied that the judge had properly considered the evidence and had valid reasons for preferring the evidence of the claimant's experts.

In *Lakey v Merton, Sutton and Wandsworth Health Authority*,[72] the claimant appealed against a finding that a decision by the hospital not to X-ray the patient's leg had not been negligent. The argument was that the judge had failed to evaluate the evidence of the two experts and to make clear findings as to what part of the evidence of each he accepted and what part he rejected. The Court of Appeal gave this issue careful consideration, stating that in order to weigh the submissions *it was necessary to analyse the manner in which the judge expressed his conclusions*. The court concluded that in fact the judge had explained his reasoning very fully and had 'explained himself at considerable length', relying on at least six specific reasons. It is interesting to note that towards the end of his judgment, Thorpe LJ said:

> I suspect that in this field of litigation it is not uncommon for the forensic experts to take relatively extreme positions in the hope of securing an outcome for the party by whom each is instructed. I suspect also that in this case the judge found that each was guilty of some error in presentation ... So it seems to me that it is not incumbent on a judge to explain at great length why he has found the expert contribution perhaps partisan and perhaps unhelpful. His function is to explain clearly the conclusions which he has reached, and Mr Justice Holland certainly did that in this case with exemplary clarity and logic.

In the Canterbury cervical smears case (*Penney, Palmer and Cannon v East Kent Area Health Authority*[73]) the claimants had two histopathologists, the defendant three. The two sides were in total disagreement over what the smears disclosed (the evidence about interpreting smears was immensely technical), but even more significantly over what the average screener, exercising due care, should have written in their report. By and large, the claimants' experts said the warning of 'borderline' changes should have been signalled. The defendant's experts said that writing up the reports as 'negative' was not unreasonable in circumstances where the claimants had developed invasive cancer.

The judge concluded that a proper standard of care had not been shown. He based his conclusion on the fact that at almost every point he *preferred the evidence of the claimants' experts*. Using the words of

---

71   (4 March 1999, unreported), CA.
72   [1999] Lloyd's Rep Med 119, CA.
73   [1999] Lloyd's Rep Med 123, HC; affd [2000] PNLR 323, CA.

Bolitho (see Chapter 6), he said he did not consider that the evidence of the defendants' experts stood up to logical analysis.

The Court of Appeal dismissed the defendants' appeal.

In *Ludlow v National Power plc*[74] the court said that a judge was required to give reasons for a decision so that a party was in no doubt as to why he had lost and could assess whether the decision was properly appealable. However, the particular judgment left no doubt as to why the claimant had failed to satisfy the judge that an accident at work had caused psychiatric injury. The judge had preferred the evidence of the defendant's psychiatrist on the issue, and this he had been entitled to do as he had taken the view that that expert had had a wider range of relevant experience than the claimant's expert.

Compare *Coleman v Dunlop Ltd*,[75] in which a new trial was ordered where, in a claim for repetitive strain injury sustained at work, the judge had simply stated a preference for the defendant's expert on the basis of wider relevant experience without making appropriate findings of primary fact and explaining her inferences therefrom. Henry LJ said:

> In my opinion, on trial of the action it is the duty of the judge first to resolve the issues before him and to give reasons. It is true that, in relation to matters in these courts, there is no statutory duty on the judge to give reasons. It is also true that for a long time it has been contended that the common law imposed no such duty. But the common law is a living thing, and it seems to me that the point has now come where the common law has evolved to the point that the judge, on trial of the action must give sufficient reasons to make clear his findings of primary fact and the inferences that he draws from those primary facts sufficient to resolve the live issues before him, explaining why he has drawn those inferences.

In *SmithKline Beecham Biologics SA v Connaught Laboratories Inc*,[76] the Court of Appeal said that in all cases the judge's judgment ought to provide a coherent summary of the issues, the evidence and the reasons for the decision, whether the judgment is delivered orally in open court, or handed down in open court in written form with copies available for the press and public.

In *Temple v South Manchester Health Authority*,[77] a claim for alleged mismanagement in the treatment in hospital of a child's diabetic ketoacidosis, the Court of Appeal, dismissing the claimant's appeal, said that although the reasons the judge gave for accepting the views of an expert paediatrician called for the defence were open to some criticism, such criticisms could not by themselves outweigh or undermine the positive impression made by the expert's oral testimony, supported in substantial measure by the published material. Similarly, in *Clifford v Grimley*[78] (not a medical case) the Court of Appeal said that the extent of the trial judge's duty to give sufficient reasons for his conclusions was dependent on the subject matter in each individual case. A short analysis of the evidence in this case was held to be sufficient.

---

74   (17 July 2000, unreported), CA.
75   [1998] PIQR P398, CA.
76   (1999) 51 BMLR 91.
77   [2002] 10 WLUK 486, CA.
78   [2001] EWCA Civ 1658.

In *Gow v Harker*,[79] a claim for injury caused through mismanagement of a blood test, the Court of Appeal said that, when on the evidence there were so many improbabilities and at least one apparent impossibility, and the judge did not address the issues in his judgment adequately or at all, his judgment could not be upheld, the defendant's appeal succeeded and a new trial was ordered in front of a different judge. Similarly, in *Glicksman v Redbridge Health Care NHS Trust*,[80] a claim for alleged negligent performance of the repair of a suspected incisional hernia, the Court of Appeal, discerning in the judgment below no reasoned rebuttal of any expert's view in circumstances which called for definition of the issues, marshalling of the evidence and for reasons to be stated, ordered a new trial in front of a judge experienced in medical negligence.

In circumstances where a court resorts to the burden of proof to resolve a disputed issue, the duty to give adequate reasons is even more acute. In *Stephens v Cannon*,[81] Wilson J said the following:

> ... a court which resorts to the burden of proof must ensure that others can discern that it has striven to make a finding in relation to a disputed issue and can understand the reasons why it has concluded that it cannot do so. The parties must be able to discern the court's endeavour and to understand its reasons in order to be able to perceive why they have won and lost. An appellate court must also be able to do so because otherwise it will not be able to accept that the court below was in the exceptional situation of being entitled to resort to the burden of proof.

Similarly, in *Barnett v Medway NHS* (cited above) the Court of Appeal, following *Stephens*, criticised the inadequacy of the judge's reasoning in the following terms (at [54]), but nevertheless upheld his findings on appeal:

> There is great virtue in writing judgments concisely. However, the parties do need to know sufficiently what led to the conclusions reached. In this instance, the judgment gave only the briefest explanation. The obligation is all the clearer in a case of such complexity, and in a case where a key issue is decided on the basis that a claimant has failed to discharge the burden of proof, as the passage from paragraph 46 of *Stephens v Cannon* quoted above makes clear. The learned judge is to be commended for his brevity, but on this aspect of the case at least, it went too far.

Recent appeals

The following brief survey of appeals relating to the burden of proof and their outcome may help to give some further indication of the approach of appellate courts in clinical negligence cases and, most significantly, their treatment of a judge's findings of fact. Appeals turning on points of substantive law are not considered here as they feature in other parts of the book.

---

79   [2003] 7 WLUK 928, CA.
80   [2001] 7 WLUK 326, CA.
81   [2005] EWCA Civ 222 at [46].

Successful appeals by the defendant

Marwan Nawaf Nayef Raji-Abu-Shkara v Hillingdon Health Authority[82] (Waite, Roch, Auld LJJ): the court allowed the defendant's appeal from the judge's finding that the respiratory arrest that had caused the claimant's brain damage had been due to a failure of medical and nursing care. This is a good example of the appellate court's willingness to make its own assessment of the evidence given below, form its own conclusions about its effect, and reverse the judge on the ground that he had no reason to reject the defendant's evidence and no good reason to reach the conclusions that he did.

Robertson v Nottingham Health Authority[83] (Sir Stephen Brown P, Roch, Brooke LJJ): this claim alleged perinatal brain damage due to hypoxia that should have been avoided. The judge found negligence but no causation. On appeal by both parties the court was prepared on the evidence to enlarge the period of culpable delay in delivering the child, but said that, even given the longer period, the judge would still have found that the injury had been sustained before the period of culpable delay began.

Tahir v Haringey Health Authority[84] (Leggatt, Otton LJJ, Sir Ralph Gibson): the trial judge found negligent delay in attending to the claimant's symptoms but rejected the claimant's case that the delay had caused his serious neurological injury, and she awarded modest compensation for a small increment in the extent of the injury. The defendant succeeded on appeal on the ground that there had been no evidence before the judge on which she could properly find that the delay had caused any additional injury.

Hooper v Young[85] (Stuart-Smith, Waite, Otton LJJ): the defendant succeeded on appeal on the ground that the evidence did not permit the judge to conclude that preoperative injury to a ureter by kinking of the suture had happened through negligence. It could equally have happened without negligence and there was nothing in the evidence making the former more likely. Stuart-Smith LJ observed that it was important that the court did not make facile findings of negligence against doctors.

Ratty v Haringey Health Authority[86] (Balcombe, Kennedy, Evans LJJ): the court, having undertaken a careful analysis of medical evidence adduced at first instance, set aside a finding by the judge of negligence in undertaking and performing colorectal surgery consequent upon a diagnosis of cancer. The court upheld only a minor aspect of the claim, and so reduced the award from nearly £130,000 to £5,000.

Hughes v Waltham Forest Health Authority[87] (Fox, Butler-Sloss, Beldam LJJ): the court reversed the judge's finding that there had been negligence in the management of the deceased's gastric pathology, on the basis that the evidence called by the defendant established that a body of responsible opinion would find the management to have been acceptable. And the court (*obiter*) reversed the judge's finding on causation, saying

---

82 [1997] 8 Med LR 114, CA.
83 [1997] 8 Med LR 1, CA.
84 [1998] Lloyd's Rep Med 104, CA.
85 [1998] Lloyd's Rep Med 61, CA.
86 [1994] 5 Med LR 413, CA.
87 [1991] 2 Med LR 155, CA.

that the evidence did not establish that the management, whether negligent or not, had been an effective cause of death.

Knight v West Kent Health Authority[88] (Kennedy, Morritt, Chadwick LJJ): this is a good example of how carefully the Court of Appeal will scrutinise the evidence to see whether the judge's findings of negligence can be supported. In this case a critical issue was whether the baby's head was higher in the vaginal canal at the time when the mother was admitted and whether the consultant should have intervened. This was important because two hours later the mother suffered substantial injury from a strenuous forceps delivery, and it was alleged that at the earlier time the head would have been higher and so a caesarean section and not a forceps delivery would have been indicated. The court concluded that there was insufficient evidence for the judge's finding that the baby's head would have been too high for a forceps delivery. They also said that the judge's other determinative finding, that the forceps delivery was not performed to a proper standard of care, depended upon her conclusion that the obstetrician had encountered resistance when starting to pull, which was not supported by the evidence.

Dunn v Bradford Hospital NHS Trust[89] (Beldam, Chadwick LJJ): there was no proper evidence on which the judge could base his conclusion that it was through negligence that the claimant had fallen from a hospital trolley. The Court of Appeal also strongly criticised the judge for his disparaging remarks about the defence lawyers, which it said were quite without foundation.

Unsuccessful appeals by the claimant

Scott v Wakefield Area Health Authority[90] (Beldam, Ward, Schiemann LJJ): the claimant unsuccessfully contended that the judge's conclusion that the defendant had not negligently managed his visual disability was unsupported by the evidence.

Delaney v Southmead Health Authority[91] (Dillon, Butler-Sloss, Stuart-Smith LJJ – judgment given in 1992): the claimant unsuccessfully argued that the finding of the trial judge was against the weight of the evidence when he concluded that her brachial plexus lesion had not been caused by improper placing of her arm during her cholecystectomy.

Sellers v Cooke[92] (Slade, Balcombe, Butler-Sloss LJJ): the trial judge found that neither negligence nor causation had been established in this claim for negligent obstetric attention resulting in the death of the foetus. The Court of Appeal dealt only with causation (because there had been a successful application to admit fresh evidence on appeal relating to negligence), and concluded that in any event, ie regardless of whether the fresh evidence might have persuaded them that the judge's finding on negligence could not stand, his negative conclusion on causation (that the child would have died anyway) could not be successfully challenged.

---

88   [1998] Lloyd's Rep Med 18, CA.
89   (1999, unreported), CA.
90   [1997] 8 Med LR 341, CA.
91   [1995] 6 Med LR 355, CA.
92   [1990] 2 Med LR 16, CA.

Gregory v Pembrokeshire Health Authority[93] (O'Connor, Nicholls, Taylor LJJ): the judge found that the claimant mother should have been told that her amniocentesis sample had been inadequate, but that she would have accepted what would have been the consultant's advice, namely not to risk another amniocentesis; so she failed on causation because her child, who was born with Down syndrome, would have been born in any event. The Court of Appeal felt unable to interfere with this negative finding on causation, emphasising that the judge, who had heard and seen the witnesses, was in the best position to assess the evidence and to draw inferences from and reach conclusions upon it.

Sherlock v North Birmingham Health Authority[94] (Pill, Henry, Chadwick LJJ): the Court of Appeal refused to interfere with the judge's findings that, even though the advice of the paediatric senior registrar should have been sought, he would not have advised transfer to the intensive care unit (the procedure that would probably have avoided respiratory collapse of the patient) and that it would not have been mandatory to effect such transfer.

Lavelle v Hammersmith and Queen Charlotte's Special Health Authority[95] (Hirst, Henry, Auld LJJ): where the new-born claimant was disastrously injured during a balloon atrial sepostomy (to correct his congenital heart condition) and there were two possible ways the injury could have been caused, only one of which involved negligence. The trial judge was held to have been entitled to conclude on the evidence that it had not been proved that the injury had been caused in the negligent manner.

Brown v Lewisham and North Southwark Health Authority[96] (Beldam, Morritt, Mantell LJJ): the judge had been entitled to conclude that there was no evidence to support the claimant's contention that the journey by way of transfer between a London and a Blackpool hospital had been an effective cause of the deep vein thrombosis that led to loss of a leg.

Matthews v East Suffolk Health Authority[97] (Henry, Robert Walker LJJ, Alliott J): the finding by the judge that prompt treatment with antibiotics would not have lessened the brain damage sustained by the appellant, because it had already occurred, was upheld.

Morris v Blackpool Victoria Hospital NHS Trust:[98] this was an obstetric case where it was agreed all round that a further scan would have revealed IUGR (inter-uterine growth retardation) and the child would then have been delivered promptly so as to avoid his brain injury. The judge's finding that the child had not been suffering from IUGR went wholly against the weight of the evidence and the Court of Appeal was bemused by it. But the appeal by the claimant failed notwithstanding, because the judge's other important finding, that there had been no mandatory indication to perform another scan and therefore no breach of duty (and so, of course, no causation), was reasonable, said the appeal court, and was not affected by the judge's incorrect analysis of the wholly distinct IUGR issue.

---

93 [1989] 1 Med LR 81, CA.
94 (1997) 40 BMLR 103, CA.
95 (16 January 1998, unreported), CA.
96 [1999] Lloyd's Rep Med 110, CA.
97 [2000] 2 WLUK 910, CA.
98 [2004] 10 WLUK 310, CA.

Williams v Cwm Taf University Hospital Board[99] (Underhill, King, Newey LJJ): the judge at first instance had been entitled to reject a claim that a multi-disciplinary medical team had been negligent in deciding to perform a sympathectomy on a patient suffering from critical limb ischemia, rather than first conducting an angiogram. That decision had met the standard of a responsible body of medical opinion, and there was no expert evidence to undermine that body of opinion. The burden under the *Bolitho* test will only shift to the defendant where there is expert evidence to undermine the body of medical opinion relied upon by a defendant.

Successful appeals by the claimant

Arkless v Leicestershire Health Authority[100] (Stuart-Smith, Otton, Tuckey LJJ): given the findings of fact of the Recorder as to the presence of clinical signs of congenital displacement of the hip at the six to nine months check and the view of the defendant's expert that examination should have detected such signs, the only conclusion open to the judge should have been that the health visitor had not conducted a competent examination.

Montantaro v Home Office:[101] in a claim by a prisoner that a prison doctor had negligently failed to diagnose his scaphoid fracture, the court allowed the claimant's appeal on the ground that the trial judge's interventions had been made largely against the claimant and the judge had had no warrant for finding that no fracture had been sustained by the time the doctor saw the prisoner. The claimant had therefore not had a fair trial. This was a case in which human rights featured prominently.

Starcevic v West Hertfordshire Health Authority[102] (Mantell, Hale LJJ, Dame Elizabeth Butler-Sloss P): the main issue in this appeal from Kennedy J was whether the deceased had complained of pain and swelling in his calf and on that issue whether the widow's account or the medical staff's account should be preferred. On consideration of all the evidence, the appeal court determined that the only possible conclusion was that the widow's evidence should have been accepted by the judge, the appeal was allowed and agreed damages awarded.

Webb v Barclays Bank plc and Portsmouth Hospitals NHS Trust[103] (Hale, Judge, Henry LJJ): this was not strictly a successful appeal by claimant though it resembled one. Mrs Webb sustained a fall while employed by Barclays. Upon advice from a doctor at the hospital she underwent an amputation. She sued both employer and hospital, the former for failing to provide a safe environment for work, and the latter for negligent advice causing her to have an amputation which she did not need. The bank settled the totality of her claim and served a contribution notice on the hospital alleging that the advice to accept an amputation had been negligent and that Mrs Webb would have declined an amputation had she been given proper advice. Mrs Webb did not give evidence at the trial

---

99 [2018] EWCA Civ 1745, Lawtel AC5003434.
100 (22 October 1998), Medical Litigation 11/98 p6, CA.
101 (2002, unreported), CA.
102 [2001] 2 WLUK 217, CA.
103 [2002] PIQR P8, CA.

of the contribution issue. The judge was not satisfied that causation was proved. But the Court of Appeal said that there was ample evidence to show that if she had been given proper advice she would have declined the amputation. Therefore the contribution notice was valid and the appeal was allowed.

FB v Princess Alexandra Hospital NHS Trust[104] (Jackson, King, Thirlwall LJJ): the claimant's appeal was allowed on the basis that the judge at first instance had applied the wrong standard of care. The correct standard in this case was that to be expected of a reasonably competent senior house officer in an A&E department. The judge had impermissibly applied a lower standard of care taking into account the negligent doctor's 'relative inexperience'. Applying the correct standard of care, the claimant succeeded in establishing breach of duty.

Unsuccessful appeals by the defendant

Fallows v Randle[105] (Stuart-Smith, Peter Gibson, Ward LJJ): a failed sterilisation case, where the court dismissed the defendant's appeal, saying that it had been open to the judge to prefer the evidence of the claimant's expert as to the probable reason why the clip was found not to be on the Fallopian tube.

Lybert v Warrington Health Authority[106] (Nourse, Millett, Otton LJJ): the court refused to interfere with the judge's finding that no proper warning of the failure rate had been given before a sterilisation, or that in the particular circumstances of the case where the couple were awaiting the claimant's hysterectomy they would have taken the added precaution of using a condom. It was certainly open to the appeal court on the evidence to have come to directly contrary conclusions, so this appears to be a decision sympathetic to the claimant (see further Chapter 12).

Bull and Wakeham v Devon Area Health Authority[107] (Slade, Dillon, Mustill LJJ): the defendant failed to persuade the court to reverse the judge's findings that they did not have in place an adequate system of obstetric care and that that had caused or contributed to perinatal injury. This case offers useful material on the (theoretically) limited scope for the appeal court to interfere with findings based on a judge's assessment of the oral evidence.

O'Keefe v Harvey-Kemble[108] (Swinton Thomas, Potter LJJ): the Recorder had been entitled to find that insufficient information had been given to the patient before a breast reduction operation and that she would have declined the procedure if properly informed of the risks. Reading between the lines of the judgments, one gets the impression that the Lords Justices were a little surprised at the Recorder's dismissal of the defendant's evidence, but nevertheless felt unable to interfere with his conclusions.

Briody v St Helens and Knowsley Health Authority[109] (Simon Brown, Ward, Walker LJJ): the court did not interfere with the vital finding that

104 [2017] EWCA Civ 334.
105 [1997] 8 Med LR 160, CA.
106 [1996] 7 Med LR 71, CA.
107 [1993] 4 Med LR 117, CA.
108 (1998) 45 BMLR 74, CA.
109 [1999] Lloyd's Rep Med 185.

the obstetrician had failed to satisfy himself that the head was likely to be a good fit for the pelvis.

Penney, Palmer and Cannon v East Kent Health Authority[110] (Lord Woolf MR, May, Hale LJJ): the Canterbury cervical smears case: the judge found that the *Bolam* principle did not apply because there was no dispute about acceptable or unacceptable practice, only a factual dispute about whether the cytoscreeners had given the wrong classification to smears. Even if the principle had applied, he was satisfied that the evidence of the three experts called by the defence did not stand up to logical analysis. The cytoscreeners did not have the ability to draw a distinction between benign and pre-cancerous cells, and so should have classified the smears as borderline. On the defendant's unsuccessful appeal the court said that the *Bolam* test did apply as the cytoscreeners were exercising skill and judgment in determining what report they should make, but they agreed with the judge that the logical analysis test was applicable and that it led to the conclusion that the opinion of the defendant's experts did not stand up to scrutiny.

EXP v Barker[111] (Black, Irwin and Henderson LJJ): the defendant appealed on the basis that the judge had given less weight to the defendant's expert who he found had failed to disclose a close connection with the defendant. On appeal, the court found that *Bolam* test had been correctly applied despite certain infelicities in the way the judge had set out the test. It had been appropriate for the judge to afford less weight to the defendant's expert given the undeclared connection with the defendant.

Lesforis v Tolias[112] (Patten, Hamblen and Holroyd LJJ): Martin Spencer J at first instance was entitled to conclude that a consultant neurosurgeon's practice of administering a chemo-prophylaxis drug to patients within six hours of spinal surgery was a breach of duty. The judge preferred the evidence of the claimant's expert that no reasonable body of surgeons would administer the drug within six hours. The defendant's expert had not given evidence that the defendant's approach reflected the acceptable practice of a reasonable body of surgeons. The defendant's submission on appeal that the judge had not sufficiently addressed the claimant's individual risk factors was dismissed. There was therefore no error in the finding that the individual risk factors did not justify departing from routine safe practice on the timing of administering the drug.

Note that other examples can be found in the various preceding sections dealing with appeals, particularly the section headed 'Must a judge give reasons for his conclusions?'.

---

110 [2000] Lloyd's Rep Med 41, CA.
111 [2017] EWCA Civ 63.
112 [2019] EWCA Civ 487.

Chapter 10

Consent

Tamar Burton and Andrew Buchan

INTRODUCTION

It is a general legal and ethical principle that valid consent must be obtained before starting treatment, physical investigation, or providing personal care to a person. This principle reflects the right of patients to determine what happens to their own bodies. It is also a fundamental part of good practice. A healthcare professional who does not respect this principle may be liable both to legal action by the patient and to action by their professional body. The phrase 'healthcare professional' will be used in this chapter to include physicians, doctors, nurses and other healthcare staff.

While there is no English statute that defines the general principles of consent, the common law has established that touching a patient without valid consent may constitute a criminal offence of assault and/or battery and be a trespass to the person. The failure to obtain proper consent, resulting in harm, may form the basis of a claim of negligence against the healthcare professional involved. Poor handling of the consent process may also result in complaints from patients through the NHS complaints procedure or to professional bodies (see Chapter 3 – Non legal remedies).

On 11 March 2015 the Supreme Court gave judgment in *Montgomery v Lanarkshire Health Board*[1] which formally established the existence of the doctrine of informed consent in the common law. The judgment represents a shift away from medical paternalism towards patient autonomy.

This chapter will consider legislative provisions that relate to consent, the issue of assault and battery, the law on informed consent, the GMC guidance on obtaining consent, and will conclude with the issue of capacity under the Mental Capacity Act 2005.

RELEVANT LEGISLATION

The following pieces of legislation have principles of consent at their core.

---

1   [2015] UKSC 11.

The Human Tissue Act 2004 came fully into force on 1 September 2006. It sets out the legal framework for the storage and use of tissue from the living and for the removal, storage and use of tissue and organs from the dead, including 'residual' tissue following clinical and diagnostic procedures. The Human Tissue Act 2004 makes consent a legal requirement for the removal, storage and use of human tissue or organs and sets out whose consent is needed in which circumstances. The Act also established the Human Tissue Authority (HTA). The HTA is responsible for approving the transplantation of organs from living donors and bone marrow and peripheral blood stem cells from adults who lack the capacity to consent and children who lack the competence to consent. Further guidance on consent and codes of practice are available below and on the HTA's website.[2]

The Mental Capacity Act 2005 (MCA 2005) came fully into force on 1 October 2007. It sets out a statutory framework for making treatment decisions for people who lack the capacity to make such decisions themselves (see also Chapter 24). The MCA 2005 establishes statutory principles governing these decisions, setting out who can make them and when. It sets out the legal requirements for assessing whether or not a person lacks the capacity to make a decision.

Where a person lacks the capacity to make a decision for themselves, any decision must be made in that person's best interests. The MCA 2005 introduced a duty on NHS bodies to instruct an independent mental capacity advocate (IMCA) in serious medical treatment decisions when a person who lacks the capacity to make a decision has no one who can speak for them, other than paid staff. The MCA 2005 allows people to plan ahead for a time when they may not have the capacity to make their own decisions: it allows them to appoint a personal welfare attorney to make health and social care decisions, including medical treatment, on their behalf or to make an advance decision to refuse medical treatment. Further guidance is available below and in the Mental Capacity Act (2005) Code of Practice.[3]

The Human Rights Act 1998 and the European Convention for the Protection of Human Rights and Fundamental Freedoms may also be relevant in the court's consideration of issues surrounding patient rights.

ASSAULT AND BATTERY

Any contact by a healthcare professional with the patient's body is potentially a trespass to the person because it involves an invasion of the patient's bodily integrity. This could be in the form of simply touching a patient, for example, for an operation, for an injection; or less directly, by the use of a machine directing electro-magnetic or other waves at the body (for example, radiotherapy, chemotherapy, X-rays, sound or heat treatment).[4]

---

2   See www.hta.gov.uk.
3   See   https://assets.publishing.service.gov.uk/government/uploads/system/uploads/attachment_data/file/497253/Mental-capacity-act-code-of-practice.pdf.
4   Every human being of adult years and sound mind has a right to determine what shall be done with his own body; and a surgeon who performs an operation without the patient's consent commits an assault (*per* Cardozo J in *Schloendorff v Society of New York Hospital* 105 NE 92 (NY, 1914)).

A striking example of trespass to the person in a medical context is the conduct of Ian Paterson, a consultant general surgeon, who in August 2017 was convicted of 17 counts of wounding with intent and three counts of unlawful wounding. The jury concluded that over a period of 14 years the surgeon had deliberately misrepresented the contents of pathology reports, exaggerated the risk of cancer and carried out unnecessary surgery, including mastectomies, to his patients in NHS and private hospitals.

In civil law it is not, in practice, significant whether the conduct complained of is termed a trespass, an assault or a battery. The nub of it is the unlawful, intentional application of force to the person of another:

> If a man intentionally applies force direct to another, the plaintiff has a cause of action in assault and battery, or, if you so please to describe it, in trespass to the person ... (per Lord Denning, in *Letang v Cooper* [1965] 1 QB 232, CA).

It is generally thought that the interference with a claimant's bodily integrity has to be by way of an intentional act; otherwise the cause of action lies in negligence (see *Fowler v Lanning*[5]). An intention to injure is not essential, but the act that violates the bodily integrity of the claimant, ie the contact, must be intentional. In *Wilson v Pringle*,[6] the Court of Appeal said, in the context of the 'horseplay' between schoolchildren, that the contact must be proved to be a hostile contact. Hostility was not to be equated with ill-will or malevolence, and would be a question of fact.

In bringing a clinical negligence claim, one is not required to show hostility when a surgeon operates without consent. Yet it is a battery. The 'hostility' factor must surely be limited to situations where the contact could otherwise be one of the incidents of friendly interaction (eg slapping a batsman on the back after a good innings, or part of accepted 'horseplay' among friends). One would do best to adopt the formulation of Goff LJ in *Collins v Wilcock*,[7] when he said that there was a general exception to the illegality of intentional physical contact which embraced all physical contact generally acceptable in the ordinary conduct of daily life. Goff LJ expressly disassociated himself from the antic notion that a battery is only committed where the action is 'angry, revengeful, rude or insolent' (*Hawkins Pleas of the Crown* (8th edn, 1824) Vol 1, Ch 15, section 2) – words hardly apt to describe a surgical intervention! Wood J took this view in *T v T*,[8] when he said that, as the law stood, a surgeon who performed a termination of pregnancy on a 'mentally handicapped' adult would be liable for trespass (assuming it was not a medical emergency) despite the absence of hostile intent.

Another example of a 'friendly' (non-hostile) assault is the hairdresser who, without getting proper consent, applies a 'tone rinse' to a customer's hair (*Nash v Sheen*[9]).

In *Allan v New Mount Sinai Hospital*,[10] an anaesthetist who acted without negligence was held liable in battery for unforeseeable injury

---

5   [1959] 1 QB 426.
6   [1987] QB 237.
7   [1984] 1 WLR 1172.
8   [1988] Fam 52.
9   [1953] CLY 3726.
10   (1980) 109 DLR (3d) 634.

suffered by the patient because he administered the injection that led to the injury into the patient's left arm, the patient having expressly told him not to inject into that limb. The defendant acted in accordance with normal medical procedure, but he had ignored the claimant's instructions. He was accordingly liable for trespass to the person, and for all the damage that flowed directly from that trespass.

In *Appleton v Garrett MLC*,[11] Dyson J awarded aggravated damages for trespass where the defendant had prescribed and carried out unnecessary dental treatment for the sole purpose of getting himself more work.[12]

Different causes of action: the merits of assault v negligence

A number of factors distinguish the action for assault from that for negligence:

1   Fault, as we have seen, is irrelevant. If the patient can show he did not consent to the treatment he will be able to recover damages without proof of negligence.
2   Whereas in the action for negligence the defendant is only liable for loss and injury which was foreseeable at the time of the negligent act (see Chapter 8), the tortfeasor in trespass is liable for all damage flowing directly from the assault, whether foreseeable or not. The wrongful act consists of a trespass, and for that the defendant is liable in respect of all loss and injury flowing directly from the assault, however unforeseeable (see *Allan v New Mount Sinai Hospital* (above) *per* Linden J). Nevertheless, the injury or loss must be of a type which the law recognises, and within the rules as to remoteness of damage in the sense that it must be directly caused by the assault (see Chapter 8).
3   Whereas negligence is not actionable without proof of actual damage or loss, trespass has no such requirement. Even if no injury is suffered, damages may be awarded to compensate for the fact of the assault (these are likely to be nominal in such a case, though one can envisage an award for, for example, the indignity suffered). The limitation period will therefore start to run, in the absence of special factors (see Chapter 20), when the assault takes place and not when injury is suffered, as the cause of action is complete at the time of the assault. In negligence the cause of action is not complete until damage has been suffered and the limitation period only starts to run when the claimant appreciates that, or ought to have.
4   The fact that the patient would have consented to an assault if asked does not absolve the defendant from liability, but it would seem sensible to take that fact into account in reducing damages, for otherwise a person might recover damages for an operation, carried

---

11   [1997] 8 Med LR 75.
12   In *R v Richardson* (1998) 43 BMLR 21 a criminal conviction was overturned on appeal where a dentist who had been struck off continued to treat her patients with their apparent consent but without telling them of her disqualification. The Court of Appeal said that only a mistake about the nature of the act alleged to constitute an assault of the identity of the assailant vitiated consent in criminal law, and for this purpose a person's professional status or qualifications did not constitute part of their identity. Consequently, the appeal was allowed.

out without consent, but which benefited him and which he would have agreed to if asked. If the cause of action is in negligence, the defendant is entitled to contend that the patient has suffered no injury because, even if he had not been negligent, eg even if he had explained the nature of the operation properly, the patient would still have agreed to it.

Until 2008, there was also a distinction in relation to the limitation periods of each cause of action. In *Stubbings v Webb*[13] the House of Lords concluded that the limitation period for an assault was a period of six years, rather than three. However, in 2008, the House of Lords changed its mind. A very rare event. In *A v Hoare*[14] it confirmed that the time limit for an assault claim was three years and the Limitation Act 1980, ss 11, 14 and 33 apply to assault claims.

CLINICAL NEGLIGENCE CLAIMS FOR CONSENT: THE LAW BEFORE *MONTGOMERY*

Every operation carries risks. Every drug can produce unwanted side effects. No treatment can be guaranteed to succeed. When something goes wrong the patient first asks whether the doctor has been negligent in their treatment. Has the doctor made a negligent diagnosis, or prescribed the wrong drugs when they should have known better? Or has the doctor performed the operation without due care? When it appears that, in the strictly medical context, the doctor's performance has been unimpugnable, the patient's complaint is likely to be: 'You never told me this might happen. If you had I would have declined the treatment.' Historically the English courts have had to consider which of two tests to adopt for assessing the duty upon a doctor to disclose the risks inherent in a particular treatment. The tests may be termed 'the medical standard' and 'informed consent'.

(A) THE MEDICAL STANDARD OF DISCLOSURE

Under the medical standard, the medical profession is permitted to set its own standards of disclosure without supervision by the court. The profession itself decides what disclosure is to be made in any particular case. Prior to *Montgomery* (see below), it was enough for a defendant to avoid liability if he or she shows that at the time of the treatment there was a body of responsible medical opinion, albeit a minority one, that would have done what he or she did. This enabled a defendant to succeed simply by producing one or two physicians who endorse his or her conduct, and it is of no avail for the claimant to produce evidence to a contrary effect. If the court accepted that there was such a body of medical opinion it will not be entitled to choose between the differing schools of thought. This was a unique advantage for the professionals.

This medical standard had for a long time been accepted as the test for assessing negligence in treatment and diagnosis (see Chapters 6

---

13   [1993] AC 498, HL.
14   [2008] UKHL 6.

and 9 above for a full discussion), but it was not clear before the decision of the House of Lords in *Sidaway v Board of Governors of the Bethlem Royal Hospital and the Maudsley Hospital*[15] (see below) that it would be applicable to the question of disclosure of risks.

(B) THE DOCTRINE OF INFORMED CONSENT

There had grown up across the Atlantic, in some US jurisdictions and also in Canada, a different test, whereby the court had the right to assess and delineate the extent of the duty of disclosure in any particular case. This was the test of 'informed consent'. If the patient was not given sufficient information upon which he or she could reach an informed decision whether to accept the treatment proposed or not, then he or she was not able to give a valid consent. It was for the court to decide whether he or she had been given that information, not for the doctors. The leading cases illustrating this doctrine are, in the US, *Canterbury v Spence*;[16] *Scaria v St Paul Fire and Marine Insurance*;[17] *Zelesnik v Jewish Chronic Disease Hospital*;[18] and in the Supreme Court of Canada, *Hopp v Lepp*[19] and *Reibl v Hughes*.[20] The courts have variously said:

> To bind the disclosure obligation to medical usage is to arrogate the decision on revelation to the physician alone. Respect for the patient's right of self-determination on particular therapy demands a standard set by law for physicians rather than one which physicians may or may not impose upon themselves.

> The duty to disclose or inform cannot be summarily limited to a self-created custom of the profession, to a professional standard that may be non-existent or inadequate to meet the informational needs of a patient.

> Risk disclosure is based on the patient's right to determine what shall be done with his body. Such right should not be at the disposal of the medical community.

According to the doctrine of informed consent, a risk is required to be disclosed when a reasonable person, in what the physician knows or should know to be the patient's position, would be likely to attach significance to the risk or cluster of risks in deciding whether or not to forgo the proposed therapy. The physician can plead therapeutic privilege, and show that there was a good clinical reason why a particular disclosure should not have been made.

Expert evidence of current medical practice remains cogent and persuasive evidence of the appropriate standard, but it is not conclusive. As it was neatly put in a Canadian case:

> No longer does the medical profession alone collectively determine, by its own practices, the amount of information a patient should have in order to decide whether to undergo an operation (*White v Turner* (1981) 120 DLR (3d) 269).

15   [1985] AC 871, MLC 0010, HL.
16   464 F 2d 772, MLC 0006 (1972).
17   227 NW 2d 647.
18   336 NYS 2d 163 (1975).
19   (1980) 112 DLR (3d) 67.
20   (1980) 114 DLR (3d) 1.

Anyone interested in applications of the doctrine of informed consent might wish to read some of the cases in which the Canadian reports abound: *Videto v Kennedy;*[21] *Bucknam v Kostuik;*[22] *Considine v Camp Hill Hospital;*[23] *Ferguson v Hamilton Civil Hospitals;*[24] *Casey v Provan;*[25] *Grey v Webster.*[26]

The Saskatchewan Court of Appeal's decision in *Haughian v Paine,*[27] is interesting. Although based on the doctrine of informed consent, it makes the generally valid point that a patient is entitled to be told of non-surgical alternatives to the treatment proposed.

Kitchen v McMullen,[28] New Brunswick Court of Appeal, can be used to illuminate the difference in the law on the doctor's duty to disclose the risks of an operation or treatment between Canadian law, where the patient's rights are respected, and here, where they are not. In short, the claimant was given an anti-coagulant (Hemofil) to control bleeding after a tooth extraction. Like all blood products, Hemofil carries a small risk of hepatitis, which materialised. The claimant sued for damages on the ground that he should have been warned of the risk, claiming that, if he had been warned, he would not have accepted the treatment.

Now, under the Canadian doctrine of informed consent, the doctor has a duty to disclose all 'material' or 'unusual or special' risks. Those risks are (more or less) such risks as the court feels would affect the mind of a patient when deciding whether or not to accept the treatment proposed. What is important here is that it is for the court to decide the status of the risk, not for the doctors. So if the court decides the risk was 'material', then it matters not that no doctor ever discloses it. A doctor is in breach of their duty in not doing so. In this way, the Canadian court protects the right of a patient to be properly informed about the treatment proposed..

The second aspect of the Canadian test is to decide if a reasonable patient in the claimant's position would have declined or accepted the treatment if warned. If the court decides that the risk should have been disclosed (for example, it is likely to find that the risk of failure of a sterilisation should be disclosed to the woman), it still has to decide if the patient would have nevertheless accepted the operation or the treatment (thus it might well find that the woman would have taken the 1 in 500 risk of the sterilisation failing, rather than try some other, probably even less secure, method). Canadian law has an additional requirement of whether a reasonable patient would have refused the treatment.

The actual decision in the *Kitchen* case was that all three judges found that the risk was one that should have been disclosed to the patient, but two of them then decided that he would have accepted the risk (the third said he would have waited to see if the bleeding got worse). So his action failed.

---

21 (1981) 125 DLR (3d) 127.
22 (1983) 3 DLR (4th) 99.
23 (1982) 133 DLR (3d) 11.
24 (1983) 144 DLR (3d) 214.
25 (1984) 11 DLR (4th) 708.
26 (1984) 14 DLR (4th) 706.
27 (1987) 37 DLR (4th) 624.
28 [1990] 1 Med LR 352.

In *Ellis v Wallsend District Hospital*,[29] the New South Wales Court of Appeal held that, where the patient's evidence was that if warned of the risks of an operation she would have declined it, the trial judge was not at liberty to reject that evidence unless there was contrary evidence showing the claimant's contention to be 'inherently incredible' or 'inherently improbable'.

(C) THE ENGLISH TEST FOR NEGLIGENCE

The English test for establishing negligence in matters of treatment and diagnosis is well-established. The medical standard test was set out in the direction to the jury given by McNair J in *Bolam v Friern Hospital Management Committee*.[30] This direction had become a *locus classicus* and was expressly endorsed by the House of Lords in *Whitehouse v Jordan*[31] and *Maynard v West Midlands Regional Health Authority*.[32] But did it apply to the duty to disclose material risks?

In fact, the *Bolam* case included an allegation of failure to disclose the risks inherent in the treatment undertaken, but it was generally thought that it was still arguable that the test for the duty of disclosure was not necessarily the same as the test for diagnosis and treatment.

In the seminal case of *Hunter v Hanley*,[33] a Scottish case upon which McNair J relied, Lord President Clyde had spoken only of diagnosis and treatment:

> In the realm of diagnosis and treatment there is ample scope for difference of opinion and one man clearly is not negligent merely because his conclusion differs from that of other professional men ... The true test for establishing negligence in diagnosis or treatment on the part of a doctor is whether he has been proved to be guilty of such failure as no doctor of ordinary skill would be guilty of if acting with ordinary care ..

In *Hills v Potter*,[34] Hirst J rejected any form of the doctrine of informed consent as having no place in English law and adopted the medical test (though he made it clear that the claimant would have failed in either event).

(D) THE *SIDAWAY* CASE

Prior to *Montgomery* the leading case was *Sidaway v Board of Governors of the Bethlem Royal Hospital and the Maudsley Hospital*.[35] The facts were that the claimant suffered paralysis following an operation upon her cervical vertebrae. The operation carried a small risk of untoward damage, about a 2% risk of damage to nerve root or spinal cord. Damage to the cord would produce a far more serious result, and the risk of that happening was less than 1%. The surgeon warned of the risk of damage to the nerve root but not of the risk to the spinal cord. The trial judge found

---

29 [1990] 2 Med LR 103.
30 [1957] 1 WLR 582.
31 [1981] 1 WLR 246.
32 [1984] 1 WLR 634.
33 1955 SLT 213, MLC 0002.
34 [1984] 1 WLR 641n.
35 [1985] AC 871, MLC 0010, HL.

that the patient had not been told of all material risks so as to be able to give a fully informed consent to the operation, but, as he was satisfied that the surgeon, in giving the limited disclosure that he did, was following a practice that had the backing of a body of responsible medical opinion at the time of the operation, the claimant must fail, because the test in English law was the medical standard, not informed consent.

The Court of Appeal by a majority endorsed this view.[36] Dunn LJ said a contrary result would damage the doctor/patient relationship and might well have an adverse effect on the practice of medicine. Sir Nicolas Browne-Wilkinson said that the particular quality of that relationship meant that the duty of disclosure in that context should be approached on a different basis from that applicable to ordinary professional men, that the patient must have all the information they reasonably should, but that to test the reasonableness of the disclosure made one look to the standards of the profession. However, the Master of the Rolls said that, although evidence of the medical practice was important, the definition of the duty of care was not to be handed over to the medical profession. It was a matter for the law and the courts, which could not stand idly by if the profession, by an excess of paternalism, denied their patient a real choice. In other words, he said, the law will not permit the medical profession to play God.

Although the House of Lords' judgments reveal different bases for their conclusions, it is tolerably clear that they, albeit by a bare majority, endorsed the medical test, though adding a proviso. Lord Diplock said that the *Bolam* test should be applied to the context of disclosure as to that of treatment and diagnosis. He pointed out that there might at any one time be a number of practices that satisfied the test, and he said:

> To decide what risks the existence of which a patient should be voluntarily warned [about] and the terms in which such warning, if any, should be given, having regard to the effect the warning may have, is as much an exercise of professional skill and judgment as any other part of the doctor's comprehensive duty of care to the individual patient, and expert medical evidence on this matter should be tested in just the same way.

On the question of informed consent, Lord Diplock said that the doctrine was jurisprudentially unsound as it sought to transfer to the sphere of negligence considerations as to consent that were only meaningful in the context of assault and battery (it is indeed true that the US courts had had difficulty in reconciling the absence of 'consent' with a cause of action not in battery but in negligence).

Lord Bridge, with whom Lord Keith agreed, rejecting the informed consent approach, said that a decision as to what degree of disclosure of risks is best calculated to assist a particular patient to make a rational choice as to whether or not to undergo a particular treatment must primarily be a matter of clinical judgment, and so the issue was to be decided primarily on the basis of expert medical evidence, applying the *Bolam* test; but he added (this is the proviso mentioned above) that the judge might in certain circumstances come to the conclusion that disclosure of a particular risk was so obviously necessary to an informed choice on the part of a patient that no reasonably prudent medical

---

36 See [1984] QB 493.

man would fail to make it. He instanced a 10% risk of a stroke from an operation, though he pointed out that there might even there be some cogent clinical reason militating against disclosure.

Lord Templeman's approach was different: he said that neither was the patient entitled to know everything nor the doctor to decide everything. The doctor was under an obligation to provide information adequate to enable the patient to reach a balanced judgment, subject always to the doctor's own obligation to say and do nothing which he was satisfied would be harmful to the patient: the court would award damages if satisfied that the doctor blundered and that the patient was deprived of information which was necessary for that purpose. Although Lord Templeman makes it clear that in his view the patient is not entitled to know everything, particularly if he does not ask, there is in his judgment no suggestion that the court is bound by medical evidence. He says more than once that it is for the court to decide whether sufficient information was given. This puts him on the same side of the conceptual fence as Lord Scarman, who effectively adopted the doctrine of informed consent, though holding against the claimant on the facts.

In *Moyes v Lothian Health Board*,[37] a Scottish court of first instance rejected a claim that certain risks alleged to be inherent in an angiography procedure should have been disclosed to the patient, principally because it was shown that at the time of the procedure, in 1981, it was consistent with responsible medical practice to give no warning at all.

In *Heath v West Berkshire Health Authority*,[38] the claimant failed in her allegation that she should have been warned of the risk of lingual nerve damage arising from an operation to extract a wisdom tooth because the evidence accepted by the judge was that at the time of the operation there was a responsible body of medical opinion that gave no such warning.

In *Smith v Tunbridge Wells Health Authority*,[39] a surgeon failed to inform a man of 28 sufficiently clearly before a rectopexy of the risk, sadly fulfilled, that the procedure could make him impotent. The judge held that, as his condition was not particularly serious, he would probably have declined the operation.

Similarly, in *McAllister v Lewisham and North Southwark Health Authority*,[40] a neurosurgeon had failed properly to warn his female patient of the relevant risks before surgery to correct arteriovascular malformation in her leg. What is particularly of note is that the judge held that she would probably have declined the operation if she had been warned, even though her evidence was to the effect that she really could not answer such a hypothetical question.

In *Smith v Salford Health Authority*,[41] the patient failed on causation, ie he proved that the warnings given before surgery on his neck were inadequate but the judge concluded that proper warnings would not have put him off the operation. However, he still won the case as he succeeded in proving operative negligence.

---

37   [1990] 1 Med LR 463.
38   [1992] 3 Med LR 57.
39   [1994] 5 Med LR 334.
40   [1994] 5 Med LR 343.
41   [1994] 5 Med LR 321.

In *Williamson v East London and City Health Authority*,[42] Butterfield J held a plastic surgeon liable for not giving sufficient information about the extent of the breast operation she intended to perform.

In *Webb v Barclays Bank and Portsmouth Hospitals NHS Trust*,[43] the Court of Appeal said that, where a doctor through ignorance brought about by his negligent failure to inform himself fully about the pathology of the patient's knee, that did not absolve him from the consequences of his negligent advice which resulted from such ignorance. Had he conducted a proper investigation and given the patient the appropriate advice, she would not then have consented to the amputation.

In *Enright v Kwun*,[44] Morland J held that the medical attendants of a 37-year-old pregnant woman had failed to tell her of the one in 250 risk of Down's syndrome and the option of an amniocentesis. If they had, she would have had the amniocentesis which would have shown the defect and she would then have opted for a termination.

However, the High Court of Australia has explicitly refused to follow *Sidaway*. In *Rogers v Whittaker*,[45] the evidence showed that a responsible body of medical practitioners would not have disclosed to the claimant the risk to her good left eye from sympathetic ophthalmitis if her defective right eye were removed. This would have been enough to lose her the case if *Sidaway* had been applied. However, it was held that it was for the courts to adjudicate on what was the appropriate standard of care after giving weight to 'the paramount consideration that a person is entitled to make his own decision about his life'; that breach of duty of care was not to be concluded on the basis of the expert medical evidence alone; that evidence of accepted medical practice was a useful (but not a conclusive) guide for the courts; and that the factors according to which a court determined whether a medical practitioner was in breach of the standard of care would vary according to whether it was a case involving diagnosis, treatment, or the provision of information and advice: the different cases raised varying difficulties which required consideration of different factors. The finding of the courts below that the defendant had been negligent in not disclosing the risk was upheld.

(E) PEARCE V UNITED BRISTOL HEALTHCARE NHS TRUST

The claimant mother maintained an unusual contention. She had tragically given birth to a dead child in December 1991. The consultant had advised her a few days before the birth, some two weeks after the estimated date of delivery, to wait yet longer, rather than be induced. It was not suggested that his advice that induction would be dangerous was negligent. But it was alleged that he should have disclosed the small additional risk involved in waiting, and, if he had done so, the mother would have sought and obtained a Caesarean section. Lord Woolf, who gave the only reasoned judgment, gave detailed consideration to the *prudent doctor* proviso. Lord Woolf described these words in the speech of Lord Bridge (in *Sidaway*) as 'particularly apposite':

---

42 [1998] Lloyd's Rep Med 6.
43 [2001] Lloyd's Rep Med 500.
44 [2003] MLC 1017.
45 [1993] 4 Med LR 79.

... even in a case where, as here, no expert witness in the relevant medical field condemns the non-disclosure as being in conflict with accepted and responsible medical practice, I am of opinion that the judge might in certain circumstances come to the conclusion that disclosure of a particular risk was so obviously necessary to an informed choice on the part of the patient that no reasonably prudent medical man would fail to make it. The kind of case I have in mind would be an operation involving a substantial risk of grave adverse consequences, as, for example, the 10 per cent risk of a stroke from the operation which was the subject of the Canadian case of Reibl *v Hughes*. In such a case, in the absence of some cogent technical reason why the patient should not be informed, a doctor, recognising and respecting his patient's right of decision, could hardly fail to appreciate the necessity for an appropriate warning.

Lord Woolf expressed himself in terms much more consistent with the Canadian, American and Australian law of disclosure of material risks (ie where, put loosely, the court is the arbiter of what needs to be disclosed and not the medical profession), rather than the far more doctor-oriented English law. He said:

In a case where it is the alleged that a plaintiff has been deprived of the opportunity to make a proper decision as to what course he or she should take in relation to treatment, it seems to me to be the law, as indicated in the cases to which I have just referred, that if there is a significant risk which would affect the judgment of a reasonable patient, then in the normal course it is the responsibility of a doctor to inform the patient of that significant risk, if the information is needed so that the patient can determine for him or herself as to what course he or she should adopt.

And he said that when one refers to a 'significant risk' it is not possible to talk in precise percentages. And:

... where there is what can realistically be called a 'significant risk', then in the ordinary event, as I have already indicated, the patient is entitled to be informed of that risk.

The way in which Lord Woolf expressed himself offered an opportunity for the effective use of the prudent doctor proviso, in the sense that a patient would find it easier to argue in appropriate circumstances that a risk should have been disclosed, and the court should declare such, even though the defendants show that there is a body of medical opinion that approves of non-disclosure in the relevant circumstances.[46]

MONTGOMERY: CONFIRMATION OF THE DOCTRINE OF INFORMED CONSENT

The facts

The pursuer ("the claimant") became pregnant in 1999. She had diabetes and was likely to have a large baby. It was agreed that the risk of shoulder dystocia in these circumstances was 9–10%. The treating consultant obstetrician did not inform the claimant of the risk of shoulder dystocia because, in her view, the risk of a grave problem for the baby arising

---

46   See also in the Introduction (see Chapter 1) Lord Woolf's observations in his address to University College, London.

as a result of shoulder dystocia was very small. It was the clinician's view that most women, if told of the risk, would ask for a Caesarean section and that this was not in their best interests. Sadly, during the delivery, shoulder dystocia occurred. The baby, as a result of occlusion of the umbilical cord, was born with severe disabilities. The claimant's case was that had the risk of shoulder dystocia been discussed with her prior to labour, she would have opted for a Caesarean section. It was agreed that had she opted for a Caesarean section, the baby would have been born uninjured.

At first instance the claimant's claim was rejected on the basis that, since she had not raised specific questions of the risks involved in vaginal delivery, the clinician's omission to warn her of the inherent risks of vaginal delivery did not constitute a breach of duty of care. The Lord Ordinary, applying *Sidaway*, concluded that on the expert evidence before the court, the omission was accepted as proper by a responsible body of medical opinion. He also concluded that even if the claimant had been told about the risk of shoulder dystocia, she would not have elected to have a Caesarean section.

The Extra Division of the Inner House of the Court of Session refused the claimant's appeal.

The Supreme Court's decision[47]

The Supreme Court unanimously, with Lords Kerr and Reid giving the lead judgment, allowed the claimant's appeal.

The court held that an adult person of sound mind was entitled to decide which, if any, of the available forms of treatment to undergo, and her consent had to be obtained before treatment interfering with her bodily integrity was undertaken. Doctors are therefore under a duty to take reasonable care to ensure that patients are aware of any material risks involved in any recommended treatment, and of any reasonable alternative or variant treatments.

The analysis of the majority of the Court of Appeal in *Sidaway* was declared unsatisfactory and Lord Scarman's dissenting judgment was preferred. The starting point in Lord Scarman's analysis was that a patient has a basic human right to make his or her own decision about his medical treatment. For Lord Scarman the decision whether to consent to medical treatment did not depend solely on medical factors.

In dismissing the approach in *Sidaway* Lords Kerr and Reed stated:[48]

> Since *Sidaway's* case, however, it has become increasingly clear that the paradigm of the doctor-patient relationship implicit in the speeches in that case has ceased to reflect the reality and complexity of the way in which healthcare services are provided, or the way in which the providers and receipts of such services view their relationship. One development which is particularly significant in the present context is that the patients are now widely regarded as persons holding rights, rather than as the passive receipts of the care of the medical profession. They are also widely treated as consumers exercising choices ...

---

47 [2015] AC 1430.
48 [2015] AC 1430 at [75].

Another significant consideration was the ability of patients to access information:

> ... it has become far easier, and far more common, for members of the public to obtain information about symptoms, investigations, treatment options, risks and side-effects via such media as the internet ... patient support groups, and leaflets issued by healthcare institutions ... It would therefore be a mistake to view patients as uniformed, incapable of understanding medical matters, or wholly dependent on a flow of information from doctors.

The judgment also recognised the societal shifts that have altered the relationship between doctor and patient with the doctrine of legal paternalism being wholly rejected by the court:

> ... [social and legal developments] point away from a model based on a view of the patient as being entirely dependent on information provided by the doctor. What they point towards is an approach to the law which, instead of treating patients as placing themselves in the hands of their doctors ..., treats them so far as possible as adults who are capable of understanding that medical treatment is uncertain of success and may involve risks, accepting responsibility for the taking of risk affecting their own lives, and living with the consequences of their choices.

For Mrs Montgomery, the Supreme Court declared that the risk of shoulder dystocia was a material risk and it was incumbent on the doctor to discuss it with her. Disagreeing with the courts below, the Supreme Court – unusually – held that there was no evidential basis for concluding that had she been warned of the risk of shoulder dystocia, Mrs Montgomery would have proceeded with vaginal delivery. She was therefore successful in her appeal.

The new test

The new test for informed consent is that a doctor is under a duty to take reasonable care to ensure that the patient is aware of any material risks involved in any recommended treatment, and of any reasonable alternative or variant treatments.

The new test represents a victory for patient autonomy. However, a doctor is still entitled to withhold information from a patient if a doctor considers that informing the patient of that information would be seriously detrimental to the patient's health. Further, a doctor is not required to discuss risks of treatment with a patient who is obviously unconscious or unable to make a decision. The Supreme Court did not elaborate on specific examples of this exemption but this is unlikely to be difficult to apply in practice.

There are three further aspects for practitioners to be aware of.

First, the assessment of whether a risk is material cannot be reduced to percentages. In assessing materiality the following factors are relevant. The:

- nature of the risk;
- effect which its occurrence would have on the life of the patient;
- importance to the patient of the benefits sought to be achieved by the treatment; and
- alternatives available and the risks involved in those alternatives.

Second, the doctor's role involves dialogue. The purpose of obtaining informed consent is so that that patient understands the severity of condition, the advantages and disadvantages of treatment, and the existence of any alternative treatments:

> ... this role will only be performed effectively if the information provided is comprehensible. The doctor's duty is not therefore fulfilled by bombarding the patient with technical information which she cannot reasonably be expected to grasp, let alone by routinely demanding her signature on a consent form.[49]

Third, the therapeutic exception outlined above is a limited exception. The Supreme Court warned that the 'therapeutic exception should not be abused'. In other words the therapeutic exception:

> ... is not intended to subvert that principle by enabling the doctor to prevent the patient from making an informed choice where she is liable to make a choice which the doctors considers to be contrary to her best interests.[50]

Impact of *Montgomery*

The prediction by many commentators that *Montgomery* would lead to an increased number of consent claims is borne out by even a cursory glance at the law reports. Since 2015, there has been an array of reported decisions applying *Montgomery*. The following cases demonstrate a successful application of the *Montgomery* test.

In *Spencer v Hillingdon Hospital NHS Trust*[51] the claimant was successful in establishing that there was a failure to warn him of the risk of a deep vein thrombosis or pulmonary embolism prior to surgery of an inguinal hernia.

In *FM v Ipswich Hospital NHS Trust*[52] the claimant sustained a brachial plexus injury during his birth. His mother brought a claim in circumstances that were very similar to the facts of *Montgomery*, namely that if the risk of shoulder dystocia was discussed with her prior to labour, she would have elected for a Caesarean section and her child would have been born uninjured. *Montgomery* was handed down during the trial and the claimant succeeded in her claim, proving that the failure to discuss shoulder dystocia was a material breach.

In *Crossman v St George's Healthcare NHS Trust*[53] it was admitted by the defendant that there was a failure to obtain informed consent for surgery in circumstances where a patient and his doctor had agreed to continue to treat the claimant's spinal problem conservatively but the claimant was erroneously added to a surgical list and, despite his protestations, was told to attend for surgery or lose his slot. It is likely, even prior to *Montgomery*, that a defendant would be in difficulties with these unusual facts.

In *Webster v Burton Hospitals NHS Foundation Trust*[54] the Court of Appeal reversed the trial judge's rejection of the claimant's claim.

---

49   [2015] AC 1430 at [90].
50   [2015] AC 1430 at [91].
51   [2015] EWHC 1058.
52   [2015] EWHC 775 (QB).
53   [2016] EWHC 2878 (QB).
54   [2017] EWCA Civ 62.

Montgomery had been handed down after the trial judge gave judgment and his application of the *Bolam* test in relation to the advice given to the claimant about being induced was an unsustainable error of law.

In *Hassell v Hillingdon Hospital NHS Foundation Trust*[55] the claimant brought a claim for the failure to obtain informed consent after she sustained a spinal cord injury during surgery. At trial the risk of permanent paralysis was found to be between 1 in 500 and 1 in 1000. The risk of spinal 'cord damage' was first mentioned to the claimant on the day of the operation. The judge held that the timing of this information and the lack of detail given to the claimant, in addition to the absence of advice on conservative options, rendered the advice given to her inadequate.

Montgomery has also been successfully utilised in claims about post-operative treatment. For example, in *Gallardo v Imperial College Healthcare NHS Trust*[56] the judge at [70] applied the principle of patient autonomy by analogy to post-treatment discussions and concluded that the claimant had the right to be informed of the outcome of any treatment, the prognosis, and the options for follow-up care and treatment as soon as they were well enough to participate in the discussion.

However, not all consent claims brought since *Montgomery* have been successful.

The following case demonstrates the difficulty for claimants to prove the second aspect of a consent claim: what would have happened in the non-negligent scenario, namely that a patient would not have consented to the surgery or treatment if he or she had been properly consented. In *MC and JC v Birmingham Women's NHS Foundation Trust*[57] the claimant's claim for a failure to give informed consent to be induced was rejected by the judge. He concluded that the claimant's evidence, with no deliberate intention to mislead, had probably shifted over time from: 'I should not have consented' to 'I would not have consented'. The judge noted the absence of detailed witness evidence about what the claimant should have been told about the advantages and disadvantages of induction, and there was no evidence in her witness statement about what she would have decided if she had been given an account containing the advantages and disadvantages of inducement.

Similarly in *Holdsworth v Luton and Dunstable University Hospital NHS Foundation Trust*[58] the consent claim failed when the judge concluded that the claimant's evidence had been 'inevitably coloured by the outcome of the surgery'.

In 2018 the Court of Appeal considered the application of *Montgomery* in *Duce v Worcester Acute Hospitals NHS Trust*.[59] The claimant's case was that her treating clinician had failed to warn her of the risk of post-operative pain (specifically chronic post-surgical pain, 'CPSP') following a total abdominal hysterectomy and bilateral salpingo-oophorectomy. She lost at first instance in relation to breach and causation, and appealed on the basis that the trial judge had failed to consider whether the risk of

---

55 [2018] EWHC 164 (QB).
56 [2017] EWHC 3147 (QB).
57 [2016] EWHC 1334 (QB).
58 [2016] EWHC 3347 (QB).
59 [2018] EWCA Civ 1307.

CPSP was material and that the judge had failed to apply the causation test in *Chester v Afshar* (see below).

The Court of Appeal disagreed: the judge had not addressed the issue of materiality of risk because the claim fell at the first hurdle; the claimant had not proven that in 2008 the risk of CPSP was sufficiently understood by gynaecologists such that there was a duty to warn of that risk. In other words, a medical professional is not under a duty to warn of a risk of which he or she could not reasonably be aware of. A similar approach was taken by the trial judge in *Bayley v George Eliot Hospital*.[60]

It is likely in the future, before considering the materiality test in *Montgomery*, the courts will first consider whether it was reasonable for the treating clinician to have been aware of the specific risk or of any alternative treatments.

Despite the obvious benefits of *Montgomery* for claimants, these cases demonstrate the continuing challenges of successfully bringing an informed consent claim. A further note of caution has recently been provided in the case of *Welsh v Walsall Healthcare NHS Trust (Costs)*[61] where Yip J departed from the usual costs order for a successful claimant, who had won her claim for the negligent performance of bariatric surgery, on the basis that the claimant had continued to pursue a weak consent claim that did not add monetary value to her case.

Consent and confidential information

In the case of *ABC v (1) St George's Healthcare NHS Trust (2) South West London & St George's Mental Health NHS Trust (3) Sussex Partnership NHS Foundation Trust*,[62] the Court of Appeal decided that it was arguable that the daughter of a patient detained under the Mental Health Act 1983 who was suffering from Huntington's disease should have been informed of a 50% chance of developing the condition. The father's doctors considered whether they should override his patient confidentiality, and his expressed wishes, and inform his children of the suspected diagnosis. However, they chose not to do so. The judgment after full argument is awaited (see further Chapter 21).

Consent and causation: Chester v Afshar

The facts in this important and controversial case[63] are easy enough to summarise. The neurosurgeon, Mr Afshar, was found by the trial judge to be in breach of duty in not warning the patient of the small risk of paralysis resulting from cauda equina compression during the lumbar operation. The risk materialised through no fault of the surgeon and the unfortunate patient suffered serious permanent injury. The judge, Sir Denis Henry, did not find for a fact that the claimant would never have had the operation if warned (that would have been an open and shut case for the patient, just as it would have been a hopeless case if the finding was that the warning would not have deterred the patient). He found that

---

60   [2017] EWHC 3398.
61   [2018] EWHC 2491.
62   [2017] EWCA Civ 336.
63   [2004] UKHL 41.

she would have declined to have it at that time, but would have sought a second or even a third opinion. He made no finding one way or another as to whether she would have had it somewhere at someone's hands at some future date. The judge concluded that that was good enough to show that the surgeon was liable for the injury. The Court of Appeal agreed.

One may think it was perfectly logical and sensible to state that, even if she did at some future time undergo the operation, the chances of the injury arising were the same as originally, ie a very great deal less than 50%, and therefore the appropriate conclusion was that the injury would not have occurred. Of course, if the fact that the patient suffered this injury was good evidence that she probably would have suffered it also in any later operation, which is sometimes the case, then she could not succeed. But that was not the case here.

Their Lordships, with the possible exception of Lord Walker, took the view that, as the surgeon's breach of duty had not increased the risk of the injury happening (ie the very fact that the chance of injury, though still very low, would remain precisely the same at any future operation), he had not caused the injury. With the possible exception of Lord Walker, who alone made the point that the scenario might well be different at a later date (in terms of surgeon, environment and maybe other more subtle factors), the House of Lords agreed that to permit the claimant to succeed in this case there would have to be an extension to the normal rules of causation (just as there was in their decision in the mesothelioma case of *Fairchild v Glenhaven Funeral Services Ltd (t/a GH Dovener & Son)*[64]).

The claimant succeeded, albeit by a bare majority (just as in the similar Australian case of *Chappell v Hart*[65]). Three of the judges supported making such an extension on policy grounds, two did not.

The policy consideration at play here is that a patient's right to disclosure of information has to be protected. If the surgeon fails to recognise those rights and the very injury against which he was required to give a warning materialises, it is only right and proper that he should be held liable, even if that amounts to putting him in the position of insurer.

The simplest expression of the minority view was put by Lord Hoffmann, who said that the claimant had failed to prove her loss as the risk would have been the same whenever or wherever the operation might have been carried out. In other words, the purpose of warning was to enable the patient, if she so wished, to take steps to remove or minimise the risk – which it had not been proved she would or could have done. Therefore the surgeon's failure to warn had not been the cause of her injury. Nor did he see any good reason for a policy extension. Lord Bingham took a similar view on both conclusions, stating that he saw no reason to provide for potentially very large damages to be paid by a defendant whose breach of duty had not been shown to have worsened the physical condition of the claimant.

Those in favour of the claimant's case were Lords Steyn, Hope and Walker. They agreed with the minority (at any rate the first two clearly did) that the application of normal principles of causation would not permit the claimant to succeed, and then went on to allow the policy extension,

---

64   [2003] 1 AC 32.
65   [1999] MLC 0067.

saying that, just as in *Fairchild*, there was in this case too, no causation proved on ordinary legal principles, but that there was a special case for making an exception and declaring that in these particular circumstances there would be a special rule for deeming causation to have been proved, or at any rate – and this is of course the important issue shorn of legal casuistry – for imposing liability on the surgeon.

What does this decision mean in practical terms to the medical negligence practitioner? In the first place it means that if the patient would have declined an operation if given a necessary but omitted warning of a risk, and the risk materialised, and the relevant injury occurred, her claim is not defeated by the fact that, though declining the operation at that time, she would probably have decided thereafter to have it anyway. But are there any limits to this? What if she would have decided, after taking a second opinion, to have it a few days later with the same surgeon in the same hospital? Perhaps the court would conclude that the chance of the risk materialising in those circumstances did not remain the same, but, as it had already been seen to have happened in virtually identical circumstances, it could be inferred that it would probably happen again. On the other hand, the risk in *Chester* was one that materialises at random, and one remembers that the chances of the tossing of a coin producing, say, a sixth consecutive tails is still 50%. There have been several unsuccessful attempts to extend the principle established in *Chester v Afshar* outside of the medical context of failure to warn cases: eg see *White v Paul Davison & Taylor*.[66]

However, *Chester v Afshar* has been successfully applied in a number of clinical negligence claims. For example, in *Birch v University College London Hospital NHS Foundation Trust*,[67] the failure to obtain consent to the risk of angiogram (ie the risk of stroke which eventuated) as opposed to other alternative tests was held to be causative of injury as the claimant would probably not have consented had he been warned.

In *Meadows v Khan*[68] a doctor was held to be negligent for failing to inform a pregnant woman of the risk of being a carrier for haemophilia. The test she underwent only confirmed that the claimant herself did not have haemophilia and was not suitable for determining whether she was a carrier. Her child was born with haemophilia and autism. It was not in dispute that, but for the negligent treatment by the doctor, the claimant would have undertaken genetic testing and would have had a termination. However, the defendant denied that it was legally responsible in relation to the needs arising from the child's autism. The trial judge disagreed: had the claimant known she was a carrier, she would have gone on to have another pregnancy which would have carried the same risk of autism (namely a risk less than 51%). Applying *Chester v Afshar*, the scope of the defendant's duty extended to preventing the child's birth and all its consequences.

This decision was reversed by the Court of Appeal.[69] It found that the judge had misapplied the 'scope of duty' test set out in *South Australia*

---

66 [2004] EWCA Civ 1511.
67 [2008] EWHC 2237.
68 [2017] EWHC 2990 (QB).
69 See [2019] EWCA Civ 152.

Asset Management Corp v York Montague Ltd.[70] The purpose of the consultation was to put the mother in a position to enable her to make an informed decision in respect of any child which she conceived who was subsequently discovered to be carrying the haemophilia gene. Given her specific enquiry, namely whether any future child of hers would carry the haemophilia gene, it would be inappropriate and unnecessary for a doctor at such a consultation to volunteer any information about other risks of pregnancy including the risk of autism. In giving such information it would be incumbent on a doctor, consistent with her/his own professional obligations, to take account of a variety of factors which on the facts of that case the doctor was unaware of. As to the apportionment of risk, the doctor would be liable for the risk of a mother giving birth to a child with haemophilia because there had been no foetal testing and consequent upon it no termination of the pregnancy. The mother would take the risks of all other potential difficulties of the pregnancy and birth. The loss which would have been sustained if the correct information had been given, and appropriate testing performed, would have been that the child would have been born with autism (at [27]). The scope of the doctor's duty was not to protect the mother from all the risks associated with becoming pregnant and continuing with the pregnancy. The doctor had no duty to prevent the baby's birth; that was a decision that could only be made by the mother and was outwith the limits of the advice/treatment which had been sought. It had not been any part of the mother's case that the doctor had a duty to advise more generally in relation to the risks of any future pregnancy. The risk of a child born with autism was not increased by the doctor's advice, and the purpose and scope of her duty was to advise and investigate in relation to haemophilia in order to provide the mother with an opportunity to avoid the risk of a child being born with haemophilia, *Parkinson v St James and Seacroft University Hospital NHS Trust*;[71] and *Groom v Selby*[72] considered.[73]

Challenges to *Chester v Afshar*

Following *Montgomery*, there have been attempts to widen the application of *Chester v Afshar*.

In *Correia v University Hospital of North Staffordshire NHS Trust*[74] the claimant had suffered from pain in her right foot and had undergone surgery twice for removal of a neuroma. Prior to her third operation, a surgeon employed by the defendant trust explained to her that the surgery would involve a three-stage process. The third stage involved the relocation of the proximal nerve ending so as to minimise the recurrence of the neuroma. The trial judge found that the operation was performed negligently because the third stage was not completed. However, the claimant lost on causation as the judge concluded that she had not shown that the substandard operation had materially contributed to her persisting pain. The claimant appealed on the basis that the judge should

---

70   [1997] AC 191, [1996] 6 WLUK 227 (SAAMCO).
71   [2001] EWCA Civ 530, [2002] QB 266, [2001] 4 WLUK 343.
72   [2001] EWCA Civ 1522, [2002] PIQR P18, [2001] 10 WLUK 513.
73   At [28].
74   [2017] EWCA Civ 356.

have found there was a failure to obtain informed consent because she was not warned of the material risks of an operation which omitted the third stage of the treatment and had she been warned, she would not have undergone the surgery. The claimant relied on *Chester v Afshar* that the failure to warn in these circumstances entitled her to damages.

The Court of Appeal rejected the argument. It held that the ratio of *Chester v Afshar* was that if there had been a negligent failure to warn of a particular risk from an operation and the injury was intimately connected to the duty to warn, then the injury was to be regarded as being caused by the breach of duty to warn. In this case, there could be no justifiable complaint about the process of consultation and consent up to the moment the operation began. The Court of Appeal found it did not follow that the negligent omission of the third stage of the procedure negated the claimant's consent. In other words, the negligent failure to deal appropriately with the nerve ending did not make it a different operation for the purposes of consent, nor did it make it an operation for which specific consent was required. The court recognised that if it found for the claimant – namely that a negligent act during surgery vitiated consent – there would be far-reaching consequences. The court distinguished the factual findings in *Chester v Afshar* from the present case. In *Chester v Afshar* it was a crucial finding that, if warned of the risk, the claimant would have deferred the surgery. In the present case, the claimant did not say she would not have had the surgery if warned of the risk.

A second attempt was made to develop *Chester v Afshar* in 2018. In *Duce v Worcester Acute Hospitals NHS Trust*[75] (considered above in relation to breach of duty), the claimant appealed to the Court of Appeal on the basis that the trial judge had failed to properly apply *Chester v Afshar*. Utilising the policy arguments of the Supreme Court in *Montgomery*, it was argued on behalf of the claimant that there were three requirements to establishing causation in consent cases that the:

1 injury was intimately involved with the duty to warn;
2 duty was owed by the doctor who performed the surgery to which the patient had consented; and
3 injury was the product of the very risk that the patient should have been warned about when they gave their consent.

This argument was rejected by the Court of Appeal. Hamblen LJ stated that Lord Hope's judgment in *Chester* does not set out a freestanding causation test but:

> ... rather the circumstances which justify the normal approach to causation being modified. That modification was to treat a 'but for' cause that was not an effective cause as a sufficient cause in law in the 'unusual' circumstances of the case.

At [69] he concluded that:

> The majority decision in *Chester* does not negate the requirement for a claimant to demonstrate a 'but for' causative effect of the breach of duty, as that requirement was interpreted by the majority, and specifically that the operation would have not have taken place when it did.

---

75 [2018] EWCA Civ 1307.

In his judgment Leggatt LJ cast doubt on whether *Chester v Afshar* was correctly decided. He described the issue as 'ripe' for consideration by the Supreme Court. This area appears set for challenge in the future, notwithstanding the Court of Appeal's rejection of a similar argument in 2017 in *Shaw v Kovac*.[76]

OBTAINING CONSENT

Having reviewed the legal landscape of the doctrine of informed consent, this part of the chapter considers the relevant guidance on obtaining consent.

The GMC's 2008 guide on consent: *Consent: patients and doctors making decisions together* remains an important source of information on consent for medical and legal practitioners. For medical practitioners the guide warns that whilst not being a statutory code 'serious or persistent failure to follow this guidance will put your registration at risk'.

The 2008 guidance sets out the expected interaction between patient and clinician at para 5:

> The doctor explains the options to the patient, setting out the potential benefits, risks, burdens and side effects of each option, including the option to have no treatment. The doctor may recommend a particular option which they believe to be best for the patient, but they must not put pressure on the patient to accept their advice. The patient weights up the potential benefits, risks and burdens of the various options as well as any non-clinical issues that are relevant to them. The patient decides whether to accept any of the options, and if so, which one.

The GMC has also provided further guidance in *Good Medical Practice* (2013) which states that it is part of the duty of a doctor to: '… listen to, and respond to, [patients'] concerns and preferences. Give patients the information they want or need in a way they can understand. Respect patients' rights to reach decisions with you about their treatment and care.'

The standards expected of healthcare professionals by their regulatory bodies may at times be higher than the minimum required at common law. It should be noted that the common law has historically been based on the standards set by the professions for their members (see further Chapter 9 – Proof of negligence); therefore where the standards required by professional bodies are rising, it is likely that the legal standards will rise accordingly.

Valid consent

For consent to be valid, it must be given voluntarily by an appropriately informed person who has the capacity to consent to the intervention in question. (This will normally be the patient but not necessarily so. It can, for example, be someone with parental responsibility for a patient under the age of 18, someone authorised to do so under a Lasting Power of Attorney (LPA) or someone who has the authority to make treatment

---

76   [2017] EWCA Civ 1028.

decisions as a court appointed deputy.) Acquiescence where the person does not know what the intervention entails is not consent.

The primary question – does the person have capacity to give consent?

Under the MCA 2005, a person must be assumed to have capacity unless it is established that they lack capacity. If there is any doubt, then the healthcare professional should assess the capacity of the patient to take the decision in question. This assessment and the conclusions drawn from it should be recorded in the patient's notes. Guidance on assessing capacity is given in Chapter 4 of the Mental Capacity Act (2005) Code of Practice.

The MCA 2005 defines a person who lacks capacity as a person who is unable to make a decision for themselves because of an impairment or disturbance in the functioning of their mind or brain. It does not matter if the impairment or disturbance is permanent or temporary. A person lacks capacity if:

- they have an impairment or disturbance (for example a disability, condition or trauma or the effect of drugs or alcohol) that affects the way their mind or brain works; and
- that impairment or disturbance means that they are unable to make a specific decision at the time it needs to be made.

An assessment of a person's capacity must be based on their ability to make a specific decision at the time it needs to be made, and not their ability to make decisions in general. A person is unable to make a decision if they cannot do one or more of the following things:

- understand the information given to them that is relevant to the decision;
- retain that information long enough to be able to make the decision;
- use or weigh up the information as part of the decision-making process;
- communicate their decision – this could be by talking or using sign language and includes simple muscle movements such as blinking an eye or squeezing a hand.

People may have capacity to consent to some interventions but not to others, or may have capacity at some times but not others.

A person's capacity to consent may be temporarily affected by a number of factors such as confusion, panic, shock, fatigue, pain or medication. However, the existence of such factors should not lead to an automatic assumption that the person does not have the capacity to consent.

Capacity should not be confused with a healthcare professional's assessment of the reasonableness of the person's decision. Under the MCA 2005 and the common law, a person is not to be treated as unable to make a decision merely because they make an unwise decision. A person is entitled to make a decision which may be perceived by others to be unwise or irrational, as long as they have the capacity to do so.

However, if the decision that appears irrational is based on a misperception of reality, as opposed to a different value system to that of the health practitioner – for example a patient who, despite the obvious evidence, denies that his foot is gangrenous, or a patient with anorexia nervosa who is unable to comprehend their failing physical condition – then it might be reasonable (ie objectively justifiable) to think that the patient cannot comprehend, weigh or make use of the relevant information and hence may lack the capacity to make the decision in question.

The MCA 2005 also requires that all practical and appropriate steps are taken to enable a person to make the decision themselves. These steps include the following:

- Providing relevant information. For example, if there is a choice – has information been given on all the alternatives?
- Communicating in an appropriate way. For example, could the information be explained or presented in a way that is easier for the patient to understand?
- Making the patient feel at ease. For example, are there particular times of the day when the person's understanding is better?
- Supporting the patient. For example, can anyone else help or support the person to understand information and to make a choice?

Guidance on how people should be helped to make their own decisions is given in Chapter 3 of the Mental Capacity Act (2005) Code of Practice.

Is any consent given voluntarily?

To be valid, consent must be given voluntarily and freely, without pressure or undue influence being exerted on the person either to accept or refuse treatment. Such pressure can come from partners or family members, as well as health or care practitioners. The healthcare professional should be alert to this possibility and where appropriate should arrange to see the person on his own in order to attempt to verify that the decision is truly his own.

When people are seen and treated in environments where involuntary detention may be an issue, such as prisons and psychiatric hospitals (see below), there is a potential for treatment offers to be perceived coercively, whether or not this is the case. Coercion invalidates consent, and care must be taken to ensure that the person makes decisions freely. Coercion should be distinguished from providing the person with appropriate reassurance concerning their treatment, or pointing out the potential benefits of treatment for the person's health. However, threats such as withdrawal of any privileges, loss of remission of sentence for refusing consent or using such matters to induce consent may well invalidate the consent given, and are not acceptable.

Consent to visual and audio recordings

Consent should be obtained for any visual or audio recording, including photographs or other visual images. The purpose and possible future use of the recording must be clearly explained to the person before their consent is sought for the recording to be made. If it is to be used for teaching, audit or research, people must be aware that they can refuse without their care being compromised and that when required or appropriate it can be anonymised. GMC guidance gives more detailed advice, including situations when permission is not required and about obtaining consent to use recordings as part of the assessment or treatment of patients and for training or research.[77]

WHO SHOULD SEEK CONSENT?

The clinician providing the treatment or investigation is responsible for ensuring that the person has given valid consent before treatment begins, although the consultant responsible for the person's care will remain ultimately responsible for the quality of medical care provided. The GMC guidance states that the task of seeking consent may be delegated to another person, as long as they are suitably trained and qualified. In particular, they must have sufficient knowledge of the proposed investigation or treatment, and understand the risks involved, in order to be able to provide any information the patient may require. The practitioner who eventually carries out the investigation or treatment must also be able to determine whether the person has the capacity to make the decision in question and what steps need to be taken if the person lacks the capacity to make that decision (see below and Chapter 24). Inappropriate delegation (for example where the clinician seeking consent has inadequate knowledge of the procedure) may mean that the 'consent' obtained is not valid. Clinicians are responsible for knowing the limits of their own competence, and should seek the advice of appropriate colleagues when necessary.

WHEN SHOULD CONSENT BE SOUGHT?

The seeking and giving of consent is usually a process, rather than a one-off event. For major interventions, it is good practice where possible to seek the person's consent to the proposed procedure well in advance, when there is time to respond to the person's questions and provide adequate information (see above). Clinicians should then check, before the procedure starts, that the person still consents. If a person is not asked to signify their consent until just before the procedure is due to start, at a time when they may be feeling particularly vulnerable, there may be real doubt as to its validity. In no circumstances should a person be given routine pre-operative medication before being asked for their consent to proceed with the treatment.

THE FORM OF CONSENT

The validity of consent does not depend on the form in which it is given. Written consent merely serves as evidence of consent: if the elements of voluntariness, appropriate information and capacity have not been satisfied, a signature on a form will not make the consent valid. For surgical procedures, a written consent is usually taken. This will refer in

---

77   GMC (2002) *Making and Using Visual and Audio Recordings of Patients*, London: GMC, https://www.gmc-uk.org/-/media/documents/making-and-using-visual-and-audio-recordings-of-patients_pdf-58838365.pdf.

short form to the operation to be undertaken, and is likely to authorise 'such further or alternative operative measures as may be found to be necessary during the course of the operation'.

In light of *Montgomery*, it is questionable whether the standard consent forms recording common risks (such as infection, bleeding and post-operative pain) only will be sufficient to demonstrate that a patient has been informed of the material risks that may affect him or her specifically.

For minor treatment involving little risk, the consent may be oral. It has been said that consent to such surgical and medical treatment as the doctors might think necessary is not to be implied simply from the fact of entering hospital (*Stoffberg v Elliott*[78]). An apparent consent, oral or written, will not be valid if the physician should have seen that the patient did not realise the significance of what he was giving his consent to (*Chatterton v Gerson*;[79] *Kelly v Hazlett*[80]).

Although completion of a consent form is in most cases not a legal requirement (exceptions include certain requirements of the Mental Health Act 1983 and of the Human Fertilisation and Embryology Act 2008) the use of such forms is good practice where an intervention such as surgery is to be undertaken. Where there is any doubt about the person's capacity, it is important, before the person is asked to sign the form, to establish both that they have the capacity to consent to the intervention and that they have received enough information to enable valid consent to be given. Details of the assessment of capacity, and the conclusion reached, should be recorded in the case notes.

In *Re C*,[81] Thorpe J held that a 68-year-old schizophrenic was entitled to an injunction preventing the hospital from amputating his leg because it had not been established that the patient's general capacity was so impaired by his illness as to render him incapable of understanding the nature, purpose and effects of the treatment advised and so his right of self-determination had not been displaced.

If the person has capacity, but is unable to read or write, they may be able to make their mark on the form to indicate consent. It would be good practice for the mark to be witnessed by a person other than the clinician seeking consent, and for the fact that the person has chosen to make their mark in this way to be recorded in the case notes. Similarly, if the person has capacity, and wishes to give consent, but is physically unable to mark the form, this fact should be recorded in the notes. Or, the person can direct someone to sign the form on their behalf, but there is no legal requirement for them to do so. If consent has been given validly, the lack of a completed form is no bar to treatment, but a form can be important evidence of such consent.

Consent may be expressed verbally or non-verbally: an example of non-verbal consent would be where a person, after receiving appropriate information, holds out an arm for their blood pressure to be taken. However, the person must have understood what examination or treatment is intended, and why, for such consent to be valid. It is good practice to obtain written consent for any significant procedure, such as

---

78   (1923) CPD 148.
79   [1981] QB 432.
80   (1976) 75 DLR (3d) 536.
81   [1994] 1 WLR 290.

a surgical operation or when the person participates in a research project or a video recording (even if only minor procedures are involved).

Special circumstances – form of consent

Requirements concerning gametes

The Human Fertilisation and Embryology Act 2008 (HFEA 2008) came into force in November 2008 and provided a fundamental review of the 1990 statute of the same name, as well as repealing the Human Reproduction Cloning Act 2001.

It is a legal requirement under the HFEA 2008 that consent must be obtained in writing before a person's gametes can be used for the treatment of others, or to create an embryo *in vitro*. Consent in writing is also required for the storage of gametes. Information and an opportunity to receive counselling must be provided before the consent is given. Where these requirements are not satisfied, it is unlawful to store or use the person's gametes for these purposes. Clinicians should ensure that written consent to storage exists before retrieving gametes.

In *ARB v IVG Hammersmith*,[82] Jay J held that the defendant IVF clinic was in breach of duty due to the failure to prevent the use of a frozen embryo without both parents' consent. It was a case where the mother had forged the father's signature on a consent form. However, the father's claim for the costs of raising the child were barred due to public policy reasons related to the costs of bringing up a healthy child: see for example *Rees v Darlington Memorial Hospital NHS Trust*.[83] (See further Chapter 12 – Wrongful birth.) Outside specialist infertility practice, these requirements may be relevant to health practitioners whose patients are about to undergo treatment that might render them sterile (such as chemotherapy or radiotherapy), where a patient may wish to have gametes, or ovarian or testicular tissue, stored prior to the procedure. Healthcare practitioners may also receive requests to remove gametes from a person who is unable to give consent.

Requirements for living donation

The Human Tissue Authority is responsible for the regulation, through a system of approvals, of the donation from living people of solid organs, bone marrow and peripheral blood stem cells for transplantation into others. Information on the legal requirements and how to proceed is available from the HTA.[84]

THE DURATION OF CONSENT

When a person gives valid consent to an intervention, in general that consent remains valid for an indefinite duration, unless it is withdrawn by the person.

---

82   [2017] EWCH 2438.
83   [2003] UKHL 52.
84   See www.hta.gov.uk.

However, if new information becomes available regarding the proposed intervention (for example new evidence of risks or new treatment options) between the time when consent was sought and when the intervention is undertaken, the GMC guidance states that a doctor or member of the healthcare team should inform the patient and reconfirm their consent. The clinician should consider whether the new information should be drawn to the attention of the patient and the process of seeking consent repeated on the basis of this information. Similarly, if the patient's condition has changed significantly in the intervening time, it may be necessary to seek consent again, on the basis that the likely benefits and/ or risks of the intervention may also have changed.

If consent has been obtained a significant time before undertaking the intervention, it is good practice to confirm that the person who has given consent (assuming that they retain capacity) still wishes the intervention to proceed, even if no new information needs to be provided or further questions answered. The position of those who lack capacity is covered below and in Chapter 24.

WHEN CONSENT IS REFUSED OR WITHDRAWN

If an adult with capacity makes a voluntary and appropriately informed decision to refuse treatment (whether contemporaneously or in advance), this decision must be respected, except in certain circumstances as defined by the Mental Health Act 1983 (see below).

This is the case even where this may result in the death of the person (and/or the death of an unborn child, whatever the stage of the pregnancy).[85] Refusal of treatment by those under the age of 18 is covered below.

In *St George's Healthcare NHS Trust v S*,[86] a 36-year-old mother, suffering from pre-eclampsia, refused medical advice to have a Caesarean section, despite being told of the risk to her and her child from natural birth. She was then consigned to a mental hospital against her will. Transferred to a labour ward, she continued to refuse consent to a section. A judge at first instance authorised the section dispensing with her consent. A baby girl was duly born. The mother then appealed to the Court of Appeal. The court upheld her complaints. It declared that, even when his own life depended on receiving medical treatment, an adult of sound mind was entitled to refuse; that, although pregnancy increased the personal responsibilities of the woman, it did not diminish her entitlement to decide whether to undergo medical treatment; and an unborn child was not a separate person from his mother and its need for medical assistance did not prevail over her right not to be forced to submit to an invasion of her body against her will, whether her own life or that of her unborn child depended on it, and that right was not reduced or diminished merely because her decision to exercise it might appear morally repugnant; and that, unless lawfully justified, the removal of the baby from within the mother's body under physical compulsion constituted an infringement of her autonomy and amounted to a trespass, and the perceived needs

---

85   *Re B* [2002] 1 FLR 1090.
86   [1999] Fam 26, [1998] 3 All ER 673, CA.

of the foetus did not provide the necessary justification. Further, the detention under the Mental Health Act 1983 was declared unlawful because detention against the will of the party was not justified merely because his thinking process was unusual and contrary to the use of the overwhelming majority of the community at large. In any event, a patient detained pursuant to the Act could not be forced into medical procedures unconnected with his mental condition unless his capacity to consent to such treatment was diminished.

A few weeks after giving their May 1998 judgment, the court formulated guidelines for all medical practitioners applying to any case involving capacity when surgical or invasive treatment might be needed. These guidelines have been adopted by the BMA but are still sufficiently important and comprehensive to require setting out in full at this point:[87]

The guidelines depend on basic legal principles which are summarised:

1. They have no application where the patient is competent to accept or refuse treatment. In principle a patient may remain competent notwithstanding detention under the Mental Health Act 1983.
2. If the patient is competent and refuses consent to the treatment, an application to the High Court for a declaration would be pointless. In this situation the advice given to the patient should be recorded. For their own protection, hospital authorities should seek unequivocal assurances from the patient (to be recorded in writing) that the refusal represents an informed decision, that is, that she understands the nature of and reasons for the proposed treatment, and the risks and likely prognosis involved in the decision to refuse or accept it. If the patient is unwilling to sign a written indication of this refusal, this too should be noted in writing. Such a written indication is merely a record for evidential purposes. It should not be confused with or regarded as a disclaimer.
3. If the patient is incapable of giving or refusing consent, either in the long term or temporarily (eg due to unconsciousness), the patient must be cared for according to the authority's judgment of the patient's best interests. Where the patient has given an advance directive, before becoming incapable, treatment and care should normally be subject to the advance directive. However, if there is reason to doubt the reliability of the advance directive (for example, it may sensibly be thought not to apply to the circumstances which have arisen), then an application for a declaration may be made.

Concern over capacity

4. The authority should identify as soon as possible whether there is concern about a patient's competence to consent to or refuse treatment.
5. If the capacity of the patient is seriously in doubt, it should be assessed as a matter of priority. In many such cases the patient's GP or other responsible doctor may be sufficiently qualified to make the necessary assessment, but in serious or complex cases involving difficult issues about the future health and well being or even the life of the patient, the issue of capacity should be examined by an independent psychiatrist, ideally one approved under s 12(2) of the Mental Health Act 1983. If following this assessment there remains a serious doubt about the patient's competence, and the seriousness or complexity of the issues in the particular case may require the involvement of the court, the

---

87   *St George's Healthcare NHS Trust v S* [1999] Fam 26, [1998] 3 All ER 673.

psychiatrist should further consider whether the patient is incapable by reason of mental disorder of managing her property or affairs.[88]

Conclusion

There may be occasions when, assuming a serious question arises about the competence of the patient, the situation facing the authority may be so urgent and the consequences so desperate that it is impracticable to attempt to comply with these guidelines. The guidelines should be approached for what they are, that is, guidelines. Where delay may itself cause serious damage to the patient's health or put her life at risk then formulaic compliance with these guidelines would be inappropriate.

In *Ms B v An NHS Hospital Trust*,[89] Dame Elizabeth Butler-Sloss held that a seriously physically disabled patient, but one with the mental capacity to make decisions about treatment even when a consequence of such decisions could be death, had the right to decide to refuse treatment. Autonomy was a fundamental principle in English law, as was the sanctity of life.

On the other hand, in *R v Feggetter, ex p Wooder*,[90] the Court of Appeal sanctioned treatment against the will of a competent patient. It said that decisions to give a psychiatric patient treatment against his will (in this case a decision made by a second opinion appointed doctor) had, by virtue of the Human Rights Act 1998, and by virtue of the fact that medical treatment was to be given which would violate the autonomy of a competent non-consenting adult, to be accompanied by reasons given. Moreover, this decision has been followed in the case of *R (on the application of O) v West London Mental Health Trust*[91] whereby it was considered that there is a duty to give reasons when a decision is made to deprive a patient of their personal liberty.

Caesarean section cases

In a number of cases at first instance, emergency orders were made at short notice authorising Caesarean sections upon women who had not consented. The mother was not always represented and the medical evidence was often scanty. In one case, the woman refused only because she had a needle phobia (*Re L*[92]). The issues arising in this context have now been extensively considered and ruled upon twice by the Court of Appeal.

In *Re MB*,[93] the court held an emergency hearing in February 1997 that was not completed until the early hours of the morning.[94] The mother was 23. The child was presenting by the breech. Caesarean section was obviously desirable; otherwise there was a 50% risk to the child (though

---

88 The court then goes on to set out guidance which, since 1 October 2007, has been superseded by the jurisdiction of the Court of Protection (see further below and Chapter 24).

89 [2002] EWHC 429 (Fam).

90 [2002] EWCA Civ 554.

91 [2005] EWHC 604 (Admin).

92 [1997] 2 FLR 837.

93 (1997) 38 BMLR 175.

94 In view of the comprehensive and authoritative judgment in this case, the earlier cases at first instance are not detailed here. They can be found within the judgment.

none to the mother). The mother wanted a Caesarean section and consented to it, but each time she saw the anaesthetic needle, or the mask, she changed her mind. So the problem was purely one of needle phobia. Her mental state was that she was a naive, not very bright, frightened young woman, but was not exhibiting any psychiatric disorder. At first instance the judge authorised the use of reasonable force for the purpose of performing a Caesarean section.

The Court of Appeal first set out basic principles:

1   In general, it was a criminal and tortuous assault to perform physically invasive medical treatment, however minimal the invasion might be, without the patient's consent.

2   A mentally competent patient had an absolute right to refuse to consent to medical treatment for any reason, rational or irrational, or for no reason at all, even where that decision might lead to his or her own death.

3   Emergency medical treatment could be given, provided the treatment was a necessity and did no more than was reasonably required in the best interests of the patient.

The court reviewed the various Caesarean section cases at first instance, and said that, with the exception of *Re S (adult: surgical treatment)*,[95] the court had expressly decided that the mother did not have the capacity to make the decision. The Court of Appeal was alive to the objections that had been made to these orders, principally that no woman should be compelled to undergo such an invasive surgical procedure against her will, not even if it was necessary to save the life of her child.

On the issue of capacity to consent, the court offered the following guidelines:

1   Every person is presumed to have the capacity to consent to or to refuse medical treatment unless and until the presumption is reported.

2   A competent woman who has the capacity to decide may for religious reasons, other reasons, for rational or irrational reasons or for no reason at all, choose not to have medical intervention, even though the consequence may be the death or serious handicap of the child she bears, or her own death. In that event, the courts do not have the jurisdiction to declare medical intervention lawful and the question of her own best interests objectively considered does not arise.

3   Panic, indecisiveness and irrationality in themselves do not as such amount to incompetence, but they may be symptoms or evidence of incompetence.

4   A person lacks capacity if some impairment or disturbance of mental functioning renders him unable to make a decision whether to consent to or to refuse treatment. A patient will be unable to make a decision on consent when he cannot understand and retain the relevant information, or cannot assess it properly, or through confusion, shock, fatigue, pain or drugs may temporarily lose the capacity. Panic and fear may also destroy capacity.

---

95   [1993] 1 FLR 26.

In the particular case, the court concluded that the mother's needle phobia rendered her incapable at the relevant time of making a decision at all.

The court then decided that the *best interests* of the mother required the Caesarean section to be carried out. There was medical evidence that she was likely to suffer significant long-term damage if her child sustained injury or died, but, on the other hand, would suffer no lasting harm if the anaesthetic were given.[96]

The court went on to consider the important issue of whether the interests of the unborn child were relevant. The court firmly stated that there was no jurisdiction to consider the unborn child as a person whose interests needed protecting. That would need the intervention of Parliament. Finally, the court advised on the procedure to be adopted where the capacity of the patient to consent to or refuse the medical intervention was in issue.

The other case is *St George's Healthcare NHS Trust v S* (above). The guidelines formulated by the court in that case have been set out above.

Despite the Human Rights Act, it is open to the court to hold, if the circumstances are appropriate and the court so desires, that the mother is (ie must be) suffering from some impairment or disturbance of mental functioning and so unable to understand and assess the information given to her by the doctors.

The timing of the withdrawal of consent

A person with capacity is entitled to withdraw consent at any time, including during the performance of a procedure. Where a person does object during treatment, it is good practice for the practitioner, if at all possible, to stop the procedure, establish the person's concerns and explain the consequences of not completing the procedure. At times, an apparent objection may in fact be a cry of pain rather than withdrawal of consent, and appropriate reassurance may enable the practitioner to continue with the person's consent. If stopping the procedure at that point would genuinely put the life of the person at risk, the practitioner may be entitled to continue until that risk no longer applies.

Assessing capacity during a procedure may be difficult and, as noted above, factors such as pain, panic and shock may diminish capacity to consent. The practitioner should try to establish whether at that time the person has capacity to withdraw a previously given consent. If capacity is lacking, it may sometimes be justified to continue in the person's best interests (see below), but this should not be used as an excuse to ignore distress.

---

96   Consideration of what is in the patient's best interests is appropriate to the context of withdrawal of treatment, but it should not be used to give a doctor a licence to proceed in the absence of consent other than in an emergency. In *Frenchay Healthcare NHS Trust v S* [1994] 1 WLR 601, CA, Lord Donaldson MR said: 'It is, I think, important that there should not be a belief that what the doctor says is the patient's best interest is the patient's best interest. For my part I would certainly reserve to the court the ultimate power and duty to review the doctor's decision in the light of all the facts.'

Advance decisions to refuse treatment

A person may have made an advance decision to refuse particular treatment in anticipation of future incapacity (sometimes previously referred to as a 'living will' or 'advance directive'). A valid and applicable advance decision to refuse treatment has the same force as a contemporaneous decision to refuse treatment. This is a well-established rule of common law, and the MCA 2005 now puts advance decisions on a statutory basis. The Act sets out the requirements that such a decision must meet to be valid and applicable. Further details are available below and in Chapter 9 of the Mental Capacity Act (2005) Code of Practice, but in summary these are:[97]

- the person must be 18 or over;
- the person must have the capacity to make such a decision;
- the person must make clear which treatments they are refusing;
- if the advance decision refuses life-sustaining treatment, it must be in writing (it can be written by someone else or recorded in healthcare notes), it must be signed and witnessed and it must state clearly that the decision applies even if life is at risk;
- a person with capacity can withdraw their advance decision at any time.

Healthcare professionals must follow an advance decision if it is valid and applicable, even if it may result in the person's death. If they do not, they could face criminal prosecution or civil liability. The MCA 2005 protects a health professional from liability for treating or continuing to treat a person in the person's best interests if they are not satisfied that an advance decision exists which is valid and applicable. The Act also protects healthcare professionals from liability for the consequences of withholding or withdrawing a treatment if at the time they reasonably believe that there is a valid and applicable advance decision. If there is genuine doubt or disagreement about an advance decision's existence, validity or applicability, the case should be referred to the Court of Protection (see Chapter 24). The courts do not have the power to overturn a valid and applicable advance decision. While a decision is awaited from the courts, healthcare professionals can provide life-sustaining treatment or treatment to stop a serious deterioration in the patient's condition.

If an advance decision is not valid or applicable to current circumstances, healthcare professionals must consider the advance decision as part of their assessment of the person's best interests (see below). Advance decisions made before the MCA 2005 came into force may still be valid if they meet the provisions of the Act.

Some healthcare professionals may disagree in principle with a person's right to refuse life-sustaining treatment. The MCA 2005 does not change the current legal position. Healthcare professionals do not have to act in a way that goes against their beliefs; however, they must not simply abandon patients or cause their care to suffer. A patient should have the option of transferring their care to another healthcare professional or, if the patient lacks capacity, arrangements should be made for the

---

97   See   https://assets.publishing.service.gov.uk/government/uploads/system/uploads/attachment_data/file/497253/Mental-capacity-act-code-of-practice.pdf.

management of the patient's care to be transferred to another healthcare professional.[98]

Patients should always be offered measures that are essential to keeping them comfortable.[99] This is sometimes referred to as 'basic' or 'essential' care, and includes warmth, shelter, actions to keep a person clean and free from distress and the offer of food and water by mouth. The BMA's guidance advises that basic care should always be provided unless it is actively resisted by a patient, and that 'refusals of basic care by patients with capacity should be respected, although it should be continued to be offered'. Advance decisions made under the MCA 2005 cannot refuse actions that are needed to keep a person comfortable. The Act allows healthcare professionals to carry out these actions in the best interests of a person who lacks capacity. An advance decision can refuse artificial nutrition and hydration.

However, although basic/essential care would include the offer of oral nutrition and hydration, it would not cover force feeding an individual or the use of artificial nutrition and hydration. The courts have recognised that an individual with capacity has the right to choose to refuse food and drink, although this may be qualified if the person has a mental disorder. Towards the end of such a period an individual is likely to lose capacity, and the courts have stated that if the individual has, while they have capacity, expressed the desire to refuse food until death supervenes, the person cannot be force fed or fed artificially when they lack capacity. If the person is refusing food as a result of mental disorder, then detention and treatment without consent may be a possibility under the Mental Health Act 1983, different considerations may apply and more specialist guidance should be consulted.[100]

DIFFICULT CASES

Self-harm

Cases of self-harm present a particular difficulty. A competent adult, who has capacity, has the right if he or she wishes to harm him or herself. There is no duty by healthcare professionals to protect a patient from deliberate self harm: see *Savage v South Essex Partnership NHS Trust*.[101]

A duty may arise where a person is vulnerable, such as a detained individual or a child. Where the person is able to communicate, an assessment of their mental capacity should be made as a matter of urgency. If the person is judged not to have capacity, then they may be treated on the basis of temporary incapacity (see below and Chapter 24). Similarly, patients who have attempted suicide and are unconscious should be given emergency treatment if any doubt exists as to either

---

98 *Re B (adult: refusal of medical treatment)* [2002] EWHC 429 (Fam) at paras 100(viii); 9.61 of the Mental Capacity Act (2005) Code of Practice.

99 BMA, *Withholding and Withdrawing Life-prolonging Medical Treatment: Guidance for decision making* (3rd edn, 2007), Part 2.11, London: BMJ Group.

100 Mental Health Act Commission (1979) *Guidance Note 3: Guidance on the treatment of anorexia nervosa under the Mental Health Act 1983* (updated 18 November 2011).

101 [2010] EWHC 865 (QB).

their intentions or their capacity when they took the decision to attempt suicide.

However, as noted above, patients with capacity do have the right to refuse life-sustaining treatment (other than treatment for mental disorder under the Mental Health Act 1983) – both at the time it is offered and in the future. Making a decision which, if followed, may result in death does not necessarily mean that a person is or feels suicidal. Nor does it necessarily mean that the person lacks the capacity to make the decision now or in advance. If the person is clearly suicidal, this may raise questions about their capacity to make the decision. If a patient with capacity has harmed themselves, a prompt psychosocial assessment of their needs should be offered. However, if the person refuses treatment and use of the Mental Health Act 1983 is not appropriate, then their refusal must be respected.[102] Similarly, if practitioners have good reason to believe that a patient genuinely intended to end their life and had capacity when they took that decision, and are satisfied that the Mental Health Act is not applicable, then treatment should not be forced upon the person, although reasonable attempts made to encourage them to accept help cannot be criticised.

Post operation – use of removed tissue

The Human Tissue Act 2004[103] makes consent the fundamental principle underpinning the lawful retention and use of body parts, organs and tissue from the living or the deceased for specified health-related purposes and public display. It also covers the removal of such material from the deceased. (It does not cover removal of such material from living patients – this continues to be dealt with under the common law and the MCA 2005.)

The 2004 Act regulates removal, storage and use of human tissue. This is referred to in the Act as 'relevant material' and is defined as material that has come from a human body and consists of, or includes, human cells. Cell lines are excluded, as are hair and nail from living people. Live gametes and embryos are excluded as they are already regulated under the HFEA 2008.[104]

The Human Tissue Act 2004 lists the purposes for which consent is required in Sch 1, and they are referred to as 'scheduled purposes'. The consent required under the Act is called 'appropriate consent', which means consent from the appropriate person, as identified in the Act. Where there has been a failure to obtain or misuse of consent, penalties of up to three years imprisonment or a fine, or both, are provided for in the Act.

---

102 National Collaborating Centre for Mental Health, commissioned by the National Institute for Clinical Excellence (2004) National Clinical Practice Guideline 16: Self-harm, https://www.nice.org.uk/guidance/qs34.

103 The Human Tissue Act 2004 repeals and replaces the Human Tissue Act 1961, the Anatomy Act 1984 and the Human Organ Transplants Act 1989 as they relate to England and Wales. It also repeals and replaces the Human Tissue Act (Northern Ireland) 1962, the Human Organ Transplants (Northern Ireland) Order 1989 and the Anatomy (Northern Ireland) Order 1992.

104 See https://www.legislation.gov.uk/ukpga/2008/22/contents.

Full details on the requirements of the Human Tissue Act 2004 and the HTA's codes of practice are on the Human Tissue Authority's (HTA) website.[105] These should be consulted to ensure compliance.

Research and innovative treatment

The same legal principles apply when seeking consent from a person for research purposes as when seeking consent for investigations or treatment. GMC guidance advises that patients 'should be told how the proposed treatment differs from the usual methods, why it is being offered, and if there are any additional risks or uncertainties'. Clinical trials are covered by the Medicines for Human Use (Clinical Trial Regulations) 2004.[106]

If the treatment being offered is of an experimental nature, but not actually part of a research trial, this fact must be clearly explained to a person with capacity before their consent is sought, along with information about standard alternatives. It is good practice to give a person information about the evidence to date of the effectiveness of the new treatment, both at national/international levels and in the practitioner's own experience, including information about known possible side-effects.

There is a more stringent need for disclosure of risks where the treatment is to any extent experimental. In *Chadwick v Parsons*,[107] the defendant admitted liability on the basis that in his desire to find patients in need of a particular treatment, he was so enthusiastic about the prospects of success that he failed to disclose the serious risks which the operation carried.

---

105 See www.hta.gov.uk.
106 See http://www.legislation.gov.uk/uksi/2004/1031/contents/made.
107 [1971] 2 Lloyd's Rep 49, affd [1971] 2 Lloyd's Rep 322, CA.

Chapter 11

Adults without capacity

Aswini Weereratne QC, Sophy Miles and Gemma Daly

GENERAL PRINCIPLES

The Mental Capacity Act 2005 (MCA 2005) came fully into force in October 2007 and applies in England and Wales to everyone who works in health and social care and is involved in the care, treatment or support of people over 16 years of age who may lack capacity to make decisions for themselves. The individual who may lack capacity is referred to as 'P'. The MCA 2005 is largely based on previous common law and creates a single, coherent framework for decision-making, including decisions about treatment. This chapter and Chapter 24 summarise the main provisions of the MCA 2005. Detailed guidance is provided in the Code of Practice,[1] which has statutory force. The MCA 2005 imposes a duty on health professionals (and other healthcare staff) to have regard to the Code of Practice.[2]

The Mental Capacity (Amendment) Act 2019 (MC(A)A 2019) received Royal Assent on 16 May 2019. The majority of the amendments concern a new statutory scheme known as the 'liberty protection safeguards' ('LPS') to regulate the deprivation of liberty of P other than in cases where the Mental Health Act 1983 (MHA 1983) is used. This will replace the current scheme, known as deprivation of liberty safeguards ('DOLS') which applies only in hospitals and care homes.

Under English law, no one is able to give consent to the examination or treatment of an adult who lacks the capacity to give consent for himself, unless they have been authorised to do so under a lasting power of attorney or they have the authority to make treatment decisions as a court appointed deputy (see also Chapter 24) Therefore, in most cases, parents, relatives or members of the healthcare team cannot consent on behalf of such an adult. However, the MCA 2005 sets out the circumstances in which it will be lawful to carry out such examinations or treatment.

In general, the refusal to an intervention made by a person when they had capacity cannot be overridden if there is a valid advance decision that is applicable to the situation (see Chapter 10). There are certain

---

1   MCA 2005, s 42.
2   MCA 2005, s 42(4).

statutory exceptions to this principle, including treatment for mental disorder under the MHA 1983, which are set out briefly below.

The legal requirements in the MCA 2005 are underpinned by five statutory principles.[3] One of these key principles is that any act done for, or any decision made on behalf of, a person who lacks capacity must be done, or made, in that person's best interests.[4] This principle applies to health professionals as it does to anyone working with and caring for a person who lacks capacity. The Act also creates an offence of ill treatment or wilful neglect of someone who lacks capacity by someone with responsibility for their care or with decision-making powers.[5]

Information on assessing capacity is given in Chapter 10. A person's capacity (or lack of capacity) refers specifically to their capacity to make a particular decision at the time it needs to be made.

The MCA 2005 provides healthcare professionals with protection from civil and criminal legal liability for acts or decisions made in the best interests of the person who lacks capacity.[6] The Act makes it clear that when determining what is in a person's best interests a healthcare professional must not make assumptions about someone's best interests merely on the basis of the person's age or appearance, condition or any aspect of their behaviour.[7]

The Law Commission recommended an amendment to the statutory defence provided by the MCA 2005.[8] The statutory defence would not be available to someone acting in a professional capacity or for remuneration, who carries out an act pursuant to a relevant decision, unless he or she has prepared a written record concerning specified information (or a written record has been prepared by someone else). 'Relevant decisions' include the provision of serious medical treatment, the administration of 'covert' medication and the administration of treatment against a person's wishes. Although the recommendation was accepted in principle by the Government,[9] the MC(A)A 2019 does not contain this amendment.

The MCA 2005 requires that a healthcare professional must consider all the relevant circumstances relating to the decision in question. These are described as factors that the healthcare professional is aware of and which are reasonable to take into account.[10]

In considering the relevant circumstances, the MCA 2005 rules that the healthcare professionals must take the following steps:

- consider whether the person is likely to regain capacity and if so whether the decision can wait;[11]

---

3   MCA 2005, s 1.
4   MCA 2005, s 1(5).
5   MCA 2005, s 44.
6   MCA 2005, s 5.
7   MCA 2005, s 4(1).
8   The Law Commission: *Mental Capacity and Deprivation of Liberty* (Law Com no 372), para 1.36
9   *Final Government Response to the Law Commission's review of Deprivation of Liberty Safeguards and Mental Capacity: Written Statement* HCWS 542 https://www.parliament.uk/business/publications/written-questions-answers-statements/written-statement/Commons/2018-03-14/HCWS542/
10   MCA 2005, s 4(11).
11   MCA 2005, s 4(3).

- involve the person as fully as possible in the decision that is being made on their behalf;[12]
- as far as possible, consider:
  - the person's past and present wishes and feelings (in particular if they have been written down);
  - any beliefs and values (eg religious, cultural or moral) that would be likely to influence the decision in question, and any other relevant factors; and
  - the other factors that the person would be likely to consider if they were able to do so;[13]
- as far as possible, consult other people if it is appropriate to do so and take into account their views as to what would be in the best interests of the person lacking capacity, especially:
  - anyone previously named by the person lacking capacity as someone to be consulted;
  - anyone engaging in caring for or interested in the person's welfare;
  - any attorney appointed under a Lasting Power of Attorney (see below and Chapter 24);
  - any deputy appointed by the Court of Protection to make decisions for the person (see below and Chapter 24);[14]
- for decisions about serious medical treatment, where there is no one appropriate other than paid staff, healthcare professionals have to instruct an Independent Mental Capacity Advocate;[15]
- if the decision concerns the provision or withdrawal of life-sustaining treatment, the person making the best interests decision must not be motivated by a desire to bring about the person's death.[16]

The Mental Capacity Act 2005 Code of Practice makes it clear that the steps set out in the Act should form the starting point for considering all the relevant circumstances of each case, and often other factors will be important. Further guidance on interpreting best interests is provided in Chapter 5 of the Code of Practice.

Healthcare professionals should keep sufficient records to demonstrate that the decision has been based on all available evidence and has taken into account any conflicting views (Code of Practice, para 5.15). What is in a person's best interests may well change over time. This means that even where similar actions need to be taken repeatedly in connection with the person's care or treatment, the person's best interests should be reviewed regularly (Code of Practice, para 5.14).

In cases of serious doubt or dispute about an individual's mental capacity or best interests, an application can be made to the Court of Protection for a ruling (see below). The office of the Official Solicitor can

---

12 MCA 2005, s 4(4).
13 MCA 2005, s 4(6).
14 MCA 2005, s 4(7).
15 MCA 2005, s 37, discussed in more detail below.
16 MCA 2005, s 4(5) .

advise on the appropriate procedure if necessary.[17] See also Chapter 8 of the Mental Capacity Act 2005 Code of Practice for further information.

PROTECTING P'S ARTICLE 5 RIGHTS

Article 5 of the European Convention on Human Rights (ECHR) permits the deprivation of liberty of persons 'of unsound mind' when this is lawful and 'in accordance with a procedure prescribed by law'. For adults who may lack capacity to make decisions about their care and treatment arrangements, the available 'procedures prescribed by law' are:

1   the 'deprivation of liberty safeguards' ('DOLS')[18] – the statutory scheme set out in the MCA 2005, Sch A1, and which applies to those of 18 years or older who are in hospitals (other than when the MHA 1983 should be used) and registered care homes – this will be replaced by the Liberty Protection Safeguards ('LPS') once the MC(A) A 2019 is implemented. LPS applies to arrangements which give rise to a deprivation of liberty of a 'cared-for person' over the age of 16;

2   a welfare order under the MCA 2005, s 16 authorising the deprivation of P's liberty in cases where DOLS could not be used (for 16–17 year olds, or for adults living in other settings such as supported living);

3   the 'emergency provisions' at the MCA 2005, s 4B,[19] which allow a person ('D') to deprive P of his liberty for the purpose of providing life sustaining treatment or carrying out a 'vital act' whilst a decision is sought from the court and, once the MC(A)A 2019 comes into force, pending the use of LPS;

4   the MHA 1983, where the criteria are met; and

5   orders pursuant to the inherent jurisdiction of the High Court.[20]

Article 5 will be engaged when the following elements are present within a patient's proposed treatment plan:

1   *the objective element:* P is confined in a particular restricted space for a 'not negligible length of time';

2   *the subjective element:* there is no valid consent;

3   the deprivation of liberty is imputable to the state.[21]

In *P (by his litigation friend the Official Solicitor) v Cheshire West and Chester Council; P and Q v Surrey County Council,*[22] Lady Hale promulgated what has become known as the 'acid test' for assessing whether P is objectively deprived of his or her liberty by his or her living arrangements:

---

17   For details of the Official Solicitor, see https://www.gov.uk/government/organisations/official-solicitor-and-public-trustee/about.

18   Now subject to impending amendment by the LPS above.

19   Also subject to impending amendment by the MC(A)A 2019.

20   See for example *A NHS Trust v Dr A* [2013] EWHC 2442 (COP) for an example of a use of the inherent jurisdiction in relation to a patient detained under the MHA 1983, requiring treatment in his best interests which could be delivered under the MCA 2005, but who was ineligible to be deprived of his liberty under the MCA 2005 to enable that treatment to be delivered.

21   *Storck v Germany* App No 61603/00 (2006) 43 EHRR 6.

22   [2014] AC 896, [2014] UKSC 19.

49 The answer, as it seems to me, lies in those features which have consistently been regarded as 'key' in the jurisprudence which started with *HL v United Kingdom* 40 EHRR 761: that the person concerned 'was under continuous supervision and control and was not free to leave' (para 91). I would not go so far as Mr Gordon, who argues that the supervision and control is relevant only insofar as it demonstrates that the person is not free to leave. A person might be under constant supervision and control but still be free to leave should he express the desire so to do. Conversely, it is possible to imagine situations in which a person is not free to leave but is not under such continuous supervision and control as to lead to the conclusion that he was deprived of his liberty.

The effect of the judgment in *Cheshire West* was significantly to increase the numbers of persons whose care and treatment arrangements gave rise to a deprivation of their liberty and who therefore required the protection of Art 5. As well as a significant increase in the number of people made subject to DOLS, it was recognised that the judgment would also apply to many who – like P, P and Q in the *Cheshire West* case – were either living in supported accommodation or their own homes. This led the senior judiciary in the Court of Protection to develop a bespoke, 'streamlined' paper-based process for applying for authorisation from the court to detain these individuals.[23]

There was concern about the application of the *Cheshire West* 'acid test' to patients in intensive care, and the potential burden to providers of inpatient services of having to make an increased number of applications for DOLS.[24] However, in *Ferreira v HM Senior Coroner for Inner South London*,[25] the Court of Appeal distinguished *Cheshire West* (which dealt with living arrangements) from the circumstances of those receiving life-saving treatment in hospital. The court held that any deprivation of liberty resulting from the administration of lifesaving treatment falls outside Art 5, as long as the patient's acute condition does not result from action which the state wrongly chose to inflict on him and that the administration of the treatment cannot in general include treatment that could not properly be given to a person of sound mind in the same condition. By contrast if restrictions needed to be imposed on a patient in hospital which would not be required for a patient of sound mind, and which were required because of the patient's 'unsoundness of mind', then Art 5 might be engaged. An example of this appears in *NHS Trust I v G*,[26] where a hospital considered it might have to give obstetric care to a woman with schizo-affective disorder, who objected to the treatment, and where the court authorised both the deprivation of her liberty and the invasive treatment required. This case is considered in more detail below under the heading 'obstetric care'.

---

23 *Re X* [2014] EWCOP 25 and 37.
24 For an example, see the summary of the evidence of the Intensive Care Society and the Faculty of Intensive Medicine, who intervened in *Ferreira v HM Senior Coroner for Inner South London* [2017] EWCA Civ 31 noting that there were 163,000 admissions to ICUs in England and Wales in 2014/15, overwhelmingly being treated in their best interests with invasive procedures, and in many cases suffering from delirium or paranoia. Complying with DOLS would involve a significant dilution of clinical time and attention.
25 [2017] EWCA Civ 31.
26 [2015] 1 WLR 1984.

Duration of lack of capacity

It is possible for capacity to fluctuate. In such cases, it is good practice to establish, while the person has capacity, their views about any clinical intervention that may be necessary during a period of anticipated incapacity, and to record these views. The person may wish to make an advance decision to refuse treatment (see Chapter 10) or a statement of their preferences and wishes (see Chapter 10). If the person does not make a relevant advance decision, decisions about that person's treatment if they lack capacity must be made in accordance with the MCA 2005 (see above). This would include considering whether the person is likely to regain capacity and, if so, whether the decision can wait, as well as the statutory principle that all practical steps must be taken to enable the person to make their own decision.[27]

Statements of preferences and wishes

A healthcare professional must take all statements of a person's preferences and wishes into consideration as part of a best interests assessment.[28] Written statements which request specific treatments made by a person before losing capacity should be given the same consideration as those made by people who currently have capacity to make treatment decisions. However, a healthcare professional would not have to follow a written request if they thought that the specific treatment would be clinically unnecessary or not appropriate for the person's condition, and therefore not in the person's best interests. If the decision is different to a written statement, a healthcare professional should keep a record of this and be prepared to justify the decision if challenged. There is an important legal distinction between a written statement expressing treatment preferences, which a healthcare professional must take into account when making a best interests decision, and a valid and applicable advance decision to refuse treatment, which healthcare professionals must follow.

Lasting power of attorney (LPA)

The MCA 2005 enables a person aged 18 or over to appoint an attorney to look after his health and welfare decisions if they should lack the capacity to make such decisions in the future.[29] Under a personal welfare LPA, the attorney – if they have the authority to do so – can make decisions that are as valid as those made by the person themselves. The LPA must be made in the form, and meet the criteria, set out in the regulations,[30] and it must be registered with the Office of the Public Guardian before it can be used.

The LPA may specify limits to the attorney's authority, and the LPA must specify whether or not the attorney has the authority to make

---

27 MCA 2005, s 1(3).
28 MCA 2005, s 4(6)(a).
29 MCA 2005, s 9.
30 Lasting Powers of Attorney, Enduring Powers of Attorney and Public Guardian Regulations 2007, SI 2007/1253.

decisions about life-sustaining treatment.[31] Healthcare practitioners directly involved in the care or treatment of a person who lacks capacity should not agree to act as that person's attorney other than in exceptional circumstances (for example if they are the only close relative of the person). If the person lacks capacity and has created a personal welfare LPA, the attorney will have the authority to make decisions and consent to or refuse treatment as set out in the LPA. Healthcare practitioners should read the LPA if it is available, in order to understand the extent of the attorney's power.

The attorney must follow the statutory principles under the MCA 2005 and make decisions in the best interests of the person lacking capacity. If the decision is about life-sustaining treatment, the attorney must not be motivated by a desire to bring about the person's death. Attorneys also have a legal duty to have regard to the guidance in the Mental Capacity Act 2005 Code of Practice. If there is a dispute that cannot be resolved, eg between the attorney and a doctor, it may have to be referred to the Court of Protection.[32] More information about LPAs is given in Chapter 7 of the Code of Practice.

Court appointed deputies

If a person lacks capacity to make a decision relating to their personal welfare, then the Court of Protection can make an order making a decision on their behalf.[33] Alternatively, the Court of Protection can appoint a deputy to make decisions on behalf of the person who lacks capacity.[34] The MCA 2005 makes it clear that in such situations it is preferable for the Court of Protection to make the decision if at all possible, and that if a deputy is appointed, then their powers should be limited in scope to what is absolutely necessary.[35]

The court must ensure that any deputy appointed has the necessary skills and abilities and is prepared to take on the duty and responsibility of the role. Both the court and any deputy must follow the statutory principles of the MCA 2005 and make decisions in the person's best interests.

Deputies for personal welfare decisions will only be required in the most difficult cases, where important and necessary actions cannot be carried out without the court's authority or where there is no other way of settling the matter in the best interests of the person who lacks capacity. For example, a deputy could be appointed to make ongoing decisions, having consulted all relevant parties. This could be useful where there is a history of family disputes.

If a deputy has been appointed to make treatment decisions on behalf of a person who lacks capacity then it is the deputy rather than the healthcare professional who makes the treatment decision. A deputy cannot go against a decision of an attorney under an LPA made before the person lacks capacity. Deputies must follow the MCA 2005's statutory

---

31   MCA 2005, s 11(8).
32   See Chapter 24.
33   MCA 2005, s 16(2)(a).
34   MCA 2005, s 16(2)(b).
35   MCA 2005, s 16(4).

principles and must make decisions in the person's best interests. A deputy cannot refuse consent to the provision of life-sustaining treatment. More information about the powers of the Court of Protection and the role of deputies is given in Chapter 8 of the Code of Practice.

Independent mental capacity advocates (IMCAs)

The MCA 2005 has, since April 2007 in England and October 2007 in Wales (see Chapter 24), introduced a duty on NHS bodies to instruct an IMCA in serious medical treatment decisions when a person who lacks capacity to make a decision has no one who can speak for them, other than paid staff.[36] In matters that meet the definition of serious medical treatment, IMCAs are only able to represent and support people whose treatment is arranged by the NHS.[37] They do not need to be appointed where the treatment concerned is regulated by Pts 4 or 4A of the MHA 1983. They have the right to information about an individual and can see relevant healthcare records.[38]

Serious medical treatment is defined in the Mental Capacity Act 2005 (Independent Mental Capacity Advocates) (General) Regulations 2006, SI 2006/1832 as:

> treatment which involves providing, withdrawing or withholding treatment in circumstances where—
>
> (a)   in a case where a single treatment is being proposed, there is a fine balance between its benefits to the patient and the burdens and risks it is likely to entail for him,
>
> (b)   in a case where there is a choice of treatments, a decision as to which one to use is finely balanced, or
>
> (c)   what is proposed would be likely to involve serious consequences for the patient.

The duties of an IMCA[39] are to:

- support the person who lacks capacity and represent their views and interests to the decision-maker;
- ascertain what the person's wishes and feelings would be likely to be and the beliefs and values that would be likely to influence the person if he or she had capacity;
- obtain and evaluate information, both through interviewing the person and through examining relevant records and documents;
- obtain the views of professionals providing treatment for the person who lacks capacity;
- identify alternative courses of action;
- obtain a further medical opinion, if required; and
- prepare a report (that the decision-maker must consider).

IMCAs are not decision-makers for the person who lacks capacity. They are there to support and represent that person and to ensure that decision-making for people who lack capacity is done appropriately and

---

36   MCA 2005, s 37.
37   MCA 2005, s 37.
38   MCA 2005, s 35(6).
39   Mental Capacity Act 2005 (Independent Mental Capacity Advocates) (General) Regulations 2006, reg 6.

in accordance with the MCA 2005. More information is given at www. dh.gov.uk/imca and in Chapter 10 of the Mental Capacity Act (2005) Code of Practice. IMCAs have the same right to challenge a decision as any other person engaged in caring for P or interested in P's welfare.

Consent forms

Where treatment is provided to a person who lacks capacity following a best interests decision, any consent form should not be signed by someone else unless they have a personal welfare LPA that authorises them to make the decision in question, or they are a court appointed deputy with similar authority. The Code of Practice states at para 5.15 that a record should be kept on the patient's file setting out how the treatment was decided to be in the patient's best interests.

Referral to the Court of Protection

The MCA 2005 established the Court of Protection[40] to deal with decision-making for adults (and children in a few cases) who may lack the capacity to make specific decisions for themselves. The Court of Protection is a superior court of record and deals with serious decisions affecting personal welfare matters, including healthcare, which were previously dealt with by the High Court. In cases of serious dispute, where there is no other way of finding a solution or when the authority of the court is needed in order to make a particular decision or take a particular action, the court can be asked to make a decision.

In *Aintree University Hospitals NHS Trust v James*,[41] Lady Hale set out the approach that the Court of Protection will take when asked to make a decision on behalf of a patient lacking capacity.

First, the court has no power to direct a clinician to administer a particular type of treatment. But any treatment which the clinician does decide to give must be lawful. As she explained in [19]:

> Generally it is the patient's consent which makes invasive medical treatment lawful. It is not lawful to treat a patient who has capacity and refuses that treatment. Nor is it lawful to treat a patient who lacks capacity if he has made a valid and applicable advance decision to refuse it: see 2005 Act, sections 24 to 26. Nor is it lawful to treat such a patient if he has granted a lasting power of attorney (under section 10) or the court has appointed a deputy (under section 16) with the power to give or withhold consent to that treatment and that consent is withheld; but an attorney only has power to give or withhold consent to the carrying out or continuation of life-sustaining treatment if the instrument expressly so provides (section 11(8)) and a deputy cannot refuse consent to such treatment (section 20(5)).

Second, if the patient lacks capacity to consent to the treatment then the question the court will ask itself is whether the proposed treatment is in the person's best interests, looking at their best interests in the widest sense at [39]:

> not just medical but social and psychological; they must consider the nature of the medical treatment in question, what it involves and its prospects of

---

40 MCA 2005, s 45.
41 [2014] AC 591, [2013] UKSC 67.

> success; they must consider what the outcome of that treatment for the patient
> is likely to be; they must try and put themselves in the place of the individual
> patient and ask what his attitude to the treatment is or would be likely to be;
> and they must consult others who are looking after him or interested in his
> welfare, in particular for their view of what his attitude would be.

She continued at [45]

> The purpose of the best interests test is to consider matters from the patient's
> point of view. That is not to say that his wishes must prevail, any more than
> those of a fully capable patient must prevail. We cannot always have what we
> want. Nor will it always be possible to ascertain what an incapable patient's
> wishes are. … But insofar as it is possible to ascertain the patient's wishes and
> feelings, his beliefs and values or the things which were important to him, it
> is those which should be taken into account because they are a component in
> making the choice which is right for him as an individual human being.

Third, if the court finds the proposed treatment to be in the best interests
of the patient, then that treatment will be lawful. If the treatment is not
in the patient's best interests, then it will not be lawful to administer it.

The position as to *when* an application should be made has changed
as a result of the judgment of the Supreme Court in *An NHS Trust v
Y (by his Litigation Friend the Official Solicitor)*,[42] which was handed
down on 30 July 2018. At the time of writing the courts have not had an
opportunity to apply or interpret it, and it is likely that further case law
will develop.

The position before Re Y

The Code of Practice at para 6.18 identifies certain cases when the court
should be asked to make a ruling on lawfulness before a procedure is
undertaken. These are:

- decisions about the proposed withholding or withdrawal of artificial
  nutrition and hydration (ANH) from patients in a permanent
  vegetative state;
- cases involving organ, bone marrow or peripheral blood stem cell
  donation by an adult who lacks the capacity to consent (see below for
  information on children);
- cases involving the proposed non-therapeutic sterilisation of a
  person who lacks the capacity to consent to this (eg for contraceptive
  purposes); and
- all other cases where there is a doubt or dispute about whether a
  particular treatment will be in a person's best interests.

At para 8.18 of the Code of Practice, the same list of procedures is set out,
with a preface stating that the courts had decided that these healthcare
decisions were 'so serious' that only the court can make them.

Practice Direction 9E (now withdrawn) had set out the same list of
serious medical treatment cases which should be brought to court. The
Practice Direction also set out a further list of examples of cases which
could be considered serious medical treatment:

---

42 [2018] UKSC 46.

- certain terminations of pregnancy in relation to a person who lacks capacity to consent to such a procedure;
- a medical procedure for the purpose of a donation to another person where the donor lacks capacity to consent to the procedure;
- a medical procedure or treatment to be carried out on a person who lacks capacity to consent to it and which will involve a degree of force to restrain the person concerned;
- experimental or innovative treatment for a person who lacks capacity to consent to it; and
- cases involving an ethical dilemma in an untested area.

This Practice Direction was withdrawn in December 2017.

Re Y: *the judgment*

In *Re Y*, the Supreme Court was asked to rule on whether there is a common law requirement to seek the approval of the court in all cases involving the withdrawal of clinically assisted nutrition and hydration from a patient with a prolonged disorder of consciousness, even when there is no dispute between clinicians and the family, or whether an application is required by the European Convention on Human Rights.

Lady Black held that there is no such common law requirement. She noted that in *Re F (Mental Patient: Sterilisation)*,[43] Lord Brandon said that 'although involvement of the court is not strictly necessary as a matter of law, it is nevertheless highly desirable as a matter of good practice.'

In *Airedale NHS Trust v Bland*[44] the House of Lords expressed the view that an application to the court where it is proposed to withdraw ANH from a patient in persistent vegetative state was 'desirable' and that doctors would be 'well advised in each case to apply to the court'. These cases, and *Burke v General Medical Council*[45] fell short of developing a common law rule.

Lady Black rejected the argument that an application in all cases was necessary to comply with Arts 2, 6 or 14. She accepted that the legal framework governing the arrangements for decision-making (including the MCA 2005, the Code of Practice, and professional guidance, particularly that issued by the General Medical Council, which she set out in detail) satisfied the requirements of Art 2 of the European Convention on Human Rights (ECHR) (the right to life). However she went on to observe at [109] that:

> the opportunity to involve the court is available whether or not a dispute is apparent, and is of particular benefit where the decision is a finely balanced one. No one would discourage an application in any case where it is felt that the assistance of the court would be valuable. And if a dispute has arisen and cannot be resolved, it must inevitably be put before the court.

Accordingly, the guidance in the Code of Practice suggesting that cases such as Y's always had to go to court is wrong and need no longer be followed – unless there is a disagreement (perhaps between the family

---

43   [1990] 2 AC 1.
44   [1993] AC 789.
45   [2006] QB 273.

and clinicians) and it is not possible to resolve it any other way. In that case, the relevant healthcare body must make an application to the court.

However, in any case which falls within the definition of serious medical treatment, it is clear from the judgment of Lady Black that:

1   an application may be made if the guidance of the Court of Protection is felt to be of benefit; and
2   an application must be made if there is a dispute that cannot otherwise be resolved.

This is consistent with longstanding guidance from the courts: see *Re S (Hospital Patient: Court's Jurisdiction)*:[46]

> [I]n cases of controversy and cases involving momentous and irrevocable decisions, the courts have treated as justiciable any genuine question as to what the best interests of a patient require or justify.

This was echoed by Coleridge J in *A NHS Trust v D (by his Litigation Friend the Official Solicitor)*:[47]

> 'I would echo the guidance of Thorpe LJ in *Re S (Adult Patient: Sterilisation)* that if any case is considered to fall anywhere near the boundary line in relation to any one of the above criteria, it should for the avoidance of doubt be referred to the court.

Furthermore it remains advisable for consideration to be given to making an application in the types of cases which are listed in former Practice Direction 9E, because of the invasive and in some cases irreversible nature of the procedures, or the element of uncertainty involved. Thus, in *University Hospital of Derby and Burton NHS Foundation Trust v J*,[48] Williams J approved the decision of a trust to seek the approval of the court before carrying out a hysterectomy and bilateral salpingo-oophorectomy on a woman with autism and a learning disability, even though there was no dispite between the clinicians and her family that this was in her best interests.

Sterilisation for non-therapeutic purposes

In *Re F (Mental Patient: Sterilisation)*[49] Lord Brandon set out at [56] six features of the procedure which led to the conclusion that an application to the court is 'highly desirable':

> That question is whether, in the case of an operation for the sterilisation of an adult woman of child-bearing age, who is mentally disabled from giving or refusing her consent to it, although involvement of the court is not strictly necessary as a matter of law, it is nevertheless highly desirable as a matter of good practice. In considering that question, it is necessary to have regard to the special features of such an operation. These features are: first, the operation will in most cases be irreversible; secondly, by reason of the general irreversibility of the operation, the almost certain result of it will be to deprive the woman concerned of what is widely, and as I think rightly, regarded as one of the fundamental rights of a woman, namely, the right to bear children;

---

46   [1996] Fam 1 at [18].
47   [2003] EWHC 2793 (Fam).
48   [2019] EWCOP 16.
49   [1990] 2 AC 1.

thirdly, the deprivation of that right gives rise to moral and emotional considerations to which many people attach great importance; fourthly, if the question whether the operation is in the best interests of the woman is left to be decided without the involvement of the court, there may be a greater risk of it being decided wrongly, or at least of it being thought to have been decided wrongly; fifthly, if there is no involvement of the court, there is a risk of the operation being carried out for improper reasons or with improper motives; and, sixthly, involvement of the court in the decision to operate, if that is the decision reached, should serve to protect the doctor or doctors who perform the operation, and any others who may be concerned in it, from subsequent adverse criticisms or claims.

There is pre-MCA 2005 case law to the effect that neither sterilisation which is incidental to the management of the detrimental effects of menstruation nor abortion need automatically be referred to court if there is no doubt that this is the most appropriate therapeutic response (see for example *Re GF (Medical Treatment)*[50]). However, this guidance should be approached and interpreted cautiously (see *Re S (Sterilisation: Patient's Best Interests)*[51]).

It is good practice to involve as part of the decision-making process a consultant in the psychiatry of learning disability, the multidisciplinary team and the patient's family, and to document their involvement. Less invasive or reversible options should always be considered before permanent sterilisation. Where there is disagreement as to the patient's best interests, an application must be made to the court.

Given the nature of the procedure, the court will give particular attention to the requirement in the MCA 2005, s 1(6) to have regard to the least restrictive option: see *Re S (Sterilisation: Patient's Best Interests)* (above); and *A Local Authority v K (by the Official Solicitor)*;[52] *A NHS Trust v DE (by his Litigation Friend the Official Solicitor)*[53] where Eleanor King J as she then was approved a vasectomy as being in the best interests of a man with a learning disability, which would allow him to continue his relationship with his partner PQ without fear of unwanted pregnancy (her first having led to care proceedings).

In *VC v Slovakia*[54] there had been breaches of Arts 3 and 8 of the ECHR where a Roma woman had undergone sterilisation after being asked to provide her consent to the procedure without being fully informed about it and at a time when she was in labour. This emphasises the grave consequences of administering serious medical treatment without lawful authority.

Termination of pregnancy

In *D v An NHS Trust*[55] Coleridge J applied the criteria set out by Lord Brandon in *Re F* to the issue of termination of pregnancies in women lacking capacity. Noting that such situations are not uncommon, and that it would therefore impose an unsustainable burden to require court

---

50   [1992] 1 FLR 293.
51   [2000] 2 FLR 389.
52   [2013] AER (D) 166 (Feb).
53   [2013] EWHC 2562 (Fam).
54   (2011) ECtHR (N Bratza P) 8/11/2011.
55   [2004] 1 FLR 1110, [2003] EWHC 2793 (Fam).

approval in all cases, he recommended that in order to avoid any doubt as to the legitimacy of the Art 8 interference an application should be made if there is any doubt as to capacity or best interests; and that the following features would usually warrant an application to the court:

1   where there is a dispute as to capacity, or where there is a realistic prospect that the patient will regain capacity, following a response to treatment, within the period of her pregnancy or shortly thereafter;
2   where there is a lack of unanimity amongst the medical professionals as to the best interests of the patient;
3   where the procedures under the Abortion Act 1967, s 1 have not been followed (ie where two medical practitioners have not provided a certificate);
4   where the patient, members of her immediate family, or the foetus' father have opposed, or expressed views inconsistent with, a termination of the pregnancy; or
5   where there are other exceptional circumstances (including where the termination may be the patient's last chance to bear a child).

Donation for the benefit of another individual

In *Re Y (Mental Patient: Bone Marrow Donation)*,[56] Connell J approved the donation of bone marrow by P to her sister as being in P's best interests; he further indicated that such cases should involve an application to the court.

Obstetric care

In *NHS Trust 1, NHS Trust 2 v FG (by her Litigation Friend the Official Solicitor)*,[57] Keehan J was asked to give guidance on the steps to be taken when a local authority and/or medical professionals are concerned about and dealing with a pregnant woman with mental health problems who potentially lacks capacity to litigate and make decisions about her welfare and medical treatment. The guidance was provided in the context of what the judge considered to be unnecessary emergency applications to the court, in circumstances where advance planning between the statutory bodies could have obviated the need for an application to the court. Central to his guidance is the need for early identification of those to whom it might apply; regular planning and professionals' meetings between the Mental Health Trusts and Acute Trusts concerned and the local authority's social services department if required as a result of concerns about the mother's ability to care for her child, and assessing at an early stage if an application to court is likely to be needed. Unless in a genuine emergency, applications should be made no later than four weeks before the expected date of delivery and in the following cases:

*   **Category 1** – the interventions proposed by the trust(s) probably amount to serious medical treatment within the meaning of COP Practice Direction 9E, irrespective of whether it is contemplated

---

56   [1997] 2 WLR 556.
57   [2014] EWCOP 30.

that the obstetric treatment would otherwise be provided under the
MCA 2005 or MHA 1983; or

- **Category 2** – there is a real risk that P will be subject to more than
transient forcible restraint; or
- **Category 3** – there is a serious dispute as to what obstetric care is
in P's best interests whether as between the clinicians caring for P,
or between the clinicians and P and/or those whose views must be
taken into account under the MCA 2005, s 4(7); or
- **Category 4** – there is a real risk that P will suffer a deprivation
of her liberty which, absent a court order which has the effect of
authorising it, would otherwise be unlawful (ie not authorised under
the MCA 2005, s 4B or Sch A1,).

This guidance remains good law and should be followed.

Other cases where an application to the court should be made are:
cases which will require a degree of force to carry out the treatment;[58]
or deception,[59] innovative or untested treatment; or cases raising ethical
dilemmas.

Research

The MCA 2005 sets out a legal framework for involving people who lack
the capacity to consent to taking part in research.[60] The Act provides for
when such research can be carried out and for safeguards to protect people
involved in the research who lack capacity, for example ensuring that
the wishes and feelings of the person who lacks capacity are respected.
Anyone setting up or carrying out such research will need to make sure
that the research complies with the provisions set out in the Act and will
need to follow the guidance given in Chapter 11 of the Mental Capacity
Act 2005 Code of Practice. The Act does not include clinical trials, which
are covered by the Medicines for Human Use (Clinical Trials) Regulations
2004, SI 2004/1031.

The MCA 2005 requires that a family member or unpaid carer must
be consulted about any proposal and agree that the person who lacks
capacity can be part of the research.[61] If such a person cannot be identified,
then the researcher must nominate a person who is independent of the
research project to provide advice on the participation of the person who
lacks capacity in the research. The person consulted should be asked for
advice about whether the person who lacks capacity should participate
in the research project and what, in his opinion, the person's wishes and
feelings about taking part would be likely to be if he had capacity.[62] The
person's past or present wishes, feelings and values are most important
in deciding whether he should take part in research or not.[63] If the person

---

58 See for example *DH NHS Foundation Trust v PS (by her Litigation Friend the Official
Solicitor)* [2010] EWHC 1217 (Fam).
59 *University Hospital of Derby and Burton NHS Foundation Trust v J* [2019] EWCOP 16.
60 MCA 2005, ss 30–34
61 MCA 2005, s 32(1) and (2).
62 MCA 2005, s 32(4).
63 MCA 2005, s 32(5).

without capacity shows any sign that he is not happy to be involved in the research, then the research will not be allowed to continue.[64]

Healthcare professionals may be providing care or treatment for a person who is taking part in a research project, and may be asked for their views about what the person's feelings are or need to advise the researchers if the person seems upset about any aspect of the research.

CHILDREN AND YOUNG PEOPLE

The legal position concerning consent and refusal of treatment by those under the age of 18 is different from the position for adults. For the purposes of this guidance 'children' refers to people aged below 16 and 'young people' refers to people aged 16–17.

Young people aged 16–17

For children over 16, the Family Law Reform Act 1969 provides, by s 8:

> 8(1)   The consent of a minor who has attained the age of sixteen years to any surgical, medical or dental treatment which, in the absence of consent, would constitute a trespass to his person, shall be as effective as it would be if he were of full age; and where a minor has by virtue of this section given an effective consent to any treatment it shall not be necessary to obtain any consent for it from his parent or guardian.
>
> (2)   In this section 'surgical, medical or dental treatment' includes any procedures undertaken for the purposes of diagnosis, and this section applies to any procedure (including, in particular, the administration of an anaesthetic) which is ancillary to any treatment as it applies to that treatment.
>
> (3)   Nothing in this section shall be construed as making ineffective any consent which would have been effective if this section had not been enacted.

It will be seen that by virtue of s 8 of the Family Law Reform Act 1969, people aged 16 or 17 are presumed to be capable of consenting to their own medical treatment, and any ancillary procedures involved in that treatment, such as an anaesthetic. As for adults, consent will be valid only if it is given voluntarily by an appropriately informed young person capable of consenting to the particular intervention. However, unlike adults, the refusal of a competent person aged 16–17 may in certain circumstances be overridden by either a person with parental responsibility or a court (see below).

Section 8 of the Family Law Reform Act 1969 applies only to the young person's own treatment. It does not apply to an intervention that is not potentially of direct health benefit to the young person, such as blood donation or non-therapeutic research on the causes of a disorder. However, a young person may be able to consent to such an intervention under the standard of *Gillick*[65] competence, considered below.

Whilst the MCA 2005 applies to those aged 16 or 17, the Court of Appeal in *Re D (Parental Responsibility: Consent to 16-Year-old Child's*

---

64   MCA 2005, s 32(5).
65   *Gillick v West Norfolk and Wisbech Area Health Authority* [1986] AC 112.

Deprivation of Liberty[66] dismissed the approach of Keehan J at first instance that there was a clear distinction between those aged under 16 and 16 and 17 year olds, due in part to the inclusion of 16–17 year olds within the ambit of the MCA 2005. The President of the Court of Protection, Sir James Munby, undertook an extensive evaluation of the jurisprudence, concluding that the exercise of parental responsibility does not end at some fixed age, but upon the child or young person attaining *Gillick* capacity (see below) (per Sir James Munby, at [84] and [125]). Sir James Munby, with whom Irwin LJ and Richards LJ agreed, noted at [127]:

> First, that in general terms the 2005 Act does not make specific provision in relation to those aged 16 or 17. Secondly, and even more important for present purposes, that with only two (in the present context irrelevant) exceptions, the 2005 Act makes no statutory provision for the role of those exercising parental responsibility. Precisely so: the matter is left to the common law, in other words to the operation of the Gillick principles.

In that case, the court found that the parent of an incapacitous 16 or 17 year old could consent to their deprivation of liberty.

If the 16/17-year-old is capable of giving valid consent then it is not legally necessary to obtain consent from a person with parental responsibility for the young person in addition to the consent of the young person. It is, however, good practice to involve the young person's family in the decision-making process – unless the young person specifically wishes to exclude them – if the young person consents to their information being shared.

In *PD v SD, JD and X County Council*,[67] even where the local authority had a statutory duty to consult with and give information to parents of a looked after child (Children Act 1989, ss 22 and 26), Keehan J considered the correct approach was to focus on the child's and parents' competing Art 8 rights. Keehan J declared that the parents of the 16-year-old, who had disengaged from his parents due to issues around his gender transition, were not to receive any information about his day-to-day life or medical treatment.

Children under 16 – the concept of *Gillick* competence

In *Gillick v West Norfolk and Wisbech Area Health Authority*[68] an action by a parent to get declared unlawful DHSS advice permitting a doctor to prescribe the pill to children without telling their parents, the court said that the parental right to determine whether or not a child should receive medical treatment terminated when the child achieved a significant understanding and intelligence to enable him to understand fully what was proposed; but it was also said that parental rights clearly existed and did not wholly disappear until majority. Lord Scarman said:

> ... the parental right yields to the child's right to make his own decisions when he reaches a sufficient understanding and intelligence to be capable of making up his own mind on the matters requiring decision.

---

66 [2018] PTSR 1791.
67 [2015] EWHC 4103 (Fam).
68 [1986] AC 112.

This is sometimes described as being '*Gillick* competent'. A child of under 16 may be *Gillick* competent to consent to medical treatment, research, donation or any other activity that requires their consent.

The concept of *Gillick* competence is said to reflect a child's increasing development to maturity. The understanding required for different interventions will vary considerably. Thus a child under 16 may have the capacity to consent to some interventions but not to others. The child's capacity to consent should be assessed carefully in relation to each decision that needs to be made.

In some cases, for example because of a mental disorder, a child's mental state may fluctuate significantly, so that on some occasions the child appears *Gillick* competent in respect of a particular decision and on other occasions does not. In cases such as these, careful consideration should be given as to whether the child is truly *Gillick* competent at the time that they need to take a relevant decision.

If the child is *Gillick* competent and is able to give voluntary consent after receiving appropriate information, that consent will be valid and additional consent by a person with parental responsibility will not be required. It is, however, good practice to involve the child's family in the decision-making process, if the child consents to their information being shared.

Where advice or treatment relates to contraception, or the child's sexual or reproductive health, the healthcare professional should try to persuade the child to inform their parent(s), or allow the medical professional to do so. If however the child cannot be persuaded, advice and/or treatment should still be given if the healthcare professional considers that the child is very likely to begin or continue to have sexual intercourse with or without advice or treatment, and that unless they receive the advice or treatment then the child's physical or mental health is likely to suffer.

In *W v Official Solicitor*[69] the court was prepared to countenance the ordering of a blood test upon a minor to determine paternity if it was in the public interest that it should be so ordered. And, on the other side of the coin, a judge authorised an abortion upon a 15-year-old girl against the wishes of her parents because the court was satisfied that the girl both wanted and understood the implications of the operation (*Re P (A Minor)*[70]).

In *Re R (A Minor) (Wardship: Consent to Treatment)*[71] the issue was whether a psychiatrically disturbed girl of 15 in the care of the local authority could effectively refuse consent to the administration of the anti-psychotic drugs that the treating doctors thought were essential to her condition. Waite J had taken the view, which had been the generally understood view, that the *Gillick* decision meant that neither parent nor court could override the decision of a *Gillick*-competent child to accept or refuse treatment. However he also concluded that in fact the child was not *Gillick* competent and so could not give a valid refusal.

In the Court of Appeal, Lord Donaldson took a much wider view of the court's powers and a much narrower view of the child's. He said that the court in the exercise of its wardship jurisdiction, which was wider than,

---

69   [1972] AC 24.
70   (1982) 80 LGR 301.
71   [1992] Fam 11.

independent of, and not derived from the parental powers (and had, of course, not been in issue in the *Gillick* case), was entitled to override the wishes of a ward, and indeed also of the parents, whether consenting to or refusing treatment, and whether the child was *Gillick* competent or not. He also said that parents could give a valid consent to treatment in the face of the child's refusal, and that if Lord Scarman in *Gillick* had meant otherwise his words were *obiter*. The farthest Lord Donaldson went was to accord the child a right to insist on such treatment as the doctors advised even if the parents objected. However, these far-reaching observations were in themselves *obiter* as the court held that this particular patient, even though she had lucid intervals when according to the medical evidence she was in her rational mind, could not be regarded in the context of her fluctuating disease as being generally of sufficient understanding to meet the criteria for *Gillick* competence.

There is certainly ground for concern at the assumption by the court of overriding powers in the case of a *Gillick*-competent child; it can be strongly argued that the court's powers in this context should be no greater than that of a natural parent. Furthermore, what power has the court to deprive the competent child over 16 years of age of the right to consent that the child has been given by Parliament?

A year later, Lord Donaldson had occasion to repeat his assertion that, although a minor over the age of 16 has a right to consent to medical treatment in defiance of his parents' wishes, that does not include an absolute right to refuse treatment. In *Re W (A Minor) (Medical Treatment)*,[72] the Court of Appeal, in the exercise of its inherent jurisdiction to protect minors, overrode the refusal of a girl aged 16 to consent to necessary treatment for anorexia nervosa. Thorpe J had held that the child was *Gillick* competent but that the court would exercise an overriding right to order the treatment necessary to save her life. In the Court of Appeal, Lord Donaldson said that the court's inherent powers under the *parens patriae* jurisdiction were theoretically limitless and certainly extended beyond the powers of a natural parent, and it was clear beyond doubt that the court could override the wishes of a *Gillick*-competent minor, not by ordering the doctors to treat, but by authorising them to treat according to their clinical judgment of what was in the best interests of the patient.

However, in this case, too, the court doubted that the minor was able to give a valid or informed refusal because the nature of her disease would impair her judgment, in that it created a compulsion to refuse treatment or to accept only treatment that was unlikely to be effective.

Note here the decision reached by Douglas Brown J in *South Glamorgan County Council v W and B*:[73] the court authorised psychiatric treatment against the wishes of a competent 15-year-old girl.

Reference may also be made to *Re K, W and H (Minors) (Consent to Treatment)*,[74] where Thorpe J said that parents' wishes could override refusal of *Gillick*-competent minors (though all three minors in the case were in fact held not to be competent).

---

72 [1993] Fam 64.
73 (1992) 11 BMLR 162.
74 [1993] 1 FCR 240.

In *Re M (Child: Refusal of Medical Treatment)*,[75] Johnson J authorised a heart transplant operation on a 15-year-old girl against her wishes but in accordance with her mother's wishes. He said that, although there were risks attached to the surgery and thereafter, including the risk that she would carry resentment for the rest of her life at what would be done to her, those risks had to be matched against the certainty of death if the transplant was not carried out. M's refusal to consent was important but not decisive and, while there was great gravity in the decision to override M's wishes, it was necessary to do so in order to achieve what was, on balance, best for her.

In *R v Portsmouth Hospitals NHS Trust, ex p Glass*,[76] a child, considered to be in a terminal state by the hospital, was treated with diamorphine contrary to his mother's wishes. Violent scenes ensued at the hospital. After the child had been discharged from the hospital, the trust suggested to the parents that it would be better if any further treatment took place elsewhere. A misconceived claim for judicial review of the hospital's actions was then commenced. Obviously the court was not going to give directions on clinical management, particularly when the critical period was long over. However, for the present purpose it is worth noting what Scott Baker J said at first instance (the Court of Appeal agreed):

> Life and death cases, like the present one, often raise incredibly difficult issues to which there is no right answer. Anyone who doubts the potential difficulties of the issues in this case should read three documents which have been exhibited with the applicant's bundle of authorities and literature. They are: *Seeking Patients' Consent: The Ethical Considerations* by the General Medical Council; *Withdrawing and Withholding Treatment*: A consultation paper from the BMA's Medical Ethics Committee; and *Withholding and Withdrawing Life Saving Treatment in Children – a Framework for Practice* from the Royal College of Paediatric and Child Health, September 1987.

And Lord Woolf said:

> There are questions of judgment involved. There can be no doubt that the best course is for a parent of a child to agree on the course which the doctors are proposing to take, having fully consulted the parent and for the parent to fully understand what is involved. That is the course which should always be adopted in a case of this nature. If that is not possible and there is a conflict, and if the conflict is of a grave nature, the matter must then be brought before the court so the court can decide what is in the best interests of the child concerned. Faced with a particular problem, the courts will answer that problem.

> In my judgment that is the desirable way forward. Of course it does involve expense; it involves coming to the courts to obtain a ruling. The courts will do their best to reduce that expense. But the answer which will be given in relation to a particular problem dealing with a particular set of circumstances, is a much better answer than an answer given in advance. The difficulty in this area is that there are conflicting principles involved. The principles of law are clearly established, but how you apply those principles to particular facts is often very difficult to anticipate. It is only when the court is faced with that task that it gives an answer which reflects the view of the court as to what is in the best interests of the child. In doing so it takes into account the natural

---

75   (1999) 52 BMLR 124.
76   (1999) 50 BMLR 269, CA.

concerns and the responsibilities of the parent. It also takes into account the views of the doctors, and it considers what is the most desirable answer taking the best advice it can obtain from, among others, the Official Solicitor. That is the way, in my judgment, that the courts must react in this very sensitive and difficult area.

In *R (on the application of Axon) v Secretary of State for Health*,[77] a mother sought judicial review of guidance issued by the DH in 2004 which outlined the advice and treatment a health professional was to give a young person under 16 in respect of various sexual matters including contraception, sexually transmitted infections, and abortion. The guidance stated that confidential advice and treatment could be given to young people who could understand the advice and its implications without their parents being notified or consulted in the event that the young person could not be persuaded to consult their parents, given that it was in the best interests of the young person to offer confidential advice and treatment. The claim for a declaration that the guidance was unlawful was dismissed and *Gillick* was followed. In doing so, Silber J offered the following guidelines in respect of such cases:

1   that the young person, although under 16 years of age, understands *all* aspects of the advice. (In the light of Lord Scarman's comments in the *Gillick* case, at p 189c, set out in para 13(v) above, he or she must 'have sufficient maturity to understand what is involved'. That understanding includes all relevant matters and it is not limited to family and moral aspects as well as all possible adverse consequences which might follow from the advice.);

2   that the medical professional cannot persuade the young person to inform his or her parents or to allow the medical professional to inform the parents that their child is seeking advice and/or treatment on sexual matters. (As stated in the 2004 Guidance, where the young person cannot be persuaded to involve a parent, every effort should be made to persuade the young person to help find another adult, such as another family member or a specialist youth worker, to provide support to the young person.);

3   that (in any case in which the issue is whether the medical professional should advise on or treat in respect of contraception and sexually transmissible illnesses) the young person is very likely to begin or to continue having sexual intercourse with or without contraceptive treatment or treatment for a sexually transmissible illness;

4   that unless the young person receives advice and treatment on the relevant sexual matters, his or her physical or mental health or both are likely to suffer. (In considering this requirement, the medical professional must take into account all aspects of the young person's health.);

5   that the best interests of the young person require him or her to receive advice and treatment on sexual matters without parental consent or notification.

The requirement of voluntariness

Although a child or young person may have the capacity to give consent, this is only valid if it is given voluntarily. This requirement must be considered carefully. Children and young people may be subject to undue influence by their parent(s), other carers or a sexual partner (current or potential), and it is important to establish that the decision is that of the individual himself.

Child or young person with capacity refusing treatment

Where a young person of 16 or 17 who could consent to treatment in accordance with s 8 of the Family Law Reform Act 1969, or a child under 16 but *Gillick* competent, refuses treatment, it is possible that such a refusal could be overruled if it would in all probability lead to the death of the child/young person or to severe permanent injury.

In the case of *Re W (A Minor) (Medical Treatment),*[78] the court stated that it has jurisdiction to override a refusal of a child/young person, at least where they seek to refuse treatment in circumstances that will, in all probability, lead to the death of the child/young person or to severe permanent injury; or where there is a serious and imminent risk that the child/young person will suffer grave and irreversible mental or physical harm.

The courts have, in the past, also found that parents can consent to their competent child being treated even where the child/young person is refusing treatment.[79] In *Plymouth Hospitals NHS Trust v YZ,*[80] where there was '*some doubt*' as to *Gillick* competence and the views of the child fluctuated, Macdonald J drew on the following principles established in: *Re J (A Minor) (Wardship: Medical Treatment);*[81] *An NHS Trust v MB;*[82] *Wyatt v Portsmouth NHS Trust;*[83] and *Kirklees Council v RE:*[84]

(i)   The paramount consideration of the court is the best interests of the child. The role of the court when exercising its jurisdiction is to give or withhold consent to medical treatment in the best interests of the child. It is the role of the court to do so and to exercise its own independent and objective judgment;

(ii)   The starting point is to consider the matter from the assumed point of view of the patient. The court must ask itself what the patient's attitude to treatment is or would be likely to be;

(iii) The question for the court is whether, in the best interests of the child patient, a particular decision as to medical treatment should be taken;

(iv)   The term 'best interests' is used in its widest sense, to include every kind of consideration capable of bearing on the decision, this will include, but is not limited to, medical, emotional, sensory and instinctive considerations. The test is not a mathematical one; the court must do the best it can to balance all of the conflicting considerations in a particular case with a view to determining where the final balance lies. In reaching

---

78   *Re W (A Minor) (Medical Treatment)* [1993] Fam 64.
79   *Re R (A Minor) (Wardship: Medical Treatment)* [1992] Fam 11.
80   [2017] EWHC 2211 (Fam).
81   [1991] Fam 33.
82   [2006] EWHC 507 (Fam).
83   [2005] 1 WLR 3995.
84   [2015] 1 FLR 1316.

its decision the court is not bound to follow the clinical assessment of the doctors but must form its own view as to the child's best interests;

(v) There is a strong presumption in favour of taking all steps to preserve life because the individual human instinct to survive is strong and must be presumed to be strong in the patient. The presumption however is not irrebuttable. It may be outweighed if the pleasures and the quality of life are sufficiently small and the pain and suffering and other burdens are sufficiently great;

(vi) Within this context, the court must consider the nature of the medical treatment in question, what it involves and its prospects of success, including the likely outcome for the patient of that treatment;

(vii) There will be cases where it is not in the best interests of the child to subject him or her to treatment that will cause increased suffering and produce no commensurate benefit, giving the fullest possible weight to the child's and mankind's desire to survive;

(viii) Each case is fact specific and will turn entirely on the facts of the particular case;

(ix) The views and opinions of both the doctors and the parents must be considered. The views of the parents may have particular value in circumstances where they know well their own child. However, the court must also be mindful that the views of the parents may, understandably, be coloured by their own emotion or sentiment;

(x) The views of the child must be considered and be given appropriate weight in light of the child's age and understanding. (para 12)

However, it would be prudent for healthcare professionals to obtain a court declaration or decision if faced with a competent child or young person who is refusing to consent to treatment, to determine whether it is lawful to treat the child.

Where the treatment involved is for mental disorder, consideration should be given to using mental health legislation.

The changes made to s 131 of the MHA 1983 by s 43 of the Mental Health Act 2007 mean that when a young person of 16 or 17 has capacity (as defined in the MCA 2005) and does not consent to admission for treatment for mental disorder (either because they are overwhelmed, do not want to consent or refuse to consent), they cannot then be admitted informally on the basis of the consent of a person with parental responsibility (see Chapter 19 of the Code of Practice to the MHA 1983, as amended 2017[85]).

A life-threatening emergency may arise when consultation with either a person with parental responsibility or the court is impossible, or the person with parental responsibility refuses consent despite such emergency treatment appearing to be in the best interests of the child. In such cases the courts have stated that doubt should be resolved in favour of the preservation of life, and it will be acceptable to undertake treatment to preserve life or prevent serious damage to health.

Child lacking capacity

Where a child under the age of 16 lacks capacity to consent (ie is not *Gillick* competent), consent can be given on their behalf by any one person with parental responsibility (if the matter is within the 'scope of parental

---

85 See https://assets.publishing.service.gov.uk/government/uploads/system/uploads/attachment_data/file/435512/MHA_Code_of_Practice.PDF.

control')[86] or by the court. As is the case where patients are giving consent for themselves, those giving consent on behalf of child patients must have the capacity to consent to the intervention in question, be acting voluntarily, and be appropriately informed. The power to consent must be exercised according to the 'welfare principle': that the child's 'welfare' or 'best interests' must be paramount. Even where a child lacks capacity to consent on their own behalf, it is good practice to involve the child as much as possible in the decision-making process.

As set out by Baker J in *Re King (A Child)*:[87]

> it is a fundamental principle of family law in the jurisdiction that responsibility for making decisions about a child rests with his parents. In most cases, the parents are the best people to make decisions about a child and the State – whether it be the court, or any other public authority – has no business interfering with the exercise of parental responsibility unless the child is suffering or is likely to suffer significant harm as a result of the care given to the child not being what it would be reasonable to expect a parent to give.

Where necessary, the courts can overrule a refusal by a person with parental responsibility. It is recommended by the DH and British Medical Association (BMA) that certain important decisions, such as sterilisation for contraceptive purposes, should be referred to the courts for guidance, even if those with parental responsibility consent to the operation going ahead.

In *Glass v The United Kingdom*[88] the ECtHR in a case where doctors treated a child contrary to his mother's wishes, without a court order, made clear that the failure to refer such cases to the court is not only a breach of professional guidance but also potentially a breach of the ECHR. In situations where there is continuing disagreement or conflict between those with parental responsibility and doctors, and where the child is not competent to provide consent, the court should be involved to clarify whether a proposed treatment, or withholding of treatment, is in the child's best interests. Parental refusal can only be overridden in an emergency.

The Children Act 1989 sets out the meaning of and the persons who may have parental responsibility. These include:[89]

- the child's mother;
- the child's father, if he was married to the mother at the time of birth;

---

86 The concept of the 'scope of parental control' derives largely from case law from the ECtHR in Strasbourg. Chapter 19 of the Code of Practice to the MHA 1983, as amended, gives guidelines about what may fall in the scope, which will depend on the particular facts of each case.

87 [2014] EWHC 2964 (Fam) at [31].

88 61827-00 (2004) 39 EHRR 15. This is the same case as: *R v Portsmouth Hospitals NHS Trust, ex p Glass* (1999) 50 BMLR 269, CA.

89 These are just examples; for all ways of obtaining parental responsibility see The House of Commons Library's useful Briefing Paper on 'Children: parental responsibility – what is it and how is it gained and lost' (England and Wales) (Number 2827; August 2017), see https://researchbriefings.parliament.uk/ResearchBriefing/Summary/SN02827#fullreport.

- unmarried fathers, who can acquire parental responsibility in several different ways:
  - for children born before 1 December 2003, unmarried fathers will have parental responsibility if they:
    - marry the mother of their child or obtain a parental responsibility order from the court,
    - register a parental responsibility agreement with the court or by an application to court,
  - for children born after 1 December 2003, unmarried fathers will have parental responsibility if they:
    - register the child's birth jointly with the mother at the time of birth,
    - re-register the birth if they are the natural father,
    - marry the mother of their child or obtain a parental responsibility order from the court,
    - register with the court for parental responsibility;
- a second female parent, who can acquire parental responsibility, where s 43 of the Human Fertilisation and Embryology Act 2008 applies, by:
  - registering as a parent of the child,
  - register a parental responsibility agreement with the court or by an application to court;
- the child's legally appointed guardian;
- a person in whose favour the court has made a residence order concerning the child;
- a local authority designated in a care order in respect of the child;
- a local authority or other authorised person who holds an emergency protection order in respect of the child. Section 2(9) of the Children Act 1989 states that a person who has parental responsibility for a child 'may arrange for some or all of it to be met by one or more persons acting on his or her behalf'. Such a person might choose to do this, for example, if a childminder or the staff of a boarding school have regular care of their child. As only a person exercising parental responsibility can give valid consent, in the event of any doubt then specific enquiry should be made. Foster parents do not automatically have parental responsibility.
- an application for a parental order may be made under s 54 of the Human Fertilisation and Embryology Act 2008, where the requirements of s 54 are met, which includes that the applicants are husband and wife, civil partners, or living as partners in an enduring family relationship, and one of the applicants provided gametes for the creation of the embryo.

Consent given by one person with parental responsibility is valid, even if another person with parental responsibility withholds consent. However, the courts have stated that a 'small group of important decisions' should not be taken by one person with parental responsibility against the wishes of another, citing in particular non-therapeutic male circumcision and immunisation.

The Court of Appeal upheld an order of Wall J refusing permission for circumcision to be carried out on a child where the Muslim father wanted it and the mother did not (*Re J (Child's Religious Upbringing and Circumcision)*).[90]

In *Re O (A Minor) (Medical Treatment)*,[91] Johnson J authorised a blood transfusion for a two-month-old girl born 12 weeks prematurely, despite the objections of her Jehovah's Witness parents. Booth J acted similarly to overrule the wishes of the parents of a ten-month-old girl suffering from leukaemia in the case of *Camden London Borough Council v R (A Minor) (Blood Transfusion)*,[92] stating that the court could grant a specific order to permit a transfusion under s 8 of the Children Act 1989, and that it was not necessary to invoke the inherent jurisdiction of the court.

Similarly, in *Devon County Council v S*,[93] Thorpe J authorised a non-urgent transfusion to enable chemotherapy upon a boy aged four-and-a-half where there was only an even chance of success and his Jehovah's Witness parents objected.

Reference may also be made to in *Re E*,[94] in which Ward J authorised a life-saving blood transfusion for a leukaemic boy of 15 from a family of Jehovah's Witnesses.[95]

In *Re L (A Minor)*,[96] the President authorised blood transfusions for a Jehovah's Witness, a girl of 16, who had sustained severe burns, on the basis that her sheltered lifestyle as a Witness limited her understanding of her condition and the need for treatment, and that the treatment sought was in her best interests.

See also *Re T (A Minor) (Wardship: Medical Treatment)*,[97] discussed below under 'The quality of life and terminally ill patients'.

In *Re B (A Child)*,[98] the Court of Appeal upheld the judge's decision when he granted the father's applications under s 8 of the Children Act 1989 that, contrary to the mother's wishes, the children's best interests required that they receive the full MMR vaccination. Where the local authority shared parental responsibility with the parents in *C v A*,[99] and the parents did not want the children to receive the MMR vaccine, booster immunisations and the flu vaccination, but the local authority did, Theis J declared the MMR and booster vaccinations were in the

---

90 (1999) 52 BMLR 82. Female circumcision is always prohibited, under the Prohibition of Female Circumcision Act 1985 (repealed on 1 September 2005) and now the Female Genital Mutilation Act 2003 in England, Wales and NI, as amended by the Serious Crime Act 2015; *Re J* [2000] 1 FLR 571 at 577; *Re B (A Child) sub nom Re vaccination / MMR litigation*; *A v B; D v E sub nom Re C (A Child) (Immunisation: Parental Rights)*; *Re F (A Child) (Immunisation: Parental Rights)* [2003] EWCA Civ 1148.
91 [1993] 4 Med LR 272.
92 (1993) 15 BMLR 72.
93 (1992) 11 BMLR 105.
94 [1993] 1 FLR 386.
95 In *Re W (A Minor) (HIV test)* [1995] 2 FCR 184, Kirkwood J authorised a blood test on a child whose mother had died of an Aids-related illness as being in the best interests of the child. Wilson J authorised a blood test on a baby for HIV detection despite the parents' opposition (*Re C (A Child)* also *sub nom Camden London Borough Council v A, B and C*) (1999) 50 BMLR 283).
96 (1998) 51 BMLR 137.
97 [1997] 1 WLR 242, CA.
98 [2003] EWCA Civ 1148.
99 [2011] EWHC 4033 (Fam).

welfare interests of the children, although there was insufficient evidence for the flu vaccination.

A distinction was made by Baker J in *Re King (A Child)*[100] between cases where there is a 'dispute between medical authorities and parents who are insisting on a wholly unreasonable course of treatment, or withholding consent to an essential therapy for their child – for example, a blood transfusion' and cases such as Ashya King's where 'the course of treatment proposed by Mr and Mrs King is entirely reasonable.' In such cases, 'both courses are reasonable and it is the parents who bear the heavy responsibility of making the decision' (at [34]).

Re King was distinguished in *Re Gard (A Child) (Child on Life Support: Withdrawal of Treatment)*,[101] where the Court of Appeal explained the law in such cases as follows:

> 95. When thoughtful, caring, and responsible parents are putting forward a viable option for the care of their child, the court will look keenly at that option, in the same way that a court in family proceedings, when it gets to the welfare stage of any case, looks at the realistic options that are before it. The court evaluates the nitty-gritty detail of each option from the child's perspective. It does not prefer any particular option simply because it is put forward by a parent or by a local authority. The judge decides what is in the best interests of the child by looking at the case entirely through eyes focused on the child's welfare and focused upon the merits and drawbacks of the particular options that are being presented to the court.
>
> 96. If one option is favoured by a parent, that may give it weight ... Notwithstanding that that is the case, in the end it is the judge who has to choose the best course for a child. Where, as in the case of *In re King* [2014] 2 FLR 855 before Baker J, there really was nothing to choose as between the benefits and detriments of the two forms of radiotherapy, the court readily stood back and allowed the parents to make their choice.
>
> 97. Where, however, as in this case, the judge has made clear findings that going to America for treatment would be futile, would have no benefit and would simply prolong the awful existence that he found was the current state of young Charlie's life, he was fully entitled, on the basis of those findings to conclude as he did. The consequence of that conclusion is that the proposal for nucleoside therapy was not a viable option before the court.

Where persons with parental responsibility disagree as to whether these procedures are in the child's best interests, it is advisable to refer the decision to the courts. It is possible that major experimental treatment, where opinion is divided as to the benefits it may bring the child, might also fall into this category of important decisions, such as in *Re Gard* (see above) where medical opinion was unanimous except for the American doctor who proposed to provide the treatment.

For an example of the court's approach to parental disagreement and best interests in the context of contact arrangements see *Re A (Children) (Contact: Ultra-Orthodox Judaism: Transgender Parent)*.[102]

Where there is doubt about whether a parent is acting in the interest of the child or young person, then the healthcare practitioner would be

---

100 [2014] EWHC 2964 (Fam).
101 [2018] 4 WLR 5.
102 [2018] 4 WLR 60.

unwise to rely on the parent's consent, for example if a child alleges abuse and the parent supports psychiatric treatment for the child.

In the recent series of high-profile cases around the removal of life-sustaining treatment for Alfie Evans, the courts have consistently decided against the parents' wishes where these were found to be contrary to the child's best interests. In refusing permission to appeal, the Supreme Court referred to the best interests of a child as the 'gold standard' to be applied in such cases, and this principle was reiterated by the Court of Appeal (*Evans v Alder Hey Children's NHS Foundation Trust*[103]):

> There can be no derogation from the mandatory requirement to apply the gold standard, namely the best interests of the young person concerned, in determining what the outcome of any relevant application is ... (per Lord Justice McFarlane, at [32])

In order to consent on behalf of a child, the person with parental responsibility must themselves have capacity. Where the person with parental responsibility for a child is under 18, they will only be able to give valid consent for the child's treatment if they themselves are *Gillick* competent (see above). Whether or not they have capacity may vary, depending on the seriousness of the decision to be taken.

Where a child is a ward of court, no important step may be taken in the life of the child without the prior consent of the court. This is likely to include more significant medical interventions but not treatment for minor injuries or common diseases of childhood.

In an emergency, it is justifiable to treat a child who lacks capacity without the consent of a person with parental responsibility, if it is impossible to obtain consent in time and if the treatment is vital to the survival or health of the child.

Research on children or young people

Where children lack capacity to consent for themselves, parents may give consent for their child to be entered into a trial where the evidence is that the trial therapy may be at least as beneficial to the patient as the standard therapy. It may also be compatible with the welfare principle for a person with parental responsibility to give consent to a research intervention that is not strictly in the best interests of the child, but is not against the interests of the child either. Such an intervention must involve only minimal burden to the child.

Decisions about experimental treatment must be made in the child's best interests (see above).

Using children as bone marrow donors

This is covered by the Human Tissue Authority's Code of Practice on donation of allogeneic bone marrow and peripheral blood stem cells for transplantation, and healthcare professionals should consult this for detailed information on the legal requirements and how to proceed.[104]

---

103 [2018] EWCA Civ 984, at [4]–[5] and [32].
104 Human Tissue Authority (2017) Code of Practice – Donation of allogeneic bone marrow and peripheral blood stem cells for transplantation, Code G, London: Human Tissue Authority, www.hta.gov.uk/legislationpoliciesandcodesofpractice/codesofpractice.cfm.

UNITED NATIONS CONVENTION ON THE RIGHTS OF THE CHILD (CRC)

The CRC was ratified by the UK on 16 December 1991 and came into force on 15 January 1992. It is a legally binding international treaty protecting the rights of children and young people aged 17 and under. 'By ratifying a Convention a State undertakes that wherever possible its laws will conform to the norms and values that the Convention enshrines.'[105] The CRC may be relevant to the interpretation of domestic law in four ways:

1   through the Human Rights Act 1998;
2   under Art 24 of the European Charter of Fundamental Rights;
3   under specific statutory provisions; and/or
4   the common law.

There is a strong presumption in favour of interpreting a statute in a way that does not place the UK in breach of its international obligations. The CRC can be used as an aid to construction of any particular provision, in case of ambiguity or uncertainty. The spirit of the CRC is incorporated into our law through sections of the Children Act 2004, and Immigration Act 2009. International treaty obligations may guide the development of the common law, or the common law should be in harmony with them. See all the speeches in *R(SG) v Secretary of State for Work and Pensions*.[106] The CRC has also explicitly been referred to in Government guidance over many years, for example, the *Framework for the Assessment of Children and Families* and current statutory safeguarding guidance, *Working Together*.[107]

The full scope and impact of the CRC is beyond the remit of this book however, of particular relevance in the context of consent to treatment might be Arts 3, 5, 12 and 18. Article 3(1) provides that 'the best interests of the child shall be a primary consideration'. Article 3(2) provides that:

> States Parties undertake to ensure the child such protection and care as is necessary for his or her well-being, taking in to account the rights and duties of his or her parents, legal guardians, or other individuals legally responsible for him or her, and, to this end, shall take all appropriate legislative and administrative measures.

Article 5 provides:

> States Parties shall respect the responsibilities, rights and duties of parents or, where applicable, the members of the extended family or community as provided for by local custom, legal guardians, or other persons legally responsible for the child, to provide in a manner consistent with the evolving capacities of the child, appropriate direction and guidance in the exercise by the child of the rights recognised in the present Convention.

Article 12(1) requires that the views of the children are to be 'given due weight in accordance with the age and maturity of the child'. Article 18(1) provides that:

---

105 *AH v West London MHT* [2011] UKUT 74 (AAC) at [16] LJ Carnwath (as he then was).
106 [2015] 1 WLR 1449.
107 HM Government 'Working Together to Safeguard Children: A guide to inter-agency working to safeguard and promote the welfare of children' (July 2018), https://assets.publishing.service.gov.uk/government/uploads/system/uploads/attachment_data/file/729914/Working_Together_to_Safeguard_Children-2018.pdf.

States Parties shall use their best efforts to ensure recognition of the principle that both parents have common responsibilities for the upbringing and development of the child. Parents or, as the case may be, legal guardians, have the primary responsibility for the upbringing and development of the child. The best interests of the child will be their basic concern.

In *Re D (Parental Responsibility: Consent to 16-Year-old Child's Deprivation of Liberty*[108] (discussed above) the court considered the impact of relevant provisions of the CRC at [136]–[137]. Lord Justice Munby derived three key principles supporting the decision in that case, in the context of a deprivation of liberty, that parental responsibility is, in principle, exercisable in relation to a 16 or 17 year old child who, for whatever reasons, lacks *Gillick* capacity:

> The first is the recognition, for example in Arts 3(2), 5 and 18(1) of, to use the language of Art 18(1), the 'primary responsibility' of the parents for their child's care, upbringing and development. The second is the philosophy to be found, for example in Arts 5 and 12(1), which recognise, to use the language of Art 5(1), the 'evolving capacities of the child' and, to use the language of Art 12(2), the need to have regard to 'the age and maturity of the child' – precisely the philosophy which, in domestic law, is enshrined in … *Gillick*. The third is the fact that nowhere in the UNCRC or in any of the literature to which we have been taken is any explicit reference made to the different position of the 16 or 17 year old child compared with the 15 year old; there is nothing to suggest that there is some 'bright-line' distinction between the 15 and 16 year old.

LIFE-SUSTAINING TREATMENT – WITHDRAWING AND WITHHOLDING

The general principles

A healthcare professional's legal duty is to care for a patient and to take reasonable steps to prolong their life. Although there is a strong presumption in favour of providing life-sustaining treatment, there are circumstances when continuing or providing life-sustaining treatment stops providing a benefit to a patient and is not clinically indicated. There is no legal distinction between withdrawing and withholding life-sustaining treatment. A person with capacity may decide either contemporaneously or by a valid and applicable advance decision that they have reached a stage where they no longer wish treatment to continue. If a person lacks capacity, this decision must be taken in their best interests and in a way that reflects their wishes (if these are known).

The legal principles around consent are the same for all medical interventions, including decisions to withdraw or withhold life-sustaining treatment, but the issues surrounding seriously ill or dying patients are necessarily more grave and sensitive. Persons with the capacity to do so can make such decisions for themselves. If the person is an adult who lacks capacity to make such decisions then the provisions of the MCA 2005 will apply to these, as to other decisions. When making a best-interests decision in relation to life-sustaining treatment, healthcare

---

108 [2018] PTSR 1791.

professionals should be aware that the MCA 2005 requires that the healthcare professional must not be motivated by a desire to bring about the person's death.

Sometimes decisions will need to be made immediately – for example whether it is appropriate to attempt resuscitation after severe trauma.[109] In an emergency situation, where there is doubt as to the appropriateness of treatment, there should be a presumption in favour of providing life-sustaining treatment. When more time is available and the patient is an adult or child without capacity, all those concerned with the care of the patient – relatives, partners, friends, carers and the multidisciplinary team – can potentially make a contribution to the assessment. The discussions and the basis for decisions should be recorded in the patient's notes.

Legally, the use of ANH constitutes medical treatment. Thus the legal principles that apply to the use of ANH are the same as those that apply to all other medical treatments, such as medication or ventilation. Decisions about the proposed withholding or withdrawal of ANH from a patient in a permanent vegetative state or a minimally conscious state do not need to be referred to the court where clinicians and the patient's family are in agreement; but where there is any doubt or dispute as to whether this is in the patient's best interests, an application should be made (see above).

There is an important distinction between withdrawing or withholding treatment that is of no clinical benefit to the patient or is not in the patient's best interests, and taking a deliberate action to end the patient's life. A deliberate action that is intended to cause death is unlawful. Although there is a strong presumption in favour of providing life-sustaining treatment, there are circumstances when continuing or providing life-sustaining treatment stops providing a benefit to a patient and is not clinically indicated. Healthcare professionals should discuss the situation with a patient with capacity and agree if and when the patient no longer wishes treatment to continue. If the patient lacks capacity, this decision must be taken in their best interests and in a way that reflects their wishes, beliefs and values (if these are known). Suitable care should be provided to ensure that both the comfort and dignity of the patient are maintained.

Adults and children with capacity

Except in circumstances governed by the MHA 1983, if an adult with the capacity to make the decision refuses life-sustaining treatment, or requests that it be withdrawn, practitioners must comply with the person's decision, even if it may result in the person's death.

In *Re B (Adult: Refusal of Medical Treatment)*[110] the court decided that if a refusal is ignored, they will be treating the person unlawfully.

The case of *Burke v GMC*[111] established that an adult patient with capacity does not have the legal right to demand treatment that is not clinically indicated. Where a patient with capacity indicates his wish to be

---

109 See Health Service Circular 2000/28 for further guidance on resuscitation decisions. It advises that NHS trusts should have appropriate resuscitation policies in place.
110 [2002] 2 All ER 449.
111 *R (On the Application of Burke) v General Medical Council* [2006] QB 273.

kept alive by the provision of ANH, the doctor's duty of care will require them to provide ANH while such treatment continues to prolong life. A patient cannot demand that a healthcare professional does something unlawful such as assisting them to commit suicide.

If a child with capacity makes such a request or refusal it is possible that such a refusal could be overruled if it would in all probability lead to the death of the child or to severe permanent injury (see above). Moreover, a decision which may result in the individual's death requires a very high level of understanding, so that many young people who would have the capacity to take other decisions about their medical care would lack the capacity to make such a grave decision.

Refusal of treatment by a child with capacity must always be taken very seriously, even though legally it is possible to override their objections. It is not a legal requirement to continue a child's life-sustaining treatment in all circumstances. For example, where the child is suffering an illness where the likelihood of survival even with treatment is extremely poor, and treatment will pose a significant burden to the child, it may not be in the best interests of the child to continue treatment.

Adults and children lacking capacity

If a child lacks capacity, it is still good practice to involve the child as far as is possible and appropriate in the decision. The decision to withdraw or withhold life-sustaining treatment must be made in the best interests of the child. The best interests of a child in the context of the withholding of medical treatment should be interpreted more broadly than medical interests, and should include emotional and other factors. There is a strong presumption in favour of preserving life, but not where treatment would be futile, and there is no obligation on healthcare professionals to give treatment that would be futile. If there is disagreement between those with parental responsibility for the child and the clinical team concerning the appropriate course of action, a ruling should be sought from the court as early as possible. This requirement was emphasised in the judgment of *R v Portsmouth Hospitals NHS Trust, ex p Glass*[112] (see above).

A person with parental responsibility for a child or young person is legally entitled to give or withhold consent to treatment. A person with parental responsibility cannot demand a particular treatment to be continued where the burdens of the treatment clearly outweigh the benefits for the child. If agreement cannot be reached between the parent(s) and the healthcare professionals, a court should be asked to make a declaration about whether the provision of life-sustaining treatment would benefit the child. In exceptional cases, the court has been willing to authorise the withdrawal of life-sustaining treatment against the parents' wishes.[113] However, the views of the parents are given great weight by the courts and are likely to be determinative, unless they conflict with the child's best interests (see above).

---

112 (1999) 50 BMLR 269, CA.
113 *Re C (A Minor) (Medical Treatment)* [1998] 1 FLR 384.

THE QUALITY OF LIFE AND TERMINALLY ILL PATIENTS

Perhaps the most difficult and anxious decision the courts have ever been asked to take in this context arose in the conjoined twins case (*Re A (Children) (Conjoined Twins: Surgical Separation)*[114]). For a variety of reasons, the court authorised the operation that would terminate the life of one twin (a child that was in any event dependent for her vital organs on her sister) but would give the other twin a fair chance of a reasonable life. The issues raised in that unique case were more a matter of medical, and general, ethics than of medical negligence, and the lengthy judgments at least as philosophical as jurisprudential, and for that reason they are not treated in detail here. Suffice it to say that there was an issue of consent, in that the parents were not consenting to the operation, and the doomed twin had no say in the matter. The 'quality of life' of the two twins was a vital element in the court's decision.

Human rights considerations figure prominently in the context of 'quality of life' cases (such as fall to be decided after the MCA 2005 came into force). The factor of 'quality of life' arises most commonly where a patient is terminally ill or in a vegetative or minimally conscious state.

The question for the courts will be whether it is in the patient's best interests to be given the treatment. If it is, then it is lawful to give the treatment. If the treatment is not in the patient's best interests, it cannot lawfully be administered (*Aintree University Hospitals NHS Trust v James*[115]).

The principles emerging from case law on the best interests in relation to life-sustaining treatment have been recently summarised by Hayden J in *Salford Royal NHS Foundation Trust v Mrs P and Q*[116]:

- the sanctity of life is not an absolute principle, and can be outweighed by the need to respect the personal autonomy and dignity of the patient *Aintree v James* (above) at [35];
- there is no prohibition to conducting a best interests analysis of the continued provision of ANH even though Mrs P is not in a vegetative state: *W v M*,[117] per Baker J;
- there can be no further guidance beyond the wording of s 4 other than that 'decision makers must look at his welfare in the widest sense, not just medical but social and psychological; they must consider what the outcome of that treatment for the patient is likely to be; they must try and put themselves in the place of the individual patient and ask what his attitude to the treatment is or would be likely to be; and they must consult others who are looking after him or are interested in his welfare, in particular for their view of what his attitude would be.' *Aintree* at [39] per Baroness Hale;
- where the patient's condition may improve, a best interests decision may be based on the 'best case scenario' as advised by the relevant clinicians and experts: *Re Briggs (Incapacitated Person) (Medical*

---

114 [2001] Fam 147.
115 [2014] AC 591, at [19].
116 [2017] EWCOP 23 at [29].
117 [2011] EWHC 2443 (Fam) at [102].

Treatment: Best Interests Decision) (No 2),[118] overview at (25) per Charles J;

- it is incumbent on the court fully to investigate and consider the values and beliefs of the patient as well as any views the patient expressed when she had capacity that cast light on the likely choice the patient would have made and the factors that the patient would have considered relevant or important: *M v N*,[119] per Hayden J, *Briggs* at [54] per Charles J;
- where the patient's views can be ascertained with sufficient certainty, they should generally be followed (*Briggs* at [62] per Charles J) or afforded great respect (*M v N* at [28] per Hayden J), though they are not automatically determinative. '... if the decision that P would have made, and so their wishes on such an intensely personal issue can be ascertained with sufficient certainty it should generally prevail over the very strong presumption in favour of preserving life. *Briggs* at [62ii] per Charles J. ... the "sanctity of life" or the "intrinsic value of life", can be rebutted (pursuant to statute) on the basis of a competent adult's cogently expressed wish. It follows, to my mind, by parity of analysis, that the importance of the wishes and feelings of an incapacitated adult, communicated to the court via family or friends but with similar cogency and authenticity, are to be afforded no less significance than those of the capacitous.' *M v N* at [32] per Hayden J.[120]

The Royal College of Paediatrics and Child Health produced guidelines in March 2015 'Making Decisions to Limit Treatment in Life-limiting and Life-threatening Conditions in Children: A Framework for Practice'.[121] The following excerpt was referred to with approval by the Court of Appeal in *Re E (A Child)*:[122]

> The RCPCH believes that there are three sets of circumstances when treatment limitation can be considered because it is no longer in the child's best interests to continue, because treatments cannot provide overall benefit:
>
> ...
>
> **II When life is limited in quality**
>
> This includes situations where treatment may be able to prolong life significantly but will not alleviate the burdens associated with illness or treatment itself. These comprise:
>
> ...
>
> C.   Lack of ability to benefit; the severity of the child's condition is such that it is difficult or impossible for them to derive benefit from continued life ...

---

118 [2016] EWCOP 53.
119 [2015] EWCOP 76 at [70].
120 See also *ACCG v P by her litigation friend the Official Solicitor and TD* [2019] EWCOP 18.
121 Reference may be made to *R v Portsmouth Hospitals NHS Trust, ex p Glass* (1999) 50 BMLR 269, CA, which is considered in the section headed 'Children under 16 – the concept of *Gillick* competence'.
122 [2018] EWCA Civ 550.

... In other children the nature and severity of the child's underlying condition may make it difficult or impossible for them to enjoy the benefits that continued life brings. Examples include children in Persistent Vegetative State (PVS), Minimally Conscious State, or those with such severe cognitive impairment that they lack demonstrable or recorded awareness of themselves or their surroundings and have no meaningful interaction with them, as determined by rigorous and prolonged observations. Even in the absence of demonstrable pain or suffering, continuation of LST may not be in their best interests because it cannot provide overall benefit to them. Individuals and families may differ in their perception of benefit to the child and some may view even severely limited awareness in a child as sufficient grounds to continue LST. It is important, here as elsewhere, that due account of parental views wishes and preferences is taken and due regard given to the acute clinical situation in the context of the child's overall situation.

If an adult lacks capacity, and has not made a valid and applicable advance decision to refuse life-sustaining treatment, the provisions of the MCA 2005 will apply and the decision must be based on the best interests of the adult, again involving the person as far as this is possible. If the adult lacking capacity has made a valid advance decision applicable to the relevant medical treatment, this is decisive and the treatment cannot lawfully be given.

As with all decisions made under the MCA 2005 (see above), before deciding to withdraw or withhold life-sustaining treatment, the healthcare professional must consider the range of treatment options available in order to work out what would be in the person's best interests. All of the factors set out in the Mental Capacity Act 2005 Code of Practice should be considered, and in particular the healthcare professional should consider any statements that the person has previously made about their wishes and feelings about life-sustaining treatment. Healthcare professionals should also refer to relevant professional guidance when making decisions regarding life-sustaining treatment. In *Re Y*[123] the Supreme Court gave particular weight to the guidance produced by the General Medical Council, because of its statutory role in providing guidance for the medical profession.

Where a patient had indicated, while they had capacity, their wish to be kept alive by the provision of ANH, the doctor's duty of care will require the doctors to provide ANH while such treatment continues to prolong life. Where life depends upon the continued provision of ANH, ANH will be clinically indicated. If the patient lacks capacity, all reasonable steps that are in the person's best interests should be taken to prolong their life. Although there is a strong presumption in favour of providing life-sustaining treatment, there are circumstances when continuing or providing life-sustaining treatment stops providing a benefit to a patient and is not clinically indicated.[124]

Following – and drawing on – *Re Y*, the BMA and the Royal College of Physicians have produced updated guidance on ANH and adults who lack capacity.[125] This has been endorsed by the General Medical Council. It notes that:

---

123 [2018] UKSC 46.
124 *Burke v the General Medical Council* [2006] QB 271.
125 See https://www.bma.org.uk/advice/employment/ethics/mental-capacity/clinically-assisted-nutrition-and-hydration.

- clinically-assisted nutrition and hydration (ANH) is a form of medical treatment;
- treatment should only be provided when it is in the patient's best interests;
- decision-makers must start from the strong presumption that it is in a patient's best interests to receive life-sustaining treatment but that presumption can be rebutted if there is clear evidence that a patient would not want ANH provided in the circumstances that have arisen;
- all decisions must be made in accordance with the MCA 2005;
- there is no requirement for decisions to withdraw ANH to be approved by the court, as long as there is agreement upon what is in the best interests of the patient, the provisions of the MCA 2005 have been followed, and the relevant professional guidance has been observed; and
- the General Medical Council's guidance states that a second clinical opinion should be sought where it is proposed, in the patient's best interests, to stop or not start ANH and the patient is not within hours or days of death.

The guidance clearly spells out that unless the patient has made a valid and applicable advance decision, or has a health and welfare deputy with the appropriate powers, then the decision-maker is 'the person with overall responsibility for the patient's care, as part of their clinical responsibility to ensure that treatment provided is in the patient's best interests. This will usually be a consultant or general practitioner'.

The GMC guidance referred to above states that:

- where there is uncertainty or disagreement about whether ANH is in the patient's best interests informal conflict resolution options should be explored;
- where those close to the patient disagree with the decision made they should be given information about 'the process to follow to challenge the decision and directed to sources of help or support';
- where there is a disagreement about the patient's best interests, or the decision is finely balanced (ie there is ongoing uncertainty) and this is unresolved by seeking a further second opinion or mediation, the Court of Protection should be asked to resolve the matter;
- Court of Protection proceedings should be initiated and funded by the Clinical Commissioning Group or trust responsible for commissioning or providing the patient's care. Family members should be kept informed at all stages but are not responsible for initiating or funding the proceedings.

OTHER EXCEPTIONS TO THE GENERAL PRINCIPLES

The MHA 1983, MCA 2005, and the exercise of the High Court's inherent jurisdiction, involve some specific exceptions to the general principles of consent. Some examples that have arisen under these provisions are considered below. Those concerned with the operation of such statutes should consult more detailed guidance.

The court in *Nottinghamshire Healthcare NHS Trust v RC*,[126] set out three circumstances where adults may have treatment imposed on them without consent:

(i) Adults *lacking capacity* who pursue a self-destructive course may have treatment forced upon them in their best interests pursuant to the terms of the MCA.

(ii) Similarly, adults who have capacity but can be categorised as 'vulnerable' and who as a consequence of their vulnerability have been robbed of the ability to give a true consent to a certain course of action, may also have treatment or other measures imposed on them in their best interests pursuant to the inherent jurisdiction of the High Court (see *DL v A Local Authority* [2012] 3 WLR 1439, and *Re SA (Vulnerable adult with capacity: marriage)* [2006] 1 FLR 867).

(iii) Under the Mental Health Act 1983 ('MHA') a detained patient may have treatment imposed on him or her pursuant to section 63 which provides, so far as is relevant to this case:

'The consent of a patient shall not be required for any medical treatment given to him for the mental disorder from which he is suffering, ... if the treatment is given by or under the direction of the approved clinician in charge of the treatment.'

The MCA 2005 is addressed above.

The inherent jurisdiction of the court allows the court to exercise a protective jurisdiction over a vulnerable adult, who whilst not incapacitated by mental disorder or mental illness, is reasonably believed to be:

(i) under constraint; or (ii) subject to coercion or undue influence; or (iii) for some other reason deprived of the capacity to make the relevant decision, or disabled from making a free choice, or incapacitated or disabled from giving or expressing a real and genuine consent.[127]

This common law power is commonly referred to as a safety net exercised by the court to fill the gap where the MCA 2005 and MHA 1983 do not provide protection. The MCA 2005 has not ousted the inherent jurisdiction of the High Court to protect vulnerable patients (*DL v A Local Authority*).[128]

It is likely that cases such as the pre-MCA 2005 'undue influence' cases will continue to be decided under the inherent jurisdiction. In these cases the patient does not have any mental disorder or impairment or disturbance in the functioning of their mind within either the MHA 1983 or MCA 2005 respectively, which is the cause of their inability to make the relevant decision. Instead, a temporary situation may arise, for example, undue influence exerted by a third party, that may render the patient unable at the material time to make the decision (*Re T (Adult Refusal of Treatment)*).[129] In a 'needle-phobia' case the Court of Appeal held that at the moment of suffering the patient was disabled by panic through fear of needles by 'an impairment in her mental functioning' so that these

---

126 [2014] EWCOP 1317 at [13].
127 *Re SA (Vulnerable Adult with Capacity: Marriage)* [2006] 1 FLR 867 per Munby J, at [77].
128 [2013] Fam 1.
129 [1992] 3 WLR 782.

cases may arguably now fall under the MCA 2005 (*Re MB*,[130] which is considered in more detail above).

Part IV of the MHA 1983, as amended by the Mental Health Act 2007, sets out circumstances in which persons liable to be detained under the Act may be treated without consent for their mental disorder:

1   MHA 1983, s 62 allows for urgent treatment to be given to a patient without consent;

2   MHA 1983, s 63 allows for treatment to be given to a patient without consent where it is 'medical treatment given to him for the mental disorder from which he is suffering'. Medical treatment in this context is defined as 'medical treatment the purpose of which is to alleviate, or prevent a worsening of, the disorder or one or more of its symptoms or manifestations' (s 145(4)).[131]

A positive decision to impose medical treatment without consent under the MHA 1983, s 63 is a public law decision challengeable by way of judicial review, and a full merits review will be appropriate because rights guaranteed by the European Convention on Human Rights are in play: *R (On the Application of B) v Haddock (Responsible Medical Officer)*.[132] In *Nottinghamshire Healthcare NHS Trust v RC (above)*, Mostyn J held that where an approved clinician decided *not* to impose treatment under s 63 and the consequences of that decision may prove to be life-threatening, then the NHS Trust in question would be 'well-advised ... to apply to the High Court for declaratory relief' for a full-merits review (at [21]).

Certain treatments under the MHA 1983, ss 57, 58 and 58A cannot be given without consent under s 63. For example, any surgical operation for destroying brain tissue or for destroying the functioning of brain tissue always requires consent as well as a second opinion (s 57).

Specific requirements are imposed for electro-convulsive treatment under the MHA 1983, s 58A. Where a patient lacks capacity to consent to electro-convulsive treatment (ECT), it can only be given where certified that the patient lacks capacity, but that treatment is appropriate, and treatment would not conflict with a valid and applicable advance decision or a decision of a donee, deputy, or the Court of Protection in compliance with the MCA 2005. It is not permissible to use the MHA 1983 to administer ECT to a patient who has capacity to consent to it, but who does not. Additionally, if a person made an advance decision when they had capacity, saying that they never wished to receive ECT and the hospital knows about this, then the treatment cannot be given. The only exception would be in an emergency if it was immediately necessary to save a patient's life or to prevent a serious deterioration of the patient's condition.

In addition, except in emergencies, it will not be permissible to administer ECT as a treatment for mental disorder in any circumstances to any child or young person under the age 18 (whether or not they are otherwise subject to the MHA 1983) unless it has been independently

130 (1997) 2 FLR 426.
131 In *B v Croydon Health Authority* [1995] Fam 133, a declaration was obtained from the Court of Appeal that tube-feeding a mental patient who was refusing to eat did not require her consent as it constituted 'medical treatment given for the mental disorder' from which she was suffering within the meaning of the MHA 1983, s 63.
132 [2006] HRLR 40.

approved in accordance with the MHA 1983. Further guidance is given in the Mental Health Act Code of Practice.[133]

Where the proposed treatment is not specified under the MHA 1983, ss 57 or 58A as requiring consent, and more than three months have passed since the detained patient first received treatment for mental disorder, a medical practitioner must consult two other persons involved in the patient's medical treatment (s 58(4) specifies who this can be) and provide a certificate confirming the patient is not capable of consenting but it is appropriate for the treatment to be given (s 58(3)(b)).

The MHA 1983 accordingly has no application to treatment for physical disorders unrelated to the mental disorder as elaborated upon in case law, which remains subject to the common law principles described in previous chapters, where the person concerned is detained under the Act, or to the principles of the MCA 2005. Where treatment for a mental disorder is concerned, for a person lacking in relevant decision-making capacity and subject to the MHA 1983, Pt IV, a best interests decision under the MCA 2005 is precluded by the MCA 2005, s 28. The Mental Health Act Code of Practice offers guidance on consent and medical treatment in this context.

For all other forms of treatment, the patient is in the same position as a non-detained patient.

In *Nottinghamshire Healthcare Trust v RC*,[134] Mostyn J reiterated the principle that 'every citizen who is of age and of sound mind has the right to harm or (since 1961) to kill himself' (per Mostyn J, at para 8). Accordingly, where there is a valid advance decision in place, it would be 'an abuse of power' to go against that.[135] In that case, a Jehovah's Witness was found to have capacity to refuse blood products. Even if he lost such capacity, there was an advance decision in place to refuse blood transfusions, which the court found would become operative. In such circumstances, 'to impose a blood transfusion would be a denial of a most basic freedom'.[136]

In *Re A*,[137] an Iranian doctor went on hunger strike in protest against the UK Border Agency's seizure of his passport, following unsuccessful asylum applications. Dr A had been voluntarily in hospital, but during the proceedings became detained under the MHA 1983, s 3. Consequently, he was subject to a 'hospital treatment regime' and detained under that regime, such that the court found that the MCA 2005 could not permit his deprivation of liberty (MCA 2005, s 16A). Forcible feeding by nasogastric tube was not within the meaning of 'medical treatment' under the MHA 1983, because the court agreed with his treating doctors that in this case it would be treating a physical disorder of starvation and dehydration, not his mental disorder. The court distinguished cases which considered the MHA 1983, s 63, such as the important case of *B v Croydon Health Authority*,[138] permitting the force feeding by naso-gastric tube of a

---

133 Department of Health, Code of Practice: Mental Health Act 1983, ((2017, London), see https://assets.publishing.service.gov.uk/government/uploads/system/uploads/attachment_data/file/435512/MHA_Code_of_Practice.PDF.
134 [2014] EWCOP 1317.
135 [2014] EWCOP 1317, per Mostyn J, at [42].
136 [2014] EWCOP 1317, per Mostyn J, at [42].
137 [2014] Fam 161.
138 [1995] 1 All ER 683.

patient with borderline personality disorder, and *ex p Brady*,[139] where Ian Brady's hunger strike was considered to be a symptom, manifestation, or consequence of his mental personality disorder (per Baker J, at [71]). Dr A's hunger strike was not a symptom, manifestation, or consequence of his mental disorder. Ultimately the court made the requested orders under its inherent jurisdiction. Baker J provided useful guidance at [96]:

> Unless and until the court or another court clarifies the interpretation of section 16A of the 2005 Act, it will therefore be necessary, in any case in which a hospital wishes to give treatment to a patient who is ineligible under section 16A, for the hospital to apply for an order under the inherent jurisdiction where the treatment (a) is outside the meaning of medical treatment of the 1983 Act and (b) involves the deprivation of a patient's liberty.

In *R (N) v M*[140] it was determined that where a patient does not have capacity to consent to treatment, treatment under the MHA 1983 must be both in the patient's best interests and medically necessary for the purpose of it not being inhuman and degrading treatment under Art 3 of the ECHR. The Court of Appeal in that case determined the standard of proof was high: medical necessity had to be 'convincingly' shown (per Dyson LJ as he then was, at [17]–[18][141]).

The courts have considered a series of cases where medical treatment does not fall within the above categories, in particular cases relating to reproductive rights where there are proposals of sterilisation[142] or abortion.[143] Many of these cases were decided prior to the MCA 2005 and need to be read in light of the MCA 2005 as it now applies.

Since the entry into force of the MCA 2005, the Court of Protection has considered proposed sterilisation of persons without capacity under the Act. Bodey J in *A Local Authority v A*[144] set out the test to be applied to ascertain whether a woman has capacity to make decisions on contraceptive treatment at [64]:

> the test for capacity should be so applied as to ascertain the woman's ability to understand and weigh up the immediate medical issues surrounding contraceptive treatment ('the proximate medical issues'...) including:
>
> (1)   The reason for contraception and what it does (which includes the likelihood of pregnancy if it is not in use during sexual intercourse;
> (2)   The types available and how each is used;
> (3)   The advantages and disadvantages of each type;
> (4)   The possible side effects of each and how they can be dealt with;
> (5)   How easily each type can be changed; and
> (6)   The generally accepted effectiveness of each.

---

139 [2000] Lloyd's Rep Med 355.
140 [2003] 1 WLR 562.
141 Citing *Herczegfalvy v Austria* (1992) 15 EHRR 437 at [82].
142 For examples of pre-MCA 2005 sterilisation cases see: *Re D (A Minor)* [1976] Fam 185; *Re B (A Minor)* [1988] AC 199; *Re F* [1990] 2 AC 1; *Re LC (Medical Treatment: Sterilisation)* [1997] 2 FLR 258; *Re S (Adult Patient) (Sterilisation)* [2001] Fam 15; *Re A (Medical Treatment: Male Sterilisation)* (1999) 53 BMLR 66; *St George's Healthcare NHS Trust v S* [1999] Fam 26.
143 For examples of pre-MCA 2005 abortion cases see: *Re SG* [1993] 4 Med LR 75, and *An NHS Trust v D* [2004] Lloyd's Rep Med 107.
144 [2011] Fam 61.

I do not consider that questions need to be asked as to the woman's understanding of what bringing up a child would be like in practice; nor any opinion attempted as to how she would be likely to get on; nor whether any child would be likely to be removed from her care.

In *A Local Authority v K*,[145] the court was asked to consider a proposal for sterilisation of an adult lacking capacity by her parents, where the various medical professionals did not agree on what would be in her best interests; one proposing sterilisation, others suggesting contraception by way of IUD/IUS implants (a 'coil'). Importantly, in light of the MCA 2005, the court considered what would be the least restrictive option (MCA 2005, s 1(6)). During the course of proceedings, agreement was reached between the parties that it would not be in K's best interests for her to undergo sterilisation, and also that it was not at that time in her best interests for her to be provided with contraception, as she was not sexually active. Cobb J took the opportunity to remind medical practitioners of the Court of Protection's role in considering questions of non-therapeutic sterilisation:'such a treatment decision is so serious that the Court has to make it' (at [36]).

Proposed sterilisation of a man, by way of a vasectomy, was considered by the Court of Protection in *A NHS Trust v DE*.[146] Whilst there are a number of contraceptive options open to women, as discussed in *A Local Authority v K* (see above), the only options open to DE for contraception were use of a condom or a vasectomy. Furthermore, unlike K, DE was in an existing relationship. King J set out the existing 'consensus' on the issue at [84]:

(i) The decision must be made in DE's best interests, not in the interests of others although the interests of others may indirectly be a factor insofar as they relate to DE's best interests ...

(ii) The court is not tied to any clinical assessment of what is in DE's best interests and should reach its own conclusions on the evidence before it ...

(iii) Best Interests is an objective test ...

(iv) The weight to be attached to the various factors will, inevitably, differ depending upon the individual circumstances of the particular case ...

(v) There is no hierarchy in the list of factors in s 4 and the weight to be attached to the various factors will depend upon the individual circumstances ...

(vi) There may, in the particular case, be one or more features or factors which, as Thorpe LJ has frequently put it, are of 'magnetic importance' in influencing or even determining the outcome ...

(vii) Any benefit of treatment has to be balanced and considered in the light of any additional suffering or detriment the treatment option would entail ...

(viii) The declaration should not be sought if vasectomy would be disproportionate and not the least restrictive step, risk management is better than invasive treatment ...

(ix) The decision is for the judge not the expert.

On the facts of DE's case, it was 'overwhelmingly' in DE's best interests to have a vasectomy, where the only factor against the treatment was the surgical procedure itself.

---

145 [2013] EWHC 242 (COP).
146 [2013] EWHC 2562 (Fam).

Neither the existence of mental disorder nor the fact of detention under the MHA 1983 should give rise to an assumption of incapacity. The person's capacity must be assessed in every case in relation to the particular decision being made. The capacity of a person with a mental disorder may fluctuate.

Certain patients discharged from detention under the MHA 1983 can be made subject to community treatment orders (CTOs), making them liable to recall to hospital for further treatment if necessary. While patients are subject to CTOs they may only be treated for mental disorder in accordance with the MHA 1983. Unless they have been recalled to hospital, it will not be permissible to treat such patients without their consent if they have the capacity to consent to the treatment in question but do not do so. Treatment for mental disorder of patients subject to CTOs who lack capacity to consent will be permitted, subject to the rules set out in the MHA 1983, Pt 4A.

Chapter 12

Wrongful birth

Sarah Fraser Butlin

THE FAILED STERILISATION AND SIMILAR MISHAPS

An unplanned pregnancy can arise as a result of a failed sterilisation, male or female. The claim is that the woman has had to endure a pregnancy. In addition, if the pregnancy is not terminated, a child, whether disabled or not, has been born who would not have been born if there had been no negligence in or around the sterilisation. A similar claim is made where a pregnancy should have been terminated but, due to negligence, was not. For example, the termination was incompetently performed or antenatal screening negligently failed to detect foetal defects which would have resulted in a lawful termination.

There are effectively five scenarios to consider:
1   wrongful pregnancy with a healthy child due to a negligently performed sterilisation operation;
2   wrongful pregnancy with a disabled child;
3   a disabled woman's wrongful pregnancy with a healthy child;
4   wrongful birth claims, that the woman would have terminated the pregnancy if she had known that she was carrying a disabled child;
5   wrongful life claims brought by a child claiming that they would not have been born but for the negligence.

Because wrongful life claims are disallowed as being contrary to public policy (Scenario 5, and dealt with further below), it is important to remember for the purposes of limitation that the claims will be by the parents, not the child.

STERILISATION

The failure rate of sterilisation

The lifetime risk of failure for tubal occlusion is generally accepted to be one in 200. Where Filshie clips are used, on the data available, it is two to three per thousand.[1] Separate figures for operator failure and natural

---

1   Royal College of Obstetricians and Gynaecologists, *Male and Female Sterilisation, Evidence-based Clinical Guideline Number 4.*

recanalisation are not available. The failure rate for vasectomy has usually been considered to be substantially lower, though some experts say that is not proven. The failure rate for vasectomy, once the initial period for testing the semen for sperm has been successfully concluded, is generally thought to be no more than one in 2000. Failure of vasectomy discovered during the post-operative testing period is referred to as 'early recanalisation', thereafter 'late recanalisation'.

Lines of attack

In failed sterilisation claims, there are generally two separate lines of attack: first, an incompetently performed operation and second, the failure to warn the patient of potential failure of the operation.

Expert evidence will be required to establish that the operation was incompetently performed. Generally, where conception has taken place within a few months of a sterilisation by Filshie clips most, but not all, experts would say that the most likely inference is that one of the clips was not properly applied to the tube (different considerations may apply where the sterilisation was not by clips or rings). A few experts, particularly if instructed by the defence, would argue that a fistula could have formed soon after the procedure or the tube recanalised unusually quickly.

The situation is much more difficult where pregnancy takes place a considerable time after the sterilisation. If the patient may be about to undergo a Caesarean section or a further sterilisation, one should ensure that a reliable observer (this may be the treating doctor) reports on the state of the tubes.

If a clip is found on the wrong structure, such as a neighbouring ligament, there can be no proper defence. The defence expert occasionally maintains that misplacing the clip can happen in the best of hands. This is untrue. The clip should properly occlude the lumen of the tube. The doctor should be able to see this. If he is in any doubt, it is his duty to advise the woman to have a hysterosalpingogram (see *McLennan v Newcastle Health Authority*[2]). Therefore it follows that if the clip is found on the tube but not properly occluding the lumen, there is no proper defence.

There may also be further evidence about the position of the clip after the relevant parts of the tubes have been sent for histological examination.

If the clip is found not to be on any structure but lying loose in the peritoneal cavity, this will indicate negligence, as, whatever defence might be offered, properly applied clips do not fall off, at least not until sufficient time has elapsed for the tube to atrophy substantially. This sort of defence was unsuccessfully maintained in *Fallows v Randle*.[3]

The *second* line of attack is to allege that the woman was not warned of the failure rate and the proper consenting process was not undertaken. It may be helpful to refer to the guidelines produced by the Royal College of Obstetricians and Gynaecologists.[4] However this line of attack is unlikely

---

2   MLC 0615, [1992] 3 Med LR 215.
3   MLC 0591, [1997] 8 Med LR 160, CA. For the medical and evidential complexities that can arise in a case that alleges misplacement, see Popplewell J in *Taylor v Shropshire Health Authority* MLC 0048, [1998] Lloyd's Rep Med 395.
4   As at n 1 above, read together with their *Obtaining Valid Consent, Clinical Governance Advice 6* and Female Sterilisation (Consent Advice No 3).

to succeed these days as the standard consent form for sterilisation gives such a warning, and in most cases it is not reasonably open to the woman to say that she did not have time to read it. Also, most doctors will put a note in the records at some time pre-operatively to the effect that they have warned. A further difficulty will be in proving that no warning was given. This may simply be a dispute of fact between doctor and patient. However, usually a specialised form of consent for a sterilisation will be used which will warn of the risk. Assuming the patient signed the form well before the operation, it will not avail to say she did not read it.

Even where there has been a failure to warn, causation is a major hurdle. In the context of sterilisation it has virtually never been known for a woman to refuse the procedure on being told of the small failure rate.[5] Occasionally for medical reasons a further pregnancy would pose such a threat to the health of mother or child that it can be alleged that her partner would also have been sterilised, or other additional contraceptive precautions would have been taken, if she/they had been told of the failure rate.[6] Alternatively one can allege that, although a warning would not have deterred the woman from accepting the operation, she would have realised she was pregnant soon enough to enable a simple termination rather than having to undergo the more complex and, to her, unacceptable option of a late termination.[7]

Vasectomy

It is almost always impossible to show that a vasectomy has been performed incompetently. The anatomy does not usually permit that argument. Therefore any allegation has to be that the semen was improperly declared to be sperm-free. It may be that the patient was told that he was sterile when there had only been one sperm test, or perhaps the laboratory reports were misinterpreted by the doctor. However in such cases, one would expect a pregnancy to follow fairly soon after the sterilisation operation, otherwise natural recanalisation is the more likely explanation.

A claim for omission to warn of the risk of late recanalisation (ie after the successful conclusion of the post-operative testing period) is subject to the same difficulties as a similar claim in respect of female sterilisation.[8] Interestingly in *Goodwill v British Pregnancy Advisory Service*,[9] the Court of Appeal rejected a claim by a woman who sued the doctor who carried out the vasectomy for not warning his patient at the time of the failure rate. She had started a relationship with a man three years after his vasectomy. The vasectomy spontaneously reversed and the claimant

---

5   In *Ellis v Wallsend District Hospital* [1990] 2 Med LR 103, the New South Wales Court of Appeal said that a patient's evidence that she would have declined surgery if properly warned should not be rejected unless it was inherently incredible or inherently improbable.
6   Although see *Gowton v Wolverhampton Health Authority* MLC 0959, [1994] 5 Med LR 432 and *Lybert v Warrington Health Authority* MLC 0712, [1996] 7 Med LR 71, CA.
7   See *Thake v Maurice* [1986] QB 644, MLC 0011, CA, affirming [1984] 2 All ER 513.
8   For example, see *Stobie v Central Birmingham Health Authority* (1994) 22 BMLR 135. An attempt to sue the Department of Health for failing to disseminate information about failure rates to the public generally unsurprisingly failed in *Danns v Department of Health* [1996] PIQR P69.
9   [1996] 1 WLR 1397.

gave birth to a healthy daughter. The Court of Appeal said that the claim, involving as it did the allegation that the doctor had owed a duty of care to an indeterminately large class of females who might have sexual relations with his patient during the patient's lifetime, was manifestly unsustainable and frivolous, vexatious and an abuse of process. However, it should be noted that the claimant faced insurmountable difficulties on her own case: she had only removed her contraceptive coil after taking advice from her GP, who had alerted her to the possibility, albeit small, of the vasectomy failing.

Occasionally it is disputed that it was the claimant who impregnated the mother of the child, at which point paternity must be established.

SCENARIO 1: WRONGFUL PREGNANCY WITH A HEALTHY CHILD

Prior to *McFarlane* the courts had generally held that damages could be recovered for the expense of bringing up a healthy child who would not have been born had it not been for some sort of negligent mismanagement (*Emeh v Kensington, Chelsea and Westminster Area Health Authority*[10]). The claims were for economic damage and most settled for about £50,000 to £80,000. The principle was that the new child had the right to be brought up in the same standard of living as the previous children.

However, the decision by the House of Lords in *McFarlane v Tayside Health Board*[11] turned this on its head. Despite the criticism it received, it was expressly approved by the House in the *Rees* case (see below).

The position in relation to the birth of a healthy child following a negligent failed sterilisation, is that any *personal injury* to the mother caused by the negligence, for example the pregnancy and any stress or psychological damage as a result, will be recoverable. However such injury is unlikely to attract more than about £10,000. Special damages flowing directly from the fact of pregnancy could increase the award. However no damages are recoverable for the cost of bringing up the child.

This has been supplemented by the decision in *Rees v Darlington Memorial Hospital NHS Trust*[12] where it was held that a further award of £15,000 could be made for the loss of the woman's right to control the extent of her family (see below at Scenario 3).

It is important to note that one point in the decision in *Emeh* is still good law: namely that, 'save in exceptional circumstances' a woman's decision not to have an abortion was not an act that broke the chain of causation. The Court of Appeal did not explain what those exceptional circumstances might be and it is difficult to see what would be accepted as exceptional enough to effectively require a woman to have an abortion.

The *McFarlane* case

The facts in the *McFarlane* case were simple. A couple decided to have a vasectomy having had four children. They were given the all clear on the semen samples, which was admitted to have been incorrect information,

---

10   [1985] QB 1012.
11   [2000] 2 AC 59.
12   [2003] MLC 1053.

though negligence was not admitted. The mother later became pregnant and gave birth to a healthy child. They brought a claim for personal injury based on the pregnancy and the economic cost of bringing up the child.

The claim for the pregnancy

The defendants argued, astonishingly, that even the claim for the unwanted pregnancy should be disallowed on the basis that a pregnancy should not be regarded as a personal injury, not even an unwanted one. Even more surprisingly, that contention had been accepted in the Scottish court of first instance. However, on both appeals the judges had no difficulty in allowing that part of the claim (damages for that aspect of the claim had been agreed at £10,000; the economic claim was put at £100,000, a fairly usual figure for such a claim). Lord Millett suggested that about £5,000 should be allowed for the frustration of the couple's desire to restrict their family (it is not clear if this would be in addition to compensation for the pregnancy itself).

Two different approaches

As can be seen from the summary below, some of the judges favoured a policy-type approach (based on general moral and societal considerations) over a legalistic one (based on standard legal principles such as foreseeability, proximity, causation and reasonable restitution), while others vice versa. But they all agreed that the economic claim could not stand.

However, whatever the grounds they gave for their conclusions, one cannot help seeing in the outcome further evidence of a general policy decision taken at the highest level, to the effect that the amount and incidence of personal injury damages over the whole spectrum must be kept as low as possible, no doubt on the basis that that is best for society as a whole.

The judges' reasoning

Lord Slynn based his view on the standard *Caparo* rule (*Caparo Industries plc v Dickman*[13]) that economic loss is only recoverable where there was a sufficient relationship of proximity to be able to say that the defendants had assumed responsibility for the consequences in respect of which recovery was being claimed and that it was fair, just and reasonable to impose such a duty. As one knows, this 'test' gives the court an unfettered right to impose its own view of policy. Apart from 'policy', it is not easy to see why Lord Slynn decided this question in the negative. He could just as easily have decided it in the 'logical' (his word) fashion, namely that the cost of upbringing was an obviously foreseeable consequence of the negligence and impossible to dissociate from it.

Lord Steyn decided the question as a moral issue and on the grounds of 'distributive justice', which means the just distribution of burdens and losses among members of a society. Lord Steyn said that was what lay behind the negative decisions in the various jurisdictions to which

---

13   [1990] 2 AC 605, HL.

the court had been referred,[14] and said this was not a matter of public policy. He said the real reasons for the court's conclusions should not be masked by unreal and formalistic propositions along the lines of no loss, no foreseeable loss, no causative link, only reasonable restitution, etc. Judges should give real reasons for their decisions.

> The truth is that tort law is a mosaic in which the principles of corrective justice and distributive justice are interwoven. And in situations of uncertainty and difficulty a choice sometimes has to be made between the two approaches. In my view it is legitimate in the present case to take into account considerations of distributive justice. That does not mean that I would decide the case on grounds of public policy. On the contrary, I would avoid those quick sands. Relying on principles of distributive justice I am persuaded that our tort law does not permit parents of a healthy unwanted child to claim the costs of bringing up the child from a health authority or a doctor. If it were necessary to do so, I would say that the claim does not satisfy the requirement of being fair, just and reasonable.

Like Lord Slynn, Lord Steyn did not wish to base his conclusion on the 'set-off' argument (ie allow for the 'joys' of parenthood as against the economic demands).

More reasons

However, Lord Hope took the view that the benefits or set-off principle was relevant, but then said that as it was impossible to value them as against the damage by way of the cost of upkeep and therefore the logical (*sic*) conclusion was that such recovery was not permissible. Otherwise the parents would be getting more than they had lost!

He also adopted, perhaps less unreasonably, the *Caparo* test of proximity which also led him to a negative conclusion.

Lord Clyde agreed with this approach. He said that policy considerations could be found to point either way, eg sanctity of human life as against the right of parents and benefit to society of limiting families. Therefore, the decision should not be founded on policy considerations. For him the principal relevant consideration was the legal rule of reasonable restitution.

> In such a context I would consider it appropriate to have regard to the extent of the liability which the defenders could reasonably have thought they were undertaking. It seems to me that even if a sufficient causal connection exists the cost of maintaining a child goes far beyond any liability which in the circumstances of the present case the defenders could reasonably have thought they were undertaking.

But why? Why should not a defendant understand that if a child is born through their negligence they will have to shoulder the financial burden rather than the parents?

Lord Clyde also considered that the extent of these economic claims was out of proportion to the wrongdoing. Again, the rationale for this is unclear given the vast changes that will be brought to bear on the individuals impacted by the birth of a child.

---

14   Their Lordships conducted an exhaustive investigation into decisions in other jurisdictions. Although the English authorities were virtually all one way (positive), there have been a substantial amount of negative decisions elsewhere.

Lord Millett was, strangely, not prepared to assume that the reason for the couple not wanting a fifth child was financial. He then made it clear that he did not accept the set-off/benefits argument, nor the strictly legalistic ones. He took what one might term the 'moral high ground':

> There is something distasteful, if not morally offensive, in treating the birth of a normal, healthy child as a matter for compensation … I accept the thrust of both the main arguments in favour of dismissing such a claim. In my opinion the law must take the birth of a normal, healthy baby to be a blessing, not a detriment. In truth it is a mixed blessing. It brings joy and sorrow, blessing and responsibility. The advantages and the disadvantages are inseparable. Individuals may choose to regard the balance as unfavourable and take steps to forego the pleasures as well as the responsibilities of parenthood. They are entitled to decide for themselves where their own interests lie. But society itself must regard the balance as beneficial. It would be repugnant to its own sense of values to do otherwise. It is morally offensive to regard a normal, healthy baby as more trouble and expense than it is worth.

There are many arguments for and against such moralising. It may also be argued that 'distributive justice' does not necessarily suggest a negative decision to this claim: there is nothing unjust about allowing these claims (they will not bankrupt the NHS) and a deal of injustice to the parents in denying it. What would have happened if Mrs McFarlane had given birth to octuplets?

Post-*McFarlane*

It is worth nothing that since *McFarlane* the High Court of Australia has decided a similar case along the same lines. This was by a majority of four to three, after both courts below had found in favour of the claimant! (*Cattanach v Melchior*[15].)

The issue of a second pregnancy after a failed sterilisation is difficult. In *Sabri-Tabrizi v Lothian Health Board*,[16] it was held that where a woman knew she was still fertile (because she had already had one pregnancy terminated following the failed sterilisation) and had sexual intercourse with her husband, using only condoms, this broke the chain of causation between the negligent sterilisation procedure and the birth of the child. Consequently her claim was struck out. This seems a rather strange result as the defendants, through their negligence, made it impossible for the couple to have any safer intercourse than that provided by condoms. Therefore it appears to be a very harsh decision of the court to hold that she was unreasonable in having sexual intercourse.

A contractual claim in the county court, attempting to get round the limiting effect of *McFarlane* was unsurprisingly unsuccessful (*Reynolds v Health First Medical Group*[17]). The claim alleged a contract between patient and GP and sought to maintain that a claim for upbringing was based on a contractual, not tortious relationship. The judge rejected the existence of a contract between an NHS patient and her GP. Although he did not need to go further, it is clear that the contention that *McFarlane* would not apply to a contractual relationship is quite hopeless, except

---

15   [2003] MLC 0722.
16   (1998) 43 BMLR 190.
17   [2000] Lloyd's Rep Med 240.

in the highly unlikely event of the contract specifically providing that the defendant undertook responsibility for the extended economic losses. Similarly in *ARB v IVF Hammersmith Ltd*,[18] although the father established that his ex-partner had forged his signature on the consent form for IVF and the defendant had thereby breached the contract with him, legal policy precluded his claim for the costs of raising the resultant healthy child.

Another novel claim was brought in *Marian Richardson v LRC Products Ltd*.[19] The couple brought a claim pursuant to the Consumer Protection Act for the birth of a child, after a condom split during use (the teat parting from the body of the condom at about shoulder level). The claim was put in two ways: first, the condom had been exposed to the detrimental and weakening influence of ozone during the course of manufacture, and secondly that it must have been defective in some way or another because otherwise it would not have fractured. Most of the case related to scientific evidence. The judge rejected the claim in relation to ozone exposure. He also held that he was satisfied by evidence given by a defence expert that condoms occasionally failed for no known reason. This is perhaps a little harder to understand. Just because it has not been possible on occasions in the past to discover why a condom has split, that does not mean one has to conclude that it was not inherently defective.

However, the judge went on (*obiter*) to disallow the claim on quite another ground. He said that there had been a duty to mitigate the damage, and that Mrs Richardson should have sought out the 'morning-after' pill, whether by telling her GP what had happened or in some other way, which would probably have avoided the pregnancy. Failure to do this invalidated the claim. Mrs Richardson's explanation was that it was a Saturday afternoon and she did not think it was such an emergency to need to call on the out of hours service. However the judge held that she should have telephoned them. This is an extremely harsh decision, particularly given that in other circumstances, a woman is not obliged to accept a termination. In addition, the judge stated summarily that he saw no reason why *McFarlane* should not apply to a consumer product case. This actually needs a little more thought. If the rationale of the House of Lords judgment can properly be said, on the majority view, to be a matter of distributive justice, ie that the NHS or the medical profession should not have to bear the cost of raising the unplanned child, then this argument would not apply to the profit-making manufacturer. If the true rationale is that it is odious to award damages for a healthy child (or impossible to calculate them given the need to deduct the benefit of a child), then it could be conceded that it would be just as odious (or impossible) where a manufacturer would be footing the bill.

Value of the claim

In general damages, an uncomplicated, unplanned pregnancy going to term has always been worth about £6,500. If there are complications, the award of general damages can be increased. If the pregnancy was terminated, whether by abortion or miscarriage (there is, of course,

---

18   [2017] EWHC 2438.
19   [2000] Lloyd's Rep Med 280.

no obligation to terminate – *Emeh v Kensington and Westminster and Chelsea Health Authority*[20]), there may be psychological injury for which additional general damages can be sought.[21]

In terms of special damages, there may be a claim for the wasted expenses involved in preparing for the birth. This will include loss of earnings while pregnant and in the initial recovery period. However, following *McFarlane* a claim for loss of earnings when a mother had to give up work to look after her healthy, unplanned child was rejected by the Court of Appeal in *Greenfield v Irwin (aka Greenfield v Flather)*.[22]

In addition, there is the *Rees* claim of around £15,000 for the loss to the woman of her right to limit her family (see below).

SCENARIO 2: WRONGFUL PREGNANCY WITH A DISABLED CHILD

In *McFarlane*, the House implicitly left open the question of whether the cost of care and allied expenses could be claimed where the child was born disabled. This was considered by the Court of Appeal in *Parkinson v St James and Seacroft University Hospital NHS Trust*.[23] While it was approved by two judges in the House of Lords in *Rees*, one cannot be certain that should the issue be expressly considered by the House of Lords the same outcome would result.

Nevertheless the position at present is that a mother can recover the additional cost of care and additional expenses in raising an unplanned disabled child than an unplanned healthy child. A thorough analysis of the present position may be found in *Meadows v Khan*.[24] She may also recover a slightly higher award for general damages for her shock on discovering that she has given birth to a disabled child (see *Hardman v Amin* (below)).

The *Parkinson* case

Parkinson v St James and Seacroft University Hospital NHS Trust,[25] was an important case. It was the first time, post-*McFarlane*, that the Court of Appeal had considered the question of what compensation could be obtained for the unplanned birth of a disabled child.

The facts can be simply stated: a disabled child had been born due to an admittedly negligently performed sterilisation. The birth of a fifth child had been 'catastrophic' for the family and the marriage (Brooke LJ). At first instance, Longmore J had allowed only the additional costs flowing from the disability. Both sides appealed; both appeals were dismissed.

Somewhat surprisingly the court did not think it relevant to consider the earlier cases at first instance, Brooke LJ stating that the policy issues were different where the allegation was that there should have been a termination (rather than that there should never have been a

---

20 [1985] QB 1012, CA.
21 See for example *Taylor v Shropshire Health Authority* [2000] MLC 0226, where the judge awarded £15,000.
22 (2001) MLC 0341, CA.
23 [2001] MLC 0360.
24 [2017] EWHC 2990.
25 [2001] MLC 0360.

conception). The logic of this is difficult to follow, but at least it had the effect of relieving the court from entering into an analysis of the complex and inconsistent arguments deployed in those judgments.

First, how disabled does the child have to be to make a claim? Hale LJ adopted the test of disability found in s 17(11) of the Children Act 1989: a child is disabled if he is blind, deaf or dumb or suffers from mental disorder of any kind or is substantially and permanently handicapped by illness, injury or congenital deformity or such other disability as may be prescribed. Brooke LJ said that 'significant disability' (the phrase used in the *McFarlane* case) would cover disabilities of the mind, including severe behavioural disabilities, but not minor defects or inconveniences. Each case would be judged on its own facts.

Next, the response to the main issue. The effect of the decision is to allow 'the extra costs of caring for and bringing up a disabled child' in that 'a disabled child needs extra care and expenditure' (*per* Hale LJ). The award should be limited to 'the extra expenses associated with the child's disability', 'the special upbringing costs associated with rearing a child with a serious disability' (*per* Brooke LJ).

What we are not told, however, is what heads of expense or loss can properly be brought within these formulae. Does it, for example, include compensation for parental care? Does it include all the heads of claim for professional care, aids and equipment, accommodation etc that are relevant where the child's injury is caused by medical mismanagement? Also unclear is whether this court was of the view that the claim went beyond majority.

Brooke LJ offered an impressive cerebral analysis of the numerous bases currently available for admitting or rejecting a claim for compensation based on the tort of negligence (the three-fold test, proximity, assumption of responsibility, fair-just-reasonable, corrective or distributive justice, public policy, what the man on the Clapham tube train might think, and so on). He analysed the judgments in the House of Lords, saying that the task was made more difficult by the fact that the Law Lords had spoken 'with five different voices'. He concluded that there was no valid argument against parents being recompensed for the costs of extraordinary care in raising a deformed child.

Hale LJ's judgment demands careful study. The judge brought into clear and inescapable focus the very substantial changes that pregnancy brings to the physical, psychological, and social life of a woman. Along with these physical and psychological consequences goes a severe curtailment of personal autonomy. Through this part of her judgment, it appears that Hale LJ indicates that she would have expected claims for any unplanned birth to have included a claim by way of valuation of parental care.

On *McFarlane* Hale LJ said:

> Their Lordships' reasons for denying what would on normal legal principles be recoverable [ie that losses flowing directly from negligence should be compensated] were variously and elegantly expressed ... In truth they all gave different reasons for arriving at ... the same result.

Like many of us, Hale LJ found it difficult to understand why, once it is agreed that the doctor assumes some responsibility for preventing conception, he is nevertheless liable for only some of the clearly foreseeable, indeed highly probable, resulting losses. At one point, she suggested that a mother might be driven to have an abortion as a result of the *McFarlane* decision, presumably if she knew or learnt in time enough about the law to realise that she would have no claim for financial help in respect of all the 'dis-benefits' the child would bring her.

Note also that Hale LJ said that many would challenge the assumption that the benefits of having a new child outweighed the disadvantages so as to 'cancel out' the claim. She said that many would argue that the true costs to the primary carer of bringing up a child are so enormous that they easily outstripped any benefits. And the notion of a child bringing benefit to the parents is deeply suspect, smacking of commodification [*sic*] of the child, regarding the child as an asset to the parents. She suggested that a conventional sum could be deducted from a claim to allow for the so-called 'benefit' of having a child.

SCENARIO 3: A DISABLED WOMAN'S WRONGFUL PREGNANCY WITH A HEALTHY CHILD

The *Rees* case

In *Rees v Darlington Memorial Hospital NHS Trust*,[26] seven judges heard the appeal in the House of Lords. The decision went by a bare majority against the claimant. The unusual fact of this case is that the unplanned child was healthy; it was the mother who was disabled. She had very little vision and for that reason expressly had asked for a sterilisation, which was negligently performed.

Counsel for the claimant sought in the first place to convince the court to reverse *McFarlane*. The court was not convinced. They declared that it had been a good decision (it had been the unanimous decision of five Lords of Appeal in extra-ordinary including Hope, Millett and Steyn who also featured in this *Rees* case), and, further, that, even if they now harboured any doubts, which was not admitted, they would not go back on it for reasons of security (of the law).

As to simple compensation under *McFarlane* for a healthy child, this was a little surprising. In *McFarlane* Lord Millett had been the lone voice that proposed that all a *McFarlane* mother should recover should be a nominal sum of £5,000 for the loss of her right to control the extent of her family. He had not even been willing to allow what the others had been willing to allow, namely something for the pregnancy itself. In the *Rees* case, the judges, four of them – Bingham, Nicholls, Millett, Scott – who considered that the *Rees* scenario fell within the *McFarlane* rule, adopted, and adapted, the Millet suggestion. They allowed the pregnancy damages, *plus* the Millett award, which they increased (Millett agreed) to £15,000. This 'gloss' on *McFarlane*, as they called it, was heavily criticised by Lord Steyn. He said that such a gloss ran counter to the views of the majority in *McFarlane*, had not been considered in the court, was a radical and most important development which should only be embarked upon after rigorous examination of competing argument, was a solution of a heterodox nature which had neither English nor foreign juridical support, was contrary to principle, that it was a novel procedure for judges to undertake the creation of such a remedy and was beyond the permissible limits of judicial creativity, that his brethren had strayed into forbidden territory, that it was a backdoor evasion of the legal policy enunciated in *McFarlane*, and could only be effected by Parliament! Lord Hope also disliked such a 'gloss'!

Legal policy

All the judges were prepared to declare, insofar as they were supporting *McFarlane* and any of its derivatives, that (a) an orthodox application of familiar and conventional principles of the law of tort would have permitted the claimant in *McFarlane* to recover damages for the costs of bringing up her healthy child. Indeed Lord Bingham said that he did not find it surprising that that had been the law here before *McFarlane*. And (b) the denial to a *McFarlane* claimant of such otherwise clearly recoverable damages was not due to the court's view of public policy but to the court's view of legal policy.

Ratio of the McFarlane *rule*

As we have seen, this was not clear in the McFarlane speeches themselves, as the judges gave a variety of reasons. In *Rees*, although Lord Steyn remarked amusingly that he was not proposing 'to undertake the gruesome task of discussing the judgments in *McFarlane*', the *McFarlane* ratio was reasonably summarised down to two principles. The first is that a child is a God-given gift and, in respect of a healthy child at any rate, its birth should not be the subject of a claim; the second is that the benefit principle requires that the benefit a claimant receives from having a child must be set against the economic loss claimed and as that benefit is incalculable, no damages can be awarded for the economic loss. Of course, these two points can be challenged and argued over.

Does the McFarlane *rule apply to all negligent birth claims or is there an exception for the disabled child/mother? (Ie the* Parkinson *and* Rees *aspects) – per Lords Bingham, Nicholls, Millett, Scott*

Lord Bingham said he would apply the rule, without differentiation, to *all* claims. He said it was anomalous that the defendant's liability should relate to a disability which the defendant had not caused. He also said it was undesirable that parents, in order to recover compensation, should be encouraged to portray their children or themselves as disabled. And he used the argument that it would be difficult to quantify the additional costs attributable to the disability. Lord Nicholls took a similar view. He thought it was disproportionate for the NHS to bear all the costs of bringing up the child, and he said the birth of a child should not be treated as comparable to a parent suffering a personal injury. Lord Millett stuck by the nominal award in 'healthy' cases that he had advocated in *McFarlane,* but it is interesting, and important, to note that he explicitly kept an open mind about disabled child cases. He said that he would not find it morally offensive if additional costs could be recovered in a *Parkinson* case, but that did not have to be decided in the instant appeal. As to the disabled mother scenario, he stated, rightly surely, that it is a mistake to assume that, because the costs attributable to the disability are 'extras' whether the disabled party is the child or the parent, there is any symmetry between the two 'disabled' scenarios. He then said that just as there would be a range of varying circumstances for a non-disabled mother, so would there be for the disabled mother.

Lord Scott stressed the 'incalculable benefit' rule, and said that the mother's visual disability did not take the case out of the normal principle established by the *McFarlane* rule. All the features that justified creating an exception under the *McFarlane* rule were present, too, in the disabled mother scenario. On the *Parkinson* scenario, he, too, kept an open mind, but he did make the interesting suggestion that a disabled child claim should only succeed if the reasons for the original sterilisation or other procedure had included a fear that any child could be born disabled. In relation to a sterilisation where there had been no such fear, apart from the normal chance of that happening (one in a few hundred), he appears to be telling us that the birth of a disabled child would not be sufficiently foreseeable to justify a claim. Then he says that on the facts existing in *Parkinson*, the decision of the Court of Appeal was not justified.

So the *obiter* tally so far in relation to a *Parkinson* claim from the majority of four judges who rejected the *Rees* claim, is two against, one somewhat supportive (Millett), and one supportive provided there had been an actual fear of any child born being disabled.

The Parkinson *and the* Rees *aspects (per Lords Steyn, Hope and Hutton)*

These were the three judges, the minority, who accepted Mrs Rees' claim. Lord Steyn said he agreed with the decision in *Parkinson*. The policy on which the *McFarlane* principle was based simply did not apply to the seriously disabled child. However, in the case of the disabled mother, it was not possible to regard her as unaffected by the *McFarlane* principle. An exception would have to be made if she was to recover. He would favour such an exception.

Lord Hope agreed with the decision in *Parkinson* even though he had been a strong advocate of the 'incalculable benefit' argument in *McFarlane*. Presumably the additional costs of upbringing in the context of disability are for some reason not caught by that argument. And he saw no reason not to allow the exception to apply in the case of a disabled parent, too. He agreed that in all these cases care would need to be taken in calculating the additional costs, but to describe the task as one of acute difficulty seemed to him to be an over-statement. By allowing the seriously disabled parent to recover the extra costs of child-rearing which were due to her disability, the law would be doing its best to enable her to perform the task of child-rearing on equal terms with those who did not have any such disability.

Lord Hutton said: (a) that it was fair, just and reasonable to award damages for the extra costs of bringing up a disabled child; and (b) that the difficulties hypothesized by Waller LJ in the Court of Appeal should not deter the court from accepting a *Rees* claim. There was a clear distinction between a healthy mother and a disabled mother. Pointing to hard cases on the boundary of recoverability did not invalidate the principle of recovery by a disabled mother.

So in respect of a *Parkinson* scenario (the disabled child), the tally among the judges who favoured Mrs Rees' claim, three of them (as against four who did not), was, as one would expect, all in favour. Overall it was three in favour, two against, a fourth probably in favour (Millett) and one in favour, it appears, only if there had been a real fear that any further child could suffer from a congenital handicap.

Final outcome

Ultimately Mrs Rees' claim failed with four judges against the claim and three for it.

SCENARIO 4: WRONGFUL BIRTH CLAIMS

The courts have not distinguished between wrongful pregnancy cases where a disabled child is born, and wrongful birth claims in which the parents bring a claim for the additional costs of a disabled child that they would have terminated but for the negligence. There is a very great difference between a wrongful birth claim and a wrongful life claim (brought by the *child* arguing that but for the negligence they would not have been born), which is addressed below in Scenario 5.

A wrongful birth claim therefore operates in the same way as a claim in Scenario 2 above. By way of example, in *Hardman v Amin*,[27] the mother argued that she would have terminated her pregnancy because of rubella infection. Liability was admitted for the birth of a disabled child. Henriques J, in a judgment carefully considering all available authorities, felt unconstrained by *McFarlane*. He allowed general damages for the pregnancy and specifically for the shock of the mother realising that she had given birth to a disabled child. He held that the continuation of a pregnancy resulting in the birth of a disabled child was a personal injury; that the claim for upkeep was a claim for pure economic loss, but that there was sufficient proximity between the defendant GP and the patient for the birth of a disabled child to be a consequence in law of the original negligence, and that awarding compensation for that consequence would not go beyond reasonable restitution. He held that a claim for the past and future care given by the mother as a result of the disability was permissible (either on the ordinary principles of a personal injury claim including a 25% discount for non-commercial care or by way of claim for loss of amenity – as per Newman J).

In *Groom v Selby*,[28] a GP admitted negligence in not diagnosing a pregnancy in time for the mother to have found a termination to be acceptable, which she otherwise would have done. The additional factor in this claim was that the child, Megan, was born apparently healthy but, because of an infection contracted from the maternal vagina perinatally, went on to develop septicaemia and brain damage. Nevertheless, the judge at trial treated her as a child born 'unhealthy' rather than healthy. The Court of Appeal dismissed the defendant's appeal, saying that their decision recently given in *Parkinson* disposed of the instant appeal. They saw no distinction between wrongful conception and wrongful birth cases; contracting the disease was a foreseeable consequence of birth, the defendant was deemed to have accepted responsibility for

27 MLC 0369, [2000] Lloyd's Rep Med 498.
28 [2001] MLC 0483, CA (at first instance MLC 0294).

the foreseeable and disastrous consequences of her negligence, and an award of compensation limited to the special upbringing associated with rearing a child with a serious disability was fair, just and reasonable. The child was apparently to be viewed as 'born disabled' (within the meaning of expression in *McFarlane*) because, it was said, her exposure to the bacterium occurred during the process of birth. All the causes of her meningitis were in place when the umbilical cord was severed: all that remained was for the bacterium to penetrate a weak point in the child's skin or mucous membranes and the damage was done.

In *Enright v Kwun*,[29] a mother aged 37 succeeded in establishing liability for a failure by her medical attendants to offer her the option of an amniocentesis. If she had been given the option, she would have accepted the procedure, the Downs syndrome defect would have been discovered and she would have opted for a termination.

LIMITATION IN SCENARIOS 1 TO 4

The limitation period cannot begin before the woman knows she is pregnant. Even then one can reasonably argue, in cases of operator failure, that she cannot know what the relevant act or omission is (to which her pregnancy is due) until she receives some explanatory medical input (usually in the form of an expert medical report). But it is clearly safer to work from the date she knew she was pregnant.

In *Walkin v South Manchester Health Authority*,[30] the mother issued within the three-year period a writ claiming damages for personal injuries and economic loss arising from a failed sterilisation followed by the birth of a child. That writ was never served. Some two years later she issued a second writ outside the three-year limitation period, but claimed only for economic loss in an attempt to take advantage of the normal six-year period of limitation. The Court of Appeal, not surprisingly, did not endorse this ploy. They said that, whether or not she was claiming damages for the unwanted pregnancy, her claim was for 'damages in respect of personal injuries' within the meaning of s 11(1) of the Limitation Act 1980. However, Roch LJ reserved the question of the proper limitation period in the case of a failed vasectomy where the woman did not know of the vasectomy and actually wanted a child. The judge said that in those circumstances a pregnancy that was not 'unwanted' by the woman would not be a personal injury to her or anyone else and the man's loss would be purely financial.

In *Godfrey v Gloucestershire Royal Infirmary NHS Trust*,[31] a wrongful birth claim for failure to give the mother proper advice about termination was held to be a personal injury action, following *Walkin*, and therefore out of time, but Leveson J exercised s 33 discretion to permit the claim to proceed nevertheless.

---

29 [2003] MLC 1017, Morland J.
30 [1995] 1 WLR 1543, CA.
31 [2003] MLC 1010.

SCENARIO 5: WRONGFUL LIFE CLAIMS

An action on behalf of a child, whether born normal or disabled, alleging that his birth (not his injuries though) only came about because the doctors were negligent, is a non-starter.

The action for wrongful life, as it has been called in the US (in contradistinction to the action for wrongful birth), is an action by the child himself, claiming that through the doctor's negligence he has been born, where if the doctor had not been negligent he would not have been born.

The metaphysical issues raised by this contention are impossible to resolve satisfactorily in a court of law, or elsewhere for that matter. The child does not complain that the doctor's negligence has caused him to be born disabled because the doctor did not cause or contribute to the disability. But, he says, if you had sterilised or aborted my mother properly (or however the claim might arise), I would not now be living. Theoretically, a healthy child could make the same contention. But if there is any claim at all to be countenanced here, obviously it is even more difficult, perhaps even ludicrous, for a healthy child to contend that he has been injured by the mere fact of being born, whereas, in the case of a severely disabled child, there is at least some superficial attraction in the contention that his quality of life is so wretched as to amount to a continuous state of suffering, and that he should be recompensed for having to endure that. The logical fallacy is, of course, as already indicated, that the negligence, assuming there to have been negligence, is not responsible for the difference between a life of suffering and a reasonable life (this can often be recompensed under the Congenital Disabilities (Civil Liability) Act 1976 (see below)), but between a life of suffering and a state of non-life; and how can the court possibly evaluate the state of non-being?

Transatlantic cases

The US courts have almost invariably rejected this claim. The Illinois Court of Appeal said in 1963: 'Recognition of the plaintiff's claim means the creation of a new tort, a cause of action for wrongful life. The legal implications of such a tort are vast, the social impact could be staggering …' (*Zepeda v Zepeda*[32]). In a 1977 case,[33] a New York court, while permitting the parents of a deformed child to recover for pain and suffering over the birth, rejected the child's claim. It has been said by the Supreme Court: 'Thus, the threshold question here is not whether life with deformities, however severe, is less preferable than death, but rather whether it is less preferable than the "utter void of non-existence".'

In the Canadian case of *Cataford v Moreau* (above), the judge, rejecting the child's claim, said:

> La naissance d'un enfant sain ne constitue pas pour cet infant un dommage, et encore moins un dommage compensable en argent. Il est bien impossible de comparer la situation de l'enfant après sa naissance avec la situation dans laquelle il se serait trouvé s'il n'était pas né. Le seul énoncé du problème

---

32   41 Ill App 2d 240 (1963).
33   394 NYS 2d 933.

montre déjà l'illogisme qui l'habite. D'ailleurs par quelle perversion de l'esprit pourrait-on arriver à qualifier comme un dommage l'inestimable don de la vie?

[The birth of a healthy baby does not constitute a loss for that child, let alone a loss that can be compensated for by money. One cannot compare the child's position after being born with what it would have been had he not been born. Merely to state the problem demonstrates its inherently illogical nature. Moreover, by what sort of warped outlook could one put under the head of loss or damage the priceless gift of life?]

There was, however, one occasion when a New York court refused to strike out the claim of a deceased child born with a fatal kidney disease after his parents had been told that the disease would not be transmitted to the foetus. It was said by the court to be 'tortious to the fundamental right of a child to be born as a whole, functional human being'. That decision was not upheld on appeal – the reasoning of the lower court seems to have fallen into the fallacy referred to above, where the defendant is illogically held responsible for the suffering of the child.

The *McKay* case

The first and, probably, the only action in which the claim for wrongful life has been considered in the English courts came before the Court of Appeal in February 1982. The facts in *McKay v Essex Area Health Authority*,[34] were that a child was born disabled as a result of her mother having contracted German measles during the pregnancy. It was alleged, inter alia, that the medical staff were negligent in not giving the mother proper advice and information which, had it been forthcoming, would have led to an abortion. So the mother claimed on her own account. But there was also a claim on behalf of the child for her having 'suffered entry into a life in which her injuries are highly debilitating'. In other words she claimed for having been born, or at any rate, for having been born into a life of handicap and suffering.

On a preliminary hearing, the Master struck out the child's claim as disclosing no reasonable cause of action; Lawson J restored it on the ground that it was really a claim for injuries suffered and was highly arguable; the Court of Appeal was unanimously of the view that the Master's decision was right (although, as a matter of procedure, Griffiths LJ was not prepared to interfere with the judge's exercise of his discretion).

Stephenson LJ pointed out the lack of success such a claim had met with in the US, and that the Law Commission report on injuries to unborn children (Cmnd 5709), which was followed by the Congenital Disabilities (Civil Liability) Act 1976, counselled against admitting such a claim. He said that the claim must be viewed as an allegation that the defendants were negligent in allowing the child to be born at all. For the medical advisers to owe a duty to the child, over and above that which they owed the mother to give her the opportunity to terminate the child's existence, would constitute a further inroad on the sanctity of human life, which would be contrary to public policy. In addition, the judge noted the impossibility of evaluating the difference between the child's disabled existence and the non-negligent consequence, namely her non-existence.

---

34 [1982] QB 1166, CA.

Ackner LJ said that he could not accept that the common law duty of care to a person could involve the legal obligation to them, whether or not *in utero*, being to terminate their existence. Such a proposition ran wholly contrary to the concept of the sanctity of human life. On the question of damage, he said that what the doctor was blamed for was causing or permitting the child to be born at all, not for causing or contributing to her injuries. He also asked how a court could begin to evaluate non-existence. 'No comparison is possible and therefore no damage can be established which a court could recognise. This goes to the root of the whole cause of action.'

Griffiths LJ, while of the view that, procedurally, the application should fail and the matter be argued at the trial, had no doubt that the claim did not lie. 'The most compelling reason to reject this cause of action is the intolerable and insoluble problem it would create in the assessment of damages.'

All the judges expressed the view that s 4(5) of the Congenital Disabilities (Civil Liability) Act 1976, while not applying to the instant birth, because it took place prior to the Act coming into force, had the effect of abolishing this cause of action for births after that date. This, with respect, is clearly wrong, in the sense that it puts an interpretation upon the section which Parliament did not intend, and which the words cannot bear, however desirable the result may be thought to be. The Act gave a child the right to sue a tortfeasor for injuries sustained in the womb; one would therefore expect that the Act would seek to abolish any common law cause of action that might possibly exist corresponding to the new statutory cause of action, and this is exactly what it does. The action for wrongful life is not an action in respect of the child's disabilities at birth; as the court itself said in this case (as noted above) it is a claim for having been born at all. The section is simply concerned with actions for personal injury suffered before or possibly at birth. That the section does not apply to the action for wrongful life is demonstrated not only by the context of the Act and the obvious intended scope of the subsection, but also by the reflection that this action would in theory, if it existed, be open to a healthy child. The fact that the claimant may be disabled rather than healthy is not of the essence of the claim (see below for a discussion of the 1976 Act).

The New South Wales Court of Appeal has upheld the judgments dismissing three cases where a disabled child claimed damages for 'wrongful life', declaring the claims unjusticiable (*Waller v James, Harriton v Stephens, Waller v Hoolahan*[35]). Surprisingly, one of the three judges dissented.

In 2001, the French Parliament passed a law reversing the success that such a claim had enjoyed in the highest court (the *Perruche* case).

LOSS OF FERTILITY

This is the reverse side of the coin and the value of any claim will depend significantly on whether there is consequent psychiatric damage and

---

35   [2004] MLC 1104.

whether the person already has a family or not. The *Judicial Studies Board Guidelines* (9th Edition), Ch 6 provides the following:

(E) Reproductive System: Male

(a)	(i) Total Loss of Reproductive Organs	In excess of £122,640	In excess of £134,900
	(ii) Cases of orchidectomy with some psychological consequences but without loss of sexual function or impotence.	£16,000 to £18,000	£17,600 to £19,800
(b)	Impotence		
	(i) Total impotence and loss of sexual function and sterility in the case of a young man.	In the region of £118,240	In the region of £130,060
	The level of the award will depend on:		
	1. age;		
	2. psychological reaction and the effect on social and domestic life.		
	(ii) Impotence which is likely to be permanent, in the case of a middle-aged man with children.		
(c)	Cases of sterility usually fall into one of two categories: surgical, chemical and disease cases (which involve no traumatic injury or scarring) and traumatic injuries (frequently caused by assaults) which are often aggravated by scarring.	£34,280 to £62,490	£37,710 to £68,740
	(i) The most serious cases merit awards up to	£112,100	£123,310
	(ii) The bottom of the range is the case of the much older man and merits an award of about	£14,960	£16,450
(d)	An uncomplicated case of sterility without impotence and without any aggravating features for a young man without children.	£44,710 to £56,870	£49,180 to £62,550
(e)	A similar case but involving a family man who might have intended to have more children.	£18,880 to £24,950	£20,760 to £27,450
(f)	Cases where the sterility amounts to little more than an 'insult'.	In the region of £5,280	In the region of £5,810

(F) Reproductive System: Female

The level of awards in this area will typically depend on:

whether or not the affected woman already has children and/or whether the intended family was complete;

scarring;

depression or psychological scarring;

whether a foetus was aborted.

(a)	Infertility whether by reason of injury or disease, with severe depression and anxiety, pain and scarring.	£91,600 to £135,030	£100,760 to £148,540

(b)	Infertility resulting from failure to diagnose Ectopic Pregnancy not included in section (a) above but where there are resulting medical complications. The upper end of the bracket will be appropriate where those medical complications are significant.	£27,140 to £81,420	£29,850 to £89,560
(c)	Infertility without any medical complication and where the injured person already has children. The upper end of the bracket is appropriate in cases where there is significant psychological damage.	£14,320 to £29,290	£15,750 to £32,210
(d)	Infertility where the injured person would not have had children in any event (for example, because of age).	£5,280 to £10,040	£5,810 to £11,040
(e)	Failed sterilisation leading to unwanted pregnancy where there is no serious psychological impact or depression.	In the region of £8,130	In the region of £8,940
(f)	Where delay in diagnosing Ectopic Pregnancy but fertility not affected. Award dependant on extent of pain, suffering, bleeding, whether blood transfusion required, anxiety and adjustment disorder and whether there is resultant removal of one of fallopian tubes.	£2,700 to £16,280	£2,970 to £17,910

As can be seen, the amount awarded for loss of fertility will depend on the age of the woman and whether she already had the size of family she wanted. There are numerous quantum reports available throughout the spectrum of awards. However, when assessing the claim it will be important to ensure that there is expert evidence available if the claimant has suffered psychological sequelae. The claimant's intentions as to having children or having further children will need to be explored and evidenced.

In *Briody v St Helens and Knowsley Health Authority*,[36] Ebsworth J awarded £66,000, to include compensation for substantial psychiatric consequences, where a 19-year-old woman lost her first child and her womb. The costs of surrogacy were not allowed, on the basis that the chances of success were slim and the arrangement would in any event be unlawful. The Court of Appeal agreed.[37] This was followed in *XX v Whittington Hospital NHS Trust*[38] at first instance. However, the Court of Appeal re-examined the recoverability of the costs of surrogacy arrangements: they considered that the changes to the illegality doctrine in *Patel v Mirza*[39] allowed them to consider afresh the public policy aspects of surrogacy. Public policy considerations have moved on. It was significant that the claimant's proposal to seek commercial surrogacy in California was a lawful act in California, albeit that commercial surrogacy is unlawful in the UK. Consequently the Court of Appeal held that there was no policy reason to retain the bar on recovery of the

36   [2000] PIQR Q165.
37   [2001] MLC 0165.
38   [2017] EWHC 2318.
39   [2016] UKSC 42.

surrogacy costs in California and were recoverable. However, this will not invariably be the result. Although not in issue in this case, whether the attempt to have four children was reasonable in all the circumstances, or whether the various surrogacy and medical steps were the reasonable way of achieving the result would have to be proved. Moreover, the court rejected the distinction drawn in *Briody* between 'own egg' and 'donor egg' surrogacy and held that such a distinction was artificial and could not be maintained.

Chapter 13

The Congenital Disabilities Act 1976

Sarah Fraser Butlin

The Act enables a child who was injured while they were a foetus to recover damages for his disabilities from the person responsible, provided that person is in breach of duty to the parent. This applies to breaches at pre-conception and post-conception.

THE PROBLEM

What if negligent treatment harms the foetus, so that the child is born handicapped? Perhaps drugs for the pregnant woman have been manufactured, marketed or prescribed without proper care. Or perhaps her antenatal care has been deficient. And what if, before conception took place, the mother's (or the father's) reproductive capacity was, unknown to her (or to him), harmed by treatment or drugs so that later she conceived a handicapped child? Or there may have been a transmission to the mother (or father) of tainted blood, years before, or tainted semen in an artificial insemination. Or a Rhesus negative mother was not given, after the birth of a Rhesus positive child, the anti-D gamma globulin injections that would immunise her, so that in her next pregnancy her blood contaminated the foetus, with the result that her second child suffered Rhesus disease.[1] Or perhaps fertility treatment was pursued to prevent a child being born with a particular known genetic condition, but an embryo was selected which had that condition.

These are just a few of the possibilities where negligence towards a parent can result in the birth of a handicapped child.

In the post-conception case, the argument is that the child was injured, albeit when they were a foetus and without legal status, with the result

---

1   Liability was admitted in the case of *Roberts v Johnstone* [1989] QB 878, CA, where the defendants, although knowing that a mother had in 1975 mistakenly been given a blood transfusion of Rhesus positive blood, failed, her husband being Rhesus negative, to protect her child when she later, in 1981, became pregnant, so that the claimant was born severely handicapped from hemolytic disease (she recovered some £400,000 damages (see also *Lazenvnick v General Hospital of Munro City Inc*, Civ Act 78-1259, Cmnd Pa, 13 August 1980)).

that they were born disabled. In the pre-conception case, the argument is that but for the negligent treatment of father or mother, the child would not have been disabled.

THE COMMON LAW

Under English law, it is the case that a child has no rights and no standing as a litigant until birth (*Paton v British Pregnancy Advisory Service Trustees*[2]). In *C v S*,[3] the Court of Appeal ruled that an 18-week foetus was not a 'child capable of being born alive' within the meaning of the Infant Life (Preservation) Act 1929, so that an otherwise lawful termination of pregnancy at that stage under the Abortion Act 1967 was not a crime. The Appeal Committee of the House of Lords later that day rejected all the arguments of the young father who sought an injunction to stop his girlfriend from having the abortion. Therefore their Lordships, as well as agreeing with the issue decided by the Court of Appeal, must have been of the view that the father had no standing to interfere with the mother's proposed abortion and that the foetus was not a legal person for the purposes of bringing an action through his father, or indeed anyone, to restrain the act which would destroy it.

Before 1990, there was no English authority which decided whether the common law recognised the right of a child injured while a foetus to sue once they were born (although the Irish case of *Walker v Great Northern Rly Co of Ireland*[4] gave a negative answer). The thalidomide litigation did not provide an answer, as a settlement was reached, and in any event it appears that the defendants did not deny the right of the children to recover if, which they denied, there had been negligence (see *S v Distillers Co*[5]).

In the Canadian case of *Montreal Tramways v Léveillé*,[6] the court was prepared to recognise the right of a child to recover for damages negligently inflicted upon it when in the womb. At the same time they pointed out:

> The great weight of judicial opinion in the common law courts denies the right of a child when born to maintain an action for pre-natal injuries (*per* Lamont J).

Such a claim was later recognised in the South African case of *Pinchin v Santam Insurance Co*,[7] in the Australian case of *Watt v Rama*,[8] in the Canadian case of *Duval v Seguin*,[9] and in the Australian case of *X and Y v Pal*.[10]

Then in the cases of *Burton v Islington Health Authority* and *De Martell v Merton and Sutton Health Authority*,[11] the Court of Appeal held

---

2   [1979] QB 276.
3   [1988] QB 135.
4   (1890) 28 LR Ir 69.
5   [1970] 1 WLR 114.
6   [1933] 4 DLR 337.
7   1963 (2) SA 254 (Supreme Court, Witwatersrand Local Division).
8   [1972] VR 353.
9   (1972) 26 DLR (3d) 418.
10   [1992] 3 Med LR 195.
11   [1993] QB 204, MLC 0927.

that children damaged *in utero* before the Act came into operation were nevertheless entitled to sue for damages at common law.[12] The defendants argued that at the time of the damage being suffered, the claimant was still in the womb and therefore not a legal person. The Court of Appeal rejected this and held that damage to a foetus was foreseeable from the negligence. Importantly, they held that the cause of action accrued when the foetus was born injured, and, at the same time, they had the necessary legal personality to sue. The court held, approving *Montreal Tramways v Léveillé* (above), that at that point the child has all the rights of action which it would have had if the child had actually been in existence at the date of the accident. The Court of Appeal approved the reasoning of the two judges at first instance. Potts J had said in *B v Islington Health Authority*,[13] that there was a potential duty on the defendants towards the child who might later be born and that the cause of action was complete when the birth took place. Phillips J had said in *De Martell v Merton and Sutton Health Authority*:[14]

1   that the claimant's case accorded with the legislative policy and that the Act of 1976 recognised the possibility that the claimant had a valid claim at common law; and
2   that the damage was suffered by the claimant at the moment he achieved personality and inherited the damaged body for which the defendants, on the assumed facts, were responsible.

He held that the events prior to the birth in February 1967 were mere links in the chain of causation between the defendants' assumed lack of skill and care and the consequential damage to the claimant. The decision of the English Court of Appeal was followed by the Scottish appeal court in *Hamilton v Fife Health Board*.[15]

THE ACT

The Congenital Disabilities (Civil Liability) Act 1976 was based on the recommendations of the Law Commission contained in their *Report on Injuries to Unborn Children* (Cmnd 5709, August 1974). (The text of the Act is set out below in Appendix I.) The statute applies to births after 22 July 1976 (s 4(5)).

It is obvious, but crucial to remember, that the right of the child to claim compensation depends on its injuries having been caused by a tortious act ('occurrence'). There is still the usual requirement to establish fault. The statute simply resolves the disjunction between the person to whom the duty was owed, and which was breached, and the person (ie the child) who was injured. In the words of the statute, the 'child's disabilities are to be regarded as damage resulting from the wrongful act of that person and actionable accordingly at the suit of the child' (s 1(1)).

Liability may occur in two ways. First, pre-conception. Where medical treatment negligently impairs the reproductive capabilities of a woman

---

12   The *de Martell* case later failed on causation ([1995] 6 Med LR 234).
13   [1991] 1 QB 638.
14   [1991] 2 Med LR 209.
15   [1993] 4 Med LR 201.

or a man, the medical professional can be liable to any child that is born disabled as a result of that treatment, provided that neither parent knew the risk they were taking when having intercourse. Second, post-conception. Where negligent medical treatment affects the mother during her pregnancy, or the mother or the child during birth, and causes injury to the child, the medical professional can be liable to that injured child.

Put simply, the tortfeasor would be liable to the mother or father if they had suffered any damage. However it is the child that has suffered the damage. The Act allows the child to sue the tortfeasor for the damage caused by the tortfeasor's breach of duty, even though the tortfeasor did not owe them a duty and the child may not even have existed at the time of breach (s 1). It is irrelevant that the mother or father suffered no damage from the breach (s 1(3)).

However the child is not entitled to sue the tortfeasor if either parent knew 'at that time' (which presumably means when having intercourse) of the risk created by the tortious act that any child they conceived might be disabled (s 1(4)). Although where the father is the tortfeasor, this does not exclude liability where the mother was not aware of the risk (s 1(4)).

A child will have an action against any tortfeasor, except (usually) his mother.[16] This may be a 'pre-conception' tortfeasor where the tortious act has affected the ability of either parent to have a healthy child (s 1(2)(a)). Alternatively it may be a 'post-conception' tortfeasor where the tortious act has affected the mother during pregnancy, or her or the child in the course of its birth (s 1(2)(b)). While the child cannot sue his mother, save in relation to road traffic accidents (s 2), the child can sue his father for injuring his mother, for example by infecting her with a sexually transmitted disease (s 1(4)).

The Act was amended by the Human Fertilisation and Embryology Act 1990 to extend its scope to children born following fertility treatment. The provisions are effectively the same as for children born naturally but they ensure that tortious acts during the fertility treatment itself which results in the child's disabilities are actionable (s 1A). The tortfeasor is not liable to the child if at the time of insemination or placing of the embryos, either parent was aware of the risk of the child being born disabled (s 1(3)). Importantly s 1(4) provides that references to 'parent' in this context, refer to the parent concerned and s 4A confirms that it includes a person who would be a parent but for ss 27 to 29 of the Human Fertilisation and Embryology Act 1990. This is specifically in order to deal with the complexities of the meaning of 'parent' in fertility treatment, particularly where gamete donation has taken place.

The child must be born alive in order to bring the claim (s 4(2)(a)). (Section 4(4) provides that for the purpose of recovering damages for loss of expectation of life, the child must live for at least 48 hours; but for deaths after 1982, the provisions of the Administration of Justice Act 1982 have now in any event abolished the right to claim under that head.)

The child must also show that he was born disabled. The Act defines this as being born with any deformity, disease or abnormality, including

---

16   A child would have no civil claim against its mother for having injured it in the womb, for example through drug taking. However when a mother is driving, she is under the same duty to take care of her unborn child as the law imposes on her with respect to the safety of other people (s 2).

a predisposition (whether or not it is susceptible of immediate prognosis) to physical or mental defect in the future (ss 1(1) and 4(1)).

Liability to the child may be reduced or extinguished where, if the claim was brought by the parent, the defendant could take advantage of a term in a contract he made with the parent (s 4(6)). However this should now be read with s 2 of the Unfair Contract Terms Act 1977 which precludes a person, whether by contract or notice, from excluding or restricting his liability for death or personal injury resulting from negligence.

Liability may also be reduced to the extent the court thinks just and equitable where it is shown that the parent shared the responsibility for the child being born disabled (this must refer to contributory negligence or some fault on the part of the parent) (s 6(7)).

CAUSATION

As in all medical negligence claims, the 'occurrence' (tortious act) must be shown to have caused the disabilities. Causation is particularly difficult in the context of pre-natal injury and strong clear expert evidence will be required. This is likely to be the key battleground in any claim.

THE DAMAGE

The child sues in respect of the disabilities caused by the original tortious act, the 'occurrence'. This has nothing to do with the non-justiciable action for wrongful life (see Chapter 12). In other words, the Act does *not* allow a child to argue that they would not have been born at all, only that they would have been born without the disability.

The Act 'replaces any law in force before its passing, whereby a person could be liable to a child in respect of disabilities with which it might be born' (s 4(5)).

LIMITATION

It is clear from s 4(3) that the limitation period will be the same as if the injuries had been suffered at birth. It will not begin while the child is still a minor (see Chapter 20). An action could therefore be brought as of right by a claimant aged 20 years in respect of an incident that injured his mother many years before he was born. However evidence, particularly in relation to causation, will become much harder to gather the longer the time period.

EXTENSIONS AND RESTRICTIONS

By s 6(3) of the Consumer Protection Act 1987, that Act applies to the provisions of the Congenital Disabilities (Civil Liability) Act 1976, thus affording its protection to the unborn child (see Chapter 12).

Chapter 14

Psychiatric injury[1]

Andrew Buchan and Rachel Barrett

Anxiety, depression, shock, upset, disappointment or grief, not amounting to a psychiatric disorder, are not compensatable when they stand alone, but it may be taken into account to increase the award when it accompanies other, recognised injuries. Nervous shock amounting to psychiatric disorder is as much a head of damage as physical injury. To recover, the claimant has to be within the range of persons likely to be harmed by nervous shock; but even then the law permits recovery in the case of one who suffers nervous shock as a result of a person's death only where the shock is suffered by a close relative who either witnesses the death or its immediate aftermath.

PRIMARY AND SECONDARY VICTIMS

It is important first to distinguish between primary and secondary victims. This was made abundantly clear by the House of Lords in *Page v Smith*.[2] Lord Keith pointed out that the cases divided broadly into two categories, those in which the claimant was involved as a participant in the incident which gave rise to the action, and those in which the claimant was a witness to injury caused to others, or to the immediate aftermath of an accident to others. Lord Lloyd said that in the instant case the claimant was not in the secondary position of a spectator or bystander (he was alleging psychiatric, but not personal, injury as a result of a minor traffic accident), but was a participant, directly involved in the accident and well within the range of foreseeable physical injury, and so a primary victim. The judge pointed out that

---

1   Nervous shock claims can be worth a great deal of money, at any rate where the injury precludes employment. Mr Tredget, who could not return to work as a result of nervous injury sustained when he was present at the stillbirth of his child, received in the region of £300,000 by way of settlement (his case on liability is considered in detail below). Mr Peter Vernon, a successful businessman who could no longer work after seeing his daughters drown in a car accident, was awarded £1m by Sedley J for loss of earnings (plus £37,500 for general damages and £152,000 for future care): (1995) 28 BMLR 1 (liability had been admitted) – see below.
2   [1996] AC 155.

the factual distinction between primary and secondary victims of an accident was obvious and of long-standing. He said that none of the control mechanisms, by way of tests of proximity and ties of affection (as to which, see below), were required in the case of a primary victim. Although foreseeability of psychiatric injury remained a crucial ingredient when the claimant was the secondary victim, for the very reason that the secondary victim was almost always outside the area of physical impact and therefore outside the range of foreseeable physical injury, foreseeability of physical injury was sufficient to found a claim based solely upon psychiatric injury.

A case which demonstrates that for a primary victim, only physical injury need be foreseeable, is *Donachie v Chief Constable of Greater London Police*.[3] The claimant police officer was, without proper thought for his safety, given a task by his superior officer of placing a tracking device under a suspect's car while the suspect was in the pub. Due to the defective nature of the device, he had to try nine times before succeeding. All the while his fear for his own safety grew in case the suspect and friends should emerge from their drinking. As a result he developed a clinical psychiatric state, leading to an acute rise in blood pressure, which caused a stroke. The Court of Appeal, summarising the principles to be derived from *Page v Smith*, said that there was a reasonable foreseeability that the employer's breach of duty would cause physical injury to the officer, though not of the kind he actually suffered and via the unforeseeable psychiatric injury actually caused by the employer's negligence. So he was a primary victim in respect of whom there was a reasonable foreseeability of physical injury and, in consequence, in respect of whom it was not necessary to prove involvement in an 'event' in the form of an assault or otherwise. If A put B in a position, said the court, whereby A can reasonably foresee that B would fear physical injury, and B, as a result, suffers psychiatric injury and/or physical injury, B was then a primary victim.

There has been controversy as to whether the mother of a baby negligently injured at birth is a primary or secondary victim. The question is whether the negligence occurred while the baby was still *in utero*, at which time mother and baby are a single legal entity. As explained in the case of *Re (A Child) v Calderdale and Huddersfield NHS Foundation Trust*,[4] if the negligent act occurred prior to birth, then the mother can recover damages for psychiatric injury as a primary victim under the principles in *Page v Smith,* otherwise, she will be a secondary victim and the 'control mechanisms' (discussed below) must be satisfied.

This chapter is concerned principally with the claim by a secondary victim.[5]

---

3   [2004] EWCA Civ 405.
4   [2017] EWHC 824 (QB), [2017] Med LR 390.
5   For further enlightenment on the distinction between primary and secondary victims, see *Schofield v Chief Constable of West Yorkshire Police* (1998) 43 BMLR 28 CA, in which post-traumatic stress disorder was sustained by a woman police officer when her sergeant discharged a loaded firearm in the confines of a bedroom where they were making inquiries of the family.

WHAT IS PSYCHIATRIC INJURY CAUSED BY SHOCK?

Nervous shock is more than the normal emotions of distress, disappointment, unhappiness or grief: these do not constitute a head of damages in themselves but can serve to increase an award for a recognised loss, whether physical or financial (eg the 'spoilt holiday' cases where disappointment over a spoilt holiday can increase the award beyond the mere financial cost of the holiday). Nervous shock means an actual mental disorder, a 'positive psychiatric illness' (*per* Lord Bridge in *McLoughlin v O'Brian*[6]).

In *Nicholls v Rushton*,[7] the Court of Appeal restated in the clearest terms the rule that nervous reaction falling short of actual psychological illness cannot be the subject of compensation unless it is parasitic to physical injury. And in *Hicks v Chief Constable of South Yorkshire Police*,[8] the House of Lords said that horror and fear for one's own safety (as the Hillsborough stadium collapsed), not amounting to recognisable psychiatric damage, do not sound in damages.

In *Reilly v Merseyside Health Authority*,[9] an unsuccessful claim for damages for extreme claustrophobia suffered by an elderly couple trapped in a lift for over an hour, the Court of Appeal said that that was not a nervous disorder but nothing more than 'excitement of normal human emotion'. Presumably the medical report failed to identify an actual psychiatric disorder consequent upon the frightening experience.

In *Page v Smith*,[10] Lord Keith said that the decided cases indicated that 'nervous shock' meant a reaction to an immediate and horrifying impact, resulting in some recognisable psychiatric illness. There had to be some serious mental disturbance outside the range of normal human experience, not merely the ordinary emotions of anxiety, grief or fear. And Lord Jauncey said that the ordinary emotions of anxiety, fear, grief or transient shock were not conditions for which the law gave compensation.

Contra, in *M (A Minor) v Newham London Borough Council*,[11] the Master of the Rolls rejected the claim that the psychiatric damage said to have been suffered by a child as a result of allegedly incompetent diagnosis of sexual abuse was not damage which the law recognised as compensatable injury.[12] He pointed to Lord Ackner's words in the Hillsborough stadium case (*Alcock v Chief Constable of South Yorkshire Police*[13]), where the Law Lord had acknowledged that future development of the law was to be expected, and to the warning given by Lord Bridge in *McLoughlin v O'Brian* (above) against the temptation of seeking to freeze the law in a rigid posture.

At first instance in *RK and MK v Oldham NHS Trust*,[14] Simon J said that emotional responses of even the most serious type did not found a

6   [1983] 1 AC 410, HL.
7   (1992) Times, 19 June.
8   [1992] PIQR P433.
9   [1995] 6 Med LR 246.
10   [1996] AC 155, HL.
11   [1995] 2 AC 633, CA.
12   This aspect of the case does not seem to have been relevant to the appeal to the House of Lords ([1995] 2 AC 633, HL).
13   [1992] 1 AC 310.
14   [2003] Lloyd's Rep Med 1.

claim in damages and the court should not infer an injury where experts in the field did not.

In *Grieves v F T Everard & Sons*,[15] the appellant (G) had been negligently exposed to asbestos dust by the respondent employers, and had developed pleural plaques. The presence of such plaques did not usually occasion any symptoms. The plaques did not cause asbestos-related diseases, but they signalled the presence in the lungs and pleura of asbestos fibres that might independently cause life-threatening or fatal diseases. G had developed not merely anxiety but clinical depression, a recognised psychiatric illness, in consequence of being told that his pleural plaques indicated a significant exposure to asbestos and the risk of future disease. It was held that:

1   The symptomless plaques were not damage that could found a cause of action. It was not merely that the plaques caused no immediate symptoms. The important point was that, save in the most exceptional case, the plaques would never cause any symptoms, did not increase the susceptibility of G to other diseases or shorten his expectation of life. They had no effect upon his health at all. See also *Rothwell v Chemical and Insulating Co Ltd*[16] and the more recent case of *Dryden v Johnson Matthey Plc*[17] in which sensitisation to platinum exposure was held to be a physical change amounting to an actionable personal injury even though the change was hidden and symptomless.

2   G's psychiatric illness was not a reasonably foreseeable consequence of his employers' breach of duty. It was not reasonably foreseeable that the creation of a risk of an asbestos-related disease would cause psychiatric illness to a person of reasonable fortitude, *Page v Smith*[18] was distinguished.

This case would have been decided differently if the House of Lords had found that the psychiatric illness was reasonably foreseeable. But where does that leave the eggshell personality? Having succeeded on breach of duty and causation, G should have been able to recover damages upon the principle that the tortfeasor takes his victim as he finds him.

In *Eileen Corr (administratrix of the estate of Thomas Corr, deceased) v IBC Vehicles Ltd*,[19] the claimant succeeded because she was able to prove that her late husband's suicide was reasonably foreseeable following upon his injury. See further below.

The older cases

Where the nervous shock is allied to a more apparent physical injury, there has been no problem with recovery. But where it stands alone, the courts have been reluctant to permit recovery, both, in the older cases, because knowledge of mental trauma was scanty, and also because of

---

15   [2007] UKHL 39.
16   [2007] UKHL 39.
17   [2018] 2 WLR 1109.
18   [1996] AC 155.
19   [2006] EWCA Civ 331.

a feeling that public policy should draw the line at recovery for mental shock.

Thus, where a level crossing attendant negligently allowed a pregnant woman to cross the railway lines in her carriage in front of an oncoming train and she suffered nervous shock and a miscarriage, the Privy Council would not permit her to succeed. But that was in 1888 (*Victorian Railways Comrs v Coultas*[20]). A pregnant barmaid suffered nervous shock when a negligently driven van crashed into the pub. She succeeded, but only because her shock arose 'from a reasonable fear of immediate personal injury to [herself]' (*Dulieu v White & Sons*[21]). The scope of the claim was extended by the majority decision in *Hambrook v Stokes Bros*:[22] a mother suffered shock through fear that her children had been injured when she saw a runaway lorry careering down a hill from the bend round which her children had just gone out of sight (her apprehension was unhappily justified). The significance of this decision was twofold: first, it severed the link between nervous shock and fear of impact to oneself; second, it suggested extension of the claim to cases where the disaster had already occurred and the fear of what might be about to occur was no longer relevant.

The only case in which the House of Lords had considered the matter before *McLoughlin v O'Brian* (above) was *Hay (or Bourhill) v Young*.[23] The claimant heard the noise of a road accident as she alighted from a bus, went of her own volition to the scene and, seeing upon the road the blood of the dead motorcyclist (who was not known to her), suffered shock. Understandably, her claim was rejected. It could be said she as passer-by was owed no duty by the negligent driver, at least no duty as far as the infliction of injury by shock was concerned, or that the actual injury suffered was too remote, or unforeseeable.

In *Hinz v Berry*,[24] it was agreed without dispute that a mother could recover for psychiatric illness caused by her witnessing a ghastly accident to her family on the other side of the road. Lord Denning MR said that it was settled law that 'damages can be given for nervous shock caused by the sight of an accident, at any rate to a close relative'.

But recovery had not always been limited to a 'close relative'. In *Chadwick v British Railways Board*,[25] the estate of a rescuer at the Lewisham rail disaster recovered in respect of a psychiatric disorder caused by his work amid the dead and dying that night. (See also *Galt v British Railways Board*,[26] where a train driver recovered for nervous shock occasioned by his seeing in front of him two men on the track whom he then thought he went on to strike and kill.) In *Wigg v British Railways Board*,[27] Tucker J held that it was reasonably foreseeable that a train driver who stopped the train and got down to help a passenger, who had

---

20 (1888) 13 App Cas 222.
21 [1901] 2 KB 669.
22 [1925] 1 KB 141, CA.
23 [1943] AC 92.
24 [1970] 2 QB 40, CA.
25 [1967] 1 WLR 912.
26 (1983) 133 NLJ 870.
27 [1986] NLJ Rep 446n, (1986) Times, 4 February.

in fact been killed due to the negligence of the guard in giving the starting signal, might suffer nervous shock thereby.[28]

Recovery for nervous shock was extended by the House of Lords in *McLoughlin v O'Brian*,[29] where a mother was told at home by a witness that her family had just been involved in a serious road accident. She rushed to the hospital to find one child dead, two others seriously injured, and her husband in a state of shock. She herself suffered nervous shock, organic depression and a change of personality. She lost her claim at first instance and in the Court of Appeal, on the ground that her injury was not foreseeable and she herself was owed no duty of care, but the House of Lords reversed the decision. Lord Wilberforce promulgated the 'aftermath' principle. Recovery was permitted, but only where the shock came through sight or hearing of the event or its immediate aftermath. This is an example of judicial law-making – but none the worse for that. If therefore a relative visits the hospital to find a patient dying because of negligent treatment and suffers himself some psychiatric disorder as a result of nervous shock, he could recover damages. Probably also if he sees the corpse soon after, provided the relationship is sufficiently close; but not if the shock is occasioned merely by being told of the death and its circumstances, however horrible, and however close the relationship. In *Schneider v Eisovitch*,[30] recovery for shock on being so informed was permitted as an additional item of damages, where a wife, injured along with her husband in a road accident, learned that he had died. (It is of interest to note that the New South Wales legislature intervened as early as 1944 to permit recovery for this sort of injury suffered by a close relative of a person 'killed, injured or put in peril', irrespective of any spatial or temporal nexus with the accident.)

So we can summarise by saying that claims for nervous shock by witnesses, or secondary victims as they are now called, have had only slow and restricted acceptance in English law. The claim was first recognised where the claimant had been put in fear of imminent physical harm (this context should really be seen as one of primary victim, just as if the harm had materialised), then extended to shock caused by fear that imminent harm was about to befall others, to the witnessing of a shocking event (also to shock caused to a rescuer by actually participating in a horrific event), then, by the House of Lords decision in *McLoughlin v O'Brian* (above) to shock caused by coming upon the aftermath of a horrific event. Recent developments have done nothing to extend the ambit of the claim for the secondary victim.

---

28 For an example of an unsuccessful claim for shock suffered by a rescuer, see the Piper Alpha case of *McFarlane v EE Caledonia Ltd* [1994] PIQR P154, where the Court of Appeal held that there had been insufficient involvement or risk of involvement by the claimant in the tragedy (the fire-fighting vessel he was in was never in danger). Similarly, *Hegarty v EE Caledonia Ltd* (1997) Times, 13 February, CA.

29 [1983] 1 AC 410.

30 [1960] 2 QB 430.

Further development in *Alcock* – 'control' mechanisms for secondary victims

In the Hillsborough stadium case (*Alcock v Chief Constable of South Yorkshire*[31]), the House of Lords held that a claimant claiming for nervous shock over the death or injury of another must satisfy the following requirements (subsequently referred to as 'control mechanisms'):

1 the injury must have arisen from a sudden and unexpected shock to the claimant's nervous system;

2 the injury must have arisen from witnessing the death of, extreme danger to, or injury and discomfort suffered by the primary victim;

3 proximity of relationship, namely a close tie of love and affection to the primary victim;

4 proximity in space, in that the claimant must have been present at the scene or in the immediate vicinity;

5 proximity in time, in that the claimant must have witnessed the accident, or its immediate aftermath.

In relation to the test of relational proximity, it must have been foreseeable that this particular claimant might suffer nervous shock over the death of that particular relative or friend. The law would not define a class of qualifying relationships. The required proximity (to be based upon close ties of love and affection) was to be proved by evidence; it could in the case of obviously close familial ties be presumed (a presumption that could, however, be rebutted by appropriate evidence). The court was prepared to make the presumption in the case of claimants who had lost a son or a fiancé but not, in the absence of evidence of closeness, in the case of a brother, brother-in-law or grandson. Second, the court reaffirmed Lord Wilberforce's limited extension of the right of recovery to the 'aftermath' principle, ie the witnessing of the traumatic event or its immediate aftermath. It was not possible to bring within that principle the viewing of the distressing scenes on television, emphasis being laid on the fact that the television code of ethics meant that the suffering of recognisable individuals was not broadcast. Although it was not impossible that a television viewer might be sufficiently proximate in appropriate circumstances (probably where the telecast was horrifyingly graphic), the viewing of the television scenes in this case did not create the necessary degree of proximity and could not be 'equiparated' with the position of a claimant at the ground. Thus, there are two tests of proximity for the claimant to satisfy, the first relating to the victim, the second to the event – the second can be further divided into the proximity of the claimant to the accident and the means by which the shock has been caused. Lord Ackner said that 'shock' involved the sudden appreciation by sight or sound of a horrifying event which violently agitated the mind; as the law presently stood, it did not include psychiatric illness caused by the accumulation over a period of time of more gradual assaults on the nervous system. So illness caused by the stress of caring for an injured relative over a period of time would not be compensatable.

The court's decision was that none of the claimants could succeed – those at the ground failed the test of proximity of relationship, those

---

31 [1992] 1 AC 310.

elsewhere failed the test of proximity in time and space (those who came to the hospital or mortuary later were said not to be within the 'immediate' aftermath as they did not get there for some eight hours – the mother in *McLoughlin v O'Brian* (above) had arrived at the hospital within one hour).[32]

In *McFarlane v EE Caledonia Ltd*,[33] which concerned an oil rig disaster, Stuart-Smith LJ refused to extend the duty to bystanders in line with *obiter* comments in *Alcock* essentially for policy reasons.

In *Frost v Chief Constable of South Yorkshire Police*,[34] the House of Lords, reversing the decision of the Court of Appeal, held that police officers, who had suffered psychiatric injury when performing rescue duties in the aftermath of the Hillsborough football stadium disaster, could not recover damages. They were secondary victims and had to satisfy the tests for secondary victims. The fact that they were employed by the defendant did not affect that requirement. Noting that many relatives who were secondary victims had failed in earlier claims, the court said it would be unfair if police officers could recover in similar circumstances. Lord Steyn said that the law in this field was 'a patchwork quilt of distinctions which are hard to justify'; and Lord Hoffmann said that the search for principle had been called off in the *Alcock* case, that it was too late to go back on the control mechanisms stated in *Alcock*, and until there was legislative change the courts must live with them and judicial developments must take them into account.

In *W v Essex CC*,[35] which concerned an appeal from a strike-out decision, the House of Lords held that the categorisation as a primary or secondary victim would not necessarily be conclusive. In that case, foster parents were caused psychiatric injury by the negligent placement of a child with them who abused their own children. This shows that the law on secondary victims may yet develop further.

In *Liverpool Women's Hospital NHS Foundation Trust v Ronayne*,[36] Tomlinson LJ described the *Alcock* requirements for secondary victim liability as 'both arbitrary and pragmatic but ... well-understood, [and] binding on the court'.

The Law Commission has written extensively on liability for injury to secondary victims, and is generally supportive of a relaxation of the *Alcock* control mechanisms.[37]

What qualifies as the 'aftermath' of a shocking event?

Cases in which secondary victim claims have succeeded include the following.

In *North Glamorgan NHS Trust v Walters*,[38] the mother attended the last two days of her infant son's life after he had suffered a fatal injury due

---

32 Contra, *McCarthy v Chief Constable of South Yorkshire* (11 December 1996, unreported), QBD Toulson J, where a claimant had had a good view from his stand of the horrific events of the day in which his half-brother died.

33 [1994] 2 All ER 1.

34 [1998] QB 254, CA, reversed [1999] 2 AC 455, HL.

35 [2001] 2 AC 592.

36 [2015] EWCA Civ 588, [2015] PIQR P20.

37 See https://www.lawcom.gov.uk/project/liability-for-psychiatric-illness/.

38 [2002] MLC 0876, [2003] PIQR P16.

to the defendant's negligence. She was first told that brain damage was unlikely, later that he had in fact suffered severe brain injury and needed life support. The child later died in his mother's arms when the support was withdrawn. *Sunt lacrimae rerum.* The Court of Appeal, dismissing the defendant's appeal, and declaring that the only issue in the case was whether the mother's illness 'arose from the sudden appreciation by sight or sound of a horrifying event or its immediate aftermath', said that the law permitted a realistic view to be taken of what constituted an 'event'. 'Event' was for secondary victims a convenient description for the series of events which made up the entire event beginning with the negligent infliction of damage to the conclusion of the immediate aftermath, whenever that might be. Its identification was a matter of judgment from case to case depending on the facts and circumstances of each case. On the facts of this case, the court said that there was an inexorable progression from the moment when the fit causing the brain damage occurred which shortly thereafter made the child's death inevitable and the dreadful climax when he died in his mother's arms. It was a seamless tale lasting for a period of 36 hours which, for the mother, was undoubtedly one drawn-out experience. The entire event was undoubtedly a 'horrifying' event. The assault on the mother's nervous system began when she was woken by her child's convulsion and she reeled under successive blows as each was delivered. In other words, the blows were each of them a sudden assault; the picture was not of a gradual assault (some distinction!). Clarke LJ said that although the court's decision did not actually involve taking the step forward of allowing a claim for a secondary victim for psychiatric illness caused by the accumulation over a period of time of more gradual assaults on the nervous system (as opposed to a sudden assault on same), he for his part would have been willing to take that step forward on the facts of the instant case if that had been necessary.

In the highly distressing case of *Galli-Atkinson v Seghal*,[39] the Court of Appeal held that the immediate aftermath of a fatal road accident in which the claimant's daughter was killed extended from the moment of the accident until the moment the claimant left the mortuary. The visit to the mortuary, not long after the claimant had arrived at the police cordon at the site of the accident, was not merely to identify the body, which still bore the horrifying marks of the fatal injury, but also to complete the story as far as the claimant was concerned. An 'event' for the purposes of establishing a claim by a secondary victim might be made up from a number of components, as had been said in *North Glamorgan NHS Trust v Walters*.

By contrast, in the following cases the claimant was held not to have satisfied the proximity test by coming to or learning of the shocking event after its immediate aftermath.

A harsh example of the restrictions that the Court of Appeal has placed on the ambit of the nervous shock claim can be seen in *Taylorson v Shieldness Produce Ltd*.[40] Parents went immediately one morning to the hospital to which their 14-year-old son, their only child, had been admitted after being crushed under a reversing vehicle. They did not see him at the hospital, but they followed the ambulance that transferred him to

---

39 [2003] Lloyd's Rep Med 285.
40 [1994] PIQR P329, CA.

another hospital, the father glimpsing him in the ambulance, the mother seeing him briefly as he was being rushed into the intensive care unit on a trolley. They did not see him then for a few hours while he was being treated. The father saw him that evening, when he had black eyes, blood on his face and a tube attached to the top of his head to relieve pressure on the brain. The mother saw him the next day in a similar state. The boy remained unconscious for two days. Then the life support machine was switched off. The parents were with him throughout that time.

The court said that the shocking events were not sufficiently proximate and that the involvement of the parents did not come within the aftermath principle. It seems that the first conclusion was based on the lack of close contact in the first few hours and the second on the refusal of the court to adopt the reasoning in the Australian case of *Jaensch v Coffey*[41] and extend the aftermath period to include the two days waiting at the bedside of the dying child.

In *Hunter v British Coal Corpn*,[42] the claimant had suffered psychiatric injury by way of 'surviving guilt' after a pit explosion which killed his mate. As he had left the actual scene of the accident some minutes before to look for equipment (though he was still fairly close, heard the explosion and saw the cloud of dust rising), and as he was not in any danger himself, the court said his claim could not succeed. He could not be treated as a secondary victim because he had not witnessed the accident; he had (merely) suffered an abnormal grief reaction on hearing of the death, triggered by an irrational feeling of responsibility; his 'survivor's guilt' was too remote an injury. This case is an excellent illustration of how artificial and generally unsatisfactory is the current state of the law in relation to nervous shock claims.

In *Palmer v Tees Health Authority*,[43] the mother of a child murdered by a released psychiatric patient could not recover damages for nervous shock when she saw the child's body three days later, a decision upheld by the Court of Appeal.[44]

In *Monk v PC Harrington Ltd*,[45] a claimant who heard of an accident at work via portable radio immediately as it occurred and then went to the site of the accident in order to lend assistance was neither a rescuer who reasonably feared for his own safety nor was he an unwilling participant in the accident. As such the claimant did not satisfy the requirements of being a primary victim, and he was also unable to recover as a secondary victim as he did not meet the requirements laid out in *Alcock*.

In *Berisha v Stone Superstore Ltd*[46] the District Judge held that a wife arriving to see her husband in hospital at 4.00 pm following his accident at 11.30 am lacked sufficient proximity to claim.

---

41   (1984) 155 CLR 549.
42   [1999] QB 140, CA.
43   [1998] Lloyd's Rep Med 447.
44   See [1999] Lloyd's Rep Med 351, [2000] PIQR P1. In *Tranmore v T E Scudder Ltd* [1998] JPIL 336, visiting the mortuary 24 hours after his son had been killed by falling rubble took the father outside the 'aftermath' principle, even though he had visited the accident site at the time (he had not seen his son there, though).
45   [2008] EWHC 1879.
46   [2014] 12 WLUK 53, CC.

In *Wild v Southend University Hospital NHS Foundation Trust*,[47] Michael Kent QC held that a father who suffered psychiatric illness caused by hearing midwives determine that his baby had died in his wife's womb was not able to recover because his illness was not caused by witnessing an 'event' and 'there was no assault on the senses'. The mother, who had to go through a stillbirth, did succeed in recovering damages as the primary victim.

A further complexity is that the claimant must be proximate to the aftermath of the shocking event itself, and not to the ensuring consequences. In *Taylor v A Novo (UK) Ltd*[48] a daughter who was with her mother when she died some weeks after an accident at work was held not to be a secondary victim because she lacked sufficient proximity to the original accident. This distinction was applied in the context of criminal injuries compensation in *RS v Criminal Injuries Compensation Authority*[49] and in the context of negligent mental health treatment causing a claimant's husband's later attempted suicide in *Morgan v Somerset Partnership NHSFT*.[50]

Causation – must the psychiatric injury be caused by proximity to the shocking event rather than the consequences of the event itself?

In *Taylorson v Shieldness Produce Ltd*[51] the court found that causation was not proved, in that it took the view that the real cause of the psychiatric injury was the loss of their child and that the injury would have been sustained even if there had been no question of any participation in any aftermath.

In *Vernon v Bosley*[52] where the claimant had witnessed the drowning of his two children (than which a more dreadful experience could hardly be imagined),[53] the Court of Appeal held that the legal test determining recoverability was whether the claimant had suffered mental injury caused by the negligence of the defendant and not whether he had suffered post-traumatic stress disorder rather than pathological grief disorder. Accordingly, the secondary victim could recover damages for mental illness caused or at least contributed to by the actionable negligence of the defendant, notwithstanding that the illness could also be regarded as a pathological consequence of the bereavement which the claimant had inevitably suffered. It followed that damages payable to a claimant who was a secondary victim of a breach of a duty of care owed by the defendants and who suffered mental illness, which was properly regarded as a consequence both of his experience as a bystander and of an intense and abnormal grief reaction to the bereavement which he

---

47 [2014] EWHC 4053 (QB).
48 [2013] EWCA Civ 194, [2014] QB 150.
49 [2013] EWCA Civ 1040, [2014] 1 WLR 1313.
50 [2016] 2 WLUK 751, CC.
51 [1994] PIQR P329, CA.
52 [1997] 1 All ER 577, CA.
53 The judgment of Sedley J at first instance can be found at (1995) 28 BMLR 1. The initial huge award, including £1m for loss of earnings, £37,500 for general damages and £152,000 for future care, was reduced on a separate appeal upon the admission of fresh evidence indicating a better prognosis (*Vernon v Bosley* (No 2) [1997] 1 All ER 614, CA).

suffered, should not be discounted for his grief and the consequences of bereavement, even though his illness was partly so caused.

This decision appears to be inconsistent with the judgment of the Court of Appeal in *Calascione v Dixon*,[54] where they held that the trial judge had been right to distinguish between post-traumatic stress disorder suffered by a mother on seeing the corpse of her son mangled after a road traffic accident and pathological grief reaction which was not due to the accident or its aftermath.

Unusual cases

In *Attia v British Gas plc*,[55] a woman had allegedly suffered positive psychiatric illness (as opposed to 'normal' grief and distress) through seeing her home burnt down before her eyes as a result of the defendants' negligence. The Court of Appeal refused to strike out the claim for nervous shock (the claim for damage to property had been settled), saying that there was in principle no reason to preclude recovery if the injury and foreseeability were proved in the usual way. In other words, nervous shock arising out of damage to property rather than damage to the person is not for that reason alone to be irrecoverable. Scott J has doubted whether shock caused by the disclosure of confidential medical information could properly be reflected in an award of damages (*W v Egdell*[56]). See also the sharp rejection by the Court of Appeal in *Powell v Boldaz*[57] of the claim for nervous shock sustained as a result of getting certain upsetting written information in A4 rather than A5 form.

Still within the realm of the unusual, we find *Froggatt v Chesterfield and North Derbyshire Royal Hospital NHS Trust*.[58] A young wife had undergone a mastectomy followed by radiotherapy and chemotherapy, only to be told the following month that the diagnosis of cancer had been an error. She then underwent extensive reconstruction surgery, which left her cosmetically and physically impaired and with substantial psychiatric symptoms, for which she obtained appropriate damages. What was unusual is that her husband succeeded in obtaining damages as a secondary victim having suffered psychiatric injury by way of sudden shock and horror on seeing his wife undressed for the first time, and her son obtained a small amount of damages as a secondary victim for psychiatric damage suffered when he overheard a telephone conversation in which his mother discussed the fact that she had cancer and was likely to die. This is surely the far boundary of the nervous shock claim. Could the defendants have foreseen the telephone conversation or injury arising therefrom? Or the arising of the husband's psychiatric illness? The claims of husband and son were dealt with in very short measure at the end of an extensive judgment on the patient's claim. It is doubtful that these claims would stand up to a lengthier analysis.

In a medical context, judgment was given by the House of Lords based on the allegedly negligent decisions made by medical professionals during

---

54   (1993) 19 BMLR 97.
55   [1988] QB 304.
56   [1990] Ch 359.
57   [1998] Lloyd's Rep Med 116.
58   [2002] MLC 0887, Forbes J.

clinical investigation, diagnosis and reporting of a child's condition which resulted in psychiatric injury to the child's parents. In *D v East Berkshire Community Health NHS Trust*,[59] doctors believed children to have been the subject of non-accidental injury by a parent or suspected that false reporting had been given which gave rise to a risk of future non-accidental injury. It later transpired that such accusations had been unfounded and that the parents themselves had suffered psychiatric injury as a direct consequence of those accusations. The House of Lords held, by a 4:1 majority, that where the relationship between the doctor and the parents was confined to the fact that they were the parents of the doctor's patient, then the appropriate level of protection for the parents was that clinical and other investigations had to be conducted in good faith. Carelessness was not enough to create a duty of care.

What amounts to a 'shocking event'?

What if a close relative suffers psychiatric damage through being present at and around the death and/or terminal illness in hospital (or elsewhere) of a loved one, the injury being due to medical negligence? There is no reason in principle why the tests of proximity (or the 'aftermath' test) should not be satisfied in this context. Until recently, there was no English authority on the point, but several settlements of such claims had been achieved. In the Australian case of *Jaensch v Coffey*[60] (not a medical accident case), Deane J permitted recovery for nervous shock where a wife came to her injured husband's bedside in hospital, and through her constant attendance upon him and her fear that he was going to die suffered severe anxiety and depression.[61] The judge said:[62]

> The aftermath of the accident extended to the hospital to which the injured person was taken and persisted for so long as he remained in the state produced by the accident up to and including immediate post-accident treatment ... Her psychiatric injuries were the result of the impact upon her of the facts of the accident itself and its aftermath while she was present at the aftermath of the accident at the hospital.

In principle, there is no difference between claims for shock due to horrific scenes at the hospital after a road accident and the same after a medical accident, so the case of *Taylorson* (above) is also in point. However, the difficulty with the medical accident context is that horrific scenes are less likely, and so the question that immediately springs to mind is how the element of shock can be satisfied in such a case (assuming that there is no such shocking element as the relative finding the loved one dying or dead at home). In the Hillsborough case (*Alcock v Chief Constable of South Yorkshire Police*), Lord Ackner said:[63]

---

59 [2005] 2 All ER 443.
60 (1984) 155 CLR 549.
61 Note, incidentally, that the claimant's predisposition to such injury was no defence; similarly in *Brice v Brown* [1984] 1 All ER 997, Stuart-Smith LJ held that, once nervous shock was a foreseeable consequence of a breach of duty, it made no difference that the precise nature and extent of the injury were not foreseeable (the claimant had suffered particularly severely due to a basic mental instability) – see Chapter 8 under 'You must take the claimant as you find him'.
62 (1984) 155 CLR 549 at 608.
63 [1992] 1 AC 310 at 401.

'Shock', in the context of this cause of action, involves the sudden appreciation by sight or sound of a horrifying event, which violently agitates the mind. It has yet to include psychiatric illness caused by the accumulation over a period of time or more gradual assaults on the nervous system.

In *Jaensch v Coffey* (above), Brennan J said:[64]

I understand 'shock' in this context to mean the sudden sensory perception – that is, by seeing, hearing or touching – of a person, thing or event, which is so distressing that the perception of the phenomenon affronts or insults the claimant's mind and causes a recognizable psychiatric illness.

There are now, besides the judgment in *Taylorson* (set out above), recent decisions in medical negligence actions, including one from the Court of Appeal, which make it more difficult for a claim of this sort to succeed.

In *Taylor v Somerset Health Authority*,[65] Auld J rejected a claim by a widow who had come to the hospital after her husband had suffered a fatal heart attack at work (due to earlier medical mismanagement). She had not believed that he had died, not even when she was so informed by a doctor. She then saw him lying peacefully behind curtains in the basement of the hospital. The judge said that this did not fulfil the test of temporal proximity (in other words, she was too late on the scene). He also said that there had to be an external traumatic event; however, in the *Sion* case (see below) Peter Gibson LJ made it clear that an external horrific event was not a prerequisite as the crucial element in this sort of claim was a sudden awareness, violently agitating the mind, of what was occurring or what had occurred. It could, nevertheless, be argued that in the *Taylor* case what was absent was the necessary element of horror or sudden shock. One has to remember that one cannot claim merely for psychiatric injury caused by the death of a loved one. The claim is a claim for *shock*.

In *Sion v Hampstead Health Authority*,[66] the Court of Appeal struck out as doomed to fail a claim by a father who suffered psychiatric injury through attending for some two weeks by the bedside of his 23-year-old son who had been injured in a traffic accident and fatally deteriorated in hospital due, allegedly, to negligent medical treatment. The court took the view on the pleadings, having regard principally to the psychiatric report that was served with the particulars of claim, that there was no evidence of 'shock', no sudden appreciation by sight or sound of a horrifying event, but rather a continuous process that ran from the father's first arrival at the hospital to a death two weeks later that was by then not unexpected – and on then to his realisation after the inquest of the possibility of medical negligence.

This seems odd. In the first place, does it make any sort of sense that there would probably have been a good claim if the father had still been hoping for recovery when death occurred and had therefore been 'shocked' when there was a sudden fatal deterioration? Secondly, there do in fact appear to have been discrete 'shocking' events during the two-week period, such as a sudden (though not immediately fatal)

---

64   (1984) 155 CLR 549 at 567.
65   [1993] 4 Med LR 34, MLC 0025.
66   [1994] 5 Med LR 170, MLC 0027.

deterioration, sudden respiratory difficulties, cardiac arrest and transfer to the intensive care unit.

A more imaginative judgment (in the best sense) was given in the Central London County Court by Judge White on 4 February 1994 in the case of *Tredget v Bexley Health Authority*.[67] Although this was before the Court of Appeal judgment, it was after Brooke J had struck out Mr Sion's claim at first instance, and nothing that was said in the Court of Appeal invalidates Judge White's approach.

In the first place, this case concerned claims for nervous shock sustained by both parents as a result of a traumatic and frightening delivery of their fatally injured child, following negligent failure to go for an earlier Caesarean section, and as a result of attending upon their son during his short life of some two days. So the case was rather different from the usual 'attending by the bedside' case.

Judge White accepted, as did the Court of Appeal in the *Sion* case, the following requisites for a successful claim:

> The plaintiff must show he has suffered an actual psychiatric illness caused by shock (ie the sudden and direct appreciation by sight or sound of a horrifying event or events, rather than from stress, strain, grief or sorrow or from gradual or retrospective realisation of events); that there was propinquity in time or space for the causative event or its immediate aftermath; that such injury was reasonably foreseeable; and that the relationship between plaintiff and defendant was sufficiently proximate.

It is surprising that the health authority sought to argue that there had been no element of shock in the events that the parents had experienced, and disappointing that they should have chosen to contest the mother's claim on that basis. Fortunately, the judge sensibly declined to see the two-day period as lacking the element of shock. He saw the traumatic birth (in which the husband had been involved, and which had been complicated by shoulder dystocia – an obstetric emergency) and the delivery of a clearly traumatised baby and the ensuing harrowing hours as a single event ('frightening and harrowing') which satisfied the requisite of a sudden shock to the nervous system. He said:

> Of course, it was not in the nature of an immediate catastrophe which lasts only a few seconds – panic in a stadium or a motor accident – but one just as traumatic, for those immediately involved as participants, as each of the parents was ...

> In my judgment, if this is a new step in the development of the law, it is not only ... within the principles that have been set out, but has its own in-built limits, being founded on the special relationship, with all that follows, of the parent with the child at the unique human moment of birth.[68]

In *North Glamorgan NHS Trust v Walters*[69] (discussed above), the mother attended the last two days of her infant son's life after he suffered a major epileptic seizure leading to coma and irreparable brain damage. His condition was not properly diagnosed. The Court of Appeal held that

---

67 [1994] 5 Med LR 178, MLC 0024.
68 It should be noted here that in *Allin v City and Hackney Health Authority* [1996] 7 Med LR 167, a mother recovered damages for psychiatric injury sustained on being informed wrongly (and negligently) that her new-born child had died.
69 [2002] MLC 0876, [2003] PIQR P16.

an 'event' could comprise a series of shocking occurrences over a period of time. In that case, the 36 hours the claimant mother spent in hospital with her infant son leading up to his death comprised a single event.

A lamentable step backward, however, was taken by a deputy High Court judge in *Ward v Leeds Teaching Hospital NHS Trust*[70] where the defendants succeeded in their wretched argument that the psychiatric injury suffered by a mother at the death of her daughter due to a negligently handled anaesthetic was not due to the events in hospital but due to the bereavement *simpliciter*. The judge took the view that there was no shock or horrifying event for the mother as she sat by her daughter's bedside (on and off) for two days awaiting her death. The death of a loved one in hospital, he said, did not meet that description unless also accompanied by circumstances that were wholly exceptional in some way so as to shock and horrify.

The exceptionality standard was applied in *Brock v Northampton General Hospital NHS Trust*;[71] as a result, parents who witnessed their daughter pass away in hospital after the negligent insertion of an intracranial bolt were unsuccessful in a claim for the psychiatric harm they sustained. Their experience was held to be 'dreadful', but not, applying *Ward*, 'wholly exceptional'.

In *Shorter v Surrey and Sussex Healthcare NHS Trust*[72] the claimant, herself a nurse, suffered a major depressive disorder following the death of her sister in hospital due to a negligently misdiagnosed haemorrhage. Swift J found that her psychiatric injury was caused by a series of events over a two-day period of her sister's admission to hospital, some of which she was proximate to (seeing her sister in pain on a hospital trolley) and some not (being informed by telephone that her sister had deteriorated). Applying the *Alcock* control mechanisms, Swift J held that there had not been '… the sudden appreciation by sight or sound of a horrifying event which violently agitates the mind.'

Shortly afterwards, in *Liverpool Women's Hospital NHS Foundation Trust v Ronayne*,[73] the Court of Appeal held that a husband could not found a secondary victim claim on the psychiatric injury he suffered as a result of seeing his wife's deterioration in hospital following a negligently performed hysterectomy. Tomlinson LJ explained, '… the appearance of the Claimant's wife was as would ordinarily be expected of a person in hospital in the circumstances in which she found herself. What is required in order to found liability is something which is exceptional in nature.' He set out a twofold issue:[74]

(a) Whether the events concerned were of a nature capable of founding a secondary victim case, ie were they in the necessary sense 'horrifying'; and

(b) Whether the sudden appreciation of that event or those events, ie shock, caused the Claimant's psychiatric illness.

---

70 MLC 1265, [2004] Lloyd's Rep Med 530, CA.
71 [2014] EWHC 4244 (QB).
72 [2015] EWHC 614 (QB), (2015) 144 BMLR 136.
73 [2015] EWCA Civ 588, [2015] PIQR P20.
74 [2015] EWCA Civ 588, [2015] PIQR P20 at [8].

In *Owers v Medway NHS Foundation Trust*,[75] this twofold question was applied as a threshold test, and it was noted it set the bar 'very high'. Mr Owers accompanied his wife to hospital as she was suffering a stroke. However, to his distress and frustration she was discharged without being appropriately investigated or treated, and as a result he had to drive her to another hospital while her condition deteriorated. He would have suffered a depressive illness as a result of his bereavement in any event, but as a result of her missed diagnosis and premature discharge he also suffered from PTSD. Stewart J held that his experience had been 'very distressing' but not 'horrifying' as judged by objective standards and not 'wholly exceptional'. His secondary victim claim therefore failed.

A similar conclusion was reached in *O'Connor v Royal Bournemouth and Christchurch Hospitals NHS Foundation Trust*:[76] the claimant, who was ten at the time, suffered a psychiatric injury as a result of witnessing the premature birth of his younger brother and by visiting his brother in hospital before he died at 11 days old. The judge found that witnessing his brother's birth, seeing him on a ventilator every day, his death and his funeral were all distressing events but they were not shocking.

However, the test from *Ronayne* was applied and found to be satisfied in *Re (A Child) v Calderdale and Huddersfield NHS Foundation Trust*.[77] In that case, a baby was born in a severely ill condition as a result of negligence on the part of clinical staff assisting at her birth. Her grandmother was present for the birth and suffered PTSD as a result of the shock of witnessing her poor condition. The grandmother was awarded damages as a secondary victim. (The baby's mother also suffered a psychiatric injury, and recovered as a primary victim.)

Similarly in the county court case *Farnworth v Wrightington Wigan and Leigh NHS Foundation Trust*,[78] a father who held his baby daughter as she passed away was found to have experienced a shocking event and was able to recover as a secondary victim for his consequent PTSD. Mr Recorder Terence Rigby relied on part of his reasoning that the ICD 10 diagnostic criteria for PTSD describe the condition as arising in response to an event 'of an exceptionally threatening or catastrophic nature which is likely to cause pervasive distress to almost anyone'.

WHAT NEEDS TO BE PROVED?

What, then, does the claimant need to establish to succeed in this sort of claim (assuming s/he cannot show herself to have been a primary victim)?

- In the first place, the psychiatric report must certify clearly that the claimant has suffered an actual psychiatric injury, ie going beyond the normal ambit of a bereavement reaction, grief, fear or distress.
- Next, one has to show that the circumstances were such that nervous shock was foreseeable.
- Next, the claimant needs to satisfy the test of familial proximity, ie to show that nervous shock to this relative or close friend was

---

75   [2015] EWHC 2363 (QB), [2015] Med LR 561.
76   [2018] 7 WLUK 330.
77   [2017] EWHC 824 (QB), [2017] Med LR 390.
78   [2016] 12 WLUK 604.

foreseeable. Note the arbitrary treatment of this requirement by the
House of Lords in the Hillsborough case.

- Next, the claimant needs to satisfy the test of temporal and spatial
proximity, ie show that the claimant was sufficiently close in time
and space to the events that are alleged to have caused the injury.
- Next the report must identify a discrete shocking event (or events)
that constituted a sudden assault upon the nervous system of the
claimant and was responsible wholly or at any rate materially for the
injury. It may be unwise to rely on any protracted period of time as
being the horrifying event unless the sights and sounds during that
period were more or less continuously horrifying, although recent
cases (see above) indicate that the courts are applying a less severe
test in this context.
- The psychiatric report should make it clear that the injury would
probably not have been sustained simply through the loss of the
loved one, ie in the absence of the identified shocking event(s).

How far these stringent conditions can be satisfied in a claim arising
out of medical mismanagement remains unclear. It must depend on the
precise events. If the claimant was present when a shocking emergency or
a shocking deterioration in the patient occurred, or comes to the hospital
and finds the patient in a state that reasonably shocks, or perhaps is
present at an unexpected, and therefore in itself shocking, death, the
claim might well be successful. But if there is a slow process of decline
leading to a death that was not really unexpected at the time, or at any
rate was on the cards, and the death did not involve any particularly
shocking factors beyond the actual dying, the claim may fail. It would
have failed a little while ago, but now, as we have said, a more generous
judicial interpretation of the factors necessary for such a claim to succeed
may prevail. In the PIBA lecture (see above), Lord Phillips said that 'the
aftermath principle is one of considerable elasticity'.[79]

FATAL ACCIDENT AND BEREAVEMENT

On behalf of the deceased himself or herself, that is to say the estate of
the deceased, a claim lies only for funeral expenses. The claim for loss
of expectation of life, which used to be set at a formal figure of about
£1,250, was abolished by the Administration of Justice Act 1982. The
deceased also has no claim for loss of earnings during the lost years,
ie the years when s/he would have earned had s/he been alive. There
may be a small claim for his/her suffering in the interval, if there was
one, between the injury and his/her death. Apart from that, nothing. So
one can see how truer than ever is the common law saying 'It is cheaper

---

79   It is worth noting that the Australian High Court has rejected our control mechanisms.
In *Annetts v Australian Stations Pty Ltd* [2002] HCA 35, a 16-year-old died of exhaustion
alone in the outback when working as a jackaroo. His parents joined the unsuccessful
search for him, finding only his blood-stained hat. Three months later his body was
found. The parents recovered for psychiatric damage sustained over this period. In
Gifford v Strang Patrick Stevedoring Pty Ltd [2003] HCA 33, children who suffered
psychiatric injury on being told of their father's death recovered damages. Now there
is a move afoot to introduce some sort of control mechanism. Some states have already
done this by legislation.

to kill than to maim'. Had s/he been maimed, the deceased could have claimed a substantial sum for pain and suffering and loss of amenity, all lost earnings and the cost of all necessary care for the rest of his/her life.

The tortfeasor, or his insurance company, will not, however, escape scot-free if the deceased had dependants (by virtue of the Fatal Accidents Act 1976, as amended). For full details of the fatal accidents legislation, the reader is referred to the standard textbooks. The important points to note here are as follows.

First, by virtue of the amendment made to the Act by the Administration of Justice Act 1982, the spouse or civil partner of the deceased or a parent of an unmarried minor deceased (note: a child cannot claim for loss of a parent) killed by negligence can claim from the tortfeasor (regardless of any dependency) the statutory bereavement award of £12,980.[80] This is, of course, a minimal amount and is no sort of compensation for the loss of a loved one. But it has to be remembered that at common law, the general rule is that no person has a financial or indeed a legal interest in the life of another person, so that no duty of care is owed by A to B not to kill B's relative (or employee, for that matter) by negligence. So the statutory award represents a legislative exception to the common law rule in a context where no duty of care was owed to the claimant. The 'aftermath' principle represents, as we have seen, another limited exception to the rule.

Second, the general effect of the long-standing and important statutory exception to the common law rule effected by the fatal accidents legislation is that those who were or had an expectation of being financially supported by the deceased may claim their loss from the tortfeasor over the whole of the period during which they could have expected to be supported by him. Again, for the details of this legislation, the reader is referred to the standard textbooks.

In *Eileen Corr (administratrix of the estate of Thomas Corr, deceased) v IBC Vehicles Ltd*,[81] the appellant (C) appealed against the decision that she was not entitled to damages following the suicide of her husband (D) in a claim against his employer (V). D had been badly injured in a factory accident that V admitted had been caused by its negligence or breach of statutory duty. D subsequently suffered post-traumatic stress disorder and was later treated in hospital for depression. Some six years after the accident he committed suicide. C brought a claim against V on behalf of his estate and under the Fatal Accidents Act 1976. The judge held that V had been in breach of its duty of care but that that duty did not extend to a duty to take care to prevent D's suicide and that his suicide was not reasonably foreseeable. C contended that the only requirement was the foreseeability of some injury and that depression and consequent suicide lay within the scope of the employer's duty. V contended that the duty did not extend to a duty to protect D from self-harm and that the suicide broke the chain of causation between

---

80 A deceased child must have died, not merely sustained the lethal injury, before their 18th birthday for the parents' entitlement to arise (*Doleman v Deakin* (1990) Times, 30 January, CA). Following the decision in *Smith v Lancashire Teaching Hospitals NHS Foundation Trust* [2017] EWCA Civ 1916, cohabiting couples of over two years may also benefit from this provision in order to avoid discriminatory treatment contrary to Art 14 of the European Convention on Human Rights.

81 [2006] EWCA Civ 331.

the negligence and its consequences. It was held (1) On the evidence D's suicide did not break the chain of causation between V's negligence and the consequences of the suicide, *Holdlen Pty Ltd v Walsh* considered.[82] (2) C did not need to establish that at the time of the accident D's suicide was reasonably foreseeable as a kind of damage separate from psychiatric and personal injury. Responsibility for the effects of suicide depended on whether it flowed from a condition for which, by reference to appropriate foreseeability criteria, the defendant was responsible. In the instant case C founded her claim on depression, which was admitted to have been a foreseeable consequence of V's negligence, and the uncontroverted evidence was that suicide was a not uncommon consequence of severe depression. The compensatable consequences of the depression included D's eventual suicide.

DEATH OF AN INFANT

It is not easy to know how to assess damages for a stillbirth or a miscarriage. They will, of course, vary according to the time at which the miscarriage takes place and according to the degree of nervous shock (ie actual psychiatric injury) suffered by the mother. But there is little in the way of precedent.

One must first bear in mind that mental trauma unaccompanied by physical injury will not found a claim in negligence unless the mental trauma amounts to actual psychiatric damage (to be proved by a medical report). It should be possible in most cases of miscarriage or stillbirth to identify a physical injury, eg the pain of the abortion or the prolongation of labour beyond the appropriate point.[83] It may well be that damaging the child *en ventre*[84] constitutes in itself a physical injury to the mother.

In *Yah v Medway NHS Foundation Trust*,[85] Whipple J held that in a negligent birth case, the mother will be a primary victim and therefore the *Alcock* control mechanisms do not apply and there is no need to prove that a psychiatric injury is caused by shock. In that case, the mother's psychiatric injury was caused by witnessing her baby in a poor condition after the birth (she thankfully survived).

For an early miscarriage, up to a few weeks, say, the award is likely to be about £2,500 – of course, if any sequelae are proved, eg substantive psychiatric injury, or difficulty or impossibility of conception, gestation or parturition in the future, damages will be substantially increased. The estimate above applies to a miscarriage that leaves no substantive sequelae.

After the early days, the award will increase as the pregnancy advances until you have the stillbirth. The real question on assessing for a stillbirth (again, assume no substantive nervous shock, only the normal sorrow, distress and disappointment, with some identifiable physical injury on

---

82   (2000) 19 NSWCCR 629.
83   In some other contexts, it will be essential to prove nervous shock, eg where cancer is negligently diagnosed and, although the patient does not accept treatment and is therefore not physically harmed by the misdiagnosis, they suffer very great anxiety for a period of time until the diagnosis is corrected.
84   The medics prefer us to say 'in utero'.
85   [2018] EWHC 2964 (QB).

which to hang that) is whether one takes the bereavement award as a guide. However, as explained above, that is an award under the fatal accident legislation and presupposes no common law duty of care owed to the relative (the spouse or parent). So it can be viewed as a bonus added by the legislation. In the case of the stillbirth, there is of course a duty of care owed to the mother. Nevertheless, the old principle of the common law that no person has an interest in the life of another means that traditional learning would say that the mother cannot be compensated for the death of her child as such (apart from the bereavement award, which presumably cannot apply where the child is not born alive and so is never a 'person' within the meaning of the legislation).

Cases

There are a few reported cases on damages for stillbirth. In Bagley *v North Herts Health Authority*,[86] Simon Brown J acknowledged that damages could not be awarded to the mother for grief and distress as such (Lord Wilberforce had made that clear in *McLoughlin v O'Brian* (above)) or for loss of society, or for the statutory bereavement award, but he found other means of compensating her. He awarded damages for loss of satisfaction in bringing the pregnancy to a successful end, for disappointment at the shattering of her plans for a family and for being deprived of the joy of bringing up an ordinary healthy child, and he said that those damages would amount to not less than the statutory sum. In fact, the mother received some £18,000, but a lot of that was for other heads of claim such as actual physical sequelae (she suffered a substantial nervous illness as a result). Counsel in the case has said that one could probably think in terms of about £6,000 for the actual stillbirth. In *(1) CS (2) GS v Kingston Hospital NHS Trust*[87] (Lawtel) a sum of £5,000 was agreed for this head of loss. Following that case, the same figure of £5,000 was agreed for loss of satisfaction in *MD v Nottingham University Hospitals NHS Trust*[88] .

In *Kralj v McGrath and St Theresa's Hospital*,[89] where £10,000 general damages were awarded after a horrendous and agonising piece of obstetric mismanagement had caused the stillbirth of one of a pair of twins, Woolf J said that not only was the mother entitled to damages for shock at what had happened, but, if her injury was aggravated by the grief she was suffering, that could be reflected in the award. Having stated that it would be wholly inappropriate to introduce into the medical context the concept of aggravated damages, the judge awarded compensation also for the financial loss that would arise if the parents went on to implement their desire for a larger family; if they decided not to, then that award would be appropriate nevertheless to cover disappointment over the loss of their objective; £10,000 was awarded for pain and suffering, and £18,000 for loss of the mother's earnings. It is not possible to know how much of the total award was for the stillbirth pure and simple (if one may use that expression) – indeed it is probable that the judge did not assess that aspect separately in his own mind.

---

86   [1986] NLJ Rep 1014.
87   (2012, unreported).
88   (2013, unreported) (Lawtel).
89   [1986] 1 All ER 54.

In *Grieve v Salford Health Authority*,[90] Rose J awarded a woman with a pre-existing vulnerable personality £12,500 in respect of initial prolongation of labour, some additional pain, loss of her stillborn child and of the satisfaction of a successful conclusion to the pregnancy, plus psychological damage likely to endure for some four years from the date of the stillbirth. This could possibly be seen as about £6,000 for the stillbirth in itself and about £6,000 for the four-year nervous illness.

In *Kerby v Redbridge Health Authority*,[91] a twin was fatally injured before birth in 1988 by admitted negligence, and survived only three days. Ognall J said, with reference to the dicta in *Bagley* (above), that damages for 'dashed hopes' would duplicate the bereavement award, but he awarded, nevertheless, in addition to the bereavement award, £10,000 for the Caesarean section and consequent scar, a depressive illness of moderate severity lasting some six months, and the constant reminder of what might have been by the presence of the surviving twin.

If the matter were put to the test, it is likely that a court would award close to the bereavement award for a stillbirth pure and simple. The approach in some settlements has been to include an amount equivalent to the statutory bereavement award. One line of argument that might suggest that damages should not greatly exceed the bereavement award is as follows: what if the child dies shortly after birth, let us say through poor neonatal care? How does one justify any award other than the bereavement award in that case? In which event, why should the situation be radically different if the child died just before birth? No duty of care is owed by the paediatricians to the mother in respect of their care of the neonate. Probably the only way of increasing the award substantively beyond the bereavement level in such a context is to show that the mother suffered substantial nervous shock – ie an actual psychiatric injury – that comes within the 'aftermath' principle of *McLoughlin v O'Brian* (above).

---

90   [1991] 2 Med LR 295.
91   [1993] 4 Med LR 178.

Chapter 15

Economic loss

William Latimer-Sayer

INTRODUCTION

Mere economic loss, ie economic loss that is not consequent upon physical damage to person or property or the threat of it, is as a general rule not recoverable in tort, as opposed to contract. It is, however, recoverable when it arises from careless statements, provided there is a duty in the circumstances on the person making the statement to take care; that duty will arise in the context of a fiduciary relationship. Recent years have seen the formulation by the courts that recovery is also permitted where there is a sufficient relationship of proximity between the parties to permit the court to infer that the defendant voluntarily assumed a duty of care in respect of the alleged negligent activity; but it is hard to know in any particular case whether or not the court will discern such a relationship. Apart from these contexts, a line will be drawn by the court as a matter of policy to prevent recovery for economic loss that does not flow from, ie is not consequent upon, some physical damage or the threat of it.

There has never been any problem in compensating for financial loss where it accompanies injury to person or property. If your car is damaged, you can hire another pending repair; if you are injured, you can recover lost earnings. Nor has there been any difficulty in permitting recovery for economic loss consequent upon breach of contract. But, as regards liability in tort, carelessness, whether in act or word, which gives rise to foreseeable economic loss only is a different matter. 'The reluctance to grant a remedy for the careless invasion of financial or pecuniary interests is long-standing, deep-rooted and not unreasonable' (*per* Professor Heuston). The court might declare that there is no duty of care, as where a large supermarket sets up next door to a small competitor putting the latter out of business, or that the damage is too remote, or that public policy draws the line at recovery in respect of the loss claimed, or simply that mere economic loss is not recoverable.

As with so many aspects of the law of negligence, the question of recovering economic loss is one of policy. Whenever the courts draw a line to mark out the bounds of 'duty', they do it as a matter of policy so as to limit the responsibility of the defendant. Whenever the courts set bounds to the 'damages' recoverable – saying that they are, or are not, too remote – they do it as a matter of policy so as to limit the liability of the defendants (*per* Lord Denning MR in *Spartan Steel and Alloys Ltd v Martin & Co (Contractors) Ltd*[1]).

The 'electricity' cases

Where economic loss is consequent upon physical injury, it is usually recoverable. Thus, in *SCM (United Kingdom) Ltd v W J Whittall & Son Ltd*,[2] defendants who negligently cut off the electricity supply to the claimants' factory were held liable by the Court of Appeal for the loss of profit which resulted from the solidifying in the furnaces of molten metals, because it stemmed from the damage to furnace and metal, but not for further economic loss which was said to be too remote. Lord Denning said that recovery for mere economic loss was not usually permitted by the law, on the ground of public policy, rather than by the operation of any logical principle; and Winn LJ said that, apart from the special case of liability for negligently uttered false statements, there was no liability for negligent unintentional infliction of any form of economic loss which was not itself consequential upon foreseeable physical injury or damage to property.

In the similar *Spartan Steels* case (above), the defendants negligently damaged the electric cable supplying the claimants' factory, who had therefore to pour molten metal out of their furnaces, for otherwise it would have solidified and damaged the furnaces. They lost part of the value of the metal and their profit on its resale. In addition, they claimed for loss of profit on the four further melts they could have performed in the time the power was off. Though they succeeded at first instance, the Court of Appeal would not permit recovery in respect of the four melts, on the basis that whereas loss of profit on the metal that was poured out was consequential on the physical damage to that metal and the risk of damage to the furnaces, loss of profit on the four hypothetical melts was mere economic damage not consequent upon the physical damage or the risk of physical damage. Lord Denning said that the more he thought about the subject of recovery for economic loss, the more difficult he found it to put each case into its proper pigeonhole:[3]

> Sometimes I say: 'There was no duty.' In others I say: 'The damage was too remote.' So much so that I think the time has come to discard those tests which have proved so elusive. It seems to me better to consider the particular relationship in hand, and see whether or not, as a matter of policy, economic loss should be recoverable or not.

In truth, as Edmund Davies LJ pointed out in a strong dissenting judgment, there was no logical distinction between the two losses. It must simply be seen as a matter of policy that the court insisted on drawing a line to limit the defendants' liability.[4]

---

1   [1973] QB 27, CA at 36.
2   [1971] 1 QB 337.
3   [1973] QB 27, CA at 37.
4   Economic loss can be recovered where it is claimed as part of a claim which originates in a claim for physical damage: *SCM (United Kingdom) Ltd v W J Whittall & Son Ltd* [1971] 1 QB 337; *Spartan Steel and Alloys Ltd v Martin & Co (Contractors) Ltd* [1973] QB 27, CA; *Muirhead v Industrial Tank Specialities* [1986] QB 507; *Ehmler v Hall* [1993] 1 EGLR 137, CA.

Development

For a time, beginning with the decision of the House of Lords in *Anns v Merton London Borough Council*,[5] it seemed that economic loss which was foreseeable should be recoverable, as any other loss, unless there were policy considerations in the particular case militating against such recovery. This general formulation was later whittled down by the courts; the context in which it was proposed, the liability of local authority inspectors for certifying defective foundations, was itself reduced to the situation where physical damage was created or threatened; and then the very decision itself, imposing liability for economic loss in these circumstances, was declared misconceived because the court in 1978 had failed to recognise that the damage for which it was permitting compensation was mere economic loss and to do that was to introduce a wholly new and unsuitable extension to the law (see further below on this).

In *Junior* Books *v Veitchi*,[6] the House of Lords held that, assuming the facts pleaded were true, subcontractors who laid a defective floor would be liable to the claimant occupiers of the building for the cost of repair and certain financial loss flowing therefrom. This was despite the fact that there was neither a contractual nexus between the parties nor any physical damage or threat of it to the building. It was said that where there was a sufficient relationship of proximity between the parties, the duty of care extended to the duty not to inflict carelessly economic loss (Lord Roskill said that the defendants, as subcontractors, were in almost as close a commercial relationship with the plaintiff as it was possible to envisage, short of privity of contract).

Lord Brandon dissented, saying that to impose liability would be to create obligations appropriate only to a contractual relationship, and that the authorities made it clear that in the absence of physical damage or the threat of it mere economic loss was not recoverable.

Retrenchment

Recovery for mere economic loss was denied in shipping contexts – by the Court of Appeal in *Leigh and Sillavan Ltd v Aliakmon Shipping Co*,[7] where buyers sued shipowners in contract and tort for damage to goods caused by bad stowage; and by the House of Lords in *Candlewood Navigation Corpn v Mitsui OSK Lines Ltd*,[8] involving a time charterer's claim for financial loss. In *Muirhead v Industrial Tank Specialities*,[9] the Court of Appeal rejected a claim for mere economic loss by the user against the manufacturer of lobster tanks. It was said that there was not a sufficiently close relationship between the two for such a duty to arise; there had to be such a very close proximity of relationship between the parties and reliance by the claimant on the defendant that the defendant

---

5   [1978] AC 728.
6   [1983] 1 AC 520.
7   [1985] QB 350.
8   [1986] AC 1.
9   [1986] QB 507.

was to be taken voluntarily to have assumed direct responsibility to the claimant.[10]

Then came the highly significant House of Lords' decision in *Caparo Industries plc v Dickman*,[11] where it was held that auditors of a company owed no duty of care not to inflict economic loss on shareholders or potential investors who relied on the audit in deciding whether to invest (further) in the company. The court said that liability for economic loss due to negligent misstatement was confined to cases where the statement or advice had been given to a known recipient for a specific purpose of which the maker was aware, and on which the recipient had relied and on which he had acted to his detriment. As the auditors had no reason to think that their report would go to the claimant, let alone that it would be relied on by them in deciding whether to invest (further) in the company, there was no sufficient proximity between them and the claimants to found a duty of care (see also Chapter 5 for further cases).

The decisions of the House of Lords in July 1990 in *Murphy v Brentwood District Council*,[12] and *Department of the Environment v Thomas Bates & Son*[13] concerned liability for economic loss caused not by misstatement but by negligent conduct. The House of Lords made it clear that, as presently constituted, they shared the disquiet that had been voiced increasingly in the last five years or so about the wholesale extension of the law of negligence, in cases where no physical injury had been sustained, that was inherent in and threatening to develop as a logical outcome from the 1978 decision of the House of Lords (as then constituted) in *Anns v Merton London Borough Council*.[14] In our present context, the point to note is that the court made it clear that there can be no general formula for establishing when mere economic loss is recoverable – one can only look to decided cases and see if one's own case falls more or less within the factual matrix of any case where liability has been imposed.

There is, of course, scope for the court to admit a new situation, for the categories of negligence are never closed, but it would need careful argument and the court would need to be convinced that policy and justice required that liability be imposed. One such example of the court being so convinced is *Spring v Guardian Assurance plc*,[15] where the House of Lords held that an insurance company owed a duty of care to a former representative when providing him or prospective employers with a reference (the breach of duty was by way of careless statement and the damage purely economic). Another is *Welton v North Cornwall District Council*,[16] where the Court of Appeal permitted recovery for economic loss in respect of building works required, quite wrongly, to be done to a restaurant by an incompetent environmental health officer. The court said:

- that the officer had 'assumed a responsibility' to take care in respect of what he said to or required of the restaurant owner; and

---

10   See also *Virgo Steamship Co v Skaarup Shipping Corpn* [1988] 1 Lloyd's Rep 352.
11   [1990] 2 AC 605.
12   [1991] 1 AC 398.
13   [1991] 1 AC 499.
14   [1978] AC 728.
15   [1995] 2 AC 296.
16   [1997] 1 WLR 570.

- that it was fair, just and reasonable, and in accordance with public policy, that a duty of care should be imposed.

In *Hamble Fisheries Ltd v L Gardner & Sons Ltd*,[17] where damages for economic loss occasioned by the failure of marine engines was claimed in tort against the manufacturer (for not warning of that possibility), the Court of Appeal, dismissing the purchaser's appeal, said that the general rule was as set out in the *Murphy* case (above): there was no duty on a manufacturer towards a consumer for economic loss. The pertinent question was whether in a given situation there was a special relationship of proximity on the manufacturer to safeguard the consumer from economic loss. *Contra*, in *Bailey v HSS Alarms*,[18] the Court of Appeal discerned the requisite special relationship between a property owner and a company who provided security services to the property (the two parties not being in direct contractual relationship). The company was held liable to the owner for economic loss when thieves broke in and stole a substantial amount of property.

In *Commissioner of Police of the Metropolis v Lennon*,[19] the claimant police officer had asked for advice from an employee of the Commissioner who had held herself out as familiar with the ins and outs pertaining to the claimant's transfer to a new force, in particular in connection with the preservation of his housing allowance. That advice was wrong and caused the claimant economic loss. The Court of Appeal dismissed the Commissioner's appeal, saying it was irrelevant that the employee was not a professional adviser as she had expressly assumed responsibility for giving the claimant the advice in relation to possible loss of housing allowance. She had led the claimant to believe that he could leave it to her and could rely on her, and had not told him to seek advice elsewhere. No new category of duty situation had been created by the judge. It was well established that liability in tort for pure economic loss could arise from the negligent carrying out of a task undertaken pursuant to an express voluntary assumption of responsibility, given appropriate reliance by the relevant party.

The 'wrongful birth' cases (dealt with in detail in Chapter 12) have usually raised issues about the right to claim for economic loss, and the decisions of the courts have been influenced strongly by policy considerations, of which the case of *McFarlane v Tayside Health Board*[20] is the most egregious example.

COMMENT

In the absence of a special relationship of proximity and/or a voluntary assumption of risk (it is not clear what terminology to use – see eg *Reid v Rush & Tompkins Group*[21]), there is no duty of care not to inflict mere economic loss. It remains very difficult to predict if in a given situation

---

17   [1999] 2 Lloyd's Rep 1.
18   (2000) Times, 20 June.
19   [2004] 1 WLR 2594.
20   MLC 0127, [2000] 2 AC 59, HL.
21   [1990] 1 WLR 212, CA.

the court will or will not discern the requisite special relationship. The position is, of course, clear enough if a product causes *physical* injury, as the ginger beer with the decomposing snail in it taught us many years ago (*Donoghue v Stevenson*[22]).

Junior Books v Veitchi[23] must be seen now as a flash in the pan: if that case recurred today, Lord Brandon's dissenting judgment would be followed – no court is going now to hold that a subcontractor is under a duty of care in his work not to inflict mere economic loss on the building owner with whom he is not in a contractual relationship.[24] That said, the liability of subcontractors for economic loss is still a developing area of jurisprudence and therefore it may be difficult to strike out such a claim.[25]

MEDICAL CONTEXT

Most, but not all, medical negligence actions are in respect of personal injury. This may take the form of physical injury or a recognisable psychiatric disorder.[26] Within the doctor-patient relationship there is normally a sufficient proximity and reliance by the patient on the doctor to give rise to a duty not to inflict mere economic loss, so that, for example, a careless diagnosis that leads to the patient taking time off work will give rise to compensation for lost wages.[27] Where a negligently premature discharge from hospital of an infected child causes his siblings to contract the infection, resulting in financial loss to the parents, a court would probably hold the hospital liable (see on these facts *Evans v Liverpool Corpn*,[28] where the father failed in his action against the hospital, but on the basis that, as the law then, stood the hospital was not liable for the negligence of the discharging physician). Likewise, the Supreme Court has recently held that there is a general duty on receptionists in hospital accident and emergency departments to keep patients informed about likely waiting times; including a duty not to provide misleading information about waiting times.[29] However, this duty was on the facts of the case limited to taking reasonable care not to cause physical injury.

In order to establish liability, it is important that the alleged breach of duty is a 'relevant breach' of duty such that it renders the defendant liable for the state of affairs that arose (see *Brown v Lewisham and North Southwark Health Authority*[30]). In other words, the resulting damage or

---

22 [1932] AC 562.
23 [1983] 1 AC 520.
24 The House of Lords made it clear enough in *D & F Estates v Church Comrs for England* [1989] AC 177 what they thought of the *Junior Books* decision.
25 *Linklaters Business Services v Sir Robert McAlpine* [2010] EWHC 1145 (TCC), 130 Con LR 111, (2010) NPC 61.
26 For the definition of what constitutes an actionable personal injury see further *Grieves v FT Everard & Sons Ltd* [2007] UKHL 39 and *Dryden v Johnson Matthey Plc* [2018] UKSC 18.
27 The time limit for such claims is six years: see *Younger v Dorset Strategic Health Authority* [2006] Lloyd's Rep Med 489.
28 [1906] 1 KB 160.
29 *Darnley v Croydon Health Services NHS Trust* [2018] UKSC 50. See also *Kent v Griffiths No 3* [2007] QB 36 where the Court of Appeal held that the ambulance service could owe a duty of care to a member of the public on whose behalf a 999 call had been made if the ambulance failed to arrive within a reasonable time through negligence.
30 [1999] Lloyd's Rep Med 110.

type of damage must have been foreseeable from the alleged breach of duty. For example, in the case of *Thompson v Bradford*,[31] the defendant GP was held not to be liable for failing to give advice as to whether he should postpone a polio vaccination due to an unusual abscess on the claimant's buttock. A competent GP should have provided information to the claimant's parents that the abscess was unusual and might require surgery, and that it might be uncomfortable to undergo such surgery a short time after the vaccination. However, it was common ground that the GP could not have foreseen the increased risk in the claimant contracting polio. Therefore the breach of duty was not a relevant breach of duty and the Court of Appeal overturned the finding of liability against the GP.

Claims for the cost of upkeep of an unplanned child may be for economic loss only, ie where there is no claim made for any personal injury (see Chapter 12, where it is explained that, although such claims are no longer possible in the case of a healthy child, they are permitted where the unplanned child is born with a disability).

Outside the special doctor-patient relationship, the courts have generally been reluctant to impose liability for pure economic loss and recent examples of failed cases include:

* A local authority that provided care to a person injured by the negligence of an NHS trust was not able to recover the cost of care from the trust in negligence.[32]
* A local authority that had organised a horse fair was not liable to a member of the public who was seriously injured whilst at the fair for failing to take out public liability insurance.[33]
* An orthopaedic surgeon providing treatment to a football player under the terms of a medical insurance policy owed no duty of care in tort in respect of any foreseeable economic loss caused to the football club resulting from his negligent treatment.[34]
* Health authorities do not owe a duty of care in tort to proprietors of nursing homes when making applications without notice for cancellation of their registration under the Registered Homes Act 1984.[35]
* A local authority was not liable for failing to make an application for compensation to the Criminal Injuries Compensation Board in relation to a child in their care.[36]
* A bookmaker was not liable for failing to implement a telephone betting exclusion agreement preventing a compulsive gambler from continuing to place bets.[37]
* A hospital was held not to owe a non-delegable duty of care in respect of genetic testing of a tissue sample which was sent to be cultured by a reputable independent cytogenetics laboratory.[38]

---

31 [2005] EWCA Civ 1439.
32 *Islington LBC v University College London Hospital NHS Trust* [2005] EWCA Civ 556.
33 *Glaister v Appleby-in-Westmorland Town Council* [2009] EWCA Civ 1325.
34 *West Bromwich Albion Football Club Ltd v Medhat El-Safty* [2006] EWCA Civ 1299.
35 *Ashok Jain v Trent Strategic Health Authority* [2009] 1 AC 853.
36 *VL v Oxfordshire CC* [2010] EWHC 2091 (QB).
37 *Calvert v William Hill Credit Ltd* [2008] EWCA Civ 1427.
38 *Farraj v King's Healthcare NHS Trust* [2009] EWCA Civ 1203.

- A mother was held not to owe her son a duty of care to take reasonable steps to keep him safe from injury from the hands of his father, where the discharge of the duty would have involved the break-up of the family.[39]
- The Police Commissioner does not owe a duty of care to protect police officers from economic or reputational harm when conducting litigation founded on alleged vicarious liability for their actions because it would not be fair, just or reasonable to impose such a duty, and such a duty would be inconsistent with the Commissioner's freedom to act in accordance with her public duty.[40]

---

39   *XA v YA* [2010] EWHC 1983 (QB).
40   *Rod James-Bowen v Commissioner of Police of the Metropolis* [2018] UKSC 40.

Chapter 16

Product liability in a medical context

Neil Block QC, Romilly Cummerson, Emma Corkill

INTRODUCTION

In an age of rapid technological advancement, the need to balance the rights of the consumer against both the rights of the producer and the drive to innovate, presents a complex and evolving challenge for the law. This chapter considers how product liability law seeks to strike that balance in the context of claims involving medical products. For these purposes the definition of 'product' covers a vast array of medical items including drugs, devices, implants,[1] and even organic materials such as organs,[2] tissue, and blood products.[3] The claims involved may relate to manufacturing defects within the products themselves or defects that arise out of the presentation or marketing of the products and the adequacy of the information provided to the consumer. The subject matter is sufficiently broad to justify a book in its own right. Consequently, this chapter is, of necessity, restricted to providing an overview of product liability law, with a particular focus on the Consumer Protection Act 1987 (CPA 1987), the legislation at the centre of most recent medical product liability authorities, and the 2018 case of *Gee v Depuy*.[4] Chapter 2 of the judgment of Mrs Justice Andrews in *Gee v Depuy*, which sets out the legal framework for the claim, is recommended reading for all those who wish to gain a clearer understanding of the workings of, and policy behind, the CPA 1987. It is discussed in detail below.

The legal framework governing product liability in the medical context in the UK began as a response to the Thalidomide-related birth defects which came to light in the early 1960s. Across Europe, this led legislative

---

1   *Anthony Wilkes v Depuy International Ltd* [2016] EWHC 3096 and *Colin Gee v Depuy International Ltd sub nom In the Matter of Depuy Pinnacle Metal on Metal Hip Litigation* [2018] EWHC 1208 (QB).
2   For further discussion in relation to organs, see Judith M Laing, Jean V McHale (eds) *Principles of Medical Law* (4th edn, 2017), Ch 18 and Richard Goldberg, *Medicinal product liability and regulation*, Ch 9.
3   *A v The National Blood Authority* [2001] 3 All ER 289.
4   *Colin Gee v Depuy International Ltd sub nom In the Matter of Depuy Pinnacle Metal on Metal Hip Litigation* [2018] EWHC 1208 (QB).

branches of government to recognise, and respond to, a need to protect the medical consumer. In the UK[5] this resulted in the passing of the Medicines Act 1968, which provided the first comprehensive system of licensing for those manufacturing or dealing in medicines, both human and veterinary.[6] The Medicines Act 1968 was the first in a long line of statutes and statutory instruments governing the manufacture and supply of medical products, culminating in the Human Medicines Regulations 2012, SI 2012/1916, which consolidated many of the earlier statutes and regulations.[7] Medical devices are regulated separately, in accordance with the Medical Devices Regulations 2002, SI 2002/618. Following the Poly Implant Prostheses (PIP) breast implant scandal in 2012, which highlighted deficiencies with regard to the obligations and liabilities of notified bodies[8] under the Medical Devices Directive,[9] in May 2017 the European Commission published a proposal for a new regulation on medical devices, which will impose greater obligations on notified bodies.[10] The new regulation has a three year transition period, meaning that the requirements will apply in full from May 2020.

The Product Liability Directive 1985[11] represented the EU response to the challenges posed by product liability in a rapidly developing market. It was implemented into domestic law by the CPA 1987 and remains at the centre of product liability litigation, not least because its strict liability regime makes it an attractive option for those wishing to bring a claim. More recently, contractual product liability has been addressed by the Consumer Rights Act 2015 (CRA 2015), which consolidated and amended existing legislation including the Sale of Goods Act 1979, the Supply of Goods and Services Act 1982 and the Unfair Terms in Consumer Contracts Regulations 1999.[12]

Civil claims for product liability in the medical context can be brought in tort and/or contract, including under the CRA 2015 and CPA 1987. The different causes of action each have their own approach to the question of product liability. Under the contractual regime of the CRA 2015, the focus is on the condition of the product, with the court being asked to consider whether or not it is fit for purpose or of satisfactory quality. Tortious claims are concerned with the acts or omissions of the person producing or selling the product and whether reasonable care has been

---

5   The legislation being enacted in England and Wales, Scotland and Northern Ireland.
6   The regulation of veterinary medicine was subsequently hived off by virtue of the Veterinary Medicine Regulations 2005, SI 2005/2745.
7   It should be noted that vaccinations have their own legislation: Vaccine Damage Payments Act 1979 and subsequent Vaccine Damage Payments Act 1979 Statutory Sum Orders (SI 1991/939; SI 1998/1587; SI 2000/1983; and 2007/1931); Vaccine Damage Payments (Specified Disease) Orders (SI 2016/454; SI 2015/47; SI 2009/2516; SI 2008/2103; SI 2006/2066; SI 2001/1652; SI 1995/1164; and 1990/623); and Vaccine Damage Payments (Specified Disease) (Revocation and Savings) Order 2010, SI 2010/1988.
8   Bodies authorised in accordance with Part V of the Medical Devices Directives to carry out tasks of a notified body or the importing party under the Medical Devices Directives or the Mutual Recognition Agreements in respect of a conformity assessment procedure.
9   Council Directive 93/42/EEC of 14 June 1993 concerning medical devices.
10   Regulation (EU) 2017/745 of 5 April 2017 on medical devices.
11   Council Directive 85/374/EEC of 25 July 1985 on the approximation of the laws, regulations and administrative provisions of the member states concerning liability for defective products.
12   SI 1999/2083.

taken to avoid or minimise risk of injury to the consumer. As noted above, the CPA 1987 provides a strict liability regime,[13] in which the focus is on the safety of the product, irrespective of the steps taken to ensure that safety.

HISTORY OF MEDICAL PRODUCT LIABILITY CLAIMS

Commencing with the thalidomide litigation of the 1960s, a number of high profile medical product liability group actions have been brought in the courts of England and Wales, including in respect of pregnancy tests,[14] the contrast dye Myodil,[15] and the MMR vaccine[16]. In more recent years there have been claims in respect of benzodiazepines,[17] Seroxat, and Epilim[18] (an anticonvulsant drug alleged to have caused vision and birth defects in children), PIP breast implants and metal-on-metal hip replacements.[19]

Medical product liability claims are often complex and expensive. Relatively few have proceeded to a final judgment, with the result that there is a paucity of legal authority. A significant proportion of medical product liability claims are brought as group actions, with all the attendant risks of complex multi-party litigation. Claims made in respect of medical products have the added difficulty of often involving claimants with a wide variety of symptoms and pre-existing conditions, making an individual approach to causation necessary, which adds to the length and complexity of proceedings, with the associated high cost.

Obtaining and retaining funding through to trial has presented a particular difficulty for claimants in this area. Historically, the Legal Aid Board[20] was prepared to fund multi-party actions that met the Legal Aid Board eligibility criteria, which involved means-testing for the proposed claimants, a need to establish reasonable prospects of success and a costs/benefit analysis that weighed the costs of proceeding against the damages likely to be recovered. Eligibility for funding was kept under review throughout the litigation, with the result that even if the initial hurdle of obtaining funding to mount a claim was successfully surmounted, that funding could be withdrawn at any stage. One of the more high profile examples of this difficulty involved the group litigation concerning the MMR vaccine in the 1990s.[21] The Legal Aid Board initially provided funding to commence a group action against the manufacturers of the MMR vaccine in respect of physical and mental disorders alleged to have been caused by the vaccine. However, the litigation collapsed when the

---

13 Subject to statutory defences set out in the CPA 1987, s 4.
14 'Is this the forgotten Thalidomide?' (2018) The Telegraph, 29 August.
15 'Medical dye row is settled for pounds 7m', (1995) The Independent, 1 August.
16 *Sayers v Smith Kline Beecham Plc* [2007] EWHC 1346 (QB) (also known as MMR/MR Vaccine Litigation).
17 *AB v John Wyeth & Brother Ltd (No 2)* [1994] 5 Med LR 149.
18 *Multiple Claimants v Sanifo-Synthelabo Ltd* [2007] EWHC 1860 (QB).
19 *Colin Gee v Depuy International Ltd sub nom In the Matter of Depuy Pinnacle Metal on Metal Hip Litigation* [2018] EWHC 1208 (QB).
20 Forerunner to the Legal Services Commission.
21 For a detailed discussion on the MMR litigation, see Richard Goldberg, *Medicinal Product Liability and Regulation*, Ch 6 and Ch1 for background on legal aid funding in medical product cases.

research upon which the claim was largely based was widely discredited and the Legal Aid Board withdrew funding in 2003, seven months before the trial was due to commence. It has been estimated that the cost to the Legal Aid Board of the failed litigation was in the region of £15 million.[22]

Funding problems also put an end to claims made against the prescribers of benzodiazepines in the 1990s.[23] A subsequent attempt to revive the litigation also resulted in a strike out when the Legal Aid Board concluded that, on a cost to potential benefit analysis, the claims did not meet the threshold to justify further funding.[24]

In more recent years, the Paroxetine/Seroxat litigation[25] has faced similar funding difficulties. This group action was due to go to trial in 2010, but was stayed when Legal Aid funding was withdrawn on the basis that the claims had insufficient prospects of success.[26] Six years later the claim was revived when the Queen's Bench Division lifted the stay and gave directions for continuing the claim.[27] However, towards the end of 2017 Mr Justice Foskett ordered the claimants' litigation funder to give security for the defendant's costs up to trial of £1.75 million.[28] The matter came to trial in April 2019. However, an issue arose in the course of the claimant's opening submissions with regard to the scope of the claimant's pleaded case on defect. The trial was, therefore, adjourned pending resolution of this issue. On 9 May 2019 Mrs Justice Lambert resolved the preliminary issue in favour of the defendant.[29] At the time of writing an appeal against the decision of Mrs Justice Lambert is outstanding. It remains to be seen whether the claimants' funding arrangements will be sufficient to see the action through to an effective trial.

One of the last publicly funded medical product group actions concerned a claim against the producers of Epilim,[30] an anticonvulsant alleged to have caused vision and birth defects when used during pregnancy. The litigation was complex and there were over one hundred claimants. Legal Aid funding was obtained in 2005. The funding was temporarily withdrawn in 2006, but subsequently reinstated, only to be withdrawn again in late 2010, just weeks before trial, on grounds of insufficient prospects of success, at an estimated cost to the public purse of over £3 million.[31]

---

22   The Guardian (26 June 2014).
23   *AB v John Wyeth & Brother Ltd (No 4)* [1994] PIOR P109 – a group action against the prescribers of benzodiazepine drugs diazepam and lorazepam was struck out for abuse of process on the basis that the irrecoverable costs likely to be incurred by the prescribers were out of all proportion to any benefit that the claimants would obtain if successful. It should, however, be noted that claims against the manufacturers and marketers of the drugs were allowed to continue at that stage.
24   *AB v John Wyeth & Brother Ltd (No 5)* [1996] 7 Med LR 267. In striking out the claims, the court criticised the Steering Committee for the claimants and the Legal Aid Board for the inordinate and inexcusable delay caused by a failure to filter out the weaker cases at the commencement of the litigation.
25   Seroxat Group Litigation Order No 68 (29 October 2008).
26   This followed a review of the claims undertaken after service of the joint statements of the numerous experts involved in the litigation.
27   *Bailey v GlaxoSmithKline (UK) Ltd* [2016] EWHC 178 (QB).
28   *Bailey v GlaxoSmithKline UK Ltd* [2017] EWHC 3195 (QB).
29   *Sandra Bailey v Glaxosmithkline UK Ltd* [2019] EWHC 1167 (QB).
30   *Multiple Claimants v Sanifo-Synthelabo Ltd* [2007] EWHC 1860 (QB), also known as the *Fetal* Anticonvulsant Litigation.
31   'The *Epilim* case shows the flaws in the legal aid regime', (2010) The Guardian, 29 November.

Legal Aid ceased to be available for most clinical negligence claims in April 2013. The intention of the Government at that time was that it would be replaced by alternative funding arrangements in the form of Conditional Fee Agreements ('CFAs'). In practice, however, with a few notable exceptions,[32] solicitors have been understandably reluctant to enter into CFAs in respect of high-risk, complex, multi-party litigation of this nature.

Nevertheless, large-scale medical product claims have not ceased altogether. In July 2017 city law firm Wedlake Bell announced that it was building a large group litigation in conjunction with action group Sling the Mesh, in respect of injuries alleged to have been caused by transvaginal surgical mesh implants. It is intended that the claim will be issued against the manufacturers of the mesh, Johnson & Johnson.[33] When first reported, it was anticipated that that the group litigation could involve over four hundred claimants.[34] However, more recent reported estimates suggest that up to two thousand potential claimants are involved.[35] In light of the revelation that 75,000 trans-vaginal tape ('TVT') implants were fitted by the NHS between 2006 and 2016 and that more than 4,900 procedures were carried out to remove TVT implants during the same period, it seems likely that the number of potential claimants will continue to rise.

CONSUMER PROTECTION ACT 1987

The European Council first proposed a Directive to deal with product liability in 1976, but it was not until 1985 that agreement was reached on an appropriate regime. After considering a number of options, including a system of absolute liability,[36] on 25 July 1985 the Council adopted Council Directive 85/374/EEC ('the Product Liability Directive') which provided a system of no-fault liability in respect of defective products, the safety of which falls below the standard that people are generally entitled to expect, subject only to limited defences.

Domestic legislation in the form of the CPA 1987 was enacted to implement the Directive. In accordance with the Directive, Part I of the CPA 1987 provides for strict liability. The CPA 1987, s 1(1) reinforces the obligation on domestic courts to interpret domestic legislation in so far as is possible in the light of the wording and purpose of the Directive, to achieve the result intended by the Directive.

As noted by Mrs Justice Andrews in the recent case of *Gee v Depuy International Ltd*,[37] although there are numerous references to consumer

---

32 Ultamet Pinnacle litigation – *Anthony Wilkes v Depuy International Ltd* [2016] EWHC 3096 and *Colin Gee v Depuy International Ltd sub nom In the Matter of Depuy Pinnacle Metal on Metal Hip Litigation* [2018] EWHC 1208 (QB).
33 (2017) Times, The Brief, 27 July.
34 Litigation Futures (9 November 2017).
35 Sky News 18 July 2017, as reported in The Guardian (15 August 2017) *'Scandal' of Mesh Removal Rates Revealed by NHS Records*.
36 For a detailed history of the Directive and the CPA 1987 see CJ Miller, RS Goldberg, *Product Liability* (2nd edn), Pt II.
37 *Anthony Wilkes v Depuy International Ltd* [2016] EWHC 3096 and *Colin Gee v Depuy International Ltd sub nom In the Matter of Depuy Pinnacle Metal on Metal Hip Litigation* [2018] EWHC 1208 (QB).

protection in the recitals to the Directive, the first justification for the Directive is an economic one, namely the need to achieve harmonisation of product liability laws across the member states to prevent distortions in the market:

> A core objective of the Directive, reflected in its first recital, was to achieve total harmonisation of strict product liability throughout the EU, irrespective of the identity of the product. Variations in the burdens imposed on producers by different national conditions for product liability were thought to create unacceptable distortions in competition and impediments to the free movement of goods within the common market. Therefore, the first justification given for the Directive is an economic one.[38]

The central importance of harmonisation of product liability laws has been highlighted by the Court of Justice of the European Union in a number of cases in which the court has rejected the suggestion that domestic legislatures retain the power to provide consumers with a higher level of protection against damage caused by defective products than that provided by the Directive.[39]

In spite of the name given to the domestic legislation that implemented the Directive, consumer protection is not the overriding objective of the Directive. As Mrs Justice Andrews noted, several recitals to the Directive are concerned with the need to balance the needs of consumers and producers and other policy considerations, including a desire to achieve a fair apportionment of the risks associated with innovation. She concluded that:

> ... this indicates that, whilst the effective protection of consumers is a key objective of the Directive, it is not the main or overriding objective. It has equal status with the other objectives.[40]

Although detailed rules of evidence and proof are left to the domestic courts, national rules must not undermine the effectiveness of the system provided for in the Directive. The rights of consumers and producers as set out in the Directive must be effectively implemented.

Who can claim?

Any person who has sustained damage with a value in excess of £275[41] as a result of a defective product can make a claim under the CPA 1987. It is not necessary for the injured claimant to have been the purchaser of the product. This is of particular importance in claims concerning medical products when the injured party is unlikely to have purchased the product in question directly from the producer.

Damage giving rise to liability is defined by the CPA 1987, s 5(1) as 'death or personal injury or any loss of or damage to any property (including land)'. Pure economic loss is excluded. Further, no claim can be made for the loss of, or damage to, the defective product itself or for the

---

38   Ibid n 19, para 69.
39   *Commission v France* [2002] ECR 1-3827, *Commission v Greece* [2002] ECR 1-3879 and *Gonzalez Sanchez v Medicina Asturiana SA* [2002] ECR 1-3901 referenced by Mrs Justice Andrews in [76] of her judgment in *Gee v Depuy.*
40   Ibid n 19 para 73.
41   CPA 1987, s 5(4).

loss of, or damage to, the whole or part of any product supplied with the defective product or comprised in the defective product.[42] The CPA 1987 is concerned with the protection of the consumer; consequently, claims for damage to or loss of business property are excluded from the Act by virtue of s 5(3).

Identifying the appropriate defendant

The CPA 1987, s 2(2) identifies the categories of person against whom a claim can be made under the Act, namely:

* the producer of the product;
* any person who has held himself out as the producer of the product, whether by putting his name on the product or using a trademark or other distinguishing mark;
* any person who imported the product into a member state from a place outside the member states in the course of business and to supply it to another.

A 'producer' of a product is defined by the CPA 1987, s 1(2) as:

(a) the person who manufactured it;
(b) in the case of a substance which has not been manufactured but has been won or abstracted, the person who won or abstracted it;
(c) in the case of a product which has not been manufactured, won or abstracted but essential characteristics of which are attributable to an industrial or other process having been carried out (for example, in relation to agricultural produce), the person who carried out that process.

In reality it can be difficult for consumers to identify the original producer or importer of a product. The CPA 1987, s 2(3) provides a solution to this problem by placing an obligation on the supplier of the defective product to provide the injured party with the identity of one or more persons falling within the categories identified in s 2(2) on request, in default of which the supplier will be deemed liable for the damage. In this way, liability works its way up the supply chain until the producer is identified, or the buck stops with someone who does not, or cannot, identify their supplier or the producer. It should be noted that the obligation to provide this information only arises if the request is made within a reasonable period after the damage occurred and at a time when it is not reasonably practicable for the person making the request to identify the persons in question him/herself.

To establish liability, the product must have been supplied in the course of the supplier's/producer's business.[43] It is not a prerequisite that the product has been purchased; a sample product provided to a consumer free of charge would suffice for these purposes, as the product would have been provided in the course of business. The CPA 1987 does not, however, apply to a product taken without the producer's/supplier's consent or to raw materials that caused damage before being supplied and put into circulation.

---

42   CPA 1987, s 5(2).
43   CPA 1987, s 4(c).

One practical effect of the widely drawn CPA 1987, s 2 is that the injured party may have a choice of several parties against whom a claim can be made in respect of the damage in question. The liability of those parties will be joint and several.[44]

Temporal limitations

Part I of the CPA 1987 applies in respect of damage caused by any defective product supplied on or after 1 March 1988.[45] The relevant date is the date the individual product that caused the harm was supplied, not the date when that type of product first came onto the market.

With regard to claims for damages for personal injury caused by a defective medical product, the usual three year primary limitation period for a personal injury action applies. However, the CPA 1987, s 6(6) and Sch 1 operate to impose a ten-year long-stop period for bringing a claim under the CPA 1987.[46] This is achieved by an amendment to the Limitation Act 1980, adding s 11A(3), which reads:

> An action to which this section applies shall not be brought after the expiration of the period of ten years from the relevant time, within the meaning of section 4 of the said Act of 1987; and this subsection shall operate to extinguish a right of action and shall do so whether or not that right of action had accrued, or time under the following provisions of this Act had begun to run, at the end of the said period of ten years.

The ten-year period runs from the 'relevant time', as defined by the CPA 1987, s 4(2). In a case against one of the three categories of person identified in the CPA 1987, s 2(2), the relevant time is when that person supplied the product to another. In all other cases, the relevant time is the time when the product was last supplied by a person in one of those categories.

> s 4(2) In this section 'the relevant time', in relation to electricity, means the time at which it was generated, being a time before it was transmitted or distributed, and in relation to any other product, means—
>
> (a)   if the person proceeded against is a person to whom subsection (2) of section 2 above applies in relation to the product, *the time when he supplied the product to another* [author's emphasis];
>
> (b)   if that subsection does not apply to that person in relation to the product, the time when the product was last supplied by a person to whom that subsection does apply in relation to the product.

The ten-year long-stop applies throughout the member states and reflects recital 10 of the Product Liability Directive[47] which provides that:

> … a uniform period of limitation for the bringing of action for compensation is in the interests both of the injured person and of the producer …

---

44   CPA 1987, s 2(5).

45   CPA 1987, s 50(7): 'Nothing in this Act or in any order under subsection (2) above shall make any person liable by virtue of Part I of this Act for any damage caused wholly or partly by a defect in a product which was supplied to any person by its producer before the coming into force of Part I of this Act.'

46   Limitation under the Directive was considered recently in *O'Byrne v Aventis Pasteur SA* [2010] UKSC 23.

47   Council Directive 85/374/EEC.

and recital 11 which notes that:

> ... whereas products age in the course of time, higher safety standards are developed and the state of science and technology progresses whereas, therefore, it would not be reasonable to make the producer liable for an unlimited period for the defectiveness of his product; whereas, therefore, liability should expire after a reasonable length of time, without prejudice to claims pending at law ...

This long-stop on claims can present difficulties in the sphere of medical products, where defects can remain latent for periods in excess of ten years. In such cases the CPA 1987 will not assist the prospective claimant, although the possibility of a claim in common law negligence will remain.

In *O'Byrne v Aventis Pasteur SA*,[48] the Supreme Court was asked to consider the effect of the CPA longstop on an application to substitute one defendant for another, outside the ten-year limitation period. The claimant ('OB') alleged that a vaccine manufactured by Aventis Pasteur SA ('APSA') was defective and had caused him brain damage. APSA had sent a consignment of the vaccine to its wholly-owned English subsidiary, Aventis Pasteur MSD Ltd ('APMSD') in September 1992. On an unknown date in late September or early October 1992, APMSD sold part of the consignment to the Department of Health, which in turn supplied it to the medical practice that had vaccinated OB. Proceedings were commenced against APMSD on 1 August 2001. In its defence, APMSD stated that it was not the manufacturer of the product, but merely the distributor. Following a request by OB, in April 2002 APMSD identified APSA as the manufacturer of the product. In October 2002 OB issued proceedings against APSA under the CPA 1987. The APSA argued that the claim was time-barred. Faced with that defence, in March 2003, OB applied for an order in accordance with the CPR 19.5(3)(a) and the Limitation Act 1980, s 35(5)(b) that APSA be substituted as defendant in the proceedings against APMSD. APSA contended that insofar as English law might permit APSA to be substituted after expiry of the ten-year time limit, it was inconsistent with Art 11 of the Product Liability Directive.[49]

At the request of both parties, the High Court made a preliminary reference to the ECJ, which held that:[50]

- Article 11 prevented a producer being sued, unless proceedings had been taken against it within the ten-year period, and that a national rule allowing the substitution of one defendant for another could not be applied in a way which allowed a producer to be sued after expiry. That ruling effectively put an end to any argument that the claimant was entitled to rely upon the Limitation Act 1980, s 35 in order to bring proceedings after the ten-year time-limit;
- Article 11 must be interpreted as meaning that a product is put into circulation when it is taken out of the manufacturing process operated by the producer and enters a marketing process in the form in which it is offered to the public in order to be used or consumed;
- Article 11 did not prevent a producer being substituted for a wholly-owned subsidiary against which proceedings had been issued within the ten-year period, if the relationship between the producer and the

---

48 [2010] UKSC 23.
49 Council Directive 85/374/EEC.
50 *Aventis Pasteur SA v OB* (C-358/08) EU:C:2009:744.

subsidiary was such that the putting into circulation of the product had in reality been determined by the producer.

In light of the ECJ's answer, at first instance Mr Justice Teare allowed OB's application for substitution. The Court of Appeal dismissed APSA's appeal. It granted APSA leave to appeal, but due to a diversity of opinion on the appellate committee with regard to the correct interpretation of the ECJ ruling, the House of Lords made a second referral to the ECJ.

The Supreme Court[51] held that the ECJ's core ruling had been that:

> Article 11 ... must be interpreted as precluding national legislation, which allows the substitution of one defendant for another during proceedings, from being applied in a way which permit a producer, within the meaning of Article 3 of that directive, to be sued, after the expiry of the period prescribed by that article, as defendant in proceedings brought within that period against another person.[52]

It was emphasised that, for these purposes, it was irrelevant whether the failure to sue a particular producer within the ten-year period had been due to a mistake on the claimant's part. It was noted that the strict liability regime of the Directive imposed a greater burden on producers than a traditional fault-based system. The ten-year time-limit was intended to alleviate that burden.

The Supreme Court noted that, having answered the core question, the ECJ went on to provide further guidance to the referring court. In doing so the ECJ had noted that APMSD was a wholly owned subsidiary of APSA at the time it supplied the vaccine to the Department of Health. In that context, the ECJ stated that it was a matter for the national court to determine in accordance with national law whether the putting into circulation of the product was in fact determined by the parent company which manufactured it (APSA). If that was the case, Art 11 would not preclude the producer being substituted for the distributor. The fact that the distributor was a wholly-owned subsidiary of ASPA was not determinative of the issue. It was simply one of the factors to be taken into account by the national court when assessing how closely the subsidiary was involved with its parent company's business as an Art 3(1) producer. The question was whether the relationship between APMSD and APSA was such that by suing APMSD OB was, in effect, suing APSA, such that when proceedings were issued against APMSD, time stopped running against APSA. On the facts of the particular case the Supreme Court held that APSA had not determined the putting into circulation of the product. The appeal would, therefore, be upheld. It does, however, remain open to a claimant in a suitable case to argue that the relationship between the producer and the distributor is such that the producer could be substituted as the defendant in proceedings after expiry of the 10-year long-stop without undermining Art 11.

---

51 By the time the ECJ had ruled on the second referral, the House of Lords had become the Supreme Court.

52 Judgment of the ECJ cited at [10] per Lord Rodger's judgment.

Geographical/jurisdictional limitations

There is nothing in the text of the CPA 1987 to restrict its territorial operation. It is, however, doubtful whether it applies in respect of damage caused outside the EEA. This issue was considered as part of a preliminary issues hearing in the case of *Lawrence Allen v Depuy International Ltd*.[53] The case concerned personal injury claims brought by non-EU claimants in respect of allegedly defective prosthetic hip implants. The implants had been manufactured in England, by an English company, but had been implanted into the claimants in New Zealand, Australia and South Africa. It was alleged that the claimants had suffered adverse reaction to metal debris ('ARMD') as a result of the implants. Proceedings were issued in England. On a trial of three preliminary issues, Mr Justice Stewart found that English law was not applicable to the proceedings. However, he went on to determine the question of whether, if English law had been applicable, the CPA 1987 would have applied to the claims. He found that the CPA 1987 would not have been applicable. In doing so he noted that the damage had been caused outside the EEA, to claimants who had no connection to the EEA in circumstances in which the supply and marketing of the allegedly defective product occurred outside the EEA. In all the circumstances, he did not consider the CPA 1987 to be applicable in these particular claims. He did, however, leave open the possibility that, in appropriate and, crucially, undefined circumstances, the CPA 1987 could apply to damage sustained outside the EEA:

> In my judgment wherever one draws the line, consumers who suffer damage outside the EEA and who have no connection with the EEA, and where marketing and supply of the defective product was outside the EEA are not within the scope of CPA. Where and how the line should be drawn in terms of the territorial scope in difficult cases will have to be determined upon the facts of those cases. There will often be difficulties with the territorial limits of any statute/directive.[54]

What is a product?

A 'product' is defined in the CPA 1987, s 1 as:

> any goods or electricity and (subject to subsection (3) below) includes a product which is comprised in another product, whether by virtue of being a component part or raw material or otherwise.

Certain items are easily identifiable as products. For example, in the medical sphere, medicines and implants are non-contentious items. In the case of *A v National Blood Authority*,[55] blood was held to be a product for the purposes of the Act. The reference to 'a substance which has not been manufactured but has been won or abstracted' would appear to encompass human tissue and organs.[56] Historically, there has been some

---

53 [2014] EWHC 753 (QB).
54 *Lawrence Allen v Deputy International Ltd* [2014] EWHC 753 (QB), per Mr Justice Stewart at[32].
55 *A v National Blood Authority (No 1)* [2001] 3 All ER 289.
56 For further discussion in relation to organs, see Judith M Laing, Jean V McHale (eds) *Principles of Medical Law* (4th edn, 2017), Ch 18 and Richard Goldberg, *Medicinal Product Liability and Regulation*, Ch 9.

resistance to considering human body parts/tissue as products, but those reservations are not reflected in the terms of the CPA 1987 and appear, increasingly, to be out of step with modern sensitivities and medical advancements.

What makes a product defective?

The burden of proof rests on the claimant to prove that he/she has sustained damage as result of a defective product, but what constitutes a defect for the purposes of the Directive and the CPA 1987? There are a number of approaches the EC could have adopted when defining a defect for these purposes. For example, it could have chosen to focus upon the intended function of the product and fitness for purpose. However, in line with the emphasis on product safety set out in the recitals to the Directive, Art 6 focuses on the safety of the product as the key factor. This is reflected in the CPA 1987, s 3 which provides that:

> 3. Meaning of 'defect'.
>
> (1) Subject to the following provisions of this section, there is a defect in a product for the purposes of this Part *if the safety of the product is not such as persons generally are entitled to expect;*[57] and for those purposes 'safety', in relation to a product, shall include safety with respect to products comprised in that product and safety in the context of risks of damage to property, as well as in the context of risks of death or personal injury.

Unlike the US system, no distinction is made between design and manufacturing defects.[58] The test is whether or not the product itself was not safe. It will not always be possible to identify the precise mechanism by which a product has caused damage, but that will not preclude a successful claim if it can be established that the product does not meet the standard of safety that persons generally are entitled to expect. That of course gives rise to the question: what level of safety are persons generally entitled to expect?

This question is of particular significance in the context of claims concerning medical products when few, if any, of the products in question will be 100% safe for all patients in all circumstances.[59] This particular feature of medical product claims was acknowledged by Mr Justice Hickinbottom in *Wilkes v Depuy* when he noted that:

> No medicinal product is free from risk, and thus 'safety' in this field is inherently and necessarily a relative concept.[60]

A product is not necessarily deemed to be defective simply because a new, improved, product has come on to the market.[61] The level of safety the public is entitled to expect is evaluated at the time when the product is first placed on the market, by reference to the standards and knowledge

---

57   Emphasis added.
58   For a general comparison of the US and UK approaches to medical product liability see Richard Goldberg, *Medicinal Product Liability and Regulation*, Ch 2.
59   Cf *A v The National Blood Authority* [2001] 3 All ER 289 in which it was held that persons are generally entitled to expect blood products to be 100% safe.
60   *Anthony Frederick Wilkes v Depuy International Ltd* [2016] EWHC 3096, [13].
61   Article 6(1) and (2); *Worsely v Tambrands 2000* and *Wilks v Depuy 2016*.

possessed in the industry at that time.[62] However, in determining whether or not the product in question met that standard, the court is entitled to have regard to everything known about it at the time of the hearing, regardless of whether that information was available to the producer at the time the product was put on the market. As noted by Mrs Justice Andrews in *Gee v Depuy*,[63] if that were not the case, it would be impossible for any claimant to establish liability in respect of a defect that did not become evident until a number of years after the product was placed on the market.[64]

The question of what persons generally are entitled to expect is a matter of law, to be determined by the court. The court has a wide discretion in this respect. When drafting the Directive, the European Council recognised the fact that it would apply to a vast array of products with many different uses and that it was highly unlikely that one standard would be appropriate in all cases. Consequently the Directive and the CPA 1987 allow the courts sufficient flexibility to consider the appropriate safety standard in respect of each individual product, by reference to all the circumstances relevant to that product.

The test is an objective one, unconnected to either the defendant's intentions or to the state of mind or actual expectations of the particular claimant or the general public. The standard the public is entitled to expect may be a higher standard than the public or the individual claimant actually expects, or it could be lower. As noted by Mr Justice Burton in *A v National Blood Authority*[65] in respect of new products, it is possible that the public and/or the claimant would have no actual expectation.

In *Richardson v LRC Products Ltd*[66] the claimant brought a claim under the CPA 1987 against the manufacturer of a condom when she became pregnant after the condom split during use. In finding that the condom was not defective for the purposes of the CPA 1987, Mr Justice Kennedy acknowledged that of course the user of a condom would not expect it to fail. Nevertheless, nobody expects any method of contraception to be 100% effective and the producer had not made any claims that its condoms would never fail. In the circumstances, persons were not generally entitled to expect that a condom would not split and the claimant had, therefore, failed to establish a defect.

An attempt by Mr Justice Burton in *A v National Blood Authority* to import a test of legitimate expectation into the s 3 determination, as agreed by the parties in that case, was firmly rejected in the cases of *Wilkes* and *Gee*. Mr Justice Hickinbottom in *Wilkes*[67] endorsed counsel for the defendant's description of the phrase as adding an 'unnecessary and unhelpful gloss on the Act'.[68]

---

62 Endorsed by Mrs Justice Andrews *Gee v Depuy*, at [84].
63 *Colin Gee v Depuy International Ltd sub nom In the Matter of Depuy Pinnacle Metal on Metal Hip Litigation* [2018] EWHC 1208 (QB).
64 The extent to which the court is entitled or required to have knowledge of matters not known at the time the product was put on the market is discussed in further detail below.
65 See n 54.
66 [2000] PIQR P164.
67 *Anthony Frederick Wilkes v Depuy International Ltd* [2016] EWHC 3096.
68 Ibid at [71].

Similarly, the trial Judges in *Wilkes* and *Gee* rejected the approach adopted by Mr Justice Burton in *A v National Blood Authority* of distinguishing between standard and non-standard products when evaluating safety. Under Mr Justice Burton's approach, 'standard products' were products which performed as the producer intended but nevertheless carried a risk of harm. 'Non-standard products' were products that were deficient or inferior to the standard product. Different tests were proposed for the two different types of product. In *Wilkes*, Mr Justice Hickinbottom, whose analysis was firmly endorsed by Mrs Justice Andrews in *Gee*, stated that the distinction was 'unnecessary and undesirable' and that it did not derive from the Directive or the CPA 1987. In his view:

> whether a particular product is within the producer's specification, and is compliant with relevant standards ... may be relevant circumstances in relation to whether the level of safety is that to which persons generally are entitled to expect; but to raise the distinction to a rigid categorisation is positively unhelpful and potentially dangerous.[69]

Identifying the defect

Identification of the alleged defect is a prerequisite to the establishment of a claim under the CPA 1987. This does not necessarily mean identifying a specific flaw in the product, but it is essential for the claimant to identify what it is about the state or behaviour of the product or the risks that it posed that led it to fall below the requisite level of safety. In some cases the fact that a product failed following normal use, in circumstances in which it ought not to have failed, may suffice for the court to draw an inference that the product is defective.[70] In *Gee,* the example given was that if an electrical appliance bursts into flames if it is left plugged in, it clearly does not meet the requisite safety standard and it is not necessary for the claimant to establish precisely what caused it to explode.[71] However, if the injury or damage could have arisen even if the product met the s 3 standard of safety, in consequence of the manifestation of a known risk that could arise in normal use, a greater level of specificity is required. In those circumstances, the claimant will need to establish that there was something abnormal that caused the product to fail when it should not have done or that something had happened to increase the inherent risk to a level higher than the public was entitled to expect.

The latter category will often apply to medical product claims in which safety is necessarily a relative concept. Many commonly prescribed medications and medical devices/implants carry a risk of potentially harmful side effects. The public is not entitled to expect that a product known to have an inherently harmful or potentially harmful characteristic will not cause that harm: the normal risks inherent in the use of a product

---

69   Ibid at [94].
70   *Ide v ATB Sales Ltd* [2008] EWCA Civ 424.
71   *Colin Gee v Depuy International Ltd sub nom In the Matter of Depuy Pinnacle Metal on Metal Hip Litigation* [2018] EWHC 1208 (QB) at [99]. For a recent example of the application of the principle in practice, please see the case of *Al-Iqra v DSG Retail* [2019] EWHC 429 (QB).

cannot constitute a defect.[72] Neither can the product's potential to cause harm in itself be categorised as a defect for these purposes.[73]

Gee v Depuy, like *Wilkes*, was a case concerning metal-on-metal hip implants, in this case the Pinnacle Ultamet prosthesis. The claimants argued that the Pinnacle prosthesis had a tendency or propensity to cause an adverse reaction to metal debris ('ARMD'), resulting in the need for early hip revision surgery and that it was this propensity to cause harm that constituted the alleged defect.

Applying *Wilkes*, Mrs Justice Andrews rejected the claimants' argument. In order to establish liability it was necessary for the claimant both to identify and prove the defect as well as the causal relationship between the defect and the damage. The claimants' approach was 'self-evidently circular'.[74] She noted that all hip prostheses eventually wear out and fail if the patient lives long enough. The natural propensity to fail could not, therefore, be a defect for the purposes of the CPA 1987. Similarly, it was known in 2002 when the Pinnacle Ultamet was launched that all hip prostheses shed debris in the course of their normal operation and that in metal-on-metal implants this produced metal debris. It was also known that, as a consequence of metal debris entering the body, some patients would develop ARMD causing the prosthesis to fail and necessitating hip revision surgery. In the circumstances, the public had no entitlement to expect a metal-on-metal hip implant not to produce metal debris, even though that debris could cause ARMD. The development of ARMD was a normal risk inherent to the product. If that propensity was categorised as a defect, all metal-on-metal implants would be defective and no manufacturer would be able to avail itself of the development risk defence[75] because the risk was known at the time the product was placed on the market. In other words:

> the Claimants are seeking to use the actual or predicted incidence of manifestation of a known inherent risk, under normal circumstances of use, to characterise something that is normal as a 'defect'. That approach is both misconceived and contrary to the spirit and intention of the Act and Directive.[76]

It was held that there was no feature of the Pinnacle Ultamet that made it any more likely than any other metal-on-metal implant to shed debris or to increase the risk of developing ARMD. The public was not entitled to expect that the prosthesis would not shed metal debris. The vast majority of patients who had received a Pinnacle Ultamet had well-functioning hips. The alleged incidence, or predicted incidence, of ARMD in a small minority of patients, even if established, would not convert a known risk which may eventuate from normal use into a defect for the purposes of s 3.

The *Gee* claimants' secondary argument that the Pinnacle Ultamet was defective by virtue of the fact that it had an abnormal potential for damage compared with comparator non-metal-on-metal prostheses failed due to the absence of any evidence to demonstrate that there was

---

72 *Wilkes v Depuy*; *Gee v Depuy* ibid n 1.
73 *Colin Gee v Depuy International Ltd sub nom In the Matter of Depuy Pinnacle Metal on Metal Hip Litigation* [2018] EWHC 1208 (QB).
74 [2018] EWHC 1208 (QB) at [108].
75 The defences provided by CPA 1987 are discussed in detail below.
76 [2018] EWHC 1208 (QB), per Andrews J at [119].

a materially greater risk of the Pinnacle Ultamet failing within the first ten years than a comparator prosthesis.

Although the argument failed in *Gee* on the evidence, a material increase in a known inherent risk can be sufficient to constitute a defect for the purposes of the Directive. In *Boston Scientific Medizintechnik GMbH v AOK SachesnAnhalt-Die Gesundheitskasse*[77] the European Court of Justice (hereafter referred to by its modern name, CJEU) considered a referral from the German courts concerning cardiological products, defibrillators and pacemakers belonging to a batch of products in which some, but not all, of the devices suffered from a fault which might cause the device to fail. In the case of the pacemakers the risk of failure was 17–20 times greater than would normally be expected. The consequences of such failure would potentially be fatal. It was not possible to tell which products contained the fault whilst it was implanted in the patient. In the circumstances, the manufacturer had recommended surgical removal of all the devices already implanted. The claimants brought claims under the German legislation implementing the Directive. The defendant argued that in order to prove a defect, it would be necessary for each claimant to demonstrate that the specific device removed was one of the devices within the batch of products that suffered from the identified fault. The claimants on the other hand argued that it would suffice for them to establish that the device removed fell within a group of devices that carried a significant risk of failure.

Understandably, the CJEU preferred the claimants' argument. It was held that, in light of the particular function of the devices, the safety requirements persons generally were entitled to expect were particularly high. Where products belonging to the same group or forming part of the same production series have a potential defect, all products in that group or series could be classified as defective without the need to establish that the particular product in question was itself defective.

Legally relevant circumstances

The CPA 1987, s 3(2) requires the court to take into account 'all the circumstances' when determining the level of safety the public is entitled to expect. This must necessarily be interpreted to mean all relevant circumstances, but what is, or is not, a relevant circumstance for these purposes?

The relevant circumstances include, but are not restricted to, those set out in s 3(2):

(2) In determining for the purposes of subsection (1) above what persons generally are entitled to expect in relation to a product all the circumstances shall be taken into account, including—

(a)   the manner in which, and purposes for which, the product has been marketed, its get-up, the use of any mark in relation to the product and any instructions for, or warnings with respect to, doing or refraining from doing anything with or in relation to the product;

(b)   what might reasonably be expected to be done with or in relation to the product; and

(c)   the time when the product was supplied by its producer to another;

---

77   Case C-503/13 [2015] 3 CMLR 173.

and nothing in this section shall require a defect to be inferred from the fact alone that the safety of a product which is supplied after that time is greater than the safety of the product in question.In order to be taken into account, a circumstance must be factually and legally relevant to the evaluation of safety of the product. Fault on the part of the producer is legally irrelevant as it has no bearing on the condition or state of the product.

In *A v National Blood Authority*,[78] Mr Justice Burton listed factors which he considered could never be relevant to a court's assessment of the safety of a product. In that list he included:

- the avoidability of the harmful characteristic or impossibility of taking precautionary measures;
- the impracticality, difficulty or cost of taking such measures;
- the benefit to society or utility of the product (except in the context of whether, with full information and proper knowledge, the public does and ought to accept the risk).

In the case of *Wilkes v Depuy*[79] Mr Justice Hickinbottom rejected Mr Justice Burton's approach on the basis that it undermined the flexibility of the CPA 1987 and the wide discretion it gave to the court in determining what constitutes a defect:

the Court must maintain a flexible approach to the assessment of the appropriate level of safety, including which circumstances are relevant and the weight to be given to each, those factors being quintessentially dependent upon the particular facts of any case.[80]

In *Gee v Depuy*, Mrs Justice Andrews endorsed the approach of Mr Justice Hickinbottom, and rejected Mr Justice Burton's more rigid approach.

It follows from the flexible approach advocated in *Wilkes* and *Gee* that the circumstances to be taken into account must be determined on a case-by-case basis. The judges in those cases did, however, provide some useful guidance with regard to circumstances they considered could be relevant circumstances for the purposes of the CPA 1987, s 3.

Avoidability, risk-benefit and cost

The determination of whether or not a product has met the required safety standard cannot be reduced to a simple risk/benefit analysis. That approach was specifically rejected by the EC when formulating the Directive. It is, however, permissible to take into account any benefits deriving from the product that are relevant to the evaluation of safety. Whether or not the risk of harm could have been avoided or reduced will not often be relevant, straying as it does into the territory of focusing on the acts/omissions of the producer as opposed to the condition of the product. As Mrs Justice Andrews noted:

it is possible to envisage circumstances in which it might legitimately form part of a holistic evaluation of whether that level of safety falls below the

---

78 *A v National Blood Authority (No1)* [2001] 3 All ER 289, at [68].
79 [2016] EWHC 3096.
80 *Wilkes* [2016] EWHC 3096 at [78].

threshold set in section 3 of the Act – ie the level that the public generally was entitled to expect.[81]

In *Gee* the defendant provided an example of the circumstances in which such considerations might be relevant to the s 3 determination. It was submitted that if a new chemotherapy drug was produced which had proven advantages over other drugs on the market but which also carried the risk of a rare and serious side effect, in order to evaluate a claim made by a patient who had been harmed as a result of suffering that side effect, it would be essential for the court to look at the potential benefits of the drug as well as the risks in order to determine whether its safety was such as members of the public were entitled to expect. It was submitted that a proper evaluation of the safety of the product could not be made by reference only to the risks of the product, excluding the benefits. Mrs Justice Andrews endorsed that approach noting that:

> if the use to which the product can reasonably be expected to be put is a relevant consideration, as it undoubtedly is, then it cannot be objectionable for the Court to consider the benefits likely to arise from its contemplated use as part and parcel of the circumstances that have a bearing on the evaluation of the level of safety that the public generally is entitled to expect. In the example given, the additional benefit conferred by the new chemotherapy drug is plainly a relevant circumstance that would assist in the evaluation of its safety by reference to the test set out in s 3 of the Act.

Rather than importing a risk/benefit analysis, Mrs Justice Andrews argued that consideration of benefits and the avoidability of harm constituted the adoption of a holistic approach to the objective evaluation of safety.[82] The recent case of *Sandra Bailey v Glaxosmithline UK Ltd*,[83] demonstrates that although the courts have endorsed the so-called 'holistic assessment', it remains possible for a party, perhaps unwittingly, to define its case on defect in such narrow terms that the possibility of a holistic assessment of risks and benefits is excluded.

In addition, when adopting a holistic approach to the objective evaluation of safety, the court must be vigilant not to let notions of fault/negligence creep into the assessment.[84] Subject to that very important proviso, both Mr Justice Hickinbottom in *Wilkes* and Mrs Justice Andrews in *Gee* considered that in an appropriate case the ease with which, and the extent to which, a risk of harm could be eliminated or mitigated may be a relevant circumstance for the purposes of the CPA 1987, s 3. In particular, Mrs Justice Andrews noted that in an appropriate case it was possible that the court could legitimately conclude that the public is not entitled to expect a producer to achieve something in terms of safety that is scientifically impossible or prohibitively expensive, or which would be impossible to insure against. This element of the judgment in *Gee* is potentially of particular significance in the context of claims relating to medical products.

---

81   *Colin Gee v Depuy International Ltd sub nom In the Matter of Depuy Pinnacle Metal on Metal Hip Litigation* [2018] EWHC 1208 (QB), at [146].
82   See also *Bogle v McDonalds Restaurants* [2002] EWHC 490 (QB).
83   [2019] EWHC 1167 (QB). An appeal on this matter is outstanding at the time of writing.
84   *Gee* [2018] EWHC 1208 (QB), at [160].

Regulations and standards

The fact that a product is subject to a regulatory regime is a relevant circumstance to be taken into account.[85] Compliance with a regulatory regime is not a defence under the CPA 1987, but is likely to be an important factor. It is noted that when formulating the Directive the EC rejected the suggestion that compliance with a regulatory regime should be treated as prima facie evidence of the absence of a defect. The standards of the regulatory body in question cannot be taken as a substitute for the statutory test under the CPA 1987, s 3 and the level of safety which the public is entitled to expect may in any given case be higher, or lower, than a particular regulatory standard. Consequently, a product may be defective notwithstanding compliance with all relevant regulations/standards.

One example of a product in respect of which the standard of safety the public was entitled to expect fell below a regulatory standard can be found in the case of *Tesco Stores Ltd v Pollard*.[86] The case concerned a child-resistant cap ('CRC') on a bottle of dishwasher powder. A 13-month-old child had picked up the bottle of dishwasher powder, opened it and ingested the contents, sustaining injury. It was alleged that the bottle and cap were defective in that it was too easy for a child to remove the cap. At first instance the judge found the producer liable on the basis that the cap was subject to British Standards regulations for CRCs but failed to meet the required torque resistance criteria. He held that, having elected to fit a CRC, the consumer was entitled to expect the cap to function at least up to the relevant British Standard. On appeal by the producer, the Court of Appeal reversed the first instance decision, noting that the test for whether or not the product was defective under the CPA 1987 was not whether the product met the British Standard, but whether it met the level of safety persons generally are entitled to expect. In this particular case, people were entitled to expect that the CRC would be more difficult to open than an ordinary cap. The cap in question met that standard and therefore, in the circumstances, there was no breach of the CPA 1987.

The weight to be placed on compliance with regulations/standards is a matter of fact and degree to be determined on a case-by-case basis. However, in cases involving medical products, the authors consider that the courts are unlikely to accept that a product that does not comply with relevant regulatory standards nevertheless meets the standard of safety persons generally are entitled to expect.

In the medical context, NICE Guidelines (which are not a regulatory standard) are likely to be considered to be a relevant circumstance; they are, however, unlikely to be determinative.

Learned intermediaries

The existence of a so-called 'learned intermediary',[87] for example a doctor or pharmacist, and the information and warnings about use of a product provided to that intermediary are relevant circumstances for the purposes

---

85 *Boston Scientific Medizintechnik GMbH v AOK SachesnAnhalt-Die Gesundheitskasse,* Case C-503/13 [2015] 3 CMLR 173.
86 [2006] EWCA Civ 393.
87 See *Gee* at [168] and [169].

of the CPA 1987, s 3. The weight to be given to such considerations is a matter to be determined by the court on a case-by-case basis. The question remains one of the levels of safety *the public* is entitled to expect, but it is acknowledged that the expectations of health professionals may have a significant bearing on public expectations in the sphere of medical products. That is not to say, however, that any product will be rendered defective due to any fault on the part of the intermediary, such as the failure to pass on warnings provided by the producer to the intermediary.

DEFENCES

The CPA 1987, s 4 sets out six defences that may be relied upon by a producer/manufacturer/supplier, as a complete defence to any claim under the Act:

1   'the defect is attributable to compliance with any requirement imposed by or under any enactment or with any [EU] obligation';[88]

2   'the person proceeded against did not at any time supply the product to another'.[89] This could encompass a situation where a product was taken without consent. As noted above, a product can be supplied without being sold eg provided as a sample. It is noted that the phrase used in the Directive is not 'supply', but 'put into circulation'. In the case of *O'Byrne v Sanofi Pasteur* it was held that a product is put into circulation when it is taken out of the manufacturing process operated by the producer and enters a marketing process in the form in which it is offered to the public in order to be used or consumed;[90]

3   the product was supplied by the defendant 'otherwise than in the course of a business of that person's' *and* he was not the producer, trade-marker or importer of the product, or that he can only be categorised as the producer, trade-marker or importer by virtue of things done otherwise than with a view to profit.[91] This defence for non-profit making activities is slightly narrower for producers than suppliers. Suppliers have the benefit of the defence if they can show that the product was not supplied in the course of a business, whereas a producer must additionally establish that s/he never supplied the product in question with a view to making profit;

4   the 'defect did not exist in the product at the relevant time'.[92] 'Relevant time' is defined in the CPA 1987, s 4(2) but means different things in different circumstances. In medical cases, s 4(2)(a) will usually apply, meaning that the 'relevant time' will be the time when the product was supplied. This defence would be useful where, for example, medication was stored incorrectly or packaging damaged by the retailer or the user themselves and this caused the defect;[93]

---

88   CPA 1987, s 4(1)(a).
89   CPA 1987, s 4(1)(b).
90   See earlier discussion above.
91   CPA 1987, s 4(1)(c).
92   CPA 1987, s 4(1)(d).
93   See *Piper v JRI (Manufacturing) Ltd* [2006] EWCA Civ 1344 for an example of this defence in practice.

5   'the state of scientific and technical knowledge at the relevant time
     was not such that a producer of products of the same description as
     the product in question might be expected to have discovered the
     defect if it had existed in his products while they were under his
     control';[94]
6   the defect 'constituted a defect in a product ("the subsequent
     product") in which the product in question had been comprised; and
     it was wholly attributable to the design of the subsequent product
     or to compliance by the producer of the product in question with
     instructions given by the producer of the subsequent product'.[95]

The burden of proving one of the six defences rests on the defendant.
It is the fifth defence, known as the 'development risk defence', that is
of particular significance in the context of medical claims. There is a
slight difference between the wording of the Product Liability Directive
and the CPA 1987 in this respect. The Directive states that the defence
applies where 'the state of scientific and technical knowledge at the time
when he put the product into circulation *was not such as to enable*[96] the
existence of the defect to be discovered',[97] whereas the CPA 1987 uses the
wording 'might be expected to have discovered'. The Directive wording
leans towards a stricter, no fault regime whereas it could be argued that
the domestic version has undertones of a reasonableness test.

When the CPA 1987 was passed the European Commission was
concerned that the wording of s 4(2)(e) failed properly to implement
the Directive. It therefore brought proceedings in the CJEU seeking a
declaration to that effect.[98] The Commission argued that the test under
the CPA 1987 was broader and easier to satisfy than the test set out in
Art 7(e) of the Directive and that it had the effect of transforming strict
liability into a liability founded on negligence. The Commission argued
that, in accordance with the Directive, if there was a scientist anywhere
in the world who could have discovered the defect then liability should
attach.

The UK successfully argued that this represented a misinterpretation
of both the Directive and the CPA 1987. The test of the 'state of scientific
knowledge' in both Art 7(e) and the CPA 1987, s 4(2)(e) was objective. It
was a reference to the state of knowledge which producers of the class of
the producer in question may objectively be expected to have. Finding in
favour of the UK, the CJEU held that in order to have a defence under
Art 7(e) the producer of a defective product must establish that the
objective state of scientific and technical knowledge, including the most
advanced level of such knowledge, at the time the product was placed into
circulation was not such as to enable the defect to be discovered. However,
that scientific knowledge must have been accessible to the producer at
the time when the product was put into circulation. It was noted that
this particular aspect of Art 7(e) raised difficulties of interpretation, but
it was left to the national courts to resolve those difficulties on a case-by-
case basis.

---

94   CPA 1987, s 4(a)(e).
95   CPA 1987, s 4(1)(f).
96   Emphasis added.
97   Article 7(e) of the Product Liability Directive 85/374/EEC.
98   See *Commission v UK* C-300/95 (1997).

The High Court grappled with some of those difficulties in the case of *A v National Blood Authority*,[99] a case concerning the supply of blood products infected with Hepatitis C. Mr Justice Burton held that the development risk defence would not be available to a producer if there was a known risk in the generic category of product. It would not avail the defendant to establish that it did not and could not have known that there was a defect in the particular product in question. Further, when considering the interpretation of the 'state of scientific knowledge' Mr Justice Burton made obiter comments to the effect that if any hypothetical researcher could have discovered the defect the defence will not apply unless the relevant information was contained within 'an unpublished document or unpublished research not available to the general public, retained within the laboratory or research department of a particular company'.[100] These comments with regard to the state of scientific knowledge represent a rather more restrictive interpretation of the defence than that adopted by the CJEU in *Commission v UK*. It is anticipated that the correct interpretation of the 'state of scientific knowledge' will continue to be the subject of dispute and litigation for the foreseeable future.

CAUSATION

Under the CPA 1987 the claimant must prove that the product in question is defective and that the defect caused damage. Both the Directive and the CPA 1987 are, however, silent when it comes to the approach to be adopted when considering the issue of causation.

Causation is considered to be a matter for the domestic courts, subject to the proviso that the approach adopted must not undermine the effectiveness of the no-fault approach of the legislation or alter the balance of interests set by the Directive:[101]

> National courts must first ensure that the evidence adduced is sufficiently serious, specific and consistent to warrant the conclusion that, notwithstanding the evidence produced and the arguments put forward by the producer, a defect in the product appears to be the most plausible explanation for the occurrence of the damage, with the result that the defect and the causal link may reasonably be considered to be established.[102]

The law of causation in the UK and its particular application in the medical context is dealt with in Chapter 7 and will not be considered in detail here. It is, however, perhaps helpful to consider one particular causation issue frequently encountered in medical product cases. As previously noted, many medical products carry an inherent or known risk that can manifest in normal use, in the absence of any defect. In cases involving such products, it may be the claimant's case that the defect in question has caused an increase in that risk. In those circumstances, it will be extremely difficult for the claimant to prove that the damage sustained was caused by the increased risk, as opposed to the underlying risk.

---

99   [2001] 3 All ER 289.
100 [2001] 3 All ER 289 at [39].
101 *NW v Sanofi Pasteur* (Case 621/15) (2017) ECLI:EU:C:2017:484.
102 *NW v Sanofi Pasteur* (Case 621/15) (2017) ECLI:EU:C:2017:484 at [36].

In some cases the courts have adopted a rule of thumb that in order to establish causation in the circumstances described above, the claimant must demonstrate that the risk associated with the defective product was at least double the risk of the non-defective product,[103] or more than double the risk.[104] That was the position adopted by the defendant in *Gee v Depuy*. In that case, the court's finding that the product in question was not defective meant that it was not necessary for Mrs Justice Andrews to make any findings on causation. Nevertheless, it is of interest to note that she agreed that if the claimant had been able to establish that the incidence of failure of the Pinnacle Ultamet by reason of ARMD was more than double the general incidence of early failure of comparator hip prostheses, causation would 'of course' have been established. However, she went on to state that she was not persuaded that 'more than double the risk' should be adopted as a 'bright-line test'.[105] It remains to be seen whether other courts faced with this issue take the same view.

Gee v Depuy also provides a helpful demonstration of the critical importance of correctly defining both the damage and the risk in claims of this nature. It was the claimants' case that, when determining causation, the court needed to consider what would have happened if the prosthesis implanted in the claimant did not have the identified abnormal potential for damage, defined as ARMD. The correct question was, in their submission, whether the claimant would have suffered ARMD requiring early revision if a prosthesis without the potential to cause ARMD had been used. The court rejected that approach noting that by characterising the test in this way they had set themselves up to succeed.

In the opinion of Mrs Justice Andrews, the correct question for the court to determine was whether, on the balance of probabilities, the claimant would have suffered the damage complained of (early revision) if the hip had not carried an *increased risk* of early failure that made it defective. The appropriate comparison for the purposes of determining that increased risk was with the generic incidence of hip prosthesis failure, not just failure caused by ARMD.

CLAIMS IN CONTRACT

Claims in contract for medical product liability are of limited application in the UK where the majority of healthcare is provided by the NHS and there is often no contractual relationship between the manufacturer of a product and the injured person. Where the NHS has prescribed medication, there is usually no contract with the prescribing doctor or the pharmacist who dispensed the medication. Pharmacists are under a statutory obligation to dispense drugs upon presentation of a prescription so long as the relevant charge is paid.[106] Nevertheless contractual claims will be of potential relevance in the case of private patients who purchase

---

103 *XYZ v Schering Health Care Ltd* [2002] EWHC 1420 (QB).

104 *Novartis Grimsby v Cookson* [2007] EWCA Civ 1261 and *Jones v Secretary of State for Energy and Climate Change* [2012] EWHC 2936.

105 *Colin Gee v Depuy International Ltd sub nom In the Matter of Depuy Pinnacle Metal on Metal Hip Litigation* [2018] EWHC 1208 (QB), at [186].

106 *Pfizer Corpn v Ministry of Health* [1965] AC 512.

medical products directly from the manufacturer or those who purchase medication over-the-counter.

If a claimant is able to establish a contract of sale, a claim may be brought under the Consumer Rights Act 2015 (CRA 2015). The CRA 2015 consolidated numerous pieces of consumer legislation including the Sale of Goods Act 1979 and the Sale and Supply of Goods and Services Act 1982. There is limited case law to date in respect of interpretation of the CRA 2015 in the medical product liability context. It is, therefore, necessary to look to the text of the Act itself to consider how it might be applied in future.

Under the CRA 2015, s 5 a sales contract is defined as follows:

(1) A contract is a sales contract if under it—

(a)   the trader transfers or agrees to transfer ownership of goods to the consumer, and

(b)   the consumer pays or agrees to pay the price.

(2) A contract is a sales contract (whether or not it would be one under subsection (1)) if under the contract—

(a)   goods are to be manufactured or produced and the trader agrees to supply them to the consumer,

(b)   on being supplied, the goods will be owned by the consumer, and

(c)   the consumer pays or agrees to pay the price.

This may apply to privately prescribed drugs or over-the-counter medication. If it can be established that a contract was in place, the definition of 'trader' under the CRA 2015, s 2(2) is a wide one:

'Trader' means a person acting for purposes relating to that person's trade, business, craft or profession, whether acting personally or through another person acting in the trader's name or on the trader's behalf.[107]

Disputes may arise as to whether the CRA 2015 will apply when one person purchases medication for another person's use. It could be argued that the purchaser was acting as agent for the person who was injured and that the injured person is, therefore, entitled to bring a claim under the CRA 2015. It is, however, envisaged that in such cases claims under the CPA 1987 or in common law negligence will provide a more useful solution for the injured party.

The benefit of bringing a claim under the CRA 2015, as opposed to the CPA 1987, is that the CRA 1987 is not concerned solely with the safety of a product. Under the CRA 1987, liability is established if the claimant can prove that the product was not of satisfactory quality, was not fit for purpose or did not match the given description. The scope for a successful claim is therefore potentially greater than under the safety-focused CPA 1987.

Satisfactory quality

The CRA 2015, s 9 provides that:

(1) Every contract to supply goods is to be treated as including a term that the quality of the goods is satisfactory.

---

107 CRA 2015, s 2(2).

(2) The quality of goods is satisfactory if they meet the standard that a reasonable person would consider satisfactory, taking account of—

(a) any description of the goods,
(b) the price or other consideration for the goods (if relevant), and
(c) all the other relevant circumstances (see subsection (5)).

(3) The quality of goods includes their state and condition; and the following aspects (among others) are in appropriate cases aspects of the quality of goods—

(a) fitness for all the purposes for which goods of that kind are usually supplied;
(b) appearance and finish;
(c) freedom from minor defects;
(d) safety;
(e) durability.

The satisfactory quality provision includes the need for the product to be fit for purpose, so long as that purpose is one for which the product is ordinarily used. Unless some experimental procedure is being performed, most product related claims in the medical arena will fall under the CRA 2015, s 9. The test for assessing whether a product meets the satisfactory quality test is set out at s 9(2). One interesting feature of the CRA 2015 is that the standard varies depending on a number of factors, including the price paid for the product: cheaper products are reasonably expected to be of a lower standard than more expensive ones. As discussed in the section on the CPA 1987 above, no medical product is 100% safe. That factor is also taken into account under the CRA 2015. Consequently, the mere occurrence of side effects will not render a product of unsatisfactory quality if a reasonable person would still consider that medication to be satisfactory notwithstanding the risk of such side effects.

Fit for a particular purpose

The CRA 2015, s 10 sets out specific requirements to be met where the goods are required for a particular purpose:

(1) Subsection (3) applies to a contract to supply goods if before the contract is made the consumer makes known to the trader (expressly or by implication) any particular purpose for which the consumer is contracting for the goods.

(2) ...

(3) The contract is to be treated as including a term that the goods are reasonably fit for that purpose, whether or not that is a purpose for which goods of that kind are usually supplied.

(4) Subsection (3) does not apply if the circumstances show that the consumer does not rely, or it is unreasonable for the consumer to rely, on the skill or judgment of the trader or credit-broker.

The CRA 2015, s 10 could apply to cases in which a claimant and a medical practitioner had discussed the specific purpose for which the claimant intended to use a drug or the claimant had communicated information about his/her particular medical history to the prescribing doctor, or dispensing pharmacist. In order to be of relevance, the information in question must have been communicated. If, for example, a person has an allergic reaction to a medication, s 10 will not be engaged unless the doctor or pharmacist was informed about the claimant's allergy. Section 10(4) excludes liability in circumstances in which it can be shown that the claimant did not in fact rely upon the skill of the trader in question. Consequently, if a dispensing pharmacist is able to demonstrate that the claimant relied upon information/advice provided by his/her doctor, the pharmacist would avoid liability.

The CRA 2015, ss 9 and s 10 obligations cannot be restricted or excluded by the seller.[108] Specific provision is made with regard to proving defects in respect of s 9 and s 10. Section 19 provides that if the claimant can show that the goods do not meet the contractual obligations within six months of the day the goods were delivered to the consumer, there is a presumption that the goods were defective when delivered.[109] This presumption is rebuttable but the burden rests on the seller to show that the goods did in fact meet the contractual requirements on the day of delivery.[110] If an issue arises after six months from delivery, the burden rests on the claimant to show that the product was in breach of the contractual obligations at the time of delivery.

Chapter 4 of the CRA 2015 deals with services, as opposed to goods, where there is a contract for a trader to supply a service to a consumer.[111] The CRA 2015, s 49 imposes the well-known obligation:

> (1) Every contract to supply a service is to be treated as including a term that the trader must perform the service with reasonable care and skill.

Any term seeking to exclude this obligation to perform a service with reasonable care and skill would not be binding on a consumer.[112]

In the medical context, it is not uncommon for a doctor to both sell the product to the patient and to perform the service of fitting the product, so both Chapter 2 (goods) and Chapter 4 (services) of the CRA 2015 may be of relevance.

If the person with whom the claimant had a contract does not have the money to meet the breach of contract claim, it is worth bearing in mind that there may be a claim directly against the claimant's own credit card provider under the Consumer Credit Act 1974, s 75 if the product was purchased on a credit card.

CLAIMS IN NEGLIGENCE

The majority of medical product liability claims will be framed as claims under the CPA 1987 to enable the claimant to take advantage of the strict liability regime. However, there are circumstances in which the ten-year limitation long-stop under the CPA 1987 will mean that a claimant is debarred from making a claim under the CPA 1987 but will still have a potentially valid claim in common law negligence. Ordinary rules of limitation apply to product liability injury claims brought in negligence, namely that there are three years in which to bring the claim from the

---

108 CRA 2015, s 31.
109 CRA 2015, s 19(14).
110 CRA 2015, s 19(15)(a).
111 CRA 2015, s 48.
112 CRA 2015, s 57.

date the cause of action accrued or from the date of knowledge, if later.[113] Consequently, if the claimant's date of knowledge is more than ten years after the product was put into circulation, the claimant will need to frame his/her claim in negligence.

Ordinary principles of common law negligence will apply to such a claim: the claimant will need to establish that he/she was owed a duty of care by the defendant, that there was a breach of that duty and that the breach caused damage. Those principles are the subject of dedicated chapters within this book (Chapters 5 to 9) and will not be explored in detail here.

The seminal case of *Donoghue v Stevenson*[114] established the right of the ultimate consumer of a product to sue the manufacture regardless of whether or not there was a contractual relationship between the two:

> a manufacturer of products, which he sells in such a form as to show that he intends them to reach the ultimate consumer in the form in which they left him with no reasonable possibility of intermediate examination, and with the knowledge that the absence of reasonable care in the preparation or putting up of the products will result in an injury to the consumer's life or property, owes a duty to the consumer to take that reasonable care.[115]

That basic principle is of particular importance in medical product liability claims, in which a direct contractual relationship between the consumer and the manufacturer is the exception rather than the rule.

In claims of this nature there are potentially several parties in the supply/distribution line who could owe the claimant a duty of care. For example, a pharmacist who supplies the incorrect drug or the correct drug but at the wrong strength,[116] or who fails to consider the contraindications of a drug or impermissible combinations with other drugs, may be in breach of a duty of care owed to the consumer. In addition, the licensing authority might be liable in negligence if the medication or device fails but had met the relevant standards, as contemplated by the Court of Appeal in *HIV Haemophiliac Litigation*.[117]

The product does not need to have been sold for a negligence claim to bite. Here, as with the CPA 1987, samples sent out for use by a potential consumer are likely to fall within the scope of the duty.[118]

When determining whether a defendant has met the common law duty of care in respect of a particular product, a wide range of factors must be taken into account, including the magnitude of the risk involved, the probability of harm, the burden of taking precautions and the utility of the defendant's conduct. Such factors will be of particular importance in the context of medical product liability claims, and in particular those concerning design defects. In such cases producers often face an extremely difficult balancing exercise in which the potential benefits of a drug or device are weighed against the risks associated with the product. This is particularly difficult in cases where the benefits are of potential

---

113 Limitation Act 1980, s 11.
114 *Donoghue v Stevenson* [1932] AC 562.
115 *Donoghue v Stevenson*, per Lord Atkin at 599.
116 *Wooten v J Docter Ltd* [2008] EWCA Civ 1361.
117 HIV Haemophiliac Litigation 1990 WL 754830.
118 See obiter comments in *Hawkins v Coulsdon and Purley Urban District Council* [1954] 1 All ER 97 CA.

advantage to a large number of patients and the risk of significant injury will affect only a small number.

The standard of care required of the defendant is evaluated by reference to the knowledge the defendant had, or ought reasonably to have possessed, based on scientific knowledge at the relevant time;[119] knowledge gained by hindsight is not relevant. However, ignorance is not a defence and there is a positive duty on the producer/supplier of medical products to keep abreast of scientific discoveries that may affect the risk caused by the product in question.[120] This positive duty includes the duty to perform appropriate research and to design, implement and maintain a reasonable design process for products, especially if those products are inherently and obviously dangerous.[121]

For defendants, proving compliance with industry standards will provide strong evidence of reasonable care having been taken. It is not, however, determinative. There may be circumstances in which industry standards fall behind the general knowledge of an industry.

Proving that a defect in a medical product was caused by negligence is potentially difficult as it can often take years for problems to come to light. Testing of products will always be in limited numbers and may not uncover issues that become apparent when the product is distributed more widely. Unexpected reactions or unanticipated problems when given to a patient who is taking a certain combination of other drugs cannot always be predicted. Finding a balance between the need to guard against risk and appreciation of the unavoidable uncertainties involved with innovation in the medical sphere is something with which the courts have to grapple on a case-by-case basis. In doing so, they take into account the need for innovation to be encouraged in pursuit of wider benefits.

A manufacturer may escape liability if it can be established that it could reasonably be expected that examination by an intermediary ought to have revealed the defect in question.[122] For example, a dispenser of a medication can reasonably be expected to spot a broken packet.

Product liability claims in negligence are not restricted to circumstances in which there is a defect in the product itself; failure to provide instructions for use of the product or warnings with regard to known risks can be sufficient to found a claim. It is accepted that not every risk can or should be included within information leaflets. Some risks are medically complex and will need to be explained by a learned intermediary, such as a doctor or surgeon. Further, there is no requirement for products to include information that is needlessly alarming. There is, however, a duty not to mislead the user by the provision or omission of information. Consequently, where the labelling on a product listed a minor risk of 'harmful vapour', when in fact there was a risk of a serious explosion, there was a breach of duty, because users were likely to be misled by the label as they would reasonably assume that no more serious risk existed.[123]

---

119 *Vacwell Engineering Co Ltd v BDH Chemicals Ltd* [1970] 3 WLR 67.
120 *Cartwright v GKN Sankey* [1973] 14 KIR 349.
121 *Vacwell Engineering v BDH Chemicals* [1970] 3 WLR 67.
122 *Donoghue v Stevenson* [1932] AC 562.
123 *Vacwell Ltd v BDH Chemicals Ltd* [1971] 1 QB 88.

A defendant could be liable for failure to warn against the consequences of reasonably foreseeable misuse of a product, such as taking more than the recommended dose of medication, but liability is unlikely to be established if the usage in question was obscure.[124]

The manufacturer is not absolved of responsibility for the product once it has been placed on the market. A breach of duty can be established in the event of failure to act to recall a product or to issue appropriate warnings in the event that a risk of harm comes to light after the product has been supplied. In *Walton v British Leyland*,[125] British Leyland became aware of a problem involving the rear wheel bearing of Austin Allegros that caused the wheel to come off the vehicle. British Leyland had introduced a modification to the vehicle that would keep the wheel in place even if the bearing failed; however, an internal memorandum showed that they considered the risk of people driving Allegros without the modification to be intolerably high. In finding against British Leyland on the basis of a failure to take adequate steps to give instructions to dealers and other maintenance providers with regard to the known risk, the judge commented that:

> manufacturers have to steer a course between alarming the public unnecessarily, and so damaging the reputation of their products, and observing their duty of care towards whom they are in a position to protect from dangers of which they and they alone are aware.

It is noted that, in the majority of cases, warning about the potential risks associated with medical products will be a relatively inexpensive and easy exercise and the harm that could be potentially caused as a result of a failure to warn will often be severe. In the circumstances, if a defendant has failed to provide adequate warning with regard to a particular risk, good evidence will be needed to demonstrate that it was not reasonable to expect that warning to have been given.

---

124 See CJ Miller, RS Goldberg, *Product Liability* (2nd edn), Ch 17 for discussion on remoteness of damage, intervening act and the scope of the duty of care.
125 *Walton v British Leyland UK Ltd* (1978) Times, 13 July.

Part Three

Chapter 17

Procedure to service of proceedings

Hugh Johnson

PRIOR TO ISSUE

Pre-Action Investigations and the Pre-Action Protocol

The Pre-Action Protocol for the Resolution of Clinical Disputes ('the Protocol'), was first implemented in April 1999, as a means of ensuring that the Parties to proposed actions would both be able to investigate and respond to complaints at the pre-action stage. The explanatory notes in the early protocols referred to them as a set of 'ground rules' and drew reference to mistrust in healthcare disputes and the need to encourage a climate of openness and a less adversarial and more cost-effective way of resolving disputes about healthcare and medical treatment.

Against that background, the introduction to the Protocol continues to refer to a 'cards on the table' approach in which the parties are expected to set out their case in correspondence; it is the standard of normal reasonable pre-action conduct. However, whilst the Protocol could be described as the road map to follow when conducting early litigation investigations, it has never enjoyed the codified status of the Civil Procedure Rules 1998.

Almost two decades on, the Protocol remains flexible and can be applied to all sectors of healthcare: primary and secondary; and public and private.

The first significant revision to the Protocol was made in 2015. One of the frustrations of practitioners had been that the previous iteration of the Protocol 'lacked teeth' with no specific penalties for non-compliance. This was remedied, to an extent, by the 2015 revision, which stated explicitly that where either party has failed to comply with the Protocol the court *may* impose sanctions, taking into account the effect that the non-compliance has had on any other party. Any sanction is likely to be costs based[1] and will not be automatic; the court is required to

---

1 Whilst reports of such outcomes are rare, see, for example, *Nicole Chapman v Tameside Hospital NHS Trust* (2016) Lawtel LTL 18/7/2016, where the claimant (who discontinued) was award awarded costs for the defendant's failure to comply with the relevant protocol in an occupier's liability claim.

consider the effect that the non-compliance has had on any other party. More generally, the Practice Direction on Pre-Action Conduct is also applicable.[2]

The Protocol now specifically references the duty of candour imposed by the Health and Social Care Act 2008 (Regulated Activities) Regulations 2014, SI 2014/2936, reg 20 which addresses matters such as the 'culture of openness' that the original Protocol sought to facilitate. Taking into account those legislative changes and practitioner familiarity with it, the 2015 iteration was pared back, with less preamble and a focus upon the prescriptive recommended steps to be followed where litigation is in prospect. Those are addressed in turn below.

Claimant practitioners could be forgiven for overlooking the fact that the Protocol addresses pre-action rehabilitation, since it is rarely possible in healthcare claims to secure funding by agreement with the defendant for early treatment of that kind. This is, of course, in stark contrast with the position adopted by insurers in the field of personal injury. The difference can, in part, be explained by the challenges in resolving liability disputes early in clinical cases.

It is worth reflecting upon the rehabilitation provisions. Claimant practitioners should routinely invite rehabilitation input: the Protocol requires, through use of the imperative 'shall', that both parties consider rehabilitation needs and discuss them. There is, of course, a separate Rehabilitation Code[3] that provides guidance on the process of rehabilitation instructions if the parties do agree to implement early rehabilitation.

Whilst the Protocol does reference the possibility of discussions between the parties as to expert selection and regarding single joint experts, it also recognises that clinical claims are complex and does not seek to restrict the use of experts or approach to investigations. The Protocol makes clear that the court will determine which expert(s) can be relied upon (see also CPR 35.1). Put another way, whilst practitioners will need to instruct the appropriate experts at an early stage, there is no carte blanche to obtain and rely upon unlimited expert reports.

Having considered the Protocol in general terms above, it is then necessary to consider the procedural steps which the Protocol sets out. Whilst all of the steps may not be suitable for all cases, the Protocol provides a framework for the investigative process for the parties to the dispute and sets out a broad timetable for the pre-action procedures.

The prescribed steps, all of which are addressed in further detail below, include:

1   obtaining the medical records;
2   letter of notification;
3   letter of claim;
4   letter of response;

---

2   In particular, para 13 notes: The court may take into account (non)-compliance with a protocol when giving directions (CPR 3.1(4), 3.1(5)), and when making orders for costs (CPR 44.2(5)(a)).
3   The current version of the Rehabilitation Code is available, free to download, on the internet at https://www.cmsuk.org/files/CMSUK%20General/REHAB%20CODE%20 in%20full.pdf. There is also a direct 'click through' link is set out within the online version of the Protocol available from the Justice website.

5   dispute resolution;
6   stocktake; and
7   alternative dispute resolution (ADR).

Annex A of the Protocol is a helpful flow chart, which refers to each of the investigative stages of the Protocol.

Obtaining the medical records

The Protocol sets out at Annex B standard forms that can be used for clinical records requests. It should be noted, however, that the Protocol and the Annexes pre-date the General Data Protection Regulations (GDPR) and the Data Protection Act 2018 (DPA 2018), which made material changes to the law regarding the processing of personal data.

The GDPR is clear that there is no requirement to request personal data in writing. Patients can, in principle, simply ask for their notes. In practice, written requests will still need to be made. The annex to the Protocol would, ideally, have been updated in the 2019 edition of the *White Book*.[4] Since that amendment was overlooked, it is recommended that practitioners use the existing templates at Annex B (with which institutions and medical providers are already familiar) and adapt them to refer to the DPA 2018.

All requests for records should contain sufficient information to alert the healthcare provider where the adverse outcome has been serious. Copy records should be provided by the healthcare provider within *30 days*. This is a tighter timeframe than previously. Since it has long been the case that supplying healthcare providers struggled to meet the old 40 day timescale, requests for time extensions to collate and supply records are likely to continue. Reasonable requests for a time extension to copy the records (particularly if they are voluminous or still in use) are not uncommon; it will often be appropriate to accommodate them. In the event of non-compliance, an application to the court can be made.

Whereas it was once the case that computerised records were supplied for a notional cost of £10 and clinical records that required manual copying/processing were capped at a fee of £50, all records must now be supplied without charge. This is subject to limited exceptions, which include inter alia vexatious requests and repeated requests for the same information. Therefore the first request for records (and any periodic updates to obtain new records) should all be supplied without charge.

Where the patient has died, requests for records are treated differently. Despite the recent DPA 2018 the old anomaly from the 1998 Act persists. Medical records for living patients are processed under data protection provisions, whereas medical records of the deceased are processed under the provisions of the largely repealed Access to Health Records Act 1990 (AHRA 1990). There is no change to the fee structure of the AHRA 1990. Accordingly and in contrast to the DPA 2018, practitioners can expect to be charged for copy records. As there is no upper limit to that fee, most healthcare providers will levy a charge based upon the number of pages of records supplied. Those costs can be quite substantial.

---

4   *White Book Service 2019* (Sweet & Maxwell) 18 February 2019.

In all cases, the supplying healthcare provider is not expected to investigate every case where records are requested. Such is the volume of medical records requests nationwide, that it is likely to be all but impossible to investigate the background to each request. However, all healthcare providers should have a policy on what cases will be investigated. In serious cases, investigations are likely to have commenced before any records request is received for clinical reasons. Those investigations will typically be recorded in the form of a serious incident/root cause analysis report.

It may be necessary to request multiple sets of clinical records from both primary and secondary care providers and to include the ambulance service. When undertaking these initial enquiries, the claimant practitioner obtaining the relevant notes for their investigations should consider whether there are other documents that will assist the investigations, which will not necessarily be filed within the clinical notes. Depending on the facts of the case, these could include:

- hospital investigations into clinical treatment, such as serious untoward incident (SUI) or root cause analysis (RCA) reports (and any related investigation files);
- ambulance or out of hours telephone call logs/transcripts;
- patient complaints (responses and related internal memoranda);
- operating theatre and/or radiology logs; and
- hospital treatment protocols.

Whilst considering the documents that the claimant may wish to have sight of in the course of investigations, it should be noted that there is the option to apply to the court for pre-action disclosure under CPR 31.16 for disclosure prior to the commencement of proceedings. An application for pre-action disclosure can be made if, for any reason, a party has failed to provide key documents necessary to the investigations and which are likely to fall within the obligations of standard disclosure once proceedings are started. Whilst the provisions of CPR 31.16 are not confined to any party, in practice this is a tool most likely to be used by the claimant where there has been a failure to supply key clinical records, protocols or documents at an early stage.

The Protocol mirrors the High Court directions for clinical negligence matters. Once clinical records have been obtained, it is the responsibility of the claimant upon receipt of the records to collate, sort and paginate the records into bundles and to keep them updated. This is an essential step which will (if the case progresses) ensure that the claimant and defendant expert reports can helpfully refer to the same records by page numbering alone.

As a practical point, consideration should also be given to creating an expandable PDF® electronic record of the notes once collated and paginated. A number of commercial providers will now sort, paginate and create an electronic record as a single service.

Whether or not the records are held on CD-R or other means, such as Cloud storage, the existence of an electronic record facilitates the sharing of the records between experts and the parties more quickly, securely and cost-effectively, particularly if they are voluminous. NHS Resolution now require their panel solicitors to store and share clinical records electronically. This practice is becoming increasingly widespread and is likely to become the norm, reducing the risk of unencrypted paper records being lost in transit or misplaced.

Letters of notification

One of the defendant criticisms of the investigative stage of litigation was always that claimants have lavished time on their investigations, sometimes for a year or more, whilst permitting the defendant parties initially just three, and later, four months, to both investigate and prepare a letter of response to sometimes very detailed allegations of negligence. Inevitably, in some cases the defendant parties would find themselves simply unable to respond within those timescales. The letter of notification was introduced as a new step in the Protocol to counter those criticisms. In short, it is a 'heads up' to the defendant that there is an incoming claim, which should – if correctly acted upon – permit them to commence earlier investigations.

A template letter of notification forms part of the Protocol at Annex C1. It is necessarily an example and will require substantial amendment to suit the facts of any particular claim. The letter of notification should be sent where a clear case is identified (ie after analysis of the clinical records). In practice, it will often be appropriate to also await receipt of initial expert evidence, but that is not a requirement. For example, the existence of other documentary material, such as a hospital serious untoward incident investigation or a response to a patient complaint, could enable the claimant's representatives to prepare a letter of notification outlining the likely claim to follow. The core elements of the letter of notification should include:

- The claimant's details and confirmation that an initial case has been identified;
- a request for confirmation that the recipient is the correct defendant;
- an outline summary of facts;
- an outline summary of negligence alleged;
- whether expert evidence has been obtained (or the disciplines of experts likely to be required/from whom evidence is awaited);
- brief details of the injuries and their impact; and
- an index of the clinical records obtained.

The purpose of the letter of notification is only to state that it is likely that a detailed letter of claim will follow; it is an outline letter, not a pleading. A copy of the letter should be sent to NHS Resolution[5] or the relevant medical defence organisation (if known) in addition to the defendant. The letter should be acknowledged by the defendant within 14 days and details provided of the relevant claims handler if conduct of the matter is to be passed to a defence organisation or indemnifier.

Given that a detailed letter of claim will be sent at a later date, the aim should be to send the letter of notification as early as reasonably possible.

---

5   NHS Resolution will be the medical indemnifier in the majority of cases. Since 1 April 2017 the NHS Litigation Authority has operated under the name NHS Resolution. At the time of publication, all NHS Hospitals are members of the pooled indemnity scheme. Since 1 April 2019, general practitioners have also been indemnified under the NHS Resolution scheme.

If this stage is completed early, as it should be, it is inevitable that the claimant's final case will not be fully known. Some refinement by the time the letter of claim is prepared is inevitable and is unlikely to be (and should not be) criticised by the defendant party.

Letter of claim

If a letter of notification has been sent, it will normally be the case that, upon completion of the necessary investigations, the claimant will go on to set out detailed allegations of negligence in a letter of claim. Again, there is no precise formula for the content of the letter of claim or the scope of the investigations that should have been completed.

Nevertheless, given the earlier letter of notification stage is a preliminary notification of a case to answer; it follows that the letter of claim should be a thorough analysis, not generic in nature, and prepared with the benefit of expert evidence. Claimant practitioners should endeavour to send a letter of claim which is as close to their final allegations of negligence as possible. In more complex or high value cases, it is likely that a conference with counsel and experts will have taken place before the letter of claim is prepared. As before, the letter of claim should also be copied to the relevant medical indemnifier, if known. It is usually helpful to set out what clinical records have been obtained or to provide an index of the records in order that the defendant can request early disclosure of the records and/or work from the same collated set of records.

The Protocol includes a further template for the letter of claim at Annex C2. The format of the letter of claim is similar, but, inevitably, recommends greater detail is provided. The following is a useful summary of what should be included in the letter of claim:

- the patient's name, address, and date of birth;
- the dates of the alleged negligent treatment;
- the events giving rise to the claim;
- the allegations of breach of duty and the causation of the injury(ies) (which can be as complex as the circumstances require);
- the patient's injuries, condition and future prognosis;
- a request for clinical records if not previously sought or provided; and
- the likely value of the claim and/or the mains heads of loss.

The Protocol also refers to optional steps, most notably the possibility of serving the letter of claim with a CPR Part 36 settlement offer. It should be noted that the Protocol recommends that when an offer advanced in that way, condition and prognosis evidence[6] should also be served, together with details of the quantified claim in the form of a schedule of loss. Put simply, the Protocol makes clear that any offer to settle accompanying the letter of claim should be supplied with the same documentary evidence that is served when issuing proceedings (see further, Chapter 18).

The Protocol has always required the letter of claim to set out details of the funding position. That was particularly important where claimants sought to recover litigation insurance costs and additional liabilities in

---

6   Liability evidence is usually disclosed simultaneously during the proceedings, after issue. Neither the protocol nor the CPR provides for pre-action disclosure of the liability evidence.

the form of a conditional fee agreement success fee. Whilst there will now be few matters where there are funding retainers incepted prior to the changes brought in by the Legal Aid, Sentencing and Punishment of Offenders Act 2012 (LASPOA 2012) on 1 April 2013, it remains good practice to confirm the funding arrangements. It is also worth noting that the more limited additional insurance liabilities may still need to be notified, if the claimant seeks to recover them.[7]

The letter of claim is not a formal statement of case. As set out above, whilst it should reflect as closely as possible the finalised case to be set out in the particulars of claim (ie the case that the claimant intends to advance), the Protocol specifically states that no sanctions necessarily apply if the two differ. This is an important qualification that allows a claimant to expand upon or develop the allegations claimed in the letter of claim, where necessary, taking into account any response. It is, of course, a primary objective of the Protocol that issues should narrow prior to issue.

As a practical point, if, after having sent the letter of claim, an additional, new, allegation is identified, claimant practitioners would be well advised to notify the defendant of that new allegation as soon as possible. This will ensure that they have the opportunity to address the additional allegation prior to issue and avoid later delays at the defence stage.

Claimants are expected to wait four months from the sending of their letter of claim before issuing proceedings. This will permit the defendant to respond with the letter of response. The exception to this is where there is an impending limitation date. The Protocol does not extend any statutory limitations. Instead, the Protocol advocates protective issue and a stay in the proceedings. In practice, a consent order providing for an agreed time extension for the preparation of the particulars of claim, rather than a stay, will usually suffice and allow the early investigations to be completed prior to the statements of case being finalised.

Letter of response

The letter of claim should be acknowledged within 14 days and the name and details of the defendant representative provided. This is important as it is often at this juncture that the representation changes (whether to a claims handler or to external solicitors).

A template letter of response is attached to the Protocol at Annex C3. The Protocol provides that the letter of response should set out clearly what is denied, what is admitted and whether in whole or part.[8] Where there is a denial, reasons should be set out and any alternative case. There is no rigid formula, but the response will likely be clearest when responding to specific allegations in the letter of claim, if it adopts the

---

7   LASPOA 2012, s 46 provided for an amendment (s 58C) to the Courts and Legal Services Act 1990 which, with the Recovery of Costs Insurance Premiums in Clinical Negligence Proceedings (No 2) Regulations 2013, SI 2013/739, reg 3 provides that the part of any ATE premium which relates to the costs of initial expert report(s) may be recoverable inter partes.

8   Any admissions would need to be open (as distinct from made without prejudice) if they are to later be relied upon by the claimant for the purposes of securing judgment; see the CPR 14.1A(4)(a).

same numbering and headings and/or addresses each of the questions raised in turn.

The response should mirror the letter of claim in setting out what expert evidence[9] has been obtained. As may be expected, if the defendant seeks to attribute responsibility elsewhere, the details of that alternative defendant or provider should be provided. Where the defendant will rely upon hospital protocols, copies of those protocols should be provided.

Notwithstanding the four month period for the defendant to respond to the letter of claim, it is not unusual for a defendant to require additional time. The Protocol requires the defendant to give reasons and for the claimant to consider any reasonable request made.

By way of 'mirror' provisions, the Protocol envisages the possibility that the letter of response may be accompanied with settlement proposals. If that is the case, medical evidence should normally be provided.

Stocktake and alternative dispute resolution (ADR)

The Protocol has always included provision for ADR and the need to consider whether some form of dispute resolution other than litigation may provide better recourse. The detail of the Protocol is not restated here, but it may be that the 'stocktake' phase of the Protocol is the appropriate time to also consider ADR, once preliminary investigations have taken place.

Practitioners should also be aware of the NHS Resolution commitment to mediation to include, in particular, cases involving elder care or fatal cases. There is now a formal agreement between NHS Resolution and two mediation services (currently CEDR and Trust Mediation) who provide mediators for this service.

The stocktake was newly introduced as a Protocol step in 2015 and in an effort to focus the issues remaining in dispute prior to the commencement of court proceedings. The process requires each party to review their position, before co-operating to agree:

- a chronology of events which also identifies the facts/issues which are agreed and those which are disputed); and
- procedural directions for case management in the proposed litigation

The Protocol stages set out above structure the investigations process and introduce a degree of certainty regarding timescales and the steps to be undertaken by the parties, to the benefit of the parties and their representatives. The parties can begin (and in some cases) conclude investigations efficiently, having assessed the merits of their respective cases.

Where settlement is not possible and the claim is to proceed, it will do so after the stocktake process with the parties having already considered the steps likely to be required to progress the litigation.

---

9   It should be noted that the protocol makes no distinction between independent expert evidence and advisory expert evidence. Whilst the author understands that it was the intention of those on the Clinical Disputes Forum (CDF) that the evidence obtained at the protocol stage would be wholly independent, this is not an express requirement of the protocol. The defendant is therefore free to seek advice from employee, rather than an independent, expert in the field – if they so wish.

ISSUE

Starting proceedings

Clinical negligence remains a sphere of litigation recognised as involving complexity that can involve little relationship to the damages value of the claim. For that reason, such cases require greater court input and resource and are generally only appropriate for the multi-track. Whilst there continue to be proposals for reform within the civil litigation process, which include the fixing of the small claims limit[10] at the increased level of £2,000 for injury claims and proposals to fix costs for claims with a value of £25,000[11] it is worth noting that Lord Justice Jackson is on record that clinical negligence matters are unsuited to the fast track.[12]

Proceedings must be started in the High Court if the value of the claim is expected to exceed £100,000 and/or the value of the award for personal injuries is expected to exceed £50,000.[13] In forming an estimate of value, all additional claims to interest are disregarded as are reductive factors, such as contributory negligence (CPR 16.3(6)). The value of the claim will also have a bearing on the issue fee applicable to the claim (see below). There are provisions (see Practice Direction 7A, para 2.4) for starting a lower value claim in the High Court if: (a) the value of the claim is in dispute; (b) it is particularly complex; and/or (c) the outcome of the claim has importance to the public and, in the view of the claimant, it needs a High Court judge.

Claims outside London can be heard in the County Court District Registry; the circuit judge allocated the case will as a matter of course be accredited to try High Court actions.

Court fees on issue

Before considering the content of the claim form and particulars, the applicable court fees, which have risen substantially in recent years, now merit a separate note. Whilst the scale of civil litigation fees does, at least in theory, start from just £35, for clinical negligence matters the fee is likely to be far higher. The maximum fee (for claims worth more than £200,000) is now set at £100,000.

Accordingly, careful consideration should be given to the value of the claim to ensure that the commensurate fee is paid, whilst also noting that additional fees may be payable where provisional damages are sought. An application for a fee remission on Form EX160 should always be made if the court fee can be reclaimed on behalf of an

---

10   Currently limited by CPR 26.6(1)(a)(ii) to £1,000 for personal injury damages.
11   A Civil Justice Council (CJC) working group was convened in February 2018 and is now expected to prepare for the introduction of fixed recoverable costs for 'low value' clinical claims worth up to £25,000. This is now overdue, with the findings originally expected to be announced in September 2018.
12   Jackson LJ, *Review of Civil Litigation Costs: Supplemental Report Fixed Recoverable Costs*, para 9, p 9 (July 2017).
13   CPR PD 7A paras 2.1 and 2.2. See also High Court and County Courts Jurisdiction Order 1991, para 5(1).

eligible claimant.[14] The remission can be applied for prospectively and retrospectively. There are strict time limits for applying to remit the fees and appropriate evidence will need to be provided. From 1 July 2019 clinical negligence claims in the High Court became subject to e-filing for both documents and payments, see CPR PD 510. A prospective fee remission will therefore normally be essential.

Practitioners would be well advised to pay the correct court fee and to assess the value of the claim as accurately as possible. Not to do so is risky, giving rise to limitation issues and/or the restriction of the damages that may be recoverable. The authorities are somewhat contradictory. In *Page v Hewetts Solicitors*[15] and *Lewis v Ward Hadaway*,[16] claims had been brought (ie sent to the court) immediately before the limitation date but, critically, they had not yet been issued. The cases faltered on the basis that the correct fee needed to have been paid before the limitation date and in neither case had that occurred. *Lewis* is particularly notable because of a policy adopted by the solicitor to under-pay the court fee, a practice which was noted to be an abuse. By way of contrast, in *Dixon v Radley House Partnership*[17] and *Glenluce Fishing Co Ltd v Watamota Ltd*[18] the claim forms had been issued prior to the limitation date and upon payment of a fee, which it later transpired was insufficient for the value of the claim. Given the claim had been issued and paid prior to limitation, it was 'live' and not statute barred. The court found that there was then nothing to preclude an application to amend the certificate of value on the claim form if the additional information led to the claimant re-valuing the action. The proviso to that finding was that the very nature of the claim needed to be the same (ie whilst the heads of loss were likely to be revised, there was no attempt to bring a new cause of action).

It should be said that the above distinctions are marginal. In *Atha & Co Solicitors v Liddle*,[19] the most recent case to consider the point, Mr Justice Turner declined to find that the claimant's claim was statute barred, despite what appeared to be an intentional underpayment of the court fee. Whilst doing so, he acknowledged that there was conflicting case law and invited the Court of Appeal to provide definitive guidance. A case which provides that certainty is yet to be heard.

The claim form

The claim form will, of course, be well familiar to practitioners. There are no special requirements for clinical negligence matters as compared with other forms of litigation. Regard should be had to the valuation of the claim and the element of the claim relating to pain, suffering, and loss of amenity (see CPR PD 7A 3.6 and 3.8).

---

14   Note however, that there is some county court authority to suggest that the paying party will face an uphill struggle to avoid paying statutory court fees even where there has been a failure to seek remission – *Ian Cook v Malcolm Nicholls Ltd* (April 2019, unreported, Coventry County Court).
15   [2013] EWHC 2845 (Ch).
16   [2015] EWHC 3503 (Ch).
17   [2016] EWHC 2511 (TCC).
18   [2016] EWHC 1807 (TCC).
19   [2018] EWHC 1751 (QB).

CPR 16.2 states that the claim form must contain a concise statement of the nature of the claim, the remedy sought, and anything else required by any relevant practice direction. It is important to specify any representative capacity (if, for example, the claim is brought by a parent on behalf of a child or on behalf of a protected party). CPR 16.3 requires the value of the claim to be certified and it is upon this basis that the relevant court fees are payable (see above).

No claim can be initiated without setting out details of the nature of the claim (the particulars of claim) either on the reverse of the claim form itself or as a separate document. In clinical claims, it is usual to prepare particulars as a separate document given that it is usually necessary to set out a detailed medical history or to list breach allegations. Pursuant to CPR 16.2(2) reference to any separate particulars of claim must be made on the claim form CPR 16.2(2). There is a box which can be endorsed for that purpose on the back of the claim form.

Strictly speaking, if separate particulars are to be served, the claim form should be amended above the statement of truth to read 'the claimant believes the facts contained in this claim form are true' thereby deleting reference to the particulars of claim, for which there will need to be a separate declaration. The statement of truth is no empty formality. If a solicitor is to sign it, he must have authority from the claimant or risk that the proceedings will be struck out.[20] The claim form can, where time permits, be served wholly independently of the particulars of claim. Accordingly, service of the claim form is addressed first in this chapter.

Service of the claim form

The 'take home summary' is that in *all* circumstances the claim form should be served promptly. If nothing else, that will build in time to correct any error, such as sending documents to the wrong address. Even if the particulars of claim are not ready to be served (see below) far better to commence a valid claim than risk limitation. It is precisely because there is a wealth of jurisprudence highlighting the perils of service at the last minute (a number of which are referred to below) that the courts will not always be sympathetic.

As noted above, proceedings are 'brought' when the relevant documents are received by the court (thereby preventing expiry of any limitation period – even if the claim form is not sealed immediately). However, proceedings are only started when the claim form itself is sealed and thereby issued (CPR 7.2). The claim form must then be served within four months of issue (CPR 7.5(1)).[21] The normal rule is that the particulars of claim, if not served with or in the claim form, must be served within

---

20 In *Bao Xiang International Garment Centre v British Airways plc* [2015] EWC 3071 (Ch) proceedings were served on behalf of over 64,000 litigants in a class action, the claim form and particulars having been verified only by the solicitor with conduct. Significantly, the claimants had not retrospectively ratified that course of action by the time of the defendant's application to strike out. The claim was struck out for lack of authority.

21 Note that by virtue of the CPR 6.7(1) where a party has specified that their solicitor will accept service, serving the claim form on the party directly, rather than their solicitor will not constitute proper service. See *Nanglegan v Royal Free Hampstead NHS Trust* [2001] EWCA Civ 127; *Elmes v Hygrade Food Products plc* [2001] EWCA Civ 121.

14 days of service of the claim form. However, the particulars of claim cannot be served later than the last day permitted for service of the claim form (CPR 7.4). This latter caveat is highlighted in the commentary to the *White Book* as a 'trap for the unwary' and it was fatal to the claimant in *Venulum Property Investments Ltd v Space Architecture Ltd*,[22] where the particulars were served three days after the last day permitted for service of the claim form (ie four months and three days after issue).

Practitioners will note that the service provisions for documents other than the claim form (CPR 6.26) are quite different to those regarding the claim form. This will need to be borne in mind if the particulars of claim are served separately. As such, if claimant practitioners are to take the ill-advised step of attempting to serve on the last day, the particulars are best prepared as an addendum to the claim form and served as one document in the same envelope to avoid the particulars becoming subject to different service provisions. Further information relating to the contents of the particulars is provided later in the chapter.

Under CPR 7.5(1) where the claim form is served within the jurisdiction, the claimant need only complete 'the relevant step' before 12.00 midnight on the calendar day four months after the date of issue of the claim form. The effect of this rule is that service is instantly effective upon completion of the step (receipt of the claim is irrelevant). In contrast, when dispatched separately, the particulars of claim have the status of 'documents other than the claim form' and are subject to CPR 6.20. When using postal service, this means that particulars of claim sent separately will not be served until the second business day.

There are provisions for deemed service of the claim form at CPR 6.14 (on the second business day after dispatch). This initially appears to be otiose if valid service is affected merely by posting the claim form. However, this rule avoids uncertainty and is essential to defendant practitioners calculating the date upon which the acknowledgment of service or defence will be due.

The CPR 6.9(2) provides that service can be affected on an individual at their usual residential address (or, if sued in the name of a business at either the principal place of business or residential address). In the author's experience the medical indemnifiers for private practitioners make clear at an early stage that proceedings are served on them, to avoid proceedings being served on their members (whether at home or work). Conversely, the current position with healthcare services provided by the NHS seems to be that the relevant hospital trust is to be served directly. In all cases, practitioners are well advised to check the position. Checks should always be undertaken to ensure the correct party is being served at the correct address. There is a wealth of authorities to confirm that the mere involvement of a defendant solicitor in the early stages of the litigation does not equate to an authorisation to accept service of proceedings.[23]

As noted at the start of the service section of this chapter, there are a worryingly large number of cases in which the courts have grappled

---

22   [2013] EWHC 1242 (TCC) It should, however, be noted that this preceded *Denton v TH White* [2014] EWCA Civ 906. Whilst the interpretation of the CPR remains good law, it is possible that under the new test for relief from sanctions the claimant *may* have enjoyed a different outcome.

23   *Brown v Innovatorone plc* [2009] EWHC 1376 (Comm); *Woodward v Phoenix Healthcare Distribution Ltd* [2018] EWHC 2152 (Ch).

with poor service. Consideration of all of them is beyond the scope of this chapter, but it is worth noting that the rules do contain provisions for service to be dispensed with in 'exceptional circumstances' (CPR 6.16) and for service to be effected by alternative method or alternative place (CPR 6.15). Both are useful provisions, but the former provision will rarely be permitted – the courts have consistently shown reluctance to dispense with service where this was due to an error of the claimant.[24]

Service out of the jurisdiction is also beyond the scope of this chapter, not least because different countries will have different service requirements. For a recent example of the pitfalls, see *Punjab National Bank (International) Ltd v Srinivasan*[25] which addresses inter alia, deemed service, ex parte orders to extend time for service and service by alternative means.

Service by alternative means under the CPR 6.15 is a useful provision where service cannot easily be completed by post and may be a lifeline if a procedural error has been made which is capable of rectification. In *OOO Abbott v Econowall UK Ltd*[26] for example, the claimant's solicitors had misunderstood arrangements for an extension of time for service of the claim form, as a result of which the proceedings were out of time. The claimant successfully applied for an order that a photocopy of the claim form sent in earlier correspondence was alternate service. In *Abela v Baaderani*[27] the Supreme Court held that service upon the defendant's solicitor in Lebanon was to be validated as alternate service under the CPR 6.15(2) where there was evidence that the defendant himself was evading service. In all cases, it should be noted that there needs to be good reason for such an application, which will be fact specific.

Whilst a change is perhaps long overdue, it remains the case that service by email is not good service unless the requirements of CPR PD 6A 4.2 are met.

In *Barton v Wright Hassall*[28] the claimant, a litigant in person, emailed the proceedings at the end of the service period without checking to ensure that this would be valid service. The solicitors in receipt of the email subsequently argued that the claim was statute barred as they only accepted postal service. Inevitably, the claimant sought to argue that there was no prejudice to the defendant, since the claim had been received electronically. The case leapfrogged on appeal to the Supreme Court, which held that service had not been effective. Specifically, it was noted that the courts should be slow to remedy a service failure retrospectively by means of the CPR 6.15(2), where there has otherwise been good opportunity to correctly serve proceedings and where the CPR rules were not obscure or difficult to interpret.

No sooner than judgment in *Barton* was handed down, than similar issues arose again in *Woodward v Phoenix Healthcare Distribution Ltd*, albeit in relation to service by conventional means.[29] In *Woodward* a law firm tactically failed to make clear to their opponent that it had

---

24 See *Anderton v Clwyd* [2002] EWCA Civ 933 and *Bethell Group Plc v Deloitte and Touche* [2011] EWCA Civ 1321.
25 [2019] EWHC 89 (Ch).
26 [2016] EWHC 660 (IPEC).
27 [2013] UKSC 44.
28 [2018] UKSC 12.
29 [2018] EWHC 2152 (Ch).

no authority from their client to accept service. The claimant served proceedings upon the law firm, rather than upon the defendant company. By the time the error was rectified limitation had expired. At first instance, the Master was unimpressed by the defendant's solicitors. However, on appeal, the claim was held to be statute barred. In addition to the general point that the courts will be unwilling to rectify service failure after the event, *Woodward* confirms two other points: (i) there is no duty to advise an opponent of an error being made; and (ii) a failure to serve proceedings is not an issue which can be addressed as a relief from sanctions matter under the CPR 3.9.

Practitioners hoping to serve the claim form electronically will be reassured to note that *prospective* applications under the CPR 6.15(1) have been used to good effect to permit electronic service, which could assist where there are real difficulties affecting service. Whilst the provisions may not assist with 'routine service' where a party is abroad or there is uncertainty regarding postal service, service by electronic means clearly addresses the issue. The court will consider applications for service by alternate means on a case specific basis. However, service of various court proceedings and orders have previously been permitted across a range of electronic platforms. Somewhat unhelpfully, many of the cases remain unreported. Cases include, for example: *Linklaters LLP v Frank Mellish* (email);[30] *Ako Capital v TFS* (Facebook);[31] *DDF v YYZ* (Instagram);[32] and *Blaney v Persons Unknown* (Twitter).[33] Service has recently been permitted via SMS text message in the anonymised case of *NPV v QEL*.[34]

In all of the matters where electronic service was permitted it needed to be shown that: (i) the account belonged to the recipient; and (ii) was actively in use. These examples may be of practical use where a private practitioner has moved abroad and conventional service is impracticable.

Extending time for service of the claim form

The claimant may find himself in the position in which he is not ready to proceed with the litigation or is unable to effect service within the timescales available after issue.

The Court of Appeal confirmed in *Thomas v Home Office*[35] that the general provisions of the CPR 2.11 which permit the parties to agree extensions of time, do not exclude agreements relating to service of the claim form from their scope. Any agreements *must* be made by agreement in writing; it was on this latter point that the orally agreed time extension in *Thomas* was defective. The judgment provides clear guidance as to what constitutes written agreement and goes on to state that any further variation of the extended time period will also have to be agreed in writing.

Applications for extensions of time must otherwise be made under the CPR Part 7. Under the CPR 7.6(2) the court has a general discretion to

---

30   [2019] EWHC 177 (QB).
31   *Ako Capital LLP & Ako Master Fund Ltd v TFS Derivatives Ltd* (17 February 2012, unreported), Teare LJ; see also ECL Rep 2012, 12(2), 4–5.
32   (2015, unreported), Nicol J.
33   (2009, unreported) Lewinson J; See also case report, Matthew Richardson/University of London, at https://sas-space.sas.ac.uk/5370/1/1942-2747-1-SM.pdf.
34   *NPV v QEL, ZED* [2018] EWHC 703 (QB).
35   [2006] EWCA Civ 1355.

extend the time for serving a claim form, provided that the application is made prospectively, ie before the last date for service and within four months of issue. After that time, the claimant has very limited grounds to secure a time extension under the CPR 7.6(3), whilst demonstrating that they have acted promptly in applying and that, despite taking all reasonable steps, have been unable to serve the form (or that the court has been unable to serve it).

The court has no power to extend time for service of a claim form where the period prescribed for service has expired and the claimant cannot bring himself within the narrow provisions of the CPR 7.6(3). See, for example, *Vinos v Marks and Spencer plc*[36] where the claimant's solicitors had issued and filed proceedings, but not served within time.

Once out of time, the court's general discretion and powers of case management in the CPR 3.1(2)(a) cannot be utilised as an alternative basis for an application to extend the time limits for service. This is because CPR 3.1(2) stipulates 'except where these rules provide otherwise;' this has the practical effect of making the CPR 7.6 determinative.[37] Similarly, an application under the CPR 3.9 (relief from sanctions) cannot be made to secure a retrospective time extension, as was confirmed by the Court of Appeal in *Kaur v CTP Coil Ltd*.[38] In *Kaur* the court found it had not been reasonable for the claimant's solicitors to have delayed service because of difficulties preparing the schedule of loss.

Even when the claimant has a time extension from the court, they should not rest easy. In *Bayat v Cecil*,[39] the claimant intentionally delayed serving the claim form whilst he put in place a conditional fee agreement ('CFA') to fund the claim and, in particular, to obtain the necessary 'after the event' ('ATE') insurance to provide protection against adverse legal costs. A number of ex parte extensions of time were obtained, which perhaps ought to have been sufficient to put in place appropriate funding and to progress the litigation. In total there were extensions of time totalling some 11 months. Subsequently, the defendant applied to set aside the extensions of time that had been obtained (as it is permitted to do where an ex parte order has been made). Setting aside the extensions, the Court of Appeal held that whilst the applications had been made in time, ATE funding was not a good reason to delay service where the defendant should be able to take certainty from the statutory limitation and service periods. It was not for the claimant to unilaterally delay service.[40]

Bayat is but one example of how dangerous it can be to unilaterally extend time for service, despite apparently having authority from the court to do so. There are numerous examples. One can do little better than to turn to the punchy opening lines of the judgment of Mr Justice Stuart-Smith in *Lincolnshire County Council v Mouchel Business Services*.[41]

36 [2001] 3 All ER 784.
37 CPR 3.1(2) will, of course, apply in respect of extensions of time for other matters (even if retrospectively sought).
38 [2001] CP Rep 34.
39 [2011] EWCA Civ 135.
40 Burnton LJ, [100] citing with approval Browne-Wilkinson LJ in *Dagnell v J L Freedman & Co* [1993] 1 WLR 388 (HL).
41 [2014] EWHC 352 (TCC).

Where a party issues protective proceedings hard up against the expiry of the limitation period, it is expected to pursue those proceedings promptly and effectively; and if it subsequently seeks and obtains orders extending time for the service of the Claim Form or Particulars of Claim without notice to the other party, it dices with procedural death. These simple propositions should be known to all professionals conducting litigation. They were established long before the recent reforms of the Civil Procedure Rules.

Turning back to clinical matters, a not dissimilar approach was taken in *Foran v Secret Surgery Ltd*[42] where on appeal Cox LJ accepted the defendants' submissions – a time extension to serve the claim form out of jurisdiction was set aside, where that prejudiced a limitation defence. The extension should not have been permitted in the absence of good reasons.

In *Hashtroodi v Hancock*[43] the claimant's solicitor failed to serve the defendant with the claim form and supporting documents despite having previously secured an ex parte time extension. In rejecting the application to further extend time (and thereby debarring the claim) the Court of Appeal noted that the power to extend time retrospectively must be exercised in accordance with the overriding objectives. That included not permitting an extension of time, where an extension was required only by reason of the incompetence of the claimant's solicitor.

Insofar as it is possible to summarise a wealth of case law, much of it fact specific, one can draw together the common threads below:

* service of the claim form (whilst seeking time extension for other steps in the claim, such as service of the particulars of claim or schedule of losses) is likely to preferable to risking lapse of the proceedings;
* ex parte applications for extensions of time will always risk an application to set aside after the event;
* the better the reason for the time extension, the more likely it is to be granted; and solicitor error/negligence is 'a powerful reason for refusing to grant an extension of time'. Dyson LJ in *Hashtroodi* at para 35.

Particulars of claim

The CPR 16.4 states what the particulars of claim ('the particulars') must contain. Principally, it is to be a concise statement of the facts on which the claimant relies. Practitioners should also take note of the practice directions referred to. There are separate additional requirements in the practice directions for personal injury cases (most clinical claims) and cases incorporating a claim under the Fatal Accidents Act 1976 (FAA 1976).

Fatal claims are explored in detail in the sister edition of this book *Personal Injury Practice* (6th edn, 2014, Bloomsbury) at Chapter 29. For present purposes it is sufficient to note the requirements of the practice directions at the CPR PD 16 5.1–5.3 for any claim made under the FAA 1976. Details of all dependents, their ages and the specific nature of that claim must be set out within the particulars of claim.

---

42 [2016] EWHC 1029 (QB).
43 [2004] EWCA Civ 652.

In respect of any personal injury claim the requirements are that in addition to details of the injury, a schedule of loss setting out past and future expenses and losses must be served (CPR PD 16 4.2) together with a report from a medical practitioner, setting out the nature of the injury, if the claimant relies upon that evidence (CPR PD 16 4.3).

For cases where provisional damages are claimed, CPR PD 16 4.4 will apply. Those provisions require the claim to be set out explicitly, together with details of the disease or possible deterioration to their injury that the claimant may suffer. Typically, that will require the Particulars of Claim to state the condition and to cross refer to expert evidence. Practitioners should note that there is an additional fee payable on issue of the claim form where there is a provisional damages claim.

If the particulars are to be a 'concise statement of the facts' there is clearly a balance to be struck between clarity and brevity on the one hand and otiose detail on the other. See *McPhilemy v Times Newspapers Ltd*[44] and more recently, *Hague Plant Ltd v Hague*[45] where the claimant sought to re-cast his particulars into a 65 page document, five times longer than the original. In *McPhilemy*, Lord Woolf MR made the following remarks in connection with what were then new civil procedure rules:

> Pleadings are ... required to mark out the parameters of the case that is being advanced by each party. In particular they are still critical to identify the issues and the extent of the dispute between the parties ... As well as their expense, excessive particulars can achieve directly the opposite result from that which is intended. They can obscure the issues rather than providing clarification.

It may, of course, be the case that it is necessary to prepare a lengthy document if there is a particularly complex (relevant) medical history or allegations relating to multiple days or defendants. However, over reliance on precedent templates which may not be fully relevant or adopting a highly generalised view of the claim which results in putting allegations in 'for completeness' without fully analysing whether they require inclusion is, of course, to be avoided. Care should be taken in claims against multiple defendants that the allegations against each are set out clearly and in distinct terms.

Particulars that that make vague references to poor outcomes, and/or which are unclear as to dates or times – eg the defendant failed to monitor or monitor adequately the claimant during the admission – are likely to be met with a request for further information under the CPR 18 (see Chapter 18). Those will require additional work in the form of responses, often with expert input and/or additional court time if resisted in whole or part.

Key issues that the particulars should address are likely to include, inter alia, the following points:

- what action or omission was negligent;
- when it occurred;
- why it is alleged to have been negligent;
- what the claimant contends should have been done instead; and
- what the claimant says was the result to them of that negligent act or omission.

---

44   [1999] 3 All ER 775 (Woolf MR).
45   [2014] EWCA Civ 1609.

The particulars can only be adequately prepared once all of the clinical records have been reviewed and expert evidence obtained. It will usually be appropriate for there to be a conference with counsel and the experts to ensure that they are involved in shaping the allegations. In any event, the experts should have the opportunity to comment on the particulars before they are finalised ready for service.

All statements of case need to be endorsed with a statement of truth (CPR 22). The relevant practice direction – CPR PD 22 3.1 sets out clearly who can sign the declaration. This will usually be the claimant or their legal representative. It should be noted that a legal authority to control affairs (eg a power of attorney) does not confer authority to sign a statement of truth, unless also acting as litigation friend. The CPR 22.2 provides that a failure to sign a statement of truth will not lead to a served statement of case being struck out (other than on the application of the defendant) but will mean that the evidence contained within it cannot be relied upon. The usual remedy is simply to require service of a signed statement of case under the CPR 22.4.

Late service of particulars of claim

Whereas limitation is not a matter to take lightly and the courts have been relatively unforgiving where additional time is needed to serve the claim form, the position is different with the particulars of claim. Once a claim is 'up and running' a claimant is more likely to be permitted to extend time for service of the particulars than would be the case if the claim form had not been served at all. No better is this illustrated than in *Viridor Waste Management v Veolia Environmental Services Ltd*[46] where particulars were served a few days late as a result of an administrative error. Not only was relief from sanction granted, but costs were awarded against the defendant for taking the point insofar as the defendant had failed to have regard to the overriding objectives.

Applications made prospectively within time

In *Robert v Momentum Services*[47] the Court of Appeal confirmed that an application to extend time for service of particulars made within time under the CPR 3.1(2) was not a matter to which the requirements of the CPR 3.9 (relief from sanction) needed to be considered at all, nor did the court need to consider the merits of the case generally.

Applications made after the event and out of time

The CPR 3.9 (relief from sanctions) and the test established in *Denton v TH White*[48] will both need to be considered if the particulars are served late and the defendant takes issue with late service. Given the conscious decision to impose a new regime which is less forgiving of default, limited

---

46   [2015] EWHC 2321 (Comm).
47   [2003] EWCA Civ 299. Whilst determined under a previous incarnation of the CPR, Jackson LJ confirmed in *Hallam Estates v Baker* [2014] EWCA Civ 661 that this remains the correct approach.
48   [2014] EWCA Civ 906.

guidance can perhaps be garnered from precedents pre-dating 2014. Strike out is a distinct possibility. In *Chelsea Bridge Apartments v Old Street Homes Ltd*,[49] the court refused to permit late particulars in the absence of good reasons, whilst also rejecting the alternative argument that the bare details set out on the face of a claim form were sufficient in lieu of detailed particulars. In *North Midland Construction plc v Geo Networks Ltd*[50] there is a useful consideration of the issues. In that case, which considered two claims, relief was granted in respect of one claim, but not the other. A positive factor in the claim where relief was given was that steps had been taken to ameliorate the breach (the late particulars had at least been served by the date of the hearing).

Documents required to be served with the proceedings

As clinical negligence claims are cases involving personal injury, it is an essential requirement of CPR PD 16 4.1–4.3 that a medical report, and schedule of loss are served with the proceedings. In addition, the response pack (forms N9) and, if part of any ATE insurance premium is to be recoverable, form N251 should also be served. The preparation of those documents, other than the response pack, is addressed elsewhere in this book. The section below explores the position where limited or only provisional evidence is available in the form of a schedule of loss or medical report and yet proceedings need to be served.

Schedule of loss

In some cases, it will not be possible to serve a fully costed schedule of loss with the proceedings. Strictly speaking, CPR PD 16 4.2 does not make the service of a schedule mandatory, which means that the court is unlikely to strike out the entire claim unless in receipt of an application to do so. However, the claimant risks being excluded from claiming special damages without a schedule of loss.

In many cases and certainly with claims involving fatal injury, it will be possible to fully cost the losses or, to have at least costed all of the past losses with a high degree of accuracy. Service of a bare schedule may risk an application by the defendant that the claimant should be limited to the damages pleaded in the schedule or at least serve a revised schedule.

However, there are cases where there may be good reasons that a fully costed schedule cannot be prepared. Such cases may include child cases (injuries at birth) or those where there has been a catastrophic injury. Where there is a significant body of quantum expert evidence yet to be obtained it will rarely be possible to have a full and detailed schedule available at the outset. If the parties believe a split trial is appropriate, then it is likely that some experts will not even have been retained. A pragmatic view therefore needs to be taken.

---

49 *Old Street Homes Ltd (2) Anthony Donnellan v (1) Chelsea Bridge Apartments Ltd (2) Alan Ward* [2018] EWHC 1162 (Ch).
50 [2015] EWHC 2384 (TCC).

Whilst not confining his comments to the schedule of loss, but rather the statements of case, Mr Justice Smith's comments in *Gamatronic (UK) Ltd v Hamilton*[51] are apposite.

> I do not criticise the claimants for being unable at this stage to assess the amount of damages that they claim. However, they do not identify even their heads of loss beyond pleading (at para 21) that Gamatronic UK 'claims as damages from the defendants its lost profits and other losses it suffered as a result of their breaches of duty'.

Accordingly, a preliminary schedule identifying the heads of loss, which at least provides information and narrative relating to past losses and possible future expenses, if not the total sums claimed, ought to be served. In that way there is sufficient information for the receiving defendant to understand the scope of the claim in such a way that a sensible insurance reserve can be set. This is an approach which, if not quite approved, was accepted by Mr Justice Spencer in *Mark v Universal Coatings*[52] as the usual course for complex cases which will require quantification over time.

The medical report

Now that the majority of clinical negligence claims are brought by specialists in the field, it is perhaps unnecessary to emphasise that the requirement of CPR PD 16 4.3 is to only to serve 'a report from a medical practitioner about the personal injuries which he alleges in his claim.' Put simply, the report needs to address present condition and prognosis – a report commenting on liability is not required (and in the author's view, should not be served) with proceedings.

Whilst it will no doubt be referred to within the particulars of claim, the condition and prognosis report does not form part of the pleading; it should not be expected to necessarily address the entirety of the case set out in the particulars of claim. In *Sion v Hampstead Health Authority*,[53] albeit a case that pre-dates the CPR, Staughton LJ referred to the report as providing a 'general outline' of the claim only. That must be correct, as additional evidence may later become available and/or the original report updated. However, this does not mean that the contents of the report are not important. The report must contain sufficient evidence to substantiate the loss claimed. In *Sion*, the claimant's medical evidence, although evidencing a psychological injury did not establish sufficient nexus to permit a 'nervous shock' claim to be made out.

It will normally be possible to have arranged a condition and prognosis examination of the claimant by an independent specialist prior to commencing proceedings. However, occasionally, this may not be possible within available time constraints. With all of the authorities on this point, it is clear that a failure to serve any medical evidence risks strike out. Similarly, the service of *some* medical evidence is perhaps ill-advised, but likely to be a better option than proceeding with the claim unsupported by evidence.

---

51   [2013] EWHC 3287 (QB).
52   *Mark v Universal Coatings & Services Ltd* [2018] EWHC 3206 (QB) See, in particular, [49].
53   [1994] EWCA Civ 26.

In *Duce v Worcestershire Acute Hospitals NHS Trust*[54] the claimant served proceedings in the County Court without supporting medical evidence. The defendant applied to debar the claimant from relying on supporting evidence and, in fact, the claim was ultimately struck out. The case is notable for a number of procedural errors (by both the court and the claimant) which included confusion regarding exactly what reports needed to be served (all of them, liability, or condition and prognosis). Whilst the Court of Appeal did ultimately restore the claim, it is evident from the judgment that the claimant could consider herself fortunate. Unfortunately for the claimant, she was later to be unsuccessful in the substantive litigation in any event.

There are a number of reported challenges in relation to medical evidence served with proceedings which, whilst evidencing injury, do not meet the requirements of expert evidence under CPR 35. Whilst there are helpful, if now old, Court of Appeal authority to suggest that a letter from a medical practitioner may be adequate to stand as a medical report[55] those judgments are to be treated with caution, given that they refer to the County Court Rules (CCR) then applicable. In *Knight v Sage Group plc*[56] the claimant served only a letter from her GP. The court at first instance accepted that this was sufficient 'for the initial period of proceedings' but expressly noted that it was not compliant with the new CPR requirements. It should be noted, however, that before obtaining that favourable determination from the court, the claimant faced both a strike out application and the appeal of that decision. On any view, such hearings are best avoided. The Court of Appeal subsequently required a full medical report to be served within three months.

In *Dalus v Lear Corporation (Nottingham) Ltd*[57] the County Courts considered the status of an audiology test served with proceedings, rather than a report from an ENT consultant. The claim was for noise induced hearing loss. Whilst a County Court decision, it helpfully explores the CPR rules, the definition of and status of the 'medical practitioner', and the status of documents such as that served (which are clearly not to be regarded as medical reports). The claimant avoided strike out, but it should be noted that this was in no small part because the defendant had raised the point very late. By the date of the hearing a CPR Part 35 compliant report had been obtained and served.

Most recently, in *Mark v Universal Coatings & Services Ltd*[58] Mr Justice Spencer went as far to remark (at [53]) that the failure to serve a medical report may amount to a trivial breach of the rules in view of the fact that the preliminary documents served with proceedings so often are limited in scope and need later updating.

If there is no condition and prognosis report available and there is a need to serve, the safest course should still normally be to serve proceedings together with a relevant clinical letter or report. The report must, of course, be signed by a medical professional and set out as clearly as possible the injury sustained, which is the basis of the claim. Where

---

54 [2014] EWCA Civ 249.
55 *Edwards v Peter Black Healthcare (Southern) Ltd* [1999] EWCA Civ 1369.
56 [1999] EWCA Civ 1285.
57 (2018) 02/07/2018; Leeds CC; HHJ Gosnell.
58 [2018] EWHC 3206 (QB) See, in particular, [49] and [53].

possible, it may be prudent for the claimant to liaise with the defendant prior to service to agree a timetable to provide a full and detailed condition and prognosis report, rather than to disregard the issue and risk a later application.

Finally, as a practical point, care should be taken when serving the condition and prognosis report to ensure that it does not cross refer to draft statement or documents that are privileged.

THE DEFENCE

It goes almost without saying that if there is a defect with the proceedings (eg limitation or service, for example), the correct approach is to contest jurisdiction with the acknowledgment of service, not to acknowledge the service of the claim. See, for example, *Hoddinott v Persimmon Homes*.[59] Failure to contest such issues prior to the defence, risks the defendant from being unable to take the point.

Assuming that proceedings have been served appropriately, the time within which a defence must be filed (14 days after service of the particulars of claim, or 28 days if an acknowledgment of service has been filed (CPR 15.4), can be extended by agreement between the parties for a further period up to 28 days (CPR 15.5)). If agreeing to the longer extension under the CPR 15.5 the defendant must inform the court in writing).

In some cases, it may be necessary to agree by consent order to longer periods of time to accommodate expert availability or where the claimant and defendant have agreed 'mirror' time extensions to finalise their respective statements of case.

If no defence is filed on time, the claimant will be entitled to seek judgment in default. Following *Billington v Davies*[60] it is now clear that serving a defence out of time, without permission of the court, will be insufficient to preclude the claimant from obtaining default judgment as it will be 'a document purporting to be a defence' unless and until the court have permitted late service.

The CPR 16.5 provides that the defence must:

- set out which of the claimant's allegations the defendant admits or denies;
- set out which of the allegations the defendant requires the claimant to prove;
- state reasons the defendant's reasons for any denial; and
- if the defendant intends to aver a different version of events, set out those details.

If the defence deals with an issue, but does not expressly plead to an allegation of breach, the CPR 16.5(3) provides that this is sufficient for the defendant to have required that allegation to be proven. In contrast, the CPR 16.5(4) provides that if the defence is wholly silent in relation to a pleaded allegation, an admission will be inferred. It is therefore

---

59 [2007] EWCA Civ 1203.
60 *Ian Billington v Simon Davies & Sloane Capital Ltd* [2016] EWHC 1919 (Ch).

essential that care is taken by the defendant practitioner to address all aspects of the particulars and to avoid any inadvertent admissions.

As a result of the above requirements, the bare defence which consists of little more than a denial of all elements of the claim is rarely seen. If such a defence is served, it is likely that the defendant will risk an application for strike out under the CPR 3.4(2)(a). In *DIL v Commissioner of Police of the Metropolis*,[61] the court declined to strike out a defence comprising bare denials, but ordered that a new defence was filed and held that in default, the allegations would be admitted under the CPR 16.5(4).

When preparing the defence, regard should also be had to the requirements of the practice direction CPR PD 16 12.1. The defendant must state in the defence whether they agree, dispute or have no knowledge of the matters contained in the claimant's medical report. If the defendant disputes any part of the report, they must give their reasons. In practice, the defendant will often need to reserve his position pending receipt of any condition and prognosis evidence of their own.

The provision at CPR PD 16 12.1(3) is often overlooked. If the defendant has already obtained their own (condition and prognosis) report on which they intend to rely, it must be served with the defence. Since the defendant's medical experts will not often have had opportunity to examine the claimant so early on in the proceedings this rarely needs to be considered. Nevertheless, where an examination has taken place, both parties should therefore have early access to the condition and prognosis evidence and the claimant's representatives should ensure it is served.

If the claimant has served a detailed schedule of loss, the CPR PD 16 12.2 requires the defence to address the contents of the schedule served with the particulars of claim. In practice this is likely to be limited to more straightforward cases and fatal cases, for the reasons outlined above. It is, however, an important requirement if the parties are to sensibly progress to early ADR, for example. Clearly, if the claimant has served a heavily qualified schedule of loss marked 'to be confirmed' throughout or limited to narrative comment on the likely heads of loss, the defendant is unlikely to be criticised for electing not to prepare a preliminary counter-schedule, precisely because it will be similarly qualified.

Finally and without restating the references above made in connection with the particulars, it follows that the principles of (concise) good drafting practice remain common to both statements of case.

Reply to the defence

The reply to the defence is the claimant's optional opportunity to respond to any points made in the defence which were not dealt with in the claim or particulars of claim. Clearly, a reply and defence would be mandatory if a counter-claim is advanced, but that will be rare in the context of a clinical negligence matter.

A reply is likely to be considered by the claimant where the defence raises questions or issues such that a factual clarification is needed. Critically, the reply must not contradict the earlier particulars or be used to bring in any new allegations of negligence. If the claimant wishes to depart from the case set out in the particulars of claim, the correct

---

61 [2014] EWHC 2184 (QB).

approach is to apply to amend the particulars of claim, not to serve a reply to the defence.

In the absence of permission from the court, the CPR 15.9 provides that no party has a right to file or serve a statement of case after the reply. In this way, the parties are committed to the pleaded case, without multiple replies or revisions to the statements of case being served continuously.

Chapter 18

Procedure from service to trial

Hugh Johnson

INTRODUCTION

With the requirements of active case management at the CPR 1.2(4) each clinical negligence claim should, following issue, be allocated to a track and progressed in a linear fashion, to a strict timetable up to the date of trial. In practice, much depends upon the conduct of the litigation process and the nature of the evidence served.

This chapter addresses the procedures from service to trial in five separate components: (i) dealing with the steps usually directed; (ii) common applications; (iii) the toolbox of applications at the litigator's disposal to bring proceedings to a swift end; (iv) other matters; and (v) the distinct procedures specific to multi-party actions.

1   The litigation process and directions:
   • case management;
   • disclosure;
   • witness statements;
   • expert reports and discussions; and
   • trial.
2   Common applications:
   • requests for further information;
   • disclosure applications.
3   Applications to strike out (and analogous orders):
   • strike out;
   • default judgment;
   • summary judgment;
   • fundamental dishonesty.
4   Other matters:
   • civil restraint orders;
   • defendant submission of no case to answer;
   • issuing fresh proceedings after procedural defect: 'Back in play'.
5   Multi-party (group) actions – the distinct processes/procedures for these claims.

THE LITIGATION TIMETABLE AND DIRECTIONS

Case management

Allocation questionnaire

Once a defence has been filed, the parties will be sent an allocation questionnaire (Form N150) pursuant to the CPR 26, which requires further information about the claim to be provided. As noted in Chapter 17, clinical negligence matters will, almost invariably be assigned to the multi-track. The court will then fix a case management conference ('CMC') for the purpose of giving relevant directions on every aspect of the future progress of the case, per the CPR 29.2 and 29.3.

When completing the allocation questionnaire, practitioners will need to address questions relating to:

- ADR;
- the appropriate court;
- the numbers of witnesses and experts;
- the appropriate directions; and
- estimated costs.

Draft directions should be prepared and appended to or returned with the questionnaire as should an estimate of costs, subject to matters of costs budgeting.

When completing the allocation questionnaire consideration needs to be given to the costs budgeting provisions of the CPR 3.13. The approach to completion of the N150 must vary contingent upon the value of the claim (see below). If the claim is brought on behalf of a child or protected party, the claim will not subject to costs budgeting at all (CPR 3.12).

Costs and costs budgeting will be covered in more detail in Chapter 27. However, for the purposes of allocation, it should be noted that:

1 *For cases valued at £50,000 or less:*
   A costs budget must be returned with the questionnaire.
2 *For cases valued between £50,000 and £10m:*
   Since budgets do not need to be filed until 21 clear days prior to the costs and case management hearing (CPR 3.13), it is now common practice to lodge the questionnaire with no costs information provided, save for endorsing the form with the words 'a costs budget will be filed 21 days prior to the costs and case management hearing' (or similar).
3 *For cases valued in excess of £10m:*
   There will be no costs budget. Whereas this category of cases applied to only very few clinical negligence matters, the readjustment of the discount rate from +2.5% to –0.75% and from 15 July 2019, to –025% has brought many more maximum severity clinical claims within this band. The discount rate is, of course, likely to be subject to more regular review in future years.[1]

Practitioners are expected to have liaised before preparing their draft directions and appending them to the directions questionnaire. This is

---

1 Civil Liability Act 2018, s 10(2), Sch A1, para 1(3).

indicated on the N150 itself and, of course, is to be encouraged given the 'active case management' provisions of the CPR 1.4(2). It was once possible, even in the largest claims, for experienced practitioners to reach agreement as to the necessary directions, with the aim of dispensing with a hearing. Indeed, many case management hearings were agreed and vacated in that way. Where cases are not costs budgeted, that may still be achieved. However, in the majority of cases a CMC will be required, simply because it is rare that the costs budgets will be agreed. If a hearing then becomes inevitable, there may also be less incentive to try and resolve minor directions disputes.

Costs and case management conference – directions

One of the unintended consequences of the Jackson reforms that brought in costs and case management hearings has been that very few first CMCs are vacated. Additionally, all CMCs are now rather longer in duration. Whilst regional experience has varied wildly, the courts are invariably busy. It will likely be a period of months, rather than weeks, before a CMC is heard. At the High Court, six months is usual.

Whilst the early consideration of steps needed to progress the litigation is helpful, there are two clear limitations. First, any dates set out in the draft directions will need to be revisited at the CMC given the passage of time between the drafting and the likely hearing date. Second, even if directions were agreed by the parties a period of months before the CMC, neither party will have been able to complete any steps before the CMC, given that one or both parties will want to put a costs budget in place first. This often means that little can be achieved in the intervening period.

Whilst the directions will be ordered on the basis that the timetable is realistic rather than aspirational, there are such a number of variables, many outside the practitioner's control, that some delays (and extensions of time) are inevitable. For example, the clinical commitments of medical experts may impinge upon their availability to report on time. The helpful provisions of the CPR 3.8(4) permit extensions of time to be agreed by the parties of up to 28 days to an order of the court – provided the trial date is not adversely affected.[2] Those provisions codify a provision that had been routinely ordered by the clinical negligence Masters after *Andrew Mitchell MP v News Group Newspapers Ltd*.[3] Practitioners should note the pitfall that the agreement cannot be retrospective and must be in writing. In *Thomas v Home Office*[4] it was confirmed that oral agreements or time extensions not confirmed by written exchange will be inadequate. Therefore, when seeking an extension of time, which are often requests made by email, practitioners should ensure that a return email confirming the terms is received.

The case management directions will inevitably vary between cases, but generally will require the claimant to obtain and collate up-to-date clinical records and make clear each expert report required and/or expert

---

2   The time extension is permitted to any order, provided that there is no adverse effect on the trial date and it is agreed by both parties in writing. After a 28 day extension, a further order of the court is needed. Unless that court order specifies otherwise, it is then once again capable of a further 28 day extension by agreement.

3   [2013] EWCA Civ 1537.

4   [2006] EWCA Civ 1355.

permitted to give evidence. A detailed timetable will be set down for the steps below to be completed:

- disclosure of documents;
- exchange of evidence (lay witnesses);
- exchange of evidence (expert witnesses);
- expert agendas and the meeting/discussions between experts;
- expert joint reports;
- service of schedules and counter-schedules;
- an appropriate last date by which ADR needs to be considered;
- a trial period or window; and
- service of chronologies, summaries and skeleton arguments.

Unless there are directions for split trial, the directions for witness evidence and expert evidence will usually include two dates for exchange: liability evidence, which is exchanged simultaneously; and quantum evidence, which is exchanged sequentially.

Drafting the directions – practical points

The precise requirements will be case specific, but will include everything the parties and the court can reasonably contemplate at the time of making the directions. The Masters of the High Court, who are assigned to clinical negligence claims, first developed a useful set of standard clinical directions in 2002 ('the model directions'). These have been updated regularly since and are now a benchmark from which there needs to be good reason to depart in High Court clinical negligence claims. The published, current model directions are set out in full at Appendix III, but are also available online at the Justice website[5] and periodically updated.

The High Court directions are not binding on other courts, but courts outside London often use them. Whilst the comments were made in connection with just one element of the standard directions, Brooke LJ in the Court of Appeal observed the following:

> Now that so many relatively heavy clinical negligence actions in the multi-track are being conducted in county courts, in addition to district registries of the High Court, it is essential that best practice should be followed throughout the country in relation to case management directions in the multi-track in this specialist field.[6]

Whatever form directions take, it is essential that exchange of witness statements takes place two or three months before exchange of expert reports in order to allow sufficient time for the experts to consider the witness statements. As was noted by the Supreme Court in the Scottish case of *Kennedy v Cordia Services*[7] and most recently, in the pointed comments of Mr Justice Martin Spencer in *Arksey v Cambridge University Hospitals*[8] the experts need to consider the factual evidence before them. This should therefore include reference to both documents and the statements of fact.

---

5   The model directions (online), see https://www.justice.gov.uk/courts/procedure-rules/civil/standard-directions/general/list-of-cases-of-common-occurance.
6   *Wardlaw v Farrar* [2003] EWCA Civ 1719, at [24].
7   *Kennedy v Cordia (Services) LLP (Scotland)* [2016] UKSC 6, at [57].
8   *Arksey v Cambridge University Hospitals NHS Foundation Trust* [2019] EWHC 1276 (QB) at [63].

Preliminary issues

In cases where a number of quantum experts are likely to be required and liability is disputed, it may be appropriate to seek a trial of the preliminary issue (often referred to as a split trial). In this way, issues of breach of duty and causation can be dealt with at a separate trial. This will streamline the directions initially required and, importantly, avoids the often significant costs of obtaining several reports addressing quantum issues.

In the author's experience, claimants prefer a split trial if only because there is less demand to attend multiple medico-legal appointments until such time as it is known whether or not their case has been successful. If expert assessments, especially domiciliary appointments are deferred until after the liability issues are resolved, there is scope to avoid significant legal costs: in a large claim if a claim is successfully defended, a preliminary issues trial may mean that the costs of between 2–5 quantum experts for each party will have been avoided and not wasted.

If a preliminary issues trial is considered appropriate, early discussions between the parties will be required to try and agree the directions. Further, it should not be assumed that the court will automatically agree. Indeed, practitioners should consider preparing two sets of directions (and budgets) for the CMC. This will assist the parties to prepare for whichever approach the court determines to be appropriate.

Disclosure

The CPR 31 deals with the duties of disclosure. In practice, disclosure in clinical negligence matters can be the most straightforward element of the directions. By the time that the parties have had the first CMC, it is common for the clinical records to have been collated, paginated and mutually exchanged.

Therefore disclosure is likely to deal with other materials which may be available. From the defendant these could include hospital policy documents/procedures, any complaints or investigations files, surgical and/or theatre log books (if relevant) and which are yet to be disclosed. From the claimant, these could include diary excerpts, text messages, social media posts and/or emails to confirm appointment dates or symptoms, if relevant to the liability issues. Clearly, when it comes to the assessment of quantum, there may also be a number of receipts and invoices.

Disclosure is dealt with by exchange of Form N265. There should be a properly itemised list, prepared and certified by each party. It should be noted that the CPR 31.10 does not permit a solicitor to sign the disclosure statement (in contrast to the statements of case which can, of course, be signed by the legal representatives). Disclosure is not to be regarded as a mere technicality, see *Arrow Trading v Edwardian Group Ltd*[9] where lists were not correctly served by all of the respondents, nor were declarations signed to confirm that the disclosure process had been properly complied with. Where records are increasingly held by both parties in electronic

---

9   [2004] EWHC 1319 (Ch), at [43]–[45].

form, care should be taken to ensure the correct declarations are made for those documents.

At present, there remains a good deal of documentation still created and retained in hard copy form and standard disclosure is the norm. However, it is to be expected that parties will increasingly migrate to systems where records are supplied and maintained electronically with, in time, the use of the CPR e-disclosure provisions where appropriate (CPR PD 31B). The usual course is that documents should be requested (copies or inspection) within 7–14 days of service of the disclosure list and any copies are to be provided promptly thereafter. If there is any dispute over the nature or extent of the disclosure sought an application may be made to the court. Clearly any delays relating to disclosure are likely to have a consequential effect upon other directions.

Witness evidence

Witness evidence could justifiably form the subject of a book in its own right. The section below covers the service of the evidence and some of issues that arise, in particular, in relation to the liability evidence.

Evidence from the claimant and, often, family members, will be important –both in relation to the negligence alleged, but also in relation to quantum – to support the claim for the damages sought. The model directions assume the service of two sets of statements during the litigation. Liability statements will address the treatment received with the quantum evidence often addressing matters as diverse as care needs and accommodation. In most cases, the defendant medical practitioner or provider will have no quantum witness evidence to adduce. However, multiple liability statements are not uncommon.

Practitioners will note that the model directions contain the following provision:

> For the avoidance of doubt statements of all concerned with the relevant treatment and care of the claimant must be included.

Whilst this clearly cannot be interpreted as a provision requiring all hospital staff who ever treated the claimant to provide witness evidence, it can be expected that a statement will be adduced from all the key personnel involved in the claimant's care. There have been a number of cases exploring whether the absence of a witness statement from a treating clinician is a lacuna for which an adverse inference should be drawn by the court. See *Wisniewski (A Minor) v Central Manchester Health Authority*,[10] where an adverse inference was drawn – the defendant served a short Civil Evidence Act 1995 notice from the key senior house officer (SHO) on duty in a maternity claim.

The position relating to adverse inferences (more usually referred to as 'regarding the claimant's evidence benevolently and the defendant's evidence critically')[11] was perhaps expressed most clearly in *Keefe v Isle*

---

10   [1998] EWCA Civ 596.
11   [2010] EWCA Civ 683, at [19].

of *Man Steam Packet Co Ltd*[12] where Lord Justice Longmore made the following observation, citing *British Railways Board v Herrington*:[13]

> If a defendant fails to call witnesses at his disposal who could have evidence relevant to an issue in the case, that defendant runs the risk of relevant adverse findings ... Similarly a defendant who has, in breach of duty, made it difficult or impossible for a claimant to adduce relevant evidence must run the risk of adverse factual findings.

In *TW (A Child) v Royal Bolton NHS Foundation Trust*[14] there was neither a written record nor witness evidence – a hospital midwife had failed to make notes of a key telephone discussion and the defendant trust had not located and called her as a witness. It was appropriate to draw an adverse inference in the circumstances. In *Raggett*,[15] the witness had an unreliable recollection and had also failed to make notes; an adverse inference was also drawn. However, it is clear that an adverse inference will not routinely be drawn. In *Claire Manzi v King's College Hospital NHS Foundation Trust*[16] the Court of Appeal clarified that the drawing of an adverse inference is just one avenue available to the court where there is incomplete evidence. There is no obligation to draw an adverse inference simply because a witness has not been called or is unavailable. In declining to draw an inference it was noted both that the absent witness was not central to the issues in the case and that the claimant had not sought a statement from the absent witness prior to trial.

The witness statements served stand as the evidence of that witness (CPR 32.2). Put another way, just because a statement is served from a named witness, there is no license to then comment expansively on new points at trial. Specific permission from the court is required for a witness to amplify their statement at the trial and give evidence of new matters which have arisen since their statement was served on the other side. That permission will only be given where the judge considers that there is good reason not to confine their evidence to the contents of the statement (CPR 32.5).

Form and content

The CPR 32, PD 32 17.1–20.3 set out the detailed requirements for the layout and preparation of witness statements. These are relatively straightforward. Regard should be had to the CPR 32.2(3) under which the court can restrict the type of evidence that can be introduced (typically at the first CMC). Such orders may limit the numbers of witnesses, the length of witness statements or the issues that may be addressed.

It is perhaps an obvious point, but the witness statement is intended to be a factual account to the best of the recollection of the witnesses. The statements are not an opportunity to set out extensive opinion, which is the domain of the experts. In practice, there are 'shades of grey' regarding the facts as a witness perceives them. Just as it may be reasonable for

---

12 Ibid.
13 [1972] AC 877, at 930G.
14 [2017] EWHC 3139.
15 *Executors of John Raggett (Deceased) v King's College Hospital NHS Foundation Trust* [2016] EWHC 1604 (QB).
16 [2018] EWCA Civ 1882.

a witness in a personal injury road traffic claim to estimate the speed of a car based on their own experience as a driver, a mother experiencing complications in her second or third birth may opine that, in contrast to her first labour, the midwife seemed not to know what to do. Similarly, it would be artificial to expect an experienced consultant not to record the facts as he or she perceived them with reference to their prior clinical experience.

However, there can be two matters which need consideration. First, where the defendant relies upon factual witnesses who, in combination, are sufficiently well qualified that there is an inequality of arms – ie that the combined weight of the defendants factual and expert evidence wholly 'outguns' the claimant's expert. This can only be addressed by applying to introduce a second expert. See, for example the comments of Lord Justice Brooke in *ES v Chesterfield & North Derbyshire Royal Hospitals NHS Trust*.[17]

> Anybody watching the trial would be bound to be impressed by the fact that there was only one consultant obstetrician giving evidence for the claimant, while there would be three giving evidence for the defendant hospital trust, and those three would cover a much wider spectrum of personal experience than the single expert permitted to the claimant. It is not as if the medical witness of fact for the defendants is a junior hospital doctor. We were told something of Mr Downes' professional history both as a practitioner in a number of hospitals and as a teacher, and his evidence on the reasons why he believed he acted with appropriate care will be supported by two other consultants. Against them there will be a single voice speaking for the claimant.

Such applications are rare, limited to the facts of the case and, on balance, are likely to be hotly contested. Whilst the claimant was permitted additional expert evidence in *ES*, it should be emphasised that his application had failed at first instance before the Master. There appears to be just one reported case of a similar order being made since *ES* was decided in 2003.[18]

The court in *ES* was also clear that reference to opinion evidence of the type an expert may give is inevitable to some degree as it will have informed the process of clinical decision making: 'no professional person can explain or justify his or her actions and decisions save by reference to his or her training and experience' per Holman LJ at [31]. The issue will therefore be one of balance. It is clear that claimants cannot routinely expect to adduce additional expert evidence merely because the defendant (inevitably) wishes to adduce witness evidence from their professionally qualified staff.

The second, altogether different, type of statement is where the evidence adduced is from individuals who, on the face of it, are unable to give factual evidence at all. Practitioners should not do so, even where there are challenges locating witnesses. Statements served by clinicians who were never involved in the care of the claimant, commenting on the care provided by colleagues will *usually* contain impermissible quasi-expert, opinion evidence. This is because such statements will contain a retrospective analysis of the records and scans and critique or detailed

---

17 [2003] EWCA Civ 1284, at [24].
18 *VTB Capital Plc v Nutritek International Corpn* [2011] EWHC 2842 (Ch).

analysis of the pleadings (ie the trial bundle) which are the very tasks which the independent expert should undertake.

Such matters are, of course, very case specific and an absent clinician can, of course, give evidence of fact in some circumstances: For example, the on-call consultant can (and should) give evidence as to the steps that would have been taken had he or she been called in. Indeed evidence of that type was central to the facts considered in *Bolitho*[19] where the senior registrar, Dr Horn, had not attended.

The courts have been forthright when statements are deemed to stray beyond the appropriate boundaries. See, for example, *JD Wetherspoon plc v Harris*.[20] In *Harris*, the defendant sought to introduce evidence from a Mr Goldberger as a factual witness. In fact, he was unable to add any contemporaneous evidence at all. The claimant sought to exclude the non-factual evidence. The pithy findings of Sir Terence Etherton are worth restating as it is clear how a statement can stray into quasi-expert commentary.

> The vast majority of Mr Goldberger's witness statement contains a recitation of facts based on the documents, commentary on those documents, argument, submissions and expressions of opinion, particularly on aspects of the commercial property market. In all those respects Mr Goldberger's witness statement is an abuse. The abusive parts should be struck out.

The extract below from the Queen's Bench Guide ('the Guide')[21] is also helpful to define the limits.

> [witness statements should] consist only of the issues on which the party serving the witness statement wishes that witness to give evidence in chief and should not include commentary on the trial bundle or other matters which may arise during the trial or may have arisen during the proceedings

Where a party seeks to rely upon a witness statement that is not compliant with Part 35, the Guide goes on to state that the onus is on 'an opposing party to [apply to] strike out inadmissible or irrelevant material.'[22] The fact that this provision is so clearly set out in the Queen's Bench Guide is perhaps indicative of the scope for statements to stray beyond the remit of the permissible factual evidence.

Service of the statements

A witness statement may be used only for the purpose for which it is served (CPR 32.12). If the statement is not served within the time specified by the court, it is not permitted without permission from the court (CPR 32.10). Since the sanction follows the event (late service) the correct application is a relief from sanctions application under the CPR 3.9, to which the test in *Denton v TH White*[23] will apply. It is, of course, not unusual to agree modest time extensions under the CPR 3.8 or longer extension by consent, where appropriate. If necessary, a witness summary may be served (CPR 32.9) together with an application. That

---

19 *Bolitho v City and Hackney Health Authority* [1997] UKHL 46.
20 [2013] EWHC 1088 (Ch).
21 Judiciary of England and Wales, *Queen's Bench Guide 2017*, para 10.9.5(2).
22 Judiciary of England and Wales, *Queen's Bench Guide 2017*, para 10.9.5(3).
23 [2014] EWCA Civ 906.

approach preserves the possibility that a witness may be called, but the applicant party needs to demonstrate an inability to prepare a statement within time.[24]

As with any other direction of the court, repeated delays or applications by a party to extend time for service of the witness evidence may be addressed by way of a peremptory order to encourage compliance. Note that if a party does not call at trial a witness in respect of whom a statement has been served and does not put in the statement as hearsay evidence (which requires the service of a Civil Evidence Act notice with the statement under the CPR 33.2) the other party may instead put it in as hearsay evidence (CPR 32.5). This is, of course, the natural extension of the fact that there is no property in a witness.

Both parties can, and sometimes do, seek to obtain statements from the same witness(es). That is most likely where a relevant witness has changed employment within the healthcare sector or has retired. Knowledge of the employment status of witnesses may therefore be helpful in determining which witnesses may assist and with efforts to locate them.

Having served the witness statements, it can be the case that circumstances change. This is not uncommon in relation to the quantum statements; the obvious example is where there is a change in care provision because of illness or deterioration. A helpful distinction has recently been drawn by the court in relation to the introduction of new factual evidence on the basis that it did not exist at the time of the previous directions (ie it is not late, as such, since it did not exist when the original order was made), and evidence which was available but was simply served late, which would require a relief from sanctions application.[25]

Expert evidence

The success or failure of a clinical negligence action will often turn on the quality of the expert evidence. For that reason, expert evidence is addressed in detail at Chapter 22. For the purposes of this chapter, we are concerned with the directions relating to the expert evidence only. All of the expert evidence will be restricted to that which is reasonably required to resolve proceedings (CPR 35.1).

The CMC directions order will normally provide limits to the type of expert evidence and the number of experts that may be relied upon. As a practical matter, it is helpful for the order to include a provision naming the expert and their field (or containing a provision that specifies a date to name the experts). Such a provision ensures that the parties cannot engage in 'expert shopping' without disclosure of preceding reports, as was the case in *Vasiliou v Hajigeorgiou*.[26]

Whilst it is possible to retain privilege on advisory reports (see below), reports prepared for and addressed to the court (whether obtained prior to or after proceedings are issued) have a different status. In *Edwards-*

---

24   *Scarlett v Grace* [2014] EWHC 2307 (QB).
25   *Jones v Oven* [2017] EWHC 1647 (Ch).
26   [2005] EWCA Civ 236.

Tubb v JD Wetherspoon plc[27] the court held that a report addressed to
the court did not enjoy the privileged status of an advisory report. If a
second expert in the same discipline was to be relied upon, the first report
should also be disclosed. The judgment of Lord Justice Hughes analyses
the preceding authorities and does much to clarify the issue of when it
is appropriate to substitute an expert and the requirements when doing
so. As a practical step, practitioners may wish to consider obtaining any
initial expert opinion as a note of advice, rather than as a report for
the court. That is likely to preserve privilege over the expert opinions
contained therein.

It is worth noting that in *Beck v Ministry of Defence*,[28] where the
defendant lost confidence in their expert, the court permitted substitution
(subject to disclosure of the earlier report) but were clear that the reasons
for that loss of confidence did not need to be addressed in detail, where
that could provide ammunition for cross-examination. Similarly in *Dennis
Lee v Colchester University NHS Foundation Trust*[29] the defendant was
again permitted to change an expert close to trial, subject to disclosure
of the earlier report, where the defendant would otherwise have been
unfairly prejudiced by cross-examination of their expert regarding issues
unrelated to the case.

Issues arising from the examination

Condition and prognosis evidence will have been obtained by the
claimant prior to the issue of proceedings and served. If the defendant
did not obtain a condition and prognosis report of their own pre-issue,
it is likely that they will want to examine the claimant promptly. It may
not be unreasonable to refuse an examination if: (a) trial of a preliminary
issue is likely, for which no examination is required; (b) the examination
requires some test or treatment that is uncomfortable or distressing; or
(c) the requirements are particularly onerous (claimants with very severe
injuries should not generally be expected to travel long distances for
examination).

If directions are set down for trial and medical expert evidence has
been permitted, the defendant can reasonably expect the claimant to
submit to a medical examination. It has been long established that where
it can be demonstrated that there has been an unreasonable failure to
be examined, the claim may be stayed. See *Edmeades v Thames Board
Mills Ltd*[30] and, more recently *Nield-Moir v Freeman*[31] where no stay was
ordered, but an adverse inference was to be drawn if a DNA swab was
not provided.

In order to secure a stay, it is clear from *Lane v Willis*[32] that the
defendant applicant needs to establish that an examination is required
in the interests of justice (often because a defence cannot be prepared or
the case progressed). Whilst that case is pre-CPR it remains good law

---

27   [2011] EWCA Civ 136.
28   [2003] EWCA Civ 1043.
29   [2015] EWHC 1766 (QB).
30   [1969] 2 QB 67 (CA).
31   *Janice Elizabeth Nield-Moir v Lorraine Karen Freeman* [2018] EWHC 299 (Ch).
32   [1972] 1 WLR 326.

and has been followed more recently at tribunal level.[33] Needless to say, the medical evidence sought must be relevant to the dispute at issue. In *Smith v Ealing, Hammersmith & Hounslow Health Authority*[34] the claimant could not be compelled to undergo a psychiatric evaluation where the injury claim (for scarring) did not include a psychiatric injury component.

The claimant should be permitted a friend, relative (or chaperone) to be present at the examination if desired and/or appropriate. It is possible to object to a particular clinician, whilst maintaining agreement to be examined. In such circumstances it is necessary to give reasons, see *Starr v National Coal Board*.[35] In *Belkovic v DSG International plc*[36] the High Court of Northern Ireland drew together the established themes of the jurisprudence, requiring the plaintiff to submit to an examination, despite the fact that he no longer wished to rely upon medical evidence of his own. Where there were concerns regarding the influence of his McKenzie friend, he was also required to attend the appointment alone.

In general terms, however, it is difficult to see why a claimant should be made to see the defendant's doctor alone, particularly if anxious, a poor historian, or unwell. Even were that not the case, current guidance from the National Institute of Clinical Excellence (NICE) regarding the conduct of medical examinations provides for patients to be accompanied and to take notes if they wish.[37]

The concerns that some claimants have prior to the examination are, unfortunately, not always misplaced. In the extraordinary family case of *Re F (A Child)*[38] the court was critical of the expert, Dr Harper, who had incorrectly attributed controversial statements to the child's mother. Covert recordings made by the mother during the consultation showed the account set out in the report to be demonstrably false. The report of Dr Harper could not be relied upon. *Re F* gives rise to the question as to whether it is permissible or advisable for claimants to record the expert examination. Strictly speaking, the medico-legal examination is not different to any other medical examination. The assessing clinician will owe a duty to the court, but also to the claimant undergoing examination in the capacity of healthcare professional and patient. As such, whilst it may be preferable to have obtained consent, if the claimant patient undergoing an examination wishes to record it for their own purposes, they may do so. There is no provision that would prevent any recording being made covertly since the claimant would, for data protection purposes, be both the 'data subject' of the examination and the data processor of their own data. Finally, NICE have provided clear guidelines to clinicians that patients should be permitted to record their consultations, if they wish.[39]

Inevitably a claimant having undergone an examination, particularly an examination arranged by a defendant party, will want to see the

---

33 *Government Communications Headquarters v Bacchus* [2012] Eq LR 1002 (EAT).
34 [1997] 8 Med LR 290.
35 [1977] 1 WLR 63.
36 [2014] NIQB 25.
37 NICE Guideline CG138, 'Patient experience in adult NHS services: improving the experience of care for people using adult NHS services', at 1.5.16.
38 *Re F (A Child) (Care Proceedings) (Failure of Expert)* [2016] EWHC 2149 (Fam).
39 NICE Guideline CG138, 'Patient experience in adult NHS services: improving the experience of care for people using adult NHS services', at 1.5.16.

subsequent report(s) as soon as possible. Initially, the report will, of course, be subject to privilege and there is no entitlement to immediate disclosure. However, if the defendants want to rely on the report as to condition and prognosis, it will, ultimately, need to be disclosed. As set out in Chapter 17, disclosure of a condition and prognosis report is mandatory with the defence if a report has been obtained at the pre-action stage (CPR PD 16 12.1(3)).

Service

Practitioners will note that the time limits contained within the directions order are absolute, in the same way as the directions timetable for witness evidence. Late service of an expert report risks debarral from being able to rely on the expert evidence (CPR 35.13) and an application for relief from sanction under the CPR 3.9 will be required. Needless to say, applications for time extensions should always be made prospectively to prevent the automatic debarral.

There are numerous authorities that deal with the late introduction of expert evidence. A common factor in all of the applications will be a concern to preserve the trial date where possible to do so.

In *O'Connor v The Pennine Hospitals NHS Trust*[40] an effort was made by the defendant to introduce new evidence on the first day of trial, the defendant's previous expert having changed her mind. That was refused. On appeal, it was noted that the application was both late and the change of mind had occurred as a result of new evidence; it was not a proper basis to introduce a new expert. In *Chambers v Buckinghamshire Healthcare NHS Trust*,[41] the defendant (having had two extensions of time) served their expert evidence late and had failed to serve a counter-schedule of loss and damage at all at the point in which the claimant applied to debar them from relying on the evidence. The defendant was debarred from relying on the evidence and from serving a counter-schedule. The Master was unimpressed with a restriction from the client (the NHSLA) not to serve the expert reports, which prevented their solicitors complying with an order. Whilst the judgment pre-dates *Denton*,[42] the delay of one month in seeking any relief from sanction or time extension would likely still prove fatal now.

The recent case of *Hall v Derby Teaching Hospitals NHS Foundation Trust*[43] sets out clearly how not to approach an application concerning expert evidence (in this case, an application to rely upon neurosurgical evidence). When the claimant was ultimately unsuccessful in adducing additional evidence, she had to bear the cost of two interim hearings and of deleting reference to the neurosurgical evidence from the reports of the other advising experts who were permitted.

Clearly, the party seeking to introduce late expert evidence faces an uphill struggle. The issues will inevitably be fact specific. In the right circumstances, permission to rely upon expert evidence may still be given

---

40 [2015] EWCA 1244.
41 [2013] EWHC (QB).
42 *Denton v TH White* [2014] EWCA Civ 906.
43 *Sharron Denise Hall v Derby Teaching Hospitals NHS Foundation Trust* [2018] EWHC 3276 (QB).

even if the trial date will be lost. In *Liddle v Bristol City Council*[44] a personal injury claim, the claimant instructed (in error) the 'wrong' type of engineering expert, which expanded beyond engineering or surveyor comment upon the accident locus, a sea wall, but addressed instead issues of accident reconstruction. If permitted, the defendant would need to obtain new evidence. Where the claimant had alerted the defendant to the issue promptly and the evidence was likely to assist the trial judge in a high value claim, the report was allowed, despite the loss of the trial date.

Expert discussions

Once expert reports have been served, work will need to be undertaken on the agenda for expert discussions. These are addressed further at Chapter 22 which deals with the expert evidence in detail. As a practical point, it is sufficient to note that the expert's discussions are: (i) not mandatory; and (ii) are often completed later than directed. This will often occur as a result of difficulties agreeing the agenda or because of clinical commitments. For that reason, work on the agenda for joint discussions (the first draft of which is usually prepared by the claimant) should begin as soon as reasonably possible after the parties have exchanged expert evidence and considered the reports in detail. Where possible, only one agenda should be used – not least because referring to two agendas (often with similar question numbers) can be confusing at trial. If questions cannot be wholly agreed for the agendas, it will usually be helpful to merge the questions into one document, preparing a set of claimant questions and a set of defendant questions within a single agenda, whilst endeavouring to avoid duplication. See, for example, *Saunders v Central Manchester University Hospitals NHS Foundation Trust*, where Mrs Justice Yip commended the quality of the expert evidence but was highly critical of the joint statements prepared:[45]

34.   ... for reasons not explained to me, there had apparently been two separate agendas that the experts were required to consider. Both involved repetitive questions for the experts and far from producing a focus on the real issues, the result was a document that served only to confuse rather than assist.

35.   The joint statement is an important document. It ought to be possible to read it and to understand the key issues and each expert's position on those issues. Sometimes less is more as far as the agenda is concerned. Parties should adopt a common sense and collaborative approach rather than allowing this stage of the litigation to become a battleground. Frankly, the approach to the joint statement in this case achieved nothing of value.

It is possible that the experts change their view in discussion. Both the CPR PD 35 9.8 and the model directions require that a written note is produced to explain the rationale to any change of opinion, should that occur.

---

44   [2018] EWHC 1094 (QB).
45   [2018] EWHC 343 (QB), at [34]–[35].

Whilst undoubtedly a rare set of circumstances, in *Mayr v Cameron McKenna*,[46] the court excluded the evidence of an expert who twice failed to engage properly in the process of joint expert meetings, resulting in the claimant being at a material disadvantage going into trial. Whilst relief was ultimately given, it is clear that the independent expert must properly engage in the process and understand their duty to the court.

Further directions

Second CMC/pre-trial review

A second CMC or pre trial review (CPR 29.7) is generally listed for a date shortly after the exchange of expert reports and either prior to or shortly after the completion of the pre-trial checklist (Form N170), which must normally be completed ten weeks prior to trial. The CPR 29.6(3) makes provision for a claim to be struck out unless a checklist is filed. See also *British Gas Trading Ltd v Oak Cash & Carry Ltd*.[47]

If a hearing is required, it will primarily address the trial timetable, but in practice it is often dispensed with provided the case is 'on track' for trial. Nevertheless it can be useful where there have been delays to bring the parties back before the court for further directions.

Alternative dispute resolution (ADR)

The standard directions provide for ADR to take place in the period after the expert discussions and prior to trial. As a practical step, it is often helpful to secure a date for ADR well in advance of the expert discussions as it can be difficult to secure the availability of counsel, clients and insurers. Better to cancel a date for ADR than to fail to schedule ADR in the first place. It may be appropriate to cancel an ADR if, for example, the expert discussions have materially changed the litigation risks, such that one party feels that there are no concessions likely to be made or settlement to be reached. The case management directions now require witness evidence to be served where a party has declined to participate in ADR. Contingent upon the wording of the directions order, that statement will usually need to be filed within 28 days of a refusal to participate in ADR or upon a date not less than a month prior to trial.

Practitioners will now be well familiar with the established line of authorities that have criticised (and often penalised a party as to costs) where there has been a failure to consider or to engage in ADR. *Dunnett v Railtrack plc*[48] was the first judgment which penalised a *successful* party who had refused ADR and was followed by *Halsey v Milton Keynes General NHS Trust*,[49] which is a helpful judgment, exploring many of the issues arising from ADR. Importantly, whilst the defendant escaped censure in *Halsey* for a failure to mediate, there was no directions order which addressed ADR in that case. Paragraph 33 of the judgment of Lord

---

46 *Mayr v CMS Cameron McKenna Nabarro Olswang LLP* [2018] EWHC 3669 (Comm).
47 [2016] EWCA Civ 153.
48 [2002] EWCA Civ 303.
49 [2004] EWCA Civ 576.

Justice Dyson highlights the real possibility that the case could have been decided differently, had the clinical negligence directions provided that ADR should be considered – which of course they now do.

Trial bundles

It is perhaps an obvious point, but work should commence on the trial bundles at an early stage. A rushed or incomplete trial bundle assists nobody – particularly if there are numerous late additions. Further, where there are voluminous clinical records, but the negligence alleged concerns a short period (as will often be the case for surgical and birth injury claims) time should be taken to prepare and agree with the opposing party an agreed bundle of the key records. Mr Justice Spencer noted the importance of such a bundle in *Lesforis v Tolias*[50] 'although the full medical records comprising 5 lever arch files were made available, it did not become necessary at any stage to go beyond the core bundle. This made the task of the court significantly easier, for which I am grateful.'

COMMON APPLICATIONS

Requests for further information

The CPR 18 is a useful part of the CPR, commonly used for one of the purposes below:

- to obtain clarification of the other party's case or to narrow the focus of a statement that is broad or ambiguous by restricting the other party to a clarified case;
- to ascertain details of aspects of the other party's case to reduce the element of surprise (for example, after service of witness statements to anticipate issues that may arise at trial);
- to elicit any weaknesses in the other party's case;
- to obtain information as to material facts which the applicant needs to prove;
- to try and secure admissions (although a notice to admit facts (Form N266) may also be used for this purpose); or
- to narrow the issues between the parties and reduce the expense and length of trial.

Practice Direction 18 provides that, before any application is made to the court, the party desiring the information must first write to the other side asking for it. The request should be concise and strictly confined to matters which are 'reasonably necessary and proportionate to enable him to prepare his own case or to understand the case he has to meet' (the guidance that supplements the CPR 18.1 further provides that such requests should only be in relation to a 'matter which is in dispute in the proceedings').

Whilst requests may be made in a letter rather than a separate document if they are brief, generally it is preferable to set them out in a separate document containing numbered questions. The rules state clearly that

---

50   [2018] EWHC 1225 (QB), at [79].

questions should not be raised on a piecemeal basis. More often than not Pt 18 questions are addressed without the need for a party to apply to court to try and compel a response. However, questions can be raised that go beyond the scope of the rules. What information is 'reasonably necessary' for a party to prepare their case is not always totally clear, such that the response needs to be carefully considered. The recipient of a request will of course be reluctant to prepare extensive replies if they appear unmeritorious or unnecessary. However, there is the risk of an adverse costs order if the court determines that the preparation of a reply has been unreasonably refused. Deployed correctly, the request will genuinely narrow the issues in dispute and, in the case of questions raised shortly after service of a pleaded case may resolve ambiguity or restrict the scope of future argument to a narrower set of issues. There is a risk to the party raising the questions that their analysis of a case is highlighted and/or that the opponent will be able to use the replies as an opportunity to strengthen their case. The response prepared must be verified with a statement of truth and will form part of the statements of case.

The merits of a request (or more particularly, what may be permitted by the court following an application) can be difficult to assess. Clearly a high value claim case involving a number of complex issues may merit closer questioning or clarification than a modest claim. 'Fishing expeditions' to try and obtain evidence to support the pleaded statements of case will not be permitted. As an example of a disproportionate approach to the litigation, in *Lexi Holdings (In Administration) v Pannone & Partners Partners*,[51] the applicant prepared a ten page document raising some 31 questions. The questions were held to be an abuse. In *Hegglin v Google Inc*[52] some 38 questions were raised by Google after service of the witness statements. Those were regarded as 'quite onerous' by Mr Justice Edis. On his analysis the information sought would neither save time nor narrow the issues in dispute. It followed that the request was not necessary or proportionate.

Part 18 questions were, at one time, deployed to ascertain the scope of insurance cover. Insurance issues in clinical negligence (at least in relation to care provided outside the NHS) have become ever more important where established providers are in some areas withdrawing cover[53] and there are increasingly more commercial insurers in sectors that had been limited to a narrower band of major medical indemnifiers – the Medical Defence Union, Medical Protection Society and Medical and Dental Defence Union of Scotland. Whilst doctors are, of course, required by both law and professional obligation to maintain insurance cover,[54] a review of the *Paterson* litigation[55] highlights the issues that can arise if

---

51 [2010] EWHC 1416 (Ch).
52 *Hegglin v (1) Persons Unknown (2) Google Inc* [2014] EWHC 3793 (QB).
53 The Medical Defence Union (MDU) announced the withdrawal of indemnity cover for spinal surgery in the private sector.
54 Medical Act 1983, ss 44C(1) and 44C(9), and General Medical Council (Licence to Practise and Revalidation) Regulations Order of Council 2012, SI 2012/2685.
55 Whilst an extreme example, the insurance implications for payments of damages by private hospitals, individual indemnifiers and even in relation to representation are clear. See *Bradbury v Paterson* [2014] EWHC 3992 (QB) and *Spire Healthcare Ltd v Royal Sun Alliance plc* [2018] EWCA Civ 317.

there are failures to ensure inadequate cover or indemnifiers avoid or restrict cover. Unfortunately for claimants who want to ascertain early on whether the defendant could be uninsured, it is now clear that the CPR 18 may not be used to obtain insurance details, principally because the insurance issues do not relate to the issues in dispute. *Harcourt v Griffin*,[56] initially appeared to support the use of the CPR 18 to compel disclosure of insurance information, but it was subsequently followed by *West London Pipeline & Storage Ltd v Total UK Ltd*,[57] a case which concerned the explosion at the Buncefield Oil Refinery. Steel J refused to follow *Harcourt*, noting that details of the insurance policies were not disclosable under the CPR 31 and were clearly not relevant to the issues in dispute. In *XYZ v Various*,[58] which concerned the PIP breast implant litigation. Mrs Justice Thirlwall followed *West London Pipeline*, refusing the request for further information. Interestingly, she noted that the courts could make an order under the CPR 3.1(2)(m) to address the issue in the rare circumstances that it is necessary for effective case management.

Requests for disclosure

Pre-action disclosure requests may be made before the commencement of proceedings under the CPR 31.16. Typically, such applications are made by claimants where there is insufficient information to be able to understand the case that will need to be advanced. A failure to disclose medical information could be addressed with such an application, for example. This section addresses cases where, after issue, inadequate disclosure is given by a party.

The usual order is for standard disclosure, which is addressed above. In the ordinary course it will often be the defendant that is required to provide additional disclosure, since there may be a wealth of policy documents and records kept across a number of sites. It is common for the standard disclosure lists served by institutions to be limited to the clinical records that are, of course, generally disclosed prior to the commencement of proceedings. The parties will need to consider critically whether the disclosure lists set out in adequate detail all of the documents that have come into being as a result of the care provided and any other relevant documents.

If, after a reasonable request a party has refused or been unable to provide the relevant document(s) an application may be made under the CPR 31.12 for specific disclosure of documents. The court may make an order for a party to disclose specific documents or document classes and undertake searches.

In appropriate cases, specific disclosure requests (and applications if required) may be relevant for other non-clinical documents, such as theatre or scanner logs, attendance records and policy documents. The provisions of the CPR 31.14 should be noted – documents referred to in the statements of case or witness evidence should be made available or an

---

56   [2007] EWHC 1500 (QB).
57   [2008] EWHC 1296.
58   [2013] EWHC 3643 (QB).

application can be made for a court order. Such requests may be relevant to patient diaries or hospital policy/procedure.

STRIKE OUT AND ANALOGOUS ORDERS OF THE COURT

Strike out

An order to strike out may be made on application or the court's own initiative. The decision to strike out a party's statement of case is the most serious step in any proceedings, depriving that party of the opportunity to run some (or all) of their arguments at trial. Incorrectly exercised, a strike out may interfere with Art 6 rights under the European Convention on Human Rights, to a fair trial.

Despite this, the powers of the court under the CPR 3.4 to strike out a party's statement of case are broad, enabling the court to apply their discretion to the varied cases before them in meeting the overriding objectives of the CPR 1, given that unmeritorious cases should not proceed or take up unnecessary court resources. The CPR 3.4(2) provides that the court may strike out a statement of case if it: (a) discloses no reasonable ground for bringing or defending the claim; (b) is an abuse of the court's process or is otherwise likely to obstruct the just disposal of the proceedings (obstruction in this context means 'impede to a high extent'); or (c) if there has been a failure to comply with a rule, practice direction or court order. These should not be regarded as exhaustive provisions. These powers are within the court's discretion and can be made on the court's own initiative or where an application has been made.[59] The wide range of discretion available to the court is evident from the judgment in *Biguzzi v Rank Leisure:*[60]

> Under Part 3.4(c) a judge has an unqualified discretion to strike out a case such as this where there has been a failure to comply with a rule. The fact that a judge has that power does not mean that in applying the overriding objectives the initial approach will be to strike out the statement of case. The advantage of the CPR over the previous rules is that the court's powers are much broader than they were. In many cases there will be alternatives which enable a case to be dealt with justly without taking the draconian step of striking the case out.

Alternatives highlighted by the Court of Appeal, which should be considered prior to strike out include orders for costs or indemnity costs.

The rules relating to strike out where there is no reasonable ground to bring the claim are not dissimilar to the provisions relating to summary judgment under the CPR 24 (as to which, see below) and applications for strike out are often made in the alternative. When arguing for or against strike out, the court will consider primarily the overriding objectives but also the probable merits. The courts will be reluctant to strike out any claim if there is a prospect that it could ultimately succeed – even if remote. The CPR 3.4(1) permits part of a claim to be struck out if only elements of the claim advanced are defective or unlikely to succeed.

---

59 Any order made without notice will, of course, be subject to the provisions of the CPR 3.1(5) and may be set aside on application.
60 *Ricardo Biguzzi v Rank Leisure plc* [1999] 1 WLR 1926.

In *Smith v University of Leicester NHS Trust*[61] the defendant successfully applied under the CPR 3.4 to strike out a statement of case on the basis that no duty was owed to the claimants. The particulars alleged liability in relation to a failure to impart information to the claimant about a congenital medical condition. However that information had come to light as a result of treatment provided to another patient (a cousin). As a matter of law, no duty had been owed to the claimant. Whilst *Smith*, which was not appealed, demonstrates how a strike out application can be used to good effect at an early stage of the proceedings, it should be noted that in *ABC v St George's Healthcare NHS Foundation Trust*,[62] a case which turned on similar facts, the Court of Appeal reversed a strike out at first instance. Generally, practitioners should expect this most 'nuclear' of options to be rarely exercised, particularly if the application is made late in the day. See also *Fairclough Homes Ltd v Summers*[63] for consideration by the court of a strike out application after trial where there was an abuse of process (fraud).

However, the position may be different where there is a pattern of default. The CPR 3.8 provides that any sanction specified to come into effect by the rules or court order on a certain event or date, will be automatic. Thus, if the court makes a peremptory order with a penalty attached, eg 'unless the claimant serves amended particulars of claim by [date] the claim be struck out' it is clear that the non-compliance leads directly to that penalty. The parties cannot, between themselves, agree to waive the sanction. In such circumstances, the party affected would need to (promptly) make an application for relief from sanction under the CPR 3.9(2) and address the *Denton*[64] principles. There, different considerations will apply.

Default judgment

Whilst this is an issue that can only arise prior to the service of the defence and it is therefore, strictly speaking, a matter which could be included within Chapter 17 (litigation prior to service), it makes sense to address the issues here, as part of the common applications that arise in litigation. This is particularly the case where there are similarities with the rules relating to summary judgment.

If a defendant fails to return the acknowledgment of service or fails to serve a defence within the period specified in the CPR 15.4 (or any further period consented to by the parties) the CPR 12 entitles the claimant to apply to obtain default judgment. It should be noted that even where the claimant does not apply for judgment, that does not mean that the defendant is able to rely upon a defence filed late, without a relief from sanctions application. See, for example, *ADVA Optical Networking Ltd v Optron Holding Ltd*.[65]

If the defendant is in default, judgment will be given as of right on the basis of a simple request to the court under the CPR 12.4, without scrutiny

61   [2016] EWHC 817 (QB).
62   [2017] EWCA Civ 336.
63   [2012] UKSC 26.
64   *Denton v TH White* [2014] EWCA Civ 906.
65   [2017] EWHC 1813 (TCC).

of any reason for the default. As a result, there is a wealth of developed case law regarding applications to set aside judgments in default.

The relevant rules for set aside applications are found at CPR 13. There are just two evidential hurdles at the CPR 13.3 for the defendant to meet in order to set aside a default judgment, provided that the application is made promptly. Namely: (a) does the defendant have a real prospect of successfully defending the claim; and/or (b) is there some other good reason why the judgment should be set aside or the defendant permitted to defend the claim? What amounts to a 'real prospect' of a successful defence is exactly the same test as with summary judgment (see below). However, what might have been less clear until more recently (see for example, *Redbourn v Fairgate*)[66] is that the defendant may be required to seek relief from sanctions as part of the same application. The criteria in *Denton*[67] may prove to be a more insurmountable obstacle than those of the CPR 13.3.

Practitioners will note that even where default judgment has been awarded, that is not the end of the matter. Default judgments should be construed narrowly. It is clear from *Symes*[68] that such a judgment is in relation to breach of duty and the causation of *some damage* (not necessarily judgment on the whole of the claimant's pleaded injury claim). Put simply, the defendant may, by reason of the default, have a liability judgment secured against them, but such a judgment does not preclude them advancing causation arguments relating to the nature and extent of the injuries alleged.

Certain types of case may not be amenable to judgment in default. Claimants advancing a claim for provisional damages under the CPR 41 cannot be awarded a judgment in default unless the provisional damages claim is first abandoned (see CPR PD 41A at 5.1). In some cases the prospective provisional damages claim will be substantial and therefore cannot be surrendered lightly. This would, on first reading, appear to exclude some of the largest claims from the option of securing a default judgment. The CPR provisions do make sense where one cannot know if the circumstances giving rise to the provisional damages claim will eventuate nor accurately quantify a finite award in monetary terms. However, the important caveat may be precisely what judgment is sought.

The CPR 12.4 sets out the types of default judgment that may be sought. Whilst it is not wholly clear from the wording, arguably an application for judgment in unspecified form, with damages to be assessed (CPR 12.4(b)) rather than a fixed money judgment, is a matter which can be the subject of a default judgment without the need to abandon the provisional damages claim.

Summary judgment

The CPR 24 deals with summary judgment. The grounds for such an application will depend upon the party making the application. If it is the defendant making the application, it is, in effect, a striking out application. The application may be made at any time during the

---

66 *Redbourn Group Ltd v Fairgate Development Ltd* [2017] EWHC 1223 (TCC).
67 *Denton v TH White* [2014] EWCA Civ 906.
68 *Symes v St George's Healthcare NHS Trust* [2014] EWHC 2505 (QB).

litigation, but applications are often filed upon receipt of the statements of case if it is felt the opposing party has no meritorious case to run.

The court can give summary judgment against a party on the claim or on a particular issue if it considers that a party has no real prospect of succeeding on the claim/the defence or on the particular issue, and that there is no other compelling reason why the case or issue should be disposed of at a trial (CPR 24.2). The purpose of summary judgment is disposal of a claim that is so poor that it can be dealt with at an interim stage; the claim is, in essence, unsuitable for trial. It has long been understood that it is not for the court to undertake a 'mini-trial' in an interim hearing: if the respondent demonstrates sufficiently that the issues are not straightforward that will normally be sufficient to defeat a summary judgment application (ie it will normally then be a matter for trial). However, this does not prevent minor or straightforward points of law being addressed at the interim stage – if that is the case, the court is free to and should 'grasp the nettle and decide it'.[69]

It is now well established since *Swaine v Hillman*[70] that the respondent to a summary judgment application has to show some prospect that has a chance of success which must be real – the prospects must not be false, fanciful or imaginary. There are detailed notes in the *White Book* at para 24.2.3, but it is clear that the test is not that there is a good case, but merely that it is more than merely arguable. Put another way, there is a relatively low bar for a respondent to contest (and defeat) a summary judgment application. The test when applying to set aside a default judgment and demonstrating a case which should be permitted to proceed to trial is, ostensibly, the same.

Notwithstanding the apparently low threshold that applies, the respondent practitioner to a summary judgment application should not be complacent. In *Doncaster Pharmaceuticals*[71] Lord Justice Mummery remarked that assessing the merits of a summary judgment application can involve 'more difficulties ... than in trying the case in its entirety' not least because of the limited evidence available before the court. The dangers of such hearings are further set out at para 6 of his judgment:

> The outcome of a summary judgment application is more unpredictable than a trial. The result of the application can be influenced more than that of the trial by the degree of professional skill with which it is presented to the court and by the instinctive reaction of the tribunal to the pressured circumstances in which such applications are often made.

With that in mind, the parties should prepare carefully for such hearings. Whilst subsequently successfully appealed, the first instance judgment from Master Cook in *Hewes v West Hertfordshire NHS Trust*[72] remains illustrative of the care that needs to be taken when faced with an application.

The claimant had suffered from a Cauda Equina Syndrome and brought a claim against his GP, the ambulance service and the treating hospital.

---

69 *ICI Chemicals & Polymers Ltd v TTE Training Ltd* [2007] EWCA Civ 725.
70 [2000] PIQR P51, CA.
71 *Doncaster Pharmaceuticals Group Ltd v The Bolton Pharmaceutical Company 100 Ltd* [2006] EWCA Civ 661.
72 *Hewes v (1) West Hertfordshire NHS Trust (2) East of England Ambulance Service NHS Trust (3) Dr Pankaj Tanna* [2018] EWHC 1345 (QB).

The GP, the third defendant to the claim, obtained summary judgment largely on the weight of expert evidence before the court (having served his reports early specifically for that purpose). The claimant relied on very brief correspondence to inform the court that supportive evidence would be served in due course. Unfortunately that was insufficient, not least because of apparent input from the solicitor as to the terms of the letter. One must be sympathetic to the invidious decision the claimant faced: (i) serve possibly imperfect reports early (and defeat the purpose of simultaneous exchange where there were two further defendants who had not served their evidence); or (ii) try to defend an application without a comprehensive report.

It is possible that more detailed correspondence may have averted the summary judgment, sparing the claimant the need to appeal. In the event, the appeal was successful and Mr Justice Foskett went on to provide some useful observations for practitioners. In particular he made the observation below at [45] as to the timing of such applications:[73]

> I have been told that there has been no reported decision of a successful summary judgment application in a clinical negligence case. As a matter of principle there is no reason why clinical negligence cases are any different from any other case and an obviously weak case on liability or causation is vulnerable to such an application. There will be few cases, in my view, where such an application could ordinarily be contemplated before the relevant experts' reports have been exchanged and, in most cases, until after the experts have discussed the case and produced a joint statement.

He went on to note that where the pre-action correspondence and the particulars pointed to a weight of supportive expert evidence (not yet served), it was impossible at the interim stage, prior to the disclosure of a final report to support the conclusion that the matters raised within it were not arguable, such that they should not be considered by the trial judge.

The first instance judgment caused some concern amongst claimant practitioners, not least because it appeared to subvert the directed timetable. The appeal judgment restores the position that it is the exchange of independent expert evidence that will permit the merits of an arguable claim to be properly assessed. It also remains clear that, utilised at the correct stage and on the right facts, the parties will still be able to secure summary judgment.

There is, on any analysis, a degree of overlap between the CPR provisions relating to strike out and the criteria that will be sufficient for summary judgment to be given. CPR PD 3A 1.6 states that a defence may fall within the CPR 3.4(2)(a) if it consists of a bare denial or otherwise sets out no coherent statement of facts, or the facts it sets out, while coherent, would not, even if true, amount in law to a defence to the claim. The court, therefore, has the discretion of dealing with defective or 'thin' cases on either a striking out or summary judgment basis, asking itself (in relation to either mechanism) whether the relevant argument has a real prospect of success.

However, the provisions of CPR 3 and CPR 24 are not wholly the same. CPR 3 gives the court wider discretion to evaluate whether a claim or

---

73 *Hewes v (1) West Hertfordshire NHS Trust (2) East of England Ambulance Service NHS Trust (3) Dr Pankaj Tanna* [2018] EWHC 2715 (QB).

part of it should be struck out. Wider criteria than the steps/requirements to secure summary judgment under CPR 24 may be considered. Whilst it has been suggested that it is unhelpful to make an application under both the CPR Parts 3 and 24[74] it is not clear that a party should be criticised for doing so. In *Moroney v Anglo-European College of Chiropractice*[75] (an appeal of a strike out application brought under the CPR 3.4) Lord Justice Ward confirmed that the overlap between Parts 3 and 24 of the CPR meant that the court was free to determine a strike out application by analysing the merits of a case by reference to Part 24 summary judgment criteria.

Fundamental dishonesty

On 13 April 2015 the Criminal Justice and Courts Act 2015, s 57 came into force. Those provisions will be well familiar to practitioners: in summary, for the first time, where any element of a personal injury claim was fundamentally dishonest, the courts were not just permitted to, but required to, strike out the entire claim. Claimant practitioners may well hope that applications to strike out clinical negligence claims on the basis of fundamental dishonesty never become common, but it would be remiss not to address such applications here, where an application by the defendant will be both a complete defence and permit the full recovery of costs under the CPR 44.16.

No legal representative will want to represent a dishonest client. Since most injury claims are still brought by means of a conditional fee agreement and with the benefit of qualified one-way costs shifting (QOCS)[76] the claimant's legal representatives have an additional incentive to identify early on and to cease acting for a claimant that has either feigned injury or, perhaps more likely, exaggerated the full nature and extent of the injury. Whilst the reported cases since 2015 are predominantly personal injury matters, it is clear that NHS Resolution are committed to identifying fraudulent claims and will meet the cost of the necessary investigations. In *Calderdale & Huddersfield NHS Foundation Trust v Atwal*[77] the claimant was said to be unable to work following negligent facial surgery. His total claim exceeded £800,000. He subsequently accepted, out of time a Part 36 offer of £30,000, which left him with a costs liability. Relying on the damning surveillance evidence, he was sentenced to three months imprisonment for contempt.[78] Whilst *Atwal* is, perhaps, an extreme example, investigations into the possibility of dishonesty and the use of surveillance are likely to become more prevalent where the investigations are relatively cheap to undertake and cases such as this demonstrate the need for it.

In *Howlett v Davies*[79] the courts clarified that fundamental dishonesty can be raised even as late as trial and it does not have to be pleaded in the

---

74   *Independents' Advantage Insurance Company Ltd v Cook* [2003] EWCA Civ 1103 Chadwick LJ, at [8].
75   [2009] EWCA Civ 1560.
76   See further Chapter 27 on Costs.
77   [2018] EWHC 961 (QB).
78   *Calderdale & Huddersfield NHS Foundation Trust v Atwal (sentencing judgment)* [2018] EWHC 2537 (QB).
79   *Howlett v Davies & Ageas Insurance* [2017] EWCA Civ 1696.

statement of case. Since a finding of dishonesty is a complete defence, it is a very effective argument to raise where any element of the case appears to be overstated. In *LOCOG v Sinfield*[80] a fraudulent special damages claim for a gardener was sufficient for the claim to be struck out.

The need for caution by claimant practitioners when presenting the claimant's claim is clearly apparent from *Wright v Satellite Information Services Ltd*.[81] In *Wright*, the claimant had presented honestly in his witness statement an account of his past care. He was clear as to the (very limited) care he continued to require. The schedule of loss relied upon expert evidence to present a very much larger care claim that was not sustained. A £73,000 claim for care was, in the event, reduced to just £2,100. Mrs Justice Yip was critical of the way that the claim had been presented in the schedule and was sympathetic to the claimant who had, by his own admission, not fully understood it. Whilst the claimant in *Wright* was honest, he came perilously close to a finding of dishonesty because of inconsistencies in the claim and the way the evidence was presented, which arguably invited the application made by the defendant.

Considerations during and after strike out

Factors limiting dismissal

In the Seventh Edition of this work it was noted that the effects of Art 6 of the European Convention on Human Rights (right to a fair trial) meant that the courts would weigh up carefully the use of strike out, even where there appeared to be grounds to make such an order.

Article 6[82]

The starting point is that a restriction to court access will not be a breach of Art 6 rights per se. In *Ashingdane v The United Kingdom*[83] the European Court of Justice set out the position in the following terms at [57]:

> ... Certainly, the right of access to the courts is not absolute but may be subject to limitations ... a limitation will not be compatible with Article 6 para 1 (art 6-1) if it does not pursue a legitimate aim and if there is not a reasonable relationship of proportionality between the means employed and the aim sought to be achieved ...

Whether one considers the limitation provisions which prevent indefinite claims being brought or the CPR rules that permit early dismissal of unmeritorious claims so as to use court resources appropriately, it appears clear that there are legitimate aims to those requirements. The question that therefore arises is whether an absolute debarral will be appropriate in the circumstances of the claim to achieve the aim?

---

80 *London Organising Committee of the Olympic and Paralympic Games (LOCOG) v Sinfield* [2018] EWHC 51 (QB).
81 [2018] EWHC 812 (QB).
82 See further Chapter 23 on Human Rights.
83 [1985] ECHR 8.

In *Stolzenburg v CIBC Mellon Trust Co Ltd*,[84] the considerations in *Ashingdane* were considered by Lady Justice Arden in the context of an application to set aside default judgment:

> The essence of the right of access to court is not destroyed because the litigant has the opportunity to seek relief against the sanctions ... Proportionality will be satisfied if the overriding objective is met ... The essence of the right will not be destroyed even if [relief is] refused, since the appellants always had the chance to comply with the court orders and to help progress the case to trial.

In *Stolzenberg* the defendants had failed to serve a defence both on time and when faced with an unless order. They then applied to set aside judgment. Clearly there had been access to the court, because a defence could have been served on time and there had still been a relief from sanctions hearing to reconsider the issues. The refusal of relief from sanctions would not be a breach of Art 6 rights precisely because the defendants did not need to be in that position.

The overriding objectives at the CPR 1 have included since 2013 the direction that the courts consider the need to deal with cases justly and at proportionate cost (CPR 1(1)). That costs requirement is significant, having been given 'equal billing' with the former requirement to deal with cases justly. It can be expected that the courts need not give the parties endless opportunities to comply with court orders where that will introduce delay and expense. This is clearly an important provision and legitimate aim when a strike out application is made and a default or summary judgment given.

Article 6 issues were explored at some length by the Supreme Court in *Summers v Fairclough Homes*,[85] the case which immediately preceded the changes brought in by the Criminal Justice and Courts Act 2015, s 57. The appellant, Fairclough Homes, sought to strike out the claimant's case on grounds of fraud, notwithstanding that the claimant had been caused an admitted injury and been awarded damages at trial. If successful, the application, brought as a test case, would have deprived the claimant of the judgment he had secured. Noting that the provisions of the CPR 3.4 provided the court with absolute discretion to strike out a case, even if it was in part meritorious, there was then careful consideration of the Art 6 issues. In deciding that it would not be proportionate to deprive the claimant of damages despite the fraud, it was made clear that an earlier application may well have resulted in a different outcome.

OTHER MATTERS

Civil restraint orders

Wherever a statement of case is struck out for one of the reasons in the CPR 3.4(2), the court may have recourse to its jurisdiction to make a civil restraint order (CRO). It must consider whether it is appropriate to make a CRO (in accordance with the CPR 3.4(6)) when it strikes out a statement of case and, at the same time, considers it to be 'totally without merit'. A statement of case, or indeed an application, can be determined

---

84 [2004] EWCA Civ 827, at [161].
85 *Fairclough Homes Ltd v* Summers [2012] UKSC 26.

to be totally without merit where it is hopeless and bound to fail and essentially 'vexatious'. What amounts to vexatious use of proceedings is explored in *Attorney-General v Barker*[86] and in the excoriating judgment of Lord Justice Brooke set out in *Bhamjee (No 1) v Forsdick*[87] which was subsequently followed by helpful guidance to the making of a CRO, which is worth consideration, albeit that those judgments pre-date the provisions for CROs now codified in the CPR PD 3C:

> [He] was an example of a litigant who will not take no for an answer, will not consider the reasons which have been given in clear language as to why his claims have not been successful, and is willing, not only to seek to re-litigate them again and again and again, but also, to bring what, in my judgment, are completely misconceived claims for damages.

Perhaps inevitably, a CRO is most likely to be considered by the court in clinical negligence claims against an unrepresented claimant in lower value claims – possibly because of the loss of objectivity that representation can bring to understandably emotive litigation.

The CPR 3.11 is the relevant section that permits a CRO to be made. In turn, that section refers to CPR PD 3C. There it is made clear that there are three types of order:

1   limited CROs, where a party has made two or more applications which are totally without merit;
2   extended CROs, where a party has persistently issued claims or made applications which are totally without merit;
3   general CROs, which are reserved for parties that have persisted in issuing claims and/or making unmeritorious applications where an extended civil restraint order would not be sufficient.

The practice direction sets out at 2.1, 3.1 and 4.1 the specific requirements of each.

However, the effect of a CRO, once made, is broadly similar: any proceedings or application issued are to be automatically struck out or dismissed – unless permission has been given by the court. Limited CROs will tend to be limited to a single set of proceedings and are intended to prevent a party making further applications within those proceedings, subject to any further orders of the court. An order will be limited to the duration of the proceedings. In contrast, extended CROs and general CROs are limited to maximum periods of two years, renewable upon review.

Extended civil restraint orders are directed at parties who issue and make applications in multiple proceedings. See *Couper v Albion Properties*[88] where, between them, the claimant and his wife had made six prior unmeritorious applications and had a further five applications similarly dismissed at the hearing; and see *Camille Saskia Richardson v Google UK Ltd.*[89] In *Nowak v NMC*[90] the court dealt with an application for a CRO and, specifically addressed (and dismissed) the counter-argument

---

86   [2000] 1 FLR 759.
87   [2003] EWCA Civ 799.
88   [2017] EWHC 22 (Ch).
89   [2016] EWHC 1534 (QB).
90   *Nowak v (1) Nursing & Midwifery Council (2) Guys & St Thomas' NHS Foundation Trust* [2013] EWHC 1932 (QB).

that such an order infringed the claimant's Art 6 human rights. It is worth noting that where a series of claims have been instituted, a CRO may still be made even if some of the claims apparently have merit, see *Thakerar v Lynch Hall & Hornby*.[91] In those proceedings the court was at pains to point out that an application that appeared to have merit would be permitted, but permission would be required for them, the threshold for a CRO having been met.

Submission of no case to answer

More because it is right to highlight this submission as a 'weapon in the arsenal' of the defendant practitioner than because it is likely to be used, it is worth noting that it is possible to request judgment mid-trial after the claimant's evidence on the basis that no case has been made out.

Such applications will be vanishingly rare in civil, clinical negligence matters. With trial costs having already been substantially incurred, the court will need to be persuaded in the clearest terms as to why trial should not proceed, mindful of the risks of appeal and the possibility that further argument may have a bearing on the assessment of the merits at 'half time'. Indeed, if the defendant has evidence to do so before trial, an application for summary judgment would be preferable. The test for a 'real prospect of success' is broadly similar, yet fewer costs would have been incurred. Indeed, the limited precedents suggest that it may be harder to secure judgment on the basis of no case to answer. In *Benham Ltd v Kythira Investments Ltd*,[92] Lord Justice Simon Brown drew on a number of authorities to support the contention that the claimant needed 'a scintilla of evidence' to support a case to answer.

In *Saed v Ealing Hospital NHS Trust*,[93] a successful submission was made at trial. The claim concerned a failure to diagnose and treat tuberculous meningitis. The defendant made a submission of no case to answer at the close of the claimant's case. The claimant's own witness evidence suggested that it would not have been possible to introduce effective pharmacological treatment in time to prevent the injury that had occurred. As the claimant had no chance of proving negligence, judgment was entered.

'Back in play': new claims made on the same facts

For fans of the board game Monopoly™ this is the 'get out of jail free card'. Whilst such proceedings are perhaps uncommon, where a claim has expired or there is a procedural defect with service, it may be possible (and easier) to simply issue fresh proceedings – provided that the new proceedings still fall within the limitation period. After limitation, it may be possible to proceed whilst relying on the Limitation Act 1980, s 33 (see below) but will face obvious challenges.

Previously, it had been thought that issuing new proceedings in respect of the same claim amounted to an abuse of process, such that the second proceedings should be struck out. It is now established law that this need

---

91   [2005] EWHC 2751, Ch.
92   [2003] EWCA Civ 1794.
93   [2001] All ER (D) 45 (Sep).

not be the case. In *Securum Finance Ltd v Ashton (No 1)*[94] the Court of Appeal held that despite the claimant's first claim having been struck out for delay, there was no principle that precluded a new, second action commenced within the limitation period, provided that there was good reason. However, in permitting the new action consideration of court resources (CPR 1.1(2)(e)) is necessary. Essentially, there remains scope for second actions to be refused. In *Securum* it was noted that the doctrine of res judicata does not arise where a prior claim has been struck out for default or because the claim was never properly initiated (for example, if the claim form was not served). That is to say, the claim was actionable precisely because the merits of the claim had never been previously ruled upon. In the more recent case of *Davies v Carillion*,[95] where the claimant was permitted to bring fresh proceedings more than four years after the first claim, Mr Justice Morris undertook a helpful exposition of all of the authorities as to whether a second claim may be permitted to proceed in relation to the same facts.

In the cases of *Dixie v British Polythene/Atkas v Adepta*[96] which were heard together, the Court of Appeal noted that it was the will of parliament that there should be preserved the possibility of pursuing a personal injury claim after the limitation date – subject to the courts' discretion. Therefore, where claim forms had been issued but not served in time, the act of failing to serve was not an abuse – the claim was simply out of time. Further, where there is nothing in the CPR to prevent the new issue of a claim form, thereafter relying upon the discretion of the Limitation Act 1980, s 33 is not an abuse either.

MULTI-PARTY ACTIONS[97]

Whilst not every clinical negligence practitioner will be willing to or be able to undertake multi-party litigation claims, it is important to have some knowledge of the mechanisms of a multi-party action to recognise when a claimant may be a party and to provide the best advice.

A distinction needs to be drawn between the types of order that may be made in which multi-party litigation may arise:

- *general powers of the court* – CPR 3.1(2)(f) and CPR 3.1(2)(g) permit the courts to hear cases together, to consolidate proceedings and to add claimants or defendants after the commencement of proceedings, if appropriate;
- *bringing multiple claims within a single set of proceedings* – CPR 7 permits the claim form to be issued in the name of multiple claimants or defendants (although this is unlikely to be appropriate for complex clinical negligence matters);

---

94 [2000] 3 WLR 1400.
95 *Davies v (1) Carillion Energy Services Ltd; (2) HIS Energy Ltd (In Liquidation)* [2017] EWHC 3206 (QB).
96 *Atkas v Adepta and Dixie v British Polythene Industries Ltd* [2010] EWCA Civ 1170. See, in particular, at [93].
97 See also Chapter 16 on Product Liability in a Medical Context.

- *representative claims* – CPR 19.6 permits a representative to bring or defend an action on behalf of others who have the same interest in the claim; and
- *group litigation orders (GLOs)* – CPR 19.10 provides for the use of GLOs which allow the court to manage multiple claims together, provided that the claimants opt-in, only where there are common or related issues of fact or law.

Parties may choose to defer proceedings pending the outcome of test cases, rather than to proceed as one GLO. For example, whilst many hundreds of women were affected by the treatment provided by the breast surgeon, Ian Paterson, no GLO was ever made. Seven lead cases were instead identified to be pursued. The terms of the settlement on behalf of his private patients in August 2017 addressed both the extant claims, which numbered approximately 540 at that time, but also included provision for future claims, limited to a cut-off on 31 October 2018. That litigation also did not include the claims in relation to his NHS practice whilst in the employ of the Heart of England NHS Foundation Trust. Those claims are thought to number around 800, which were mostly settled earlier.

There is no restriction under the CPR to defendant parties defending in a representative capacity or under a GLO. However, it will, of course, be far more common for such actions to be brought by the claimant and that assumption is made here.

Representative actions

There is no comprehensive record of representative actions. In practice, such actions will generally be few in number. It is worth touching upon representative actions here because any party considering whether to apply for a GLO is first required to consider whether the consolidation of claims or a representative action would be more appropriate.[98] For claims involving large numbers of claimant parties a GLO is likely to be more appropriate.

A representative action requires no specific court permission, subject to limited exceptions at the CPR 19.7, which include claims on behalf of estates and claims on behalf of children. The court does, however, have powers under the CPR 19.6(2) to remove a party as representative and may order that an existing claim proceeds in a representative capacity (CPR 19.6(1)). In *Emerald Supplies Ltd v British Airways*,[99] the Court of Appeal clarified the strict requirements as to what amounted to the same interest in the litigation *and*, in particular, that the nature of qualifying representative parties. It must be possible to identify the parties that qualify for representation at the commencement of, and throughout the litigation.

In commencing a representative action, the claimant should normally set out the representative capacity on the face of the claim form, but the representatives do not need to be named as part(ies). Indeed, strictly speaking it is not necessary to have authority from the party concerned to commence a claim in a representative capacity.[100] Where a claim is

98 CPR PD 19B Group Litigation, para 2.3.
99 [2009] EWHC 741 (Ch) at [62].
100 *Independiente Ltd v Music Trading* [2003] EWHC 470.

continuing under a representative party, the day-to-day management and decisions on the running of the case will, of course, be taken by the representative. Unlike a GLO, any claimant that is represented in that way could take no active part in the claim. Critically, if that is the case, the represented party will bear no liability as to the costs of the action. Finally, it will be noted that it is possible to commence a representative action with just two claimants, but there is no maximum number.

Group litigation orders

The purpose of the GLO is to enable the court to enable it to manage multi-party litigation more effectively. The CPR 19.10 states that the court may make a GLO to provide for case management of claims where there are 'common or related issues of fact or law'. In practice, this means, of course, that there must be multiple claims or proposed claims and common, identifiable, issues which, if decided in one case, would be binding on other cases falling within the GLO. When considering whether to bring a GLO the Practice Direction encourages practitioners to contact the Law Society's Multi Party Action Information Service to obtain information relating to other cases giving rise to issues relevant to the proposed GLO.

Importantly, the interests of the claimant parties under a GLO do not need to be uniformly aligned as with representative proceedings. For complex and higher value claims the establishment of the group may promote effective case management and earlier resolution. For smaller cases, the inclusion within a group may permit claims to be brought which it otherwise may not have been possible to bring (at all) cost-effectively.

Historically, the multi-party actions which concerned healthcare provision have concerned claims relating to defective medical products or drugs. For example, GLOs have been made inter alia in connection with Sodium Valproate (fetal anti-convulsants), DePuy metal-on-metal hips[101] and the Trilucent and PIP breast implant litigation. However, multi-party actions are not restricted to such claims. Multi-party claims have been brought on behalf of special needs residents harmed in a hospital setting[102] and (as a vicarious liability claim) against an employer where patients were sexually abused by a doctor during occupational health examinations.[103]

The CPR 19 provides the framework within which GLOs can be made (CPR 19.10–19.15).

Each multi-party action will, of course, be different and some cases, even where there are overlapping issues, will not be suited to a GLO. The principles of group party litigation are relatively straightforward and broadly reflect the core principles of the overriding objectives, namely to reduce cost and limit the use of court resources.

---

101 *Gee v DePuy International Ltd* [2018] EWHC 1208 (QB).
102 See, for example, the Winterbourne View Group Litigation Order.
103 The Dr Gordon Bates (Deceased) and Barclays Bank Group Litigation Order. For the appeal judgment on the vicarious liability issue, see also *Barclays Bank plc v Various Claimants* [2018] EWCA Civ 1670 which may be of interest and practical application to clinical negligence practitioners considering the liability of private hospitals to patients, where self-employed practitioners are given practice privileges at private hospitals.

The elements that define a GLO are:

- the group register setting out all of the claims being managed under the GLO;
- the appointment of a 'management court' which manages all claims subject to the GLO;
- the creation of a list of 'GLO issues' – essentially, the common elements to the claims, which in turn establish which claims are eligible to be incorporated within the group.

The register is essential in that any judgment or order made in respect of one claim on the register will usually be binding on all the claims on the register at that time (CPR 19.12(1)). Such orders will generally also be binding on claims added to the register at a later date, unless the new addition to the group seeks permission not to be bound (CPR 19.12(3)). Note that claims cannot be registered within the group until proceedings are issued (CPR PD 19A 6.1A).

Despite the obvious importance of the register, CPR 19 sets out few requirements as to whether, when, by whom or how specific criteria should be chosen and applied to identify and add suitable claims.

The court will always direct that a register is maintained as part of the GLO. Clearly if a GLO is to serve its purpose there must also be an awareness of the existence of potential multi-party actions as early as possible, such that related claims can join the group. As such, it is usual for the court to direct that any new GLO is advertised. In view of the binding nature of the GLO, one of the most significant directions that can be made, if appropriate, is for an individual claim to proceed by way of a test case (CPR 19.15) on an issue or group of issues.

A party can apply for a GLO under the CPR 19.11. The related CPR PD 19B sets out the procedures for making that application, although the court can also make a GLO of its own initiative. Perhaps counter-intuitively, the first requirement under CPR PD 19B is to consider whether other forms of litigation are more appropriate, such as a representative claim or consolidated claim. The application procedure is somewhat onerous (see CPR PD 19B 3.2 for the list of requirements) and will require, for High Court claims), permission from the President of the Queen's Bench Division (CPR PD 19B 3.3).

A witness statement filed with the application will need to address that issue, which is no mere technicality. Failure to demonstrate that a GLO is required and/or the proportionate basis upon which to pursue the litigation will result in the refusal of the order. In *Hobson v Ashton Moreton Slack*[104] the court noted a number of failures in the way that the cases brought by the claimant had been presented, which had merely resulted in increased costs. In particular, it was noted that the applicant had failed to consider other approaches, such as a test case to address a common factual point rather than to proceed with the group claim.

There must be funding for a GLO to proceed and, perhaps obviously, a sufficient number of parties in the group. In *Austin v Miller Argent (South Wales) Ltd*[105] the Court of Appeal upheld a first instance refusal of a GLO where there was insufficient evidence that any significant element of the

---

104 [2006] EWHC 1134 (QB).
105 [2015] 1 WLR 62.

proposed claimant group could proceed with the litigation in view of the insurance position.[106] After the event (ATE) cover was unavailable to the proposed claimants, only two of the proposed group of more than 500 had alternative before the event (BTE) cover (which is self-evidently too few to constitute a group), and whilst none of the proposed claimants had issued proceedings at the time of the application, that had remained the case at the time of the appeal.

Whilst it may be an obvious point, it is worth reiterating that in complex multi-party litigation of this nature it is important to have fully prepared the application before seeking a GLO. That is likely to involve addressing any issues between the parties seeking to form a group. In *Crossley v Volkswagen*[107] the claimants were ordered to pay indemnity costs to the defendants for nearly a year's worth of additional costs thrown away after a premature GLO application and the multiple hearings that were necessitated. A stay to resolve the issues would have been appropriate.

Whilst the terms of GLOs will vary, each group will be conducted in a similar way, with the appointment of a lead firm or firm(s) under the CPR 19.13(c), often a set of generic group particulars of claim will be prepared or authorised (or parties required to include specified information within their statements of case under the CPR 19.3(d) in order to be identified as part of the group), and a generic team of lawyers (or 'steering' group/committee) will be agreed to direct strategy.

From a practical perspective, the main requirements of GLO cases are:

- that costs need to be kept to a minimum: a generic team of lawyers will work on common issues, to avoid duplication, thereafter providing guidance to individual case counsel and the solicitors;
- that the generic team must have authority and be capable of addressing tactical issues quickly on behalf of the group;
- where the generic team take on a central role, it is essential that there is good communication between the generic team and the case teams throughout the litigation;
- to identify and manage cases: new clients may need to be referred on to the generic solicitors. The GLO will usually be made with a direction that requires advertising. This is necessary because date of knowledge may be key, but also because there will be a time limit for new claims to join the group without permission of the court (CPR 19.13(e));
- to establish which issue(s) within the client group need to be addressed at a case-specific level or at a generic level;
- to consider preliminary issues: it will often be appropriate to deal with liability issues separately from quantification. This avoids unnecessary costs, such as extensive medical reports and the costs of work on schedules of loss being incurred if liability proves to be determinative. Such an approach should be addressed in the directions, which can also address the position if pecuniary settlement terms are advanced early (and the claimant then needs time to undertake quantification);

---

106 For further information about litigation funding and insurance, see Chapter 27.
107 *Crossley v Volkswagen Aktiengesellschaft (The VW NOx Group Emissions Litigation)* [2018] EWHC 2308 (QB).

- to avoid internal disputes: there will need to be a common system for resolving claims as between claimants where possible. If the claims are brought adopting different approaches it is clear that there is scope for defendant parties to 'divide and rule' by settling the stronger cases. Where possible claimants should be asked to agree to abide by advice on the terms of settlement from the generic counsel common to the group. Unnecessary infighting within the group leaves the group vulnerable – if only as to costs. In *Crossley* referred to above, internal disputes between claimant firms would appear to have led to delay and significant costs exposure;
- ensure that a scheme is set up for the distribution of any damages so that it properly and fairly reflects the loss suffered and the strengths and weaknesses in each case or type of case within the group. Any settlement will, of course, need approval where claimant(s) lack capacity (see Chapters 10, 11 and 24.)

Quantifying claims under a GLO

Many multi-party actions settle. If a defendant is willing to settle, the question then arises as to how one can accurately, quickly and cost-effectively calculate the true value of all of the many claims within the group. Two approaches are may be used, neither of which is perfect.

The broad brush approach

In the first approach, damages calculations can be based on the hypothetical average group member's damage, rather than a specific assessment of each individual claimant. Naturally, that sum is then multiplied by the number of claimants within the group to produce a global sum. The obvious flaw with this approach is that it over-compensates claimants with weaker claims (and, in particular, the claimants with the weakest claims of all) and under-compensates claimants with very strong claims.

Whether or not it is appropriate to approach the quantification in this way will depend upon the cases within the group. Sufficient numbers of much stronger, potentially significantly higher value cases as supposed to a few outliers or modest variations in levels of harm may mean an alternative approach is preferable.

Aggregation

The second approach is to aggregate damage awards, where the management court or defendants consider what injury has been done to the group without having to resolve matters per individual claim. So long as the evidence is reliable and a reasonable degree of accuracy can be achieved, this method does avoid some of the criticisms of the broad brush approach and yet still avoids a multiplicity of hearings on damages.

Distribution of damages

Whichever of the above approaches is adopted, both methodologies gives rise to either an actual conflict of interest between claimant group members, between clients and claimant law firms – both in calculation of the central pot and in its distribution. Those challenges must, of course, be balanced against the cost (time and money) of not reaching a swift conclusion or limitations specific to the litigation.

By way of a practical settlement example (albeit not a GLO), the *Paterson* litigation was concluded on an aggregated basis. There, the medical indemnifier had withdrawn their discretionary indemnity cover,[108] the private hospital group had reached the limit of their commercial insurance policy[109] and was therefore required to pay damages from its reserves. The £37.2m damages amounts to a sum that the defendants will pay, rather than an assessment of individual claims, not all of which were before the court. The terms offered contained a restriction that the settlement incorporated provision for future claims (potential claimants may register a claim until 31 October 2018). Thus it would not be possible to adopt a broad-brush approach. The limitations of awards which are not individually quantified do, of course, need to be balanced with the benefit of achieving earlier settlement and certainty.

Costs

The costs of multi-party litigation will undoubtedly be significant. The courts have long been willing to make costs capping orders, placing ceilings on GLO costs. Whilst the matters in dispute can be complex, the existence of a GLO does not obviate the need to costs budget; the courts can and will make budgeting orders. See, for example, *Various Claimants v Sir Robert McAlpine*[110] for an example of the multiple budgets filed and considered as part of the GLO case management.

The approach adopted by the courts to the apportionment of costs tends to be the same for both legally aided and privately funded claimants in that costs of lead actions are borne equally (on a several basis) by all members of the group register at the time the order is made. More specifically, in most cases, the court will separate and apportion those costs which are 'common costs' (ie costs which are incurred: (a) in relation to the GLO issues; (b) in a claim while it is proceeding as a test claim; or (c) by the lead solicitor in administering the group litigation) and those which are individual costs (ie those costs incurred in relation to an individual claim on the group register). However, where the court does not do so, that will then need to be addressed at detailed assessment; see the CPR 46.6(5) – 'Costs where the court has made a group litigation order' and CPR PD 19B 16.5. The court may, of course, depart from the usual order if there are conduct issues to consider.[111]

Legal Aid was always available only restrictively for claims involving medical products and even then rarely without a declaration by the relevant regulator that such a product is dangerous in its normal

---

108 See *Bradbury v Ian Paterson* [2014] EWHC 3992 (QB) at [10] where the Official Solicitor withdrew as litigation friend, upon the MDU no longer willing to indemnify the defendant.
109 *Spire Health Care v Royal & Sun Alliance* [2018] EWCA Civ 317.
110 [2015] EWHC 3543 (QB).
111 *Bairstow v Queens Moat Houses Plc (Assessment of Costs)* [2001] CP Rep 59.

conditions of use.[112] The changes to Legal Aid funding[113] now mean that such cases are highly unlikely to receive Legal Aid funding. That being the case, some claims which would previously have benefited from public funding, will now be all but impossible to bring under a GLO unless funded by way of a conditional fee agreement. As the market develops, third party litigation funding may be available if the merits are deemed strong enough.

---

112 In the Fetal Anti-Convulstant litigation (which did have the benefit of Legal Aid funding) cover was withdrawn by the Legal Services Commission (as was) just six weeks before trial.
113 See Chapter 27.

Part Four

Part Four

Chapter 19

The inquest – the law, procedure and funding

Linda Jacobs
Caron Heyes – Funding and the recoverability of costs

INTRODUCTION

It is of fundamental importance that a system exists to investigate the cause and circumstances of a death. If there is going to be an inquest, efforts should be made to make the most of the opportunity to find out what the hospital, and/or GP say about the circumstances surrounding the death. Hospital staff and/or GPs should also use the opportunity to provide an explanation, and to allay any rumour or suspicion the family or wider community may have. This chapter focuses on healthcare related deaths; such deaths do not automatically give rise to an inquest.

Reform

The last decade saw two major reviews of the coronial service and system of death certification. One review was carried out by the Fundamental Review of Death Certification and Investigation Committee (Luce Committee 2003) which declared that:

> neither the certification system nor the investigation system is 'fit for purpose' in modern society. Both need substantial reform.[1]

The Shipman Inquiry: Death Certification and the Investigation of Death by Coroners, chaired by Dame Janet Smith reported in July 2003, declaring:

> there must be radical reform and a complete break with the past, as to organisation, philosophy, sense of purpose and mode of operation. The new Coroner Service that I shall recommend will be barely recognisable as the offspring of its parent.

Critically, the Shipman Inquiry concluded that the systems for death registration, cremation certification, and coronial investigation failed to

---

1 *Death Certification and Investigation in England, Wales and Northern Ireland: A Report of a Fundamental Review 2003* (28 April 2003: Chairman Tom Luce) (Cm 5831).

deter Dr Shipman from committing multiple murders and failed to detect his crimes.[2]

These reviews and other commentators identified a plethora of deficiencies and inadequacies in the coronial system. The draft Coroners Bill, seeking to address these shortcomings, was prefaced by a scathing description of the then current coronial service:

> The coroners' system at present is fragmented, non-accountable, variable in its processes and its quality, ineffective in part, archaic in its statutory basis, and very much dependant on the good people working in, or resourcing it, at present to its continued ability to respond to the demands we place on it.[3]

The Coroners and Justice Act 2009 received Royal Assent on 12 November 2009. It represents a long overdue reform of the coronial system and death certification systems in England and Wales. The previous legislation is based on the Coroners Act 1887, and the Coroners and Justice Act 2009 represents the first substantial reform of the law and procedure since that time. Many of the provisions in the new Act re-enact provisions in the Coroners Act 1988. The new provisions address some of the weaknesses identified by the Luce Committee and the Shipman Inquiry. However, there is no nationally funded coroner's service; a service that most commentators (including the Chief Coroner)[4] opine is a necessity.

Statutory framework and subordinate legislation

Coronial law is governed in England and Wales by the Coroners and Justice Act 2009 (CJA 2009). Under ss 43 and 45, new rules and regulations were introduced, as follows.

1   Coroners (Investigations) Regulations 2013;[5]
2   Coroners (Inquests) Rules 2013;[6]
3   Coroners Allowances, Fees and Expenses Regulations 2013.[7]

The CJA 2009 and the subordinate legalisation all came into force on 25 July 2013. Parts of the CJA 2009 have yet to take effect.

Section 13 of the Coroners Act 1988 remains in force providing a mechanism to challenge decisions by coroners in the High Court, including seeking a fresh inquest and a decision not to hold an inquest.

OVERVIEW

The CJA 2009 introduced wide-ranging and fundamental reforms to the death certification system and coronial service. In reforming the coronial service, the Government stated that it aimed to deliver an improved service for bereaved people; introduce national operational leadership

---

2   The Shipman Inquiry Third Report: *Death Certification and the Investigation of Death by Coroners* (14 July 2003: Chairman Dame Janet Smith DBE) (Cm 5854), p 489.
3   The Shipman Inquiry Third Report: *Death Certification and the Investigation of Death by Coroners* (14 July 2003: Chairman Dame Janet Smith DBE) (Cm 5854).
4   Report of the Chief Coroner to the Lord Chancellor, Fifth Annual Report : 2017–2018, para 15.
5   SI 2013/1629.
6   SI 2013/1616.
7   SI 2013/1615.

whilst ensuring that the system was better embedded locally; and ensured that investigations and inquests were more effective.[8]

The CJA 2009 distinguishes between a coroner's duty to investigate a death, and the duty to hold an inquest. The investigation process does not automatically result in an inquest, which is viewed as the last and most formal stage in the overall investigative process. The Government stated that the change of emphasis was intended to reflect the reality that an inquest was only required in a small proportion of cases.[9]

The number of inquests held annually is significantly smaller than the number of deaths referred to coroners. In 2018, 220,648 deaths were reported to coroners; representing 41% of all registered deaths. However, inquests were only opened in approximately 13% of all cases reported to coroners. The percentage of cases involving post-mortem examination, as a percentage of all deaths reported to coroners in 2018, was approximately 39%. Since 1995, the proportion of deaths in which a post-mortem examination was ordered has steadily declined from 61% to 36% in 2016, but has recently increased (37% in 2017 and 39% in 2018).[10]

As part of its reforms, the Government introduced a *Charter for Bereaved People Who Come Into Contact With a Reformed Coroner System*. This was republished by the Ministry of Justice in February 2014 as the *Guide to Coroner Services* and is available online.[11] The *Guide* is issued by the Lord Chancellor under the CJA 2009, s 42, and therefore has statutory force on how the coronial service operates in relation to the family of the deceased.

Coronial areas

England and Wales is divided into coroner areas, and at the date of writing there were 88 areas. This is a decrease from 110 since the CJA 2009 came into force as the Lord Chancellor has exercised his/her powers under the CJA 2009, Sch 2 to combine smaller coroner areas. Each area continues to be funded and resourced by a local authority or authorities. There is no new funding available and as a result, the facilities and resources available in different coroner areas vary.

Chief Coroner

As a result of the CJA 2009, the coronial system is led by a Chief Coroner, who must be a High Court or Circuit Judge.[12] The Chief Coroner provides national leadership, coordinates and supervises the coronial service, and is responsible for improving the consistency of standards and taking measures to reduce unnecessary delays. The current Chief Coroner is His

---

8   Ministry of Justice, 'Reform of the Coroner System – Next Stage: Preparing for Implementation' (Consultation Paper, March 2010), p 4.
9   Secretary of State for Constitutional Affairs and Lord Chancellor, 'Coroner Reform: The Government's Draft Bill: Improving Death Investigation in England and Wales' (Cm 6849), (2006), p 8.
10 Ministry of Justice, Coroners Statistics Annual 2018 (9 May 2018).
11 See   https://assets.publishing.service.gov.uk/government/uploads/system/uploads/attachment_data/file/363879/guide-to-coroner-service.pdf.
12 CJA 2009, s 35 and Sch 8, para 1(2).

Honour Judge Mark Lucraft QC. The first Chief Coroner was His Honour Judge Peter Thornton QC. He retired from office on 30 September 2016 and is an Assistant Coroner in the City of London. In January 2019, the appointed two deputy chief coroners: Derek Winter, Senior Coroner for the Sunderland Coroner Area; and HHJ Alexia Durran.

Criticisms expressed by the Shipman Inquiry were that coroners differ significantly in their practices and there was a lack of uniformity in the interpretation of the statutory provisions. To improve the consistency of standards between coroners, the Chief Coroner has published numerous guidance notes, including *Guidance No 25: Coroners and the media*; and law sheets, including *Law Sheet No 1: Unlawful killing*.[13]

Other functions of the Chief Coroner include:

1   keeping a register of investigations lasting more than 12[14] months and taking steps to reduce necessary delays;
2   overseeing transfer of cases between coroners[15] and directing a coroner to conduct an investigation;[16]
3   approving the appointment of coroners[17]
4   providing an annual report on the coroner system of the Lord Chancellor;[18] and
5   monitoring reports to prevent future deaths.[19]

The Chief Coroner may conduct investigations and inquests.[20]

CORONERS

The CJA 2009 created three types of coroner: senior coroner; area coroner; and assistant coroner ('coroners'). In order to be appointed as a coroner, the applicant must:

- be under 70 years of age;
- satisfy the 'judicial-appointment eligibility condition' on a five year basis;[21]
- have the Lord Chancellor and Chief Coroner consent to their appointment.[22]

The 'judicial-appointment eligibility condition' requires the applicant to be a qualified barrister, solicitor[23] or fellow of the Chartered Institute of Legal Executives[24] for five years and have experience in law for five

---

13   These are available on the Chief Coroner's website: https://www.judiciary.uk/related-offices-and-bodies/office-chief-coroner/. At the date of writing there are five law sheets and 31 guidance notes.
14   CJA 2009, s 16(3).
15   CJA 2009, s 2.
16   CJA 2009, s 3.
17   CJA 2009, Sch 3, para 1(3).
18   CJA 2009, s 36.
19   CJA 2009, Sch 5, para 7.
20   CJA 2009, s 41 and Sch 10, para 1(1).
21   CJA 2009, Sch 2, para 3.
22   CJA 2009, Sch 3, para 1(3).
23   Tribunal, Courts and Enforcement Act 2007, s 50.
24   Judicial Appointments (Amendment) Order 2013, SI 2013/3022, art 3.

years. Applicants with only a medical qualification are unable to satisfy the 'judicial-appointment eligibility condition' and are not eligible for appointment under the CJA 2009. However, this does not affect doctors already appointed as coroners, although they would not be eligible to apply for a different office.

Coroners are appointed by the local authority or lead authority, if more than one. To enhance consistency, the Chief Coroner has issued guidance: *Chief Coroner's Guidance: No 6 The Appointment of Coroners*. The guidance clearly states that the coroner is 'an independent judicial office holder', responsible to the Crown. Local authorities appoint coroners, but that they do not employ them (although the pay the coroner's salary or fees). The independence of the coroner as a judicial officer is particularly important. They are charged with investigating sudden, violent or unnatural death involving numerous authorities, including the NHS, police and local authorities. Therefore it is important that they are not subject to central or local government control. Further, coroners are under a duty to make reports to prevent future deaths, which may involve changes of practice and/or additional costs.

The Chief Coroner is responsible for making regulations to train coroners[25] and has issued several guidelines to assist coroners:

1   *Guidance No 20: Core Competencies for Assistant Coroners*, tasks include – knowing when a doctor can provide an Medical Certificate Cause of Death, authorising post-mortems, histology, toxicology; and approval of organ or tissue donation;
2   *Guidance No 19: Mentors for Coroners.*

Coroners officers

The CJA 2009, s 24 stipulates that the relevant local authority 'secure the provision of whatever officers and staff are needed by the coroners for the area to carry out their functions – but only to the extent that such officers and staff are not provided by a police authority'. Consequently, coroners are assisted by coroner's officers whom are often retired police officers or police officers on secondment. There is recognition that coroner's officers should be employed from backgrounds that are more diverse as part of a change in emphasis from a coronial service focussed on crime towards a wider medical and social function.[26]

The functions of coroner's officers vary from district to district, and include a wide range of non-standardised duties and practices. The Chief Coroner is responsible for making regulations about training coroners' officers and general staff.[27] Coroners' officers are often the first point of contact for representatives of those who are involved in the investigation and inquest process, and many are exceptionally helpful.

---

25 CJA 2009, s 37.
26 The Shipman Inquiry Third Report: *Death Certification and the Investigation of Death by Coroners* (14 July 2003: Chairman Dame Janet Smith DBE) (Cm 5854), Chapter 8.
27 CJA 2009, s 37.

CORONIAL INVESTIGATION STAGES

The CJA 2009 distinguished between a coroner's duty to investigate a death, and the duty to hold an inquest; thereby signalling the arrival of a new investigative ethos in the coronial service. Under this more transparent decision making approach, an inquest is viewed as the last and most formal stage in the overall investigative process. The stages are:

1   a pre-investigation inquiry;
2   the investigation;
3   the inquest.

The investigation is governed by the Coroners (Investigations) Regulations 2013.

Pre-investigation inquiry

A coroner may make 'whatever enquiries seem necessary in order to decide'[28] if there is a duty to investigate a death in the following circumstances:

1   if the coroner has 'reason to suspect' the deceased died a violent or unnatural death; the cause of death is unknown; or the deceased died whilst in custody or in state detention;[29] and
2   if the coroner has 'reason to believe' that a death occurred in or near the coroners area, the circumstances of the death require investigation and there is no duty to investigate because of the destruction, loss or absence of the body.[30]

The phrase 'reason to suspect' is not defined in the CJA 2009. 'Reason to suspect' does not require positive proof or even formulated evidence; any information giving 'reason to suspect' will suffice.[31]

In healthcare deaths, preliminary inquiries are likely to include obtaining information from the family, GP or hospital and obtaining the medical notes. A post-mortem examination may be required.

The investigation

Coroners may continue their investigations as a formal investigation where the preliminary investigation reveals:

1   an unnatural death; or
2   a natural cause of death, but there may have been neglect or culpable human failure in medical treatment (this is where a natural death becomes an unnatural death).

If a post-mortem examination was not carried out under the preliminary enquiry, it will be carried out at this stage. It is likely that the coroner will request further information from the hospitals and/or GP. The CJA 2009, Sch 5 includes a range of powers available to the coroner, including the

---

28   CJA 2009, s 1(7).
29   CJA 2009, s 1(2).
30   CJA 2009, s 1(4).
31   *R v Inner London Coroner, ex p Linnane* [1989] 1 WLR 395, at 398.

power to require a person within such a period as the coroner thinks reasonable to:

1 provide evidence in the form of a witness statement;
2 produce any documents in the custody or control of the person which relate to a matter that is relevant to the inquest;
3 produce for inspection, examination or testing any other thing in the custody or control of the person which relate to a matter that is relevant to the inquest.[32]

Once an investigation into death is commenced, there are two potential outcomes:

1 an inquest into the death;[33] or
2 discontinuing the investigation before an inquest is opened, if:

- the post-mortem examination and results from the investigations reveal a natural cause of death; and
- the coroner 'thinks it is not necessary to continue the investigation'.[34]

Importantly, an inquest must be held where the coroner has reason to suspect that the death was violent, or unnatural, or occurred in custody or state detention.[35] In healthcare deaths, a coroner will consider whether the circumstances of the death raise a reason to suspect neglect or culpable failure in medical treatment and care. If an investigation is discontinued, the coroner must record the cause of death and inform the next of kin.[36]

The Chief Coroner has recommended to the Lord Chancellor that coroners should also be able to discontinue an investigation where the cause of death is revealed by means other than a post-mortem examination (for example, through reviewing the medical records), provided there is no statutory requirement to hold an inquest.[37]

The inquest

Any inquest must be opened as soon as practicable once the coroner has concluded that there is a duty to hold the inquest.[38] Once opened an inquest must be concluded.

REPORTING DEATHS TO THE CORONER

Coroners can only investigate deaths that are reported to them. At present, there is no statutory duty on doctors or other heath service personnel to report a death to the coroner.

---

32 CJA 2009, Sch 5(2).
33 CJA 2009, s 6.
34 CJA 2009, s 4(1).
35 CJA 2009, s 4(2).
36 Coroners (Investigations) Regulations 2013, SI 2013/1629, reg 17.
37 Report of the Chief Coroner to the Lord Chancellor, Fifth Annual Report: 2017–2018, para 181.
38 Coroners (Inquests) Rules 2013, SI 2013/1616, r 5.

Medical practitioners are often uncertain when they are required to report a death. However, in the healthcare environment, doctors report deaths to the coroner where the cause of death is unknown, or where the deceased was not attended by a doctor during their last illness (which is not defined and open to interpretation).[39] In such circumstances, the doctor is unable to complete the Medical Certificate of Cause of Death ('MCCD'). Without the MCCD, the death cannot be registered with the Registrar of Births, Deaths and Marriages. Referrals to coroners are made electronically by using a template. As the Chief Coroners *Guidance: No 23* states:

> A referral form provides a permanent written and early record in the words of the doctor (not in the words of a coroner's officer interpreting a doctor's words on the phone). It concentrates the doctor's mind on the important details in advance of communication with the coroner.

Even if a doctor does not report a death to the coroner, the Registrar of Births, Deaths, and Marriages must report certain deaths to the coroner, including a death occurring during an operation or before recovery from an anaesthetic; a death that appears to be unnatural, or to have been caused by violence, neglect, abortion, or occurred in suspicious circumstances; and a death where the attending doctor had not seen the deceased within the 14 days preceding death or had not seen the body after death.[40]

There is a common law duty to report a death to the coroner in circumstances that might require an inquest.[41] Consequently, anyone can report a death to the coroner, including the family of a patient who dies in hospital. If a report is to be made, it is preferable to do so at the earliest opportunity so that the coroner can collate all the essential evidence before it is no longer available. If the family have specific concerns about the treatment or care of the deceased, it is advisable to write to the coroner at an early stage setting out their concerns. Such information often assists the coroner in the pre-investigation/ investigation and helps identify witnesses that may be asked to provide evidence. These issues can always be developed and refined as the investigation progresses.

Medical examiners and reportable death reforms

The CJA 2009 introduces a system of secondary certification of deaths not referred to the coroner, and a new statutory duty to report deaths.[42] The intention is to move away from a system that allows a single doctor to issue a MCCD. It was this weakness in the system that Dr Shipman exploited. The key change is the introduction of the post of Medical

---

39 Births Deaths and Registration Act 1953, s 22(1) – Certificates of cause of death: in the case of the death of any person who has been attended during their last illness by a registered medical practitioner, that practitioner shall sign a certificate in the prescribed form stating to the best of his knowledge and belief the cause of death and shall forthwith deliver that certificate to the registrar.

40 Registration of Births and Deaths Regulations 1987, SI 1987/2088, reg 41(2)(d)–(e).

41 *R v Clerk* (1702) 1 Salk 377.

42 CJA 2009, s 18(1).

Examiner (ME) appointed by Primary Care Trusts in England and Local Health Boards in Wales.[43] Medical Examiners will work alongside coroners, with the aim of providing a more comprehensive independent system of death investigation in England and Wales.

According to the CJA 2009, the ME will scrutinise the MCCD that was completed by the medical practitioner. Once informed about the death, the ME will make 'whatever enquires appear to be necessary in order to confirm or establish the cause of death'.[44] The ME will be entitled to have full access to medical notes and patient records.[45] The ME will also be empowered to discuss the circumstances of the death with the attending medical practitioner and the family,[46] but cannot insist that an individual or a specific organisation provides any information.[47] The ME will not be able to order a post-mortem examination, but can make such recommendations to the coroner. Following enquires to establish or confirm the cause of death, the ME will issue a medical examiners certificate stating the cause of death to the best of the examiner's knowledge and belief, or refer the case back to the coroner if the cause of death remains undetermined.[48] At the time of writing, it is understood that the government will draw on the CJA 2009 to establish regulations, including free-standing regulations identifying reportable deaths. However, the relevant provisions regarding the ME and statutory reporting duties in the CJA 2009 will not be fully enacted.

The Department of Health and Social Care indicated in June 2018 that medical examiners will start to scrutinise deaths from April 2019 and that a national medical examiner would be in post from December 2018. It is proposed that medical examiners will be employed within the NHS, but with a separate line of accountability. A national medical examiner will oversee the system to ensure independence and provide guidance to medical examiners. It is understood that medical examiners will gradually extend their coverage from hospital deaths, to deaths in homes, care homes, and other settings. At the time of writing a national medical examiner is yet to be appointed.

JURISDICTION

A coroner is under a duty to investigate a death where made aware that the body of a deceased person is within their area if they have reason to suspect:

- the deceased died a violent or unnatural death;
- the cause of death is unknown;
- the deceased died whilst in custody or otherwise in state detention.[49]

---

43   CJA 2009, s 19(1).
44   CJA 2009, s 20(1)(e).
45   Access to Health Records Act, s 3, as amended by the CJA 2009, Sch 21, para 29.
46   CJA 2009, s 20(1)(k)(i).
47   CJA 2009, Explanatory Notes, para 176.
48   CJA 2009, s 20(1)(h)(i), (ii).
49   CJA 2009, s 1(2).

The evidence considered by a coroner is not limited to admissible evidence.[50]

Violent death

A violent death involves an injury, caused by a traumatic event that is accidental or deliberate, and with or without human intervention, for example, a road traffic accident or lightning strike. The traumatic event might be self-inflicted, such as suicide. The time between the traumatic event and death is not a relevant consideration.

Natural death/unnatural death

There is no statutory definition of natural or unnatural death. The Court of Appeal stated that the word 'unnatural' should be given its ordinary meaning, and that the question of natural or unnatural depends upon the cause of death, which was essentially a practical question of fact.[51] Therefore, a death that appears to be ostensibly from natural causes may be an unnatural death for the purposes of coronial law.

In *R on the application of Touche v Inner North London Coroner*,[52] the Court of Appeal considered whether the failure to monitor a mother's blood pressure after giving birth to twins delivered by caesarean section that resulted in her death from a cerebral haemorrhage was an unnatural death. An experienced anaesthetist with an interest in obstetric anaesthesia gave expert evidence, and opined that the failure of the hospital staff to monitor Mrs Touche's blood pressure whilst she was receiving post-operative analgesics was 'astonishing' and described the level of neglect as 'starkly apparent'. The Court of Appeal held that an unnatural death could be the result of neglect. The requirements are the need for basic medical attention to be obvious at the time; the patient to be dependent on others to provide that attention; and a gross failure to provide or procure the attention.

Alternatively, for cases that fall outside the 'neglect' category, an unnatural death is a 'wholly unexpected death from natural causes which would not have occurred but for some culpable human failure'. It is the combination of the unexpectedness of the death and the culpable human failing that allows the death to occur which renders such deaths unnatural.[53]

It is not necessary to prove a causative link between the death and the improper behaviour or treatment as this exceeds the requirement of suspecting that the deceased died an unnatural death, as required by the CJA 2009, s 1(2).[54] As a result of the investigative process, coroners will be able to make inquiries into the adequacy of care prior to any inquest and families should highlight their concerns in as much detail as possible.

---

50   *R v South London Coroner, ex p Weeks* CO595 (6 December 1996, unreported), per Scott Baker J.
51   *R v HM Coroner for Inner London North District, ex p Thomas* [1993] QB 610 (also referred to as *R v Poplar Coroner, ex p Thomas*), per Simon Brown LJ.
52   [2001] EWCA Civ 383, [2001] 3 WLR 148, [2001] 2 All ER 752.
53   *R v Inner London North Coroners, ex p Touche* [2001] EWCA Civ 383.
54   *Bicknell v HM Coroner for Birmingham/Solihull* [2007] EWHC 2547 (Admin).

If a coroner refuses to hold an inquest on the ground that it was a natural death, the family of the deceased are likely to need expert evidence of the circumstances that renders a death an unnatural death. This was the approach taken in *Canning v HM Coroner for the County of Northampton*.[55] In *Canning* the expert evidence failed to persuade the coroner to hold an inquest; a decision that was upheld by the Court of Appeal.[56]

The cause of death is unknown

The cause of death may be unknown if it is not positively identified as natural[57] or a doctor cannot certify the death.[58] This may occur where the terminal event was known, but the underlying condition that was the real cause of death had not been identified, or the terminal cause of death is unknown.

One of the fundamental purposes of the CJA 2009 is to determine the cause of death where it is unknown. In the pre-investigation or investigation phases, the coroner is likely to order a post-mortem examination to enable them to determine the cause of death.[59] If the cause of death is identified as natural the coroner will cease pre-investigation enquires. If the formal investigation has begun but an inquest has not been started, the coroner must discontinue the investigation unless it is considered as necessary to continue the investigation.[60] Preliminary inquiries and an investigation cannot be discontinued if the coroner has reason to suspect that the deceased died a violent or unnatural death or died whilst in custody or state detention.[61] Where an investigation into a death is discontinued, an inquest will not be held,[62] there is no discretion for a coroner to hold an inquest.

The deceased died in custody or otherwise in state detention

A person is in state detention if they are compulsorily detained by a public authority within the meaning of the Human Rights Act 1998, s 6.[63] This includes deaths of persons who are compulsory detained in police stations, prisons, mental health hospitals/wards (detained for assessment under s 2 or for treatment under s 3 of the Mental Health Act 1983) and immigration detention centres. If a prisoner dies in hospital having been transferred from custody, it remains a death in state detention.[64]

In the case of *R (on the application of Ferreira) v HM Senior Coroner for Inner South London*,[65] the Court of Appeal considered whether a death in the intensive care unit of a hospital was a death in state detention. The

---

55 [2006] EWCA Civ 1225, [2006] All ER (D) 187 (Nov).
56 See also *Bickness v HM Coroner for Birmingham / Solihull* [2007] EWHC 2547 (Admin), [2007] All ER (D) 166 (Nov) for a decision that went the other way.
57 *R v Greater Manchester Coroner, ex p Worch* [1998] QB 513.
58 *R (on the application of Kasperowicz) v HM Coroner for Plymouth* [2005] EWCA Civ 44.
59 CJA 2009, s 14(1).
60 CJA 2009, s 4(1).
61 CJA 2009, s 4(2).
62 CJA 2009, s 4(3).
63 CJA 2009, s 48(2).
64 *R v HM Coroner for Inner North London, ex p Limmane* [1989] 1 WLR 395.
65 [2017] EWCA Civ 31.

deceased was being treated for pneumonia and heart problems. She had been sedated and intubated but managed to dislodge the endotracheal tube with her mittened hand which resulted in a cardiac arrest and death. The Court of Appeal held that a death in an intensive care unit was not a death in state detention for the purpose of the CJA 2009. Arden LJ stated:

> no one would ordinarily regard a patient who is in intensive care as deprived of their liberty because their treatment and condition results in their being physically unable to leave the ICU.[66]

Permission to appeal to the Supreme Court was refused.

For a death that occurred after 3 April 2017, a person is not in state detention when he or she is deprived of liberty under the Mental Capacity Act 2005.[67] This amendment to the CJA 2009 dealt with the significant number of referrals to coroners of people who were subject to a deprivation of liberty safeguarding order ('DoLS') when they died (ie those in hospital or care homes who were proved on the balance of probabilities to lack capacity and who might be subject to restrictions amounting to a deprivation of liberty). However, if there is a concern about the death and/or care or treatment before death or the medical cause of death is uncertain, there is a duty on the coroner to investigate. The Chief Coroner's *Guidance No 16A* considers the effect of DoLS and deprivation of liberty on coronial jurisdiction.

Stillbirth

A stillbirth is defined as 'a child which has issued forth from its mother after the 24th week of pregnancy (ie 24 weeks + 0 days of gestation) and which did not at any time breathe or show any other signs of life',[68] for example, a heartbeat. As a stillborn baby has no independent life, there is no death. Consequently, a coroner has no jurisdiction to investigate.

As a result of calls for the law to be changed, a Private Members Bill (Civil Partnerships, Marriages and Deaths (Registration etc) Bill 2017–19) was introduced that would 'give coroners the power to investigate stillborn deaths'. The purpose of the amendment is set out in the explanatory notes:

> In November 2017, the then Secretary of State for Health and Social Care announced that the Healthcare Safety Investigation Branch would conduct independent investigations into all English cases of term intrapartum still-birth, neonatal and maternal death and birth-related brain injuries (as defined by the Royal College of Obstetricians and Gynaecologists' 'Each Baby Counts' criteria). There is however a question of whether coroners should have a role to play in investigating still-births to contribute to learning and reducing the still-birth rate.[69]

On 26 March 2019, the Civil Partnerships, Marriages and Death (Registration etc) Act 2019 received Royal Assent. Section 4(1) states: 'The Secretary of State must make arrangements for the preparation of

---

66   [2017] EWCA Civ 31 at [110].
67   CJA 2009, s 48(2A).
68   Births and Deaths Registration Act 1953, s 1(1).
69   See https://publications.parliament.uk/pa/bills/lbill/2017-2019/0140/18140en03.htm.

a report on whether, and if so how, the law ought to be changed to enable or require coroners to investigate still-births'.[70] In March 2019, the Department of Health and Social Care and the Ministry of Justice began a Consultation on Coronial Investigations of Stillbirths, it concluded on 18 June 2019.[71] The Government's response to the consultation is expected in September 2019.

Once the report has been published, the Lord Chancellor may by regulations amend Part 1 of the Coroners and Justice Act 2009 to:

(a) enable or require coroners to conduct investigations into still-births (whether by treating still-births as deaths or otherwise);

(b) specify the circumstances in which those investigations are to take place (including by limiting the duty or power to investigate to certain descriptions of still-birth);

(c) provide for the purposes of those investigations;

(d) make provision equivalent or similar to provision in that Part relating to investigations into deaths.[72]

Where there is doubt that a baby was stillborn, a coroner may investigate whether the baby was born alive as part of the pre-investigation inquiry and investigation; it is not necessary for the coroner to be satisfied in information gathered before they open an investigation that the baby was probably born alive.[73] If an investigation is begun but the coroner concludes that the baby was stillborn, there can be no findings as to a cause of death because the duty of the coroner to investigate in respect of the 'body of a deceased person', a stillborn child was never alive.

POST-MORTEM EXAMINATION

A post-mortem examination may be required to ascertain the medical cause of death. A coroner has the power to order a post-mortem examination under the CJA 2009, s 14(1)(a) if there is a duty to investigate a death or the coroner is undertaking preliminary inquiries to determine if there is a duty to investigate a death.[74] Regulations 11 to 16 of the Coroners (Investigation) Regulations 2013[75] regulates the practice and procedure of ordering a post-mortem examination. Where religion requires burial within a short time after death, any post-mortem examination and release of the body should be expedited.[76]

---

70 Civil Partnerships, Marriage and Deaths (Registration etc) Act 2019, s 4(1).

71 See https://consult.justice.gov.uk/digital-communications/coronial-investigations-of-stillbirths/supporting_documents/Consultation%20on%20coronial%20 investigations%20of%20stillbirths%20web.pdfhttps://consult.justice.gov.uk/digital-communications/coronial-investigations-of-stillbirths/supporting_documents/ Consultation%20on%20coronial%20investigations%20of%20stillbirths%20web.pdf.

72 See https://publications.parliament.uk/pa/bills/lbill/2017-2019/0158/18158.pdf.

73 *R (on the application of T) v HM Senior Coroner for the County of West Yorkshire (Western Area)* [2017] EWCA Civ 318.

74 CJA 2009, s 14(1)(a) and (b).

75 SI 2013/1629.

76 *Adath Yisroel Burial Society v Senior Coroner for Inner North London* [2018] EWHC 969 (Admin); Chief Coroner's *Guidance No 28: Report of Death to the Coroner: Decision Making and Expedited Decisions*.

Coroners should consider whether the cause of death could be established without a post-mortem examination. Post-mortem examinations were carried out on 39% of all death reported to coroners in 2018.[77] Since 1995, the proportion of deaths for which a post-mortem examination was ordered by coroners has steadily declined, although 2017 and 2018 saw slight increases.[78] In 2018, there were 3326 post-mortems conducted using less invasive techniques (such as computerised tomography (CT) scan), an increase from 1671 in 2017.[79] Any post-mortem examination should take place as soon as practicable,[80] and the coroner is required to notify several persons of the date, time and place of the post-mortem examination.[81] It may be possible to talk to the coroners' pathologist (or Coroners' radiologist if a CT scan was performed) about the results of the post-mortem examination before the inquest, but the permission of the coroner must be sought in advance.

Wishes of the family

Some relatives strongly oppose a post-mortem examination on religious or cultural grounds; and/or if deeply distressed by the thought of an invasive procedure being carried out on the body of the deceased. *The Guide to Coroner Services* states:

> where possible, coroners will take account of your religious and cultural needs whilst acting in accordance with the law when ordering a post-mortem examination and the type of examination to be performed.[82]

However, a coroner does not require the consent of the family to order a post-mortem examination, and can be contrasted to a hospital post-mortem examination which requires the consent of the next of kin. The Human Tissue Authority Code of Practice states that the coroner should explain the reasons for the post-mortem examination and the process to the family.[83]

Arguably, Art 8(1) of the European Convention on Human Rights (right to respect for private and family life) imposes a duty on coroners to consider whether a post-mortem examination is necessary and proportionate to ascertain how a person came by their death; and this requires coroners to make reasonable efforts to contact the family and inquire about their views on a post-mortem examination.[84] A decision by a coroner to order a post-mortem examination where the family oppose such an examination will only be lawful if it is proportionate to the aims in Art 8(2), including: public safety; the protection of health; or to investigate a potential crime.

---

77   Ministry of Justice, *Coroners Statistics Annual 2018* (9 May 2018).
78   Ministry of Justice, *Coroners Statistics Annual 2018* (9 May 2018).
79   Ministry of Justice, *Coroners Statistics Annual 2018* (9 May 2018), p 5.
80   Coroners (Investigations) Regulations 2013, SI 2013/1629, reg 11.
81   Coroners (Investigations) Regulations 2013, SI 2013/1629, reg 13(1).
82   Ministry of Justice, *Guide to Coroner Services,* p 8.
83   Human Tissue Authority Code of Practice. https://www.hta.gov.uk/sites/default/files/Code%20B.pdf.
84   *Death Certification and Investigation in England, Wales and Northern Ireland: A Report of a Fundamental Review 2003* (28 April 2003: Chairman Tom Luce), Cm 5831, Chapter 13.

Practical arrangements

The coroner must notify certain people and bodies of the date, hour, and place at which the post-mortem examination will take place, unless it is impractical or would cause unreasonable delay to the post-mortem examination[85] This includes the deceased's next of kin or personal representative of the deceased, the deceased's regular GP or other interested persons whom have notified the coroner of a desire to be represented at the post-mortem examination, and the hospital if the deceased died in hospital.[86] Representation by a doctor at a post-mortem examination may incur a separate fee, payable by the instructing interested person.[87]

The post-mortem examination

There is no statutory definition of 'post-mortem examination'. The Explanatory Notes to the CJA 2009 make it clear that the post-mortem examination is not limited to an invasive examination by a pathologist, but 'will include an examination made of the deceased including non-invasive examination, for example, using Magnetic Resonance Imaging (MRI) Scans'.[88]

Unlike the Coroners Act 1988, there is no distinction between a post-mortem and 'special examination', which is a more specific examination, eg toxicology. Consequently, the coroner can specify the specify the kind of examination, eg particular examination of a tissue or organ or toxicology screen, which seems most relevant to the cause of death if a full post-mortem examination is not considered necessary.[89]

Pathologist

The coroner can request a 'suitable practitioner' to perform the post-mortem examination, which includes a pathologist, a radiologist and a toxicologist.[90] Most post-mortem examinations are carried out by pathologists working in the NHS. Some pathologists specialise in particular fields, and in appropriate cases, coroners may choose to appoint a specialist pathologist, for example, a cardiac pathologist where death is the result of a sudden cardiac event in a young person without apparent heart disease. A coroner's post-mortem examination is separate to the pathologist's NHS work, and the coroner pays a fee for each examination: this is currently £96.80 for a coroner's post-examination and report.[91]

If the deceased died in hospital, coroners may request pathologists employed by, or associated with, the hospital staff to conduct the post-mortem examination. Pathologists must be aware of possible conflicts of

---

85 Coroners (Investigations) Regulations 2013, SI 2013/1629, reg 13 (1), (2).
86 Coroners (Investigations) Regulations 2013, SI 2013/1629, regs 13(3)(a)–(c).
87 *Standards for Coroners' pathologists in post-mortem examinations of deaths that appear not to be suspicious* (February 2014).
88 CJA 2009, Explanatory Notes, para 136.
89 CJA 2009, s 14(2).
90 CJA 2009, s 14(3).
91 See https://www.bma.org.uk/advice/employment/fees/coroners.

interest which should be disclosed to the coroner.[92] A registered medical practitioner or person implicated in the death of the person by improper or negligent treatment must not make or assist on the examination of the body, but is entitled to be represented at the examination.[93]

Autopsy: invasive examination

A post-mortem examination normally involves an external examination of the body, followed by dissection and removal of the major internal organs (autopsy), including the heart, lungs, liver, kidneys, spleen and lungs; and may include the brain. Samples may be taken for further analysis, such as blood, urine, vitreous humour, or tissue. The histological examination of tissue, toxicology and sample analysis may provide further relevant information as to the medical cause of death. Following most post-mortem examinations, the internal organs and body material will be returned to the body. There are specific procedures for the retention of organs or body material.

The extent of the post-mortem examination and any further special investigations depend upon the circumstances of each case and coroners often ask the pathologist to use their experience and judgment to determine the extent of the autopsy so that they can opine on the cause of death. The pathologist should perform an examination according to the clinical context, reflecting standards and guidance issued by the Royal College of Pathologists and must be able to justify the examination, or indeed the omission of any part of an examination.[94]

Standards of post-mortem examination

Standards of post-mortem examinations have been criticised by: the courts;[95] the Shipman Inquiry;[96] and the *Report of a Fundamental Review* (Luce Report).[97] In the Report of the National Confidential Enquiry into Patient Outcome and Death (2006): *The Coroners' autopsy: do we deserve better?*, the quality of post-mortem reports was considered to be unacceptable in 26% of cases, where unacceptable meant that the post-mortem report did not sufficiently explain the cause of death, or was evidently wrong.[98] Some of the particular issues that the advisors to the study considered important were:

92　*Standards for Coroners' pathologists in post-mortem examinations of deaths that appear not to be suspicious* (February 2014).
93　CJA 2009, s 14(4).
94　*Standards for coroners' pathologists in post-mortem examinations of deaths that appear not to be suspicious* (February 2014), see https://www.rcpath.org/uploads/assets/uploaded/5831a505-4c50-4867-86e9f41065eba473.pdf.
95　*R v Clark* [2003] EWCA Crim 1020, at paras 169–170.
96　The Shipman Inquiry Third Report: *Death Certification and the Investigation of Death by Coroners* (14 July 2003: Chairman Dame Janet Smith DBE), (Cm 5854), Ch 10.
97　*Death Certification and Investigation in England, Wales and Northern Ireland: A Report of a Fundamental Review 2003* (28 April 2003: Chairman Tom Luce) (Cm 5831), Ch 13.
98　*National confidential enquiry into patient outcome and death, the coroner's autopsy: do we deserve better?* (2006), Ch 4 (the study group was 1,691 in size with a median age of 74 years).

1   that there was poor communication between coroners and pathologists;

2   that there were apparent gaps in the information provided to the pathologists by the coroners;

3   that in almost 20% of cases the cause of death stated seemed questionable;

4   that in 6.25% of cases it was determined that samples for histology should have been taken to determine or further elucidate the cause of death; and

5   that the very elderly may not have been examined as carefully as younger subjects.

In 2014, the Royal College of Pathologists published its document entitled *Standards for coroners' pathologists in post-mortem examination of deaths that appear not to be suspicious*.[99] This is a helpful guide in reviewing the post-mortem report as it sets out standards at several stages of the post-mortem examination, including before the examination, the post-mortem examination, further investigations, the pathologists' report and disposal or retention of retained material on completion of the coroner's involvement. The following points in the guidance are of particular note:

*   if the pathologist does not think they have the relevant expertise to conduct the post-mortem examination, they should advise the coroner;
*   where the deceased died in hospital or following a period of hospitalisation immediately preceding death, the clinical notes should be obtained under the authority of the coroner, and considered by the pathologist prior to the post-mortem examination. If indicated, other records such as the GP notes and ambulance notes should be requested from the coroner;
*   the pathologist should discuss with the coroner if other expertise or investigations are required, such as radiology and the retention of human material;
*   the pathologist should remain aware that the death may not be natural;
*   body features that reveal something out of the ordinary, whether or not they appear relevant to the cause of death should be noted.

The Royal College of Pathologists has also issued documents in its Autopsy Guidelines Series.[100] The guidelines may assist on reviewing the post-mortem report and questioning the pathologist at the inquest; and it is a breach of the procedural limb of Art 2 of the European Convention on Human Rights for a post-mortem examination to be ineffective.[101] Current/future guidelines include:

*   Guidelines on autopsy practice: Sudden death with likely cardiac pathology (January 2016).

---

99   See https://www.rcpath.org/uploads/assets/uploaded/5831a505-4c50-4867-86e9f41065 eba473.pdf.

100 See https://www.rcpath.org/profession/guidelines/autopsy-guidelines-series.html.

101 *Kakouli v Turkey* (App No 38595/97) (Fourth Section ECHR) 22 November 2005, at 122–128.

- Guidelines on autopsy practice: Autopsy when drugs or poisoning may be involved (December 2018).
- Guidelines on autopsy practice: postoperative deaths (May 2019).
- Guidelines on autopsy practice: deaths following known or suspected hanging (in development).
- Guidelines on autopsy practice: Sudden unexpected death in infancy (SUDI) (in development).
- Guidelines on autopsy practice: Autopsy after tissue and organ donation (in development).

Non-invasive techniques

In *Kasperowicz,* the Court of Appeal stated that if the cause of death could be ascertained by less invasive means, then that was a matter of common decency and good practice as opposed to a matter of law.[102] If the death is not suspicious, the coroner should consider evidence from the family and medical practitioners that might enable the coroner lawfully to avoid ordering a post-mortem examination.[103]

Alternatively, it might be possible to use less invasive techniques, such as MRI and CT scanning, to ascertain the medical cause of death;[104] although the coroner, with advice from the pathologist and radiologist, will need to consider the efficacy of alternative investigations considering the particular circumstances of the death.[105] For example, post-mortem imaging cannot reliably diagnose coronary artery disease, pulmonary thromboembolism and pneumonia, some of the most common causes of death.[106] The Chief Coroner issued *Guidance No 1: The Use of Post-Mortem Imaging (Adults).* This guidance sets out the procedure once it has been decided that non-invasive techniques should be used. The guidance was updated in January 2016 highlighting the case of *R (on the application of Rotsztein).*[107]

In *R (on the application of Rotsztein)* the court gave guidance as to the approach coroners should take on whether a non-invasive post-mortem examination should be used where the cause of death is unknown and the deceased's family expressed religious objections to an invasive post-mortem examination. The guidance is unlikely to apply where the deceased died a violent or unnatural death, as the court acknowledged an invasive post-mortem examination will almost always be required and that this will almost always override any religious objection.

---

102 *R (on the application of Kasperowicz) v HM Coroner for Plymouth* [2005] EWCA Civ 44 at [15].
103 See also *R (on the application of Kasperowicz) v HM Coroner for Plymouth* [2005] EWCA Civ 44 at [13].
104 See *R (on the application of Kasperowicz) v HM Coroner for Plymouth* [2005] EWCA Civ 44 at [14]–[15].
105 An MRI scan may not provide as much detail as a dissection post-mortem examination and there are a number of research studies examining the efficacy of MRI scanning versus a conventional post-mortem examination in identifying the cause of death.
106 Royal College of Pathologists REC/RCPPath Statement on 'Standard for Medici-legal post-mortem cross-sectional imaging in adults' (October 2012), see https://www.rcr.ac.uk/system/files/publication/field_publication_files/FINALDOCUMENT_PMImaging_Oct12.pdf.
107 *R (on the application of Rotsztein) v HM Senior Coroner for Inner London* [2015] EWHC 2764 (Admin).

In order for the coroner to fulfil their duty under the CJA 2009, s 1(2)(b) (investigation where the coroner has reasons to suspect that the cause of death is unknown) in cases of religious objections to an invasive post-mortem examination, the coroner's conduct should be guided by the following propositions:

1 there must be an established religious tenet that an invasive autopsy was to be avoided before any question of avoidance on the ECHR, Art 9 grounds could arise;
2 there must be a realistic possibility (not more than 50:50 chance) that non-invasive procedures would establish the cause of death and would permit the coroner to fulfil his duty under the CJA 2009, s 5(1) (matters to be ascertained by the coroner);
3 the whole post-mortem examination must be capable of being undertaken without undue delay to fulfil the statutory obligation under the Coroners (Investigations) Regulations 2013, reg 11;
4 the performance of non-invasive or minimally-invasive procedures must not impair the effectiveness of an invasive autopsy if one was ultimately required; and
5 non-invasive procedures could be adopted without imposing an additional cost burden on the coroner.

The post-mortem report

The person who performed the post-mortem examination must complete a post-mortem report as soon as practical.[108] There is no standardised format for the report, but in general the report will include a record of the information provided prior to the post-mortem examination, the examination findings and conclude with an opinion of the medical cause of death. The Royal College of Pathologists has provided a general standard for the pathology report, indicated that the conclusion should be supported by reasons, detailing all the material and literature in support and explain why any unusual features have been discounted.[109] The report should include a schedule of all material retained as part of the examination and the reason for retention.[110] The post-mortem report may be 'provisional' in that the person performing the post-mortem examination may alter their conclusions having heard the evidence at any inquest.

The format of the conclusion follows guidelines issued by the World Health Organisation (WHO). Part I sets out the chain of causation resulting in death. Part II lists other significant conditions or diseases contributing to death, but not causally related.

---

108 CJA 2009, s 14(5) and the Coroners (Investigations) Regulations 2013, SI 2013/1629, reg 16(2).
109 *Standards for Coroners' pathologists in post-mortem examination of deaths that appear not to be suspicious* (February 2014).
110 *Standards for Coroners' pathologists in post-mortem examination of deaths that appear not to be suspicious* (February 2014).

In my opinion the cause of death was:

I

1(a): Disease or condition directly causing death

1(b): Disease or condition that led to the immediate cause of death (antecedent causes)

1(c): Morbid conditions (if any)

II

Other significant conditions contributing to the death, but not related to the disease or condition causing it.

The practitioner performing the post-mortem examination must only provide the coroner with the post-mortem report, unless the coroner gave written authority to disclosure to 'any other person'.[111] *The Guide to Coroners Services* indicates that the post-mortem report can be provided to 'interested persons', including the family of the deceased, although the report must be requested and there may be a fee.[112]

Coroners are not under a duty to disclose a post-mortem report to interested persons before the inquest without an application, and there is no duty on the coroner to disclose the post-mortem report if there is good reason not to do so.[113]

Second post-mortem examination

If the deceased's family are dissatisfied with the result of the coroner's postmortem examination, they are entitled to a second post-mortem examination,[114] at their expense. If the coroner is still in possession of the deceased's body, the coroner's permission will be required; and such permission should be given unless there are reasonable grounds to refuse.[115] Otherwise, a second post-mortem examination can be carried out once the coroner has released the body, although that might not be until the inquest has concluded and therefore is of little practical assistance. If a post-mortem examination or further tests are carried out after the coroner has released the body, the coroner's permission is not required.[116] In the alternative, the family may instruct their own pathologist to review the post-mortem examination results or any specimens that may have been collected. The pathologist instructed by the family can be called as a witness to give evidence at the inquest to rebut the findings and conclusions of the coroner's pathologist.

After the post-mortem examination

The coroner has the right and duty to take possession of the deceased's body once they have acquired jurisdiction, and can retain possession until

---

111 Coroners (Investigations) Regulations 2013, SI 2013/1629, reg 16(2).
112 *Guide to the Coroners Service*, No 13.1.
113 *R (on the application of McLeish) v HM Coroner for the Northern District of Greater London* [2010] EWHC 3624 (Admin), CO/4224/2009.
114 *R v HM Coroner for Greater London (Southern District), ex p Ridley* [1985] 1 WLR 1347.
115 *R v HM Coroner for Greater London (Southern District), ex p Ridley* [1985] 1 WLR 1347.
116 *R ((1) Heinonen (2) Sawko v Coroner for Inner South District of greater London)* [2017] EWHC 1803 (Admin).

completion of the inquest.[117] However, most coroners will release the body to the family so that the funeral can be organised as soon as possible after the conclusion of the post-mortem examination. Some families may wish to delay the funeral until all the specimens are returned to the body. This decision may depend upon whether complete organs or small specimens, such as blood or tissue samples, have been retained; or whether further investigations on the body may be necessary. Where small specimens have been taken, relatives are often reassured by the fact that the specimens are miniscule.

Removal and retention of organs and tissue

In most cases, small samples of tissues and organs will be taken by the pathologist, although on occasions an entire organ is removed and retained. The retention of any material should be recorded on the post-mortem report. In some circumstances, the family may want tissues or blood samples retained by the pathologist in case further testing becomes necessary, particularly if they instruct their own pathologist. The rules relating to the retention of materials removed during post-mortem examination are located at regs 14–16 of the Coroners (Investigations) Regulations 2013.

The pathologist must preserve material that in their opinion is relevant to the cause of death or identification of the deceased, and must notify the coroner in writing that material has been retained.[118] The coroner responds to the notification, specifying the time for which the material must be preserved.[119] The coroner must notify the deceased's next of kin or personal representative and any other relative who notified the coroner of their intention to attend the post-mortem examination, that material has been retained; the time of retention; and the prescribed options for disposal when the material is no longer required.[120] The options for disposal include burial, cremation, other lawful disposal by the pathologist. There is no requirement for the pathologist to seek the family's view about the method of disposal, but it is likely that the coroner will ask the family for an indication. Alternatively, the material can be returned to the next-of-kin, personal representative or other family member upon their request,[121] or can be retained for research or other purposes, but only with the consent of one of the deceased's relatives.[122] Once the date for preserving the material has passed, the pathologist must record the method of disposal, that the material has been delivered to the specific person, or that the material has been retained on behalf of a specified person.[123]

117 *R v Bristol Coroner, ex p Kerr* [1974] QB 652.
118 Coroners (Investigations) Regulations 2013, SI 2013/1629, reg 14(1).
119 Coroners (Investigations) Regulations 2013, SI 2013/1629, reg 14(4).
120 Coroners (Investigations) Regulations 2013, SI 2013/1629, reg 14(6).
121 Coroners (Investigations) Regulations 2013, SI 2013/1629, reg 14(6).s
122 Coroners (Investigation) Regulations 2013, SI 2013/1629, reg 14(6)(c).
123 Coroners (Investigations) Regulations 2013, SI 2013/1629, reg 15(5).

THE INQUEST

As a result of the new investigative regime under the CJA 2009, coroners are more likely to reach a decision of death by natural causes without an inquest. In summary, an inquest is not required:

1　where the coroner makes preliminary inquiries under the CJA 2009, s 1(7), including a request for a post-mortem examination under s 14(1)(b), and concludes that there is no duty to investigate under s 1(1). There will be no inquest because there was no investigation;[124]

2　where the coroner decides to conduct an investigation into the death, the coroner may discontinue the investigation where the cause of death is revealed by the post-mortem examination and there is no statutory requirement to hold an inquest.[125]

The coroner is under a duty, where reasonably practicable, to complete an inquest within six months of the date on which the coroner was made aware of the death.[126] In cases under the ECHR, Art 2 there is 'a requirement of promptness and reasonable expedition' in the investigation.[127] Coroners must notify the chief coroner if an investigation and inquest are not completed within 12 months of being made aware of the body within the coroner's area. The Coroners (Inquests) Rules 2013[128] regulate the practice and procedure of inquests conducted under the CJA 2009.

Statutory questions

The function of an inquest is to seek out and record as many of the facts concerning the death as the public interest requires.[129] The proceedings and evidence at an inquest are directed towards ascertaining the statutory matters set out in the CJA 2009, s 5(1):

- who the deceased was;
- where the deceased came by their death;
- when the deceased came by their death;
- how the deceased came by their death; and
- the particulars (if any) required by the Births Deaths and Registration Act 1953 to be registered concerning the death.

For deaths that engage Art 2 of the ECHR, the question of 'how' is treated more broadly and includes ascertaining in what circumstances the deceased came by their death (CJA 2009, s 5(2)). This follows the principles set out in *R (Middleton) v HM Coroner for Western Somerset*.[130]

　　Section 5(3) of the CJA 2009 prohibits the coroner or jury from expressing an opinion on any other matter that is not included in the CJA 2009, ss 5(1) and (2).

---

124 CJA 2009, s 6.
125 CJA 2009, s 4.
126 Coroners (Inquests) Rules 2013, SI 2013/1616, r 8.
127 *Jordan v UK* (2001) 37 EHRR 913.
128 SI 2013/1616.
129 *R v South London Coroner, ex p Thompson* (1982) 126 Sol Jo 625.
130 [2004] 2 AC 182.

Interested persons

There are no parties to an inquest, only 'interested persons'. Section 47 of the CJA 2009 introduced a statutory definition of an 'interested person' that expanded the list of interested persons. The list includes a spouse, civil partner, partner, parent, child, siblings, a personal representative of the deceased, and a person who may by an act or omission have caused or contributed to the death of the deceased, or whose employee or agent may have done so.

PREPARING FOR THE INQUEST

Inquest opening

The coroner must open the inquest as soon as reasonably practicable after the date on which the coroner considers that the duty to hold an inquest applies.[131] To enhance consistency between different coroners, the Chief Coroner issued *Guidance No 9: Opening Inquests*, stating: 'the new procedures and this guidance are designed for greater openness and accessibility and with a view to providing more consistent practice'.[132] The coroner must inform the family of the deceased of the time, date and place of the opening of the inquest.[133]

It is generally a brief hearing and the primary purpose is to identify the deceased. Many coroners do not require the family to attend (although they may if they wish) and the identification of the deceased is provided on oath by the coroner's officer, or in written form complying with the Coroners (Inquests) Rules 2013, r 23. The coroner may also hear brief evidence of the finding of the body, the general circumstances of the death, whether a post-mortem examination has taken place and the provisional medical cause of death if known.[134] However, no conclusions should be reached on any issue.[135] The coroner may give directions, including a timetable for the provision of reports and statements. Coroners have the power to require evidence to be produced pursuant to the CJA 2009, Sch 5, but this power is unlikely to be exercised at an inquest opening as it is used when all other requests have failed.

The inquest is then adjourned and ideally the coroner will fix a date for either a pre-inquest review or the resumed inquest.[136] During the adjournment the coroner is likely to undertake further investigations, collate evidence, and/or organise a pre-inquest review hearing or the full hearing. Alternatively, criminal investigations may be carried out and the inquest will be suspended until those investigations and any proceedings have finished.

---

131 Coroners (Inquests) Rules 2013, SI 2013/1616, r 5(1).
132 Chief Coroner's *Guidance No 9*, para 2.
133 Chief Coroner's *Guidance No 9*, para 9.
134 Chief Coroner's *Guidance No 9*, para 22.
135 *R (Coker) v HM Coroner for Inner South District of Greater London* [2006] EWHC 614 (Admin).
136 Coroners (Inquests) Rules 2013, SI 2013/1616, r 5(2).

Pre-inquest review hearing 'PIR'

Coroners are increasingly holding pre-inquest hearings, particularly in complex cases, although such a hearing is held at the discretion of the coroner. This procedure has been codified in the Coroners (Inquests) Rules 2013, r 6. To enhance consistency between coroners, the Chief Coroner has issued *Guidance No 23: Pre-Inquest Review Hearings*. A pre-inquest hearing is a case management conference primarily to review procedural matters that should result in a more focussed inquiry.

The Chief Coroner identified three essential elements of a PIR:

1   an agenda;
2   the hearing;
3   rulings (with reasons).

The agenda

In advance of the PIR, the coroner should distribute to all potentially interested persons an agenda. Ideally, it should be sent out 14 days in advance of the hearing, but otherwise should be sent out 'in good time'.[137] The agenda issues may include the following topics, and will be specific to the individual case:

- identity of interested persons;
- scope of the inquest;
- whether the ECHR, Art 2 is engaged (see Chapter 23);
- whether jury required;
- matters for further investigation;
- provisional list of witnesses;
- disclosure;
- bundle/jury bundle;
- date of next PIR hearing;
- date and length of inquest;
- venue for hearings;
- anonymity of witnesses;
- special measures for witnesses (including video links and screens);
- apparent bias;
- need for an interpreter;
- CCTV evidence;
- other matters.

The coroner will often indicate their provisional view on any issues included in the agenda. The Chief Coroner's Guidance indicates that coroner should disclose relevant statements and documents to interested persons in good time before the PIR, so that informed representations can be made.[138]

The pre-inquest hearing also provides an opportunity to explain and clarify with the coroner and the other representatives the family's concerns and the relevant issues that they would like explored at the inquest. If detailed submissions are to be made the coroner is likely to

---

137 Chief Coroner's *Guidance No 22*, para 6.
138 Chief Coroner's *Guidance No 22*, para 10.

be assisted by a skeleton argument lodged with authorities in advance of the pre-inquest hearing. If the coroner does not hold a pre-inquest hearing, the issues will need to be raised in correspondence or telephone discussions with the Coroner's Officer in sufficient time prior to the inquest. It is unhelpful to raise issues on the day of the inquest that should have been raised earlier.

The PIR hearing

A pre-inquest hearing is usually held in public unless there are 'cogent reasons' for holding it in private.[139] The Chief Coroner has indicated that, where possible, video-conferencing (or telephone conferencing) should be made available at PIRs for those who wish to use it,[140] although hearings are more likely to be in person. No evidence will be called at the PIR.

Rulings

The coroner will make a decision and give an oral ruling at the PIR, or in writing within seven days of the PIR.[141] The ruling should include 'brief reasons' justifying the coroner's decision, although are not required where there is general agreement between the interested persons or for most 'housekeeping' decisions.[142] In complex mattes, it is not unusual for a further PIR to be listed, particularly to deal with further disclosure, expert witnesses or new issues.

Bias

Coroners must be fair and impartial. An apparent bias by a coroner is sometimes used as a reason for a coroner to recuse themselves, or to quash an inquisition. In *R v Inner London West Coroner, ex p Dallaglio and Lockwood Croft*,[143] Sir Thomas Bingham, MR stated that the coroners' 'central and dominant role in the conduct of an inquest might be said to call for a higher standard since those interested in the proceedings are, to an unusual extent, dependent on his sense of fairness'.[144]

When considering the issue of apparent bias, the court must first ascertain the circumstances that had a bearing on the suggestion that the coroner was biased. The court must then apply an objective question, 'whether the fair-minded and informed observer, having considered the facts, would conclude that there was a real possibility that the tribunal was biased'.[145] An example of bias that has been successful is a case in which a coroner committed himself to the outcome on a particular issue that remained to be adjudicated.[146] The Chief Coroner's *Guidance No 15:*

---

139 See *R (on the application of Coker) v HM Coroners for South London* [2006] EWHC 614 (Admin) at paras 18–19. See also see Coroners (Inquests) Rules 2013, r 11(3).
140 Chief Coroner's *Guidance No 22*, para 15.
141 Chief Coroner's *Guidance No 22*, para 20.
142 Chief Coroner's *Guidance No 22*, para 22.
143 [1994] 4 All ER 139.
144 [1994] 4 All ER 139 at 163.
145 *Porter v Magill* [2001] UKHL 67, [2002] 2 AC 357 at [103].
146 *Hemsworth Application (Collette), An Application for Judicial Review by Collette Hemsworth* [2009] NIQB 33.

Dealing with the Possibility of Apparent Bias provides a helpful guide and advises coroners to disclose the interest at the earliest opportunity, in writing; not to wait to any pre-inquest review hearing.

Evidence

The coroner will collate documentary evidence and any other evidence that is considered relevant to the particular death. In the healthcare context, this is likely to include the hospital and/or GP notes and witness evidence of GP and/or hospital staff; these are usually produced by agreement.

Coroners have the power under the CJA 2009, Sch 5, para 1 to summon witnesses and to compel the production of evidence including a written statement for the purposes of an investigation[147] or an inquest[148] by way of written notice. This power is limited, for example, the coroner does not have the power to require anything to be provided to them that a person could not be required to provide to a civil court.[149] Evidence may also be withheld on grounds of public interest immunity.[150] The penalties for a failure to comply with the written notice are included in the CJA 2009, Sch 6, including a fine not exceeding £1000.[151] The Chief Coroner has indicated that this power should only be used when 'other methods of request have failed'.[152] The additional powers of coroners to order enter, search and seizure in the CJA 2009, Sch 5 are not in force.

Documents and statements provided to the coroner should not be provided on the assumption that they are confidential, as the coroner may disclose the documents to the other interested persons. Coroners have different practices on the documents that they will disclose. It is usually helpful for the legal representative of the family to write to the coroner and the hospital/GP setting out the issues of concern. On occasions, coroners will disclose the letter from the family to the hospital or GP. However, these letters often include information that is not relevant to the inquest, and the coroner may write to the hospital or GP with a summary of the concerns of the family.

The hospital or GP surgery should consider whether all the documents that may have been generated as a result of the death of the deceased should be disclosed to the coroner. Such documents include an adverse incident report, a serious untoward incident report, an internal investigation report, or a report prepared as a result of a complaint by the family following the death of the deceased. Only documents that are relevant to the inquest should be disclosed. It is advisable to disclose such documents early in the investigation, as disclosure on the day of the inquest is likely result in an adjournment.

It is often advantageous to provide a carefully prepared statement, which may save time during the inquest. A prepared statement also ensures that the coroner receives all the relevant evidence, as most witnesses are nervous giving oral testimony. Representatives for the

---

147 CJA 2009, Sch 5, para 1(2).
148 CJA 2009, Sch 5, para 1(1).
149 CJA 2009, Sch 5, para 2(1).
150 CJA 2009, Sch 5, para 2(2).
151 CJA 2009, Sch 6, para 6.
152 Chief Coroner's *Guidance No 9*, para 37.

family may wish to provide a statement; particularly if there may be factual disputes in relation to the deceased's mental or physical health prior to death, or the care received in hospital.

Representatives of the hospital and GP will usually prepare statements at the request of the coroners' officer. It is helpful if the witness includes their qualifications and experience in working within a particular speciality (if relevant) and at the hospital where the deceased died. The statement should be chronological, setting out the professional's involvement with treating and caring for the deceased, including references (where appropriate) to the healthcare notes and an explanation of any medical treatments and terminology; and focused on the issues that are relevant to the inquest. If the hospital or GP surgery has made any changes to practice as a result of the death of the deceased, evidence of such changes should be included. The legal advisor for the hospital or GP should consider whether any of the information in the statement is subject to the privilege from self-incrimination or legal professional privilege that should not be waived.

If representatives believe that all the relevant evidence has not been requested by the coroner or disclosed to the coroner, the coroner can be asked to seek disclosure. A coroner who refuses to request disclosure of relevant evidence and thereby fails to investigate a death fully may be subject to judicial review proceedings.

Expert evidence

Healthcare deaths usually involve consideration of the practices of a doctor, nurse, midwife, or other healthcare professional, systems of healthcare, and the safety of buildings where patients are detained under mental health legislation. An important consideration for the coroner is whether independent medical evidence should be obtained, and this should be considered at an early stage in the investigation.

Many coroners call and rely upon the evidence of the consultant, senior nurse/midwife, other healthcare professional, and/or hospital manager so that the coroner may express a view on the adequacy of the treatment provided by the hospital and/or system of healthcare. Understandably, families often find this approach objectionable for a number of reasons: the expert is not independent; the professional giving evidence may have caused or contributed to the death; they may not have had any in involvement in the patient's care; or the issues maybe outside their area of expertise.

In some cases, a coroner may instruct an independent expert, either on their own initiative or at the request of an interested party, which is usually the family of the deceased. However, there is no principle that independent expert evidence is always required to render an inquest an effective investigation; it depends upon the circumstances of the case, including the expertise of the coroner and the issues and evidence before them.[153] This is consistent with the principle that the coroner has a

---

153 *R (on the application of Goodson) v Bedfordshire and Luton Coroner (Luton and Dunstable Hospital NHS Trust, interested party)* [2004] EWHC 2931 (Admin), [2006] 1 WLR 432, [2005] 2 All ER 792 at [71].

wide discretion in deciding which witnesses to call.[154] The reality is that independent experts are retained in only a small proportion of healthcare deaths,[155] and this is often attributed to the underfunding of the coronial service.

A failure to call expert evidence is reviewable by judicial review proceedings, illustrated by the case of *Jones v HM Coroner for the Southern District of Greater London*.[156] In *Jones*, the administrative court held that there had been insufficient inquiry into the means by which the deceased died from Fentanyl toxicity (an opioid analgesic) that had been prescribed by an out of hours doctor's service. The coroner had been satisfied that the question of how the deceased came by his death was discharged by establishing that it was due to a fatal dose of Fentanyl. The administrative court stated that the scope of the inquest was too narrow, relying on *R v HM Coroner for Inner West District, ex p Dallagio*,[157] where it was held that an investigation into the means by which the deceased came by his death would not necessarily be limited to the last link in the chain of causation. The court did not make any specific findings about expert evidence; although it is likely that such evidence would be required.

If there are available funds, the family of the deceased may obtain independent expert evidence. Communications with an expert for the purpose of obtaining information or advice in connection with existing or contemplated litigation are privileged, but only when the following conditions are satisfied:

1   the litigation must be in progress or in contemplation when the document/evidence was created;
2   the communications must have been made for the sole or dominant purpose of conducting that litigation; and
3   the litigation must be adversarial, not investigative or inquisitorial.[158]

It is noteworthy that the families of two soldiers found dead at Co Down Barracks failed in a recent High Court application challenging the order of the coroner for them to disclose a psychiatric report. The coroner said that if the report had been obtained for civil or criminal litigation he would have upheld the claim for privilege.[159]

If the report plainly indicates substandard treatment and care, it may be advisable to disclose it to the coroner. However, the interested party must waive privilege (not his lawyer), and the expert must agree to this

---

154 *Takoushis* at [61] and *R (Warren) v HM Assistant Coroner for Northamptonshire* [2008] EWHC 966 (Admin) at [41].
155 In *R (on the application of Goodson) v Bedfordshire and Luton Coroner (Luton and Dunstable Hospital NHS Trust, interested party)* [2004] EWHC 2931 (Admin), [2006] 1 WLR 432, [2005] 2 All ER 792 the coroner assessed this to be in the region of 5–6% of inquests, although it was accepted that practice varied across the coronial districts (at [36]).
156 [2010] EWHC 931 (Admin).
157 [1994] 4 All ER 139.
158 *Three Rivers District Council v Governor and Company of the Bank of England (No 6)* [2004] UKHL 48 at 102.
159 See   https://www.belfasttelegraph.co.uk/news/northern-ireland/mothers-of-soldiers-found-dead-in-co-down-fail-in-coroner-challenge-over-psych-report-37725273.html. *In the Matter of an Application by (1) Linda Ketcher (2) Carol Mitchell for Leave to Apply for Judicial Review* [2019] NIQB 4 updated reference.

course of action. If the evidence assists the investigation, the coroner can adopt the expert witness and call them to give evidence at the inquest.[160] In such circumstances, the defendant will have advance notice of the expert evidence for the claimant in any subsequent civil claim.

Alternatively, the family may instruct an expert to provide a report to identify the issues and areas of concern that should be explored with the witnesses by the advocate for the family at the inquest. Such information often includes NICE standards or guidance of one of the medical colleges. This document is also privileged if it has been communicated to the interested party.[161]

Advance disclosure

In healthcare deaths, the deceased's medical notes and x-rays, internal investigation reports, adverse incident reports, serious untoward incident reports, hospital policy and procedure documents and the witness statements of the hospital staff and GP are likely to be required by the family of the deceased. Medical records can be obtained by the deceased's personal representative under the Access to Health Records Act 1990.[162]

Interested persons can request the disclosure of documents from the coroner during or after the course of an investigation, pre-inquest review or inquest.[163] The coroner must provide the documents or a copy of the documents as soon as reasonably practicable, including the post-mortem examination report, any other report that has been provided to the coroner during the course of an investigation and any other document that the coroner considers relevant to the inquest.[164] A coroner may refuse to supply a document or copy of a document in the following circumstances:

1   there is a statutory or legal prohibition on disclosure;
2   the consent of any author or copyright owner cannot reasonably be obtained;
3   the request is unreasonable;
4   the document relates to contemplated or commenced criminal proceedings; or
5   the coroner considers the document irrelevant to the investigation.[165]

Interested persons are unlikely to obtain disclosure of documents supplied to the coroner in confidence. In *Worcestershire County Council and Worcestershire Safeguarding Children Board v HM Coroner for the County of Worcestershire*,[166] it was held that the coroner was entitled to disclosure of reports obtained by the local safeguarding children board investigating the death of a 16 year old girl hanging from a tree. Baker J

---

160 *R (on the application of Nicholls) v Coroner for the City of Liverpool* [2001] EWHC Admin 922.
161 *Three Rivers District Council v Governor and Company of the Bank of England (No 6)* [2004] UKHL 48 at 115.
162 Access to Health Records Act 1990, s 3(f): where the patient has died, the patient's personal representative and any person who may have a claim arising out of the patient's death.
163 Coroners (Inquests) Rules 2013, SI 2013/1616, r 12.
164 Coroners (Inquests) Rules 2013, SI 2013/1616, r 13.
165 Coroners (Inquests) Rules 2013, SI 2013/1616, r 15.
166 [2013] EWHC 1711 (QB).

held that the coroner was entitled to full disclosure so that he could decide the issues to be considered at the inquest and the witnesses to be called to give evidence. Any onward disclosure to interested persons was a matter for the coroner considering the Coroners (Inquests) Rules 2013 and case law, for example, the *Worcestershire* case and *Inner West London Assistant Deputy Coroner v Channel Four Television Corporation*.[167]

The Chief Coroner has indicated in *Law Sheet No 3: The Worcestershire Case: Disclosure to the Coroner, not the Public*, dated January 2014, that the process of disclosure is a two stage process.[168] The first stage is for the document to be disclosed to the coroner, for the purpose of deciding the scope of the inquest and/or the witnesses to be called to give evidence. The second stage the coroner decides whether there can and should be onward disclosure of the document to interested persons.

Scope of the inquiry including Art 2 of the ECHR

Human rights law has profoundly influenced coronial law, and there has been much discussion of the scope of Art 2 of the ECHR and the function of the inquest in discharging the United Kingdom's obligations under it. The majority of the jurisprudence has focussed on violent deaths, and deaths of detainees in police or prison custody as opposed to healthcare deaths. Article 2 is one of the most fundamental provisions in the ECHR. Article 2, which by virtue of s 6 of the Human Rights Act 1998 binds all public authorities in the United Kingdom, provides that:

> Everyone's right to life shall be protected by law. No one shall be deprived of his life intentionally save in the execution of a sentence of a court following his conviction of a crime for which the penalty is provided by law.

The European Court of Human Rights and domestic courts have interpreted Art 2 of the ECHR as imposing the following obligations:

1   not to take life without justification;
2   to establish a framework of laws, precautions, procedures and means of enforcement which will, to the greatest extent reasonably practicable, protect life; and
3   a procedural obligation to initiate an effective independent public investigation into any death occurring in circumstances in which it appears that one of the foregoing substantive obligations have been, or may have been, violated and it appears that agents of the state are, or may have been, in some way implicated.[169]

In the Court of Appeal case of *R (on the application of Humberstone) v Legal Services Commission* (The Lord Chancellor intervening),[170] Lady Justice Smith explained the obligations under Art 2, as follows:

> Article 2(1) provides that: 'Everyone's right to life shall be protected by law'. That primary duty imposes on the state a duty not to take life and also a duty to take appropriate legislative and administrative steps to protect life, for example by the provision of a police force and criminal justice system. It

---

167 [2007] EWHC 2513 (QB).
168 See   https://www.judiciary.uk/wp-content/uploads/2016/02/law-sheets-no-3-the-worcestershire-case.pdf.
169 *R (Middleton) v West Somerset Coroner* [2004] UKHL 10, [2004] 2 AC 182 at [2]–[3].
170 [2010] EWCA Civ 1479 at [21].

imposes on state authorities such as the police and prison authorities the duty to protect those in their immediate care from violence either at the hands of others or at their own hands: see *LCB v United Kingdom* [1998] 27 EHRR 212; *Osman v United Kingdom* [1998] 27 EHRR; *Edwards v United Kingdom* [2002] 35 EHRR 487 and *R (Amin) v Secretary of State for the Home Department* [2004] 1 AC 653, [2003] UKHL 51. The duty also extends to organs of the state, such as hospital authorities, to make appropriate provision and to adopt systems of work to protect the lives of patients in their care: see *Savage v South Essex Trust* [2009] 1 AC 681.[171]

In *Lopes de Sousa Fernandes v Portugal* the Grand Chamber took the opportunity to clarify the law.[172] The court held that there had been no violation of Art 2 where hospital staff failed to diagnose meningitis at an early stage. It was alleged that there was dysfunction in the hospital services between the ear, nose and throat ('ENT') department and hospital emergency department that resulted in the death of the deceased. The Grand Chamber gave further guidance on the systemic duty to protect the lives of patients. *Fernandes* was considered in *R (Parkinson) v Kent Senior Coroner*[173] and the court used the case to restate the law on Art 2 and system failure (see later).

When considering the scope of the inquiry, the coroner must consider Art 2. Representatives of all interested persons should also consider the scope of the inquest and make representations to the coroner as appropriate. Healthcare staff may wish to narrow the scope of the investigation to avoid criticism, to deter subsequent civil claims, and to prevent any adverse publicity. However, it has been held that 'an inquiry which leaves too many questions unanswered and too many issues unresolved is not a sufficient inquiry',[174] and may be the subject of a successful judicial review.

One difficulty in considering the potential scope of the inquiry is that imprecise language has been used in relation to the engagement of Art 2 leading to failure to consider the correct issues. In the Court of Appeal case of *Humberstone*, Lady Justice Smith, giving the judgment of the court, provided welcome clarity to the state's duties to investigate deaths under the ECHR. Essentially, all inquests are Art 2 inquests. Article 2 of the ECHR may be engaged in two senses.[175]

Traditional (Jamieson) inquests

First, Art 2 imposes an obligation on the state to provide a legal system by which the citizen may access an open and independent investigation of the circumstances of the death (ie a general investigative obligation). The coroner's inquest, the availability of criminal and civil proceedings, and disciplinary proceedings will satisfy the general obligation.[176] These inquests are often described as traditional, ordinary, domestic, or

---

171 [2010] EWCA Civ 1479 at [21].
172 (App No 56080/13) (2018) 66 EHRR 28.
173 [2018] EWHC 1501 (Admin).
174 *R (Reilly) v HM Coroner for Coventry* [1996] 35 BMLR 48 at [53].
175 *R (on the application of Humberstone) v Legal Services Commission* [2011] EWCA Civ 1479; [2010] All ER (D) 225 (Dec) at [58].
176 *R (on the application of Humberstone) v Legal Services Commission* [2011] EWCA Civ 1479, [2010] All ER (D) 225 (Dec) at [58].

Jamieson type inquests after the Court of Appeal decision in *R v North Humberside and Scunthorpe Coroner, ex p Jamieson*.[177]

The inquest is directed towards ascertaining the statutory questions. However, in traditional *Jamieson* inquests, 'how' the deceased came by his death is narrowly interpreted as meaning 'by what means' the deceased came by his death.[178] The scope of the inquest will be determined by the coroner, and in *Jamieson*, it was explained that:[179]

> It is the duty of the coroner ... whether he is sitting with a jury or without, to ensure that the relevant facts are fully, fairly and fearlessly investigated ... He must ensure that the relevant facts are exposed to public scrutiny ... He fails in his duty if his investigation is superficial, slipshod or perfunctory. But the responsibility is his. He must set the bounds of the inquiry ...

The investigation and inquest should not be 'limited to the last link in the chain of causation' as this would 'defeat the purpose of holding an inquest at all if the inquiry were to be circumscribed'.[180] In addition, the investigation should not be limited to matters that caused the death, but should include the relevant systems at the hospital and the safeguards that were in place; and how the system operated on the day in question.[181] If, during the course of an inquest, it becomes apparent that a systemic defect may be to blame for the death of the deceased, the coroner should convert the traditional *Jamieson* inquest into an enhanced *Middleton* inquest in order to discharge the states' obligations under the ECHR.

Enhanced (Middleton) *inquests*

Second, Art 2 imposes a procedural obligation on the state to conduct an effective investigation 'where there was ground for suspicion that the state might have breached a substantive obligation under Article 2'[182] (ie the enhanced obligation). Inquests that arise out of the procedural obligation are often described as Art 2,[183] enhanced, or *Middleton* inquests, after the leading case of *R (Middleton) v West Somerset Coroner*.[184] The enhanced *Middleton* inquest, criminal proceedings, and public inquiries satisfy the procedural obligation. In such cases, the obligation is proactively to initiate a thorough investigation into all the circumstances of the death.[185]

The enhanced *Middleton* inquest is directed at ascertaining the same statutory questions. However, 'how' the deceased came by their death is broadly interpreted to mean 'by what means and in what circumstances'

---

177 *R v North Humberside and Scunthorpe Coroner, ex p Jamieson* [1994] 3 All ER 972.
178 *R v North Humberside and Scunthorpe Coroner, ex p Jamieson* [1994] 3 All ER 972.
179 *R v North Humberside and Scunthorpe Coroner, ex p Jamieson* [1994] 3 All ER 972 at para 14 of the conclusions. Adopted in *Dallaglio*, at 154–155 by Simon Brown LJ.
180 *R v Inner West London Coroner, ex p Dallaglio and Lockwood Croft* [1994] 4 All ER 139 at 164.
181 *R (on the application of Takoushis) v Inner North London Coroner* [2005] EWCA Civ 1440, [2006] 1 WLR 461 at [49]–[51].
182 *R (on the application of Smith) v Oxfordshire Assistant Deputy Coroner (Equality and Human Rights Commission Intervening)* [2010] UKSC 29, [2010] 3 WLR 223.
183 The use of Art 2 in this context is misleading.
184 *R (on the application of Middleton) v West Somerset Coroner* [2004] UKHL 10, [2004] 2 AC 182.
185 *R (on the application of Middleton) v West Somerset Coroner* [2004] UKHL 10, [2004] 2 AC 182 at [20].

the deceased came by their death.[186] This ensures that the inquest considers the circumstances alleged to have caused the breach of Art 2. The scope of the conclusion is also wider compared to the traditional *Jamieson* inquest, as indicated in *R (on the application of Hurst) v London Northern District Coroner*:[187]

> Of course, the scope of the inquiry is ultimately a matter for the coroner. The 'conclusion' and findings, however, are not. The *Jamieson* construction of 'how' severely circumscribes these. But where the *Middleton* construction applies, the conclusion and findings are not merely permitted, but *required* to be wider: section 11 dictates that the inquisition 'shall set out, so far as such particulars have been proved ... how ... the deceased came by his death'. If in every case that means 'in what circumstances' as well as 'by what means', the coroner will inevitably in many cases have to widen the scope of the inquiry beyond that which, under the *Jamieson* approach, he would otherwise regard to be appropriate.

In *R (on the application of Amin) v Secretary of State for the Home Department*, Lord Bingham explained the purposes of the procedural duty:[188]

> The purposes of such an investigation are clear: to ensure so far as possible that the full facts are brought to light; that culpable and discreditable conduct is exposed and brought to public notice; that suspicion of deliberate wrongdoing (if unjustified) is allayed; that dangerous practices and procedures are rectified; and that those who have lost their relative may at least have the satisfaction of knowing that lessons learned from his death may save the lives of others.

To comply with the Art 2 procedural duty, the investigation must be:

1 independent;
2 effective;
3 reasonably prompt;
4 involve a sufficient element of public scrutiny; and
5 the next-of-kin must be involved to an appropriate extent.[189]

Engagement of Article 2

As all inquests engage Art 2, the proper approach is to identify the obligations that arise. In *R (Parkinson) v Kent Senior Coroner*[190] Singh LJ summarised the law on substantive and procedural obligations on the state in healthcare:

> (1) Article 2 imposes both substantive positive obligations on the state and procedural obligations.
> (2) The primary substantive positive obligation is to have in place a regulatory framework compelling hospitals, whether private or public, to adopt appropriate measures for the protection of patients' lives.

---

186 CJA 2009, s 5(2).
187 [2007] UKHL 13, [2007] 2 WLR 726 at [51].
188 [2003] UKHL 51, [2004] 1 AC 653 at [31].
189 *Jordan v UK* [2001] 37 EHRR 52 at [106]–[107] adopted in R *v Home Secretary, ex p Amin* [2004] 1 AC 653 at [25].
190 [2018] EWHC 1501 (Admin).

(3)   The primary procedural obligation is to have a system of law in place, whether criminal or civil, by which individual failures can be the subject of an appropriate remedy. In the law of England and Wales that is achieved by having a criminal justice system, which can in principle hold to account a healthcare professional who causes a patient's death by gross negligence; and a civil justice system, which makes available a possible civil claim for negligence. We note that, in the present case, there is in fact an extant civil claim which has been brought by the claimant against the NHS Trust which ran the hospital.

(4)   The enhanced duty of investigation, which falls upon the state itself to initiate an effective and independent investigation, will only arise in medical cases in limited circumstances, where there is an arguable breach of the state's own substantive obligations under Article 2.

(5)   Where the state has made adequate provision for securing high professional standards among health professionals and the protection of the lives of patients, matters such as an error of judgment on the part of a health professional or negligent co-ordination among health professionals in the treatment of a particular patient are not sufficient of themselves to call the state to account under Article 2.

(6)   However, there may be exceptional cases which go beyond mere error or medical negligence, in which medical staff, in breach of their professional obligations, fail to provide emergency medical treatment despite being fully aware that a person's life would be put at risk if that treatment is not given. In such a case the failure will result from a dysfunction in the hospital's services and this will be a structural issue linked to the deficiencies in the regulatory framework.

(7)   At the risk of over-simplification, the crucial distinction is between a case where there is reason to believe that there may have been a breach which is a 'systemic failure', in contrast to an 'ordinary' case of medical negligence.

Identifying what will amount to a 'dysfunction in the hospital's services and this will be a structural issue linked to the deficiencies in the regulatory framework' is difficult. In *Takoushis,* the court considered that the triage system in a hospital might be defective requiring investigation under Art 2.[191] In *Humberstone*, Lady Justice Smith considered that there was an issue with the resources and operational system of the Yorkshire Ambulance Service that were deficient requiring investigation under Art 2.[192]

This is a developing area of law. However, the procedural duty in healthcare deaths arises where death arguably results in the following circumstances:

1   Following *Parkinson:* where system 'dysfunction' denies a person emergency medical treatment despite being aware that the person's life is at risk if the treatment is not given. Whether this will include a failure to provide systems, rules and procedures to protect life, for example, a systemic failure in the provision of medical care (*Takoushis*),[193] or the failure to provide suitable facilities, adequate

---

191 *R (on the application of Takoushis) v Inner London North Coroner* [2005] EWCA Civ 1440.
192 *R (on the application of Humberstone) v Legal Services Commission* [2011] EWCA Civ 1479, [2010] All ER (D) 225 (Dec) at [58].
193 *R (on the application of Takoushis) v Inner London North Coroner* [2005] EWCA Civ 1440.

staff, or appropriate systems of operation (*Humberstone*)[194] remains to be seen. When considering whether the enhanced obligation under Art 2 is engaged practitioners should consider the judgments in both *Fernandes* (Grand Chamber) and *Parkinson*.

2   Where the deceased was detained in hospital under the Mental Health Act 1983 and there was a real and immediate risk of suicide, of which the authorities knew or ought to have been aware. In such circumstances there is an operational obligation and the staff are required to do all that could reasonably be expected of them to prevent the patient committing suicide (*Savage v South Essex Partnership NHS Foundation Trust*).[195]

3   In *Rabone v Pennine Care NHS Trust*,[196] the Supreme Court held that Art 2 imposed an operational duty to take reasonable steps to protect an informal psychiatric patient from the 'real and immediate risk' of suicide. There were particular features that brought the deceased within the operational duty: she had been admitted as a suicide risk; she as extremely vulnerable; the hospital had assumed responsibility, and was under its control, even though not detained.

4   Where the deceased arguably died as a result of grossly negligent medical care.[197] By gross negligence, the Court of Appeal in *Takoushis* stated (*obiter*) that it meant the kind of negligence that would be sufficient to sustain a charge of manslaughter.[198]

Simple or ordinary negligence in the care and treatment of a patient in hospital is insufficient to amount to a breach of the state's positive obligation to protect life.[199] In *Humberstone*, Lady Justice Smith cautioned against dressing up allegations of individual negligence as systemic failures.[200] However, she acknowledged that it is not always easy to distinguish between individual negligence and systemic failures.[201] For example, in *Takoushis* the allegations related to the nature of the

---

194 *R (on the application of Humberstone) v Legal Services Commission* [2011] EWCA Civ 1479, [2010] All ER (D) 225 (Dec) at [58].

195 *Savage v South Essex Partnership NHS Foundation Trust* [2008] UKHL 74, [2009] 1 AC 681, at [49]; and see *R (on the application of Smith) v Oxfordshire Assistant Deputy Coroner (Equality and Human Rights Commission Intervening)* [2009] EWCA Civ 441, [2009] 3 WLR 1099 at [102]–[103].

196 [2012] UKSC 2.

197 This issue was mentioned in *R (on the application of Takoushis) v Inner London North Coroner* [2005] EWCA Civ 1440, [2005] All ER (D) 461 (Nov) at [96] and *R (on the application of Humberstone) v Legal Services Commission* [2011] EWCA Civ 1479, [2010] All ER (D) 225 (Dec) at [71], but no decisions were made on this point. Both courts referred to the decision in *R (on the application of Khan) v Secretary of State for Health* [2003] EWCA Civ 1129, [2004] 1 WLR 971. Also see on this point *R (on the application of Moss) v HM Coroner for the North and South Districts of Durham and Darlington* [2008] EWHC 2940 (Admin), [2008] All ER (D) 292 (Nov) at [24]–[25].

198 *R (on the application of Takoushis) v Inner London North Coroner* [2005] EWCA Civ 1440; [2005] All ER (D) 461 (Nov) at [96].

199 *R (on the application of Goodson) v Bedfordshire and Luton Coroner* [2004] EWHC 2931 Admin, [2005] All ER (D) 122 (Oct), at [5]; approved in *R (on the application of Humberstone) v Legal Services Commission* [2011] EWCA Civ 1479, [2010] All ER (D) 225 (Dec) at [58].

200 *R (on the application of Humberstone) v Legal Services Commission* [2011] EWCA Civ 1479, [2010] All ER (D) 225 (Dec) at [71].

201 See also *R (on the application of JL) v Secretary of State for Justice* [2008] UKHL 68, [2009] 2 All ER 521 at [88] for a helpful discussion on systemic negligence and operational negligence.

triage system in the Accident and Emergency Department at St Thomas' Hospital,[202] and in *Humberstone* the allegations related to the resources and operational services of the Yorkshire Ambulance Service.[203] It is advisable to consider and collate evidence of systemic failings as early as possible, and to raise this issue at a pre-inquest hearing.

Summoning a jury

Once the Coroner has determined the scope of the inquest, a decision must be made as to whether a jury is required.[204] The coroner must carry out sufficient investigations before deciding whether a jury is required, and any relevant documentary and witness evidence should be provided before the decision to call or not to call a jury is made.[205] The coroner also has the power to reconsider the decision not to call a jury at any time during the inquest. Where an inquest starts without a jury but is subsequently summoned, the validity of anything done by the Coroner before the jury was summoned is still effective.[206] If a jury is summoned, it will consist of between seven and eleven people.[207] Rules 28 to 31 of the Coroners (Inquests) Rules 2013 set out the practical procedure for summoning a jury.

There is a presumption that the coroner will sit without a jury,[208] except in certain circumstances. These circumstances are set out in the CJA 2009, s 7(2):

> (2) An inquest into a death must be held with a jury if the senior coroner has reason to suspect—
> (a)   that the deceased died while in custody or otherwise in state detention, and that either—
>   (i)   the death was a violent or unnatural one, or
>   (ii)   the cause of death is unknown,
> (b)   that the death resulted from an act or omission of—
>   (i)   a police officer, or
>   (ii)   a member of a service police force,
>   in the purported execution of the officer's or member's duty as such, or
> (c)   that the death was caused by a notifiable accident, poisoning or disease.

The phrase 'reason to suspect' is not defined in the CJA 2009. A 'reason to suspect' does not require positive proof or even formulated evidence; any information giving 'reason to suspect' will suffice: *R v Inner London Coroner, ex p Linnane*.[209] In *R (Fullick) v HM Senior Coroner for Inner North London*[210] the Chief Coroner (Peter Thornton) adopted the approach

---

202 *R (on the application of Takoushis) v Inner London North Coroner* [2005] EWCA Civ 1440, [2005] All ER (D) 461 (Nov).
203 *R (on the application of Humberstone) v Legal Services Commission* [2011] EWCA Civ 1479, [2010] All ER (D) 225 (Dec).
204 *R (on the application of Paul) v Deputy Coroner of the Queens's Households and the Assistant Deputy Coroner for Surrey* [2007] EWHC 408 (Admin), [2008] QB 172 at [42].
205 *R (on the application of Takoushis) v Inner London North Coroner* [2005] EWCA Civ 1440, [2005] All ER (D) 461 (Nov) at [55].
206 Coroners (Inquests) Rules 2013, SI 2013/1616, r 32.
207 CJA 2009, s 8(1).
208 CJA 2009, s 7(1).
209 [1989] 1 WLR 395 at 398.
210 [2015] EWHC 3522 (Admin).

of Hickinbottom J in *R (Davey) v HM Coroner for Leicester City and South Leicestershire*[211]:

> 'Reason to suspect' is a low threshold for the triggering of the obligation to empanel a jury, 'suspicion' for these purposes being a state of conjecture or surmise arising at the start of an investigation in which obtaining a prima facie proof is the end (*Hussien v Chong Fook Kam* [1970] AC 942).[212]

If Art 2 of the ECHR is engaged, it does not automatically following that the coroner must sit with a jury. Indeed, jury inquests are no longer required where the deceased died in custody, but from natural causes.

A 'notifiable accident' is if notice of it is required under any Act to be given to a government department, to any inspector or other officer of a government department or to an inspector appointed under the Health and Safety at Work etc Act 1974, s 19.[213] Deaths are reportable by employers or a person in control of premises to the Health and Safety Executive by virtue of the Reporting of Injuries Diseases and Dangerous Occurrences Regulations 2013 (RIDDOR 2013).[214] Regulation 14 of RIDDOR 2013 excludes deaths that occur out of an examination, treatment or operation carried out or supervised by a registered medical practitioner or registered dentist.

However, other healthcare related deaths may be reportable requiring the Coroner to sit with a jury. The HSE Information Sheet Number 1: *Reporting Injuries, Diseases and Dangerous Occurrences in Health and Social Care (revision 3)*,[215] includes several reportable accidents in the healthcare environment. Some examples are:

- a confused patient falls from a hospital window on an upper floor;
- a service user falls out of bed. The assessment identified the need to bedrails, but they or other preventative measures were not taken;
- a patient suffered a serious injury as a result of a power failure during an operation (not caused by the conduct of the operation).

The information sheet includes examples of accidents that are not reportable. Some examples are:

- a patient commits suicide;
- a service user falls out of bed. There was a detailed assessment in the care plan identifying that fall protection was not required;
- a service user is admitted to hospital and contracts Legionnaires disease and dies. The death has to be caused by an accident to be reportable. Consequently poor maintenance of a hot water system is not reportable.

The coroner continues to have the discretion to summon a jury if the coroner 'thinks that there is sufficient reason for doing so'.[216] In making a decision, the coroner will take into consideration the view of the deceased's family, the complexity/amount of documentation, whether the

---

211 [2014] EWHC 3982 (Admin).
212 [2014] EWHC 3982 (Admin), at [7].
213 CJA 2009, s 7(4).
214 Reporting of Injuries Diseases and Dangerous Occurrences Regulations 2013, SI 2013/1471.
215 See http://www.hse.gov.uk/pubns/hsis1.pdf.
216 CJA 2009, s 7(3).

facts of the case resemble the type of situation covered by the mandatory jury provisions, including the policy considerations underpinning the provisions, and the benefit of a reasoned explanation for his conclusions (a jury is only able to give brief answers to a limited number of questions).[217] Therefore, it is vital for representatives to take instructions in relation to summoning a jury. The factors that may be relevant include the increased length of the inquest if a jury is summoned, that a jury may be more willing to return a conclusion that criticises the hospital/GP; and the fact that a coroner can provide a reasoned explanation for the conclusion.

THE INQUEST HEARING

The resumed hearing

The coroner will list the inquest for a full hearing once the investigations are complete and criminal proceedings (if any) are finished. The inquest should be completed within six months of the date that the coroner is made aware of the death, or as soon as reasonably practicable after that date.[218] Coroners must inform the Chief Coroner if the investigation has not been concluded within 12 months.[219]

The inquest is an inquisitorial process. However, inquests are often not entirely inquisitorial as representatives of the interested persons try to advance particular cases or agendas. The inquest will be heard in public; although the coroner has the power to direct that the public be excluded from an inquest or part of an inquest if it is considered to be in the interests of national security to do so.[220] This is unlikely to arise in the healthcare context.

The relatives of the deceased will usually expect the inquest to reveal and explain all the circumstances surrounding the death and to apportion blame. However, the inquiry is limited to the four statutory questions, and the CJA 2009, s 10(2) prohibits apportioning of criminal or civil liability. Therefore, the expectations of the family and friends must be managed at an early stage in the process. Healthcare staff are often anxious about giving evidence and the practical effect of a critical conclusion in relation to their employment and professional standing.

Witnesses called to give evidence

The coroner is the sole arbiter of evidence heard at an inquest. In *Le Page v HM Assistant Deputy Coroner for Inner South London,*[221] the court comprehensively reviewed the authorities on the coroner's power, duty and discretion in relation to the witnesses to be called. The coroner will decide which lay and expert witnesses are to be called to give oral evidence and a list of witnesses that will be called should be provided in advance

---

217 *R (Paul) v Deputy Coroner of the Queen's Household* [2007] EWHC 408 (Admin), [2008] QB 172, and *R (Shafi) v HM Senior Coroner for East London* [2015] EWHC 2106 (Admin) at [69].
218 Coroners (Inquests) Rules 2013, SI 2013/1616, r 9.
219 Coroners (Investigations) Regulations 2013, SI 2013/1629, reg 26.
220 Coroners (Inquests) Rules 2013, SI 2013/1616, r 11.
221 [2012] EWHC 1485.

of the inquest. The coroner can compel a witness to attend the inquest and give evidence,[222] although it is unlikely that a coroner would need to exercise this power in a healthcare related death. Interested persons are not entitled to call witnesses. However, the coroner can be invited to call any witness who might assist, and representatives should alert the coroner if they believe a witness will be able to assist, or whose conduct will be called into question.

The case of *R (Mack) v HM Coroner for Birmingham and Solihull*[223] is illustrative of the importance of calling appropriate witnesses. In *Mack*, the inquest was quashed because the coroner failed to call the consultant gastro-enterologist who had been responsible for the patient over the nine days before his death. During these last days, there were a number of criticisms of the quality of the care and treatment, for example, defects in recording fluid balance, and tests which had been requested had not been carried out. Instead, the coroner called the consultant who had been responsible for the deceased immediately before the consultant gastro-enterologist, and did not work on the ward about which the family raised most of their concerns. Therefore, whilst the witness could say, for example, that the patient's drug charts where unsatisfactory, he could not say if it was a one-off problem or a systematic problem on the ward. The practical point is that the coroner had accepted the witness nominated by the hospital. Therefore, hospitals must ensure that it nominates witnesses who have cared for and/or treated the patient. The administrative court accepted that it is not possible to call every doctor or nurse who could give material evidence. However, the effect of the judgment may be that coroners call more witnesses from hospitals to ensure that the investigation is sufficient.

Another example is *R (Bentley) v Coroner's District of Avon*,[224] in which Sullivan J accepted the applicant's submissions that an inquest which does not hear evidence from the actual witness whose behaviour was said to lack competence could not be described as a sufficient inquest. Consequently, the conclusion of an inquest in which a coroner made a number of criticisms about the GP, but where the GP was not called to give evidence, did not attend the inquest, was not notified of the inquest, and was not represented at the inquest, was quashed.[225]

The coroner will decide the order that the witnesses will give evidence, but if a family member is giving evidence, they will usually be called first. In an inquest that will be heard over several days or longer, the coroner usually provides a list of the order that the witnesses will be called.

In healthcare deaths, coroners usually hear the factual evidence first before the medical evidence, and the evidence of the pathologist is often heard last. This enables the pathologist to revise their opinion when the facts and circumstances of death are known. This occurred in *Hopkins and Ryan v HM Coroner for Swansea, Neath and Port Talbot*,[226] where

---

222 CJA 2009, Sch 5, para 1(1)(a).
223 [2011] EWCA Civ 712.
224 [2001] EWHC Admin 170, [2002] ACD 1.
225 *R (on the application of Dowler) v Coroner for North London* [2009] EWHC 3300 (Admin), [2010] 11 BMLR 124.
226 [2018] EWHC 1604 (Admin).

the pathologist amended his initial opinion on the medical cause of death upon hearing witness evidence. The family of the deceased were concerned by the change of opinion of the pathologist and obtained a medical report from a consultant pathologist. The expert supported the initial opinion on the medical cause of death. A new inquest was ordered.

Other coroners call the pathologist to give evidence first, and the remainder of the evidence is directed to ascertaining how the deceased came by their death. If the pathologist is the first witness, the coroner can be invited to recall the pathologist should any new evidence or issue arise that might alter the coroner's opinion. On occasions, the pathologist is not called to give evidence and the post-mortem report is admitted under the Coroners (Inquests) Rules 2013, r 23 (see below); although this is unlikely to occur in healthcare deaths, unless the evidence is uncontroversial.

Family members may not wish to hear the evidence of the post-mortem examination and may prefer to sit outside court whilst the pathologist gives evidence. Instructions should be taken on this issue before the hearing, and it is often helpful to inform the coroner's officer that the family wish to sit outside court for that part of the hearing.

Witnesses are examined under oath or affirmation.[227] The coroner will ask question of the witnesses first, and if the witness is represented, their advocate will ask questions of that witness last.[228] Coroners usually use the written statement or report prepared by the witness in advance of the hearing as a basis of asking questions to elicit the relevant evidence in open court. The coroner must examine any inconsistencies in a witness statement and seek an explanation.[229]

Interested persons (through their advocate or in person) are entitled to question the witnesses at an inquest.[230] Questions must be relevant to the particular issues that are raised by the inquest and within the scope of the inquiry. Coroners will disallow any question that is not relevant or any improper question.[231] Although some coroners allow the advocate for the family a degree of latitude, it is preferable for advocates to identify any issues that are important to the family but are not relevant to the inquest before the hearing and liaise with the representative for the hospital or GP to obtain the required information. Leading questions can be asked as an inquest is not a trial, but such questions are usually only suitable where the issue is not contentious. There is no right to re-examine a witness, although coroners often exercise discretion to allow follow up questions.

In an inquest into a healthcare death, it is usual for all the witnesses to sit in court to hear the evidence of the other witnesses before they are called. However, coroners have discretion to exclude witnesses from the court (as in criminal proceedings) if there is a risk that a witness may alter their evidence as a result of the evidence that has already been heard.

---

227 Coroners (Inquests) Rules 2013, SI 2013/1616, r 20.
228 Coroners (Inquests) Rules 2013, SI 2013/1616, r 21.
229 *R v Inner North London Coroner, ex p Cohen* (1994) 158 JP at 650–651.
230 Coroners (Inquests) Rules 2013, SI 2013/1616, r 19(1).
231 Coroners (Inquests) Rules 2013, SI 2013/1616, r 19(2).

Self-incrimination

A witness is not obliged to answer any question that tends to incriminate them. The Coroners (Inquests) Rules 2013, r 22(1) provides:

(1) No witness at an inquest shall be obliged to answer any question tending to incriminate him or her.

(2) Where it appears to the coroner that a witness has been asked such a question, the coroner must inform the witness that he or she may refuse to answer it.

The risk of self-incrimination is in relation to criminal proceedings, not civil proceedings.[232] The coroner does not have the power to impose a blanket prohibition against relevant questions on behalf of the family, particularly when the witness has already waived privilege on factual matters in answering the coroner's questions.[233] Witnesses are also not obliged to answer questions that are covered by legal professional privilege, although privilege may be waived by the witness.

Evidential points

Notes of evidence

Inquest and pre-inquest hearings should be recorded.[234] Interested persons can apply for a copy of the recording, and the various procedural rules and guidance are set out in the Chief Coroner's *Guidance No 4: Recordings*. A copy of one recording disc incurs a fee of £5[235] and inquests may last longer than one recording disc. Evidence given at the inquest may assist parties in subsequent civil claims and the coroner must keep all documents (a disc is a document) for at least 15 years.[236]

Uncontested documentary evidence

Under the Coroners (Inquests) Rules 2013, r 23, a coroner has discretion to admit documentary evidence in the absence of the person who made the statement if it is relevant to the inquest and in the coroner's opinion is unlikely to be disputed.[237] However, interested persons may object to the admission of documentary evidence.[238] This usually results in the witness being called to give evidence, unless the maker of the document is unable to give oral evidence within a reasonable period.[239]

Documentary evidence admitted under r 23 is read out by the coroner in court, unless the coroner directs otherwise.[240] Rule 23(2) provides the procedure that coroners must follow to admit documentary evidence without the witness attending to give evidence at the inquest:

---

232 Civil Evidence Act 1968, s 14(1)(a).
233 *R v Lincolnshire Coroner, ex p Hay* [1999] All ER (D) 173 at para 57.
234 Coroners (Inquests) Rules 2013, SI 2013/1616, r 26.
235 Coroners Allowances, Fees and Expenses Regulations 2013, SI 2013/1615, reg 12(4).
236 Coroners (Investigations) Regulations 2013, SI 2013/1629, reg 27(1).
237 Coroners (Inquests) Rules 2013, SI 2013/1616, r 23 (1).
238 Coroners (Inquests) Rules 2013, SI 2013/1616, r 22(2)(c).
239 Coroners (Inquests) Rules 2013, SI 2013/1616, r 23(1)(a).
240 Coroners (Inquests) Rules 2013, SI 2013/1616, r 23(4).

(2) Before admitting such written evidence the coroner must announce at the inquest hearing—

(a)   what the nature of the written evidence to be admitted is;
(b)   the full name of the maker of the written evidence to be admitted in evidence;
(c)   that any interested person may object to the admission of any such written evidence; and
(d)   that any interested person is entitled to see a copy of any written evidence if he or she so wishes.

The coroner should disclose the documentary evidence (or a brief summary of the evidence) that he believes is uncontested and can be admitted under r 23 in advance of the inquest, asking for the views of the interested persons. It is unlikely that the coroner has discretion to admit documentary evidence under r 23 if there is an objection.[241]

Coroners have the power to admit into evidence a document made by a deceased person if the contents of the document are relevant to the purpose of the inquest,[242] and the Coroners (Inquests) Rules 2013 do not provide for any objection by the interested persons. This rule covers suicide notes that may be helpful in assessing the deceased's mental disposition before death. Where such notes exist, coroners may elect not read out the full note, but confirm that a suicide note was written and summarise the deceased's state of mind.

The case of *Mueller v Area Coroner for Manchester West*[243] is an important case of what is to be read into the record of the inquest and the accuracy of a summary of a suicide note. Sir Brian Leveson P, gave guidance on inquests on written evidence at para 30, as follows:

> Where, as in this case, a coroner sets out with an intention of dealing with the inquest by reading the statements, it is equally important to explain to all concerned, in advance, exactly what that will mean. The coroner should indicate which statements and documents are likely to be read or summarised at the public hearing, and which parts (if any) of the statements or documents are not to be read. Statements of witnesses often include relevant and non-relevant matters and may refer to documents. In cases involving suicide it is particularly important to indicate to all concerned whether any note has been found, what is says and whether any other evidence is connected to the note that may shed light on the contents of the note. The family should be alerted to the contents of any statement or document that may cause them concern. Equally where a coroner does not intend to include part of a statement or document, and the family wish it to be included, then subject to relevance, the coroner should have regard to their wishes.

The Chief Coroner's *Guidance No 23: Document Inquests (also known as Short Form of Rule 23 Inquests)* provide further guidance on documentary inquests, also referred to as 'fast-track inquests'.

Hearsay

A coroner's inquest is not bound by the strict laws of evidence.[244] There is no rule preventing the admission of hearsay evidence (oral or written) at an inquest.[245] If admitted and the evidence is material, the coroner should warn the jury about the weight and reliability of such evidence.[246]

Closing speeches

An advocate should advise the interested party that they represent on the possible conclusions before the start of the inquest. Some families and healthcare staff express the hope that the coroner or jury will reach a particular conclusion at the end of the evidence. However, it is inadvisable for an interested party to focus on the conclusion alone. An approach that is conclusion driven potentially restricts the evidence. An inquest is an opportunity for the family to ask questions and for an explanation of the events that resulted in the death of the deceased. It is also an opportunity for healthcare staff to provide an explanation, and to allay any rumour or suspicion the family or wider community may have.

Representatives of the interested persons may make legal submissions to the coroner. If a jury has been empanelled, the submissions are made in the absence of the jury and before the coroner sums up the evidence. The submissions must be directed to the law (ie the conclusion), and not to the facts as r 27 of the Coroners (Inquests) Rules 2013 states that: 'No person may address the coroner or the jury as to the facts of who the deceased was and how, when and where the deceased came by his or her death'. Consequently, an advocate cannot ask the coroner to prefer one person's evidence to another where there is a dispute.

However, in *R (on the application of Lin) v Secretary of State for Transport*,[247] the administrative court stated obiter that an advocate was entitled to make submissions of law, in particular:

1 how the coroner should direct the jury;
2 the form of the questionnaire; and
3 recommendations pursuant to a report to prevent future deaths.

The court stated obiter that such submissions 'would merely be beating in the wind unless they were founded on the facts of the instant inquiry'.[248] It is difficult to make submissions on the sufficiency of the evidence and appropriate conclusions, and in particular on a narrative conclusion, without referring to the facts. However, some coroners will accept skeleton arguments that include the relevant facts.

Summing up to the jury

The coroner will sum up the evidence to the jury and direct them as to the law before they consider their conclusion.[249] This includes drawing

---

244 *R v Divine, ex p Walton* [1930] 2 KB 29 at 36.
245 *R v Greater Manchester Coroner, ex p Tal* [1985] QB 67.
246 *R v Greater Manchester Coroner, ex p Tal* [1985] QB 67.
247 [2006] EWHC 2575 (Admin), [2006] All ER D 472 (Jul).
248 [2006] EWHC 2575 (Admin), [2006] All ER D 472 (Jul) at [56].
249 Coroners (Inquests) Rules 2013, SI 2013/1616, r 33.

the attention of the jury to the statutory questions to be answered (the identity of the deceased, how, when and where the deceased came by their death), that the jury must not express an opinion on any other matter (CJA 2009, s 5(1)) and that the conclusion should not be framed in such a way as to appear to determine any question of criminal liability on the part of a named person, or civil liability (CJA 2009, s 10(2)).

The rules are not prescriptive about the issues that must be covered in summing up, and coroners typically include the following issues:

- a reminder of the purpose of the inquest;
- an explanation of the CJA 2009, ss 5(3) and 10(2);
- an explanation of the questions to be answered on the inquisition form, the conclusions which the jury is to consider and any relevant law, and the necessary standard of proof;
- a summary of the important points of evidence;
- instruction on how the jury might approach assessing the evidence;
- a direction on causation;
- a direction that the conclusion must be unanimous (initially); and
- brief advice as to how the task should be approached.[250]

The summing up, particularly on the law, must be clear;[251] and there are numerous examples where the inquisition has been quashed because of misdirection on the law. Today, coroners often use specimen directions in relation to potential conclusions, but the content should be agreed first with the advocates for the interested persons.

CONCLUSIONS

At the end of the evidence, the coroner or jury must set out their findings on the disputed facts and give a conclusion in Form 2 of the Coroners (Inquests) Rules 2013.[252] This is the answer to the four statutory questions: who the deceased was; and how; when; and where the deceased came by his death. Form 2: Record of an inquest is as follows:

1   The name of the deceased (if known).
2   Medical cause of death.
3   How, when and where, and for investigations where the CJA 2009, s 5(2) applies, in what circumstances the deceased came by his death.
4   Conclusion of the jury/Coroner as to the death.
5   Particulars required by the Births and Deaths Registration Act 1953:

   (a) date and place of death;
   (b) name and surname of deceased;
   (c) sex;
   (d) maiden surname of woman who has married;
   (e) date and place of birth; and
   (f) occupation and usual address.

---

250 See C Dorries *Coroners' Courts: A Guide to Law and Practice* (3rd edn, Oxford University Press), para 8.90.
251 *R v Inner South London Coroner, ex p Douglas-Williams* [1999] 1 All ER 344.
252 Coroners (Inquests) Rules 2013, SI 2013/1616, r 34.

The 'injury or disease causing death' is the medical cause of death set out in the World Health Organisation (WHO) format. Coroners usually following the medical cause of death given by the pathologist, unless there is other evidence to take into account. The 'time, place and circumstances at or in which injury was sustained' is analogous to when, where and how the decreased came by his death.

Conclusion: adequacy of the evidence

At the conclusion of the evidence, the coroner must decide what conclusions are open to the coroner or the jury. In determining whether a particular conclusion is open to reach on the evidence, the test is similar to that laid down in the criminal case of *R v Galbraith*: whether taking the evidence at its highest a jury, properly directed, could reach that particular conclusion.[253] However, in inquests, this test has been described as *'Galbraith* plus' as the *Galbraith* test on its own is insufficient. There are two formulations of the *Galbraith* plus test.

First, in *R v Inner South London Coroner, ex p Douglas-Williams*,[254] the Court of Appeal endorsed the use of the *Galbraith* test at inquests. However, the court qualified its application and indicated that the coroner had a broad discretion:

> ... in deciding whether to leave a possible conclusion to the jury, the coroner had a broad discretion, and he did not need to leave all possible conclusions just because there was technically evidence to support them, since to do so could in some situations merely confuse and overburden the jury; it was sufficient if he left those conclusions which realistically reflected the thrust of the evidence as a whole.

Second, in *R (Secretary of State for Justice) v HM Deputy Coroner for the Eastern District of West Yorkshire*,[255] Haddon-Cave J held that the coroner must be satisfied that it was safe to leave a particular conclusion to the jury. It was stated at [23]:

> It is clear, therefore, that when coroners are deciding whether or not to leave a particular verdict to a jury, they should apply a dual test comprising both limbs and 'schools of thought':
> (a)   'Is there evidence on which a jury properly directed could properly convict', plus
> (b)   'Would it be safe for the jury to convict on the evidence before it?'

It was said that the second limb of the test was required because the inquest is inquisitorial rather than adversarial, and the rights of interested persons to engage in the proceedings are necessarily curtailed.

However, in the recent case of *R (Chidlow) v HM Senior Coroner for Blackpool*,[256] which focussed on the safety of evidence and in particular statistical evidence, the court acknowledged that 'in many cases, there may be little difference between *Galbraith Plus* and pure *Galbraith*. Where there is evidence upon which a jury properly directed could

---

253 [1981] 1 WLR 1039.
254 [1999] 1 All ER 344.
255 [2012] EWHC 1634 (Admin).
256 [2019] EWHC 581.

properly reach a particular conclusion or finding then it is likely to follow that the jury could safely reach such conclusion or finding'.[257]

Where there are two almost identical conclusions, it has been stated that one can be discarded if leaving both conclusions would confuse and over burden the jury.[258] Conclusions that incorporate the adjective 'gross', such as neglect and gross negligence manslaughter, import a value judgment, to be assessed by a jury.[259]

Limits to conclusions

Coroners are entitled to give a conclusion and judgment relevant to matters falling within their jurisdiction, but must not infringe the CJA 2009, ss 5(3) and 10(2).

Section 5(1)–(3) provides that:

(1) The purpose of an investigation under this Part into a person's death is to ascertain—
(a)   who the deceased was;
(b)   how, when and where the deceased came by his or her death;
(c)   the particulars (if any) required by the 1953 Act to be registered concerning the death.
(2) Where necessary in order to avoid a breach of any Convention rights (within the meaning of the Human Rights Act 1998 (c. 42)), the purpose mentioned in subsection (1)(b) is to be read as including the purpose of ascertaining in what circumstances the deceased came by his or her death.
(3) Neither the senior coroner conducting an investigation under this Part into a person's death nor the jury (if there is one) may express any opinion on any matter other than—
(a)   the questions mentioned in subsection (1)(a) and (b) (read with subsection (2) where applicable);
(b)   the particulars mentioned in subsection (1)(c).

In *R (on the application of Farah) v HM Coroner for Southampton and New Forest District of Hampshire*,[260] the administrative court held that comments made by the coroner that:

1   do not relate to any of the matters falling within his or her jurisdiction;
2   are matters of opinion; and
3   are sufficiently critical and offensive of any party,

were unlawful.

In *Farah*, the coroner not only criticised the deceased's behaviour before his death, he criticised the solicitors representing the deceased's family for pursuing an allegation of racism. The administrative court granted declarations that some comments made by the coroner were unlawful.

The CJA 2009, s 10 provides that:

---

257 *R (Chidlow) v HM Senior Coroner for Blackpool* [2019] EWHC 581at [35].
258 See the case of *R v Inner South London Coroner, ex p Douglas-Williams* [1999] 1 All ER 344 for a discussion between the verdict of neglect and gross negligence manslaughter.
259 In the case of neglect see *R (on the application of Commissioner of Police for the Metropolis) v HM Coroner for Southern District of Greater London* [2003] EWHC 1892 (Admin), CO/222/2003 at para 60. In the case of gross negligence manslaughter see *R v Adomako* [1995] 1 AC 171 at 197 D/E.
260 [2009] EWHC 1605 (Admin), [2009] Inquest Law Reports 220.

(1) After hearing the evidence at an inquest into a death, the senior coroner (if there is no jury) or the jury (if there is one) must—
(a)   make a determination as to the questions mentioned in section 5(1)(a) and (b) (read with section 5(2) where applicable), and
(b)   if particulars are required by the 1953 Act to be registered concerning the death, make a finding as to those particulars.
(2) A determination under subsection (1)(a) may not be framed in such a way as to appear to determine any question of—
(a)   criminal liability on the part of a named person, or
(b)   civil liability.

In *R v North Humberside Coroner, ex p Jamieson*,[261] Sir Thomas Bingham, MR considered the potential conflict between the statutory duty to establish how the deceased came by his death and the prohibition on appearing to determine any question of criminal and civil liability:

> It may be accepted that in case of conflict the statutory duty to ascertain how the deceased came by his death must prevail over the prohibition in rule 42. But the scope for conflict is small. Rule 42 applies, and applies only, to the conclusion. Plainly the coroner and the jury may explore facts bearing on criminal and civil liability. But the conclusion may not appear to determine any question of criminal liability on the part of a named person nor any question of civil liability.[262]

Therefore, it is essential that the CJA 2009, s 10(2) is not interpreted in a way that is over-extensive, particularly when directing a jury. Conclusions can be judgmental and imply blame without breaching the CJA 2009, s 10(2), otherwise there is the risk that there will be omissions in the findings regarding the circumstances of death. A finding by a coroner or jury that there was a failure to carry out a task, or that precautions were inadequate or inappropriate, or that the illness causing death was treatable are not prohibited by the CJA 2009, s 10(2) as such findings do not determine any criminal or civil liability.

However, in an application for judicial review in the case of *My Care (UK) Ltd v HM Coroner for Coventry*, Mr Justice Langstaff stated that the narrative conclusion could name My Care (UK) Ltd without appearing to determine any question of criminal and civil liability.[263] My Care (UK) Ltd had provided care to Mrs Pearson. At the end of the inquest, the coroner reached a conclusion that neglect had been causative of her death, and stated in a narrative conclusion:

> The deceased died from sepsis caused by sacral pressure ulcer. The ulcer developed as a result of neglect in that, notwithstanding 4 visits 7 days per week, including dressing and undressing and toiletry needs, it had not been recognised by her carers that she had a developing pressure sore. The discovery of the pressure sore was made by her friend Iris Payne rather than her carers on or about the 15th December 2007. The matter was reported to her GP and district nurses attended on 17 December 2008. At that stage it was noted to be a grade 4 pressure sore.

My Care (UK) Ltd complained that the conclusion was a breach of the prohibition on appearing to determine any question of criminal and civil

---

261 *R* [1995] QB 1.
262 [1995] QB 1 at 24E.
263 *My Care (UK) Ltd v HM Coroner for Coventry* [2009] EWHC 3630 (Admin), CO/11963/2009 at [5] and [6].

liability as it identified the company as being responsible for the death. Mr Justice Langstaff disagreed, and stated that even if My Care (UK) Ltd had been named, it was not a breach, and the application for judicial review was refused. Consequently, a submission can be made to the coroner about naming the individual or company/organisation responsible for neglect in a narrative conclusion, and arguably any conclusion, except a conclusion of unlawful killing. However, coroners remain reluctant to name an individual or company/organisation.

The prohibitions on appearing to determine any question of criminal and civil liability and a conclusion of unlawful killing was the subject of an application for judicial review in 2010. In *R (on the application of Evans) v HM Coroner for Cardiff and the Vale of Glamorgan*,[264] the coroner returned a conclusion of unlawful killing (gross negligence). The conclusion contained in the inquisition did not name the nurse who accidently administered an overdose of insulin causing death, but a document prepared by the coroner entitled 'Summing up and Conclusion' referred to the nurse by name on numerous occasions. The administrative court gave permission for a hearing on whether the rule was breached,[265] but a full hearing was not pursued.

Conclusions and causation

For causation of death to be proved, the event or conduct said to have caused the death must on the balance of probabilities have 'more than minimally, negligibly or trivially contributed to the death'.[266]

In *R (Lewis) v HM Coroner for the Mid and North Division of the County of Shropshire*,[267] the Court of Appeal considered the extent to which causation is relevant to the conclusion. This is a significant issue because inquests usually investigate issues that are not subsequently included in the conclusion. The issue in *Lewis* was whether a coroner is obliged to leave to the jury a fact or circumstance that could have caused or contributed to the death, but it cannot be shown on the balance of probability to have done so.

Karl Lewis, who had a history of self-harm, was serving a prison sentence in a young offenders institution. One night, Lewis hanged himself from a light fitting; and was found by Officer Support Grade Knowles during a routine check. OSG Knowles had not received any suicide prevention or first aid training, and was not equipped with a 'fishknife', which is a special tool designed to enable suicide victims to be cut down promptly without further injury. OSG Knowles summoned assistance, but used the incorrect procedure so that the assistance took longer than it should have done to arrive. By the time Lewis was cut down, he was dead. It could not be determined on the balance of probability that more appropriate and swifter intervention by OSG Knowles would have saved Lewis; although it might have done. The coroner prepared a questionnaire to elicit the jury's findings on the central matters. However, the jury was not asked

---

264 [2010] EWHC 3478 (Admin).
265 [2010] EWHC 3478 (Admin), [2010] Inquest LR 217.
266 See eg *R (Dawson) v HM Coroner for East Riding and Kingston upon Hull Coroners District* [2001] Inquest LR 233.
267 [2009] EWCA Civ 1403, [2010] All ER 858.

to make any findings of fact about the actions of the prison staff that occurred after the body was discovered.

The Court of Appeal held that there was a power but not a duty to allow a jury to make findings of fact on non-causative matters. If non-causative matters are not left to the jury, this may hamper the coroner's ability to make recommendations to prevent future fatalities at the end of the inquest. This is because Reports to Prevent Future Deaths are based on factual findings, and in a jury inquest, the jury makes the findings of fact. In *Lewis*, the Report to Prevent Future Deaths was based on uncontested evidence that OSG Knowles did not have the required training or equipment. Therefore, the fact that the coroner did not ask the jury to make findings of fact on these issues was irrelevant; the coroner was able to submit a Regulation 28 Report on the uncontested evidence. However, where the evidence is disputed and a Regulation 28 Report is required to discharge the state's obligations under Art 2, the coroner will need to put a non-causative issue to the jury or alternatively make findings on whether the State failed to comply with its obligation to protect life, irrespective of whether the failure resulted in death in order to exercise the Regulation 28 power.

However, in the case of *R (Tainton) v HM Coroner for Preston & West Lancashire Care NHS Trust (Interested Party)*,[268] the divisional court reached a different view that in an enhanced Art 2 case, where a shortcoming in care had been admitted, the jury should be directed to record it even if it is only possibly causative of death. The court stated at [80]:

> ... it was not reasonable or lawful for the admitted shortcomings in (the deceased's) medical care to be excluded from the Record of the Inquest, so that the conclusion as to the death was merely described as natural causes. The material facts leading up to the deceased's death included substandard care by agents of the state which, if they were to pass unmentioned, would render the bland short form 'natural causes' verdict inadequate to describe properly the circumstances in which the deceased met his death.

This leaves some uncertainly on how coroners will exercise their discretion regarding whether the circumstances by which the deceased came by their death are only recorded if they are causative (*Lewis*), or recorded if they are admitted but remain only a possible cause (*Tainton*).

Conclusions: standard of proof

The facts to support most conclusions at an inquest must be proved to the civil standard of proof. There has been a recent shift from finding a conclusion of suicide on the criminal standard to the balance of probabilities.[269] The conclusion of unlawful killing requires the facts to be found to the criminal standard. An open conclusion reflects the fact that the evidence has not met the requirements for any other conclusions, and arguably does not require any standard of proof.

---

268 [2016] EWHC 1396 (Admin).
269 *R (Maughan) v HM Senior Coroner Oxfordshire, the Chief Coroner as an Intervener and INQUEST as an Interested Party* [2019] EWCA Civ 809.

Conclusions in healthcare deaths

There are short-form conclusions and a narrative conclusion. Short-form conclusions are viewed as traditional conclusions. They are set out in Form 2, in the Schedule to the Coroners (Inquests) Rules 2013. The Form 2 list of potential conclusions is non-exhaustive, and is merely guidance.[270] The relevant short-form conclusions in relation to healthcare deaths are: natural causes; suicide; accidental death/misadventure; stillbirth; lawful/unlawful killing; and an open conclusion. In addition to announcing a short-form conclusion, the coroner must record the facts that he or she has found on the relevant issues.

The alternative to the short-form conclusion is a narrative conclusion, where the coroner explains what happened, although a short-form conclusion may have a narrative conclusion appended to it.[271] The Chief Coroner's *Guidance No 17: Conclusions: Short Form and Narrative*, indicated that 'wherever possible coroners should conclude with a short-from conclusion'.[272] The reason is that it has the advantage of simplicity, that it is accessible for the bereaved, the public and clerk for statistical purposes. Such statistics are often used to inform future healthcare provision.

Natural causes

A conclusion of 'natural causes' is given were a suspected 'unnatural' death is found at the inquest to be the result of a natural disease process without significant human intervention. At the inquest, other potentially causative matters will be investigated, such as whether a delay in ordering a CT scan had caused or materially contributed to the death of a child.[273] In 2018, a conclusion of natural causes made up 13% of all conclusions.[274]

Suicide

> Suicide is voluntarily doing an act for the purpose of destroying one's life whilst one is conscious of what one is doing, in order to arrive at a conclusion of suicide there must be evidence that the deceased intended the consequence of the act.[275]

Suicide can never be presumed,[276] and evidence that the deceased intended to take their own life is required. In the absence of a letter left by the deceased, circumstantial evidence can be used to draw an inference of an intention to end life. For example, whether the deceased may have

---

270 *R v HM Coroner for Inner London North District, ex p Thomas* [1993] QB 610 (also referred to as *R v Poplar Coroner, ex p Thomas*).
271 *R (on the application of P) v HM Coroner for the District of Avon* [2009] EWCA Civ 1367, 112 BMLR 77 at 28.
272 Chief Coroner's *Guidance No 17: Conclusions: Short Form and Narrative*, para 26.
273 *R v HM Coroner for Avon, ex p Smith* [1998] EWHC 174, (1998) 162 JP 403. This case actually arose out of the refusal of a coroner to hold an inquest on the basis that the death was the result of natural causes (a cerebella haematoma).
274 Ministry of Justice, Coroners Statistics Annual 2018, p 11.
275 *R v Cardiff Coroner, ex p Thomas* (1970) 3 All ER 469 at 472.
276 *R v Cardiff Coroner, ex p Thomas* (1970) 3 All ER 469.

anticipated being found before death occurred, or whether survival was unlikely, such as jumping from a high building. Therefore, before reaching a conclusion of suicide, a question that must be considered is 'whether other possible explanations were totally ruled out'.[277]

In *R (Maughan) v HM Senior Coroner Oxfordshire, the Chief Coroner as an Intervener and INQUEST as an Interested Party*[278] the Court of Appeal held that the civil standard of proof applies to finding of suicide, whether expressed as a short-form conclusion or a narrative conclusion. The Court of Appeal highlighted five reasons that the standard of proof should be the civil standard, including that since 1961 suicide has ceased to be a crime, that the inquest is primarily inquisitorial, and is not concerned to make findings of guilt or liability, and that the application of the civil standard to a conclusion of suicide expressed in a narrative conclusion would cohere with the standard applicable to other potential aspects of a narrative conclusion.[279]

Coroners rarely record a death as 'suicide', preferring 'the deceased took his or her own life, or killed him/herself'. A conclusion of suicide was found in 11% of all inquests in 2018; representing a relatively static trend.[280]

Accidental death/misadventure

There is some debate as to whether 'accidental death' and 'misadventure' are the same conclusions, although the majority of opinion is that it is a distinction 'without purpose or effect'.[281] 'Accidental' death is often used when the death results from an unintended act with unintended consequences. A conclusion of 'misadventure' is often used where a deliberate act has unintended consequences, for example, a patient who dies following an operation. Conclusions of death by accident or misadventure have been declining, from 47% of all conclusions returned in 1994 to 26% in 2018.[282]

A more important distinction is between accidental death/misadventure and death from natural causes in the medical context. This was considered in *R v HM Coroner for Birmingham and Solihull, ex p Benton*,[283] a case in which a child died in hospital following a bronchoscopy. The court made the following distinction in relation to healthcare deaths:

Natural Causes

The first is where a person is suffering from a potentially fatal condition and medical intervention does no more than fail to prevent that death. In such circumstances the underlying cause of death is the condition that proved fatal and in such a case, the correct conclusion would be death from natural causes. This would be the case even if the medical treatment that had been given was viewed generally by the medical profession as the wrong treatment. All the

---

277 *R v HM Coroner for the County of Essex, ex p Hopper* [1988] Crown Office Digest 7.
278 [2019] EWCA Civ 809.
279 *R (Maughan) v HM Senior Coroner Oxfordshire, the Chief Coroner as an Intervener and INQUEST as an Interested Party* [2019] EWCA Civ 809 at [74].
280 Ministry of Justice, Coroners Statistics Annual 2018, p 10.
281 *R v Portsmouth Coroners Court, ex p Anderson* [1987] 1 WLR 1640 as 1646 (obiter).
282 Ministry of Justice, Coroners Statistics Annual 2018, p 10.
283 (1997) 8 Med LR 362 at 366.

more so is the case where such a person is not treated at all, even if the failure to give the treatment was negligent.

Accident/Misadventure

Where a person is suffering from a condition which does not in any way threaten his life and such person undergoes treatment which for whatever reason causes death, then, assuming that there is no question of unlawful killing, the conclusion should be death by accident, misadventure.

Want of attention at birth

This is an ancient conclusion, which is a form of neglect. It is unlikely that such a conclusion would be given today.

Lawful/unlawful killing

A conclusion of unlawful killing includes murder and manslaughter, including:

1   wrongful act/constructive involuntary manslaughter; and
2   gross negligence manslaughter.

The standard of proof in unlawful killing is the criminal standard,[284] although practitioners should consider the instructive obiter comments of Lord Justice Davis on a civil standard of proof in *R (Maughan) v HM Senior Coroner Oxfordshire, the Chief Coroner as an Intervener and INQUEST as an Interested Party*. Unlawful killing is an infrequent conclusion in the coroners' court. However, the fact that the Crown Prosecution Service has decided not to prosecute,[285] or that the prosecution resulted in an acquittal, does not bar the possibility of such a conclusion in the coroners' court. A practitioner considering addressing a coroner on such a conclusion is advised to refer to a specialist criminal practitioner textbook.

Unlawful act manslaughter

The requirements for unlawful act manslaughter were set out by the Court of Appeal in *R v Inner South London Coroner, ex p Douglas-Williams*:[286]

1   there must be an unlawful act (in this case an assault);
2   that act must be dangerous in the sense that any reasonable and sober person would recognise that the assault exposed the victim to risk of some harm, albeit not necessarily serious harm; and
3   that the unlawful act caused death in the sense that it more than minimally, negligibly or trivially contributed to the death.

---

284 [2019] EWCA Civ 809 at [90]–[96]. *R v West London Coroner, ex p Gray* [1998] 1 QB 467.
285 See the inquest before the HM Coroner for Cardiff and the Vale of Glamorgan. A nurse administered an overdose of insulin causing death. The verdict of the coroner was that it was an unlawful killing, and the CPS indicated that it would review its decision not to prosecute. See news.bbc.co.uk/1/hi/wales/south_east/7967862.stm.
286 [1999] 1 All ER 344 at 350.

Gross negligence manslaughter

The requirements for gross negligence manslaughter were set out by the House of Lords in the criminal case of *R v Adomako*.[287] In *Adomako*, the defendant anaesthetist failed to notice that a tube supplying oxygen to the patient (who had been paralysed for the operation) had become disconnected from a ventilator during an eye operation. The disconnection lasted some six minutes, and the patient suffered a cardiac arrest from which he subsequently died. Two expert witnesses gave evidence for the prosecution. One described the standard of care by the defendant as 'abysmal'. The other stated that a competent anaesthetist should have recognised the signs of disconnection within 15 seconds, and that the defendant's conduct amounted to 'a gross dereliction of care'.

The House of Lords held that the requirements for gross negligence manslaughter are:

1   the existence of a duty of care;
2   a breach of that duty of care;
3   the breach caused the death of the deceased; and
4   a finding by the jury that the breach was 'gross' and consequently criminal.

Lord Mackay stated that a finding of gross negligence would depend upon the seriousness of the breach of duty committed by the defendant in all the circumstances in which the defendant was placed when it occurred. The jury needs to consider whether, having regard to the risk of death involved, the conduct of the defendant was so bad in all the circumstances as to amount to a criminal act or omission.[288]

Gross negligence manslaughter was considered by the Court of Appeal in the context of the coroners' court in *R v Inner South London Coroner, ex p Douglas-Williams*.[289] The Court of Appeal set out the requirements for a conclusion of killing by gross negligence manslaughter:

1   negligence consisting of an act or failure to act;
2   that negligence must have caused the death in the sense that it more than minimally, negligibly or trivially contributed to the death; and
3   the degree of negligence has to be such that it can be characterised as gross in the sense that it was of an order that merits criminal sanctions rather than a duty merely to compensate the victim.

Open conclusion

An open conclusion is a decision by the coroner or the jury that there is insufficient evidence to reach any of the short-form conclusions, or the evidence does not meet the required standard of proof for a short-form conclusion. Although an open conclusion reflects the fact that the exact circumstances of how the deceased came by their death remain unknown, it is preferable for a narrative conclusion to be given, setting out the facts

---

287 [1995] 1 AC 171.
288 *R v Adomako* [1995] 1 AC 171 at 187.
289 [1999] 1 All ER 344 at 350.

that have been determined. The Chief Coroner has stated that 'open conclusions are to be discouraged'.[290]

Stillbirth

This has been an uncommon conclusion in coroners' courts and in 2018, there were no conclusions recorded.[291] However, this is likely to change if proposed changes to the jurisdiction of coroners to investigate stillbirths is indicated.

Neglect

A finding of 'contributed to by neglect' may be attached to conclusions of natural causes, want of attention at birth, suicide and accident/misadventure, or could be included in a narrative conclusion. It is not a conclusion in itself. Many families want neglect to be considered during the inquest where the deceased died in contentious circumstances. On the other hand, some families want reassurance that nothing more could have been done by the healthcare team to prevent the deceased from dying. Neglect is not a common conclusion in inquests concerned with healthcare deaths. However, where a narrative conclusion is given, coroners can include failings that contributed to the death.

The leading case on neglect is *R v North Humberside Coroner, ex p Jamieson*.[292] Michael Jamieson was serving a long sentence of imprisonment. During his incarceration, Jamieson attempted suicide, and had received hospital treatment for depression. Whilst detained in the hospital wing, Jamieson exhibited worrying behaviour for some days and then committed suicide by hanging. The question for the Court of Appeal was whether the coroner had wrongly directed the jury not to consider whether his death had been caused or contributed to by a lack of care by the prison authorities who had placed Jamieson in a single cell in a prison hospital without special supervision.

The Court of Appeal held that, at its highest, the applicant's case suggested that the doctors and the prison authorities gave the deceased an opportunity to take his life. The court provided guidelines for the conduct of cases involving the possibility of neglect:[293]

> Neglect in this context means a gross failure to provide adequate nourishment or liquid, or provide or procure basic medical attention or shelter or warmth for someone in a dependent position (because of youth, age, illness or incarceration) who cannot provide it for himself. Failure to provide medical attention for a dependent person whose physical condition is such as to show that he obviously needs it may amount to neglect. So it may be if it is the dependent person's mental condition which obviously calls for medical attention (as it would, for example, if a mental nurse observed that a patient had a propensity to swallow razor blades and failed to report this propensity to a doctor, in a case where the patient had no intention to cause himself injury but did thereafter swallow razor blades with fatal results). In both cases the crucial consideration will be

290 Chief Coroner's *Guidance No 17*, para 68.
291 Ministry of Justice, *Coroners Statistics Annual 2018*.
292 [1995] QB 1.
293 *R v North Humberside and Scunthorpe Coroner, ex p Jamieson* [1994] 3 All ER 972 at 990–991.

what the dependent person's condition, whether physical or mental, appeared to be.

Initially, the *Jamieson* test was interpreted as requiring a complete absence of care, or the failure to take an obviously necessary step. The requirements were the need for basic medical attention to be obvious, the patient to be dependent on others to provide that attention, and a gross failure to provide or procure that attention.

In two cases following *Jamieson*, poor medical treatment and care was held not to satisfy these requirements. In *R v HM Coroner for Birmingham, ex p Cotton*,[294] the court held that where death resulted from a clinical judgment (wrong medical treatment), which might or might not be negligent, a conclusion of neglect could not be left to the jury. The issue arose again in *R v HM Coroner for Surrey, ex p Wright*,[295] which was an application for judicial review where an anaesthetist failed to maintain the deceased's airway during minor dental surgery. Tucker J held that a conclusion of neglect was not open to the coroner, despite the coroner's finding of fact that death resulted from a lack of care. Further, he held that neglect must be 'continuous or at least non-transient', and that was not an appropriate description of the negligent lack of care in this case.

Recent decisions indicate a widening of the *Jamieson* test, and that errors in diagnosis and treatment are capable of amounting to neglect. In *R (Davies) v Birmingham Deputy Coroner*[296] the court held that an error by a nurse in deciding that an inmate's condition did not require further assistance until the following day could amount to neglect. In *R (Nicholls) v Coroner for City of Liverpool*[297] the court considered the alleged failure of a police medical examiner to properly recognise the fact that the deceased had swallowed drugs, believed to be heroin. Sullivan J said:

> Notwithstanding [Counsel's] submission that neglect and negligence are two different 'animals', there is, in reality, no precise dividing line between 'a gross failure to provide ... basic medical attention' and a 'failure to provide ... medical attention'. The difference is bound to be one of degree, highly dependent on the facts of the particular case.[298]

Neglect does not need to be confined to the acts or omissions of one person; and acts of omissions by different individuals and systemic failures may combine to form a 'total picture that amounts to neglect'.[299] Neglect may also be a 'continuous sequence of shortcomings'.[300] Not every failure in treatment or care will amount to neglect and it will depend upon the facts and circumstances of the case. However, the failure must be a 'gross failure'. Matters that may amount neglect in healthcare settings include:

---

294 [1995] 160 JP 123.
295 [1997] QB 786.
296 [2003] EWCA Civ 1739.
297 [2001] EWHC Admin 992.
298 *R (Nichols) v Coroner for City of Liverpool* [2001] EWHC Admin 992 at [52], Sullivan J and Rose LJ agreed.
299 *R (on the application of S) v Inner West London Coroner* [2001] EWHC Admin 105 at paras 13 and 29; 61 BMLR 222.
300 *R v HM Coroner for Wiltshire, ex p Clegg* (1997) 161 JP 521.

1　the failure to monitor a patient's condition;[301]
2　the failure to provide effective medical treatment; [302]
3　the failure to properly recognise the deceased's medical condition;[303] and
4　the failure to take into account relevant and reasonably obtainable information in care and treatment.[304]

Neglect and causation

The original test in *Jamieson* was for a 'clear and direct' causal connection between the neglect and the death.[305] However, this is a difficult test to satisfy and on occasions the test has been modified by the courts.[306] In *R (on the application of Khan) v HM Coroner for West Herefordshire*, Richards J reviewed recent authorities on neglect and causation.[307] He concluded that it was sufficient to establish on the balance of probabilities that the conduct made a material contribution to death; it must be shown that care would have been rendered and that it would have saved or prolonged life[308] Neglect does not need to be the sole or predominant cause of death.[309]

Narrative conclusion

A narrative conclusion is the conclusion by a coroner or a jury on the main issues arising out of the circumstances by which the deceased came by his death and is often associated with enhanced *Middleton* inquests. There is no guidance for coroners on the form and content of a narrative conclusion, but the main issues arguably include the matters that caused or contributed to death, any systemic failings, and any relevant circumstantial matters in enhanced *Middleton* inquests.[310] A narrative conclusion in a *Middleton* inquest must be a 'judgemental conclusion of a factual nature, directly relating to the circumstances of death'.[311] However, the prohibition on expression of opinion on matters outside the statutory question and avoiding any criminal and civil liability remain. A narrative

---

301 *R v Inner London North Coroner, ex p Touche* [20001] EWCA Civ 383, [2001] 2 All ER 752.
302 *R v HM Coroner for Wiltshire, ex p Clegg* (1997) 161 JP 521.
303 *R v HM Coroner for Greater London (Inner West), ex p Scott* [2001] EWHC Admin 105, 165 JP 417.
304 *R v HM Coroner for Greater London (Inner West), ex p Scott* [2001] EWHC Admin 105, 165 JP 417.
305 *R v North Humberside and Scunthorpe Coroner, ex p Jamieson* [1994] 3 All ER 972 at 991.
306 See *R v HM Coroner for Coventry, ex p Chiefly Constable of Staffordshire* (2000) 164 JP 655; and *R (Nicholls) v HM Coroner for the City of Liverpool* [2001] EWHC Admin 922.
307 [2002] EWHC (Admin) 302, [2002] All ER (D) 68 (Mar).
308 *R (on the application of Khan) v HM Coroner for West Herefordshire* [2002] All ER (D) 68 (Mar) at 43(i).
309 *R (on the application of Commissioner of Police for the Metropolis) v HM Coroner for Southern District of Greater London* [2003] EWHC 1892 (Admin), CO/222/2003 at 57.
310 *R (on the application of Middleton) v HM Coroner for West Somerset* [2004] 2 AC 182.
311 *R (on the application of Middleton) v HM Coroner for West Somerset* [2004] 2 AC 182 at [37].

conclusion is not required if a short-form conclusion encapsulates the jury's conclusions on all the main issues.[312]

Narrative conclusions may also be (and often are) used in traditional *Jamieson* inquests,[313] particularly where death results from more than one cause.[314] The type of narrative findings that may be made is uncertain.[315] However, in a *Jamieson* inquest, the narrative conclusion should be a brief, neutral, factual statement that does not include any judgment or opinion.[316]

It is for the coroner to determine how best to elicit the jury's conclusion on the central issues in the inquest,[317] and in healthcare deaths it is likely that the jury will require assistance with complex medical evidence to ascertain the issues that must be decided. Some coroners use questionnaires prepared by the coroner and the advocates to elicit the conclusions of the jury, although care must be taken to ensure that the jury are not restricted in their answers. It is helpful if advocates prepare a draft questionnaire in advance of the hearing that can be refined as the inquest progresses.

Reports to prevent future deaths

Schedule 5 of the CJA 2009 and regs 28 and 29 of the Coroners (Investigation) Regulations 2013 provide coroners with the duty to make reports to a person or organisation where the coroner believes that action should be taken to prevent the recurrence of fatalities. In *Middleton* it was stated that the coroners procedural obligation under Art 2 is most effectively discharged if the coroner publicly announces an intention to issue a report to prevent future fatalities and the broad terms of the contents of the report.[318]

The Chief Coroner's *Guidance No 5: Reports to Prevent Future Deaths* indicates the purpose of such reports:

> Broadly speaking, reports should be intended to improve public health, welfare and safety. They should not be unduly general in their content; sweeping generalisations should be avoided. They should be clear, brief, focussed, meaningful and, wherever possible designed to have practical effect.[319]

The coroner can issue a Regulation 28 Report in relation to a matter revealed in any part of the investigation and it must only be made once the coroner has considered all the documents, evidence and information

---

312 For example, in *Middleton* a short-form verdict of suicide was insufficient as the jury were unable to express its conclusion on the central issues of whether the deceased should have been recognised as a suicide risk and whether appropriate precautions should have been taken to prevent him taking his own life: *R (on the application of Middleton) v HM Coroner for West Somerset* [2004] UKHL 10, [2004] 2 AC 182.

313 *R (on the application of Longfield Care Homes) v HM Coroner for Blackburn* [2004] EWHC 2467 (Admin).

314 *R (Longfied Care Homes) v HM Coroner for Blackburn* [2004] EWHC 2467 (Admin) at 28–31.

315 *R (on the application of Hurst) v Commissioner of Police for the Metropolis* [2007] UKHL 13, [2007] 2 AC 189.

316 *Jamieson* at [24].

317 *R (on the application of Middleton) v HM Coroner for West Somerset* [2004] 2 AC 182 at [36].

318 *R (on the application of Middleton) v HM Coroner for West Somerset* [2004] 2 AC at [38].

319 Chief Coroner's *Guidance No 5: Reports to Prevent Future Deaths*, para 5.

that in the opinion of the coroner are relevant to the investigation.[320] This is usually at the conclusion of the inquest, but can be at the conclusion of the investigation if an inquest is not necessary.

The person or organisation that receives a report is under a duty to provide the coroner with a written response within 56 days,[321] although an extension of time may be granted.[322] The response must contain details of any actions that have been, or will be, taken, or an explanation as to why no action is proposed. If a person or organisation fails to respond, the coroner should make reasonable attempts to follow the matter up. However, there is no sanction for a failure to respond. In such circumstances, coroners may retain this information and should a death occur in similar circumstances, there is evidence of a failure to take action.

The coroner must send a copy of the report to the Chief Coroner, any interested person and any person who the coroner believes may find it useful or of interest,[323] which arguably includes the media. The Chief Coroner publishes the reports on his website (redacted as necessary) and they can be viewed by category in chronological order. Unfortunately, at present there is no key word search facility.

Closure of the inquest, media, and publicity

At the conclusion of the inquest, the coroner must send to the Registrar of Deaths a certificate of all the relevant information concerning the death for the death to be registered. The coroner's officer will often assist with information in relation to collecting the final death certificate.

Representatives of the media frequently attend inquests, often the initial and final days. At the conclusion of the inquest, they will usually ask whether the family or the hospital/GP would like to make a statement for publication. It is advisable to have discussed this with the client before the conclusion of the inquest so that a decision can be made whether a statement will be given by the family/hospital staff/GP or their legal representatives, and the latter is usually preferable. A statement can be prepared for the final day, or the media can be asked to contact the solicitor's office the following day. If relevant, the hospital or GP should consider whether to make an apology (and often this is done at the start of an inquest); and outline any changes in practice to prevent deaths in similar circumstances.

FUNDING AND THE RECOVERABILITY OF COSTS

Caron Heyes

When it comes to obtaining legal representation, the family will have to consider carefully how they will meet the costs. As the hearing is an inquisitorial process and there is no notion of winning or losing, the costs

---

320 Coroners (Investigations) Regulations 2013, SI 2013/1629, reg 28(3).
321 Coroners (Investigations) Regulations 2013, SI 2013/1629, reg 29(4).
322 Coroners (Investigations) Regulations 2013, SI 2013/1629, reg 29(5).
323 Coroners (Investigations) Regulations 2013, SI 2013/1629, reg 29(6).

of having legal representation are generally not recoverable unless the representation is deemed to have advanced a wider civil action. The options to fund the case are, in short:

1   legal help funding for preparation for an inquest;
2   exceptional funding from the Legal Aid Agency for provision of advocacy services;
3   the client privately funds the case;
4   the deceased had legal expenses insurance that will cover the costs of attending the inquest;
5   CFA funding;
6   pro bono.

Inquests are costly hearings to prepare for and run, and are very time consuming, often over a very short space of time. Moreover, the likely cost of inquest representation is unpredictable at the outset of the matter. For most families the costs present an insuperable barrier to obtaining representation and deciding how to meet the costs of an inquest is a difficult issue for the family.

Public funding can only be obtained for advocacy at inquests deemed to engage Art 2 of the ECHR, or which have a wider public interest. Thus it must be possible to demonstrate an arguable case that the state has been in breach of its substantive duty to protect life, ie a *Middleton* inquest. Even then, public funding is not guaranteed. Obtaining that funding is an uphill struggle and is rarely granted. Once granted it can be withdrawn at any time and it is unlikely to cover even core costs of attending the inquest.

The alternative to legal aid funding is primarily CFA funding. This can only come into play where a wider civil claim is envisaged, and the work done at inquest is expected to be recovered as part of the overall investigatory costs for that civil claim. There is a range of case law on this, the most recent having been heard in 2018. Solicitors can ask the family to privately fund the inquest. Where there is no civil claim to be pursued then privately financing legal services is the family's only option, unless they can persuade a charitable organisation to provide pro bono inquest services. The British Legion has an inquest service that assists with providing representation and assistance at inquests, as does AvMA.

Public funding

Generally

If you have already obtained an investigative certificate for a civil claim and there is also to be an inquest it will not cover representation at the inquest itself but will cover all the usual investigative stages that must be gone through to prepare for an inquest, so long as these are actions that would have been taken to investigate the claim itself. Funding for representation at the inquest itself is only available under exceptional funding.

Legal help has been retained to provide advice and assistance for the preparatory work associated with the inquest, including preparing submissions to the coroner. However that does not generally provide funding for representation at the inquest itself, for the following reasons:[324]

> ... because an inquest is a relatively informal inquisitorial process ... There are no defendants, only interested persons, and witnesses are not expected to present legal arguments. An inquest cannot determine civil rights of obligations or criminal liability, so Article 6 ECHR is not engaged.

The 'Lord Chancellor's Exceptional Case Funding Guidance (Inquests)'[325] provides that legal aid funding is likely to be awarded for inquests where there has been a non-natural death or suicide of a person detained by police, in prison or in a mental health unit. When assessing means they only now take into account the means of the applicant and not the whole family, and discretion has been given the legal aid cases workers to waive the means test if Art 2 of the ECHR is engaged.

At the time of writing the government is considering the outcome of its consultation looking into the provision of legal aid for inquests. It has yet to report but may lead to further changes to the legal aid funding system. If it does, it is unlikely to introduce funding for cases not engaging Art 2 and therefore will exclude the majority of inquests arising out of suspected medical negligence.

Exceptional funding is available if it can be shown that the inquest is to be the way in which the state complies with its Art 2 obligation to investigate cases where the state has been in breach of its substantive duty to protect life, ie Article 2 of the ECHR is engaged and representation of the family is required to discharge the state's procedural obligations.

This obligation does not arise routinely in clinical negligence inquests. It is generally the case that inquests raising allegations around medical care will not trigger the state's Art 2 procedural duty, primarily because the case would not involve allegations of a systemic nature. However there have been cases, such as *R (Letts) v The Lord Chancellor*[326] that have held that: (a) the suicide of an involuntary psychiatric patient, depending on the facts, was capable of triggering the investigative duty under Art 2 of the ECHR, irrespective of whether the state, arguably or otherwise, was in breach of its substantive duties; and (b) that same duty may arise in other circumstances including the suicide of a voluntary psychiatric patient.

There is a second option to obtain legal aid funding pursuant to the Legal Aid, Sentencing and Punishment of Offenders Act 2012, s 10(4). This grants the Lord Chancellor the power to direct funding for advocacy where the applicant qualifies for legal aid, and there is a wider public interest determination that in the particular circumstances of the case, the provision of advocacy for the individual at the inquest is likely to produce significant benefits for a class of person other than that applicant and members of the applicant's family. That discretion will only be exercised if it can be established that funded representation is necessary to assist

---

324 'Lord Chancellor's Exceptional Funding Guidance (Inquests)' (June 2018), para 4, see   https://assets.publishing.service.gov.uk/government/uploads/system/uploads/attachment_data/file/715441/legal-aid-chancellor-inquests.pdf.
325 See   https://assets.publishing.service.gov.uk/government/uploads/system/uploads/attachment_data/file/715441/legal-aid-chancellor-inquests.pdf.
326 [2015] EWHC 402 (Admin).

the coroner to investigate the case effectively, and establish the facts, not just that there is wide public interest in the hearing itself.

Applying for exceptional funding for provision of advocacy at hearings

The application must provide evidence of the following:

1   the applicant's relationship with the deceased. Only family members of the deceased are eligible to apply for legal aid funding;
2   why representation is necessary to enable the deceased's family to play an effective part;
3   why the family cannot participate effectively without advocacy services;
4   why the family could not attend and understand proceedings without advocacy services;
5   why the family would not be able to raise any particular matter of concern with the coroner without advocacy services;
6   an explanation as to why the issues of medical, legal or factual complexity cannot be explained by the available witnesses such as the pathologist and treating doctors without the input of legal representation;
7   that there has been no family involvement in other investigations;
8   that there are no other represented agencies who might be able to present the same point of view as that of the relatives;
9   that the family or a family member may be at risk of prosecution if they do not have representation;
10   an estimate of costs based on the anticipated number of pre-inquest review and inquest hearing dates.

The application for exceptional funding should be made using a CIV ECF1 (Application for Exceptional Case Funding) form and is submitted to the Exceptional Case Funding Team.[327]

Refusal of public funding

It is possible to ask for reconsideration of the refusal by a Legal Aid Agency senior policy adviser. If the application is still refused, even with coronial support, the only option is to challenge by judicial review.

Extent of funding

Funding is for inquest advocacy against a budget submitted by the legal advisor. The legal advisor's budget should cover advocacy and immediate inquest preparation only. Other investigative work has to be financed separately, probably under the legal help scheme if there is no civil claim. Once funding has been granted it will contain a binding costs limitation and that limitation cannot be exceeded without prior agreement from the Legal Aid agency. Updated estimates for additional funding should be done before further work outside of the binding limitation is carried out, and can be applied for using paper form CIV APP8.

---

327 13th Floor, 102 Petty France, London SW1H 9AJ.

Unlike legal aid for normal case work, no funding certificate is issued and payment is made on submission in a letter setting out the finalised details of the claim. The legal advisor is paid as a one-off grant less a contribution assessed from relatives. That contribution is for the solicitor to collect from the family.

Payment rates

The remuneration rates are set out in the Civil Legal Aid (Remuneration) Regulations 2013[328] in the main but there are circumstances in which remuneration may be paid in accordance with the Criminal Defence Service (Very High Cost Cases) (Funding) Order 2013, Sch 2, Pt 2[329] for instance where the inquest is going to last a very long time, or there is an unusually high volume of papers. In some cases the length and complexity of the inquest may justify payment of counsel at a higher rate.

The funding will generally not cover attendance of a senior solicitor and counsel, but would allow a junior fee earner to attend with counsel.

The commission will consider any representations made on this point at the time of the application.

More detailed information is found on the www.gov.uk website in an 'Inquests – Exceptional Cases Funding – Provider Pack'.[330]

Contribution

Pursuant to the Civil Legal Aid (Financial Resources and Payment for Services) Regulations 2013,[331] reg 44, where funding is granted to provide advocacy at an inquest into the death of a member of the client's family, the Agency may require a financial contribution from the represented party if their monthly disposable income exceeds £315 (note this sum may change if the regulations are amended). Thus, although the grant of exceptional funding is not means tested, the applicant's financial circumstances are taken into account. It is therefore important to set out:

- expenses already incurred;
- the applicant's financial circumstances;
- the level of the proposed contribution;
- any hardship that contribution may cause to the applicant;
- the identity of the relatives; and
- the interests of the relatives in participating in and being represented at the inquest.

The contribution is collected by the interested parties' solicitor and deducted from the payment to that solicitor made by the LAA.

Legal expenses insurance (LEI)

Many families have legal expenses insurance attached to a housing contents policy. In the writer's experience, most policies do not

---

328 SI 2013/422.
329 SI 2013/2804.
330 See   https://www.gov.uk/government/publications/legal-aid-exceptional-case-funding-form-and-guidance.
331 SI 2013/480.

specifically include inquest representation, and sometimes specifically exclude representation at an inquest. However, where a policy will cover the investigations for a civil claim, and if it can be demonstrated that participation in and attendance at the inquest is required to fully investigate the claim (and even save the insurer money), then cover for the inquest may be obtained by negotiation with the LEI provider. It will generally not be available for inquests where no civil claim is intended. The policy needs to be reviewed in each case.

Conditional fee agreements (CFAs)

There are cases where it would appear that there may be a civil claim arising out of the wrongful death of the deceased. In those circumstances, solicitors can take on the case under a conditional fee agreement. No special CFA is required for a civil claim including an inquest. Note that the case law as to recoverability of inquest costs assumes that only costs incurred to progress the civil claim are recoverable. It is therefore necessary to be very clear when advising a client that if there are aspects of the inquest that do not progress the claim (for example, the family is seeking answers to questions that are about conduct of clinicians and that have no bearing on the alleged negligence, or expert evidence is obtained for the inquest not later relied on for the civil claim) the costs of those aspects will remain payable by the family.

Recovering costs of the inquest after the conclusion of the civil claim

This section only applies where the lawyer has acted for a family in an inquest as part and parcel of pursing a civil claim for damages, and where the civil claim is successful.

Section 51 of the Supreme Court Act 1981 (SCA 1981) provides the court with a wide discretion to award costs that it has judged as being 'of and incidental to' court proceedings. It is worth noting s 51(1) and (3) here:

51 Costs in civil division of Court of Appeal, High Court and county courts

(1) Subject to the provisions of this or any other enactment and to rules of court, the costs of and incidental to all proceedings in –
(a)   the civil division of the Court of Appeal;
(b)   the High Court; and
(ba)   the family court;
(c)   the county court,
shall be in the discretion of the court.

...

(3) The court shall have full power to determine by whom and to what extent the costs are to be paid.

Thus in principle, the costs of attending an inquest where the lawyer has a valid retainer with the client that allows the lawyer to charge for the costs of providing legal services, are recoverable as costs 'incidental to' civil proceedings. The text of *Re Gibson's Settlement*

Trusts[332] provides that to recover costs incidental to civil proceedings the work done must:

1   have been of use and service in the claim; and
2   relevant to the matters in issue in the claim; and
3   attributable to the defendant's conduct.

All three tests must be established and each test is of equal significance.

Case law has also reinforced the principle that costs of attendance at inquests are capable of being recovered as costs incidental to subsequent civil proceedings.

In *King v Milton Keynes General NHS Trust*[333] the courts accepted the approach to costs applied in *Bowbelle*,[334] ruling they were recoverable in the civil claim.

The case of *Roach v Home Office*,[335] followed. Here the Home Office sought to overturn those earlier decisions and argued costs incurred in a prior proceeding (in this case the inquest) could not be recovered in later proceedings. The court held that the position is governed by the SCA 1981, s 51, and CPR 44.4(1) and the inquest costs were recoverable. The impact of CPR 44.4(1) was noted to restrict the recovery of costs which have been unreasonably incurred or are unreasonable in amount. CPR 44.3(5) also applies, so that costs that are disproportionate could be disallowed or reduced even if reasonably or necessarily incurred.

A recent case of *Douglas v Ministry of Justice*[336] raised this issue again in the context of the defendant having made an admission of liability pre-inquest. The defendant said it had made a full unqualified admission of liability to every claim on the claim form (including breaches of ECHR) and therefore the claimant did not need representation at the inquest to investigate the negligence claim and the costs were irrecoverable. The claimant sought to rebut that argument by saying there was good reason for the claimant to need representation and there was still a question of the amount of damages to be awarded. The Senior Courts Costs Office ('SCCO') held that some of the costs were recoverable, as the claimant should be entitled to recover the reasonable and proportionate costs of gathering evidence that would allow her to present her case against the defendant, subject to the proviso that the costs should not be dealt with as if no admission had been made and the work had to have sufficient connection to the claim against the defendant. The court also held that hindsight should not be used when applying the *Gibson* principles (above).

Breaking down the allocation of costs, the court held:

1   costs of attending the inquest in order to participate in obtaining disclosure and evidence from the defendant is recoverable;
2   costs of attending the inquest in order to participate in obtaining disclosure and evidence from any third party is not recoverable;
3   costs of attributing blame between multiple participants in the inquest are not recoverable;

---

332 [1981] Ch 179.
333 (13 May 2004) SCCO AGS 04000350.
334 *Deborah Jane Ross v Owners of Ship 'Bowbelle'* [1997] EWCA Civ 1343 (26 March 1997).
335 [2009] EWHC 312 (QB) (25 February 2009).
336 [2018] Inquest LR 71.

4   costs of participating in general procedural matters of the inquest
are not recoverable, although making submissions to secure a verdict
are (but note *Lynch v Chief Constable of Warwickshire*[337]). Costs of
attending the inquest in order to participate in obtaining disclosure
and evidence from the defendant is recoverable;

5   costs of attending the summing up and waiting for a jury verdict are
not recoverable, but attending for the actual verdict is;

6   all other costs of the inquest are recoverable depending on the extent
to which the work done on a given day contributed to securing
disclosure or witness evidence from the defendant.

When claiming costs at the end of the civil claim, it would be helpful to see
the role of lawyers in attending an inquest fall into two equal parts: first
assisting the coroner; and second obtaining evidence from the defendant
that is necessary to pursue the civil claim. Costs arising out of obtaining
evidence from the defendant to pursue the claim are recoverable inter-
partes. So for example, a lawyer may attend an inquest where the family
instruct them to ask questions on an issue that it is clear will not advance
a civil claim. Those costs will most likely not be recoverable.

During the course of conduct of a civil claim that includes attendance at
an inquest, it is advisable to make a careful contemporaneous note of why
the work being carried out is relevant to the claim. Instructions should
be provided to experts and/or counsel that make clear whether they have
been instructed for the purposes of the civil claim or the inquest. The
family should be clearly advised from the outset that all of the costs of the
inquest may not be recovered and whether they will be expected to meet
those costs in full or part from any damages they recover.

As *Douglas* illustrates, there is always a risk that the defendant
may admit liability prior to the inquest hearing. If that happens the
justification for attending the hearing will need to be carefully considered
with the family, and the risk that if attendance does not advance the case
then the costs will not be recoverable inter-partes.

POST-INQUEST REMEDIES[338]

Decisions of coroners can be challenged by way of judicial review and
under s 13 of the Coroners Act 1988. Both procedures can be used,
provided the qualifying criteria for each procedure are satisfied.

Judicial review

The coroner's powers are set out in statute and secondary legislation,
and the office of the coroner performs public duties. Therefore, coronial
decisions and proceedings are amenable to judicial review. The people
that are likely to have sufficient standing to bring judicial review
proceedings are the 'interested persons', and any individual/organisation
whose conduct is called into question at the inquest. In the healthcare

---

337 [2014] Inquest LR 247.
338 This section written by Linda Jacobs.

context, this will include the family of the deceased, the hospital and/or GP, and healthcare staff.

In order to bring judicial review proceedings, there must be a public law error or failing by the coroner. The grounds for challenging include:

1   A decision that was unlawful because the coroner did not have the power to make the decision (*ultra vires*). The starting point is to consider the CJA 2009, the Coroners (Investigation) Regulations 2013 and the Coroners (Inquests) Rules 2013.
2   To identify the provision under which the purported decision was made.
3   A decision that was irrational (*Wednesbury* unreasonable[339]). This is a decision that is so perverse that no reasonable coroner properly directing him/her self to the law to be applied could have reached.
4   An error of law. Errors of law include misinterpreting a statute or secondary legislation, taking irrelevant considerations into account, failing to take relevant considerations into account, and failing to follow the proper procedures required by law.
5   An act was incompatible with a Convention right.[340] In coronial law, this is likely to include Art 2 and Art 8 of the ECHR.
6   The proceedings were conducted in breach of procedural fairness or natural justice. These principles include the right to an unbiased decision maker and a right to a fair hearing.

The types of decisions by coroners that have been the subject of judicial review proceedings include refusing to hold an inquest, failing to order a post-mortem examination, wrongfully limiting the scope of the inquest, failing to leave a particular conclusion to the jury or an error of law in directing the jury on a conclusion, failing to obtain expert evidence, failing to hear legal submissions on behalf of interested persons, and insufficiency of investigation.

Judicial review is a discretionary remedy. Therefore, even if there is an error in the decision-making process, the administrative court retains discretion as to whether it should grant the relief sought. Following a successful judicial review, the administrative court can quash the decision of the coroner (quashing order) and order a new inquest, possibly before another coroner. Alternatively, the court may impose a prohibiting order, preventing a coroner from acting unlawfully or issue a mandatory order, to compel the coroner to act in a particular way. In addition, or instead of the above orders, the administrative court might make a declaration.

Procedural points

Judicial review proceedings are subject to the CPR 54. A claim should normally comply with the pre-action protocol for judicial review, must be made promptly, and in any event within three months of the date when the grounds of the claim first arose.[341] Early consideration must be given to the cost of such proceedings, including the costs of any intervening party.

---

339 *Associated Provincial Picture House Ltd v Wednesbury Corp* [1948] 1 KB 223.
340 Human Rights Act 1998, s 6(1).
341 CPR 54.5.

A key decision in coronial proceedings is whether to make the application before the inquest has concluded. The administrative court is able to consider urgent applications, and Form N463 'Application for urgent consideration of judicial review claim' must be completed. The coroner or administrative court may grant a stay of the inquest for the application to be heard in the administrative court.[342] A decision to bring judicial review proceedings whilst the inquest is ongoing is likely to be finely balanced: should the inquest continue, although potentially defective in some way with a risk of a re-hearing; or should proceedings be interrupted, causing a delay and possible difficulties for all the persons involved?

In *R (Khan) v HM Coroner for West Hertfordshire*, the coroner rejected a submission to leave conclusions of unlawful killing and death contributed to by neglect to the jury. The coroner adjourned the inquest to enable the deceased's wife to challenge that ruling. Richards J dismissed the application for judicial review and opined:

> In adjourning the inquest to enable his ruling to be challenged, the coroner acted with great fairness and with a view to avoid the unsatisfactory position which can arise where an inquest conclusion is challenged after the event, on the grounds that the coroner [sic] erred in the conclusions he left or did not leave to the jury. The course adopted, however, has disadvantages, since four months will have elapsed since the jury will have heard the evidence. It is highly undesirable for there to be a long break at such a stage in proceedings. A further disadvantage is that the court did not have the benefit of the coroners' summing up as a means of putting the evidence in perspective. That suggests that the court ought to entertain considerable caution about entertaining a challenge to an interlocutory ruling of this kind.[343]

Coroners Act 1988, s 13

Section 13 of the Coroners Act 1988 provides an alternative route to challenging inquest proceedings. Unlike judicial review proceedings, there is no time limit for bringing proceedings. It is therefore particularly suitable if fresh evidence is discovered at a later time. Early consideration must be given to costs, as the court has a power to award costs on appeal.[344]

An application under s 13 requires the permission (fiat) of the Attorney-General. The application for a fiat should be addressed to the Attorney-Generals' Office.[345] If permission is granted, an application can be made by way of a Part 8 claim form to administrative court. The grounds of challenge[346] are that:

1   the coroner refused to hold an inquest (s 13(1)(a));
2   an inquest was held, but by reason of fraud, rejection of evidence, irregularity of proceedings, insufficiency of inquiry, the discovery of new evidence or otherwise, it is necessary or desirable in the interests of justice that another inquest should be held (s 13(1)(b)).

---

342 CPR 54.10.
343 [2002] All ER (D) 68 (Mar).
344 Supreme Court Act 1981, s 51 and CPR 54.10(2)(e).
345 Attorney-General's Office, 5–8 The Sanctuary, London SW1P 3JS; tel: 020 7271 2492; website: www.atorneygeneral.gov.uk.
346 Coroners Act 1988, s 13(1).

If one of the grounds is made out, the Attorney-General and the administrative court will consider whether it is necessary or desirable in the interests of justice that the inquest conclusion should be quashed and another inquest ordered. The court does not have the power to quash part of the Record of Inquest or substitute its own conclusion.

The 'interests of justice' is a broad concept, demonstrated by *R (on the application of Sutovic) v Northern District of Greater London Coroner*:[347]

> Notwithstanding the width of the statutory words, its exercise by courts shows that the factors of central importance are an assessment of the *possibility* (as opposed to the probability) of a different conclusion, the number of shortcomings in the original inquest, and the need to investigate matters raised by new evidence which had not been investigated at the inquest.

However, the possibility of a different conclusion is not necessarily conclusive.[348] Other matters that the administrative court will take into account when considering whether to order a new inquest is the interest of the people who will be affected by the decision. Although the administrative court will consider the possibility of a different conclusion at a new inquest, it must not usurp the functions of the coroner and/ or jury by reaching its own conclusion.[349] If there is a problem with the conclusion, for example, a potential conclusion should not have been left to the jury, or the jury direction on the conclusion were incorrect, the administrative court may quash part of the conclusion.

Civil proceedings

A civil claim can arise out of a wrongful death. The evidence given at an inquest should assist both parties in assessing the strength of their respective cases. Even if the family are not represented at the inquest, a representative of their legal team should attend and take notes of the evidence, particularly the evidence given by the witnesses for the hospital or GP surgery. If the coroner has recorded the inquest, a copy of the recording or written transcript can be obtained upon payment of a fee.

The coroners' court is inquisitorial. Therefore, the parties to a civil claim are not bound by the findings of the coroner, and a finding that death was due to natural causes does not preclude a civil claim. The coroner's conclusion is not admissible within civil proceedings. Consequently, if the conclusion was death by natural causes contributed to by neglect, this cannot be pleaded as proof of the fact that there was neglect. However, the transcript is a record of the evidence given by the witnesses at the inquest, and can be put in cross-examination if a witness gives inconsistent evidence during a subsequent civil trial.

Coroners must provide interested persons with any document put into evidence at the inquest, which includes statements read into evidence under the Coroners (Inquests) Rules 2013, r 23, and any document referred to during the inquest. Coroners must retain documents in

---

347 [2006] EWHC 1095 (Admin), [2006] 5 WLUK 443, [2006] Inquest LR 104.
348 See *Sutovic* at [94] and [98] and *R (on the application of Aineto) v Brighton and Hove Coroner* [2003] EWHC 1896 (Admin) at [12].
349 *R (Khan) v HM Coroner for West Hertfordshire* [2002] EWHC Admin 302 at [45].

connection with an inquest or post-mortem examination for at least 15 years, unless a court directs otherwise.[350]

Criminal proceedings

Consideration of whether to prosecute an individual for a criminal offence arising out of the death usually occurs before the inquest. This is because the CJA 2009, Sch 1, paras 1 and 2 provide that if a coroner is informed that a person may be charged/has been charged with certain offences the investigation must be suspended.

The possibility of criminal proceedings may need to be reconsidered after the inquest if the coroner or jury return a conclusion of unlawful killing, and in such circumstances coroners refer the matter to the Director of Public Prosecutions. In *R v DPP, ex p Manning and Melbourne*,[351] the administrative court considered the case of a person who died in prison custody whilst restrained by prison officers. The inquest jury returned a conclusion of unlawful killing but a prosecution did not follow the inquest. The court held that where 'an inquest following a proper direction to the jury culminates in a lawful conclusion of unlawful killing implicating a person who, although not named in the conclusion, is clearly identified, who is living and whose whereabouts are known, the ordinary expectation would naturally be that a prosecution would follow.' The court further held that it would expect the Director of Public Prosecutions to give reasons if a prosecution did not taken place in such circumstances.[352]

In *R v Bawa-Garba (Hadiza)*,[353] the Court of Appeal noted that Dr Hadiza Bawa-Garba and Nurse Isabel Amaro were convicted of gross negligence manslaughter following the death of a six-year old boy, Jack Adcock. The inquest was adjourned part-heard as Dr Bawa-Garba and Nurse Amaro were charged and tried at the Crown Court in Nottingham.

Disciplinary/professional misconduct proceedings

The evidence given at an inquest may result in internal disciplinary proceedings initiated by the hospital or GP surgery, and coroners can refer matters as part of their report to prevent future deaths. Although internal disciplinary proceedings may take place before the inquest, the employer may wish to hear all the evidence, including any expert evidence before proceedings are fully considered.

Professional disciplinary proceedings may take place before the inquest. However, after an inquest, coroners and members of the public may make a complaint about an individual to any of the professional bodies, including the General Medical Council, the General Dental Council and the Nursing and Midwifery Council. If disciplinary proceedings take place after the inquest, the professional bodies may take evidence given at an inquest into account when considering whether the healthcare professional is guilty of misconduct. An inquest may also lead to an

---

350 Coroners (Investigations) Regulations 2013, SI 2013/1629, reg 27(1).
351 [2001] QB 330 at [30].
352 *R v DPP, ex p Manning and Melbourne* [2001] QB 330 at [30]. Also see *R (on the application of Da Silva) v DPP* [2006] EWHC 3204 (Admin), CO/8477/2006 for a discussion about giving reasons in relation to the death of Jean Charles de Menezes.
353 [2016] EWCA Crim 1841.

investigation by the Care Quality Commission. An example is the death of David Gray, who died when a locum doctor from Germany supplied by Take Care Now providing out-of-hours cover for GPs, administered a dose of morphine that was ten times the normal therapeutic dose.[354]

---

354 Care Quality Commission, *Investigation into the out-of-hours service provided by Take Care Now* (July 2010). See www.cqc.org.uk/_db/_documents/20100714_TCN_Summary.pdf.

Chapter 20

Limitation

Lisa Sullivan

INTRODUCTION

Limitation is entirely a creature of statute. It has existed since 1623. Its purpose is to prevent prejudice to the defendant in having to face stale claims. The majority of clinical negligence actions will fall under the Limitation Act 1980. The relevant provisions have been the subject of much judicial consideration at appellate level in recent years; resulting in changes to and clarification of the application of the relevant provisions.

The importance of understanding limitation in clinical negligence cases cannot be underestimated. Issues of limitation arise in clinical negligence cases more frequently than in other areas of personal injury. There are many reasons why a claimant might not initially realise that they have a claim, ranging from not realising that the outcome of treatment was worse than it should have been because the injury is not apparent for a number of years, to trust in the medical profession that what happened was just one of those things.

THE PERIOD OF LIMITATION

Most clinical negligence actions are actions for negligence or breach of duty where the damages claimed consist of or include damages for personal injuries and are therefore subject to a three-year limitation period, by virtue of s 11 of the Limitation Act 1980. The limitation period starts to run from the date the cause of action accrues, or the date of knowledge of the claimant (as defined in s 14 of the Act) if later. It can be disapplied at the court's discretion under s 33 of the Act. Claims resulting in death are dealt with under s 12 of the Act and have a few differences which are set out in the section on Fatal Accidents below.

The limitation period provided under s 11 of the Limitation Act does not extinguish the claimant's claim. It provides a defence to it. That has two consequences. The first is that a defendant can agree to waive that defence in advance and the second is that they can chose not to rely on it. In the case of waiver, the defendant must expressly declare that the limitation period will not be relied upon in order for the waiver to be effective. If a claim form has been issued very shortly after the limitation period has expired, a defendant will sometimes decide not to pursue the defence, based on the likely success of an application to extend time, or argument about date of knowledge.

Although most will involve a personal injury, a clinical negligence action is not necessarily an action for personal injuries. It may be that the only claim is for financial loss, as where a patient is negligently told not to work any longer. If that was the case, the limitation period would not be three years under s 11, but would be a six-year period under s 2 (if the claim was brought in tort) or s 5 if brought in contract. In either case, the limitation period starts to run when the cause of action accrues. Where the damage is latent, the period may be extended to three years after the relevant knowledge is acquired under s 14A of the 1980 Act, subject to a 15-year longstop from the date of negligence. The provisions as to knowledge for latent damage are essentially the same as under s 14.

WHAT AMOUNTS TO A PERSONAL INJURY ACTION?

'Personal injuries' are defined by the interpretation section of the 1980 Act, s 38, as including 'any disease and any impairment of a person's physical or mental condition'.

A claim in which the negligence does not cause personal injury, even if it involves consideration of injuries, is not a personal injury action for these purposes. So the following situations have been found not to be claims for personal injury:

In *Ackbar v C F Green & Co*,[1] it was held that a claim against an insurance broker for failing to obtain cover for the claimant was not a claim for damages for personal injuries, although the claim in fact arose out of the claimant's having suffered personal injuries.

Where an injured party claimed under the Third Parties (Rights against Insurers) Act 1930 against the insurers of his employers, who had been wound up, this was held by the Court of Appeal in the context of pre-action disclosure not to be a claim in respect of personal injuries (*Burns v Shuttlehurst Ltd*[2]).

A claim against a solicitor for not pursuing a clinical negligence action would not be a claim in respect of personal injuries. In *Broadley v Guy Clapham & Co*,[3] it appears to have been accepted without argument that a six-year period applied.

In *Pattison v Hobbs*,[4] the Court of Appeal held that where, following an allegedly negligently performed vasectomy, damages were claimed only for the cost of raising a healthy child, the action was not one which included a claim for personal injuries.

A claim against employers for failing to advise of the possibility of getting benefits for injury suffered during employment was not a personal injury action (*Gaud v Leeds Health Authority*[5]).

---

1   [1975] QB 582.
2   [1999] 1 WLR 1449.
3   [1994] 4 All ER 439, CA.
4   (1985) Times, 11 November.
5   (1999) 49 BMLR 105, CA.

But where the negligence is a cause of the personal injury, even if it is not the direct cause, it is a personal injury action. In *Norman* v *Aziz*,[6] the Court of Appeal held that an action against the owner of a motor vehicle for permitting someone to drive it uninsured, the driver then injuring the claimant, was an action in respect of personal injuries and so subject to a three-year limitation period.

Sometimes it may not be clear if an undisputed consequence is to be regarded as an injury or not; for example, there is judicial authority to support the proposition that an unwanted pregnancy is an 'injury', whereas, if the pregnancy was welcome, it is not an injury.

In *Walkin v South Manchester Health Authority*,[7] the Court of Appeal held that a claim for an unwanted pregnancy following a failed sterilisation and for the consequent costs involved in raising the unplanned child was a claim for 'damages in respect of personal injuries', and it was not possible for the claimant to abandon a claim for personal injury, ie the claim for compensation for the unwanted pregnancy, and in that way to assert a six-year period of limitation as for a claim simply for economic loss. In the circumstances of this particular case the decision can be readily understood because the claimant had already issued, but not served, a writ in the usual form before the expiry of the three-year period. It was only when she realised that a second writ would be outside that period (but within the six-year period) that the claim was reduced to one for economic loss only. However, it is to be noted that Roch LJ said that he had some difficulty in perceiving a normal conception, pregnancy and the birth of a healthy child as 'any disease or any impairment of a person's physical or mental condition' in cases where the only reasons for the pregnancy and subsequent birth being unwanted were financial. He also reserved the question of the proper limitation period in cases of failed male sterilisation because in those circumstances there would be no personal injury to the claimant. Neill LJ also reserved the question whether any personal injury at all would be suffered where a woman who desired to have a child became pregnant as a result of a failed vasectomy. This decision was followed in *Godfrey v Gloucestershire Royal Infirmary NHS Trust*.[8]

In *Rothwell v Chemical and Insulating Co Ltd*,[9] it was held that the development of pleural plaques as a result of exposure to asbestos did not amount to a personal injury. Pleural plaques, although a physical change to the lungs as they are fibrous thickening of the pleural membrane, do not, save for exception circumstances, cause any symptoms or any adverse effect on health. They were therefore held not to amount to damage.

In the dyslexia case of *Phelps v Hillingdon London Borough Council*,[10] held that the prolongation of a congenital defect (here dyslexia) could amount to a personal injury.

---

6   [2000] PIQR P72.
7   MLC 0731, [1995] 1 WLR 1543.
8   [2003] MLC 1010.
9   [2007] UKHL 39.
10   MLC 0228, [1999] 1 WLR 500, CA, on appeal [2000] 3 WLR 776, HL.

Assault

A quick note on claims for assault: this may arise in the clinical negligence context as the result of a procedure being undertaken without proper consent from the patient or inappropriate examination amounting to an assault.

Before 2008, a distinction was drawn between actions for personal injury arising out of assault and those arising out of negligence.[11] Since the House of Lords decision in *A v Hoare*,[12] this distinction is no longer relevant. Actions for personal injury arising out of assault also fall within s 11 of the Act and are subject to a three-year (extendable) limitation period. When does the limitation period begin?

Normally, the limitation period begins when the cause of action accrues (ie when negligent conduct gives rise to injury) subject to the claimant's date of knowledge.

Capacity

Time for limitation will not begin to run if, at the time the cause of action arises (when the negligent conduct has given rise to injury), the claimant is under a disability (s 28 of the Act). Section 38 of the Act defines persons under a disability as a child (not yet 18) or a person who lacks capacity to litigate within the meaning of the Mental Capacity Act 2005. For a detailed discussion of whether a person lacks capacity see Chapter 10.

The limitation period does not start to run until the claimant ceases to be under a disability, so when a claimant turns 18, or regains capacity. Once that occurs, the limitation period starts to run from the date of gaining capacity as if that was the date on which the cause of action arose.

If a claimant loses capacity after the cause of action arises (a supervening disability), the limitation period is not stopped from running, but the disability should be taken into account on a s 33 application. See *Kirby v Leather*[13] and *Rogers v Finemodern Ltd*.[14]

Deliberate concealment

Under s 32(1)(b) of the Act, deliberate concealment of relevant facts by a defendant may operate to delay the commencement of the limitation period; see *Williams v Fanshaw Porter Williams*.[15] By s 32(2), a *deliberate* commission of a breach of duty in circumstances in which it is unlikely

---

11 The leading case prior to 2008 was *Stubbings v Webb* [1993] AC 498, HL. That was a claim brought by a woman who was abused by her family before she was 15. She suffered psychological damage but did not bring a claim until she was 30. It was held that assault claims were subject to the non-extendable six-year limitation period in s 2 of the Act rather than s 11 and therefore her claim was statute barred. The difficulty of this distinction was demonstrated in *Seymour v Williams* [1995] PIQR P470, CA, where a claim against an abusive father was statute barred under s 2 of the Act, but claims against the mother, who had not been abusive, but had known of the abuse and done nothing to protect her child, was allowed to continue under s 11.

12 [2008] UKHL 6.

13 (1965) 2 QB 367.

14 [1999] All ER (D) 1193.

15 [2004] EWCA Civ 157.

to be discovered for some time equates with deliberate concealment (see *Cave v Robinson Jarvis and Rolf*[16]).

KNOWLEDGE

Section 14 of the Limitation Act 1980 defines the necessary knowledge:

(1) Subject to subsection (1A) below, in sections 11 and 12 of this Act references to a person's date of knowledge are references to the date on which he first had knowledge of the following facts —
(a)   that the injury in question was significant; and
(b)   that the injury was attributable in whole or in part to the act or omission which is alleged to constitute negligence, nuisance or breach of duty; and
(c)   the identity of the defendant; and
(d)   if it is alleged that the act or omission was that of a person other than the defendant, the identity of that person and the additional facts supporting the bringing of an action against the defendant;
and knowledge that any acts or omissions did or did not, as a matter of law, involve negligence, nuisance or breach of duty is irrelevant.

Knowledge can be actual knowledge of the claimant or it can be constructive knowledge. Section 14(3) sets out the test for constructive knowledge:

(3) For the purposes of this section a person's knowledge includes knowledge which he might reasonably have been expected to acquire —
(a)   from facts observable or ascertainable by him; or
(b)   from facts ascertainable by him with the help of medical or other appropriate expert advice which it is reasonable for him to seek;
but a person shall not be fixed under this subsection with knowledge of a fact ascertainable only with the help of expert advice so long as he has taken all reasonable steps to obtain (and where appropriate, to act on) that advice.

Difficulty with knowledge of the identity of the defendant is unlikely to arise in a medical claim, though it is conceivable that it might prove difficult, for example, to identify the GP who treated. If the wrong GP has been sued, the mistake could probably be corrected pursuant to the CPR 19.2, 19.5 or 17.4. In *Gregson v Channel Four Television Corpn*,[17] the court said, echoing the previous law, that the CPR 19.5 applied where the application was to substitute a new party for a party who was named in the claim form in mistake for the new party, and the CPR 17.4(3) applied where the intended party was named in the claim form, but there was a genuine mistake as to the name of the party and no-one was misled. The court said there was no significant conflict between the two rules. In this case CPR 17.4 applied: it was not a question of substituting a new party, and the judge's discretion in favour of the claimant had been correctly exercised.

Actual knowledge

The claimant has to *know* that he has suffered a *significant* injury that is *attributable* to the alleged negligent act or omission. It is expressly

16   [2003] 1 AC 384, HL.
17   (2000) Times, 11 August, CA.

provided that knowledge of *fault*, ie that the relevant act or omission was negligent, is irrelevant (s 14(1)).[18]

'Know'

What amounts to 'knowledge' of the facts? Must a claimant know for certain, or is a lesser level of knowledge enough? It is clear that certainty is not required and mere suspicion is not enough, but is a belief enough?

In *Davies v Ministry of Defence*,[19] May LJ held that:

> 'knowledge' is an ordinary English word with a clear meaning to which one must give full effect: 'reasonable belief' or 'suspicion' is not enough.

In *Halford v Brookes*,[20] Donaldson MR distinguished *Davies* as an exceptional case where, despite the claimant's initial belief that his dermatitis was attributable to the act or omission of an employee, he received medical and legal advice, which he accepted, that it was not attributable to the act or omission of the employer. He held that 'knowledge' means 'know with sufficient confidence to justify embarking on the preliminaries to the issue of a writ, such as submitting a claim to the proposed Defendant, taking legal and other advice and collecting evidence'. On that basis, he held that 'suspicion, particularly if it is vague and unsupported, will indeed not be enough, but reasonable belief will normally suffice.'

These two approaches were considered in *Nash v Eli Lilly & Co.*[21] The Court of Appeal said that there was in fact no conflict between the two approaches and that:

> Knowledge is a condition of mind which imports a degree of certainty and ... the degree of certainty which is appropriate for these purposes is that which, for the particular claimant, may reasonably be regarded as sufficient to justify embarking upon the preliminaries to the making of a claim for compensation such as the taking of legal or other advice.

> Whether or not a state of mind for these purposes is properly to be treated by the court as knowledge seems to us to depend, in the first place, upon the nature of the information which the claimant has received, the extent to which he pays attention to the information as affecting him, and his capacity to understand it. There is a second stage at which the information, when received and understood, is evaluated. It may be rejected as unbelievable. It may be regarded as unreliable or uncertain. The court must assess the intelligence of the claimant; consider and assess his assertions as to how he regarded such information as he had; and determine whether he had knowledge of the facts by reason of his understanding of the information.

In the clinical negligence context, it is not easy to see why embarking on the preliminaries to the making of the claim for compensation, ie going to see a solicitor, implies knowledge on the part of the claimant. The claimant may go to see a solicitor – in fact often does – for the very

---

18   This means, among other things, that where one expert reports that there is no cause of action and later another says the opposite, that does not mean that the limitation period begins only with the second report (*Jones v Liverpool Health Authority* [1996] PIQR P251, CA).

19   (26 July 1985, unreported), CA (Civil Division) Transcript No 413 of 1985.

20   [1991] 1 WLR 428 at 443.

21   [1993] 1 WLR 782, MLC 0021.

reason that they do not know where they stand or where the truth lies. The claimant may be asking the solicitor to seek clarification of their lack of understanding of what happened.[22] On the other hand, the court did envisage the possibility that a particular claimant might have been taking the view that, although they had received information on which knowledge could be based, they needed expert confirmation before their belief could attain that degree of firmness to amount to knowledge. At the other end of the spectrum there may be a claimant who has a firm belief that their condition is attributable to an act or omission of the defendant, but that belief is incorrect.

The issue of what amounts to 'knowledge' was revisited by the Supreme Court in *AB v Ministry of Defence*.[23] In a majority decision, the decision of Donaldson MR was endorsed. The degree of confidence required is that the belief is held 'with sufficient confidence to justify embarking on the preliminaries to the issue of a writ, such as submission the claim to the proposed Defendant, taking legal and other advice and collecting evidence'. It was however recognised that it does not automatically follow that by the date a claimant first takes legal advice they will have acquired the requisite knowledge. The same goes for instructing experts; the court has to have regard to the confidence with which a claimant has held the belief. Where an expert is giving assistance as to facts required by s 14, for example advising they have a medical condition of which they were previously unaware, that is different to an expert providing evidence to substantiate a claim. Prior to the former, a claimant is unlikely to have sufficient belief, prior to the latter they may well do.

It will be a matter for decision upon the facts of the individual case whether expert confirmation was required for knowledge to be had. *Spargo v North Essex District Health Authority*[24] is an example of a case where the Court of Appeal held, not unreasonably, that the judge's finding that expert confirmation had been needed could not be supported.[25] In *Spargo*, the claimant was wrongly committed to a mental hospital with a mistaken diagnosis of permanent brain damage. She had always taken the view that she had been wrongly committed. That was her view without the benefit of medical evidence, despite her treating doctors maintaining their diagnosis was correct. That was her clear view when she attended her solicitors. The following is said, in the context of knowledge of attributability (for which see below) about the level of knowledge needed:

> A plaintiff has the requisite knowledge when she knows enough to make it reasonable for her to begin to investigate whether or not she has a case against the defendant. Another way of putting this is to say that she will have such knowledge if she so firmly believes that her condition is capable of being attributed to an act or omission which she can identify (in broad terms) that she goes to a solicitor to seek advice about making a claim for compensation.

---

22 At another point in the judgment, the court said a claimant would have knowledge where he had sought advice *and taken proceedings* [emphasis added]. This case should not be taken as authority for the proposition that merely going to a solicitor for advice about a possible claim constitutes knowledge (and see below the commentary on the case of *Sniezek*).

23 [2012] UKSC 9.

24 MLC 0651, [1997] 8 Med LR 125.

25 So, too, *Skitt v Khan and Wakefield Health Authority* [1997] 8 Med LR 105.

On the other hand, she will not have the requisite knowledge if she thinks she knows the acts or omissions she should investigate but in fact is 'barking up the wrong tree': or if her knowledge of what the defendant did or did not do is so vague or general that she cannot fairly be expected to know what she should investigate, or if her state of mind is such that she thinks her condition is capable of being attributed to the act or omission alleged to constitute negligence, but she is not sure about this, and would need to check with an expert before she could be properly be said to know that it was.

On the other hand, in *Ali v Courtaulds Textiles Ltd*,[26] the Court of Appeal, reversing the trial judge, held that the claimant, who had taken all reasonable steps to obtain expert knowledge, could not have known that his deafness was attributable to noise rather than age until he got his expert report.

In *Rowbottom v Royal Masonic Hospital*,[27] the Court of Appeal held, by a majority, that a claimant who was alleging that he had suffered injury from a failure to administer antibiotics could only have had the relevant knowledge when he received his second expert report. That report told him that lack of antibiotics was responsible for his injury; up till then he had thought it was failure to install a drain. Two other cases at first instance on this issue of no knowledge until expert report received are *Mirza v Birmingham Health Authority*[28] and *Burton v St Albans and Hemel Hempstead NHS Trust*.[29]

In *Sniezek v Bundy (Letchworth) Ltd*,[30] another case that focused on the meaning of the word 'know', the court equated with knowledge a firm, consistent and convinced belief on the part of the claimant, despite repeated contrary medical advice, that his respiratory problems were caused by his work conditions. On the one hand, the court put much emphasis on the third of Brooke LJ's principles in *Spargo*,[31] the first paragraph set out above, to the effect that a claimant with a firm belief who goes to a solicitor to seek advice about making a claim for compensation has knowledge (unless – principle four – she is in fact barking up the wrong tree; or her knowledge remains vague, so that she cannot be fairly expected to know what should be investigated; or she believes but is not sure and needs to check with an expert). On the other hand, all three judges deprecated the mountain of past authority analysing and re-analysing the ordinary word 'know'. Simon Brown LJ suggested a simple distinction between a claimant who was a mere believer and one who was a firm believer, whilst recognising that the decision as to which side of the line the claimant fell would be a difficult one. Bell J similarly distinguished between a firm belief, which a claimant retained whatever expert advice he received, and a claimant who believed that he may have or even probably had a significant injury attributable to his working conditions but was not sure and felt it necessary to have expert advice on those questions. Judge LJ clearly supported a simple test. He said that the question was one of fact in each case. He doubted whether any considerable legal refinement was necessary or appropriate. He thought

---

26   [1999] Lloyd's Rep Med 301.
27   MLC 0553, [2002] Lloyd's Rep Med 173.
28   [2001] MLC 0412.
29   [2002] MLC 0856.
30   [2000] PIQR P213, [2000] MLC 0225 (Simon Brown, Judge LJJ, Bell J).
31   [1997] PIQR P235.

that five or ten minutes of argument should enable the judge to make up his mind rather than a long trawl through the authorities, treating a question of fact as a question of law.

In *AB v Ministry of Defence,* Lord Walker referred to the case *of Driscoll-Varley v Parkside Health Authority*[32] where a claimant thought injury to her leg had been caused by a surgeon's negligence during an operation but later discovered the real cause was removal of the leg from traction during subsequent treatment. That was said to be an example of a claimant 'barking up the wrong tree' and therefore not having requisite knowledge until she learned of the issue with traction. However, Lord Walker referred to that as a 'rather marginal example of barking up the wrong tree'.

Once knowledge has been obtained, it cannot be lost. In *Young v Catholic Care (diocese of Leeds),*[33] the claimant was sexually abused as a child and had subsequently blocked out the memory. He made a claim for psychiatric injury and it was held that he must have known that he suffered injury whilst the abuse was happening and therefore his date of knowledge was whilst the abuse was occurring – his understandable psychological reaction was something to take into account under s 33 of the Act.

So what is the requisite level of knowledge?

Firm belief can amount to knowledge in appropriate circumstances. It can even amount to knowledge despite contrary negative expert advice in appropriate circumstances. But it needs to be firm enough to amount more or less to an enduring conviction, and although going to a solicitor would normally suggest the necessary knowledge, the inference does not inexorably follow (note that in *Sniezek,* Judge LJ explicitly said that nothing in the authorities or in the Act supported a conclusion that time automatically started to run against a claimant who had taken legal advice). The circumstances in which firm belief will amount to knowledge depend on the particular facts of the case and do not call for further defining. It is however worth bearing in mind that once a claimant has been to see a solicitor, it will be more difficult to deny actual knowledge.

Adult claimants with capacity in birth injury cases

In *Appleby v Walsall Health Authority,*[34] Popplewell J found that a claimant born in 1971 with cerebral palsy affecting only motor control did not acquire actual knowledge until 1996. Even if his mother had actual knowledge years earlier, that knowledge could not be imputed to him.[35] A similar issue arose in *Whiston v London Strategic Health Authority.*[36] The claimant was born in 1974 and again suffered with cerebral palsy affecting only motor control. The claimant was 21 in 1995. He issued proceedings in 2006. It was argued by the defendant that the claimant

---

32 [1991] 2 Med LR 346.
33 [2008] UKHL 6.
34 [1999] Lloyd's Rep Med 154, MLC 0020.
35 Note that the reasoning in this case on constructive knowledge is no longer good law following *Adams v Bracknell* BC.
36 [2010] EWCA Civ 195.

had actual knowledge as he knew that the disability was linked to the circumstances of his birth; his parents had told him his disability was due to forceps delivery, but had said nothing about the competence of the obstetrician using them (which was one of the allegations of negligence). The claimant, on the other hand, said that he had got on with life and never thought of himself as disabled, he had gone to school on a scholarship and to Cambridge University, where he got his undergraduate degree and a PhD in mathematics. He had only investigated further when his condition deteriorated, within three years of issue. The claimant was found not to have actual knowledge. He was however found to have constructive knowledge (see further below).

'Significant' injury

Section 14(2) of the Act defines what 'significant injury' is:

> For the purposes of this section an injury is significant if the person whose date of knowledge is in question would reasonably have considered it sufficiently serious to justify his instituting proceedings for damages against a defendant who did not dispute liability and was able to satisfy a judgment.

The wording of the section raises the question of whether this is a subjective test, an objective test or a combination of the two; the consideration is whether the actual claimant (with their knowledge) would reasonably have considered it sufficiently serious.

If it is partly subjective, is account taken of the claimant's personal characteristics (his intelligence, his character etc) and if so, how much? The House of Lords in *A v Hoare*[37] considered the issue and (although doubted by Baroness Hale) held that it was a purely objective test. The test is applied to what the claimant knows of their injury, probably including their constructive knowledge, but the test is whether a reasonable person with that knowledge would have considered the injury sufficiently serious to justify instituting proceedings. The personal characteristics of a claimant, including their injury, are irrelevant to that question.[38]

So when, objectively, is an injury significant? Sometimes there may be argument about what constitutes an injury.

Although even minor injuries are usually enough to be considered serious, *Harding v People's Dispensary for Sick Animals*[39] is an example of a claimant reasonably believing for a considerable time after an accident (some 18 months) that her back and leg pain were not significant, because she reasonably thought it was a temporary sprain of the back. In *Field v British Coal Corpn*,[40] the claimant suffered from slight hearing loss which he believed was due to a build-up of wax and infection – essentially an intermittent condition which was temporary in nature. It was held that given that knowledge (no further knowledge was to be imported to him), a reasonable person would not have considered the injury sufficiently serious. In fact, Mr Field had noise-induced hearing loss for about five years before he knew he had such hearing loss.

---

37 [2008] UKHL 6.
38 See Lord Hoffmann at para 34.
39 [1994] PIQR P270, CA.
40 [2008] EWCA Civ 912.

A patient is unlikely to succeed in an argument that, although she knew of a minor (but still significant) injury, time did not run in respect of a deterioration of, or more serious consequence of, that same original injury of which she did not know (*Roberts v Winbow*[41]). If the claim is not for an original injury but for an exacerbation of that injury, the question then is: When did the claimant first have knowledge that the exacerbation was significant?[42]

Where a patient knows that he is suffering adverse effects from a drug prescribed by his doctor, he cannot argue that that is not a significant injury because the benefit he is getting from it balances out the equation.[43]

Attributability

What is it that the claimant has to *know*? He has to know that the significant injury is reasonably *attributable* to the act or omission alleged to constitute negligence. So, in addition to the requirement that he should *know* that he has suffered a *significant injury*, he must also be able to identify a particular act or omission, on which he will later rely as being negligent, as a reasonably possible cause of his injury. This question of attributability has often been the central issue in the reported cases. With what degree of precision must he be able to identify the relevant act or omission?

Knowledge of 'negligence' not necessary

The Act provides in s 14(1) that the claimant's knowledge of whether or not the relevant act or omission constituted a breach of duty is not relevant; in other words he does not need to know that the defendant has been negligent.[44]

Omission cases

In the case of an omission to treat, it is clear that he needs to know not merely that treatment did not take place, but that there was or may well have been a missed opportunity for him to benefit from treatment.

Smith v West Lancashire Health Authority,[45] was a case where the allegation was one of omission rather than commission (ie that the doctors had failed to do something they should have done, rather than had done something they should not have done). The patient was treated conservatively at A&E in 1981 for a simple fracture at the base of a ring finger. After two months he was told they would have to operate. He ended up with a disability and lost his job in 1989. Having consulted a solicitor, he obtained a positive medical report in 1991. The court applied the principle of specificity: the question was when did the patient know, or when should he have found out, that he had suffered a significant injury from the act or omission alleged to constitute negligence? Clearly

---

41 MLC 0074, [1999] Lloyd's Rep Med 31, CA.
42 *McManus v Mannings Marine Ltd* [2001] EWCA Civ 1668.
43 *Briggs v Pitt-Payne and Lias* MLC 0073, [1999] Lloyd's Rep Med 1, CA.
44 See *Fennon v Anthony Hodari & Co* [2000] All ER (D) 1917.
45 [1995] PIQR P514, CA.

the omission consisted in not operating immediately. The Court of Appeal, reversing the trial judge, said that the patient did not know that was the relevant omission until he got the expert report, nor was there any reason for him to have found it out earlier. He knew he had not had an operation at the outset, but 'he did not know that his problem was in any way associated with the absence of an operation at that time'. The important point is that, although this patient ended up with a disability, there was no reason for him to suspect it was attributable to anything done or not done by the doctors (remember that knowledge of fault is irrelevant). This reasoning was endorsed in *Forbes v Wandsworth Health Authority*,[46] where a delay of less than 24 hours in operating (therefore an omission rather than a positive act) caused the claimant's leg to be amputated. The claimant could not be expected to know that the injury was attributable to the omission without medical advice as it was a matter of medical science of which he was unaware. Also relevant is *Hayward v Sharrard*[47] (patient unaware that an X-ray had been misinterpreted as showing no fracture), and *James v East Dorset Health Authority*,[48] where Sedley LJ said:

> I do not believe that in enacting section 14 Parliament intended to reward those alert to assume that every misfortune is someone else's fault and to place at a disadvantage those who do not assume the worst when there is nothing to alert them to it.

In *Oakes v Hopcroft*,[49] the claimant, having suffered an accident at work, settled her claim on the basis of a report from the defendant doctor. Years later, after continuing disability and then a further report from a different specialist, she sued the first expert for negligent diagnosis. The court, reversing the judgment below, said that she had not known of the essence of her complaint, nor could have been expected to discover it, until she received the second report.[50]

Attributable to what?

How precisely must the act or omission be known? With what degree of precision must the claimant be able to identify the act or omission? Is it enough to know that the operation or treatment has resulted in an injury, or must the patient know more precisely how it happened?

Two cases which raised concerns that claimants would be fixed with knowledge of attributability when in fact they did not actually have knowledge were *Broadley v Guy Clapham & Co*[51] and *Dobbie v Medway Health Authority*.[52] In fact, they did not pose such problems for the patient as some people thought at the time. In *Broadley*, the claimant knew she

---

46   [1997] QB 402, MLC 0671, [1996] 7 Med LR 177, CA.
47   MLC 0061, [1998] JPIL 326.
48   [1999] MLC 0129.
49   [2000] Lloyd's Rep Med 394, CA.
50   In *Smith v National Health Service Litigation Authority* [2001] Lloyd's Rep Med 90, [2001] MLC 0286, Andrew Smith J held that a claimant born in 1973 with a congenitally displaced hip had not known that her disability might be reasonably attributable to an omission in her medical treatment (failure to examine her properly as a baby) until 1994 (however the claim failed on the facts).
51   [1994] 4 All ER 439, MLC 0043, [1993] 4 Med LR 328, CA.
52   [1994] 1 WLR 1234, MLC 0038, [1994] 5 Med LR 160.

had come out of an operation on her knee with an unlooked-for result, namely a foot-drop.

Legatt LJ said it was not necessary that the claimant should have knowledge of the *mechanics* of damage; it was enough that soon after the operation she knew something was wrong with her foot which was not an inevitable consequence of it, and therefore she should reasonably have made inquiries. Had she done so she would have been told a nerve and been damaged in a way that was not inevitable. It is the knowledge of the injury to the nerve that was the relevant knowledge.

In *Dobbie*, the claimant went into hospital to have a lump removed from her breast. The surgeon, wrongly believing the lump to be cancerous, removed the whole breast. The claimant had not given her consent for the breast to be removed. Soon after the operation she knew that her breast had been removed and that the breast they had removed had turned out to be non-cancerous. She was led to believe that the practice was usual and proper. She argued that she didn't have the requisite knowledge of attributability because she did not know that excision of the lump for microscopic examination could and should have preceded removal of the breast (which was the essential allegation of negligence). The judge in fact found that she knew that she had been admitted for excision of the lump, that the breast had been removed, that the lump was not malignant and that the decision to remove the breast had been taken before microscopic examination had been carried out. It was held that she knew of her injury and that it was attributable to the removal of her breast. The fact that she did not know that the removal of the breast before the microscopic examination had been undertaken was blameworthy was irrelevant. The difficulty seen with this decision is that Mrs Dobbie acquired knowledge before she found out that the treatment was unjustified – she believed that it had been proper treatment. But she did have a significantly worse outcome than she had expected and one can hardly quarrel with the argument that she should have investigated the matter given the disparity in outcome to what was expected. It would be different if she had consented to the possibility of the removal of her breast in advance of the operation. Then she would not have known that the outcome was worse than anticipated.

In *Spargo v North Essex District Health Authority*,[53] the Court of Appeal reversed the trial judge's finding that the plaintiff did not have actual knowledge more than three years before the commencement of proceedings. The brief facts were that at the age of four in 1975 the plaintiff was confined to a psychiatric hospital on a mistaken diagnosis of permanent brain damage. Her difficulty on limitation was that, when cross-examined, she said that she knew that she had suffered in hospital for a long time and that she firmly believed that that was because of the mistaken diagnosis. In her mind, all her suffering was attributable to the mistaken diagnosis of organic brain damage, and that was her clear view when she first saw her solicitor in October 1986. The trial judge held that this was one of those cases, foreseen by the Court of Appeal in *Nash v Eli Lilly*,[54] where the patient's belief about the attributability of her problem cannot amount to knowledge until an expert report confirms her

53 [1997] MLC 0651.
54 [1993] 1 WLR 782, MLC 0021.

view. The Court of Appeal disagreed: this plaintiff on her own evidence was convinced that the diagnosis of brain damage had caused her injury (through being confined as a result for a substantial period of time to a mental hospital). She had that conviction as early as 1986 at which time she also had a report on an intelligence test she had taken which indicated that the original diagnosis had been mistaken. The trial judge had actually found that 'she was clear in her mind that the connection was there between the disturbances and what she had suffered'. In those circumstances, the decision of the Court of Appeal which held that she had actual knowledge no later than 1986 is readily understandable.

In coming to the decision, Brooke LJ reviewed the preceding case law, including *Dobbie* and set out the following principles, which have been followed in subsequent cases:

(1)   The knowledge required to satisfy section 14(1)(b) is a broad knowledge of the casually relevant act or omission to which the injury is attributable;

(2)   'Attributable' in this context means 'capable of being attributed to', in the sense of being a real possibility;

(3)   A plaintiff has the requisite knowledge when she knows enough to make it reasonable for her to begin to investigate whether or not she has a case against the defendant. Another way of putting this is to say that she will have such knowledge if she so firmly believes that her condition is capable of being attributed to an act or omission which she can identify (in broad terms) that she goes to a solicitor to seek advice about making a claim for compensation;

(4)   On the other hand she will not have the requisite knowledge if she thinks she knows the acts or omissions she should investigate but in fact is barking up the wrong tree; or if her knowledge of what the defendant did or did not do is so vague or general that she cannot fairly be expected to know what she should investigate; or if her state of mind is such that she thinks her condition is capable of being attributed to the act or omission alleged to constitute negligence, but she is not sure about this, and would need to check with an expert before she could properly be said to know that it was."

This was followed in the non-medical case of *Hallam-Eames v Merrett Syndicates*,[55] which was a decision upon one of the economic claims in the Lloyd's Names saga. The limitation provisions of s 14A of the Limitation Act 1980, inserted by the Latent Damage Act 1986, are to all intents and purposes identical with the personal injury provisions of s 14. In short form, the allegation was that the defendants had negligently written contracts for the claimants which involved them in substantial liabilities without having the material on which to assess the potential liabilities. The act was identified as the act that was 'causally relevant' for the purpose of an allegation of negligence so that the claimant 'must have known the facts which can fairly be described as constituting the negligence of which he complains'.

It was therefore held that it was not enough for the claimants to have known that the contracts had been written, because they also needed to know that they had been written at a time when the potential liabilities of the parties were impossible to assess. *Dobbie* was analysed on the same principle, the act which would constitute negligence was not that

---

55   MLC 0703, [1996] 7 Med LR 122.

the breast had been removed but that a *healthy* breast had been removed. That was the essence of her complaint, and she had knowledge of those broad facts.

Rowbottom v Royal Masonic Hospital,[56] is an example of a claimant who is 'barking up the wrong tree'. There will be no knowledge of attributability if the claimant has not identified the facts which would constitute negligence. The relevant act constituting negligence was a failure to administer antibiotics. The Court of Appeal held he could only have had the relevant knowledge when he received his second expert report. That report told him that lack of antibiotics was responsible for his injury; up till then he had thought it was failure to install a drain. He had been 'barking up the wrong tree'.

In *Harrison v Isle of Wight NHS Primary Care Trust*[57] the claimant had a shoulder surgery from which her recovery was not as expected. She thought that too much bone had been removed during the operation but following investigation with medical experts and lawyers was advised that the amount of bone that had been taken would be Bolam defensible. By the time of that advice, limitation extensions had been agreed with the defendant and a letter of claim had been sent and letter of response received. She then had surgery to her shoulder by her treating doctors who found that her deltoid muscle was not attached to the acromion. A claim was later brought on that basis. Limitation was raised and the question was in essence: *what* was it that the claimant had to have knowledge of; that something done at the operation had caused injury or the particular mechanism by which the injury had occurred? *Driscoll-Valley* and *AB v Ministry of Defence* were considered.

The judge found the 'essence of the claim' was the attachment of the deltoid muscle. It was noted that replacing the excess bone would not resolve the damage. Although the claimant suspected the operation was in some way the cause, the claimant and her advisors were initially 'barking up the wrong tree'.

That does not necessarily sit easily with the dicta of Legatt J in *Broadley* that that claimant need not know the mechanics of the damage. However in *Broadley* the relevant knowledge was that the nerve was damaged; she did not need to know the mechanics of *how* the nerve was injured and similarly here the knowledge was of injury to the deltoid muscle not how it was injured. Nonetheless that is a fairly fine distinction and it is perhaps illustrative of the fact that these are marginal, difficult, cases.

Constructive knowledge

If the claimant does not have actual knowledge, they may still be fixed with constructive knowledge. The burden of proof is on the defendant to prove the date of constructive knowledge. Section 14(3) provides:

> For the purposes of this section a person's knowledge includes knowledge which he might reasonably have been expected to acquire—
> (a) from facts observable or ascertainable by him; or
> (b) from facts ascertainable by him with the help of medical or other appropriate expert advice which it is reasonable for him to seek;

---

56 MLC 0553, [2002] Lloyd's Rep Med 173.
57 [2013] EWHC 422 (QB).

but a person shall not be fixed under this subsection with knowledge of a fact ascertainable only with the help of expert advice so long as he has taken all reasonable steps to obtain (and, where appropriate, to act on) that advice.[58]

For a number of years, there were two lines of cases coming to different conclusions as to what, if any, individual characteristics of the claimant can be taken into account in deciding what knowledge a person might reasonably be expected to acquire. In other words, is this an objective or subjective test of reasonableness?

The first line of cases followed *Nash v Eli Lilly & Co.*[59] The test was said to be to enquire what the particular claimant should have observed or ascertained, asking of him no more than is reasonable. In deciding what is reasonable, the particular position, circumstances, character and intelligence of the individual claimant should be taken into account.

The second followed *Forbes v Wandsworth Health Authority.*[60] The test was said to be an objective one, and the character and intelligence of the claimant were therefore irrelevant.

The House of Lords has now clarified the issue and the test is an objective one.

In *Adams v Bracknell Forest Borough Council,*[61] the claimant brought a claim against his local education authority for negligently failing to help him with dyslexia between 1981 and 1988. He was born in March 1972. He issued the claim in June 2002, aged 30. There were no useful medical notes extant, nor, it appears, much in the way of useful evidence any teacher could give so long after the event. The claimant said he first knew he probably was dyslexic when he was speaking to a friend at a dancing class in November 1999, who happened to be an educational psychologist. She said she thought he was dyslexic and, as a result, he went to see a solicitor in January 2000. An expert confirmed severe dyslexia and severe psychological symptoms including panic attacks and social phobia, consequent upon undiagnosed and untreated learning difficulties. Mr Adams, an intelligent man, had not sought any advice about his literacy problems because he wanted to hide them. He did not want people to think he was stupid. He spoke to his doctor about the psychological problems but not about his inability to read and write. Yet, said Lord Hoffmann, 'on a social occasion on 19th November 1999 he spilled out the entire story to Ms Harding, a lady nearly 20 years his senior whom he says he hardly knew and had no reason to believe had any expertise in the matter. After talking to her the first thing he did was to consult a solicitor'. The trial judge had found that Mr Adams had known since childhood that he had psychological problems and that they were 'linked in some way to his problems with reading and writing'. But he did not know that the education authority could have helped him. It was this finding that led both courts below to find that he did not have

---

58   In *Henderson v Temple Pier Co* [1998] 1 WLR 1540, the Court of Appeal held that the claimant was fixed with the knowledge that her solicitors should have acquired earlier about the identity of the defendants. This, incidentally, was the case the absence of knowledge of which by counsel led the Court of Appeal to utter harsh admonitions in *Copeland v Smith* [2000] 1 WLR 1371, about the need for counsel to be aware of the relevant authorities!

59   [1993] 1 WLR 782.

60   [1997] 1 QB 402, CA.

61   [2004] UKHL 29.

actual earlier knowledge (accepted by the defendants) but which also led them to conclude that there was no reason why he should have got it (before speaking to his lady friend) – which was the issue on which the defendants were to appeal successfully to the House of Lords.

The issue was: is the question as to what the claimant should reasonably be expected to have done in the line of making enquiries or seeking expert help to be answered on a subjective or an objective basis; that is, do you factor in all the personal characteristics of the particular claimant or do you ask what would your average sufferer reasonably have done? Their Lordships concluded (by a majority) that the test was an objective one, but there were different formulations as to the objective test.

Lord Hoffmann said that the claimant must be assumed to be the person who has suffered the injury in question, but that the particular character or intelligence of the particular claimant was not relevant. The normal expectation is that a person suffering from a significant injury will be curious about its origins. But, if the injury itself would reasonably inhibit a claimant from seeking advice, that would be a relevant factor to be taken into account, but no other personal characteristic would be relevant. In the case of dyslexia, in order for it to be taken into account he would expect medical evidence to show that the dyslexia itself would have caused such inhibition; such evidence was not present in *Adams*. Lord Phillips agreed with Lord Hoffmann. Lord Scott also agreed with Lord Hoffmann's conclusions but added that the test should be 'mainly objective'; 'what would a reasonable person placed in the situation in which the claimant was placed have said or done?'.[62] However, it is not clear what the person's 'situation' would cover. It would cover a brain injury in issue in the case, but what about a pre-existing learning disability short of a lack of capacity?

Baroness Hale pointed out that it had rarely, if ever, been necessary to resolve the difference between the two tests to decide the case and she wondered if there was in practice much difference between the two approaches. She did not want to rule out that personal characteristics might be relevant to knowledge, and in particular that the qualifications, training and experience would probably be relevant whilst intelligence may not. But she agreed that strictly personal characteristics such as shyness or embarrassment were not relevant.

Lord Walker thought that Baroness Hale's distinction between personal characteristics which affect a person's ability to acquire information and personal characteristics which affect a person's reaction to the information once acquired would be useful in some cases, but that characteristics such as shyness, embarrassment and lack of assertiveness might fall under both categories.

The test for s 14(3) was considered again by the House of Lords in *A v Hoare*.[63] The argument in *A v Hoare* was around s 14(2), what the test for the significance of an injury is; that section was compared to s 14(3). Lord Hoffmann described s 14(3) as a test for imputing knowledge by reference to what a claimant ought to have done, as opposed to s 14(2) which is a standard of seriousness applied to what the claimant knew or must be treated to have known. He said that because s 14(3) turns on what the

---

62 Para 73.
63 [2008] UKHL 6.

claimant ought reasonably to have done, it must take into account the injury which the claimant has suffered. 'You do not assume that a person which has been blinded could have reasonably acquired knowledge by seeing things'.

It is notable that this more restrictive approach to s 14 knowledge is contrasted with the s 33 discretion. Lord Carswell said:

> If, as I think to be the case, section 14 should be construed in that manner, which is less favourable to the claimant, there requires to be a more liberal approach to the exercise of discretion than has always been the case. For the reason which my noble and learned friends and I have set out, that less favourable construction of section 14 is correct in principle, but it must follow that the favourable factors which have hitherto been taken into account in reaching a conclusion under section 14 should form a part, and in appropriate cases a very significant part, of the judge's determination in exercising his desertion under section 33.[64]

The courts have, since *Adams* and *Hoare*, construed s 14(3) as a strictly objective test (save for the claimant's injuries) and have considered the factors which used to be considered in this section under s 33. For example, in *Whiston v London Strategic Health Authority*,[65] the test applied at first instance was 'when would a reasonable person in the circumstances of the claimant, suffering from cerebral palsy and with the same level of disability have the curiosity to begin investigating with expert help whether his injury could be considered capable of being attributed to something the hospital staff did or didn't do at the time of his birth?'[66]

A dispute arose about whether it was relevant, when looking at the circumstances of the claimant, to take into account the difference between a claimant who is injured at birth, and therefore has known nothing else, and a claimant who is injured as an adult. It was argued that the latter would be much more likely to be curious about the cause of his injuries than the former.

In the Court of Appeal, Lord Justice Dyson said 'In my judgement, the ratio of *Adams* is that section 14(3) requires an objective test to be applied …The importance of *Adams* is that it settled the difference between the objective (or mainly objective) test applied in *Forbes* and the subjective test enunciated in the earlier cases to which I have referred in favour of the former'.[67] He agreed that the fact that a claimant has been suffering the injury since he was born is a relevant circumstance of the case when assessing the extent to which someone is reasonably to be expected to be curious about the cause of his disability.

It is now therefore settled that it is an objective test: when would a reasonable person in the circumstances of the claimant, suffering from the same injury as the claimant, have the curiosity to begin investigating, with expert help, whether their injury could be considered as capable of being attributed to something the defendant did or did not do?

In *Lewin v Glaxo Operations UK Ltd*,[68] the claimant suffered from back pain from the age of 14 for which, in 1973 aged 15 or 16, he underwent

---

64   Para 70.
65   [2010] EWCA Civ 195.
66   Paras 32–33.
67   Para 54.
68   [2016] EWHC 3331(QB).

a diagnostic myelogram during which his spine was injected with a drug called Myodil. No abnormality was shown and he went on to suffer with back problems which were investigated through the 1970s with no cause found. He continued to suffer increasing lower and cervical back problems in the 1980s and 1990s. Between 1990 and 1995 there was group litigation about Myodil causing adhesive arachnoiditis which the claimant, a solicitor, read about. He looked up adhesive arachnoiditis but the symptoms were not the same as the symptoms he was suffering from. He started to suffer more severe symptoms of pain in 2007 and further deteriorating condition including urinary urgency in 2012. He was referred for an MRI and in October 2012 the possibility of a link between the Myodil and his condition was raised by his doctors. He then contacted solicitors to pursue a claim. The defendant argued his date of knowledge was in the late 1970s or around 1980 as his medical records showed a discussion of possible arachnoiditis in 1977 and that should have given rise to investigation and relevant knowledge. The judge found that was not sufficient; he had undergone many investigations and was told they did not know what the cause of his problems was, and even had he taken on board that he might have arachnoiditis, that was not something he, or a reasonable person, should have been sufficiently curious about that he should have started investigating the cause of it. He also found that he did not have constructive knowledge in the 1990s when he knew about the group litigation as there was no reason for him, or any reasonable person, to connect that litigation with his symptoms. His date of knowledge was later, when he was told he had adhesive arachnoiditis in around 2012.

SECTION 33 DISCRETION

Section 33 of the Limitation Act 1980 provides:

> 33.—(1) If it appears to the court that it would be equitable to allow an action to proceed having regard to the degree to which—
> (a)   the provisions of section 11 or 11A or 12 of this Act prejudice the plaintiff or any person whom he represents; and
> (b)   any decision of the court under this subsection would prejudice the defendant or any person who he represents;
>
> the court may direct that those provisions shall not apply to the action, or shall not apply to any specified cause of action to which the action relates.
>
> ...
>
> (3) In acting under this section the court shall have regard to all the circumstances of the case and in particular to—
> (a)   the length of, and the reasons for, the delay on the part of the plaintiff;
> (b)   the extent to which, having regard to the delay, the evidence adduced or likely to be adduced by the plaintiff or the defendant is or is likely to be less cogent than if the action had been brought within the time allowed by section 11, by section 11A or (as the case may be) by section 12;
> (c)   the conduct of the defendant after the cause of action arose, including the extent (if any) to which he responded to requests reasonably made by the plaintiff for information or inspection for the purpose of ascertaining facts which were or might be relevant to the plaintiff's cause of action against the defendant;

(d)   the duration of any disability of the plaintiff arising after the date of the accrual of the cause of action;

(e)   the extent to which the plaintiff acted promptly and reasonably once he knew whether or not the act or omission of the defendant, to which the injury was attributable, might be capable at that time of giving rise to an action for damages;

(f)   the steps, if any, taken by the plaintiff to obtain medical, legal or other expert advice and the nature of any such advice he may have received.

These are not the only factors to which the court must pay attention. The overall consideration is where the balance of prejudice lies and whether a fair trial is still possible.[69]

There are a plethora of cases on this section, but as each case is dependent on the circumstances of that particular case, they are often helpful more as examples than strict precedent. It is often possible to find two cases with similar facts and differing outcomes. However, since the tightening of the requirements for knowledge in s 14, some consideration has been given to the purpose of s 33 which does provide useful general guidance as to the proper approach to the s 33 discretion.

In *Cain v Francis*,[70] the Court of Appeal had to consider the issue of whether any weight should be given in the balancing exercise to the defendant's loss of a 'windfall defence'. That is to say, when a defendant suffers no other prejudice as a result of the claim being issued outside the limitation period (should the claim be allowed to proceed) save for the loss of the limitation defence. In a case where, for example, the defendant has admitted liability prior to the expiry of limitation, this defence has been described as a windfall. In order to decide whether that should be a consideration to be put in the balance, the court considered the history and purpose of the discretion. The leading judgement was given by Lady Justice Smith. Her Ladyship said:

> It is a fundamental precept of the common law that a tortfeasor should compensate the victim of the tort. At common law, the victim, now the claimant, could sue the tortfeasor at any time, without limitation. It is also a fundamental precept that any person who is sued in respect of a tort should have a fair opportunity to defend himself. In 1623, a uniform limitation period of six years was introduced for all actions. The rationale behind the limit was to protect defendants from stale claims. It was not fair and just to impose liability on a defendant who had not had a proper opportunity to investigate the allegations against him and to assemble the evidence necessary to defend himself. There may have been other policy reasons for the provision, such as the desirability of finality but, as between the parties, the reason was to protect the defendant form a stale claim.[71]

> ... Any limitation bar is arbitrary ... The imposition of an arbitrary limit could only ever hope to do rough justice ... Parliament introduced ... section 33 ... The only rationale which would have underlain the introduction of this provision was a desire to refine the rough justice of the old arbitrary provision. Instead of a limitation rule of thumb, the courts would be required to consider what was fair and just in all the circumstances of the individual case. In my view the words of section 33 must be construed against that background. The operation of section 11 has given him a complete procedural defence which

---

69   *Cain v Francis* [2008] EWCA Civ 1451.

70   [2008] EWCA Civ 1451.

71   Para 64.

removes the obligation to pay. In fairness and justice, he only deserves to have that obligation removed if the passage of time has significantly diminished his opportunity to defend himself (on liability and/or quantum). So the making of a direction, which would restore the Defendant's obligation to pay damages, is only prejudicial to him if his right to a fair opportunity to defend himself has been compromised.[72]

... It seems to me that, in the exercise of discretion, the basic question to be asked is whether it is fair and just in all the circumstances to expect the Defendant to meet the claim on the merits, notwithstanding the delay in commencement. The length of delay will be important, not so much for itself, as to the effect it has had. To what extent has the Defendant been disadvantaged in his investigation of the claim and/or assembly of the evidence, in respect of the issues of both liability and quantum? But it will also be important to consider the reasons for the delay. Thus there may be some unfairness to the defendant due to the delay in issue but the delay may have arisen for so excusable a reason that, looking at the matter in the round, on balance it is fair and just that the action should proceed. On the other hand, the balance may go in the opposite direction, partly because the delay has caused procedural disadvantage and unfairness to the defendant and partly because the reasons for the delay (or its length) are not good ones.[73]

In summary, the purpose of s 33 is to do fairness between the parties, balancing the *effects* of the delay on the defendant and the *reasons* for the delay on the part of the claimant. In *Carroll v Chief Constable of Greater Manchester Police*[74] the Court of Appeal have set out a useful general summary of the principles derived from the cases and the factors which have to be considered, both those expressly listed in s 33 and other circumstances which should be considered.

Here it is useful however to consider the issues that might arise in the clinical negligence context.

(A) THE LENGTH OF AND REASONS FOR THE DELAY

The period of delay in question is that after the expiry of the limitation period, however any delay before the expiry of the limitation period is a relevant factor to be taken into account in all the circumstances of the case.[75] In looking at whether the reasons are 'good' ones or not, the test is subjective.[76]

In *Whiston v London Strategic Health Authority*,[77] the fact that a claimant who was injured at birth, suffering cerebral palsy affecting mobility only, had got on with his life, obtaining a PhD in mathematics from the University of Cambridge and employment as a qualitative analyst and who didn't consider himself disabled, was given permission to proceed with his claim, despite, in considering his knowledge, a finding that he had not displayed the curiosity of a reasonable person in his

---

72 Paras 67–68.
73 Para 73.
74 [2017] EWCA Civ 1992.
75 *Donovan v Gwentoys* [1990] 2 All ER 1018.
76 *Coad v Cornwall and Scilly Isles Health Authority* [1997] 1 WLR 189.
77 [2010] EWCA Civ 195.

position. His approach to his disability was a good reason for not bringing a claim.[78]

In *Godfrey v Gloucestershire Royal Infirmary*,[79] where the negligence led to the birth of a child with severe disabilities requiring continuous care, the fact that the claimant mother and her family were 'having to cope with a severely disabled baby which will have imposed its own emotional, physical and financial constraints on the single minded pursuit of litigation' was relevant to the delay. The delay was four and a half years after the limitation expired. The discretion was exercised.

In *Berry v Calderdale Health Authority*,[80] the court refused to exercise the discretion because no reason was given for the delay. The delay was about a year.

(B) THE EFFECT OF DELAY ON COGENCY OF EVIDENCE

In *Farthing v North East Essex Health Authority*,[81] Simon Brown LJ and Hale J said, in respect of an allegation of negligence around a hysterectomy in 1981, that the case did not turn on the recollection of witnesses as to precisely what was done, but upon the contemporaneous records. The delay was 15 years from the damage but the discretion was exercised. In *Smith v Leicestershire Health Authority*,[82] the Court of Appeal (Roch, Mantell LJJ, Sir Patrick Russell) reversed a decision of May J whereby he held that a spina bifida patient, born in 1943, who claimed in respect of clinical negligence going back some 40 years, had constructive knowledge in 1983 and that it would not be equitable to exercise discretion in her favour. The appeal court held that there was no proper ground for a finding of constructive knowledge and, further, that the judge's exercise of discretion was flawed as he had given too much weight to the mere passage of time and insufficient weight to the fact that a defendant's evidential disadvantage was not great where a case will turn on the extant medical records, and so it pales into insignificance beside the prejudice to the claimant if not permitted to proceed. In such a situation, the experts could still make proper analyses. However, in *Skitt v Khan and Wakefield Health Authority*,[83] where a relevant witness had died and the defendant doctor's health was such he would be unable to give evidence, there was prejudice to the defendant due to the non-availability of the witnesses. The delay was four years. The discretion was not exercised.

In *Conry v Simpson*,[84] the defendant had properly destroyed relevant documents, which meant the evidence was less cogent.

In *Mossa v Barbara Wise*,[85] it was held a fair trial was still possible despite the death of the defendant doctor shortly after issue in a case where the issue was the adequacy of the consent. The records still existed

---

78 Similarly in *Coad v Cornwall and Scilly Isles Health Authority* [1997] 1 WLR 189, genuine ignorance of legal rights was found to be a good reason for the delay.
79 [2003] EWHC 549 (QB).
80 [1998] Lloyd's Rep Med 179, CA.
81 [1998] Lloyd's Rep Med 37, MLC 0053.
82 [1998] Lloyd's Rep Med 77.
83 [1997] 8 Med LR 105.
84 [1983] 3 All ER 369.
85 [2017] EWHC 2608.

and it was thought unlikely his witness statement would have added much to those records.

In *The Pennine Acute Hospitals NHS Trust v Mr Simon De Meza*[86] the age and infirmity of the defendant doctor was put in issue. It was held that although age and infirmity may be relevant to the cogency of the evidence, they are not in themselves factors to weigh in the balance. The judge at first instance had erred in taking age, infirmity and the fact the defendant was an individual not an institution in to account in the balancing exercise.

(c) THE CONDUCT OF THE DEFENDANT

In *Hammond v West Lancashire Health Authority*,[87] x-rays were destroyed despite the defendant having been notified of the claim and medical records had been requested. The prejudice to the defendant in not having those x-rays was discounted significantly as a result.

(d) DISABILITY

This refers to disability arising after the cause of action. Section 28, which suspends time running whilst a claimant lacks capacity, only applies where the lack of capacity is present at the time the cause of action arises. The disability being referred to is capacity rather than physical disability.[88]

(e) THE EXTENT TO WHICH THE CLAIMANT ACTED REASONABLY ONCE THEY KNEW OF A POTENTIAL CLAIM

This is an objective test.[89] In *Buckler v J F Finnegan Ltd*,[90] the Court of Appeal reversed the judge who disapplied the limitation period where a workman who had decided originally not to sue for so slight an injury as pleural thickening to one lung, changed his mind years later when he mistakenly thought his condition had deteriorated. This can be compared to *Doughty v North Staffordshire Health Authority*[91] where, unrelated to the claim, the claimant had a severely handicapped daughter. Her husband blamed her for their daughter's handicap and had left leaving her bringing her daughter up alone and going through a divorce. She had been injured 28 years before issue, as a child, and the delay was 11 years. The discretion was exercised to disapply the limitation period.

---

86 [2017] EWCA Civ 1171.
87 [1998] Lloyd's Rep Med 146.
88 *Yates v Thakenham Tiles Ltd* [1995] PIQR P135 CA; but an impairment of the claimant's health short of 'disability' may be given due weight by the court: *Davis v Jacobs and Camden and Islington Health Authority* MLC 0071, [1999] Lloyd's Rep Med 72, CA at 86.
89 *Coad v Cornwall and Scilly Isles Health Authority* [1997] 1 WLR 189.
90 [2004] EWCA Civ 920.
91 [1991] 4 WLUK 21; [1992] 3 Med LR 81.

(F) THE STEPS TAKEN TO OBTAIN ADVICE

In *Roberts v Winbow*,[92] where the claimant instructed solicitors prior to the limitation period, but the expert reported after expiry of the primary limitation period (18 months after instructions were sent), the discretion to extend was exercised. The solicitor had not issued as the claimant was funded by legal aid and it was thought not appropriate to issue in the circumstances of the case with no causation report.

In addition, the court must consider the whole of the circumstances. Relevant factors include the apparent merits of the claim,[93] whether it would be proportionate for the claim to proceed,[94] whether the issues depend on recollection[95] or extant medical records, whether the claimant has a claim against his solicitors,[96] whether the defendant had reasonably early notice of a possible claim,[97] and the personal situation of the claimant in having to cope with the injuries sustained.[98] Factors which have found not to be relevant include the fact that a defendant is insured (*Kelly v Bastible*[99]) and any other financial prejudice to the defendant.[100] The discretion must be exercised reasonably: refusing to allow a case to proceed where it is one day out of time is not reasonable (*Hartley v Birmingham City District Council*)[101].

Other cases on discretion

The discretion is an unfettered one, and the Court of Appeal should be loath to interfere with its exercise by the judge (see *Conry v Simpson*;[102] *Firman v Ellis*;[103] *Bradley v Hanseatic Shipping*[104]).

In *Mold v Hayton and Newson*,[105] the court reversed the exercise of the judge's discretion whereby he permitted an action for failure to examine timeously for vaginal cancer to proceed 18 years out of time, on the ground that it was not appropriate to grant such a huge extension without giving clear reasons for doing so, and the judge had not given clear reasons.

---

92 [1997] PIQR P77.
93 But a cast iron case is not a passport to proceed: an untruthful claimant should not be given discretion (*Long v Tolchard & Sons Ltd* (2000) Times, 5 January, CA).
94 *Adams v Bracknell Forest Borough Council* [2004] UKHL 29.
95 The court can infer impairment of recollection from the lapse of time – *Price v United Engineering Steels Ltd* [1998] PIQR P407, CA – specific evidence of impairment is not required.
96 *Thomson v Brown Construction (Ebbw Vale) Ltd* [1981] 1 WLR 744, HL; *Ramsden v Lee* [1992] 2 All ER 204, CA; *Das v Ganju* [1999] PIQR P260, CA.
97 See *Long v Tolchard & Sons Ltd* [2001] PIQR P18, CA.
98 See *Godfrey v Gloucestershire Royal Infirmary* [2003] EWHC 549, QB and *Khairule v North West Strategic Health Authority* [2008] EWHC 1537.
99 [1997] 8 Med LR 15, CA.
100 *Cain v Francis* [2008] EWCA Civ 1451.
101 [1992] 1 WLR 968, CA.
102 [1983] 3 All ER 369.
103 [1978] QB 886.
104 [1986] 2 Lloyd's Rep 34.
105 (17 April 2000, unreported), [2000] MLC 0207, CA.

The rule in *Walkley v Precision Forgings* and the effect of *Horton v Sadler*

The rule in *Walkley v Precision Forgings* that if a claim form was issued within time, and not validly served, or was struck out or the claim otherwise discontinued, an application could not be made under s 33 to disapply the limitation period in respect of a second claim form issued outside the limitation period was overruled in *Horton v Sadler*.[106] A second claim form can therefore be issued. In *McDonnell v David Walker (Executor of the Estate of Richard Walker, deceased)*,[107] Waller LJ held that the tension between the (stringent) terms of the CPR 7.6, which only allows an extension of time for service of a claim form if the claimant has taken all reasonable steps to do so within the limitation period, even if no prejudice has been suffered by a defendant and the broad discretion under s 33 is a relevant factor to be taken into account in the s 33 discretion.

It was argued in *Atkas v Adepta*[108] that to issue a second claim form when the first had not been served through the claimant's solicitor's negligence was an abuse of process and such a claim form should be struck out. That argument was rejected. Whilst issuing a second claim form can be an abuse of process (in the same way as it can be if done within the limitation period), the mere act of doing so is not an abuse of process. The relevance of the 'tension' referred to by Lord Justice Waller is also doubted.

Preliminary trial

Although a preliminary trial on limitation is frequently desirable, it should not be ordered where the limitation issues are intricately bound up in the substantive issues (*Fletcher v Sheffield Health Authority*;[109] see also *Roberts v Winbow*[110] and *Worsley v Tambrands*[111]). If limitation is not dealt with as a preliminary issue but at the conclusion of the evidence, the decision on whether to allow the s 33 applications should be made before consideration of the merits of the claim itself.[112]

FATAL ACCIDENT CLAIMS

The limitation period provided by s 12 of the 1980 Act for actions under the Fatal Accidents Act 1976 (amended by s 3 of the Administration of Justice Act 1982) is three years from the date of death, or the date of 'knowledge' of the dependant for whose benefit the action is brought, whichever is the later. If, at the date of death, the deceased's right of action was already time-barred by s 11, then the dependants' action is also barred, no account being taken of the possibility that the deceased might have got leave to proceed under s 33; but provided the limitation

---

106 [2006] UKHL 27.
107 [2009] EWCA Civ 1257.
108 [2010] EWCA Civ 1170.
109 [1994] 5 Med LR 156, MLC 0035.
110 MLC 0074, [1999] Lloyd's Rep Med 31, CA at 39.
111 [2000] MLC 0186, CA.
112 *KR v Bryn Alyn Community (Holdings) Ltd (in liquidation)* [2003] EWCA Civ 85.

period had not expired at the date of death, the dependants can on their own account ask for their action to be permitted to proceed under s 33 (by virtue of s 12(1) and (3)).

Although only one action can be brought on behalf of all dependants,[113] dependants are to be considered separately for the purpose of limitation. Therefore one dependant may be barred where another is within the limitation period because his knowledge arose later, or because he is under a disability (s 13(1)). The court has power to exclude a dependant from participating in the action if their claim would be outside the limitation period (s 13(2)). That power is limited by s 13(3), which provides that no direction to exclude shall be given if it is shown that if the action were brought exclusively for the benefit of that dependant, it would not be defeated by a defence of limitation.

A fatal accident claim may often include a claim for, for example, terminal suffering or care given to the deceased while he was still alive. That is not a fatal accident head of claim, but is a claim pursuant to the Law Reform (Miscellaneous Provisions) Act 1934, and the limitation period in respect of that claim is not necessarily the same. The relevant provision is s 11(5) of the Limitation Act 1980, which provides that the three-year period runs from the date of death or the date of the personal representative's 'knowledge'. In many cases, the distinction will not be important, but it could be. For example, the personal representative may have acquired the relevant 'knowledge' years before, which will prevent him claiming on behalf of the estate or as a dependent (subject to any application for s 33 discretion), whereas the claim by any dependent children will not be affected.

AMENDING A CLAIM

Amending the statement of claim

The issue sometimes arises that a claimant needs to add a new party after proceedings have been begun. Perhaps the culprit appears to be a different GP from the current defendant, or perhaps a GP or health authority needs to be added to the frame. Alternatively, a new allegation of negligence may need to be made against the existing defendants following, for example, an expert seeing new records. The legislative provisions are not particularly easy to understand, but can usefully be summarised by saying that the judge has no general power to add a defendant (or a new cause of action) out of time, except by exercising discretion under s 33 (see s 35(3)). Section 35(4) and (5) lays down guidelines for the enaction of rules of court to permit new claims to be added, but provides that the rules can be more restrictive than the guidelines. Therefore, it is to the rules of court that one has to look upon any such application.

The CPR 17.4 (amendments to statements of case after the end of a relevant limitation period) enables amendments to be made where the effect will be to add or substitute a new claim, provided the new claim arises out of the same facts or substantially the same facts as a claim in respect of which the party applying for permission has already claimed

---

113 Fatal Accidents Act 1976, s 2(3).

a remedy in the proceedings. Genuine mistakes over identity may be corrected under this rule provided the mistake was genuine and not one which would cause reasonable doubt as to the identity of the party in question.[114]

The CPR 19.5 provides that for the addition or substitution of a party, the relevant limitation period must have been current at the start of the proceedings and the amendment must be necessary, which means that the court must be satisfied that the substitution arises out of a mistake, or the change must be made to enable the claim to be properly carried on. There is, of course, power to amend where the court directs, under s 33, that the time limits under s 11 or 12 shall be disapplied (and it is specifically provided that the issue whether those sections apply is to be determined at trial). These powers arise from s 35 of the Limitation Act.

The mistake under the CPR 19.5 must be a mistake as to the name of the party rather than the identity of the party, so the sort of mistake where the claimant gives the right description of the defendant (in the body of the pleading) but the wrong name.[115]

In *Sayer* v *Kingston and Esher Health Authority*,[116] the Court of Appeal endorsed the judge's decision to permit an amendment of the claim on the eve of the trial whereby the previous case alleging mishandling of the Caesarean section was replaced by allegations of mismanagement earlier in the labour and after delivery. The court said that as the new claims arose out of substantially the same facts as those already pleaded, the judge had discretion to allow the amendment under s 35(5) of the Limitation Act 1980.[117] Whether a similar amendment would be allowed now on the facts given the lateness of the amendment is another matter.

In *Welsh Development Agency* v *Redpath Dorman Long Ltd*,[118] the Court of Appeal held that leave could not be given to add a new claim after the expiry of the limitation period unless it fell within one of the stated exceptions in the Act and the then current rules of court, and that the relevant date for when a new claim should be taken to be made was not the date when the application for leave to amend was issued, but when the amendment was actually made. Reference may also be made to *Howe* v *David Brown Tractors (Retail) Ltd*.[119]

In *Sion* v *Hampstead Health Authority*,[120] the defendants' counsel took an obviously bad point on adding a claim after the expiry of the limitation period. It was agreed that the rules permitted a new claim to be added where it arose out of substantially the same facts as a cause of action in respect of which relief had already been claimed in the action, but he said that as the statement of claim in fact disclosed no cause of action, the

---

114 See *International Distillers* v *J F Hillebrand (UK) Ltd* (2000) Times, 25 January. See also the commentary above (under 'Knowledge') on *Gregson* v *Channel Four Television Corpn* (2000) Times, 11 August, CA.

115 See *Adelson* v *Associated Newspapers Ltd* [2007] EWCA Civ 701 and *Lockheed Martin Corporation* v *Willis Group Limited* [2010] EWCA Civ 927.

116 (1989) Independent, 27 March, CA.

117 It is useful to note that the Court of Appeal have said that there is no need to amend the pleading every time the medical condition changes, provided that notice in the form of appropriate medical evidence is given to the defendants (*Oksuzoglu* v *Kay* [1998] Lloyd's Rep Med 129).

118 [1994] 1 WLR 1409.

119 [1991] 4 All ER 30, CA.

120 MLC 0027, [1994] 5 Med LR 170, CA.

rule did not apply. The court gave the obvious response, namely that if the pleading could be amended to disclose a cause of action substantially on the facts as pleaded, the pre-condition to adding a new cause of action was satisfied.

The patient seeking to add a party should try to show that the relevant knowledge was not acquired more than three years before such date as the amendment is likely to be made if it is granted; failing which, she may be able to show a genuine mistake (on this, see *Evans Construction Co Ltd v Charrington & Co Ltd and Bass Holdings Ltd*,[121] approved in *Signet Group plc v Hammerson UK Properties plc*[122]); failing that possibility, discretion must be sought under s 33. See also *SmithKline Beecham plc v Horne-Roberts*,[123] where an application within the MMR litigation to substitute Smithkline as defendants in place of Merck was permitted because there had been a 'mistake' within the meaning of s 35 of the Limitation Act 1980 and the ten-year time limit applicable to the claim was a 'period of limitation' within the CPR 19.5(3). See also *Parsons v George*,[124] where the mistake related to the identity of the claimants' landlord.

In *Senior v Pearsons and Ward*,[125] the court said that the question whether or not the new claim arose out of the same facts as the existing claim was a matter of impression. The Act and the CPR both focused on the particular facts in each case as being relevant. See also *Savings and Investment Bank v Fincken*.[126] In the RTA claim of *Goode v Martin*,[127] the Court of Appeal allowed an amendment of the claim out of time whereby the claimant was permitted to plead the different facts alleged in the defence. Although this new claim was, on a strict interpretation of the rule (CPR 17.4), impermissible as not arising out of the same facts as the original claim, the court said that, the Human Rights Act 1998 having come into operation since the Master's original order disallowing the application, to prevent the claimant from now putting her case on the basis of the facts as pleaded in the defence would constitute an impediment on her access to the court.

---

121 [1983] QB 810, CA.
122 [1998] 03 LS Gaz R 25, CA.
123 [2001] MLC 0667.
124 [2004] EWCA Civ 1912.
125 (26 January 2001, unreported), CA.
126 (2001) Times, 2 March.
127 [2002] PIQR P333.

Chapter 21

The medical records

Andrew Buchan and Dr Thomas Boyd

THE RECORDS OF TREATMENT

The patient's medical records are the backbone of almost all clinical negligence claims. They must be obtained, intelligently sorted and read. After that, they will be submitted to an expert, who will make his report based on them and any other relevant information, such as witness statements from patient and family. The pre-action protocol sets out pro formas for requesting records and for responding to such a request. It is not mandatory to use the pro forma, but it would be unwise not to (see Appendix II). The box that asks the patient to give grounds for his claim need not be taken too seriously. It is not a legal requirement, and is in any event unlikely to be able to be clearly answered at such a preliminary stage.

All relevant records should be obtained. Records of treatment at other hospitals earlier or later than the impugned treatment may well illuminate aspects of the claim. On the other hand, they may relate to conditions not pertinent to the claim, in which case one would expect the expert solicitor not to spend money getting them. GP records are almost always relevant.

Copy records should be checked against the originals. Originals will often yield a better insight into the medical events by revealing more clearly the appearance of the entries (eg colours, writing pressures). Often the photocopying will not extend to the dates in the left margin of the nursing notes, or will show only the last of the two digits for the day of the month – which creates confusion. In one case, the parties were misled in that way when the hole-puncher had obliterated the first digit (*Johnson v John and Waltham Forest Health Authority*[1]).

Often certain records will be missing. If relevant, they should be chased up with vigour. It is amazing what turns up eventually. The law on getting such documents is explained below. But what if records have been lost for good or destroyed?

---

1   (1998) MLC 0244, CA.

Records lost or destroyed

HC(80)7 advises a minimum retention period of 25 years for obstetrics records; until the 25th birthday or eight years after the last entry for children and young people; for mentally disordered persons 20 years from the date of cure; and in any other case eight years.

In *Malhotra v Dhawan*,[2] the Court of Appeal, considering the maxim *omnia praesumuntur contra spoliatorem*, indicated that inferences could be drawn against a party who had destroyed relevant evidence (although the court said the maxim only applied where that had been done to stop the other party showing how much of his property had been taken).[3] In *Le Page v Kingston and Richmond Health Authority*,[4] John Samuels QC, sitting as a Deputy Judge of the Queen's Bench Division, said that the defendants could not properly complain if he drew inferences from surviving documentation which might have been contradicted by other records which they had improperly destroyed.

In *Skelton v Lewisham and North Southwark Health Authority*,[5] the inadequacy of the anaesthetic notes (brief, unsigned, without a record of key events and pressures), although not causative of the damage, was said by the judge to be indicative of an unexplained carelessness. In *Rhodes v Spokes and Farbridge*,[6] Smith J said:

> A doctor's contemporaneous record of a consultation should form a reliable evidential base in a case such as this. I regret to say that Dr Farbridge's notes of the plaintiff's attendances do not provide any such firm foundation. They are scanty in the extreme. He rarely recorded her complaints or symptoms; he rarely recorded any observations; usually he noted only the drug he prescribed ... The failure to take a proper note is not evidence of a doctor's negligence or of the inadequacy of treatment. But a doctor who fails to keep an adequate note of a consultation lays himself open to a finding that his recollection is faulty and someone else's is correct. After all, a patient has only to remember his or her own case, whereas the doctor has to remember one case out of hundreds which occupied his mind at the material time.

Do the records prove themselves?

The answer is no, strictly. But normally in a trial it is tacitly accepted that they are not going to be challenged, unless one party has put the other side on notice that the timing or content or authoring of a particular note is not accepted. In *Arrowsmith v Beeston*,[7] it was said that GP records are not evidence of the correctness of the diagnosis made unless the maker of the record is called to give evidence. In *Steele v Millbrook Proving Ground Ltd*,[8] the relevant issue was whether the rotator cuff syndrome from which the claimant in an employment accident case was suffering was due to the accident or not. In concluding that it was, the judge had relied to an

---

2   [1997] 8 Med LR 319.
3   In *Dobson v North Tyneside Health Authority* [1997] 1 WLR 596, the Court of Appeal said that for the maxim to apply it had to be shown that the spoliator was a 'wrongdoer'.
4   MLC 0610, [1997] 8 Med LR 229.
5   [1999] MLC 0662, [1998] Lloyd's Rep Med 324.
6   MLC 0640, [1996] 7 Med LR 135.
7   (18 June 1998, unreported), CA.
8   (6 May 1999, unreported), CA.

extent on GP records which tended to confirm the claimant's account. Upon objection by the defendants, the Court of Appeal said that there was no doubt that medical records were evidence of the facts recorded in them, and the weight to be attached to the records in this case, given that neither party called the GP to give evidence, was a matter for the judge.

Occasionally a party to a clinical negligence action will serve a notice to admit medical records (the Treasury Solicitor has been known to do this). As has been indicated, that is probably the correct procedure, strictly speaking.

The Data Protection Act 1998 and the Freedom of Information Act 2000

The Act of 1998, intended to implement Directive 95/46/EC,[9] repealed the Data Protection Act 1984 and the Access to Health Records Act 1990 with effect from 1 March 2000, except to the extent that it applied to deceased patients. So the new Act is the route for access to medical records. It has its own jargon. A patient is a 'data subject', the holder of the records is a 'data controller', and the records are 'information constituting data'. Clinical records include 'all paper and computer records whenever created'.[10] A health record means any record which consists of information relating to the physical or mental health or condition of an individual and which has been made by or on behalf of a health professional in connection with the care of that individual (s 68). A health professional includes, by s 69, all forms of medical practitioners (eg doctors, dentists, opticians, nurses, midwives, osteopaths, chiropractors, speech therapists, physiotherapists) and anyone registered as a member of a profession supplementary to medicine (within the catchment of the Professions Supplementary to Medicine Act 1960). Under s 7, an individual or his representative has a right to access and get a copy of his clinical records on making a request in writing with the prescribed fee. Copies are to be supplied within 40 days unless such supply would involve disproportionate effort. An explanation must be supplied where the records contain terms otherwise unintelligible. There are provisions for an application to the court by either party.

The Act is drafted in general terms. The Data Protection (Subject Access Modification) (Health) Order 2000, SI 2000/413 sets out specific rules concerning health records. Disclosure may be refused where serious harm might be caused to the physical or mental health of the patient. Medical records that have been created in the expectation that they would not be disclosed to the person making the request are exempt from the Act. In *Hubble v Peterborough Hospital NHS Trust*,[11] a Recorder held that X-rays fell within the Act and so no extra charge for copying them could be levied. Although not expressly decided, the same reasoning

---

9   Note that the human rights aspect of accessing medical records is considered in Chapter 23.
10 The Data Protection Act 1984 did not apply to paper records; one had to turn to the Access to Health Records Act 1990 for them. (See the Court of Appeal's judgment in *R v Mid-Glamorgan Family Health Services Authority, ex p Martin* [1994] 5 Med LR 383.) The 1984 Act was also limited to records created after October 1991.
11 (2001) MLC 0347.

would seem to apply to the CTG traces, in respect of which an additional charge had already been paid.

The Freedom of Information Act 2000 applies, by and large, to non-personal data. Although most documents which might be helpful to a clinical negligence claim can be obtained under normal disclosure rules, it is not difficult to see that some might fall outside the ambit of those rules in the more complex or wide-ranging claim, and the Act of 2000 could be particularly useful in accessing information previously undivulged relating (for example) to Trust or health authority systems and data or Department of Health and government management, thus assisting in the investigation and formulation of a claim. This might well be particularly helpful to group claims, where the budget for such an investigation is so much greater than for the single claim. Though on the surface exceptionally wide-ranging, the Act is complex and hedged about with exceptions. This is not the place to offer more than a brief summary.

Individuals already have the right to access information about themselves (personal data) which is held on computer and in some paper files under the Data Protection Act 1998. The Act of 2000 extends this right of access (as far as public authorities are concerned) to allow access to all the types of information held, whether personal or non-personal. This may include information about third parties, although the public authority will have to take account of the Data Protection Act 1998 before releasing any personal information. The Act gives two related rights:

- the right to be told whether the information exists; and
- the right to receive that information.

The right to access the information held by public authorities can be exercised by anyone, worldwide. The Act is also retrospective. This right to access information came into effect on 1 January 2005.

The Act is 'challenged with the task of reversing the working premise that everything is secret, unless otherwise stated, to a position where everything is public unless it falls into specified excepted cases' (Lord Chancellor's first Annual Report on the implementation of the Act, November 2001). As indicated, it gives a general right of access to all types of recorded information held by public authorities, sets out exemptions from that right and places a number of obligations on public authorities (health bodies are, of course, included in the term 'public authority'). The Act also makes appropriate amendments to the Data Protection Act 1998 and the Public Records Act 1958. Subject to the exemptions, any person who makes a request to a public authority for information must be informed whether the public authority holds that information. If it does, that information must be supplied, subject to certain conditions.

Every public authority is required to adopt and maintain a publication scheme setting out how it intends to publish the different classes of information it holds, and whether there is a charge for the information. Some trusts have already put their publication schemes online. Two codes of practice issued under the Act provide guidance to public authorities about responding to requests for information and records management. The Act is enforced by the Information Commissioner and was brought into force in two parts, with full implementation on 1 January 2005. The requirement to publish and maintain a publication scheme was phased in during 2003 and 2004. Individual rights of access to information came into force across all public authorities in January 2005.

Before 2005, there were Codes that gave the public access to some information held by government departments. These were little used and were considered to be exclusive rather than inclusive. The Freedom of Information Act covers over 100,000 public bodies. It is proclaimed that the Act will ensure that much more information will be routinely and freely available about the way in which we are governed and the way decisions that affect all our lives are reached, at both national and local levels. With the introduction of publication schemes in 2003/04, a vast amount of information not previously accessible became available as a matter of routine. Publication schemes mean that public bodies have to ensure that information which they say is available through their publication scheme is truly and easily available, and they will have to indicate in their schemes how they will achieve this. The legislation allows for public bodies to charge for access subject to certain restrictions but this too should be notified in the publication scheme.

The main features of the individual right of access are:

1   Every written request for information, including emails, will be considered to be an access request under the Freedom of Information Act. There is no set format, nor is there any requirement to justify the request. There are no citizenship or residency restrictions and the only requirement is that applicants provide a name and address.
2   Access requests must be dealt with within 20 working days.
3   If the information is not available or the information is not supplied, the applicant must be told why.
4   In cases where either the precise information covered by the request is unclear or where the scope is so wide as to make it likely that the request would be refused on the grounds of cost, public bodies are encouraged to discuss with the applicant the nature of their request to see whether it can be redefined to lead to a positive outcome.
5   The Act requires public bodies to set up an appeals procedure to review refusals at the request of the applicants and, if the applicant remains unhappy at the refusal, there is an avenue of recourse to the Information Commissioner.

The modest hope has been offered to the effect that the Act will encourage transparency in decision-making, leading to a re-establishment of the trust between national and local public bodies and the people they serve.

THE RIGHT TO PRE-ACTION DISCLOSURE

The Access to Health Records Act 1990 did not apply to records created before November 1991, as to which the old law remained in force. Given that the 1998 Act applies to all clinical records whenever created, the old law has assumed considerably less significance in clinical negligence claims. However, there may from time to time be documents the patient wants to see which do not comprise data caught by the Act. For example, in *Hewlett-Parker v St George's Healthcare NHS Trust*,[12] Owen J ordered

---

12   [1998] MLC 0072.

disclosure of an NHS complaints file (pursuant to the then current RSC Ord 24, r 8). It is therefore useful to summarise the old law.

Pre-action disclosure is provided for by s 33 of the Supreme Court Act 1981, s 52 of the County Courts Act 1984, and CPR 31.16. Note that this facility is only available against a likely party to future proceedings. Disclosure against a non-party can only be obtained after action is commenced[13] – apart of course from any rights under the 1998 Act. Disclosure against a non-party is governed by s 34 of the Supreme Court Act 1981, s 53 of the County Courts Act 1984, and CPR 31.17.

Pre-action disclosure is no longer limited to personal injury cases. In *Burrells Wharf Freeholds Ltd* v *Galliards Homes Ltd*,[14] the court rejected the submission that Art 5 of the Civil Procedure (Modification of Enactments) Order 1998, which removed the former restriction to personal injury cases, was *ultra vires.*

Any application must be supported by evidence. The applicant must show that he and the respondent are likely to be parties to proceedings, that the documents he seeks fall within the ambit of disclosable documents under the general provisions of CPR 31.6, and that early disclosure is desirable in order to dispose fairly of the anticipated proceedings or to assist the dispute to be resolved without proceedings or to save costs.

On an application for disclosure against a non-party, it must be shown that the documents sought are likely to support the case of the applicant or adversely affect '*another*' [our emphasis] party's case, and that disclosure is necessary in order to dispose fairly of the claim or to save costs.[15]

The Court of Appeal considered the ambit of the Act of 1981 and the new rules in the case of *American Home Products Corpn and Professor Sir Roy Calne* v *Novartis Pharma AG*.[16] This was an action for alleged infringement of a patent for the use of rapamycin in the preparation of a drug for inhibiting organ or tissue transplant rejection. The court found a similar limitation to the Act's 'any documents which are relevant to an issue' in the words of the CPR 31.17, enabling the court to make an order 'only where the documents … are likely to support the case for the applicant or adversely affect the case of one of the other parties to the proceedings'.

Confidentiality of medical records

It goes without saying that a person's medical records are confidential and normally not to be disclosed to anyone but his doctors. The main exception to this is that in a personal injury action or a clinical negligence action he is taken to have waived his right to confidentiality so that the defendants are entitled to see all relevant records (and in most cases that will embrace all his records). Any unacceptable disclosure is likely also to be a contravention of the right to privacy under Art 8 of the Convention.

---

13   It is not permissible to join a party simply to get disclosure (*Douihech* v *Findlay* [1990] 1 WLR 269).
14   [1999] 33 EG 82.
15   The House of Lords considered the relevant principles in *O'Sullivan* v *Herdmans Ltd* [1987] 1 WLR 1047.
16   (2001) IPD 24021.

In *R v Plymouth City Council, ex p Stevens*,[17] where a mother sought to see the medical records of her adult son who was in the guardianship of the respondent council, the court said that, although there was a legitimate interest in protecting the confidentiality of personal information about a person in the guardianship of his local authority, his nearest relative was entitled to have direct access to that information when she needed it in order to determine whether she should oppose the renewal of the guardianship. This reasoning was followed by Sumner J in *Re R (A Child)*,[18] where the judge made an order for pre-action disclosure under CPR 31.16, subject to conditions, in respect of a potential claim by a child against the respondent Trust for failing to diagnose his condition. The judge said that the balance came down in favour of full disclosure even though the Trust's notes contained sensitive material about the applicant's mother.[19]

In *A Health Authority v X*,[20] the Court of Appeal said that a judge who had ordered the disclosure to a health authority of case material used in care proceedings and GP patient records had correctly balanced the public interest in effective disciplinary procedures for the investigation and eradication of medical malpractice against the confidentiality of the documents, and had correctly used his power to attach conditions to the disclosure. In the absence of exceptional circumstances, an application for the release of papers in care proceedings should be determined by the trial judge.

In *A v X & B (non-party)*,[21] a defendant who had admitted causing injury by his negligent driving sought to reduce the victim's damages by proving, by way of disclosure of the medical records of the victim's brother, that the victim's brain disability was familial (genetic) and would have arisen in any event. Morland J, refusing the application, said that only in a very exceptional factual situation would a court be justified in civil proceedings in ordering disclosure of a non-party's confidential medical data and that this was not such a case. In *Bennett v Compass Group UK*,[22] defendants to a claim in respect of an accident at work had sought, reasonably enough one would have thought, to obtain disclosure of the employee's medical records. The records had been referred to in an expert medical orthopaedic report served on behalf of the claimant. The Court of Appeal said that the judge had had jurisdiction to make his order that the claimant provide the defendant with a signed form of authority for release of her GP and hospital records direct to the defendant, although care was to be taken in the exercise of that jurisdiction. The defendant

---

17 [2002] EWCA Civ 388.
18 [2004] EWHC 2085 (Fam).
19 It is also worth noting the costs point: the judge said that ordinarily a party required to provide pre-action disclosure would be awarded his costs but in the circumstances each side should pay its own costs. It is not the practice in my experience that a party who successfully challenges the refusal of a likely party to proceedings bears the costs of the application.
20 [2001] EWCA Civ 2014.
21 [2004] EWHC 447 (QB).
22 [2002] EWCA Civ 642.

had a right to inspect the records under CPR 31.3, and also as records relied on by the claimant's expert in his report, under CPR 31.14(e).[23]

In *Ashworth Security Hospital v MGN Ltd*,[24] the House of Lords agreed with the Court of Appeal in upholding the judge's order that a journalist's employer at the *Daily Mirror* should disclose the identity of an intermediary as a means of identifying the source of information on a patient detained under the Mental Health Act 1983. The court said that the disclosure of confidential medical records to the press was misconduct which was not merely of concern to the individual establishment in which it occurred; it was an attack on an area of confidentiality which should be safeguarded in any democratic society and the protection of patient information was of vital concern to the National Health Service. However, when the hospital sought to compel the intermediary journalist who had originally obtained the information from hospital sources, ie information derived from the patient's records, to disclose the identity of those sources, the Court of Appeal, managing to distinguish the House of Lords decision, declined to make the order sought, saying that protection of journalistic sources was one of the basic conditions of press freedom and there was no overriding requirement in the case to allow what would otherwise be a breach of Art 10 of the European Convention on Human Rights (*Ackroyd v Mersey Care NHS Trust*).[25]

For guidance concerning the disclosure of medical records of patients detained under the Mental Health Act 1983 in Mental Health Review Tribunal proceedings, see *Dorset Healthcare NHS Trust v MH*.[26]

Consent and confidential information

In the case of *ABC v (1) St George's Healthcare NHS Trust (2) South West London & St George's Mental Health NHS Trust (3) Sussex Partnership NHS Foundation Trust*,[27] the respondents were responsible for treating the appellant's father, who was detained under the Mental Health Act 1983. It was suspected that he might be suffering from Huntington's disease. The child of a parent with Huntington's disease had a 50% chance of developing the condition. The father's doctors considered whether they should override his patient confidentiality, and his expressed wishes, and inform his children of the suspected diagnosis. However, they chose not to do so. In late 2009, the appellant informed her father that she was pregnant. Again, his doctors considered whether to inform his children of the provisional diagnosis, but decided against it. Genetic testing subsequently confirmed the diagnosis in him. The appellant gave birth in April 2010. Later that year, she was accidentally informed of her father's condition by one of his doctors. She underwent genetic testing

---

23   Note that in care proceedings it will generally be the case that the court should be provided with medical records of parents (see *Re B (disclosure to other parties)* (2001) 2 FLR 1017 and *Re B, R and C (Children)* 12 November 2002, CA).
24   (2002) MLC 0800.
25   [2003] Lloyd's Rep Med 379. There is some fear for confidentiality as the Government proposes at huge expense to put all health records on a central database. But such fear is unwarranted. If the Government's track record on IT is taken into account, in the civil service and defence, for example, as well as in health, it will not work.
26   (2010) BMLR 1.
27   [2017] EWCA Civ 336.

and was diagnosed as suffering from the disease. She brought her claim in negligence on the basis that the respondents should have informed her of her father's diagnosis: they knew of the 50% risk to her and knew that a diagnosis would have a direct effect on her health, welfare and life. The judge struck out the claim, holding that there was no reasonably arguable duty of care owed to the appellant.

The appellant relied on clinical guidance given by the Royal College of Physicians, the Royal College of Pathologists and the British Society of Human Genetics (April 2006) entitled *Consent and Confidentiality in Genetic Practice, Guidance on Genetic Testing and Sharing Genetic Information*. She submitted that the guidance made it clear that there were professional obligations towards those who, although not in an existing doctor/patient relationship with a clinician, had a vital interest in genetic information which the clinician had obtained. She argued that those obligations were a good foundation for an extension of the legal duty of care to individuals affected in that way. It was held to be arguably fair, just and reasonable to impose on the respondents a duty of care towards the appellant on the facts alleged. The policy reasons (no public interest to counterbalance obvious public interest in preserving doctor/patient confidentiality/subjecting doctors to conflicting duties/ duty to disclose information to third parties would undermine trust and confidence/'Floodgates'/the extension of a doctor's duty of care was not consonant with the incremental development of the common law) relied on by the respondents to argue against any extension of the duty of care were not persuasive in a strike out. They were all arguable. At the time of writing the judgment of the Court of Appeal after hearing the full arguments is awaited.

Misleading disclosure

Where a health authority had grossly misled the claimant's medical and legal advisers in their disclosure of X-rays, the Court of Appeal ordered a new trial (*Cunningham v North Manchester Health Authority*[28]).

OTHER PRE-ACTION FACILITIES

By s 33(1) of the Act of 1981, the court may make orders for:

- the inspection, photographing, preservation, custody and detention of property which by s 35(5) includes any land chattel or other corporeal property of any description [possibilities of inspection of hospital premises and machines here] that appears to the court to be property which may become the subject matter of subsequent proceedings or as to which any question may arise in any such proceedings; and
- taking samples of any such property and carrying out any experiment on or with it.

In *Ash v Buxted Poultry Ltd*,[29] Brooke J held that the court had power to order one party to a personal injury action to permit the other to make

---

28 [1997] 8 Med LR 135.
29 (1989) Times, 29 November.

a video recording of a relevant industrial process so as to facilitate the judge's understanding of the case. This power could be of use in the odd clinical negligence case, eg to film the process of a machine in hospital.

In *Dobson v North Tyneside Health Authority*,[30] the Court of Appeal held that there was no right of property in the brain of a deceased and that there was no duty to preserve the brain after *post mortem* and after the rest of the body had been buried. The claim was therefore struck out.[31] In *AB v Leeds Teaching Hospital NHS Trust and Cardiff and Vale NHS Trust*,[32] an imaginative group action by parents of deceased children whose organs had been removed at post-mortem, the claim was for psychiatric injury caused on discovery of the removal of the organs. Gage J held that the parents had no possessory rights in the organs (although a duty of care could exist in such circumstances – see Chapter 5).[33]

The reverse side of the coin

Subject to any conflict with human rights (see Chapter 23), we may note *Dunn v British Coal Corpn*,[34] in which the Court of Appeal held that where a claim for damages for an industrial accident included a substantial claim for loss of earnings, the claimant was obliged to disclose all his medical records and not just those relating to the accident (the Court of Appeal has confirmed that the duty to disclose medical records in this type of situation was a duty to disclose not only to the medical advisers for the other party but also to the legal advisers – *Hipwood v Gloucester Health Authority*[35]).

In the Irish case of *Irvin v Donaghy*,[36] where the application by the defendants for the claimant's medical records was made direct to the GP and hospital, it was said that a sensible practice had grown up of providing that the documents were in the first instance to be inspected by the claimant who could object to the production on grounds of privilege. The court had to seek to ensure that only the relevant parts of confidential documents were made available to the applicant. There was no objection in principle to the claimant having a right to object to the production of irrelevant material and he should have the opportunity to cover up entries in the medical records which were irrelevant, just as the claimant could in the traditional context of discovery between parties.

Section 35(1) provides that the court is not to make an order for disclosure if it considers that compliance with the order would be likely to be injurious to the public interest. As the court has a general discretion whether to exercise its power to order disclosure or not, this provision seems otiose.

---

30   [1997] 1 WLR 596.
31   In *R v Kelly* (1998) 51 BMLR 142, it was held that parts of a dead body can be property within s 4 of the Theft Act 1968 if they have acquired different attributes as a result of the application of skill, such as dissection or preservation techniques, for exhibition or teaching purposes.
32   (2004) MLC 1101.
33   A breach of the human right to family life under Art 8 was included in the plea, of course.
34   [1993] PIQR P275.
35   MLC 0708, [1995] 6 Med LR 187.
36   [1996] PIQR P207.

Disclosure should not be refused on the ground that the claim is time-barred unless that is clear beyond reasonable argument, particularly as discovery might reveal material which would affect the position (*Harris v Newcastle upon Tyne Health Authority*[37]).

PRIVILEGE

Privileged documents must be disclosed but can be withheld from inspection. Rule 31(3) acknowledges this, but, if challenged, the existence of privilege has to be proved. The two classes of privilege that are likely to be relevant to disclosure of medical records are legal professional privilege and public interest.

Legal professional privilege

Correspondence and other communications between a solicitor and his client are privileged from production even though no litigation was contemplated or pending at the time, provided that they are of a confidential nature and the solicitor was acting in his professional capacity for the purpose of giving legal advice or getting it on behalf of the client, as from counsel. If a document to which legal professional privilege attaches does find its way into the hands of the defendant, he may use it as desired, regardless of the privilege, but if he has not yet made use of it, he can be restrained from so doing (*Goddard v Nationwide Building Society*;[38] *English and American Insurance Co v Herbert Smith & Co*;[39] and see also *Guinness Peat Properties v Fitzroy Robinson Partnership*[40] – and see below the section on documents obtained by mistake).

But it is in the class of documents that are only privileged if made when litigation was contemplated or pending that any problems on disclosure of medical records are likely to arise. The general principle is that communications between a solicitor and third party, whether directly or through an agent, which come into existence after litigation is contemplated or commenced and are made with a view to such litigation, either for the purpose of giving or obtaining advice in regard to that litigation, or of obtaining or collecting evidence to be used in it, or obtaining information which may lead to the obtaining of such evidence, are privileged. This privilege includes documents which are obtained by a solicitor with a view to enabling him to prosecute or defend an action, or to give advice with reference to existing or contemplated litigation, but does not include copies he obtains of documents that are not themselves privileged. It is with reference to reports of accidents and similar documents which are made before litigation is commenced and generally have the purpose of putting the senior personnel or the solicitors of the potential defendants fully in the picture that problems have arisen. Such reports have a dual purpose at least, that of producing as clear an account of the incident as possible and as soon as possible so that the facts may

---

37 [1989] 1 WLR 96, CA.
38 [1987] QB 670, CA.
39 [1988] FSR 232.
40 [1987] 1 WLR 1027, CA.

be ascertained and any necessary action taken, and that of providing a basis on which solicitors may be instructed if necessary and proceedings defended (or settled) if they are instituted. It is not easy to discern in the shifting sands of the law what the legal rules are for defining the test of 'made with a view to litigation'. Similarly, it is not clear at what point litigation may be said to have begun to be 'contemplated'.[41]

Dominant purpose

In *Waugh v British Railways Board*,[42] the defendants sought privilege for an internal report that was made in accordance with their usual practice after an accident. It contained contemporary accounts from witnesses. The defendants deposed that one of the principal purposes in preparing it had been so that it could be passed to their chief solicitor to enable him to advise the Board on their legal liability and defend any proceedings if so advised. After considerable dissension below, the House of Lords, agreeing with Lord Denning MR's judgment in the Court of Appeal, said that the due administration of justice strongly required that a contemporary report such as this, which would almost certainly be the best evidence as to the cause of the accident, should be disclosed, and that for that important public interest to be overridden by a claim of privilege the purpose of submission to the party's legal advisers in anticipation of litigation must be at least the dominant purpose for which it had been prepared; that in that particular case that purpose had been of no more than equal weight with the purpose of facilitating proper railway operation and safety. Therefore, the claim to privilege failed. The court added that the fact that the report stated on its face that it had finally to be sent to the solicitor for advice could not be conclusive as to what in fact the dominant purpose of its creation was.[43]

This principle was applied to a health authority report in *Lask v Gloucester Health Authority*.[44] The Court of Appeal held that a confidential accident report, which NHS circulars required to be completed by health authorities, both for the use of solicitors in case litigation arose in respect of the accident and also to enable action to be taken to avoid a repetition of the accident, was not privileged since the dominant purpose of its preparation had not been for submission to solicitors in anticipation of litigation, and this was so decided even though both health authority and solicitor had deposed that that had in fact been its dominant purpose and the report itself referred only to that purpose (the court saw in the wording of the relevant Health Circular material which enabled it to reject the sworn statements in the affidavits). This may be contrasted with

---

41 Privilege does not attach to pre-existing documents obtained, but not created, for the purposes of litigation (*Ventouris v Mountain* [1991] 1 WLR 607, CA). Note also that the Court of Appeal stated that just because a document had to be disclosed, it did not automatically follow that production or inspection would be ordered. Privilege, as opposed to admissibility, becomes irrelevant once a document has in fact been disclosed (*Black & Decker Inc v Flymo Ltd* [1991] 1 WLR 753.

42 [1980] AC 521.

43 In *Secretary of State for Trade and Industry v Baker* [1998] Ch 356, the Vice-Chancellor said that it would not be enough to establish 'dominant purpose' if production of the document did not involve a risk of impinging upon the inviolability of lawyer/client communications.

44 [1991] 2 Med LR 379.

McAvan v London Transport Executive[45] in which reports that had been prepared by a bus crew and an inspector after an accident had occurred were held by the court to be privileged as the dominant purpose in their preparation was to ascertain blame in the event of a claim being made.

In *Green v Post Office*,[46] the Court of Appeal ordered disclosure of an accident report brought into existence by an employer for the dual purpose of providing information not only on which legal advice could be obtained if a claim for personal injuries was made by the employee but also on which the employer could consider whether any remedial action was required to avoid a repetition of the accident at work.

Medical reports

Although Lord Woolf wanted all communications between patients' solicitors and medical experts to be disclosed, that has fortunately not become the law.[47] Medical reports, whether on liability or prognosis, and indeed any expert report that a party has commissioned, are privileged and he cannot be required to produce them (*Worrall v Reich*;[48] *Causton v Mann Egerton (Johnsons) Ltd*[49]). If you want a sight of the defendants' doctor's report when you show them yours or agree to send the client to a medical examination, you must get their agreement first. It is not safe to rely on an implied agreement, even though Lord Denning MR said in the *Causton* case in a strong dissenting judgment:

> I hope that in future the solicitors for every plaintiff will refuse to allow any defendants to have any medical examination of the plaintiff except on the terms that the defendants will disclose the medical reports following the examination. This has become so usual in practice that I think it may be said to have become the 'usual terms'. This is most desirable. We know that the medical men of this country give their reports honestly and impartially by whichever side they are instructed, and it is only fair that if one side shows his the other should reciprocate.

The usual order for disclosure of medical reports on the claimant's condition and prognosis means only that if a party does in fact intend to produce such evidence in court, he must disclose it first.

If the reports are not prepared in anticipation of litigation, eg where they have been made by an employer in order to establish whether an employee is able to return to work, the court may order disclosure if that is necessary for the fair disposal of the case (*Ford Motor Co v X Nawaz*[50]).

In *Jackson v Marley Davenport Ltd*,[51] the Court of Appeal said that CPR 35.13 did not provide the courts with the power to order disclosure of earlier reports made by experts in preparation of a final report. Where an expert made a report for legal advisers for the purposes of a conference, such a report was subject to litigation privilege at the time it was made. It was not intended that the CPR should abrogate privilege,

---

45 (1983) 133 NLJ 1101, CA.
46 (15 June 1987, unreported).
47 Note, however, that in certain circumstances the court can order disclosure of an expert's instructions under r 35(10)4 (see Chapter 22).
48 [1955] 1 QB 296, CA.
49 [1974] 1 WLR 162, CA.
50 [1987] ICR 434, EAT.
51 [2004] 1 WLR 2926.

and references to the disclosure of experts' reports in CPR 35.10(2) had to be references to the expert's actual evidence and not to earlier draft reports (*Carlson v Townsend* applied[52]). A bold attempt had already been made in *Linstead v East Sussex, Brighton and Hove Health Authority*[53] to consign legal professional privilege to the waste bin using the ubiquitous human rights plea, here under Art 6, the right to a fair trial. The claimant sought to force disclosure of an earlier statement made by a midwife to the defendants at a time when clearly proceedings were pending. Forbes J refused the application, saying that the privilege was paramount and absolute when not waived or abrogated. The right to a fair trial did not entitle interference with the right to legal confidentiality. The Human Rights Act did not alter the nature and effect of legal privilege, which was not subject to any balancing exercise of weighing competing public interests.

The House of Lords has three times recently had occasion to consider legal professional privilege. In *B v Auckland District Law Society*,[54] a case on appeal from New Zealand, they held that privilege had not been waived where documents had voluntarily been made available expressly for limited purposes. In *Medcalf v Weatherill*,[55] they held that it was unfair to make wasted costs orders against counsel for pursuing allegations of fraud where legal professional privilege prevented counsel from adducing evidence as to whether they had any reasonably credible material before them to prove those allegations. Reference may also be made to *Dempsey v Johnstone*,[56] where the Court of Appeal held that the question whether counsel had been negligent in pursuing a claim could only be resolved by a sight of counsel's written advice and that was not permitted as the document was privileged.

The third House of Lords decision is *Three Rivers Council v Bank of Credit and Commerce International*.[57] The court said that legal advice privilege attached to advice given by solicitors about the preparation and presentation of evidence to be submitted to an inquiry since legal advice for the purposes of privilege included advice as to what should prudently and sensibly be done in the relevant legal context. Legal professional privilege was not an extension of litigation privilege, but a single integral privilege whose sub-heads were legal advice privilege and litigation privilege; it was litigation privilege that was restricted to proceedings or anticipated proceedings in a court of law.

Proceedings contemplated

The other question – at what point can one say that proceedings are contemplated? – can also give rise to difficulties. It can be said that as soon as any accident has occurred, there is a prospect of litigation. Some cases have endorsed that approach, principally *Seabrook v British Transport*

---

52   [2001] PIQR P346.
53   [2002] 3 WLR 172.
54   [2003] 2 AC 736.
55   *Medcalf v Mardell (wasted costs order)*, sub-nom *Medcalf v Weatherill* [2002] UKHL 27, [2003] 1 AC 120.
56   [2003] EWCA Civ 1134.
57   [2004] 3 WLR 1274.

Commission[58] ('I think that, whenever a man is fatally injured in the course of his work on the railway line, there is at least a possibility that litigation will ensue', *per* Havers J); but it is doubtful if that case is authority for anything anymore in view of *Waugh v British Railways Board* (above) and *Alfred Crompton Amusement Machines Ltd v Customs and Excise Comrs (No 2)*,[59] which would appear to be authority for the proposition that, where a decision needs to be taken by a potential defendant before solicitors are instructed, documents coming into existence before that decision is taken cannot be said to have been made when litigation was in contemplation and are therefore not privileged. There would appear to be scope for arguing on that basis for the disclosure of a great many accident reports (the documents in the *Alfred Crompton* case comprised material collected for the purpose of preparing a valuation of the claimant's goods for an assessment to purchase tax, but the principle is equally applicable to accident or medical reports).

Whose privilege?

The general rule is that the privilege is that of the client and of no-one else; only the client can waive the privilege (though the privilege is not lost by reason of the death of the client). The somewhat complex facts of *Lee v South West Thames Regional Health Authority*,[60] illustrate what appears to be an exception to the principle that privilege may be claimed only by the party for whose benefit the document was prepared, or at any rate a limit upon that principle.

> Pre-action disclosure was sought on behalf of a small boy who suffered brain damage, probably through lack of oxygen when he was on a respirator either in hospital or in the ambulance. The health authority for the hospital had, after litigation was contemplated against them, required from the defendants, who were responsible for the ambulance service, a report on what had or might have happened. That report was agreed by the parties to be privileged as far as the hospital health authority was concerned; but its disclosure was sought against the defendants, it being argued that the privilege was not theirs to assert. The Court of Appeal refused to order disclosure, saying that, although the defendants appeared to be advancing the other authority's claim to privilege, the cause of action being asserted against the defendants was not a wholly independent cause of action, but arose out of the same incident as that which rendered the hospital authority a likely defendant. However, that conclusion was 'reached with undisguised reluctance because we think that there is something seriously wrong with the law if Marlon's mother cannot find out exactly what caused this brain damage'.

Public interest privilege

It is all too easy for a public body that wishes to avoid embarrassing disclosures, or to create or preserve a sense of mystique, to claim that disclosure of certain important documents would be damaging to the public interest. Where the claim is based on the ground of national

---

58 [1959] 1 WLR 509.
59 [1974] AC 405, HL.
60 [1985] 1 WLR 845, CA.

security, it may well succeed as that is an argument which our courts take very seriously. So, too, where the interests of children are involved. But in all cases, such a claim must be carefully scrutinised so that public bodies that are seeking to take the easy way out should not be encouraged to expect to succeed.

Strictly, this is not a claim for privilege that a party may advance, but rather an immunity from production that the court should invoke of its own accord if the party does not, on the basis that such production would be injurious to the public interest, ie that withholding the documents is necessary to the proper functioning of the public service. It features most frequently in the area of governmental decisions or policy, and police or similar investigations, but it could be found occasionally in the clinical negligence action. Every potential claim to immunity will be considered on its own facts, but a decision as to a particular type of document is likely to be of persuasive authority when a similar situation occurs later. There are many reported cases on public interest privilege. One example, in the medical field, must suffice here.

> In September 1990 haemophiliacs seeking compensation for having been infected with the HIV virus from contaminated clotting agents secured in the Court of Appeal the release of many important documents that the government were unjustly trying to withhold from them on the factitious ground, so dear to government, that the public interest demanded that they remain secret (see *Re HIV Haemophiliac Litigation* (1990) 41 BMLR 171, [1990] NLJR 1349).

Documents obtained by mistake

It is not unusual to find privileged documents among the medical records, such as memos or letters from the 'accused' doctor to the hospital administrator, health authority solicitor or MDU, which have clearly been included through oversight – someone has simply copied everything in the file without properly scrutinising the documents. In such a case, the general rule is that you cannot take advantage of their oversight and must send back the documents and any copies, though that rule seems to admit of the strange exception that if you did not realise when you saw the document that it had been supplied by mistake, you need not give it back (see *Guinness Peat Properties Ltd v Fitzroy Robinson Partnership*[61] and *Derby & Co v Weldon (No 8)*[62]). In *Kenning v Eve Construction Ltd*,[63] Michael Wright J refused to order the return of a clearly privileged covering letter from an expert which had been inadvertently disclosed along with his report, on the ground that if the defendants were going to call that expert, they were in any event obliged to disclose all his evidence, warts and all. Where defendants had no reason to suspect a mistake when certain documents had been included by the claimants in the trial bundle, they were entitled to assume that they were documents on which the claimants intended to rely, whether privileged or not, and that any privilege had been waived (*Derby & Co v Weldon (No 10)*[64]).

---

61   [1987] 1 WLR 1027, CA.
62   [1991] 1 WLR 73.
63   17 [1989] 1 WLR 1189.
64   [1991] 1 WLR 660.

Where the defendant's solicitor in a claim for industrial injury reasonably believed that the claimant's advisers had waived privilege in sending him a copy of a medical report, the claimant was entitled to make use of it at the trial (*Pizzey v Ford Motor Co Ltd*[65]).

In *IBM Corpn v Phoenix International*,[66] Aldous J held that the question whether the disclosure was understood by the solicitor for the other party to be a mistake should be adjudged according to the likely reaction of the reasonable solicitor.

The rules remain the same despite the new CPR: *Breeze v John Stacey & Sons*[67] (where the mistake was not obvious there was no duty on the receiving party to inquire further).[68]

In *Fayed v Commissioner of Police for the Metropolis*,[69] the Court of Appeal, reviewing the principles involved, said that an injunction to prevent the use of documents that were subject to legal professional privilege or public interest immunity but had been voluntarily, though mistakenly, sent to the other side for inspection, should only be granted where the mistake would have been obvious to a reasonable solicitor.

CONTENTS OF THE RECORDS[70]

The medical records are likely to contain some or all of the following:

* accident and emergency department record card;
* GP's referral letter;
* admitting doctor's notes on examination;
* ward doctor's clinical notes;
* operating record;
* anaesthetic record;
* daily nursing notes;
* laboratory reports on blood and other bodily samples;
* radiographs and reports on radiographs;
* electrocardiograms (ECG) and reports;
* electroencephalograms (EEG) and reports;
* temperature, pulse and respiration charts;
* fluid balance charts;
* head injury charts;
* partogram (midwifery only);
* foetal heart trace (maternity only);
* correspondence to and from other hospitals involved in treatment and with the GP.

A GP's notes will include medical record cards, correspondence from hospitals and the results of tests.

---

65   [1994] PIQR P15, CA.
66   [1995] 1 All ER 413.
67   (1999) Times, 8 July, CA.
68   Where a prima facie case of fraud against a party has been made out, the court may overrule an otherwise properly made claim to privilege (*Derby & Co v Weldon (No 7)* [1990] 1 WLR 1156).
69   [2002] EWCA Civ 780.
70   The sections that follow explain content for non-computerised records.

NHS records belong to the Secretary of State. Records maintained by private hospitals do not include doctors' notes, which are their own property, and may often be kept separately by the treating doctor. Unlike NHS hospitals, private hospitals may not be responsible for the default of consultants, as opposed to nursing staff (see Chapter 4).

GP RECORDS

The primary purpose of a general practice record is to aid in the continuity of care of the patient. A recent systematic review[71] has shown that increased continuity of care is associated with lower mortality rates in addition to greater patient satisfaction and fewer avoidable admissions to hospital. However, there is no evidence that 'continuity of record', which has been advocated as a subsitute for personal care, has the same beneficial effects. Ideally the notes should allow a GP to reconstruct previous consultations without recourse to memory or questioning of the patient and to take over care seamlessly from a colleague. Unfortunately few GP records live up to this ideal. The doctors' regulatory body, the General Medical Council (GMC), specifies[72] a basic standard:
   Clinical records should include:

1   relevant clinical findings;
2   the decisions made and actions agreed, and who is making the decisions and agreeing the actions;
3   the information given to patients;
4   any drugs prescribed or other investigation or treatment;
5   who is making the record and when.

General practice records have several secondary functions, including the defence of the doctor should he later be the subject of criticism. The medical defence organisations repeatedly remind their members of the importance of good records and give examples in their case reports of poor records which have made the defence of a claim impossible and good records which have enabled criticism to be dispelled. There is a loose correlation between the standard of the notes and quality of care: it is extremely rare to encounter a GP who practices excellent medicine and makes poor notes and, conversely, to come across a GP with a poor standard of clinical practice and good record-keeping.

Many GPs who are the subject of a claim will, when their notes are inadequate, rely in their defence on statements of their usual practice. Claimant lawyers may assert that what has not been noted has not been done. Defences based on usual (or even invariable) practice are inevitably flawed. A paper[73] from the Netherlands (which has a rather similar system of general practice to that in the UK) elegantly demonstrated that performance, what doctors actually do, is very poorly correlated with

71 Pereira Gray DJ, Sidaway-Lee K, White E et al *Continuity of care with doctors—a matter of life and death? A systematic review of continuity of care and mortality* (BMJ Open 2018;8:e021161. doi: 10.1136/bmjopen-2017-021161).
72 General Medical Council *Good Medical Practice* (London: GMC, 2013).
73 Rethans J et al *Does competence of general practitioners predict their performance? Comparison between examination setting and actual practice* (BMJ 1991; 303:1377–80).

competence, what they are capable of doing. It also showed that doctors performed significantly below standard in actual practice. A good clinical record remains the best defence against an allegation of substandard practice.

The electronic patient record (EPR)

Most general practices started to keep computer records in the 1990s and computer records have become universal since the introduction of the new GP contract in 2004. The contract introduced the Quality and Outcomes Framework (QOF), which included financial incentives for GPs to make and maintain up-to-date clinical summaries of their patients' medical histories, which should now be present in the majority of records. There are also incentives to record items such as blood pressure, smoking status and ethnicity.

The enthusiasm for computer records has been very variable both between and within practices, leading to a situation where paper and computer records often operated in tandem. Many doctors have embraced the new technology so wholeheartedly that there is a widespread perception amongst patients that their GP is more interested in his computer than he is in them. The undesirable practice of using both computer and paper records, with obvious potential deleterious effects on clinical care, operated in many practices during the 1990s and persists in some practices today. Dual systems of record-keeping also complicate the task of lawyers and experts in ensuring that they have gathered all the available evidence and in constructing chronologies.

General practitioners use one of the computer systems approved by the Department of Health, from one of the suppliers in the 'GP Systems of Choice' (GPSoC) scheme (details are available at https://digital.nhs.uk/ services/gp-systems-of-choice). There are four principal system suppliers. The systems use different software, are different in operation and generate different records. This creates difficulties for doctors working in more than one practice, when records are transferred between practices and for lawyers and experts who may lack any knowledge of the system being used by a doctor who is the subject of a claim against him.

The Department of Health issued detailed guidelines[74] to general practitioners on the use of computer systems. The guidance specifies in detail how GPs should use, maintain and transfer electronic records. GP computer systems all include an 'audit trail', separate from the electronic patient record (EPR), which enables one to establish who made a record, when that record was made and whether there have been any changes to the record. The guidance states:

> It is the audit trail that enables a record to be taken back to any date and viewed as it was on that date. Audit trails are of great medico-legal importance in determining the true state of entries in the EPR at any time in the past.

The audit trail of the computer of the notorious mass-murderer Harold Shipman showed that many of his records were fabricated and was one of

---

74 See www.dh.gov.uk *Good practice guidelines for general practice electronic patient records* (v 3.1, June 2005).

the factors which led to his detection.[75] Proving that an entry is false or has been made non-contemporaneously in a negligence action is likely to involve the employment of considerable information technology expertise.

A GP computer record will typically include registration details, a summary of the medical history, basic data relating to prevention such as smoking status, blood pressure, a record of consultations, a list of all prescriptions issued, a record of drugs available on repeat prescription and the records of investigations performed. Many practices now scan correspondence into the electronic record, where it should be visible as an attachment. When requesting records from practices it is important to specify that complete disclosure is required: it is not uncommon, for example, for the printout generated by a practice to include only the latest issue of a drug on repeat prescription rather than all prescriptions or to fail to include attachments. Sometimes a case may generate the need for a record whose existence is not obvious: the crucial evidence relating to an abnormal test result which has negligently not been acted upon may be lurking within an undisclosed part of the electronic mailbox in which such results are sent from the local hospital laboratory to the GP.

The fact that different parts of the record appear on different screens is a potential source of error in general practice medicine because important information may not be easily visible or may be difficult to access. Important information from a recent hospital attendance, for example, might only be accessible if an attachment is opened in a new screen.

If a patient has moved practices after a medical error, the details transferred to the new practice might be an incomplete record. It may therefore be necessary to approach the original practice to obtain complete disclosure.

The record of each consultation will include at least one Read code, a coded term used in clinical practice. The codes are arranged in hierarchical structure and allow clinical entries to be searched for the purposes of audit or reporting. Read codes are arranged in chapters for items such as symptoms, examination findings, diagnostic and therapeutic procedures and diagnoses. A doctor who wished to record the fact that a patient had a heart attack might use the Read code 'G30 Acute myocardial infarction' or might explore the hierarchy to be more specific and enter 'G301 Anterior myocardial infarction'. Many GPs find Read codes difficult to use and inappropriate or incorrect Read codes are frequently encountered. Alternatively, doctors may resort to the use of a small repertoire of easily remembered codes for every consultation, such as 'had a chat to patient' or 'patient reviewed'. The codes are regularly updated to include, for example, new drugs, diseases or procedures.

In addition to the Read code, each clinical entry should identify the date of the consultation, the author of the record and it should contain a free text narrative. This will typically include the symptoms of which the patient complained (sometimes preceded by 'S' for subjective), examination findings (sometimes preceded by 'O' for objective), a diagnosis (often Read coded), any treatment prescribed and details of other management, such as a referral. The poor keyboard skills of many general practitioners cause some of them to write shorter records than when writing, even though

---

75   See www.the-shipman-inquiry.org.uk.

the written notes of general practitioners were frequently criticised for their brevity.

GPs should also routinely record their telephone consultations with patients, although there is evidence[76] that documentation of telephone advice is particularly poor. If a patient's telephone records show a telephone call of significant length to a GP practice then an explanation may be required if there is no corresponding record.

Computer records may enhance patient safety. Prescribing systems flag up warnings of potential drug interactions or contraindications, though some GPs find that these appear so frequently when they are clinically irrelevant that they routinely override them. The systems can incorporate reminders and prompts to tell the GP that the patient needs, for example, to have his blood pressure checked, his medication reviewed or his thyroid function measured.

Many GPs use computerised appointment systems linked to the EPR. In theory, these might allow one to determine the precise length of a consultation. However, the complexity of the systems and the varying ways in which doctors use them mean that this is frequently not possible. Nonetheless, asking for disclosure of computer appointment system records might allow one to establish that a patient did in fact attend on a specific day at a particular time.

GPs make electronic referrals through 'Choose and Book', a national service which allows patients to book their own appointments from a choice of 'providers' either over the internet or by telephone. These referrals are allocated a unique reference number, which will appear in the record with the prefix 'UBRN'. Referral letters are sent and may be retrieved electronically.

Telephone recordings

Many GP out of hours services record the telephone conversations between call-handlers, triage nurses or doctors and patients. The recordings of such calls may be invaluable evidence, for either the doctor or the patient, in a clinical negligence case. The following is a verbatim transcript of the essential part of the history given to an out of hours doctor by a 23-year-old man:

> Yesterday, I mean I've been bad anyway, I've had like a cold and that, but yesterday I went out for a walk with my dog and like one minute I was all right and suddenly I had a pain at the back of my neck and the back of my head ... And my hearing went funny, I couldn't hear properly ... like I was kneeling on the floor and throwing up and everything and like all night, I've been, my head's been hurting, like nausea and I've been throwing up all night.

This young man clearly gave a history of the sudden onset of a severe headache accompanied by vomiting and other symptoms. This constitutes a subarachnoid haemorrhage (bleeding into the subarachnoid space around the brain) until proved otherwise and requires that the patient be admitted immediately to hospital. This young man was not admitted to hospital and died five weeks later when he suffered a more severe haemorrhage. The second haemorrhage would have been prevented by

---

76   Car J, Sheikh A *Telephone consultations* (BMJ 2003; 326:966-9).

competent management. The existence of the telephone recording made a claim against the doctor impossible to defend.

Paper records: the Lloyd George record

Most patients born before 2004, and some born after 2004, will have an envelope of Lloyd George records containing continuation cards, correspondence and results of investigations. There might in addition be a summary card, a card detailing repeat prescriptions, a record of immunisations and a new patient questionnaire, completed by the patient on registering. It was not uncommon for GP records to be a chaotic jumble of cards and paper, making effective use of the information contained impossible. An effective doctor will have ordered records with a summary. Once this summary has been incorporated into a computer record the Lloyd George envelope may remain unused.

Doctors have notoriously bad handwriting and entries on the Lloyd George continuation cards may be very difficult to read. However, a written record allows doctors to incorporate items like diagrams of the abdomen and highlight parts of the record, which is usually not possible with current GP computer software. There is abundant anecdotal evidence that it is easier to overlook important data on a computer screen than on a paper record.

Many GPs use idiosyncratic abbreviations and shorthand. A list of the more common abbreviations appears at Appendix IV. The idiosyncratic nature of GP records means that there is no infallible method for interpreting an entry such as 'O/E SOB++' (on examination short of breath ++). How short of breath is '++'? Most doctors would use '++' to signify 'very' but it would be difficult to challenge a GP who claimed otherwise.

Written records should be contemporaneous and non-contemporaneous entries should be clearly identified as such. It may be difficult to identify an amendment to a written record or a non-contemporaneous entry. However, more than one doctor has been trapped by not knowing that Lloyd George continuation cards bear the date of printing in the bottom right-hand corner. Making an entry for a consultation that took place before the printing of the card is quite likely to lead to investigation by the GMC.

Other records

There may be other sources of evidence relevant to a clinical negligence claim whose existence is not obvious but whose disclosure would assist the claim. General practitioners and their staff usually keep a daybook and/or a telephone log and a book or electronic record of requests for visits, which usually contain some details of the symptoms or condition underlying the request. There may also be separate records of two-week wait referrals (for suspected cancer). Records of complaints and complaints correspondence should be kept separate from the patient record. There may also be minutes of a significant event analysis or other meetings relating to a medical error. No two general practices operate identical information systems, so it is desirable to make requests for disclosure as open and broad as possible.

The summary care record

The National Programme for Information Technology was established in 2005 and introduced the summary care record (SCR). This was originally intended to make quite a lot of clinical information about patients, including discharge summaries and out of hours GP records, available to authorised NHS staff throughout England but the database currently includes only prescribed drugs, adverse reactions to drugs and allergies in addition to the patient's name, address, date of birth and NHS number. The SCR is being rolled out to community pharmacies. GPs should also add information about patients identified as having 'information or communication needs' and those who are moderately or severely frail, after seeking consent to do so. The information is automatically uploaded to the 'Spine web portal' by GP practices. Patients may choose to add information such as significant medical history to the SCR. Patients should be contacted before their records are uploaded and are given the option to opt-out, but only about 1% do so. However, it appears that many patients treat communications about the SCR as junk mail and many are unaware that their details have been uploaded.

HOSPITAL RECORDS

National Health Service hospital records are more ordered and more consistent in their quality than are the records kept by GPs. They are usually in A4 size folders and are divided into sections. There is some variation in the nature of these sections and their order, but the usual principles are as follows.

The folder contains records kept by nurses as well as those kept by doctors, but these are usually arranged in separate bundles, each in chronological order. In the medical notes, each admission to hospital is filed as a complete unit, which usually opens with an 'admission sheet' on which various particulars are recorded by a clerk as soon as possible after the patient enters the hospital. These include name, address, date of birth, next of kin and consultant responsible.

There should follow a thorough record of the patient's complaints and an appraisal of their current clinical state made by the FY1 (Foundation Year 1) doctor (formerly called a house officer), the most junior of the team of doctors that is to care for the patient during his admission. This is called the 'clerking' and it constitutes a most important and valuable record, both because it is done at a most crucial time in a patient's care, especially in the case of emergency admissions, and because custom dictates that it is carried out with a great degree of thoroughness and in a certain order. Thus, this record should allow readers, if it has been done properly, to have a full understanding of the patient's clinical state at that time, if they can 'read' the traditional system of layout and abbreviation which medical students are taught to use.

In the next section, an example with a glossary is presented to help 'translate' records. It is possible to attempt this because doctors throughout the UK are taught to use much the same system – the clarity and thoroughness of their clerking of patients is one of the chief ways in which a consultant, who is responsible for their training, will assess the competence of the junior doctor, so the junior will wish to make his records comprehensible and useful to the consultant. Therefore, the adequacy of the hospital records is some indication of the quality of care patients have received. A junior doctor who is neglectful or overworked will keep less thorough and comprehensible records, and if his seniors, the specialist registrar or consultant, are also neglectful, this failure will not be corrected.

After the FY1 doctor has thus recorded the admission of the patient to the hospital, the doctor who is immediately responsible for supervising his work may write in the notes, usually using the same format, but more briefly. Thus, frequently in hospital records the same clinical findings are recorded again under the same date, in a different handwriting, which may be that of an FY2 (Foundation Year 2) doctor or a specialist registrar.

There follows a sequential series of entries by one or other of the team members, the frequency of which is, in general, a reflection of how acutely ill the patient is. In an intensive care unit, the junior doctors or more senior colleagues may write in the notes several times a day, recording the hour at which they have assessed the patient; as well as the team of doctors responsible for the patient's care, other consultants whose opinion has been sought may write in the notes. On the other hand, the medical records kept in a long-stay ward, in a psychiatric hospital for example, may be written in only a few times a year.

Next will be filed the results of investigations carried out during that hospital admission, which are generally arrayed by sticking them in date sequence on a card, each card representing a different department – histology (the microscopic examination of tissues), biochemistry (blood levels of hormones and drugs, and of compounds the levels of which are indices of the function of the liver and kidneys), haematology (the characteristics of the cells in the blood), or X-ray. If electrocardiograms have been done, these too should be arranged, in a pattern which enables the trace to be interpreted, and kept in the notes.

If an operation is performed while a patient is in hospital, this should be recorded by a junior doctor, but there will also be a separate sheet which has been filled in immediately after the operation by the surgeon and the anaesthetist.

The admission notes are ended by a junior doctor, who should write a list of the drugs which a patient has been given to take at home. There will also be a typed discharge summary, which is usually written to the patient's GP by the specialist registrar or the consultant; this document is often not written until several weeks or even months after the patient has been sent home.

In between hospital admission notes, but occasionally filed separately, there will be handwritten notes made in the out-patient clinic by the consultant, registrar or FY2 doctor who has seen the patient in the clinic; also there will usually be a letter sent to the GP after each clinic visit, and copies of these letters will be kept in sequence in the patient's hospital notes.

Hospital records will contain many records kept by nurses, which may be of medico-legal importance: chief among these is the patient's 'Kardex' record: this is a system of notes kept in a single folder in the sister's office on the ward, each patient having a card which is folded into a specially designed folder which allows the patients' names to be displayed in the same sequence as their beds are arranged on the ward. When the patient leaves the hospital, the card is removed and kept in the patient's hospital records folder. The nursing staff make an entry in the Kardex for each patient every day, noting the basic observations (temperature, pulse rate and blood pressure) and commenting briefly on the patient's progress.

Also filed with the nursing records will be all the charts which have been kept at the end of the patient's bed during the admission. These will include a chart of recordings made of the patient's temperature, pulse rate and blood pressure, which may be measured hourly, four-hourly or daily, according to how acutely ill the patient is. There may also be fluid balance charts which record the volumes of fluid which the patient has been given, orally or intravenously, and the volumes they have excreted.

With these charts will be found a 'treatment card', a new one of which is made out for each hospital admission. This is kept by the patient's bed, and is written on by one of the doctors whenever he wishes to prescribe a drug. The name of the drug should be written clearly, with instructions as to dose and frequency and route of administration, with the doctor's signature. The nurse in charge of the ward, whenever she administers the drug, will sign the card again in a column which gives the date and time.

Most patients require the services of some other professional workers, whether they are social workers, physiotherapists or occupational therapists, while they are in hospital. However, the notes of their activities kept by these other professionals are not usually assembled to be kept with the other records in the patient's hospital record folder, for reasons that are historical rather than logical.

EXAMPLES OF THE FORM AND ABBREVIATION IN MEDICAL RECORDS

Medicine has its own language. In the past, when the knowledge and skill of physicians and surgeons were relatively limited, the dignity of their profession was enhanced and their distance above the patient increased by the use of terms the meaning of which was apparent only to their fellow trained doctors. To what extent that is no longer true today is a moot point.

However, there are other important factors as well as the plethora of 'medical' words – many derived from Latin and Greek – which are still used in notes and make them difficult to understand. NHS doctors making records, whether GPs in the community or junior doctors in hospitals, often work in situations of pressure in which it is inappropriate to spend a high proportion of time in writing. This leads not only to poor legibility,[77] but also to the proliferation of a large number of abbreviations. In using these abbreviations, doctors assume that their colleagues will be able to interpret them, and they sacrifice the possibility of non-doctors being able to understand. This follows from the prevailing attitude to

---

77 In *Prendergast v Sam & Dee Ltd* [1989] 1 Med LR 36, MLC 0018, CA, a GP was held 25% liable for injury caused when the pharmacist (held 75% liable) misread his prescription and dispensed Daonil instead of Amoxil.

records throughout the medical profession, which is that they are written for the benefit of other doctors who may be treating the same patient in future; they are certainly not written for the patient to be able to understand them.

In recent decades, advances in diagnostic methods and in treatment have led to a vast proliferation of specialities and of kinds of data that can be assembled about a particular patient. These are often presented using new codes and new words, which are hard to understand unless you have a thorough knowledge of the particular techniques.

To read medical records, one needs a medical dictionary which is up-to-date. Even if the technical words are translated, however, there remains the problem of abbreviations. In the section which follows, one may see what a house surgeon might typically write in the notes when clerking a previously fit woman with acute appendicitis. The purpose is to give an example, not only of commonly used abbreviations, but also of the way in which a doctor's notes are generally laid out and organised in a certain sequence.[78]

Form and abbreviation in hospital records: an annotated example

	DATE TIME	NAME ADDRESS DATE OF BIRTH
Complains of . . (Presenting complaint) (duration)	C O	Abdominal pain 3 days
History of presenting complaint RIF = right lower quadrant of the abdomen 1/52 = 1 week (1/12 = 1 month, 1/7 = 1 day)	HPC	Off food with central abdo pain 3 days ago, then pain moved to RIF, and became more severe with nausea and anorexia. Some diarrhoea, 1/52
Previous medical history	PMH	Tonsillectomy age 12

Previous obstetric history
  P = Parity (number of pregnancies).
  Figures represent number of births
  followed by number of miscarriages
  or abortions (= TOPs)
LSCS = caesarean section
	POH	P 1 + 1 (TOP 1980)
		LSCS (elective) 1983 for pre-
		eclampsia

Social history	S H	Mother and part-time worker Non-smoker Drinks socially
Family history A & W = alive and well Ca = cancer	F H	Mother A & W, age 67 Father died age 68 Ca Lung 2 sibs A & W Daughter age 4 well

---

78   Further hieroglyphs may be found set out in Appendix IV.

Systematic enquiry	S E	
Gastro-intestinal system (tract)	GIT	Appetite normal until 3 days ago
B O = bowels open		B O regular
° Diarrhoea = no diarrhoea		° Diarrhoea previous few months
° Melaena = no blood in motions that is black		° Melaena
P R = per rectum		° Fresh blood P R
Weight Ý = weight constant		Weight
Genito-urinary tract	G U	° Haematuria
Dysuria = pain on urinating		° Dysuria
Nocturia = arising from sleep to urinate		° Frequency
		° Nocturia
Gynaecological	Gynae	K 5/27–32
K = menstrual cycle – number of days of bleeding / number of days of whole cycle		
Cardiovascular system	CVS	° Palpitations
SOBOE = short of breath on exertion		° SOBOE
Orthopnoea = short of breath on lying flat		° Orthopnoea
PND = paroxysmal nocturnal dyspnoea (attacks of waking up very breathless)		° PND
Oedema = swelling with fluid especially of ankles		° Oedema
Respiratory system	R S	° Cough
° Haemoptysis = coughing blood		° Haemoptysis
		° Wheezing
Neurological system	Neuro	° Headaches – occasional
		° Fits
LOC = episode of loss of consciousness		° LOC
Vision 4 = no problem with visions	Vision 4 Hearing 4	
List of regular medication	Drugs	Nil
List of drugs to which the patient thinks she is allergic	Allergy	Penicillin
ON EXAMINATION	O/E	
General description		Distressed
Not anaemic, cyanosed or jaundiced		°An, °Cy, °J
No clubbing (deformity of nails)		
No palpable lymph nodes		° C I
		° L Ns
		Temp 37.8°C
Cardiovascular system	CVS	
Pulse rate and rhythm		p 90 reg

Blood pressure (arterial)

B P 120/70

JVP = venous pressure estimated by observing jugular vein

JVP

H S = heart sounds (diagram used as visual representation of the sounds)
R = L = findings same on both sides, ie normal

H S

° Oedema
Pulses R = L

Respiratory system
T • = trachea in centre (normal)

R S

T •

P N = findings on percussion of chest
B S = breath sounds, heard with stethoscope. (Added sounds may be crackles (= creps, crepitations) or wheezes)

Expansion R = L
P N resonant R = L
B S vesicular, nil added

Abdominal examination
LSKK° = liver, spleen and kidneys number palpable (ie not enlarged)
° Masses = no lumps in abdomen

Abdo

LSKK°

° Masses

Guarding = reflex muscle spasm

Tender, with guarding & rebound

Rebound = pain on removal of pressure
B S = bowel sounds
P R = rectal examination
NAD = nothing abnormal detected

P R

B S 4
NAD

P V = per vaginam examination of the pelvis
N/S = normal size (if abnormal, uterine size is often expressed as equivalent of a certain gestational age in pregnancy, eg 14/40 meaning the same as the size of a normal pregnant uterus at 14 weeks after the last period began)
A/V = anteverted (alternative uterine positions are axial or retroverted)
V/V = vulva and vagina
Adnexae = areas at either side of uterus

P V

Uterus N/S A/V
Adnexae NAD

Cervix NAD
V/V – NAD

Central nervous system
Examination (this part of the examination is often highly abbreviated or omitted)
PERLA = pupils are equal and react to light and accommodation
Fundi = contents of the eyeballs are seen by the ophthalmoscope

CNS

Cranial nerves

PERLA

Fundi NAD

Motor = examination of the motor aspect of the nervous system in each limb	Motor	Power Tone R = L Co-ordination NAD Reflexes
Sensory = examination of the different modalities of sensation in the limbs and trunk	Sensory	Pain Light touch R = L Temperature NAD Position sense Vibration
SUMMARY	ANALYSIS	Previously fit mother aged – years with acute abdominal pain and fever
Δ = diagnosis		Δ appendicitis
NBM = nil by mouth	Plan	NBM
Hourly obs = instructions to nursing staff to record pulse, temp and bp every hour		hourly obs
IVI = intravenous drip N saline = salt solution of similar concentration to that of plasma. (Other fluids are Dextrose saline, or 5% dextrose, which contain a sugar for energy)	IVI	N saline 1L in 6 hours
FBC = full blood count (haematology) U&E = urea and electrolytes (biochemistry) LFT = liver function tests (biochemistry)	FBC U&E LFTs	

Abbreviations and hieroglyphs

For a list of common abbreviations and hieroglyphs, see Appendix IV.

Chapter 22

Experts

Patricia Hitchcock QC and Tom Gillie

Ein Fachmann ist ein Mann, der einige der grössten Fehler kennt, die man in dem betreffenden Fach machen kann und der sie deshalb zu vermeiden versteht.

[An expert is someone who is aware of a few of the worst mistakes that can be made in his field, and so understands how to avoid them.]

Werner Heisenberg *Der Teil und das Ganze* (1969)

WHY DO YOU NEED EXPERTS?

The role of the expert in a clinical negligence case will vary case by case, but the success or failure of the case will invariably depend in very large part on the intellect, competence and communication skills of the expert witness. Amongst the expert's most crucial functions are:

- to assess the evidence and to advise on breach of duty and/or causation, to enable the lawyers to assess the merits and the litigation risks prior to issue;
- to identify gaps in the medical records and, when vital medical records are missing (as they often seem to be), to reconstruct the chain of events insofar as this is possible;
- to provide practical tips, such as where to look for documents in a hospital filing system, what records should exist, what scans should have been retained, etc;
- to review the medical literature, Royal College guidelines and internal hospital protocols and where possible provide independent support for their expert analysis;
- to review the pleadings prior to service, to catch any medical idiocies inadvertently introduced by counsel and to identify at the outset any allegation that cannot be supported;
- once a case has been formulated on the basis of the expert's views, to support and explain that case – in writing, at the experts' meeting and in the witness box;
- to remain independent throughout, keep an open mind – and tell the lawyers of any change of mind as soon as possible, with reasons.

It is no part of the expert's role to decide factual issues, nor to act as an advocate for one of the parties, tempting though this may be. Usurping either the judge's or the advocate's role in the proceedings will draw trenchant criticism from any judge and is likely to be fatal to the cause of the instructing party.

Expert evidence is needed to prove both breach of duty and causation, and very often causation requires a different specialism from breach. An expert for GP liability, for example, will never be able to give authoritative evidence on causation. In a claim for obstetric injury to the foetus, the obstetrician is seldom used to prove causation, and never without the support of a paediatric neurologist or neonatologist. In some areas, however, and especially in straightforward cases, a single expert may suffice: for example, in a claim for inadequate orthopaedic management, where the orthopaedic consultant may be able to speak to both breach of duty and causation.

In cases in which the injury was long in the past, such as birth brain damage, it may well be necessary to instruct two experts, simply because of the lapse of time: the breach of duty expert will need to have been in practice at the date of the injury and be able to comment in the context of what was standard medical practice at that time, to avoid the use of the 'retrospectoscope' rightly reviled by judges. The causation expert must, however, be totally up to date and normally will be in current clinical practice; although the wisdom and continuing professional interest of some eminent experts enables them to continue to give authoritative views on causation long after retirement, this is only rarely a good idea.

The onward march of medical knowledge can cut both ways, however: in *CJL v West Midlands Strategic Health Authority*,[1] for example, Tugendhat J had to decide the issue of how long it would have taken a reasonably competent obstetrician to deliver the claimant by forceps following onset of fetal bradycardia in 1987, and decided on a total of six minutes; some commentators have queried whether a modern doctor, less used to using forceps, could be expected to achieve delivery that fast.[2]

Medical experts will also be needed on quantum, as for any personal injury action, for condition and prognosis, and crucially life expectancy; often, the causation expert will also be able to provide an opinion on both these topics. In larger cases, expertise will be needed from a wide range of related specialisms, which will now need to be identified at an early stage. The specialisms will vary case by case but also with judicial fashion; 30 years ago employment experts were ubiquitous and financial advisors almost unheard of but the advent first of the Woolf reforms and then of periodical payment orders (and the court's duty to assess the form of damages under CPR 41) have reversed that position. Legal teams should invariably direct their minds at every stage to whether or not a given specialism is really cost-effective and necessary to prove the case and be prepared to justify and fight for their choices at cost and case management hearings.

Consideration should be given at the outset to the possibility of using a joint expert in any given specialism, so that if the decision is taken to

---

1   (2009) MLC 1595.
2   See, for example, the article by Andrew Farkas, consultant obstetrician, *Decision to Delivery Interval* (commentary on CJL case) on *Medical Litigation* website (May 2009).

instruct a single party expert, the legal team will be able to explain the need for this at a directions hearing.

WHAT THE COURT EXPECTS OF THE EXPERT

The importance in an expert of independence of mind and the ability to rise above the fray has long been identified and emphasised and, even in the bad old days of partisan warhorses and little judicial control, the judges were not slow to comment. In *Loveday v Renton*,[3] Stuart-Smith LJ set out ten attributes of an expert that assist the court in assessing the weight to be attributed to that expert's opinion. The list would not be out of place in today's rules:

- eminence;
- soundness of opinion;
- internal consistency and logic;
- precision and accuracy of thought;
- response to searching and informed cross-examination;
- ability to face up to logic and make concessions;
- flexibility of mind and willingness to modify opinions;
- freedom from bias;
- independence of thought; and
- demeanour.

It is essential for the legal advisors thoroughly to explore the profiles of all the experts, on both sides, to cover background, training, experience, extent of any original research, qualifications, publications, and clinical and forensic experience, for the purpose of evaluating comparative stature.

In *The Ikarian Reefer*,[4] Cresswell J said that the expert witness had a duty to give independent evidence, uninfluenced as to form or content by the exigencies of litigation, and to provide objective, unbiased opinion to the court on matters within his expertise, never assuming the role of advocate.

In *Sharpe v Southend Health Authority*,[5] Cresswell J commented further:

> An expert witness should make it clear in his or her report that, although the expert would have adopted a different approach or practice, he or she accepted that the approach or practice adopted by the defendant was in accordance with an approach or practice accepted as proper by a responsible body of practitioners skilled in the relevant fields.

And Thorpe LJ said in *Vernon v Bosley*:[6]

> The area of expertise in any case may be likened to a broad street with the plaintiff walking on one pavement and the defendant on the opposite one. Somehow the expert must be ever mindful of the need to walk straight down the middle of the road and to resist the temptation to join the party from whom his instructions come on the pavement.

---

3   [1990] 1 Med LR 117.
4   [1993] 2 Lloyd's Rep 68 at 81.
5   [1997] 8 Med LR 299.
6   [1997] 1 All ER 577, CA.

THE BAD OLD DAYS

The judge went on to wonder whether the practising clinician might find it easier to maintain that detachment than the professional expert witness, who has retired and may spend his life doing medico-legal reports. Sadly, the tenets set out by the judges were often honoured in the breach by expert witnesses, many of whom frankly declared themselves to be available to act only for one party – whether defendant or claimant – in every case. The same faces regularly appeared in both the civil and the criminal courts, and many abandoned clinical practice in favour of becoming a full-time expert witness. As Stuart-Smith LJ observed in *Vernon v Bosley* (above), the judge had not been assisted, as he should have been, by disinterested evidence from the medical professional witnesses, who were allowed to range unchecked into almost every aspect of the case, and he added, with a degree of prescience:

> In my opinion in this type of case in particular there is much to be said for the practice sometimes adopted in the Family Division of there being a psychiatrist appointed by the court. In the field of psychiatry it may be more difficult for those who have treated the plaintiff to approach the case with true objectivity. That was certainly the case here ... Certain it is that the case would have been much shorter and would have been kept in more manageable bounds. But at present the rules of court do not permit this course. Unless the parties agree on a psychiatrist – these parties never would have – the court has no power to make such an order.

REFORM

The Civil Procedure Rules now enshrine the foregoing jurisprudence into a formal code, providing that it is the duty of an expert to help the court on the matters within his expertise and that that duty overrides any obligation to the person from whom experts have received instructions or by whom they are paid (CPR 35.3). The rules also enable the court to restrict the number of experts instructed by the parties (CPR 35.1, 35.4), to order that a given issue be dealt with by a single joint expert where appropriate (CPR 35.7), and to appoint an assessor to assist the judge in dealing with an issue in which the assessor has skill and experience (CPR 35.15). (For good reasons, this latter power has not been much taken up in the clinical negligence context.) The introduction of the rules has not eliminated old-style partisan experts but it has significantly reduced their number and made them somewhat easier to identify.

It should be noted that 'expert' is defined by the CPR 35.2 as a person 'who has been instructed to give or prepare evidence for the purpose of proceedings'. A preliminary report for a potential claimant at the investigative stage is never intended for disclosure, and so should not be considered to have been prepared for the purpose of court proceedings. The notes to r 35.2 make clear that a distinction is to be drawn between advisory experts (at any stage of the claim) and experts instructed to provide written reports for the court. In practice, this can be a difficult line to draw, especially where, as is commonplace, the expert has advised pre-issue and then has to change roles when proceedings are brought. The CPR 35.3 and CPR PD 35 2.1, 2.2 and 3.1 make clear that the court expert's overriding duty is to the court: the distinction lies in the presenting of the expert's opinion to the court; if an expert merely advises a party and never advances a view, in person or in writing, to the court then the duty will not arise – but it is a distinction without much of a difference, since a party will not be well served by any advice that seeks to please the client and does not meet the criteria for court evidence. Reliance on such advice is likely merely to delay recognition of the real risks of litigation and to increase the risk of ambush.

By the CPR 35.10, the report must contain a declaration that the expert understands his or her duty to the court and has complied with that duty. A set form of words is provided in CPR PD 35 3.3 and further guidance for solicitors is to be found in the Guidance for the Instruction of Experts in Civil Claims 2014, available at www.judiciary.uk.

The report is to be addressed to the court and not to the instructing party, and where there is a range of possible opinion that range must be summarised and reasons given for the expert's preference. The report should contain a summary of all relevant instructions received, both written and oral, and a statement of truth.[7]

It should also be remembered that the court expects an expert to take responsibility for his or her role in the process and to be proactive. There is an under-used power under the CPR 35.14 for an expert formally to ask the court for directions, with copies in advance to the instructing party and to the other side. It is to be hoped that such requests will normally be resolved by the solicitor instructing the expert but in the last resort the expert does not have to put up with unreasonable, unworkable or incomprehensible instructions.

CODES OF GUIDANCE

Current guidance on the use of experts pre-issue is available in the Pre-action Protocol for the Resolution of Clinical Disputes, which was the first major work of the Clinical Disputes Forum ('CDF') and was revised following wide consultation in 2010: see Appendix II.[8] The amended version of the Protocol has been in force since 2015, and deals with the use of experts at section 4, emphasising the need for economy and a less adversarial culture.

The first code to guide lawyers instructing experts working under CPR 35 was produced by the Academy of Experts in 2000. A second code was published by the Expert Witness Institute in December 2001. The Civil Justice Council then produced a very detailed authoritative code, drawing on both the EWI and the AoE codes. The CJC Code, together with suggestions and draft guidelines produced by the CDF, was used as the basis for a formal Protocol for the Instruction of Experts to Give Evidence in Civil Claims. A revised version of

---

7   See www.judiciary.uk.
8   See www.judiciary.uk.

the guidance was produced in 2009, and again in 2014, when it was renamed: Guidance for the Instruction of Experts in Civil Claims and is available at https://www.judiciary.uk/related-offices-and-bodies/advisory-bodies/cjc/cjc-publications/guidance-for-the-instruction-of-experts-in-civil-claims/. Its provisions should be carefully studied (and experts should be provided with a copy) as it covers all steps from selection and initial instruction of experts to trial and provides a useful and detailed gloss on CPR 35.

WHAT THE LAWYER EXPECTS OF THE EXPERT

In essence, lawyers expect medical experts to take their cases as seriously as they do themselves, and to exhibit the same level of courtesy and commitment to the lay client. An expert must review the treatment the patient has received carefully, thoughtfully and in full detail. A quick skim through the records and a short declaration that there was no negligence will not do. The expert – like the lawyer – is providing a professional service, and this calls for courtesy to the lay client and high professional standards in written or oral advice. To agree to act is to commit to the case, to undertake to take it seriously and complete work within a reasonable time throughout the currency of the case; only in an emergency is it acceptable to plead supervening clinical commitments to explain late delivery of reports or inadequate preparation for a conference or – worse still – an experts' meeting.

What the lawyer does *not* want is an expert determined to support a party's position, regardless of the facts. It does the instructing party no favours if a claim or defence initially supported by the expert has to be discontinued at a later stage when the expert is facing cross-examination and resiles from their report. What is needed is a clear, authoritative, well-grounded opinion on the issues on which the expert is instructed to comment, whether or not that provides the party with a case, or a defence. If it does not, it should wherever possible provide the client with a greater understanding of what happened, the need for which is often the primary motivation for a claimant seeking legal advice.

Many reports are inadequate. Some do not address the right questions or provide clear answers, and others are deficient in their presentation. In either case, it is the lawyer's task to explain the shortcomings to the expert and seek amendments prior to service. Some experts are very resistant to making any amendment to a report once written, but there is nothing whatever improper in this, provided that the expert is not being asked to amend their true opinion: the CJC Guidance makes this clear at para 65. It is even possible that the lawyer may raise points or provide references that cause the expert to alter their opinion, in which case it is perfectly proper for the expert to amend the report accordingly, provided that they acknowledge and explain the thought process, if appropriate.

The Practice Direction to the CPR 35 provides guidance as to the content of expert reports at para 3; see also the Guidance at paras 52–60.

Models for written reports are available from the Academy of Experts and the Expert Witness Institute, and there is plenty of training available, so there is little excuse for an unclear or poorly presented report.

One basic structure can be used for most reports:

1   Expert's qualifications and experience – the level of detail needed will vary with the complexity of the case; often it is sufficient to state the specialism and append a curriculum vitae.

2   Instructions – summary stating when the expert was asked to advise, by whom, on behalf of which party and on what issues.

3   Facts – the history may be as per the medical records or as per the patient's account, as the two are not always consistent. The expert needs to set out the salient extracts from both (with page references – bear in mind questions may be asked about the report months or years after it was written), and must draw attention to any important discrepancies without assuming either source to be right, questions of fact being for the judge to resolve. Exceptionally, an expert may be able to say from clinical experience or medical knowledge that only one version of events is capable of belief; in that case only is it appropriate to express that view, explaining the medical basis for it.

4   The expert's commentary and opinion can take the form of observations appended after each section of the facts has been set out, or by way of an opinion section at the end of the report. In either case, it should be clear on what fact (or variant version of the facts) the opinion relies.

5   Medical literature references, where appropriate – conclusions need to be supported by appropriate reasoning and, where relevant, texts (NB texts published later than the incident will normally be relevant only on causation, not on liability). Full copies of the sections of relevant texts relied on should be supplied and the significant passages highlighted, to enable the lawyers to explore their own understanding of the background literature and to raise any necessary points with the expert.

It is the expert who has to explain the medical case to the judge, whether in person or on the page, so the ability to communicate clearly is crucial. An expert will be expected to write clearly, grammatically and as succinctly as possible, with sub-headings and numbered paragraphs and pages for ease of reference. The report will be expected to read consistently: the conclusions must tally with the observations and argument in the main body of the report. An expert must also be able to explain his or her opinion verbally in conference with sufficient clarity and jargon-free English that both the lawyers and the lay client can understand. If this proves a problem, the expert will flounder in the witness box when trying, under considerably greater stress, to explain the same opinion to the judge.

SELECTING AN EXPERT

The starting point for the lawyer is to identify the specialism(s) needed to investigate the case and then to set about finding a suitable individual within that specialism. Suitability will depend on the nature, complexity and value of the case: whereas it may be worth waiting six months for the leading expert to advise on a multi-million pound case with a long life expectancy, in a simpler case the criteria may be cost and speed of turnaround. Finding the right expert is not the problem it used to be. The lawyers on both sides will be experienced in the field. They will have their own lists of experts, many of whom they will know personally, and they will know where to seek help if stuck for an expert. An extensive database of medical experts is kept by Action against Medical Accidents (AvMA), which provides a search service for members. Recommendations are made but AvMA emphasise in their expert protocol that the database is not a warranty of expertise nor any form of accreditation – the duty remains on the lawyers to check out anyone they instruct. The Association of Personal Injury Lawyers (APIL) similarly compiles and distributes to members a list of experts but this is in much broader categories and contains fewer names. Professional organisations can also be a useful source: for example, the College of Occupational Therapists Specialist Section (COTSS-IP) publishes a searchable online directory of independent practitioners. Commercial sites abound on the internet. It is crucial to check the site sponsor before relying on any information provided.

It is important to check that the expert has the right sub-specialism: not every orthopaedic consultant is an expert on hand surgery; not every paediatrician is an expert on meningitis; not every anaesthetist is expert on anaphylactic reactions. Experts commenting on breach of duty will need to be drawn from the same specialism as the clinician whose act or omission is under investigation. In *Hutton v East Dyfed Health Authority*,[9] Bell J criticised the claimant's presentation of specialist evidence to assess the management of a generalist (at 349, 352). See also the Chinese herbalist case of *Shakoor v Situ*,[10] where the claimant did not call an expert in Chinese medicine.

Defendants, with the resources of the Trust and of NHS Resolution at their disposal, are notorious for identifying, and producing, the top expert for the precise matter in issue (a perfectly proper procedure, of course). It is at that point one glances at the claimant's expert who has brought the case thus far to see if he is showing any sign of strain! Sometimes it may be necessary to look far afield to find an expert with the requisite level of expertise. In one case in which the author was instructed, the allegations were against the leading Welsh practitioner of an esoteric procedure (isolated limb perfusion), who was calling the leading practitioner in England as his expert witness. Those instructing intelligently sought out the leading expert in Holland, where the procedure had first been developed.

It is worth remembering the general rule that there is no property in a witness, particularly where an issue arises about what a treating doctor would have done, had circumstances been different. Either party can see to interview and call the other side's witness, if he wishes. In *Lilly Icos LLC v Pfizer Ltd*,[11] Jacob J held that an alleged contract with a party under which an expert was said to have bound himself not to act for the other party was unenforceable as contrary to public policy.

---

9 [1998] Lloyd's Rep Med 335.
10 [2000] 4 All ER 181.
11 (17 August 2000, unreported), Ch D.

The Expert Witness Institute and the Academy of Experts

The EWI,[12] set up in 1996 as a direct result of encouragement from Lord Woolf, exists to support, encourage and improve the quality of expert evidence and to act as a voice for experts. It is first and foremost an educational body and its fellows are drawn from a range of disciplines. Its founding funders include both the Medical Defence Union and the Medical Protection Society. It should not be confused with the Academy of Experts, of earlier provenance and originally concerned principally with the construction industry, although it now offers a searchable online database[13] that includes a (rather limited) medical section. There is now a fair degree of amicable interbreeding between the two bodies.

Clinical Disputes Forum

Also distinct from the EWI is the Clinical Disputes Forum,[14] Lord Woolf being again the progenitor of this organisation, whose stated aim is to bring together the 'key people in clinical negligence litigation' to work on practical improvements to procedure and reduce the need for litigation. It was registered as a charity in 2000. As its name suggests, the CDF is concerned with all aspects of clinical disputes. It has produced very detailed Guidelines for Experts' Discussions in the Context of Clinical Disputes. The forum is currently composed of the heads of NHS Resolution and of AvMA and representatives of the judiciary, the Law Society, the Bar, the GMC, the Legal Aid Agency, doctors and medical insurers.

INSTRUCTING AN EXPERT

Ground rules on the contents of letters of instruction are given at section 20 of the Guidance, and experts are enjoined by para 23 to refuse to act until instructions have been fully clarified. Basic requirements set out in the Guidance are:

- name, address, telephone numbers, dates of incident and claim reference numbers;
- nature of expertise called for;
- purpose of requesting advice or report – matters to be investigated, known issues, identities of all parties;
- whether proceedings are contemplated and, if so, whether the expert is asked only for advice or for a court report;
- outline programme for the completion and delivery of each stage of the expert's work;
- if issued, the court and claim number, any known or projected court dates or deadlines and the track to which the case has been allocated.

It is suggested that experts should also be provided with whatever statements of case, relevant disclosed documents and witness statements are available. It will also be necessary to deal with funding – whether public funding is available or is being sought, and whether there are any

---

12   See www.ewi.org.uk.
13   See www.academy-experts.org.
14   See www.clinical-disputes-forum.org.uk.

restrictions on the hourly rate or total fee chargeable and whether the court has set a specific budget for experts' fees.

Most experts will also need a brief summary of the relevant law (eg the civil standard of proof; *Bolam* and *Bolitho*; in an oncology causation case, *Gregg v Scott*, etc) and of their own duties to the court, including a warning as to the perils of stepping outside the expert's specialism. Shrewd solicitors will also include the location of the treatment(s) complained of and the names of treating clinicians, if known. The letter of instruction must provide sufficient detail about the parties for the expert to identify any conflict of interest. Finding out later on can be an expensive mistake. In *Toth v Jarman*,[15] the Court of Appeal emphasised the need for early disclosure of any interest in the case and recommended that, as a matter of practice, experts should add to their declaration of truth that there is no such conflict. In smaller cases, treating doctors are not infrequently asked to give expert evidence on condition and prognosis, but their involvement with the patient may undermine the weight of, or even render inadmissible, comment on wider issues: see, for example, *Re B (A Minor) (Sexual Abuse: Expert's Report)*,[16] where a psychiatrist treating a child was held insufficiently independent to provide forensic evidence on issues relating to the father; but compare the treatment of Gill Levett's evidence in *Williams v Jervis*.[17]

An integral part of proper instruction in a medical case is to provide a complete set of sorted, paginated medical records. Some solicitors still obtain the medical records and pass them on as received, with no intervening process; this is virtually never cost-effective, as each expert and counsel must then wade through sorting them out from his or her own perspective, at what is usually a rather higher hourly rate than that of a junior solicitor. If the solicitor does not have the expertise or the time to sort out the records, specialist paginators charge less than medical experts to do this task, and are likely to be more methodical. Once the records are properly prepared, the paginated set can be disclosed and used by experts in every discipline and by counsel, for all parties. Failure to sort the records at an early stage not only creates expensive make-work later but also significantly increases the risk that a crucial point will be missed.

DO THE LAWYERS NEED MEDICAL KNOWLEDGE?

The answer is yes, to an extent. That is why the Lord Chancellor set up specialist panels and why one of the criteria for admission to the specialist panels is attendance at medical and medico-legal courses. The lawyer is not expected to be medically trained, but a general understanding of the medical issues in a case is essential. A small number of lawyers in the field are doubly qualified. The medically trained lawyer needs to be careful not to set up by way of challenge to the expert, but rather to use his own medical knowledge to understand, test and explore the expert's opinion. Another potential pitfall for the doctor-lawyer to watch for is

---

15 [2006] EWCA Civ 1028.
16 [2000] 1 FLR 871A.
17 [2008] EWHC 2346 (QB).

allowing their own understanding to blind them to the need for fuller expert explanation for non-medics, such as the judge.

In March 2010, *Clinical Risk* published a comparative survey of the conduct and outcome of clinical cases conducted by specialist (ie AvMA or SRA panel) and non-specialist solicitors,[18] based on a random sample of 180 cases drawn from one eminent expert's medico-legal practice over 23 years (some 5,800 cases). From this inevitably selective sample, the authors conclude that there is clear evidence that specialist firms perform better in the conduct of cases and have a significantly lower discontinuance rate (after initial assessment) than non-specialist firms. It is less clear whether outcomes are improved, although it is interesting that specialist panel members had a slightly higher settlement rate and that the only cases that went to trial (two!) were panel member cases.

Far more necessary than a general medical training is familiarity with medico-legal litigation. This embraces a number of aspects. The claimant lawyer needs to be familiar with the way this litigation is practised and the way in which different defendants (trusts, health authorities, different firms of solicitors, the medical protection societies) respond to different stimuli, and the various ploys they practise; the defence firm needs to get a grip on the issues at a sufficiently early stage to be able to assess the claim and push for resolution or discontinuance of the claim.

Most claims fall within perhaps a dozen categories, within which the issues are not very different. The lawyer needs to be familiar with the medical focus of each type of claim and the medical issues and arguments that usually arise. Take one example: if a lawyer is processing a claim for perinatal brain damage leading to cerebral palsy, it is obviously useful to have a general grounding in obstetrics. But it will be enough, and in fact more relevant, if the lawyer understands the terminology and outline concepts relating to likely medical issues in the *forensic* context: antenatal ultrasound scan, estimated date of delivery, absolute and relative disproportion, prematurity, intrauterine events, cardiotocograph (CTG), early and late deceleration, induction, syntocinon, lie, presentation, partogram, fetal distress, relative duties of midwives, SHOs, registrar and consultant, and a lot more besides. After a number of such cases, the lawyer will know on what issues to focus and will understand without further instruction what the obstetric experts are saying, but must be careful not to make assumptions about what this individual case is about; the lawyer must keep an open mind to all possible issues and encourage the experts to do the same.

When we come to the issue of causation, the situation becomes even more technical. It is not enough for the lawyer to understand that his causation expert is saying that the child would or would not have been uninjured if delivered at a certain time. The lawyer needs to be familiar with the medical arguments on causation and on discussion documents and research in current circulation, and with the general medical consensus as to what factors need to be established if the damage is to be deemed to have been caused by, for example, perinatal asphyxia. A lawyer who is not familiar with the interpretation of CTG traces, Apgar scores, hypoxic ischemic encephalopathy, the different types of

---

18   Julian Brigstocke, David Shields and John Scurr 'Clinical negligence lawyers: specialists versus non-specialists – the evidence' (*Clinical Risk* Vol 16, No 2).

cerebral palsy and their possible aetiologies and alternative causation possibilities, is going to be at a very substantial disadvantage, and therefore so also is the lay client. After doing two or three cases of the same sort (eg cerebral palsy, shoulder dystocia, amputation, delayed diagnosis of cancer) the lawyer is likely to have gathered enough information to ask the right questions and to assess the strength of the proposed case. Before that stage, attending medico-legal conferences is an excellent way of achieving a similar type of knowledge, albeit at a less immediate level; such conferences also provide an essential update for experienced practitioners and an opportunity to see and hear medical experts whom the lawyer has yet to instruct.

INTERLOCUTORY USE OF EXPERTS

Contact with experts is an expensive hobby and a careful cost-conscious eye needs to be kept at all times, but in larger cases it is far more cost-effective to involve the experts as the case progresses rather than saving them up for a pre-trial conference at which all manner of worms emerge from the can. It is good practice where proportionality permits for counsel and the experts to meet in conference before proceedings are drafted, and for the experts to see and approve the proposed particulars of claim before service, or to propose amendments if necessary. Conferences on difficult issues, especially where perusal of the medical records during the discussion is necessary, are usually far more productive when all parties attend in person. In the long run, this may well be more cost-effective than telephone conferencing, regarded by some experts as a meeting that can be attended from a moving car, an office not containing the papers, a home with audible children or animals, or a range of other variously unsuitable venues. Video links resolve these problems to a limited extent but can present their own time-wasting technical problems. Sitting across the table from fellow experts, and from the injured person, concentrates the mind and produces answers and agreements at an early stage that may otherwise not emerge till far too late (in serious cases, at court).

Experts are only human and if instructed to write a report in 2013 and then summoned at short notice to court in 2018 are likely to under-perform. Keeping experts in the loop – copying lay evidence and other experts' reports to them, keeping them regularly informed of significant developments in the case, giving them prompt and adequate notice of court deadlines for reports, expert joint meetings and hearing dates – is not only courteous, but also likely to ensure optimum support for the lay client. The expert who is thinking about the case will flag up problems before they become insurmountable and retain a lively interest in the issues.

JUDICIAL OVERSIGHT: THE EFFECT OF THE WOOLF AND JACKSON REFORMS

In the early post-Woolf days, there were numerous cases, some of which were cited in the last edition of this work, that demonstrated the court flexing its new case management muscles, sometimes despite agreement between the parties, and by no means always in the interests of justice.

As the jurisdiction has bedded in, while it is of course still possible to cite some maverick decisions – and case management decisions are notoriously difficult to rectify on appeal – overall the early zeal has come to be tempered by common sense and by the overriding principle, especially in the specialist Masters' corridor of the High Court, and amongst the more experienced (and now specialist) district judges on circuit.

It is still not always easy to get permission from some courts for all the necessary experts for a clinical case to be presented properly, especially in smaller cases. If the case for a given expert is clearly and forcefully made, and the instruction is proportionate, multiple experts are frequently permitted in complex cases. After all, claimant solicitors are not allowed to act in any legally aided clinical negligence cases if they have not proved themselves expert in the field and obtained entry to one of the accredited panels, and they have the expertise to select similarly competent specialist counsel. It is arguably a paradox to create an expert panel and then tell judges, many of them less experienced than the lawyers, to supervise their work. Some district judges, and even on occasion the specialist Masters, still impose impossible deadlines and refuse reasonable requests for necessary experts. The Court of Appeal is unlikely to interfere in a case management decision unless it is very plainly wrong, so the best defence is a well-prepared argument at the initial directions hearing. Co-operative working in case management, recognising the considerable pressures on those managing cases to hold down costs, is more likely to secure a just outcome and one beneficial to the lay client than hostility and confrontation.

CUTTING DOWN ON EXPERTS

Twenty years ago it was common for parties to call two or even three experts apiece on the main contentious issues, but for many years the trend has been for the number of experts to be reduced. Lord Woolf was highly critical of the over-use and the high expense of experts and judicial scrutiny of expert-related costs has been growing ever since. Despite the best efforts of defendants, the cost-capping powers under CPR 44.18(5) were rarely exercised in clinical negligence cases, partly because judges perceived this as unjust to injured claimants, and partly because the necessary assessment exercise would tie up a costs judge for almost as long as a final assessment (see eg *Willis v Nicolson*[19]). Prospective cost budgeting was regarded by Lord Woolf as 'artificial and unworkable' in his final report in July 1996. A pilot scheme for cost budgeting in defamation cases came into force in October 2009 under CPR PD 51D. Costs budgeting was implemented more widely in 2013 under CPR Part 3.12 and 3.12, which now covers most Part 7 multi-track cases where the claim was commenced on or after 22 April 2014. The new rules follow Jackson LJ's Review of Civil Litigation Costs, which focused on reducing expert costs by a number of means, including targeting prolixity, closer case management and increasing the use of single joint experts.

---

19   [2007] EWCA Civ 199.

It can be unjust to limit the number of experts permitted to a party too closely: *E S v Chesterfield and North Derbyshire Royal NHS Trust*[20] was a claim for cerebral palsy as a result of perinatal asphyxia – a fairly common claim, unfortunately – and is a good example of a fairly common problem for claimants. A junior doctor (by the time of trial a consultant) and a consultant were in the frame, both obstetricians. The claimant wanted two forensic obstetric experts, on the basis that it would not be a level playing field if their single expert was faced not only with a single independent expert for the defence but also with two consultants who would naturally be giving their opinions even though they were, strictly speaking, witnesses of fact. The district judge took the unimaginative view but the appeal succeeded. The court said the case was very important, complex and of high value. The parties would not be on an equal footing if the order of the district judge prevailed. Not only was it not disproportionate to allow the claimant to call two obstetric experts; it was actually necessary for the achievement of justice. Although *E S's case* is still good law, it was distinguished in *Beaumont v Ministry of Defence*,[21] in which the court again required to be persuaded of 'exceptional circumstances' before allowing a second expert (and on the facts found there were none). Beaumont's case was itself distinguished in the first instance chancery case of *VTB Capital plc v Nutritek*,[22] in which two experts were held not to be disproportionate, citing Brooke LJ in *E S's* case.

WHEN IS AN EXPERT NOT AN EXPERT?

The CPR provides by CPR 35.4 that all expert evidence, written or oral, requires the court's permission, and that the specialty and, if possible, the name of the desired expert should be identified. The court makes a clear distinction these days between permission to put in an expert report and permission to call its maker, and of course the use of experts is also tightly controlled by cost budgeting.

The CPR 32.1 gives the court an overriding and comprehensive power with regard to evidence generally and is considerably less draconian: calling witnesses as to fact does not normally require permission from the court. The court may give directions as to the issues on which it requires evidence, the nature of that evidence and its form of presentation. It may also exclude evidence which would otherwise be admissible (and may limit cross-examination). The desire for both strict equality of arms and costs saving that informs case management of experts under the CPR 35 runs into difficulties when clinicians with expert-level expertise are called as witnesses of fact, thus ducking that tight control and coming under the lighter rein of the CPR 32.

The trite rule that factual witnesses cannot give evidence of opinion is ripe for reconsideration in this context and is, in practice, being stretched to breaking point already. It is commonplace in clinical negligence actions for the defendant to call as factual witnesses one or more consultants in

---

20   MLC 1051, [2003] EWCA Civ 1284.
21   [2009] EWHC 1258 (QB).
22   [2011] EWHC 2842.

the specialism at issue in the case (in addition to the forensic experts allowed under the CPR 35). Both parties will often call specialist solicitors as 'lay' witnesses on the issue of Court of Protection costs, and treating therapists and case managers may also come perilously close to opining as experts in projecting their future costs. When the treating doctor alleged to have been negligent, or his supervising consultant gives evidence about why he did or did not do the crucial act, this is essentially giving evidence of expert opinion. The problem in which claimants frequently find themselves is that their own experts are governed by the strict rules of the CPR 35 while equally august consultants are called by the defence under the rather looser control of CPR 32. This was exactly the problem that the court recognised in *E S v Chesterfield* and sought to remedy by allowing the claimant an extra forensic expert (although that still left him 3:2 down).

In *Kirkman v Euro Exide Corporation (CMP Batteries) Ltd*,[23] unusually it was the claimant who sought to call a consultant orthopaedic surgeon as a witness of fact: Mr Kirkman had injured his knee in an accident at work and needed surgery; he claimed for the above-knee amputation that followed a perioperative infection. He had a long history of knee problems and D alleged that he would have needed the surgery (and so would have run the risk of infection and amputation) anyway. In addition to forensic experts on both sides, C sought to call his treating surgeon to state, as a matter of fact, whether he would have recommended surgery in the absence of the index accident. The district judge directed that the witness be called at trial, for the trial judge to assess whether his evidence constituted fact or opinion; D appealed and the circuit judge reversed the decision, excluding the evidence. On appeal to the Court of Appeal, Buxton and Smith LJJ held that the statement was one of fact and, should the witness be tempted in cross-examination to stray into giving an opinion, it would be for the trial judge to decide whether or not to permit this.

Outside the clinical negligence context, there has been a franker admission of expert evidence under the guise of evidence of fact. In *Multiplex Constructions (UK) Ltd v Cleveland Bridge UK Ltd*,[24] Jackson J sitting in the Technology and Construction Court held that it was perfectly proper for the defendant sub-contractor to call one of his employees, a highly qualified and experienced engineer, as a witness of fact and for that witness to proffer statements of opinion that were reasonably related to the facts within his knowledge and that, as a matter or practice, technical and expert opinions were frequently expressed by factual witnesses in that court without objection being taken. Similar latitude has been allowed to brain injury case managers in some cases: see for example *C v Dixon*.[25]

---

23   [2007] EWCA Civ 66.
24   [2008] EWHC 2220 (TCC).
25   [2009] EWHC 708 (QB).

JOINT EXPERTS

Section 7 of Practice Direction 35, the latest revision of which came into force on 22 November 2017, sets out the criteria that the court should consider when asked to give permission for the parties to rely on expert evidence. It is arguable (and in a talk to the 2009 JPIL conference, specialist clinical negligence master, Master Roberts, as he then was, considered this a real possibility) that the section creates a presumption in favour of the appointment of joint single experts, at least in smaller cases. This emphasis carries through to the CJC Guidance for the Instruction of Experts, which notes (at para 34) that 'Single joint experts are the norm in cases allocated to the small claims track and the fast track' and should be used 'wherever possible'. It remains open to the parties to rely on the complexity of the issue, the importance to the parties, the existence of a range of expert opinion, the need to discuss the issues in conference or the fact that one party has already instructed an expert to oppose such a direction. Jointly instructed single experts can undoubtedly save costs and may be able to provide fair and comprehensive evidence in uncontentious areas. In such cases, it is increasingly possible for this simply to be agreed between the parties. It is highly unlikely that joint single experts will ever be appropriate on issues such as complex causation, high-cost care programmes, or breach of duty.

Legal aid for most clinical negligence cases was withdrawn by the Legal Aid, Sentencing and Punishment of Offenders Act 2012 (LASPOA 2012). Since 2013, legal aid has been restricted to children who have suffered severe disability due to a neurological injury sustained during the mother's pregnancy, the child's birth or the first eight weeks of the child's life. This change makes it even more difficult for claimants to obtain suitable separate medical evidence and may increase the use of joint experts for all the wrong reasons, especially following the limiting of Conditional Fee Agreements (CFAs) through capping success fees and removing the right to recover the success fee and the After the Event (ATE) premium from the losing defendant. LASPOA 2012 explicitly allows for partial recovery of an ATE premium to protect against the risk of a claimant becoming liable for expert reports that address the issue of liability. In November 2017 the Court of Appeal confirmed in *Peterborough and Stamford Hospitals NHS Trust v McMenemy*[26] that it was clear that the government had decided for reasons of public policy to exclude ATE insurance premiums relating to the cost of expert reports in clinical negligence cases from the general abolition of the recovery of such premiums. Lewison LJ set out that the concern was that claimants might not be able to afford the 'upfront' costs of such expert reports, and thus access to justice might be unduly restricted. Further, the government had intended not to disturb the practice of claimants taking out an ATE policy at the same time as entering a CFA. It remains permissible for ATE insurance to be taken out as soon as a claimant enters a CFA.

The withdrawal of public funding is strongly opposed by many, including Lord Justice Jackson himself, who has pointed out that his reform recommendations were put forward in the context of legal aid being available for clinical negligence cases and that maintenance of legal aid for

---

26 [2017] EWCA Civ 1941.

clinical negligence is both sensible and in the public interest. In a speech to Cambridge University in March 2018 Lord Justice Jackson stated that he deplored and regretted cuts to civil legal aid. NHS Resolution has also opposed the withdrawal of legal aid in this area.[27]

Where a single joint expert's report is unclear (or unhelpful to a party), the CPR 35.6 provides that a party may put written questions about his report to an expert, whether joint or not (once only, within 28 days of the report, and for the purpose of clarifying the report – unless the court or the other party permits otherwise). Single joint experts are, like all experts, under a duty to notify those instructing them if they take the view that their expertise is insufficient to cover all the issues on which they are instructed to comment.[28]

Challenging a report from a joint expert

If a topic was thought uncontentious (or the court ordered a single joint expert) but a joint report proves unsatisfactory or damaging and questioning has failed to resolve this, it is open to either party to apply to the court for a new, single party expert. If this is permitted, the other party may and often does retain the expert originally instructed jointly as its own single party expert. This saves costs and provides that party with the tactical advantage that the expert was originally mutually accepted as having the necessary expertise. Careful, and helpful, treatment of the position when a party wishes to reject a jointly instructed expert may be found in Lord Woolf's judgment in *Daniels v Walker*.[29] In that case, the defendants wanted to instruct their own care expert because they thought that the joint expert had estimated far too much care in the joint report that they had agreed should be obtained. The claimant maintained that the defendants were effectively bound by it. Lord Woolf, emphasising that the overriding objective was to deal with cases justly, disagreed. He said that, although in small value cases the objecting party might have to be restricted to asking the joint expert questions, in cases of substantial value it might well be appropriate to permit the objecting party to put his own report in evidence, and even to call the new expert at trial, provided that the issues could not be resolved simply by the experts meeting.

If unopposed it is unusual for a joint expert to be called and cross-examined at trial, the whole purpose of a joint expert being to avoid calling experts on the issue in question. This was emphasised by Lord Woolf's observations in *Peet v Mid-Kent Healthcare Trust*,[30] suggesting that the evidence of the joint expert should not normally be subject to cross-examination, in the context of ruling that it is not acceptable for one party, without the consent of the other(s), to have access to the single joint expert. In *Popek v Natwest*,[31] the Court of Appeal said that it was not generally open to parties to cross-examine the single joint expert, particularly where written questions had been asked and answered after

---

27 See https://www.judiciary.gov.uk/wp-content/uploads/2018/03/speech-lj-jackson-was-it-all-worth-it-mar2018.pdf at para 3.20.
28 See, in a different context, *Re W (A Child) (Non-accidental Injury: Expert Evidence)* [2007] EWHC 136 (Fam).
29 [2000] 1 WLR 1382, CA.
30 [2002] 1 WLR 210.
31 [2002] EWCA Civ 42.

the expert's report was made. In *Yorke v Katra*,[32] the Court of Appeal said that there was no rule that a party should be bound by the instruction given to a joint expert by the other side. Where a defendant's solicitor had communicated with a joint expert without the claimant's consent or knowledge, that expert was tainted and the claimant was entitled to a fresh expert: *Edwards v Bruce & Hyslop (Brucast) Ltd*.[33] If it is regarded as useful for a joint expert to attend a conference with one party's single party experts, it is good practice to offer the other party access to that section of the conference or consultation, either by the solicitor attending in person, or by a full tape-recorded transcript being disclosed. Where this occurs, it is of course essential to forewarn all single-party experts and lay clients that the other party will be listening in to that part of the discussion.

MEDICAL LITERATURE

Experts often rely on medical literature to support their arguments but only the most experienced and most carefully instructed collate all the papers on which they propose to rely in good time before trial. This dilatoriness can cause a range of different problems. Any counsel who has been presented with 17 highly technical medical papers the day before the expert is to be called at trial will readily identify the first problem: the lawyers have to have time to understand and assimilate the literature so that it can be admitted, explained to the judge as necessary and used as a basis for cross-examination. The opposing expert is also entitled not to be ambushed and this creates the other potential problem: the evidence may be excluded. In *Wardlaw v Farrar*,[34] the Court of Appeal refused an application to use further medical texts on appeal and gave guidance on the orderly deployment of the literature on which experts sought to rely. The best practice, as found on the standard form of directions used by the specialist Masters of the High Court, should be followed throughout the country: this requires experts to identify the literature on which they propose to rely at an early stage and to provide copies of any material that is unpublished or not widely available, so that they can be disclosed as well as provided to counsel in good time.

An eloquent example of the problems caused if this practice is not followed is provided by *Breeze v Ahmad*.[35] The judge decided Mrs Breeze's case on the basis of two medical papers that were not before the court but were summarised for him by the defendant's expert. On that summary, the literature supported D's position and the judge found for him expressly on that basis. On appeal, the two papers were shown by C's counsel to be at worst neutral and at best to support C's position. D's expert had unwittingly summarised the papers inaccurately and/or incompletely and inadvertently misled the trial judge. The judge had placed much emphasis on his belief that, whereas one expert was wholly unsupported

---

32   [2003] EWCA Civ 867.
33   [2009] EWHC 2970 (QB).
34   [2004] Lloyd's Rep Med 98.
35   [2005] EWCA Civ 223.

by the literature, the other's view was 'compellingly supported' by it. The matter was remitted for retrial.

DISCLOSURE

The secretive nature of litigation has been opened out by the Woolf reforms and the cards-on-the-table approach broadly in use in clinical negligence actions in England and Wales is beginning to trickle into other related areas: rules for exchange of expert medical and non-medical evidence in clinical negligence cases came into force in Northern Ireland in July 2009.[36] A statutory duty of candour has been in force since 2014 and applies to all health care organisations which are registered with the Care Quality Commission (CQC); this follows AvMA's long campaign for a statutory duty of candour on medical professionals ('Robbie's Law') and Sir Robert Francis's recommendations after the Mid-Staffordshire Hospitals Inquiry.

There are, however, still good grounds for retaining legal professional privilege over documents prepared in contemplation of litigation. CPR 35 appears to offer inroads into the principle, specifically stating at the CPR 35.10(4) that the material instructions on the basis of which the report was written shall not be privileged. Solicitors on both sides have frequently demanded to see statements of witnesses and any other documents referred to in the expert report but the courts have been slow to ride a coach and horses through established case law on legal privilege, except where there is good reason to think that the instructions were incomplete, inaccurate or misleading. (Lord Woolf had advocated total disclosure of all documents generated by an expert and all instructions, but, wisely, in the final report that was thought a bridge too far.)

Toulson J in *General Mediterranean Holding SA v Patel*[37] (where the issue was legal professional privilege) held that if an order for disclosure is made, the court may permit cross-examination on the instructions (para 3 of Practice Direction 35). In *Morris v Bank of India*,[38] Hart J ordered disclosure of an expert's instructions on the ground (under the CPR 35.10) that the expert report was patently defective in failing to reveal all material instructions.

In *B v John Wyeth & Brother Ltd*,[39] a judgment given within the benzodiazepine group litigation, the Court of Appeal said that although each claimant's medical history relied on by the medical expert in preparing his report is disclosable, waiver of privilege in respect of documents containing that information should not be inferred; the manner of disclosure lies within each claimant's discretion. Two months earlier (October 1991), Tucker J had reached a similar conclusion in *Booth v Warrington Health Authority*.[40] But in *Clough v Tameside and Glossop Health Authority*,[41] Bracewell J, having held that service of a witness statement waives any privilege previously enjoyed by that statement,

36   Rules of the Supreme Court (Northern Ireland) (Amendment No 2) 2009, SI 2009/230.
37   [2000] 1 WLR 272.
38   (15 November 2001), Ch D.
39   [1992] 1 WLR 168.
40   [1992] PIQR P137.
41   [1998] 1 WLR 1478.

ordered disclosure by the defendants of a statement by a treating doctor referred to in an expert report served by the defendants. She said that a party should not be forced to meet an expert opinion based on documents he could not see. This decision was distinguished in *Bourns v Raychem Corporation (No 3)*,[42] where it was held that documents disclosed for a specific purpose (on the facts, taxation of costs) did not constitute waiver of privilege for collateral purposes. See also the report of an interlocutory appeal in *Forbes v Wandsworth Health Authority* in [1995] *Clinical Risk* (vol 1, p 153), where it was held that privilege was not lost merely because the pleadings had referred to receipt of a document in support of the argument on limitation. In *Bourns v Raychem*, the Court of Appeal held that in order for privilege to be waived, there had to be something more than bare reference to a document in the report, or there had to be reliance by the expert in his report on that document.

One must also bear in mind the CPR 31.14, which provides that a party may inspect a document mentioned in a statement of case, a witness statement, a witness summary, an affidavit, or, subject to the CPR 35.10(4), an expert's report (CPR 35.10(4), as explained above, relates to the power to order disclosure of instructions given to an expert for the preparation of his report). It is not clear to what extent this rule is intended to go further than the previous RSC, Ord 24, r 10, which gave the court a discretion to order or not to order disclosure.

This rule first came before the Court of Appeal in *Lucas v Barking, Havering and Redbridge Hospitals NHS Trust*.[43] The court considered the interplay between the different rules. The CPR 31.14, as amended, states a party 'may inspect' a document mentioned in a statement of case, a witness statement or summary, or an affidavit, but, in respect to a document mentioned in an expert report, it says a party 'may apply for an order for inspection' *but* subject to the CPR 35.10(4). The CPR 35.10(3) requires the expert to 'state the substance of all material instructions, whether written or oral, on the basis of which the report was written, and the CPR 35.10(4), having dramatically declared that the instructions shall not be privileged against disclosure, states that the court will not, in relation to those instructions order disclosure of a document unless it is satisfied that the expert's statement of instructions under the CPR 35.10(3) is 'inaccurate or incomplete'. The defendants sought sight of documents mentioned in an expert's report on the basis not that the statement of instructions from the expert was inaccurate or incomplete, but on the basis that the documents in question did not form part of his instructions and therefore they had an unfettered right to see them under the CPR 31.14(2) – because the words 'subject to rule 35.10(4)' did not apply. The Master acceded to their application, but the Court of Appeal disagreed, holding that the documents did form a part of the instructions and there was no ground for thinking the expert's statement of instructions was inaccurate or incomplete. Waller LJ said the appeal raised a quite fundamental question as to what effect the new CPR were intended to have on the issue of privilege. It is important to note first that there are very strong indications in the judgments, albeit *obiter*, that the judges did not think that the CPR 31.14(1) gave an unfettered

---

42   [1999] 3 All ER 154.
43   MLC 1037, [2003] Lloyd's Rep Med 57, CA.

right to inspect a document mentioned in a statement of case, witness statement or summary, or affidavit. Waller LJ said it was unlikely that the rule had intended to abolish privilege in such cases at a stroke and without saying so. However, the main issue in the case was whether the documents referred to in the expert's report were part of his instructions. As the court found that they were, the CPR 31.14(1) was not relevant, only CPR 31.14(2), and as there was no suggestion from the defendants that the expert's statement of instructions was inaccurate or incomplete, they were not entitled to disclosure. Waller LJ made the clear observation that 'material supplied by the instructing party to the expert as the basis on which the expert is being asked to advise should be considered as part of the instructions and thus subject to CPR 35.10(4)'. Further, his lordship said there was no need to set out all the information contained in a statement referred to or all the material that had been supplied to an expert; the only obligation on the expert was to set out *'material instructions'* (the judge's emphasis). Laws LJ said that the purpose of the rule was to ensure that the factual basis on which the expert had prepared his report was patent. In the ordinary way the expert was to be trusted to comply with this obligation.

So we see that the other party does not have an unfettered right to see documents referred to in pleadings, affidavits or witness statements. The other party will be entitled to see documents referred to in an expert report only if the court finds that the statement of his instructions given by the expert is inaccurate or incomplete.

This judgment was echoed the following year in *Jackson v Marley Davenport Ltd*,[44] in which the Court of Appeal held that CPR 35.13 did not empower the courts to order disclosure of draft reports; service of the final report waived privilege in that report only and not in the drafts.

The situation will be otherwise where there is an evidential basis to attack the summary of instruction: In *Morris v Bank of India*,[45] Hart J ordered disclosure of an expert's instructions on the ground (under the CPR 35.10) that the expert report was patently defective in failing to reveal all material instructions. Disclosure may also be ordered where a party seeks at a late date to change its expert.

The situation is different when a change of expert is needed, however it will now normally be necessary to disclose the report of the expert originally instructed in order to obtain the court's permission to rely on the second expert. In *Beck v Ministry of Defence*,[46] the defendant sought to change its psychiatric expert as it had, it said, lost all confidence in its original expert as having proper knowledge of the relevant psychiatric issues in the case. Naturally the claimant's solicitors refused access for a new psychiatric examination. The defendant succeeded in the two lower courts in gaining permission to start again. The single judge then gave leave for a further appeal in this interlocutory matter, a most unusual event. In the Court of Appeal, Simon Brown LJ had some sympathy with the defendant's position, in that this was a high value case, involving allegations against their psychiatric personnel, and without a further report they would be proceeding with an expert in whom they had no

---

44 [2004] EWCA Civ 1225.
45 Ch D, 15 November 2001.
46 [2004] PIQR P1, CA.

confidence. He said that, though it would be unfair to require a defendant upon such an application to argue in detail as to why the original report and the original expert were now deemed to be unsatisfactory because that would give the claimant unfair ammunition for cross-examination of their expert if the application were refused, nevertheless, once it had been decided that the defendant should be permitted to instruct another expert, there were very good reasons why the original report should be disclosed. Ward LJ agreed, saying that expert shopping was to be discouraged and requiring the report to be disclosed was a check against possible abuse. The Master of the Rolls, agreeing, said that a claimant can properly object in any personal injury case to submitting to a second examination without good reason being shown for it. No second examination should be permitted if it appears to be 'a possibility' that the reason a defendant wants a fresh expert is that the first expert has reached a conclusion more favourable to the claimant than the defendant expected. This logic was followed (in the rather different context of restaurant valuation) in *Hajigeorgiou v Vassiliou*[47] and in a personal injury case in *Edwards-Tubb v JD Wetherspoon plc*.[48] In the latter case it was the claimant who wanted to change experts: he had instructed an orthopaedic surgeon (one of three named by him under the protocol, not objected to by the defendant but not jointly instructed); that surgeon examined him and wrote a report, which was never disclosed or relied upon, pre-issue; D admitted liability prior to issue; C served particulars supported by the report of a different expert, who referred in passing to the fact of the earlier examination. D applied for disclosure of the first report, on the basis that the court should require its disclosure as a condition of allowing C to rely on a new expert, relying on the CPR 35.4 ('No party may call an expert or put in evidence an expert's report without the court's permission') and the personal injury pre-action protocol (C2-001). The court confirmed that:

- the first, undisclosed report was subject to legal professional privilege;
- it was not open to the court to infer from C's refusal to waive that privilege that the report was adverse to his case;
- it was however open to the court under CPR 35.4 to require disclosure of the first expert's report as a condition of allowing C to rely on the second expert – this did not override the privilege, but gave C a choice as to whether or not to waive it (although the court accepted that C would realistically be unable to proceed without medical evidence, and so would be forced to waive privilege if he wanted to do so);
- the principle is that, in order to discourage expert shopping, the court should attach a condition of disclosure to permission to change expert, whenever it had power to do so;
- there is no distinction between expert reports acquired pre- and post-issue, or between cases in which the court on case management has identified named experts and those in which it has merely given permission for an expert in a given discipline, in all of which the court should usually exercise its discretion to attach a condition of disclosure;

---

47 [2005] EWCA Civ 236, CA.
48 [2011] EWCA Civ 136.

- expert advice acquired by a party pre-protocol, before the parties have 'engaged with each other in the process of the claim', by contrast, should normally not be subject to disclosure;
- it may be appropriate in some cases to require a party seeking to rely on an opponent's report disclosed in this context to call its author, to enable cross-examination by the original instructing party.

C's counsel had argued that the power under the CPR 35.4 existed only in the context of an expert approved by the court post-issue and that pre-issue opinions not relied upon were privileged, and accordingly on these facts there was no such power; Judge Denyer QC (on appeal from the District Judge) had agreed but the Court of Appeal did not, restoring the ruling of the District Judge. Hughes LJ, giving the leading judgment with which Lord Neuberger MR and Richards LJ agreed, reviewed the authorities, including setting out and distinguishing some obiter dicta from *Carlson v Townsend*[49] that might appear to support the claimant respondent's position in this case. The court held that *Beck* was not distinguishable and that the issue of privilege had been fully explored in *Vasiliou*.

It is an unfortunate side-effect of the *Edwards-Tubb* judgment that parties may now, where there is sufficient time before the limitation period expires, be advised to obtain full medical evidence before entering into the protocol, to ensure that any adverse report will be protected by legal privilege. This, of course, would undermine the spirit of the Woolf reforms and the purpose of the protocols but may be seen as a necessity in what is, after all, still an adversarial system. The alternative of being permitted to cross-examine one's own initial choice of expert is not one that will appeal greatly to either party. It should also be noted that Hughes LJ specified that pre-protocol advice would fall outside the CPR 35.2 (and so the CPR 35.4) because the expert had been 'consulted at that time and not instructed to write a report for the court'; so that he could not be said to have 'been instructed to give or prepare expert evidence for the purpose of proceedings'. Given that the pre-protocol privilege is based on evidence being prepared in contemplation of proceedings, this may prove to be a fine distinction where an expert has been instructed to produce a full written report pre-protocol.

JOINT EXPERT DISCUSSIONS

By the CPR 35.12 (amended in October 2009), the court may direct experts' discussions for identifying relevant issues and, if possible, reaching agreement, and may direct a written statement of the meeting identifying what was and what was not agreed, and why. The content of the discussion between the experts is not disclosable without agreement (ie is privileged), and any agreement by the experts does not bind a party unless he agrees – although of course the practical reality is otherwise and the rules have been amended expressly to forbid parties from instructing their experts not to make agreements, and experts from accepting any such instruction. The note of the joint discussion, once agreed by the

---

49   [2001] EWCA Civ 511.

experts, is disclosable and will be put before the court. It was originally intended that lawyers should not be present at these discussions but initial experience suggested that this might be necessary and the Clinical Disputes Forum proposed that lawyers should be present at experts' meetings (unless agreed or ordered otherwise) but not normally intervening, save to answer questions put to them by the experts or to advise them on the law. An explanation for this view is to be found in *Clinical Risk* July 2000, p 149. In practice now, attendance of lawyers at medical expert meetings is vanishingly rare, the case management courts having taken the view that such attendance increases rather than reduces costs. This is not always the case – as when the medics have a cosy chat about the medically interesting points but fail to address the legal issues – but a properly drawn agenda goes a long way to remedying this. There will always be exceptions, too: in *Woodall v BUPA Hospitals Ltd*,[50] Judge Hindley QC, sitting as a High Court judge, allowed an appeal by which he gave permission for lawyers to attend a complex series of expert meetings in a relatively high value case. He said:

> It seems to me that in a complex case such as this involving different specialities it is extremely important for all of the lawyers concerned to have an understanding as to why measures of agreement have been achieved and, more importantly, why there has not been agreement on certain issues, so that the lawyers themselves have an opportunity of considering the cogency of arguments, because only on that basis can they properly advise their clients in terms of either narrowing issues or compromising the case.

He added that the costs of the lawyers' attendance would not be disproportionate to the issues and values of the particular claim.

In *Hubbard v Lambeth Southwark and Lewisham Health Authority*,[51] claimants unsuccessfully objected to a meeting of experts on the highly original basis that their own experts, overawed by the high standing of the defence expert, would feel unable to contradict him. The Court of Appeal, pointing out that the claimants' experts had already committed their views to paper in the knowledge that they might have to go to court to support those views, dismissed the argument, adding that there was no issue under Art 6 of the Convention. The court also said that lawyers would not normally attend such a meeting: a well-drafted agenda and a recording would suffice.

Agendas

Agendas are problematic. Some experts need little guidance; others, left to their own devices, are perfectly capable of omitting to consider all or most of the issues in the case. The problem arises from the difference in approach of lawyers and doctors presented with the same problem – lawyers seek a legal answer, doctors a clinical solution. Lengthy agendas, however, make things worse rather than better, and some firms undoubtedly run up costs (inadvertently or otherwise) by the sort of to-ing and fro-ing that goes on with commercial agreements before the final draft is agreed. An agenda should be short, simple and neutral. Provided

---

50 MLC 0340.
51 MLC 0503, [2002] Lloyd's Rep Med 8.

that the experts are clear about the purpose of the meeting, all they need is some tolerably precise guidance as to what they should be looking at, and then let them get on with it. The agenda should not be seen as a means of cross-examining the other expert, and thus requiring many pages of subtly worded questions (and consequent increased expenditure of time and money). Unfortunately, it is still not unusual to see agendas containing 50 and more questions – sometimes one from each party, because no compromise could be agreed. The effect of this is confusion, often involving inconsistent responses at some point, each side always having tried, by questions sly and subtle, to winkle some useful response out of the opposing expert, and then to put an interpretation on the answers that assists their cause.

The Masters are increasingly unsympathetic to this process and seek to bring agendas in bounds through the Model Direction, now echoed in section 9 of Practice Direction 35, which emphasises:

- expert meetings are not mandatory and should take place only if they are likely to serve a useful purpose;
- the purpose is not for experts to settle cases but to agree and narrow issues and identify what action, if any, may be taken to resolve outstanding points of disagreement;
- if a meeting is to happen, the parties should consider whether an agenda is necessary; and
- if so, an agenda should be agreed if possible, to help the experts focus on the legal issues – *the agenda must not be in the form of leading questions or hostile in tone.*

Lawyers should note that under the CPR 35.12(2) the court has power to set the agenda itself, although this is an invitation that the Masters, at least, have been reluctant to take up.

Lengthy agendas often result from (sometimes legitimate) concern on the part of lawyers that the experts will simply carve up the case in their absence. Defendants have often met this by instructing their experts not to agree anything without checking back – this practice is now outlawed by the Rules. A careful, short preamble to the agenda goes a long way to minimising the risk, as does a conference with the expert before the meeting, where costs allow. The points to stress are:

- the purpose of the meeting is to identify the outstanding issues and provide brief reasons for continuing disagreement, to focus the issues for trial;
- the experts are not being asked to reach a compromise settlement;
- no expert should feel pressured to agree or compromise any issue;
- if persuaded to change their mind on any issue, the expert should provide full reasons for this in the joint note;
- experts should approach factual issues in the alternative – resolution of these is for the judge;
- experts should approach causation issues on the balance of probabilities, and not apply a medical standard of proof;
- the expert must never sign a joint note that does not completely and accurately reflect their true opinion.

When the expert gives the case away

Every experienced clinical negligence lawyer has known that heart-sinking moment when you read the joint expert note and realise that it damages or even apparently finishes the case. This moment is often followed by a telephone call to the expert in which one of the following responses is made:

- 'I didn't think it was important, so I let him have that one';
- 'I didn't really mean that/that's not what I said'; or
- 'I've always thought that – didn't you know?'.

Sometimes (at least in the first two instances) the situation can be rescued by a supplementary report, letter or discussion. Sometimes a speedy recourse to alternative dispute resolution has a great deal to be said for it. Otherwise, application may need to be made for a change of expert. The expert meeting is usually one of the later stages in the case, so this is always going to be difficult, but it is not necessarily always hopeless. Where an expert's view of the case had changed radically, to the detriment of the party instructing him and without any clear reason, following a discussion with his opposite number, a second expert has been allowed: *Stallwood v David*.[52] C claimed on the basis that her back and neck injuries prevented her working full-time as a self-employed accountant and claimed about £200,000. An orthopaedic surgeon supported the claim and accepted that she had continuing pain at the four-year point, some of which would be permanent. D's expert stated that full resolution had been achieved by six to 12 months and that C was now malingering. After the joint meeting, C's expert changed his view to recovery at two years post-accident (significantly, D's expert was prepared to agree disadvantage on the labour market up to that point), with all continuing symptoms not accident-related. C lost all confidence in her expert and instructed a new expert, who supported her case. At first instance, the judge refused permission to change experts on the basis that the trial was imminent and the accident was five years ago, without any apparent consideration of the unfairness to the claimant. Teare J noted that case management decisions 'will rarely be the subject of appeal because they are the result of an exercise of discretion', and that 'a party to a claim cannot usually be afforded a second expert merely because his or her first expert has altered his opinion after having discussed it with the opponent's expert', but still allowed the claimant her new expert. After a careful consideration of the matters properly to be considered when seeking to avoid an experts' agreement under the CPR 35.12(5), his lordship cited the *White Book* note – that the agreement could be set aside where an expert has clearly stepped outside his expertise or brief or otherwise shown himself to be incompetent – and the overriding objective and held that the judge had not considered all relevant matters (such as the extent of any delay if the application were to be granted) and had considered irrelevant matters (such as his own backache, despite which he worked full time). The judge had accepted an invitation to recuse himself. Note that no enquiry had been made of the first expert as to his reasons for changing his mind: as Teare J observed, 'they might have been shown to be sound reasons,

---

in which case there could be no ground for seeking additional expert evidence', so the court found that C could not show good reason for needing an additional expert (but then found for her on other grounds).

Much the same point came before Irwin J in *Read v Superior Seals Ltd*.[53] C claimed for a back injury at work; C's expert reported five times over four years, consistently concluding that while there was some psychological overlay (ie unconscious exaggeration) there was a genuine, permanent and disabling injury; D alleged malingering; at the experts' meeting C's expert decided for the first time that the damage was merely a two to three-year acceleration. C's lawyers immediately instructed a third expert, who entirely supported the case. Permission to change experts was refused at first instance, but allowed on appeal. Irwin J observed that such cases would be rare but the overriding objective applied and the court should not permit C to be ambushed by his own expert. (It may well be significant that, unusually, this case was at an early stage when the experts' meeting took place.)

The court will be less sympathetic where the expert's change of heart is understandable: compare *Singh v CS O'Shea & Co Ltd*,[54] where Macduff J failed to take pity on a claimant whose expert's altered view was based on service of surveillance evidence that showed C walking, jogging, sprinting and driving without any apparent disability.

The more usual approach of the courts is to disallow a change of expert at a later stage (see for example *Jones v Kaney*,[55] a ground-breaking negligence action against an expert (of which more below) following the court's refusal to allow such a late change). Where an expert's late change of heart can be shown to be in breach of duty to the instructing party, this is now actionable.

SPA LITIGATION

The Review of Civil Litigation Costs by Jackson LJ proposed the idea of expert evidence being given in a new forum, now widely referred to as 'in the hot tub' – the judge chairing a discussion between the experts, with counsel having an opportunity to ask questions, in preference to sequential cross-examination. A 'hot tub' pilot scheme obtained broad support from those involved; judges unanimously found that hot-tubbing assisted the court and over 90% of practitioners agreed. The pilot scheme resulted in a change to the Practice Direction to CPR Part 35 with effect from November 2017. Section 11 of the Practice Direction provides that at any stage in the proceedings the court may direct that some or all of the evidence of experts from like disciplines shall be given concurrently. Where expert evidence is to be given concurrently, three stages should be followed. First, the judge will initiate the discussion by asking the experts in turn for their views about the issues on the agenda. Once an expert has expressed a view the judge may ask questions about it. The judge may also invite other experts to comment or ask that expert's own questions of the first expert at appropriate points. Second, after the first

---

53   [2008] QBD (Winchester) CLY 267.
54   [2009] EWHC 1251 (QB).
55   [2011] UKSC 13.

stage has been completed for any or all issues, the judge will invite the parties' representatives to ask questions of the experts. Representatives' questions should be directed towards testing the correctness of an expert's view; seeking clarification of an expert's view; or eliciting evidence on any issue which has been omitted from consideration up to that point. Third, after the second stage has been completed in relation to any or all issues, the judge may summarise the experts' different positions on the issue and ask them to confirm or correct that summary.

Where expert evidence is not to be given concurrently, the Practice Direction confirms the long-standing practice of practitioners in larger clinical negligence cases by permitting the court to direct that the evidence is given in any appropriate manner, including for cross-examination of experts to proceed on an issue-by-issue basis. The rules now provide that the court, rather than the parties, may set an agenda for the taking of expert evidence. Alternatively, the court may direct that the parties agree an agenda subject to the court's approval. In any event, the agenda should be based on the areas of disagreement in the experts' joint statements.

This is a radical, and apparently welcome, step away from the traditional adversarial approach to clinical cases. Recent jurisprudence has described the 'hot tub' approach positively as 'a valuable and efficient exercise' (*Socrates Training Ltd v The Law Society of England and Wales*[56]). A hybrid approach of 'partial' hot-tubbing was used in *M v N*,[57] where Hayden J heard evidence from three experts individually in the witness box but also encouraged discussion between the three whilst each gave their evidence. The judge remarked[58] that: 'though there are differences between them, much of which focuses on nomenclature, I was impressed by their respect for each others' views and their willingness continually to re-evaluate the available evidence'.

It should be noted that 'hot-tubbing' does not (at least, not yet) replace a joint expert meeting; and various problems with joint expert discussion still remain. Already the parties' lawyers are losing control of the process to the extent that issues are decided in joint expert discussions to which they have no access; lawyers are now expressly forbidden to instruct their experts not to reach agreement on a material issue in the course of the meeting (Guidance para 77) and they are very seldom permitted to be in attendance. Often the outcome of the joint expert meeting determines the outcome of the case, if only by leaving one party in so weak a position that a settlement or even withdrawal of the case is inevitable.

JUDICIAL PREFERENCE

Where there are warring experts, part of the judge's task will inevitably be to choose between them (or, as in some cases, to ignore all of them). The law reports are full of medical (and other) cases decided simply on the ground of the judge 'preferring' one side's expert to the other. The judge may give detailed reasons for such preference, based on the evidence, or

---

56   [2017] CAT 10.
57   [2015] EWCOP 76.
58   [2015] EWCOP 76 at [36].

may restrict himself to one or two general criticisms, or may simply state that he prefers the evidence of X to Y. This last may be appealable (see Chapter 9). Full, detailed explanations of why a judge considers that an expert has got it wrong and another has got it right are infrequent. More common is general denigration. In *Hutchinson v Leeds Health Authority*,[59] Bennett J said of an expert haematologist:

> I find Dr R's evidence to be illogical and unsustainable ... Regrettably I did not have the same confidence in Dr R [as in the other experts]. I gained the impression of an expert witness who was clearly allied to Dr C [the impugned doctor] probably because of a shared speciality in medicine ...'

In just one issue of *Medical Litigation* (January 2000), judicial criticisms in no fewer than four different cases appear along the lines of 'spend an undue amount of their time in medico-legal work', 'not entirely detached in their analysis of the evidence', 'a degree of inflexibility which is not entirely becoming', 'unwillingness to make concessions', 'changes in the course of his evidence ... do not give me confidence', 'his evidence starts on a precarious basis', 'forensic considerations had overridden those of objectivity', 'serious allegations placed before the court on a casual and flimsy basis'.

The problem has not gone away, although partisan experts are dwindling in number. More recently, Roderick Evans J observed of a defence neurologist that:

> Although [he] has dealt with the claimant's case voluminously there are clear indications of a lack of thoroughness and a failure to spend adequate time in properly analysing the case. It may be that his heavy workload ... has prevented this. It is equally likely in my judgement that he approached the case with a set view of the claimant and looked at the claimant and her claimed symptomology through the prism of his own disbelief. From that unsatisfactory standpoint he unfortunately lost the focus of an expert witness and sought to argue a case. I am driven to the conclusion that I am unable to place reliance on [his] evidence.[60]

Clearly, experts need to bear in mind that anything other than a courteous, moderated and impartial response to questioning in court will damage their credibility.

Even where an expert is a sound clinician and experienced forensic expert, inattention or slack preparation can result in reputation-ending judicial criticism: see eg *Loughlin v Singh*,[61] where the claimant's neurologist so angered Kenneth Parker J that he wrote an entire separate annexe to his judgment to set out his reasons for regarding the expert's evidence as 'so unreliable that it should be rejected'. Sometimes an expert may succeed in learning from gruelling forensic experience and rehabilitating their reputation: for example, an obstetrician roundly criticised by the judge in *Sardar v NHS Commissioning Board*[62] had the courage to return to the fray and, despite some judicial caution about both obstetric experts from

---

59   [2000] MLC 0287.
60   *Williams v Jervis* [2008] EWHC 2346 (QB) at [119].
61   [2013] EWHC 1641.
62   [2014] EWHC 38.

Garnham J, successfully resisted the next attack on his character, in *Cox v Secretary of State for Health*.[63]

The hegemony of medical over non-medical experts is no longer automatic, either (and not before time, some may think): in *HJ v Burton Hospital NHS Foundation Trust*,[64] Turner J upheld the trial judge's preference for the claimant's care expert despite, or perhaps because of, her having relied on her own expert assessment of the claimant's needs rather than that of a jointly instructed orthopaedic expert.

Perhaps reflecting the occasional shortfalls in expert independence, it is clear that judges are not bound to accept expert evidence, even where it is uncontradicted: see, for example, (in another context) *A County Council v M*.[65] The court, it was said, should be cautious of declining to follow uncontradicted expert evidence but was not bound by it – the approach in *Loveday v Renton (No 1)*[66] would be followed. Three more recent decisions underline that there are no hard and fast rules governing judicial preference and that the judge has a very broad discretion. In *Huntley v Simmons*,[67] Waller LJ, giving the unanimous judgment of the Court of Appeal, approved the decision of Underhill J to reject the evidence of the care experts on both sides and award an intermediate regime (that coincided with preliminary costings by the claimant's expert) and to prefer the view of one neurospychiatrist to the joint view of the parties' neuropsychologists as to the likelihood of improvement through rehabilitation. Similarly, in *Masterman-Lister v Jewell*,[68] the Court of Appeal had no difficulty with Wright J's preference for the evidence of the defence neuropsychiatrist's view, although it was not only opposed by three eminent experts for the claimant but was not supported by either of the other two defence experts. These are judgments well within the discretion of the trial judge. Similarly, the Court of Appeal of New South Wales upheld a judge's decision to prefer an expert argued on appeal to have less expertise than his opponent, and to form his own view on causation, differing from both the parties' experts.[69] Ipp JA emphasised (citing the court's judgment in the leading NSW case of *Strinic v Singh*[70]) that a judge should not reach a judgment on findings of fact based on his own knowledge or experience rather than the evidence, but rejected an allegation that this had occurred in the instant case.

The preference must, however, be fair, and rational. In *Hewes v West Hertfordshire Hospitals NHS Trust*,[71] Foskett J allowed an appeal against a decision of a specialist QB Master to grant summary judgment on the basis of the defendant's expert evidence (served without permission). The claimant also had expert evidence, supportive of the claim, but the time for exchange of that evidence had not yet arrived and so only a letter from the expert, confirming that he continued to support the claim had been served. Perhaps unsurprisingly, Foskett J held that in

---

63 [2016] EWHC 924 (QB).
64 [2018] EWHC 1227 (QB).
65 [2005] EWHC 31 (Fam).
66 [1989] 1 Med LR 117.
67 [2010] EWCA Civ 54.
68 [2003] 3 All ER 162.
69 *Sydney SW Area Health Service v Stamoulis* [2009] NSWCA 153.
70 [2009] NSWCA 15.
71 [2018] EWHC 2715 (QB).

those circumstances it was not permissible for the Master to treat the defendant's expert as conclusive on the issue of liability; but it is salutary to note that the Master's reasons for his decision ran to 18 pages.

AN EXPERT'S IMMUNITY

The position of expert witnesses sued by their own clients was expressly considered in 1992 in *Palmer v Durnford Ford*,[72] when Simon Tuckey QC, sitting as a deputy High Court judge, ruled that the expert was immune from suit in respect of work done in or in preparation for court. This decision was made in the context of a centuries-long tradition that all those directly taking part in litigation are immune from civil suit, which has since been confirmed in the House of Lords: see *Darker v Chief Constable of the West Midlands Police*[73] and *Arthur JS Hall & Co v Simons*.[74] Witnesses could be sued for malicious prosecution or misfeasance in public office, or prosecuted for perjury or contempt of court, but were protected by witness immunity from any action in general negligence. Until very recently, this blanket immunity extended to expert witnesses but the cloak was lifted in *Jones v Kaney*,[75] in which a 5:2 majority of the Supreme Court abolished the immunity and also addressed the concern that to do so would cause a serious expert shortage. In 2006, the Chief Medical Officer, Sir Liam Donaldson, carried out a survey of expert medical evidence in family cases[76] in response to a number of highly publicised cases in which medical experts had been heavily criticised for causing miscarriages of justice (similarly trenchant concerns had also caused review of a large number of criminal cases). Amongst his findings was that there was a shortage of suitable experts, caused in part by a widespread fear that the doctor would be sued or prosecuted for expressing an honest view in cases that, as one respondent put it, 'required the wisdom of Solomon'. Witness immunity was regarded as clearly necessary in appropriate circumstances to keep and increase the pool of experts that AvMA and others have fought so hard to build up. This concern was echoed and underlined by Thorpe LJ in *Meadow v General Medical Council*.[77] Many commentators argued, however, that there will be circumstances in which it is right that there should be accountability, whether through professional disciplinary proceedings, civil suit or an application for costs; even before the *Jones* case, the courts have shown themselves willing to impose costs sanctions, to endorse regulatory controls and where possible to find routes around the blanket ban on civil suit.

In *Landall v Dennis Faulkner & Alsop*,[78] an orthopaedic surgeon was sued in respect of advice given in a personal injury action to the effect that the claimant's condition could be ameliorated by a spinal fusion. The action was settled on that basis. The claimant contended that the advice

---

72   [1992] QB 483.
73   [2001] 1 AC 435.
74   [2002] 1 AC 615.
75   [2011] UKSC 13.
76   *Bearing Good Witness: Proposals for reforming the delivery of medical expert evidence in family law cases* (30 October 2006), Ch 3 'Key issues and challenges'.
77   [2007] QB 462.
78   [1994] 5 Med LR 268.

was negligent and that the operation had damaged him further. Holland J held that the expert was immune from suit, as the report in question had been given for the purpose of assisting the lawyers to conduct the claimant's case, and not for the purpose of advising the claimant about medical treatment. The Court of Appeal expressed a contrary view, however, in the somewhat legally similar case of *Hughes v Lloyds Bank plc*.[79] Following a road traffic accident, the injured party's GP wrote a letter for her detailing her injuries to be sent to the third party's insurers. As the letter was provided before proceedings had been issued and purely for negotiation purposes, the GP was not covered by the immunity of a witness in respect of the allegation that he had not taken reasonable care in describing the injuries.

In *Stanton v Callaghan*[80] the Court of Appeal, in a comprehensive review of the ambit of expert witness immunity, held that witness immunity attached not only to oral evidence given at trial but also to preliminary work, including the joint statement produced after discussions between experts, so that no claim could be made against an expert for negligence in agreeing issues or backtracking on his original report in the experts' meeting.

This principle was necessarily followed by Blake J at first instance in *Jones v Kaney*,[81] a negligence action arising out of a road traffic case. Mr Jones was stationary on his motorcycle when (in 2001) he was knocked down by a drunk driver, Mr Bennett. Mr Jones sued and Bennett's MIB-appointed insurer admitted liability. Kirwans, solicitors for Mr Jones, instructed an orthopaedic surgeon, who suggested that a clinical psychologist be instructed. Kirwans instructed Dr Kaney, who advised that Mr Jones currently suffered from post-traumatic stress disorder. The quantum case was brought on this basis. The defendant then instructed a consultant psychiatrist, Dr El-Assra, who expressed the view that Mr Jones was exaggerating his symptoms. At their subsequent telephone discussion, Dr Kaney agreed with Dr El-Assra that the injury did not amount to PTSD but only to a short-lived adjustment disorder; that Mr Jones was deceitful and that he was consciously exaggerating his symptoms. She then signed a written joint statement (prepared by D's expert) to the same effect. When challenged by Mr Jones' solicitors to explain her change of heart, Dr Kaney stated that she had not seen Dr El-Assra's reports prior to the experts' meeting; that she had felt that the draft joint statement did not reflect what she had agreed but that she had felt under pressure to sign it; that she believed Mr Jones to be evasive rather than deceptive; that she did believe he had suffered PTSD, although this had now resolved; and that she was content for the joint statement to be amended by the solicitors. Kirwans applied for permission for a change of expert, which was refused. They then settled the case for a sum significantly lower than the claim and sued Dr Kaney in negligence, arguing that the expert witness immunity rule could not stand in the face of the Human Rights Act 1998, in that the expert's actions had precluded a fair trial. Blake J struck out the claim, holding that *Stanton* remained good law, having been cited without criticism in the House of Lords in

---

79 [1998] PIQR P98.
80 [2000] 1 QB 75.
81 [2010] EWHC 61 (QB).

Arthur J S Hall & Co v Simons[82] and *Darker v Chief Constable of the West Midlands.*[83] *Obiter*, however, his lordship observed that so broad and indiscriminate a protection might well be held by a superior court to be disproportionate to the public policy justification for it and granted an application for a certificate under s 12 of the Administration of Justice Act 1969 for the matter to be referred direct to the Supreme Court.

The Supreme Court accepted that this was a point of general public importance and conducted a review of the law in this area, and of the policy considerations driving it. Lord Phillips (with whom Lords Brown, Collins, Kerr and Dyson agreed) put and answered seven central questions (para 38) and then overruled *Stanton* and abolished the immunity from suit previously enjoyed by expert witnesses in respect of their involvement in legal proceedings. The court opined that the principal purpose of the historic immunity was to ensure honest and independent opinion at all stages of litigation (paras 44–45, 55–57), to protect all participants in litigation from 'unjustified and vexatious claims from disgruntled litigants' (paras 15, 58–60) and to ensure a suitable pool of experts would be available (paras 52–54); that any exception to the general rule that every wrong should have a remedy would however need to be justified and kept under review; and that there was no longer any such justification in this context. The court noted that the parallel immunity protecting barristers had been abolished in 2001 (in *Hall v Simons*), that there was no evidence that following that decision there had developed either a shortage of barristers or a rash of vexatious litigation; and that removing the immunity would not create any conflict with the expert witness's duty to the court (see para 49 and for example para 99, per Lord Dyson). It was noted that expert witnesses, like barristers, would continue to enjoy an absolute privilege against claims in defamation arising out of statements made in the course of legal proceedings (para 62).

Lord Hope (who had previously considered these issues in *Darker's* case) and Lady Hale, dissenting, raised concerns that so long-standing a rule of law should be amended without consideration by the Law Commission and the intervention of parliament, Lady Hale expressing the view (at para 190) that it was 'irresponsible to make such a change on an experimental basis'. It was possible that the pool of experts would diminish, and that indemnity insurance premiums – and so expert fees – would rise, but the primary concern for Lady Hale was the risk of what Lord Hope (para 165) described as 'worthless but possibly embarrassing and time-consuming claims' brought by disappointed litigants (para 189). Lord Hope further expressed concern about defining the demarcation line between lay and expert witnesses, where one enjoys immunity and the other does not (para 172). Lord Phillips stated that the distinction can be made on the basis of voluntary assumption of risk in entering into a contract for reward, expressly departing from Lord Hoffmann's view in *Hall v Simons* (at p 698 of that report) that an expert owes no duty to his client once he gets in a witness box (paras 18 and 46). Lord Brown expressly distinguished expert witnesses from treating doctors or other experts called to give factual evidence, who may be asked for their professional opinions without having been retained by any party,

---

82   [2002] 1 AC 615.
83   [2001] 1 AC 435.

and who retain witness immunity in respect of those opinions (para 64). The expert's contract will normally be with the solicitor rather than the lay client, but it will normally be to the lay client (possibly as well as to the professional client) that a duty of care is owed. It is possible to envisage cases in which a party may be damaged by the negligently formed or expressed view of an expert instructed by another party, or of a medical witness called as a lay witness, in which case the immunity/duty of care boundary will no doubt fall to be tested further. It is interesting in this context that most of the commonwealth cases cited by Lord Collins (para 75) related to claims against adverse or independent experts. Even before *Jones v Kaney*, experts have been held responsible for at least part of the costs of a case: *Phillips v Symes (A Bankrupt) (Expert Witnesses: Costs)*,[84] in which an expert's 'flagrant reckless disregard of his duties to the court' caused significant expense and he was held to have no immunity against an order for costs. It is also worth bearing in mind that, even while the expert remained immune from civil suit, he was not protected from professional conduct proceedings arising out of evidence given to a court: see *Meadow v General Medical Council*.[85]

Lawyers who should not have relied on an expert's report or should have known that the case was not strong enough to bring, can also be held liable for wasted costs. A full understanding of this important issue can be obtained by study of the following cases: *Locke v Camberwell Health Authority*;[86] *Scott v Bloomsbury Health Authority*;[87] *Ridehalgh v Horsefield*;[88] *Tolstoy-Miloslavsky v Aldington*;[89] *Medcalf v Mardell*[90] but note *Jones v Chief Constable of Bedfordshire Police*,[91] where the Court of Appeal said that a hopeless case does not necessarily mean that the lawyers have been negligent, because properly conducted and apparently reasonable cases can turn out to be hopeless. Those using dodgy or incompetent experts, however, may find themselves censured in costs: see *Williams v Jervis*,[92] in which costs were awarded on an indemnity basis in respect of the time taken to deal with the evidence of two of the defendant's medical experts, who had unreasonably alleged that the claimant was malingering.

There may be other sanctions available to the disappointed litigant, too. In *Moran v Heathcote*,[93] a claimant's orthopaedic expert gave a negative opinion which resulted in the discharge of the legal aid certificate. The patient continued on his own and lost at trial. He then told the expert he was going to publish an account of his dealing with the expert on the internet. The expert, fearing he would be defamed, sought an injunction against publication. Eady J declined to grant one, being satisfied that the limited ambit of the patient's commentary, as explained to him by the patient, would not attack the expert's integrity. This issue may be

---

84   [2004] EWHC 2330 (Ch).
85   [2006] EWCA Civ 1390.
86   [1990] 1 Med LR 253; revsd [1991] 2 Med LR 249, CA.
87   [1990] 1 Med LR 214.
88   [1994] Ch 205, CA.
89   [1996] 1 WLR 736, CA.
90   [2001] 05 LS Gaz R 36, CA.
91   (30 July 1999).
92   [2009] EWHC 1838 (QB).
93   MLC 0344 (2001, unreported elsewhere).

differently approached now in light of some of the extreme and potentially defamatory material appearing on some websites although, unless a 'super-injunction' can be justified, the further publicity relating to the application for an injunction may serve only to add fuel to the flames.

Chapter 23

Human rights

Dr Jonathan Cook

INTRODUCTION

It is clearly impossible, and inappropriate, to attempt in this chapter any sort of general overview of human rights law. Instead this chapter will provide an introduction to the use of human rights arguments, and free-standing and parallel human rights claims, in the context of a clinical negligence practice.

The chapter is in two parts. The first part of the chapter will introduce the mechanics of the domestic human rights statutory framework: the important nuts and bolts you need to know to initiate and successfully run a human rights argument or claim. The second part of the chapter consists of a review of relevant English and European human rights case law, with the emphasis on highlighting where clinical negligence claims are reasonably likely to be assisted by resort to the Human Rights Act 1998.

Although the review of case law will necessarily consider relevant European cases, which must be taken into account by our domestic courts when determining any question relating to rights enshrined in the European Convention on Human Rights ('ECHR'), this chapter is specifically focused on the domestic human rights framework implemented by the Human Rights Act 1998 (HRA 1998). Any wider consideration of international human rights is outside the remit of this chapter. A final note of caution: this chapter should be regarded only as an introduction, and should be supplemented where appropriate by reference to one of the many excellent and comprehensive human rights practitioner textbooks.

THE EUROPEAN CONVENTION ON HUMAN RIGHTS AND FUNDAMENTAL FREEDOMS

The ECHR opened for signature by the Council of Europe in Rome on 4 November 1950. All new member states of the Council of Europe are required to sign and ratify the Convention. The Convention sets out 'human rights and fundamental freedoms' to be universally recognised by the states signatory to it. Under Art 1, it provides a mechanism by which European states are required to secure legal rules to determine when and how the Convention rights can be recognised and in which circumstances derogations will apply. It also establishes a supranational legal institution which citizens can individually petition to have their allegations that a state has violated their rights determined: the European Court of Human Rights (ECtHR) in Strasbourg. Established in 1959, the ECtHR has developed a very substantial body of human rights jurisprudence which sets the standards to be expected of the States Parties to the Convention.

The United Kingdom was heavily involved in the drafting of the ECHR, and was one of the first signatories. The ECtHR has always been available as a direct forum for UK applicants in circumstances where breaches of human rights are alleged. Accordingly, numerous cases against the UK were considered and decided in the ECtHR prior to the enactment of the HRA 1998. However, before the passing of the HRA 1998 the Convention operated solely in the sphere of international law, and accordingly could not be applied to overrule domestic law (*R v Secretary of State for the Home Department, ex p Brind*[1]). By the 1990s, both domestically within the UK and internationally there was a climate of increasing political pressure directed at ensuring the recognition of fundamental human rights. Specifically, there was a growing call for the direct incorporation of the Convention into domestic law, a call that was met by the passage into law of the HRA 1998.

THE HUMAN RIGHTS ACT 1998

The HRA 1998 came into force on 2 October 2000. The HRA 1988 does not simply incorporate the Convention into domestic law, but is a domestic statute that creates domestic rights. In *Re McKerr*,[2] Lord Hoffmann explained the effect of the Act at [63]:

> Although people sometimes speak of the Convention as having been incorporated into domestic law, that is a misleading metaphor. What the Act has done is to create domestic rights expressed in the same terms as those contained in the Convention. But they are domestic rights, not international rights. Their source is the statute, not the Convention. They are available against specific public authorities, not the United Kingdom as a state. And their meaning and application is a matter for domestic courts, not the court in Strasbourg.

The aim of the HRA 1998 was to comply with the ECHR, and it achieves that end by two principal means. First, it imposes an interpretative obligation on the courts to read all legislation, insofar as it is possible to do so, compatibly with the Convention rights. To the extent that primary legislation is incompatible with Convention rights, the primary legislation is preserved (although the court has the power to make a declaration of incompatibility under s 4 of the HRA 1998). Second, the HRA 1998 imposes an obligation on public authorities to act compatibly with Convention rights. Directly enforceable rights against public bodies were created, and a ground of illegality was introduced into judicial review (that of acting incompatibly with a Convention right). Furthermore, even when

---

1   [1991] 1 AC 696.
2   [2004] 1 WLR 807, HL (NI).

neither party to proceedings is a public authority, a court is still required, so far as possible, to read legislation compatibly with the Convention rights, and, as a public authority itself, a court must act compatibly with Convention rights.

Under s 1 of the HRA 1998, certain rights are defined as 'Convention rights', and it is only those rights which are given domestic effect by the Act. The 'Convention rights' (Arts 2–12 and 14 of the Convention, Arts 1–3 of the First Protocol and Art 1 of the Thirteenth Protocol, as read with Arts 16–18 of the Convention) are set out in Sch 1 of the HRA 1998.

Interpretation of primary and subordinate legislation

All legislation, whenever enacted, must be read and given effect in a way that is compatible with the Convention rights so far as possible (s 3 of the HRA 1998). 'So far as possible' has been held to mean 'unless it is plainly impossible' (*R v A (No 2)*[3]). This is a very strong interpretative obligation and amounts to a presumption that Parliament always has, and always will, enact legislation that is compatible with Convention rights. In this way, respect for Convention rights is made central to any consideration of domestic law. The obligation to read legislation compatibly with the HRA applies not only to the courts, but to all legal persons, natural or corporate, and so this provision has important repercussions for anyone taking decisions by reference to a statutory framework.

Public authorities: the duty to act compatibly with Convention rights

Section 6 to the HRA 1998 makes it unlawful in most circumstances for a public authority to act incompatibly with a Convention right (the very limited circumstances where it may act incompatibly are where it is acting under legislation that cannot be read compatibly with the convention). It is important to note that the statutory duty to act compatibly includes not only refraining from interfering with the individual's enjoyment of the right, but also, where appropriate, taking positive steps to protect the enjoyment of that right. These duties are reinforced by the inclusion in s 7 of the HRA 1998 of new causes of action through which the new statutory duties can be directly enforced by 'victims' of breaches or anticipated breaches. Even where no free-standing human rights claim has been brought per se, human rights arguments can be relied upon in any proceedings, for example as a shield in response to legal proceedings brought against an individual by the state (in respect of which there is no time limitation).

Public authorities: what is a 'public authority'?

The question of what is a 'public authority' is of crucial significance for the purposes of HRA 1998 claims. It is helpful to bear in mind that the underlying logic behind the term 'public authority' is that it is intended to capture *emanations of the state* in their many and varied forms. In the modern state, many functions of government are delegated to private

---

3   [2002] 1 AC 45.

bodies, and the HRA 1998 quite properly attempts to draw within its protection delegated public functions as well as direct acts and omissions of the government.

Parliament is not a 'public body' for the purposes of the HRA 1998, and so no domestic claim under s 6 lies in respect of a failure to legislate to give effect to Convention rights (s 6(3) of the HRA 1998). Courts and tribunals are public authorities (HRA 1998, s 6(3)(a)).

There are some other public bodies which are clearly and obviously public authorities. Often termed 'core public authorities', the relevant members of this group for present purposes include: local authorities; government ministers and departments; NHS Trusts; coroners; and the General Medical Council. These bodies are subject to the statutory duty under s 6 in respect of all their functions and activities, whether public or private.

There is then a further group of public authorities that are only subject to the s 6 duty in terms of their public functions (for example providing education services) and not in respect of their private functions (for example concluding employment contracts). This group is sometimes referred to as 'mixed function', 'hybrid' or 'functional' public authorities.

The question of whether a private entity like a commercial care home should be considered to be exercising public functions when providing care bought by local authorities in the exercise of its public functions is a much more difficult one. The leading authority on the question of what are 'functions of a public nature' in this context is *YL v Birmingham City Council*,[4] in which the House of Lords by a majority of 3:2 (with powerful and detailed dissenting opinions by Lord Bingham and Lady Hale) determined that a privately-owned commercial care home, when providing care to a resident pursuant to agreements made with a local authority under ss 21 and 26 of the National Assistance Act 1948, was not exercising functions of a public nature within the meaning of s 6(3)(b) of the HRA 1998.[5]

The decision in *YL* was controversial and the subject of some sustained criticism for allowing organisations which are essentially 'standing in the shoes of the state' to proceed unfettered by the prospect of HRA 1998 liability. Arguably this allows the state to contract out of its duties under the HRA 1998 insofar as recipients of state assistance provided by private organisations are concerned. This, it was feared, could contribute to a serious gap in the protection that the Act was intended to confer, and in respect of some of the most vulnerable members of society – those entitled to care under the National Assistance Act 1948. Parliament took prompt steps to fill this gap to some extent, by enacting s 145 of the Health and Social Care Act 2008, which provides that a care home is to act compatibly with the HRA 1998 in respect of a person placed in a care home under Part III of the 1948 Act (but, of course, this only protects recipients of care provided under those particular statutory arrangements). Section 73 of the Care Act 2014 does now allow, in certain defined circumstances,

---

4   [2008] 1 AC 95.
5   For further cases dealing with this issue, see: *Poplar Housing and Regeneration Community Association Ltd v Donoghue* [2001] EWCA Civ 595 and *R (on the application of Heather) v Leonard Cheshire Foundation* [2002] EWCA Civ 336.

adult residents of care homes to bring HRA 1998 claims against the care provider.

The question of whether a particular function is public or private is ultimately to be decided on the facts. Privatised companies or commercial bodies that undertake contracted-out work which would ordinarily have been governmental work (unless caught by the specific exceptions referenced in the preceding paragraph) are unlikely to be subject to the HRA 1998 in the carrying out of those activities (however, see *London & Quadrant Housing Trust v R (on the application of Weaver)*,[6] where a social housing trust that had charitable status was exercising public and not purely commercial functions in the allocation of housing resources).

No free-standing claim can be brought under the HRA 1998 against a private defendant (or against a mixed body in respect of a private function).

Appropriate forum and procedure: bringing a claim under HRA 1998

There is no special discrete human rights claims procedure, and human rights claims should be pursued under the Civil Procedure Rules, with some minor modifications.

A person who claims that a public authority has acted (or proposes to act) in a way that violates a Convention right may bring proceedings against the public authority in the appropriate court or tribunal. In general, claims that a public authority has acted in a way incompatible with a Convention right will be most appropriately progressed in the Administrative Court by way of judicial review (see the CPR 54 and PD 54D). The HRA 1998 itself does not oblige human rights claimants to proceed by way of judicial review (HRA 1998, s 7), and proceedings against a public authority may also be brought in the Chancery Division, Queen's Bench Division or in the County Court.

Where a human rights claim is limited to seeking damages and no other remedy, the claim cannot be brought as a judicial review.[7] Where the claim is for damages for maladministration it must be brought as an ordinary claim in the Administrative Court (*Anufrijeva v London Borough of Southwark*).[8]

A claim under s 7(1)(a) of the HRA 1998 in respect of a judicial act may only be brought in the High Court, but any other claim under s 7(1)(a) may be brought in any court (CPR PD 7A 2.10). In England and Wales, pursuant to the HRA 1998, s 4(5), only the High Court, Court of Appeal or Supreme Court can make a declaration of incompatibility.[9]

Where the claimant seeks to raise any issue under the HRA 1998 or seeks a remedy under that Act this must be specified in the claim form and details given in the statement of case (see CPR PD 54A 5.3 and PD 16 15).

---

6   [2010] 1 WLR 363, CA.
7   *Andrews v Reading Borough Council* [2004] EWHC 970 (Admin).
8   [2004] QB 1124, CA.
9   See CPR 19.4A and CPR PD 19A 6 for the procedure relating to claims for a declaration of incompatibility.

In *Barclays Bank plc v Ellis*,[10] the Court of Appeal said that mere reference to the Convention did not help the court. Counsel wishing to rely on the Act had a duty to have available decisions of the ECtHR upon which he relied or which might help the court (see further CPR PD 39A 8 for directions relating to citation of authorities on human rights).

The Court of Appeal has expressed concern about the high and often disproportionate costs of litigating human rights damages claims. *Anufrijeva v London Borough of Southwark* provided guidance on the procedures that parties should follow.

Limitation

Proceedings against a public authority under the HRA 1998, s 7(1)(a) must be brought 'before the end of the period of one year beginning with the date on which the act complained of took place; or such longer period as the court or tribunal considers equitable having regard to all the circumstances' (HRA 1998, s 7(5)). In practical terms, this means that a claimant wishing to bring a human rights claim for damages against an allegedly negligent NHS trust or other entity would be prudent to issue all claims arising out of the same facts within the applicable one-year basic limitation period. This means being alive to the possibility of an HRA claim at what is usually regarded as a very early stage in the progression of a potential clinical negligence claim.

This creates obvious problems, particularly in complex and high value claims, given the importance of complying with the pre-action protocol and the need to obtain appropriate supporting expert evidence.

The one-year basic limitation period is 'subject to any rule imposing a stricter time limit in relation to the procedure in question' which is relevant if, for example, the claim is being brought by way of judicial review – in which case the stricter time limit of bringing the claim within three months of the act complained of will apply.

The Supreme Court recently made clear in *O'Connor v Bar Standards Board*[11] that where a continuing course of unlawful conduct is relied upon to found a HRA claim, time will run from the last act in the chain.

O'Connor was a discrimination case founded upon a very different factual matrix to most clinical negligence claims. However, there is no reason, in principle, where a course of conduct is relied upon as the basis for an HRA claim in the clinical negligence context, that time should not run from the last act or omission in that course of conduct. Practitioners should nevertheless be cautious about relying upon the availability of such an extension unless the essence of the complaint is undeniably an ongoing course of conduct rather than a series of discrete incidents.

In fatal cases, where there may be significant delays in the coroner's court (particularly if an Art 2 right to life compliant inquest needs to be held), a sensible way to proceed is to protectively issue all claims and negotiate an extension of time to serve until after the coroner has given his or her verdict.

There is provision to apply for an equitable extension of time, in respect of which the courts have wide discretion. In *Rabone v Pennine*

---

10   (2000) Times, 24 October, CA.
11   [2017] 1 WLR 4833.

NHS Trust,[12] Lord Dyson said at [75] that the factors in the Limitation Act 1980, s 33 may be relevant to the decision to extend time in HRA 1998 claims. However, he expressly endorsed the approach taken by the Court of Appeal in *Dunn v Parole Board*,[13] where it was held that a court should examine all the relevant factors in the circumstances of each case and look at the matter broadly and attach such weight as is appropriate. Consequently, there is no requirement for a court to rigidly apply the factors in the Limitation Act 1980, s 33 when considering the extension of time in a HRA 1998 claim.

In *Rabone* in the Supreme Court, Lord Dyson departed from the more rigid approach taken by the High Court and Court of Appeal. In the Court of Appeal,[14] Jackson LJ had held that if a claim was 'doomed to failure' it would not be appropriate to extend time and the burden was on the claimant to show that it was equitable to extend time. However exercising the discretion in favour of the extension of time in the Supreme Court, Lord Dyson emphasised the fact that the required extension was short, the defendant had suffered no prejudice by the delay, the claimant had acted reasonably, and, most importantly, the claimant had a good claim for breach of Art 2 (see paras [73]–[79]).

Standing: who can bring a claim under HRA 1998?

Only a person who is, or would be, a 'victim' of an act made unlawful by the HRA 1998 may bring a claim under the HRA 1998, s 7 against a public authority (s 7(7)). The definition includes those who are at risk of being affected by a violation as long as the risk is sufficiently real and immediate. The meaning of 'victim' in the HRA 1998 is defined by reference to Art 34 ECHR, whereby 'any person, non-governmental organisation or group of individuals' can bring proceedings where they can show they have been (or will be) actually directly affected by the act or omission complained of.[15] A victim can be any legal or natural person, including a company, but a core public authority cannot be a victim for the purposes of the act and an NHS Trust is not a victim for the purposes of the Act.[16]

For present purposes, it is relevant to note that the concept of 'victim' clearly and obviously differs from the familiar concept of 'claimant' in clinical negligence claims as one who has suffered injury and loss caused by a breach of duty by the defendant. One practical effect of this is that persons who have not suffered injury, but have been otherwise directly affected, are able to bring claims complaining of human rights violations by, for example, a hospital. An example of this wide application of the victim test is *R (Hooper) v Secretary of State for Work and Pensions*[17] in which the House of Lords considered (*obiter*) that the applicants were victims for the purposes of the Art 34 test because they could establish they would have claimed the benefits alleged to have breached Art 14 (protection

---

12 [2012] 2 AC 72.
13 [2009] 1 WLR 728.
14 [2011] QB 1019.
15 *Klass v Germany* (1978) EHRR 214.
16 See *Frame v Grampian University Hospitals NHS Trust* [2004] HRLR 18, HC (Scotland).
17 [2005] 1 WLR 1681.

from discrimination) if they had been allowed to do so. A further example is that potential recipients of information can be 'victims' in relation to claims of Art 10 (freedom of expression) violations[18]. See also *R (on the application of Holub) v Secretary of State for the Home Department*[19] in which it was held that a child's parents have standing to bring a claim of breach of Convention rights on the child's behalf.

The ECtHR has held that an individual whose life is put at risk but survives can be a victim for Art 2 purposes.[20] It has considered relatives of the deceased to be 'victims' in relation to complaints of violations of Art 2.[21] Domestically, this point became somewhat confused in the wake of *obiter* comments of Lord Scott in *Savage v South Essex Partnership NHS Foundation Trust*[22] to the effect that it was doubtful whether a close family member could claim to be a victim of an omission in breach of the positive Art 2 obligation that had led to an individual's death. However, clarity has been restored on this point by Court of Appeal in *Rabone* in which the point was fully argued and Jackson LJ, after reviewing the ECtHR and domestic authorities, including clear statements of principle on this point by the ECtHR,[23] confirmed that relatives of a deceased person have standing to claim violation under Art 2. That aspect of the Court of Appeal's decision was upheld by the Supreme Court[24] where Lord Dyson expressly stated that Lord Scott's observations in *Savage* were not correct and appeared to have been made without reference to the ECtHR jurisprudence on that point.

The availability of alternative remedies and in particular the settlement of a civil law claim for damages can have an impact on standing (*Powell v UK;*[25] *Hay v UK* (App No 41894/98). Also in *Rabone*, in the Court of Appeal, Jackson LJ considered the authorities on this point and teased out the following general principles: first that where the applicant brings a claim in his domestic courts in respect of matters which form the basis of his Convention claim and succeeds, that success may deprive him of the status of victim under Art 34; second, in order to ascertain whether the settlement or award has that consequence, it is necessary to consider all the circumstances of the domestic litigation and to determine whether it affords effective redress for the Convention breach; finally, it is necessary to consider: (a) whether liability for the offending conduct has been accepted by the state authority or found proven by the court; and (b) the adequacy of any compensation awarded by the domestic court. In *Rabone*, Jackson LJ said that taking all the factors into account, including the fact that an apology had been given by the defendant, there had been effective redress and therefore the claimants had lost their standing to bring claims.

In the Supreme Court, Lord Dyson adopted a more flexible approach. At [54] he rejected the contention that *Powell* and *Rowley v United*

---

18 See *Open Door Counselling & Dublin Well Woman v Ireland* (1992) 15 EHRR 244.
19 [2001] 1 WLR 1359, CA.
20 *Osman v UK* (2000) 29 EHRR 245.
21 *Brecknell v UK* (App No 324 57/04), 27 November 2007; *Yasa v Turkey* (1999) 28 EHRR 408; *McShane v UK* (2002) 35 EHRR 23, para [93].
22 [2009] 1 AC 681.
23 *Kats v Ukraine* (App No 29971/04) and *Micallef v Malta* (2010) 50 EHRR 37.
24 In [2013] 2 AC 72 at [48].
25 (2000) 30 EHRR CD 362.

Kingdom[26] clearly showed that the ECtHR took the view that acceptance of compensation in settlement of a domestic law cause of action arising from a death necessarily meant that an individual could no longer be regarded as a victim for the purposes of an Art 2 claim arising from the same death. Lord Dyson went on, however, to emphasise that other cases, such as *Caraher v United Kingdom*,[27] fell on the other side of the line. Consequently, Lord Dyson determined (at [57]) that it was difficult to divine any clear statement of principle from ECtHR jurisprudence on whether the settlement of a domestic law claim would preclude an Art 2 claim being litigated. He noted that the ECtHR seemed to adopt a broad approach to determining the true meaning and effect of a settlement.

Consequently, the true legal effect of the settlement of a domestic claim remains unclear and highly fact specific. It is nevertheless important for practitioners to be aware that any settlement may result in standing being lost to pursue the human rights claim. The best way to guard against this is to carefully frame the settlement to exclude the human rights claim from its ambit. However, there can be no certainty about the approach the courts will take, so a great deal of care is required.

In the recent case of *Daniel v St George's Healthcare NHS Trust*[28] the High Court considered the extension of standing in HRA 1998 claims to individuals who would not typically be regarded as belonging to the 'immediate family'. The deceased in *Daniel* was a 37-year-old prisoner who had died on remand at HMP Wandsworth following alleged negligence. The first claimant had been the deceased's foster mother for three years during his childhood, while the second claimant described himself as the deceased's 'foster brother'. The claimants sought to bring claims for breach of Arts 2 and 3 of the ECHR against the defendants. Lang J identified four factors which she considered to be relevant to standing:

1   the nature of the legal/family relationship between the claimants and the deceased;
2   the nature of the personal ties between the claimants and the deceased;
3   the extent to which the alleged violations of the convention (1) affected them personally and (2) caused them to suffer;
4   involvement in the proceedings arising out of the deceased's death.

While the claims failed on other bases, Lang J was prepared to accept, having applied the facts to the legal framework she identified, that the deceased's former foster mother (but not his 'foster brother') did have standing to bring an action under the HRA 1998.

Remedies

In relation to any unlawful act (or proposed act) of a public authority, the court or tribunal may grant any relief or remedy or make any order as it considers just and appropriate (HRA 1998, s 8(1)). Damages may be awarded if, taking into account all the circumstances of the case, including any other relief or remedy granted, and the consequences of any decision

---

26   (Application No 31914/03), February 2005.
27   (2000) 29 EHRR CD 119.
28   [2016] 4 WLR 32.

taken in respect of that act, the court is satisfied that an award of damages is necessary to award 'just satisfaction' to the person in whose favour it is made (HRA 1998, s 8(3)). 'Just satisfaction' is a Convention concept which arises under Art 41 of the ECHR, and the domestic court must take into account the principles applied by the ECtHR in relation to the award of compensation under Art 41 (HRA 1998, s 8(4)). 'Just satisfaction' can be achieved by means other than compensatory damages; for example by way of a declaration of violation, an apology or by settlement. Indeed, damages are to be regarded a remedy of last resort under the HRA 1998, because compensation is of secondary importance to the primary aim of bringing the unlawful interference with the Convention right to an end (*Greenfield v Secretary of State for the Home Department*[29] and see also *Commissioner of Police of the Metropolis v DSD*;[30] and *Van Colle v Chief Constable of Hertfordshire*[31]).

Damages are, therefore, not awarded as of right where an HRA 1998 claim succeeds. The question of whether to make an award, and if so how much, is a matter within the broad discretion of the court. The guiding principle for an award of damages is to place the claimant so far as possible in the same position he would have been in if his convention rights had not been violated. If damages are awarded, the assessment should be informed by the approach of the ECtHR, and damages awarded for breaches in the domestic courts should be roughly comparable to those awarded by the Strasbourg Court.

While, however, there is a duty to take Strasbourg jurisprudence into account, it is very difficult to extract clear legal principles from the ECtHR's judgments on just satisfaction. Lord Reed expressly commented upon the absence of coherent principles in *R (on the application of Faulkner) v Secretary of State for Justice*.[32]

When assessing damages, the court will take into account a range of factors including the seriousness and manner of the violation (see, for example, *Baiai v Secretary of State*[33] in which it was said that a 'high threshold of harm was required before a damages award would be made' and *R (on the application of B) v DPP*[34] regarding the specific nature of the harm being a relevant factor).The overall approach is an equitable one, but several cases have emphasised the need to establish causation between the violation and the loss and damage caused (see *Re C*[35]). The decision to award damages needs to strike a balance between the rights of the individual and the rights of the public as a whole.

Damages for non-pecuniary loss, including: distress and anxiety; pain and suffering; humiliation; inconvenience; loss of love and support; and invasion of privacy are available, but the case law does not provide any consistent or coherent approach to their assessment. The levels of damages awarded in respect of torts as set out in the Judicial College Guidelines, the Criminal Injuries Compensation Board Scheme and the levels of awards made by the Parliamentary Ombudsman and the

29   [2005] 1 WLR 673, HL.
30   [2018] UKSC 11.
31   [2009] 1 AC 225.
32   [2013] 2 AC 254 at [34].
33   [2006] EWHC 1035 (Admin).
34   [2009] 1 WLR 2072, HC (DC).
35   [2007] HRLR 14, CA.

Local Government Ombudsman may all provide some rough guidance where the consequences of the infringement of human rights are similar to that being considered in the comparator selected (see: *Anufrijeva v Southwark London Borough Council* per Lord Woolf at [74]). The ECtHR has awarded pecuniary loss in respect of past and future lost earnings, pension rights, medical expenses, funeral costs and loss of future career prospects.

The ECtHR does not award punitive or exemplary damages and in *R (KB) v Mental Health Review Tribunal*,[36] Burnton J held at [60] that 'section 9(3) of the 1998 Act, by prohibiting any award of damages otherwise than by way of compensation, expressly prohibits the award of exemplary damages' at least as regards human rights proceedings in respect of a judicial act done in good faith.[37]

In *McGlinchey v UK*,[38] the ECtHR awarded damages for a breach of Art 3 (prohibition of torture) in circumstances where no award could have been made under English law as the requirements of injury caused by breach of duty could not be satisfied. The claim was brought by the children of M, a heroin addict, who had died while imprisoned. The applicants were awarded damages of €22,900 in respect of non-pecuniary damage (of which €11,500 was awarded to M's estate, and M's children received €3,800 each) and €7,500 for costs and expenses.

In *Rabone*, where the suicide of a voluntary patient was argued to have been caused by systemic failures by the NHS hospital, the judge at first instance said that if actionable breaches of Art 2 had been established, the proper award would have been a modest £1,500 in the case of each claimant (the parents of the patient who committed suicide). On appeal to the Court of Appeal,[39] Jackson LJ said that if the case had succeeded in his view the proper level of award would have been £5,000 for each parent.[40] The Supreme Court upheld the Court of Appeal's conclusion, as the appellants had not challenged the quantum of damages awarded. However, Lord Dyson at [88] noted that there was 'real force' in counsel for the appellants' argument that the £5,000 awarded by the Court of Appeal was too low.

In *Van Colle* (a failed claim for breach of Art 2) the court said it would have awarded £10,000 to the deceased's estate for the distress suffered by the deceased, and £7,500 to each of the deceased's parents for their own grief and suffering.

The ECtHR's awards of damages are generally a lot lower than we are accustomed to in the context of clinical negligence. General damages are often not awarded at all by the ECtHR which is justified by the notion that the finding of the court in favour of the applicant is sufficient compensation. When general damages are awarded, they rarely exceed £15,000. There are some circumstances where some damages will be available in circumstances where no damages would be available under common law negligence or other available statutory remedies (for example where no physical or psychological injury can be evidenced beyond

---

36 [2004] QB 936, HC.
37 See also *Watkins v Secretary of State for Home Department* [2006] 2 AC 395.
38 [2003] Lloyd's Med Rep 264.
39 [2010] EWCA Civ 698.
40 *Rabone v Pennine NHS Trust* [2010] EWCA Civ 698.

anxiety, distress and loss of dignity, or where relatives do not qualify for bereavement awards), but in the vast majority of clinical negligence cases the common law continues to provide the most adequate compensation for injury and loss.

Taking a case to Strasbourg

As this is a route that will be unlikely to be relevant or useful to the vast majority of clinical negligence practitioners and clients, it is dealt with only briefly here. However it is important to note at least that such a route is available in the prescribed circumstances. An applicant is able to take a claim to the ECtHR in Strasbourg if their rights have arguably been breached by the state and they have exhausted all domestic remedies. The application must be made within six months of the final domestic decision. Some legal aid funding is available from the ECtHR. The conclusion of any settlement is likely to affect the admissibility of an application to the ECtHR.

THE CONVENTION RIGHTS

Interpretation of Convention Rights

Any court or tribunal determining a question which has arisen in relation to a Convention right must take into account any relevant jurisprudence of the ECtHR (HRA 1998, s 2). Therefore, practitioners of domestic human rights need to understand the Strasbourg approach and have a good working knowledge of the case law.

In order to set the scene for the review of relevant human rights jurisprudence that follows, it is necessary to understand some of the terminology and underlying legal concepts preferred by the ECtHR.

Absolute rights

In ordinary language, a 'right' to something is normally understood as an absolute entitlement. The Convention does include some 'absolute' rights that cannot be derogated from, and in respect of which no interference can ever be justified in the public interest. The Convention supplies an absolute right not to be subjected to torture (Art 3), or to be held in slavery or servitude (Art 4), or to be subjected to a retrospective criminal offence (Art 7(1)). If a claimant can prove a state has acted in violation of an absolute right, that conduct cannot be justified in any circumstances. In the UK this has proven controversial in the arena of deportation of suspected terror suspects to their home country in circumstances where the deportation presents a risk of torture. The ECtHR has consistently refused to countenance any reduction in the privileged protection afforded to these few absolute rights, despite attempts by states to alter the court's approach (see the intervention of the UK Government in *Saadi v Italy*)[41].

---

41   (2008) 24 BHRC 123.

Limited rights

The absolute Convention rights are in a clear minority; most of the Convention rights are expressly or impliedly limited. For example, Art 5 (right to liberty and security) which in general terms protects the individual's right to liberty, expressly references certain circumstances in which a citizen can be lawfully detained without violating their Art 5 rights. Further implied limits on rights can and have been determined by the ECtHR on a case by case basis, but such implied restrictions are generally interpreted narrowly by the court and are subject to the same general principles that govern the qualified rights.

Qualified rights

Interference with a right that is 'qualified' can be justified by proportionate reliance on a legitimate aim. The qualified rights are drafted in two limbs, the first setting out the substantive right, and the second qualifying that right by prescribing circumstances in which that right may lawfully be interfered with (see Arts 8 (right to privacy), 9 (freedom of thought, conscience and religion), 10 (freedom of expression), 11 (freedom of assembly and association), and Art 1 of Protocol 1 (protection of property)). A legitimate aim is one that is prescribed in accordance with the law and necessary in a democratic society. The concept of 'proportionality' is extremely important. An interference with a substantive right can only be justified to the extent that the interference is necessary to achieve the legitimate aim, and no further (see: *Silver v UK;*[42] *Handyside v UK;*[43] *Sporrong v Sweden*[44]). There is a balancing act that needs to be carried out between the rights of collective society (the legitimate social aim) and the rights of the individual. A balancing act also frequently needs to be carried out between competing Convention rights, such as in circumstances where the individual's right to respect for private and family life under Art 8 needs to be balanced against the freedom of expression under Art 10.

Margin of appreciation

The 'margin of appreciation' is a European law concept which describes the ambit of discretion given to different sovereign states in terms of how they are allowed to comply with the requirements of an international treaty using different but equally valid means to achieve an appropriate balance of protection of citizens' rights. If a course of action (or inaction) is determined by the court to fall within the state's 'margin of appreciation', this simply means that the state has acted compatibly with the Convention.

Positive obligations

In addition to the specific obligations set out in the body of the text itself (for example Art 5(2) 'everyone who is arrested shall be informed

---

42 (1983) 5 EHRR 347.
43 (1976) 1 EHRR 737.
44 (1982) 5 EHRR 35.

promptly in a language which he understands of the reasons for his arrest and any charge against him'), some of the rights have been interpreted by the ECtHR as impliedly giving rise to further positive and negative obligations on the state. It is generally accepted that the Convention positively obliges the state to adopt sufficient and adequate legal systems to deter and punish individuals guilty of violating the Convention rights of others (for example an obligation to create, maintain and put into practice an effective system of criminal law to deter the commission of offences against the person). Specific arms of the state such as the police or other relevant public bodies have been found to be under positive operational duties to take steps to prevent a violation of individuals' rights under Arts 2 or 3 (for police see *Osman v UK*;[45] for local authorities see *Z v UK*[46]). Where such obligations have been determined to exist in relation to Convention rights, and are relevant to the present exercise, they are set out further below.

Article 2: The right to life

1. Everyone's right to life shall be protected by law. No-one shall be deprived of his life intentionally [....]

2. Deprivation of life shall not be regarded as inflicted in contravention of this Article when it results from the use of force which is no more than is absolutely necessary

(a)   In defence of any person from unlawful violence;
(b)   In order to effect a lawful arrest or to prevent the escape of a person lawfully detained;
(c)   In action lawfully taken for the purpose of quelling a riot or insurrection.

Article 2 is one of the 'most fundamental provisions in the Convention' which 'together with Article 3 enshrines one of the basic values of the democratic societies making up the Council of Europe'.[47] The right imposes substantive positive and negative obligations on the state (to refrain from taking and to protect life) as well as significant procedural obligations to investigate the taking of life; in particular where the state or its agents are implicated in the loss of life.

How does Article 2 affect the unborn child?

In the UK, a foetus has no legal rights or interests before birth. However, this is not the position across Europe. Some states, such as Ireland, do recognise a pre-natal right to life. The vexed philosophical question of when life begins is one to which there is no common or universal answer among the state parties to the Convention, and for that reason the ECtHR has allowed a generous margin of appreciation to state parties in terms of when they identify Art 2 rights may begin to apply (see *Evans v UK*[48] in which it was held that the destruction of embryos did not engage Art 2 in the UK).

---

45   (2000) 29 EHRR 245.
46   (2002) 34 EHRR 3.
47   *McCann v UK* (1996) 21 EHRR 97.
48   (2007) 22 BHRC 190.

To date, no Strasbourg case has found a breach of Art 2 in respect of a foetus, however a number of cases have suggested that this may not necessarily remain the case in future. In a case held inadmissible on other grounds, the ECtHR held that in principle a foetus could be a 'victim' under Art 34 in relation to a breach of Art 2 (*Boso v Italy*[49]), and in *Vo v France*[50] the Grand Chamber of the ECtHR specifically noted that 'the court has yet to determine the "beginning" of "everyone's right to life" within the meaning of this provision and whether the unborn child has such a right'. The question of when life begins remains firmly within the state's margin of appreciation, as does the balancing of the conflicting interests of the foetus and the mother (see Grand Chamber judgment in *A, B and C v Ireland*[51] which concerned three women who were resident in Ireland and travelled to the UK to have lawful abortions for health and social reasons).

Substantive prohibition on taking life – how does this provision affect end of life decisions and clinical decisions that result in death?

It has been held by the ECtHR that the Article does not require that passive euthanasia, by which a person is allowed to die by not being given treatment, be a crime. In *Widmer v Switzerland*,[52] it was sufficient that Swiss law provided liability for negligent medical treatment causing death.

In the UK there have been several major challenges to the lawfulness of prohibitions on assisted suicide. Diane Pretty brought proceedings seeking an undertaking from the DPP that her husband would not be prosecuted if he assisted her suicide. She was terminally ill with Motor Neurone Disease and wished to establish in advance whether her husband would be prosecuted if he assisted her to die with dignity at a time when she judged her mental and physical suffering had become utterly unbearable. Her claim raised issues under Arts 2, 3 and 8. The House of Lords and the ECtHR held that a 'right to die' could not be read into the Art 2 protection of life (*R (on the application of Pretty) v DPP*,[53] *Pretty v UK*[54]) but that the ambit of Art 8 was wide enough to encompass the right to self-determination in terms of life and death issues. The ECtHR held that while a blanket ban on assisted suicide did engage Art 8, the interference was a legitimate and proportionate one that was 'designed to safeguard life by protecting the weak and vulnerable and especially those who are not in a condition to take informed decisions against acts intended to end life or to assist in ending life'. The interference was reasonable and objectively justified, and there was no violation by the state of Art 8.

In *R (on the application of Purdy) v DPP*,[55] the House of Lords revisited this context in the case of a woman terminally ill with multiple sclerosis who sought clarification of the DPP policy in relation to prosecutions for assisted suicide in order to make an informed decision about whether to

---

49 (App No 50490/99) 5 September 2002.
50 [2004] 2 FCR 577.
51 (App No 25579/05).
52 (App No 20527/92) 1993, unreported.
53 [2002] 1 AC 800.
54 (2002) 35 EHRR 1.
55 [2010] 1 AC 345.

ask her husband to assist her in travelling to a country where suicide was lawful in order to die. The House of Lords found the Code for Prosecutors was insufficient in this context to meet the requirements under Art 8 of foreseeability and accessibility, and ordered the DPP to promulgate an offence specific policy to identify the facts and circumstances that would be taken into account in deciding whether to prosecute in such a case (since *Purdy*, s 59 of the Coroners and Justice Act 2009 has been enacted which amends and clarifies to some extent the offence of 'encouraging or assisting suicide', without meaningfully altering the substance of the offence).

Recently, the blanket ban on assisted suicide in the Suicide Act 1961, s 2(1) was upheld by the Court of Appeal in *R (on the application of Conway) v Secretary of State for Justice*[56] as a necessary and proportionate interference with the claimant's Art 8 rights; and a provision that lay clearly within the state's margin of appreciation.

One can, however, contrast *Pretty*, *Purdy* and *Conway* with *Ms B v An NHS Trust*[57] (a case about mental capacity in which there is no reference to human rights), in which a competent tetraplegic patient wished to refuse life sustaining artificial ventilation in order to die naturally, but no doctor at her hospital would carry out her wishes. Dame Butler-Sloss P warned against the 'serious danger exemplified in this case of a benevolent paternalism which does not embrace recognition of the personal autonomy of the severely disabled patient'. Ms B was judged to have capacity to make the decision to refuse treatment that would end her life, and ultimately a doctor was identified outside the defendant NHS trust who was prepared to carry out her wishes.

The domestic courts have also held that where responsible medical professionals take the view that further treatment is not in the patient's best interests, withdrawal of artificial hydration and nutrition will not violate Art 2. In *National Health Service Trust A v M* and *National Health Service Trust B v H*,[58] Butler-Sloss P held that, if artificial nutrition and hydration were withdrawn from two patients who had been for years in permanent vegetative state, there would not be a breach of the Article. She said that the Article did not impose an absolute obligation to treat if such treatment would be futile. The Article only imposed a positive obligation to give life-sustaining treatment in circumstances where, according to responsible medical opinion, such treatment was in the best interests of the patient. See *Re O T*[59] for a more recent illustration of the balancing exercise the court will undertake to make an assessment of the patient's best interests.

In *R (on the application of Burke) v General Medical Council*,[60] the claimant suffered from the progressively degenerative disease of cerebellar ataxia. He was of full capacity, but there would come a time when he could only survive by artificial nutrition. His cognitive facilities would remain intact, however. He did not want artificial nutrition to be withdrawn until he died of natural causes. He based his arguments on

56 [2018] EWCA Civ 1431.
57 [2002] All ER 449, HC (Fam).
58 [2001] Fam 348 (HC).
59 [2009] EWHC 633 (Fam).
60 [2006] QB 273, CA.

a number of Articles in the Convention. The Court of Appeal confirmed that where a competent patient indicated his wish to be kept alive by the provision of artificial nutrition and hydration (ANH), any doctor who deliberately brought that patient's life to an end by discontinuing the supply of artificial nutrition and hydration would not merely be in breach of duty but would be guilty of murder. However Art 2 did not impose a continuing obligation on health authorities to continue treatment to patients in a permanent vegetative state in all cases. The question of whether or not the withdrawal of ANH would be in his best interests after he had lost capacity was not a question that could be prejudged in advance by application of a simple test. The guidance on withholding and withdrawing life prolonging treatment produced by the GMC did not violate the Convention in the particular way alleged by the claimant.

The issue has been further clarified in a number of recent cases. In *Lambert v France*[61] the ECtHR held the Art 2, 3 and 8 rights of a patients whose ANH had been withdrawn had not been infringed. The ECtHR was prepared to give significant latitude to domestic authorities in this area of law, and in the factual circumstances of the case the authorities had complied with the obligations flowing from Art 2.

In *NHS Trust v Y*,[62] the Supreme Court held that is no mandatory requirement, either at common law or under the ECHR, for a court order to be obtained before ANH can be withdrawn. If the provisions of the Mental Capacity Act 2005 are followed, the relevant guidelines are followed, and there is agreement on what is in the best interests of the patient, the patient can be treated in accordance with that agreement without reference to the court. However, it seems that in circumstances where there is no clear agreement on whether ANH should be withdrawn, or complex considerations are involved, an application to the court will still be required.

The domestic courts have held that the value of life under Art 2 is not absolute; in appropriate cases a balance has to be struck, as in the vexing case of the conjoined twins.[63] The conjoined twins required surgical separation which would inevitably result in the death of the weaker twin, for which the parents understandably could not give their consent. It was held by the domestic courts both that this was an appropriate case in which to override the parents' decision, and that the operation would not violate the Art 2 prohibition on the taking of life. The ratio was that the doctors' *intention* was not to kill the weaker, but to increase the life chances of the stronger twin. A plea of quasi self-defence, modified for the exceptional circumstances, could be available to the doctor acting to save J's life by removing M, who in reality was killing J.

In summary, an adult with capacity may lawfully: travel to a country where assisted suicide is legal; decide to refuse treatment even where that will certainly result in harm or even death; take active steps to commit suicide; and dictate by way of advance directive (see Mental Capacity Act 2005) that treatment is to be refused when he loses capacity. It remains unlawful to take life by assisting suicide (whether by medicine or by assisting travel abroad for that purpose) unless either the assistance has

---

61   (2016) 62 EHRR 2.
62   [2018] UKSC 46.
63   [2000] Fam Law 16; affirmed [2001] Fam 147, CA.

the primary effect of some form of palliative care and only secondarily hastens death (the doctrine of 'double effect') or the taking of life fulfils the requirements of one of the express exceptions to Art 2 (for example 'self-defence').

Substantive positive obligation to protect life

The Commission has stated that the Article 'enjoins the state not only to refrain from taking life intentionally but, further, to take appropriate steps to safeguard life' (*X v UK*[64]).

Primarily, the substantive positive obligations under Art 2 refer to general or systemic duties to establish and apply an effective criminal law system to deter and punish the taking of life and to take appropriate measures to prevent deaths in custody. The ECtHR has confirmed that the duty on the state to take appropriate steps to protect life applies to public health, in the sense of requiring states to regulate hospitals to adopt appropriately high professional and practice standards (see *Calvelli and Ciglio v Italy*[65] and *Powell v UK*[66]). The House of Lords revisited this general duty under Art 2 in *Savage v South Essex Partnership NHS Trust*,[67] per Lord Rodger at [68]–[69]:

> In terms of Article 2, health authorities are under an overarching obligation to protect the lives of patients in their hospitals. In order to fulfil that obligation, and depending on the circumstances, they may require to fulfil a number of complementary obligations.
>
> In the first place, the duty to protect the lives of patients requires health authorities to ensure that the hospitals for which they are responsible employ competent staff and that they are trained to a high professional standard. In addition, the authorities must ensure that the hospitals adopt systems of work which will protect the lives of patients. Failure to perform these general obligations may result in a violation of Article 2.

Where mental health is concerned, the general duty includes putting in place appropriate systems to prevent patients from taking their own lives. In *Savage*, Lord Rodger continued at [69]:

> If for example a health authority fails to ensure that a hospital puts in place a proper system for supervising mentally ill patients and as a result a patient is able to commit suicide, the health authority will have violated the patient's right to life under Article 2.

(See also *Herczegfalvy v Austria*.[68])

There is an important distinction to be drawn between a systemic failure that will engage the state's responsibility under Art 2, and a failure which is the result of the act or omission of an individual or individuals which will not. The ECtHR in *Powell v UK*[69] stated that it could not accept that 'matters such as errors of judgment on the part of a health professional or negligent coordination among health professionals in the treatment of

---

64 (App No 7154/75), 14 DR 31 (1978).
65 (App No 32967/96).
66 (2000) 30 EHRR CD 362.
67 [2009] 1 AC 681.
68 (1992) 15 EHRR 437.
69 (2000) 30 EHRR CD 362.

a particular patient are sufficient of themselves to call a contracting state to account [under Article 2]'. This was in essence the approach adopted by the Divisional Court (Singh LJ and Foskett J) in *R (on the application of Parkinson) v HM Senior Coroner for Kent*.[70] In *Parkinson*, the court held that a coroner had been entitled to find that the enhanced investigative duty under Art 2 did not arise. The court determined that the enhanced investigative duty only arises where there is an arguable breach of the state's own substantive obligations under Art 2.

The logic appears to be that the state must be culpable in some way before it can be held responsible. If the state properly trains, regulates and provides facilities for healthcare professionals, the fact that a doctor then acts negligently and/or not in accordance with his training is not a matter which should engage the state's liability under Art 2. In such circumstances the individual doctor may be personally liable in negligence for the clinical misjudgement or failure to implement the system in place, and the health authority will probably be vicariously liable, but there will be no breach of the state's general duty under Art 2 to have a proper system in place.

In *Lopes de Sousa Fernandes v Portugal*,[71] the ECtHR Grand Chamber took the opportunity to reaffirm the status quo, reversing a previous ruling of the ECtHR Chamber and holding that 'merely' negligent medical treatment is insufficient to engage the substantive limb of Art 2.

The ECtHR has held that in certain prescribed circumstances the state will be obliged to take preventive operational measures (distinct from and additional to the general systemic obligations) to protect the lives of specific individuals. In *Osman v UK*,[72] those circumstances were described as where 'the authorities knew or ought to have known at the time of the existence of a real and immediate risk to the life of an identified individual or individuals … and that they failed to take measures within the scope of their powers which, judged reasonably, might have been expected to avoid that risk'. In *Osman*, the ECtHR rejected the submission made by the UK Government that the failure must amount to gross negligence or wilful disregard of the duty to protect life before it could be said to breach the operational duty.

The 'real and immediate' risk has been described as a high threshold (Lord Carswell, *Re Officer L*[73]); but see comments by Lord Bingham in *Van Colle* (at [30]) and Baroness Hale in *Savage* (at [78]) warning against treating this as a refinement of the test. In *Van Colle*, where a prosecution witness had been murdered by a criminal at whose trial he was about to be a witness, the House of Lords reaffirmed and applied the *Osman* test, but found on the facts of that case that, despite evidence of intimidation by the accused, there was no real and immediate risk in circumstances where there had been no actual death threats and the trial was for a relatively minor offence. In *Rabone* in the Supreme Court, the evidence of one of the deceased's treating psychiatrists that there was a 20% risk that she might commit suicide was sufficient to satisfy the 'real and immediate risk' test.

---

70 [2018] 4 WLR 106, HC.
71 (2018) 66 EHRR 28.
72 (2000) EHRR 245.
73 [2009] 1 WLR 2135, HL.

The *Osman* Art 2 operational duty to a specific individual has been extended to the protection of individuals in custody from suicide (*Keenan v UK*[74]) to individuals in immigration detention (*Slimani v France*[75]) and in the domestic courts to detained mental health patients (*Savage v South Essex Partnership NHS Trust*).

In *Osman* at [116], the court said that the obligation under the Convention to take appropriate steps to safeguard life must be interpreted in a way that does not impose an impossible or disproportionate burden on the authorities. In the healthcare context, this is a necessary qualification, as it would be impossible to run the NHS if patients were entitled to any life-saving operation or medication without regard to resources. In *Savage*, Baroness Hale also drew attention to the fact that in the case of mental health detention, where the objectives are therapeutic and protective rather than penal, steps taken by the state to protect life must be proportionate and must take into account properly the competing values in the Convention, in particular the liberty and autonomy rights protected by Arts 5 (right to liberty and security) and 8 (right to respect for private and family life).

There was speculation in the wake of *Savage* (inspired in part by *obiter* comments by Baroness Hale at [101]) that the operational duty might also be extended by analogy to circumstances outside detention, such as to voluntary mental health patients, or indeed to non-mental health patients in public hospitals dependent on physical care and assistance. That point was considered by the Supreme Court in *Rabone* where it was held that health authorities do owe Art 2 operational duties to voluntary patients in hospitals. Lord Dyson observed at [22] that a critical factor in determining whether a duty arose was the assumption of responsibility by the state for the individual's welfare. In reaching this conclusion, Lord Dyson relied upon the judgment of Lord Rodger in *Mitchell v Glasgow City Council*[76] at [66] where it was said that the duty was not restricted to cases of detention but can arise whenever the state assumes responsibility for the individual. Lord Dyson also identified, at [23]–[24], the vulnerability of the victim and the nature of the risk as relevant factors in determining whether an operational duty under Art 2 arises.

The state's positive obligations can extend to the provision of information, where appropriate, to protect the lives of persons in their jurisdiction. In *Oneryildiz v Turkey*,[77] the state's failure to provide sufficient information about the danger of landslides as well as failure to take appropriate steps to avoid landslides was held by the ECtHR to be a breach of the Art 2 rights of residents of slum housing killed by landslides. A further line of argument under Art 2 could be a complaint that the state failed to give adequate warnings about life threatening dangers to health, for example from radiation (see *LCB v UK*[78]), or contaminated food, or a medical product or medical treatment such as a vaccination programme. These challenges are likely to fall under the general systemic Art 2 duty.

---

74   (2001) 33 EHRR 913.
75   (2004) 43 EHRR 1068.
76   [2009] AC 874.
77   (2004) 18 BHRC 145.
78   (1998) 27 EHRR 212.

Procedural obligation

The state's obligation under Art 2 includes the responsibility to establish an effective independent judicial system to promptly and effectively determine responsibility for the deaths of patients receiving medical treatment. The prompt examination of deaths in hospitals is considered to be important for the safety of all users of health services. A breach of Art 2 was found in *Silih v Slovenia*,[79] where, following the death of the claimant's son during hospital treatment, resolution of the civil proceedings was still pending 13 years later and the extent of the delays could not be explained by the complexity of the case or other factors. The court was also critical of the frequent replacement of the trial judge that had contributed to the delay (on this point see also: *Dvoracek v Slovakia*;[80] and *Byrzykowski v Poland*[81]).

In an ordinary clinical negligence case where there is no evidence of any systemic failures, the Art 2 procedural obligation is likely to be met by the availability of internal hospital investigations, with opportunity to pursue a civil negligence suit, as well as disciplinary or regulatory proceedings where appropriate. The inquest system is the principal means for investigating deaths in the UK. The scope of enquiry in an inquest is quite narrowly controlled by coronial rules and law. However, in circumstances where the state or its agents are implicated in a death, the scope of both the nature of the coroner's inquiry and the verdict that may be given are increased to give effect to the Art 2 procedural duty (see further Chapter 19 – The inquest the law, procedure and funding).

The inquest system does not have power to investigate cases where death has not in fact occurred, but these circumstances can also invoke the Art 2 duty (see: *R (JL) v Secretary of State for Justice*[82]). In these and other cases where the standard domestic inquest system is unable to fulfil the investigative function adequately, the Art 2 procedural duty may require the state to set up prompt and effective internal or public investigations ('enhanced investigations') with varying degrees of public scrutiny appropriate depending on the circumstances (*R (on the application of Khan (Mohammed Farooq) v Secretary of State for Health*[83]) and indeed, in a rare case, even to set up a full public inquiry (*Scholes v Home Secretary*,[84] death in custody). Practitioners should also note *R (on the application of Claire Humberstone) (claimant) v Legal Services Commission (defendant) & HM Coroner for South Yorkshire (West) (interested party)*[85] in which the Court of Appeal dismissed an appeal against a decision of the High Court quashing a decision of the LSC to deny funding for representation at an inquest into the claimant's son's death by asthma attack in which the ambulance service, hospital and GP were interested parties, and where the mother had initially been charged with manslaughter (based on allegations she had failed to appropriately administer asthma medication). It was the view of Hickinbottom J that

---

79 (2009) 49 EHRR 37.
80 (App No 30754/04).
81 (2008) 46 EHRR 32.
82 [2009] 1 AC 588.
83 [2004] 1 WLR 971, CA.
84 [2006] HRLR 44, CA.
85 [2011] 1 WLR 1460.

in the circumstances of that case an 'effective investigation', which was necessary to meet Art 2 obligations arising in the case, could not be conducted unless the mother was represented. The Court of Appeal commented that the Lord Chancellor's guidance on funding was 'less than satisfactory' and that 'the decision must focus on the effective participation of the family and not on the needs of the Coroner' (paras [73]–[75], [78]–[79]).

Article 3: Freedom from inhuman treatment

No-one shall be subjected to torture or to inhuman or degrading treatment or punishment.

Although this provision is clearly aimed at quite different contexts than the purely medical (it speaks of torture, degrading treatment and punishment), the ECtHR has held 'the suffering which flows from naturally occurring illness, physical or mental, may be covered by Article 3 where it is, or risks being, exacerbated by treatment, whether flowing from conditions of detention, expulsion or other measures, for which the authorities can be held responsible' (*Pretty v UK*). For a more recent example finding inadequate medical treatment in detention in breach of Art 3, see *Paladi v Moldova*.[86]

In one UK case, the ECtHR found that detention conditions for a severely disabled woman breached Art 3 in circumstances where she was dangerously cold and was unable to use her bed or toilet or wash without great difficulty. Judge Bratza in his opinion held the judicial authorities primarily responsible for the breach, because they had sentenced her to imprisonment without establishing that appropriate and adequate facilities for her care existed in detention.

In respect of medical treatment, whether in a detained or open setting, the crucial issue under Art 3 will be whether the conduct complained of reaches 'a minimum level of severity' (*Ireland v UK*[87]). The threshold for breach of Art 3 is very high. In a case brought by the family of a deceased prisoner who had been handcuffed during his treatment for chemotherapy and who had suffered humiliation and distress throughout his treatment (*R (on the application of Faizovas) v Secretary of State for the Home Department*[88]), the Court of Appeal held that the threshold for breach of Art 3 had not been crossed (but cf *Mouisel v France*[89] in which the ECtHR found that Art 3 had been breached when a severely ill man with lymphocytic leukaemia was chained by both feet and wrists during his treatment in hospital). In *R (on the application of MD (Angola)) v Secretary of State for the Home Department*[90] the Court of Appeal held that there was no basis for a human rights claim of breach of Arts 2 or 3 based on the failure of the Home Secretary to adopt the guidance from the British HIV Association, or something equivalent, as a legal standard for the management of the needs of detainees who were HIV positive.

---

86   (App No 398061/05) judgment in March 2009.
87   (1978) 2 EHRR 25.
88   [2009] ACD 58.
89   (2004) 38 EHRR 34.
90   [2011] EWCA Civ 1238.

In *Paposhvili v Belgium*[91] the ECtHR relaxed, to a degree, the position set out in its prior jurisprudence about the removal of seriously ill migrants to their country of origin and emphasised the importance of a substantive assessment of risk of ill-treatment in such circumstances. The impact of the judgment was considered by the Court of Appeal in *AM (Zimbabwe) v Secretary of State for the Home Department*.[92] Sales LJ held that *Paposhvili* had relaxed the test for violation of Art 3 set by the House of Lords in *N v Secretary of State for the Home Department*[93] to only a very modest extent. Following *Paposhvili*, the prohibition against removal in medical cases is not solely confined to deathbed cases where death is already imminent when the applicant is in the removing country. It now extends to cases where:

> substantial grounds have been shown for believing that [the applicant], although not at imminent risk of dying, would face a real risk, on account of the absence of appropriate treatment in the receiving country or lack of access to such treatment, of being exposed to a serious, rapid and irreversible decline in his or her state of health resulting in intense suffering or to a significant reduction in life expectancy (see *AM* at [38] and *Paposhvili* at [183].

It appears likely that the issue will be considered by the Supreme Court in the near future.

The question of whether the threshold has been breached in a particular case will depend on a number of factors including the type and duration of treatment, and sometimes the individual characteristics (age, sex, health) of the victim of the violation, but it is clear that in all but the most extreme cases, examples of hospital neglect, such as failing to keep a patient clean, warm, fed, appropriately dressed, provided with analgesia, or provided with optimum care, are unlikely to breach the threshold of Art 3. However there is an important overlap here with Art 8, which concerns not only the private and family life of the individual but also extends to such concepts as dignity, autonomy and physical and psychological integrity.

Forcible medical treatment of detainees will not be a breach of the Article 3 where it is reasonably required to preserve physical and mental health, because 'as a general rule, a measure which is a therapeutic necessity cannot be regarded as inhuman or degrading' (*Herczegfalvy v Austria*[94]). The court must however be satisfied that the therapeutic need for the treatment exists (see *R (on the application of B) v Ashworth Hospital Authority*,[95] and *B v UK*[96] in relation to the psychiatric treatment of a Broadmoor patient).

In *Hegarty v University Hospitals Birmingham NHS Foundation Trust*[97] the claimant alleged that her treatment by nursing staff had been negligent and also amounted to a breach of Arts 3 and 8 of the ECHR. HHJ Platts (sitting as a judge of the High Court) found at [72] that the nursing care had been negligent but that the allegations raised by the

---

91 [2017] Imm AR 867.
92 [2018] EWCA Civ 64.
93 [2005] 2 AC 296.
94 (1993) 15 EHRR 437.
95 [2005] 2 AC 278.
96 (App No 6870/75) 32 DR 5 (1981).
97 [2017] EWHC 2115 (QB).

claimant fell well short of the minimum level of severity required to come within the scope of Art 3. Furthermore, the judge noted that the allegations under Arts 3 and 8 of the ECHR were largely co-extensive with the common law allegations of breach of duty and that even if the HRA 1998 claims had succeeded he could not see that any further award beyond the claimant's entitlement at common law would be necessary to provide the claimant with just satisfaction. The case neatly illustrates the reality that the common law will continue to provide the most appropriate and effective remedy in the vast majority of clinical negligence cases.

Experimental treatment without full consent could also come within the terms of Art 3 (*X v Denmark*[98]); but in such a case there would presumably be a claim in negligence anyway (though the claim under the Act might obviate possible defences, such as the contention that consent would have been given if properly sought, or that the treatment was in fact beneficial).

As well as the obvious negative obligation to not engage in conduct in breach of Art 3, the ECtHR has developed implied positive obligations on the state to prevent conduct that violates Art 3. In *A v UK*,[99] the UK was found to be in breach of Art 3 for failing to adequately protect a child from corporal punishment amounting to conduct in breach of Art 3 by insufficiently defining what constituted 'reasonable' (and therefore legal) punishment of a child by a parent. The ECtHR found breaches of Art 3 in two cases where the UK authorities had failed to take steps that 'could have had a real prospect of mitigating the harm' to children at real risk of abuse or neglect (*Z v UK*;[100] *E v UK*[101]).

However, these positive obligations are not without limit – the terminally ill applicant in *Pretty v UK* argued that the state's positive obligation to prevent suffering in breach of Art 3 should extend to allowing lawful assistance with suicide where otherwise she faced significant mental and physical torment before death, but this was rejected by the ECtHR (*Pretty v UK*[102]).

Article 6: The right to a fair trial

> In the determination of his civil rights ... everyone is entitled to a fair and public hearing within a reasonable time by an independent and impartial tribunal ...

The greater part of Art 6 deals with the requirements of a fair criminal trial, but the protections of Art 6(1) apply to the determination of civil rights and obligations as well. There are some significant points to note in relation to civil procedure and substantive access to civil justice.

There are a number of general entitlements that have been held by the ECtHR to be implicit in the notion of a fair trial, for example the right to real and effective access to a court, without unreasonable delay, and a real and effective opportunity to present one's case to an impartial and fair court or tribunal, in public, and to receive a decision which is

98   (1988) 32 DR 282.
99   (1998) 5 BHRC 137.
100 (2002) 34 EHRR 97.
101 (2003) 36 EHRR 519.
102 (2002) 35 EHRR 1.

clear and supported by reasons. The ECtHR has held that because the recognition and protection of all human rights depends on a fair and effective judicial process, the right to a fair trial holds a prominent place in a democratic society, and there can be no justification for interpreting Art 6(1) restrictively (*Moreira de Azevedo v Portugal*[103]).

Does Article 6 have any part to play in fair case management?

The basic elements of the right to a fair trial set out above are really no more or less than what should be expected by any litigant in England and Wales. Our civil justice system was reformed in 2000 by the coming into force of the Civil Procedure Rules. The rules are bound together by the 'overriding objective' set out in CPR 1, which is to 'deal with cases justly and at proportionate cost'. The CPR was obviously drafted with the Convention in mind, and broadly, post the Jackson reforms, continues to satisfy the requirements of Art 6.

If the expectation among personal injury lawyers had, not unreasonably, been that the procedural constraints on the proper preparation of cases could be challenged under Art 6, it appeared to be rudely dispelled by the trenchant observations of Lord Woolf in *Daniels v Walker*.[104] The claimant had been severely injured in a road traffic accident. A joint care report was obtained by consent. The defendants wanted to challenge the report by obtaining their own expert report, as they considered that the existing report recommended far more care than was needed. A careful argument was compiled to the effect that to deny them their request would be a breach of Art 6. Lord Woolf said:

> I will deal with the Human Rights Act point first. It was raised in a supplementary skeleton argument on behalf of the defendant. It relies on Article 6 of the Convention. It refers to *Mantovanelli v France* (1996) 24 EHRR 370, and suggests that, having regard to the provisions of Article 6, the order of the judge in this case conflicted with Article 6 because it amounted either to barring the whole claim of the defendant or barring an essential or fundamental part of that claim ... Article 6 has no possible relevance to this appeal. Quite apart from the fact that the [HRA] is not in force, if the court is not going to be taken down blind alleys it is essential that counsel, and those who instruct counsel, take a responsible attitude as to when it is right to raise a Human Rights Act point. The point was raised in this case and was supported by a skeleton argument which referred to different authorities under the Convention. It covered four pages. It resulted in a supplementary skeleton argument ...

> Article 6 could not possibly have anything to add to the issue on this appeal. The provisions of the Civil Procedure Rules, to which I have referred, make it clear that the obligation on the court is to deal with cases justly. If, having agreed to a joint expert's report a party subsequently wishes to call evidence, and it would be unjust having regard to the overriding objective of the Civil Procedure Rules not to allow that party to call that evidence, they must be allowed to call it.

...

---

103 (1990) 13 EHRR 721.
104 [2000] 1 WLR 1382, CA.

It would be unfortunate if case management decisions in this jurisdiction involved the need to refer to the learning of the European Court of Human Rights in order for them to be resolved. In my judgment, cases such as this do not require any consideration of human rights issues, certainly not issues under Article 6. It would be highly undesirable if the consideration of case management issues was made more complex by the injection into them of Article 6 style arguments. I hope that judges will be robust in resisting any attempt to introduce those arguments ... When the Act of 1998 becomes law, counsel will need to show self-restraint if it is not to be discredited.

In effect, Lord Woolf was saying that considerations of a fair trial in respect of procedural issues have nothing to do with the right to a fair trial under Art 6 and everything to do with the overriding objective under CPR 1. Justice in this context would be justice under the Rules, not under the Convention. Clearly, he was worried that the restraints placed on the preparation of cases in the interests of cutting costs and delays could be the subject of innumerable challenges under the HRA 1998 as the Convention does not explicitly recognise that what is the just solution in a procedural context must be heavily affected by considerations of expense and delay (something that CPR 1 makes abundantly clear).

The right to a fair trial includes the 'right to equality of arms'. This has been expressed by saying that a party must have a reasonable opportunity of presenting his case to the court under conditions which do not place him at substantial disadvantage *vis-à-vis* his opponent. In *Dombo Beheer v Netherlands*[105] a breach was found where one party was not allowed to call a factual witness relevant to the factual evidence called by the other side. It has been held in other cases that equality of arms requires that the parties be allowed to cross-examine witnesses and be allowed access to facilities on equal terms. This is unlikely in practice to afford any greater protection than that afforded by the overriding objective in CPR 1 (see *Daniels v Walker*, above).

A fair hearing also requires a reasoned judgment, albeit only a brief statement of reasons would probably suffice (*Hiro Balani v Spain;*[106] cf *Stefan v GMC;*[107] see also *Hyams v Plender*,[108] where the court said that the judge should properly have identified in what way a Practice Direction had not been complied with, rather than leaving it to the claimant to conjecture why his application for permission to appeal had been refused, and *English v Emery Reimbold*[109] where the Court of Appeal held that ECtHR jurisprudence required that a judge give reasons for his decision but they did not need to be spelt out *in extenso*).

There have been several decisions condemning the failure to allow a party to comment on a report prepared for the court. In *McMichael v UK*,[110] the ECtHR unanimously held that the refusal at a children's hearing under Scots law (where the mother was seeking to avoid her child going into care), and on appeal at the Sheriff's Court, to disclose to her 'vital' documents, including social reports, was a breach of her right to a fair trial. Compensation of £5,000 was awarded. Meanwhile, her child

---

105 (1994) 18 EHRR 213.
106 (1994) 19 EHRR 565.
107 [1999] 1 WLR 1293, PC.
108 [2000] 1 WLR 32, CA.
109 [2002] 1 WLR 2409.
110 (1995) 20 EHRR 205.

had been adopted without her consent. The court said that a litigant should have an opportunity to have knowledge of and to comment on observations filed and evinced by another party.

Where a sufficient procedure is provided but not used, there is no breach of Art 6. In *McGinley v UK*,[111] where ex-servicemen complained, in relation to the Christmas Island nuclear tests, that the Ministry of Defence had not disclosed available medical records, the court held that there had been no violation of Art 6. It was not established that the UK had in its possession documents relevant to the questions at issue in the pension appeals of the applicants and, in any case, it was open to them to apply for disclosure of the relevant documents under r 6 of the Pensions Appeals Tribunals (Scotland) Rules 1981. Since this procedure was provided and the applicants had failed to use it, they were not denied a fair hearing or effective access to the Pensions Appeal Tribunal.

In *S v Gloucestershire County Council*,[112] the court said that a summary hearing could be a fair hearing within the meaning of the Article. Nevertheless, our courts have already changed their approach to applications for a claim to be struck out as disclosing no cause of action (see *Barrett v Enfield London Borough Council*[113]). It appears that the approach the House of Lords adopted in *Barrett*, and in other cases, has been due to the influence of the 'fair trial' provisions in the Convention (see, for example, *Waters v Metropolitan Police Commissioner*[114]).

In *Fairclough Homes Ltd v Summers*[115] Lord Clarke said the following with reference to Article 6 at [48]:

> It is in the public interest that there should be a power to strike out a statement of case for abuse of process, both under the inherent jurisdiction of the court and under the CPR, but the court accepts the submission that in deciding whether or not to exercise the power the court must examine the circumstances of the case scrupulously in order to ensure that to strike out the claim is a proportionate means of achieving the aim of controlling the process of the court and deciding cases justly.

There is, therefore, an obligation on courts to consider the proportionality of sanctions under the CPR arising from Art 6. However, even the most draconian case management sanctions that debar a party from pursuing litigation will not necessarily breach the convention, because a breach of Art 6(1) can be justified where proportionate and necessary for a legitimate purpose. The court's power to impose sanctions on parties exists in order to enable fair trials to be achieved. Therefore, in cases where a party's right to proceed is debarred or made subject to onerous conditions, the court must consider whether the appropriate balance has been struck in the individual case. But assuming it has, the sanction will be convention compliant. To hold otherwise would undermine the ability of the civil justice system to manage cases at all.

It seems that although there has perhaps been some perceptible rise in the threshold for application of the most draconian case management powers (see *Waters* above; *Goode v Martin*,[116] where the Court of Appeal,

---

111 (1998) 42 BMLR 123.
112 [2001] 2 WLR 909, CA.
113 [2001] 2 AC 550.
114 [2000] ICR 1064, HL.
115 [2012] 1 WLR 2004, SC.
116 [2002] PIQR P333.

influenced by Art 6, took a more relaxed view of an application to amend a statement of case after the expiry of the relevant period of limitation; and *Cachia v Faluyi*[117] in relation to relaxing the procedural bar in s 2(3) of the Fatal Accidents Act 1976 to comply with Art 6) broadly speaking any matter arising out of case management will be decided in the domestic courts according to the provisions of the CPR.

Overall, the CPR holds firm as a Convention compliant procedural code and it will be an unusual case indeed where facts will support a complaint of breach of Art 6 where the domestic courts have acted in accordance with the CPR. The Court of Appeal in *Woodhouse v Consignia plc*[118] stated that provided judges make their decision within the general framework provided by CPR 1.1 (and in that case specifically CPR 3.9), they are unlikely to fall foul of Art 6 (for further examples see, in relation to relief from debarring sanctions under CPR 3.9, *Momson v Azeez*;[119] and, in relation to default judgment, *Akram v Akram*[120]).

Article 6 and expert evidence

Under the CPR, the court has power to appoint a single joint expert in circumstances where two or more parties wish to submit expert evidence on a particular issue (CPR 35.7), and the power extends to choosing that expert (from an agreed list) if the parties are unable to agree on an individual. The appointment of experts by the court is not objectionable *per se* under Art 6, but such experts must be free from actual and apparent bias (*Bradnsletter v Austria*;[121] *Bonisch v Austria*;[122] *Eggertsdottir v Iceland*[123]) and the parties must be able to take part in the process of preparation of expert evidence, insofar as is necessary to ensure the parties are on an equal footing and have had opportunity to provide evidence and comment where appropriate to the expert.

In *Mantovanelli v France*,[124] the parents of a 20-year-old woman who died in hospital after contracting jaundice applied for a declaration that the hospital was responsible for her death. They complained that she had been given excessive doses of halothane during anaesthesia. In the course of the proceedings, the parents applied for the appointment of an expert. The appointment was refused. The application was renewed and an expert was appointed by the court. The applicants complained there had been a breach of Art 6 as the expert prepared his report for the court without the parties having an opportunity to make representations to him. In particular, the expert had interviewed hospital doctors without the parties being present, and without the applicants having an opportunity to examine the accounts of those witnesses or some of the documents available to the expert. The ECtHR found that:

> ... while Mr and Mrs Mantovanelli could have made submissions to the Administrative Court on the content and findings of the report after receiving

---

117 [2001] 1 WLR 1966, CA.
118 [2002] 1 WLR 2558 at [43].
119 [2009] EWCA Civ 202.
120 [2004] EWCA Civ 1601.
121 (1993) 15 EHRR 378.
122 (1987) 9 EHRR 191.
123 (2009) 48 EHRR 32.
124 (1996) 24 EHRR 370.

it, the court is not convinced that this afforded them a real opportunity to comment effectively on it. The question that the expert was instructed to answer was identical with the one that the court had to determine ... it pertained to a technical field that was not within the Judge's knowledge. Thus, although the Administrative Court was not bound by the expert's findings, his report was likely to have a preponderant effect on the assessment of the facts by that court. Under such circumstances, and in the light also of the Administrative Court's refusal of their application for a fresh expert report, Mr and Mrs Mantovanelli could only have expressed their views effectively before the expert report was lodged ... they were prevented from participating in the interviews ... As to the documents taken into consideration by the expert, the applicants only became aware of them once the report had been completed and transmitted. Mr and Mrs Mantovanelli were thus not able to comment effectively on the main piece of evidence. The proceedings were therefore not fair as required by Article 6(1) of the Convention.

In *H v France*,[125] the European Court considered whether a court's refusal to allow a party to call an expert should constitute a breach of Art 6. On the facts of that case, it was found that no breach had occurred, as it was reasonable for the administrative court to reject the application for a medical expert's report when the applicant had failed to make out a prima facie case on the existence of a causal link between the treatment he received and the alleged damage. The court said:

> ... the Conseil d'Etat's decision not to order an expert's report might at first sight seem open to criticism in a case concerning medical treatment with a controversial drug ... However, having regard to all the circumstances ... the fact that it did not order an expert's report did not infringe the applicant's right to a fair trial.

Therefore it seems there is no right under Art 6(1) to call expert evidence where the court considers that such evidence would serve no useful purpose.

Although a claim would seem to be possible along the lines that, for example, there was a breach of the right to fair trial on the equality of arms principle because the patient was only allowed one expert, whereas the defendants had, in addition, the treating doctors to offer their views, the courts would be likely to give such an argument short shrift. A claim in respect of restrictions imposed on the specialties for expert reports allowed to a party seems equally unlikely to succeed where the CPR has been appropriately applied.

Does Article 6 create substantive rights?

The right to a fair trial includes the right of access to a court (*Golder v UK*;[126] *Osman v UK*). This is not, however, an absolute right. Within the margin of appreciation allowed to the state, restrictions on the right of access to a court may be implied where they can be justified as a proportionate response to a legitimate need (for example the limitation on access to court for persons of unsound mind was considered and found to be justifiable by the ECtHR in *Ashigdane v UK*[127]). In *Z v UK*[128] the ECtHR recognised

125 (1989) 12 EHRR 74.
126 (1975) 1 EHRR 524.
127 (1985) 7 EHRR 528 at [57].
128 [2002] 2 FCR 246.

that the right to a hearing was concerned with procedural obstacles to a hearing and not situations where the substantive law precluded any basis for a hearing, quietening speculation that Article 6 would catalyse development of new substantive rights to action in UK tort law (see also *Matthews v Ministry of Defence;*[129] *Thompson v Arnold*[130]).

Impartiality of the tribunal

It remains to be seen whether any challenge under the Act will be permitted in respect of alleged dependence or partiality of the court or tribunal. There are several decisions from the ECtHR in respect of the impartiality of tribunals and the need for a hearing in open court. But as our appeal courts are in any event scrupulous in their application of the bias principle (see, for example, the *Locabail* case;[131] *Roylance v General Medical Council;*[132] *Taylor v Lawrence*[133]), it is probable that reference to European decisions would not add anything to existing domestic jurisprudence.

Article 8: The right to respect for private and family life, home and correspondence

1. Everyone has the right to respect for his private and family life, his home and his correspondence.

2. There shall be no interference by a public authority with the exercise of this right except such as is in accordance with the law and is necessary in a democratic society in the interests of ... public safety, ... for the protection of health or morals, or for the protection of the rights and freedom of others.

The impact of Art 8 on domestic law has been more extensive than many of the Convention rights, and has led to the establishment of a free standing right to privacy under UK law where none existed before. Article 8 encompasses a wide ranging sphere of concerns important to the individual, not only the obvious protection of family life and privacy, but also the protection of identity, dignity, autonomy, self-determination, physical and moral integrity.[134] It is a right expressly qualified by the second limb, as set out above, as interference with Art 8 can be justified in appropriate circumstances. It has been recognised as involving an increasing number of positive, as well as negative obligations on the state.

The ambit of Article 8

In *Pretty v UK* the ECtHR recognised the 'notion of personal autonomy is an important principle underlying the interpretation of its guarantees'. The court held that an individual has a right to choose how and when to die that was protected by Art 8, but that the existence of laws prohibiting

---

129 [2003] 1 AC 1163.
130 [2007] EWHC 1875 (QB).
131 [2000] QB 451, CA.
132 (1999) 47 BMLR 63, PC.
133 (25 January 2001, unreported), CA.
134 *Connors v UK* (2005) 40 EHRR 9.

assisted suicide were a justified and proportionate interference with that right that was within the state's margin of appreciation.

Threats to physical and psychological integrity can engage Art 8. In *Bensaid v UK*,[135] the ECtHR held that 'treatment which does not reach the severity of Article 3 treatment may none the less breach Article 8 in its private life aspect where there are sufficiently adverse effects on physical and moral integrity'. In *Tysiac v Poland*,[136] the court found an unjustified breach of Art 8 in circumstances where the national law failed to provide an effective mechanism for determining whether the preconditions for a lawful abortion had been met and a visually impaired applicant had been refused a certificate for lawful abortion in circumstances where continuing the pregnancy put her own health at significant risk.

In *R v North and East Devon Health Authority, ex p Coughlan*,[137] the Court of Appeal set aside a decision by the health authority to close a home for disabled residents, on the ground that, having told the residents at an earlier date that it would be a permanent home for them, there was no sufficient 'over-reaching public interest' which would justify the health authority breaking that 'home for life promise'. The court was also satisfied that to move the elderly applicant from her home, which was likely to be 'emotionally devastating and seriously anti-therapeutic' would, in circumstances where the financial benefit to be gained by such a move would be small, be in breach of Art 8(1) and disproportionate and accordingly not justifiable under Art 8(2). For a more recent case where this balance has been considered, see *R (on the application of Elaine McDonald) v Kensington & Chelsea Royal London Borough Council*,[138] in which a local authority's decision to replace an overnight carer who assisted the applicant to a commode with incontinence pads and/or absorbent bedding was found not to breach Art 8. The ECtHR subsequently held in *McDonald v UK*[139] that the initial decision to withdraw the right to toileting assistance was a breach of Art 8, but that the breach was subsequently justified by a local authority assessment that the use of incontinence pads met the applicant's needs. The ECtHR observed that the state had a wide margin of appreciation in setting economic, social and healthcare policy; especially when deciding how to allocate scarce resources.

In the unhappy case of *Glass v United Kingdom*,[140] there was a significant dispute between parents and doctors about the treatment of a seriously ill child. The doctors wanted to give morphine as analgesia, but the parents refused consent as this would have been likely to hasten his death. The ECtHR held that a claim under Art 2 was manifestly ill-founded and should be declared inadmissible (claims under Arts 6, 13 and 14 met a similar fate) but the claim under Art 8 was not struck out and later succeeded: the failure to seek authorisation from a court in relation to providing treatment that the parents refused consent for, and in respect of which it was known by the hospital that there would be significant opposition from the parents, was a breach of Art 8. This

135 (2001) 33 EHRR 205.
136 (2007) 22 EHRR 155.
137 [2000] 2 WLR 622.
138 [2011] HRLR 36, SC.
139 (2015) 60 EHRR 1.
140 (2004) 39 EHRR 15.

case is often cited as support for the proposition that even if there is no legal requirement to do so, it is best practice for doctors to seek a court declaration in relation to proposed treatment where the legality of that treatment is in dispute, a position that has not changed following the recent decision of the Supreme Court in *NHS Trust v Y*.

In the recent and highly publicised case of *Gard v United Kingdom (Admissibility)*[141] concerning the withdrawal of ANH contrary to the express wishes of Charlie Gard's parents, the ECtHR ruled that the parents' complaints of breaches of Arts 2, 3 and 8 of the ECHR were 'manifestly ill-founded'. The ECtHR held that the essential purpose of Art 8 was to protect the individual against arbitrary action by the public authorities. The legal system in the United Kingdom was appropriate to deal with such complaints and the authorities had a significant margin of appreciation. In the circumstances of the case, the ECtHR held that the UK courts, at three different levels, had dealt with the issues in a way that was meticulous and thorough. All the relevant parties, including the parents, Charlie's court-appointed guardian, and the treating doctors had been given an opportunity to make representations, and significant regard was had to expert evidence. It could not therefore be said that the process that had been followed infringed Art 8 or any other provision of the ECHR. The same result on admissibility was reached in the case of Alfie Evans (*Evans v UK*, App No 14238/18).

Access to treatment

The Convention rights do not create a 'right' to any particular treatment on the NHS at any time, but have had some impact on the scrutiny of state decisions about funding choices for treatment. In *R v North West Lancashire Health Authority, ex p A, D and G*,[142] the Court of Appeal invalidated the policy of the health authority in relation to the treatment it was or was not prepared to provide to transgender individuals, to the effect that gender reassignment surgery would be refused unless there were exceptional circumstances over and above the clinical need. However, the court was not prepared to find that the refusal of treatment had been in breach of Art 8, because that imposed no positive obligations on the authority to provide treatment and there had been no interference with the applicants' private lives or their sexuality.

R (on the application of Watts) v Bedford Primary Care Trust[143] was a claim by a patient to obtain reimbursement for the cost of a replacement hip operation carried out in France. She had been unwilling to wait several months for the operation under the NHS. Insofar as her claim was based on her Convention rights, she relied on Arts 3 and 8. Munby J held that there was no positive obligation to provide treatment, as decided by the *North West Lancashire* case. Article 3 was not engaged unless the ill-treatment in question attained a minimum level of severity and involved actual bodily injury or intense physical or mental suffering, and in any event did not apply as it was not designed to apply to challenges in relation to policy decisions on the allocation of resources. This case was taken to

---

141 (2017) 65 EHRR SE9.
142 [2000] 1 WLR 977.
143 [2003] EWHC 2228 (Admin).

the European Court of Justice by the applicant,[144] where it was held that a patient could, pursuant to Council Regulation 1408/71, Art 22, go to another member state to receive medical treatment and be reimbursed the cost where there would, on an objective medical assessment of the medical circumstances, be an unacceptable delay before treatment could be provided in the UK by reason of waiting lists.

In *R (on the application of Condliff) v North Staffordshire Primary Care Trust*[145] the Court of Appeal held that a primary care trust's individual funding request policy, which provided that non-clinical, social factors could not be taken into account when determining exceptionality, did not breach Art 8. As a result, the trust was entitled to refuse funding for a morbidly obese individual to have a gastric by-pass. The claimant's obesity was having a seriously adverse effect on his private and family life in the most basic ways, which, without surgery, would continue and was likely to become worse. However, the court held that the application of the policy did not involve a lack of respect for C's private and family life. The policy of allocating scarce medical resources on a basis of the comparative assessment of clinical needs was intentionally non-discriminatory. Performing the function of allocating limited resources strictly according to the trust's assessment of medical need was to do no more than to apply the resources for the purpose for which they were provided without giving preferential treatment on non-medical grounds. The court noted that any attempts made to impose a positive obligation on the state to provide support for an individual under Art 8 had been unsuccessful (in *McDonald* in the Supreme Court and *Anufrijeva* in the Court of Appeal) and concluded that Art 8 could not be relied upon as giving rise to a positive duty to take into account welfare considerations wider than the comparative medical conditions and medical needs of different patients. The trust was entitled to set a policy which reflected what it reasonably considered to be the fairest way of treating patients.

In *R (on the application of Tracey) v Cambridge University Hospitals NHS Foundation Trust*[146] the Court of Appeal determined that even though there was no ECtHR authority on whether a decision to impose a 'do not resuscitate notice' engaged Art 8, that did not mean that Art 8 was not engaged in such circumstances. A decision as to how one managed death touched a patient's personal autonomy, dignity and quality of life in an immediate and obvious way. While the absence of a mandatory national do not resuscitate policy did not infringe Art 8, the Court of Appeal accepted that the hospital had breached the patient's Art 8 rights by failing to consult the patient before imposing a do not resuscitate order.

In *R (on the application of A (A Child) v Secretary of State for Health*[147] a majority of the Supreme Court held that whilst NHS England's refusal to provide free abortion services to patients from Northern Ireland, where abortion remains illegal, engaged Art 8, the difference in treatment was justified and did not breach the prohibition on discrimination in Art 14. The Supreme Court decision in *In the matter of an application by the Northern Ireland Human Rights Commission for Judicial Review*

---

144 *R (on the application of Watts) v Bedford Primary Care Trust* [2006] QB 667.
145 [2011] PTSR 460.
146 [2015] QB 543.
147 [2017] 1 WLR 2492.

(Northern Ireland)[148] determined that the criminalisation of abortion in Northern Ireland was incompatible with Art 8. However, the appeal brought by the Northern Ireland Human Rights Commission failed on the basis that the Commission did not have standing to bring judicial review proceedings.

It should also be noted that while the Supreme Court's judgment on the duty to advise and inform a patient of material risks before undertaking medical treatment in *Montgomery v Lanarkshire Health Board*[149] was based upon common law principles, Lord Reed and Lord Hodge specifically referenced the importance of the duties imposed by Art 8 in the following passage at [80]:

> In addition to these developments in society and in medical practice, there have also been developments in the law. Under the stimulus of the Human Rights Act 1998, the courts have become increasingly conscious of the extent to which the common law reflects fundamental values. As Lord Scarman pointed out in *Sidaway's* case, these include the value of self-determination (see, for example, *S (An Infant) v S* [1972] AC 24, 43 per Lord Reid; *McColl v Strathclyde Regional Council* 1983 SC 225, 241; *Airedale NHS Trust v Bland* [1993] AC 789, 864 per Lord Goff of Chieveley). As well as underlying aspects of the common law, that value also underlies the right to respect for private life protected by article 8 of the European Convention on Human Rights. The resulting duty to involve the patient in decisions relating to her treatment has been recognised in judgments of the European Court of Human Rights, such as *Glass v United Kingdom* (2004) EHRR 341 and *Tysiac v Poland* (2007) 45 EHRR 947, as well as in a number of decisions of courts in the United Kingdom.

Confidentiality of medical records

What follows should be read with the treatment on confidentiality under domestic law found in Chapter 21.

In *MS v Sweden*[150] the ECtHR acknowledged that the protection of personal data, particularly medical data, is of fundamental importance to a person's enjoyment of his or her right to respect for private and family life. Any state measures which compel disclosure of such information without the consent of the patient call for the 'most careful scrutiny'. Article 8 is a qualified right, and whether an interference can be justified will depend upon the reason for disclosure and the safeguards surrounding its use.

The collection of medical data and the maintenance of medical records fall within the sphere of 'private life' (*Chave née Jullien v France*[151]). Unauthorised collection and dissemination of medical information on an individual is likely to engage Art 8 and can only be justified if the circumstances of the collection and/or dissemination is a proportionate response that serves a legitimate social purpose.

Although parties are only required to disclose evidence which is relevant, a defendant may not be entitled to inspect all of a claimant's medical/personal records, as this may be unjustified and disproportionate. The court indicated that the right to privacy is not automatically waived

148 [2018] UKSC 27.
149 [2015] AC 1430.
150 (1999) 28 EHRR 313.
151 No 14461/88, 71 DR 141, 155 (1991).

by the mere fact of commencing proceedings, and observed that the disclosure required was limited to the extent that the evidence was material.[152] Although the Article might seem to permit a claimant to refuse to undergo a medical examination requested by the defendant, in such circumstances the Art 8 rights of the claimant have to be balanced against the fair trial rights of the defendant. In such cases, where the defendant is unable to understand the whole case it has to meet or to prepare its own case without such an examination, it has been held not to be a breach of the Convention to stay the proceedings pending consent to examination or, where possible, to delimit and strike out the particular claims unable to be fairly assessed without the examination (*James v Baily Gibson*[153]). The rationale underlying this is that if a person sues another for damages for personal injuries he must be prepared to submit to such examination of his records and person as is necessary to enable a fair trial of the issues to be achieved (see also *OCS Group Ltd v Wells*,[154] application for pre-action disclosure of medical records).

In *Woolgar v Chief Constable of Sussex Police*,[155] an injunction was unsuccessfully sought by the matron of a nursing home to restrain the Chief Constable of Sussex Police from disclosing, to the United Kingdom Central Council for Nursing, Midwifery and Health Visiting (UKCC), the contents of an interview between her and the police which had taken place at Worthing Police Station. The court said that when someone was arrested and interviewed by the police, the content of the interview was confidential, otherwise than in the course of a criminal trial. Article 8 of the ECHR indicated that, to protect private and family life, where information had been obtained in confidence, there should be no disclosure. However, there were exceptional circumstances, recognised by Art 8, where disclosure was justified as being necessary in a democratic society in the interests of national security, public safety or economic well-being of the country, for the prevention of crime and disorder, for the protection of health and morals, or for the protection of rights and freedoms of others. Where a regulatory body such as the UKCC, operating in the field of public health, sought access to confidential material in the possession of the police, being material which the police were reasonably persuaded was of some relevance to the subject matter of the inquiry being conducted by the regulatory body, the police were entitled to disclose the material on the basis that, save insofar as it may be used by the regulatory body for the purposes of its own inquiry, the confidentiality which already attached to the material would be maintained. Even if there was no request from the regulatory body, if the police came into possession of confidential material which in their reasonable view, in the interests of public health or safety, should be considered by a professional or regulatory body, then the police were free to pass that information to the relevant regulatory body for its consideration.

In *General Dental Council v Rimmer*[156] Sales J held that when investigating allegations by an insurance company of possible

---

152 See also *Z v Finland* (1997) 25 EHRR 371.
153 [2003] CP Rep 24, CA.
154 [2009] 1 WLR 1895 (HC).
155 [2000] 1 WLR 25, CA.
156 [2010] EWHC 1049 (Admin).

fraudulent claims concerning treatment of patients by their dentist, the General Dental Council was entitled to pass on patients' records to its investigating committee and, if necessary, practice committee. Given that there was a strong public interest in allowing disclosure of the records for the GDC's investigation, and there were safeguards in place to ensure that the records were used only for that purpose, the GDC did not need to seek a declaration from the court that it was entitled to disclose patients' records before it did so, even where the patients had refused to consent to the disclosure.

In *R v Secretary of State for Home Department, ex p Kingdom of Belgium*,[157] the Divisional Court ordered disclosure, limited to four named states who had unsuccessfully sought General Pinochet's extradition, of the medical reports which had led the Home Secretary to refuse extradition. The court, while confirming the basic right to confidentiality, said that in the circumstances the integrity of the international criminal justice system needed to be demonstrated, and that the governing interest was the public interest in operating a procedure which would be perceived and accepted by the great majority to be fair. This imperative outweighed any private interest. The disclosure fell within the exceptions of Art 8 of the Convention as being both 'in accordance with the law' and 'necessary in a democratic society ... for the prevention of disorder or crime'.

In *Ashworth Hospital Authority v MGN Ltd*[158] the Court of Appeal held that there was no breach of the Convention when they upheld an order requiring a journalist to disclose the source of his information gained from medical records held at Ashworth on one of the Moors murderers. The court said only in exceptional circumstances, where vital public or individual interests were at stake, could an order requiring journalists to disclose their sources be justified (as *per Goodwin v UK*[159]), but this was an exceptional case because the disclosure of confidential medical records to the press was misconduct which was not merely of concern to the individual establishment in which it occurred; it was an attack on an area of confidentiality which should be safeguarded in any democratic society and the protection of patient information was of vital concern to the NHS. This decision was upheld by the House of Lords,[160] which confirmed that only in exceptional circumstances could the disclosure of journalists' sources be justified, but that 'the care of patients at Ashworth is fraught with difficulty and danger. The disclosure of the patients' records increases that difficulty and danger and to deter the same or similar wrongdoing in the future it was essential that the source should be identified and punished. This was what made the orders to disclose necessary and proportionate and justified.'

A related issue that is of the utmost importance to clinical negligence practitioners, is that of the now burgeoning surveillance evidence trade. In *Jones v University of Warwick*,[161] the defendant obtained surveillance evidence by instructing an agent to use deception to gain access to the claimant's home and film covertly. The evidence obtained was highly

---

157 [2000] EWHC 293 (Admin).
158 [2001] 1 WLR 515.
159 (1996) 22 EHRR 123.
160 [2002] 1 WLR 2033.
161 [2003] 1 WLR 954, CA.

damaging to the claimant's case and was seen by both experts who said it was apparent she had significantly exaggerated her claim. The Court of Appeal said that there were competing public interests to consider, on one hand the public interest in discouraging invasion of privacy and on the other hand public interest in discouraging exaggerated or inflated claims. They concluded that the evidence was admissible. The claimant's Art 8 rights were clearly engaged but on balance the interference was justified in pursuit of a legitimate aim and therefore there was no breach of Art 8 (although the defendant was penalised in costs to mark the court's disapproval of this 'improper and unjustified' conduct). It should be noted that this is not an authority setting a principle that all evidence gained covertly will be admissible, but that in each case a balancing act must be carried out by the court. The existence of features aggravating the breach such as the nature of deception used, the severity of the invasion of privacy (for example if the claimant was naked or semi-dressed or engaged in very private functions), the presence of children in the film, and indeed the probative value of the evidence obtained, will all have to be weighed and in some cases the result must be that the interference cannot be justified and the evidence is not admissible.

The issue was considered by the ECtHR in *Vukota-Bojic v Switzerland*[162] where it was held that the surveillance of an insurance claimant was a breach of Art 8, but that the use of the evidence obtained at a hearing was not a breach of Art 6. The applicant was awarded compensation in respect of the infringement of Art 8 rights only. In reality it seems the substance of the decision will have a minimal practical impact domestically, but it reinforces the need for the courts to be sensitive to the competing interests of Art 6 and Art 8 rights in similar contexts.

Article 10: Freedom of expression

> Everyone has the right to freedom of expression. This right shall include freedom to hold opinions and to receive and impart information and ideas without interference by public authority and regardless of frontiers.

Article 10 encompasses both the right to express opinions, and to receive opinions and information. However, there is no general right to freedom of information established under this Article; a right to free information only arises in consequence of protecting another right (for example, see *Gaskin v UK*,[163] where a right to access social services files was considered in relation to an alleged interference with Art 8).

The right of freedom of information is enshrined in the General Data Protection Regulation and the Data Protection Act 2018.

Article 10 has been used to found arguments against holding inquiries in private on a number of occasions. In *R v Secretary of State for Health, ex p Wagstaff*,[164] the Divisional Court found a decision by the Secretary of State to hold the Shipman inquiry in private was irrational *inter alia* because there was a breach of Art 10 in that there was a reasonable expectation based on prior practice that when many lives were lost

---

162 [2017] IRLR 94.
163 (1989) 12 EHRR 36.
164 [2001] 1 WLR 292.

as a consequence of a major public disaster, a public inquiry would be held. Further, the court held that holding the inquiry in private constituted unjustified governmental interference with the reception of information that others wished or might be willing to impart. But in *R (on the application of Howard) v Secretary of State for Health*,[165] a case concerning a government decision to hold inquiries into the serious malpractice and criminal misconduct of a GP and consultant in private rather than in public, Scott Baker J distinguished *Wagstaff* on the basis that it was a special and unusual case which had not established any general principle of law, and held that the minister's decision in *Howard* did not breach the claimants' right to freedom of expression under Art 10. His reasoning was that the claimants in *Howard* were complaining about an interference with their right to receive information, rather than to impart information, and the Convention did not afford a right to receive information that others were not willing to impart (*Leander v Sweden*;[166] *R v Bow County Court, ex p Pelling*[167]). In those circumstances, therefore, holding an inquiry in private did not breach the claimant's rights under Art 10.

In *Kennedy v Information Commissioner*[168] the Supreme Court held by a 5:2 majority that the Freedom of Information Act 2000, s 32(2) provided an absolute exemption from disclosure under the Act by any public body of information placed in the custody of that body for the purposes of an inquiry, and Art 10 did not require s 32(2) to be interpreted differently.

Article 12: The right to marry and have a family

> Men and women of marriageable age have the right to marry and to found a family, according to the national laws governing the exercise of this right.

In *Briody v St Helens and Knowsley Area Health Authority*[169] where the claimant, who had been made infertile as a result of negligent hospital treatment, claimed damages for the cost of surrogacy, and Art 12 was prayed in aid, Hale LJ giving the judgment of the Court of Appeal said that while everyone has the right to try to have their own children by natural means, Art 12 does not confer the right to be provided with a child. Damages in respect of surrogacy were not awarded.

In *R v SSHD, ex p Gavin Mellor*[170] the Court of Appeal held that there was no breach of Art 12 where the Secretary of State had refused a prisoner permission to artificially inseminate his wife. The Court of Appeal held that the consequences of imprisonment on the exercise of human rights were justifiable provided that they were not disproportionate to the aim of maintaining a penal system designed both to punish and deter. The restriction on a prisoner's Art 12 right to found a family was a punitive restriction justifiable in the penal context, and in the absence of exceptional circumstances making the refusal disproportionately unfair, the prison authorities would not infringe Art 12 by declining to provide

---

165 [2003] QB 830, HC.
166 (1987) 9 EHRR 433.
167 [2001] 1 UKHRR 165.
168 [2014] AC 455.
169 [2002] QB 856, CA.
170 [2002] QB 13.

assistance with artificial insemination. However, the Grand Chamber of the ECtHR has since considered a number of complaints by prisoners relating to refusals of artificial insemination and reached a different conclusion: that the Home Office policy of allowing artificial insemination only in 'exceptional circumstances' did not afford sufficient weight to the prisoners' Art 12 and 8 rights (*Dickson v UK*[171]). As a direct result, Home Office policy has been amended: the Secretary of State continues to make decisions based on the individual merits of each case, but with a more inclusive consideration of the rights of prisoners.

CONCLUSION

Clinical negligence claimants are often as concerned with achieving a thorough investigation of incidents and deaths as with damages awards, and the development of the domestic law on Art 2 procedural obligations is particularly welcome in this context.

Domestic human rights law as currently constituted is unlikely to supplant the primacy of the common law in terms of providing an effective remedy for the victims of clinical negligence. Damages, *if awarded at all* under the HRA 1998, are rarely comparable to domestic common law compensatory awards. In many areas, the Convention protections overlap with existing areas of tortious liability and the clinical negligence claimant's most effective and comprehensive remedy is under the common law. Indeed, where the common law provides an adequate remedy, no further remedy is likely to be available pursuant to the convention principle of 'just satisfaction'. However, there are areas to which tort liability does not extend and it is in these areas that the Convention may have a significant role to play. It is important to note that Convention remedies are directly available under Art 2 to distressed and grieving relatives (without need to fulfil the 'secondary victim' requirements of *Alcock v Chief Constable of South Yorkshire*[172]), and to persons who have suffered consequences that would not sound in damages under the common law (*Wainwright v Home Office*;[173] *Wainwright v UK*[174]). The ability to bring a claim under the HRA 1998 is therefore likely to be useful where there may be issues over establishing a duty of care, or in the absence of a dependency, as well as in securing an adequate and thorough investigation in an appropriate case.

---

171 (2008) 46 EHRR 41.
172 [1992] 1 AC 310.
173 [2004] 2 AC 406.
174 [2006] ECHR 807.

Chapter 24

Court of Protection and issues involving capacity

Aswini Weereratne QC and Sophy Miles

MENTAL CAPACITY ACT 2005

The Mental Capacity Act 2005 (MCA 2005) governs decision-making on behalf of adults (16 and over) who have lost the capacity to make a particular decision at a particular time in their lives or where their incapacity has existed since birth. The MCA 2005 refers to the person concerned as 'P'. It implements most of the recommendations of the Law Commission in its report on *Mental incapacity*,[1] which was published in February 1995 after extensive consultation. The Government consulted further and published a policy statement, *Making decisions*,[2] in October 1999, in which it set out proposals to reform the law in order to improve and clarify the decision-making process for people unable to make decisions for themselves.

On 27 June 2003, the Government published a draft Mental Incapacity Bill and accompanying notes (Cm 5859-I & II) which was subject to pre-legislative scrutiny by a joint committee of both Houses. The joint committee published their report on 28 November 2003.[3] The Government's response to the joint committee report was presented to Parliament in February 2004.[4]

The renamed Mental Capacity Bill was introduced in Parliament on 17 June 2004 and the Act received Royal Assent on 7 April 2005. Sections 35 to 41 (on independent mental capacity advocates, or IMCAs), 42 and 43 (on the code of practice), and 44 (on ill-treatment and neglect) came into force on 1 April 2007, and the remainder of the Act came into force on 1 October 2007.

On 1 April 2009 the Mental Health Act 2007 came into force. As well as amending the provisions of the Mental Health Act 1983, this also brought into force Sch A1 to the MCA2005, together with amendments to ss 4, 16,

---

1   *Mental Incapacity* (Law Com no 231).
2   *Who decides? Making Decisions on behalf of Mentally Incapacitated Adults* (Cm 3803).
3   HL Paper 189-I and HC 1083-I.
4   *Government Response to the Scrutiny Committee's Report on the draft Mental Incapacity Bill* (HLP 189 Session 2002–03), (Cm 6121).

21 and 39 of the Act. Schedule A1 provides a statutory code known as the 'Deprivation of Liberty Safeguards' or 'DoLS' which permits hospitals and registered care homes to deprive adults lacking capacity to consent to their living arrangements of their liberty in their best interests, when 'qualifying requirements' are fulfilled. On 16 May 2019 the Mental Capacity Amendment Act 2019 (MCAA 2019) received Royal Assent, completing a process which started in 2014, when the Law Commission was asked to make recommendations about a replacement for the 'DoLS'. The MCAA 2019 inserts Sch AA1 into the MCA 2005, and introduces 'Liberty Protection Safeguards'. The MCAA 2019 is expected to come into force in October 2020.

The MCA 2005 is supported by two Codes of Practice: the 'Mental Capacity Act Code of Practice' and the 'Mental Capacity Act 2005: Deprivation of Liberty Safeguards Code of Practice'. A replacement Code is being prepared at the time of writing.

The MCA 2005 codifies the common law test for capacity and the doctrine of necessity. These had been developed following the landmark decision in *Re F (Mental Patient: Sterilisation)*,[5] where the House of Lords held that the defence of the doctrine of necessity meant that it was lawful for professionals and carers to do what was in the best interests of a person who lacked capacity to decide for him or her self whether it should be done; and that the High Court could use its inherent jurisdiction to make declarations that a particular course of action (such as, for example, an operation) would, or would not be lawful.

There are apparent tensions between the MCA 2005 and the UN Convention on the Rights of Persons with Disabilities (UNCRPD),[6] which was adopted by the UN in 2006 and ratified by the UK in 2009, and has been described as a 'new paradigm' of human rights. This reflects a social model of disability, which focuses on the enjoyment and promotion of a disabled person's life on an equal footing with an able-bodied or person with full capacity, by the removal of barriers between the individual and society. It contains a number of substantive rights, such as the right to life, freedom from torture, equal treatment before the law, liberty and security of the person, and independent living.

Whilst the UNCRPD is not incorporated into domestic law, it is binding on the UK as a matter of international law. Importantly for the purpose of the MCA 2005, Art 12 (the right to equal recognition before the law) requires states parties to provide support to persons with disabilities to exercise their legal capacity, and that measures relating to legal capacity respect the 'rights, will and preferences of the person'. Article 14 (the right to liberty) and security of the person) provides that a person's disability 'shall in no case justify a deprivation of liberty'. The UNCRPD Committee has raised concerns as to whether the provisions of both the MCA 2005 and the Mental Health Act 1983 comply with the UNCRPD, and has called on the UK to abolish all forms of substituted decision-making (such as the MCA 2005) and adopt new legislation.[7]

---

5   [1990] 2 AC 1, [1989] 2 WLR 1025.
6   Discussed *Joint Committee on Human Rights Report* 'The Right to Freedom and Safety: Reform of the Deprivation of Liberty Safeguards' (HC 890, HL Paper 161).
7   United Nations Committee on the Rights of Persons with Disabilities, 'Concluding observations on the initial report of the United Kingdom of Great Britain and Northern Ireland' (29 August 2017, UN Doc CRPD/C/GBR/CO/1, 2017.

The principles of the MCA 2005

Section 1 of the MCA 2005 sets out key principles applying to all decisions and actions taken under the Act. The starting point is a presumption of capacity. A person must be presumed to have capacity unless it is established that they lack capacity (s 1(2)). A person must also be supported to make their own decision, as far it is practicable to do so. The Act provides that a person is not to be treated as unable to make a decision unless 'all practicable steps' to help them do so have been taken without success (s 1(3)). This could include, for example, making sure that the person is in an environment in which they feel comfortable, or involving an expert in helping them express their views. It is expressly provided that a person is not to be treated as lacking capacity to make a decision merely because they make an unwise decision (s 1(4)). This means that a person with capacity has the ability to make unwise decisions which others may not consider to be in their best interests. Any act done or decision made under the Act for a person who lacks capacity must be done or made in that person's best interests (s 1(5)). The concept of 'best interests' is described in greater detail in s 4 of the Act. Finally, any substitute decision-maker must have regard to whether the intended objective can be achieved in a way that is less restrictive of the person's rights and freedom of action (s 1(6)).

Lack of capacity

Section 2(1) of the MCA 2005 defines a lack of capacity as follows:

> For the purposes of this Act, a person lacks capacity in relation to a matter if at the material time he is unable to make a decision for himself in relation to the matter because of an impairment of, or a disturbance in the functioning of, the mind or brain.

As can be seen from this definition, there has to be both a diagnostic threshold, and a resultant inability to make a decision. In *PC v City of York Council*,[8] the Court of Appeal stressed the importance of establishing the 'causative nexus' between the impairment and the inability to make the decision. The decision itself is both 'matter specific' and 'time specific'.

Section 3(1) provides that for the purposes of s 2:

> a person is unable to make a decision for himself if he is unable –
> (a)   to understand the information relevant to the decision,
> (b)   to retain that information,
> (c)   to use or weigh that information as part of the process of making the decision, or
> (d)   to communicate his decision (whether by talking, using sign language or any other means).

This definition largely replicates the tests developed at common law before the Act came into force.

Section 3(2) states that a person is not to be regarded as unable to understand the information relevant to a decision if that person is able to understand an explanation of it given to them in a way that is appropriate to their circumstances (using simple language, or visual aid,

---

8   [2013] EWCA Civ 478, [2014] Fam 10, at [58].

for example). The person does not need to understand all the peripheral details as long as he or she is able to able to understand the 'salient details'.[9] The information relevant to a decision includes information about the reasonably foreseeable consequences of deciding one way or another, or of failing to make the decision altogether. Section 3(3) states that the fact that a person is able to retain information relevant to a decision for a short period only does not prevent that person from being regarded as able to make the decision.

Best interests

If a person ('P') is incapable of making a decision by reference to the test above, whoever makes the decision on P's behalf must do so in their best interests (s 1(5)). The MCA 2005 does not actually define 'best interests', but s 4 sets out a non-exhaustive checklist of things that must be done (in other words, it is mandatory, and not discretionary) when determining what is in P's best interests. The checklist is as follows:

- the determination must not be made merely on the basis of P's age or appearance, or a condition, or aspect of P's behaviour, which might lead others to make unjustified assumptions about what might be in P's best interests (s 4(1));
- all the relevant circumstances must be considered (s 4(2)). 'Relevant circumstances' are those of which the substitute decision-maker is aware, and which it would be reasonable to regard as relevant (s 4(11)). In particular, the following steps must be taken;
- the decision-maker must consider whether it is likely that P will at some time have capacity in relation to the matter in question, and, if it appears likely that P will, when that is likely to be (s 4(3)). This is in case the decision can be put off until P is able to make it. Even if the decision cannot be put off, the decision is likely to be influenced by whether P will always lack capacity or is likely to regain capacity (Explanatory Notes to the MCA 2005, para 29);
- the decision-maker must, so far as reasonably practicable, permit and encourage P to participate, or to improve their ability to participate, as fully as possible in any act done for them and any decision affecting them (s 4(4));
- the decision-maker must not be motivated by a desire to bring about P's death, where the determination relates to life-sustaining treatment, and the substitute decision-maker is considering whether the treatment is in P's best interests (s 4(5));
- the decision-maker must consider, so far as is reasonably practical, P's past and present wishes and feelings, and, in particular, any relevant written statement made by P when they had capacity (s 4(6)(a));
- the decision-maker must consider, so far as is reasonably practical, P's beliefs and values that would be likely to influence P's decision if they had capacity (s 4(6)(b)). These would include, for example, P's cultural background, religious beliefs, political convictions, and past behaviour and habits (Code of Practice, para 5.46);

---

9 *L v J* [2010] EWHC 2665 (Fam), [2011] 1 FLR 1279.

- the decision-maker must consider, so far as is reasonably practical, the other factors that P would be likely to consider if they were able to do so (s 4(6)(c)). This might include the effect of the decision on other people, obligations to dependants, or the duties of a responsible citizen (Code of Practice, para 5.47);
- the decision-maker must take into account, if it is practicable and appropriate to consult them, the views of anyone named by P as someone to be consulted on the matter in question or on matters of that kind, or anyone engaged in caring for P or who is interested in P's welfare, as to what would be in P's best interests, and as to what P's wishes and feelings, and beliefs and values would be (s 4(7)(a) and (b));
- the decision-maker must take into account, if it is practicable and appropriate to consult them, the views of any other donee of a lasting power of attorney granted by the donor, as to what would be in P's best interests, and what P's wishes and feelings, and beliefs and values would be (s 4(7)(c)).

Section 4 does not provide for a hierarchy of factors. The weight to be attached to each factor will vary with the individual circumstances of the case, in which there may be a factor or factors of 'magnetic importance.'[10]

The courts have given anxious consideration to the role of the incapacitated person's wishes and feelings. In *Aintree University Hospitals NHS Foundation Trust v James*[11] (a case concerning the continued provision of life-sustaining treatment) Lady Hale commented (at [24]) that:

> This is, as the Explanatory Notes to the Bill made clear, still a 'best interests' rather than a 'substituted judgment' test, but one which accepts that the preferences of the person concerned are an important component in deciding where his best interests lie. To take a simple example, it cannot be in the best interests to give the patient food which he does not like when other equally nutritious food is available.

She continued at [45]:

> The purpose of the best interests test is to consider matters from the patient's point of view. That is not to say that his wishes must prevail, any more than those of a fully capable patient must prevail. We cannot always have what we want. Nor will it always be possible to ascertain what an incapable patient's wishes are. Even if it is possible to determine what his views were in the past, they might well have changed in the light of the stresses and strains of his current predicament ... But insofar as it is possible to ascertain the patient's wishes and feelings, his beliefs and values or the things which were important to him, it is those which should be taken into account because they are a component in making the choice which is right for him as an individual human being.

In *Re M, ITW v Z*,[12] an early case on the weight to be given to the incapacitated person's wishes and feelings, Munby J set out the following helpful formulation:

---

10   Munby J (as he then was) in *Re M, ITW v Z* [2009] EWHC 2525 (Fam), [2009] COPLR Con Vol 828.
11   [2013] UKSC 67, [2013] AC 591.
12   [2009] EWHC 2525 (Fam), [2009] COPLR Con Vol 828.

i) First, P's wishes and feelings will always be a significant factor to which the court must pay close regard: see *Re MM; Local Authority X v MM (by the Official Solicitor) and KM* [2007] EWHC 2003 (Fam), [2009] 1 FLR 443, at paras [121]–[124].

ii) Secondly, the weight to be attached to P's wishes and feelings will always be case-specific and fact-specific. In some cases, in some situations, they may carry much, even, on occasions, preponderant, weight. In other cases, in other situations, and even where the circumstances may have some superficial similarity, they may carry very little weight. One cannot, as it were, attribute any particular *a priori* weight or importance to P's wishes and feelings; it all depends, it must depend, upon the individual circumstances of the particular case. And even if one is dealing with a particular individual, the weight to be attached to their wishes and feelings must depend upon the particular context; in relation to one topic P's wishes and feelings may carry great weight whilst at the same time carrying much less weight in relation to another topic. Just as the test of incapacity under the 2005 Act is, as under the common law, 'issue specific', so in a similar way the weight to be attached to P's wishes and feelings will likewise be issue specific.

iii) Thirdly, in considering the weight and importance to be attached to P's wishes and feelings the court must of course, and as required by section 4(2) of the 2005 Act, have regard to *all* the relevant circumstances. In this context the relevant circumstances will include, though I emphasise that they are by no means limited to, such matters as:

a) the degree of P's incapacity, for the nearer to the borderline the more weight must in principle be attached to P's wishes and feelings: *Re MM; Local Authority X v MM (by the Official Solicitor) and KM* [2007] EWHC 2003 (Fam), [2009] 1 FLR 443 , at para [124];

b) the strength and consistency of the views being expressed by P;

c) the possible impact on P of knowledge that her wishes and feelings are not being given effect to: see again *Re MM; Local Authority X v MM (by the Official Solicitor) and KM* [2007] EWHC 2003 (Fam), [2009] 1 FLR 443, at para [124];

d) the extent to which P's wishes and feelings are, or are not, rational, sensible, responsible and pragmatically capable of sensible implementation in the particular circumstances; and

e) crucially, the extent to which P's wishes and feelings, if given effect to, can properly be accommodated within the court's overall assessment of what is in her best interests.

Particular importance has been given to P's wishes and feelings in cases concerning older people lacking capacity but whose consistent wishes to live at home rather than in a residential care setting has countered the potential risks involved (*Re GC*;[13] *Re M*;[14] *Westminster City Council v Sykes*[15]). Past wishes have been held to be particularly significant where the court has considered the continuation of life-sustaining treatment for those in persistent vegetative or minimally conscious state: for example, *Briggs v Briggs*;[16] *Salford Royal NHS Foundation Trust v Mrs P and Q*.[17]

With a view to aligning the MCA 2005 closer to the principles of the United Nations Convention on the Rights of Persons with Disabilities,

13 *Re GC* [2008] EWHC 3402 (Fam).
14 *Re M (Best Interests: Deprivation of Liberty* [2014] COPLR 35, [2013] EWHC 3456 (COP).
15 [2014] 2 WLUK 729, (2014) 17 CCL Rep 139, COP.
16 [2016] EWCOP 53, [2017] 4 WLR 37.
17 [2017] EWCOP 23, [2018] COP LR 120.

the Law Commission proposed an amendment to s 4 which would require a decision-maker to give 'particular weight' to the wishes and feelings of the person without capacity. However this does not appear in the MCAA 2019.

Life-sustaining treatment

The principles emerging from case law on the best interests in relation to life-sustaining treatment have been helpfully summarised by Hayden J in *Salford Royal NHS Foundation Trust v Mrs P and Q* (at [29]):

i)   The sanctity of life is not an absolute principle, and can be outweighed by the need to respect the personal autonomy and dignity of the patient: *Aintree v James* [2013] UKSC 6 at [35];

ii)   There is no prohibition to conducting a best interests analysis of the continued provision of CANH even though Mrs P is not in a vegetative state: *W v M* [2011] EWHC 2443 (Fam) at [102] per Baker J;

iii) There can be no further guidance beyond the wording of s 4 other than that 'decision makers must look at his welfare in the widest sense, not just medical but social and psychological; they must consider what the outcome of that treatment for the patient is likely to be; they must try and put themselves in the place of the individual patient and ask what his attitude to the treatment is or would be likely to be; and they must consult others who are looking after him or are interested in his welfare, in particular for their view of what his attitude would be.' *Aintree* at [39] per Baroness Hale.

iv)   Where the patient's condition may improve, a best interests decision may be based on the 'best case scenario' as advised by the relevant clinicians and experts: *Briggs*[18] overview at (25) per Charles J;

v)   It is incumbent on the court fully to investigate and consider the values and beliefs of the patient as well as any views the patient expressed when she had capacity that cast light on the likely choice the patient would have made and the factors that the patient would have considered relevant or important: *M v N* at [70] per Hayden J, *Briggs* at [54] per Charles J;

vi)   Where the patient's views can be ascertained with sufficient certainty, they should generally be followed (*Briggs* at [62] per Charles J) or afforded great respect (*M v N* at [28] per Hayden J), though they are not automatically determinative. '... if the decision that P would have made, and so their wishes on such an intensely personal issue can be ascertained with sufficient certainty it should generally prevail over the very strong presumption in favour of preserving life. *Briggs* at [62ii] per Charles J. '...the "sanctity of life" or the "intrinsic value of life", can be rebutted (pursuant to statute) on the basis of a competent adult's cogently expressed wish. It follows, to my mind, by parity of analysis, that the importance of the wishes and feelings of an incapacitated adult, communicated to the court via family or friends but with similar cogency and authenticity, are to be afforded no less significance than those of the capacitous.' *M v N* at [32] per Hayden J;

For a more detailed discussion see also Chapter 11, under the heading 'Life-sustaining treatment – withdrawing and withholding'.

---

18   *Briggs v Briggs* [2016] EWCOP 53, [2017] 4 WLR 37.

The MCA 2005, s 4A permits a person (D) to deprive P of P's liberty if either:

1   D is giving effect to a decision of the court; or
2   the deprivation of liberty is authorised by the MCA 2005, Sch A1.

Section 4B permits deprivation of P's liberty to administer life-sustaining treatment or carry out a 'vital act' whilst a relevant decision is sought from the court.

See the section below, 'Protecting P's Article 5 rights'.

The general defence in ss 5 and 6

Section 5 of the MCA 2005 contains what was originally described by the Law Commission, when it prepared the first draft of the legislation, as a 'general authority to act reasonably'. It is also referred to as 'the general defence'. Its purpose is to offer a statutory defence against liability for acts done in connection with the care or treatment of P, provided that the person doing the act or making the decision:

*   has taken reasonable steps to determine whether P lacks capacity in relation to the matter in question;
*   reasonably believes that P lacks capacity;
*   reasonably believes that it will be in P's best interests for the act to be done.

In such circumstances, provided the person doing the act is not acting negligently, the action is to be treated as if P lacked capacity in relation to the matter and had consented to the act being done.

Section 6 provides that the s 5 defence can apply to an act 'that is intended to restrain P' as long as D reasonably believes that it is necessary to do the act in order to prevent harm to P and that the act is a proportionate response to the likelihood of P suffering harm and the seriousness of that harm. Section 6 defines restraint as the use or threat of force to secure the doing of an act which P resists, or restricting P's liberty of movement, whether or not P resists. Section 6 does not permit the deprivation of P's liberty: see the section below, 'Protecting P's Article 5 rights'.

The extent of the general defence, however, is unclear. The Code of Practice gives guidance at paras 8.8, and 8.18–8.24 as to the serious healthcare and treatment decisions which should be brought to court. These include:

1   cases involving organ or bone marrow donation by a person who lacks capacity to consent;
2   cases involving non-therapeutic sterilisation of a person who lacks capacity to consent to this;
3   cases where there is a dispute or doubt about whether a particular treatment is in the person's best interests; or those involving ethical dilemmas.

At para 6.18, the Code states that the Court of Protection must be asked to make decisions about the proposed withholding or withdrawal of artificial nutrition and hydration from a patient in a persistent vegetative state. On 30 July 2018 the Supreme Court ended years of uncertainty about whether an application to the court is in fact required before withdrawing clinically assisted nutrition and hydration from a patient in a prolonged disorder of consciousness, and where there is no dispute between clinicians and the patient's family. In *An NHS Trust v Y (by his litigation friend the Official Solicitor)*,[19] Lady Black concluded that:

- there is no common law requirement for the court's approval to be sought in all such cases;
- the combined effect of the MCA 2005, the Code of Practice and the professional guidance (particularly that of the General Medical Council) is to create a regulatory framework and, taken together with the requirement of decision-makers to take account of the views of the patient and those close to him/her and the opportunity to seek the court's guidance where there is doubt or dispute, that framework complies with the requirements of Art 2 of the ECHR (set out in *Lambert v France*).[20]

Lady Black found the availability of the court is a key feature, even though it does not need to be invoked in all cases:

> 125. If, at the end of the medical process, it is apparent that the way forward is finely balanced, or there is a difference of medical opinion, or a lack of agreement to a proposed course of action from those with an interest in the patient's welfare, a court application can and should be made. As the decisions of the ECtHR underline, this possibility of approaching a court in the event of doubts as to the best interests of the patient is an essential part of the protection of human rights. The assessments, evaluations and opinions assembled as part of the medical process will then form the core of the material available to the judge, together with such further expert and other evidence as may need to be placed before the court at that stage.

The impact of this judgment is considered in more depth in Chapter 11.

Who should make the application?

The Code states at para 8.8 that 'for cases about serious or major decisions concerning medical treatment ... the NHS Trust or other organisation responsible for the patient's care will usually make the application'. In relation to decisions about the incapacitated adult's welfare, as opposed to healthcare decisions, the Code states at para 8.8 that 'If social care staff are concerned about a decision that affects the welfare of a person who lacks capacity, the relevant local authority should make the application'.

In *London Borough of Hillingdon v Neary*,[21] Peter Jackson J (as he then was) stated that:

> The ordinary powers of a local authority are limited to investigating, providing support services, and where appropriate referring the matter to the court. If a local authority seeks to regulate, control, compel, restrain, confine or coerce it must, except in an emergency, point to specific statutory authority for what it is doing or else obtain the appropriate sanction of the court ...

> Significant welfare issues that cannot be resolved by discussion should be placed before the Court of Protection, where decisions can be taken as a matter of urgency where necessary.

---

19   [2018] UKSC 46.
20   [2016] 62 EHRR 2, App No 46043/14.
21   [2011] EWHC 1377 (COP), [2011] 4 All ER 584.

He further commented at §142 that:

> Where a dilemma exists, the court provides an accessible forum. Often, parties will have a clear view of what they are proposing, but if a party needs more evidence or is uncertain about the best outcome in a difficult case, it is no shame to say so. Proceedings in the Court of Protection need not be adversarial.

The Law Commission recommended an amendment to the statutory defence provided by the MCA 2005. The statutory defence would not be available to someone acting in a professional capacity or for remuneration who carries out an act pursuant to a relevant decision, unless he or she has prepared a written record concerning specified information (or a written record has been prepared by someone else). The purpose of the amendment was to provide greater protection to those lacking capacity in the case of decisions which represent significant interferences with P's rights under Art 8 of the ECHR. 'Relevant decisions' include:

- a decision by a public authority to meet P's needs by a move to long term accommodation;
- a decision to restrict or prevent P's contact with named individuals or a specified class of individuals;
- the provision of serious medical treatment;
- the administration of 'covert' medication;
- the administration of treatment against a person's wishes.

Although the recommendation was accepted by the government, and may have provided greater clarity, the MCAA 2019 does not contain the amendment.

In the absence of legislation professionals seeking to give effect to a decision listed above would be well advised to consider an application to the court; and should make such an application in a disputed case of this nature or one which is finely balanced.

See further in Chapter 11.

Lasting powers of attorney

Sections 9 to 13 and Sch 1 to the MCA 2005 make it possible for individuals to create a lasting power of attorney (LPA). There was previously an Enduring Powers of Attorney Act 1985, which allowed for the creation of an enduring power of attorney (EPA), which endured, or remained in force, after the donor of the power had lost the capacity to manage his property and financial affairs. The LPA was intended to be an improved version of the EPA, and enables a donor to appoint an attorney to make any health and welfare decisions that the donor is incapable of making at the material time, as well as decisions relating to their property and financial affairs.

There are two prescribed forms of LPA: one for property and financial affairs; and the other for health and welfare. An attorney cannot act on the authority conferred on them in the LPA until the LPA has been registered by the Public Guardian. A formal application for registration should be made, in respect of which a fee of £82 is payable.

LPAs are mainly, though not exclusively, executed by older people, who are planning for the possibility that they may become mentally incapacitated as a result of some age-related mental disorder. It is questionable whether they are appropriate vehicles for the management of a substantial damages award for personal injury or clinical negligence, essentially because there is no formal oversight or monitoring of the attorney's actions by an independent third party.

Advance decisions to refuse treatment

Sections 24, 25 and 26 of the MCA 2005 placed advance decisions to refuse (medical) treatment on a statutory footing for the first time. They codify and clarify the existing common law rules, and integrate them into the broader scheme of the Act. An 'advance decision' is a decision, made by a person who had capacity to make it at the relevant time, that specified treatment is not to be carried out or continued if, at some time in the future, that person lacks the capacity to consent to that treatment.

An advance decision must specify the treatment that is being refused, though this can be expressed in layman's terms. It may also specify the particular circumstances in which the refusal will apply, again in layman's terms. A person can change or completely withdraw the advance decision if they have capacity to do so, and the withdrawal, including a partial withdrawal, of an advance decision does not need to be in writing and can be by any means.

Section 25 of the Act introduces the two important safeguards in relation to advance decisions to refuse treatment: (i) validity; and (ii) applicability. Section 25(2) provides that an advance decision is not valid if the person who made it has:

*   withdrawn it;
*   subsequently created an LPA, which gives the attorney the authority to consent or refuse consent to the treatment to which the advance decision relates (other LPAs will not override the advance decision); or
*   done anything else that is clearly inconsistent with the advance decision remaining his fixed decision.

An example of inconsistent conduct arose in a case in 2003, *HE* v *A Hospital NHS Trust*[22] where a former Jehovah's Witness became engaged to a Turkish man, and agreed to convert to Islam. Even though she had forgotten to destroy the Jehovah's Witnesses' standard advance decision refusing blood transfusion, her actions could be taken into account in determining whether that earlier refusal remained her fixed decision.

Section 25(3) and (4) provide that advance decision will not be applicable if:

*   the person actually has capacity to make the decision when the treatment concerned is proposed;
*   the proposed treatment is not the treatment specified in the advance decision;
*   any circumstances specified in the advance decision are absent; or
*   there are reasonable grounds for believing that the current circumstances were not anticipated by the person who made the

---

22   [2003] EWHC 1017 (Fam), [2003] 2 FLR 408.

advance decision, and if they had been anticipated, it would have affected the decision made.

An advance decision will not apply to life-sustaining treatment unless it is in writing, and contains a statement that the decision is to apply to that treatment 'even if life is at risk', and is signed and witnessed (s 25(5) and (6)).

If an advance decision to refuse treatment is both valid and applicable it has the same effect as a contemporaneous refusal of treatment by a person with full capacity (s 26(1)). That means the treatment cannot lawfully be given. If the treatment is given, the person refusing would be able to claim damages for the tort of battery and the treatment-provider might face criminal liability for assault. A treatment-provider may safely treat unless satisfied that there is a valid and applicable qualifying advance refusal; and a treatment-provider may safely withhold or withdraw treatment as long as he has reasonable grounds for believing that there is a valid and applicable qualifying advance decision.

If there is doubt or a dispute about whether an advance decision exists, is valid or is applicable to a treatment, the Court of Protection can determine the issue and make a declaration (s 26(4)). Action may be taken to prevent the death of the person concerned, or a serious deterioration in his condition, whilst any such doubt or dispute is referred to the court. In *A Local Authority v E (by her litigation friend the Official Solicitor) v A Health Authority, E's Parents*[23] Peter Jackson J (as he then was) observed that:

> ... for an advance decision relating to life-sustaining treatment to be valid and applicable, there should be clear evidence establishing on the balance of probability that the maker had capacity at the relevant time. Where the evidence of capacity is doubtful or equivocal it is not appropriate to uphold the decision.

Excluded decisions

Certain decisions are excluded from the MCA 2005 by s 27. This provides that no person can make a decision on another's behalf in matters involving intimate or family relationships (including consent to sexual relationships, marriage, divorce or dissolution of a civil partnership on the basis of two years' separation and consenting to a child being placed for adoption).

Section 28 prohibits the use of the MCA 2005 to give medical treatment for a mental disorder, or consent to such treatment on a person's behalf, where that person's treatment is regulated by the Mental Health Act 1983, Pt 4.

Protecting Article 5, Right to liberty

Article 5(1)(e) of the ECHR permits the deprivation of liberty of persons 'of unsound mind' when this is lawful and 'in accordance with a procedure prescribed by law'. P's rights under Art 5 will be engaged when the following elements are present:

---

23   [2012] EWHC 1639 (COP).

1   the objective element: P is confined in a particular restricted space
     for a 'not negligible length of time';
2   the subjective element: there is no valid consent;
3   the deprivation of liberty is imputable to the state.

In *P (by his litigation friend the Official Solicitor) v Cheshire West
and Chester Council; P and Q v Surrey County Council*,[24] Lady Hale
promulgated what has become known as the 'acid test' for assessing
whether P is objectively deprived of his or her liberty by his or her living
arrangements and thereby entitled to safeguards under Art 5(4):

> [49] The answer, as it seems to me, lies in those features which have consistently
> been regarded as 'key' in the jurisprudence which started with *HL v United
> Kingdom* 40 EHRR 761: that the person concerned 'was under continuous
> supervision and control and was not free to leave' (para 91). I would not go so
> far as Mr Gordon, who argues that the supervision and control is relevant only
> insofar as it demonstrates that the person is not free to leave. A person might
> be under constant supervision and control but still be free to leave should he
> express the desire so to do. Conversely, it is possible to imagine situations in
> which a person is not free to leave but is not under such continuous supervision
> and control as to lead to the conclusion that he was deprived of his liberty.

In *Ferreira v HM Senior Coroner for Inner South London*,[25] the Court
of Appeal distinguished *Cheshire West* (which dealt with living
arrangements) from the circumstances of those receiving life-saving
treatment in hospital. Article 5 will not normally be engaged in such
cases. See Chapter 11 for a more detailed discussion of this issue.

The MCA 2005 provides a 'procedure prescribed by law' for the purpose
of the ECHR, Art 5(1)(e) through three mechanisms:

1   the 'Deprivation of Liberty Safeguards' ('DoLS') – the statutory
     scheme set out in the Mental Capacity Act 2005, Sch A1, and which
     applies to those of 18 years or older who are in hospitals (other than
     when the Mental Health Act 1983 should be used) and registered
     care homes (to be placed by the Liberty Protection Safeguards in
     2020);
2   a welfare order under the MCA 2005, s 16 authorising the deprivation
     of P's liberty in cases where DoLS could not be used (for 16–17 year
     olds, or for adults living in other settings such as supported living);
3   the 'emergency provision' in the MCA 2005, s 4B to deprive P of the
     liberty to administer life-sustaining treatment or carry out a vital
     act while a relevant decision is sought from the court.

P's rights under the ECHR, Art 5(4) (the right to bring proceedings
in a court to challenge the lawfulness of a deprivation of liberty) are
protected via:

1   the MCA 2005, s 21A, which allows the court to hear challenges
     to an authorisation under the MCA 2005, Sch A1 (DoLS) (broadly
     replicated in the MCAA 2019);
2   a bespoke 'streamlined' procedure by which P's deprivation of liberty
     can be authorised by the court under the MCA 2005, s 16, and which
     ensures that P is consulted and can be represented if there is any

---

24   [2014] UKSC 19, [2014] AC 896.
25   [2017] EWCA Civ 31, [2018] QB 487.

dispute.[26] It is intended that the vast majority of such applications will become redundant when the MCAA 2019 comes into force because the new scheme, LPS, can be used in any setting.

THE COURT OF PROTECTION

The MCA 2005, s 45 provides for a superior court of record, known as the Court of Protection, to make decisions in relation to the property and financial affairs and healthcare and personal welfare of adults (and children in a few cases) who lack capacity to make such decisions themselves.

The court also has the power to make declarations about whether someone has the capacity to make a particular decision (MCA 2005, s 15). Where the court finds that a person lacks capacity to make a decision the court can make it for them or appoint a deputy to do so (MCA 2005, s 16) The court has the same powers, rights, privileges and authority in relation to mental capacity matters as the High Court (MCA 2005, s 47). In effect, the current Court of Protection represents an amalgamation of the former office of the same name, which had jurisdiction over the property and financial affairs of persons who were incapable, by reason of mental disorder, of managing and administering their property and affairs, with the health and welfare jurisdiction that had been progressively developed by puisne judges of the Family Division since the late 1980s. The Court of Protection is also the forum for challenges to authorisations made under the MCA 2005, Sch A1 (deprivation of liberty safeguards), and must authorise any deprivation of liberty other than in a hospital or care home under s 16.

The Court of Protection can only make decisions that P would be able to make for him or herself if s/he had capacity to make the decision: *Re N (An Adult) (Court of Protection's Jurisdiction)*.[27]

Article 8 and the Court of Protection

Article 8 of the ECHR protects respect for a person's home, family and private life.

Private life has been held to cover the physical and psychological integrity of the person; the right to personal development and to establish relationships with other human beings in the outside world.[28]

The Article 8 rights of P and those close to him or her will often be engaged by cases before the Court of Protection: first, by the very process of a declaration that P lacks capacity in the first place;[29] and second by the nature of the 'best interests' questions that the court may determine, such as medical treatment, where to live, and the contact P has with others, including close relatives. As such, the 'safe approach of the trial judge in Mental Capacity Act cases is to ascertain the best interests of

---

26 *Re X (Deprivation of Liberty)* [2014] ECOP 25, [2015] 1 WLR 2454; *Re X (Deprivation of Liberty)* [2014] EWCOP 37, [2015] 1 WLR 2454.
27 [2017] UKSC 22, [2017] AC 549.
28 *R (Razgar) v SSHD* [2004] UKHL 27, [2004] 2 AC 368.
29 *Shtukaturov v Russia* [2012] 54 EHRR 27, App No 44009/05.

the incapacitated adult on the application of the section 4 checklist. The judge should then ask whether the resulting conclusion amounts to a violation of Article 8 rights and whether that violation is nonetheless necessary and proportionate'.[30]

Judges of the Court of Protection

The President of the Court of Protection is Lord Justice Macfarlane, who is also the President of the Family Division. The Vice President is Mr Justice Hayden. The day-to-day running of the court is the responsibility of the senior judge, currently Her Honour Judge Hilder. The President has nominated a number of additional High Court, Circuit and District Judges to hear Court of Protection cases.

There are several district judges who hear cases full-time and part-time at the court's central registry.[31] The other judges hear cases on a part-time basis in the courts where they sit across England and Wales. The Court of Protection (Amendment) Rules 2011[32] provide for the jurisdiction of the court to be exercised in specified circumstances by authorised court officers.

Appeals lie from the decision of a first instance judge to a prescribed higher judge of the Court of Protection. Any second appeal from a first instance decision of a district judge or circuit judge lies to the Court of Appeal (MCA 2005, s 53, and the Court of Protection Rules 2017, r 20.4).

Court of Protection Rules 2017

The court's procedures are governed by the Court of Protection Rules 2017[33] and the accompanying Practice Directions. These rules were made by the President of the Court of Protection (the judicial office holder nominated by the Lord Chief Justice) who, with the agreement of the Lord Chancellor, makes the following Rules in exercise of the powers conferred by the MCA 2005, ss 49(5), 50(2), 51, 53(2) and (4), 55, 56 and 65(1), and in accordance with the Constitutional Reform Act 2005, Sch 1, Pt 1.[34]

Part 1 of the rules sets out the overriding objective that is to be applied whenever the court exercises its powers under the rules, or interprets any rule or practice direction. It also addresses the participation of P in all cases before the court. Part 2 contains provisions for interpreting the Rules and for the Civil Procedure Rules 1998 and the Family Procedure Rules 2010 to be applied insofar as may be necessary to further the overriding objective. Part 3 sets out the court's general case management powers, and includes the power to dispense with the requirement of any rule. Part 4 deals with hearings including the publication of information and privacy and publicity of hearings. Part 5 makes provision as to court documents, including the requirement for certain documents to be verified by a statement of truth. The Rules provide procedures for serving

---

30   *K v A Local Authority* [2012] EWCA Civ 79, [2012] 1 FCR 441 at [35].
31   At First Avenue House, 42–49 High Holborn, London WV1V 6NP.
32   SI 2011/2753.
33   SI 2017/1035.
34   The rules can be found at https://www.legislation.gov.uk/uksi/2017/1035/contents/made.

documents (Pt 6), notifying the person who lacks capacity and who is the subject matter of the application of certain documents and events (Pt 7), seeking permission to start proceedings (Pt 8), starting proceedings (Pt 9), and making interim applications and applications within proceedings (Pt 10).

Part 11 deals with applications to deprive P of his of her liberty in settings other than hospitals or care homes, as well as challenges to authorisations under the MCA 2005, Sch A1. Part 12 addresses applications raising human rights issues. Part 13 covers matters such as jurisdiction, participation, withdrawal and reconsideration.

The rules set out procedures to be followed in relation to evidence (Pt 14), experts (Pt 15), disclosure (Pt 16), appointment of litigation friends and other representatives for P, (Pt 17), change of solicitor (Pt 18), costs (Pt 19), appeals (Pt 20), the enforcement of orders (Pt 21), civil restraint orders (Pt 22), cross-border matters (part 23) and miscellaneous matters (Pt 24).

Practice directions

Practice directions are directions given by the President of the Court of Protection, with the concurrence of the Lord Chancellor, on the practice and procedure of the court (MCA 2005, s 50). The following practice directions have been issued. Practice Direction 3B should always be consulted before considering an application in the Court of Protection because it sets out the pre-issue requirements on would-be applicants:[35]

- 1A: Participation of P – effective from 1 December 2017;
- 2A: Levels of judiciary – effective from 1 December 2017;
- 2B: Authorised court officers – effective from 1 December 2017;
- 2C: Application of Civil Procedure Rules 1998 and the Family Procedure Rules 2010 – effective from 1 December 2017;
- 3A: Court's jurisdiction to be exercised by certain judges – effective from 1 December 2017;
- 3B: Case pathways – effective from 1 December 2017;
- 4A: Hearings (including reporting restrictions) – effective from 1 December 2017;
- 4B: Court bundles – effective from 1 December 2017;
- 4C: Transparency – effective from 1 December 2017;
- 5A: Court documents – effective from 1 December 2017;
- 5B: Statements of truth – effective from 1 December 2017;
- 6A: Service of documents – effective from 1 December 2017;
- 6B: Service out of the Jurisdiction – effective from 1 December 2017;
- 7A: Notifying P – effective from 1 December 2017;
- 8A: Permission – effective from 1 December 2017
- 9A: The application form – effective from 1 December 2017;
- 9B: Notification of other persons that an application form has been issued – effective from 1 December 2017;
- 9C: Responding to an application – effective from 1 December 2017;

---

35 The Practice Directions can be found at https://www.judiciary.uk/publications/court-of-protection-practice-directions/.

- 9D: Applications by currently appointed deputies, attorneys and donees in relation to P's property and affairs – effective from 1 December 2017;
- 9E: Applications relating to statutory wills, codicils, settlements and other dealings with P's property – effective from 1 December 2017;
- 9F: Applications to appoint or discharge a trustee – effective from 1 December 2017;
- 9G: Applications relating to the registration of enduring powers of attorney – effective from 1 December 2017;
- 10A: Applications within proceedings – effective from 1 December 2017;
- 10B: Urgent and interim applications – effective from 1 December 2017;
- 11A: Deprivation of liberty applications – effective from 1 December 2017;
- 12A: Human Rights Act 1998 – effective from 1 December 2017;
- 13A: Procedure for disputing the court's jurisdiction – effective from 1 December 2017;
- 14A: Written evidence – effective from 1 December 2017;
- 14B: Depositions – effective from 1 December 2017;
- 14C: Fees for examiners of the court – effective from 1 December 2017;
- 14D: Witness summons – effective from 1 December 2017;
- 14E: Section 49 reports – effective from 1 December 2017;
- 15A: Expert evidence – effective from 1 December 2017;
- 17A: Litigation friend – effective from 1 December 2017;
- 17B: Rule 1.2 representatives – effective from 1 December 2017;
- 18A: Change of solicitor – effective from 1 December 2017;
- 19A: Costs – effective from 1 December 2017;
- 19B: Fixed costs in the Court of Protection – effective from 1 December 2017;
- 20A: Appeals – effective from 1 December 2017;
- 20B: Allocation of appeals – effective from 1 December 2017;
- 21A: Contempt of court – effective from 1 December 2017;
- 22A: Civil Restraint Orders – effective from 1 December 2017;
- 23A: International protection of adults – effective from 1 December 2017;
- 24A: Request for directions where notice of objection prevents the Public Guardian from registering an Enduring Power of Attorney – effective from 1 December 2017;
- 24B: Where P ceases to lack capacity or dies – effective from 1 December 2017;
- 24C: Transitional provisions – effective from 1 December 2017.

Forms

The following forms can also be found at https://www.gov.uk/government/collections/court-of-protection-forms:

1   Form COP DLA: Deprivation of liberty application form – for urgent consideration;
2   Form COP DLB: Deprivation of liberty – declaration of exceptional urgency;

3   Form COP DLD: Deprivation of liberty certificate of service/non service, Certificate of notification/non notification;

4   Form COP DLE: Acknowledgment of service/notification;

5   Form COP1: Apply to make decisions on someone's behalf;

6   Form COP1A: Apply to make decisions on someone's behalf (property and finance);

7   Form COP1B: Apply to make decisions on someone's behalf (personal welfare);

8   Form COP1C: Apply to make decisions on someone's behalf (finances);

9   Form COP1D: Apply to make decisions on someone's behalf (appoint or discharge a trustee);

10 Form COP1E: Apply to make decisions on someone's behalf (supporting information);

11 Form COP3: Make a report on someone's capacity to make decisions;

12 Form COP4: Apply to become someone's deputy (make a declaration);

13 Form COP5: Apply to be part of Court of Protection proceedings ('acknowledgment of service');

14 Form COP7: Application to object to the registration of a Lasting Power of Attorney;

15 Form COP8: Application relating to the registration of an enduring power of attorney (EPA);

16 Form COP9: Apply to make decisions on someone's behalf ('application notice');

17 Form COP10: Application notice for applications to be joined as a party;

18 Form COP DOL10: Apply to authorise a deprivation of liberty;

19 Form COPDOL11: Application to authorise a deprivation of liberty (Sections 4A(3) and 16(2)(a) of the Mental Capacity Act 2005;

20 Form COP12: Special undertaking by trustee;

21 Form COP14: Proceedings notification (Court of Protection);

22 Form COP15: Confirmation of proceedings (Court of Protection);

23 Form COP1F: Annex F – Supporting information relating to validity or operation of enduring power of attorney (EPA) or lasting power of attorney (LPA);

24 Form COP20A: Certificate of Notification/Non-Notification of the person to whom the proceedings relate;

25 Form COP20B: Certificate of Service/Non-Service Notification/Non-Notification;

26 Form COP22: Certificate of suitability of Litigation Friend;

27 Form COP23: Certificate of failure or refusal of witness to attend before an examiner;

28 Form COP24: Give a witness statement about a person who lacks capacity;

29 Form COP25: Affidavit;

30 Form COP28: Notice of hearing;

31 Form COP29: Notice of hearing for Committal Order;

32 Form COP30: Notice of change of solicitor;

33 Form COP31: Notice of intention to file evidence by deposition

34 Form COP35: Appellant's notice;

35 Form COP36: Respondent's notice;

36 Form COP37: Skeleton argument;

37 Form COP44A: Apply for help with Court of Protection fees;

38   Form EX343A: Complaint form;
39   Form LPA 008: Notice to the Office of the Public Guardian of an application to object to registration of a lasting power of attorney made to the Court of Protection.

Fees

The MCA 2005, s 55 enables the Lord Chancellor to prescribe fees in respect of anything dealt with by the Court of Protection. The relevant orders are the Court of Protection Fees Order 2007[36] and the Court of Protection, Civil Proceedings, and Court Fees (Miscellaneous Amendments) Order 2018,[37] which reduced the application and appeal fees. There are only five fees, namely:

Application fee	art 4	£365
Appeal fee	art 5	£230
Hearing fee	art 6	£485
Copy of a document fee	art 7(1)	£5
Certified copy of a document fee	art 7(2)	£25

Article 8 of the fees order makes provision for exemptions where a person is in receipt of a qualifying benefit, as defined, and art 9 makes provision for fee reductions and remissions in exceptional circumstances.

Costs

The MCA 2005, s 55(1) provides that, subject to the Court of Protection Rules 2017, the costs of and incidental to all proceedings in the Court of Protection are in its discretion. The rules may in particular make provision for regulating matters relating to the costs of those proceedings, including prescribing scales of costs to be paid to legal or other representatives (s 55(2)), and the court has full power to determine by whom and to what extent the costs are to be paid (s 55(3)).

Rule 19.2 of the Court of Protection Rules 2017[38] sets out the following general rule for property and affairs cases:

> Where the proceedings concern P's property and affairs the general rule is that the costs of the proceedings, or of that part of the proceedings that concerns P's property and affairs, shall be paid by P or charged to his estate.

Rule 19.3 sets out the following general rule for personal welfare cases:

> Where the proceedings concern P's personal welfare the general rule is that there will be no order as to the costs of the proceedings or that part of the proceedings that concerns P's personal welfare.

---

36   SI 2007/1745.
37   SI 2019/1063.
38   SI 2017/1035.

Rule 19.4 provides that:

> Where the proceedings concern both property and affairs and personal welfare the court, insofar as practicable, shall apportion the costs as between the respective issues.

Rule 19.5 enables the court to depart from rr 19.2 to 19.5 if the circumstances so justify, and in deciding whether departure is justified the court will have regard to all the circumstances. This would include the conduct of the parties; whether a party has succeeded on part of their case, even if not wholly successful; and the role of any public body involved in the proceedings.

Practice Direction 19B sets out the fixed costs which solicitors may claim for various categories of work in order to avoid a detailed assessment of their costs. The Practice Direction also sets out the scale of remuneration that a public authority deputy may receive.

Making an application to the Court of Protection

In a case in which there is likely to be a compensation for clinical negligence or personal injury, the solicitor acting on behalf of the claimant in the proceedings ('P') usually makes an application to the Court of Protection for the appointment of a deputy to manage the compensation award on P's behalf. The court has produced a booklet, COP 42 *Making an application to the Court of Protection*.

The application consists of:

- Form COP1, the application form itself, which asks the applicant to state what order they are seeking;
- Form COP1A, which sets out information regarding P's property and financial affairs, such as an inventory;
- Form COP3, assessment of capacity, which needs to be completed by a medical practitioner or any other person who specialises in assessing mental capacity;
- Form COP4, deputy's declaration, in which the deputy provides important information about themselves; and
- the application fee of £385.

P will be notified of the application, and so will P's relatives and other persons closely involved in P's care, and they can signify their consent or opposition to the application on an acknowledgment of service form (COP5). If there is an objection, a judge will set a date for an oral hearing to consider the application and the objection, but in 97% of applications, there are no objections, and the application is dealt with by paperwork alone.

Appointment of a deputy

Although this is not laid down in the MCA 2005 itself, judicial precedent generally recognises an order of preference of persons who might be considered suitable for appointment as a deputy. Generally speaking, this order of preference is:

- P's spouse or partner;
- any other relative who takes a personal interest in P's affairs;

- a close friend;
- a professional adviser, such as P's solicitor or accountant;
- a local authority's social services department; and finally, as a last resort,
- a deputy from a panel maintained by the Office of the Public Guardian.

Adherence to any order of preference would, of course, have the effect of negating the court's discretion in deciding whom or whom not to appoint. Accordingly, the court takes into account a wide range of other relevant factors. These include:

- the applicant's own financial track-record;
- the applicant's criminal record;
- the size and complexity of the estate;
- the degree of contact the applicant has with P;
- any particular ethnic or religious considerations;
- P's own wishes and feelings on the matter, so far as they are ascertainable;
- the ability of the applicant to interact successfully with P and P's carers;
- any conflicts of interest;
- any special qualities of the applicant;
- any special features of the case;
- whether there are any matters to be investigated, such as alleged fraud or financial abuse; and
- the expense involved in managing P's property and affairs.

Orders appointing deputies for property and affairs purposes

The order appointing a deputy to make decisions relating to P's property and affairs:

- names the deputy;
- if there is more than one deputy, it states whether they can act jointly and severally, or whether they must act jointly at all times;
- states whether there is any time limit to the appointment – for example, for three years from the date of the order;
- sets out the scope of the deputy's authority, and any restrictions or conditions;
- may require the deputy to keep within a specified budget by limiting the amount the deputy can spend each year, without the need for further authorisation by the court;
- may provide that the deputy cannot buy, sell, mortgage, lease or dispose of P's residence without the prior approval of the court;
- may require the deputy to take professional advice on the investment of P's funds;
- usually requires the deputy to provide accounts and reports to the Public Guardian, when required;
- sets out the terms on which a professional deputy may be remunerated; and
- usually requires the deputy to give security to cover any defalcations by the deputy of up to a specified sum. The premium

for this security guarantee is payable each year and in most cases amounts to 0.2% of the payment guaranteed. So, for example, in the case of a guaranteed payment of up to £200,000, the annual premium would be £400.

Duties of a deputy

A deputy takes on a number of duties and responsibilities. These are set out in the Deputy's Declaration (Form COP4) in the form of an undertaking:

1 I will have regard to the Mental Capacity Act 2005 Code of Practice and I will apply the principles of the Act when making a decision. In particular I will act in the best interests of the person to whom the application relates and I will only make those decisions that the person cannot make themselves.

2 I will act within the scope of the powers conferred on me by the court as set out in the order of appointment and I will apply to the court if I feel additional powers are needed.

3 I will act with due care, skill and diligence, as I would do in making my own decisions and conducting my own affairs. Where I undertake my duties as a deputy in the course of my professional work (if relevant), I will abide by professional rules and standards.

4 I will make decisions on behalf of the person to whom the application relates as required under the court order appointing me. I will not delegate any of my powers as a deputy unless this is expressly permitted in the court order appointing me.

5 I will ensure that my personal interests do not conflict with my duties as a deputy, and I will not use my position for any personal benefit.

6 I will act with honesty and integrity, and will take any decisions made by the person to whom the application relates while they still had capacity, into account when determining their best interests.

7 I will keep the person's financial and personal information confidential (unless there is a good reason that requires me to disclose it).

8 I will comply with any directions of the court or reasonable requests made by the Public Guardian, including requests for reports to be submitted.

9 I will visit the person to whom the application relates as regularly as is appropriate and take an interest in their welfare.

10 I will work with the person to whom the application relates and any carer(s) to achieve the best quality of life for him or her within the funds available.

11 I will co-operate with any representative of the court or the Public Guardian who might wish to meet me or the person to whom the application relates to check that the deputyship arrangements are working.

12 I will immediately inform the court and the Public Guardian if I have any reason to believe that the person to whom the application relates no longer lacks capacity and may be able to manage his or her own affairs.

The following further undertakings are required if someone is applying to be appointed as a property and affairs deputy:

13 I understand that I may be required to provide security for my actions as deputy. If I am required to purchase insurance, such as a guarantee bond, I undertake to pay premiums promptly from the funds of the person to whom the application relates.

14   I will keep accounts of dealings and transactions taken on behalf of the person to whom the application relates.

15   I will keep the money and property of the person to whom the applicant relates separate from my own.

16   I will ensure so far as is reasonable that the person to whom the application relates receives all benefits and other income to which they are entitled, that their bills are paid and that a tax return for them is completed annually.

17   I will take reasonable steps to maintain the property of the person to whom the application relates (if applicable), for example arranging for insurance, repairs or improvements. If necessary, I will arrange and oversee a sale or letting of property with appropriate legal advice.

The Office of the Public Guardian (OPG)

When the Court of Protection has appointed a deputy, the responsibility for monitoring the deputy passes to the Office of the Public Guardian. The MCA 2005, s 57 provides that there is to be an officer known as the Public Guardian, and their functions are set out in s 58. These functions include:

* supervising deputies appointed by the court;
* directing visits by a Court of Protection visitor;
* receiving the security which the court requires a deputy to give for the discharge of their functions;
* receiving accounts and other reports from deputies and donees of lasting powers of attorney; and
* investigating complaints about deputies and donees of lasting powers of attorney.

The OPG now operates two levels of supervision:

1   general supervision – allocated to all cases in their first year; and
2   minimal supervision – deputies managing total assets of less than £19,000 will usually be moved down to this level after the deputyship's first year.

Statutory wills

Since 1970, the Court of Protection has had jurisdiction to authorise the execution of a will on behalf of a person who lacks testamentary capacity. This jurisdiction can now be found in the MCA 2005, s 18(1)(i), (2) and Sch 2.

Since the MCA 2005 came into force, there have been two important decisions on statutory will applications which have been of general importance.

In *Re P*,[39] Mr Justice Lewison considered the difference between substituted judgment and best interests, and held that the earlier law regarding the making of statutory wills, including the landmark decision of Sir Robert Megarry V-C in *Re D(J)*,[40] is no longer good law because it

---

39   [2009] LS Law Med 264, [2009] WTLR 651.
40   [1982] Ch 237, [1982] 2 All ER 37.

applied a substituted judgment test. Lewison J went on to note that for many people, it is in their best interests to be remembered after their death as having 'done the right thing' in their will.

In *Re M, ITW v Z*,[41] Mr Justice Munby considered a statutory will application in a case in which an older woman had been the victim of financial abuse by a neighbour. He held that the weight to be attached to P's wishes and feelings will always be case-specific and fact-specific. In some cases, in some situations, they may carry much, even, on occasions, preponderant, weight. In other cases, in other situations, and even where the circumstances may have some superficial similarity, they may carry very little weight. Just as the test of incapacity under the MCA 2005 is, as under the common law, 'issue specific', so in a similar way the weight to be attached to P's wishes and feelings will likewise be issue specific. He said that there was no hierarchy of factors in the MCA 2005, s 4, though there may be a single factor of 'magnetic importance'.

In *Re Meek*[42] HHJ Hodge said that in referring to 'doing the right thing' in *Re P*, Lewison J had in mind the perspective of the well-informed, objective bystander: however following the judgment of Lady Hale in *Aintree* (see above), this should now be judged according to the standards of the incapacitated person themselves.

In *Re Jones*,[43] District Judge Eldergill observed that the onset of mental incapacity is not an 'opportunity for moral correction', but in the absence of clear evidence to the contrary, most people would want to do the right thing by their family and loved ones and a judge is entitled to take that view.

CODES OF PRACTICE

Sections 42 and 43 of the MCA 2005 provide for a Code of Practice, the first edition of which was issued on 1 April 2007, six months before the rest of the Act came into force. A second Code of Practice was issued in April 2009 to support the deprivation of liberty safeguards (MCA 2005: Deprivation of Liberty Safeguards Code of Practice).

The purpose of the Code of Practice is to supplement the MCA 2005 by considering in depth a number of important issues, which are not in themselves suitable matters for inclusion in primary or secondary legislation. It provides practical guidance on how the provisions of the MCA 2005 should be applied in ordinary, everyday situations. For example, when:

1. assessing whether someone has capacity in relation to a particular matter;
2. helping them to make decisions for themselves;
3. deciding whether a particular course of action is in a person's best interests;
4. acting as a carer or a treatment provider, and in emergency situations;
5. acting as an attorney under a lasting power of attorney or as a court-appointed deputy; or

---

41 [2009] EWHC 525 (Fam), [2009] WLR 1791.
42 [2014] EWCOP 1, [2014] COPLR 535.
43 [2014] EWCOP 59.

6   carrying out intrusive research on a patient who lacks the capacity to consent to such research.

Although the MCA 2005 requires certain people, such as deputies and professional carers, to 'have regard to' the code, it does not impose a legal duty on them to 'comply with' the code, nor does it impose specific penalties if they fail to comply with it. The code should be regarded as guidance rather than instruction. But, anyone with a duty to have regard to the code must have cogent reasons for departing from it.[44] At the time of writing a new Code of Practice is being prepared with a view to a public consultation in late 2019.

---

44   *R (Munjaz) v Mersey Care Trust* [2005] UKHL 58, [2006] 2 AC 148.

Chapter 25

Wales

Linda Jacobs

COMPLAINTS HANDLING AND REDRESS FOR LOW VALUE CLINICAL NEGLIGENCE CLAIMS IN WALES

Wales has an alternative compensation scheme for low value clinical negligence claims against Welsh NHS hospitals which co-exists with the traditional civil court system. The Speedy Resolution Pilot Scheme, which also provided an alternative dispute resolution mechanism for low value clinical negligence claims against NHS Trusts in Wales, is no longer in operation. It was never formalised and was superseded by the National Health Service (Concerns, Complaints and Redress Arrangements) (Wales) Regulations 2011, SI 2011/704.

NATIONAL HEALTH SERVICE (CONCERNS, COMPLAINTS AND REDRESS ARRANGEMENTS) (WALES) REGULATIONS 2011

The National Health Service (Concerns, Complaints and Redress Arrangements) (Wales) Regulations 2011[1] referred to as the 'Putting Things Right' scheme, was enacted under the NHS Redress (Wales) Measure 2008. The Regulations were laid before the National Assembly for Wales on 7 February 2011 for approval by resolution.[2] The majority of the Regulations came into force on 1 April 2011, and Part 7 (the cross border arrangements) came into force on 1 April 2012.[3] The Regulations are supplemented by Guidance prepared by the Welsh Assembly Government entitled *Putting Things Right – Guidance on dealing with concerns about the NHS from 1 April 2011*, which will be updated as necessary. Version 3 dated November 2013 is available online.[4]

The Regulations provide an integrated approach, combining common arrangements for handling and investigating complaints, and dealing with patient safety issues at a local level. The Regulations apply to Welsh NHS bodies (the seven Local Health Boards, Velindre NHS Trust,

---

1   SI 2011/704.
2   The Regulations were laid under s 11(6) of the NHS Redress (Wales) Measure 2008.
3   SI 2011/1706.
4   SI 2011/704, reg 2(1).

the Welsh Ambulance Services NHS Trust and Public Health Wales NHS Trust); primary care practitioners; and independent providers in Wales (collectively called 'Responsible Bodies' in the Regulations).

The Regulations also incorporate redress arrangements, including financial compensation for claims against Welsh NHS bodies that do not exceed the current limit of £25,000. Redress is not available against primary care practitioners and independent providers, unless the primary care practitioner is employed within a health board managed practice.

Redress arrangements will also apply when Welsh NHS bodies enter into arrangements with NHS organisations in England, Scotland, or Northern Ireland for treatment and care provided on behalf of the NHS in Wales.

Background

On 11 January 2010, the Welsh Assembly Government published a consultation document entitled *Putting Things Right – A better way of dealing with concerns about health services*. The consultation followed interim guidance issued to NHS Trusts in Wales in October 2009.[5] The *Putting Things Right* project was established by the Welsh Assembly Government to examine the way that the NHS in Wales handled concerns/complaints. The project suggested common methods of investigation, with an emphasis on resolving concerns in a timely fashion, openly and honestly; and included a philosophy to 'investigate once, investigate well'. The stated aims were to ensure that the patient remained at the heart of the investigation, to ensure that that the investigation was proportionate to the issue in question, and result in appropriate remedies for patients and service users; 'appropriate remedies' includes financial compensation.[6] The new system envisaged an integrated team handling and investigating concerns/complaints, incident reporting, claims management, and patient safety issues. In terms of patient safety, it was hoped that the new system would drive improvements in quality, and reduce adverse events and avoidable harm to patients and service users both locally and on an all-Wales basis.

The arrangements for Responsible Bodies

Each organisation operates with a single point of entry for handling all concerns, and a single address, telephone number, mailbox, fax or text service must be clearly published for raising a concern.[7] The system is managed by a Responsible Officer (who must be an executive director or officer; chief executive officer; sole proprietor or partner, depending upon the nature of the Responsible Body[8]), taking overall responsibility for the effective day-to-day operation of the arrangements for dealing

---

5   Welsh Assembly Government, *Putting Things Right – Dealing with concerns (Interim Guidance on the handling of concerns in the new NHS Structure)* (October 2009).

6   Welsh Assembly Government, *Putting Things Right – A better way of dealing with concerns about health services* Background Policy Paper (11 January 2010).

7   Welsh Assembly Government, *Putting Things Right – Guidance on dealing with concerns about the NHS from 1 April 2011* (Version 3, November 2013), para 5.1.

8   SI 2011/704, reg 7(3).

with concerns in an integrated manner.[9] A Senior Investigations Manager is responsible for handling and investigating concerns.[10] The Senior Investigations Manager should be supported by staff of varied experience and skill sets,[11] collectively called the 'concerns team'.[12] The Regulations state that staff should be appropriately trained in the operation of the arrangements for reporting, handling, and investigating concerns.[13] The Guidance includes examples of relevant training, including, *Being Open* training; records management; equality and diversity; safeguarding children and vulnerable adults; and legal training and awareness.[14] The availability of the arrangements must be published and advertised in a variety of media, formats, and languages;[15] and examples are available on the Welsh Assembly Government's *Putting Things Right* website,[16] and as part of the Guidance.

Each organisation must include arrangements to act upon and monitor deficiencies identified in the investigation process.[17] This is part of the ethos of 'learning from concerns' to maximise the opportunities to improve services, thereby avoiding future deficient treatment or care. Responsible Bodies must share any lessons learnt with other service providers to improve the wider provision of services and avoid the recurrence of similar concerns in other areas.[18] Responsible Bodies must also monitor the arrangements,[19] and prepare an annual report.[20]

The Annual Reports can be found online. The Annual Report of Cardiff and Vale University Health Board indicated 92 new clinical negligence and 61 new PI claims in 2017–2018.[21] The report acknowledges an annual increase in concerns and identifies five general themes: pressure areas; patient falls; patients with learning disabilities; missed opportunity to diagnose cancer; and a failure to recognise a deterioration in a patient's condition, such as sepsis.

Potential drawbacks

The most significant issue raised in the consultation process was the lack of independence in relation to investigating a potential claim of negligence. Independence is an important aspect in patients and service users having confidence in a system of investigation. Concern was also raised in relation to the wide discretion given to Responsible Bodies resulting in a potential lack of consistency in investigations.

---

9   SI 2011/704, reg 7(1).
10 SI 2011/704, reg 8(1).
11 SI 2011/704, reg 8(2).
12 Welsh Assembly Government, *Putting Things Right – Guidance on dealing with concerns about the NHS from 1 April 2011* (Version 3, November 2013), para 2.10.
13 SI 2011/704, reg 9.
14 Welsh Assembly Government, *Putting Things Right – Guidance on dealing with concerns about the NHS from 1 April 2011* (Version 3, November 2013), para 3.5.
15 SI 2011/704, reg 5.
16 See www.wales.nhs.uk/sites3/page.cfm?orgid=932&pid=50738.
17 SI 2011/704, reg 49(1).
18 Welsh Assembly Government, *Putting Things Right – Guidance on dealing with concerns about the NHS from 1 April 2011* (Version 3, November 2013), para 9.5.
19 SI 2011/704, reg 50.
20 SI 2011/704, reg 51.
21 See http://www.cardiffandvaleuhb.wales.nhs.uk/sitesplus/documents/1143/Putting%20Things%20Right%20Annual%20Report.pdf.

The Welsh Assembly Government responded that guidance was to be developed about 'how teams within the organisation will work and their accountability arrangements, to ensure that they can act independently within the organisation'.[22]

In 2014, a 12-week independent review of the Regulations was commissioned by the Welsh government, led by Keith Evans, former Chief Executive and Managing Director of Panasonic UK and Ireland, supported by Dr Andrew Goodall, Chief Executive of Aneurin Bevan University Health Board. The review, entitled 'A Review of Concerns (Complaints) Handling in NHS Wales', also referred to as 'Using the Gift of Complaints', identified 109 recommendations to improve the management of concerns. The report acknowledged that 'Putting Things Right' had been well received. However, there remained concerns as to implementation of the Regulations, including inconsistency in practice across Wales.

The major themes from those dissatisfied with the service included:

- that the complainant did not feel listened to;
- timelines were not adhered to and complainants were not informed of delays;
- there was a lack of clinical engagement in reviewing concerns;
- a lack of openness and honesty;
- there was little evidence of learning and a lack of accountability when things went seriously wrong.

In terms of concerns that raised issues of liability, it was felt that these were not being addressed appropriately and that organisations appeared hesitant of admitting that further investigations were being undertaken. One specific recommendation was that there should be a statutory duty of candour. In response, the Welsh government set up working groups to further explore some of the identified concerns in the report. It is anticipated that the Regulations and Guidance will be updated.

The Regulations 2011

The National Health Service (Concerns, Complaints and Redress Arrangements) (Wales) Regulations 2011 are divided into ten parts. The Guidance includes ten templates to standardise some aspects of the process. In addition, there is guidance on particular issues, such as the grading of concerns and an investigation checklist; a legal fees framework; and a financial tariff for the assessment of claims below £25,000.

The Regulations provide a number of general principles that are to be applied in handling and investigating concerns; and are set out in reg 3 and the Guidance as follows:

(a) there is a single point of entry for the submission of concerns;
(b) concerns are dealt with efficiently and openly;
(c) concerns are properly investigated;

---

22   Welsh Assembly Government, *Putting Things Right – A better way of dealing with concerns about health services*, Consultation Report (2 August 2010), p 4.

(d) provision should be made to establish the expectations of the person notifying the concern and to seek to secure their involvement in the process;

(e) persons who notify concerns are treated with respect and courtesy;

(f) persons who notify concerns are advised of—

(i) the availability of assistance to enable them to pursue their concern;

(ii) advice as to where they may obtain such assistance, if it is required; and

(iii) the name of the person in the relevant Responsible Body who will act as their contact throughout the handling of their concern;

(g) a Welsh NHS body must give consideration to the making of an offer of redress in accordance with Part 6 where its investigation into the matters raised in a concern reveal that there is a qualifying liability;

(h) persons who notify concerns receive a timely and appropriate response;

(i) persons who notify concerns are advised of the outcome of the investigation;

(j) appropriate action is taken in the light of the outcome of the investigation; and

(k) account is taken of any guidance that may be issued from time to time by the Welsh Ministers.

When do the Regulations apply?

The Regulations apply to:

1   a complaint (an 'expression of dissatisfaction');

2   the notification of an incident concerning patient safety ('any unexpected or unintended incident which did lead to or could have led to harm for a patient'); and

3   a claim for compensation.[23]

Complaints and the notification of incidents concerning patient safety can be made against a 'Responsible Body', defined as:

1   a Welsh NHS body (a Local Health Board, or a NHS Trust managing a hospital or other establishment or facility wholly or mainly in Wales);

2   a primary care provider (GPs, dentists, persons providing ophthalmic services and pharmacists who provide services under arrangements with Local Health Boards); and

3   an independent provider (a person or body who (a) provides health care in Wales under arrangements made with a Welsh NHS body; and (b) is not an NHS body or primary care provider).[24]

Claims for compensation (redress) under Pts 6 and 7 of the Regulations can only be made against Welsh NHS bodies.

If a concern involves more than one Responsible Body, the Responsible Body that received the concern must inform the complainant/

---

23   SI 2011/704, reg 2.
24   SI 2011/704, reg 2(1).

representative that another Responsible Body is or may be involved in their concern and seek their consent to notifying the other Responsible Body about the concern. This must be done within two days of receiving the concern.[25] Once consent has been received, the Responsible Body must inform the second Responsible Body about the concern within two working days of receiving the consent.[26] All the Responsible Bodies involved with the concern should cooperate and agree who will lead the investigation, who will communicate with the complainant/representative; to share information; and to issue a joint response to the concern.[27]

Who can raise a concern?

The category of people that can raise a concern is wide. The Responsible Body is under a duty to consider whether the concern can be investigated and to handle a concern in accordance with the provisions set out in the Regulations. Regulation 12 provides that a concern may be raised by:

1   a person who is receiving or has received services from a Responsible Body;
2   any person who is affected or likely to be affected by the actions, omissions, or decisions of a Responsible Body;
3   a member of staff of the Responsible Body;
4   an independent member (non-executive director or non-officer member) of the Responsible Body);
5   partners in a Responsible Body (for example a partner in a GP Practice);
6   a third party acting on behalf of a person who is unable to raise a concern, for example, a child, a person who lacks capacity within the meaning of the Mental Capacity Act 2005, or a person who has died; and
7   a third party acting on behalf of a person who wants a representative to act on their behalf.

Members of staff should report incidents concerning patient safety, which in turn should raise a concern with the Responsible Body. The *Putting Things Right* project utilised work by the National Patient Safety Agency entitled *Being Open* that was re-launched on 19 November 2009. *Being Open* encourages staff to report errors and concerns; and involves acknowledging, apologising and explaining when errors occur. The advice is based on research that 'shows that patients are more likely to forgive medical errors when they are discussed in a timely manner; and that being open can decrease the trauma felt by patients following a patient safety incident'.[28]

---

25   SI 2011/704, reg 17(2)(a).
26   SI 2011/704, reg 17(2)(b).
27   SI 2011/704, reg 17(3), (4); and Welsh Assembly Government, *Putting Things Right – Guidance on dealing with concerns about the NHS from 1 April 2011* (Version 3, November 2013), para 6.4.
28   Research by Vincent, C A and Counter, A 'Patient Safety: what about the patient?' Qual Saf Health Care (2003) 11: 76–80; and Vincent, C A, Pincus, T and Schurr, J H 'Patients' experience of surgical accidents' Qual Saf Health Care (1993) 2: 77–82. Quoted in The National Patient Safety Agency Patient Safety Alert: NPSA//2009/PSA003 – Being Open Supporting Information (November 2009).

Although the Regulations introduce an ethos of openness, the Welsh Assembly Government did not go as far as incorporating a duty of candour into the Regulations. This issue was raised in responses to the *Putting Things Right* consultation. The Welsh Assembly Government replied that it was unable to introduce a duty of candour, and stated '[w]e believe that we have addressed this issue as far as we can in the powers available to the Assembly. We are keeping a watching brief on development in England, where we know this matter is being further discussed'.[29]

It is regrettable that a duty of candour (and a duty to report a concern) has not been introduced as research undertaken by the National Audit Office in 2004/05 established that only 24% of Trusts routinely inform patients that they were involved in a patient safety incident and 6% of Trusts did not inform patients at all.[30] This is a significant number given that in the same year there were approximately 974,000 reported adverse incidents and near misses.[31] In 2005, the National Audit Office concluded, 'there is still more to do to achieve a fully open and fair culture with regard to communicating with patients'.[32]

Methods for raising a concern

A concern can be raised with the Responsible Body in numerous ways, either in writing, electronically (email, fax or text[33]), or verbally, either by telephone or in person.[34] For concerns that are raised verbally, but are not 'on the spot concerns', that is concerns that are raised and resolved at the point of service delivery, the person to whom the concern is made must make a written record, and provide a copy to the person who raised the concern.[35] The Guidance includes a template for recording verbal concerns that will be handled under the Regulations (see Appendix E of the Guidance).

What concerns can be raised?

Concerns can be raised about any service, decision, care and treatment provided by a Responsible Body in Wales,[36] provided it is not excluded under reg 14. Concerns that that are specifically excluded include:

---

29 Welsh Assembly Government, *Putting Things Right – A better way of dealing with concerns about health services*, Consultation Report (2 August 2010), p 10.
30 National Audit Office (Department of Health) *A Safer Place for Patients: Learning to improve patient safety* (Report by the Comptroller and Auditor General) (3 November 2005), p 15.
31 National Audit Office (Department of Health) *A Safer Place for Patients: Learning to improve patient safety* (Report by the Comptroller and Auditor General) (3 November 2005), p 1 (96% response rate).
32 National Audit Office (Department of Health) *A Safer Place for Patients: Learning to improve patient safety* (Report by the Comptroller and Auditor General) (3 November 2005), p 15.
33 Welsh Assembly Government, *Putting Things Right – Guidance on dealing with concerns about the NHS from 1 April 2011* (Version 3, November 2013), para 5.2.
34 SI 2011/704, reg 11.
35 SI 2011/704, reg 11(2).
36 SI 2011/704, reg 13.

1   concerns that are the subject of court proceedings (ie proceedings have been issued). If court proceedings are issued when a concern is under investigation, the investigation must stop;[37]
2   concerns that are raised and resolved at the point of service delivery 'on the spot'. The concern must be resolved to the satisfaction of the complainant/representative no later that the next working day after the concern was notified.[38] On the spot concerns must be recorded and Appendix A of the Guidance sets out a template;
3   where a person attempts to re-open a concern that they have already agreed was dealt with satisfactorily on the spot, unless the Responsible Body considers it needs to look into the issue again;[39]
4   concerns that have already been considered under either a complaints procedure operating before 1 April 2011 or the new Regulations;[40]
5   a concern about an individual patient funding treatment request.[41] This situation is dealt with under the All-Wales Policy: Making Decisions on Individual Patient Funding Requests.[42]

There is no right to legal assistance funded by the Responsible Body at this stage. Some concerns may involve medically complex issues, and be difficult for a person with no legal or medical knowledge to articulate in writing. This may be compounded by the fact that patients and service users may not be provided with all the necessary information, relying on an ethos of openness, rather than being owed a duty of candour.

Time limits for notification of a concern to the Responsible Body

In order for the Regulations to apply, the Responsible Body must be notified of a concern no later than: (i) 12 months after the date on which the concern occurred; or (ii) if later, 12 months after the date the person raising the concern realised they had a concern.[43] The Responsible Body has discretion to disapply the time limit if it is satisfied that (i) the person raising the concern had a good reason for not notifying the Responsible Body within the time limit, and (ii) it is still possible to investigate the concern effectively and fairly.[44] In the case of a patient that is being represented under reg 12(2)(d), it is the patient's date of knowledge, not the representative's date of knowledge that is relevant.[45]

There is a time limit longstop of three years. Therefore, a concern cannot be notified three or more years from the date the concern occurred; or three or more years from the date the person realised they had a

---

37   SI 2011/704, reg 14(1)(i).
38   SI 2011/704, reg 14(1)(f).
39   SI 2011/704, reg 14 (1)(f) and (g).
40   SI 2011/704, reg 14(1)(h).
41   SI 2011/704, reg 14(1)(j).
42   See   http://www.wales.nhs.uk/sitesplus/documents/866/NHS%20Wales%20IPFR%20 Policy%20-%20June%202017%20-%20Final.pdf.
43   SI 2011/704, reg 15(1).
44   SI 2011/704, reg 15(2).
45   SI 2011/704, reg 15(4).

concern.[46] A period of three years was chosen as it is consistent with the limitation period in clinical negligence claims.[47]

There are no provisions within the Regulations to disapply the time limits for any reason, including the fact that the person raising the concern is a child, or lacks capacity under the Mental Capacity Act 2005. However, the Guidance suggests that there are exceptions to the three year limitation[48] period as follows:

1   where the person raising the complaint is a child at the time of injury, the three-year period does not begin to run until the individual reaches 18 years of age;
2   where the person raising the concern lacks capacity under the Mental Capacity Act 2005, the three-year period may never begin to run, but it can start to run at the date of any recovery.

Where there is an exception to the time limit, the Responsible Body may limit the investigation, based upon the information available, particularly if key staff have left the organisation.[49]

Withdrawal of concerns

There is no obligation on the complainant/representative to continue with the investigation process and a concern that has been notified to the Responsible Body may be withdrawn at any time by the complainant/representative. The concern can be withdrawn in writing, electronically or verbally, either by telephone or in person.[50] If the concern is withdrawn verbally, the Responsible Body should write to that person as soon as practicable to confirm the decision.[51] Although a concern may be withdrawn, the Responsible Body can continue to investigate the concern if the Responsible Body considers it necessary.[52]

Initial response by the Responsible Body

Additional requirements for children, third party representatives, and staff

Where a child or young person raises a concern, the Responsible Body must provide reasonable support to the child/young person in order for him to pursue the concern.[53] Advocacy support can be arranged by Local Health Boards in accordance with the Welsh Assembly Government's *Model for Delivering Advocacy Services to Children and Young People*

---

46   SI 2011/704, reg 15(3).
47   Welsh Assembly Government, *Putting Things Right – Guidance on dealing with concerns about the NHS from 1 April 2011* (Version 3, November 2013), para 5.18.
48   Welsh Assembly Government, *Putting Things Right – Guidance on dealing with concerns about the NHS from 1 April 2011* (Version 3, November 2013), para 5.18.
49   Welsh Assembly Government, *Putting Things Right – Guidance on dealing with concerns about the NHS from 1 April 2011* (Version 3, November 2013), para 5.20.
50   SI 2011/704, reg 16(1).
51   SI 2011/704, reg 16(2).
52   SI 2011/704, reg 16(3).
53   SI 2011/704, reg 12(4).

in Wales.[54] If the concern is raised on behalf of a child, the Responsible Body must satisfy itself that there are reasonable grounds for the concern being notified by a representative as opposed to the child.[55] If the Responsible Body is not satisfied, the concern must not be investigated, and the Responsible Body must notify the representative giving reasons for its decision.[56]

Where a concern is raised on behalf of a child, young person or person who lacks capacity within the meaning of the Mental Capacity Act 2005, the Responsible Body must consider whether the third party representative is a suitable representative, and is pursuing the concern in the best interests of that person.[57] In circumstances where a determination has been made that the representative is not suitable, the Responsible Body may continue with the investigation if it is satisfied that it is necessary to do so.[58] However, the Reasonable Body is not under an obligation to provide a detailed response to the representative, unless it is reasonable to do so.[59]

Members of staff of Responsible Bodies can raise concerns, including reporting errors in treatment/untoward events as a 'patient safety incident'. An initial assessment of the concern will be undertaken in accordance with the principles in reg 23 to determine the parameters of the investigation and the severity of the concern.[60] If the initial investigation reveals that the patient suffered moderate or severe harm (which is not defined in the Regulations or the Guidance[61]) or death, the Responsible Body must inform the patient or his representative that a report has been made,[62] unless, in the opinion of the Responsible Body, it is not in the best interests of the patient.[63] The Guidance states that it would not be in the patient's best interests if 'involving them could cause a deterioration in their physical or mental health'.[64] Therefore, it seems that a patient or his representative will not be informed if the harm is judged to be relatively low; which does not accord with the *Being Open* principle. If the patient or his representative is told that a concern has been raised, the Responsible Body must involve the patient/representative in the investigation unless it is not in the interests of the patient.[65]

---

54   Welsh Assembly Government, *Putting Things Right – Guidance on dealing with concerns about the NHS from 1 April 2011* (Version 3, November 2013), paras 4.30 and 5.8.
55   SI 2011/704, reg 12(3)(a).
56   SI 2011/704, reg 12(3)(a), (b).
57   SI 2011/704, reg 12(5).
58   SI 2011/704, reg 12(5).
59   SI 2011/704, reg 12(6).
60   Welsh Assembly Government, *Putting Things Right – Guidance on dealing with concerns about the NHS from 1 April 2011* (Version 3, November 2013), para 6.49.
61   SI 2011/704, reg 2(1) states that 'moderate or severe harm determined in accordance with guidance issued for the purpose of these regulations by the Welsh Ministers'.
62   SI 2011/704, reg 12(7).
63   SI 2011/704, reg 12(8).
64   Welsh Assembly Government, *Putting Things Right – Guidance on dealing with concerns about the NHS from 1 April 2011* (Version 3, November 2013), para 6.32.
65   SI 2011/704, reg 12(7).

Acknowledgement by the Responsible Body

The Responsible Body must acknowledge receipt of the notification of concerns, except for 'on the spot' concerns, and concerns involving primary care providers. The period for the Responsible Body to acknowledge receipt of a concern is limited, and must be made no later than two working days after the day on which the notification was received.[66] The acknowledgement must be in writing even if the notification was made verbally;[67] but if the notification was received electronically, it may be acknowledged electronically.[68] Appendix G to the Guidance sets out the templates for acknowledgment letters. The date that the Responsible Body receives the notification of the concern is important as it is the date from which the limitation for claims for negligence will be suspended.

As part of its acknowledgement, the Responsible Body must provide the complainant/representative with the name of the contact person who will be handling the concern, and details of how to contact that person.[69] The acknowledgment letter or electronic communication must include an offer for the complainant/representative to discuss the following issues by telephone or at a meeting:

1   the manner in which the investigation will be handled, including consent to the use of medical records;
2   the availability of advocacy and support services in relation to the concern:
     –   Advocacy services may be provided by the Community Health Council to anyone over 18 years of age; and for children or young people, advocacy services can be arranged by Local Health Boards in accordance with the Welsh Assembly Governments' *Model for Delivering Advocacy Services to Children and Young People in Wales*;[70]
3   how long the investigation is likely to take and when a response can be expected;
4   any specific needs that the representative may have which should be taken into account as the investigation proceeds; and
5   what the complainant/representative expects as an outcome.[71]

The complainant/representative should be given the opportunity to bring a friend, relative or an advocate to the meeting.[72] If the concern is resolved at the meeting, no further investigation is required. The Responsible Body must write to the complainant/representative after the meeting including a full written response based on the discussions and confirmation that

---

66   SI 2011/704, reg 22(1).
67   SI 2011/704, reg 22(3).
68   SI 2011/704, reg 22(2).
69   Welsh Assembly Government, *Putting Things Right – Guidance on dealing with concerns about the NHS from 1 April 2011* (Version 3, November 2013), para 6.24.
70   Welsh Assembly Government, *Putting Things Right – Guidance on dealing with concerns about the NHS from 1 April 2011* (Version 3, November 2013), paras 44.30.
71   SI 2011/704, reg 22(4); and Welsh Assembly Government, *Putting Things Right – Guidance on dealing with concerns about the NHS from 1 April 2011* (Version 3, April 2013), para 6.24.
72   Welsh Assembly Government, *Putting Things Right – Guidance on dealing with concerns about the NHS from 1 April 2011* (Version 3, November 2013), para 6.26.

the concern has been resolved.[73] If the offer of a discussion is refused by the complainant/representative, the Responsible Body must determine how to manage the concern and inform the complainant/representative about the proposed action plan, including details about the availability of advocacy and support services.[74]

If a concern has been raised about a primary care provider (by a complainant/representative directly or by the primary care provider forwarding on a concern) to a Local Health Board, the Local Health Board must consider whether it or the primary care provider is in the best position to investigate.[75] Once the Local Health Board has decided that it will conduct the investigation, it will send an acknowledgement letter.[76] If the Local Health Board decides that it is more appropriate for the primary care provider to investigate, it will inform the complainant/representative and the primary care provider.[77]

Effect of a conditional fee agreement or insurance premium

If it is apparent to the Responsible Body when they receive a concern that the patient has entered into a conditional fee agreement or insurance premium, the Guidance indicates that they must liaise with Legal and Risk Services immediately, which will support them in dealing with a concern.[78]

Part 5 of the Regulations: Investigation of concern

Obtaining medical records and consent

In most cases, medical records will be required in order for the concern to be investigated; and Appendix H to the Guidance sets out information about the circumstances in which consent is required. Where a patient raises a concern, he is deemed to have given implied consent to the investigation.[79] This principle applies if a concern is raised by a representative who proves that they are legally entitled to act for the patient/service user.[80] However, the patient/representative may refuse access to their records. If the Responsible Body judges that the concern is not sufficiently serious to merit an investigation without access to the medical records, the concern will not be investigated.[81]

---

73 Welsh Assembly Government, *Putting Things Right – Guidance on dealing with concerns about the NHS from 1 April 2011* (Version 1, April 2011), para 6.27.
74 SI 2011/704, reg 22(4).
75 SI 2011/704, regs 19(1) and 20(1).
76 SI 2011/704, reg 22(1).
77 SI 2011/704, reg 21(2).
78 Welsh Assembly Government, *Putting Things Right – Guidance on dealing with concerns about the NHS from 1 April 2011* (Version 3, November 2013), para 14.3.
79 Welsh Assembly Government, *Putting Things Right – Guidance on dealing with concerns about the NHS from 1 April 2011* (Version 3, November 2013), para 6.36.
80 Welsh Assembly Government, *Putting Things Right – Guidance on dealing with concerns about the NHS from 1 April 2011* (Version 3, November 2013), para 6.36.
81 Welsh Assembly Government, *Putting Things Right – Guidance on dealing with concerns about the NHS from 1 April 2011* (Version 3, November 2013), para 6.39.

Grading the concern

Once the medical records/other records have been obtained, the concern will be graded by the Responsible Body in terms of severity.[82] This will determine the level and scope of the investigation[83] as all investigations are required to be proportionate to the severity of the concern.[84] In addition, grading determines the number and knowledge/competency of the investigators.[85] The aim of the grading framework is to promote a consistent approach across NHS Wales. Appendix I of the Guidance sets out five grades of concern. It is a framework based on a risk matrix developed by the Patient Safety Agency used to assess and manage risks and incidents.[86]

- *Grade 1 – no harm:* where the potential for qualifying liability and redress is 'highly unlikely'. Examples include a patient fall, where there is no harm or time off work, a delay in an outpatient appointment with no adverse health consequences; and difficulty in parking nearby.
- *Grade 2 – low harm:* where the potential to qualifying liability/ redress is 'unlikely'. Examples include concerns regarding care and treatment which span a number of different aspects/specialities; a patient fall requiring treatment; concerns involving a single failure to meet internal standards with minor implications for patient safety and requiring time off work of three days.
- *Grade 3 – moderate harm:* where the potential for qualifying liability/ redress is 'possible in some cases'. Examples include clinical/process issues that have resulted in avoidable, semi-permanent injury or impairment of health or damage that requires intervention; a RIDDOR reportable incident; moderate patient safety implications and requiring time off work for four to 14 days.
- *Grade 4 – severe harm:* where the potential for qualifying liability/ redress is 'likely in many cases'. Examples include clinical/process issues that have resulted in avoidable, semi-permanent injury or impairment of health or damage leading to incapacity or disability; concerns outlining non-compliance with national standards with significant risk to patient safety; a RIDDOR reportable incident and requiring time off work of more than 14 days.
- *Grade 5 – death:* where the potential for qualifying liability and redress is 'very likely'. Examples include concerns leading to unexpected death, multiple harm or irreversible health effects; concerns outlining gross failure to meet national standards; and clinical/process issues that have resulted in avoidable, irrecoverable

---

82 Welsh Assembly Government, *Putting Things Right – Guidance on dealing with concerns about the NHS from 1 April 2011* (Version 3, November 2013), para 6.49.
83 Welsh Assembly Government, *Putting Things Right – Guidance on dealing with concerns about the NHS from 1 April 2011* (Version 3, November 2013), para 6.49.
84 Welsh Assembly Government, *Putting Things Right – Guidance on dealing with concerns about the NHS from 1 April 2011* (Version 3, November 2013), para 6.49.
85 Welsh Assembly Government, *Putting Things Right – Guidance on dealing with concerns about the NHS from 1 April 2011* (Version 3, November 2013), paras 6.50.
86 Welsh Assembly Government, *Putting Things Right – Guidance on dealing with concerns about the NHS from 1 April 2011* (Version 3, November 2013), Appendix I.

injury or impairment of health, having a lifelong adverse effect on lifestyle, quality of life, physical and mental wellbeing.[87]

The website Patient Safety Wales includes information on grading and learning lessons from concerns, and can be accessed online.[88]

Investigation: reg 23

Regulation 23 is the key provision in terms of investigating a concern. The Regulations provide that concerns must be investigated in the most appropriate, efficient and effective way.[89] Regulation 23 includes a list of matters that Responsible Bodies must have regard during the investigation. The issues include the involvement of the complainant/ representative in the investigation; whether independent or other advice is required; and whether the concern can be resolved by ADR. Where the Responsible Body is a Welsh NHS body (but not primary care providers or independent providers) and the concern includes an allegation of harm that has or may have been caused, the Welsh NHS body is under a duty to consider whether there is any qualifying liability in negligence.

Appendix P of the Guidance sets out an 'investigation checklist' for the investigator to follow; including an instruction to copy only records that are relevant to the concern; identifying the healthcare professionals who provided the care and/or treatment; and considering whether there is any merit in obtaining a report on breach of duty and/or causation and, condition and prognosis. The investigators are encouraged to use various tools such as chronologies; the '5 Whys' and other investigation tools provide by the Patient Safety Wales website[90] to investigate the concern, and to fulfil the intention to 'investigate once, investigate well'.[91] Responsible Bodies must also consider whether the concern raises issues requiring a referral to other bodies, including the Welsh Government (serious incidents); professional bodies, such as the General Medical Council or Nursing and Midwifery Council; the Healthcare Inspectorate Wales; the Health and Safety Executive (RIDDOR); the Medicines Healthcare and Regulatory Agency; the Information Commissioners Office; the Police; HM Coroner; and the Local Children's Safeguarding Board.[92]

Independent expert advice

Investigators will be able to obtain independent medical or other advice.[93] At the investigation stage, that advice is limited to:

---

87 Welsh Assembly Government, *Putting Things Right – Guidance on dealing with concerns about the NHS from 1 April 2011* (Version 3, November 2013), pp 150–151.
88 See   http://www.patientsafety.wales.nhs.uk/sitesplus/documents/1104/How%20to%20 learn%20lessons%20from%20concerns22.pdf.
89 SI 2011/704, reg 23(1).
90 See   http://www.patientsafety.wales.nhs.uk/sitesplus/documents/1104/How%20to%20 learn%20lessons%20from%20concerns22.pdf.
91 Welsh Assembly Government, *Putting Things Right – Guidance on dealing with concerns about the NHS from 1 April 2011* (Version 3, November 2013), para 6.52.
92 Welsh Assembly Government, *Putting Things Right – Guidance on dealing with concerns about the NHS from 1 April 2011* (Version 3, November 2013), para 6.69.
93 SI 2011/704, reg 23(1)(e).

1 obtaining a second opinion to aid a patient's understanding of their own care, or to identify any other issues that should be explored in terms of the provision of care and treatment;

2 where an allegation of harm has been made, and where a Welsh NHS body is unable to determine if there is a qualifying liability in negligence, an advice dealing with breach of duty and/or causation'.[94]

By this stage, patients and service users are still not entitled to legal advice paid for by the Responsible Body, or to jointly instruct an expert unless the redress arrangements are triggered. A suggestion raised in the consultation was that legal advice should be available to the complainant/representative at an early stage. However, the Welsh Assembly Government replied that this would be disproportionate and increase costs. Independent medical experts can only be commissioned from a database held by the Legal & Risk Services (redress@wales. nhs.uk).[95] The Guidance includes general terms and conditions that are applicable to all independent expert advisors (Appendix K of the Guidance), although additional terms and conditions may be agreed.[96] A template letter of instruction is included in Appendix J of the Guidance.

Duty to consider whether there might be any qualifying liability in tort

Where a concern includes an allegation of harm that has or may have been caused, a Welsh NHS body is under a duty to consider the likelihood of any qualifying liability in negligence,[97] and may obtain expert evidence on breach of duty and causation to assist in this determination. This requirement does not apply to primary care providers or independent providers, unless the primary care practitioner is employed within a Health Board managed practice. The threshold to considering liability is that harm has or may have been caused. It is a low threshold; there is no requirement that harm was probably caused. The Regulations and Guidance do not provide any definition of 'harm'.

'Qualifying liability' is defined as:

> liability in tort owed in respect of, or consequent upon, personal injury or loss arising out of or in connection with breach of a duty of care owed to any person in connection with the diagnosis of illness, or in the care or treatment of any patient:
>
> (a) in consequence of any act or omission by a healthcare professional; and
>
> (b) which arises in connection with the provision of qualifying services.[98]

Therefore, qualifying liability is the traditional fault-based system which was criticised in the consultation phase.[99]

---

94 Welsh Assembly Government, *Putting Things Right – Guidance on dealing with concerns about the NHS from 1 April 2011* (Version 3, November 2013), para 6.57.

95 Welsh Assembly Government, *Putting Things Right – Guidance on dealing with concerns about the NHS from 1 April 2011* (Version 3, November 2013), para 6.58.

96 Welsh Assembly Government, *Putting Things Right – Guidance on dealing with concerns about the NHS from 1 April 2011* (Version 3, November 2013), Appendix K.

97 SI 2011/704, reg 23(1)(i).

98 SI 2011/704, reg 2(1).

99 AvMA (Response to Welsh Assembly Consultation on Proposed NHS Redress (Wales) Measure September 2007). AvMA proposed an 'avoidability test' as opposed to a fault or no-fault based system to determine eligibly for redress.

In cases where harm was alleged, but the Welsh NHS body determines that there is no qualifying liability, it must respond to the complainant/ representative denying any liability and provide reasons for that decision.[100] In addition, it must provide a Final Response under reg 24.[101]

In cases where harm was alleged but damages would exceed £25,000, the Welsh NHS body must issue a Final Response under reg 24, explaining that the quantum of any potential claim arising out of the concern exceeds the financial threshold in the Regulations and so the redress arrangement under Part 6 of the Regulations will not be entered into.[102]

The Guidance acknowledges that it can be difficult at the beginning of an investigation under reg 23 to be certain about the financial value of the claim. Therefore, it will be inevitable that some cases that proceed down the redress route (because it was originally considered that if liability was proved the value would be less that £25,000) transpire on investigation to exceed £25,000. In such cases, an offer of settlement can be made outside the Regulations;[103] the Regulations are silent on the limit the amount of compensation that might be paid in such circumstances. An offer made outside the Regulations must be approached with some caution, as the provisions for paid legal and medical advice do not apply. The Guidelines address this issue as follows:

> Welsh NHS bodies might at this stage, and in the spirit of the Regulations, consider offering to pay the patient's legal costs associated with obtaining advice on any such out of court settlement. However, there is no obligation for them to do so.[104]

In cases where a qualifying liability exists or may exist, and qualifying liability would attract a damages award of £25,000 or less, the concern requires further consideration. The Welsh NHS body must issue an Interim Response under regulation 26, and is under a duty to consider redress.[105]

Following an investigation under regulation 23 where a qualifying liability exists or may exist and the complainant is seeking redress, he is entitled to legal advice.[106] The legal advice must be obtained from firms of solicitors with recognised expertise in clinical negligence, for example, a partner or employee who is a member of the Law Society Clinical Negligence Panel or the AvMA Clinical Negligence Panel.[107] The legal advice is funded by the Welsh NHS body[108] and may be obtained in relation to the joint instruction of medical experts, including clarification of issues arising in their reports; an offer of redress; the refusal to make an offer of redress; and any settlement agreement that is proposed.[109] Appendix O

---

100 SI 2011/704, reg 24(2).
101 SI 2011/704, reg 24(1).
102 Welsh Assembly Government, *Putting Things Right – Guidance on dealing with concerns about the NHS from 1 April 2011* (Version 3, November 2013), para 6.73.
103 SI 2011/704, reg 29(3).
104 Welsh Assembly Government, *Putting Things Right – Guidance on dealing with concerns about the NHS from 1 April 2011* (Version 3, November 2013), para 7.35.
105 SI 2011/704, reg 25(1).
106 SI 2011/704, reg 32(1).
107 SI 2011/704, reg 32(2).
108 SI 2011/704, reg 32(4).
109 SI 2011/704, reg 32(3)(a)–(d).

of the Guidance provides the legal fees framework, and includes capped hourly rates and fixed fees. Any experts instructed at this stage must be instructed as a joint expert by the complainant/representative and the Welsh NHS body.[110] Expert evidence can be obtained on breach of duty, causation, condition and prognosis and/or quantum. The cost of obtaining medical evidence must be paid for by the Welsh NHS body.[111]

Response from the Responsible Body to the complainant / representative

There are two written reports that can be made in response to a concern: an Interim Response issued under reg 26, which only applies to concerns raised against a Welsh NHS bodies where there is, or may be, a qualifying liability in tort; and a Final Response, issued under reg 24.

An Interim Response report is issued where a Welsh NHS body considers that there is or may be qualifying liability in tort and the financial compensation would be at or below the current limit of £25,000. The timeframe for issuing an Interim Response report is similar to the timeframe for a Final Response. An Interim Response report should be issued within 30 working days beginning on the day on which the concern was received.[112] If the Welsh NHS body cannot reply within this timeframe, it must notify the complainant/representative, providing reasons for the delay. It must send the response as soon as reasonably practicable, and within six months beginning on the day on which the concern was received.[113] In exceptional circumstances, the written response report can be issued after six months. However, the complainant/representative must be informed about the reason for the delay and given an expected date for the report.[114] Appendix N of the Guidance includes an Interim Report template.[115]

The Interim Response report must include a summary of the nature and substance of the concern; explain the investigation, include relevant medical records (if appropriate), the reasons that there is or might be qualifying liability, an explanation of how to access legal advice without charge, the availability of advocacy and support services, the process for considering liability and redress, and offer to discuss the response to the concerns with the executive officer or his nominated representative.[116]

A Final Response report is issued by all Responsible Bodies, but in the case of Welsh NHS bodies, a final response will only be issued if there is no qualifying liability in tort to which the redress arrangements could apply. The timeframe is limited, and a Final Response report should be issued within 30 working days, beginning on the day on which the concern was received.[117] If the Responsible Body cannot reply within this timeframe, it must notify the complainant/representative, providing reasons for

---

110 SI 2011/704, reg 32(1)(b).
111 Welsh Assembly Government, *Putting Things Right – Guidance on dealing with concerns about the NHS from 1 April 2011* (Version 3, November 2013), para 6.57.
112 SI 2011/704, reg 26(2).
113 SI 2011/704, reg 26(3).
114 SI 2011/704, reg 26(4).
115 Welsh Assembly Government, *Putting Things Right – Guidance on dealing with concerns about the NHS from 1 April 2011* (Version 3, November 2013), p 164.
116 SI 2011/704, reg 26(1).
117 SI 2011/704, reg 24(3).

the delay. It must send the response as soon as reasonably practicable, and within six months beginning on the day in which the concern was received.[118] In exceptional circumstances, the written response report can be issued after six months. However, the complainant/representative must be informed about the reason for the delay and given an expected date for the report.[119] The Final Response report is provided to the complainant/representative, except where the concern was raised by a third party, but only if it is reasonable to do so.[120] When the issue is a patient safety incident that was reported by a member of staff and the patient was not informed, a final written response must be sent to the appropriate committee.[121]

The Final Response report must include a summary of the nature and substance of the concern; explain the investigation; include relevant medical records (if appropriate); identify any actions taken as a result of the investigation; include an apology (if appropriate); and an offer to discuss the response to the concerns with the executive officer or his nominated representative.[122] The report must contain copies of any expert opinion obtained as part of the investigation;[123] and where there is no qualifying liability, a Welsh NHS body must give its reasons for reaching that conclusion.[124] Appendix M of the Guidance includes a Final Response report template.[125]

Part 6 of the Regulations: redress

If there is or may be a qualifying liability against a Welsh NHS body, it is under a duty to consider redress.[126] An offer of redress may be made by a Welsh NHS body where there is a qualifying liability in accordance with the Regulations.[127] Redress under the Regulations is wider than financial compensation, and reg 27 provides:

(1)   Redress under this Part comprises—
    (a)   an offer of compensation in satisfaction of any right to bring civil proceedings in respect of a qualifying liability;
    (b)   an explanation;
    (c)   a written apology; and
    (d)   a report on the action which has been, or will be, taken to prevent similar cases arising.
(2)   The compensation that may be offered in accordance with regulation 27(1)(a) can take the form of entry into a contract to provide care or treatment or of financial compensation, or both.

---

118 SI 2011/704, reg 24(4).
119 SI 2011/704, reg 24(5).
120 Welsh Assembly Government, *Putting Things Right – Guidance on dealing with concerns about the NHS from 1 April 2011* (Version 3, November 2013), para 5.7.
121 Welsh Assembly Government, *Putting Things Right – Guidance on dealing with concerns about the NHS from 1 April 2011* (Version 3, November 2013), para 6.77.
122 SI 2011/704, reg 24(1).
123 SI 2011/704, reg 24(1)(c).
124 SI 2011/704, reg 24(2).
125 Welsh Assembly Government, *Putting Things Right – Guidance on dealing with concerns about the NHS from 1 April 2011* (Version 3, November 2013), p 163.
126 SI 2011/704, reg 25(1).
127 SI 2011/704, reg 25(2).

Redress can be one or a combination of the above. There are no further details about a 'contract to provide care or treatment' in the Regulations. However, the Guidance states that remedial treatment would try to improve their condition, 'to restore them, as far as possible, to the position that they would have been in had the treatment complained of or negligent care not occurred'.[128]

The full Investigation Report

Where a complainant/representative is seeking redress, the findings of the investigation must be recorded in an Investigation Report.[129] Following the Interim Response report, the complainant/representative seeking redress will be provided with a copy of the full Investigation Report, which will include a copy of any medical evidence commissioned to determine liability and/or condition and prognosis, and a reasoned decision by the Welsh NHS body on qualifying liability.[130] However, the full Investigation Report need not be provided before an offer of redress; before a decision not to make an offer of redress is communicated; if the investigation of redress is terminated; or where the report contains information likely to cause the complainant significant harm or distress.[131]

Communication of a decision about redress

On the conclusion of the investigation, the Welsh NHS body must communicate its decision to either offer redress by way of compensation, care and/or treatment, or, if there is no qualifying liability, its decision not to make an offer.[132] The decision must be communicated to the complainant within 12 months of the date that the Welsh NHS body was notified of the concern.[133] In exceptional circumstances, where the Welsh NHS body is unable to make a decision within 12 months, the complainant/representative should be told in writing the reason for the delay and the expected date for the decision.[134]

The complainant/representative has six months to respond to the decision.[135] However, if the complainant/representative cannot respond within six months, they must write to the Welsh NHS body providing a reason for the delay. The time limit for response can be extended to nine months from the date of the offer/decision.[136] However, if no response is received the limitation period (which is suspended under reg 30) will start again.[137] When an offer of redress is accepted, the complaint/representative must sign a waiver of any right to bring civil proceedings in respect of the qualifying liability to which the settlement relates.[138]

128 Welsh Assembly Government, *Putting Things Right – Guidance on dealing with concerns about the NHS from 1 April 2011* (Version 3, November 2013), para 74.
129 SI 2011/704, reg 31(1).
130 SI 2011/704, reg 31(1), (2).
131 SI 2011/704, reg 31(4).
132 SI 2011/704, reg 33.
133 SI 2011/704, reg 31(4).
134 SI 2011/704, reg 33(a).
135 SI 2011/704, reg 33(b).
136 SI 2011/704, reg 33(d).
137 SI 2011/704, reg 30(3), (5).
138 SI 2011/704, reg 33(e).

The quantification of damages for redress

The financial limit of £25,000 includes both general and special damages.[139] The assessment of general damages for pain, suffering, and loss of amenity will be calculated on a common law basis,[140] and will be made in accordance with the tariff included at Appendix Q of the Guidance.[141] The stated aim is that this approach will lead to appropriate and consistent awards,[142] although it is accepted that individual factors will increase or decrease the awards.[143] Some tariff awards refer to the Joint Studies Board Guidelines (now the Judicial College Guidelines for the Assessment of General Damages in PI cases) and/or the criteria selected for the brackets is the same or similar. However, a comparison of the awards under the JC Guidelines and the All-Wales Tariff indicates that on multiple occasions the All-Wales tariff awards are lower.[144] Up-to-date figures can be obtained from the Legal & Risk Services.[145] However, it is unclear if the 10% uplift following *Simmons v Castle*[146] on general damages awards will be included.

The tariff also includes summaries of case law reports for some injuries, and the Guidance makes it clear that offers may be made above or below the case law examples.[147] The reported quantum cases include out of court settlements, which may be lower than court awards. The awards have been calculated to take account of inflation. The Guidance states that the awards will need to be updated to take account of inflationary increases,[148] but this has been done before publication of the Guidance in

---

139 SI 2011/704, Explanatory note; and Welsh Assembly Government, *Putting Things Right – Guidance on dealing with concerns about the NHS from 1 April 2011* (Version 1, April 2011), para 7.226.
140 SI 2011/704, reg 29(1), (4).
141 SI 2011/704, reg 29(1), (5).
142 Welsh Assembly Government, *Putting Things Right – Guidance on dealing with concerns about the NHS from 1 April 2011* (Version 3, November 2012), para 7.36.
143 Welsh Assembly Government, *Putting Things Right – Guidance on dealing with concerns about the NHS from 1 April 2011* (Version 3, November 2012), page 169.
144 For example:

JC Guidelines (14th edition)		All-Wales Tariff (2013)	
Serious injury to ring or middle finger (fractures or serious injury to tendons casing stiffness, deformity and permanent loss of grip or dexterity):	£13,080 –£14,330	Fracture or serious injuries to tendons causing stiffness, deformity, and permanent loss of gip or dexterity of ring or middle fingers.	
		Total loss of middle finger with be at top of bracket:	£8.000– £9,000
Total loss of the middle finger:	In the region of £13,710		

145 Welsh Assembly Government, *Putting Things Right – Guidance on dealing with concerns about the NHS from 1 April 2011* (Version 3, November 2013), p 169.
146 [2012] EWCA Civ 1039 and [2012] EWCA 1288.
147 Welsh Assembly Government, *Putting Things Right – Guidance on dealing with concerns about the NHS from 1 April 2011* (Version 3, November 2013), p 169.
148 Welsh Assembly Government, *Putting Things Right – Guidance on dealing with concerns about the NHS from 1 April 2011* (Version 3, November 2013), p 169.

November 2013, and therefore does not represent the up–to-date value of the awards at the date of publication.

Any claim for loss of earnings must be supported with evidence, such as wage slips, P60, etc.[149] A deduction will be made from the loss of earnings award for any relevant recoupable state benefits.[150] There is no mention of a claim for gratuitous care and assistance, but in principle, there is no reason why this cannot be included. However, there is no mention in the Guidance for offsetting any relevant benefits in relation to gratuitous care and assistance.

Court approval of settlement

Where the settlement agreement has been made on behalf of a child or a person who lacks capacity, the approval of the court will be required.[151] The Welsh NHS body must pay the reasonable legal costs of obtaining the approval of the court.[152]

Limitation

If an application for redress is made, the relevant limitation period under the Limitation Act 1980 for bringing a civil claim is suspended.[153] The start date is that date on which the initial concern which became an application for redress was received by the Welsh NHS body.[154] The date that the limitation period restarts is as follows:

1   where the Welsh NHS body considers after an investigation that there is no qualifying liability, the complainant/representative has nine calendar months from the date that the Welsh NHS body communicated its decision.[155] The intention is that the complainant and/or his legal adviser will have time to prepare and issue civil proceedings if they do not agree with the decision of the Welsh NHS body;[156]

2   where an offer of redress is made, the complaint/representative has up to nine calendar months to accept/reject an offer of financial compensation. After that nine months, limitation restarts;[157]

3   where court approval of a settlement is required, limitation is suspended until the date upon which the court approves the settlement.[158]

---

149 Welsh Assembly Government, *Putting Things Right – Guidance on dealing with concerns about the NHS from 1 April 2011* (Version 3, November 2013), para 7.27.
150 Welsh Assembly Government, *Putting Things Right – Guidance on dealing with concerns about the NHS from 1 April 2011* (Version 3, November 2013), para 7.25.
151 SI 2011/704, reg 33(f).
152 SI 2011/704, reg 33(g).
153 SI 2011/704, reg 30(1).
154 SI 2011/704, reg 30(2)(a).
155 SI 2011/704, reg 30(5).
156 Welsh Assembly Government, *Putting Things Right – Guidance on dealing with concerns about the NHS from 1 April 2011* (Version 3, November 2013), para 7.12.
157 SI 2011/704, reg 30(3).
158 SI 2011/704, reg 30(4).

*Cross border arrangements of the handling and investigation concerns
including redress*

The Regulations provide cross border arrangements for concerns
about treatment and care provided on behalf of the NHS in Wales by
organisations outside Wales. The concern should be handled in accordance
with the relevant complaints procedure that applies to the organisation
in question. If, during the investigation, a qualifying liability in tort exists
or may exist, then the redress provisions in Pt 7 of the Regulations may
apply. The Guidance notes that care is not routinely commissioned by
Welsh NHS bodies from NHS bodies in Scotland and Northern Ireland.[159]

---

159 Welsh Assembly Government, *Putting Things Right – Guidance on dealing with
concerns about the NHS from 1 April 2011* (Version 3, November 2013), para 10.4.

Part Five

Chapter 26

Funding

Nick Knowles

Without adequate funding there can be no access to justice for the victim of a medical 'accident'. In recent years there has been an enormous amount of activity in this crucial area for the clinical negligence practitioner.

Funding and costs go hand in hand. Together they determine the bigger picture, the financial context in which the specialist practitioner must operate.

At the present time, as can be seen below, the dust is even now still settling after yet another period of tumultuous flux and there will undoubtedly always be further changes for the practitioner to contend with in this politically-sensitive area of work.

Medical 'accidents' generate high emotions. The client has suffered a violation of mind and body and can naturally be demanding, sometimes to the point of obsession. The defendant affects outrage that the integrity of the medical profession is at stake and goes to extreme lengths to defeat the claim. The substantive law leaves it to the medical profession, or those clinicians who are prepared to spend the time in court, to determine whether there is a breach and causation. Experts have to be constantly chased to stick to the timetable and to answer the question. Their views determine the success or failure of the claim but they can always change their mind. The more serious the claim, the harder it will be fought, not only to the doors of the court but later also to the doors of the Senior Court Costs Office, invariably following preparation of a detailed bill of costs.

Although much of the work is necessarily done pro bono and some is legally aided, the practitioner is pilloried in the press as a 'fat cat lawyer' and 'ambulance chaser', a prime beneficiary of the compensation culture which is mistakenly believed to exist in this field.

Unless they or their loved ones have suffered a medical 'accident', members of the public will display surprise, even disgust that claims should be brought against the NHS, a public body paid to do good. Fanned by the turgid media headlines, the perception is that the larger the compensation paid out, the more the squeeze on NHS resources to provide proper care for the public.

The myriad tensions generated by medical 'accidents', the strong feelings concerned, but more importantly the financial ramifications, the vagaries of the economic climate, and crucially the political agenda of the changing governments (all of them driven to reduce public expenditure), all of these things have accounted for the constant tinkering in recent times with the methods by which clinical negligence funding is provided.

The specialist practice has to keep abreast of all these nuances and upheavals if it is to remain in business so as to be able to pursue justice for the victims of medical 'accidents'.

It is particularly because of this great uncertainty and the enormity of the changes that it will be of some benefit to take a brief look back at what has been happening in the past as this may enable some sense to be made out of the present and of what the future holds in store.

To the extent that there may still be older cases yet to enter the costs process, (and quite legitimately in clinical negligence where a claim might be held up, say, for the better prognosis of a child), the rules of earlier funding schemes could still be relevant.

HISTORICAL BACKGROUND

The legislation for the welfare state created after the Second World War was concerned with its four pillars of health, housing, social security and education.

Access to justice was a younger sibling, having its birth in the report of the cross-party Rushcliffe Committee published in 1945 which proposed a system of legal aid providing for 'those of slender means and resources'.

Whereas the proposals for the creation of the National Health Service were met with fierce opposition from the medical profession, the legal aid scheme was embraced by the lawyers. The Legal Aid and Advice Act 1949 set up a scheme funded by the state but administered by the Law Society.

In contrast to the proposed status of lawyers in the legal scheme, however, and to be fair to the doctors, the NHS scheme proposed that they should become employees of the state.

It was not until 1989 that the Legal Aid Board took over control of legal aid from the Law Society. By this stage the increasing costs of the legal aid service was becoming an issue for all the political parties to deal with. The costs of criminal work (involving the liberty of the individual and the right to a fair trial) was taking up an increasingly larger share of the legal aid budget.

Eventually legal aid became available only to the poorer of society and from 1994 much reduced 'prescribed rates' were introduced for unsuccessful civil cases.

The Courts and Legal Services Act 1990 first introduced the startling concept of the conditional fee agreement into this jurisdiction. Lawyers were permitted to conduct cases on the basis that they would take an uplift to their fees out of any damages recovered for the client, but if the case was not successful they would get nothing. This was a revolutionary idea and completely contrary to the traditional ethos of the legal profession which did not permit lawyers to be financially interested in the outcome of a case (at least, not openly). The lawyer became under pressure to get a settlement.

However, few people foresaw the vigour with which the legal aid system would be attacked by Lord Mackay's successor, the Labour Lord Irvine, upon taking office in 1997. As a result, legal aid for personal injury claims became virtually unobtainable. That would also have been the fate of clinical negligence claims, had he not been forced to accept that to abolish legal aid would deprive medical accident victims of access to justice because such claims require significant expenditure on investigation in order to find out whether there is a viable claim. The risks involved in the new conditional fee system would not provide adequate means of funding for the work concerned in such front-loaded cases. These legal aid reforms introduced by the Access to Justice Act 1999 and its supporting legislation required solicitor firms wishing to undertake such category of work to obtain a 'clinical negligence' franchise. In order to obtain such a franchise each firm had to have a category supervisor who belonged to one of the two specialist panels of clinical negligence solicitors. One panel is run by the Law Society (now by the SRA) and the other is administered by AvMA[1] (then 'AVMA'), the charity which has done so much to support medical accident victims and to empower them, if need be, to litigate successfully for compensation through the courts.

It has to be said that some form of accreditation was necessary for solicitors (and remains necessary for barristers). History is full of horror stories of cases abandoned, lost or simply left to wither because of the lack of experience, enthusiasm and effort of the lawyers involved. So the need for specialist lawyers alone to handle clinical negligence cases was clear.

What had previously been known as 'medical negligence' thereafter generally became known as 'clinical negligence' even outside of legal aid circles. One story was that the medical profession was irked that doctors should be labelled generally as the tortfeasors in the provision of healthcare when other non-medical providers could also be at fault. Cynics wondered whether the new tag could serve to confuse potential claimants amongst members of the public.

It is something of a coincidence that a lot of these changes were going on at the same time as the Woolf reforms were implemented following his report 'Access to Justice' published in 1997. These far-reaching procedural changes were intended to ameliorate the expense and delays of litigation. (It is arguable whether the reforms have had a beneficial effect on the reduction of costs and indeed in some areas these have resulted in an increase in the costs involved. How many claims have successfully settled at an advanced stage post-issue despite the initial service of robustly defensive Pre-action Protocol letters of response! Generally, however, greater case management by the courts has appreciably speeded up the litigation process and other reforms proposed by Lord Woolf have undoubtedly assisted in the fairer disposal of claims.

In 2003, the Chief Medical Officer, Professor Sir Liam Donaldson, published his report *Making amends: A consultation paper setting out proposals for reforming the approach to clinical negligence in the NHS*. Practitioners in this field anxiously awaited its publication during the two long years of the consultation period, particularly as one of the proposals was a no-fault compensation scheme. They need not have worried. The suggestion of such a scheme was firmly dismissed. Given that a staggering proportion of medical untoward incidents never see the light of day and, on the basis of a duty to disclose all incidents, the scheme would be massively and prohibitively costly. Furthermore, to be affordable any compensation paid would probably not meet the needs of the severely injured patient, difficult issues of causation might also arise even with the removal of 'fault' and, finally, such a scheme would not be conducive to the need to learn from past mistakes (a priority for the improvement of patient care).

The report made various recommendations, the most important of which was the NHS Redress Scheme whereby redress was to involve investigation and an explanation of the incident, the provision of a package of care where needed and payments for pain and suffering and expenses and for any care or treatment which the NHS could not provide. Any avoidable harm caused by serious shortcomings in NHS care would be eligible for payments in this way up to a maximum of £30,000. Such a scheme, intended to be closely aligned to changes to the NHS Complaints Procedure, got as far as the enactment of the NHS Redress Act 2006. (As late as July 2009, the House of Commons Select Committee on Health expressed concern about the absence of the regulations which have yet to be drawn up to implement the scheme.)

In recognition of the particular difficulties in pursuing birth injury claims Sir Liam also proposed a separate redress scheme for compensation for these, effectively on a no-fault basis.

Also in line with another of Sir Liam's recommendations, the current NHS Complaints Procedure, (dealt with in Chapter 3), was altered so that the patient's complaint would still be investigated, notwithstanding that the patient intended also to seek compensation through the courts. As is covered in Chapter 25 on Wales the NHS complaints procedure in Wales was replaced in 2008 by its own NHS redress measure. This pilot scheme was subsequently substantively enacted in Wales in April 2010 known as the 'Putting Things Right' scheme intended to provide quick, proportionate and fair resolution of simple, low value clinical negligence claims up to £25,000.

THE JACKSON REPORT

Later in December 2008, the then Master of the Rolls, Sir Anthony Clarke, commissioned Lord Justice Jackson to 'review the rules and principles governing the costs of civil litigation and to make recommendations in order to promote access to justice at proportionate cost'. His preliminary report (663 pages long) was published in May 2009 and after very wide consultation with all concerned. His (monumental) *Review of civil litigation costs: final report* (557 pages long) was published on 14 January 2010.

Jackson looked at the amount of litigation, all the methods of funding, those discussed below, as well as third-party funding, contingency legal aid funds (CLAFs) and supplementary legal aid schemes (SLASs), contingency fees (in other jurisdictions) and fixed costs. He devoted 70 pages to personal injuries litigation and discussed other specific types of litigation, including clinical negligence. He looked at methods of controlling costs and the procedures, including the assessment of costs.

What Jackson termed his 'major' recommendations and those of particular relevance to the funding of clinical negligence work included the irrecoverability of success fees and after the event (ATE) premiums from unsuccessful defendants.

Jackson considered that conditional fee agreements (CFAs) were the major contributors to disproportionate costs in civil litigation in England and Wales, the two key drivers being the lawyer's success fee and the ATE insurance premium. Their irrecoverability, he felt, would lead to significant savings, whilst providing access to justice. Clients could still enter into 'no win, no fee' agreements, but they would have to bear the success fees, payable likely out of their damages.

To ensure proper compensation and that the damages would not be substantially eaten into by the legal fees, Jackson recommended that general damages be increased by 10% and that the maximum amount of damages that lawyers might deduct for success fees be capped at 25% (excluding any damages for future care or future losses). Jackson felt that in the majority of cases, successful claimants should be no worse off than under the current regime.

Another counter-balance for the claimant recommended by Jackson were enhanced rewards for claimants who beat their Part 36 offers who should receive a 10% uplift on total damages.

ATE insurance premiums, Jackson felt, added considerably to the costs of litigation, which could be reduced by taking away the need for insurance. He recommended the introduction of qualified one way costs shifting so that the claimant would not have to pay the defendant's costs if the claim was unsuccessful but the defendant would have to pay the claimant's costs if it was successful. However, a different costs order might be appropriate where conduct or financial resources justified this.

Jackson also recommended that contingency fee agreements for contentious business (damages-based agreements) should be legitimised. Under such agreements, the lawyer is only be paid where the client's case succeeds and on the basis of a percentage of the sum awarded or agreed. However, Jackson recommended that the losing party should only be responsible for the normal between the parties costs and the balance of the fee should be paid by the winning party (with a similar 25% cap applying in personal injury cases as in CFAs). He further recommended that the terms of contingency fee agreements should be regulated.

THE IMPLEMENTATION OF JACKSON

As is set out later in this chapter, Jackson's 'major' proposals were broadly implemented by the Legal Aid, Sentencing and Punishment of Offenders Act 2012 (LASPOA 2012).This provided for: the abolition of legal aid for clinical negligence (save for claims relating to serious birth injury); the abolition of referral fees in personal injury cases; the transfer of payment of success fees from the losing opponent to the client, subject to a cap; the irrecoverability of the ATE premium (save for a modest concession in clinical negligence cases); the ability to use damages-based agreements in clinical negligence claims.

LASPOA 2012 was brought into effect on 1 April 2013.

Jackson's other proposals relevant to clinical negligence claims and which did not require primary legislation were mainly implemented by new or amended Civil Procedure Rules. These included, a new test for proportionality, the introduction of qualified one way costs shifting ('QOCS'), the changes to claimant Part 36 offers, and other measures, such as, the docketing of clinical negligence cases, the introduction of costs budgeting and the 'hot-tubbing' of expert evidence.

The 10% increase in general damages was achieved through the two decisions of the Court of Appeal in late 2012 in the case of *Simmons v Castle*.[1]

In the event, the recommendations put forward by Jackson which were not introduced included the abolition of the indemnity principle (although worn away in some respects) and the retention of legal aid (save for clinical negligence claims for injuries suffered at birth).

THE FUNDING OPTIONS

One of the most important decisions facing a solicitor in relation to any potential client is whether to take on their case at all and funding considerations will be pre-eminent in the decision-making process.

It is of extreme importance to both solicitor and client that for any given claim the correct method of funding is chosen. Obviously the means of funding have to be affordable and appropriate for the client, but from the solicitor's perspective the professional rules of conduct impose a comprehensive duty to fully advise the client as to the funding options available and as to the nature and extent of the costs involved to the client.

In addition, however, the solicitor has to ensure that any claim is profitably undertaken and in particular that its loss would not have any untoward implications for the firm's practice. Even if a claim is successful, the solicitor may well have to go through a lengthy costs assessment process before the final bill can be reckoned. The defendant will be quick to pounce on any solicitor and own client retainer problems. The paying party's liability is to reimburse the winning party only in respect of the latter's liability for costs, ('the indemnity principle', which is still in force despite increasing objection). If the winning party has no liability for costs then there is nothing for the losing party to indemnify.

The Solicitors Regulation Authority (SRA) issued a new Handbook for solicitors implemented on 6 October 2011. Version 21 was published on 6 December 2018. The Code of Conduct contained in the Handbook reflected the SRA's fresh, flexible approach to regulation which was outcome-focussed and risk-based. The emphasis is on solicitors running their businesses properly and in a way that best suits the needs of their particular clients.

There are ten all-pervasive Principles which set out the fundamental ethical and professional standards which are expected of solicitors. There are the mandatory outcomes which must be achieved so as to comply with the principles and to provide a proper standard of service for the benefit of the clients and the general public. These outcomes are supplemented by indicative behaviours which, although not mandatory, assist in assessing whether an outcome has been achieved.

The outcomes are expressed in general terms and those particularly relevant to funding include:

---

1   [2012] EWCA Civ 1288, [2013] 1 WLR 1239.

O (1.6)   you only enter into fee agreements with your clients that are legal, and which you consider are suitable for the client's needs and take account of the client's best interests;

O (1.12) clients are in a position to make informed decisions about the services they need, how their matter will be handled and the options available to them;

O (1.13) clients receive the best possible information, both at the time of engagement and when appropriate as their matter progresses, about the likely overall cost of their matter.

Relevant indicative behaviours include under the following headings:

Dealing with the client's matter
IB (1.4)   explaining any arrangements, such as fee sharing or referral arrangements, which are relevant to the client's instructions;

IB (1.5)   explaining any limitations or conditions on what you can do for the client, for example, because of the way the client's matter is funded;

Fee arrangements with your client
IB (1.13) discussing whether the potential outcomes of the client's matter are likely to justify the expense or risk involved, including any risk of having to pay someone else's legal fees;

IB (1.14) clearly explaining your fees and if and when they are likely to change;

IB (1.15) warning about any other payments for which the client may be responsible;

IB (1.16) discussing how the client will pay, including whether public funding may be available, whether the client has insurance that might cover the fees, and whether the fees may be paid by someone else such as a trade union;

IB (1.17) where you are acting for a client under a fee arrangement governed by statute, such as a conditional fee agreement, giving the client all relevant information relating to that arrangement;

IB (1.18) where you are acting for a publicly funded client, explaining how their publicly funded status affects the costs;

IB (1.19) providing the information in a clear and accessible form which is appropriate to the needs and circumstances of the client;

IB (1.20) where you receive a financial benefit as a result of acting for a client, either:
   (a) paying it to the client;
   (b) offsetting it against your fees; or
   (c) keeping it only where you can justify keeping it, you have told the client the amount of the benefit (or an approximation if you do not know the exact amount) and the client has agreed that you can keep it;

IB (1.21) ensuring that disbursements included in your bill reflect the actual amounts spent or to be spent on behalf of the client.

A specific example of how not to achieve the outcomes and therefore not to comply with the principles is as follows:

Accepting and refusing instructions
IB (1.27) entering into unlawful fee arrangements such as unlawful contingency fee.

This all having been said, practitioners should be aware that the SRA Handbook will be replaced on 25 November 2019 by the SRA Standards and Regulations. Practitioners are urged to prepare for the changes in good time beforehand as there will apparently be an immediate seamless transition from old to new and there will be no transitional honeymoon period for compliance.

The different methods of funding a claim are as follows:

1   private retainer;
2   legal expense insurance (LEI);
3   public funding (legal aid);
4   conditional fee agreement (CFA);
5   damages-based agreements (contingency fees).

There are some instances where a client has the availability of funding through his employment or as a member of an organisation such as a trade union, but these are not very common.

PRIVATE RETAINER

As even a fairly straightforward clinical negligence claim might cost upwards of something in the order of £50,000 to litigate to trial, this is rarely chosen by clients as a method of funding. Few would choose to take that risk and substantially compound their losses. It is more commonly used in limited aspects of the litigation process, for instance, for costs of investigation, often only for disbursements, where the merits of a claim are very uncertain in the absence of specific expert advice. Sometimes it might be used, where appropriate, for representation at an inquest, which can be a useful vehicle for the investigation of the merits of a claim, but always depending, of course, upon the means of the client.

The introduction of QOCS has done away with the added risk for the clinical negligence claimant of having to pay the costs of the successful defendant.

LEGAL EXPENSE INSURANCE

In his final report Jackson recommended that the public should be encouraged to take out legal expense insurance (or before the event insurance or 'BTE') as a beneficial method of funding litigation.

However, the market in BTE appears to have since declined, perhaps because householders have preferred to minimise the cost of their insurance premiums and the introduction of QOCS has made it less important. Also the LASPOA 2012 ban on referral fees may have reduced the financial incentive for the insurance industry to offer such insurance.

Nevertheless, BTE can still provide useful back-up cover for a claimant's liability for disbursements or adverse interlocutory or CPR Part 36 costs. It can also fund the interim payment of disbursements throughout the case (and even, from the solicitors' perspective, profit costs under some policies).

It is certainly a method of funding which needs to be explored, discussed and decided upon with the client. Pursuant to the decision of the Court of Appeal in *Sarwar v Alam*[2] it is (still) an important part of the initial interview with all clients that every policy of insurance which they own

---

2   [2001] EWCA Civ 1401.

is investigated for the availability of legal expenses cover. It is an add-on feature of insurance of which clients may be unaware.

Legal expense cover is often to be found in household contents policies, car insurance (though it is rare for the legal costs covered to be more than those relating to a road traffic accident) and sometimes in banking and credit card agreements.

The period of cover needs to be checked to ensure that the negligence occurred within that time frame, and there is often a stringent time limit for reporting as a precondition of the insurer's liability to indemnify under the policy. BTE policies often provide for periods of reporting of between 90 and 180 days after the insured knew or ought of have known of the incident giving rise to the claim.

Sometimes clinical negligence claims are wholly excluded from legal expense cover. In other policies, however, death or bodily injury only is covered and there may be specifically excluded 'any illness or bodily injury which happens gradually or is not caused by a specific or sudden event'. This wording would apparently exclude from cover many claims of clinical negligence which involve a delay in the diagnosis and treatment of a medical condition which occurs over a period of probably anything longer than 24 hours.

There will also be a maximum indemnity under the policy, frequently of £50,000 but sometimes of £100,000, which is to cover both the practitioner's and the opponent's costs. The insurer will often seek also to impose a much smaller 'authorised costs limit'. This will probably be unrealistic in amount but sometimes the insurer seeks to impose such a limit even if it is not included as a term within the policy.

The policy will also require that the claim should at all times have reasonable prospects of success whilst it is on-going.

The solicitor must advise the client of the terms of the BTE and provide all necessary information in relation to all other funding options so that the client can make an informed decision as to which method or methods they wish to use. Such a decision in the context of BTE will invariably include deciding which solicitors should represent them.

In the case of a clinical negligence claim of more than little worth it may well be beneficial for the specialist practitioner to deal with it, subject to any necessary safeguarding of the client's liability for any costs shortfall, particularly if the limit of indemnity is insufficient to cover the client's potential liabilities at the end of the day. It may also be that the solicitor's special expertise is able to add significant value to the claim or would increase the chance of success in a difficult liability issue.

The free choice of the client to instruct whom he may under a BTE policy has been a particularly contentious issue throughout the years and the legal position is far from settled to the satisfaction of all concerned.

Even after the insurers agree to indemnify the client, often the specialist practitioner will be faced with the insistence of the insurer that if the client wishes to have the benefit of their policy the claim will have to be handled by a firm which is a member of their own panel of solicitors. (Prior to the abolition of referral fees some personal injury solicitors would pay a not insignificant fee for membership of an insurer's panel as a means of obtaining work in this increasingly competitive market.) It is often the case that the firm designated by the insurer does not have specialist clinical negligence expertise.

Confronted with this situation, the specialist practitioner will have to seek to persuade the insurer of the need for their special expertise and may well have to agree to abide by the insurer's terms in so far as they affect the practitioner.

The situation could be assisted by the solicitor offering the client a discounted CFA where there will be any shortfall in the indemnity in respect of the solicitor's costs. In this situation the CFA will provide for the solicitor's full hourly rate if the claim is successful but the lower discounted rates will apply if the case is not: this was approved by the Court of Appeal in *Gloucester County Council v Evans*.[3]

The client will, of course, have to give informed consent to such an arrangement, particularly if their damages are at risk of a deduction regarding any success fee or ATE insurance premium and where the BTE insurance would not have this effect. The funding advice would have to be very clear, comprehensive and well-documented.

Alternatively the solicitor might consider offering a CFA lite so that the client's liability is limited strictly to the amount recovered from their losing opponent. There is no win no fee if the claim fails but no liability by the client for costs or disbursements if the claim succeeds.

The right of freedom of choice of solicitor is enshrined in an EU Directive of 1987 put into UK law by the Insurance Companies (Legal Expenses Insurance) Regulations 1990.[4] Two European cases are quoted in support of such choice but are also distinguished. However, the current guidance from the Financial Ombudsman is clear that it is expected that the insurer would choose their solicitor to act 'in preparing the claim form and any other work needed to start the proceedings'. Only in exceptional cases would the insured be able to instruct their own solicitor up to this stage, otherwise the insured is only free to choose 'after legal proceedings have become necessary'.

However, one commentator relies on another EU case, *Nobile v DAS Rechtsschutz-Versicherungs AG*[5] as authority for the insured to choose their solicitor as early as 'the stage of notification of the claim ... or any instruction of a lawyer to assess the legal and factual situation'.

Once permitted to act the practitioner will find that there will invariably be tight reporting restrictions regarding the progress of the claim, sometimes required as often as once a month. All the costs involved in this work may well prove irrecoverable between the parties and it will not be funded by the insurer.

Often the insurer will discriminate between the panel member and the non-panel- member by imposing upon the latter, in comparison to the former, more stringent requirements in the terms of appointment.

It should never be forgotten, of course, that a contract of insurance is one of 'utmost faith' and as such any matter must be reported which any prudent insurer would wish to take into account in deciding whether or not to assume the risk or to continue covering the risk under the policy or upon what terms. The failure to report any such material matter will entitle the insurer to avoid the policy altogether.

---

3   [2008] EWCA Civ 21.
4   SI 1990/1159.
5   Case E-21/16.

It should also be remembered, however the insurer decides to word the policy, that the retainer for the legal work is still that between a solicitor and client in the usual way and the policy is simply to indemnify the client in respect of liability for the solicitor's costs.

The legal expense insurer expects not to have to pay anything under the policy if the case is won, save where any adverse costs have been ordered (where the risk for these particular costs was explicitly assumed by the insurer beforehand). The policy will not usually provide for the payment of interim profit costs but disbursements authorised beforehand can be met, although this is increasingly rare. Some insurers unrealistically demand that all experts and counsel accept deferred payment and limit themselves to fees recovered.

One unusual advantage of BTE cover which is rarely encountered is the insertion of a reverse indemnity provision whereby the insurer agrees to pay any judgment sum and costs awarded to the insured in the proceedings in the event that these are not satisfied by the opponent. It is a peculiar feature of clinical negligence claims that, unlike other litigation, the successful claimant does not usually encounter any enforcement problems in obtaining payment of all compensation and costs due in the action. However, increasingly in private care, practitioners come across clinicians who may not have professional indemnity cover or the means to satisfy any award obtained by the client.

LEGAL AID (PUBLIC FUNDING)

As stated above the Access to Justice Act 1999 effectively abolished legal aid for general personal injury work but retained such funding for clinical negligence claims.

At the same time, the right to conduct these claims on legal aid was restricted to firms that had a solicitor on one of the two specialist clinical negligence panels and had a 'clinical negligence franchise'. The panel run by AvMA[6] had been going a long time. The Law Society Clinical Negligence Panel published a set of criteria, which were originally drafted with the help of AvMA so, not surprisingly, the two sets of criteria are similar. They are not easy to satisfy and many able solicitors have been refused admission on the ground of failure to satisfy the criteria. There is much duplication between the panel members but they currently number about 350 on the Law Society Panel. These solicitors tend to gravitate towards larger firms as it is not easy to run a clinical negligence practice as a sole practitioner or as the only fee earner doing that sort of work in the firm (assuming the firm has already been able to satisfy the criteria relating to backup).

Under the Access to Justice Act 1999 the Legal Services Commission (LSC) took the place of the Legal Aid Board. To qualify for funding, the client had to show (further reduced) financial eligibility and merit for the

---

6   AVMA is a charitable organisation which from minimal beginnings has campaigned with considerable success since its inception in 1982 to improve the lot of the patient in litigation and generally. It has acquired considerable influence in various important quarters, such as with the legal aid authority and conditional fee insurers (CFIs). It recently changed its name, in line with the mood of the times and the spirit of the age, to Action against Medical Accidents (AvMA).

claim. Investigative help would be available where the prospects of success of a significant claim were uncertain, and substantial investigative work was required.

Once the investigation supported a claim with at least moderate prospects of success (50–60%), full representation would be available but subject to strict cost benefit ratios, on the basis that the better the prospects of success the lower the ratio of the likely damages in relation to the likely amount of costs required.

Very high cost civil cases were referred to the Special Cases Unit, who required a detailed costed case plan, reviewable at every stage.

The LSC compiled detailed statistics of clinical negligence claims and assessed the performance of each specialist firm, even transferring cases to the more successful 'green flag' firms.

The Special Cases Unit also worked in co-operation with specialist practitioners to compile a 'template' for a standard case plan for the investigation of a cerebral palsy claim, the most costly claim to investigate and to litigate. This sort of claim also made up the most significant proportion of the potentially massive bill facing the NHS in terms of compensation and costs. The template was consulted on from June 2006.

In late 2008 the Special Cases Unit unveiled the clinical negligence funding checklist, an alternative to the detailed costs schedules. However, at the end of 2008, as has been seen, Jackson was commissioned to review the costs of civil litigation. His final report published in January 2010 set out his concern (at page 68) that although legal aid was not within the remit of his report, the diminishing financial eligibility for legal aid was inhibiting access to justice. He went to say that it was 'vital' that legal aid remained for the key areas of litigation, which included clinical negligence.

Unfortunately, by dint of the very same legislation that enacted the major part of his recommendations, LASPOA 2012, Pt 1, in fact withdrew legal aid even for clinical negligence cases, save for those concerning neurological injuries caused at birth.

Since 1 April 2013 pursuant to LAPSOA 2012, Sch 1, Pt 1, s 23(2), (3) the Legal Aid Agency, (which replaced the Legal Services Commission), can only grant legal aid 'to a claim for damages in respect of clinical negligence which caused a neurological injury to an individual ("V") as a result of which V is severely disabled' (either physically or mentally) but only on two conditions:

(2) The first condition is that the clinical negligence occurred—
(a)   while V was in his or her mother's womb, or
(b)   during or after V's birth but before the end of the following period—
   (i)   if V was born before the beginning of the 37th week of pregnancy, the period of 8 weeks beginning with the first day of what would have been that week;
   (ii)   if V was born during or after the 37th week of pregnancy, the period of 8 weeks beginning with the day of V's birth.
(3) The second condition is that—
(a)   the services are provided to V, or
(b)   V has died and the services are provided to V's personal representative.

The client, most often a child but possibly an adult protected party, will likely come within the financial eligibility criteria. Similarly, unless there are clear factors pointing against the likelihood of a viable claim, it should not be difficult to satisfy the merits criteria, or at least to show the need for limited expenditure so as to investigate whether there is a likely claim. Furthermore, such claims are very unlikely to fall at the proportionality or the cost benefit hurdle, bearing in mind that the likely damages of a viable claim will many times outstrip the likely costs.

The clinical negligence checklist[7] sets out the proposed cost limitations/contract prices to cover all work in these cases. Where likely final costs exceed £25,000 a very high cost case contract will be necessary, though its terms are unaffected by the funding checklist.

The sums specified at each of the six stages of the case will be the maximum likely to be paid by the Legal Aid Agency if the case is unsuccessful. However, these sums will be revised downwards if necessary to keep within the cost benefit ratios of the Civil Legal Aid (Merits Criteria) Regulations 2013: (1:4 for cases with 50–60% prospects; 1:2 for cases with 60–80% prospects and 1:1 for cases with 80% plus prospects).

The solicitors' rates for the first £25,000 costs are £108 per hour and this rate reduces thereafter to £70 and counsel suffer even more severely reduced fees. Medical experts' authorised rates are set out in the Civil Legal Aid (Remuneration) Regulations 2013.[8] (These are often below the level of fees which reputable medical experts will seek especially in the important area of cerebral palsy claims where the pool of experts is tiny.)

The basic principle for the simplified payment at each stage under the funding checklist is the number of experts used so that whatever the authorised limit, payment will be pegged to the sum allowed for any lesser number of experts actually used.

The current clinical negligence checklist, limited as it is effectively to cerebral palsy claims, follows almost precisely the previous checklist in terms of the stages, although it very slightly reduces the sums allowed in respect of each stage as follows:

1	Investigative help (5–6 experts)	£4,500–£22,500
2	Issue of proceedings – mutual exchange(5 experts)	£6,750–£19,000
3	Settlement (5 experts)	£6,750–£21,750
4	Trial – full trial or liability only (5 experts)	£6,750–£40,000
5	Quantum investigations (8–10 quantum experts)	£34,000
6	Quantum trial (8–10 quantum experts and 5 day trial)	£41,000

At each stage, all relevant information is to be provided and particular risks are to be highlighted. The information is to include, though tailored to each stage, a report on the issues in the case, of breach and causation, risk factors, the number and nature of experts to be used, the likely costs both past and future, the prospects of success, a likely timetable and quantum, together with the supply of any relevant documents.

An amount of costs within the range is allowed in respect of each stage, but depending, of course, upon the number of experts actually used. The cost amounts are cumulative and it is stated in the checklist that the

---

7   This and other documents are downloadable at: www.gov.uk/government/publications/high-cost-cases-non-family-civil.
8   SI 2013/422.

Legal Aid Agency is likely to authorise a maximum of £178,250 in total for a fully contested cerebral palsy case (split trial) with five liability and ten quantum experts where all six stages are completed.

There is very little scope for the solicitor to charge the client in respect of any solicitor and own client costs (previously the 'statutory charge' which will attach to the damages). It is hoped that the solicitor will be satisfied with the monies which the client recovers from the defendant.

If there is any risk of the client's damages being reduced by reason of adverse costs, particularly with multiple defendants and also CPR Part 36, it would be wise for the solicitor to consider with the client the possible need for taking out ATE insurance cover to guard against the risk and to safeguard the damages. In the current austere financial climate, defendants may be readier to enforce orders for costs in their favour.

As is clear above, the Solicitors' Code of Conduct requires that the solicitor should include in the discussions with their client, which will more probably be the Litigation Friend, as to how the case will be funded, the question as to 'whether public funding may be available' (see above IB (1.16)). Providing the client is fully advised as to the funding options, and depending on the circumstances, including the terms of any CFA on offer and the pros and cons of each alternative, the client may well feel better served by funding the claim by CFA rather than under a legal aid certificate.

There have been conflicting decisions regarding cases in which, for instance, legal aid funding has been switched to CFAs, an important Court of Appeal decision on this issue is dealt with under the CFA heading later in this chapter.

ADR

Alternative dispute resolution (ADR) is very much encouraged. As stated in LASPOA 2012, s 1(5), the criteria for legal aid set by the Lord Chancellor '... must reflect the principle that, in many disputes, mediation and other forms of dispute resolution are more appropriate than legal proceedings'.

Exceptional cases funding

Even if a case would otherwise fall outside the scope of legal aid services (as set out in LASPOA 2012, Sch 1, Pt 1), it may be possible to qualify for exceptional case funding (ECF).

To qualify for ECF, LASPOA 2012, s 10(2) and (4), and also the Lord Chancellor's Funding Guidance issued under LASPOA 2012, s 4(3) have to be complied with. Also the legal financial eligibility criteria and the merits criteria must be satisfied.

The Lord Chancellor has issued separate exceptional funding guidance[9] for inquests and for non-inquests.

Funding for inquests is dealt with in Chapter 19 of this work but suffice it to say here, preparatory work for a hearing is within the scope of legal aid and legal help covers advice, assistance and preparation, including experts' reports (for preparatory work only).

---

9   This and other documents are downloadable at: www.gov.uk/government/publications/legal-aid-exceptional-case-funding-form-and-guidance.

An inquest is deemed to be a relatively informal inquisitorial process, rather than a contentious adversarial exercise, and advocacy at inquests is therefore outside scope. However, instructing an advocate or providing advocacy at an inquest can be covered by ECF if one of two grounds are met:

1   that advocacy is required by the ECHR, Art 2 concerning advocacy into the death of a member of the applicant's family; and
2   where the director of legal aid casework makes a 'wider interest determination' in relation to the individual and the inquest.

Article 2 of the ECHR relates to the right to life, and imposes on states the 'substantive obligation' not to take life without justification and to do everything reasonable to avoid a risk to life where the state is implicitly aware of a risk of a breach of Art 2 and to establish a legal framework and means of enforcement to protect life. A 'procedural obligation' is also imposed to conduct a public investigation into a death where there are 'circumstances that give ground for suspicion that the State may have breached a substantive obligation imposed by Article 2.' The case law is complex and developing but a procedural duty is automatically triggered in all intentional killings by the state and all non-natural deaths or suicides of detainees in police custody or prison or mental institutions. Cases concerning allegations against hospital authorities will not be a breach of a substantive obligation where only ordinary clinical negligence is involved, as opposed to allegations of systemic failure.

'Wider public interest' must be significant and includes determining, for instance, that the advocacy at the inquest is likely to benefit a wider class of persons other than the applicant or their family members (probably more than 100 people!) or relates to a systemic failure requiring radical overhaul.

There is some discretion for inquest work to waive the usual legal aid financial eligibility criteria.

Non-inquest ECF is available when civil legal services, other than those set out in LASPOA 2012, Sch 1, Pt 1, are necessary to be made available in order for the state to comply with the individual's Convention rights (within the meaning of the Human Rights Act 1998) or any rights of the individual to the provision of legal services that are enforceable EU rights. (Article 6(1) of the ECHR guarantees the right to a fair hearing and the right of access to the court for the purposes of the determination of a person's rights and obligations.) The 'overarching question', as stated in the Lord Chancellor's Guidance, 'is whether the withholding of legal aid would mean that the applicant is unable to present his case effectively and without obvious unfairness'.[10]

In clinical negligence cases, paras 47 and 48 in the Annex to the Guidance for Non-Inquests state as follows:

47. Clinical negligence claims will generally involve the determination of civil rights and obligations.

48. Where a case involves the determination of civil rights and obligations, caseworkers should consider whether the withholding of legal aid would mean

---

10   See p 5, para 19.

the applicant will be unable to present his or her case effectively or lead to an obvious unfairness in proceedings, having regard to the general factors described above. The following matters may be particularly relevant:

- In relation to the complexity of the case, how complex is the case at hand bearing in mind the complexity and volume of any medical expert evidence and any medico-legal arguments in issue in the case?
- In relation to the ability of the applicant to present their own case, how able is the applicant or litigation friend to do this:
  - bearing in mind any caring responsibilities they have due to caring for a disabled child or family member?
  - bearing in mind any disabilities or medical problems they have?
- In relation to the importance of the matter at stake, is the applicant a disabled person who is seeking to recover damages which would, in whole or in part, cover adjustments, adaptations, equipment and care?

CONDITIONAL FEE AGREEMENTS (CFAS)

The history

Previously at common law, any sort of contingency or conditional fee agreement (CFA) between solicitor and client was anathema. It was said by the courts time and again that it was totally unacceptable for the lawyer to have a financial interest in the outcome of a case. This applied equally to the simple situation where it was agreed or understood that the solicitor would only get paid or would only get his full fee if he won the case as to the obviously more contentious situation where he would get more than his full fee if he won and less or nothing if he lost.

Maintenance and champerty

Maintenance consisted in supporting a case financially when having no proper interest to do so ('improperly stirring up litigation and strife by giving aid to one party to bring or defend a claim without just cause or excuse').[11] It was permissible if the person concerned had a legitimate interest in supporting the action, whether financial or social or whatever. Champerty was a form of maintenance whereby the person maintaining the action took as a reward a share in the property recovered (ie it adds to maintenance 'the notion of a division of the spoils').[12]

Both used to be both tortious and criminal until the Criminal Law Act 1967. However, that Act preserved the common law rule that they were contrary to public policy.

Lord Denning more than once expressed his horror of champerty, particularly in respect of the lawyer who charged a fee that would only be payable if his client was successful, whether as a portion of the damages recovered or merely his normal fee payable only if he won, or by way of uplift to his normal fee.

---

11 Per Lord Denning in *Re Trepca Mines Ltd (No 2)* [1963] Ch 199 at 219, CA.
12 Per Lord Mustill in *Giles v Thompson* [1994] 1 AC 142 at 161, HL.

The Introduction of CFAs

Conditional fees were first introduced by the Courts and Legal Services Act 1990, which by s 58 (which came into force in July 1993) provided that a lawyer could agree in writing for fees and expenses to be payable only in specified circumstances and any increase above normal fees, ie any uplift, had to be specified as a percentage of them. The situations in which a conditional fee agreement was permissible were first specified by the Conditional Fee Agreements Order 1995 (CFA Order 1995) which permitted this type of funding in personal injury and insolvency cases. The CFA Order 1998 extended such funding to cover all civil proceedings in 1998.

The solicitors' normal or base costs were to be reimbursed by the losing opponent but the success fee was to be paid for by the client out of the damages obtained. The success fee was not to exceed 100% of the base costs but the Law Society recommended to its members that the success fee should not be more than 25% of the client's damages.

During the ensuing period there were not many personal injury claims funded by CFA and indeed the new insurance market needed to provide cover for any necessary liabilities, after the event or 'ATE', was in its infancy. The CFA was just an alternative new funding method when legal aid was still available for personal injury clients who satisfied the financial eligibility criteria.

The era of recoverability

The Labour government assuming power in 1997, as with previous governments, were anxious to reduce the spiralling legal aid bill but at the same time they felt that the tortfeasor should pay for all the consequences of their wrongdoing. The Access to Justice Act 1999 removed legal aid for almost all personal injury cases, save for clinical negligence. However, the Act also provided that the CFA success fee should now be recoverable from the losing party, along with the ATE premium (even if the case was not funded by CFA). CFAs were clearly the way forward. Seemingly unaware how complex the situation was that they were creating, that Labour government would have abolished legal aid for clinical negligence claims also had they not been forced by persistent lobbying to acknowledge that, although removing legal aid support for clinical negligence claims would certainly have reduced the legal aid bill, it was going to leave many wrongly injured patients without a remedy. The cost of investigating whether there was a viable clinical negligence claim was more than the average client could pay or specialist solicitor could afford to risk.

As the success fee was no longer payable by the client out of their damages the Law Society was no longer concerned that the success fee should be capped at the maximum of 25% of the damages awarded.

Furthermore, as it was now the responsibility of the losing party, there was no longer the same pressing need for the solicitor to keep the level of the success fee to the absolute minimum. Indeed in clinical negligence work, because of the need for initial detailed investigation, it became the practice of some specialist practitioners to offer a CFA at an early stage and to apply a 100% success fee on the basis that they were assuming a substantial risk of failure in the absence of the relevant facts which prevented them from properly assessing the merits of the claim.

Although there was no requirement for a client with a CFA to obtain ATE insurance cover it was prudent to protect them from liability for their opponent's costs and for their own disbursements in the event the case was lost. The solicitor was, of course, required to advise the client on ATE insurance.

Even if a claim were successful overall, there might still be adverse costs ordered against the client, for instance, if a Part 36 offer was not beaten or if there were multiple defendants and one or more was successful in defending the case. Most ATE policies would cover these risks and as the premium was likely to be self-insuring the client would never be liable for it even if they lost the case.

Whilst there has been much success in personal injury claims in keeping ATE premiums to manageable proportions, those sought by insurers prepared to fund clinical negligence work were very high in comparison to the amount of liability covered because of the high risks and costs of such claims.

Conditional Fee Agreements Regulations 2000

For a CFA to be enforceable it had to be in writing and to specify a percentage success fee but it had also to comply with the regulations issued by the Lord Chancellor pursuant to s 58 of the Courts and Legal Services Act 1990 (as amended by the Access to Justice Act 1999 (AJA 1999)).

The Conditional Fee Agreements Regulations 2000[13] were effective from 1 April 2000, at the same time as the AJA 1999 came into force. The regulations set out the requirements concerning the form and contents of particular types of CFAs and the information to be given to the client before the CFA was entered into.

The detailed requirements of these regulations provided much ammunition for the attacks upon the validity of the CFA launched in so many cases by the losing defendant. The important consequence was, of course, that if the client had no liability for costs to their own solicitor, then under the indemnity principle the losing opponent had nothing to reimburse.

These assaults mushroomed into the vast amount of satellite litigation which became known as 'the costs wars'. The challenges to the validity of the CFAs in the many cases ranged throughout all the regulations, particularly regarding reg 4, which governed the information to be given to the client before the CFA was entered into. Some of this was to be given orally and some of it both orally and in writing.

In *Hollins v Russell*,[14] the Court of Appeal held that only those departures which had a 'materially adverse effect' upon the protection afforded to the client or upon the 'proper administration of justice' could invalidate a CFA.

Sadly, despite this appeal for calm, the challenges continued.

---

13 SI 2000/692.
14 [2003] 4 All ER 590.

In 2003, in an effort towards an improvement, the government introduced a regulation providing for the 'CFA lite', whereby the solicitor agreed not to charge the client any more than the amount recovered from the losing opponent (save where the client defaulted under the CFA).

The CFA Regulations 2005

It was generally felt that the situation had become intolerable and it was concluded that the regulations were too complicated to understand and too complex to explain to lay clients. As from 1 November 2005, the regulations were quite simply revoked by the Conditional Fee Agreements (Revocation) Regulations 2005.[15]

The very basic statutory provisions remain, effectively in relation to clinical negligence, that in order to be valid the CFA must be in writing and, if it has a success fee, it must specify the percentage success fee uplift, which must be limited to 100%. However, the current additional requirements for the making of CFAs were thenceforth dictated by the SRA's Code of Conduct.[16]

As shown above, the Code's principles and mandatory outcomes in relation to client care and funding are of general application. However, outcome O (1.6) requires solicitors to only enter into fee arrangements that are legal and which cater for the client's needs and best interests. Otherwise the sole reference to a CFA is in the non-mandatory indicative behaviour IB (1.17) which exhorts a solicitor acting under a CFA to give the client 'all relevant information relating to that arrangement' in order that the client might give their informed consent to the method of funding to be agreed.

Non-compliance with the Code of Conduct would not be fatal to the validity of the CFA but would be a disciplinary matter.

Ever since the AJA 1999 ushered in the era of recoverability of the additional liabilities, if the validity of the CFA itself could not be attacked, the major victims of assault by the losing opponent would be the reasonableness of the success fee and the amount of the ATE premium.

There was much satellite litigation concerning the reasonableness of success fees in personal injury cases, particularly in Road Traffic Act cases. The various decisions of the Court of Appeal in *Callery v Gray*,[17] (albeit in the context of RTA claims) and later cases suggested that for those cases which were not expected to settle until a later stage of the litigation, a two-stage success fee might be used. It was held that a solicitor who sought a lower success fee if the case settled at an early stage in the process might be better able to justify a higher success fee if the case progressed to a more advanced stage of the litigation. (Indeed the Law Society model CFA 2005 made provision for a two-stage success fee.)

The merits of a clinical negligence case, however, are particularly much more uncertain and difficult to assess at the outset where often the only material to hand would be the client's statement, which might be of little,

---

15 SI 2005/2305.
16 Then 2011 but as now updated in Version 21 of the SRA Handbook published on 6 December 2018.
17 [2001] EWCA Civ 1117, [2001] 1 WLR 2112.

if any, assistance. Indeed, there were somewhat conflicting first instance authorities regarding the practice of setting 100% success fees at the outset in clinical negligence cases.

However, even these two issues, previously hotly contested by the losing party, are now really matters for discussion and agreement with the client.

The current position post-Jackson

As has been seen earlier in this chapter, the major reforms recommended by Jackson, principally the removal of recoverability of the success fee and the ATE premium (save for a meagre clinical negligence concession), were put into effect on 1 April 2013 by LASPOA 2012, Pt 2, s 44 (which amended the CLSA 1990, ss 58 and 58A). LASPOA 2012 also withdrew legal aid for clinical negligence claims save for neurological injury at birth. On the same date QOCS was brought in, amongst other of Jackson's lesser reforms, by amendment to the Civil Procedure Rules.[18] However, this protection against having to pay the successful opponent's costs will be lost where:

1   the claim is fundamentally dishonest;
2   the claimant has failed to beat a defendant's Part 36 offer (but the costs ordered against him will be limited to the amount of his damages awarded);
3   the case was struck out for want of cause of action or abuse of process or because the claimant's conduct was likely to obstruct the just disposal of the proceedings.

At the same time the Conditional Fee Agreements Order 2013[19] was effected which revoked and replaced the Conditional Fee Agreements Order 2000.[20] Although the maximum success fee claimable was 100% of base costs, in personal injury claims (including clinical negligence) the maximum success fee (now chargeable to the client) was 25% of general damages for pain and suffering and loss of amenity and of past financial losses. (This cap is net of any payment to the Compensation Recovery Unit and will also include VAT and counsel's success fee payable under the CFA. Also the cap does not apply to appeals.)

Additionally in force on 1 April 2013 was Jackson's intended softening of the blow for personal injury claimants, the 10% increase in general damages (which had been implemented by the Court of Appeal's decisions in *Simmons v Castle*,[21] unless the claimant had already entered into the CFA prior to 1 April 2013).

The further sop for the clinical negligence claimant regarding ATE is that they can recover from the losing opponent that part of the premium which relates to cover for their experts' reports relating to liability or causation.[22]

---

18   See CPR Pt 44.13.
19   SI 2013/689.
20   SI 2000/823.
21   [2012] ECWA Civ 1039 and also 1288.
22   See the Recovery of Costs Insurance Premiums in Clinical Negligence Proceedings (No 2) Regulations 2013, SI 2013/739.

As previously, the form of the post-Jackson CFA must simply be in writing. It need not provide for a success fee but if it does it should be expressed as a percentage of the solicitor's base costs and at no more than 100% of them.

The Law Society introduced a model CFA for use in personal injury and clinical negligence cases only and it has been updated, the latest following the Jackson reforms. It is very short and sets out what work and associated proceedings are covered and what is not covered. It sets out the circumstances in which the client's liability for any costs might arise, if there is a win and if there is a loss. The percentage amount of success fee and the cap is set out in Schedule 1; and Schedule 2 sets out the base costs and any fixed fee and overall cap agreed by the solicitor. The Law Society's Conditions are attached to the model CFA and form part of the agreement.

Since 1 October 2008, the CFA and any retainer will need to include the notice of a right to cancel the agreement within seven days if the retainer or CFA was made or offered at the client's or another person's home or at the client's place of work.[23] This can be found at Schedule 3 of the model CFA.

Indeed, the practitioner will need to be aware of all changes in any other areas of the law which may impact upon CFAs. (The practitioner is again reminded that the SRA Handbook will be replaced on 25 November 2019 by the new SRA Standards and Regulations.)

Practical considerations

Whether or not to take on a case funded by a success fee is an important financial decision for the firm and often a committee of partners would be involved in weighing up the merits and participating in the risk assessment process whereby the success fee uplift is fixed.

There is no set formula for the calculation but when the success fee was recoverable, the risk of losing the case as a percentage was commonly converted into a percentage success fee, and the reasons in support of the risk assessment (at least, if not also the CFA itself) had be disclosed on assessment as the stated risks would necessarily come under critical scrutiny in the costs court by the losing opponent.

As the solicitor has to justify their success fee to their client (and possibly also to the costs court), it is good practice to have a detailed note as to how it was calculated. As previously stated a two, or even more, stage success fee will more likely meet with the court's approval upon any challenge.

If the CFA actually provides for no or reduced costs if a defendant's Part 36 is not beaten, then the success fee can reflect this. Also deferment of the solicitor's costs and disbursements can also justify a higher success fee (and in the early days this was normally set at 10%).

Counsel's fees can be dealt with as a disbursement under the CFA, but normally counsel would be working under a corresponding CFA. A model CFA for use in personal injury and clinical negligence cases has been

---

23 See the Cancellation of Contracts made in a Consumer's Home or Place of Work etc Regulations 2008, SI 2008/1816.

prepared jointly by the Association of Personal Injury Lawyers and the Personal Injuries Bar Association.

On the death of the client, the retainer will cease, but the solicitor may enter into a new CFA with the personal representatives (but any such CFA after 1 April 2013 will not attract recoverable additional liabilities).

If the client was a minor at the inception of the CFA, the position when they reach 18 years is not entirely clear. If the CFA is deemed a contract for 'necessaries' and the Litigation Friend signed it as agent for the minor, the minor can formally adopt the CFA without a new agreement. If, however, the Litigation Friend signed personally as the principal contractor then a new CFA will be needed for the client.

A change in the mental capacity of the client is another complication where the law is similarly unclear. If capacity is in doubt at the outset then it would be sensible to have the CFA signed by both client and Litigation Friend. It has been decided that where the client protected party subsequently regains capacity, this will not automatically terminate the retainer, which will become merely voidable.

CFAs can be retrospective, in that the date when it is deemed to have come into effect can be an earlier date, although the CFA itself must not be backdated.

It is particularly important to fully use up any BTE cover that might exist before seeking any ATE cover. Although it is not as significant as previously, before the introduction of QOCS, BTE will still have a part to play in possibly providing funding for disbursements throughout the progress of the case and/or to provide cover for any adverse costs of an interlocutory nature or for any liability by the client for costs under an unbeaten Part 36 offer.

It is essential that on the one hand the solicitor should keep the cost of the client's insurance cover to a minimum, particularly as the opponent's liability therefor will be scrutinised later, but on the other hand, the solicitor must ensure that the whole of the client's potential liability (for their own disbursements and any adverse costs) should be fully covered by insurance,

Nowadays, because of QOCS, the ATE premium will be only a very small fraction of what it is likely to have been previously, as the level of cover does not, of course, include the opponent's likely costs including trial.

Since LASPOA 2012 it is not necessary to serve notice of any additional liability, as none are recoverable, save as to an ATE premium in clinical negligence cases (partly relating to liability for payment of experts fees for reports on liability or causation). If taken out after 1 April 2013, CPR PD 48 4.1 enables the court to make the necessary costs order in respect of such liability therefor and although not required it is good practice for a Form N251 to be served as soon as possible after obtaining the policy.[24]

There are other matters which need to be considered as a result of the many changes made to CFAs since their introduction. The legal effect

---

24   Pre-LASPOA 2012 notices of funding were ripe subjects for litigation after April 2000 as notice had to be given of any additional liabilities and in October 2009 further information as to these was required to be provided at various stages. Any failure was punished by the inability to charge any additional liabilities for the period in default and relief from sanctions would have to be applied for.

of a CFA will depend to a large extent on its date and the particular regime which was in force at the time. Hopefully arguments concerning the CFA Regulations of 1995 and 2000 will effectively now be long past.

However, the vast financial consequences for the parties as a result of the Jackson reforms will continue to reverberate for a while to come as a result of the end of recoverability of success fees and ATE premiums on 1 April 2013.

Although Jackson's final report came out in January 2010 it was not known until very late in 2012 that virtually all his proposals would in fact have full force of law, and would come into effect on 1 April 2013. During this period there was much activity to sign up clients and/or counsel to CFAs and also to change funding methods (for instance, from legal aid to CFA) in order to retain the benefits of recoverability.

Furthermore, there was much reorganisation of the legal market for some while beforehand, as bigger firms appeared, businesses were bought up or firms merged and smaller firms taken over or went out of business altogether, along with the consequential movement of individual practitioners to different firms.

The assignment of CFAs is another complex area of the law which requires special mention. This received some clarity in the recent long-awaited case of *Budana v The Leeds Teaching Hospitals* NHS Trust.[25] Firm A acted for Ms Budana under a pre-LASPOA 2012 CFA with a 100% success fee. By 22 March 2013 it had decided to cease its personal injury work and it wrote to Ms Budana explaining this. It had already entered into an agreement with Firm B for the purchase of its business, including Ms Budana's claim. She consented and all relevant paperwork was signed including a deed of assignment whereby Firm B was to provide Firm A's legal services under the CFA.

The defendant insurer objected that it was not possible to assign the burden of a contract for personal services such as a CFA and the agreement was therefore a novation, a new contract. The Court of Appeal, however, found that there was no reason in principle why rights and benefits under solicitors' contracts with their clients could not be capable of assignment in today's business environment. The client merely wanted a competent practitioner. Further, even if the agreement was a novation (as found by the majority of the court) it did not matter as the retainer was not affected by LASPO as the transitional provisions of the Act preserved vested rights arising from the previous law and also all three parties consented to the CFA remaining in force. It should be pointed out that all the paperwork regarding the arrangement and the intention of the parties was in pristine order.

As regards the change of funding in March 2013, a national specialist firm changed the method of funding for three of their clients who were on legal aid to CFAs and in all the cases liability had been admitted by the defendants. In *Surrey v Barnet and Chase Farm Hospitals NHS Trust, AH v Lewisham Healthcare NHS Trust and Yesil v Doncaster and Bassetlaw Hospitals NHS Foundation Trust*[26] the Court of Appeal held that the additional liabilities were not recoverable on the ground that the clients were not given adequate advice about the funding changes.

---

25 [2017] 6 Costs LR 1135.
26 [2018] EWCA Civ 451.

Lewison LJ felt that the advice given to the clients had exaggerated (and in two cases, misrepresented) the disadvantages of remaining with legal aid funding. The clients were not told that moving to CFAs would result in their losing the benefit of a 10% uplift in damages. The court further approved the District Judge's finding that, 'Where one of two or more options available to a client is more financially beneficial to the solicitor, the need for transparency becomes ever greater'.

Doubtless there will be many more issues to be heard in the costs courts as a result of the end of recoverability brought about by LASPOA 2012.

In relation to costs assessments, in *Hollins* (see above), the Court of Appeal stated that 'where a genuine issue is raised … in which there is a real chance that the CFA is unenforceable as a result of failure to satisfy the applicable conditions', the costs judge will have to investigate the solicitors' relevant papers. Although the court suggested that ordinarily the CFA should be disclosed, under the relevant Costs Practice Direction, the receiving party could elect to rely on other evidence of compliance rather than to disclose the CFA itself.

In some costs assessments, particularly involving pre-LASPOA 2012 CFAs, details might still need to be provided by the ATE insurer as to how the premium was calculated in order to justify its reasonableness.

As complex and as time-consuming as funding issues can be, especially in discussing them with the client, unfortunately the costs of arranging the funding of the action are not recoverable against the losing party. In the Court of Appeal decision *Motto v Trafigura Ltd*,[27] in the context of CFA funding, the Master of the Rolls stated that such costs 'are ultimately attributable to the need of a litigant to fund the litigation as opposed to the actual funding of the litigation itself'.

DAMAGES BASED AGREEMENTS (CONTINGENCY FEES)

For many years, as with CFAs, these were outlawed as providing the lawyer with a financial stake in the outcome of the case.

CFAs were a very English compromise whereby the loser was still obliged to pay and any success fee for the risk of losing was to be linked to the base costs and not to the amount of damages achieved.

Damages based agreements are similarly a 'no win, no fee' agreement but are fixed in accordance with the amount of damages awarded, more in the mould of a US contingency fee. Jackson describes them in his Final Report as 'fees which (a) are payable if the client wins and (b) are calculated as a percentage of the sum recovered'. They have been in employment tribunals for a long while but mainly because tribunals do not normally order the payment of costs between the parties.

Even after the introduction of CFAs, it was not permissible for solicitors to act on the basis of contingency fees whilst conducting contentious business.

When Jackson came to research funding in other jurisdictions he noted the stark difference between the English 'loser pays' and the US parties bearing their own costs position. He was more attracted to the Ontario

---

27   [2011] EWCA Civ 1150.

model of contingency fees which was applied in a similar system where costs were recoverable between the parties.

Jackson set out the pros and cons of contingency fees in his Interim Report and in his Final Report he concluded that lawyers should be permitted to enter into contingency fee agreements on the Ontario model: 'In other words, costs shifting is effected on a conventional basis and in so far as the contingency fee exceeds what would be chargeable under a normal fee agreement, that is borne by the successful litigant'. Jackson went on to say, however, that: 'It is desirable that as many funding methods as possible should be available to the litigants'.

In due course, contingency fees on Jackson's narrow basis, as damages based agreements (DBAs) became lawful under LASPOA 2012, s 45 which effectively amended the CLSA 1990, s 58A.

Accordingly a DBA must be in writing, entered into after 1 April 2013 and comply with the Damages-Based Agreements Regulations 2013[28] (DBA Regulations 2013). Regulation 3 requires the DBA to specify the proceedings to which it relates, the circumstances in which the solicitors' fees are payable and the reason for setting the percentage. The maximum in personal injury (including clinical negligence claims) is 25% of general damages and past losses as with CFAs. (Just pausing here, how are the amounts of these heads of damage to be worked out in practice to provide fairness between client and solicitor with the onus on the solicitor to fully advise the client on the basis of full transparency, particularly where damages are usually arrived at between the parties on the basis of a horse-trade?)

Unfortunately it is generally agreed that the DBA Regulations 2013 are poorly drafted. As early as December 2014 the Government was requesting that the Civil Justice Council look into improving the Regulations. If the changes discussed since by the Working Party were implemented these would show a significant departure from what had been understood to have been proposed previously. Furthermore, Jackson's favoured 'hybrid' DBA option was studiously ignored and the Government's response to the CJC's report is still awaited.

Unfortunately, in view of the complete lack of clarity in relation to DBA funding, this is as yet not an option which solicitors can sensibly advise their clients about, nor prudently consider for themselves.

Indeed, in February 2019 the Ministry of Justice's long-awaited Post-Implementation Review of Part 2 of LASPOA 2012, the Government confirmed it would give careful consideration to the way forward following the independent review of the drafting of the DBA Regulations 2013 being undertaken by Professor Rachael Mulheron and Nicholas Bacon QC. Their report is expected later in 2019.

THE VERDICT ON JACKSON SO FAR

In July 2017 Jackson published his Supplementary Report on 'Fixed Recoverable Costs'[29] setting out further recommendations for 'FRCs' for

---

28   SI 2013/609.
29   See   https://consult.justice.gov.uk/digital-communications/fixed-recoverable-costs-consultation/supporting_documents/fixedrecoverablecostsconsultationpaper.pdf.

fast track cases, a new intermediate track for other less complex cases up to £100,000 claimed and for clinical negligence cases claiming up to £25,000.

As for Jackson's own verdict on his reforms so far, he has voiced these in a lecture he delivered to the Cambridge Law Faculty on 5 March 2018 and in an interview given in *Litigation Funding* in April 2018.[30]

In terms of clinical negligence funding he highlighted his successes as the ending of recoverable success fees and ATE premiums, and the introduction of QOCS, all of which he felt reduced the costs of litigation and therefore permitted wider access to justice. He also thought the abolition of referral fees reduced litigation costs and the 10% increase in general damages provided a balance for claimants.

Jackson saw DBAs as the main failure of his reforms. He rued the refusal to abolish the indemnity principle, the failure to implement his suggestion for 'hybrid" DBAs and considered that the unsatisfactory DBA Rules required reform.

Jackson was particularly distressed by the savage cutbacks in legal aid availability and eligibility, which took place wholly contrary to and despite his warnings against these: 'I regret and deplore those cutbacks'.

Jackson looked forward to the implementation of his recommendations regarding FRCs and regretted the resistance, particularly in the field of clinical negligence. It seems that he has later scaled back his suggestions for FRCs from cases up to £250,000 down to £100,000.

He also wished to see case management control over pre-action costs which he had also recommended and would like to see more guidance on proportionality.

Over many months the Ministry of Justice carried out a post-implementation review of Part 2 of LASPOA 2012. (Separate reviews of legal aid generally under Part 1 of LASPOA 2012 and also of legal aid for inquests were also undertaken.)

The Law Society's Response of September 2018 to the Ministry of Justice's online survey felt that overall the balance had been tipped in favour of the defendants, irrecoverability had reduced access to justice and claimants were being undercompensated. Further, the defendants' behaviour was driving up costs, QOCS were an inadequate replacement for ATE and DBAs needed extensive reform. There was felt to be a lack of policing of the defendants' failure to beat claimants' Part 36 offers.

Interestingly, the Law Society strongly advocated that where a CFA was not available on reasonably affordable terms, legal aid ought to be provided for clinical negligence claims.

Probably more surprising was the response of the Medical and Dental Defence Union of Scotland (MDDUS) dated 27 August 2018 in which they welcomed the reduction in the size of claimants' bills of costs but considered this was outweighed by negative features where QOCS had led to an increase in the number of claims and defendants' costs, all of which would be more effectively assisted by the reintroduction of legal aid more widely in clinical negligence. They felt that this would provide greater scrutiny of claimant's costs and more rigorous review of the merits of claims with an opportunity for them to make representations to 'an objective third party' where cases lack merit.

---

30   At pp 6–9.

THE MINISTRY OF JUSTICE'S VERDICT ON JACKSON

In June 2018 the Ministry of Justice published its initial assessment of the LASPOA 2012 changes in conjunction with a Civil Justice Council seminar and invited the views of all stakeholders to an online survey. After consideration of the views of 155 participants, of courts and published data, and independent analysis by Professors Fenn and Rickman of the impacts of the changes, on 7 February 2019 the Ministry of Justice published its post-implementation review ('PIR') of Pt 2 of LASPOA 2012. (On the same day it also published a separate review of legal aid generally under Pt 1 of LASPOA 2012 and a further review of legal aid for inquests.)

In its PIR of Pt 2 of LASPOA 2012, the Government announced its conclusion that the Pt 2 reforms had been successful in that they had achieved the overall objectives '... to reduce the costs of civil litigation and to rebalance the costs liabilities between claimants and defendants while ensuring that parties with a valid case could still bring or defend a claim'.[31] Unmeritorious claims would be discouraged by the reforms and meritorious claims would be resolved at proportionate cost.

The Government proposed therefore that no changes to Pt 2 of LASPOA 2012 were to be made. However, in relation to two areas of concern, it conceded that the DBA Regulations 2013 would benefit from 'additional clarity and certainty' and it would also look cautiously into extending QOCS to other categories of case beyond personal injury.

The Ministry of Justice's PIR of Pt 1 of LASPOA 2012 attracted mixed reviews from the bodies concerned regarding general civil legal aid funding. The Government appeared to accept the need in principle for review of the means test and of solicitors' remuneration but proposed yet further reviews and future pilot evaluations.

In the Ministry of Justice's 'Final Report: Review of legal aid for inquests',[32] to bitter disappointment from those advising bereaved families, the Government refused to introduce automatic public funding where the state was represented.

THE FUTURE

It requires to be stressed that the irrecoverability of the CFA success fee and of the ATE premium will have significant adverse consequences for the more seriously injured clients. Whilst Jackson anticipated that in the majority of low value cases the claimant may be even better off than at present, the flipside is that in the higher value cases, those suffering serious injuries, the claimant would be much worse off than pre-LASPOA 2012.

Suppose a claim for tetraplegia could likely involve substantial past losses of £320,000 and general damages of £280,000. The solicitors' basic costs could well approach £250,000 (with liability and then quantum issues fought separately to the doors of the court). As compensation for

---

31   At p 8, para 26.
32   February 2019, see https://assets.publishing.service.gov.uk/government/uploads/system/uploads/attachment_data/file/777034/review-of-legal-aid-for-inquests.pdf.

his success fee liability of £150,000, (capped at 25% of £600,000), Jackson merely awards the claimant a 10% increase in his general damages, a paltry £28,000!

General damages have always been appallingly low, as the Law Commission recognised 20 years ago when it recommended an increase of up to 50%.[33]

Even if a 10% increase were fair, that so much of the reform is reliant upon such an imprecise figure as 10% of general damages is wholly unsatisfactory. The Judicial College Guidelines are expressed in large bands of figures and the parties are often way too far apart in their assessments of the appropriate figures.

However, in order to preserve true equality of arms, it is true that some additional form of legal aid must be retained for the funding of costly claims, particularly of vulnerable claimants, or requiring heavy investigation work, or of uncertain merit or issues of major public interest. These would not at all come within the current criteria for exceptional case funding.

The fear is that in the anxiety to cut costs yet further, the extension of fixed costs to more substantial claims will be seen as the panacea and this would have an extremely detrimental effect upon access to justice for the most vulnerable in society.

---

33   *Damages for Non-Pecuniary Loss* (Law Com no 257) (1999).

Chapter 27

Costs

Martyn McLeish

There are only two bases upon which lawyers provide their services. They are either paid or they offer their services for free: *pro bono publico*. Legal Services Commission (LSC) funding, Conditional Fee Agreements (CFAs), insurance-funded and private client work, are species of retainer providing for payment under certain agreed terms. Funding itself is the subject of its own chapter in this book. However, the essential point made at the outset of this chapter is as simple as it is complex: litigation costs money. How a case is funded and who pays the costs incurred, are fundamental to clinical negligence practice.

This chapter can only scratch the surface of the issues and at best aspire to provide an introduction rather than a definitive analysis. Discussion is limited to a short summary of the basic principles, the twin pillars of costs jurisprudence: the costs-shifting rule and the indemnity principle. This chapter then considers general rules about costs, including qualified one way costs shifting ('QOCS') and Part 36. Reasons of space prohibit any discussion of either detailed or summary assessment, but there is a section on the principles of assessment and, in particular, proportionality.

THE TWIN PILLARS OF COSTS JURISPRUDENCE

The twin pillars of costs jurisprudence provide simplicity and symmetry which in the ordinary case will cause little confusion.

The first pillar is the costs-shifting rule by which the 'loser' pays the winner's costs, ie the costs' burden *shifts* from the unsuccessful party to the successful party. Although a fact of everyday life in the context of clinical negligence, it is important to bear in mind that the costs-shifting rule is a historical artefact of the common law and not a principle of universal application. Many other jurisdictions – the USA in particular – do not have such a system, and in the UK itself there are 'no costs' jurisdictions such as the Employment Tribunal. The existence of the costs-shifting rule is one of the unique features of clinical negligence litigation in England and Wales.

The second pillar of costs jurisprudence is the indemnity principle. The costs the losing party pays have to be based upon and cannot exceed the amount the winning party is obliged to pay his legal representatives. In effect the losing party 'indemnifies' the winning party's legal obligations to pay his solicitor's costs.

Applying these principles, the general position at the end of a case will be that the losing party will pay the winning party's costs and those costs will be assessed on the basis of the fees the winning client is charged by his solicitor. Some moments of reflection will lead us to realise the potential problems with the general position: are there not cases in which it is impossible to say who has 'won'? What happens when a party wins on some issues but not others? What happens when a party 'wins' but his conduct has unnecessarily prolonged the litigation or otherwise made it more expensive? What happens when a party beats or fails to beat a Part 36 offer? There may be cases in which it is unjust to allow the losing party to pay the full scale of the fees the lay client is prepared to incur. The process of assessment must limit *inter partes* recovery to those costs which are reasonable, but how does the court determine what is 'reasonable' and what principles apply to this assessment?

SOME RULES ABOUT COSTS

Historically courts have had a wide discretion relating to costs. CPR 44.2(1) provides that the court:

> has discretion as to –
> (a)   whether costs are payable by one party to another;
> (b)   the amount of those costs; and
> (c)   when they are paid.

The 'general rule' is that 'the unsuccessful party will be ordered to pay the costs of the successful party' (CPR 44.2(2)(a)) but 'the court may make a different order' (CPR 44.2(2)(b)).

The overriding objective of the CPR and its costs provisions allow the court to take a forensic and nuanced view of costs. Costs orders can be subtle enough to take into account the 'measure' of success as well as success itself. A party can be awarded a proportion of its costs where it has achieved only partial success. The order can reflect success or failure on a particular issue.

In making a costs order the court *must* have regard to *all* the circumstances of the case including:

1   the conduct of all the parties;
2   whether a party has succeeded on part of its case, even if that party has not been wholly successful; and
3   any admissible offer to settle made by a party which is drawn to the court's attention, and which is not an offer to which costs consequences under Part 36 apply. (CPR 44.2(4))

In considering cases when the general rule does not apply, the most important factors to consider will be the conduct of the parties, the nature of 'success' in the particular case, and the nature and consequences of any offer.

The conduct of parties as set out in the CPR 44.2(5) includes conduct before as well as during proceedings (CPR 44.2(5)(a)) and:

(b)   whether it was reasonable for a party to raise, pursue or contest a particular allegation or issue;

(c)   the manner in which a party has pursued or defended its case or a particular allegation or issue; and

(d)   whether a claimant who has succeeded in the claim, in whole or in part, exaggerated its claim.

Although the wide discretion of the court allows for no hard and fast rules, it is possible to comment on some of the circumstances in which the general rule will not apply or applies in some modified form.

Multiple defendants

The introduction of QOCS gives rise to particular issues in relation to claims against multiple defendants which are considered below. However, the earlier authorities provide some assistance in outlining the general approach taken prior to this change.

Bringing claims against multiple defendants makes litigation more complicated and expensive. Damages recovered against an unsuccessful defendant may be wiped out by the expense of meeting the costs of other successful defendants. Historically the courts have recognised the injustice that the strict application of the general rule creates in these circumstances and the wide discretion the court enjoys in relation to costs includes the power to order that the unsuccessful defendant bear the burden of the successful defendant's costs. This can be achieved in one of two ways: the unsuccessful party pays the successful defendant's costs directly to him following *Sanderson v Blyth Theatre Company*;[1] or the claimant pays the successful defendant's costs which he then recovers from the unsuccessful defendant as part of the costs of the action following *Bullock v London General Omnibus Co.*[2]

The fact that the court *can* make either a *Bullock* or *Sanderson* order does not mean that the court *will* make such an order, and the court will have regard to all the circumstances of the case.

In cases where one defendant blames another potential defendant for the claimant's injury, a *Bullock* or *Sanderson* order may be appropriate. Where the allegations made by a defendant against another potential defendant amount to a complete defence to the claim, it may be reasonable for the claimant to sue both defendants. However, the fact that one defendant blames another is only one factor to be taken into account and the court has to consider whether or not it had been reasonable for the claimant to pursue the allegations against the successful defendant; see *Irvine v Commissioner of Police for the Metropolis*,[3] cf *Moon v Garrett*.[4]

The CPR is a complete procedural code. Active case management is intended to root out unmeritorious causes of action at an early stage, and where such claims are continued they are more likely to result in adverse costs orders. The fact that a party has succeeded at a hearing either in whole or in part is still a powerful indicator of where the costs burden should fall. The courts will not readily accept that it is fair for an

---

1   [1903] 2 KB 533, CA.
2   [1907] 1 KB 264, CA.
3   [2005] EWCA Civ 129.
4   [2006] EWCA Civ 1121.

unsuccessful party to bear the additional burden of a successful party's costs without good reason.

The consequences of bringing proceedings against multiple defendants are particularly relevant to clinical negligence practice when claims may proceed against a number of clinicians or health care providers, for example an NHS trust and a GP. In *Ganz v Childs*[5] the court had to determine whether or not the claimant or an unsuccessful defendant ought to be liable for the successful defendant's case. In this case, although the claim against the GP succeeded, that against the hospital failed. Foskett J ordered that the claimant should pay the hospital's costs.

Partial success

Partial success in clinical negligence cases is common. The claimant may succeed in proving negligence but only modest damages may be awarded by comparison with the large sums claimed, invariably because the claimant fails in some aspect of the case in relation to causation. In *Oksuzoglu v Kay*,[6] the claimant failed to satisfy the court that the negligence of the defendants caused the loss of his right leg. However, their negligence had resulted in a period of pain and suffering prior to the correct treatment being given, justifying a claim for general damages and some care. The defendants effectively 'won' the case.

In most cases defendants can protect themselves against the costs consequences of partial success by making appropriate Part 36 offers. However, if no effective offers are made the courts have to consider who the real 'winner' is, and in this respect there are several competing arguments. Applying the general rule, if the claimant is awarded damages, even if he did not recover as much as had been hoped, success has still been achieved. The circumstances may be that the claimant would still have had to come to court to recover even those damages recovered, and the partial success made no or little difference to the costs incurred. If it was reasonable for the claimant to proceed in this way, he should be entitled to his costs. At the other extreme, a claimant may win and recover a substantial amount of damages but certain allegations may have failed or been abandoned at trial. In complex litigation, a successful party may well fail in one or more issues and it would be inappropriate to award only part of the successful party's costs. The successful party's costs should not be reduced simply because he had not recovered as much as had been hoped.

Where a claimant's success is only partial, the court has to have regard to the issues in dispute at trial and to what extent the costs incurred relate to the failure. Where the claimant's failure in respect of some aspects of the claim had little relevance or impact on the defendant's conduct, the usual costs consequences will follow. Where the true nature of the case is that the defendant has essentially won on the main or essential issues, the claimant can expect an adverse costs order.

A recent case illustrates the issues discussed above. In *Medway Primary Care Trust v Marcus*,[7] the claimant lost before the trial judge on

---

5   [2011] EWHC 13.
6   [1998] Lloyd's Rep Med 129, CA.
7   [2011] EWCA Civ 750.

his central allegation that the negligence of the defendants had resulted in the amputation of his left leg. However there had been breaches of duty which caused delay during which the claimant suffered pain and injury compensatable by a modest award of £2,000 general damages. Having achieved judgment for this sum the judge awarded the claimant 50% of his costs. This decision was reversed on appeal and the defendants recovered 75% of their costs. The award of £2,000 was 'insignificant' in the context of the claim itself:

> it was in truth a last minute addition to salvage something (0.25%) from an action which the respondent had lost.

The essential issue in the claim was causation and the defendants had succeeded on that point. Moreover, the defendants had maintained the same defence in relation to causation from the outset of the claim. The fact that no Part 36 or Calderbank offers had been made was not relevant to the issue of who had *won* the case. The decision in the Court of Appeal is notable for the dissenting judgment of Jackson LJ. In characteristically blunt terms at the end of his speech he pointed out that:

> The defendants made no Part 36 offer in this case and in my view they should accept the consequences.

Underlying this assertion were important public policy considerations:

> Part 36 ... affords protection for defendants who have a weak case on liability but a strong case on quantum. Such defendants can and should protect their position on costs by making an appropriate Part 36 offer at an early stage. If only defendants and their insurers would take this course, a large amount of unnecessary litigation would be avoided.

Issues-based costs orders

The CPR allows the court to make costs orders that accurately reflect the outcome of the adjudication of distinct issues within the case as well as success in the case itself. However, a balance needs to be struck between an unsuccessful argument put forward which is an integral part of the claim and where a wholly separate and distinct but unsuccessful position is pursued. In the latter case, the court will have regard to what extent the unsuccessful arguments took up the court's and the parties' time and resulted in a measureable increase in the costs of the claim.

In some cases costs can be made in relation to a discrete issue. For example, in *Webster v Ridgeway Foundation School*,[8] Nicol J allowed the defendant the costs of defending a human rights claim to be assessed on an indemnity basis. The judge found that the claim was hopeless. The claim was a discrete issue in the proceedings, and there was sufficient clarity as to which costs were attributable to it to treat it differently from the other costs.

In some cases the court could award a successful claimant a percentage of his costs to reflect the fact that some allegations were unsuccessful or not pursued. In *Devon County Council v Clarke*,[9] the Court of Appeal allowed the claimant 70% of his costs. Although the trial judge had allowed

---

8   [2010] EWHC 318 (QB).
9   [2005] EWCA Civ 266.

the claimant 100% of his costs, the allegations pursued against different professionals employed by the defendant local authority at different times were distinct claims in their own right and could be considered as discrete aspects of the claim.

It is inappropriate to judge the success or failure of a claim at an interlocutory stage. So where the claimant amended his particulars of claim to plead fresh allegations of negligence, it was inappropriate for the judge to award the defendant its costs of defending the original case up until the amendment, see *Chadwick v Hollingsworth*.[10] These were matters that were properly considered after trial.

Mediation

The leading case is *Halsey v Milton Keynes General NHS Trust*.[11] This was a fatal accident claim brought by a widow arising from the death of her husband in hospital. Her solicitors wrote a number of letters, including one to the Secretary of State for Health, asking for mediation. The trust refused to mediate. The Court of Appeal held that there was no presumption that a party will mediate. The failure to mediate would not displace the general costs rule unless the failure to mediate had been unreasonable. In order to show that the failure to mediate was unreasonable, the party would have to show that mediation had reasonable prospects of success. The court will have regard to all the circumstances of the case: the nature of the dispute; the merits in the case; attempts to settle the claim by other means; the value of the claim and the costs incurred by mediation; and any delay caused by mediation. In *Halsey*, the court found that there was reason to believe that mediation would have been successful. The defendant was intent on defending the claim and was entitled to take it to trial with the usual costs consequences.

CPR PART 36

A new Part 36 came into force on 6 April 2015 and applies only to offers made after that date.[12] Part 36 is a self-contained procedural code which governs such offers.[13]

Form and content

The form and content of a Part 36 offer are set out at CPR 36.5 as follows:

(1) A Part 36 offer must—
(a)   be in writing;
(b)   make clear that it is made pursuant to Part 36;
(c)   specify a period of not less than 21 days within which the defendant will be liable for the claimant's costs in accordance with rule 36.13 or 36.20 if the offer is accepted;

---

10   [2010] EWHC 2718 (QB).
11   [2004] 1 WLR 3002, CA.
12   Civil Procedure (Amendment No 8) Rules 2014, SI 2014/3299.
13   CPR 36.1(1).

(d)   state whether it relates to the whole of the claim or to part of it or to an issue that arises in it and if so to which part or issue; and

(e)   state whether it takes into account any counterclaim.

(2) Paragraph (1)(c) does not apply if the offer is made less than 21 days before the start of a trial.

(3) In appropriate cases, a Part 36 offer must contain such further information as is required by rule 36.18 (personal injury claims for future pecuniary loss), rule 36.19 (offer to settle a claim for provisional damages), and rule 36.22 (deduction of benefits).

(4) A Part 36 offer which offers to pay or offers to accept a sum of money will be treated as inclusive of all interest until—

(a)   the date on which the period specified under rule 36.5(1)(c) expires; or

(b)   if rule 36.5(2) applies, a date 21 days after the date the offer was made.

The specific requirements that apply to personal injury claims are set out at the CPR 36.18 and relate specifically to issue in relation to future loss and periodical payments. The requirements are as described below.

The defendant's offer

Under the CPR 36.6 a Part 36 offer by a defendant to pay a sum of money in settlement of a claim must be an offer to pay a single sum of money. A defendant's offer that includes an offer to pay all or part of the sum at a date later than 14 days following the date of acceptance will not be treated as a Part 36 offer unless the offeree accepts the offer.

Timing of a Part 36 offer

A Part 36 offer may be made at any time, including before the commencement of proceedings and is made when it is served on the offeree (CPR 36.7).

Clarification of a Part 36 offer

CPR 36.8 sets out the procedure for a party to clarify a Part 36 offer:

1   the offeree may, within seven days of a Part 36 offer being made, request the offeror to clarify the offer;

2   if the offeror does not give the clarification requested under paragraph 1 within seven days of receiving the request, the offeree may, unless the trial has started, apply for an order that the offeror do so;

3   if the court makes an order under paragraph 2, it must specify the date when the Part 36 offer is to be treated as having been made.

Withdrawing a Part 36 offer

A Part 36 offer may be withdrawn under the CPR 36.9:

(1)   A Part 36 offer can only be withdrawn, or its terms changed, if the offeree has not previously served notice of acceptance.

(2)   The offeror withdraws the offer or changes its terms by serving written notice of the withdrawal or change of terms on the offeree.

(3)   Subject to rule 36.10, such notice of withdrawal or change of terms takes effect when it is served on the offeree.

(4)   Subject to paragraph (1), after expiry of the relevant period—

    (a)   the offeror may withdraw the offer or change its terms without the permission of the court; or

    (b)   the offer may be automatically withdrawn in accordance with its terms.

(5)   Where the offeror changes the terms of a Part 36 offer to make it more advantageous to the offeree—

    (a)   such improved offer shall be treated, not as the withdrawal of the original offer; but as the making of a new Part 36 offer on the improved terms; and

    (b)   subject to rule 36.5(2), the period specified under rule 36.5(1)(c) shall be 21 days or such longer period (if any) identified in the written notice referred to in paragraph (2).

Changes or withdrawal of a Part 36 offer before the expiry of the relevant period

Under the CPR 36.10 a party may withdraw or change the terms of a Part 36 offer within the relevant period if the following apply:

(1)   Subject to rule 36.9(1), this rule applies where the offeror serves notice before expiry of the relevant period of withdrawal of the offer or change of its terms to be less advantageous to the offeree.

(2)   Where this rule applies—

    (a)   if the offeree has not served notice of acceptance of the original offer by the expiry of the relevant period, the offeror's notice has effect on the expiry of that period; and

    (b)   if the offeree serves notice of acceptance of the original offer before the expiry of the relevant period, that acceptance has effect unless the offeror applies to the court for permission to withdraw the offer or to change its terms—

        (i)   within 7 days of the offeree's notice of acceptance; or

        (ii)   if earlier, before the first day of trial.

(3)   On an application under paragraph (2)(b), the court may give permission for the original offer to be withdrawn or its terms changed if satisfied that there has been a change of circumstances since the making of the original offer and that it is in the interests of justice to give permission.

Acceptance of a Part 36 Offer

By the CPR 36.11(1) a Part 36 offer is accepted by serving written notice of acceptance on the offeror. A Part 36 offer may be accepted at any time (whether or not the offeree has subsequently made a different offer), unless it has already been withdrawn under the CPR 36.11(2).

Under the CPR 36.11(3) the court's permission is required to accept a Part 36 offer where: (a) CPR 36.15(4) (multiple defendants); and (b) CPR 36.22(3)(b) (deduction of benefits) apply, the relevant period has expired and further deductible amounts have been paid to the claimant since the date of the offer (CPR 36.15(4) and 36.22(3)); and also when (c) an apportionment is required under the CPR 41.3A, apportionment in proceedings under the Fatal Accidents Act 1976 and Law Reform (Miscellaneous Provisions) Act 1934); or (d) a trial is in progress. Where the court gives permission, unless all the parties have agreed costs, the court must make an order dealing with costs, and may order that the costs consequences set out in the CPR 36.13 apply.

Costs consequences of accepting a Part 36 offer

Other than in cases to which the rules of fixed costs apply, the basic rule is that where a Part 36 offer is accepted within the relevant period the claimant will be entitled to the costs of the proceedings (including their recoverable pre-action costs) up to the date on which notice of acceptance was served on the offeror under the CPR 36.13(1), subject to:

> (2)   Where—
>   (a)   a defendant's Part 36 offer relates to part only of the claim; and
>   (b)   at the time of serving notice of acceptance within the relevant period the claimant abandons the balance of the claim, the claimant will only be entitled to the costs of such part of the claim unless the court orders otherwise.

and

> (4)   Where—
>   (a)   a Part 36 offer which was made less than 21 days before the start of a trial is accepted; or
>   (b)   a Part 36 offer which relates to the whole of the claim is accepted after expiry of the relevant period; or
>   (c)   subject to paragraph (2), a Part 36 offer which does not relate to the whole of the claim is accepted at any time,
>   the liability for costs must be determined by the court unless the parties have agreed the costs.

Under the CPR 36.13(5) and (6):

> (5) Where paragraph (4) (b) applies but the parties cannot agree the liability for costs, the court must, unless it considers it unjust to do so, order that—
> (a)   the claimant be awarded costs up to the date on which the relevant period expired; and
> (b)   the offeree do pay the offeror's costs for the period from the date of expiry of the relevant period to the date of acceptance.
> (6) In considering whether it would be unjust to make the orders specified in paragraph (5), the court must take into account all the circumstances of the case including the matters listed in rule 36.17(5).

For further discussion of CPR 36.17(5), see below.

Acceptance of a Part 36 offer made by one or more but not all defendants

The CPR 36.15 applies when the claimant wishes to accept a Part 36 offer made by one or more, but not all, of a number of defendants. The relevant provisions (CPR 36.15(2), (3), (4)) are as follows:

> (2) If the defendants are sued jointly or in the alternative, the claimant may accept the offer if—
> (a)   the claimant discontinues the claim against those defendants who have not made the offer; and
> (b)   those defendants give written consent to the acceptance of the offer.
> (3) If the claimant alleges that the defendants have a several liability to the claimant, the claimant may—
> (a)   accept the offer; and
> (b)   continue with the claims against the other defendants if entitled to do so.
> (4) In all other cases the claimant must apply to the court for permission to accept the Part 36 offer.

Costs consequences following judgment

The CPR 36.17(1) applies where judgment is entered and either: (a) a claimant fails to obtain a judgment more advantageous than a defendant's Part 36 offer; or (b) judgment against the defendant 'is at least as advantageous' to the claimant as the proposals contained in a claimant's Part 36 offer.

Under the CPR 36.17(2):

> in relation to any money claim or money element of a claim, 'more advantageous' means 'better in money terms by any amount, however small, and 'at least as advantageous' shall be construed accordingly.

Where the claimant fails to beat the offer: CPR 36.17(3)

Unless it considers it unjust to do so, the court can order that the defendant is entitled to: (a) costs (including any recoverable pre-action costs) from the date on which the relevant period expired; and (b) interest on those costs.

Where the claimant's offer 'is at least as advantageous' as a claimant's Part 36 offer, CPR 36.17(1)(b) applies and the court must, unless it considers it unjust to do so, order that the claimant is entitled to:

(a)   interest on the whole or part of any sum of money (excluding interest) awarded, at a rate not exceeding 10% above base rate for some or all of the period starting with the date on which the relevant period expired;

(b)   costs (including any recoverable pre-action costs) on the indemnity basis from the date on which the relevant period expired;

(c)   interest on those costs at a rate not exceeding 10% above base rate; and

(d)   provided that the case has been decided and there has not been a previous order under this sub-paragraph, an additional amount, which shall not exceed £75,000, calculated by applying the prescribed percentage set out below to an amount which is—

  (i)   the sum awarded to the claimant by the court; or

  (ii)   where there is no monetary award, the sum awarded to the claimant by the court in respect of costs—

Amount awarded by the court	Prescribed percentage
Up to £500,000	10% of the amount awarded
Above £500,000	10% of the first £500,000 and (subject to the limit of £75,000) 5% of any amount above that figure.

Factors to be taken into account in making an award under CPR 36.17(3) and (4)

In considering whether it would be unjust to make the orders referred to in paragraphs (3) and (4), the court must take into account all the circumstances of the case including:

(a)   the terms of any Part 36 offer;

(b)   the stage in the proceedings when any Part 36 offer was made, including in particular how long before the trial started the offer was made;

    (c)   the information available to the parties at the time when the Part 36 offer was made;

    (d)   the conduct of the parties with regard to the giving of or refusal to give information for the purposes of enabling the offer to be made or evaluated; and

    (e)   whether the offer was a genuine attempt to settle the proceedings.

Interest: CPR 36.17(6)

Awards of interest are considered in the CPR 36.17(6). Where the court awards interest under the CPR 36, and also awards interest on the same sum and for the same period under any other power, the total rate of interest must not exceed 10% above base rate.

Exceptions: CPR 36.17(7)

CPR 36.17(3) and (4) do not apply to a Part 36 offer—

(a) which has been withdrawn;

(b) which has been changed so that its terms are less advantageous to the offeree where the offeree has beaten the less advantageous offer;

(c) made less than 21 days before trial, unless the court has abridged the relevant period.

Personal injury claims and future pecuniary loss

CPR 36.18 applies to a claim for damages for personal injury which is or includes a claim for future pecuniary loss and under CPR 36.18(3) provides that:

> A Part 36 offer to which this rule applies may contain an offer to pay, or an offer to accept—
>   (a)   the whole or part of the damages for future pecuniary loss in the form of—
>   (i)   a lump sum;
>   (ii)   periodical payments; or
>   (iii) both a lump sum and periodical payments;
>   (b)   the whole or part of any other damages in the form of a lump sum.

Under the CPR 36.18(4)(a) a Part 36 offer to which this rule applies must state the amount of any offer to pay or to accept the whole or part of any damages in the form of a lump sum, and further:

>   (b)   may state—
>   (i)   what part of the lump sum, if any, relates to damages for future pecuniary loss; and
>   (ii)   what part relates to other damages to be paid or accepted in the form of a lump sum;
>   (c)   must state what part of the offer relates to damages for future pecuniary loss to be paid or accepted in the form of periodical payments and must specify—
>   (i)   the amount and duration of the periodical payments;
>   (ii)   the amount of any payments for substantial capital purchases and when they are to be made; and

(iii)   that each amount is to vary by reference to the retail prices index (or to some other named index, or that it is not to vary by reference to any index); and

(d)   must state either that any damages which take the form of periodical payments will be funded in a way which ensures that the continuity of payments is reasonably secure in accordance with section 2(4) of the Damages Act 1996 or how such damages are to be paid and how the continuity of their payment is to be secured.

(5) Rule 36.6 applies to the extent that a Part 36 offer by a defendant under this rule includes an offer to pay all or part of any damages in the form of a lump sum.

(6) Where the offeror makes a Part 36 offer to which this rule applies and which offers to pay or to accept damages in the form of both a lump sum and periodical payments, the offeree may only give notice of acceptance of the offer as a whole.

(7) If the offeree accepts a Part 36 offer which includes payment of any part of the damages in the form of periodical payments, the claimant must, within 7 days of the date of acceptance, apply to the court for an order for an award of damages in the form of periodical payments under rule 41.8.

Part 36 and provisional damages

Under the CPR 36.19 a Part 36 offer can be made in respect of a claim which includes a claim for provisional damages. The offer must specify whether or not the offeror is proposing that the settlement shall include an award of provisional damages (CPR 36.19(2)). When such an offer is made the offer must also comply with CPR 36.19(3) and state that:

(a)   that the sum offered is in satisfaction of the claim for damages on the assumption that the injured person will not develop the disease or suffer the type of deterioration specified in the offer;

(b)   that the offer is subject to the condition that the claimant must make any claim for further damages within a limited period; and

(c)   what that period is.

QUALIFIED ONE WAY COSTS SHIFTING (QOCS)

The QOCS is a significant innovation to the Civil Procedure Rules. A fundamental pillar of the common law is the costs-shifting rule: the rule by which the 'loser' pays the winner's costs, ie the costs burden *shifts* from the unsuccessful party to the successful party. One-way costs shifting means the general principle and expectation that if the claimant wins the defendant will pay the claimant's costs, but if the defendant wins the claimant will not incur a practical liability to pay the defendant's costs: the costs shift but only in one direction, to the claimant. The key innovation that creates complexity is the fact that the one way costs shifting rule is 'qualified'.

Under QOCS orders for costs may be made against a claimant in the ordinary way, however, they may only be enforced in certain circumstances, with or without the permission of the court and are 'capped' at the aggregate amount of the order for damages and interest made in favour of the claimant (CPR 44.14(1)). Orders for costs made against a claimant may only be enforced after the proceedings have been concluded and the costs have been assessed or agreed (CPR 44.14(2)). An order for costs which is enforced only to the extent permitted by CPR 44.14(1) shall not be treated as an unsatisfied or outstanding judgment for the purposes of any court record.

Where the permission of the court is not required: CPR 44.15

Orders for costs made against the claimant may be enforced to the full extent of such orders without the permission of the court where the proceedings have been struck out on the grounds that:

(a) the claimant has disclosed no reasonable grounds for bringing the proceedings;
(b) the proceedings are an abuse of the court's process; or
(c) the conduct of –
    (i)   the claimant; or
    (ii) a person acting on the claimant's behalf and with the claimant's knowledge of such conduct,

is likely to obstruct the just disposal of the proceedings.

Where permission of the court is required: CPR 44.16

Orders for costs made against the claimant may be enforced to the full extent of such orders with the permission of the court where the claim is found on the balance of probabilities to be fundamentally dishonest, see CPR 44.16(1).

QOCS and interlocutory costs orders, including Part 36

The CPR 44.14 does not contain any express reference to Part 36. However, an order for costs made against a successful claimant can be enforced against a successful claimant subject to the cap. For example, any interlocutory costs orders made against a claimant during the course of proceedings can be enforced against the successful claimant. Likewise any order made against a claimant who fails to 'beat' the defendant's Part 36 offer can be enforced against the claimant subject to the cap.

QOCS and multiple defendants

How does QOCS apply in a case where the claimant succeeds against one or more but not all defendants? Is the claimant liable to pay the costs of the successful defendant? The short answer to these questions is: yes (see *Cartwright v Venduct Engineering Ltd*[14]). A claimant who has an order for damages and interest payable by a defendant is liable to pay out of that amount any adverse costs orders in favour of a successful defendant, but only up to the limit of the order for damages and interest payable by the unsuccessful defendant. In that case the claimant compromised the claim against three defendants by way of a Tomlin order and served a notice of discontinuance on the remaining defendant. The Tomlin order

---

14 [2018] EWCA Civ 1654.

was not an order 'for damages and interest in favour of the claimant' for the purposes of the CPR 44.14(1). Payments under a Tomlin order do not fall within the scope of the CPR 44.14 because the order setting out the agreement is not part of the order but a record of the agreement reached between the parties.

PRINCIPLES OF COSTS ASSESSMENT

Standard and indemnity costs

Costs fall to be assessed either on the standard or the indemnity basis, but in either case the court will not allow costs which have been unreasonably incurred or are unreasonable in amount (CPR 44.3(1)).

When assessed on a standard basis, the court will have regard to whether the costs were: (i) proportionately and reasonably incurred; or (ii) proportionate and reasonable in amount (CPR 44.4(1)(a)).

The CPR 44.3(2) provides that where the amount of costs is to be assessed on the standard basis, the court will:

(a) only allow costs which are proportionate to the matters in issue. Costs which are disproportionate in amount may be disallowed or reduced even if they were reasonably or necessarily incurred; and
(b) resolve any doubt which it may have as to whether costs were reasonably and proportionately incurred or were reasonable and proportionate in amount in favour of the paying party.

When costs are to be paid on an indemnity basis, the court will have regard to whether the costs were: (i) unreasonably incurred; or (ii) unreasonable in amount (CPR 44.4(1)(b)).

CPR 44.3(3) provides that when the amount of costs is to be assessed on the indemnity basis, the court will resolve any doubt which it may have as to whether costs were reasonably incurred or were reasonable in amount in favour of the receiving party.

Standard costs: proportionality

CPR 44.3(5) provides that costs incurred are proportionate 'if they bear a reasonable relationship to':

(a) the sums in issue in the proceedings;
(b) the value of any non-monetary relief in issue in the proceedings;
(c) the complexity of the litigation;
(d) any additional work generated by the conduct of the paying party; and
(e) any wider factors involved in the proceedings, such as reputation or public importance.

Factors to be taken into account in determining the amount of costs

CPR 44.4(3) sets out the factors the court will have regard to in determining the amount of costs, including:

(a) the conduct of all the parties, including in particular –
  (i) conduct before, as well as during, the proceedings; and
  (ii) the efforts made, if any, before and during the proceedings in order to try to resolve the dispute;
(b) the amount or value of any money or property involved;
(c) the importance of the matter to all the parties;
(d) the particular complexity of the matter or the difficulty or novelty of the questions raised;
(e) the skill, effort, specialised knowledge and responsibility involved;
(f) the time spent on the case;
(g) the place where and the circumstances in which work or any part of it was done; and
(h) the receiving party's last approved or agreed budget.

PRO BONO COSTS ORDERS

From 1 October 2008, the Legal Services Act 2007 allows for the recovery of costs in pro bono cases. Section 194 allows the court to make an order against a party who is unsuccessful against a party represented pro bono. The costs awarded are not payable to the successful litigant but to the Access to Justice Foundation ('the prescribed charity'). CPR 46.7 sets out the relevant procedure including that the order must specify that payment by the paying party is to be made to the prescribed charity (CPR 46.7(2)). The Costs Practice Direction provides that the assisted party must file and serve a written statement setting out the sum of costs 'that party would have been claimed for that legal representation had it not been provided free of charge' (CPR PD 46 4.1).

Appendices

All Statutes, Civil Procedure Rules, Practice Directions and Protocols are published with the kind permission of the Ministry of Justice.

Appendices

Appendix I

Statutes

Contents

1. DAMAGES

[The sections reproduced below are printed as amended, where appropriate.]

Law Reform (Personal Injuries) Act 1948 (11 & 12 Geo 6 c 41)

2. *Measure of damages ...*

(4) In an action for damages for personal injuries (including any such action arising out of a contract), there shall be disregarded, in determining the reasonableness of any expenses, the possibility of avoiding those expenses or part of them by taking advantage of facilities available under the [the National Health Service Act 2006 or the National Health Service (Wales) Act 2006] or the National Health Service (Scotland) Act 1978, or of any corresponding facilities in Northern Ireland.

[NOTE: there is a growing lobby for the repeal of this section. If ever enacted, this would have the effect of substantially reducing compensation in many cases.]

Administration of Justice Act 1982 (1982 c 53)

Abolition of certain claims for damages etc

Abolition of right to damages for loss of expectation of life

1.–(1) In an action under the law of England and Wales or the law of Northern Ireland for damages for personal injuries –

  (a) no damages shall be recoverable in respect of any loss of expectation of life caused to the injured person by the injuries; but

  (b) if the injured person's expectation of life has been reduced by the injuries, the court, in assessing damages in respect of pain and suffering caused by the injuries, shall take account of any suffering caused or likely to be caused to him by awareness that his expectation of life has been so reduced.

(2) The reference in subsection (1)(a) above to damages in respect of loss of expectation of life does not include damages in respect of loss of income.

Abolition of actions for loss of services etc

2. No person shall be liable in tort under the law of England and Wales or the law of Northern Ireland –

  (a) to a husband on the ground only of his having deprived him of the services or society of his wife;

  (b) to a parent (or person standing in the place of a parent) on the ground only of his having deprived him of the services of a child; or

  (c) on the ground only –

   (i) of having deprived another of the services of his menial servant;

   (ii) of having deprived another of the services of his female servant by raping or seducing her; or

   (iii) of enticement of a servant or harbouring a servant.

Fatal Accidents Act 1976

3. The following sections shall be substituted for sections 1 to 4 of the Fatal Accidents Act 1976 –

  '...

Bereavement

1A.–(1) An action under this Act may consist of or include a claim for damages for bereavement.

(2) A claim for damages for bereavement shall only be for the benefit –
(a)   of the wife or husband [or civil partner] of the deceased; and
(b)   where the deceased was a minor who was never married [or civil partner]
–

   (i)   of his parents, if he was legitimate; and
   (ii)   of his mother, if he was illegitimate.
(3) Subject to subsection (5) below, the sum to be awarded as damages under this section shall be [£12,980].
(4) Where there is a claim for damages under this section for the benefit of both the parents of the deceased the sum awarded shall be divided equally between them (subject to any deduction falling to be made in respect of costs not recovered from the defendant).
(5) The Lord Chancellor may by order made by statutory instrument, subject to annulment in pursuance of a resolution of either House of Parliament, amend this section by varying the sum for the time being specified in subsection (3) above.
...'

Claims not surviving death

Exclusion of Law Reform (Miscellaneous Provisions) Act 1934

4.–(1) The following subsection shall be inserted after section 1(1) of the Law Reform (Miscellaneous Provisions) Act 1934 (actions to survive death) –

'(1A) The right of a person to claim under section 1A of the Fatal Accidents Act 1976 (bereavement) shall not survive for the benefit of his estate on his death.'.

(2) The following paragraph shall be substituted for subsection (2)(a) –

'(a) shall not include –

   (i)   any exemplary damages;
   (ii)   any damages for loss of income in respect of any period after that person's death;'.

Maintenance at public expense

Maintenance at public expense to be taken into account in assessment of damages

5. In an action under the law of England and Wales or the law of Northern Ireland for damages for personal injuries (including any such action arising out of a contract) any saving to the injured person which is attributable to his maintenance wholly or partly at public expense in a hospital, nursing home or other institution shall be set off against any income lost by him as a result of his injuries.

2. LIMITATION

Limitation Act 1980 (1980 c 58)

[The sections reproduced below are printed as amended, where appropriate.]

An Act to consolidate the Limitations Acts 1939 to 1980.
[13th November 1980]

Part I

Ordinary Time Limits for Different Classes of Action

Time limits under Part I subject to extension or exclusion under Part II

Time limits under Part I subject to extension or exclusion under Part II

1.–(1) This Part of this Act gives the ordinary time limits for bringing actions of the various classes mentioned in the following provisions of this Part.

(2) The ordinary time limits given in this Part of this Act are subject to extension or exclusion in accordance with the provisions of Part II of this Act.

Actions founded on tort

Time limit for actions founded on tort

2. An action founded on tort shall not be brought after the expiration of six years from the date on which the cause of action accrued.

Actions founded on simple contract

Time limit for actions founded on simple contract

5. An action founded on simple contract shall not be brought after the expiration of six years from the date on which the cause of action accrued.

Actions in respect of wrongs causing personal injuries or death

Special time limit for actions in respect of personal injuries

11.–(1) This section applies to any action for damages for negligence, nuisance or breach of duty (whether the duty exists by virtue of a contract or of provision made by or under a statute or independently of any contract or any such provision) where the damages claimed by the plaintiff for the negligence, nuisance or breach of duty consist of or include damages in respect of personal injuries to the plaintiff or any other person.

(1A) This section does not apply to any action brought for damages under section 3 of the Protection from Harassment Act 1997.

(2) None of the time limits given in the preceding provisions of this Act shall apply to an action to which this section applies.

(3) An action to which this section applies shall not be brought after the expiration of the period applicable in accordance with subsection (4) or (5) below.

(4) Except where subsection (5) below applies, the period applicable is three years from –
    (a)   the date on which the cause of action accrued; or
    (b)   the date of knowledge (if later) of the person injured.

(5) If the person injured dies before the expiration of the period mentioned in subsection (4) above, the period applicable as respects the cause of action surviving for the benefit of his estate by virtue of section 1 of the Law Reform (Miscellaneous Provisions) Act 1934 shall be three years from –
    (a)   the date of death; or
    (b)   the date of the personal representative's knowledge;
whichever is the later.

(6) For the purposes of this section 'personal representative' includes any person who is or has been a personal representative of the deceased, including an

executor who has not proved the will (whether or not he has renounced probate) but not anyone appointed only as a special personal representative in relation to settled land; and regard shall be had to any knowledge acquired by any such person while a personal representative or previously.

(7) If there is more than one personal representative, and their dates of knowledge are different, subsection (5)(b) above shall be read as referring to the earliest of those dates.

Actions in respect of defective products

11A.–(1) This section shall apply to an action for damages by virtue of any provision of Part I of the Consumer Protection Act 1987.

(2) None of the time limits given in the preceding provisions of this Act shall apply to an action to which this section applies.

(3) An action in which this section applies shall not be brought after the expiration of the period of ten years from the relevant time, within the meaning of section 4 of the said Act of 1987; and this subsection shall operate to extinguish a right of action and shall do so whether or not that right of action had accrued, or time under the following provisions of this Act had begun to run, at the end of the said period of ten years.

(4) Subject to subsection (5) below, an action to which this section applies in which the damages claimed by the plaintiff consist of or include damages in respect of personal injuries to the plaintiff or any other person for loss of or damage to any property, shall not be brought after the expiration of the period of three years from whichever is the later of –

    (a)   the date on which the cause of action accrued; and

    (b)   the date of knowledge of the injured person or, in the case of loss of or damage to property, the date of knowledge of the plaintiff or (if earlier) of any person in whom this cause of action was previously vested.

(5) If in a case where the damages claimed by the plaintiff consist of or include damages in respect of personal injuries to the plaintiff or any other person the injured person died before the expiration of the period mentioned in subsection (4) above, that subsection shall have effect as respects the cause of action surviving for the benefit of his estate by virtue of section 1 of the Law Reform (Miscellaneous Provisions) Act 1934 as if for the reference to that period there were substituted a reference to the period of three years from whichever is the later of –

    (a)   the date of death; and

    (b)   the date of the personal representative's knowledge.

(6) For the purposes of this section 'personal representative' includes any person who is or has been a personal representative of the deceased, including an executor who has not proved the will (whether or not he has renounced probate) but not anyone appointed only as a special personal representative in relation to settled land; and regard shall be had to any knowledge acquired by any such person while a personal representative or previously.

(7) If there is more than one personal representative and their dates of knowledge are different, subsection (5)(b) above shall be read as referring to the earliest of those dates.

(8) Expressions used in this section or section 14 of this Act and in Part I of the Consumer Protection Act 1987 have the same meanings in this section or that section as in that Part; and section 1(1) of that Act (Part I to be construed as enacted for the purpose of complying with the product liability Directive) shall apply for the purpose of construing this section and the following provisions of this Act so far as they relate to any action by virtue of any provision of that Part as it applies for the purpose of construing that part.

Special time limit for actions under Fatal Accidents legislation

12.–(1) An action under the Fatal Accidents Act 1976 shall not be brought if the death occurred when the person injured could no longer maintain an action and recover damages in respect of the injury (whether because of a time limit in this Act or in any other Act, or for any other reason).

Where any such action by the injured person would have been barred by the time limit in section 11 or 11A of this Act, no account shall be taken of the possibility of that time limit being overridden under section 33 of this Act.

(2) None of the time limits given in the preceding provisions of this Act shall apply to an action under the Fatal Accidents Act 1976, but no such action shall be brought after the expiration of three years from –

    (a)   the date of death; or

    (b)   the date of knowledge of the person for whose benefit the action is brought;

whichever is the later.

(3) An action under the Fatal Accidents Act 1976 shall be one to which sections 28, 33, 33A, 33B and 35 of this Act apply, and the application to any such action of the time limit under subsection (2) above shall be subject to section 39; but otherwise Parts II and III of this Act shall not apply to any such action.

Operation of time limit under section 12 in relation to different dependants

13.–(1) Where there is more than one person for whose benefit an action under the Fatal Accidents Act 1976 is brought, section 12(2)(b) of this Act shall be applied separately to each of them.

(2) Subject to subsection (3) below, if by virtue of subsection (1) above the action would be outside the time limit given by section 12(2) as regards one or more, but not all, of the persons for whose benefit it is brought, the court shall direct that any person as regards whom the action would be outside that limit shall be excluded from those for whom the action is brought.

(3) The court shall not give such a direction if it is shown that if the action were brought exclusively for the benefit of the person in question it would not be defeated by a defence of limitation (whether in consequence of section 28 of this Act or an agreement between the parties not to raise the defence, or otherwise).

Definition of date of knowledge for purposes of sections 11 and 12

14.–(1) Subject to subsection (1A) below, in sections 11 and 12 of this Act references to a person's date of knowledge are references to the date on which he first had knowledge of the following facts –

    (a)   that the injury in question was significant; and

    (b)   that the injury was attributable in whole or in part to the act or omission which is alleged to constitute negligence, nuisance or breach of duty; and

    (c)   the identity of the defendant; and

    (d)   if it is alleged that the act or omission was that of a person other than the defendant, the identity of that person and the additional facts supporting the bringing of an action against the defendant;

and knowledge that any acts or omissions did or did not, as a matter of law, involve negligence, nuisance or breach of duty is irrelevant.

(1A) In section 11A of this Act and in section 12 of this Act so far as that section applies to an action by virtue of section 6(1)(a) of the Consumer Protection Act 1987 (death caused by defective product) references to a person's date of knowledge are references to the date on which he first had knowledge of the following facts –

    (a)   such facts about the damage caused by the defect as would lead a reasonable person who had suffered such damage to consider it sufficiently serious to justify his instituting proceedings for damages against a defendant who did not dispute liability and was able to satisfy a judgment; and

(b)   that the damage was wholly or partly attributable to the facts and circumstances alleged to constitute the defect; and

(c)   the identity of the defendant;

but, in determining the date on which a person first had such knowledge there shall be disregarded both the extent (if any) of that person's knowledge on any date of whether particular facts or circumstances would or would not, as a matter of law, constitute a defect and, in a case relating to loss of or damage to property, any knowledge which that person had on a date on which he had no right of action by virtue of Part I of that Act in respect of the loss or damage.

(2) For the purposes of this section an injury is significant if the person whose date of knowledge is in question would reasonably have considered it sufficiently serious to justify his instituting proceedings for damages against a defendant who did not dispute liability and was able to satisfy a judgment.

(3) For the purposes of this section a person's knowledge includes knowledge which he might reasonably have been expected to acquire –

(a)   from facts observable or ascertainable by him; or

(b)   from facts ascertainable by him with the help of medical or other appropriate expert advice which it is reasonable for him to seek;

but a person shall not be fixed under this subsection with knowledge of a fact ascertainable only with the help of expert advice so long as he has taken all reasonable steps to obtain (and, where appropriate, to act on) that advice.

Actions in respect of latent damage not involving personal injuries

Special time limit for negligence actions where facts relevant to cause of action are not known at date of accrual

14A.–(1) This section applies to any action for damages for negligence, other than one to which section 11 of this Act applies, where the starting date for reckoning the period of limitation under subsection (4)(b) below falls after the date on which the cause of action accrued.

(2)   Section 2 of this Act shall not apply to an action to which this section applies.

(3)   An action to which this section applies shall not be brought after the expiration of the period applicable in accordance with subsection (4) below.

(4) That period is either –

(a)   six years from the date on which the cause of action accrued; or

(b)   three years from the starting date as defined by subsection (5) below, if that period expires later than the period mentioned in paragraph (a) above.

(5) For the purposes of this section, the starting date for reckoning the period of limitation under subsection (4)(b) above is the earliest date on which the plaintiff or any person in whom the cause of action was vested before him first had both the knowledge required for bringing an action for damages in respect of the relevant damage and a right to bring such an action.

(6) In subsection (5) above 'the knowledge required for bringing an action for damages in respect of the relevant damage' means knowledge both –

(a)   of the material facts about the damage in respect of which damages are claimed; and

(b)   of the other facts relevant to the current action mentioned in subsection (8) below.

(7) For the purposes of subsection (6)(a) above, the material facts about the damage are such facts about the damage as would lead a reasonable person who had suffered such damage to consider it sufficiently serious to justify his

instituting proceedings for damages against a defendant who did not dispute liability and was able to satisfy a judgment.

(8) The other facts referred to in subsection (6)(b) above are –

(a) that the damage was attributable in whole or in part to the act or omission which is alleged to constitute negligence; and

(b) the identity of the defendant; and

(c) if it is alleged that the act or omission was that of a person other than the defendant, the identity of that person and the additional facts supporting the bringing of an action against the defendant.

(9) Knowledge that any acts or omissions did or did not, as a matter of law, involve negligence is irrelevant for the purposes of subsection (5) above.

(10) For the purposes of this section a person's knowledge includes knowledge which he might reasonably have been expected to acquire –

(a) from facts observable or ascertainable by him; or

(b) from facts ascertainable by him with the help of appropriate expert advice which it is reasonable for him to seek;

but a person shall not be taken by virtue of this subsection to have knowledge of a fact ascertainable only with the help of expert advice so long as he has taken all reasonable steps to obtain (and, where appropriate, to act on) that advice.

Overriding time limit for negligence actions not involving personal injuries

14B.–(1) An action for damages for negligence, other than one to which section 11 of this Act applies, shall not be brought after the expiration of fifteen years from the date (or, if more than one, from the last of the dates) on which there occurred any act or omission –

(a) which is alleged to constitute negligence; and

(b) to which the damage in respect of which damages are claimed is alleged to be attributable (in whole or in part).

(2) This section bars the right of action in a case to which subsection (1) above applies notwithstanding that –

(a) the cause of action has not yet accrued; or

(b) where section 14A of this Act applies to the action, the date which is for the purposes of that section the starting date for reckoning the period mentioned in subsection (4)(b) of that section has not yet occurred;

before the end of the period of limitation prescribed by this section.

PART II

EXTENSION OR EXCLUSION OF ORDINARY TIME LIMITS

Disability

Extension of limitation period in case of disability

28.–(1) Subject to the following provisions of this section, if on the date when any right of action accrued for which a period of limitation is prescribed by this Act, the person to whom it accrued was under a disability, the action may be brought at any time before the expiration of six years from the date when he ceased to be under a disability or died (whichever first occurred) notwithstanding that the period of limitation has expired.

(2) This section shall not affect any case where the right of action first accrued to some person (not under a disability) through whom the person under a disability claims.

(3) When a right of action which has accrued to a person under a disability accrues, on the death of that person while still under a disability, to another person under a disability, no further extension of time shall be allowed by reason of the disability of the second person.

(4) No action to recover land or money charged on land shall be brought by virtue of this section by any person after the expiration of thirty years from the date on which the right of action accrued to that person or some person through whom he claims.

(4A) If the action is one to which section 4A of this Act applies, subsection (1) above shall have effect –

    (a)   in the case of an action for libel or slander, as if for the words from 'at any time' to 'occurred' there were substituted the words 'by him at any time before the expiration of one year from the date on which he ceased to be under a disability'; and

    (b)   in the case of an action for slander of title, slander of goods or other malicious falsehood, as if for the words 'six years' there were substituted the words 'one year'.

(5) If the action is one to which section 10 of this Act applies, subsection (1) above shall have effect as if for the words 'six years' there were substituted the words 'two years'.

(6) If the action is one to which section 11 or 12(2) of this Act applies, subsection (1) above shall have effect as if for the words 'six years' there were substituted the words 'three years'.

(7) If the action is one to which section 11A of this Act applies or one by virtue of section 6(1)(a) of the Consumer Protection Act 1987 (death caused by defective product), subsection (1) above –

    (a)   shall not apply to the time limit prescribed by subsection (3) of the said section 11A or to that time limit as applied by virtue of section 12(1) of this Act; and

    (b)   in relation to any other time limit prescribed by this Act shall have effect as if for the words 'six years' there were substituted the words 'three years'.

Extension for cases where the limitation period is the period under section 14A(4)(b)

28A.–(1) Subject to subsection (2) below, if in the case of any action for which a period of limitation is prescribed by section 14A of this Act –

    (a)   the period applicable in accordance with subsection (4) of that section is the period mentioned in paragraph (b) of that subsection;

    (b)   on the date which is for the purposes of that section the starting date for reckoning that period the person by reference to whose knowledge that date fell to be determined under subsection (5) of that section was under a disability; and

    (c)   section 28 of this Act does not apply to the action;

the action may be brought at any time before the expiration of three years from the date when he ceased to be under a disability or died (whichever first occurred) notwithstanding that the period mentioned above has expired.

(2) An action may not be brought by virtue of subsection (1) above after the end of the period of limitation prescribed by section 14B of this Act.

Fraud, concealment and mistake

Postponement of limitation period in case of fraud, concealment or mistake

32.–(1) Subject to subsections (3) and (4A) below, where in the case of any action for which a period of limitation is prescribed by this Act, either –

(a)   the action is based upon the fraud of the defendant; or

(b)   any fact relevant to the plaintiff's right of action has been deliberately concealed from him by the defendant; or

(c)   the action is for relief from the consequences of a mistake;

the period of limitation shall not begin to run until the plaintiff has discovered the fraud, concealment or mistake (as the case may be) or could with reasonable diligence have discovered it.

References in this subsection to the defendant include references to the defendant's agent and to any person through whom the defendant claims and his agent.

(2) For the purposes of subsection (1) above, deliberate commission of a breach of duty in circumstances in which it is unlikely to be discovered for some time amounts to deliberate concealment of the facts involved in that breach of duty.

(3) Nothing in this section shall enable any action –

(a)   to recover, or recover the value of, any property; or

(b)   to enforce any charge against, or set aside any transaction affecting, any property;

to be brought against the purchaser of the property or any person claiming through him in any case where the property has been purchased for valuable consideration by an innocent third party since the fraud or concealment or (as the case may be) the transaction in which the mistake was made took place.

(4) A purchaser is an innocent third party for the purposes of this section –

(a)   in the case of fraud or concealment of any fact relevant to the plaintiff's right of action, if he was not a party to the fraud or (as the case may be) to the concealment of that fact and did not at the time of the purchase know or have reason to believe that the fraud or concealment had taken place; and

(b)   in the case of mistake, if he did not at the time of the purchase know or have reason to believe that the mistake had been made.

(4A) Subsection (1) above shall not apply in relation to the time limit prescribed by section 11A(3) of this Act or in relation to that time limit as applied by virtue of section 12(1) of this Act.

(5) Sections 14A and 14B of this Act shall not apply to any action to which subsection (1)(b) above applies (and accordingly to the period of limitation referred to in that subsection, in any case to which either of those sections would otherwise apply, is the period applicable under section 2 of this Act).

Discretionary exclusion of time limit for actions in respect of personal injuries or death

Discretionary exclusion of time limit for actions in respect of personal injuries or death

33.–(1) If it appears to the court that it would be equitable to allow an action to proceed having regard to the degree to which –

(a)   the provisions of section 11 or 11A or 12 of this Act prejudice the plaintiff or any person whom he represents; and

(b)   any decision of the court under this subsection would prejudice the defendant or any person whom he represents;

the court may direct that those provisions shall not apply to the action, or shall not apply to any specified cause of action to which the action relates.

(1A) The court shall not under this section disapply –

(a)   subsection (3) of section 11A; or

(b)   where the damages claimed by the plaintiff are confined to damages for loss of or damage to any property, any other provision in its application to an action by virtue of Part I of the Consumer Protection Act 1987.

(2) The court shall not under this section disapply section 12(1) except where the reason why the person injured could no longer maintain an action was because of the time limit in section 11 or subsection (4) of section 11A.

If, for example, the person injured could at his death no longer maintain an action under the Fatal Accidents Act 1976 because of the time limit in Article 29 in Schedule 1 to the Carriage by Air Act 1961, the court has no power to direct that section 12(1) shall not apply.

(3) In acting under this section the court shall have regard to all the circumstances of the case and in particular to –

    (a)   the length of, and the reasons for, the delay on the part of the plaintiff;

    (b)   the extent to which, having regard to the delay, the evidence adduced or likely to be adduced by the plaintiff or the defendant is or is likely to be less cogent than if the action had been brought within the time allowed by section 11, by section 11A or (as the case may be) by section 12;

    (c)   the conduct of the defendant after the cause of action arose, including the extent (if any) to which he responded to requests reasonably made by the plaintiff for information or inspection for the purpose of ascertaining facts which were or might be relevant to the plaintiff's cause of action against the defendant;

    (d)   the duration of any disability of the plaintiff arising after the date of the accrual of the cause of action;

    (e)   the extent to which the plaintiff acted promptly and reasonably once he knew whether or not the act or omission of the defendant, to which the injury was attributable, might be capable at that time of giving rise to an action for damages;

    (f)   the steps, if any, taken by the plaintiff to obtain medical, legal or other expert advice and the nature of any such advice he may have received.

(4) In a case where the person injured died when, because of section 11 or subsection (4) of section 11A, he could no longer maintain an action and recover damages in respect of the injury, the court shall have regard in particular to the length of, and the reasons for, the delay on the part of the deceased.

(5) In a case under subsection (4) above, or any other case where the time limit, or one of the time limits, depends on the date of knowledge of a person other than the plaintiff, subsection (3) above shall have effect with appropriate modifications, and shall have effect in particular as if references to the plaintiff included references to any person whose date of knowledge is or was relevant in determining a time limit.

(6) A direction by the court disapplying the provisions of section 12(1) shall operate to disapply the provisions to the same effect in section 1(1) of the Fatal Accidents Act 1976.

(7) In this section 'the court' means the court in which the action has been brought.

(8) References in this section to section 11 or 11A include references to that section as extended by any of the provisions of this Part of this Act other than this section or by any provision of Part III of this Act.

PART III

MISCELLANEOUS AND GENERAL

New claims in pending actions: rules of court

35.–(1) For the purposes of this Act, any new claim made in the course of any action shall be deemed to be a separate action and to have been commenced –

    (a)   in the case of a new claim made in or by way of third party proceedings, on the date on which those proceedings were commenced; and

    (b)   in the case of any other new claim, on the same date as the original action.

(2) In this section a new claim means any claim by way of set-off or counterclaim, and any claim involving either –

    (a)   the addition or substitution of a new cause of action; or

    (b)   the addition or substitution of a new party;

and 'third party proceedings' means any proceedings brought in the course of any action by any party to the action against a person not previously a party to the action, other than proceedings brought by joining any such person as defendant to any claim already made in the original action by the party bringing the proceedings.

(3) Except as provided by section 33 of this Act or by rules of court, neither the High Court nor any county court shall allow a new claim within subsection (1)(b) above, other than an original set-off or counterclaim, to be made in the course of any action after the expiry of any time limit under this Act which would affect a new action to enforce that claim.

For the purposes of this subsection, a claim is an original set-off or an original counterclaim if it is a claim by way of set-off or (as the case may be) by way of counterclaim by a party who has not previously made any claim in the action.

(4) Rules of court may provide for allowing a new claim to which subsection (3) above applies to be made as there mentioned, but only if the conditions specified in subsection (5) below are satisfied, and subject to any further restrictions the rules may impose.

(5) The conditions referred to in subsection (4) above are the following –

    (a)   in the case of a claim involving a new cause of action, if the new cause of action arises out of the same facts or substantially the same facts as are already in issue on any claim previously made in the original action; and

    (b)   in the case of a claim involving a new party, if the addition or substitution of the new party is necessary for the determination of the original action.

(6) The addition or substitution of a new party shall not be regarded for the purposes of subsection (5)(b) above as necessary for the determination of the original action unless either –

    (a)   the new party is substituted for a party whose name was given in any claim made in the original action in mistake for the new party's name; or

    (b)   any claim already made in the original action cannot be maintained by or against any existing party unless the new party is joined or substituted as plaintiff or defendant in that action.

(7) Subject to subsection (4) above, rules of court may provide for allowing a party to any action to claim relief in a new capacity in respect of a new cause of action notwithstanding that he had no title to make that claim at the date of the commencement of the action.

This subsection shall not be taken as prejudicing the power of rules of court to provide for allowing a party to claim relief in a new capacity without adding or substituting a new cause of action.

(8) Subsections (3) to (7) above shall apply in relation to a new claim made in the course of third party proceedings as if those proceedings were the original action, and subject to such other modifications as may be prescribed by rules of court in any case or class of case.

(9) *[Repealed]*

Interpretation

38.–(1) In this Act, unless the context otherwise requires –

'action' includes any proceedings in a court of law, including an ecclesiastical court;

'personal injuries' includes any disease and any impairment of a person's physical or mental condition, and 'injury' and cognate expressions shall be construed accordingly;

(2) For the purposes of this Act a person shall be treated as under a disability while he is an infant, or [lacks capacity (within the meaning of the Mental Capacity Act 2005) to conduct legal proceedings].

(5) Subject to subsection (6) below, a person shall be treated as claiming through another person if he became entitled by, through, under, or by the act of that other person to the right claimed, and any person whose estate or interest might have been barred by a person entitled to an entailed interest in possession shall be treated as claiming through the person so entitled.

(9) References in Part II of this Act to a right of action shall include references to –

    (a) a cause of action;

(10) References in Part II to the date of the accrual of a right of action shall be construed –

    (a) in the case of an action upon a judgment, as references to the date on which the judgment became enforceable; and

[Note: Words in italic repealed and words in square brackets substituted by the Care Standards Act 2000, from a date to be appointed.]

3. CONGENITAL DISABILITIES (CIVIL LIABILITY) ACT 1976

(1976 Administration of Justice Act 1982 c 28)

An Act to make provision as to civil liability in the case of children born disabled in consequence of some person's fault; and to extend the Nuclear Installations Act 1965, so that children so born in consequence of a breach of duty under that Act may claim compensation.

[22nd July 1976]

Civil liability to child born disabled

1.–(1) If a child is born disabled as a result of such an occurrence before its birth as is mentioned in subsection (2) below, and a person (other than the child's own mother) is under this section answerable to the child in respect of the occurrence, the child's disabilities are to be regarded as damage resulting from the wrongful act of that person and actionable accordingly at the suit of the child.

(2) An occurrence to which this section applies is one which –
  (a) affected either parent of the child in his or her ability to have a normal, healthy child; or
  (b) affected the mother during her pregnancy, or affected her or the child in the course of its birth, so that the child is born with disabilities which would not otherwise have been present.

(3) Subject to the following subsections, a person (here referred to as 'the defendant') is answerable to the child if he was liable in tort to the parent or would, if sued in time, have been so; and it is no answer that there could not have been such liability because the parent suffered no actionable injury, if there was a breach of legal duty which, accompanied by injury would have given rise to the liability.

(4) In the case of an occurrence preceding the time of conception, the defendant is not answerable to the child if at that time either or both of the parents knew the risk of their child being born disabled (that is to say, the particular risk created by the occurrence); but should it be the child's father who is the defendant, this subsection does not apply if he knew of the risk and the mother did not.

[(4A) In the case of a child who has a parent by virtue of section 42 or 43 of the Human Fertilisation and Embryology Act 2008, the reference in subsection (4) to the child's father includes a reference to the woman who is a parent by virtue of that section.]

(5) The defendant is not answerable to the child, for anything he did or omitted to do when responsible in a professional capacity for treating or advising the parent, if he took reasonable care having due regard to then received professional opinion applicable to the particular class of case; but this does not mean that he is answerable only because he departed from received opinion.

(6) Liability to the child under this section may be treated as having been excluded or limited by contract made with the parent affected, to the same extent and subject to the same restrictions as liability in the parent's own case; and a contract term which could have been set up by the defendant in an action by the parent, so as to exclude or limit his liability to him or her, operates in the defendant's favour to the same, but no greater, extent in an action under this section by the child.

(7) If in the child's action under this section it is shown that the parent affected shared the responsibility for the child being born disabled, the damages are to be reduced to such extent as the court thinks just and equitable having regard to the extent of the parent's responsibility.

Extension of section 1 to cover infertility treatments

1A.–(1) In any case where –
  (a) a child carried by a woman as the result of the placing in her of an embryo or of sperm and eggs or her artificial insemination is born disabled,

(b)   the disability results from an act or omission in the course of the selection, or the keeping or use outside the body, of the embryo carried by her or of the gametes used to bring about the creation of the embryo, and

(c)   a person is under this section answerable to the child in respect of the act or omission,

the child's disabilities are to be regarded as damage resulting from the wrongful act of that person and actionable accordingly at the suit of the child.

(2) Subject to subsection (3) below and the applied provisions of section 1 of this Act, a person (here referred to as 'the defendant') is answerable to the child if he was liable in tort to one or both of the parents (here referred to as 'the parent or parents concerned') or would, if sued in due time, have been so; and it is no answer that there could not have been such liability because the parent or parents concerned suffered no actionable injury, if there was a breach of legal duty which, accompanied by injury, would have given rise to the liability.

(3) The defendant is not under this section answerable to the child if at the time the embryo, or the sperm and eggs, are placed in the woman or at the time of her insemination (as the case may be) either or both of the parents knew the risk of their child being born disabled (that is to say, the particular risk created by the act or omission).

(4) Subsections (5) to (7) of section 1 of this Act apply for the purposes of this section as they apply for the purposes of that but as if references to the parent or the parents affected were references to the parent or parents concerned.

[Note: Section 1A was inserted by s 44(1) of the Human Fertilisation and Embryology Act 1990.]

Liability of woman driving when pregnant

2. A woman driving a motor vehicle when she knows (or ought reasonably to know) herself to be pregnant is to be regarded as being under the same duty to take care for the safety of her unborn child as the law imposes on her with respect to the safety of other people; and if in consequence of her breach of that duty her child is born with disabilities which would not otherwise have been present, those disabilities are to be regarded as damage resulting from her wrongful act and actionable accordingly at the suit of the child.

Disabled birth due to radiation

3.–(1) Section 1 of this Act does not affect the operation of the Nuclear Installations Act 1965 as to liability for, and compensation in respect of, injury or damage caused by occurrences involving nuclear matter or the emission of ionising radiations.

(2) For the avoidance of doubt anything which –

(a)   affects a man in his ability to have a normal, healthy child; or

(b)   affects a woman in that ability, or so affects her when she is pregnant that her child is born with disabilities which would not otherwise have been present,

is an injury for the purposes of that Act.

(3) If a child is born disabled as the result of an injury to either of its parents caused in breach of a duty imposed by any of sections 7 to 11 of that Act (nuclear site licensees and others to secure that nuclear incidents do not cause injury to persons, etc), the child's disabilities are to be regarded under the subsequent provisions of that Act (compensation and other matters) as injuries caused on the same occasion, and by the same breach of duty, as was the injury to the parent.

(4) As respects compensation to the child, section 13(6) of that Act (contributory fault of person injured by radiation) is to be applied as if the reference there to fault were to the fault of the parent.

(5) Compensation is not payable in the child's case if the injury to the parent preceded the time of the child's conception and at that time either or both of

the parents knew the risk of their child being born disabled (that is to say, the particular risk created by the injury).

Interpretation and other supplementary provisions

4.–(1) References in this Act to a child being born disabled or with disabilities are to its being born with any deformity, disease or abnormality, including predisposition (whether or not susceptible of immediate prognosis) to physical or mental defect in the future.

(2) In this Act –
   (a) 'born' means alive (the moment of a child's birth being when it first has a life separate from its mother), and 'birth' has a corresponding meaning; and
   (b) 'motor vehicle' means a mechanically propelled vehicle intended or adapted for use on roads;
[and references to embryos shall be construed in accordance with section 1 of the Human Fertilisation and Embryology Act 1990 and any regulations under section 1(6) of that Act.]

(3) Liability to a child under section 1 [or 1A] or 2 of this Act is to be regarded–
   (a) as respects all its incidents and any matters arising or to arise out of it; and
   (b) subject to any contrary context or intention, for the purpose of construing references in enactments and documents to personal or bodily injuries and cognate matters,
as liability for personal injuries sustained by the child immediately after its birth.

(4) No damages shall be recoverable under [any] of those sections in respect of any loss of expectation of life, nor shall any such loss be taken into account in the compensation payable in respect of a child under the Nuclear Installations Act 1965 as extended by section 3, unless (in either case) the child lives for at least 48 hours.

(4A) In any case where a child carried by a woman as the result of the placing in her of an embryo or of sperm and eggs or her artificial insemination is born disabled, any reference in section 1 of this Act to a parent includes a reference to a person who would be a parent but for sections 27 to 29 of the Human Fertilisation and Embryology Act 1990 [or sections 33 to 37 of the Human Fertilisation and Embryology Act 2008].

(5) This Act applies in respect of births after (but not before) its passing, and in respect of any such birth it replaces any law in force before its passing, whereby a person could be liable to a child in respect of disabilities with which it might be born; but in section 1(3) of this Act the expression 'liable in tort' does not include any reference to liability by virtue of this Act, or to liability by virtue of any such law.

(6) References to the Nuclear Installations Act 1965 are to that Act as amended; and for the purposes of section 28 of that Act (power by Order in Council to extend the Act to territories outside the United Kingdom) section 3 of this Act is to be treated as if it were a provision of that Act.

[Note: Sub-s (4A) was inserted by s 35 of the Human Fertilisation and Embryology Act 1990 and subsequently amended by the Human Fertilisation and Embryology Act 2008, Sch 6(1), and the words in square brackets in sub-ss (2), (3) and (4) were substituted by s 44 of the Human Fertilisation and Embryology Act 1990]

Crown application

5. This Act binds the Crown.

Citation and extent

6.–(1) This Act may be cited as the Congenital Disabilities (Civil Liability) Act 1976.

(2) This Act extends to Northern Ireland but not to Scotland.

Appendix II

Practice Directions and Protocols

Contents

1 PRACTICE DIRECTION – PRE-ACTION CONDUCT AND PROTOCOLS

Introduction

1. Pre-action protocols explain the conduct and set out the steps the court would normally expect parties to take before commencing proceedings for particular types of civil claims. They are approved by the Master of the Rolls and are annexed to the Civil Procedure Rules (CPR). (The current pre-action protocols are listed in paragraph 18.)

2. This Practice Direction applies to disputes where no pre-action protocol approved by the Master of the Rolls applies.

Objectives of pre-action conduct and protocols

3. Before commencing proceedings, the court will expect the parties to have exchanged sufficient information to—

    (a)   understand each other's position;

    (b)   make decisions about how to proceed;

    (c)   try to settle the issues without proceedings;

    (d)   consider a form of Alternative Dispute Resolution (ADR) to assist with settlement;

    (e)   support the efficient management of those proceedings; and

    (f)   reduce the costs of resolving the dispute.

Proportionality

4. A pre-action protocol or this Practice Direction must not be used by a party as a tactical device to secure an unfair advantage over another party. Only reasonable and proportionate steps should be taken by the parties to identify, narrow and resolve the legal, factual or expert issues.

5. The costs incurred in complying with a pre-action protocol or this Practice Direction should be proportionate (CPR 44.3(5)). Where parties incur disproportionate costs in complying with any pre-action protocol or this Practice Direction, those costs will not be recoverable as part of the costs of the proceedings.

Steps before issuing a claim at court

6. Where there is a relevant pre-action protocol, the parties should comply with that protocol before commencing proceedings. Where there is no relevant pre-action protocol, the parties should exchange correspondence and information to comply with the objectives in paragraph 3, bearing in mind that compliance should be proportionate. The steps will usually include—

    (a)   the claimant writing to the defendant with concise details of the claim. The letter should include the basis on which the claim is made, a summary of the facts, what the claimant wants from the defendant, and if money, how the amount is calculated;

    (b)   the defendant responding within a reasonable time – 14 days in a straight forward case and no more than 3 months in a very complex one. The reply should include confirmation as to whether the claim is accepted and, if it is not accepted, the reasons why, together with an explanation as to which facts and parts of the claim are disputed and whether the defendant is making a counterclaim as well as providing details of any counterclaim; and

    (c)   the parties disclosing key documents relevant to the issues in dispute.

Experts

7.   Parties should be aware that the court must give permission before expert evidence can be relied upon (see CPR 35.4(1)) and that the court may limit the fees recoverable. Many disputes can be resolved without expert advice or evidence. If it is necessary to obtain expert evidence, particularly in low value claims, the parties should consider using a single expert, jointly instructed by the parties, with the costs shared equally.

Settlement and ADR

8.   Litigation should be a last resort. As part of a relevant pre-action protocol or this Practice Direction, the parties should consider whether negotiation or some other form of ADR might enable them to settle their dispute without commencing proceedings.

9.   Parties should continue to consider the possibility of reaching a settlement at all times, including after proceedings have been started. Part 36 offers may be made before proceedings are issued.

10.   Parties may negotiate to settle a dispute or may use a form of ADR including—

    (a)   mediation, a third party facilitating a resolution;

    (b)   arbitration, a third party deciding the dispute;

    (c)   early neutral evaluation, a third party giving an informed opinion on the dispute; and

    (d)   Ombudsmen schemes.

(Information on mediation and other forms of ADR is available in the Jackson ADR Handbook (available from Oxford University Press) or at—

- http://www.civilmediation.justice.gov.uk/
- http://www.adviceguide.org.uk/england/law_e/law_legal_system_e/law_taking_legal_action_e/alternatives_to_court.htm)

11.   If proceedings are issued, the parties may be required by the court to provide evidence that ADR has been considered. A party's silence in response to an invitation to participate or a refusal to participate in ADR might be considered unreasonable by the court and could lead to the court ordering that party to pay additional court costs.

Stocktake and list of issues

12.   Where a dispute has not been resolved after the parties have followed a pre-action protocol or this Practice Direction, they should review their respective positions. They should consider the papers and the evidence to see if proceedings can be avoided and at least seek to narrow the issues in dispute before the claimant issues proceedings.

Compliance with this Practice Direction and the Protocols

13.   If a dispute proceeds to litigation, the court will expect the parties to have complied with a relevant pre-action protocol or this Practice Direction. The court will take into account non-compliance when giving directions for the management of proceedings (see CPR 3.1(4) to (6)) and when making orders for costs (see CPR 44.3(5)(a)). The court will consider whether all parties have complied in substance with the terms of the relevant pre-action protocol or this Practice Direction and is not likely to be concerned with minor or technical infringements, especially when the matter is urgent (for example an application for an injunction).

14.   The court may decide that there has been a failure of compliance when a party has—

    (a)   not provided sufficient information to enable the objectives in paragraph 3 to be met;

(b) not acted within a time limit set out in a relevant protocol, or within a reasonable period; or

(c) unreasonably refused to use a form of ADR, or failed to respond at all to an invitation to do so.

15. Where there has been non-compliance with a pre-action protocol or this Practice Direction, the court may order that

(a) the parties are relieved of the obligation to comply or further comply with the pre-action protocol or this Practice Direction;

(b) the proceedings are stayed while particular steps are taken to comply with the pre-action protocol or this Practice Direction;

(c) sanctions are to be applied.

16. The court will consider the effect of any non-compliance when deciding whether to impose any sanctions which may include—

(a) an order that the party at fault pays the costs of the proceedings, or part of the costs of the other party or parties;

(b) an order that the party at fault pay those costs on an indemnity basis;

(c) if the party at fault is a claimant who has been awarded a sum of money, an order depriving that party of interest on that sum for a specified period, and/or awarding interest at a lower rate than would otherwise have been awarded;

(d) if the party at fault is a defendant, and the claimant has been awarded a sum of money, an order awarding interest on that sum for a specified period at a higher rate, (not exceeding 10% above base rate), than the rate which would otherwise have been awarded.

Limitation

17. This Practice Direction and the pre-action protocols do not alter the statutory time limits for starting court proceedings. If a claim is issued after the relevant limitation period has expired, the defendant will be entitled to use that as a defence to the claim. If proceedings are started to comply with the statutory time limit before the parties have followed the procedures in this Practice Direction or the relevant pre-action protocol, the parties should apply to the court for a stay of the proceedings while they so comply.

Protocols in force

18. The table sets out the protocols currently in force and from which date.

Protocol	Came into force
Personal Injury	6 April 2015
Resolution of Clinical Disputes	6 April 2015
Construction and Engineering	9 November 2016 2nd Edition
Defamation	02 October 2000
Professional Negligence	16 July 2000
Judicial Review	6 April 2015
Disease and Illness	8 December 2003
Housing Disrepair	6 April 2015
Possession Claims by Social Landlords	6 April 2015
Possession Claims for Mortgage Arrears	6 April 2015
Dilapidation of Commercial Property	1 January 2012
Low Value Personal Injury Road Traffic Accident Claims	30 April 2010 extended from 31 July 2013
Low Value Personal Injury Employers' and Public Liability Claims	31 July 2013

2 PRE-ACTION PROTOCOL FOR THE RESOLUTION OF CLINICAL DISPUTES

1　INTRODUCTION

1.1　This Protocol is intended to apply to all claims against hospitals, GPs, dentists and other healthcare providers (both NHS and private) which involve an injury that is alleged to be the result of clinical negligence. It is not intended to apply to claims covered by—

(a)　the Pre-Action Protocol for Disease and Illness Claims;

(b)　the Pre-Action Protocol for Personal Injury Claims;

(c)　the Pre-Action Protocol for Low Value Personal Injury Claims in Road Traffic Accidents;

(d)　the Pre-Action Protocol for Low Value Personal Injury (Employers' Liability and Public Liability) Claims; or

(e)　Practice Direction 3D – Mesothelioma Claims

1.2　This Protocol is intended to be sufficiently broad-based and flexible to apply to all sectors of healthcare, both public and private. It also recognises that a claimant and a defendant, as patient and healthcare provider, may have an ongoing relationship.

1.3　It is important that each party to a clinical dispute has sufficient information and understanding of the other's perspective and case to be able to investigate a claim efficiently and, where appropriate, to resolve it. This Protocol encourages a cards-on-the-table approach when something has gone wrong with a claimant's treatment or the claimant is dissatisfied with that treatment and/ or the outcome.

1.4　This Protocol is now regarded by the courts as setting the standard of normal reasonable pre-action conduct for the resolution of clinical disputes.

1.5

1.5.1　This Protocol sets out the conduct that prospective parties would normally be expected to follow prior to the commencement of any proceedings. It establishes a reasonable process and timetable for the exchange of information relevant to a dispute, sets out the standards for the content and quality of letters of claim and sets standards for the conduct of pre-action negotiations.

1.5.2　The timetable and the arrangements for disclosing documents and obtaining expert evidence may need to be varied to suit the circumstances of the case. Where one or more parties consider the detail of the Protocol is not appropriate to the case, and proceedings are subsequently issued, the court will expect an explanation as to why the Protocol has not been followed, or has been varied.

Early Issue

1.6

1.6.1　The Protocol provides for a defendant to be given four months to investigate and respond to a Letter of Claim before proceedings are served. If this is not possible, the claimant's solicitor should give as much notice of the intention to issue proceedings as is practicable. This Protocol does not alter the statutory time limits for starting court proceedings. If a claim is issued after the relevant statutory limitation period has expired, the defendant will be entitled to use that as a defence to the claim. If proceedings are started to comply with the statutory time limit before the parties have followed the procedures in this Protocol, the parties should apply to the court for a stay of the proceedings while they so comply.

1.6.2　The parties should also consider whether there is likely to be a dispute as to limitation should a claim be pursued.

Enforcement of the Protocol and sanctions

1.7 Where either party fails to comply with this Protocol, the court may impose sanctions. When deciding whether to do so, the court will look at whether the parties have complied in substance with the Protocol's relevant principles and requirements. It will also consider the effect any non-compliance has had on any other party. It is not likely to be concerned with minor or technical shortcomings (see paragraph 4.3 to 4.5 of the Practice Direction on Pre-Action Conduct and Protocols).

Litigants in Person

1.8 If a party to a claim does not seek professional advice from a solicitor they should still, in so far as is reasonably possible, comply with the terms of this Protocol. In this Protocol "solicitor" is intended to encompass reference to any suitably legally qualified person.

If a party to a claim becomes aware that another party is a litigant in person, they should send a copy of this Protocol to the litigant in person at the earliest opportunity.

2 THE AIMS OF THE PROTOCOL

2.1 The general aims of the Protocol are –
  (a) to maintain and/or restore the patient/healthcare provider relationship in an open and transparent way;
  (b) to reduce delay and ensure that costs are proportionate; and
  (c) to resolve as many disputes as possible without litigation.

2.2 The specific objectives are–
  (a) to encourage openness, transparency and early communication of the perceived problem between patients and healthcare providers;
  (b) to provide an opportunity for healthcare providers to identify whether notification of a notifiable safety incident has been, or should be, sent to the claimant in accordance with the duty of candour imposed by section 20 of the Health and Social Care Act 2008 (Regulated Activities) Regulations 2014;
  (c) to ensure that sufficient medical and other information is disclosed promptly by both parties to enable each to understand the other's perspective and case, and to encourage early resolution or a narrowing of the issues in dispute;
  (d) to provide an early opportunity for healthcare providers to identify cases where an investigation is required and to carry out that investigation promptly;
  (e) to encourage healthcare providers to involve the National Health Service Litigation Authority (NHSLA) or their defence organisations or insurers at an early stage;
  (f) to enable the parties to avoid litigation by agreeing a resolution of the dispute;
  (g) to enable the parties to explore the use of mediation or to narrow the issues in dispute before proceedings are commenced;
  (h) to enable parties to identify any issues that may require a separate or preliminary hearing, such as a dispute as to limitation;
  (i) to support the efficient management of proceedings where litigation cannot be avoided;
  (j) to discourage the prolonged pursuit of unmeritorious claims and the prolonged defence of meritorious claims;
  (k) to promote the provision of medical or rehabilitation treatment to address the needs of the claimant at the earliest opportunity; and

(l)   to encourage the defendant to make an early apology to the claimant if appropriate.

2.3   This Protocol does not—

(a)   provide any detailed guidance to healthcare providers on clinical risk management or the adoption of risk management systems and procedures;

(b)   provide any detailed guidance on which adverse outcomes should trigger an investigation; or

(c)   recommend changes to the codes of conduct of professionals in healthcare.

3   THE PROTOCOL

3.1   An illustrative flowchart is attached at Annex A which shows each of the stages that the parties are expected to take before the commencement of proceedings.

Obtaining health records

3.2   Any request for records by the claimant should–

(a)   provide sufficient information to alert the defendant where an adverse outcome has been serious or has had serious consequences or may constitute a notifiable safety incident;

(b)   be as specific as possible about the records which are required for an initial investigation of the claim (including, for example, a continuous copy of the CTG trace in birth injury cases); and

(c)   include a request for any relevant guidelines, analyses, protocols or policies and any documents created in relation to an adverse incident, notifiable safety incident or complaint.

3.3   Requests for copies of the claimant's clinical records should be made using the Law Society and Department of Health approved standard forms (enclosed at Annex B), adapted as necessary.

3.4

3.4.1   The copy records should be provided within 40 days of the request and for a cost not exceeding the charges permissible under the Access to Health Records Act 1990 and/or the Data Protection Act 1998. Payment may be required in advance by the healthcare provider.

3.4.2   The claimant may also make a request under the Freedom of Information Act 2000.

3.5   At the earliest opportunity, legible copies of the claimant's medical and other records should be placed in an indexed and paginated bundle by the claimant. This bundle should be kept up to date.

3.6   In the rare circumstances that the defendant is in difficulty in complying with the request within 40 days, the problem should be explained quickly and details given of what is being done to resolve it.

3.7   If the defendant fails to provide the health records or an explanation for any delay within 40 days, the claimant or their adviser can then apply to the court under rule 31.16 of the Civil Procedure Rules 1998 ('CPR') for an order for pre-action disclosure. The court has the power to impose costs sanctions for unreasonable delay in providing records.

3.8   If either the claimant or the defendant considers additional health records are required from a third party, in the first instance these should be requested by or through the claimant. Third party healthcare providers are expected to co-operate. Rule 31.17 of the CPR sets out the procedure for applying to the court for pre-action disclosure by third parties.

Rehabilitation

3.9 The claimant and the defendant shall both consider as early as possible whether the claimant has reasonable needs that could be met by rehabilitation treatment or other measures. They should also discuss how these needs might be addressed. An immediate needs assessment report prepared for the purposes of rehabilitation should not be used in the litigation except by consent.

(A copy of the Rehabilitation Code can be found at: http://www.iua.co.uk/IUA_ Member/Publications)

Letter of Notification

3.10 Annex C1 to this Protocol provides a template for the recommended contents of a Letter of Notification; the level of detail will need to be varied to suit the particular circumstances.

3.11

3.11.1 Following receipt and analysis of the records and, if appropriate, receipt of an initial supportive expert opinion, the claimant may wish to send a Letter of Notification to the defendant as soon as practicable.

3.11.2 The Letter of Notification should advise the defendant that this is a claim where a Letter of Claim is likely to be sent because a case as to breach of duty and/or causation has been identified. A copy of the Letter of Notification should also be sent to the NHSLA or, where known, other relevant medical defence organisation or indemnity provider.

3.12

3.12.1 On receipt of a Letter of Notification a defendant should—
- (a) acknowledge the letter within 14 days of receipt;
- (b) identify who will be dealing with the matter and to whom any Letter of Claim should be sent;
- (c) consider whether to commence investigations and/or to obtain factual and expert evidence;
- (d) consider whether any information could be passed to the claimant which might narrow the issues in dispute or lead to an early resolution of the claim; and
- (e) forward a copy of the Letter of Notification to the NHSLA or other relevant medical defence organisation/indemnity provider.

3.12.2 The court may question any requests by the defendant for extension of time limits if a Letter of Notification was sent but did not prompt an initial investigation.

Letter of Claim

3.13 Annex C2 to this Protocol provides a template for the recommended contents of a Letter of Claim: the level of detail will need to be varied to suit the particular circumstances.

3.14 If, following the receipt and analysis of the records, and the receipt of any further advice (including from experts if necessary – see Section 4), the claimant decides that there are grounds for a claim, a letter of claim should be sent to the defendant as soon as practicable. Any letter of claim sent to an NHS Trust should be copied to the National Health Service Litigation Authority.

3.16 This letter should contain—
- (a) a clear summary of the facts on which the claim is based, including the alleged adverse outcome, and the main allegations of negligence;
- (b) a description of the claimant's injuries, and present condition and prognosis;
- (c) an outline of the financial loss incurred by the claimant, with an indication of the heads of damage to be claimed and the scale of the loss, unless this is impracticable;

(d) confirmation of the method of funding and whether any funding arrangement was entered into before or after April 2013; and

(e) the discipline of any expert from whom evidence has already been obtained.

3.17 The Letter of Claim should refer to any relevant documents, including health records, and if possible enclose copies of any of those which will not already be in the potential defendant's possession, e.g. any relevant general practitioner records if the claimant's claim is against a hospital.

3.18 Sufficient information must be given to enable the defendant to focus investigations and to put an initial valuation on the claim.

3.19 Letters of Claim are not intended to have the same formal status as Particulars of Claim, nor should any sanctions necessarily apply if the Letter of Claim and any subsequent Particulars of Claim in the proceedings differ.

3.20 Proceedings should not be issued until after four months from the letter of claim.

In certain instances it may not be possible for the claimant to serve a Letter of Claim more than four months before the expiry of the limitation period. If, for any reason, proceedings are started before the parties have complied, they should seek to agree to apply to the court for an order to stay the proceedings whilst the parties take steps to comply.

3.21 The claimant may want to make an offer to settle the claim at this early stage by putting forward an offer in respect of liability and/or an amount of compensation in accordance with the legal and procedural requirements of CPR Part 36 (possibly including any costs incurred to date). If an offer to settle is made, generally this should be supported by a medical report which deals with the injuries, condition and prognosis, and by a schedule of loss and supporting documentation. The level of detail necessary will depend on the value of the claim. Medical reports may not be necessary where there is no significant continuing injury and a detailed schedule may not be necessary in a low value case.

Letter of Response

3.22 Attached at Annex C3 is a template for the suggested contents of the Letter of Response: the level of detail will need to be varied to suit the particular circumstances.

3.23 The defendant should acknowledge the Letter of Claim within 14 days of receipt and should identify who will be dealing with the matter.

3.24 The defendant should, within four months of the Letter of Claim, provide a reasoned answer in the form of a Letter of Response in which the defendant should—

(a) if the claim is admitted, say so in clear terms;

(b) if only part of the claim is admitted, make clear which issues of breach of duty and/or causation are admitted and which are denied and why;

(c) state whether it is intended that any admissions will be binding;

(d) if the claim is denied, include specific comments on the allegations of negligence and, if a synopsis or chronology of relevant events has been provided and is disputed, the defendant's version of those events;

(e) if supportive expert evidence has been obtained, identify which disciplines of expert evidence have been relied upon and whether they relate to breach of duty and/or causation;

(f) if known, state whether the defendant requires copies of any relevant medical records obtained by the claimant (to be supplied for a reasonable copying charge);

(g) provide copies of any additional documents relied upon, e.g. an internal protocol;

(h) if not indemnified by the NHS, supply details of the relevant indemnity insurer; and

(i) inform the claimant of any other potential defendants to the claim.

3.25

3.25.1 If the defendant requires an extension of time for service of the Letter of Response, a request should be made as soon as the defendant becomes aware that it will be required and, in any event, within four months of the letter of claim.

3.25.2 The defendant should explain why any extension of time is necessary.

3.25.3 The claimant should adopt a reasonable approach to any request for an extension of time for provision of the reasoned answer.

3.26 If the claimant has made an offer to settle, the defendant should respond to that offer in the Letter of Response, preferably with reasons. The defendant may also make an offer to settle at this stage. Any offer made by the defendant should be made in accordance with the legal and procedural requirements of CPR Part 36 (possibly including any costs incurred to date). If an offer to settle is made, the defendant should provide sufficient medical or other evidence to allow the claimant to properly consider the offer. The level of detail necessary will depend on the value of the claim.

3.27 If the parties reach agreement on liability, or wish to explore the possibility of resolution with no admissions as to liability, but time is needed to resolve the value of the claim, they should aim to agree a reasonable period.

3.28 If the parties do not reach agreement on liability, they should discuss whether the claimant should start proceedings and whether the court might be invited to direct an early trial of a preliminary issue or of breach of duty and/or causation.

3.29 Following receipt of the Letter of Response, if the claimant is aware that there may be a delay of six months or more before the claimant decides if, when and how to proceed, the claimant should keep the defendant generally informed.

4 EXPERTS

4.1 In clinical negligence disputes separate expert opinions may be needed—
- on breach of duty;
- on causation;
- on the patient's condition and prognosis;
- to assist in valuing aspects of the claim.

4.2 It is recognised that in clinical negligence disputes, the parties and their advisers will require flexibility in their approach to expert evidence. The parties should co-operate when making decisions on appropriate medical specialisms, whether experts might be instructed jointly and whether any reports obtained pre-action might be shared.

4.3 Obtaining expert evidence will often be an expensive step and may take time, especially in specialised areas of medicine where there are limited numbers of suitable experts.

4.4 When considering what expert evidence may be required during the Protocol period, parties should be aware that the use of any expert reports obtained pre-action will only be permitted in proceedings with the express permission of the court.

5 ALTERNATIVE DISPUTE RESOLUTION

5.1 Litigation should be a last resort. As part of this Protocol, the parties should consider whether negotiation or some other form of alternative dispute resolution ('ADR') might enable them to resolve their dispute without commencing proceedings.

5.2 Some of the options for resolving disputes without commencing proceedings are—
- (a) discussion and negotiation (which may or may not include making Part 36 Offers or providing an explanation and/or apology)
- (b) mediation, a third party facilitating a resolution ;

(c)   arbitration, a third party deciding the dispute;

(d)   early neutral evaluation, a third party giving an informed opinion on the dispute; and

(e)   Ombudsmen schemes.

5.3 Information on mediation and other forms of ADR is available in the Jackson ADR Handbook (available from Oxford University Press) or at—

* http://www.civilmediation.justice.gov.uk/
* http://www.adviceguide.org.uk/england/law_e/law_legal_system_e/law_ taking_legal_action_e/alternatives_to_court.htm

5.4 If proceedings are issued, the parties may be required by the court to provide evidence that ADR has been considered. It is expressly recognised that no party can or should be forced to mediate or enter into any form of ADR, but a party's silence in response to an invitation to participate in ADR might be considered unreasonable by the court and could lead to the court ordering that party to pay additional court costs.

6   STOCKTAKE

6.1

6.1.1   Where a dispute has not been resolved after the parties have followed the procedure set out in this Protocol, the parties should review their positions before the claimant issues court proceedings.

6.1.2   If proceedings cannot be avoided, the parties should continue to co-operate and should seek to prepare a chronology of events which identifies the facts or issues that are agreed and those that remain in dispute. The parties should also seek to agree the necessary procedural directions for efficient case management during the proceedings.

3 THE PRE-ACTION PROTOCOL FORM FOR REQUESTING MEDICAL RECORDS

Consent form
(Releasing health records under the Data Protection Act 1998)

About this form

In order to proceed with your claim, your solicitor may need to see your health records. Solicitors usually need to see all your records as they need to assess which parts are relevant to your case. (Past medical history is often relevant to a claim for compensation.) Also, if your claim goes ahead, the person you are making the claim against will ask for copies of important documents. Under court rules, they may see all your health records. So your solicitor needs to be familiar with all your records.

Part a – your, the health professionals' and your solicitor's or agent's details

Your full name:	
Your address:	
Date of birth:	
Date of incident:	
Solicitor's or agent's name and address:	
GP's name and address (and phone number if known):	
Name (and address if known) of the hospitals you went to in relation to this incident :	
If you have seen any other person or organisation about your injuries (for example, a physiotherapist) or have had any investigations (for example, x-rays) please provide details.	

Part b – your declaration and signature

Please see the 'Notes for the client' over the page before you sign this form.

To health professionals

I understand that filling in and signing this form gives you permission to give copies of all my GP records, and any hospital records relating to this incident, to my solicitor or agent whose details are given above.

Please give my solicitor or agent copies of my health records, in line with the Data Protection Act 1998, within 40 days.

Your signature:		Date:	/ /

Part c – your solicitor's or agent's declaration and signature

Please see the 'Notes for the solicitor or agent' over the page before you sign this form.

To health professionals

I have told my client the implications of giving me access to his or her health records. I confirm that I need the full records in this case.   I enclose the authorised fee for getting access to records.

Solicitor's or agent's
signature:

Date: /   /

Notes for the client

Your health records contain information from almost all consultations you have had with health professionals. The information they contain usually includes:

- why you saw a health professional;
- details of clinical findings and diagnoses;
- any options for care and treatment the health professional discussed with you;
- the decisions made about your care and treatment, including evidence that you agreed; and
- details of action health professionals have taken and the outcomes.

By signing this form, you are agreeing to the health professional or hospital named on this form releasing copies of your health records to your solicitor or agent. During the process your records may be seen by people who are not health professionals, but they will keep the information confidential.

If you are making, or considering making, a legal claim against someone, your solicitor will need to see copies of all your GP records, and any hospital records made in connection with this incident, so he or she can see if there is anything in your records that may affect your claim. Once you start your claim, the court can order you to give copies of your health records to the solicitor of the person you are making a claim against so he or she can see if any of the information in your records can be used to defend his or her client.

If you decide to go ahead with your claim, your records may be passed to a number of people including:

- the expert who your solicitor or agent instructs to produce a medical report as evidence for the case;
- the person you are making a claim against and their solicitors;
- the insurance company for the person you are making a claim against;
- any insurance company or other organisation paying your legal costs; and
- any other person or company officially involved with the claim.

You do not have to give permission for your health records to be released but if you don't, the court may not let you go ahead with your claim and, in some circumstances, your solicitor may refuse to represent you.

If there is very sensitive information in the records, that is not connected to the claim, you should tell your solicitor. They will then consider whether this information needs to be revealed.

Notes for the solicitor or agent

Before you ask your client to fill in and sign this form you should explain that this will involve his or her full health records being released and how the information in them may be used. You should also tell your client to read the notes above.

If your client is not capable of giving his or her permission in this form, this form should be signed by:

- your client's litigation friend;
- someone who has enduring power of attorney to act for

  your client; or
- your client's receiver appointed by the Court of Protection.

When you send this form to the appropriate records controller please also enclose the authorised fees for getting access to records.

If you find out at any stage that the medical records contain information that the client does not know about (for example, being diagnosed with a serious illness), you should discuss this with the health professional who provided the records.

Unless your client agrees otherwise, you must use his or her health records only for the purpose for which the client signed this form (that is, making his or her claim). Under the Data Protection Act you have responsibilities relating to sensitive information. The entire health record should not be automatically revealed without the client's permission and you should not keep health records for any longer than you need them. You should return them to the client at the end of the claim if they want them. Otherwise, you are responsible for destroying them.

Notes for the medical records controller

This form shows your patient's permission for you to give copies of his or her full GP record, and any hospital records relating to this incident, to his or her solicitor or agent. You must give the solicitor or agent copies of these health records unless any of the exemptions set out in The Data Protection (Subject Access Modification) (Health) Order 2000 apply. The main exemptions are that you must not release information that:

- is likely to cause serious physical or mental harm to the patient or another person; or
- relates to someone who would normally need to give their permission (where that person is not a health professional who has cared for the patient).

Your patient's permission for you to release information is valid only if that patient understands the consequences of his or her records being released, and how the information will be used. The solicitor or agent named on this form must explain these issues to the patient. If you have any doubt about whether this has happened, contact the solicitor or agent, or your patient.

If your patient is not capable of giving his or her permission, this form should be signed by:

- a 'litigation friend' acting for your patient;
- someone with 'enduring power of attorney' to act for your patient; or
- a receiver appointed by the Court of Protection.

You may charge the usual fees authorised under the Data Protection Act for providing the records.

The BMA publishes detailed advice for doctors on giving access to health records, including the fees that you may charge. You can view that advice by visiting
http://bma.org.uk/practical-support-at-work/ethics/confidentiality-and-health-records

This form is published by the Law Society and British Medical Association. (2nd edition, October 2004)

 BMA

The Law Society

Appendix III

Directions

MODEL DIRECTIONS FOR CLINICAL NEGLIGENCE CASES (2018) – BEFORE MASTER YOXALL AND MASTER COOK

Introductory note

These are the Model Directions for use in the first Case Management Conference in clinical negligence cases before the Masters.

A draft order in Word format, adopting the Model Directions as necessary, is to be provided by e-mail to the Master at least 2 days before the hearing.

Parties are required to use the form of order at the end of this document – adapted as necessary. The CPR requires parties to take as their starting point any relevant Model or Standard Directions

The e-mail addresses of the clinical negligence Masters are:

master.yoxall@ejudiciary.net
master.cook@ejudiciary.net
master.surname@ejudiciary.net

The Model Directions allow the court and the parties to be flexible. For example, sequential exchange of quantum statements (say, with schedule and counter-schedule of loss) may be appropriate. The sequential exchange of expert evidence on breach of duty and causation may sometimes be appropriate.

It would be helpful if dates appeared in **bold** type.

Please note: Solicitors must ensure that the claimant is accurately described in the title to the order: e.g., "JOHN SMITH (a child and protected party by his mother and Litigation Friend, JOAN SMITH). It is never permissible to refer to such a claimant as "JOHN SMITH".

The order should make it clear that it is made pursuant to a Case Management Conference or an application or both.

Please note the role of experts in the preparation of Agendas.

The Model Directions

Warning: you must comply with the terms imposed upon you by this order otherwise your case is liable to be struck out or some other sanction imposed. If you cannot comply you are expected to make formal application to the court before any deadline imposed upon you expires.	
ON a [Costs and] Case Management Conference AND ON hearing solicitor/counsel for the Claimant and solicitor/counsel for the Defendant IT IS ORDERED that	*A Costs and Case Management Conference may well be attended by a costs lawyer or costs draughtsman. If so, this should be stated*
(1) The Claim is allocated to the Multi-Track and is assigned to Master Xxxx for case management.	*All claims issued in the High Court must be allocated to the Multi-track and may well have been allocated earlier. This merely confirms allocation for the avoidance of doubt and confirms the 'docketing' of the claim to the assigned Master.*
(2) At all stages the parties must consider settling this litigation by any means of Alternative Dispute Resolution (including round table conferences, early neutral evaluation, mediation and arbitration); any party not engaging in any such means proposed by another is to serve a witness statement giving reasons within **21 days** of receipt of that proposal. That witness statement must not be shown to the trial judge until questions of costs arise. Such means of Alternative Dispute Resolution adopted shall be concluded not less than 35 days before trial.	*The object is to reduce 'door of the court' settlements which are wasteful of costs, resources and judicial time. '21 days' can be altered. The words 'and not less than **28 days** before trial' can always be added after the word 'proposal' by the managing judge if appropriate. Not necessary for every Order.*
(3) Documents are to be retained as follows: (a) the parties must retain all electronically stored documents relating to the issues in this Claim. (b) the Defendant must retain the original clinical notes relating to the issues in this Claim. The Defendant must give facilities for inspection by the Claimant, the Claimant's legal advisers and experts of these original notes on 7 days written notice. (c) legible copies of the medical and educational records of the Claimant/Deceased/Claimant's Mother are to be placed in a separate paginated bundle by the Claimant's Solicitors and kept up to date. All references to medical notes are to be made by reference to the pages in that bundle.	

This and any additional paragraphs to be inserted here may cover various case management directions:

Amendments

The following is suggested:

Permission to Claimant/ Defendant to amend the Particulars of Claim/Defence in terms of the draft initialled by the Master [or the draft served on xxxx]; the Defendant to serve an amended Defence by xxxx. Costs of and occasioned by the amendments to be borne by (usually, the party seeking permission to amend). [Where no draft is available, but the form of the amendments is not contentious] (Party wishing to amend) to serve draft amended [Statement of Case] by xxxx. If no objection to the draft amendments, response to be served by xxxx, if objection is taken to the draft, permission to restore.

Judgment *(The following is suggested)*:

Judgment for the Claimant an amount to be decided by the court being xx% of the damages due on a full liability basis.

Split Trial

[An order "That there be a split trial" is inappropriate. The following is suggested.]

A preliminary issue shall be tried between the Claimant and the Defendant as to whether or not the Defendant is liable to the Claimant by reason of the matters alleged in the Particulars of Claim and, if so, whether or not any of the injuries described were so caused; and, if any such injuries were so caused, the extent of the same.

(4) Disclosure of documents relevant to the issues of breach of duty and causation and quantification of damages will be dealt with as follows: (a) **By 4pm on xxxx** both parties must give to each other standard disclosure of documents by list and category. (b) **By 4pm on xxxx** any request must be made to inspect the original of, or to provide a copy of, a disclosable document. (c) Any such request unless objected to must be complied with within 14 days of the request. (d) **By 4pm on xxxx** each party must serve and file with the court a list of issues relevant to the search for and disclosure of electronically stored documents, or must confirm there are no such issues, following Practice Direction 31B; or confirm in writing that there are no electronically stored documents.]	*The words 'and category' are optional. Where there is a large number of documents all falling into a particular category, the disclosing party may list those documents as a category rather than individually. See: para 3.2 to Practice Direction 31A.*
(5) Evidence of fact will be dealt with as follows: (a) **By 4pm on xxxx** both parties must serve on each other copies of the signed statements of themselves and of all witnesses on whom they intend to rely in respect of breach of duty and causation and all notices relating to evidence, including Civil Evidence Act notices. (b) For the avoidance of doubt statements of all concerned with the relevant treatment and care of the Claimant must be included. (c) **By 4pm on xxxx** both parties must serve on each other copies of the signed statements of themselves and of all witnesses on whom they intend to rely in respect of condition, prognosis and loss and all notices relating to evidence, including Civil Evidence Act notices. (d) Oral evidence will not be permitted at trial from a witness whose statement has not been served in accordance with this order or has been served late, except with permission from the Court. (e) [Evidence of fact is limited to xx witnesses on behalf of each party.] (f) [Witness statements must not exceed xx pages of A4 in length.]	

(6)	Expert evidence is directed as follows.	*The following text is not designed to be prescriptive, but will cover the essential directions for expert evidence. The directions will identify the disciplines of expertise on which it proposed to rely and, preferably, the names of each expert (or a direction requiring the expert to be named by a date). Where necessary the specific issues which the expert is to address can be identified.*
(7)	The parties have permission in respect of breach of duty and causation and quantification of damages to rely on the following jointly instructed written evidence of an expert xxxx	*Delete as necessary* *OR* experts in the following fields:
	(a) By xxxx the expert should be agreed and instructed, and if no expert has been instructed by that date the Claimant must apply to court by 4pm the following day for further directions.	
	(b) By xxxx the expert will report to the instructing parties.	*Where it is necessary to confine an expert to specific issues the following subparagraph is appropriate:*
	(c) By xxxx the parties may put written questions to the expert.	(a) The expert's report will be confined to the following issues
	(d) By xxxx the expert will reply to the questions.	(i) xxxxx
	(e) A copy of this order must be served on the expert by the Claimant with the expert's instructions.	(ii) xxxxx
	(f) A party seeking to call the expert to give oral evidence at trial must apply for permission to do so before pre-trial check lists are filed.	*Whether questions are to be put to the single joint expert is a matter for case management. If they are not required the subparagraphs can be deleted.*
	(g) Unless the parties agree in writing or the Court orders otherwise, the fees and expenses of the expert shall be paid by the parties giving instructions for the report equally.	*The following optional subparagraph can be used:* The expert may apply direct to the court for directions where necessary under Rule 35.14 Civil Procedure Rules. *Note: The Claimant is directed to serve a copy of the order as we are dealing with joint experts. Otherwise, it is the instructing party who serves the expert with the copy order.*

(8)	In respect of breach of duty and causation the parties each have permission to rely on the following written expert evidence:	*The following can be added for each expert:* confined to the following issues:

(a) The Claimant:

    (i) an expert in xxxx, namely Mr A, whose report must be served by xxxx.

    (ii) an expert in xxxx, namely Dr B, whose report must be served by xxxx.

    (iii) an expert in xxxx, namely Ms C, whose report must be served by xxxx

(b) The Defendant:

    (i) an expert xxxx, namely Mr AA, whose report must be served by xxxx.

    (ii) an expert xxxx, namely Mr BB, whose report must be served by xxxx.

    (iii) an expert xxxx, namely Ms CC, whose report must be served by xxxx.

(9)	In respect of condition, prognosis and quantification of damages the parties (the Defendants acting jointly *where there are several defendants*) each have permission to rely on the following written expert evidence:	*When there are several defendants consideration must always be given to the defendants sharing expert evidence.*

(a) The Claimant:

    (i) an expert in xxxx, namely Mr A, whose report must be served by xxxx.

    (ii) an expert in xxxx, namely Dr B, whose report must be served by xxxx.

    (iii) an expert in xxxx, namely Ms C, whose report must be served by xxxx.

(b) The Defendant:

    (i) an expert in xxxx, namely Mr AA, whose report must be served by xxxx.

    (ii) an expert in xxxx, namely Mr BB, whose report must be served by xxxx.

    (iii) an expert in xxxx, namely Ms CC, whose report must be served by xxxx.

| (10) | Unless the reports are agreed, there must be a without prejudice discussion between the experts of like discipline by 4pm on xxxx in which the experts will identify the issues between them and reach agreement if possible. The experts will prepare for the court and sign a statement of the issues on which they agree and on which they disagree with a summary of their reasons in accordance with Rule 35.12 Civil Procedure Rules, and each statement must be sent to the parties to be received by 4pm on xxxx and in any event no later than 7 days after the discussion. | *A guide is **8 weeks** after the exchange of reports for the discussion and **7 days** to produce their statement.*

The following direction may be used as appropriate:

Discussions between experts are not mandatory. The parties should consider, with their expert, whether there is likely to be any useful purpose in holding a discussion and should be prepared to agree that no discussion is in fact needed.

Where it is necessary to identify more specifically the areas of discussion, the following may be used (numbering not formatted):

The purpose of the discussions is to identify:

The extent of the agreement between the experts;

The points of disagreement and short reasons for disagreement;

Action, if any, which may be taken to resolve the outstanding points of disagreement;

Any further material points not raised in the Agenda and the extent to which these issues are agreed |
| (11) | xxxx | **Agendas**

The use of an agenda is not necessary in every case.

Claimants' solicitors and counsel should note the obligation to prepare the draft Agenda jointly with the relevant expert. Experts should note that it is part of their overriding duty to the court to ensure that the Agenda complies with the following direction which may be used (numbering not formatted):

The use of agendas is not mandatory. Solicitors should consult with the experts to ensure that agendas are necessary and, if used, are reasonable in scope. The agenda should assist the experts and should not be in the form of leading questions or hostile in tone. An agenda must include a list of the outstanding issues in the preamble. |

The preamble should state: the standard of proof: the Bolam test: remind the experts not to attempt to determine factual issues: remind them not to stray outside their field of expertise and indicate the form of the joint statement. It will also be helpful to provide a comprehensive list of the materials which each expert has seen, perhaps in the form of an agreed supplementary bundle (it is assumed that experts will have been provided with the medical notes bundle).

Otherwise *the following direction may be used (numbering not formatted):*

Unless otherwise agreed by all parties' solicitors, after consulting with the experts, a draft Agenda which directs the experts to the remaining issues relevant to the experts' discipline, as identified in the statements of case shall be prepared jointly by the Claimant's solicitors and experts and sent to the Defendant's solicitors for comment at least **35 days** before the agreed date for the experts' discussions.

The Defendants shall **within 21 days** of receipt agree the Agenda, or propose amendments.

7 days thereafter all solicitors shall use their best endeavours to agree the Agenda. Points of disagreement should be on matters of real substance and not semantics or on matters the experts could resolve of their own accord at the discussion. In default of agreement, both versions shall be considered at the discussions. Agendas, when used, shall be provided to the experts not less than **7 days** before the date fixed for discussions.

Where it has been impossible to agree a single agenda, it is of assistance to the experts if the second agenda is consecutively numbered to the first, i.e. if the first agenda has 16 questions in it, the second agenda is numbered from 17 onwards.

(14)	A copy of this order must be served on each expert by the instructing party.	
(15)	The parties have permission to call oral evidence of the experts of like discipline limited to issues that are in dispute.	**OR** A party seeking to call oral expert evidence at trial must apply for permission to do so before pre-trial check lists are filed.
(16)	Any unpublished literature upon which any expert witness proposes to rely must be served at the same time as service of his report together with a list of published literature. Any supplementary literature upon which any expert witness relies must be notified to all parties at least one month before trial. No expert witness may rely upon any publications that have not been disclosed in accordance with this order without the permission of the trial judge subject to costs as appropriate.	
(17)	Experts will, at the time of producing their reports, incorporate details of any employment or activity which raises a possible conflict of interest.	
(18)	For the avoidance of doubt, experts do not require the authorisation of solicitor or counsel before signing a joint statement.	
(19)	If an expert radically alters an opinion previously recorded, the joint statement should include a note or addendum by that expert explaining the change of opinion.	*Note: This does not affect Rule 35.12 which provides that where experts reach agreement on an issue during their discussions, the agreement shall not bind the parties unless the parties expressly agree to be bound by the agreement.*
(20)	Schedules of Loss must be updated as follows:	*Periodical Payments. Parties should, at the first case management conference, be prepared to give their provisional view as to whether the case is one in which the periodical payment of damages might be appropriate.*
	(a) **By 4pm on xxxx** the Claimant must send an up to date schedule of loss to the Defendant.	*Schedules. Parties are encouraged to exchange Schedules in a form which enables the Counter schedule to be based on the Claimant's Schedule i.e. by delivering a disk with the hard copy, or by sending it as an e-mail attachment.*
	(b) **By 4pm on xxxx** the Defendant, in the event of challenge, must send an up to date counter-schedule of loss to the Claimant.	
	(c) The schedule and counter-schedule must contain a statement setting out that party's case on the issue of periodical payments pursuant to Rule 41.5 Civil Procedure Rules.	

(21)　The trial will be listed as follows.	*The Queen's Bench Judges' Listing, in order to maintain the necessary degree of flexibility for listing, will give a 'trial period' rather than a fixed date, but, in order to accommodate the parties' need for certainty as to dates for experts to attend, will, if an approach is made closer to the beginning of the trial period, confirm the date for the trial to begin as the first day of the trial period.*
	The trial period will usually be directed to begin at least 2-3 clear months after the last event besides Alternative Dispute Resolution (this is to allow for Alternative Dispute Resolution).
	In relatively modest claims (in term of damages only), the Master may direct:
	If the parties reach agreement upon breach of duty and causation, the parties are to immediately restore the case before the Master so that alternative directions on the assessment of damages may be considered.
	The following subparagraph may be added:
	Certified fit for High Court Judge, if available
(a)　A copy of this sealed order will be sent to the Queen's Bench Judges Listing Office who will notify all parties of a listing appointment for a trial date or period within the trial window, which will usually be six weeks from the date the order is sealed. If parties have any queries in relation to the listing appointment they should contact Queen's Bench Judges Listing on qbjudgeslistingoffice@hmcts.gsi.gov.uk.	
(b)　Trial: Judge alone; London	
(c)　Category: B [Fit for trial by High Court Judge]	
(d)　Trial window: from xxxx to xxxx inclusive.	
(e)　Time estimate: × days	
(f)　The parties shall file Pre-Trial Check Lists as directed by the Queen's Bench Judges' Listing.	

(22)	Pre-trial directions are as follows:
	
	(a) There will be a review case management conference in [Room E119/E112] on [**date**] at [**time**] with a time estimate of [ ]
	
	(b) If there are no substantial issues between the parties and all parties agree, one party may email the Master to request that the hearing be conducted by telephone and in accordance with Practice Direction 23A Civil Procedure Rules.
	
	(c) At least **3 clear days** before the case management conference the Claimant must file and send to the Defendant preferably agreed and by email:
	
	    (i) any draft directions;
	
	    (ii) a case summary.
	
	(d) The case management conference MUST be vacated by giving direct notice to the Master in the event that no further directions are required and all directions have been complied with or the claim has settled.
		Delete Room number as appropriate
		
		It is not appropriate to include this provision in all cases. Most quantum only claims or preliminary issues will not require a further hearing and permission to restore should be included. This hearing may be vacated by consent provided that all directions have been complied with; no further directions are required; and the Master is given reasonable notice. The hearing must be vacated by giving direct notice to the Master in the event the claim settles. The hearing will not be vacated in the event a consent order settling the action is sent to the court unless the order specifically so provides.

(23)	The parties are to agree the trial bundle not less than 10 days before trial	
(24)	Not more than **7 nor less than 3 clear working days** before the trial, the Claimant must file at court and serve an indexed and paginated bundle of documents which complies with the requirements of Rule 39.5 Civil Procedure Rules and Practice Direction 39A. The bundle will include a case summary and a chronology.	
(25)	The parties must file with the court and exchange skeleton arguments at least three working days before the trial, by email.	
(26)	The Parties may, by prior agreement in writing, extend time for a direction in this order by up to 28 days and without the need to apply to Court. Beyond that 28-day period any agreed extensions of time must be submitted to the Court by email including a brief explanation of the reasons, confirmation that it will not prejudice any hearing date and with the draft Consent Order in Word format. The Court will then consider whether a formal application and hearing is necessary.	*Note that it is by prior agreement in writing. This provision is designed to prevent unnecessary applications being made to the court seeking extensions of time for service of witness statements and expert's reports.*

(27) Permission to restore. The parties may email the Master direct.	*Note: A party may request the restoration of a CMC or application by letter or e-mail to the assigned Master. If possible the Master should be provided with an agreed list of dates to avoid. Where the application is urgent and the time estimate is no more than 30 minutes, the Master will endeavour to list a hearing at 10.00am as soon as possible. Applications estimated to take more than 30 minutes should be applied for as private room appointments in the usual way.]* *[The Central Office of the Queen's Bench Division is not a telephone enabled court see PD 23A 6.1. Both Masters are willing, in appropriate cases, to hear applications by telephone link, provided sufficient notice is given directly to the Master concerned and the relevant papers are provided in advance. E-mails are an acceptable means of communication, provided that they are copied to all parties.]* *[NOTE: The Court File in cases proceeding before the Masters will not routinely be placed before the Master. Parties wishing for it to be produced should notify the Case Management Section FIVE CLEAR DAYS in advance of the appointment. In all other cases parties should bring with them copies of any filed documents upon which they intend to rely.]*
(28) Costs in case.	*Or other costs order*
(29) Claimant to serve sealed order.	*Usually the court will send sealed CMC orders to the Claimant's solicitors so that they can serve.* *Where trial directions are not given, it may be appropriate to direct that the Claimant draw, file and serve the order.*

DRAFT ORDER

IN THE HIGH COURT OF JUSTICE   Case No.

QUEEN'S BENCH DIVISION

MASTER [YOXALL/COOK]

B E T W E E N

JOAN SMITH

Claimant

And

THE GREAT SCOTT HOSPITAL NHS TRUST

Defendant

ORDER

ON a [Costs and] Case Management Conference

AND ON hearing solicitor/counsel for the Claimant and solicitor/counsel for the Defendant

IT IS ORDERED that

(1) The Claim is allocated to the Multi-Track and is assigned to Master Xxxx for case management.

(2) At all stages the parties must consider settling this litigation by any means of Alternative Dispute Resolution (including round table conferences, early neutral evaluation, mediation and arbitration); any party not engaging in any such means proposed by another is to serve a witness statement giving reasons within **21 days** of receipt of that proposal. That witness statement must not be shown to the trial judge until questions of costs arise.

Such means of Alternative Dispute Resolution adopted shall be concluded not less than 35 days before trial.

(3) Documents are to be retained as follows:

(a) the parties must retain all electronically stored documents relating to the issues in this Claim.

(b) the Defendant must retain the original clinical notes relating to the issues in this Claim. The Defendant must give facilities for inspection by the Claimant, the Claimant's legal advisers and experts of these original notes on 7 days written notice.

(c) legible copies of the medical and educational records of the Claimant/Deceased/Claimant's Mother are to be placed in a separate paginated bundle by the Claimant's Solicitors and kept up to date. All references to medical notes are to be made by reference to the pages in that bundle.

(4) Disclosure of documents relevant to the issues of breach of duty and causation and quantification of damages will be dealt with as follows:

(a) **By 4pm on xxxx** both parties must give to each other standard disclosure of documents by list and category.

(b) **By 4pm on xxxx** any request must be made to inspect the original of, or to provide a copy of, a disclosable document.

(c) Any such request, unless objected, to must be complied with within 14 days of the request.

(d)   [**By 4pm on xxxx** each party must serve and file with the court a list of issues relevant to the search for and disclosure of electronically stored documents in accordance with Practice Direction 31B; or confirm in writing that there are no electronically stored documents.]

(5)   Evidence of fact will be dealt with as follows:

(a)   **By 4pm on xxxx** both parties must serve on each other copies of the signed statements of themselves and of all witnesses on whom they intend to rely in respect of breach of duty and causation and all notices relating to evidence, including Civil Evidence Act notices.

(b)   For the avoidance of doubt statements of all concerned with the relevant treatment and care of the Claimant upon which the Defendant wishes to rely must be served at this stage.

(c)   **By 4pm on xxxx** both parties must serve on each other copies of the signed statements of themselves and of all witnesses on whom they intend to rely in respect of condition, prognosis and loss and all notices relating to evidence, including Civil Evidence Act notices.

(d)   Oral evidence will not be permitted at trial from a witness whose statement has not been served in accordance with this order or has been served late, except with permission from the Court.

(e)   [Evidence of fact is limited to xx witnesses on behalf of each party.]

(f)   [Witness statements must not exceed xx pages of A4 in length.]

(6)   Expert evidence is directed as follows.

(7)   The parties have permission in respect of breach of duty and causation and quantification of damages to rely on the following jointly instructed written evidence of an expert xxxx

(a)   By **xxxx** the expert should be agreed and instructed, and if no expert has been instructed by that date the Claimant must apply to court by 4pm the following day for further directions.

(b)   By **xxxx** the expert will report to the instructing parties.

(c)   By **xxxx** the parties may put written questions to the expert.

(d)   By **xxxx** the expert will reply to the questions.

(e)   A copy of this order must be served on the expert by the Claimant with the expert's instructions.

(f)   A party seeking to call the expert to give oral evidence at trial must apply for permission to do so before pre-trial check lists are filed.

(g)   Unless the parties agree in writing or the Court orders otherwise, the fees and expenses of the expert shall be paid by the parties giving instructions for the report equally.

(8)   In respect of breach of duty and causation the parties each have permission to rely on the following written expert evidence:

(a)   The Claimant:

(i)   an expert in xxxx, namely Mr A, whose report must be served by **xxxx**.

(ii)   an expert in xxxx, namely Dr B, whose report must be served by **xxxx**.

(iii)   an expert in xxxx, namely Ms C, whose report must be served by **xxxx**.

(b)   The Defendant:

(i)   an expert xxxx, namely Mr AA, whose report must be served by **xxxx**.

(ii)   an expert xxxx, namely Mr BB, whose report must be served by **xxxx**.

(iii)   an expert xxxx, namely Ms CC, whose report must be served by **xxxx**.

(9) In respect of condition, prognosis and quantification of damages the parties [the Defendants acting jointly where there are several defendants] each have permission to rely on the following written expert evidence:

    (a) The Claimant:
        (i) an expert in xxxx, namely Mr A, whose report must be served by **xxxx**.
        (ii) an expert in xxxx, namely Dr B, whose report must be served by **xxxx**.
        (iii) an expert in xxxx, namely Ms C, whose report must be served by **xxxx**.
    (b) The Defendant:
        (i) an expert in xxxx, namely Mr AA, whose report must be served by **xxxx**.
        (ii) an expert in xxxx, namely Mr BB, whose report must be served by **xxxx**.
        (iii) an expert in xxxx, namely Ms CC, whose report must be served by **xxxx**.

(10) Unless the reports are agreed, there must be a without prejudice discussion between the experts of like discipline by 4pm on **xxxx** in which the experts will identify the issues between them and reach agreement if possible. The experts will prepare for the court and sign a statement of the issues on which they agree and on which they disagree with a summary of their reasons in accordance with Rule 35.12 Civil Procedure Rules, and each statement must be sent to the parties to be received by 4pm on **xxxx** and in any event no later than 7 days after the discussion.

(11) Unless otherwise agreed by all parties' solicitors, after consulting with the experts, a draft Agenda which directs the experts to the remaining issues relevant to the experts' discipline, as identified in the statements of case shall be prepared jointly by the Claimant's solicitors and experts and sent to the Defendant's solicitors for comment at least 35 days before the agreed date for the experts' discussions.

(12) The Defendants shall within 21 days of receipt agree the Agenda, or propose amendments.

(13) 7 days thereafter all solicitors shall use their best endeavours to agree the Agenda. Points of disagreement should be on matters of real substance and not semantics or on matters the experts could resolve of their own accord at the discussion. In default of agreement, both versions shall be considered at the discussions. Agendas, when used, shall be provided to the experts not less than 7 days before the date fixed for discussions.

(14) A copy of this order must be served on each expert by the instructing party.

(15) The parties have permission to call oral evidence of the experts of like discipline limited to issues that are in dispute.

(16) Any unpublished literature upon which any expert witness proposes to rely must be served at the same time as service of his report together with a list of published literature. Any supplementary literature upon which any expert witness relies must be notified to all parties at least one month before trial. No expert witness may rely upon any publications that have not been disclosed in accordance with this order without the permission of the trial judge subject to costs as appropriate.

(17) Experts will, at the time of producing their reports, incorporate details of any employment or activity which raises a possible conflict of interest.

(18) For the avoidance of doubt, experts do not require the authorisation of solicitor or counsel before signing a joint statement.

(19) If an expert radically alters an opinion previously recorded, the joint statement should include a note or addendum by that expert explaining the change of opinion.

(20) Schedules of Loss must be updated to the date of trial as follows:

    (a) **By 4pm on xxxx** the Claimant must send a schedule of loss to the Defendant.

    (b) **By 4pm on xxxx** the Defendant, in the event of challenge, must send a counter-schedule of loss to the Claimant.

    (c) The schedule and counter-schedule must contain a statement setting out that party's case on the issue of periodical payments pursuant to Rule 41.5 Civil Procedure Rules.

(21) The trial will be listed as follows.

    (a) A copy of this sealed order will be sent to the Queen's Bench Judges Listing Office who will notify all parties of a listing appointment for a trial date or period within the trial window, which will usually be six weeks from the date the order is sealed.
    If parties have any queries in relation to the listing appointment they should contact Queen's Bench Judges Listing on *qbjudgeslistingoffice@ hmcts.gsi.gov.uk*.

    (b) Trial: Judge alone; London

    (c) Category: B [Fit for trial by High Court Judge, if available]

    (d) Trial window: from **xxxx** to **xxxx** inclusive.

    (e) Time estimate: × days

    (f) The parties shall file Pre-Trial Check Lists as directed by the Queen's Bench Judges' Listing.

(22) Pre-trial directions are as follows:

    (a) There will be a review case management conference in Room E119/ E112 on [*date*] at [*time*] with a time estimate of [ ]

    (b) If there are no substantial issues between the parties and all parties agree, one party may email the Master to request that the hearing be conducted by telephone and in accordance with Practice Direction 23A Civil Procedure Rules.

    (c) At least 3 clear days before the case management conference the parties must provide the Master with:
        (i) any draft directions in Word;
        (ii) a succinct case summary in Word setting out the remaining factual and legal issues between the parties.

    (d) The case management conference MUST be vacated by giving direct notice to the Master in the event that no further directions are required and all directions have been complied with or the claim has settled.

(23) The parties are to agree the trial bundle not less than 10 days before trial.

(24) Not more than **7 nor less than 3 clear working days** before the trial, the Claimant must file at court and serve an indexed and paginated bundle of documents which complies with the requirements of Rule 39.5 Civil Procedure Rules and Practice Direction 39A. The bundle will include a case summary and a chronology.

(25) The parties must file with the court and exchange skeleton arguments at least three working days before the trial, by email.

(26) The Parties may, by prior agreement in writing, extend time for a direction in this order by up to 28 days and without the need to apply to Court. Beyond that 28-day period any agreed extensions of time must be submitted to the Court by email including a brief explanation of the reasons, confirmation that it will not prejudice any hearing date and with the draft Consent Order in Word format. The Court will then consider whether a formal application and hearing is necessary.

(27) Permission to restore. The parties may email the Master direct.

(28) Costs in the case.

(29) Claimant to serve sealed order.

Dated the

Common hieroglyphs and abbreviations

COMMON HIEROGLYPHS AND ABBREVIATIONS

Here is a list of common abbreviations and hieroglyphs, reproduced by kind permission of Ann Winyard.

Common hieroglyphs

+++	much/many
#	fracture
Δ	diagnosis
diff. Δ or ΔΔ	differential diagnosis
R	treatment
J° (no jaundice)	nil/nothing/no
↑	up, increasing
N, →	constant, normal or lateral shift (eg of apex of heart)
↓	down, decreasing
⊥	central (of the trachea)
$\frac{1}{7}$	one day
$\frac{2}{52}$	two weeks
$\frac{3}{12}$	three months
T38.6°C	temperature 38.6
T–14	term (ie date baby due) less two weeks
T+7	term plus one week
$\frac{35+4}{40}$	35 weeks and 4 days
$\frac{37+3}{40}$	37 weeks and 3 days

Common abbreviations

AAL	Anterior axillary line
ATCH	Adrenocorticotrophic hormone
AE	Air entry
AFB	Acid fast bacillus (TB)
AFP	Alpha-fetoprotein (maternal serum and occasionally amniotic fluid levels tested in pregnancy to screen for neural tube defect in foetus).
AJ	Ankle jerk (reflex: see also BJ, KJ, SJ, TJ)
Anti-D	This gamma globulin must be given by injection to Rhesus negative mother who delivers/aborts Rhesus positive child/foetus to prevent mother developing antibodies which could damage a subsequent Rhesus positive baby.
Apgar	Apgar score: means of recording baby's condition at birth by observing and 'scoring' (0, 1 or 2) 5 parameters
A/V	Anteverted
BJ	Biceps jerk (reflex: see AJ)
BNF (plus date)	British National Formulary (prescriber's 'bible' supplied free to all NHS doctors). New edition each year. You can buy one (about £10 from medical bookshops).
BO	Bowels open
BP (plus date)	British pharmacopoeia
BP	Blood pressure
BS	(a) Breath sounds
	(b) Bowel sounds
	(c) Blood sugar
c	With (Latin: cum)
C_2H_5OH	Alcohol
Ca	(a) Carcinoma/cancer
	(b) Calcium
Caps	Capsules
CAT scan	Computed axial tomograph
CNS	Central nervous system
CO	Complaining of
CO_2	Carbon dioxide
COETT	Cuffed oral endotracheal tube (see COT and ETT)
COT	Cuffed oral tube (endotracheal tube used for ventilating a patient who cannot breath unaided)
CPD	Cephalo-pelvic disproportion (baby too big to fit through pelvis)

CSF	Cerebrospinal fluid
CTG	Cardiotocograph (trace during labour of baby's heart and mum's contractions)
CVA	Cerebrovascular accident (stroke)
CVS	Cardio-vascular system
Cx	Cervix
CXR	Chest X-ray
DNA	(a) Did not attend
	(b) Deoxyribonucleic acid
D & V	Diarrhoea and vomiting
DOA	Dead on arrival
DVT	Deep vein thrombosis
Dx	Diagnosis
EGG	Electro-cardiogram/graph (electric heart recording)
ECT	Electro-convulsive therapy
EDC	Expected date of confinement
EDD	Expected date of delivery
EEG	Electroencephalogram/graph (brain scan)
ERCP	Endoscopic retrograde choledochopancreatico/graphy/scopy
ERPC	Evacuation of retained products of conception
ESR	Erythrocyte sedimentation rate (blood)
EtOH	Another code for alcohol
ETT	Endotracheal tube (see COT above)
FB	Finger's breadth
FBC	Full blood count
FBS	Fetal blood sampling (carried out during labour to check baby's condition)
FH	Family history
FHH	Fetal heart heard
FHHR	Fetal heart heard regular
FHR	Fetal heart rate
FLK	(Used by paediatricians) Funny looking kid
FMF	Fetal movements felt
FSE	Fetal scalp electrode
FSH	(a) Family and social history
	(b) Follicle-stimulating hormone (produced in pregnancy)
GA	General anaesthetic
GFR	Glomerular filtration rate

GIT	Gastro-intestinal tract
GTT	Glucose tolerance test (for diabetes)
GUT	Genito-urinary tract
Hb	Haemoglobin (blood)
HPC	History of presenting complaint
HS	Heart sounds
HVS	High vaginal swab
Hx	History
ICS	Intercostal space (usually as xICS, where x = a number from 1 to 11)
IJ	Internal jugular vein
IM	Intramuscular
IVI	Intravenous infusion (drip)
JVP	Jugular vein pressure
K	Potassium
KJ	Knee jerk (reflex: see AJ)
kPa	Kilopascal, approximately 7.5 mmHg
L	Litre
LA	Local anaesthetic
LFTs	Liver function tests
LIH	Left inguinal hernia
LMP	Last menstrual period
LN	Lymph node
LOA	Left occiput anterior (position of baby's head at delivery; see also LOP, ROA, ROP)
LOC	Loss of consciousness
LOL	Left occipitolateral
LOP	Left occiput posterior (see LOA above)
LSCS	Lower segment caesarean section (the 'normal' type of caesarean)
LSKK	Liver, spleen and kidneys
mcg	Microgram
MCL	Mic clavicular line
µg	Microgram
mg	Milligram
mist	Mixture
ml	Millilitre
mmHG	Millimetres of mercury (pressure)

mMOL	Milimol
N & V	Nausea and vomiting
Na	Sodium
NaHCO₃	Sodium bicarbonate (alkaline substance: *inter alia* given to counteract metabolic acidosis following oxygen deprivation)
NAD	Nothing abnormal diagnosed/detected
NBM	Nil by mouth
ng	Nanogram
NG	Carcinoma/cancer (neoplastic growth)
NMCS	No malignant cells seen
NOF	Neck of femur
N/S	Normal size
O₂	Oxygen
OA	Occipito-posterior
P	Pulse
π	Period
Pco₂	Partial pressure of carbon dioxide (normally in blood)
PERLA	Pupils are equal and react to light and accommodation
PE	(a) Pulmonary embolism
	(b) Pre-eclampsia
PET	Pre-eclamptic toxaemia
pg	Pictogram
pH	Negative log of hydrogen icon activity: 'acidity and alkalinity' scale. Low is acidic. High is alkaline. pH7 is about neutral
PH	Past/previous history
PID	(a) Pelvic inflammatory disease
	(b) Prolapsed intervertebral disc
PMH	Past/previous medical history
PN(R)	Percussion note (resonant)
PO₂	Partial pressure of oxygen (normally in blood)
POH	Past/previous obstetric history
po	Per os (by mouth)
pr	Per rectum (by the rectum)
prn	As required – of, eg, pain killers
pv	Per vaginam (by the vagina)
RBC	Red blood cell (erythrocyte)

Rh	Rhesus (blood type, can cause problems in pregnancy if mother is Rhesus *negative* and father Rhesus *positive*)
RIH	Right inguinal hernia
ROA	Right occiput anterior (see LOA above)
ROL	Right occipito-lateral
ROM	Range of movement
ROP	Right occiput posterior (see LOA above)
RS	Respiratory system
RTI	Respiratory tract infection
s	Without (Latin: sine)
S/B	seen by
S/D	Systolic/diastolic (heart and circulation)
SH	Social history
SJ	Supinator jerk (reflex: see AJ)
SOA	Swelling of ankles
SOB (OE)	Short of breath (on exertion)
SOS	(a) si opus sit (if necessary)
	(b) see other sheet
SROM	Spontaneous rupture of membranes (labour)
SVC	Superior vena cava
SVD	Spontaneous vaginal delivery
SVT	Supraventricular tachycardia
TCI/52	To come in, in 2 weeks' time
TGH	To go home
THR	Total hip replacement
TIA	Transient ischemic attack
TJ	Triceps jerk (reflex: see AJ)
TVF	Tactile vocal fremitus
U & E	Urea and electrolytes (biochemical tests)
URTI	Upper respiratory tract infection
UTI	Urinary tract infection
VE	Vaginal examination
VF	Ventricular fibrillation
VT	Ventricular tachycardia
V/V	Vulva and vagina
WBC	White blood corpuscle/white blood cell count
XR	X-ray

Appendix V

The Hippocratic oath

This oath, taken at the time of graduation by medical students at some universities, dates back to the 4th century BC. It was handed down as part of the *Hippocratic Collection*, a philosophy developed by the Greeks from the writings of Hippocrates and others, from which the whole of their science grew. One version of the oath states:

> I will look upon him who shall have taught me this Art even as one of my parents. I will share my substance with him, and I will supply his necessities, if he be in need. I will regard his offspring even as my own brethren, and I will teach them this Art, if they would learn it, without fee or covenant. I will impart this Art by precept, by lecture and by every mode of teaching, not only to my own sons, but to the sons of him who taught me, and to disciples bound by covenant and oath, according to the Law of Medicine.
>
> The regimen I adopt shall be for the benefit of my patients according to my ability and judgment, and not for their hurt or for any wrong. I will give no deadly drug to any, though it be asked of me, nor will I counsel such, and especially I will not aid a woman to procure abortion. Whatsoever house I enter, there will I go for the benefit of the sick, refraining from all wrongdoing or corruption, and especially from any act of seduction of male or female, of bond or free. Whatsoever things I see or hear concerning the life of men, in my attendance on the sick, or even apart therefrom, which ought not to be noised abroad, I will keep silence thereon, counting such things to be as sacred secrets.

Appendix VI

Letters of instruction to expert

1 EXAMPLE LETTER OF INSTRUCTION TO CLAIMANT'S EXPERT

Our Ref: XXX/YYY/Z
Your Ref:

[Date] 2019

FIRST CLASS
Dr CCC
[address]

Private and Confidential

Dear Dr CCC,
Mr XXX
ADDRESS:
DOB:

I refer to previous correspondence regarding this matter. You wrote on ....
confirming that you could report in this case. I now enclose my instructions to you
to prepare a report on [liability and/or causation and/or condition and prognosis].

Accordingly, I now enclose the following documents to assist you in preparing
your report(s):-

1   Chronology
2   Medical records
     (a) GP records
     (b) ....
     (c) ....
3   Statement of ....
4   Protocols/Guidelines
5   Draft previous reports obtained (if relevant)
6   Complaint documentation

Some general issues

As I am sure you appreciate, it is partly on the basis of your report that a decision
will be taken about the prospects of successful litigation for Mr XXX. Therefore
the report needs to address the medical treatment received with reference to the

legal tests that we have to meet to pursue a claim successfully. The legal tests require that we establish at least one incident of breach of duty, or substandard treatment, and then that that breach caused an injury to the Claimant. Even if an injury was not wholly the result of substandard care it is possible to argue that it was materially contributed to by the breach. The test is whether the breach's contribution to the Claimant's injuries was more than insignificant.

In order to establish breach we must show that the investigation or treatment in question probably fell below medically acceptable standards of a reasonably competent practitioner in the relevant field practicing at the relevant time. To establish causation we must show that any substandard treatment probably caused or materially contributed to the injury sustained.

You will be aware that it is a defence to an allegation of professional negligence to show that a substantial body of reputable practitioners in the relevant field at the relevant time would have carried out the treatment the same way that the Defendant did in this case. However the Courts look to our experts to provide evidence-based support for their opinions as to why a treatment may be substandard, and so providing academic texts etc as well as your advice on whether a method of treatment adopted was reasonable to use is very helpful.

Thus the test for assessing criticisms of Dr YYY's treatment will be whether the allegations can be justified on the balance of probabilities, ie is it more likely than not that the treatment fell below a medically acceptable standard.

I would be grateful if in your report you could refer to at least one contemporary academic published standard for each main criticism of Dr YYY's technique and where referring to such text(s) please provide a copy of the whole of the chapter(s) from which your reference(s) is extracted along with a copy of the front sheet showing details of the author, publisher and date of publication.

I have provided you with my client's statement. In forming your opinion on issues of liability and causation please consider my client's version of events as accurate. If you find for any reason that you are unable to do so, please advise any specific comments which you have discounted and why this was necessary.

If after your review you are of the opinion that a medical expert in a field other than your own should be asked to report in order to examine further issues of liability or causation, please state so specifically in your report so I can advise my client and consider appropriate next steps.

In terms of expert immunity from being sued, I am sure that you have heard of the case of *Jones v Kaney*, where the Supreme Court abolished the immunity from suit for breach of duty by expert witnesses in relation to their participation in legal proceedings. I would like to reassure you that your duty to the client and the Court remains unchanged, to perform your function as an expert with the reasonable skill and care of an expert drawn from the relevant discipline. This includes a duty to perform the overriding duty of assisting the Court. The Court held in *Jones* that:

> If the expert gives an independent and unbiased opinion which is within the range of reasonable expert opinions, he will have discharged his duty both to the court and his client.

(Lord Dyson SCJJ).

The Court went on to find that in this case the expert had no immunity from being sued. As a consequence you need to carry indemnity insurance to cover you for carrying out medico-legal work. It would be appreciated if you could confirm that you do hold such cover.

Finally, this report will not be disclosed to the Defendant. It is a preliminary report intended for myself, my client and counsel if or when instructed as an indication of the evidence you would give if it became necessary to call you as an expert witness.

History of treatment

[Refer expert to relevant documents and highlight here the key aspects of the treatment that you want him to focus on, or that you think are particularly important, making clear why you hold that opinion.]

INSTRUCTIONS

Report on liability

Would you please comment in general on the standard of care of the medical management and treatment given to Mr XXX by Dr YYY, summarising those aspects of his treatment which you feel relevant to this particular claim. It is of course essential for this claim to be successful that I establish causation ie was any failure in the treatment of Mr XXX's condition the probable cause of his pain and suffering. Therefore wherever you identify substandard care can you advise what treatment should have been provided, and what difference that may have made to the patient.

Please also consider the following particular issues [*examples of issues to be raised follow*]:

1   Was any aspect of the treatment provided inappropriate? If yes, would you please describe that treatment and on what grounds you advise that that treatment should not have been provided. What difference would it have made if different treatment had been provided?

2   Was there any omission of treatment, eg should they have .... and if they had would that have led to a different outcome?

3   Was there a failure to adequately diagnose or recognise ....? If the condition had been diagnosed earlier, what action should have been taken, and what difference would that have made to the Claimant?

4   Do you think there are any consent issues here? Was Mr XXX adequately consented with respect to the treatment that was provided, and were there any known risks of it that he should have been warned of? Also was there any alternative treatment he could have had that carried less risk, and that he was not advised of?

5   Do you think there was any aspect of the aftercare provided to Mr XXX that fell below a medically acceptable standard?

If you are of the opinion that Mr XXX's care was managed negligently in any respect would you also consider the possible arguments that may be raised by the Defendant. For instance, what reason could the other side be expected to use to back up an argument that the treatment carried out in this case was appropriate.

Report on condition and prognosis

I would like you to also arrange to see my client in order to prepare a condition and prognosis report. This should be a stand alone document from the report(s) on liability and causation, as if proceedings are commenced this report will be served on the Defendant with the pleadings.

In considering Mr XXX's condition and prognosis please could you advise on the following:

[Set out questions regarding the impact of the injuries and how severe they are.]

I have raised a number of questions in my instructions to you. However, there may be issues that I have not raised that you feel should be considered. If so please raise these in your report. If there are any aspects of this case that you would like to discuss with me before finalising your report please do not hesitate to contact me.

Finally, I would be grateful if you or your secretary could confirm receipt of these instructions and all the documents so that I know you have received everything safely. I thank you for accepting instructions and look forward to hearing from you further.

Yours sincerely

2   EXAMPLE LETTER OF INSTRUCTION TO DEFENDANT'S EXPERT

Our Ref:
Your Ref: yyy/zzz/1

[Date] 2019

FIRST CLASS
Dr DDD
[address]

Private and Confidential

**REPORT REQUIRED BY [DATE] ON
[BREACH OF DUTY/CAUSATION/CONDITION AND PROGNOSIS]**

Dear Dr DDD,
Mr YYY
ADDRESS:
DOB:
I am instructed by .... to act on behalf of the Defendant, ..., to investigate allegations of clinical negligence by the above named Claimant, ... The Claimant alleges the Trust was negligent in that it ....

I am grateful to you for confirming that you are able to accept instructions on behalf of the trust to consider the allegations and report on by [insert date].

Factual background

....

Procedural background

....

Breach of duty

I refer you to the allegations in the Claimant's witness statement [if Defendant – Letter of Claim/Particulars of Claim] dated .... where the Claimant alleges ....

Causation

It is alleged that but for the Trust's negligence ....

The law

As you are aware, in order to succeed in any clinical negligence claim, the Claimant must show:
(a)   the Defendant [clinician/nurse/midwife] breached their duty of care to the Claimant by failing to provide the required standard of care; and
(b)   their breach of duty caused injury, loss or damage.

It is a defence to any allegation of professional negligence to show a responsible body of opinion would have treated the Claimant in the same way. The term '*responsible*' means the Court must be satisfied the body of opinion relied upon can demonstrate the opinion has a logical basis. Furthermore, in terms of the standard to be applied, it is the standard of care applicable at the time of the incident [insert year] rather than the standard of care applicable at the time you write your report.

If the Claimant cannot show that on the balance of probabilities (more than 50% likely) that but for the alleged breach of duty he would have avoided injury, the claim will fail as causation will not be established.

Documents

I enclose copies of the following documents for your consideration:

Volume One
Pleadings (if available)
Claim Form dated ....
Particulars of Claim dated ....
Schedule of Loss dated ....
Claimant's expert evidence
Condition and prognosis report of [insert discipline] dated ....
Letter from [insert discipline] dated ....
Defendant's evidence (not disclosed)
Condition and prognosis report of [insert discipline] dated ....
Letter from [insert discipline] dated ....
Miscellaneous
Guidelines for experts
Letter from Tom Fothergill (NHS Litigation Authority's Director of Finance) regarding experts' fees

Volumes Two and Three: medical records
Claimant's GP records
Claimant's medical records from King's College Hospital NHS Foundation Trust medical records
2 ¥ CD-Rom of Radiography

Instructions

I should be grateful if you would please consider the Claimant's medical records and report on [the standard of care the Claimant received from the Trust and whether, on the balance of probabilities, this has caused the Claimant's current condition]. In particular, I should be grateful if you would provide comments on the following:

It is important your report is supported by medical literature where relevant. I should be grateful if you would attach a list of references, together with copies of any extracts to your report.

As you know, your report may be disclosed to the Claimant [and/or Co-Defendant] and you may need to attend a conference with counsel in due course. More importantly please bear in mind when preparing your evidence that you may be required to give evidence at trial and be cross examined on the contents of your report.

[The documents in enclosure .... are privileged from disclosure to the Claimant's solicitors. Please do not refer to them in your report unless your opinion is based on this document.]

I confirm my client will be responsible for your reasonable fees in preparing your report.

Statement of truth

It is a requirement of the Civil Procedure Rules that your report must be verified by a Statement of Truth in the following form:

> I confirm that I have made clear which facts and matters referred to in this report are within my own knowledge and which are not. Those that are within my own knowledge I confirm to be true. The opinions I have expressed represent my true and complete professional opinions on the matters to which they refer.

I should be grateful to receive your report by .... If this deadline causes difficulty, please advise me at your earliest opportunity. If you require any additional information or documentation, please do not hesitate to contact me.

Please kindly acknowledge safe receipt of these instructions by email.

Thank you again for your assistance and I look forward to receiving your report by ....

Kind regards.

Yours sincerely

....

Enc

Appendix VII

Example of an agenda for the experts

Claim No: ...

IN THE HIGH COURT OF JUSTICE
QUEENS BENCH DIVISION
(IF ANY DISTRICT REGISTRY)

xxx

Claimant

-and-
YYY

Defendant

AGENDA FOR [INSERT] EXPERTS

1 Objectives

The purpose of the discussion is to assist the Parties, their solicitors and the Court to identify:

(a) the extent of agreement between the experts;

(b) the points of disagreement and the reasons for disagreement;

(c) any further material points not raised in the Agenda, and the extent to which there is agreement or disagreement with respect to them;

(d) the steps, if any, which might usefully be taken by the parties, with a view to resolving the outstanding points of disagreement.

This Agenda is intended to provide a guide to the experts' discussion. It is not intended to be exhaustive and the experts should feel free to discuss any other issue that they consider to be relevant.

2 Basic legal principles

(a) When considering the answers to the questions relating to the standard of care or management, regard should be had to the standards applicable at the relevant time and not (if different) to the standards of the present day.

(b) The actions of medical or nursing staff should be judged by the standards of the 'reasonably competent' practitioner; substandard management is therefore management which falls below that to be expected from the 'reasonably' competent practitioner; alternatively it is management which would not be adopted or condoned by a 'responsible body of professional opinion' in the particular field.

(c)   A 'material contribution' to injury or damage is a contribution which is not 'de minimis' and is therefore a contribution which is of more than trifling importance.

(d)   When an answer depends on facts which are understood to be in dispute, that should be expressly indicated, and it should be explained whether (and, if so, to what extent) the answer would be different, if the facts were different.

(e)   When considering causation or questions of hypothetical fact (eg what might the findings or outcome have been if certain steps had been taken) the question should be answered on the balance of probabilities – 'what probably would have been found/happened'. The Court considers an event or outcome to have been a probability if there was a greater than 50% chance that it would have occurred, so the approach should be 'what is more likely than not to have been found/happened'. Certainty is not required nor expected.

(f)   No attempt should be made by any expert to deal with matters outside that expert's particular area of expertise.

(g)   It should be remembered that the experts' overriding duty is to the Court, and not to the party instructing him or her.

(h)   It is not intended that the experts should arrive at a compromised view during the discussion or otherwise attempt to 'settle the case'.

3   Outcome

At the beginning of the discussion one of the experts should be nominated to prepare the experts' joint statement for the Court, recording the conclusion of each part of the discussion. At the end of the discussion the joint statement should be signed by each individual participating in the discussion, setting out in respect of each question (whether arising from the agenda or because it has been separately identified by the experts as being material):

(a)   those matters on which there is agreement as to the answer;

(b)   those matters on which there is disagreement and a summary of the reasons for disagreement;

(c)   a note of any steps which might usefully be taken by the Parties to resolve any areas of disagreement;

(d)   any further material points not raised in the Agenda and the extent to which those issues are agreed.

A copy of the joint statement should be signed by both experts and forwarded to their instructing solicitors within seven days of the experts' discussion.

QUESTIONS THAT THE PARTIES WOULD LIKE TO BE ADDRESSED BY THE EXPERTS

1

2

3

4

etc

[dd.mm.yyyy]

Index

[all references are to page number]

A

A&E departments
ambulance services, 25–26
generally, 26
Access to medical treatment
human rights, and, 654–656
Absence of non-negligent explanation
res ipsa loquitur, and, 133–135
Academy of Experts
Code of Guidance, 592
generally, 596
model reports, 594
Accidental death
inquest verdicts, and, 511–512
Acquiescence
consent to treatment, and, 255
Action Against Medical Accidents (AvMA)
See also **Non-legal remedies**
database of experts, and, 595
legal aid, and, 32
Actual knowledge
adult claimants with capacity in birth
injury cases, 539–540
attributability
degree of precision required to identify
act or omission, 542–545
generally, 541
knowledge of 'negligence', 541
omission cases, 541–542
generally, 535–536
'know', 536–539
requisite level, 539
significant injury, 540–541
Adults without capacity
consent to treatment, and
consent forms, 277
court appointed deputies, 275–276
duration of lack of capacity, 274
general principles, 269–272
IMCAs, 276–277
lasting powers of attorney, 274–275
protection of P's rights, 272–284
referral to Court of Protection, 277–
283

Adults without capacity – *contd*
consent to treatment, and – *contd*
research, 283–284
statements of preferences and wishes,
274
**Advance decisions to refuse
treatment**
consent to treatment, and, 265–266
mental incapacity, and, 672–673
Advance disclosure
inquests, and, 489–490
Adverse outcome
res ipsa loquitur, and, 133
Advice given in legal proceedings
duty of care, and, 109–110
After-the-event insurance
funding, and, 714–715
'Aftermath' principle
doctor's duty to insurers and employers,
and, 107
foreseeability, and, 195
psychiatric injury, and
bereavement, 354–358
generally, 344–347
medical accident, 349–353
proof, 353–354
Agency workers
vicarious liability, and, 64–65
Aggravated damages
assault and battery, 236
death of an infant, 357
Allocation questionnaires
generally, 424–425
**Alternative dispute resolution
(ADR)**
directions, 437–438
generally, 406
public funding, and, 724
Alternative therapies
breach of duty of care, and, 129–130
Ambulance services
emergency and urgent care, and, 25–26
Amendment of proceedings
statements of claim, and, 556–558
Antenatal care
congenital disabilities, and, 332